FREE MOVEMENT OF PERSONS IN THE ENLARGED EUROPEAN UNION

FREE MOVEMENT OF PERSONS IN THE ENLARGED EUROPEAN UNION

SECOND EDITION

By

Nicola Rogers, Rick Scannell
and
John Walsh

SWEET & MAXWELL   THOMSON REUTERS

First Edition 2005
Second Edition 2012

Published in 2012 by Sweet & Maxwell, 100 Avenue Road, London NW3 3PF part of Thomson Reuters (Professional) UK Limited
(Registered in England & Wales, Company No 1679046. Registered Office and address for service:
Aldgate House, 33 Aldgate High Street, London EC3N 1DL)

For further information on our products and services, visit
www.sweetandmaxwell.co.uk

Typeset by YHT, London
Printed and bound by CPI Group (UK) Ltd, Croydon, CR0 4YY

No natural forests were destroyed to make this product, only farmed timber was used and re-planted.

ISBN 9780414023079

©
Sweet & Maxwell/Thomson Reuters

EU statutory material is acknowledged as © European Union, http://eur-lex.europa.eu/. Only European Union legislation printed in the paper edition of the Official Journal of the European Union is deemed authentic.

A CIP catalogue record for this book is available from the British Library

All rights reserved. Thomson Reuters and the Thomson Reuters Logo are trademarks of Thomson Reuters. Sweet & Maxwell is a registered trademark of Thomson Reuters (Legal) Limited. Crown Copyright material is reproduced with the permission of the Controller of the HMSO and the Queen's Printer for Scotland.

No part of this publication may be reproduced or transmitted in any form or by any means, or stored in any retrieval system of any nature without prior written permission, except for permitted fair dealing under the Copyright, Designs and Patents Act 1988, or in accordance with the terms of a licence issued by the Copyright Licensing Agency in respect of photocopying and/or reprographic reproduction. Application for permission for other use of copyright material including permission to reproduce extracts in other published works shall be made to the publishers. Full acknowledgment of author, publisher and source must be given.

PREFACE

The right of freedom of movement for persons is the cornerstone of the principle of European integration lying at the heart of the European Union. Since the Maastricht Treaty the right has been given articulation by the establishment of citizenship of the Union and the right of every citizen of the Union to move and reside freely within the Union now contained in the Treaty on the Functioning on the European Union.

There are at present 27 Member States of the European Union. When the 10 new States[1] joined on May 1, 2004 the scale of the enlargement of the European Union went far beyond what had gone before. In more than a 30-year period the four previous Accession Treaties had accounted for a total of nine new Member States[2]: In 2007 Bulgaria and Romania also became full members. At the present time the prospect of Albania, Bosnia and Herzegovina, Croatia, Iceland, Macedonia, Montenegro, Serbia and Turkey becoming members of the European Union is on the horizon.

Enlargement provided justification for the timing of the first edition of this book written by Nicola Rogers and Rick Scannell. The prospect of further enlargement as well as the overhaul of secondary legislation at EU level on free movement motivated the writing of this second edition.[3] However, sufficient time needed to pass to allow the CJEU to develop its jurisprudence on this legislation.

This book provides comprehensive analysis of the EU legislation and CJEU case law on freedom of movement of persons for both EU nationals and their family members. It deals also with the Association Agreements.

Although we have devoted a chapter to social security, this is intended to be only an outline and general guide to social security provisions in EU law. In the absence of harmonisation amongst Member States of social security provisions, a more detailed analysis is beyond the scope of this work.

---

[1] Cyprus, the Czech Republic, Estonia, Hungary, Latvia, Lithuania, Malta, Poland, the Slovak Republic and Slovenia.
[2] Under the terms of the first accession treaty signed on January 22, 1972, Denmark, Ireland, Norway and the United Kingdom joined the six Member States from January 1, 1973 to make a Community of nine Member States; the second accession treaty saw the Member States grow to 10 with the admission of Greece with effect from January 1, 1981; the third accession treaty accounted for Portugal and Spain who became full members from January 1, 1986 and with effect from January 1, 1995 the 12 Member States became 15 with the fourth accession treaty by which Austria, Finland and Sweden became full members.
[3] In April 2006 Directive 2004/38 on the rights of Union citizens and their family members to move freely and reside in the territory of the Member States (commonly referred to as the Citizens' Directive) came into force. It repealed and amended much of the existing secondary legislation in this area.

PREFACE

Our intention has been to focus on EU law, rather than the UK's implementation and application of it. We have in fact devoted Part IV of the book to the UK's approach, although that Part is not intended to be used in isolation.

Our hope is to engender a discipline which regrettably appears all too often to be lacking, of having primary regard to substantive EU law provisions, rather than the UK's interpretation of those provisions. In examining the scope of the right of the freedom of movement of persons the supremacy of EU law must always be kept in mind, as must the fact that most relevant concepts, procedures and rights are spelt out in detail by EU law itself.

The lack of regard to principles of EU law has had regrettable results. One only needs to look at the frequency with which the UK Government appears to lose its arguments in this area before the CJEU to appreciate that something must be going wrong both at decision making level and before the UK courts. Perhaps there is no better illustration of this than the position taken by the English Court of Appeal in *Lui and others*[4] in which the Court expressed its disquiet at being presented with arguments based on arts 20 and 21 TFEU which would have resulted in an EU citizen child being able to live with her non-EU national parent in the UK. Following an observation of the then House of Lords that such arguments were obviously wrong, the Court of Appeal judgment included a stern warning.

> "It is to be hoped that the professions, and the Legal Services Commission, will take good note of that observation, and that these appeals will be the last occasion on which the AIT, and this court, is troubled with these issues."

Those arguments were substantially the same as those which the CJEU subsequently accepted in *Zambrano*.[5]

The book is divided into four parts.

Part I identifies in four chapters the fundamental principles of EU law. Perhaps the most significant question in the context of the freedom of movement of persons is the true reach of arts 20 and 21 TFEU. Chapter 4 is a special chapter co-authored by Professor Steve Peers and Nicola Rogers. In Ch.4 (Union Citizenship) two questions are considered. First, whether anything of value has been added to the rights of individuals by the creation of Union citizenship. Secondly, the impact on the free movement rights of Union citizens made by the inclusion of the "right to move and reside freely."

Part II examines the substantive provisions in EU law for the free movement of Union citizens and their family members. We deal with the economically active free movers in Chs 6 and 7 (workers and those exercising the freedom of establishment and the freedom to provide and receive services) and those who are economically inactive in Ch.8 (the self-sufficient exercising a general

---

[4] *Liu and Others v Secretary of State for the Home Department* [2007] EWCA Civ 1275.
[5] *Ruiz Zambrano Office National de l'Emploi (ONEM)* (C–34/09) [2011] E.C.R. I-0000.

right of residence, retired persons and students). In addition we consider the rights of family members of all free movers in Ch.9. Separate chapters are devoted to the right of entry and residence, to discrimination and other obstacles to freedom of movement, to access to social security (as observed in outline and in general) and to exclusion and expulsion.

Part III deals with agreements with third countries insofar as they impact on the freedom of movement of persons. Since the early 1990s the EU has broadened its relations to include a degree of co-operation with nearly all regions of the world and signed agreements and conventions with a wide range of partners. Detailed consideration however is limited to the Stabilisation and Association Agreements (concluded with the Western Balkan States) and the EC-Turkey Association Agreement. It is these agreements which have most significance (at the present time for nationals of Macedonia, Croatia, Albania, Montenegro and Turkey) in the context of the freedom of movement of persons.

Part IV deals with UK law and practice implementing EU law provisions on the free movement of persons. However as already made clear it is not intended to be able to be used in isolation of the analysis of EU law contained in Parts I–III. The focus of Part IV is on contentious areas where UK law and practice appears to diverge from EU law standards.

We are indebted to Steve Peers for his contribution in this book. His knowledge of EU law is vast and respect for him in the field is enormous.

Nicola and Rick are very pleased indeed to welcome as co-author John Walsh. As they leave practice after years of specialising in this area, John remains in full swing at Doughty Street Chambers. In leaving the profession a huge debt of acknowledgement and gratitude is owed to all former colleagues, in particular Professors Elspeth Guild and Steve Peers, others from the ILPA European Sub-Committee and colleagues at Garden Court Chambers.

The law is as stated as at March 2012.

Nicola Rogers, Rick Scannell and John Walsh

CONTENTS

Preface	v
Table of European Cases	xxiii
Table of UK Cases	xxxvii
Table of EU Legislation	xxxix
Table of EU Agreements	xlvii
Table of International Treaties and Conventions	li
Table of Statutes	liii
Table of Statutory Instruments	lv

PART ONE—FUNDAMENTAL PRINCIPLES OF EU LAW

Chapter 1: Treaty Foundations and Institutions

1. Treaty Foundations	1–01
(a) Introduction	1–01
(b) The Treaty establishing the European Coal and Steel Community	1–07
(c) The Treaty establishing the European Atomic Community	1–07
(d) The Treaty establishing the European Economic Community	1–10
(e) The Single European Act	1–17
(f) The Maastricht Treaty	1–19
(g) The Amsterdam Treaty	1–23
(h) Treaty of Nice	1–26
(i) The Treaty of Lisbon	1–29
2. The EU Institutions	1–35
(a) Introduction	1–35
(b) The European Parliament	1–39
(c) The Council of the European Union	1–51
(d) The European Commission	1–62

Chapter 2: The European Legal Order

1. Sources of European Union	2–01
(a) Treaties	2–02
(b) Secondary legislation	2–03

(c) Agreements with third countries	2–08
(d) Rulings by the Court of Justice of the European Union and the General Court	2–13
2. Principles of European Union Law	2–27
(a) Introduction	2–27
(b) Supremacy	2–29
(c) Direct effect	2–36
(d) Indirect effect	2–55
(e) General principles	2–58

Chapter 3: Relationship between EU and Human Rights Law

1. The Sources and Content of Human Rights in EU Law	3–01
(a) The Treaty on European Union (TEU)	3–01
(b) The Charter of Fundamental Rights	3–05
(c) ECHR and the Charter	3–09
(d) The Court of Justice of the European Union	3–14
(e) EU secondary legislation	3–23

Chapter 4: Union Citizenship
Written by Professor Steve Peers and Nicola Rogers

1. Introduction	4–01
2. Union Citizenship	4–03
(a) Historical background	4–03
3. A New Form of Citizenship	4–09
(a) Introduction	4–09
(b) Rights and benefits flowing from Union citizenship	4–12
(c) Tension between Union and national citizenship	4–35
4. Article 21 TFEU: The Right of Union Citizens to Move and Reside	4–44
(a) Introduction	4–44
(b) A restrictive interpretation	4–46
(c) An interpretative obligation	4–48
(d) A free standing right	4–56
(e) The future of art.21 TFEU	4–64

CONTENTS

PART TWO—FREE MOVEMENT PROVISIONS FOR UNION CITIZENS AND THEIR FAMILY MEMBERS

Chapter 5: Beneficiaries of Free Movement Provisions

1. Citizenship of the Union — 5–01
   - (a) The Union citizen — 5–01
   - (b) Nationals of Member States — 5–04
   - (c) The situation of dual nationals — 5–22
   - (d) Third country nationals — 5–28

Chapter 6: Workers

1. Introduction — 6–01
   - (a) Fundamental importance of free movement for workers — 6–01
   - (b) Treaty provisions on workers — 6–02
   - (c) Secondary legislation — 6–05
   - (d) The Union concept of worker — 6–06
   - (e) Union concept of worker depends on context — 6–07

2. The Definition of Worker — 6–08
   - (a) Generally — 6–08
   - (b) Services of economic value — 6–09
   - (c) Services for and under the direction of another person — 6–12
   - (d) Remuneration — 6–13
   - (e) Application of principles — 6–16
   - (f) Work seekers — 6–47
   - (g) Previous employment — 6–54
   - (h) Frontier workers — 6–67
   - (i) The public service exception — 6–69

Chapter 7: Establishment and Services

1. Treaty Provisions and Subsidiary Legislation on Establishment — 7–01
   - (a) General Treaty aims and relationship with provisions on workers — 7–01
   - (b) Secondary legislation — 7–04

2. Concept of Establishment — 7–05
   - (a) Definition of economic activity — 7–06
   - (b) Cross-border character — 7–08
   - (c) Stable and continuous nature of economic activity — 7–12

[xi]

3. Establishment of Persons	7–15
4. Establishment of Companies	7–21
(a) Primary establishment—head office	7–22
(b) Secondary establishment—branches, subsidiaries and agencies	7–24
(c) Nationality of the company	7–27
(d) Nationality of the employees	7–29
5. Meaning of Freedom of Establishment "Without Restrictions"	7–30
6. Treaty Provisions and Subsidiary Legislation on Service Provision and Recipients of Services	7–33
(a) General Treaty aims and relationship with established provisions	7–37
(b) Articles 56—62 TFEU	7–41
(c) Secondary legislation	7–43
7. Service Providers	7–47
(a) Economic activity	7–47
(b) Cross-border element	7–52
(c) Temporary character	7–55
(d) Nationality of natural persons	7–57
8. Companies as Service Providers	7–59
(a) Nationality of company	7–59
(b) Personnel of company	7–61
9. Recipients of Services	7–71
(a) Concept of recipients of services	7–71
(b) Personal scope of recipients of services	7–72

Chapter 8: The Economically Inactive

1. Introduction: Beyond the Economically Active	8–01
2. General Requirement of the Provisions Relating to the Economically Inactive	8–06
(a) The concept of self-sufficiency	8–12
(b) Sickness insurance	8–23
3. The General Right of Residence	8–27
4. The Retired Person	8–29
5. Students	8–32
(a) Generally	8–32

(b) Specific provisions relating to the right of residence of students   8–37

Chapter 9: Family Members

1. Introduction   9–01
   (a) General European Union law principles   9–01
   (b) Inter-relationship with the right to family life in human rights law   9–08
   (c) Which family members can be installed with the Union citizen?   9–23

2. Spouses and Register Partners   9–30
   (a) Legal spouse   9–30
   (b) Registered partnerships   9–36
   (c) Transsexuals   9–42
   (d) Sham marriages/registered partnerships   9–50

3. Descendants   9–53
   (a) Under the age of 21   9–53
   (b) Dependency   9–55
   (c) Adopted and foster children   9–61

4. Relatives in the Ascending Line   9–64
5. Other Family Members   9–66
   (a) Other dependants   9–67
   (b) Living as part of the household   9–70
   (c) Serious health grounds   9–71
   (d) Durable relationships   9–73
   (e) Beyond the scope of the Directive   9–77
   (f) Without the EU national   9–85

Chapter 10: Rights of Entry and Residence

1. Introduction   10–01
   (a) Right of entry and residence as a corollary of right to move   10–01
   (b) Deriving the right of residence from the Treaty   10–02
   (c) Human rights and proportionality   10–03

2. Specific Rights of Residence for EU Nationals and their Family Members under Directive 2004/38   10–06
   (a) The rights of residence for up to three months   10–06
   (b) The rights of residence for more than three months   10–07

(c) Retained right of residence	10–09
(d) Right to permanent residence	10–10

3. Formalities — 10–13
    (a) Declaratory effect of residence documents and visas — 10–15
    (b) Member States cannot ask for more than permitted in legislation — 10–18
    (c) Failure to comply with formalities — 10–25
    (d) Time-limits for providing visas and residence permits — 10–29
    (e) Time limits imposed on applicants to comply with administrative formalities — 10–35
    (f) Fees — 10–37
    (g) Visas — 10–38
    (h) Residence documents — 10–43
    (i) Permanent residence documents — 10–52

4. Obtaining and Retaining Specific Residence Documents — 10–54
    (a) Registration certificates as a worker or self-employed person — 10–54
    (b) Self-sufficient persons — 10–60
    (c) Students — 10–71
    (d) Permanent registration certificate for Union citizens after five years' residence — 10–76
    (e) Permanent registration certificates after less than five years' residence — 10–86
    (f) Family members — 10–89
    (g) Remaining beyond the Union citizen — 10–107

Chapter 11: Discrimination and Other Obstacles to Freedom of Movement

1. General Principle of Non-discrimination in the European Union Law Context — 11–01
    (a) Introduction — 11–01
    (b) The scope and application of art.18 TFEU — 11–04
    (c) Inter-relationship with other non-discrimination provisions — 11–12
    (d) Indirect discrimination — 11–19
    (e) Justification — 11–21

2. Obstacles to the Free Movement of Workers — 11–25
    (a) Introduction — 11–25
    (b) The provisions of Regulation 492/2011 — 11–26

(c) Personal scope	11–32
(d) Material scope	11–39
(e) Prohibited forms of discrimination	11–50
(f) Justification	11–56
3. Obstacles to Establishment	11–58
(a) Definition of restrictions of freedom of establishment	11–58
(b) Prohibited discrimination based on nationality	11–63
(c) Non-prohibited restrictions	11–68
4. Mutual Recognition of Diplomas/Training	11–75
5. Obstacles to Service Provision	11–90
6. Obstacles to the Exercise of Free Movement by the Economically Inactive	11–97
(a) Introduction	11–97
(b) Application to the economically inactive	11–100

Chapter 12: Access to Social Security

1. Introduction	12–01
(a) Regulation 883/2004	12–03
(b) Underlying principles	12–07
(c) Non-discrimination, equal treatment	12–08
(d) Structure and content of Regulation 883/2004	12–17
2. Conclusions	12–33

Chapter 13: Exclusion and Expulsion

1. Introduction	13–01
2. EU Law Provisions on the Expulsion and Exclusion of Free Movers	13–02
3. Grounds for Exclusion/Expulsion of Free Movers	13–10
(a) General observations	13–10
(b) Public policy	13–18
(c) Public security	13–30
(d) Public health	13–34
4. Safeguards Against Exclusion or Expulsion of Free Movers	13–36
(a) Heightened protection from expulsion	13–36
(b) Notification of decision to expel or exclude	13–48
(c) Legal remedies	13–53

5. The Exclusion/Expulsion of Other EU Nationals   13–59

PART THREE—ASSOCIATION AGREEMENTS WITH THIRD COUNTRIES

Chapter 14: Agreements with Third Countries

1. Treaty Provision for Agreements with Third Countries   14–01
2. EEA Agreement   14–11
   (a) Background   14–11
   (b) Free movement of persons   14–16

3. Agreement with Switzerland   14–21
   (a) Background   14–21
   (b) Free movement rights   14–22

4. Agreement with Turkey   14–26
   (a) Background   14–26
   (b) Free movement of persons   14–29

5. Agreements with Western Balkan States   14–30
   (a) Background   14–30
   (b) Free movement provisions   14–36

6. Agreements with Other European and Central Asian Countries   14–45
   (a) Background   14–45
   (b) Free movement provisions   14–49

7. Euro-Mediterranean Agreements   14–57
   (a) Background   14–57
   (b) Free movement provisions   14–59

8. Agreements with African, Caribbean and Pacific Countries   14–66
   (a) Background   14–66
   (b) Free movement provisions   14–70

9. Association Agreement with Chile   14–73
   (a) Background   14–73
   (b) Free movement provisions   14–76

Chapter 15: Association Agreements in Community Law

1. Introduction	15–01
2. Mixed Agreements	15–02
3. The Agreements as a Tool to Accession	15–10
4. Jurisdiction of the CJEU	15–15
5. Direct Effect	15–24

Chapter 16: Workers under the Stabilisation and Association Agreements

1. Introduction	16–01
2. Non-discrimination of Workers	16–05
(a) Introduction	16–05
(b) Direct effect	16–06
(c) Relationship with national laws permitted by art.62	16–09
(d) Meaning of the non-discrimination provision	16–13
(e) Indirect discrimination	16–16
(f) Scope of non-discrimination provision	16–18
(g) The meaning of "legally employed"	16–22
(h) The meaning of "worker"	16–25
(i) Temporal effect of the non-discrimination provision for workers	16–27
3. Family Members	16–29
4. Key Personnel	16–32
5. Supply of Services	16–39

Chapter 17: Introduction to the Ankara Agreement

1. Background to the Agreement	17–01
2. The Structure and Content of the Ankara Agreement and the Additional Protocol	17–07
(a) The Ankara Agreement	17–07
(b) The Additional Protocol	17–08
3. The Objectives of the Ankara Agreement and its Protocol	17–09
(a) Preamble to the Agreement	17–10
(b) Other provisions in the Agreement and its Protocol	17–13
4. Decisions of the Association Council	17–18
(a) Decisions relating to free movement	17–18
(b) The direct effect of decisions of the Council of Association	17–31

Chapter 18: Workers under the Ankara Agreement

1. Introduction: the Provisions — 18–01
   (a) The Ankara Agreement and Additional Protocol — 18–01
   (b) Relevant provisions of the Decisions of the Council of Association — 18–04

2. The Worker's Right to Continued Employment — 18–10
   (a) The concept of "worker" — 18–14
   (b) The concepts of "legal employment" and being "duly registered as belonging to the labour force — 18–20
   (c) Employment for one of three requisite time periods — 18–43
   (d) The right of residence — 18–64
   (e) The right of non-discrimination — 18–69
   (f) The standstill clause — 18–76

Chapter 19: Establishment under the Ankara Agreement

1. Provisions of the Ankara Agreement and Additional Protocol — 19–01
   (a) Ankara Agreement provisions relating to establishment and services — 19–01
   (b) Additional Protocol relating to establishment and services — 19–05

2. Right of Establishment and Right to Provide Services Under the Agreement — 19–08
   (a) Entry and establishment — 19–08
   (b) Lawful residence and establishment — 19–13

3. The Standstill Provision — 19–17
   (a) The concept of a standstill provision — 19–17
   (b) Applicability of the standstill clause — 19–21
   (c) The scope of the standstill clause — 19–24

4. Non-discrimination — 19–33

Chapter 20: Family Members under the Ankara Agreement

1. Provision for Family Members in the Ankara Agreement and the Decisions of the Council of Association — 20–01
   (a) The Agreement — 20–01
   (b) Decisions of the Council of Association — 20–05

Contents

2. The Rights of Family Members of Turkish Workers	20–07
(a) Direct effect of art.7 of Decision 1/80	20–09
(b) Right of entry for family members of workers	20–11
(c) Right of residence for family members during the first three years	20–16
(d) Right of residence of family members of workers after three years' residence	20–20
3. Children	20–38
(a) Provisions in Decision 1/80 relating to children	20–38
(b) Children who have completed vocational training	20–41
(c) Children and education	20–52
4. Family Members of Those Established in Business	20–55

Chapter 21: Expulsion under the Ankara Agreement

1. Workers and Their Family Members	21–01
(a) Workers and their family members with accrued rights under arts 6 and 7 of Decision 1/80	21–01
(b) Workers and their family members without accrued rights	21–12
2. Self-employed Turkish Nationals	21–13
(a) The self-employed in a regular position	21–13
(b) Self-employed covered by the standstill provision	21–15

Chapter 22: Introduction to UK Law and Practice

Chapter 23: Incorporation of European Union Law into UK Law

1. Relevant Legislation	23–01
2. The Legal Framework for Union Law in the United Kingdom	23–02
(a) Introduction	23–02
(b) Main provisions of the European Communities' Act 1972	23–04
3. Reference to the CJEU from UK Courts	23–09
(a) Circumstances in which a case will be referred from a UK court	23–09
(b) Which English courts or tribunals are entitled to refer questions to the CJEU	23–11
(c) The final court	23–14

(d) Appeals against the making of a reference	23–15
(e) Costs	23–16

Chapter 24: Free Movement of Union Citizens and Their Families

1. Relevant Primary and Secondary Legislation	24–01
(a) Incorporation of EU law into UK law	24–01
2. UK Nationals for the Purposes of EU Law	24–02
3. General Scheme for EEA Nationals and their Family Members	24–05
(a) Introduction	24–05
(b) Immigration (European Economic Area) Regulations 2006	24–08
(c) Controversial points	24–14
(d) Extended family members	24–15
(e) Right to permanent residence	24–18
(f) Surrinder Singh principle	24–21
(g) Common law partners	24–23
(h) Change in circumstances—loss of EU status	24–24
(i) Evidential problems	24–25
(j) Primary carers of children	24–28
(k) Accession	24–31

Chapter 25: Agreements with Third Countries

1. Swiss Agreement	25–01
(a) Relevant legislation	25–01
(b) General provisions	25–02
2. EC-Turkey Association Agreement	25–03
(a) Residence of Turkish workers under art.6 of Decision 1/80	25–03
(b) Self-employed Turkish nationals	25–07
3. The Stabilisation and Association Agreements (SAAs)	25–32
4. Partnership and Co-operation Agreements	25–33

CONTENTS

PART FOUR—APPENDICES

PRIMARY EUROPEAN LEGISLATION

Appendix 1—	Treaty on European Union (excerpts): arts 1–19	A1–01
Appendix 2—	The Treaty on the Functioning of the European Union (excerpts): arts 18–22, 45–47, 49–52, 56–57, 216–218, 267 and 288	A2–01
Appendix 3—	Directive 2004/38/EC of the European Parliament and of the Council	A3–01
Appendix 4—	Regulation (EU) No 492/2011 on freedom of movement for workers within the Union	A4–01
Appendix 5—	Regulation (EC) No 883/2004 of the European Parliament and of the Council of 29 April 2004 on the coordination of social security systems	A5–01
Appendix 6—	Agreement on the European Economic Area (excerpts): arts 28–35	A6–01
Appendix 7—	Agreement between the European Community and its Member States, of the one part, and the Swiss Confederation, of the other, on the free movement of persons (excerpts): Preamble, arts 1–25, Annex I	A7–01
Appendix 8—	Agreement Establishing an Association between the European Economic Community and Turkey (excerpts): Preamble, arts 7, 12–14	A8–01
Appendix 9—	Additional protocol to the EU Turkey Agreement (excerpts): arts 36–41, 58–59	A9–01
Appendix 10—	Decision No 1/80 of the Association Council of 19 September 1980 on the Development of the Association (excerpts): preamble, arts 7–19	A10–01
Appendix 11—	Stabilisation and Association Agreement between the European Communities and their Member States, of the one part, and the former Yugoslav Republic of Macedonia, of the other part (excerpts): Premable, arts 1, 44–57, and 61–63	A11–01

UK LAW

Appendix 12—	European Communities Act 1972 c.68 (excerpts): ss.1–3	A12–01
Appendix 13—	Immigration Act 1988 (excerpts): s.7	A13–01
Appendix 14—	Immigration (European Economic Area) Regulations 2006 (SI 2006/1003)	A14–01
Appendix 15—	The Immigration (European Economic Area) (Amendment) Regulations 2011 (SI 2011/1247)	A15–01
Appendix 16—	The Accession (Immigration and Worker Authorisation) Regulations 2006 (SI 2006/3317)	A16–01

Contents

Appendix 17— The Accession (Immigration and Worker Registration) (Revocation, Savings and Consequential Provisions) Regulations 2011 (SI 2011/544)   A17–01
Appendix 18— Immigration (Swiss Free Movement of Persons) (No.3) Regulations 2002 (SI 2002/1241)   A18–01

Index   *Page* 687

TABLE OF EUROPEAN CASES

Abatay and Nadi Sahin v Bundesanstalt für Arbeit (C–317/01 & C–369/01) [2003]
 E.C.R. I–12301; [2005] All E.R. (D) 342 .... 18–79, 19–22, 19–27, 19–29
Adoui v Belgium (115/81) [1982] E.C.R. 1665; [1982] 3 C.M.L.R. 631 .... 6–27, 13-21
Ajoke Alarape (Olaitan), Olukayode Azeez Tijani v Secretary of State for the Home
 Department (C-529/11) September 17, 2011 9-79
Akman v Oberkreisdirektor des Rheinisch Bergischen Kreises (C–210/97) [1998] E.C.R.
 I–7519; [2001] 1 C.M.L.R. 17 .... 20–22, 20–47, 20–48, 20–49, 20–53
Aladzhov v Zamestnik direktor na Stolichna direktsia na vatreshnite raboti kam Ministerstvo na vatreshnite raboti (C–434/10) Unreported November 17, 2011 13–20
Alassini v Telecom Italia SpA (C–317/08) Unreported March 18, 2010 3–06
Albert Ruckdeschel & Co v Hauptzollamt Hamburg-St Annen (117/76) [1977] E.C.R.
 1753; [1979] 2 C.M.L.R. 445 11–03
Albore, Re (C–423/98) [2000] E.C.R. I–5965; [2002] 3 C.M.L.R. 10 .... 13–30, 13–31
Al-Faqih v Council (T–135/06) Unreported September 29, 2010 GC 2–17
Alim v Russia (39417/07) Unreported September 27, 2011 ECHR 9–74
Allue v Universita degli Studi di Venezia (33/88) [1989] E.C.R. 1591; [1991] 1 C.M.L.R.
 283 6–73
Alpine Investments BV v Minister van Financien (C–384/93) [1995] All E.R. (EC) 543;
 [1995] E.C.R. I–1141; [1995] 2 B.C.L.C. 214; [1995] 2 C.M.L.R. 209 7–53
Altun v Stadt Boblingen, (C–337/07) [2008] E.C.R. I-10323 ECJ. 18–61, 20–33, 20–35
Asscher v Staatssecretaris van Financien (C–107/94) [1996] All E.R. (EC) 757; [1996]
 S.T.C. 1025; [1996] E.C.R. I–3089; [1996] 3 C.M.L.R. 61; [1996] C.E.C. 834 6–12
Association de Soutien aux Travailleurs Immigrés (ASTI) v Chambre des Employés
 Privés (C–213/90) [1991] E.C.R. I–3507; [1993] 3 C.M.L.R. 621 18–73
ASTI I. *See* Association de Soutien aux Travailleurs Immigrés (ASTI) v Chambre des Employés Privés (C–213/90)
ASTI II. *See* Commission of the European Communities v Luxembourg (C–118/92)
Avello v Belgium (C–148/02) [2004] All E.R. (EC) 740; [2003] E.C.R. I–11613; [2004] 1
 C.M.L.R. 1 .... 4–22, 4–30, 5–23, 5–25, 11–11
Ayaz v Land Baden-Württemberg (C–275/02) [2004] E.C.R. I–8765; [2005] 1 C.M.L.R.
 50; [2004] All E.R. (D) 188 .... 9–64, 20–36, 20–37, 21–04
B (C–101/09) Unreported November 9, 2010 3–06
Baumbast v Secretary of State for the Home Department (C–413/99) [2002] E.C.R.
 I–7091; [2002] 3 C.M.L.R. 23; [2003] I.C.R. 1347; [2003] I.N.L.R. 1 ECJ ... 3–22, 4–15,
  4–47, 4–48, 4–53, 4–54, 4–55, 4–57, 4–58, 4–59, 4–68, 4–76, 8–08, 8–10, 8–23, 8–24,
  8–25, 8–26, 8–40, 8–42, 9–06, 9–21, 9–54, 9–62, 9–78, 9–79, 9–80, 10–05, 10–67,
  10–109, 10–116, 13–69, 20–53, 24–27, 24–28
Bekleyen v Land Berlin (C–462/08) [2010] 2 C.M.L.R. 35 20–50
Bela-Mühle Josef Bergmann KG v Grows Farm GmbH & Co KG (114/76) [1977]
 E.C.R. 1247; [1977] E.C.R. 1269; [1977] E.C.R. 1211; [1979] 2 C.M.L.R. 83 2–60
Belgian State v Fatna Mesbah (C-179/98) [1999] E.C.R. I-7955 14–65
Belgium v Humbel (C–263/86) [1988] E.C.R. 5365; [1989] 1 C.M.L.R. 393 ...... 7–49, 7–75
Belgium v Royer (48/75) [1976] E.C.R. 497; [1976] 2 C.M.L.R. 619; [1977] I.C.R. 314
 ECJ 6–51, 10–02, 10–15, 10–16,
  10–25, 10–27, 13–02, 13–11, 13–14, 19–17
Bergemann v Bundesanstalt für Arbeit (C–236/87) [1988] E.C.R. 5125; [1990] 1
 C.M.L.R. 525 6–67
Bernini v Netherlands Ministry of Education and Science (C–3/90) [1992] E.C.R.
 I–1071 .... 6–64, 18–16
Bettray v Staatssecretaris van Justitie (344/87) [1989] E.C.R. 1621; [1991] 1 C.M.L.R.
 459 ECJ 6–16, 6–26, 6–40, 6–41, 6–43, 6–44, 6–45, 6–46, 18–16
Bicakci (C–89/00) Unreported September 19, 2000 21–06
Biehl v Administration des Contributions du Grand-Duché de Luxembourg (C–175/88)
 [1991] S.T.C. 575; [1990] E.C.R. I–1779; [1990] 3 C.M.L.R. 143 11–49

TABLE OF EUROPEAN CASES

Birden v Stadtgemeinde Bremen (C–1/97) [1998] E.C.R. I–7747; [1999] 1 C.M.L.R.
  420 .... 16–23, 6-44, 18–06, 18–11, 18–15, 18–16, 18–18, 18–32,
                              18–34, 18–35, 18–36, 18–39, 18–40, 18–64
Bond van Adverteerders v Netherlands (352/85) [1988] E.C.R. 2085; [1989] 3 C.M.L.R.
  113 7–51
Bonsignore (Angelo), Cologne v Oberstadtdirektor of the City of Cologne (67/74) [1975]
  E.C.R. 297; [1975] 1 C.M.L.R. 472 .... 13–22, 13–25
Borowitz v Bundesversicherungsanstalt für Angestellte (21/87) [1988] E.C.R. 3715;
  [1990] 1 C.M.L.R. 34 ECJ 12–03
Boultif v Switzerland (54273/00) [2001] 2 F.L.R. 1228; (2001) 33 E.H.R.R. 50; [2001]
  Fam. Law 875 ECHR 9–12, 13–29
Bozkurt v Staatssecretaris van Justitie (C–434/93) [1995] E.C.R. I–1475 ..... 17–20, 18–04,
          18–15, 18–21, 18–39, 18–41, 18–42, 18–54, 18–56, 20–17, 20–20, 20–28, 20–32
Bressol v Gouvernement de la Communauté Française (C–73/08) [2010] 3 C.M.L.R. 20;
  [2011] C.E.C. 80 ECJ 4–30
Broekmeulen v Huisarts Registratie Commissie (C246/80) [1981] E.C.R. 2311; [1982] 1
  C.M.L.R. 91 ECJ 23-11
Brown v Secretary of State for Scotland (197/86) [1988] E.C.R. 3205; 1989 S.L.T. 402;
  [1988] 3 C.M.L.R. 403 6–09, 6–64, 8–41, 8–44, 11–43, 11–103, 18–16
Bussone v Italian Ministry for Agriculture and Forestry (31/78) [1978] E.C.R. 2429;
  [1979] 3 C.M.L.R. 18 ECJ 2–44
Butterfly Music Srl v Carosello Edizioni Musicali e Discografiche Srl (CEMED) (C–60/
  98) [1999] E.C.R. I–3939; [2000] 1 C.M.L.R. 587; [2000] C.E.C. 200; [2000]
  E.C.D.R. 1; [1999] E.M.L.R. 847 ECJ 16–28
Caisse Regionale d'Assurance Maladie (Lille) v Diamente Palermo (Toia) (C–237/78)
  [1979] E.C.R. 2645; [1980] 2 C.M.L.R. 31 12–10
Campus Oil Ltd v Minister for Industry and Energy (72/83) [1984] E.C.R. 2727; [1984] 3
  C.M.L.R. 544 13–31
Carpenter v Secretary of State for the Home Department (C–60/00) [2003] Q.B. 416;
  [2003] 2 W.L.R. 267; [2003] All E.R. (EC) 577; [2002] E.C.R. I–6279; [2002] 2
  C.M.L.R. 64; [2003] 2 F.C.R. 711; [2002] I.N.L.R. 439 ECJ3–22, ... 3–22, 5–20, 5–21,
               9–03, 9–08, 9–16, 9–21, 9–22, 9–49, 9–83, 10–04, 10–116, 20–03
Centre Public d'Aide Sociale, Courcelles v Lebon (316/85) [1987] E.C.R. 2811; [1989] 1
  C.M.L.R. 337 9–55, 9–56, 11–35, 11–37
Centro di Musicologia Walter Stauffer v Finanzamt München für Korperschaften
  (C–386/04) [2008] S.T.C. 1439; [2006] E.C.R. I–8203; [2009] 2 C.M.L.R. 31; [2009]
  B.T.C. 651; [2006] S.T.I. 2203 7–30
Centros Ltd v Erhvervs- og Selskabsstyrelsen (C–212/97) [2000] Ch. 446; [2000] 2 W.L.R.
  1048; [2000] All E.R. (EC) 481; [1999] E.C.R. I–1459; [1999] B.C.C. 983; [2000] 2
  B.C.L.C. 68; [1999] 2 C.M.L.R. 551; [2000] C.E.C. 290 ECJ 7–30
Chahal v United Kingdom (22414/93) (1997) 23 E.H.R.R. 413; 1 B.H.R.C. 405 ECHR 13–51
Chen v Secretary of State for the Home Department (C–200/02) [2005] Q.B. 325; [2004] 3
  W.L.R. 1453; [2005] All E.R. (EC) 129; [2004] E.C.R. I–9925; [2004] 3 C.M.L.R. 48;
  [2004] C.E.C. 503; [2004] Imm. A.R. 754; [2005] I.N.L.R. 1 .... 4–38, 4–67, 4–68,
                              4–69, 4–70, 4–71, 8–19, 8–21, 9–55, 9–79
Chuck v Raad van Bestuur van de Sociale Verzekeringsbank (C–331/06) [2009] P.T.S.R.
  131; [2008] E.C.R. I–1957; [2008] 2 C.M.L.R. 36 12–03
CILFIT Srl v Ministero della Sanita (283/81) [1982] E.C.R. 3415; [1983] 1 C.M.L.R.
  472 .... 2–26, 23–10
Collins v Secretary of State for Work and Pensions (C–138/02) [2005] Q.B. 145; [2004] 3
  W.L.R. 1236; [2004] All E.R. (EC) 1005; [2004] E.C.R. I–2703; [2004] 2 C.M.L.R. 8;
  [2004] C.E.C. 436; [2005] I.C.R. 37 ECJ 4–34, 6–08, 6–53, 11–20, 11–35,
                                                11–37, 11–53, 11–57
Commission of the European Communities v Austria (C–393/05) [2007] E.C.R. I–10195;
  [2008] 1 C.M.L.R. 42 ↲ 7–52
Commission of the European Communities v Austria (C–161/07) [2008] E.C.R. I–10671;
  [2009] 2 C.M.L.R. 16 .... 7–05, 7–31
Commission of the European Communities v Austria (C–477/08); Commission of the
  European Communities v France (C–468/08); Commission of the European Com-
  munities v Germany (C–505/08); Commission of the European Communities v
  Greece (C–465/08); Commission of the European Communities v Luxembourg

TABLE OF EUROPEAN CASES

(C–51/08); Commission of the European Communities v United Kingdom (C–556/08) Unreported September 24, 2009 ECJ 11–88
Commission of the European Communities v Austria (C–53/08); Commission of the European Communities v Belgium (C–47/08); Commission of the European Communities v Germany (C–54/08); Commission of the European Communities v Greece (C–61/08); Commission of the European Communities v Portugal (C–52/08) Unreported May 2, 2011 11–89
Commission of the European Communities v Belgium (No.1) (149/79) [1980] E.C.R. 3881; [1981] 2 C.M.L.R. 413. .... 6–70, 6–71, 6–72
Commission of the European Communities v Belgium (321/87) [1989] E.C.R. 997; [1990] 2 C.M.L.R. 492 10–19, 10–21, 10–22, 10–23
Commission of the European Communities v Belgium (C–278/94) [1996] E.C.R. I–4307; [1997] 1 C.M.L.R. 1040 .... 11–36, 11–37
Commission of the European Communities v Belgium (C–408/03) [2006] All E.R. (EC) 725; [2006] E.C.R. I–2647; [2006] 2 C.M.L.R. 41; [2006] C.E.C. 850. . . 4–69, 8–19, 8–20, 10–36, 10–62, 10–70
Commission of the European Communities v France (270/83) [1986] E.C.R. 273; [1987] 1 C.M.L.R. 401 .... 7–21, 7–30
Commission of the European Communities v France (307/84) [1986] E.C.R. 1725; [1987] 3 C.M.L.R. 555. 6–70
Commission of the European Communities v France (C–496/01) [2008] E.C.R. I–2351 ECJ 11–92
Commission of the European Communities v France (C–389/05) [2008] E.C.R. I–5337; [2008] 3 C.M.L.R. 36. 7–52
Commission of the European Communities v France (C–468/08) [2009] E.C.R. I–160. 11–88
Commission of the European Communities v Germany (C-205/84) [1986] E.C.R. 3755; [1987] 2 C.M.L.R. 69 11-92
Commission of the European Communities v Germany (249/86) [1989] E.C.R. 1263; [1990] 3 C.M.L.R. 540 9–09
Commission of the European Communities v Germany (C–341/02) [2005] 3 C.M.L.R. 4 7–66
Commission of the European Communities v Germany (C–244/04) [2006] E.C.R. I–885; [2006] 2 C.M.L.R. 23 7–65, 7–69
Commission of the European Communities v Germany (C–318/05) [2008] All E.R. (EC) 556; [2008] S.T.C. 1357; [2007] E.C.R. I–6957; [2007] S.T.I. 2188 4–30
Commission of the European Communities v Germany (C–404/05) [2007] E.C.R. I–10239; [2008] 1 C.M.L.R. 43 7–52
Commission of the European Communities v Germany (C–490/04) [2007] E.C.R. I-6095. .... 7–59, 7–66, 11-92
Commission of the European Communities v Greece (305/87) [1989] E.C.R. 1461; [1991] 1 C.M.L.R. 611 ECJ 2–16, 11–17
Commission of the European Communities v Greece (C–398/98) [2001] E.C.R. I–7915; [2001] 3 C.M.L.R. 62. 13–31
Commission of the European Communities v Greece (C–140/03) [2005] E.C.R. I–3177; [2005] 3 C.M.L.R. 5; [2006] C.E.C. 16. 7–32
Commission of the European Communities v Ireland (C–13/00) [2002] E.C.R. I–2943; [2002] 2 C.M.L.R. 10; [2002] E.C.D.R. 30 .... 15–05, 15–09
Commission of the European Communities v Italy. *See* Freedom of Establishment, Re (168/85)
Commission of the European Communities v Italy (225/85). *See* Employees of the Consiglio Nazionale delle Ricerche, Re (225/85)
Commission of the European Communities v Italy (3/88) [1989] E.C.R. 4035; [1991] 2 C.M.L.R. 115 11–70
Commission of the European Communities v Italy (C–58/90) [1991] E.C.R. I–4193 . . 11–60
Commission of the European Communities v Italy (C–424/98) [2000] E.C.R. I–4001 . 8–15, 8–16, 8–18, 8-48, 10–62, 10–73, 10–74
Commission of the European Communities v Italy (C–279/00) [2002] E.C.R. I-1425; [2003] 2 C.M.L.R. 20 ECJ 11-92
Commission of the European Communities v Luxembourg (C–111/91) [1993] E.C.R. I–817; [1994] 2 C.M.L.R. 781 11–43
Commission of the European Communities v Luxembourg (C–118/92) [1994] E.C.R. I–1891 18–73

Table of European Cases

Commission of the European Communities v Luxembourg (C–299/01) [2002] E.C.R.
I–5899 11–43
Commission of the European Communities v Luxembourg (C–445/03) [2004] E.C.R.
I–10191; [2005] 1 C.M.L.R. 22; [2005] C.E.C. 529.................... 7–65, 7–67
Commission of the European Communities v Luxembourg (C–319/06) [2009] All E.R.
(EC) 1049; [2008] E.C.R. I–4323; [2009] I.R.L.R. 388 7–66
Commission of the European Communities v Netherlands (C–68/89) [1991] E.C.R.
I–2637; [1993] 2 C.M.L.R. 389 10–20
Commission of the European Communities v Netherlands (C–50/06) [2007] E.C.R.
I–4383; [2007] 3 C.M.L.R. 8; [2008] C.E.C. 98 .... 13–18, 13–23
Commission of the European Communities v Netherlands (C–398/06) Unreported April
10, 2008 10–62
Commission of the European Communities v Spain (C-157/03) [2005] E.C.R. I-2911;
[2005] 2 C.M.L.R. 27 ECJ 13-15
Corsten (C–58/98) [2000] ECR I–7919 7–50
Costa v Ente Nazionale per l'Energia Elettrica (ENEL) (6/64) [1964] E.C.R. 585; [1964]
C.M.L.R. 425 .... 2–32, 2–33
Council of Ministers of the European Communities v European Parliament (C–295/90)
[1992] E.C.R. I–5299 4–05
Council of the European Union v Hautala (C–353/99 P) [2002] 1 W.L.R. 1930; [2001]
E.C.R. I–9565; [2002] 1 C.M.L.R. 15; [2002] C.E.C. 127 3–06
Cowan v Trésor Public (186/87) [1989] E.C.R. 195; [1990] 2 C.M.L.R. 613 .... 4–12, 11–91,
13–09
Criminal Proceedings against Arcaro (C–168/95) [1997] All E.R. (EC) 82; [1996] E.C.R.
I–4705; [1997] 1 C.M.L.R. 179; [1998] Env. L.R. 39 2–57
Criminal Proceedings against Bickel (C–274/96) [1998] E.C.R. I–7637; [1999] 1 C.M.L.R.
348; [1999] C.E.C. 119 ECJ............ 4–12, 4–61, 7–74, 11–07, 11–10, 11–21, 11–22
Criminal Proceedings against Calfa (C–348/96) [1999] All E.R. (EC) 850; [1999] E.C.R.
I–11; [1999] 2 C.M.L.R. 1138; [1999] C.E.C. 477; [1999] I.N.L.R. 333; (1999) 96(19)
L.S.G. 30 .... 6–27, 13–12, 13–24
Criminal Proceedings against Gervais (C–17/94) [1995] E.C.R. I–4353.......... 7–52
Criminal Proceedings against Neno. See Nino, Re (C–54/88, C–91/88 & C–14/89)
Criminal Proceedings against Placanica (C–338/04) [2007] All E.R. (EC) 827; [2007]
E.C.R. I–1891; [2007] 2 C.M.L.R. 25................................. 7–50
Crispoltoni v Fattoria Autonoma Tabacchi (C–133/93) [1994] E.C.R. I–4863....... 2–62
Customs and Excise Commissioners v Schindler (C–275/92) [1994] Q.B. 610; [1994] 3
W.L.R. 103; [1994] 2 All E.R. 193; [1994] E.C.R. I–1039; [1995] 1 C.M.L.R. 4 .. 7–50
D v Council of the European Union (C–122/99 P) [2001] E.C.R. I–4319; [2003] 3
C.M.L.R. 9; [2001] Emp. L.R. 956 9–41
D v United Kingdom (30240/96) (1997) 24 E.H.R.R. 423; 2 B.H.R.C. 273; (1998) 42
B.M.L.R. 149 ECHR.. 3–08
Da Silva v Netherlands (50435/99) [2006] 1 F.C.R. 229; (2007) 44 E.H.R.R. 34 ECHR 9–14
Da Veiga v Staatssecretaris van Justitie (9/88) [1989] E.C.R. 2989; [1991] 1 C.M.L.R.
217... 18–41
De Cuyper v Office National de l'Emploi (ONEM) (C–406/04) [2006] All E.R. (EC) 947;
[2006] E.C.R. I–6947; [2006] 3 C.M.L.R. 44; [2006] C.E.C. 937; [2007] I.C.R. 317 4–30
De Groot v Staatssecretaris van Financien (C–385/00) [2004] S.T.C. 1346; [2002] E.C.R.
I–11819; [2004] 3 C.M.L.R. 21; [2004] B.T.C. 437; 5 I.T.L. Rep. 711; [2003] S.T.I.
172... 6–68
Demirel v Stadt Schwabisch Gmund (12/86) [1987] E.C.R. 3719; [1989] 1 C.M.L.R. 421
ECJ 15–03, 15–04, 15–05, 15–16, 15–18, 15–19, 15–28, 18–02,
18–03, 19–04, 19–09, 20–01, 20–02
Demirkan v Germany (C–221/11) Unreported.............................. 19–31
Denkavit Internationaal BV v Ministre de l'Economie, des Finances et de l'Industrie
(C–170/05) [2007] S.T.C. 452; [2006] E.C.R. I–11949; [2007] 1 C.M.L.R. 40; [2007]
C.E.C. 172; [2007] Pens. L.R. 1; [2008] B.T.C. 418; 9 I.T.L. Rep. 560; [2007] S.T.I.
109... 7–30
Dereci v v Bundesministerium für Inneres (C–256/11) [2012] All E.R. (EC) 373; [2012] 1
C.M.L.R. 45 .... 1–25, 4–43, 5–15, 5–16, 5–17, 5–18, 9–10, 9–16, 9–82, 24–13
Derin v Landkreis Darmstadt-Dieburg (C–325/05) [2007] E.C.R. I–6495; [2007] 3
C.M.L.R. 41; [2007] I.C.R. 1706 .... 20–20, 20–28, 20–34, 20–51, 21–07

TABLE OF EUROPEAN CASES

Deutscher Handballbund eV v Kolpak (C–438/00) [2003] E.C.R. I–4135; [2004] 2
C.M.L.R. 38 .... 14–52, 14–62, 16–13, 16–15, 18–75
D'Hoop v Office National de l'Emploi (C–224/98) [2003] All E.R. (EC) 527; [2002]
    E.C.R. I–6191; [2002] 3 C.M.L.R. 12; [2002] C.E.C. 642; [2004] I.C.R. 137 ECJ .   4–15,
                             4–60, 4–61, 4–62, 4–63, 4–65, 4–76, 5–20, 11–57, 11–99
Di Leo v Land Berlin (C–308/89) [1990] E.C.R. I–4185 .... 8–38, 9–03
Diatta v Land Berlin (267/83) [1985] E.C.R. 567; [1986] 2 C.M.L.R. 164 ECJ . . . 9–05, 9–33,
                                                            9–34, 9–62
Dodl v Tiroler Gebietskrankenkasse (C–543/03) [2005] E.C.R. I–5049; [2005] 3
    C.M.L.R. 41 6–07
Dogan v Sicherheitsdirektion für das Bundesland Vorarlberg (C–383/03) [2005] E.C.R.
    I–6237; [2005] 3 C.M.L.R. 45 .... 18–05, 18–53, 18–62
Dona v Mantero (13/76) [1976] E.C.R. 1333; [1976] 2 C.M.L.R. 578 .... 6–09 11–91
Dorr v Sicherheitsdirektion für das Bundesland Kärnten (C–136/03) [2005] E.C.R.
    I–4759; [2005] 3 C.M.L.R. 11 ECJ 21–11
Dorsch Consult Ingenieurgesellschaft mbH v Bundesbaugesellschaft Berlin mbH (C–54/
    96) [1998] All E.R. (EC) 262; [1997] E.C.R. I–4961; [1998] 2 C.M.L.R. 237.....   23–11
Dory v Germany (C–186/01) [2004] All E.R. (EC) 884; [2003] E.C.R. I–2479; [2003] 2
    C.M.L.R. 26 13–30
Echouikh v Secretaire d'état aux anciens combatants (C–336/05) [2006] E.C.R I-5223   14–64
Eker (C–386/95) [1997] E.C.R. I–2697 18–44
Elgafaji v Staatssecretaris van Justitie (C–465/07) [2009] 1 W.L.R. 2100; [2009] All E.R.
    (EC) 651; [2009] E.C.R. I–921; [2009] 2 C.M.L.R. 45; [2009] C.E.C. 785; [2009]
    Imm. A.R. 477; [2009] I.N.L.R. 235 3–24
Elsen v Bundesversicherungsanstalt für Angestellte (C–135/99) [2000] E.C.R. I–10409;
    [2002] 3 C.M.L.R. 32 ECJ 4–21, 4–34, 11–10
El-Yassini v Secretary of State for the Home Department (C–416/96) [1999] All E.R.
    (EC) 193; [1999] E.C.R. I–1209; [1999] 2 C.M.L.R. 32; [1999] I.N.L.R. 131; (1999)
    96(31) L.S.G. 43 ECJ 14–53, 14–61, 14–62, 14–63, 14–72, 15–01, 16–18, 23-12
Employees of the Consiglio Nazionale delle Ricerche, Re (225/85) [1988] E.C.R. 2271;
    [1987] E.C.R. 2625; [1988] 3 C.M.L.R. 635 6–69
Er v Wetteraukreis (C–453/07) [2008] E.C.R. I–7299; [2009] 1 C.M.L.R. 6; [2009] I.C.R.
    326; [2009] Imm. A.R. 246; [2009] I.N.L.R. 501 ECJ..................... 20–45
Ergat v Stadt Ulm (C–329/97) [2000] E.C.R. I–1487 ..... 20–09, 20–11, 20–29, 20–30, 20–31
Eroglu v Land Baden-Württemberg (C–355/93) [1994] E.C.R. I–5113 . . 20–09, 20–21, 20–42,
                                                             20–45
Ertanir v Land Hessen (C–98/96) [1997] E.C.R. I–5179 . . . 18–16, 18–27, 18–39, 18–48, 18–64
European Commission v Germany (C–546/07) [2010] I-438; [2010] 2 C.M.L.R. 36
    ECJ 7–59, 11–92
European Commission v Netherlands (C–92/07) [2010] E.C.R. I-3683 . . . 2–17, 17–13, 17–14,
                                                      18–70, 19–32, 19–33, 25–04
European Commission v Spain (C–211/08) [2011] All E.R. (EC) 285; [2010] 3 C.M.L.R.
    48; [2011] C.E.C. 645 12–15
European Commission v Spain (C–400/08) [2011] 2 C.M.L.R. 50 .... 7–32, 11–59
European Parliament v Council (C–377/98). See Netherlands v European Parliament
    (C–377/98)
European Parliament v Council of Ministers of the European Communities (13/83)
    [1987] E.C.R. 1513; [1985] E.C.R. 1513; [1986] 1 C.M.L.R. 138 2–19
Eyup v Landesgeschaftsstelle des Arbeitsmarktservice Vorarlberg (C–65/98) [2000]
    E.C.R. I–4747; [2000] 3 C.M.L.R. 1049 20–37
Finalarte Sociedade de Construcao Civil Lda v Urlaubs- und Lohnausgleichskasse der
    Bauwirtschaft (C–49/98) [2001] E.C.R. I–7831; [2003] 2 C.M.L.R. 11 7–67
Finanzamt Köln-Altstadt v Schumacker (C–279/93) [1996] Q.B. 28; [1995] 3 W.L.R. 498;
    [1995] All E.R. (E.C.) 319; [1995] S.T.C. 306; [1995] E.C.R. I–225; [1996] 2
    C.M.L.R. 450 11–49
Försakringskassan v Bergström (C–257/10) Unreported December 15, 2011......... 14–24
Forster v Hoofddirectie van de Informatie Beheer Groep (C–158/07) [2009] All E.R.
    (EC) 399; [2008] E.C.R. I–8507; [2009] 1 C.M.L.R. 32; [2009] C.E.C. 473; [2009]
    P.T.S.R. (C.S.) 23 4–30
Foster v British Gas Plc (C–188/89) [1991] 1 Q.B. 405; [1991] 2 W.L.R. 258; [1990] 3 All
    E.R. 897; [1990] E.C.R. I–3313; [1990] 2 C.M.L.R. 833; [1991] I.C.R. 84; [1990]
    I.R.L.R. 353 2–53

Table of European Cases

Francovich v Italy (C–6/90) [1991] E.C.R. I–5357; [1993] 2 C.M.L.R. 66; [1995] I.C.R. 722; [1992] I.R.L.R. 84 ECJ 2–51, 2–52
Freedom of Establishment, Re (168/85) [1986] E.C.R. 2945; [1988] 1 C.M.L.R. 580 . . 2–44
Fritz Werner Industrie Ausrustungen GmbH v Germany (C–70/94) [1995] E.C.R. I–3189 13–31
Gattoussi v Stadt Rüsselsheim (C–978/05) Unreported. 14–63
GBC Echternach v Minister van Onderwijs en Wetenschappen (389/87) [1989] E.C.R. 723; [1990] 2 C.M.L.R. 305. .... 8–38, 8–40
Gebhard v Consiglio dell'Ordine degli Avvocati e Procuratori di Milano (C–55/94) [1996] All E.R. (EC) 189; [1995] E.C.R. I–4165; [1996] 1 C.M.L.R. 603; [1996] C.E.C. 175 ECJ 7–05, 7–14, 7–17, 7–18, 7–37, 7–38, 7–41, 7–56, 11–68, 13–07
Gebroeders Beentjes BV v Netherlands (31/87) [1988] E.C.R. 4635; [1990] 1 C.M.L.R. 287... 11–67
Genc v Land Berlin (C–14/09) [2010] 2 C.M.L.R. 44; [2010] I.C.R. 1108 . .6–20, 18–17, 18–68
Germany v Commission of the European Communities (278/84) [1987] E.C.R. 1; [1988] 1 C.M.L.R. 632 ECJ 16–28
Germany v Sagulo (8/77) [1977] E.C.R. 1495; [1977] 2 C.M.L.R. 585 .... .2–60, 10–02, 10–26
Giagounidis v Reutlingen (C–376/89) [1991] E.C.R. I–1069; [1993] 1 C.M.L.R. 537 . . 10–46
Goodwin v United Kingdom (28957/95) [2002] I.R.L.R. 664; [2002] 2 F.L.R. 487; [2002] 2 F.C.R. 577; (2002) 35 E.H.R.R. 18; 13 B.H.R.C. 120; (2002) 67 B.M.L.R. 199; [2002] Fam. Law 738; (2002) 152 N.L.J. 1171 ECHR 9–44
Gottwald v Bezirkshauptmannschaft Bregenz (C–103/08) [2009] E.C.R. I–9117; [2010] 1 C.M.L.R. 25 ECJ 4–30, 4–32
Graf and Engel v Landratsamt Waldshut (C–506/10) Unreported October 6, 2011 . . . 14–24
Granaria BV v Council and Commission (116/76). *See* Bela-Muhle Josef Bergmann KG v Grows Farm GmbH & Co KG (114/76)
Gravier v Liège (293/83) [1985] E.C.R. 593; [1985] 3 C.M.L.R. 1 .... .8–05, 8–32, 8-45
Greece v Commission of the European Communities (30/88) [1989] E.C.R. 449 15–20
Grunkin v Grunkin-Paul (C–353/06) [2008] E.C.R. I–7639; [2009] 1 C.M.L.R. 10; [2009] C.E.C. 263 ECJ 4–30, 4–31, 11–104
Grzelczyk v Centre Public d'Aide Sociale d'Ottignies Louvain la Neuve (C–184/99) [2003] All E.R. (EC) 385; [2001] E.C.R. I–6193; [2002] 1 C.M.L.R. 19; [2002] I.C.R. 566 ECJ 2–61, 4–15, 4–24, 4–46, 4–48, 4–49, 4–50, 4–51, 4–61, 4–70, 8–08, 8–09, 8–11, 11–102, 13–14, 13–63, 13–68, 18–19
Gülbahce v Freie und Hansestadt Hamburg (C–268/11) Unreported.............. 18–75
Gunaydin v Freistaat Bayern (C–36/96) [1997] E.C.R. I–5143; [1998] 1 C.M.L.R. 871 ECJ 6–35, 16–21, 18–11, 18–16, 18–28, 18–29, 18–64, 18–65
Gurol v Bezirksregierung Köln (C–374/03) [2005] E.C.R. I–6199; [2005] 3 C.M.L.R. 44 18–05
Haim v Kassenzahnarztliche Vereinigung Nordrhein (C–424/97) [2000] E.C.R. I–5123; [2002] 1 C.M.L.R. 11 ECJ 7–52
Halliburton Services BV v Staatssecretaris van Financien (C–1/93) [1994] E.C.R. I–1137; [1994] 3 C.M.L.R. 377 11–64
Harrow LBC v Ibrahim (C–310/08) [2010] P.T.S.R. 1913; [2010] E.C.R. 1065; [2010] 2 C.M.L.R. 51; [2011] C.E.C. 127; [2010] I.C.R. 1118; [2010] Imm. A.R. 474; [2010] H.L.R. 31; [2010] E.L.R. 261 ECJ........... 6–68, 8–40, 9–79, 10–09, 10–113, 24-28
Hartmann v Freistaat Bayern (C–212/05) [2008] All E.R. (EC) 1166; [2007] E.C.R. I–6303; [2008] 3 C.M.L.R. 38 .... 11–34, 11–55
Hoeckx v Openbaar Centrum voor Maatschappelijk Welzijn (249/83) [1985] E.C.R. 973; [1987] 3 C.M.L.R. 638 .... 6–62, 6–63, 11–43
Hoekstra v Netherlands. *See* Unger v Bestuur der Bedrijfsvereniging voor Detailhandel en Ambachten (75/63)
Idryma Koinonikon Asfaliseon (IKA) v Ioannidis (C–326/00) [2004] Q.B. 137; [2003] 3 W.L.R. 1540; [2003] All E.R. (EC) 548; [2003] E.C.R. I-1703; [2003] 1 C.M.L.R. 33; (2004) 75 B.M.L.R. 1 ECJ 12-24
Ilonka Sayn-Wittgenstein v Landeshauptmann von Wien (C–208/09) Unreported December 22, 2010 ECJ 4–30, 4–31
innoventif Ltd (C–453/04) [2006] E.C.R. I-4929... 7–24
Institut National d'Assurances Sociales pour Travailleurs Indépendants (INASTI) v Kemmler (C–53/95) [1996] E.C.R. I–703 .... 7–23, 7–55
International Transport Workers' Federation v Viking Line ABP (C–438/05) [2008] All E.R. (EC) 127; [2007] E.C.R. I–10779; [2008] 1 C.M.L.R. 51; [2008] C.E.C. 332; [2008] I.C.R. 741; [2008] I.R.L.R. 143 3–06

Table of European Cases

Internationale Handelsgesellschaft mbH v Einfuhr- und Vorratsstelle für Getreide und
 Futtermittel (11/70) [1970] E.C.R. 1125; [1972] C.M.L.R. 255 ....2–34, 3–17
Investrand BV v Staatssecretaris van Financien (C-435/05) [2008] S.T.C. 518; [2007]
 E.C.R. I–1315; [2009] B.V.C. 733; [2007] S.T.I. 340 ECJ 3-06
Inze v Austria (A/126) (1988) 10 E.H.R.R. 394 ECHR 10–116
Inzirillo v Caisse d'Allocations Familiales de l'Arrondissement de Lyon (63/76) [1976]
 E.C.R. 2057; [1978] 3 C.M.L.R. 596 11–46
Irish Farmers Association v Minister for Agriculture, Food and Forestry (Ireland)
 (C–22/94) [1997] E.C.R. I–1809; [1997] 2 C.M.L.R. 621................... 3–22
Italy v Watson and Belmann (118/75) [1976] E.C.R. 1185; [1976] 2 C.M.L.R. 552 ECJ 5–19,
6–36, 6–37, 10–01
ITC Innovative Technology Center GmbH v Bundesagentur für Arbeit (C–208/05)
 [2007] All E.R. (EC) 611; [2007] E.C.R. I–181; [2008] 1 C.M.L.R. 15......... 12–16
J Nold Kohlen- und Baustoffgrosshandlung v Commission of the European Commu-
 nities (4/73) [1975] E.C.R. 985; [1974] E.C.R. 491; [1974] 2 C.M.L.R. 338...... 3–18
Jany v Staatssecretaris van Justitie (C–268/99) [2003] All E.R. (EC) 193; [2001] E.C.R.
 I–8615; [2003] 2 C.M.L.R. 1; [2003] C.E.C. 561 ....6–27, 7–06, 7–07, 7–16, 15–14
Jia v Migrationsverket (C–1/05) [2007] Q.B. 545; [2007] 2 W.L.R. 1005; [2007] All E.R.
 (EC) 575; [2007] 1 C.M.L.R. 41; [2007] C.E.C. 349; [2008] 3 F.C.R. 491; [2007] Imm.
 A.R. 439; [2007] I.N.L.R. 336 ECJ 9–57, 9–58, 9–60, 10–100
Johnston v Chief Constable of the Royal Ulster Constabulary (222/84) [1987] Q.B. 129;
 [1986] 3 W.L.R. 1038; [1986] 3 All E.R. 135; [1986] E.C.R. 1651; [1986] 3 C.M.L.R.
 240; [1987] I.C.R. 83; [1986] I.R.L.R. 263; (1987) 84 L.S.G. 188; (1986) 130 S.J. 953 2–53
Kadiman v State of Bavaria (C–351/97) [1997] E.C.R. I–2133 ECJ ..20–09, 20–10, 20–11, 12,
20–14, 20–15, 20–18, 20–22, 20–23, 20–24, 20–25
KB v NHS Pensions Agency (C–117/01) [2004] All E.R. (EC) 1089; [2004] E.C.R. I–541;
 [2004] 1 C.M.L.R. 28; [2004] I.C.R. 781; [2004] I.R.L.R. 240; [2004] 1 F.L.R. 683;
 [2004] O.P.L.R. 145; [2004] Pens. L.R. 191; [2004] Fam. Law 249 .... 9–43, 9–44, 9–49
Kempf v Staatssecretaris van Justitie (139/85) [1986] E.C.R. 1741; [1987] 1 C.M.L.R.
 764...6–19, 6–26
Knoors v Secretary of State for Economic Affairs (115/78) [1979] E.C.R. 399; [1979] 2
 C.M.L.R. 357 11–62
Kocak v Landesversicherungsanstalt Oberfranken und Mittelfranken (C–102/98) [2000]
 E.C.R. I–1287; [2004] 2 C.M.L.R. 46................................. 17–29
Kol v Land Berlin (C–285/95) [1997] E.C.R. I–3069; [1997] 3 C.M.L.R. 1175 .. 18–21, 21–08
Kraus v Land Baden-Württemberg (C–19/92) [1993] E.C.R. I–1663 .....7–10, 11–58, 11–69
Kreil v Germany (C–285/98) [2000] E.C.R. I–69; [2002] 1 C.M.L.R. 36............ 13–30
Kurz v Land Baden-Württemberg (C–188/00) [2002] E.C.R. I–10691 .... 6–06, 6–35, 18–06,
18–15, 18–16, 18–38, 18–39, 18–40
Kus v Landeshauptstadt Wiesbaden (C–237/91) [1992] E.C.R. I–6781; [1993] 2
 C.M.L.R. 887 .... 15–22, 16–23, 17–34, 18–24, 18–26, 18–36, 20–22, 21–08
Lair v Universität Hannover (39/86) [1988] E.C.R. 3161; [1989] 3 C.M.L.R. 545 ECJ. 6–64,
11–42, 11–43, 11–103
Land Baden-Württemberg v Tsakouridis (C–145/09) [2011] 2 C.M.L.R. 11; [2011]
 C.E.C. 714; [2011] Imm. A.R. 276; [2011] I.N.L.R. 415.... 13–31, 13–32, 13–41, 13–42,
13–43, 13–46, 24–30
Land Nordrhein-Westfalen v Pokrzeptowicz-Meyer (C–162/00) [2002] E.C.R. I–1049;
 [2002] 2 C.M.L.R. 1 ECJ 16–06, 16–12, 16–17, 16–28
Land Nordrhein-Westfalen v Uecker (C–64/96) [1997] E.C.R. I–3171; [1997] 3 C.M.L.R.
 963; [1997] I.C.R. 1025; [1998] I.N.L.R. 300.................................. 5–12
Laval un Partneri Ltd v Svenska Byggnadsarbetareforbundet (C–341/05) [2008] All E.R.
 (EC) 166; [2007] E.C.R. I–11767; [2008] 2 C.M.L.R. 9; [2008] C.E.C. 438; [2008]
 I.R.L.R. 160 5–31
Lawrie-Blum v Land Baden-Württemberg (66/85) [1986] E.C.R. 2121; [1987] 3 C.M.L.R.
 389; [1987] I.C.R. 483 ....6–02, 6–08, 6–11, 6–31, 6–32, 6–33, 6–42, 6–73, 18–16
Leclere v Caisse Nationale des Prestations Familiales (C–43/99) [2001] E.C.R. I–4265;
 [2001] 2 C.M.L.R. 49... 6–65
Leichtenstein v Guatemala (1995) I.C.J. Reports p.4 5–02
Levin v Staatssecretaris van Justitie (53/81) [1982] E.C.R. 1035; [1982] 2 C.M.L.R. 454
 ECJ 6–02, 6–06, 6–09, 6–13, 6–17, 6–26, 6–28,
6–29, 6–33, 6–51
Liga Portuguesa de Futebol Profissional v Departamento de Jogos da Santa Casa da

Table of European Cases

Misericordia de Lisboa (C-42/07) [2009] E.C.R. I-7633; [2010] 1 C.M.L.R. 1; [2010] C.E.C. 399 7-50
Luisi v Ministero del Tesoro (286/82) [1984] E.C.R. 377; [1985] 3 C.M.L.R. 52 . . 7-38, 7-54, 7-71, 7-74
Malgoata Runevic-Vardyn (C-391/09) Unreported May 12, 2011 .... 4-30, 4-31
Marckx v Belgium (A/31) (1979-80) 2 E.H.R.R. 330 ECHR 9-13, 9-14
Marleasing SA v La Comercial Internacional de Alimentación SA (C-106/89) [1990] E.C.R. I-4135; [1993] B.C.C. 421; [1992] 1 C.M.L.R. 305 2-55
Marshall v Southampton and South West Hampshire AHA (152/84) [1986] Q.B. 401; [1986] 2 W.L.R. 780; [1986] 2 All E.R. 584; [1986] E.C.R. 723; [1986] 1 C.M.L.R. 688; [1986] I.C.R. 335; [1986] I.R.L.R. 140; (1986) 83 L.S.G. 1720; (1986) 130 S.J. 340 .... 2-50, 2-53
Matteucci v Communauté Française de Belgique (235/87) [1988] E.C.R. 5589; [1989] 1 C.M.L.R. 357 ECJ 11-43
Matthews v United Kingdom (24833/94) (1999) 28 E.H.R.R. 361; 5 B.H.R.C. 686 ECHR 3-15, 5-02
Maurissen v Court of Auditors of the European Communities (193/87) [1989] E.C.R. 1045 3-22
McB v E (C-400/10 PPU) [2011] Fam. 364; [2011] 3 W.L.R. 699; [2011] All E.R. (EC) 379; [2011] I.L.Pr. 24; [2011] 1 F.L.R. 518; [2011] 2 F.C.R. 382; [2011] Fam. Law 8 9-10
McCarthy (Shirley) v Secretary of State for the Home Department (C-434/09) [2011] All E.R. (EC) 729; [2011] 3 C.M.L.R. 10; [2011] Imm. A.R. 586; [2011] I.N.L.R. 450ECJ 4-43, 5-13, 5-14, 5-15, 5-17, 5-24, 5-25, 5-27, 9-16, 9-82, 24-19
ME v Secretary of State for the Home Department (C-493/10) Unreported December 21, 2011 3-12
Megner v Innungskrankenkasse Vorderpfalz (C-444/93) [1995] E.C.R. I-4741; [1996] C.E.C. 516; [1996] I.R.L.R. 236 6-19
Meints v Minister van Landbouw, Natuurbeheer en Visserij (C-57/96) [1997] E.C.R. I-6689; [1998] 1 C.M.L.R. 1159 .... 6-60, 11-43
Mesbah (C-179/98) [1999] E.C.R. I-7955 20-36
Metock v Minister for Justice, Equality and Law Reform (C-127/08) [2009] Q.B. 318; [2009] 2 W.L.R. 821; [2009] All E.R. (EC) 40; [2008] E.C.R. I-6241; [2008] 3 C.M.L.R. 39; [2009] C.E.C. 286; [2008] 3 F.C.R. 425; [2009] Imm. A.R. 113; [2009] I.N.L.R. 75 ECJ 9-01, 9-04, 9-07, 9-08, 9-19, 9-69, 10-17, 24-07, 24-08, 24-11, 24-14, 24-16
Micheletti v Delegacion del Gobierno en Cantabria (C-369/90) [1992] E.C.R. I-4239. 5-04
Minister voor Vreemdelingenzaken en Integratie v Eind (C-291/05) [2008] All E.R. (EC) 371; [2007] E.C.R. I-10719; [2008] 2 C.M.L.R. 1; [2008] C.E.C. 366; [2008] Imm. A.R. 422; [2008] I.N.L.R. 533 .... 8-21, 9-18, 9-19
Minister voor Vreemdelingenzaken en Integratie v Sahin (C-242/06) [2009] E.C.R. I-8465; [2010] 1 C.M.L.R. 8 .... 18-65, 18-79, 18-80, 18-82
Ministère Public v Even and Office National des Pensions pour Travailleurs Salariés (207/78) [1979] E.C.R. 2019; [1980] 2 C.M.L.R. 71 11-41
Ministère Public v Mutsch (137/84) [1985] E.C.R. 2681; [1986] 1 C.M.L.R. 648 ..... 11-10, 11-41, 11-43, 11-45
Ministerio Fiscal v Brea (C-330/90) [1992] E.C.R. I-323; [1992] 2 C.M.L.R. 397 11-90
Ministerul Administratiei si Internelor - Directia Generala de Pasapoarte Bucuresti v Jipa (C-33/07) [2008] E.C.R. I-5157; [2008] 3 C.M.L.R. 23 13-04
Ministre de l'Intérieur v Oteiza Olazabal (C-100/01) [2002] E.C.R. I-10981; [2005] 1 C.M.L.R. 49; (2003) 147 S.J.L.B. 178 .... 13-16, 13-20, 13-27, 13-30
Morson v Netherlands (35/82) [1982] E.C.R. 3723; [1983] 2 C.M.L.R. 221 5-11
Mouvement contre le Racisme, l'Antisemitisme et la Xenophobie ASBL (MRAX) v Belgium (C-459/99) [2003] 1 W.L.R. 1073; [2002] E.C.R. I-6591; [2002] 3 C.M.L.R. 25 ECJ 9-04, 9-05, 9-09, 9-17, 9-27, 10-16, 10-25, 10-39, 10-40, 13-14
Nazli v Stadt Nürnburg (C-340/97) [2000] E.C.R. I-957 ...... 13-28, 18-15, 18-52, 18-63, 18-66, 18-73, 21-02, 21-03, 21-04, 21-05, 21-08, 21-10
Nerkowska v Zaklad Ubezpieczen Spolecznych Oddzial w Koszalinie (C-499/06) [2008] All E.R. (EC) 885; [2008] E.C.R. I-3993; [2008] 3 C.M.L.R. 8 .... 4-30, 4-32
Netherlands v European Parliament (C-377/98) [2002] All E.R. (EC) 97; [2001] E.C.R. I-7079; [2001] 3 C.M.L.R. 49; [2002] F.S.R. 36; (2002) 68 B.M.L.R. 1 3-06
Netherlands v Reed (59/85) [1986] E.C.R. 1283; [1987] 2 C.M.L.R. 448... 9-31, 9-40, 11-43

Table of European Cases

Neukirchinger v Bezirkshauptmannschaft Grieskirchen (C–382/08) [2011] 2 C.M.L.R. 33; [2011] C.E.C. 1060 ECJ. 11–20
Ninni-Orasche v Bundesminister für Wissenschaft, Verkehr und Kunst (C–413/01) [2004] All E.R. (EC) 765; [2003] E.C.R. I–13187; [2004] 1 C.M.L.R. 19 ..... 6–25, 6–29
Nino, Re (C–54/88, C–91/88 & C–14/89) [1990] E.C.R. I–3537; [1992] 1 C.M.L.R. 83   7–08
NS v Secretary of State for the Home Department (C–411/10) pending. 3–12
NV Algemene Transport- en Expeditie Onderneming van Gend en Loos v Nederlandse Administratie der Belastingen (26/62) [1963] E.C.R. 1; [1963] C.M.L.R. 105 .... 2–30, 2–37, 2–41, 15–24, 15–25
Office national de l'Emploi v Deak (94/84) [1985] E.C.R. 1873 .... 11–46, 11–47
Office National de l'Emploi v Kziber (C–18/90) [1991] E.C.R. I–199............. 14–64
Office National de l'Emploi v Ioannidis (C–258/04) [2006] All E.R. (EC) 926; [2005] E.C.R. I–8275; [2005] 3 C.M.L.R. 47; [2006] C.E.C. 960 .... 11–37, 11–54, 12–24
O'Flynn v Adjudication Officer (C–237/94) [1996] All E.R. (EC) 541; [1996] E.C.R. I–2617; [1996] 3 C.M.L.R. 103; [1998] I.C.R. 608; (1997) 33 B.M.L.R. 54. . 11–20, 11–52
Oguz v Secretary of State for the Home Department (C–186/10) [2012] 1 W.L.R. 709; [2012] I.C.R. 335; [2011] Imm. A.R. 843 .... 19–26, 25-13, 25–14, 25–15
Olsson v Sweden (A/250) (1994) 17 E.H.R.R. 134......................... 10–68
Omega Spielhallen- und Automatenaufstellungs GmbH v Bundesstadt Bonn (C–36/02) [2004] E.C.R. I–9609; [2005] 1 C.M.L.R. 5; [2005] C.E.C. 391 3–22
Ordre des Advocats au Barreau de Paris (Paris Bar Council) v Rechtsanwalt Onno Klopp (107/83) [1985] Q.B. 711; [1985] 2 W.L.R. 1058; [1984] E.C.R. 2971; [1985] 1 C.M.L.R. 99; (1985) 82 L.S.G. 2088; (1985) 129 S.J. 347 ECJ 7–23
Orfanopoulos v Land Baden-Württemberg (C–482/01) [2004] E.C.R. I–5257; [2005] 1 C.M.L.R. 18 ECJ 13–13, 13–23, 13–25, 13–27
Oulane v Minister voor Vreemdelingenzaken en Integratie (C–215/03) [2005] Q.B. 1055; [2005] 3 W.L.R. 543; [2005] E.C.R. I–1215......................... 10–100
P v S and Cornwall CC (C–13/94) [1996] All E.R. (EC) 397; [1996] E.C.R. I–2143; [1996] 2 C.M.L.R. 247; [1996] C.E.C. 574; [1996] I.C.R. 795; [1996] I.R.L.R. 347; [1996] 2 F.L.R. 347; [1997] 2 F.C.R. 180; [1996] Fam. Law 609 9–42
Pavlov v Ausschuss der Rechtsanwaltskammer Wien, (C–101/10) Unreported July 7, 2010 ECJ 16–20
Payir v Secretary of State for the Home Department (C–294/06) [2008] 1 W.L.R. 1910; [2009] All E.R. (EC) 964; [2008] E.C.R. I–203; [2008] 2 C.M.L.R. 14; [2008] I.C.R. 1005; [2008] Imm. A.R. 330; [2008] I.N.L.R. 207 ECJ. . 6–21, 6–38, 18–12, 18–18, 18–19, 18–30, 25–05
Pehlivan v Staatssecretaris van Justitie, (C–484/07) Unreported June 16, 2011 . 17–12, 17–36, 20–08, 20–18, 20–19
Petersen v Arbeitsmarktservice Niederösterreich (C–228/07) [2008] E.C.R. I–6989; [2009] 1 C.M.L.R. 2; [2009] C.E.C. 214 ECJ 12–11
PI v Oberburgermeisterin der Stadt Remscheid (C–348/09) March 27, 2011 .... 13-32, 13-37
Pla v Andorra (69498/01) [2004] 2 F.C.R. 630; (2006) 42 E.H.R.R. 25; 18 B.H.R.C. 120 ECHR 10–116
PM v United Kingdom (6638/03) [2005] S.T.C. 1566; [2005] 3 F.C.R. 101; (2006) 42 E.H.R.R. 45; 18 B.H.R.C. 668; 7 I.T.L. Rep. 970 ECHR 10–116
Poirrez v Caf de la Seine Saint-Denis (C–206/91) [1992] E.C.R. I–6685 14–72
Poland v European Parliament (C–460/05) Unreported July 18, 2007 11–86
Portugaia Construcoes Lda, Re (C–164/99) [2002] E.C.R. I–787; [2003] 2 C.M.L.R. 35   7–67
Prais v Council of Ministers of the European Communities (130/75) [1976] E.C.R. 1589; [1976] 2 C.M.L.R. 708; [1977] I.C.R. 284........................... 3–18
Proceedings Brought by Penarroja Fa (C–372/09) [2011] 2 C.M.L.R. 49; [2012] C.E.C. 3.   11–84
Pusa v Osuuspankkien Keskinainen Vakuutusyhtio (C–224/02) [2004] All E.R. (EC) 797; [2004] S.T.C. 1066; [2004] E.C.R. I–5763; [2004] 2 C.M.L.R. 23; [2004] S.T.I. 1167... 4–21, 11–100
R&V Haegeman Sprl v Belgium (181/73) [1974] E.C.R. 449; [1975] 1 C.M.L.R. 515. . 15–17, 15–19
R. (on the application of Barkoci) v Secretary of State for the Home Department (C–257/99) [2001] All E.R. (EC) 903; [2001] E.C.R. I–6557; [2001] 3 C.M.L.R. 48; [2002] I.N.L.R. 152 .... 14–41, 15–33, 16–10
R. (on the application of Bidar) v Ealing LBC (C–209/03) [2005] Q.B. 812; [2005] 2 W.L.R. 1078; [2005] All E.R. (EC) 687; [2005] E.C.R. I–2119; [2005] 2 C.M.L.R. 3; [2005] C.E.C. 607; [2005] E.L.R. 404 ECJ 4–30, 8–35, 11–43, 11-103

[xxxi]

Table of European Cases

R. (on the application of Gloszczuk) v Secretary of State for the Home Department
 (C–63/99) [2002] All E.R. (EC) 353; [2001] E.C.R. I–6369; [2001] 3 C.M.L.R. 46;
 [2001] C.E.C. 358; [2002] I.N.L.R. 357.................................. 15–08
R. (on the application of Kondova) v Secretary of State for the Home Department
 (C–235/99) [2001] E.C.R. I–6427; [2001] 3 C.M.L.R. 47.............. 14–41, 15–06
R. v Bouchereau (Pierre Roger) (30/77) [1978] Q.B. 732; [1978] 2 W.L.R. 250; [1981] 2
 All E.R. 924; [1977] E.C.R. 1999; (1978) 66 Cr. App. R. 202; [1977] 2 C.M.L.R. 800;
 (1978) 122 S.J. 79 .... 13–18, 13–21
R. v HM Treasury Ex p. Daily Mail (81/87) [1989] Q.B. 446; [1989] 2 W.L.R. 908; [1989]
 1 All E.R. 328; [1988] S.T.C. 787; [1988] E.C.R. 5483; [1989] B.C.L.C. 206; [1988] 3
 C.M.L.R. 713; (1989) 133 S.J. 693 ECJ.................. 7–23, 7–25, 7–27, 11–61
R. v Immigration Appeal Tribunal Ex p. Antonissen (C–292/89) [1991] E.C.R. I–745;
 [1991] 2 C.M.L.R. 373; (1991) 135 S.J. 6 . . . 6–51, 6–52, 6–53, 7–19, 7–20, 10–57, 18–58,
 18–60
R. v Immigration Appeal Tribunal Ex p. Secretary of State for the Home Department
 (C–370/90) [1992] 3 All E.R. 798; [1992] E.C.R. I–4265; [1992] 3 C.M.L.R. 358;
 [1993] 1 F.L.R. 798; [1992] Imm. A.R. 565; [1993] Fam. Law 294 .... 5–19, 5–20,
 9–01, 9–50, 10–02, 24–21, 24–22
R. v Ministry of Agriculture, Fisheries and Food Ex p. Agegate Ltd (3/87) [1990] 2 Q.B.
 151; [1990] 3 W.L.R. 226; [1991] 1 All E.R. 6; [1989] E.C.R. 4459; [1990] 1 C.M.L.R.
 366.. 6–14
R. v Pieck (157/79) [1981] Q.B. 571; [1981] 2 W.L.R. 960; [1981] 3 All E.R. 46; [1980]
 E.C.R. 2171; [1981] E.C.R. 2171; [1980] 3 C.M.L.R. 220; (1981) 125 S.J. 342 ... 10–02,
 10–25, 10–28, 10–38
R. v Secretary of State for the Home Department Ex p. Cheung Chiu Hung (C–256/99)
 Unreported July 12, 2001 ECJ 4–37, 5–09
R. v Secretary of State for the Home Department Ex p. Gallagher (C–175/94) [1995]
 E.C.R. I–4253; [1996] 1 C.M.L.R. 557; [1996] C.E.C. 667 13–55
R. v Secretary of State for the Home Department Ex p. Kaur (Manjit) (C–192/99) [2001]
 All E.R. (EC) 250; [2001] E.C.R. I–1237; [2001] 2 C.M.L.R. 24; [2001] I.N.L.R.
 507.. 4–37, 5–10, 24–04
R. v Secretary of State for the Home Department Ex p. Savas (C–37/98) [2000] 1 W.L.R.
 1828; [2000] All E.R. (EC) 627; [2000] E.C.R. I–2927; [2000] 3 C.M.L.R. 729; [2000]
 C.E.C. 624; [2000] I.N.L.R. 398 .... 15–28, 17–11, 19–15, 19–16, 19–19,
 19–22, 19–25, 21–14, 25–09
R. v Secretary of State for the Home Department Ex p. Shingara (C–65/95) [1997] All
 E.R. (EC) 577; [1997] E.C.R. I–3343; [1997] 3 C.M.L.R. 703............... 13–58
R. v Secretary of State for Transport Ex p. Factortame Ltd (C–221/89) [1992] Q.B. 680;
 [1992] 3 W.L.R. 288; [1991] 3 All E.R. 769; [1991] 2 Lloyd's Rep. 648; [1991] E.C.R.
 I–3905; [1991] 3 C.M.L.R. 589; (1991) 141 N.L.J. 1107................7–12, 11–65
Raccanelli v Max-Planck-Gesellschaft zur Forderung der Wissenschaften eV (C–94/07)
 [2008] E.C.R. I–5939; [2008] 3 C.M.L.R. 25....................... 6–08, 6–35
Rahman v Secretary of State for the Home Department (C–83/11) Unreported ECJ . 9–29,
 9–69, 10–103, 10–106, 24-16
Ramrath v Ministre de la Justice (C–106/91) [1992] E.C.R. I–3351; [1995] 2 C.M.L.R.
 187; [1992] 3 C.M.L.R. 173.. 7–17
Raulin v Minister van Onderwijs en Wetenschappen (C–357/89) [1992] E.C.R. I–1027;
 [1994] 1 C.M.L.R. 227 ECJ 4–62, 6–23, 6–24, 6–64, 8–34, 18–16
Razanatsimba, Re (65/77) [1977] E.C.R. 2229; [1978] 1 C.M.L.R. 246............ 14–72
Reed v Netherlands. See Netherlands v Reed (59/85)
Reina v Landeskreditbank Baden-Württemberg (65/81) [1982] E.C.R. 33; [1982] 1
 C.M.L.R. 744 ECJ..11–41, 11–43, 11–45
Reiseburo Broede v Sandker (C–3/95) [1996] E.C.R. I–6511; [1997] 1 C.M.L.R. 224. . 7–52
Reyners v Belgium (2/74) [1974] E.C.R. 631; [1974] 2 C.M.L.R. 305 .... 11–73, 11–76
Rinner-Kuhn v FWW Spezial-Gebäudereinigung GmbH & Co KG (171/88) [1989]
 E.C.R. 2743; [1993] 2 C.M.L.R. 932; [1989] I.R.L.R. 493 .... 6–19, 12–10
Ritter-Coulais v Finanzamt Germersheim (C–152/03) [2006] All E.R. (EC) 613; [2006]
 S.T.C. 1111; [2006] E.C.R. I–1711; [2006] 2 C.M.L.R. 31; [2006] C.E.C. 531; [2006]
 S.T.I. 529 .... 6.68
Rottmann v Freistaat Bayern (C–135/08) [2010] Q.B. 761; [2010] 3 W.L.R. 1166; [2010]
 All E.R. (EC) 635; [2010] 3 C.M.L.R. 2; [2011] C.E.C. 35................4–39, 4–40
Roux v Belgium (C–363/89) [1991] E.C.R. I–273; [1993] 1 C.M.L.R. 3 13–14

[xxxii]

TABLE OF EUROPEAN CASES

Rush Portuguesa Lda v Office National d'Immigration (C–113/89) [1990] E.C.R. I–1417;
    [1991] 2 C.M.L.R. 818 ECJ 5–31, 7–62, 7–63, 7–64, 7–65, 7–66
Rutili v Ministre de l'Intérieur (36/75) [1975] E.C.R. 1219; [1976] 1 C.M.L.R. 140
    ECJ 3–18, 13–04, 13–10, 13–49, 13–50
Ruzius-Wilbrink v Bestuur van de Bedrijfsvereniging voor Overheidsdiensten (102/88)
    [1989] E.C.R. 4311; [1991] 2 C.M.L.R. 202. 6–19
S v Cornwall CC. *See* P v S and Cornwall CC (C–13/94)
Sager v Dennemeyer & Co Ltd (C–76/90) [1991] E.C.R. I–4221; [1993] 3 C.M.L.R. 639
    ECJ 7–50, 11–93
Sala (Martinez) v Freistaat Bayern (C–85/96) [1998] ECR I–2691 ECJ 4–18, 4–19, 4–20,
                4–26, 4–28, 4–30, 4–76, 6–07, 6–54, 6–57, 11–07, 11–11, 11–32, 11–43
Saldanha v Hiross Holding AG (C–122/96) [1998] All E.R. (EC) 238; [1997] E.C.R.
    I–5325; [1997] I.L.Pr. 766. 5–22
Schilling v Finanzamt Nürnberg Süd (C–209/01) [2005] S.T.C. 1756; [2003] E.C.R.
    I–13389; [2003] S.T.I. 2121 6–68
Schmid v Belgium (C–310/91) [1993] E.C.R. I–3011; [1995] 2 C.M.L.R. 803 11–43
Scholz v Opera Universitaria di Cagliari (C–419/92) [1994] E.C.R. I–505; [1994] 1
    C.M.L.R. 873 11–17
Schöning-Kougebetopoulou v Freie und Hansestadt Hamburg (C–15/96) [1998] All E.R.
    (E.C.) 97; [1998] E.C.R. I–47; [1998] 1 C.M.L.R. 931; [1998] C.E.C. 280. . . 11–20, 11–21
Scrivner and Cole. *See* Hoeckx v Openbaar Centrum voor Maatschappelijik Welzijn
    (249/83)
Seco SA v Etablissement d'Assurance contre la Vieillesse et l'Invalidité (62/81) [1982]
    E.C.R. 223 11–94
Secretary of State for the Home Department v Akrich (C–109/01) [2004] Q.B. 756; [2004]
    2 W.L.R. 871; [2004] All E.R. (EC) 687; [2003] E.C.R. I–9607; [2003] 3 C.M.L.R.
    26; [2004] I.N.L.R. 36 ECJ. 6–29, 9–50, 10–17, 23-12, 24–22
Secretary of State for Work and Pensions v Dias (C–325/09) [2012] All E.R. (EC) 199;
    [2011] 3 C.M.L.R. 40; [2011] Imm. A.R. 855; [2011] I.N.L.R. 772 ECJ. . . 10–44, 10–82,
                                            10–85, 13-37, 24-19, 24–24, 24-28
Secretary of State for Work and Pensions v Lassal (C–162/09) [2011] All E.R. (EC) 1169;
    [2011] 1 C.M.L.R. 31; [2011] Imm. A.R. 134 .... 10–80, 10–81, 24-19
Sedef v Freie und Hansestadt Hamburg (C–230/03) [2006] All E.R. (D) 7 (Jan) ECJ. 18–49
Segers v Bestuur van de Bedrijfsvereniging voor Bank- en Verzekeringswezen, Groothandel en Vrije Beroepen (79/85) [1986] E.C.R. 2375; [1987] 2 C.M.L.R. 247. . . 7–21,
                                                                             11–66
Semeraro Casa Uno Srl v Sindaco del Comune di Erbusco (C–418/93) [1996] E.C.R.
    I–2975; [1996] 3 C.M.L.R. 648 11–58
Sen v Netherlands (31465/96) (2003) 36 E.H.R.R. 7 ECHR 9–14
Sevic Systems AG v Amtsgericht Neuwied (C–411/03) [2006] All E.R. (EC) 363; [2005]
    E.C.R. I–10805; [2006] 2 B.C.L.C. 510; [2006] 1 C.M.L.R. 45; [2006] C.E.C. 355. 7–26
Sevince v Staatssecretaris van Justitie (C–192/89) [1990] E.C.R. I–3461; [1992] 2
    C.M.L.R. 57 ECJ 15–06, 15–20, 15–26, 15–29, 15–30, 17–18, 17–21,
                                            17–32, 18–06, 18–21, 18–23, 18–24, 18–77
Simutenkov v Ministerio de Educacion y Cultura (C–265/03) [2006] All E.R. (EC) 42;
    [2005] E.C.R. I–2579; [2005] 2 C.M.L.R. 11 . . 14–52, 15–26, 15–33, 16–08, 16–13, 16–15
Sirdar v Secretary of State for Defence (C–273/97) [1999] All E.R. (EC) 928; [1999]
    E.C.R. I–7403; [1999] 3 C.M.L.R. 559; [1999] C.E.C. 554; [2000] I.C.R. 130; [2000]
    I.R.L.R. 47; 7 B.H.R.C. 459. 13–30
Société française des Biscuits Delacre v Commission of the European Communities
    (C–350/88) [1990] ECR I–395 2–62
Sotgiu v Deutsche Bundepost (152/73) [1974] E.C.R. 153. .... 6–69, 11–51
Soysal v Germany (C–228/06) [2009] E.C.R. I–1031; [2009] 2 C.M.L.R. 47; [2009]
    I.N.L.R. 545 19–30, 19–31
Spain v United Kingdom (C–145/04) [2007] All E.R. (EC) 486; [2006] E.C.R. I–7917;
    [2007] 1 C.M.L.R. 3 2–17
Spotti v Freistaat Bayern (C–272/92) [1993] E.C.R. I–5185; [1994] 3 C.M.L.R. 629 . . 16–16,
                                                                             16–17
Staatsseretaris van Justitie v Oguz and Toprak (C–300/09 & C–301/09) Unreported
    December 9, 2010 .... 18–80, 19–18
Stamatelaki v NPDD Organismos Asfaliseos Eleftheron Epangelmation (OAEE)
    (C–444/05) [2007] E.C.R. I–3185; [2007] 2 C.M.L.R. 44. 11–95

TABLE OF EUROPEAN CASES

Stauder v City of Ulm (29/69) [1969] E.C.R. 419; [1970] C.M.L.R. 112 3–16
Stewart v Secretary of State for Work and Pensions (C–503/09) [2012] P.T.S.R. 1; [2012] 1 C.M.L.R. 13. 12–12
Steymann v Staatssecretaris van Justitie (196/87) [1988] E.C.R. 6159; [1989] 1 C.M.L.R. 449. . . . . 6–15, 7–07, 7–13
Stichting Collective Antennevorrziening Gouda v Commissariaat voor de Media (288/89) [1991] E.C.R. I–4007 ECJ 11–74
Stoss v Wetteraukreis (C–316/07) [2011] All E.R. (EC) 644; [2011] 1 C.M.L.R. 20 . . . 7–50
Surinder Singh. *See* R. v Immigration Appeal Tribunal Ex p. Secretary of State for the Home Department (C–370/90)
Svensson v Ministre du Logement et de l'Urbanisme (C–484/93) [1995] E.C.R. I–3955; [1996] C.E.C. 598 ECJ 7–58
Szeja v Land Berlin (C-425/10) December 21, 2011 10-81
Taflan-Met v Bestuur van de Sociale Verzekeringsbank (C–277/94) [1996] E.C.R. I–4085; [1997] 3 C.M.L.R. 40 17–28
Teixeira v Lambeth LBC (C-480/08) [2010] P.T.S.R. 1913; [2010] 2 C.M.L.R. 50; [2010] I.C.R. 1118; [2010] Imm. A.R. 487; [2010] H.L.R. 32; (2010) 160 N.L.J. 352. . . . 24-28
Terhoeve v Inspecteur van de Belastingdienst Particulieren/Ondernemingen Buitenland (C–18/95) [1999] E.C.R. I–345; [2001] 1 C.M.L.R. 12; (1999) 96(19) L.S.G. 30 . . 11–49
Tetik v Land Berlin (C–171/95) [1997] All E.R. (E.C.) 464; [1997] E.C.R. I–329; [1997] 2 C.M.L.R. 245 . . . . 18–15, 18–50, 18–51, 18–55, 18–58, 18–59, 18–60, 18–64
Thieffry v Conseil de l'Ordre des Avocats a la Cour de Paris (71/76) [1978] Q.B. 315; [1977] 3 W.L.R. 453; [1977] E.C.R. 765; [1977] 2 C.M.L.R. 373; (1977) 121 S.J. 677. . . . . 11–69, 11–72
Thijssen v Controledienst voor de Verzekeringen (C–42/92) [1993] E.C.R. I–4047. . . . 11–73
TI v United Kingdom (Admissibility) (43844/98) [2000] I.N.L.R. 211 ECHR. 5–02
Trojani v Centre Public d'Aide Sociale de Bruxelles (CPAS) (C–456/02) [2004] All E.R. (EC) 1065; [2004] E.C.R. I–7573; [2004] 3 C.M.L.R. 38; [2005] C.E.C. 139 ECJ . 4–24, 4–25, 4–29, 4–30, 4–33, 6–08, 6–13, 6–45, 11–08, 11–11, 13–14, 13–68
Tsiotras v Landeshauptstadt Stuttgart (C–171/91) [1993] E.C.R. I–2925 6–53
Tum v Secretary of State for the Home Department (C–16/05) [2008] 1 W.L.R. 94; [2007] E.C.R. I–7415; [2008] 1 C.M.L.R. 2; [2008] Imm. A.R. 175; [2007] I.N.L.R. 473 ECJ 19–20, 19–26, 19–27, 25-11, 25–12
Uecker v Land Nordrhein-Westfalen. *See* Land Nordrhein-Westfalen v Uecker (C–64/96)
Ufficio Henry Van Ameyde Srl v Ufficio Centrale Italiano di Assistenza Assicurativa Automobilisti in Circolazione Internazionale (90/76) [1977] E.C.R. 1091; [1978] R.T.R. 8; [1977] 2 C.M.L.R. 478. 11–16
Unal v Staatssecretaris van Justitie (C–187/10) Unreported September 29, 2010 . 18–31, 18–33
Unger v Bestuur der Bedrijfsvereniging voor Detailhandel en Ambachten (75/63) [1964] E.C.R. 177; [1964] C.M.L.R. 319 ECJ 6–06, 6–18, 6–61
Union Royale Belge des Sociétés de Football Association (ASBL) v Bosman (C–415/93) [1996] All E.R. (EC) 97; [1995] E.C.R. I–4921; [1996] 1 C.M.L.R. 645; [1996] C.E.C. 38 ECJ 7–07, 7–11, 11–61, 14–52, 16–14, 16–15, 18–75
Ursaff v Srl Hostellerie Le Manoir (C–29/91) [1991] E.C.R. I–5531. 6–35
Van Duyn v Home Office (41/74) [1975] Ch. 358; [1975] 2 W.L.R. 760; [1975] 3 All E.R. 190; [1974] E.C.R. 1337; [1975] 1 C.M.L.R. 1; (1974) 119 S.J. 302 . . . 2–49, 2–50, 13–10, 13–19, 18–03
Van Gend en Loos. *See* NV Algemene Transport- en Expeditie Onderneming van Gend en Loos v Nederlandse Administratie der Belastingen (26/62)
Van Pommeren-Bourgondien v Raad van Bestuur van de Sociale Verzekeringsbank (C–227/03) [2005] E.C.R. I–6101; [2005] 3 C.M.L.R. 24. 6–68
Vander Elst v Office des Migrations Internationales (OMI) (C–43/93) [1994] E.C.R. I–3803; [1995] 1 C.M.L.R. 513 ECJ 7–65, 7–66, 7–67, 7–69, 7–71
Vatsouras v Arbeitsgemeinschaft (ARGE) Nürnberg 900 (C–22/08) [2009] All E.R. (EC) 747; [2009] E.C.R. I–4585; [2009] C.E.C. 1024 12–15
Vlassopoulou v Ministerium für Justiz, Bundes- und Europaangelegenheiten Baden-Württemberg (C–340/89) [1991] E.C.R. I–2357; [1993] 2 C.M.L.R. 221; (1991) 135 S.J.L.B. 92 11–59
Vougioukas v Idrima Koinonikon Asphalisseon (C–443/93) [1995] E.C.R. I–4033; [1996] I.C.R. 913 ECJ 6–07
Wachauf v Germany (5/88) [1989] E.C.R. 2609; [1991] 1 C.M.L.R. 328 3–20

Table of European Cases

Wahlergruppe Gemeinsam Zajedno/Birlikte Alternative und Grüne Gewerkschafter-
   Innen/UG (C–171/01) [2003] E.C.R. I–4301; [2003] 2 C.M.L.R. 29...... 18–71, 18–72,
      18–73, 18–74
Walrave v Association Union Cycliste Internationale (36/74) [1974] E.C.R. 1405; [1975]
   1 C.M.L.R. 320 ECJ 6–09
Watson and Belmann. *See* Italy v Watson and Belmann (118/75)
Wirth v Landeshauptstadt Hannover (C–109/93) [1993] E.C.R. I–6447 7–49
Wood v Fonds de Garantie des Victimes des Actes de Terrorisme et d'Autres Infractions
   (C–164/07) [2008] E.C.R. I–4143; [2008] 3 C.M.L.R. 11.................... 4–30
X v Belgium and Netherlands Unreported July 10, 1975 ECHR................ 9–63
X v France Unreported October 5, 1982 ECHR 9–63
X, Y and Z v United Kingdom Unreported April 22, 1997 ECHR 9–63
Yildiz v Austria (37295/97) [2003] 2 F.C.R. 182; (2003) 36 E.H.R.R. 32 ECHR..... 9–12
Yoshikazu Iida v City of Ulm (C–40/11) January 28, 2011..................... 9-10
Zablocka-Weyhermuller v Land Baden-Württemberg (C–221/07) [2008] E.C.R. I–9029;
   [2009] 1 C.M.L.R. 37 ECJ 4–30, 4–32
Zambrano v Office National de l'Emploi (ONEM) (C–34/09) [2011] All E.R. (EC) 491;
   [2011] 2 C.M.L.R. 46; [2011] 2 F.C.R. 491; [2011] Imm. A.R. 521; [2011] I.N.L.R.
   481.................. 4–43, 5–12, 5–13, 5–14, 5–15, 5–17, 5–18, 8-21, 9–16, 9–78,
      9–80, 9–81, 9–82, 12–15, 24–12, 24–13
Zaoui v Caisse Regionale d'Assurance Maladie de l'Ile de France (147/87) [1987] E.C.R.
   5511; [1989] 2 C.M.L.R. 646......................................5–11, 11–36
Zeturf Ltd v Premier Ministre (C–212/08) [2011] 3 C.M.L.R. 30................. 7–50
Ziebell v Land Baden-Württemberg (C–371/08) Unreported December 8, 2011 17-13,
   21–09
Ziolkowski (Tomasz) v Land Berlin (C–424/10) Unreported September 14, 2011 10–81,
   24-24, 24-28

TABLE OF UK CASES

Aladeselu v Secretary of State for the Home Department [2011] UKUT 253 (IAC); [2011] Imm. A.R. 765. 24–16
Amos v Secretary of State for the Home Department [2011] EWCA Civ 552; [2011] 1 W.L.R. 2952; [2011] 3 C.M.L.R. 20; [2011] Imm. A.R. 600; [2011] I.N.L.R. 662 . 24–25
Bigia v Entry Clearance Officer [2009] EWCA Civ 79; [2009] 2 C.M.L.R. 42; [2009] Eu. L.R. 688; [2009] Imm. A.R. 515; [2009] I.N.L.R. 351; (2009) 153(8) S.J.L.B. 29. . 24–15
C v Secretary of State for the Home Department [2010] EWCA Civ 1406 24–29
EK (Turkey) v Secretary of State for the Home Department [2010] UKUT 425 (IAC); [2011] Imm. A.R. 212. 25–17
FS (Turkey) v Secretary of State for the Home Department [2008] UKAIT 66; [2009] Imm. A.R. 7 25–12
HR (Portugal) v Secretary of State for the Home Department [2009] EWCA Civ 371; [2010] 1 W.L.R. 158; [2010] 1 All E.R. 144; [2009] 3 C.M.L.R. 9; [2009] I.N.L.R. 370. 24–29
Islam v Secretary of State for the Home Department [1999] 2 A.C. 629; [1999] 2 W.L.R. 1015; [1999] 2 All E.R. 545; 6 B.H.R.C. 356; [1999] Imm. A.R. 283; [1999] I.N.L.R. 144; (1999) 96(17) L.S.G. 24; (1999) 143 S.J.L.B. 115 HL 2–63
McCarthy v Secretary of State for the Home Department [2008] EWCA Civ 641; [2008] 3 C.M.L.R. 7; [2008] Eu. L.R. 768; [2009] Imm. A.R. 83; [2009] I.N.L.R. 631 24–18
MG v Secretary of State for the Home Department [2006] UKAIT 53; [2006] Imm. A.R. 619. 24–30
Moneke (EEA: OFMs: Nigeria) [2011] UKUT 341 (IAC); [2011] Imm. A.R. 928. . . . 24–28
MR (Bangladesh) v Secretary of State for the Home Department [2010] UKUT 449 (IAC). 24–16
OB (Morocco) v Secretary of State for the Home Department [2010] UKUT 420 (IAC); [2011] Imm. A.R. 221; [2011] I.N.L.R. 615. 24–22
Oguz v Secretary of State for the Home Department [2010] EWCA Civ 311 . . . 25–13, 25–14
Okafor v Secretary of State for the Home Department [2011] EWCA Civ 499; [2011] 1 W.L.R. 3071; [2011] 3 C.M.L.R. 8 24–24
OY (Ankara Agreement) Turkey [2006] UKAIT 28. 25–05
Patmalniece v Secretary of State for Work and Pensions [2011] UKSC 11; [2011] 1 W.L.R. 783; [2011] P.T.S.R. 680; [2011] 3 All E.R. 1; [2011] 2 C.M.L.R. 45; (2011) 108(13) L.S.G. 23; (2011) 155(11) S.J.L.B. 31 12–12
PR (Sri Lanka) v Secretary of State for the Home Department [2011] EWCA Civ 988; [2012] 1 W.L.R. 73; [2011] C.P. Rep. 47; [2011] Imm. A.R. 904 23–14
R. (on the application of A) v Secretary of State for the Home Department [2002] EWCA Civ 1008; [2002] 3 C.M.L.R. 14; [2002] Eu. L.R. 580. 23-15
R. (on the application of Bessuroglu) v Secretary of State for the Home Department [2009] EWHC 327 (Admin). 25–03
R. (on the application of Lee Ling Low) v Secretary of State for the Home Department [2010] EWCA Civ 4; [2010] 2 C.M.L.R. 34; [2010] Eu. L.R. 415; [2010] I.C.R. 755 7-70
R. (on the application of LF (Turkey)) v Secretary of State for the Home Department [2007] EWCA Civ 1441 25–12
R. (on the application of NS) v Secretary of State for the Home Department (Reference to ECJ) [2010] EWCA Civ 990 3–12
R. (on the application of Tum) v Secretary of State for the Home Department [2003] EWHC 2745 (Admin); [2004] 1 C.M.L.R. 33; [2004] Eu. L.R. 298; affirmed [2004] EWCA Civ 788; [2004] 2 C.M.L.R. 48; [2004] I.N.L.R. 442. ...... 25–10, 25–11, 25–12
R. (on the application of Zagorski) v Secretary of State for Business, Innovation and Skills [2010] EWHC 3110 (Admin); [2011] Eu. L.R. 315; [2011] H.R.L.R. 6; [2011] A.C.D. 33 3–12
R. v Immigration Appeal Tribunal Ex p. Joseph [1977] Imm. A.R. 70; (1977) 121 S.J. 203 DC. 25–16
R. v International Stock Exchange of the United Kingdom and the Republic of Ireland

Table of UK Cases

Ltd Ex p. Else (1982) Ltd [1993] Q.B. 534; [1993] 2 W.L.R. 70; [1993] 1 All E.R. 420; [1993] B.C.C. 11; [1993] B.C.L.C. 834; [1993] 2 C.M.L.R. 677; (1994) 6 Admin. L.R. 67; [1993] C.O.D. 236. .... 2–26, 23–09
R. v Intervention Board for Agricultural Produce Ex p. Fish Producers Organisation (No.2) [1993] 1 C.M.L.R. 707 CA (Civ Div). 23–16
R. v Secretary of State for Transport Ex p. Factortame Ltd (No.2) [1991] 1 A.C. 603; [1990] 3 W.L.R. 818; [1991] 1 All E.R. 70; [1991] 1 Lloyd's Rep. 10; [1990] 3 C.M.L.R. 375; (1991) 3 Admin. L.R. 333; (1990) 140 N.L.J. 1457; (1990) 134 S.J. 1189 HL 2–35
Samsam v Secretary of State for the Home Department [2011] UKUT 165 (IAC); [2011] Imm. A.R. 563; [2011] I.N.L.R. 745 25–25
Secretary of State for Work and Pensions v Dias [2009] EWCA Civ 807; [2010] 1 C.M.L.R. 4 24-19
Secretary of State for Work and Pensions v Lassal [2009] EWCA Civ 157. 24–19
Sonmez v Secretary of State for the Home Department [2009] EWCA Civ 582; [2010] 1 C.M.L.R. 7; [2010] Imm. A.R. 94; [2010] I.N.L.R. 85 .... 25–12, 25–13
VP (Italy) v Secretary of State for the Home Department [2010] EWCA Civ 806 24–30
Webb v EMO Air Cargo (UK) Ltd (Reference to ECJ) [1993] 1 W.L.R. 49; [1992] 4 All E.R. 929; [1993] 1 C.M.L.R. 259; [1993] I.C.R. 175; [1993] I.R.L.R. 27; (1992) 142 N.L.J. 1720; (1993) 137 S.J.L.B. 48 HL. 2–56
ZZ v Secretary of State for the Home Department [2011] EWCA Civ 440. 13–51

TABLE OF EU LEGISLATION

Treaties
1951 Treaty establishing the
European Coal and Steel
Community (ECSC)..... 1–03,
1–07, 6–01
Ch.VIII 1–07
art.69............... 1–07, 6–01
(1) 1–07
(3) 1–07
1957 Treaty establishing the
European Economic
Community....... 1–03, 1–07,
1–15, 1–24, 2–30, 4–03, 7–50,
8–01, 23–03
Pt II 4–49
art.2 .... 1–10, 6–01, 6–31
art.3 6–31
(1)(c) .. 1–12, 4–04, 6–01, 11–79
(q) 6–31
art.4 6–31
art.5 1–13
art.7 1–13
art.8 4–06
arts 8a—8e............. 4–06
art.10............... 2–52, 10–34
art.17................. 24–04
art.34(2)............... 11–03
art.39................. 10–02
art.43................. 10–02
art.47(1)............... 11–79
art.53............ 19–17, 19–19
art.131............... 14–66
art.232(1)............... 1–07
(2) 1–08
art.238............... 14–04
art.310............... 14–04
1957 Treaty establishing the
European Atomic Energy
Community (Euratom)... 1–03,
1–08, 6–01, 23–03
art.96............... 1–09, 6–01
1961 European Social Charter
art.28................ 3–05
1965 Merger Treaty 1–06
1972 Treaty of Accession to the
European Communities
(Denmark, Ireland, United
Kingdom)....... 23–02, 23–03,
24–02
1979 Treaty of Accession to the
European Communities
(Greece) Act of Accession
arts 44—47 11–27

1985 Treaty of Accession to the
European Communities
(Spain and Portugal)
art.55................ 6–14
art.56................ 6–14
art.216(1)............. 11–27
1986 Single European Act.... 1–06, 1–17,
2–02, 4–05
art.13................ 1–17
1992 Treaty on European Union... 1–03,
1–04, 1–19, 1–30, 2–28, 2–29,
10–01, 11–97, 23–04
art.1 11–01
arts 1—19 .... **A1–01**
art.3 6–01
art.3a................ 10–34
art.4(3)......... 2–30, 2–52, 2–55
art.5(4)............... 2–60
art.6 ..... 3–01, 3–03, 3–07, 3–14
Title II................ 1–20
art.9 3–01
Title III 1–20
art.13................ 1–35
art.14............... 1–37, 1–39
(1) 1–39
(2) 1–39
(3) 1–39
art.15................ 1–33
art.16..... 1–30, 1–37, 1–51, 1–63
(2) 1–52, 1–53
art.17............... 1–37, 1–46
(3) 1–65
(7) 1–46
(8) 1–46
art.19................ 1–38
Title IV 1–20
Title V................ 1–21
Title VI 1–22
art.166............... 1–51
1997 Treaty of Amsterdam ... 1–06, 1–22,
1–23, 1–24, 1–29, 4–08, 4–36
art.17................ 4–09
2000 Charter of Fundamental Rights 1–33,
3–01, 3–03, 3–04, 3–05, 3–06,
3–07, 3–14, 3–24, 5–03, 9–10,
9–16, 9–37, 10–116, 12–07, 24–23
Title I 3–07
art.1 .... 3–08, 3–12
art.3(2)............... 3–12
art.4 3–12
Title II................ 3–07
art.7 ..... 9–10, 9–11, 9–15, 9–22
art.9 3–11
art.12................ 3–09

	art.14 3–09	4–20, 4–21, 4–22, 4–24, 4–25,
	art.15 3–09	4–28, 4–29, 4–30, 4–31, 4–34,
	art.18 3–12	4–73, 8–34, 8–35, 11–01, 11–02,
	art.20 4–31	11–04, 11–06, 11–08, 11–10,
	Title III 3–07	11–11, 11–12, 11–16, 11–17,
	art.21 2–66	11–18, 11–19, 11–21, 11–43,
	art.22 4–31	11–99, 11–100, 11–103, 12–01,
	art.23 3–05	12–08, 18–69
	Title IV 3–07	(1) 4–63
	arts 27—38 3–12	arts 18—19 (ex arts 12—13
	art.28 3–06	EC) A2–01
	art.30 3–12	arts 20—22 (ex arts 17—19
	Title V 3–07	EC) A2–01
	art.41 3–05	arts 18—25 4–02
	Title VI 3–07	art.19 (ex art.13 EC) 2–66,
	art.47 . . . . 3–12, 13–50, 13–56	11–05
	(2) 3–11	Pt II 4–07, A2–01
	art.51 . . . . 3–10, 3–11	art.20 (ex art.17 EC) 1–20,
	art.52 . . . . 3–10, 3–11	4–01, 4–08, 4–09, 4–18, 4–36,
	(3) 3–11, 3–12	4–73, 5–01, 5–08, 5–09, 5–10,
	Title VII 3–07	5–12, 5–15, 5–16, 5–26, 8–21,
	Protocol 30 3–12	9–81, 11–08, 24–12, 24–13
2001	Treaty of Nice 1–06, 1–26, 1–27,	art.21 (ex art.18 EC) 1–20,
	1–28, 1–29, 1–30, 2–02, 2–13,	4–01, 4–02, 4–15, 4–20, 4–24,
	3–07	4–34, 4–44, 4–47, 4–52, 4–56,
2003	Treaty of Accession to the	4–57, 4–58, 4–64, 4–65, 4–70,
	European Union (Czech	4–75, 5–26, 8–03, 8–06, 8–07,
	Republic, Estonia, Cyprus,	8–08, 8–11, 8–019, 11–97,
	Latvia, Lithuania,	11–99, 11–102, 14–20
	Hungary, Malta, Poland,	(1) 4–06, 4–44, 4–45, 4–46,
	Slovakia and Slovenia) . . . 5–34,	4–48, 4–49, 4–50, 4–58, 4–74,
	5–36, 7–59, 24–32, 24–33	4–75, 5–03, 10–05
	art.24 5–36	art.22 (ex art.19 EC) 4–07
2004	Treaty establishing a	(1) 5–03
	Constitution for Europe . . 1–06,	art.23 4–07
	1–33	art.24 . . . . 4–07, 4–08
2005	Treaty of Accession to the	art.26 . . . . 1–17, 6–01
	European Union (Bulgaria	art.40 11–03
	and Romania) 5–34, 5–37,	Title IV 7–38
	24–32	art.45 (ex art.39 EC) 2–42,
	art.20 5–37	2–43, 4–19, 4–57, 6–02, 6–03,
	Annex VI 5–37	6–07, 6–08, 6–17, 6–28, 6–33,
	Annex VIII 5–37	6–47, 6–51, 6–68, 7–02, 7–19,
2007	Treaty of Lisbon . . 1–06, 1–16, 1–29,	11–17, 11–25, 11–49, 11–54,
	1–30, 1–31, 1–32, 1–33, 1–34,	17–20, 18–03, 18–15, 18–18,
	1–36, 1–41, 1–56, 1–72, 2–13,	18–58, 18–59, 20–21
	3–07, 4–08, 13–09	(1) 6–02, 6–71
	art.1 1–29	(2) . . . 6–02, 11–02, 11–12, 11–25,
2008	Treaty on the Functioning of	11–28, 11–49, 16–13, 16–14,
	the European Union 1–06,	16–16, 16–17, 18–73, 18–74
	1–16, 1–34, 2–28, 2–29, 7–11,	(3) . . . 4–77, 13–02, 13–07, 21–01,
	7–12, 7–21, 7–27, 7–37, 7–48,	21–02, 21–11
	7–61, 9–16, 9–63, 10–01, 10–02,	(d) 6–55, 6–56
	10–25, 10–44, 10–89, 11–07,	(4) 6–69, 6–72, 6–73, 11–31,
	11–32, 11–39, 11–92, 13–08,	11–50, 11–89
	13–09, 13–10, 13–15, 13–29,	arts 45—47 (ex arts 39—41
	15–05, 18–14, 18–41	EC) A2–01
	arts 2—6 1–13	arts 45—48 (ex arts 39—42
	arts 3—6 1–16	EC) 1–14
	art.18 (ex art.12 EC) 1–13,	art.46 (ex art.40 EC) 6–03,
	2–58, 2–66, 4–10, 4–12, 4–14,	17–20, 18–15
	4–15, 4–16, 4–17, 4–18, 4–19,	

Table of EU Legislation

art.47 (ex art.41 EC) 6–04,
        6–05, 17–20, 18–15
art.48 (ex art.42 EC) . . . 6–04, 6–07
Title V 14–01
  Ch.4 13–09
  Ch.5 13–09
art.49 (ex art.43 EC) 2–42,
    5–07, 6–12, 7–01, 7–02, 7–03,
    7–05, 7–15, 7–24, 7–25, 7–26,
    7–30, 7–31, 7–32, 7–39, 7–52,
    7–55, 9–60, 11–16, 11–58,
    11–59, 11–60, 11–61, 11–62,
    11–63, 11–64, 11–66, 11–69,
         11–89, 19–17
arts 49—52 (ex arts 43—46
  EC) **A2–01**
arts 49—54 (ex arts 52—58
  EEC) 1–14
art.51 (ex art.45 EC) 11–72,
          11–89
arts 51—54 (ex arts 45—48
  EC) 7–41, 7–59
art.52 (ex art.46 EC) 11–96,
      13–02, 13–07, 21–09
art.53 (ex art.47 EC) 11–75,
     11–76, 11–78, 11–79
art.54 (ex art.48 EC) 7–41
art.56 (ex art.49 EC) 2–42,
    5–21, 7–33, 7–41, 7–50, 7–52,
    7–54, 7–55, 7–58, 7–59, 7–63,
    7–66, 7–67, 7–68, 7–69, 7–74,
    9–16, 9–23, 10–04, 11–16,
       11–90, 11–93
arts 56—57 (ex arts 49—50
  EC) **A2–01**
arts 56—62 (ex arts 59—66
  EEC) 1–14, 7–41
art.57 (ex art.50 EC) 7–35,
    7–38, 7–42, 7–47, 7–63, 7–66,
       7–71, 19–16
art.62 . . . . 7–41, 7–59
art.165 (ex art.149 EC) 4–65,
       8–36
art.166 (ex art.150 EC) 8–34,
       8–45
art.216 . . . . **A2–01**
  (1) 14–01
  (2) 14–01
art.217 (ex art.310 EC) 14–02,
    15–03, 15–15, 15–16, 15–17,
       A2–01
art.218 (ex art.300 EC) 14–03,
    15–03, 15–15, 15–16, 15–17,
       A2–01
  (2)—(5) 14–03
  (6)(a) 14–03
    (b) 14–03
  (8) 14–03
arts 223—234 1–39
art.234 1–46
arts 237—243 1–51
arts 244—250 1–63

art.256 2–22
art.257 2–13
art.258 . . . . 1–76, 2–14, 2–16
art.259 . . . . 2–14, 2–16, 2–17
art.260 1–78
art.263 . . . . 2–15, 2–18, 2–61
art.265 2–19
art.267 (ex art.234 EC) 2–14,
    2–24, 15–15, 15–17, 15–21,
    17–33, 17–34, 23–09, 23–11,
       23–14, **A2–01**
art.268 . . . . 2–15, 2–20
art.278 2–23
art.279 2–23
art.285 1–38
art.288 . . . . 2–03, 2–44, 2–48, 2–54,
       24–28, **A2–01**
art.294 1–42
  (7)(b) 1–43
    (c) 1–44
  (8)(b) 1–44
  (9) 1–44
  (10) 1–44
  (11) 1–44
  (12) 1–44
  (13) 1–44
  (15) 1–45
art.310 1–49
art.314 1–49
art.340 2–20
art.346(1)(a) 13–50, 13–51

Regulations
1958 Reg.3/58 on social security for
     migrant workers [1958] JO
     561 . . . . 6–06, 6–61
1968 Reg.1612/68 on freedom of
     movement of workers
     [1968] OJ L257/2 6–05,
      6–28, 6–67, 7–63, 8–01, 8–33,
        9–23, 15–21
   arts 1—6 . . . . . . 5–36, 6–14, 11–27
   art.3(1) 11–36
   art.7(1) 11–51
    (2) 4–19, 11–54, 11–57
    (3) 8–32
    (4) 11–51
   art.10 . . . . 4–63, 6–05
    (3) 9–33
   art.11 6–05
   art.12 . . . . 4–62, 4–63, 8–32, 10–09,
     10–109, 10–113, 24–28
   arts 13—23 11–27
1970 Reg.1251/70 on right of
     workers to remain in
     Member State [1970] OJ
     L142/24 8–29
   art.2 6–67
1971 Reg.1408/71 on social security
     schemes [1971] OJ L149/2. 12–03,
     12–05, 12–06, 12–16, 17–27
   art.1(b) 6–67

	art.2 12–17		art.43. 12–29
	art.4(1)(h). 4–19		arts 44—49. 12–30
	art.10. 12–12		arts 61—65. 12–31
	art.19(1). 8–25		art.71. 12–02
1972	Reg.574/72 implementing Reg.1408/71 on social security schemes . . 17–27, 17–28	2007	Reg.168/2007 establishing EU Agency for Fundamental Rights [2007] OJ L53/1 . . 3–02
2000	Reg.2725/2000 establishing Eurodac [2000] OJ L316/1 1–25	2009	Reg.987/2009 implementing Reg.883/2004 on social
2001	Reg.539/2001 establishing visa list [2001] OJ L81/1 . . . . . 1–25, 19–30		security [2009] OJ L284/1 . 12–01 art.1(2)(c). 12–06 art.25. 12–24
2001	Reg.2414/2001 amending Reg.539/2001 on visas [2001] OJ L327/1 1–25	2010	Reg.1091/2010 amending Reg.539/2001 on visas [2010] OJ L329/1 1–25
2002	Reg.407/2002 implementing Reg.2725/2000 establishing Eurodac [2002] OJ L62/1. 1–25	2011	Reg.492/2011 on freedom of movement for workers [2011] OJ L141/1 . . . 6–05, 8–01, 8–38, 11–12, 11–25, 11–26, 11–37, **A4–01**
2003	Reg.343/2003 on asylum applications [2003] OJ L50/1 . . . . 1–25, 3–12 art.3(2). 3–12		preamble . . . . 11–26 recital 4 . . . . 6–05 art.1 . . . . 11–27, 11–38
2003	Reg.453/2003 on visa list [2003] OJ L69/10. 1–25		art.2 . . . . 11–28, 11–38 art.3(1). 11–36
2003	Reg.1560/2003 implementing Reg.343/2003 on asylum applications [2003] OJ L222/3 1–25		art.6(1). . . . . 11–27 art.7(1). . . . . 11–28, 11–39 (2) 11–29, 11–34, 11–35, 11–39, 11–40, 11–48, 11–49,
2004	Reg.883/2004 on social security systems [2004] OJ L166/1 . 6–04, 8–24, 8–25, 8–26, 10–65, 10–66, 12–01, 12–03, 12–05, 12–06, 12–07, 12–16, 12–17, 12–33, 17–25, **A5–01**		11–51 (3) . . . . 8–32, 8–43, 11–30, 11–39 (4) . . . . 11–30, 11–39, 11–51 art.8 . . . . 11–31 art.9 11–31
	art.1 . . . . 12–19 art.2 . . . . 12–17, 12–19 art.3 12–19		art.10. . . . . 4–62, 8–32, 8–37, 8–40, 8–41, 20–52, 24–28

Directives

	(5) 12–15	1962	Dir. on skilled employment in
	art.4 12–08		nuclear energy [1962] OJ
	art.5 12–20		1650. 1–09
	art.6 12–20	1964	Dir.64/221 [1964] OJ 56/850 . . 13–24,
	art.10. 12–20		13–55, 13–58, 21–02, 21–04
	art.11. 12–21		art.3 2–49
	art.13(2). 12–21		(1) 13–22
	art.14. 12–21		(2) 13–22
	Title III Ch.1 . . . . 8–24, 8–25		art.6 13–49
	art.17. . . . . 12–22, 12–26		art.8 . . . . 13–55, 21–11
	art.18. 12–26		art.9 . . . . 13–55, 21–11
	art.19. . . . . . . 8–24, 12–24, 12–26	1968	Dir.68/360 on abolition of
	art.21. 12–22		restrictions on movement
	arts 22—30. 12–27		for workers [1968] OJ
	art.23. 12–27		L257/13 . . . . 6–05, 6–28, 10–14,
	art.25. 12–27		10–20, 10–26, 10–44
	art.32. 12–28		art.3 10–16
	arts 32—35. 12–28		art.4(3). 9–60
	art.33. 12–28	1973	Dir.73/148 on right of
	art.34. 12–28		establishment and services
	art.35. 12–28		[1973] OJ L172/14 . . 7–04, 7–43,
	arts 36—38. 12–28		7–72, 10–14, 10–20
	art.41. 12–28		art.1 7–72
	art.42. 12–29		art.3 10–16

Table of EU Legislation

1975	Dir.75/34 on right of self-employed to remain in another Member State [1975] OJ L14/10....... 8–29		preamble 4–76
1977	Dir.77/249 on lawyers' freedom to provide services [1977] OJ L78/17............ 11–80	1990	Dir.90/366 on right of residence for students [1990] OJ L180/30 .... 4–05, 8–02
1977	Dir.77/452 on mutual recognition of diplomas for nurses [1977] OJ L176/1 .. 11–80	1992	Dir.92/51 on mutual recognition of diplomas and education [1992] OJ L209/25 11–80
1977	Dir.77/453 on co-ordination of activities of nurses [1977] OJ L176/8............ 11–81	1993	Dir.93/16 on free movement of doctors [1993] OJ L165/1 .. 11–80
1978	Dir.78/686 on mutual recognition of diplomas for dentists [1978] OJ L233/1 11–80	1993	Dir.93/96 on right of residence for students [1993] OJ L317/59 ..... 4–05, 4–50, 4–65, 8–32, 8–33, 8–48, 9–23, 11–102 preamble .... 4–76 art.1 ....4–50, 8–32, 10–73 art.3 4–50
1978	Dir.78/687 on co-ordination of activities of dentists [1978] OJ L233/10............ 11–80	1996	Dir.96/71 on posted workers [1997] OJ L18/1.... 5–31, 7–29, 7–66
1978	Dir.78/1026 on mutual recognition of diplomas for vets [1978] OJ L362/1 . 11–80		art.3 .... 7–66 (1) .... 7–66 (a)................ 7–66
1978	Dir.78/1027 on co-ordination of activities of vets [1978] OJ L362/7............ 11–80	1998	art.10................ 7–66 Dir.98/5 on practice of the profession of lawyer on a permanent basis [1998] OJ L77/36 11–80
1980	Dir.80/154 on mutual recognition of diplomas for midwives [1980] L33/1 11–80	1999	Dir.1999/42 on mutual recognition of diplomas [1999] OJ L201/77 11–80
1980	Dir.80/155 on co-ordination of activities of midwives [1980] L33/8 11–80	2001	Dir.2001/55 on temporary protection [2001] OJ L212/ 12 1–25
1985	Dir.85/384 on mutual recognition of diplomas for architects [1985] OJ L223/15 11–80	2003	Dir.2003/9 on reception standards for asylum seekers [2003] OJ L31/18 . 1–25, 3–23, 3–24 art.11................. 3–24
1985	Dir.85/432 on co-ordination of activities of pharmacists [1985] OJ L253/34 11–80	2003	Dir.2003/86 on right to family reunification [2003] OJ L251/12 .... 1–25, 9–30
1985	Dir.85/433 on mutual recognition of diplomas for pharmacists [1985] OJ L253/37 11–80	2004	Dir.2003/109 on status of long-term migrants [2004] OJ L16/44 1–25
1989	Dir.89/48 on mutual recognition of higher education diplomas [1989] OJ L19/16....... 11–80, 11–89	2004	Dir.2004/38 on free movement of citizens [2004] OJ L158/ 77 ..... 1–09, 2–17, 3–23, 3–24, 4–68, 5–27, 5–29, 6–05, 6–47, 6–48, 8–01, 8–08, 8–11, 8–13, 8–17, 8–24, 8–28, 9–07, 9–10, 9–19, 9–30, 9–39, 9–41, 9–63, 9–75, 10–21, 10–44, 10–70, 10–80, 10–81, 11–99, 13–15, 14–20, 24–08, 24–11, 24–14, 224–15, 24–16, 24–18, 24–23, 24–24, 24–25, 24–29, **A3–01** preamble recital 3 .... 10–17 recital 5 .... 9–02, 10–111 recital 6 ..... 9–02, 9–59, 9–76 recital 9 .... 6–49 recital 10......... 4–76, 10–02
1990	Dir.90/364 on right of residence [1990] OJ L180/26 .. 4–05, 4–50, 4–53, 4–54, 4–68, 4–68, 4–69, 4–71, 8–02, 8–10, 8–13, 8–15, 8–18, 8–20, 8–23, 8–28, 8–48, 9–23, 10–70, 13–69 preamble .... 4–76 art.1(1)............4–53, 8–19 art.3 24–20		
1990	Dir.90/365 on right of residence of employees no longer in occupational activity [1990] OJ L180/28 .. 4–05, 4–50, 4–69, 8–02, 8–13, 8–15, 8–18, 8–23, 8–30, 8–48		

[xliii]

recital 14. . . . . 10–18, 10–45,
   10–102
recital 15. . . . . 9–85, 10–111
recital 16. . . . 4–76, 6–49, 10–68,
   13–14, 13–60
recital 17. . . . 9–85, 10–76, 24–18
recital 20. 11–13
recital 22. 13–03
recital 23. . . 13–03, 13–36, 13–41
recital 24. . . . . 13–36, 13–41
recital 28. 9–51
recital 31. . . 9–37, 9–38, 10–116,
   11–13
art.2 . . . . . 8–42, 9–70, 9–80, 9–82
(2) 5–17, 9–23, 9–26, 9–27,
   9–31, 9–36, 9–54, 9–61, 9–65,
   9–66, 9–69, 9–71, 10–106
(b) 9–29
art.3 . . . . 9–80, 9–82, 10–19, 10–22
(1) 5–27
(2) 9–23, 9–26, 9–27, 9–28,
   9–29, 9–37, 9–66, 9–76,
   10–08, 10–103, 11–48,
   24–16
(a). 9–28, 9–29, 10–101,
   10–103, 10–104
(b) 9–31, 9–73, 10–97
art.4 10–14
art.5 . . . . 10–14, 10–21
(2) 10–29, 10–37
(4) 10–24, 10–25, 10–39
art.6 . . . . . 6–50, 7–43, 7–71, 7–76,
   8–14, 10–14, 13–48, 13–59,
   13–61
(1) 6–49, 10–02
(2) 10–02
art.7 . . . . . 4–76, 6–50, 6–57, 6–58,
   8–10, 8–12, 8–16, 8–30, 10–81,
   13–48, 13–61, 24–28
(1) . . . 7–04, 10–02, 10–05, 10–07,
   10–75, 10–81, 10–109, 10–112,
   10–114, 24–24
(a). . . 6–58, 7–61, 8–46, 10–54
(b) . . . 8–14, 8–19, 8–22, 8–23,
   8–48, 10–60
(c). . . . 8–22, 8–23, 8–32, 8–47,
   8–48, 10–71, 10–75, 11–101
(d) 8–42
(2) 10–08
(3) 6–66, 10–09, 10–56
(a). 6–58
(b) 6–50, 6–58
(c). 6–50, 6–58
(d) 6–58, 8–46
(4) 9–25, 10–08
art.8 . . . 8–12, 8–30, 10–14, 10–45,
   13–48
(2) 10–27, 10–30, 10–35
(3) 10–46, 10–55, 10–60,
   10–72
(4) 8–13, 8–14, 8–16, 8–22,
   8–48, 10–61

(5) 10–46
(a). 10–92, 10–98
(b) 10–92, 10–98
(c). 10–92, 10–98
(e). 10–104
(d) 10–98
art.9 13–48
(2) 10–35
(3) 10–25, 10–27
arts 9—11 10–14
art.10. . . . . 10–45, 13–48
(1) 10–30
(2) 10–48
(a). 10–92, 10–98
(b) 10–92, 10–98
(c). 10–92, 10–98
(d) 9–60, 10–98
(e). 9–60, 10–104
art.11. 20–24
(1) 10–49
(2) 10–50
art.12. . . . . 6–50, 9–85, 13–61
(1) 10–02, 10–109
(2) 10–02, 10–12, 10–109
(3) 10–04, 10–109
art.13. . . . 6–50, 9–35, 9–85, 13–61
(1) 10–05, 10–114
(2) 10–12, 10–116
(a). 10–09, 10–114
(b) . . . 10–09, 10–114, 10–116
(c). 10–09, 10–114
(d) . . . 10–09, 10–114, 10–116
art.14. . . . . 4–76, 7–76, 13–61
(1) 6–50, 13–61
(2) 6–50, 10–75
(3) 10–69, 13–62, 13–63
(4) 6–50, 6–53, 7–20, 10–58,
   13–62, 13–64
(a). 6–50, 10–56
(b) 6–48, 7–20
art.15. . . . . 13–65, 24–28
(1) 13–65
(2)—(3). 13–65
art.16. . . . . . . 6–56, 10–44, 10–77,
   10–81, 10–82, 13–39, 24–20,
   24–28
(1) 10–81
(2) 10–10
(3) 10–79
(4) 10–44, 10–84, 13–41,
   13–43
arts 16—18. 9–85
art.17. . . . . 6–56, 8–29
(1) 10–86, 10–87
(a). 6–56, 6–57, 10–11,
   10–86
(b) 6–56, 6–57, 10–11,
   10–86
(c). 6–56, 6–67, 10–11,
   10–86
(4)(a) 10–11, 10–110
(b) 10–11, 10–110

TABLE OF EU LEGISLATION

  (c). 10–11, 10–110
  art.18. 10–12
  art.19. . . . . . .10–47, 10–52, 10–78,
    10–88
  (1) 10–31
  art.20. . . . . 10–51, 10–52
  (1) 10–31
  (3) 10–53
  art.21. 10–83
  art.24. . . . . . .11–14, 11–98, 12–09,
    12–13
  (1) 11–15
  (2) 4–76, 12–15
  art.25. 10–25
  (2) 10–37, 13–39
  Ch.VI 13–03, 13–04
  art.27. . . . . . .10–40, 13–05, 13–07,
    13–17
  (1) 13–14
  (2) . . .2–49, 13–11, 13–17, 13–18,
    13–22, 13–23
  (3) 13–48
  arts 27–33 24–29
  art.28. . . . . . .13–01, 13–06, 13–07,
    13–17, 13–36, 13–45. 21–09
  (1) 13–17
  (2) 13–39
  (3) 13–31, 13–32, 13–33,
    13–37, 13–40, 13–46, 13–54,
    21–05, 21–09, 24–29
  (a). 13–40, 13–41, 13–43
  (b) 13–41, 13–47
  art.29(1). 13–34
  (2) 13–35
  (3) 13–35
  (a). 13–32
  art.30. 13–65
  (1) 13–49, 13–55
  (2) 13–49, 13–50, 13–51
  (3) 13–52, 13–55
  arts 30—33. 21–11
  art.31. . . . . . .13–52, 13–53, 13–55,
    13–65, 21–11
  (1) 13–53
  (2) 13–54
  (3) 13–56
  (4) 13–54, 13–57
  art.32. 13–58
  (1) 13–58
  (2) 13–58
  art.35. . . . . .9–50, 9–52, 13–37
2004 Dir.2004/83 on minimum
  standards for qualification
  of refugees [2004] OJ
  L304/12 . . . . . 1–25, 3–06, 3–23,
    3–24
  art.15. 3–24
2004 Dir.2004/114 on admitting
  third country nationals for
  studies [2004] OJ L375/12. 1–25
2005 Dir.2005/36 on recognition of
  professional qualifications

  [2005] OJ L255/22 11–79,
    11–82, 11–84,
    11–88, 11–89
  preamble recital 1 11–79
  recital 9 11–82
  recital 41. 11–89
  art.1. 11–83
  art.2(1) 11–83
  art.3(1) 11–83
  (a). 11–83
  Title II 11–85
  Title III Ch.I. 11–87
  Ch.III 11–85
  art.33(2) 11–86
  art.43(3) 11–86
2005 Dir.2005/85 on asylum
  procedures [2005] OJ
  L326/13 . . . . 1–25, 3–23
2006 Dir.2006/123 on services in
  internal market [2006] OJ
  L376/36 . 7–44, 7–45, 7–71, 7–73
  preamble recital 1 7–45
  recital 36. . . . . 7–54, 7–73
2009 Dir.2009/50 on entry
  conditions for third
  country nationals for
  highly qualified
  employment [2009] OJ
  L155/17 1–25
2010 Dir.2010/64 on right to
  interpretation in criminal
  proceedings [2010] OJ
  L280/1 . . . . 1–55, 13–09
2011 Dir.2011/36 on preventing
  trafficking in human
  beings [2011] OJ L101/1 . . 1–55,
    13–09

Decisions
2000 Dec.2000/204 concluding Euro-
  Mediterranean Agreement
  with Morocco [2000] OJ
  L70/1 14–57
2000 Dec.2000/384 concluding Euro-
  Mediterranean Agreement
  with Israel [2000] OJ L147/
  1 14–57
2000 Dec.2000/596 on European
  Refugee Fund [2000] OJ
  L252/12 1–25
2002 Dec.2002/309 on concluding
  seven Agreements with
  Swiss Confederation [2002]
  OJ L114/1. 14–21
2004 Dec.2004/635 concluding Euro-
  Mediterranean Agreement
  with Egypt [2004] OJ
  L304/38 14–57
2005 Dec.2005/690 concluding Euro-
  Mediterranean Agreement
  with Algeria [2005] OJ
  L265/1 14–57

2006	Dec.2006/356 concluding Euro-Mediterranean Agreement with Lebanon [2006] OJ L143/1 14–57		
2008	Dec.2008/157 on Accession Partnership with Turkey [2008] OJ L51/4........ 17–03		

EEC–Turkey Association Council Decisions

1976	Dec.2/76 ...... 17–18, 17–19, 17–20, 18–77, 18–80, 21–13		
	art.2 17–19		
	art.5 17–19		
	art.7 21–13		
1980	Dec.1/80 ...... 14–62, 16–22, 17–18, 17–20, 17–21, 17–26, 18–04, 18–10, 18–41, 18–50, 21–05, 25–04, 25–05, 25–06, **A10–01**		
	art.6 .... 18–10, 18–12, 18–23, 18–25, 18–54, 18–56, 18–59, 18–81, 20–21, 20–43, 21–07, 21–10, 21–12, 25–03		
	(1) ... 6–44, 16–22, 17–22, 17–35, 18–05, 18–06, 18–07, 18–10, 18–15, 18–21, 18–24, 18–25, 18–27, 18–29, 18–30, 18–33, 18–38, 18–43, 18–44, 18–47, 18–48, 18–49, 18–52, 18–53, 18–55, 18–57, 18–63, 18–64, 18–65, 18–67, 18–71, 18–78, 18–79, 19–13, 20–26, 20–35, 20–44, 20–49, 21–08		
	(2) 17–35, 18–07, 18–47, 18–48, 18–49, 18–50, 18–53, 18–54, 18–55		
	(3) 18–07		
	art.7 .... 16–31, 17–23, 18–08, 20–06, 20–07, 20–08, 20–09, 20–10, 20–11, 20–12, 20–13, 20–16, 20–17, 20–18, 20–19, 20–20, 20–21, 20–23, 20–24, 20–25, 20–26, 20–27, 20–28, 20–29, 20–30, 20–31, 20–32, 20–33, 20–34, 20–35, 20–36, 20–37, 20–38, 20–39, 20–41, 20–42, 20–43, 20–44, 20–45, 20–46, 20–47, 20–48, 20–49, 20–50, 20–54, 21–07, 21–10, 21–12		
	(1) 17–35		
	(2) 17–35		
	art.9 .... 20–40, 20–52, 20–53, 20–54, 25–04		
	art.10. 18–70		
	(1) 18–70, 18–71, 18–72, 18–73, 18–74, 25–04, 25–05		
	art.13. .... 17–24, 17–35, 18–09, 18–76, 18–77, 18–79, 21–12, 21–13		
	art.14. 20–28		
	(1) 18–67, 21–01, 21–02, 21–03, 21–07, 21–08, 21–09, 21–11		
1980	Dec.3/80 ...... 17–18, 17–25, 17–26, 17–27, 17–28, 17–29, 17–30		
	art.2 17–29		
	art.3(1). 17–29		
1995	Dec.1/95 17–02		
2000	Dec.2/2000 17–18		
2000	Dec.3/2000 17–18		

TABLE OF EU AGREEMENTS

1961 Association Agreement with
   Greece 15–11, 15–17, 15–20,
   15–23
1963 Association Agreement with
   Turkey . . 2–09, 6–06, 6–20, 6–35,
   6–38, 6–44, 14–05, 14–10, 14–26,
   14–29, 15–01, 15–03, 15–10,
   15–11, 15–18, 15–19, 15–20,
   15–21, 15–23, 15–26, 15–29,
   16–02, 16–18, 16–21, 16–22,
   16–23, 16–25, 16–26, 16–31,
   17–01, 18–01, 19–01, 20–01,
   21–01, 25–03, 25–04, 25–05,
   A8–01
   preamble 15–10, 17–09, 17–10
   recital 4 17–11
   art.2(1)................ 17–13
   arts 2—5 17–07
   art.7 17–07
   art.9 ...... 17–14, 18–69, 18–70,
   19–31, 19–33, 19–34
   art.12....... 15–28, 17–07, 17–15,
   18–01, 18–02, 18–03, 18–15,
   19–03, 19–04, 19–09, 20–03
   art.13....... 17–07, 17–15, 19–01,
   19–03, 19–04, 19–08, 19–09,
   19–15, 19–16, 19–31, 20–56
   art.14....... 17–07, 17–15, 19–02,
   19–03, 19–04, 19–08, 19–09,
   19–16
   art.22............ 15–20, 17–07
   art.23............ 15–20, 17–07
   art.28............ 15–11, 17–11
   art.30................ 17–07
   Additional Protocol
   (1970) 14–27, 14–29, 15–11,
   17–06, 17–12, 17–21, 18–25,
   19–01, 20–04, 15–07
   Title I................ 17–08
   Title II 17–08, **A9–01**
   Title III 17–08
   art.36..... 15–11, 17–16, 18–01,
   18–02, 18–03, 18–15, 19–10
   art.39 17–08
   (1)................ 17–30
   art.41..... 19–03, 19–05, 19–07,
   19–31
   (1)...... 15–28, 17–08, 19–06,
   19–19, 19–20, 19–22,
   19–24, 19–25, 19–26,
   19–27, 19–30, 19–32,
   19–33, 20–55, 20–56, 21–15
   (2)...... 17–08, 19–10, 19–15
   Title IV 17–08
   art.50............... 17–08
   arts 58—59 .... **A9–07**
   art.59 .... 18–82, 19–32
   art.60 17–08
1963 Yaoundé I Convention 14–67
1969 Yaoundé II Convention 14–67
1975 Lomé I Convention . . . 14–67, 14–68,
   14–72
   art.65................ 14–72
1977 Maghreb Co-operation
   Agreements...... 14–53, 14–58,
   14–64, 15–01
1979 Lomé II Convention... 14–67, 14–72
1984 Lomé III Convention .. 14–67, 14–72
1985 Schengen Agreement......... 1–18
1989 Partnership and Co-operation
   Agreement with Georgia . 2–10,
   14–09, 14–45, 14–47, 14–60,
   25–33
1989 Partnership and Co-operation
   Agreement with Moldova. 2–10,
   14–09, 14–45, 14–47, 14–60,
   25–33
1989 Partnership and Co-operation
   Agreement with Ukraine . 2–10,
   14–09, 14–45, 14–47, 14–60,
   25–33
1989 Partnership and Co-operation
   Agreement with
   Uzbekistan . 2–10, 14–09, 14–45,
   14–47, 14–60, 25–33
1989 Lomé IV Convention .. 14–67, 14–72
1990 Schengen Convention 1–18
1992 European Economic Area
   Agreement 14–06, 14–11,
   14–12, 14–13, 14–52
   Pt III................ 14–16
   art.28................ 14–16
   arts 28—35............. **A6–01**
   art.31................ 14–18
   art.36................ 14–19
   Annex 5............... 14–17
   Annex 8............... 14–19
   Protocol 15 art.5......... 14–20
   Protocol 28 15–09
1994 Association Agreement with
   Hungary........ 15–12, 16–01
1994 Association Agreement with
   Poland 15–12, 16–06, 16–01
1994 Europe Agreement establishing
   an association between the
   European Economic
   Communities and their
   Member States, of the one

Table of EU Agreements

- 1994 part, and Romania, of the other part
  - art.45(1)............... 14–40
- 1994 Partnership and Co-operation Agreement with Russian Federation . 2–10, 14–09, 14–45, 14–47, 14–49, 14–60, 16–15, 25–33
  - art.23............ 14–51, 14–52
  - (1)....... 14–52, 14–78, 15–26
  - art.28................. 14–55
- 1995 Association Agreement with Bulgaria ... 15–12, 25–32, 16–01
  - art.38(1)................ 16–20
  - art.45.................. 15–08
  - (1)................... 15–32
  - art.59.................. 15–08
- 1995 Association Agreement with Czech Republic... 15–12, 16–01, 16–10
- 1995 Association Agreement with Israel...... 2–09, 14–09, 14–57
- 1995 Partnership and Co-operation Agreement with Belarus.. 14–45, 14–47, 25–33
- 1995 Partnership and Co-operation Agreement with Kazakhstan....... 2–10, 14–09, 14–45, 14–47, 14–60, 25–33
- 1995 Partnership and Co-operation Agreement with Kyrgyzstan....... 2–10, 14–09, 14–45, 14–47, 14–60, 25–33
- 1995 Association Agreement with Romania... 15–12, 16–01, 25–32
- 1995 Association Agreement with Slovakia ... 15–12, 16–01, 16–32
- 1996 Association Agreement with Morocco... 2–09, 14–09, 14–57, 14–58, 15–01, 16–18
  - art.40............. 14–61, 14–62
  - art.64................ 14–61
  - art.65(1)............... 14–64
- 1996 Partnership and Co-operation Agreement with Armenia . 2–10, 14–09, 14–45, 14–47, 14–60, 25–33
- 1996 Partnership and Co-operation Agreement with Azerbaijan....... 2–10, 14–09, 14–45, 14–47, 14–60, 25–33
- 1996 Partnership and Co-operation Agreement with Mongolia 14–45, 14–47, 25–33
- 1996 Partnership and Co-operation Agreement with Tajikstan. 2–10, 14–09, 14–45, 14–47, 14–60, 25–33
- 1996 Partnership and Co-operation Agreement with Turkmenistan 14–45, 25–33
- 1997 Association Agreement with Jordan 2–09, 14–09, 14–57
  - art.80(1)—(2)............ 14–58
- 1998 Association Agreement with Estonia......... 15–12, 16–01
- 1998 Association Agreement with Latvia.......... 15–12, 16–01
- 1998 Association Agreement with Lithuania 15–12, 16–01
- 1999 Agreement with Swiss Confederation on Free Movement of Persons ... 5–32, 14–21, 14–22, 14–23, 14–24, 14–25, **A7–01**
  - art.1 14–22
  - art.4 14–23
  - art.5 14–23
  - art.8(d) 14–24
  - (e) 14–24
  - art.9 14–23
  - art.10(1)................ 14–24
  - (2) 14–24
  - Annex I art.15(1) 14–24
- 2000 Partnership Agreement with African, Caribbean and Pacific States (Cotonou).. 1–79, 14–69
  - art.13(3)................ 14–71
- 2001 Association Agreement with Egypt...... 2–09, 14–09, 14–57
  - art.62................. 14–58
- 2001 Stabilisation and Association Agreement with Croatia.. 2–09, 14–07, 14–08, 14–34, 14–60
  - preamble 15–10
  - art.45....... 14–08, 14–38, 16–05, 16–08, 25–32
  - art.47.................. 14–44
  - arts 48—49......... 14–08, 25–32
  - art.49........... 14–39, 16–32
  - (4) 14–41, 16–01, 16–32
  - art.54(1)............ 14–42, 16–32
  - art.56.................. 16–39
  - (2) 16–01, 16–40
  - (3) 16–01, 16–39
  - art.62(1)................ 16–37
  - art.63.................. 16–36
- 2002 Agreement with Chile on Scientific and Technological Co-operation 14–74
- 2002 Association Agreement with Algeria 2–09, 14–09, 14–57, 14–58, 14–64
  - art.67(1)................ 14–59
- 2002 Association Agreement with Chile 14–73, 14–74, 14–75
  - Title III Ch.III 14–76
  - art.132............ 14–76, 14–78
  - art.134........... 14–77, 14–78
  - Annex X 14–76

Table of EU Agreements

2002	Association Agreement with Lebanon 2–09, 14–09, 14–57		2006	Stabilisation and Association Agreement with Albania. . 2–09, 14–07, 14–34, 14–60, 25–32

- 2002 Association Agreement with Lebanon 2–09, 14–09, 14–57
  - art.64. 14–58
- 2002 Association Agreement with Tunisia 2–09, 14–09, 14–57, 14–58
  - art.64(1). 14–63
  - art.65(1). 14–64
- 2002 Euro-Mediterranean Agreements. 2–09, 14–58
- 2004 Stabilisation and Association Agreement with Macedonia 2–09, 14–07, 14–34, 14–36, 14–37, 14–43, 14–44, 14–56, 14–60, 25–32, **A11–01**
  - preamble 15–10
  - art.38(1). 16–29
  - art.44. . . . . 16–11, 16–29
    - (1) 14–37, 14–38, 16–12, 16–19, 16–22, 16–24, 16–31
  - art.44. . . . . . . 16–05, 16–10, 16–11
  - art.46. 14–44
  - art.48. 14–42
    - (1) 14–40
    - (3) 14–39, 14–40, 14–41, 16–01, 16–32
    - (4) 14–41, 16–32
  - art.53. 16–32
    - (1) 14–42, 16–36
    - (2) 14–43, 16–33
    - (3) 16–35
  - art.55. 16–39
    - (2) 16–01, 16–40
    - (3) 16–01, 16–39
  - art.61(1). 16–37
  - art.62. . . . . . . 15–06, 16–09, 16–10, 16–12, 16–36, 16–37
- 2005 Horizontal Agreement with Chile on Air Transport . . 14–74
- 2006 Stabilisation and Association Agreement with Albania. . 2–09, 14–07, 14–34, 14–60, 25–32
  - preamble 15–10
  - art.46. . . . . . . 14–38, 16–05, 16–08
  - art.48. 14–44
  - art.50. . . . . 14–39, 16–32
    - (4) 14–41, 16–01, 16–32
  - art.55(1). 14–42, 16–32
  - art.57. 16–39
    - (2) 16–01, 16–40
    - (3) 16–01, 16–39
  - art.63(1). 16–37
  - art.64. 16–36
- 2007 Stabilisation and Association Agreement with Montenegro 14–34, 14–60, 25–32
  - art.49. . . . . . . 14–38, 16–05, 16–08
  - art.51. 14–44
  - art.53. . . . . 14–39, 16–32
    - (4) 14–41, 16–01, 16–32
  - art.58(1). 14–42, 16–32
  - art.59. 16–39
    - (2) 16–01, 16–40
    - (3) 16–01
  - art.65(1). 16–37
  - art.66. 16–36
- 2008 Stabilisation and Association Agreement with Bosnia and Herzegovina . . . 2–09, 14–07, 14–34
- 2009 Stabilisation and Association Agreement with Serbia. . . 2–09, 14–07, 14–34
- 2009 Stabilisation and Association Agreements with Western Balkan States 14–30, 14–31, 14–32, 14–33, 14–34, 14–36

TABLE OF INTERNATIONAL TREATIES AND CONVENTIONS

1886	Convention for the Protection of Literary and Artistic Works 15–09		art.3 .... 3–12, 3–24
			art.6 3–11
1948	Universal Declaration on Human Rights 2–63		art.8 ..... 3–05, 9–09, 9–12, 9–13, 9–47, 9–63, 9–74, 9–80, 10–106, 13–29, 16–30, 24–23
	art.1 2–63		(1) 9–10, 9–11
	art.2 .... 2–63, 11–04		(2) 9–11, 9–15
	art.7 2–63		art.12 .... 3-11, 9–44, 9–47
	art.16(2) 9–30		art.14 .... 2–65, 10–116, 11–04
1949	Geneva Convention	1953	European Convention on Social and Medical Assistance 4–18, 13–64
	art.26 3-05		
1950	European Convention on Human Rights 2–65, 3–03, 3–04, 3–09, 3–11, 3–13, 3–14, 3–15, 9–09, 9–16, 9–48, 9–49, 9–69, 9–83, 11–05, 11–23, 13–64	1979	Convention to Eliminate All Forms of Discrimination Against Women art.16(1)(b) 9–30
	art.1 9–13	1994	General Agreement on Tariffs and Trade 2–11
	art.2 3–05		

TABLE OF STATUTES

1971	Immigration Act (c.77) . . .6–52, 24–01, 24–07, 25–08	1994	European Union Accessions Act (c.38) 23–01, 23–04
	s.3(5)(a) 25–29	1997	Special Immigration Appeals Act (c.68) 13–49
	s.7 10–38		
	s.15(1)(a) 25–30	1998	European Communities (Amendment) Act (c.21). . 23–01, 23–04
	Sch.2 para.8 25–24		
1972	European Communities Act (c.68) 23–01, 23–01	1999	Immigration and Asylum Act (c.33) . . . .
	s.1 . . . . 23–03, 23–04		s.10(1)(a) 25–31
	ss.1—3 . . . . **A12–01**	2002	European Communities (Amendment) Act (c.3). . . 23–01, 23–04
	s.2 23–05		
	(1) 23–05, 23–06		
	(2) 23–07	2002	British Overseas Territories Act (c.8) 24–03
	(4) 23–07		
	s.3 23–08	2002	Nationality, Immigration and Asylum Act (c.41)
	(1) 23–08		
	(2) 23–08		s.88(2)(d) 25–06
1981	British Nationality Act (c.61) . 24–02	2003	European Union (Accessions) Act (c.35) 23–01, 23–04
1985	European Communities (Spanish and Portuguese Accession) Act (c.75) 23–01, 23–04		
		2004	Civil Partnership Act (c.33). . . 24–23
		2006	European Union (Accessions) Act (c.2) 23–01, 23–04
1986	European Communities (Amendment) Act (c.58). . 23–01, 23–04		
		2006	Immigration, Asylum and Nationality Act (c.13) . . .
1988	Immigration Act (c.14) 24–01, 24–06, 25–30		s.36 24–26
		2007	Tribunals, Courts and Enforcement Act (c.15)
	s.7 . . . . **A13–01**		s.13(6) 23–14
	(1) 24–06		
	(2) 24–07	2007	UK Borders Act (c.30) ss.40—42 24–26
1993	European Communities (Amendment) Act (c.32). . 23–01, 23–04		
		2008	European Union (Amendment) Act (c.7) 23–01, 23–04
1993	European Economic Area Act (c.51) 23–01, 23–04	2011	European Union Act (c.12) . . . 23–01

[liii]

TABLE OF STATUTORY INSTRUMENTS

1998	Civil Procedure Rules (SI 1998/3132)		Pt 4............. 24–11, 24–29
			reg.21 .... 24–11, 24–29
	Pt 68 23–13		(2) 24–29
2002	Immigration (Swiss Free Movement of Persons) (No.3) Regulations (SI 2002/1241) 24–01, 25–01, 25–02, **A18–01**		(3) 24–29
			(4) 24–29
			(5)(b) 24–29
			(c) 24–29
			(e) 24–29
2004	Accession (Immigration and Worker Registration) Regulations (SI 2004/121). 24–01, 24–31, 24–32, 24–33		Pt 5 24–11
			Pt 6 24–11
			reg.26 24–11
		2006	Accession (Immigration and Worker Authorisation) Regulations (SI 2006/3317) 24–01, 24–31, 24–32, 24–34, **A16–01**
2004	Immigration (European Economic Area) and Accession (Amendment) Regulations (SI 2004/1236) 24–31		
2005	Asylum and Immigration (Procedure) Rules (SI 2005/23)	2009	Immigration (European Economic Area) (Amendment) Regulations (SI 2009/1117) 24–01
	r.45 24–26		
	r.51 24–26	2009	Immigration ((European Economic Area) (Amendment) Regulations (SI 2011/1247) 24–07, 24–11, **A15–01**
2006	Immigration (European Economic Area) Regulations (SI 2006/1003) 24–01, 24–08, 24–12, 24–15, 24–28, 24–30, 24–31, 24–32, 24–33, 25–01, 25–02, 25–03, **A14–01**		
		2011	Accession (Immigration and Worker Registration) (Revocation, Savings and Consequential Provisions) Regulations (SI 2011/544). 24–31, **A17–01**
	Pt 1 24–10		
	reg.2 24–10		
	reg.4 24–10		
	reg.6 24–10	2011	Treaty of Lisbon (Changes in Terminology) Order (SI 2011/1043) 23–01
	reg.7 24–10		
	reg.8 .... 24–10, 24–16	2011	Immigration (European Economic Area) (Amendment) Regulations (SI 2011/1247) 24–01
	(2) 24–14, 24–16		
	(5) 24–23		
	reg.9 24–21		
	(2) 24–22	2011	Accession (Immigration and Worker Authorisation) (Amendment) Regulations (SI 2011/2816) 24–34
	reg.10 ...... 24–10, 24–27, 24–28		
	Pt 2 24–11		
	reg.11 24–11		
	reg.12 .... 24–11, 24–14	2011	First-tier Tribunal (Immigration and Asylum Chamber) Fees Order (SI 2011/2841) 23–17
	Pt 3 24–11		
	reg.13 24–11		
	reg.14 24–11		
	reg.15 .... 24–11, 24–18		

Part One
FUNDAMENTAL PRINCIPLES OF EU LAW

CHAPTER 1

TREATY FOUNDATIONS AND INSTITUTIONS

This chapter examines the foundation stones of European Union law and charts the development of the Treaties establishing (originally) the European Community and the European Union. The principal European Union institutions are described, as are their powers.

1. TREATY FOUNDATIONS

(a) *Introduction*

The creation of the European Union as a political and economic collective of States has been a gradual process that began in 1950 in the wake of the Second World War. The six original Member States[1] of the European Coal and Steel Community (ECSC) aimed to use European integration to ensure that the events of the Second World War would not be repeated.[2] **1–01**

The European Union is now a body comprising of 27 Member States.[3] It represents one of the most powerful trading blocs in the world, with a total population of just under half a billion people. Whilst originally the ECSC and then the European Economic Community were concerned principally with economic co-operation, leaving civil and political co-operation to the Council of Europe, the European Union is now involved in a range of political areas including freedom, security and justice, defence and environmental protection. **1–02**

Co-operation between the Member States of the European Union is based on four founding Treaties: **1–03**

(a) The Treaty establishing the European Coal and Steel Community (ECSC), which was signed on April 18, 1951 in Paris, entered into force on July 23, 1952 and expired on July 23, 2002 (see para.1–07 below);

(b) The Treaty establishing the European Atomic Energy Community (EAEC), which was signed (along with the EEC Treaty) in Rome on March 25, 1957, and entered into force on January 1, 1958 (see paras 1–08 to 1–09 below);

---

[1] Germany, France, Belgium, Netherlands, Luxembourg and Italy.
[2] It was first proposed by the French Foreign Minister Robert Schumann in a speech on May 9, 1950. This date, the "birthday" of what is now the EU, is celebrated annually as Europe Day.
[3] Denmark, Ireland and the United Kingdom joined in 1973, Greece in 1981, Spain and Portugal in 1986, Austria, Finland and Sweden in 1995. On May 1, 2004 the largest enlargement took place with 10 new countries joining: Estonia, Latvia, Lithuania, Slovenia, Slovakia, Czech Republic, Malta, Cyprus, Poland and Hungary. Enlargement continued on January 1, 2007 when Bulgaria and Romania joined. Croatia, the Former Yugoslav Republic of Macedonia and Turkey are also candidates for membership.

(c) The Treaty establishing the European Economic Community (EEC) ("the Treaty of Rome") (see paras 1–10 to 1–16 below); and

(d) the Treaty on European Union, which was signed in Maastricht on February 7, 1992, entered into force on November 1, 1993 ("the Maastricht Treaty") (see paras 1–19 to 1–22 below).

Each of these Treaties is analysed in further detail below.

1–04 The Maastricht Treaty changed the name of the European Economic Community to simply "the European Community" ("the EC"). It also introduced new forms of co-operation between the Member State governments—for example on defence and in the area of "justice and home affairs". By adding this intergovernmental co-operation to the existing "Community" structure, the Maastricht Treaty created a new structure with three "pillars", and expanded the scope of that co-operation to include political as well economic areas. This is the European Union ("the EU").

1–05 The founding Treaties have been amended on several occasions, in particular when new Member States acceded in 1973 (Denmark, Ireland and the United Kingdom), 1981 (Greece), 1986 (Spain and Portugal), 1995 (Austria and Finland, Sweden), 2004 (Estonia, Latvia, Lithuania, Slovenia, Slovakia, Czech Republic, Malta, Cyprus, Poland and Hungary) and in 2007 (Bulgaria and Romania).

1–06 There have also been more far-reaching reforms bringing major institutional changes and introducing new areas of responsibility for the European institutions through further Treaties:

(a) The Merger Treaty, signed in Brussels on April 8, 1965, in force since July 1,1967, provided for a single Commission and a single Council of the then three European Communities.

(b) The Single European Act (SEA), signed in Luxembourg and the Hague, entered into force on July 1, 1987, provided for the adaptations required for the achievement of the internal market (see paras 1–17 to 1–18 below).

(c) The Treaty of Amsterdam, signed on October 2, 1997, entered into force on May 1, 1999, amended and renumbered the EU and EC Treaty. The Treaty of Amsterdam changed the articles of the EU Treaties, identified by letters A to S, into numerical form (see paras 1–23 to 1–25 below).

(d) The Treaty of Nice, signed on February 26, 2001, entered into force on February 1, 2003, amended certain provisions in the EU and EC Treaties (see paras 1–26 to 1–28 below).

(e) The Treaty of Lisbon, signed on December 13, 2007, entered into force on December 1, 2009, provided for the European Union to have legal personality acquiring the competences previously conferred on the European Community and for it to be founded on the Treaty on

European Union and on the Treaty on the Functioning of the European Union (with each to have the same legal value) (see paras 1–29 to 1–34 below).[4]

(b) *The Treaty establishing the European Coal and Steel Community*

The Treaty establishing the European Coal and Steel Community (ECSC) was signed on April 18, 1951 in Paris and entered into force on July 23, 1952. It contained a chapter on workers and movement of workers (Chapter VIII). The provisions were restricted to those employed in the coal and steel industries. Although provisions relating to discrimination in remuneration and working conditions are replicated throughout subsequent Treaty of Rome provisions, the free movement provisions themselves were much weaker than those contained in the Treaty of Rome. In the ECSC Treaty Member States retained their competence as regards the free movement of workers whereas in the Treaty of Rome competence in this area was ceded to the Community.[5] The ECSC Treaty expired on July 23, 2002 and its significance is now only historical.[6]

1–07

(c) *The Treaty establishing the European Atomic Energy Community*

The Treaty establishing the European Atomic Energy Community (EAEC) was signed along with the Treaty of Rome on March 25, 1957, and entered into force on January 1, 1958. As with the ECSC Treaty, art.232(2) of the Treaty of Rome provides that its provisions do not derogate from those of the Euratom Treaty.

1–08

In the field of free movement of persons, art.96 EAEC contains a provision on the free movement of those working in the field of nuclear energy. Member States were required to abolish all restrictions on the free movement of workers in the nuclear industry. In 1962 a directive was adopted by the Euratom Council to give effect to art.96.[7] Its scope is limited to those in skilled employment in the field of nuclear energy. Skilled employment is confined to those with specialist knowledge or undertaking particular tasks in the industry. The 1962 Directive is a very short directive and provides only that Member States will adopt measures for the "automatic granting of authorisations" of any skilled employment in the field. The Directive makes clear that all other aspects of free movement are to be regulated by measures

1–09

---

[4] The Treaty in part replaced the Treaty Establishing a Constitution for Europe which had been signed by the then 25 EU Member States on October 29, 2004. Although later ratified by 18 Member States, rejection by French and Dutch voters at referenda in May and June 2005 ended the ratification process and consigned the Treaty Establishing a Constitution for Europe to the annals of history.

[5] art.69(1) and (3) of the ECSC Treaty.

[6] art.232(1) of the Treaty of Rome stated that its provisions did not affect those of the ECSC Treaty. Thus whilst the ECSC Treaty remained in force, those falling within the personal scope of art.69 of that Treaty would not be governed by the Treaty of Rome or more recently the EC Treaty.

[7] EAEC Council Directive on freedom to take skilled employment in the field of nuclear energy [1962] O.J. P 057 1650.

(d) *The Treaty establishing the European Economic Community*

1–10 The Treaty establishing the European Economic Community is more commonly referred to as the Treaty of Rome[9]. It was the central plank of the European Economic Community ("the EEC"). Article 2, which was amended by the Maastricht Treaty, laid down the objectives of the EEC: to establish a common market and economic and monetary union in order to promote throughout the Community development of economic activities, social cohesion, high levels of employment and social protection, and to raise the standard of living in the Member States.

1–11 The creation of a "common market" would involve the elimination of obstacles to trade between Member States to create conditions as close as possible to an internal market. National frontiers therefore were intended to be abolished as regards the transaction of commerce.

1–12 Article 3(c) set out the four freedoms which are the cornerstone of the creation of that internal market:

(a) free movement of goods;

(b) free movement of persons;

(c) free movement of services; and

(d) free movement of capital.

1–13 Article 5 directed Member States to take all appropriate measures to ensure the fulfilment of the obligations arising out of the Treaty or resulting from actions taken by the institutions of the Community.[10] Article 7 contained a general prohibition on non-discrimination on grounds of nationality in areas of application of the Treaty.[11]

1–14 It is the provisions which originated in the Treaty on the free movement of persons which are of principal interest in this book. Free movement rights were clearly confined to areas of economic activity. Articles 48 to 50[12] provided for the free movement of workers which are discussed in detail in Ch.6. Articles 52 to 58[13] contained provisions relating to the right of

---

[8] In principle this means that the free movement of those employed in the nuclear energy industry is governed by Directive 2004/38/EC other than where the 1962 Directive applies.
[9] References which follow in this section are to the Treaty's articles as then in force. The Treaty was renamed by the Maastricht Treaty and post-Lisbon Treaty is now the Treaty on the Functioning of the European Union (see para.1–29, below).
[10] See further discussion in paras 2–27 to 2–35 on the Community legal order. See now post-Lisbon Treaty art.2–6 of the TFEU defining the categories and areas of Union competence.
[11] Now art.18 TFEU post-Lisbon Treaty. See further discussion in paras 2–63 to 2–66 on non-discrimination.
[12] Now arts 45 to 48 TFEU post-Lisbon Treaty.
[13] Now arts 49 to 54 TFEU post-Lisbon Treaty.

establishment. Articles 59 to 66[14] provided for the freedom to provide services. Both the freedom of establish-ment and freedom to provide services are discussed in detail in Ch.7.

1–15 The Treaty contained provisions establishing the institutions of the European Community including the European Commission and the European Court of Justice. The principal Community institutions are discussed in para.1–35 et seq., below.

1–16 Many of the subsequent Treaties amended wording and numbering of the provisions contained originally in the Treaty of Rome, which following the Lisbon Treaty became the Treaty on the functioning of the European Union (TFEU). Nevertheless, the Rome Treaty's principal provisions relating to the four freedoms remain at the heart of the European Union's legal order today. Whilst the core activities have expanded[15] and the creation of the European Union has added a political dimension to the co-operation between the Member States, the internal market remains of key interest.

(e) *The Single European Act*

1–17 The Single European Act was signed in February 1986. The principal objective of the Act was the completion of the internal market by the end of 1992. To that end art.13 of the Act inserted art.8a[16] into the Treaty of Rome which stated that the Community would adopt measures with the aim of progressively establishing the internal market over a period expiring on December 31, 1992. It further stated that:

> "The internal market shall comprise an area without internal frontiers in which the free movement of goods, persons, services and capital is ensured in accordance with the provisions of this Treaty".

Article 13 of the Act has been the cause of considerable controversy since there is a divergence in understanding of that provision between Member States. The UK Government maintains the position that the provision means that since not all persons are covered by the internal market principle, border checks must remain in place. Other Member States considered it meant the abolition of all checks.

1–18 To some extent this controversy has been alleviated by the creation of the Schengen Agreement (1985) and the Schengen Convention (1990) which create a border free area for the participating Member States.

---

[14] Now arts 56–62 TFEU post-Lisbon Treaty.
[15] See now post-Lisbon arts 3–6 TFEU.
[16] See now post-Lisbon art.26 TFEU.

(f) *The Maastricht Treaty*

1–19 The Treaty on European Union was signed in Maastricht on February 7, 1992 and entered into force on November 1, 1993 (the "Maastricht Treaty"). The Maastricht Treaty created the European Union which was founded on the European Communities and was to represent "a new stage in the processing of creating an ever closed union".

1–20 Title II of the Maastricht Treaty contained provisions amending the Treaty of Rome with a view to establishing the European Community ("the EC"). Thereafter the Treaty of Rome was to be referred to as the Treaty establishing the European Community. The most significant amendment to that Treaty was the inclusion of art.8[17] which signified the creation of the European Union citizen and art.8a[18] which granted the right of every citizen of the European Union to move freely within the territory of the Union. These provisions are discussed in detail in Ch.4 below. Together with Titles III and IV of the Maastricht Treaty which contained amended provisions of the ECSC Treaty and the EAEC this constituted the "first pillar" of the European Union.

1–21 The second pillar was set out in Title V which contained provisions on common foreign and security policies. Member States agreed to co-operate in areas of foreign policy and security and to support the Union's external foreign and securities policies.

1–22 The third pillar was set out in Title VI which contained provisions on co-operation in the fields of justice and home affairs. Of principal interest was the creation of a list of areas of common interest for the Member States including asylum policies, immigration policies relating to external borders and admission of third country nationals and matters relating to policing and judicial co-operation in both civil and criminal matters. The inclusion of this third pillar was significant since it demonstrated a broadening of the areas of interest beyond the internal market. As a result of the inclusion of Title VI the Member States made a number of resolutions in the areas of justice and home affairs such as the London Resolutions on asylum.[19] However third pillar measures made under Title VI were considered as soft law and did not fall within Community competence until the Amsterdam Treaty.

---

[17] See now post-Lisbon art.20 TFEU.
[18] See now post-Lisbon art.21 TFEU.
[19] The London Resolutions include the conclusion on countries in which there is generally no serious risk of persecution; Resolution on manifestly unfounded applications for asylum; and Resolution on a harmonised approach to questions concerning host third countries: London, November 30, and December 1, 1992 (SN 2836/93 (WGI 1505)).

(g) *The Amsterdam Treaty*

The Treaty of Amsterdam was signed on October 2, 1997 and entered into force on May 1, 1999. It amended both the Maastricht Treaty and the Treaty establishing the European Community.[20] To avoid confusion we refer to these Treaties as the EU Treaty and the EC Treaty, respectively, following the Amsterdam Treaty since a significant number of the changes were in the numbering of both the EU and EC Treaty provisions.

1–23

Under the Amsterdam Treaty the third pillar of the Maastricht Treaty was moved to be included in the Treaty establishing the European Community thus bringing the areas of justice and home affairs within the competence of the Community. The Community would thus be able to make directives and regulations in areas such as asylum and the immigration of third country nationals. This significantly broadened the scope of the EC Treaty.

1–24

These provisions are not the subject of this book since they are not generally concerned with the rights of free movement within the EU or the rights of EU citizens. Rather they are concerned with the movement and rights of third country nationals from outside the European Union to within it. To date the Council has adopted a number of asylum measures.[21] As regards immigration measures these have included measures relating to the common visa list,[22] the rights of long-term resident third country nationals in the European Union,[23] the right to family reunification for certain third country nationals resident in the European Union,[24] and the conditions of admission for students and volunteers[25] and highly qualified employment.[26]

1–25

---

[20] Originally the Treaty of Rome, renamed by Maastricht Treaty.
[21] Asylum measures adopted under Title IV include:
   1. Dec.2000/596/EC on European refugee fund [2000] O.J. L252/12.
   2. Regulation 2725/2000 on Eurodac [2000] O.J. L316/1: applied from January 15, 2003.
   3. Directive 2001/55 on temporary protection [2001] O.J. L 212/12): implement by December 31, 2002.
   4. Regulation 407/2002 implementing Eurodac Regulation [2002] O.J. L62/1.
   5. Directive 2003/9 on reception conditions [2003] O.J. L31/18.
   6. Dublin II Regulation 343/2003 [2003] O.J. L50/1: in force September 1, 2003.
   7. Regulation 1560/2003 implementing Dublin II [2003] O.J. L222/3: in force September 6, 2003.
   8. Directive 2004/83/EC [2004] O.J. L304/2 on the definition of a refugee and person in need of subsidiary protection.
   9. Directive 2005/85/EC on asylum procedures [2005] O.J. L326/13.
[22] Regulation 539/2001 establishing visa list [2001] O.J. L81/1; see also Regulation 2414/2001 moving Romania to "white list" not requiring visas [2001] O.J. L327/1, Regulation 453/2003 on visa list [2003] L69/10 and Regulation 1091/2010 [2010] O.J. L 329/1 on Albania and Bosnia Herzegovina. The UK and Ireland have opted out of all these measures.
[23] Long term migrants directive [2004] O.J. L16/44. The UK has opted out of this measure.
[24] Directive 2003/86 on family reunification ([2003] O.J. L251/12). The UK has opted out of this measure. In *Dereci v Bundesministrium für Inneres* (C-256/11) [2012] E.C.R. I-0000 the CJEU specifically found that this directive does not apply to Union citizens and their family members.
[25] Directive 2004/114/EC on the conditons of admissions of third country nationals for the purposes of studies, pupil exchange, unremunerated training or voluntary service. The UK has opted out of this measure.
[26] Directive 2009/50/EC on the conditions of entry and residence of third country nationals for the purposes of highly qualified employment. The UK has opted out of this measure.

(h) *Treaty of Nice*

1–26 The Treaty of Nice was signed on February 26, 2001 and entered into force on February 1, 2003. It amended a number of provisions of the EC and EU Treaties. The Treaty of Nice was prepared anticipating the accession of 10 new Member States due in May 2004 and thus it made particular institutional amendments which would incorporate those Member States into the Council and Parliament.

1–27 Revision of the Treaties took place in four key areas:

(a) size and composition of the Commission;

(b) weighting of votes in the Council;

(c) extension of qualified-majority voting; and

(d) enhanced co-operation.

1–28 There were no major institutional or legal changes brought about by the Treaty of Nice but rather adjustments to address deficiencies in the functioning of the Community and possible imbalance which could result from enlargement by 10 new Member States.

(i) *The Treaty of Lisbon*

1–29 The Treaty of Lisbon was signed on December 13, 2007 and entered into force on December 1, 2009. As noted in the preamble, the aim of the Treaty was "to complete the process started by the Treaty of Amsterdam and by the Treaty of Nice with a view to enhancing the efficiency and democratic legitimacy of the Union and to improving the coherence of its action". The Treaty amends the Treaty on European Union (TEU or the EU Treaty) and the Treaty establishing the European Community (the EC Treaty), with the later being renamed the Treaty on the Functioning of the European Union (TFEU). Each is stated to have "the same legal value").[27]

1–30 Modifications made by the Lisbon Treaty to the Maastricht Treaty set out in the TEU affect the institutions, enhanced co-operation, foreign and security policy and defence policy. The Treaty of Lisbon merged the three pillars created by the Maastricht Treaty and as a consolidated entity the Union succeeded the legal personality of the European Communities, enabling the Union to sign international treaties in its own name. From November 1, 2014 a new rule of double majority voting will be introduced ("a qualified majority shall be defined as at least 55 per cent of the members of the Council, comprising at least 15 of them and representing Member States comprising at least 65 per cent of the population of the Union"[28]). Until that date arrangements under the Treaty of Nice remain in place. Qualified majority voting is extended to new areas, including external

---

[27] art.1 of the Lisbon Treaty.
[28] art.16 TEU.

border control, asylum and immigration (where the UK and Ireland enjoy opt out clauses).

The Lisbon Treaty for the first time explicitly recognizes the possibility for a Member State to withdraw from the Union. 1–31

The Treaty creates the position of a High Representative of the Union for Foreign Affairs and Security Policy, also Vice-President of the Commission (with back up and support provided by a European External Action Service). 1–32

The Charter of Fundamental Rights is made legally binding.[29] Whereas the rejected Treaty establishing a constitution for Europe had integrated the Charter as part of that treaty itself, the Lisbon Treaty incorporates the Charter by reference and gives it legal status without it forming part of the treaties. 1–33

Modifications to the Rome Treaty set out in the TFEU include the determination and the delimitation of the Union's competences, thereby clarifying the distribution of power between the union and its Members States. There are three categories of competence. The Union's exclusive competence in areas where it legislates alone include the customs union, competition rules for the functioning of the internal market, and monetary policy for Members States whose currency is the euro. Shared competence between the Union and Member States (with States exercising their competence if the Union is not exercising its own) include the area of freedom, security and justice. Finally, areas where Members States have exclusive competence but in which the Union can provide support or co-ordination include the protection and improvement of healthcare, culture and tourism. 1–34

2. THE EU INSTITUTIONS

(a) *Introduction*

Article 13 of the TEU provides that "the Union shall have an institutional framework which shall aim to promote its values, advance its objectives, serve its interests, those of its citizens and those of the Member States, and ensure the consistency, effectiveness and continuity of its policies and actions". There are seven institutions. These are the European Parliament, the European Council, the Council of the European Union, the European Commission, the Court of Justice of the European Union, the European Central Bank, and the Court of Auditors. 1–35

---

[29] Poland, the United Kingdom and the Czech Republic have a Protocol on the application of the Charter of Fundamental Rights. Article 1 of that Protocol provides: "The Charter does not extend the ability of the Court of Justice of the European Union, or any court or tribunal of Poland or of the United Kingdom (and the Czech Republic), to find that the laws, regulations or administrative provisions, practices or action of Poland or of the United Kingdom (or the Czech Republic) are inconsistent with the fundamental rights, freedoms and principles that it reaffirms".

1-36 The "European Council" is not to be confused with the Council of the European Union. Whilst (jointly with the European Parliament—see further below) the latter exercises legislative and budgetary functions, the former is charged by the Lisbon treaty with providing the Union with "the necessary impetus for its development" and with defining its "general political directions and priorities".[30]

1-37 The EU's decision-making process involves three main institutions:

(a) the European Parliament which represents the European Union's citizens and is directly elected by them;[31]

(b) the Council of the European Union which represents the individual Member States;[32] and

(c) the European Commission, which seeks to uphold the interests of the Union as a whole[33].

These three bodies together produce the policies and laws (directives, regulations and decisions) that apply throughout the European Union. In principle, it is the Commission that proposes new EU laws and it is the Parliament and Council that adopt them.

1-30 There are two other institutions of principal importance:

(a) the Court of Justice of the European Union which upholds the rule of law in the European Union[34]; and

(b) the Court of Auditors which checks the financing of the Union's activities[35].

These institutions were set up under the Treaties outlined above. The Treaties themselves are agreed by the key political figures in the Member States and ratified by their national Parliaments. They lay down the rules and procedures that the EU institutions must follow.

---

[30] art.15 TEU. Although established as an informal body in 1960, the European Council became an official EU institution for the first time in 2009 on entry into force of the Lisbon Treaty.
[31] art.14 TEU.
[32] art.14 TEU (referred to as "the Council").
[33] art.17 TEU.
[34] art.19 TEU.
[35] art.285 TFEU.

(b) *The European Parliament*[36]

The Parliament is composed of "representatives of the Union's citizens."[37] The representatives are known as Members of the European Parliament (MEPs). They are elected for terms of five years.[38] The number of MEPs (which shall not exceed 750[39]) is currently 736, organised into seven political rather than national groups.

1–39

The European Parliament operates from France, Belgium and Luxembourg. The monthly plenary sessions, which all MEPs attend, are held in Strasbourg, France. Parliamentary committee meetings and any additional plenary sessions are held in Brussels (Belgium), whilst Luxembourg is home to the administrative offices (the "General Secretariat").

1–40

Parliament has three main roles. First, it shares with the Council the power to legislate. Secondly, it exercises *democratic supervision* over all EU institutions, and in particular the Commission. It has the power to approve or reject the nomination of Commissioners, and it has the right to censure the Commission as a whole (by calling on the Commission to resign). Finally, it shares with the Council *authority over the EU budget* and can therefore influence EU spending. The powers of the European Parliament were significantly increased by the Lisbon Treaty by bringing over 40 new fields within the co-decision procedure under which Parliament has equal rights with the Council. Moreover, post-Lisbon Parliament has a bigger role in setting budgets (on equal footing with the Council). MEPs will now also have to consent to a range of international agreements negotiated by the EU given its new legal personality post-Lisbon.

1–41

(i) *The Power to Legislate*

The majority of EU laws are enacted by the "ordinary legislative procedure" whereby the European Parliament acts—together with the Council—following submission to each of a proposal by the Commission.[40]

1–42

On receipt of a legislative proposal from the Commission the European Parliament adopts its position at first reading which is then communicated to the Council. If approved by the Council the Act is adopted in the wording corresponding to the position of the European Parliament. If not approved by the Council, the Council adopts its position at first reading (which is then communicated to the European Parliament). On second reading within three months the European Parliament may approve the Council's position at first reading (the Act is deemed adopted in the wording corresponding to the position of the Council). However, if the European Parliament by majority rejects the Council's position then "the proposed act shall be deemed not to have been adopted".[41]

1–43

---

[36] The Parliament is provided for in art.14 TEU and arts 223–234 TFEU.
[37] art.14.2 TEU.
[38] art.14.3 TEU.
[39] art.14.1 TEU.
[40] art.294 TFEU.
[41] art.294.7(b) TFEU.

1–44 Short of rejection, the European Parliament can amend the Council's position (forwarding the amended text to both the Council and the Commission, whereby the latter shall "deliver an opinion on those amendments".[42]) On receipt the Council (acting by a qualified majority) may approve all amendments whereby the Act is deemed adopted. If not all are approved the Presidents of the Parliament and Council are obliged to convene a meeting of the "Conciliation Committee."[43] Composed of the members of the Council (or their representatives) and an equal number of members representing the European Parliament, the Conciliation Committee is tasked with coming up with a joint text.[44] If no joint text is approved within six weeks the proposed act is deemed not to have been adopted.[45] If such joint text is approved, both Parliament and Council have six weeks (extendable by two weeks) to adopt the act in accordance with the approved joint text at third reading. If they fail to do so, the proposed Act is deemed not to have been adopted.[46]

1–45 Special provisions apply as regards the role of the European Commission where a legislative Act is submitted to the ordinary legislative procedure on the initiative of a group of Member States, on a recommendation by the European Central Bank or at the request of the Court of Justice.[47]

(ii) *Democratic supervision*

1–46 Parliament exercises democratic supervision over the other European institutions. It does so in several ways. First, the Commission as a body is "responsible to the European Parliament".[48] Parliament elects the President of the Commission (following nomination of a candidate by the Council).[49] Also, such President, together with the High Representative of the Union for Foreign Affairs and Security Policy and the other members of the Commission are subject as a body to a vote of consent by the European Parliament. Secondly, the Commission is politically answerable to Parliament, which can pass a "motion of censure" on the activities of the Commission which if passed by a two-thirds majority of the votes cast (representing a majority of MEPs) requires the resignation of the Commission "as a body". Also, the High Representative of the Union for Foreign Affairs and Security Policy is required to resign from duties that he or she carries out in the Commission.[50] Following a censure motion they

---

[42] art.294.7(c) TFEU.
[43] art.294.8(b) TFEU. Note that the Council is required to act unanimously on the amendments on which the Commission has delivered a negative opinion (art.294.9 TFEU).
[44] art.294.10 TFEU; voting on such joint text is by qualified majority of the members of the Council (or their representatives) and by a majority of the members representing the European Parliament. The Commission is obliged to take part in the Conciliation Committee's proceedings and to take "all necessary initiatives with a view to reconciling the (respective) positions" (art.294.11 TFEU).
[45] art.2 94.12 TFEU.
[46] art.294.13 TFEU.
[47] art.294.15 TFEU.
[48] art.17.8 TEU.
[49] art.17.7 TEU. If such candidate does not obtain a majority of support from MEPs the Council must propose another candidate within one month.
[50] art.234 TFEU.

remain in office to deal with current business until replaced in accordance with art.17 TEU (although the term of office of the replacement members of the Commission expires on the date on which the members of the Commission required to resign as a body would have expired).

More generally, Parliament exercises control by regularly examining reports sent to it by the Commission (general reports, reports on the implementation of the budget, the application of European Union law, etc.). Moreover, MEPs regularly ask the Commission written and oral questions. The members of the Commission attend plenary sessions of Parliament and meetings of the parliamentary committees, maintaining a continual dialogue between the two institutions. Parliament can also exercise democratic control by examining petitions from citizens and setting up temporary committees of inquiry. 1–47

Finally, Parliament provides input to every EU summit (the European Council meetings). At the opening of each summit, the President of Parliament is invited to express Parliament's views and concerns about topical issues and the items on the European Council's agenda. 1–48

(iii) *The budgetary powers*

Parliament decides on the Union's annual budget with the Council.[51] Post Lisbon Parliament has a bigger role in setting budgets because of the abolition of the old distinction between "compulsory" and "non-compulsory" expenditure. The procedure for adoption of the Union's annual budget is set out in art.314 TFEU and in the event of disagreement between Parliament and the Council involves the use of a "Conciliation Committee" (similar to the use of a conciliation committee within the ordinary legislative procedure[52]). 1–49

Parliament's Committee on Budgetary Control (COCOBU) monitors how the budget is spent, and each year Parliament decides whether to approve the Commission's handling of the budget for the previous financial year. This approval process is technically known as "granting a discharge". 1–50

(c) *The Council of the European Union*[53]

(i) *Organisation of the Council*

The Council is the EU's main decision-making body responsible for policy and legislative decisions (as regards the latter sharing the final say on new EU laws with Parliament). The Council meets in different configurations.[54] It represents the Member States, and its meetings are attended by one minister from each of the EU's national governments. Attendance by 1–51

---

[51] art.310 TFEU.
[52] See above at para.1–44.
[53] The Council is provided for in art.16 TEU and arts 237–243 TFEU.
[54] art.166 TEU.

particular ministers at meetings depends on the configuration of the Council meeting and what subjects are on the agenda.

1–52 Altogether there are 10 different Council configurations:

(a) General Affairs;

(b) Foreign Affairs;

(c) Economic and Financial Affairs ("ECOFIN");

(d) Justice and Home Affairs (JHA);

(e) Employment, Social Policy, Health and Consumer Affairs;

(f) Competitiveness (internal market, industry, research and space);

(g) Transport, Telecommunications and Energy;

(h) Agriculture and Fisheries;

(i) Environment; and

(j) Education, Youth and Culture and Sport.

Nevertheless, the Council remains one single institution. Each minister in the Council is empowered to commit their government.[55] In other words, the minister's signature is the signature of the whole government. Moreover, each minister in the Council is answerable to their national parliament and to the citizens whom that parliament represents. This ensures the democratic legitimacy of the Council's decisions.

(ii) *Powers of the Council*

1–53 Article 16.2 TEU states: The Council shall, jointly with the European Parliament, exercise legislative and budgetary functions. It shall carry out policy-making and co-ordinating functions as laid down in the Treaties. The legislative process is examined in paras 1–42 to 1–45, above. In principle, the Council acts on a proposal from the Commission, and the Commission normally has responsibility for ensuring that EU legislation, once adopted, is correctly applied.

1–54 Each year the Council "concludes" (i.e. officially signs) a number of agreements between the European Union and non-EU countries, as well as with international organisations. These agreements may cover broad areas such as the environment, trade, development, textiles, fisheries, science, technology and transport.

1–55 EU member countries have decided that they want an overall economic policy for Europe, co-ordinated by the economics and finance ministers of each country. It is the Council's duty to co-ordinate such economic policy.

---

[55] art.16.2 TEU.

The Council approves the EU's budget with the Parliament. The Council is also charged with developing the European Union's Common Foreign and Security Policy and co-ordinating co-operation between the national courts and police forces in criminal matters.[56]

(iii) *The Council Presidency*

The Presidency of the Council rotates every six months amongst all Member States. During its Presidency each EU Member State in turn takes charge of the Council agenda and (with one exception) chairs all the meetings for a six-month period, promoting legislative and political decisions and brokering compromises between the Member States. The exception is the Foreign Affairs Council whose meetings are always chaired by the EU's High Representative for foreign and security policy (the post having been created by the Lisbon Treaty).

1–56

(iv) *Decision-making in the Council*

Decisions in the Council are taken by vote. The bigger the country's population, the more votes it has. However, the number is not strictly proportional: it is adjusted in favour of the less populated countries.

1–57

The number of votes is as follows:

1–58

Germany, France, Italy and the United Kingdom	29
Spain and Poland	27
Romania	14
Netherlands	13
Belgium, Czech Republic, Greece, Hungary and Portugal	12
Austria, Bulgaria and Sweden	10
Denmark, Ireland, Lithuania, Slovakia and Finland	7
Cyprus, Estonia, Latvia, Luxembourg and Slovenia	4
Malta	3

TOTAL: 345

---

[56] A number of measures have been adopted and proposed in this area. See for instance Directive 2010/64/EU on right to interpretation and translations in criminal proceedings [2010] O.J. L280/1 and Directive 2011/36/EU of the European Parliament and of the Council on preventing and combating trafficking in human beings and protecting its victims. Both apply in the UK.

Treaty Foundations and Institutions

1–59   The most common voting procedure in the Council is "qualified majority voting" (QMV). A qualified majority is reached when:

- a majority (sometimes even two thirds) of the 27 EU countries vote in favour; and
- at least 255 of the possible 345 votes are cast.

Furthermore, a member country can ask for a check to see whether the majority represents minimum 62 per cent of the total population. If this is not the case, the proposal cannot be adopted.

1–60   In votes concerning sensitive topics—like security and external affairs and taxation—decisions by the Council have to be unanimous. This means that one single country can veto a decision.

1–61   From 2014 a system known as "double majority voting" will be introduced. For a proposal to go through, it will need the support of two types of majority: a majority of countries (at least 15) and a majority of the total EU population (the countries in favour must represent at least 65 per cent of the EU population).

(d) The European Commission

1–62   The Commission is the politically independent institution that represents and upholds the interests of the European Union as a whole. It is the driving force within the European Union's institutional system: it proposes legislation, policies and programmes of action and it is responsible for implementing the decisions of Parliament and the Council.

1–63   Like the Parliament and the Council, the European Commission was set up in the 1950s under the EU's founding Treaties. It is now provided for in art.16 TEU and arts 244 to 250 TFEU.

(i) Constitution and organisation of the Commission

1–64   The term "Commission" is used in two senses. First, it refers to the members of the Commission—namely the team ("College of Commissioners") appointed by the Member States and Parliament to run the institution and take its decisions. Secondly, the term "Commission" refers to the institution itself and to its staff.

1–65   Informally, the members of the Commission are known as "commissioners". Generally they will have all held political positions in their countries of origin, and many have been government ministers, but as members of the Commission they are committed to acting in the interests of the Union as a whole and not taking instructions from national governments. They must be chosen (on the ground of their general competence and European commitment) "from persons whose independence is beyond doubt". Commissioners shall "neither seek nor take instructions from any Government or other institution".[57]

---

[57] art.17.3 TEU.

1–66 A new Commission is appointed every five years. There are 27 members of the Commission, as each Member State has one commissioner. The Commission remains politically answerable to Parliament, which has the power to dismiss it by adopting a motion of censure.[58] The Commission attends all the sessions of the European Parliament, where it must clarify and justify its policies. It also replies regularly to written and oral questions posed by MEPs. The day-to-day work of the Commission is done by its administrative officials, experts, translators, interpreters and secretarial staff. The Commission is based in Brussels although it has representations in all EU Member States and delegations in other countries around the world.

1–67 The Commission's staff are organised into departments, known as "Directorates-General" (DGs) and "services" (such as the Legal Service). Each DG is responsible for a particular policy area and is headed by a Director-General who is answerable to one of the commissioners.

(ii) *The functions of the Commission*

1–68 The European Commission has four main roles:

(a) to propose legislation to Parliament and the Council;

(b) to manage and implement EU policies and the budget;

(c) to enforce European law (jointly with the Court of Justice); and

(d) to represent the European Union on the international stage, for example by negotiating agreements between the Eurpoean Union and other countries.

Proposing new legislation

1–69 As guardian of the Treaties and defender of the general interest the Commission has been given a "right of initiative" which empowers and requires it to make legislative proposals on the matters contained in the Treaties, either because explicitly provided for or because the Commission considers it necessary in order to protect the interests of the EU and its citizens. When proposing a new law the Commission seeks to satisfy the widest possible range of interests.

1–70 The Commission's proposal is the result of an extensive consultation process, which may be conducted in various ways including conducting impact assessment, reports by experts, consultation of national experts, international organisations and non-governmental organisations. A consultation process is also launched among the different Commission departments in order to ensure that all aspects of the matter in question are taken into account.

1–71 The Commission's proposal is adopted by the College of Commissioners on the basis of either a written procedure (no discussion among Commissioners) or an oral procedure (the dossier is discussed by the College of

---

[58] See para.1–46, above.

Commissioners), and is published in the Official Journal of the European Union ("C" Series). The proposal is forwarded simultaneously to the European Parliament and to the Council but also to all National Parliaments and, where applicable, to the Committee of the Regions and the Economic and Social Committee.

1–72   A new important element introduced by the Lisbon Treaty is the strengthened role of the national Parliaments in the legislative process. In particular, the national Parliaments will act as "watchdogs" of the principle of subsidiarity at an early stage of the decision-making procedure. All proposals from the Commission, initiatives from a group of Member States, initiatives from the European Parliament, requests from the Court of Justice, recommendations from the European Central Bank, and requests from the European Investment Bank for adoption of a legislative act are to be sent to the national Parliaments at the same time as they are sent to the co-legislator (Council and Parliament). National Parliaments then have eights weeks to send their reasoned opinions on compliance of draft legislative texts with the subsidiarity principle to the Council, the European Parliament and the Commission. Except in urgent cases, an eight-week period shall elapse between a draft legislative Act being made available to national Parliaments in the official languages of the Union and the date when it is placed on a provisional agenda for the Council for its adoption of a position under a legislative procedure.

Implementing EU policies and the budget

1–73   As the European Union's executive body, the Commission is responsible for managing and implementing the EU budget and the policies and programmes adopted by Parliament and the Council. Most of the actual work and spending is done by national and local authorities, but the Commission is responsible for supervising it.

1–74   The Commission handles the budget under the supervision of the Court of Auditors. Both institutions aim to ensure good financial management. Only if satisfied with the Court of Auditors' annual report does the European Parliament grant the Commission discharge for implementing the budget.

Enforcing European law

1–75   As "guardian of the Treaties" the Commission, together with the Court of Justice of the European Union, is also responsible for making sure EU law is properly applied in all of the Member States.

1–76   If the Commission considers that a particular Member State has failed to fulfil a particular obligation under the Treaty, it may take action against that Member State by initiating the procedure provided for in art.258 TFEU.

1–77   In the first stage of the procedure, the Commission sends the Member State a letter of formal notice inviting it to submit its observations within two months.

Where the observations submitted by the Member State fail to persuade the Commission to change its point of view or where the Member State fails to respond to the request, the Commission may issue a reasoned opinion, allowing the Member State an additional two-month period within which to comply. At this stage the Commission issues a press release informing the EU's citizens of the purpose of the procedure.

If a Member State fails to conform with Community law, the Commission can take the case to the Court of Justice, whose judgment is binding. If the Member State fails to comply with Court's judgment, the Commission may, after sending a further letter of formal notice and reasoned opinion, bring the matter before the Court of Justice for a second time, seeking the imposition of a penalty payment under art.260 of the TFEU. **1–78**

Representing the EU on the international stage

A central aspect of the Commission's functions revolves around its conduct of EU's external trade relations. The Commission also has the responsibility of negotiating international agreements on behalf of the European Union.[59] **1–79**

---

[59] The Contonou Agreement discussed in para.14–69 was negotiated by the Commission for instance.

CHAPTER 2

THE EUROPEAN UNION LEGAL ORDER

This chapter examines the sources of European Union law and the system and context in which Union law operates. The inter-relationship between Union law and national legal systems is considered as are fundamental principles which are applied in the European Union legal order.

1. Sources of European Union Law

Before considering the way in which Union law interacts with the legal systems of the individual Member States of the European Union it is necessary briefly to examine the five sources of European Union law. These include: 2–01

(a) Treaties.

(b) Secondary legislation including regulations, directives and decisions.

(c) Agreements with third countries.

(d) Rulings of the Court of Justice of the European Union and the General Court.

(e) General Principles of European Union law.

(a) *Treaties*

Sources of European free movement law were the EU and EC Treaties as amended by various other Treaties such as the Single European Act and the Treaty of Nice. Following amendments made by the Lisbon Treaty these sources became the Treaty on European Union (TEU) and the Treaty on the Functioning of the European Union (TFEU). These Treaties and their evolution are discussed in detail in Ch.1.   2–02

(b) *Secondary legislation*

The Union institutions are given the power under art.288 TFEU to adopt three types of secondary legislation in order to give effect to the provisions of the Treaty and to adopt recommendations and opinions: 2–03

Article 288 TFEU

To exercise the Union's competences, the institutions shall adopt regulations, directives, decisions, recommendations and opinions.

A regulation shall have general application. It shall be binding in its entirety and directly applicable in all Member States.

A directive shall be binding, as to the result to be achieved, upon each Member State to which it is addressed, but shall leave to the national authorities the choice of form and methods.

A decision shall be binding in its entirety. A decision which specifies those to whom it is addressed shall be binding only on them.

Recommendations and opinions shall have no binding force.

2–04 There is a considerable volume of secondary legislation in general in European Union law and the field of free movement of persons is no exception to that. Part II of this book will focus on the primary and secondary legislation which specifically relates to the free movement of persons within the European Union. As is evident the three different types of secondary legislation are different in their effect.

2–05 *Regulations* are the most powerful form of secondary legislation that the institutions can make. As is discussed further in paras 2–44 to 2–47 below, regulations are directly applicable in all the Member States. Regulations are not addressed to Member States or private individuals specifically. They do not require any implementation into the national legal systems of the Member States in order to make them effective. In fact, as will be seen, Member States are not permitted to adopt national implementing measures unless the regulation itself requires it or it is necessary in order to give effect to the regulation in the national legal system.

2–06 *Directives* in contrast are weaker forms of secondary legislation. They are addressed to the Member States and impose an obligation on the Member States to which they are addressed to adopt all the measures necessary to ensure that the objectives of the directive are given full effect. Member States are entitled to choose how to implement a directive and therefore implementing measures do vary from Member State to Member State. The direct effect of directives is discussed in paras 2–48 to 2–53 below.

2–07 *Decisions* of the Union institutions are addressed to specific Member States or particular individuals. They take effect upon communication to the person or Member State to whom they are addressed. Decisions addressed to a Member State are binding on all the organs of that State, including the courts. Decisions differ from regulations in that they are addressed to specific States or individuals. Only the addressees are bound by the decision. Decisions differ from directives in that they are directly effective rather than merely setting out the objectives to be achieved. Examples of where decisions may be passed are in relation to competition policy, State aid and imposition of fines.

(c) *Agreements with third countries*

2–08 The European Union is not simply a supranational body confined to internal activities, it interacts considerably within the international arena representing both a powerful trade bloc as well as an influential political body. The European Union concludes agreements with third countries as well as international bodies to give effect to its trade, customs, social, political and economic aims within the international arena. There are three types of agreements which are of particular importance: Association Agreements, Co-operation Agreements and Trade Agreements.

Association agreements have been concluded with a wide variety of non-EU countries. Such agreements go beyond mere trade or aid agreements and are expressions of political and economic co-operation between Member States. Association agreements are often used as a pre-accession tool to prepare third countries to possible accession to the European Union. The European Union has Association Agreements with Algeria, Egypt, Israel, Jordan, Lebanon, Morocco, Tunisia[1] and Turkey[2]; the EU has Stabilisation and Association Agreements with Albania, Croatia[3] and Macedonia; and (although not yet in force) has also signed Stabilisation and Association Agreements with Bosnia and Herzegovina and Serbia.

2–09

Co-operation agreements are not as far reaching as association agreements in that they are only aimed at economic co-operation at an intensive level. Since the end of the 1990s the European Union has concluded 10 similar partnership and co-operation agreements (PCAs) with Armenia, Azerbaijan, Georgia, Kazakhstan, Kyrgyzstan, Moldova, Russia, Ukraine, Uzbekistan, and Tajikistan.

2–10

Trade agreements have been concluded with a very large number of countries and international bodies. The most important trade agreements are with the World Trade Organisation (WTO) and the multilateral agreements deriving from it including the General Agreement on Trade and Tariff (GATT).

2–11

Part Three of this book will focus on agreements with third countries. It will examine agreements which have provisions which potentially impact on the free movement of persons and provide detailed analysis of certain association agreements.

2–12

(d) *Rulings by the Court of Justice of the European Union and the General Court*

The Court of Justice of the European Union is the judicial institution of the European Union (and EURATOM). It is made up of three courts: the Court of Justice, the General Court[4] and the Civil Service Tribunal.[5]

2–13

---

[1] The Union concluded Euro-Mediterranean Association Agreements with these seven countries between 1998 and 2005.
[2] The Ankara Association Agreement was signed in 1963.
[3] Accession negotiations with Croatia were closed on June 30, 2011 and accession is anticipated for July 1, 2013.
[4] The "General Court" is a creation of the Treaty of Lisbon, From its inception on January 1, 1989 to November 30, 2009 it was known as the Court of First Instance (CFI).
[5] The Treaty of Nice provided for the creation of judicial panels in certain specific areas. This provision was amended and codified in art.257 TFEU (allowing for the establishment of "specialised courts attached to the General Court to hear and determine at first instance certain classes of action or proceeding brought in specific areas". The Civil Service Tribunal's special field is disputes involving the European Union civil service.

Judgments of the Court of Justice of the European Union (CJEU) and the General Court (GC) are binding on nationals courts. They are the only courts with judicial authority over Union law. The CJEU is the highest judicial authority. Since the Treaty of Nice the GC has had jurisdiction to determine a wider range of actions in order to alleviate the pressure on the CJEU.

2–14   There are a several types of action that can be brought before the CJEU and GC. It is important to note that there is no mechanism for individuals to take direct action against Member States for failure to act in conformity with Union law.[6] An individual with a complaint that a Member State has failed to implement European Union law correctly or has breached Union law would have two mechanisms for bringing the matter before the CJEU. The individual could either bring the matter to the attention of the Commission (or another Member State) in order that the Commission (or the other Member State) might bring infringement proceedings against the offending State under arts. 258 and 259 TFEU or the individual would have to bring legal proceedings in the national legal system and request a reference by the national court under art.267 TFEU.

2–15   There are however two exceptions to the principle that individuals may not bring direct actions in the CJEU or GC. First where a decision is individually directed at a person an action for annulment under art.263 TFEU might be brought. Secondly, where the person has suffered damage as a result of the action of EU staff an action for damages under art.268 TFEU would be appropriate. All procedures before the CJEU and GC, including those mentioned above, are described briefly below.

(i) *Treaty infringement proceedings (arts 258 and 259 TFEU)*

2–16   These are proceedings for establishing whether a Member State failed to fulfil an obligation imposed upon it by Union law. These must be preceeded by a preliminary procedure in which the Member State concerned is given an opportunity to defend its action or lack of action. If the matter is not settled at this stage either the Commission (art.258) or another Member State (art.259) can institute proceedings against the Member State concerned in the CJEU. The CJEU will then determine whether the Member State has breached an obligation of Union law. Where the CJEU finds infringement the offending Member State is obliged to take the necessary measures to conform (or possibly face a fine[7]). Most actions are brought by the Commission.

---

[6] This is entirely different from the procedures before the European Court of Human Rights where for instance an aggrieved individual who has exhausted all possible domestic remedies has a right of individual petition to that court against a Contracting State.

[7] See for instance *Commission v Greece* (C-38/97) where the CJEU ordered Greece to pay a penalty payment of €20,000 per day for its failure to comply with judgments requiring Greece to take the necessary measures to dispose of toxic and dangerous waste in the area of Chania.

The Commission has brought a number of infringement proceedings against 2–17
the Member States in the free movement field.[8] This mechanism is unsatisfactory for an individual aggrieved by the infringement of European Union law by a Member State since it will result in no compensation or individual determination regarding their particular situation.[9]

(ii) *Actions for annulment (art.263 TFEU)*

These actions can be brought against a Union institution in order to annul a 2–18
legally binding measure. If an action is brought by an individual it must be brought in the GC. Actions for annulment may be brought by a Member State, the Council, the Commission, the European Parliament, the Court of Auditors or the European Central Bank. Individuals or companies can only bring such direct action against decisions personally addressed to them.[10] Actions must be based on allegations of ultra vires, breach of procedural requirements or breach of Union law. Actions for annulment must be brought within two months of the impugned decision.

(iii) *Complaints for failure to act (art.265 TFEU)*

Complaints for failure to act in infringement of the Treaties may be taken 2–19
against certain institutions of the Union (the European Parliament, the European Council, the Commission or the European Central Bank) and against bodies, offices and agencies of the Union which fail to act.[11] Such actions before the CJEU may be brought by the Member States or the other institutions of the Union. The complainant must first put the institution on notice to perform its duty. The order sought in such an action is a declaration that the body concerned has infringed the Treaty by neglecting to take a decision required of it. Complaints may also be similarly brought by individuals or companies on the basis that an institution, body, office or agency of the Union has failed to address to such individual or company any act (other than a recommendation or an opinion). In such cases the order sought is a declaration that the institution has infringed the Treaty by neglecting to address an individual decision to them.

---

[8] For instance, *Commission v Netherlands* (C-92/07) [2010] E.C.R. I-3683. See Commission's Second Report to the Council and Parliament on the implementation of Directives 90/364, 90/365 and 93/96 (right of residence) COM/2003/0161 final where the Commission describes the number of proceedings that were commenced for incorrect implementation of the self-sufficient directives (now replaced by Directive 2004/38). For an example of a case under art.259 TFEU taken by a Member State *Spain v United Kingdom* (C-145/04) where Spain took proceedings against the UK in respect of voting rights in European Parliament elections for Commonwealth citizens in Gibraltar.
[9] Complaints to the Commission take a considerable time to be examined and thus resolution for the individual is by no means expeditious.
[10] A person named on the Taliban sanctions list might for instance bring such action if they considered that the inclusion of their name on that list was ultra vires or procedurally incorrect, see for instance, *Al-Bashir Mohammed Al-Faqih v Council* (T-135/06), September 29, 2010.
[11] See for instance, *Parliament v Council* (C-13/83) [1985] E.C.R. 1513 where Parliament instituted proceedings before the Court of Justice alleging the Council's failure to implement a Union transport policy.

(iv) *Actions for damages (arts 268 and 340 TFEU)*

2–20 Individuals and companies who suffer damage caused by the Union's institutions or by its servants in the performance of their duties can bring actions before the GC. Member States which suffer such damage may bring actions before the CJEU. The complainant would need to demonstrate that there had been an unlawful act by a Union institution or a member of its staff in the exercise of their functions. Actual harm must have been suffered.

(v) *Actions by European Union staff (art.270 TFEU)*

2–21 This is a mechanism for European Union staff to bring actions before the GC in relation to disputes regarding their employment relationship.

(vi) *Appeals procedure (art.256 TFEU)*

2–22 There is a right of appeal against decisions of the GC to the CJEU, although "on points of law only". The appeal must be on grounds of lack of competence by the GC, a breach of procedure or a breach of European Union law.

(vii) *Provisional legal protection (arts 278 and 279 TFEU)*

Article 278 TFEU provides that actions brought before the Court of Justice of the European Union shall not have suspensive effect. However, the Court may order that application of the contested act be suspended if it considers that the circumstances so require.

2–23 Applications for such provisional legal protection will be considered on the basis of prospects of success of the main action, urgency of the order and weighing of the interests of the complainant against the interests of the Union in implementation of the measure and any third parties' interests. Article 279 TFEU provides that the CJEU may in any case before it "prescribe any necessary interim measures".

(viii) *Preliminary rulings (art.267 TFEU)*

2–24 This is the mechanism whereby national courts can seek the guidance of the CJEU on matters of European Union law. The national court will stay proceedings pending reference to the CJEU on questions of interpretation of Union law or regarding the validity of a European Union law measure. The CJEU responds with a judgment which is a mandatory ruling binding on all Member States whether or not they were party to proceedings. The objective of the preliminary ruling procedure is to ensure uniform application of Union law across the Member States. It is a mechanism whereby individuals and companies can ensure the proper application of Union law before national courts. Once the CJEU has given its judgment the matter returns to the national court for final ruling on the case and determination of issues such as costs and damages.

2–25 The subject-matter of a preliminary reference must be confined to European Union law measures only. The CJEU will not entertain references concerning the interpretation or application of national law.

The reference procedure is available to all courts of the Member States. In this sense "court" means any independent institution which is empowered to resolve disputes under due process of law. Thus a "court" may range from the Constitutional court to a tribunal or adjudicator. Whether a court makes a reference to the CJEU will depend on a number of factors, primarily whether the matter is "acte clair"[12] and therefore whether the Union law measure requires any further interpretation by the CJEU.[13] Where a question of European Union law is considered by the final court of appeal in any Member State that court is obliged to refer to the CJEU unless the referral would make no material difference to the outcome of proceedings, or if the question has already been answered by the CJEU or if the interpretation of the European Union law provision is not open to reasonable doubt.[14]

2-26

2. Principles of European Union Law

(a) Introduction

The legal system created by the European Union is unique and the inter-relationship between the European Union legal order and national legal systems is not reflective of any other supranational arrangements. A national legal system is self-contained. By contrast the European Union legal order relies on the support of the national legal systems. It is the national legal systems which bring Union law into the lives of people living within the Member States.

2-27

European Union law is founded on a number of basic principles which assist in understanding the inter-relationship between the Member States and the Union. It clearly imposes obligations on Member States as well as the Union and it is important that those obligations as well as the system for enforcement are defined and adhered to. The CJEU has played a very significant role in defining the principles which guide the interpretation and application of Union law. Equally the Treaty on European Union and the Treaty on the Functioning of the European Union themselves codify many of the principles which underpin Union law.

2-28

(b) Supremacy

Numerous provisions of the TEU the TFEU and secondary legislation impose obligations on Member States requiring them to ensure that their

2-29

---

[12] The term "acte clair" means that national courts, bearing in mind the risk of divergences in judicial decisions within the Union, must be convinced that the interpretation or resolution of an issue taken by the national court is equally obvious to the court of the other Member States or the CJEU: see *CILFIT* (283/81) [1982] E.C.R. 3415.
[13] For the test to be applied by UK courts, see *R. v International Stock Exchange Ex p. Else* [1993] 1 All E.R. 420.
[14] The procedure for preliminary references to the CJEU is not the subject-matter of this book. Readers are referred to the comprehensive book entitled, References to the European Court by D. Anderson QC and M. Demetriou, 2nd edn (London: Sweet and Maxwell, 2002).

national legislation is in conformity with these obligations. Either the Commission or another Member State could bring an action before the CJEU for breach of such obligations by a Member State. Failure by the Member State to abide by the order of the CJEU will result in a financial penalty.

2–30   Article 4.3 TEU states:

> 3. Pursuant to the principle of sincere cooperation, the Union and the Member States shall, in full mutual respect, assist each other in carrying out tasks which flow from the Treaties.
>
> The Member States shall take any appropriate measure, general or particular, to ensure fulfilment of the obligations arising out of the Treaties or resulting from the acts of the institutions of the Union.
>
> The Member States shall facilitate the achievement of the Union's tasks and refrain from any measure which could jeopardise the attainment of the Union's objectives.

Whilst it was not made express in the Treaty of Rome (or subsequent amendments to that Treaty) or the TFEU, the CJEU has repeatedly referred to the supremacy of European Union law. According to the CJEU national courts of Member States are under an obligation to make their judgments in line with those of the CJEU. In a number of decisions the CJEU has established the primacy of European Union law.

2–31   In *Van Gend en Loos*[15] the CJEU stated:

> "... the Community constitutes a new legal order of international law for the benefit of which the states have limited their sovereign rights, albeit within limited fields ... ".

2–32   The doctrine of supremacy was further explained in *Costa v ENEL*[16] where the CJEU held:

> "By creating a Community of unlimited duration, having its own institutions, its own personality, its own legal capacity and capacity of representation on the international plane and, more particularly, real powers stemming from a limitation of sovereignty or a transfer of powers from the States to the Community, the Member States have limited their sovereign rights, albeit within limited fields, and have thus created a body of law which binds both their nationals and themselves.
>
> The integration into the laws of each Member State of provisions, which derive from the Community, and more generally the terms and the spirit of the Treaty, make it impossible for the States, as a corollary, to accord precedence to a unilateral and subsequent measure over a legal system accepted by them on the basis of reciprocity."

---

[15] *Van Gend en Loos v Nederlandse Administratie der Berlastingen* (26/62) [1963] E.C.R.1.
[16] *Costa v ENEL* (6/64) [1964] E.C.R. 585.

As the CJEU stated in *Costa v ENEL*, the Treaty: 2–33

"... has created its own legal system which ... became an integral part of the legal systems of the Member States and which their courts are bound to apply."

The CJEU went even further in *Internationale Handelsgesellschaft*[17] in making clear that national courts will be obliged to disapply any national law provision or practice which contradicts a Treaty provision. As put by the CJEU "the law born from the Treaty ... [cannot] ... have the courts opposing to it rules of national law of any nature whatever". 2–34

The consequence of the doctrine of supremacy is that European Union law has a very significant impact both on the legislation and the administrative and judicial practices of the Member States. Where a Union law provision has direct effect any provision of domestic law that conflicts with that Union law is rendered automatically inapplicable. This principle applies regardless of whether the national law takes the form of primary or secondary legislation and whether the national law came into force before or after the Union law provision. National courts are prevented from applying any national law which conflicts with the European Union law provision. Any provision of domestic law, and any administrative or judicial practice, which might prevent European Union laws from taking their full effect must be set aside.[18] 2–35

(c) *Direct effect*

(i) *Meaning of "direct effect"*

It is well established in European Union law that in certain instances Union law has primacy over Member States' domestic laws. This is where the provisions of Union law are said to have direct effect. The consequence of a provision having direct effect is that it grants rights to natural and legal persons. The provision can be relied upon by that individual before the national courts and authorities of the Member States regardless of any other provisions in domestic law and without the need for incorporation of the provision into domestic law. 2–36

The doctrine of direct effect was established by the CJEU in *Van Gend en Loos*.[19] In order for a provision of European Union law to be considered to be directly effective the following three conditions must be satisfied: 2–37

(1) the provision must be clear and precise;

---

[17] *Internationale Handelsgesellschaft v Einfuhr-und Vorratssteelle für Getreide und Futtermittel* (11/70) [1970] E.C.R. 1125.
[18] In *R. v the Secretary of State for Transport Ex p. Factortame Ltd (No.2)* [1991] A.C. 603, the UK courts granted an interim injunction suspending the application of primary English law pending the outcome of a legal suit based on an argument that that English law was contrary to European Union law.
[19] *Van Gend en Loos v Nederlandse Administratie der Berlastingen* (26/62) [1963] E.C.R.1. [1983] O.J. C177/13.

(2) the provision must be capable of conferring rights on individuals; and

(3) its operation must not be dependent on further action being taken by the European Union or the national authorities or any other body and is thus "unconditional".

2–38 In essence the criteria seek to identify whether a provision is capable as it stands of judicial enforcement. Not all provisions of EU law will be directly effective. Provisions which lay down general objectives for instance will not be directly effective.

2–39 Where the individual seeks to rely on the direct effect against other individuals, the provision is described as being *horizontally* effective. Where on the other hand the reliance is against a Member State, the provision is described as being *vertically* effective. In the area of free movement of persons it is primarily the vertical effect of a provision that is of concern as it is in the main State authorities and courts which may facilitate or frustrate free movement rights. However the actions of private individuals such as employers might interfere with directly effective free movement rights.[20]

2–40 It is important to distinguish between a provision which may be "directly applicable" and one which may be "directly effective". A provision may be directly applicable in that it requires no further enactment to before it becomes part of national law. It is therefore a procedural concept concerned with how a law is enacted. All Regulations are directly applicable. Direct effect on the other hand is a remedial concept referring to whether individuals can directly rely upon a provision and enforce it in a national court.[21] The direct effect of various EU law provisions are discussed below.

(ii) *Treaty Provisions*

2–41 In *Van Gend en Loos* the CJEU said that certain provisions of European Union law create "... individual rights which national courts must protect". In that case the CJEU concluded that a "new legal order" had been created by the Treaty establishing the European Community which "... independently of the legislation of Member States ... not only imposes legislation upon individuals but is also intended to confer upon them rights which become part of their legal heritage".

2–42 The CJEU has determined that a large number of EC Treaty provisions are directly effective. Of particular importance in the free movement field, the CJEU has held art.39 EC Treaty on the free movement of workers,[22] art.43

---

[20] It is to be noted that directives do not have horizontal effect. See further, para.2–53 below.
[21] There is considerable academic debate about the true distinction between "direct applicability" and "direct effect". Some have argued that the drafters of the Treaty must have intended that regulations alone had direct effect. However the CJEU has gone out of its way to find that other measures and provisions are capable of direct effect so the distinction between the Treaty reference to "applicability" which applies only to regulations and "direct effect" is drawn. See for instance P. Craig and G. de Búrca, *The Evolution of EU law*, 2nd edn (Oxford: OUP, 2011).
[22] See now art.45 TFEU.

EC Treaty on the freedom of establishment,[23] and art.49 EC Treaty on the freedom to provide services[24] to have direct effect.

This means that not only do the relevant Treaty provisions provide the framework for the free movement of persons, they also provide specific rights that can be relied upon by individuals before their national courts and authorities to assert specific rights. This can be significant particularly where there is no secondary legislation to cover the area of concern or the secondary legislation itself is not directly effective.[25] Thus for instance the free movement of work-seekers is said to derive directly from art.45 TFEU in the absence of any secondary legislation specifically referring to the situation of work-seekers.[26]

2–43

(iii) *Regulations*

Article 288 TFEU provides that a regulation "shall be binding in its entirety and directly applicable in all Member States". There is therefore no need for national implementation of regulations. Regulations are automatically part of national law. Any national implementing legislation must be consistent with the meaning given to the regulation by the CJEU. In *Bussone*[27] the CJEU stated:

2–44

> "The direct applicability of a regulation requires that its entry into force and its application in favour of or against those subject to it must be independent of any measure of reception into national law".

2–45

In *Commission v Italy*[28] the CJEU held for the first time that national implementing measures can be considered contrary to European Union law because the European Union nature of the provision is obscured by national implementation. That is not to say that the CJEU considers that national implementation of any regulation is generally impermissible but in general best practice would dictate that the national measure reflects accurately the precise wording of the regulation it purports to implement.[29]

2–46

Not all regulations will have direct effect. All will depend on the terms of the regulation itself. Where for example a regulation itself provides for implementing measures to be taken by a European Union institution or Member State then its terms may mean that it, although binding and directly applicable, may not have direct effect. This would be the position where a provision of a regulation is not sufficiently precise or is too conditional.

2–47

---

[23] See now art.49 TFEU.
[24] See now art.56 TFEU.
[25] This might be the case with certain directives. For further discussion of the direct effect of directives, see below at paras 2–48 to 2–53.
[26] See further, paras 6–47 to 6–53 on work seekers.
[27] *Bussone v Ministère Italien de l'agriculture* (31/78) [1978] E.C.R. 2429.
[28] *Commission v Italy* (168/85) (1986) E.C.R. 2945.
[29] See generally, T.C. Hartley, *The Foundations of European Union Law: An Introduction to the Constitutional and Administrative Law of the European Community*, 7th edn (Oxford: OUP, 2010), pp.215–218.

(iv) *Directives*

2–48   Article 288 TFEU provides that:

> "... a directive shall be binding, as to the result to be achieved, upon each Member State to whom it is addressed, but shall leave to the national authorities the choice of form and methods".

At first sight the wording of art.288 TFEU might suggest that directives could not have direct effect because although binding, implementation is at the choice of each Member State. But this does not mean that Member States can chose not to implement a directive, nor to do so in diluted form.

2–49   In *Van Duyn v Home Office*,[30] the CJEU found that it would be incompatible with the binding effect of a directive to exclude the possibility that an obligation which a directive imposes may be invoked by the individuals concerned. Ms Van Duyn had sought to rely on art.3 of Directive 64/221 which provided that measures taken on grounds of public policy shall be based exclusively on the personal conduct of the individual concerned.[31] She had been refused leave to enter the United Kingdom to take up employment as a secretary to the Church of Scientology on the basis of a general government policy that the activities of the Church of Scientology were socially harmful. Article 3 of Directive 64/221 had not been implemented anywhere in UK law and the decision in her case was not sought to be justified by reference to her own conduct.

2–50   The CJEU held that Ms Van Duyn could rely on art.3 of Directive 64/221 because it was sufficiently precise and unconditional. Remarking generally on the status of directives the CJEU stated:

> "where the Community authorities have, by directive, imposed on Member States the obligation to pursue a particular course of conduct, the useful effect of such an act would be weakened if individuals were prevented from relying on it before their national courts and if the latter were prevented from taking it into consideration as an element of Community law".

The direct effect of directives is not the norm. This is because the Member State to whom the directive is addressed must incorporate that directive into its own national law. The position thus contrasts with regulations which are directly applicable without the need for national implementing measures. Only the failure to implement a directive correctly or within the time-frame required by the directive will result in the individual being able to (or indeed needing to) rely on the provisions of the directive.[32]

2–51   In *Francovich*,[33] the CJEU held that provisions of a directive would be directly effective if they contained rights which were both identifiable and

---

[30] *Van Duyn v Home Office* (41/74) [1974] E.C.R. 1337.
[31] See now art.27.2 Directive 2004/38/EC of April 29, 2004 ("Citizen's Directive").
[32] *Marshall v Southampton and South-West Hampshire Area HA* (152/84) [1986] E.C.R. 723. If there is ambiguity in the meaning of a particular provision the national implementing measure, then the European Union law interpretation should be applied.
[33] *Francovich v Italy* (C-6 & 9/90) [1991] E.C.R. I-5357.

were attributable to individuals. Where the delay in implementation causes loss, the individual affected can bring an action based on the provisions of the directive. In certain circumstances a Member State would have to recompense an individual for the loss suffered by that individual due to the failure to implement a directive correctly. In that case the directive in question dealing with the rights of employees upon insolvency had not been implemented by Italy. It was not directly effective as it was not sufficiently precise as to who was to pay the sums it had guaranteed in the case of insolvency.

However, the CJEU relied on art.10 EC Treaty[34] which provided that: 2–52

> "Member States shall take all appropriate measures, whether general or particular, to ensure fulfilment of the obligations arising out of this Treaty ...".

The CJEU laid down three conditions that must be met before the individual can successfully claim damages against the Member State which fails to implement a directive correctly or in time.

(1) The result laid down by the directive involves the attribution of rights attached to individuals.

(2) The contents of those rights must be capable of identification from the provisions of that directive.

(3) A causal link must exist between the failure to implement and the damage suffered.

Directives do not have horizontal direct effect. This was confirmed by the CJEU in the case of *Marshall*[35] in which it stated: 2–53

> "With regard to the argument that a directive may not be relied upon against an individual, it must be emphasized that according to Article ... [288 TFEU] ... the binding nature of a directive, which constitutes the basis for the possibility of relying on the directive before a national court, exists only in relation to 'each Member State to which it is addressed'. It follows that a directive may not of itself impose obligations on an individual and that a provision of a directive may not be relied upon as such against such a person ..."

The definition of "Member State" in this context however is broadly defined and thus all directives are binding upon all public bodies including nationalised industries,[36] police authorities[37] and health authorities.[38]

---

[34] Repealed; replaced, in substance, by art.4 para.3 TEU.
[35] *Marshall v Southampton and South-West Hampshire Area HA* (152/84) [1986] E.C.R. 723.
[36] *Foster v British Gas plc* (C-188/89) [1990] E.C.R. I-3313, at [20].
[37] *Johnston v Chief Constable of the Royal Ulster Constabulary* (222/84) [1986] E.C.R. 1651.
[38] *Marshall v Southampton and South West Hampshire Area HA* (C-152/84) [1986] E.C.R. 723, at [48].

(v) *Decisions*

2–54 According to art.288 TFEU a decision is "binding in its entirety upon those to whom it is addressed". The provision makes no reference to the direct effect of decisions. However, the CJEU has held that decisions can be directly effective.[39]

(d) *Indirect effect*

2–55 Where provisions of European Union law are found not to have direct effect they must still be taken into account by national courts when interpreting relevant national legislation. This reflects the obligation of good faith imposed on the Member States by art.4.3 TEU. This concept of "indirect effect" was relied upon by the CJEU in *Marleasing*[40] where the action was between private operators. The CJEU reiterated that directives cannot impose obligations on individuals. However, the CJEU qualified this by holding that the authorities of the Member States have an obligation to give effect to the aims and objectives laid down in a directive, and this obligation is binding on all authorities in the State, including the courts. Therefore when applying national law, whether passed before or after the directive, a national court is required to interpret national law as far as possible so as to be in conformity with the directive.

2–56 The obligation on the national courts is thus to construe a national law in accordance with European Union law as far as it is possible to do so. Where there are two possible interpretations of a provision in national law, only the one which is consistent with the European Union law provision should be adopted.[41]

2–57 The duty to interpret national law in accordance with European Union law extends beyond the strict scope of the European Union law provision in question. The national court will be required to interpret national law in accordance with all the general principles of European Union law which are discussed below.[42]

(e) *General principles*

2–58 When the CJEU examines the application or interpretation of the Treaties or secondary legislation it does so by reference to a number of general principles. These general principles are derived from the Treaties[43] themselves and other acts of the European Union including resolutions of the Parliament and decisions of the CJEU and General Court. General principles may not be expressly recognised in the legal systems of all Member

---

[39] See discussion in P. Craig and G. de Búrca, *EU Law: Text, Cases and Materials*, 5th edn, 2011, p.178.
[40] *Marleasing SA v La Comercial Internacional de Alimentación SA* (C-106/89) [1990] E.C.R. I-4135.
[41] *Webb v Emo Air Cargo (UK) Ltd* [1993] W.L.R. 49.
[42] *Lucian Arcaro* (C-168/95) [1996] E.C.R. I-4705.
[43] For instance art.18 TFEU on non-discrimination.

States. However, they reflect the principles generally accepted in the legal systems of the majority of Member States.

(i) *Proportionality*

The principle of proportionality is one which underpins many of the CJEU's decisions. The principle requires that individuals are not subjected to excessive burdens or interferences. The means employed to achieve a particular aim must therefore correspond to the importance of that aim and must be necessary to achieve that aim. Consideration must also be given to whether there was a less intrusive or harsh manner of achieving the aim.   2–59

Although the principle of proportionality was first developed by the CJEU in cases such as *Granaria*[44] and *Sagulo*[45] the principle is now embodied in art.5.4 TEU itself which provides that "under the principle of proportionality, the content and form of Union action shall not exceed what is necessary to achieve the objectives of the Treaties".   2–60

The principle of proportionality may be used to challenge measures adopted by European Union institutions and the legislation enacted by Member States to give effect to European Union law.

(ii) *Legal certainty and legitimate expectation*

The principles of legal certainty and legitimate expectation are closely related. The principle of legal certainty means that those subject to European Union law should not be placed in a situation of uncertainty as to their legal rights and obligations. Therefore measures directed at individuals or companies must be clear and precise. They must be able to ascertain the time at which the measure comes into effect so that they may bring annulment proceedings under art.263 TFEU within the strict two-month time-limit. Linked to this principle is the principle of non-retroactivity. This provides that EU measures should not take effect before they are published. There are exceptions to this rule where there is justification for retroactivity. It should be noted however that nearly all judgments of the CJEU are retroactive unless the CJEU expressly limits the retroactive effect under the doctrine of temporal effects.[46]   2–61

The principle of legitimate expectation dictates that an individual should be able to act in reliance that European Union law will be properly applied to him.[47] The principle is generally used whether decisions are directed at individuals or companies for instance in cases concerning the recovery of State aid, pension levels for Union staff and compensation. Additionally it may have a more general application where for instance the individual had an expectation that a directive would be given proper effect through national   2–62

---

[44] *Granaria BV v Council of Ministers and Commission of the EC* (116/76) [1977] E.C.R. 1247.
[45] *Re (Criminal Proceedings) Sagulo* (8/77) [1977] E.C.R. 1495.
[46] See, for instance, *Grzelczyk and Centre public d'aide sociale d'Ottignies-Louvain-la-Neuve* (C-184/99) [2001] E.C.R. I-6193.
[47] See, for instance, *Société française des Biscuits Delacre v Commission* (350/88) [1990] E.C.R. I-418 and *Crispoltoni v Fattoria Autonoma Tabacchi* (C-368/89) [1991] E.C.R. I-3715.

measures. However, where the Member State has a degree of discretion in Union law, there can be no legitimate expectation of how that discretion will be exercised.

(iii) *Non-discrimination*

2–63 The fundamental character and importance of the principle of equal treatment (or "equality" or "non-discrimination"[48]) is beyond doubt. The principle is reflected in the preamble to the Universal Declaration of Human Rights (UDHR) which characterises the "equal and inalienable rights of all members of the human family" as the foundation of freedom, justice and peace in the word. The principle is confirmed by art.1 UDHR which provides that "all human beings are born free and equal in dignity and right"and by art.2 UDHR which provides the entitlement of "everyone ... to all rights and freedoms without distinction of any kind" (such as race, colour, sex, language, religion, political or other opinion, national or social origin, property, birth or other status). Further, art.7 UDHR provides that "all are equal before the law and are entitled without any discrimination to equal protection of the law." Moreover the right is a rule of customary international law and is the cornerstone of international human rights law.[49]

2–64 The importance of the fundamental principle of non-discrimination to the people of the European Union was revealed by the result of a 1997 Eurobarometer poll.[50] Such results might be thought to be surprising since—despite the fundamental importance of the principles in the context of human rights protection—there is a counter-tradition at work. As explained by Gerard Quinn, this counter-tradition can be described as an archaic European tendency to "exclude those who are significantly different, and consign them to the margins of the social and economic mainstream".[51] Quinn continues:

> "Our societies seem to be constructed on concentric circles of graduated exclusion ... In large measure this process is unconscious...and therefore has the appearance of naturalness and inevitability, [and this] makes it all the hard to reveal the implicit exclusion, much less reform it".[52]

2–65 There is at least one other reason why the importance ascribed to the principle by Europeans is surprising. This is that although the principle is rightly regarded as a cornerstone of all human rights protection it is correct

---

[48] The principle is variously described as "the principle of equality", "equal treatment" or "nondiscrimination", used herein without distinction.
[49] For an example of a case decided in the refugee context by the House of Lords in the UK on the basis of the fundamental principle on non discrimination, see *Islam v Secretary of State for the Home Department; R. v Immigration Appeal Tribunal and Secretary of State for the Home Department Ex p. Shah* [1999] 2 A.C. 629.
[50] The poll revealed that 90% of Europeans ranked equality in the eyes of the law as a right to be respected at all times, and more than 80% believed in a right to legal protection against discrimination. By contrast, a mere 66% thought the right to vote should be respected under all circumstances (source: Eurobarometer OP No.47 (1997), 1).
[51] See G. Quinn, "The Human Rights of People with Disabilities Under EU Law" in P. Alston (ed.) *The EU and Human Rights* (Oxford: Oxford University Press, 1999), Ch.9.
[52] See G. Quinn, "The Human Rights of People with Disabilities Under EU Law" in *The EU and Human Rights* (Oxford: Oxford University Press, 1999), Ch.9.

to observe that the principle generally finds articulation through other rights. Thus in the context of the European Convention on Human Rights for example, non-discrimination is not a free-standing right itself, but rather one linked to the enjoyment of the other discrete Convention rights.[53]

However, the poll result does indeed reflect the importance of the principles in the context of the European Union legal order. The non-discrimination principle lies at the very heart of the European Union. The Charter of Fundamental Rights reaffirms the European Union's commitment to the principle of non-discrimination. Article 21 of the Charter bans discrimination on the six grounds listed in art.19 of the TFEU, as well as seven additional grounds (social origin, genetic features, language, political or other opinion, membership of a national minority, property and birth). Like art.18 TFEU, art.21 of the Charter also prohibits discrimination on grounds of nationality. The principle underpins the exercise of free movement rights conferred on persons by the TFEU. The application of the principle in the context of free movement rights will be dealt with in detail in Ch.11. **2–66**

(iv) *Fundamental human rights*

Fundamental human rights have been recognised expressly in the Treaties and by the CJEU on a number of occasions. In the field of the free movement of persons, fundamental human rights have a significant impact and will be examined in detail in Ch.3. **2–67**

---

[53] art.14 ECHR provides that "the enjoyment of the rights and freedoms set forth in this Convention shall be secured without discrimination on any grounds such as sex, race, colour, language, religion, political or other opinion, national or social origin, association with a national minority, property, birth or other status".

CHAPTER 3

RELATIONSHIP BETWEEN EU AND HUMAN RIGHTS LAW

This chapter examines the impact on EU law of international human rights law and specific EU provisions on human rights. Over recent years human rights law has come to play an ever more significant role in decisions concerning free movement of persons.

1. THE SOURCES AND CONTENT OF HUMAN RIGHTS IN EU LAW

(a) *The Treaty on European Union (TEU)*

The protection of fundamental human rights is clearly provided for in art.6 TEU. 3–01

It provides:

(1) The Union recognises the rights, freedom and principles set out in the Charter of Fundamental Rights of the European Union of December 7, 2000, as adapted at Strasbourg, on December 12, 2007, which shall have the same legal value as the Treaties.
(2) The Union shall accede to the European convention for the Protection of Human Rights and Fundamental Freedoms. Such accession shall not affect the Union's competencies as defined in the Treaties.
(3) Fundamental rights, as guaranteed by the European Convention for the Protection of Human Rights and Fundamental Freedoms and as they result from the constitutional traditions common to the Member States, shall constitute general principles of the Union's law.

Article 9 provides:

> "In all its activities, the Union shall observe the principle of the equality of its citizens, she shall receive equal treatment from its institutions, bodies, offices and agencies."

By Council Regulation in 2007, a new body was established, the Agency for Fundamental Rights, which has been charged with providing EU institutions and the Member States with: 3–02

> "information, assistance and expertise in order to support them when they take measures or formulate courses of action within their respective spheres of competence to fully respect fundamental rights."

As is plain from art.6, the Charter of Fundamental Rights of the European Union (the Charter) and the European Convention on Human Rights (ECHR) are central to the Union's legal system. As all Member States of the 3–03

Union are parties to the Council of Europe and ECHR which has legally binding implications, it is to be expected that the ECHR will be an important source of Union human rights law. Article 6 goes much further of course and provides for the Union's accession to the ECHR. Primary place in human rights instruments goes to the Charter which is given equal status in the Union legal scheme as the founding treaties of the Union.

3–04 There is scope for tension between the Union, ECHR and the Charter, not least because the ECHR is already supervised and enforced by other international bodies, namely the Council of Europe and the European Court of Human Rights. The relationships between the Charter, ECHR and the Union will be discussed below.

(b) *The Charter of Fundamental Rights*

3–05 Accompanying Explanations relating to the Charter state the sources of the Charter rights as follows:

(a) ECHR (e.g. art.2, right to life; art.8, right to respect for private and family life)
(b) Other international agreements: Geneva Convention (art.26, right to asylum; European Social Charter—art.28, right of collective bargaining).
(c) EU Treaties (e.g. art.23, gender equality).
(d) CJEU case law (e.g. art.41, right to good administration).

3–06 The Charter as adopted in December 2000 was, at most, considered "soft law", not binding on Member States or EU institutions and purely aspirational. Soon however it found its way into Opinions of the Advocate Generals to bolster reliance on arguments drawing on fundamental rights arguments.[1] The CJEU referred at some length to the Charter in *Parliament v Council*[2]:

> "While the Charter is not a legally binding instrument, the EU legislature did, however, acknowledge its importance by stating, the second recital in the Directive, that the Directive observes the principles recognised not only by Article 8 of the ECHR but also in the Charter."

The Court in *Investrand BV v Staatssecretaris van Financien*[3] referred to the right to strike as a fundamental right "which forms an integral part of the general principles of EU law" and which is "reaffirmed by Article 28

---

[1] See, for example, *Council of European Union v Heidi Hautala* (C-353/99) [2001] E.C.R. I-9565, Opinion of A.G. Leger referring to the Charter as "a privileged instrument for identifying fundamental rights"
[2] *Netherlands v European Parliament* (C-377/98) [2002] All E.R. (EC) 97.
[3] (C-435/05) [2007] E.C.R. I-1315; *The International Transport Workers' Federation and the Finnish Seamen's Union v Viking Line ABP and OÜ Viking Line Eesti* (C-438/05) [2007] E.C.R. I-10779 at [41].

of the Charter". Post the Lisbon Treaty 2007 there were increasing references to the "Charter.[4]

The Charter is a statement of principles, values and rules which underpin the European Union. No reference to the Charter was included in the Treaty of Nice which post dated its adoption in December 2000. The Treaty of Lisbon 2007 put it at the heart of the Union legal order as now clear from art.6 TEU. The Charter is broad in content bringing together in one document all of the rights previously found in a variety of legislative instruments, including national laws and international conventions from the Council of Europe, the United Nations and the International Labour Organisation. It contains a preamble and 54 articles, grouped into seven chapters:

3–07

(1) Chapter I: Dignity (human dignity, the right to life, the right to the integrity of the person, prohibition of torture and inhuman or degrading treatment or punishment, prohibition of slavery, and forced labour).

(2) Chapter II: Freedoms (the right to liberty and security, respect for private and family life, protection of personal data, the right to marry and found a family, freedom of thought, conscience and religion, freedom of expression and information, freedom of assembly and association, freedom of the arts and sciences, the right to education, freedom to choose an occupation and the right to engage in work, freedom to conduct a business, the right to property, the right to asylum, protection in the event of removal, expulsion or extradition).

(3) Chapter III: Equality (equality before the law, non-discrimination, cultural, religious and linguistic diversity, equality between men and women, the rights of the child, the rights of the elderly, and integration of persons with disabilities).

(4) Chapter IV: Solidarity (workers' right to information and consultation within the undertaking, the right of collective bargaining and action, the right of access to placement services, protection in the event of unjustified dismissal, fair and just working conditions, prohibition of child labour and protection of young people at work, family and professional life, social security and social assistance, health care, access to services of general economic interest, environmental protection, and consumer protection).

(5) Chapter V: Citizens' rights (the right to vote and stand as a candidate at elections to the European Parliament, the right to vote and stand as a candidate at municipal elections, the right to good administration, the right of access to documents, the ombudsman, the right to petition, freedom of movement and residence, diplomatic and consular protection).

---

[4] See *Alassini* (C-317 & 320/08) on the principle of effective judicial protection and art.47 of the "Charter; (C-101/09 B) on requirement to interpret Directive 2004/83/EC of April 29, 2004 on minimum standards for the qualification and status of third country nationals or Stateless persons as refugees or as persons who otherwise need international protection and the content of the protection granted", O.J. L304, September 30, 2004 in accordance with the Charter.

(6) Chapter VI: Justice (the right to an effective remedy and a fair trial, the presumption of innocence and the right of defence, principles of legality and proportionality of criminal offences and penalties, and the right not to be tried or punished twice in criminal proceedings for the same criminal offence).

(7) Chapter VII: General provisions (including rights specifically relating to citizenship of the European Union such as free movement rights).

3–08 The central role of "dignity" in the Charter puts the concept well beyond that which exists in previous EC legislative provisions or case law of the CJEU. Article 1 provides that dignity "must be respected and protected". The following four articles of the Charter provide for concrete expression of the concept (right to life, right to be free from torture, etc.). Does art.1 add anything? One commentator states in respect of the concept of dignity:

> "It can never be more than one of a number of values, principles and policies which pull decision-makers in different directions".[5]

The same author goes on to recognise that it could become a useful and legitimate instrument for national courts in construing legislation touching on social and economic values.[6] Dignity does not carry the force of such things as autonomy, security or even integrity when balancing competing rights. However, it can act as an important underpinning for the promotion of human rights.[7]

(c) ECHR and the Charter

3–09 Whilst the text of the Charter largely mirrors that of the ECHR, it is more generous than the ECHR with respect to certain rights, particularly social and economic rights, such as the right to engage in work (art.15), the right to education (art.14), and collective labour rights (art.12). For historical and political reasons the ECHR did not originally have at its core any social or economic rights. However, with the passing of time such rights have come to be seen as increasingly fundamental.

3–10 There are inherent limits to the Charter. In particular, art.51 of the Charter states:

> "1. The provisions of this Charter are addressed to the institutions and bodies of the Union with due regard for the principle of subsidiarity and to the Member States only when they are implementing Union law. They shall therefore respect the rights, observe the principles and promote the application thereof in accordance with their respective powers.

---

[5] D. Feldman, "Human Dignity as a Legal Value—Part 2", *Public Law*, Spring 2000, 76.
[6] One can think of the case law in respect of the removal of AIDS sufferers from the EU to their home countries where they would face certain death within a relatively short period: *D v UK*, (1997) 24 E.H.R.R. 423.
[7] C. McCrudden, "Human Dignity and Judicial Interpretation of Human Rights," Legal Research Paper Series, July 2008.

2. This Charter does not establish any new power or task for the EU or the Union, or modify powers and tasks defined by the Treaties."

Article 52 Charter states:

"1. Any limitation on the exercise of the rights and freedoms recognised by this Charter must be provided for by law and respect the essence of those rights and freedoms. Subject to the principle of proportionality, limitations may be made only if they are necessary and genuinely meet objectives of general interest recognised by the Union or the need to protect the rights and freedoms of others.

2. Rights recognised by this Charter which are based on the EU Treaties or the Treaty on European Union shall be exercised under the conditions and within the limits defined by those Treaties.

3. In so far as this Charter contains rights which correspond to rights guaranteed by the Convention for the Protection of Human Rights and Fundamental Freedoms, the meaning and scope of those rights shall be the same as those laid down by the said Convention. This provision shall not prevent Union law providing more extensive protection."

Articles 51 and 52 make clear that the EU Charter does not alter the system of rights conferred by the EU and EC Treaties and is not applicable in situations not covered by the Treaties. Article 52(3) defines the relationship between the EU Charter and ECHR. Its purpose is to ensure the necessary consistency between the Charter and the ECHR by establishing the principle that, in so far as the rights in the present Charter also correspond to rights guaranteed by the ECHR, the meaning and scope of those rights, including authorised limitations, are the same as those laid down by the ECHR. However, as seen, the scope of the EU Charter is clearly broader than the ECHR, with greater emphasis on social and economic rights than the ECHR. Article 52 does not in any way prohibit this more extensive protection of rights. Article 51 is simply stating the subsidiarity principle to the effect that Member States will come within the scope of the Charter when implementing EU law. In areas such as immigration where the EU has a developed body of law and regulations it is likely that the Courts would consider that actions by Member States affecting the free movement of Union nationals and non-nationals alike would come within the scope of the Charter. As suggested by Beal and Hickman,[8] lawyers will undoubtedly argue that the scope of some of the common rights in the Charter and ECHR such as the right to marry and found a family (art.9 of the Charter and art.12 ECHR), the right to a fair trial (art.47(2) of the Charter and art.6 ECHR) have a wider scope in the Charter. It is easier to see how art.9 could be relied on by same sex couples to maintain a right to marry that art.12. Article 47(2) and art.6 both provide for a right to fair trial but, unlike the latter, it is not limited to the determination of civil rights and obligations—an important point potentially for immigration cases.

3–11

---

[8] K. Beal and T. Hickman, "Beano No More: The EU Charter of Rights After Lisbon", 16 *Judicial Review*, 2, 113–141.

3–12   The potential in the Charter for support for novel arguments is demonstrated in a case that came soon after the ratification of the Charter: *NS v Secretary of State for the Home Department*.[9] The English Court of Appeal referred *NS* to the CJEU which concerned the application of Council Regulation 343/2003/EEC on the criteria for determining which Member State is responsible for examining an asylum application. NS was an asylum applicant in the UK from Afghanistan who spent some time in Greece on his journey. The UK decided to return him to Greece where his claim would be assessed in accordance with Council Regulation 343/2003. He challenged that decision on the grounds that it frustrated his right to claim asylum and right to dignity as contained in the Charter (arts 1 and 18). Among the questions asked by the Court of Appeal was whether discretionary power afforded to a Member State by art.3(2) of the Regulation to take responsibility for an asylum claim notwithstanding that under the Regulation the duty to do so was on another State fell within the scope of EU law. Advocate General Trstenjak stated in her Opinion in the linked case of *ME*[10] that "particular significance and high importance" are to be given to case law of the ECtHR and she attached great significance to art.18 of the Charter-the right to claim asylum—and art.1—the right to dignity, and art.4—prohibition of torture and inhuman or degrading treatment of asylum seekers. Drawing on those rights, the Advocate General concluded that a Member State may not remove an asylum seeker to another Member State where there is serious risk of a breach of rights contained in the Charter including the right to effectively claim asylum. She considered that the exercise of discretion contained in art.3(2) of Regulation 343/2003 had to be exercised in accordance with fundamental human rights and was within the scope of EU law. She also considered that the application of a conclusive presumption that the removal of an asylum applicant by a Member State to another Member State would not lead to a breach of human rights was contrary to EU law. She went on to consider Protocol 30 to the Charter, which (it was argued by the governments of Poland and the UK) was a general opt-out for them from any new obligations arising under the Charter. The Advocate General rejected this argument while leaving open the argument whether specific rights under the Charter (the so-called social rights in arts 27–38 of the Charter) were binding on the UK and Poland.[11] The CJEU in its judgment agreed with the Advocate General.[12] As to the

---

[9] *NS v Secretary of State for the Home Department* (C-411/10), December 21, 2011.

[10] *ME v Secretary of State for the Home Department* (C-493/10), opinion of Advocate General dated September 22, 2011.

[11] A domestic case considered in which novel arguments were derived from the Charter is *R (on the application of Zagorski and Baze) Secretary of State for Business, Innovation and Skills* [2010] EWCA Civ 3110 (Admin) it was argued before the Administrative Court that the failure of the UK government to block the export of pharmaceuticals used for capital punishment from the UK to the US would be a breach of the UK's duty under the Charter (art.4—prohibition of inhuman or degrading treatment). As the prisoner was not within the jurisdiction of the UK it was agreed by all that art.3 ECHR could not be relied on as its jurisdiction under art.?? did not extend to the above circumstances. There is no such express jurisdictional restriction in the Charter and so it was argued art.4 of the Charter could be relied on. Relying on art.52(3) of the Charter which provides that in so far as the Charter contains rights that correspond to ECHR rights, "the meaning and scope of their application shall be the same as those laid down by the said Convention", the Court implied such a restriction.

[12] paras 75–108.

question whether the rights protected by the Charter in art.1, concerning human dignity, art.18, concerning the right to asylum, and art.47, concerning the right to an effective remedy, is wider than conferred by art.3 ECHR, the Court did not fully answer the question. It limited itself to concluding that the decision to remove the asylum seeker in that case amounted to a breach of art.3 and arts 1, 18 and 47. Whichever right was pleaded led to the same answer. As the answer to the question was not necessary, the CJEU plainly considered that its response was adequate. It leaves open the question for another day. Like the Advocate General, the Court did not consider that the opt out contained in art.30 of the Charter absolved the UK from the duties that arose as a result of the above provisions.[13]

In view of the currency of ECHR and the vibrant case law of the CJEU, a legitimate question to ask is, what added value or what purpose does the Charter serve? One response is that the Union sees itself as a complete entity with expanding aims well beyond narrow economic ones. Expanding competencies as a matter of principle and utility require provision for standards in all related areas. The rapid expansion of the Union incorporating less and more recently developed democracies demanded the identification by the Union of its own set of norms consistent with its aims. After all, the ever increasing union of the peoples of Europe could be more easily achieved if there existed a common set of values to all participants. 3–13

(d) *The Court of Justice of the European Union*

(i) *The protection of human rights in the Court of Justice of the European Union (CJEU)*

Article 6 TEU draws on the case law of the CJEU as a distinct source of the human rights law of the Union (along with the Charter and ECHR). In its early case law the CJEU did not see itself as a guardian of human rights and rejected any submission that a EU measure should be struck down for non-compliance with human rights provisions enshrined in national constitutions or in international agreements to which the relevant Member State was a signatory. Member States were thus left to ensure compliance with their own human rights obligations even in areas falling within the scope of the Treaties. 3–14

This position taken in its early cases was clearly not sustainable in light of the CJEU's view of the primacy of EU law and its precedence over national law. Such supremacy could only be maintained if EU law was itself able to guarantee the protection of basic human rights in compliance with Member States' international obligations. It was only a matter of time before the 3–15

---

[13] A conclusion expected, as by the stage the case reached the Court of Appeal before the matter was referred to the CJEU, the UK government accepted that the opt out did not prevent the Charter from applying to the UK: *R (NS) v SSHD* [2010] EWCA Civ 990.

ECHR asserted its scrutiny of compliance with ECHR standards and found that the transfer of power to a supranational body would not absolve a contracting party to the ECHR from its obligations under the ECHR.[14]

3–16 The potential then for conflict between the CJEU and the ECtHR would be great if the CJEU continued to assert the supremacy of EU law without regard to human rights. The first attempt by the CJEU to resolve this potential conflict was in the case of *Stauder*[15] where it referred to "fundamental human rights enshrined in the general principles of EU law and protected by the Court". Although on its facts the CJEU did not consider that the question of a violation of fundamental rights was necessary to determine, this judgment represented a significant shift in the CJEU's approach to the protection of human rights in EU law.

3–17 In the years that followed, the CJEU began to develop its protection of human rights. Initially this was by reference to the constitutions of the Member States. In *Internationale Handelsgesellschaft*,[16] the CJEU referred to the fact that its protection of fundamental rights was "inspired by the constitutional traditions common to the member states". On the facts the CJEU stated that the impugned regulation should have its validity judged by reference to the fundamental rights which it said formed "an integral part of the general principles of EU law protected by the Court of Justice".

3–18 In *Nold*,[17] the CJEU went slightly further in referring to "international treaties for the protection of human rights" as representing an additional source of the Court's new general principles. In the years that followed the CJEU was presented with arguments which hinged on the application of specific provisions of both constitutional human rights and international human rights instruments.[18]

3–19 These incremental developments culminated within about a decade in the position reached in *Cinetheque*[7] by which time the CJEU saw itself as duty bound to ensure the observance of fundamental rights in the field of EU law. This was in an era prior to the EU Treaty and therefore prior to a time when human rights were even alluded to in the Treaties governing the EU. As commentators have observed

> "respect for and protection of human rights were, thus, conceived as an integral, inherent, transverse principle forming part of all objectives, functions, and powers of the EU"[19]

albeit without any discernable Treaty basis for such principle.

---

[14] Indeed in 1999 in the case of *Matthews v United Kingdom* (Application no.24833/94) February 18, 1999) the European Court of Human Rights stated unequivocally that Member States will be responsible for Community Acts under ECHR.
[15] *Stauder v City of Ulm* (C-26/69) [1969] E.C.R.419.
[16] *Internationale Handelsgesellschaft v Einfuhr-und Vorrtssteelle für Getreide und Futtermittel* (C-11/70) [1970] E.C.R. 1125.
[17] *Nold KG v Commission* (C-4/73) [1974] E.C.R. 491.
[18] In both *Rutili v Minister of the Interior* (C-36/75) [1975] E.C.R.1219 and *Prais v Council* (C-130/75) [1976] E.C.R. 1589, the CJEU made references to specific provisions of ECHR.
[19] J.H.H. Weiler and S.C. Fries, "EC law and EU Competencies in Human Rights", in P. Alston (ed.), *The EU and Human Rights* (Oxford: OUP, 1999), p.157.

Of further significance is *Wachauf*,[20] where the CJEU held that as a consequence of the place that fundamental human rights held in the EU legal order the EU could not accept measures which were incompatible with observance of human rights protected by national constitutions and international human rights standards.

3–20

From this line of case law, it is clear that the CJEU considered itself competent to identify fundamental rights over and above those contained in the founding treaties which were binding on Member States. Individuals were not seen or treated as economic actors only. In the words of one commentator:

3–21

"Well before any European Treaty amendment making reference to fundamental rights, the CJEU, in its case law over the years, referred to (and by judicial fiat incorporated) a substantial number of legal principles which the Count nominated 'fundamental rights', recognised and protected as a matter of EU law.[21]"

The development of human rights law by the CJEU did not stop at reference and general reliance only on principles. It went on to derive from a number of sources specific hard edged rights such as the right to respect for family life,[22] the right to respect for human dignity,[23] the right to peaceful possession of property and possessions,[24] the right to join a trade union,[25] and the right of a child to education with derived right of a parent to reside in a Member State for that purpose.[26]

3–22

(e) *EU secondary legislation*

While the Union has been slow in adopting or creating its own human rights instrument, it has through the Council legislated in the area of immigration law throughout the first decade of the century in a way that aimed to be cognisant of core human rights but at the same time aware of the interests of Member States.[27] The most important of the measures adopted are: Directive 2003/9/EC on "laying down minimum standards for the reception of asylum seekers"; Directive 2004/83/EC on "minimum standards for the qualification of third country nationals or stateless persons as refugees or as persons who otherwise need intentional protection and the content of the

3–23

---

[20] *Wachauf v Federal Republic of Germany* (C-5/88) [1989] E.C.R. I-2609 at [19].
[21] A. O'Neill, "The EU and Fundamental Rights-Part 1" [2011] *Judicial Review* 216–247, at p.225.
[22] *Carpenter v Secretary of State for the Home Department* (C-60/00) [2002] E.C.R. I-6279.
[23] *Omega Spielhallen-und Automatenaufstellunga-GmbH* (C-36/02) [2004] E.C.R. I-9609.
[24] *IFA and others Minister of Agriculture, Food and Forestry, Ireland and another* (C-22/94) [1997] E.C.R.-1-1809 at [27].
[25] *Maurissen and another v Court of Auditors* (C-193 & 194/87) [1990] E.C.R. 1-95.
[26] *Baumbast and R* (C-413/99) [2002] E.C.R. I-7091 at [63]. For a comprehensive list of the rights recognised by the Court of Justice see A. O'Neill, "The EU and Fundamental Rights—Part 1" [2011] *Judicial Reivew* 225–230.
[27] The Council of Europe at a meeting in Tempere on October 15 and 16, 1999 agreed to work towards establishing a Common European Asylum Scheme with the aim of approximation of procedural rules for the assessment of asylum applications. The Council accepted that this would take place against an acceptance of the non-refoulement provisions of the Refugee Convention.

protection granted" ("the Qualification Directive"); and Directive 2004/38/EC "The Citizens' Directive"; and Directive 2005/85/EC "on minimum standards on procedures in Member States for granting and withdrawing refugee status ("the Procedures Directive")".

3–24 Directive 2004/38 is the subject of detailed consideration in Part 2 of this book. Neither this or the other Directives are human rights documents as such but they reflect the core fundamental principles that are already part of EU law in the relevant areas. All of them declare that they observe the principles of the Charter and seek to ensure full respect for human dignity. Directive 2003/9/EC is important as it brought to the centre of European Union the treatment on reception of asylum applicants within the Union. It provides for minimum standards for the treatment of such including in the provision of information, freedom of movement within the Member States, respect for family life, education, health care and special needs. Article 11 provided for the right to work after one year if no decision had been made on an asylum application. The Qualification Directive provides for the grant of refugee status and subsidiary protection from injurious acts if required to leave the host Member State. The Court of Justice in *Elgafaji*[28] held that art.15 of the Qualification Directive went further than art.3 ECHR or refugee jurisprudence in holding that indiscriminate violence in an area of armed conflict can found a claim for subsidiary protection. The Directive goes on to require that family life is maintained and that social welfare at least at the level granted to nationals is granted to refugees and those in need of subsidiary protection.

---

[28] *Meki Elgajaji and Noor Elgafaji Stastssecretarius Van Justitie* (C-465/07), February 17, 2009 [2009] E.C.R. I-00921.

CHAPTER 4

UNION CITIZENSHIP

written by Professor Steve Peers[*] and Nicola Rogers

This chapter examines the creation of Union citizenship and the rights given to Union citizens flowing from such citizenship. The interpretation given by the ECJ to these rights will determine the true reach of free movement rights for persons throughout the EU.

Article 20, Treaty on the Functioning of the European Union (TFEU)

1. Citizenship of the Union is hereby established. Every person holding the nationality of a Member State shall be a citizen of the Union. Citizenship of the Union shall be additional to and not replace national citizenship.

2. Citizens of the Union shall enjoy the rights and shall be subject to the duties provided for by the Treaties. They shall have, *inter alia*:

(a) the right to move and reside freely within the territory of the Member States;
(b) the right to vote and to stand as candidates in elections to the European Parliament and in municipal elections in their Member State of residence, under the same conditions as nationals of that State;
(c) the right to enjoy, in the territory of a third country in which the Member State of which they are nationals is not represented, the protection of the diplomatic and consular authorities of any Member State on the same conditions as the nationals of that State;
(d) the right to petition the European Parliament, to apply to the European Ombudsman, and to address the institutions and advisory bodies of the Union in any of the Treaty languages and to obtain a reply in the same language.

These rights shall be exercised in accordance with the conditions and limits defined by the Treaties and by the measures adopted thereunder.

Article 21 TFEU

1. Every citizen of the Union shall have the right to move and reside freely within the territory of the Member States, subject to the limitations and conditions laid down in this Treaties and by the measures adopted to give them effect.

2. If action by the Union should prove necessary to attain this objective and the Treaties have not provided the necessary powers, the European Parliament and the Council, acting in accordance with the ordinary legislative procedure, may adopt provisions with a view to facilitating the exercise of the rights referred to in paragraph 1.

3. For the same purposes as those referred to in paragraph 1 and if the Treaties have not provided the necessary powers, the Council, acting in accordance with a

---

[*] Professor of Law, Law School, University of Essex.

special legislative procedure, may adopt measures concerning social security or social protection. The Council shall act unanimously after consulting the European Parliament.

1. Introduction

4-01 The principal concern of this chapter is the analysis of the impact on the rights of nationals of the Member States of the establishment of Union citizenship conferred by art.20 TFEU and of the right of Union citizens to move and reside freely contained in art.21 TFEU. The uniqueness and potential enormity of these provisions—based on the creation of the novel concept of citizenship of a supranational body—should be acknowledged.

4-02 As well as examining the historical background to inclusion in the EU Treaties of a discrete part of the TFEU entitled "Non-Discrimination and Citizenship of the Union" (arts 18–25 TFEU), two questions are considered. First, whether the creation of Union citizenship has added anything of value to the rights of nationals of Member States. Secondly, whether the right to move and reside contained in art.21 TFEU Treaty creates discrete rights for Union citizens beyond those already contained elsewhere in the EU Treaties or secondary legislation.

2. Union Citizenship

(a) *Historical background*

4-03 As already acknowledged, Union citizenship and the rights accompanying it marked a huge advance on the ethos and dynamics of the process of European integration launched by the Treaty establishing the European Economic Community signed in Rome in 1957 (see generally Ch.1). Originally the right to move freely within the European Community (as it then was) was linked closely to the performance by nationals of Member States in the territories of other Member States of economic activity—whether as employee, self-employed or service provider.

4-04 However, as observed by the Commission[1] such a state of affairs could not be allowed to continue indefinitely since it did not fully comply with the objective contained in art.3(c) of the Treaty of Rome of "the abolition, as between Member States, of obstacles to the free movement of ... persons". Such objective is not one linked to the performance of economic activity. Moreover, such state of affairs did not meet the political aspiration

---

[1] See Report from the Commission to the Council and the European Parliament of March 17, 1999 on the implementation of Directives 90/364, 90/365 and 93/96 (Right of Residence) (COM(99) 127 final).

expressed at the Paris Summit in 1974 to move towards a "citizens' Europe"[2]

The first step away from the necessity to carry out economic activity as the precondition of the exercise of free movement rights was the Commission proposal of 1979[3] to extend the freedom of movement of persons to those *not* economically active. The proposal—later withdrawn—was seen by the Commission as an important step towards the completion of the internal market. But it was the adoption of the Single European Act signed in February 1986[4] which provided the impetus towards the adoption of directives providing for the right of residence for the economically non-active. In 1989 the Commission put forward three proposals covering students, retired persons and others not engaged in economic activity[5] which culminated in the adoption on June 28, 1990 of Directives 90/364, 90/365 and 90/366.[6]

4–05

The final stage in attaining the general right to movement and residence now contained in art.21(1) TFEU Treaty was the incorporation of the provisions on Union Citizenship contained in Pt II of the EC Treaty, as amended by the Maastricht Treaty signed on February 7, 1992. The provisions (originally arts 8 and 8a–e of the EC Treaty, as amended by the Maastricht Treaty) came into force on November 1, 1993. After the signing of the Treaty, the Declaration by the Birmingham European Council in October 1992 stated that

4–06

> "... citizenship of the Union brings our citizens additional rights and protection without in any way taking the place of their national citizenship".

A Declaration attached to the Treaty setting up the European Community noted that

> "the question whether an individual possesses the nationality of a Member State shall be settled solely by reference to the national law of the Member State concerned".

However, the rights of free movement and residence throughout the Union do not represent the totality of rights enjoyed by Union citizens. Specific provision is made also in Pt II of the TFEU for:

4–07

---

[2] Report from the Commission to the Council and the European Parliament of March 17, 1999 on the implementation of Directives 90/364, 90/365 and 93/96 (Right of Residence) (COM(99) 127 final), above and Report from the Commission on the Citizenship of the Union of December 21, 1993 (COM(93) 702 final).
[3] (COM(79) 215 final), [1979] O.J. C207.
[4] The single European Act stated that the Community would adopt measures with the aim of progressively establishing an internal market by December 31, 1992 and wrote provisions into the Treaty of Rome to establish an area without frontiers and to abolish checks on persons at internal frontiers.
[5] [1989] O.J. C207.
[6] Directive 90/364 on the right of residence; Directive 90/365 on the right of residence of employees and self-employed persons who have ceased their occupational activity and 90/366 on the right of residence for students (the latter replaced by Directive 93/96 after annulment of Directive 90/366 by the ECJ in *Parliament v Council* (C-295/90) [1992] E.C.R. I-4193).

- the right of every Union citizen residing in another Member State to vote and stand as a candidate in municipal elections and in elections to the European Parliament in the State where the Union citizen resides (art.22 TFEU);
- the right of every Union citizen in the territory of a third country to protection by the diplomatic or consular authorities of any Member State where the State of which the person is a national is not represented in the non-member third country (art.23 TFEU); and
- the rights of every citizen of the Union to petition the European Parliament, to apply to the Ombudsman and to write to EU institutions or bodies in their own language and have an answer in the same language, along with provision for a European citizens' initiative (art.24 TFEU).

4–08 Moreover, citizens of the Union, and indeed third country nationals residing in the European Union, also enjoy fundamental rights. Such rights, and their inter-relationship with the EU legal order, are considered in Ch.3. The Amsterdam Treaty added to the list of civic rights of Union citizens and clarified the link between national citizenship and European citizenship, while the Lisbon Treaty added another civic right.[7]

3. A New Form of Citizenship

(a) *Introduction*

4–09 The creation of the Union citizen in art.17 of the Amsterdam Treaty (now art.20 TFEU) was heralded as the dawn of a new era in Community law, with Union citizenship "destined to be the fundamental status of nationals of the Member States". Two particular questions arise in relation to Union citizenship.

4–10 First, what rights and benefits are there for holders of Union citizenship over and above those that accrue as a result of other rights contained in the EU Treaties? In summary the answer to this question is that under certain circumstances Union citizens will enjoy the protection of the non-discrimination provision contained in art.18 TFEU whether or not they are exercising free movement rights.

4–11 Secondly, what is the relationship between Union citizenship and national citizenship? Whilst Union citizenship is not intended to replace national

---

[7] art.17 EC Treaty (now art.20 TFEU) was amended by the Treaty of Amsterdam to clarify the link between European and national citizenship with the addition of the unequivocal text that "citizenship of the Union shall complement and not replace national citizenship". Further the Treaty of Amsterdam established the new right (contained now in art.24) for EU citizens to write to the European Parliament, the Council, the Commission, the Court of Justice, the Court of Auditors, the Economic and Social Committee, the Committee of the Regions or the Ombudsman in one of the languages of the Treaties and receive an answer in the same language. The Treaty of Lisbon clarified the latter right (amending it to refer to all EU institutions or bodies) and added the provisions concerning the citizens' initiative.

citizenship, if rights accrue to its holders then Union citizenship plainly enhances national citizenship. At the same time, however, Union citizenship undoubtedly also creates a potential tension with national authorities, particularly where such citizenship has consequences for Member States which are wider than anticipated.

(b) *Rights and benefits flowing from Union citizenship*

(i) *Non-discrimination and art.18 TFEU*

Union citizens may find themselves residing in Member States other than that of their nationality for different reasons. Where unambiguously exercising Treaty free movement rights the obligations consequently imposed on Member States in which they reside is the subject matter of Pt II of this book and, for the most part is laid down in the EU's primary law and secondary legislation. At the very least Union citizens who exercise free movement rights provided for in the EU Treaties enjoy the right to equal treatment entailing the right (as stated by the ECJEU in *Bickel and Franz*[8]) to "be placed on an equal footing with nationals of the [host] Member State". 4–12

However, where Union citizens do not fall within such primary rules or secondary legislation due to the exercise of Treaty free movement rights, their rights and the obligations owed to them by the Member States in which they reside are far more contentious. Prior to the inclusion of the EU citizenship provisions in the Treaties, such persons obtained no rights as a matter of Community law (as it then was) since their status in such other Member State had no Community nexus. Moreover, still less were Member States under any obligation to treat such persons any differently than they would other foreign nationals. 4–13

There is no doubt that the creation of Union citizenship has fundamentally changed this position. Union citizenship now provides the EU law nexus through which Union citizens gain the protection of art.18 TFEU and are thereby able to access a range of benefits and rights on a non-discriminatory basis in other Member States. This protection arises without the Union citizen needing to establishing an EU law right of residence in those States. 4–14

---

[8] *Bickel and Franz* (C-274/96) [1998] E.C.R. I-7637. The case concerned the trials in Italy of (respectively) an Austrian lorry driver charged with driving while under the influence of alcohol and a German tourist charged with possession of a prohibited knife. The issue was whether Mr Bickel and Mr Franz could rely on the principle of non-discrimination on grounds of nationality in order to be granted the right to have the criminal proceedings conducted in a language other than Italian where that right is granted to certain Italian nationals. Although the Advocate General had pointed to the lack of any obvious link with Community law[8] the ECJ—basing itself on its earlier decision in *Cowan* (*Cowan v Trèsor public* (186/87) [1989] E.C.R. 195) held that the situations of both Mr Bickel and Mr Franz fell within the scope of the Treaty. This was because the situations governed by Community law included those covered by the freedom for the recipients of services to go to another Member State in order to receive services there under art.59 EC Treaty (as it then was). As such they were "entitled, pursuant to art.6 [now 18] of the Treaty, to treatment no less favourable than that accorded to nationals of the host State so far as concerns the use of languages which are spoken there". (para.16)

4–15 Since the creation of Union citizenship, the ECJ has consistently affirmed the importance of this interrelationship between arts 18 and 21 TFEU.[9] As the ECJ stated in *D'Hoop*:

> "Union citizenship is destined to be the fundamental status of nationals of the Member States, enabling those who find themselves in the same situation to enjoy with the scope *ratione materiae* of the Treaty the same treatment in law irrespective of their nationality, subject to such exceptions as are expressly provided for."

4–16 In spite of such affirmation, however, the protection against discrimination for Union citizens is not without its limits. To date the CJEU has found that Union citizens only benefit from art.18 TFEU when they are "lawfully resident", albeit that such lawful residence may result from the application of national laws and practices and need not result from the exercise of a free movement right in EU law. As discussed below "lawful residence" is a difficult concept to define bearing in mind that the CJEU is here deferring to national State practice and there is huge variation in practice between Member States.[10]

4–17 Furthermore, Union citizens will only receive protection from discrimination in areas which fall within the scope of the EU Treaties. Whether a matter falls within the scope of the Treaty is a difficult question which will plainly be answered in a more limited way where the Union citizen is not exercising a free movement right. For those that *are* exercising free movement rights EU law places an overriding obligation on Member States to facili-tate the exercise of such rights. In this context the scope of art.18 TFEU will extend to any matter which affects the exercise of the free movement right concerned. By contrast, for those *not* exercising free movement rights but who are nevertheless resident in another Member State, the scope of art.18 TFEU Treaty is potentially more limited because of the absence of the exercise of any underlying Treaty free movement right.

4–18 The case of *Sala*[11] was the first to identify the benefit that art.20 TFEU (as it now is), taken together with art.18 TFEU, would bring to Union citizens. *Sala*[12] concerned a Spanish national who had lived in Germany since 1968. Although in employment doing various jobs until 1989, she had since then been in receipt of social assistance. In January 1993 an application made for child-raising allowance was refused on the ground that she did not have German nationality, a residence entitlement or a residence permit.[13]

---

[9] See, for instance, *Grzelczyk v Centre Public d'aide sociale d'Ottignies-Louvain-la-Neuve* (C-184/99) [2001] E.C.R.I-6193; *Baumbast and R. v Secretary of State for the Home Department* (C-413/99) [2002] E.C.R. I-7091; and *D'Hoop v Office national de l'emploi* (C-224/98) [2002] E.C.R. I-6191, at [28].

[10] See paras 4–25 to 4–29 below.

[11] *Martinez Sala v Freistat Bayern* (85/96) [1998] E.C.R. I-2691.

[12] *Martinez Sala v Freistat Bayern* (85/96) [1998] E.C.R. I-2691.

[13] Until May 19, 1984 Mrs Sala obtained residence permits running more or less without interruption; thereafter she obtained only documents certifying that the extension of her residence permit had been applied for. However, the European Convention on Social and Medical Assistance of December 11, 1953 did not allow her to be deported. A residence permit expiring on April 18, 1995 was issued on April 19, 1994 (which was extended for a further year on April 20, 1995).

The CJEU had no doubt that child-raising allowance fell within the material **4–19** scope of EU law. This was the case both as a family benefit within the meaning of art.4(1)(h) of Reg.1408/71 (which then set out the basic rules concerning the coordination of social security for EU citizens who exercised economic free movement rights) and as a social advantage within the meaning of art.7(2) of Reg.1612/68 (which then set out the basic rules concerning free movement of workers within the EU).[14] As regards personal scope, if the referring court were to conclude either that Mrs Sala retained the status of worker[15] or of employed person[16] her unequal treatment would be unlawful. But what if Mrs Sala retained neither status? The Commission had argued that Mrs Sala would be able to rely on her Treaty right to citizens' free movement without more to bring herself within the personal scope of the Treaty.[17] However, according to the CJEU it was not necessary to decide whether Mrs Sala could rely on that right to obtain recognition of "a new right to reside" in Germany since she had "already been authorised to reside there".[18] According to the CJEU she was within the personal scope of the Treaty provisions on Union citizenship as a national of a Member State lawfully residing in the territory of another Member State. As such she was entitled under art.18 TFEU not to suffer discrimination on grounds of nationality in matters falling within the material scope of the Treaty (which as stated included child raising allowance). In the words of the CJEU:

> "63... [A] citizen of the European Union, such as the appellant in the main proceedings, lawfully resident in the territory of the host Member State, can rely on Article [18] of the Treaty in all situations which fall within the scope ratione materiae of [Union] law, including the situation where that Member State delays or refuses to grant to that claimant a benefit that is provided to all persons lawfully res-ident in the territory of that State on the ground that the claimant is not in possession of a document which nationals of that same State are not required to have and the issue of which may be delayed or refused by the authorities of that State."

Sala was novel insofar as it provided the link between arts 18 and 21 TFEU **4–20** with the consequence that Union citizens lawfully residing in other Member States fail to be treated on an equal footing with own nationals. It is to be emphasised that *Sala* concerned a benefit that was expressly provided for in

---

[14] *Martinez Sala v Freistat Bayern* (85/96) [1998] E.C.R. I-2691, at [57].
[15] Within the meaning of art.39 EC Treaty (as it then was) and of Regulation 1612/68.
[16] Within the meaning of Regulation 1408/71.
[17] A.G. La Pergola also focussed on this provision of the Treaty. In his opinion since the entry into force of that provision:
"The right of residence can no longer be considered to have been created by [Directive 90/364]... The right to move and reside freely throughout the whole of the Union is enshrined in an act of primary law and does not exist or cease to exist depending on whether or not it has been made subject to limitations under other provisions of Community law, including secondary legislation. The limitations in Art.[21] itself concern the actual exercise but not the existence of the right ... Art.[21] extracted the kernel from the other freedoms of movement—the freedom which we now find characterised as the right, not only to move, but also to reside in every Member State: a primary right, in the sense that it appears as the first of the rights ascribed to citizenship of the Union". (para.18).
[18] *Martinez Sala v Freistat Bayern* (85/96) [1998] E.C.R. I-2691, at [60]: see discussion at paras 4–25 to 4–29 for the relevance and meaning of being "authorised" to reside in the host Member State.

secondary legislation and therefore that the benefit fell within the scope of the Treaties was less open to question. However, more difficult questions would arise if the Union citizen sought protection against discrimination in an area which did not so obviously fall within the scope of the Treaties.

4–21 Where a Union citizen is exercising free movement rights in another Member State that Member State is expected to comply with EU law, and in particular to prevent discrimination, even when exercising competence in areas that fall outside EU law and within the exclusive competence of the Member States themselves.[19] But how should this principle apply in situations where the Union citizen is not exercising free movement rights?

4–22 The CJEU had to grapple with this question in *Avello*.[20] The case concerned a dispute between Mr Avello and the Belgian State concerning an application to change the surname of his children who were dual Belgian and Spanish nationals.[21] The CJEU expressly acknowledged that the subject-matter of the dispute (namely the rules governing a person's surname) was one falling within the exclusive competence of the Member States rather than the EU.[22] However, according to the CJEU the fact that the Union citizen children were residing in another Member State provided them with a sufficient link to EU law enabling them to be afforded protection under art.18 TFEU. Such a conclusion was not undermined by the fact that they also held the nationality of the host Member State to which the host Member State wished to give preference to.[23]

4–23 Whilst the Belgian authorities were entitled to apply their own rules as regards surnames to their own nationals, where those nationals also held the nationality of a second Member State, the Belgian authorities were not entitled to treat them as if they were Belgian nationals alone without permitting them to benefit from the holding of their second State nationality. If a Spanish national were residing in Belgium he would be entitled to have his surname conferred in accordance with Spanish law. A dual Belgian/Spanish national should not be in a *worse* position by virtue only of holding such dual nationality.

---

[19] *Pusa v Osuuspankkien Keskinäinen Vakuutusyhtiö* (C-224/02) [2004] E.C.R. I-5763 concerned the taxation of a Union citizen who was exercising the right to move and reside in another Member State. Whilst personal taxation is not generally harmonised at EU law level and therefore is normally said to fall with the exclusive competence of the individual Member States, the ECJ held that such competence must be exercised in compliance with EU law and thus art.18 TFEU. Similarly in *Elsen* (*Elsen v Bundesversicherungsanstalt für Angestellte* (C-135/99)) the ECJ considered the rules relating to the calculation of old age pension allowance fell within the competence of Member States. However, such legislation must be compatible with EU law. If national legislation is disadvantageous to those who have exercised their free movement rights such legislation would be incompatible with EU law.
[20] *Avello v Belgium* (C-148/02) [2003] E.C.R. I-11613.
[21] Mr Garcia Avello, a Spanish national, and Ms I. Weber, a Belgian national reside in Belgium where they married in 1986. Applying provisions of Belgian law the registrar entered the patronymic surname of their father ("Garcia Avello") on their certificates as their own surname. An application to change the surname to "Garcia Weber" (in accordance with well-established usage in Spanish law) was refused.
[22] *Avello v Belgium* (C-148/02) [2003] E.C.R. I-11613, at [25].
[23] For a discussion on dual nationality, see Ch.5 below.

Further development of the relationship between arts 18 and 21 TFEU is to be found in the decision of the ECJ in *Trojani*.[24] The case concerned a French national residing at a Salvation Army hostel in Belgium where he undertook various jobs in return for board, lodging and some "pocket money". He approached the Belgian authorities for payment of the minimum subsistence allowance (the minimex) which was refused on the grounds that he was not Belgian and was not a worker. The CJEU left the determination of the question whether Mr Trojani was a worker to the national court.[25] In the event that the national court were to conclude that Mr Trojani was not a worker, and since due to his lack of resources he could not derive any other benefit from art.21 TFEU, the CJEU considered his position as a Union citizen alone. Mr Trojani was in possession of a residence permit issued to him by the Belgian authorities. The CJEU held that a Union citizen in such a situation could rely on art.18 TFEU in order to be granted a social assistance benefit such as the minimex. The CJEU canvassed the possibility of the Member State taking measures to remove a person who has recourse to public funds.[26] However, any such measures could be undertaken by the Member State only subject to two important caveats. First, the CJEU recalled that removal must not be the automatic consequence of having recourse to public funds.[27] Secondly, and most importantly in the present context, the CJEU emphasised that whilst the person continues to reside in the host Member State they are entitled to benefit from the fundamental principle of equal treatment.

4–24

(ii) *Lawful residence*

The CJEU appears to make as a precondition to the benefit of the principle of equal treatment guaranteed by art.18 TFEU that the Union citizen is "lawfully resident" in the host Member State.[28] Lawful residence for these purposes is defined by reference to national laws and practices. Inevitably therefore there is scope for significant divergence of approach as regards what constitutes lawful residence as between the various Member States. If "lawful residence" is an absolute precondition to access art.18 TFEU protection there is a potential for Member States with restrictive immigration laws and practices to limit the benefits of Union citizenship for Union citizens residing in their territories. Whether the CJEU would countenance such divergence is doubtful. Moreover, the case law suggests that lawful residence is not to be strictly construed.

4–25

In *Sala*,[29] Mrs Sala at the relevant time could not be removed by virtue of provisions contained in the European Convention on Social and Medical

4–26

---

[24] *Trojani v Centre public d'aide sociale de Bruxelles (CPAS)* (C-456/02) [2004] E.C.R. I-7573, at [43].
[25] See further Ch.7.
[26] *Trojani v Centre public d'aide sociale de Bruxelles (CPAS)* (C-456/02) [2004] E.C.R. I-7573, at [45].
[27] See *Grzelczyk v Centre Public d'aide sociale d'Ottignies-Louvain-la-Neuve* (C-184/99) [2001] E.C.R. I-6193.
[28] See further, *Trojani v Centre public d'aide sociale de Bruxelles (CPAS)* (C-456/02) [2004] E.C.R. I-7573, at [39].
[29] *Martinez Sala v Freistat Bayern* (85/96) [1998] E.C.R. I-2691.

Assistance. She had only documents confirming that an application had been made for a residence permit. Although the CJEU describes her as having been "authorised to reside", her situation was in fact not one of authorisation, but rather one of toleration on the part of the host Member State.

4–27 There may be a wide variety of situations in which Union citizens reside in the territories of other Member States without having fulfilled administrative formalities and in which their presence there is apparently tolerated. First, bearing in mind the administrative difficulties of actually seeking to enforce the removal of Union citizens who do not possess residence permits, such toleration is likely to be common in Member States. Secondly, in light of the breadth of the concepts of (for example) worker and work seeker, there will frequently be a very fine line between who is and who is not in fact exercising free movement rights. Thirdly, it may also occasionally be the case that Union citizens will have moved to Member States *intending* to exercise a particular free movement right, without ever actually doing so.

4–28 The *Sala*[30] decision therefore apparently includes in the beneficiaries of protection of art.18 TFEU a broad spectrum of Union citizens residing in Member States who are not in possession of residence permits. Plainly this is to be welcomed if Union citizens are not to be socially excluded and disadvantaged in other Member States.

4–29 Even however if the foregoing analysis of residence and toleration is too broad, and lawful residence *is* required, such lawful residence need not have been continuous or for a predetermined period of time in order that the Union citizen is able to benefit from the protection of art.18 TFEU. In *Trojani* the CJEU expressly stated that the benefit of art.18 TFEU was to be enjoyed by those who have been lawfully resident in a Member State "for a certain period of time".[31] Thus for example, a person whose residence was initially lawful as a work seeker, but who fails within a reasonable period to find work and who thereafter ceases to fall within the scope of the free movement provisions, should on the CJEU's analysis nonetheless benefit from art.18 TFEU.

(iii) *Scope of art.18 TFEU*

4–30 The scope of situations in which Union citizens have benefited from the equal treatment provision contained in art.18 TFEU has been both broad and varied. It has included non-discriminatory access to: the minimex (*Trojani*); child-raising allowance (*Sala*); unemployment benefit[32]; free travel for disabled persons (*Gottwald*);[33] benefits for relatives of crime victims[34];

---

[30] *Martinez Sala v Freistat Bayern* (85/96) [1998] E.C.R. I-2691.
[31] *Trojani v Centre public d'aide sociale de Bruxelles (CPAS)* (C-456/02) [2004] E.C.R. I-7573, at [43].
[32] See, for instance, *De Cuyper* (C-406/04) [2006] E.C.R. I-6947.
[33] *Arthur Gottwald v Bezirkshauptmannschaft Bregenz* (C-103/08) [2009] E.C.R. I-9117. In this case, the discrimination on grounds of nationality was indirect, since it was based on residence.
[34] *James Wood v Fonds de garantie des victimes des actes de terrorisme et d'autres* infractions (C-164/07) [2008] E.C.R. I-4143.

benefits for war victims[35]; access to education[36] including related tax and benefits[37]; and the ability to change surnames (*Avello, Grunkin-Paul, Sayn-Wittgenstein* and *Runevic-Vardyn*). Moreover as the latter three cases make clear,[38] the CJEU has even been prepared to extend the scope of art.18 TFEU for Union citizens into areas that fall within the exclusive competence of Member States.

However, the protection provided by art.18 TFEU is not absolute and is subject to objective justification invoked by Member States, which are proportionate the legitimate aim pursued. For instance, in *Grunkin-Paul*,[39] the Court ruled that various German justifications for imposing its ban on "double-barrelled" names for German nationals were legitimate, but that they were not justified in the circumstances (the child concerned had no siblings, the national rule would not prevent an obstacle to his free movement and anyway German law permitted a divergent approach to this issue in some other cases). On the other hand, the Court ruled in *Sayn-Wittgenstein* that the Austrian ban on refusing to accept its nationals' use of noble titles conferred pursuant to another Member State's law was justified, given that it was consistent with the objective of equality set out in art.20 of the EU Charter of Fundamental Rights and Freedoms and was part of the "national identity" of the State in question (as a republic).[40] Similarly, in *Runevic-Wardyn* the Court ruled a measure restricting free movement which had the aim of protection of a national language was consistent with the protection of linguistic diversity set out in art.22 of the Charter, as well as (again) the protection of national identity.

4–31

As regards social policy, the case law permits Member States to limit benefits to cases where there is a sufficient link with national territory. For example, in *Gottwald*,[41] the Court ruled that the Austrian government could justify a residence requirement, on the facts of that case. But in other cases, Member States could not justify discriminatory requirements.[42]

4–32

---

[35] *Halina Nerkowska v Zakład Ubezpieczeń Społecznych Oddział w Koszalinie* (C-499/06) [2008] E.C.R. I-3993 and *Krystyna Zablocka-Weyhermüller v Land Baden-Württemberg* (C-221/07) [2008] E.C.R. I-9229.
[36] *Nicolas Bressol and Others, Céline Chaverot and Others v Gouvernement de la Communauté française*, (C-73/08) [2010] E.C.R. I-2735. Again, the discrimination on grounds of nationality was indirect since it was based on residence.
[37] For instance, see *Jacqueline Förster v Hoofddirectie van de Informatie Beheer Groep* (C-158/07) [2008] E.C.R. I-8507; *Commission v Germany* (C-318/05) [2007] E.C.R. I-6957; and *The Queen, on the application of Dany Bidar v London Borough of Ealing and Secretary of State for Education and Skills* (C-209/03) [2005] E.C.R. I-2119.
[38] *Avello v Belgium* (C-148/02) [2003] E.C.R. I-11613, at [25]; *Leonhard Matthias Grunkin-Paul* (C-353/06) [2008] E.C.R. I-7639; *Ilonka Sayn-Wittgenstein v Landeshauptmann von Wien* (C-208/09) judgment of December 22, 2010, not yet reported; and *Małgožata Runevic-Vardyn*, (C-391/09) judgment of May 12, 2011, not yet reported.
[39] *Leonhard Matthias Grunkin-Paul* (C-353/06) [2008] E.C.R. I-7639.
[40] *Ilonka Sayn-Wittgenstein v Landeshauptmann von Wien* (C-208/09) judgment of December 22, 2010, not yet reported.
[41] *Arthur Gottwald v Bezirkshauptmannschaft Bregenz* (C-103/08) [2009] E.C.R. I-9117.
[42] See, for instance, *Halina Nerkowska v Zakład Ubezpieczeń Społecznych Oddział w Koszalinie* (C-499/06) [2008] E.C.R. I-3993 and *Krystyna Zablocka-Weyhermüller v Land Baden-Württemberg* (C-221/07) [2008] E.C.R. I-9229.

4-33 It appears from this case law that where the Union citizen seeks non-discriminatory access to a right or benefit whose provisions do not have financial ramifications for the Member State concerned the CJEU requires objective justification for the discriminatory treatment. Where on the other hand there are financial consequences for the host Member State from the provision of any such right or benefit, the CJEU examines instead the question of whether the person concerned is sufficiently integrated into the territory of the Member State concerned, inter alia examining the validity of residence requirements in many cases. Such analysis is not contradicted by the CJEU's decision in *Trojani*[43] which concerned non-discriminatory access to the minimex (a non-contributory means-tested benefit), since the minimex is a benefit guaranteeing only a minimum level of subsistence which if not given arguably engages the Member State's human rights obligations.

4-34 Whilst the development of the relationship between arts 18 and 21 TFEU is to be welcomed, it remains the case that it will normally better avail the Union citizen if able to bring themselves within the scope of a free movement right. The material scope of art.18 TFEU is plainly broader if the Union citizen is exercising free movement rights since, as already emphasised, in those cases it is the obligation of Member States to facilitate the exercise of such rights and to eliminate any obstacles to free movement.[44] All rights or benefits which in any way impact on the ability of Union citizens to exercise the right to move and reside in other Member States must fall within the scope of art.18 TFEU since such Union citizens must not be disadvantaged by their having moved.[45]

(c) *Tension between Union and national citizenship*

4-35 As identified above, the creation of citizenship of a supranational body undoubtedly creates a potential tension with national authorities, particularly where such citizenship has consequences for Member States which might be considered to be wider than anticipated. Such tension will be at its most acute where Member States are obliged to shoulder additional financial responsibility.

4-36 In its original form as it was inserted into the EC Treaty by the Maastricht Treaty art.8(1) EC [now art.20 TFEU] contained no reference to Union citizenship complementing rather than replacing national citizenship. It was the Amsterdam Treaty, signed more than five years later,[46] which clarified the link between European Union and national citizenship adding to art.17(1) EC Treaty (now art.20 TFEU) the unequivocal statement that

---

[43] *Trojani v Centre public d'aide sociale de Bruxelles (CPAS)* (C-456/02) [2004] E.C.R. I-7573.
[44] See, for example, *Collins v Secretary of State for Work and Pensions* (C-138/02) [2004] E.C.R. I-2703, where the ECJ held that a work seeker was entitled to job-seeker's allowance on a non-discriminatory basis.
[45] See *Elsen v Bundesversicherungsanstalt für Angestellte* (C-135/99) [2000] E.C.R. I-10409, at [34].
[46] The Amsterdam Treaty was signed on October 2, 1997 and came into force on May 1, 1999: see Ch.1 above.

"citizenship of the Union shall complement and not replace national citizenship".

If such clarification was not reassurance enough for Member States, the CJEU has reaffirmed the sovereignty of Member States as regards the right of Member States to determine the acquisition of nationality and also the conferal of the status of Union citizenship.[47] As made clear in Ch.5, the nationality of the Member States is determined by reference to the domestic law of the individual Member States alone. A Member State may change its laws relating to the acquisition of nationality without reference to any EU or other body, and it is permissible also for Member States to define which of their nationals are to be considered EU citizens for the purposes of EU law. Nationality is thus a matter exclusively within the competence of the Member States, although where a Member State wishes to preclude some of its nationals from obtaining EU law benefits it must do so by means of a declaration.[48]

4-37

Despite such reassurance however the tension remains. It is well shown by the June 11, 2004 citizenship referendum in Ireland which was proposed by Irish Justice Minister Michael McDowell to end what he claimed was an incentive for foreign mothers to give birth in Irish hospitals, so called "baby tourists".[49] When the Advocate General gave his opinion in *Chen*[50] Mr McDowell took the opportunity to appeal to voters to support the Government's referendum stating that the Advocate General's decision sent out a clear message that if people do not want to be sent home, "all they have to do is get to either part of Ireland and have a child there".[51] It is not inconceivable that the holding of the Irish referendum was motivated in part by pressure put on the Irish by other Member States.

4-38

Moreover, the CJEU has confirmed that Member States are *not* exclusively competent to regulate the *loss* of their nationality. For an example see the *Rottmann* judgment.[52] In this case, Mr Rottmann, an Austrian citizen, had

4-39

---

[47] See *Cheung Chiu Hung* (C-256/99) judgment of July 12, 2001 and *The Queen v Secretary of State for the Home Department Ex p. Manjit Kaur* (C-192/99) [2001] E.C.R. I-1237.
[48] The UK's declaration means that the following are to be considered as "nationals" for the purposes of EU law: (a) British citizens; (b) British subjects with the right of abode in the UK; and (c) British Dependant Territories citizens who acquire that citizenship as a result of a connection to Gibraltar. January 28, 1983 [1983] O.J. C23, p.1, (Cmnd 9062, 1983).
[49] See article "Baby tourist' vote in June" by D. Condon (posted on April 7, 2004 on the website *http://www.irishhealth.com*). On April 11, 2004 in an article by M. Brennock in *The Irish Times* ("McDowell spells out plans to restrict rights to citizenship"). Mr Brennock refers to Mr McDowell having "shifted his argument for the holding of the referendum, saying it was necessary 'to protect the integrity of the Irish citizenship law'." The article continues:
"Last month he and his Department based their case for change on suggestions the growing number of non-national births in Ireland to 'citizenship tourists' was causing a crisis in maternity hospitals. Yesterday, however, he said: 'This is not an issue about maternity hospitals. Ireland could not be the only EU state offering national—and therefore EU-wide—citizenship rights to babies whose parents came here solely for this purpose'."
[50] *Man Lavette Chen v Kunqian Catherine Zhu v Secretary of State for the Home Department* (C-200/02) [2004] E.C.R. I-9925.
[51] See D. Condon, "Ruling 'justifies' citizenship referendum" (posted on May 19, 2004 on the website *http://www.irishhealth.com*).
[52] *Janko Rottmann v Freistaat Bayern* (C-135/08) [2010] E.C.R. I-1149.

moved from Austria to Germany and then obtained German citizenship, with the result that he lost Austrian citizenship. Subsequently the German authorities found out about proceedings against him in Austria and revoked his German citizenship, leaving him Stateless—and extinguishing his rights as a citizen of the Union. The CJEU stated that even national competences over citizenship had to be exercised in accordance with EU law, and that in the circumstances, Mr Rottmann's situation fell within the "ambit" of EU law. The consequence of the application of EU law was that a decision withdrawing naturalisation, "in so far as it affects the rights conferred and protected by the legal order of the Union," had to be "amenable to judicial review carried out in the light of European Union law". The Court distinguished Mr Rottmann from Mrs Kaur, in that the latter had *never* held the nationality of a Member State (in light of the relevant UK declarations), perhaps implicitly suggesting that issues relating to the original acquisition of nationality still remained within absolute national competence.

4-40 Applying these principles to the facts, the Court ruled that it was in principle acceptable to withdraw naturalisation "because of deception", since this corresponded "to a reason relating to the public interest". Presumably other public interest grounds for withdrawing naturalisation might be conceivable—but the CJEU would implicitly insist on its jurisdiction to rule on whether a particular ground set out in national law was accepted. In this context, the Court ruled that "it is legitimate for a Member State to wish to protect the special relationship of solidarity and good faith between it and its nationals and also the reciprocity of rights and duties, which form the bedrock of the bond of nationality." This rule was also consistent with relevant international treaties—begging the question of what would happen if a Member State had not ratified one or both of those treaties, and/or had acted inconsistently with them as regards its rule on the loss of citizenship. The knock-on effect upon the loss of EU citizenship was not as such objectionable—although the national court would have to examine whether the loss of each of EU and national citizenship was proportionate.

4-41 More specifically, the national court would have to examine the impact of the loss of citizenship for the person concerned, including the impact on their family members, and to consider "the gravity of the offence committed", the lapse of time between the naturalisation and withdrawal decisions and the possibility of recovering the original nationality. As to that, a Member State would not be prevented from withdrawing its nationality just because the original nationality had not been recovered; but the national court has to determine whether the principle of proportionality requires granting that person a reasonable period of time to try to recover their original nationality before withdrawing the newer nationality. Finally, the Court did not rule on whether the original Member State of nationality had to restore that nationality, but did state that the issue of *re-acquiring* that nationality fell within the scope of EU law, and that the original Member State would have to apply the principles set out in the judgment.

4-42 In theory a Member State could seek to prevent its citizens from obtaining the benefits of Union citizenship the greater such benefits become. However, whilst such concerns might well dictate the wishes of certain national authorities to curtail rights, the reality is that it is too late. It is not possible[53] to dissociate Union citizenship from the citizenship of Member States so as to create categories of persons who could enjoy the free movement rights of the economically active and inactive, but not the rights associated with Union citizenship. This does not mean, however, that a Member State might not seek to enter a declaration which would have the effect of depriving its nationals of all benefits of EU law (as for example in the case of the UK's declarations), nor that a Member State would not seek to amend its citizenship laws as Ireland has done.

(i) *Deprivation of the substance of citizenship rights*

4-43 In recent judgments, the CJEU has also developed the principle that Member States lack the power to deprive EU citizenship of its essential substance. This principle appears to apply, according to the case law to date, only where a child with EU citizenship would be compelled to leave the territory of the Union due to an expulsion order issued to its third-country national parents, even where that child has not exercised free movement rights.[54] It does not however apply unless the refusal to admit or the expulsion of a third country national family member of the citizen who has not exercised free movement rights would effectively deprive that citizen of his or her right to move and reside in the EU, by forcing that citizen to leave the EU in practice. It also does not apply where an EU citizen who holds the nationality of two Member States has not exercised free movement rights.[55] It remains to be seen what further impact the concept of deprivation of the substance of citizenship rights might have.

4. ARTICLE 21 TFEU: THE RIGHT OF UNION CITIZENS TO MOVE AND RESIDE

(a) *Introduction*

4-44 The insertion of art.8a (now art.21(1) TFEU) into the EC Treaty by the Maastricht Treaty was symbolically important. It placed at the heart of the EC Treaty (now the TFEU) a right for all Union citizens to move and reside freely in the Member States. Whilst free movement rights had always been core to the Treaty of Rome, the original intended beneficiaries were the economically active. Until the Maastricht Treaty, the substance of free movement rights for the economically inactive was described only by secondary legislation.

4-45 The extent to which art.21(1) TFEU was more than merely symbolic is a question that the ECJ is still answering. There is potentially a range of interpretations which could be given to art.21(1) TFEU:

---

[53] Subject of course to Treaty amendment.
[54] *Ruiz Zambrano v Office National de l'Emploi (ONEM)* (C-34/09) [2011] E.C.R. I-0000.
[55] *Dereci and others v Bundesministerium für Inneres* (C-256/11) [2012] E.C.R. I-0000 judgment of November 15, 2011, not yet reported and *Shirley McCarthy v Secretary of State for the Home Department* (C-434/09) [2011] E.C.R. I-0000 and further Ch.5.

- art.21(1) TFEU adds nothing of substance to free movement rights which are conferred exclusively by (other) existing Treaty provisions and secondary legislation. The conditions and limitations laid down in those other provisions are to be strictly construed and applied (a "restrictive interpretation");

- art.21(1) TFEU provides an interpretative obligation requiring Member States to apply such limitations and conditions in compliance with the limits imposed by EU law and in accordance with the general principles of that law, in particular the principle of proportionality. Thus the "limitations and conditions" that are found in Treaty provisions and secondary legislation are to be construed against a backdrop of the fundamental right to move and reside contained in Art. 21(1) TFEU Treaty (an "interpretative obligation"); and

- art.21(1) TFEU itself founds the right to move and reside without reference to any need to establish that the right is already provided for elsewhere in the pre-existing specific provisions contained in the Treaty or secondary legislation relating to free movement (a "free standing right").

Each is considered in turn below.

(b) A restrictive interpretation

4-46 The narrowest interpretation of art.21(1) TFEU would deprive the provision of any legal impact at all, in effect characterising it as having little more than political significance. Such approach is reflected by (for example) the submissions made to the CJEU in *Grzelczyk*[56] by the Belgian and Danish Governments that Union citizens did not obtain through art.21(1) TFEU rights that were "new" or "more extensive" than those already derived from the Treaty and secondary legislation. As the CJEU itself characterised their submissions: "The principle of citizenship of the Union has no autonomous content, but is merely linked to other provisions in the Treaty".[57]

4-47 The CJEU's response to such exhortations by some Member States has been one of resounding rejection. As stated by the CJEU in *Baumbast*[58] (and as consistently restated thereafter), art.21 TFEU grants a right to reside which is conferred directly on every Union citizen. Although the CJEU acknowledges that the right conferred is subject to limitations and conditions, the application of those limitations and conditions is subject to judicial review. The narrow approach advocated by some Member States is thus plainly not one which the CJEU approves.

---

[56] *Grzelczyk v Centre Public d'aide sociale d'Ottignies-Louvain-la-Neuve* (C-184/99) [2001] E.C.R. I-6193.
[57] *Grzelczyk v Centre Public d'aide sociale d'Ottignies-Louvain-la-Neuve* (C-184/99) [2001] E.C.R. I-6193, at [21].
[58] *Baumbast and R. v Secretary of State for the Home Department* (C-413/99) [2002] E.C.R. I-7091.

(c) *An interpretative obligation*

4–48 The majority of the cases to date in which the CJEU has considered art.21(1) TFEU reflect "the interpretative approach". This approach sees the "limitations and conditions" referred to in art.21(1) TFEU as those provided for in existing primary law and secondary legislation, but insists that they must be construed against the backdrop of the fundamental right to move and reside. The cases of *Grzelczyk*[59] and *Baumbast*[60] provide good examples of this approach.

4–49 *Grzelczyk*[61] concerned a French student studying in Belgium who during the final year of his studies was refused payment of the minimum subsistence allowance known as the minimex because he was not a Belgian national. The CJEU emphasised that Union citizenship was

> "destined to be the fundamental status of nationals of the Member States, enabling those who find themselves in the same situation to enjoy the same treatment in law irrespective of their nationality, subject to such exceptions as are expressly provided for".[62]

Such situations included those involving the exercise of the fundamental freedoms guaranteed by the Treaty and those involving the exercise of the right to move and reside freely in another Member State as conferred by art.21(1) TFEU.

4–50 In the context of art.21(1) TFEU the limitations and conditions relevant to Mr Grzelczyk were those contained in the Student Directive.[63] However, reading those limitations in conjunction with art.21(1) TFEU the CJEU emphasised the following features of the Directive:

- whilst art.3 of the Directive makes clear that it does not establish any right to payment of maintenance grants, there are no provisions in the Directive that preclude those to whom it applies from receiving social security benefits;
- as to resources, art.1 of the Directive does not require resources of any specific amount, nor that they be evidenced by specific documents:

---

[59] *Grzelczyk v Centre Public d'aide sociale d'Ottignies-Louvain-la-Neuve* (C-184/99) [2001] E.C.R. I-6193.
[60] *Baumbast and R. v Secretary of State for the Home Department* (C-413/99) [2002] E.C.R. I-7091.
[61] *Grzelczyk v Centre Public d'aide sociale d'Ottignies-Louvain-la-Neuve* (C-184/99) [2001] E.C.R. I-6193.
[62] *Grzelczyk v Centre Public d'aide sociale d'Ottignies-Louvain-la-Neuve* (C-184/99) [2001] E.C.R. I-6193, at [31]. Such aspirational statement has been repeated frequently by the ECJ since first used in this case. However, there are no transitional provisions contained in Pt II of the EC Treaty and whilst perhaps understandable that the ECJ's attitude to art.21(1) TFEU should reflect incremental change, it is difficult to see what possible justification there could be for any notion that Union Citizenship should be confined to something aspirational as opposed to some-thing which is real and effective.
[63] Directive 93/96 [1993] O.J. L317/59.

rather the article refers merely to a declaration (or equivalent alternative means) enabling the student to satisfy the national authority as to the availability of sufficient resources (the truthfulness of which fell to be assessed only as at the time when made); and

- the directive thereby differed from Dirs 90/364 and 90/365 which do indicate the necessary minimum level of available income.

4–51 Such factors did not prevent a Member State from taking the view that a student who has recourse to social assistance no longer fulfils the conditions of their right of residence or from taking measures, within the limits imposed by EU law, either to withdraw their residence permit or not to renew it. However, according to the ECJ

> "in no case may such measures become the automatic consequence of a student who is a national of another Member State having recourse to the host Member State's social assistance system."

In these circumstances the ECJ held that:

> "Articles 6 [now 18] and 8 [now 20] of the Treaty preclude entitlement to a non-contributory social benefit, such as the minimex, from being made conditional, in the case of nationals of Member States other than the host State where they are legally resident, on their falling within the scope of Regulation No 1612/68 when no such condition applies to nationals of the host Member State".[64]

4–52 Whilst Member States might have previously construed the Student Directive as placing an absolute bar on access to social assistance, the CJEU has made clear by reference to art.21 TFEU that such a narrow interpretation is no longer open.

4–53 In *Baumbast*[65] the CJEU considered the limitations found in the general right of Residence Directive.[66] The limitations and conditions contained in that Directive require that those wishing to enjoy the right to reside (and members of their families) must be covered by sickness insurance in respect of *all* risks in the host Member State and have sufficient resources to avoid becoming a burden on the social assistance system of the host Member State during their period of residence.[67]

4–54 Mr Baumbast satisfied the condition relating to sufficient resources. At issue was whether his sickness insurance covered all risks.[68] However, whatever the actual position as regards sickness insurance (a matter for determination

---

[64] *Grzelczyk v Centre Public d'aide sociale d'Ottignies-Louvain-la-Neuve* (C-184/99) [2001] E.C.R. I-6193, at [46].
[65] *Baumbast and R. v Secretary of State for the Home Department* (C-413/99) [2002] E.C.R. I-7091.
[66] Directive 90/364 [1990] O.J. L180/26.
[67] Directive 90/364 art.1(1).
[68] It had been found by the UK first instance court that Mr Baumbast's sickness insurance could not cover emergency treatment given in the UK: *Baumbast and R. v Secretary of State for the Home Department* (C-413/99) [2002] E.C.R. I-7091, at [89].

by the national tribunal), the CJEU acknowledged that the limitations and conditions laid down by Directive 90/364 were based on the notion that the exercise of the right of residence could be sub-ordinated to the legitimate interests of the Member States which (according to the fourth recital in the preamble to Directive 90/364) included the requirement that beneficiaries of the right must not become an "unreasonable" burden on the public finances of the host Member State.

However, reflective of the interpretative approach the CJEU held that such limitations and conditions were to be applied "in compliance with the limits imposed by [EU] law and in accordance with the general principles of that law, in particular the principle of proportionality".[69] This meant that national measures adopted were required to be both necessary and appropriate to attain the objective pursued. Applying the principle of proportionality the CJEU stated:[70]

4–55

> "92. In respect of the application of the principle of proportionality to the facts of the *Baumbast* case, it must be recalled, first, that it has not been denied that Mr Baumbast has sufficient resources within the meaning of Directive 90/364; second, that he worked and therefore lawfully resided in the host Member State for several years, initially as an employed person and subsequently as a self-employed person; third, that during that period his family also resided in the host Member State and remained there even after his activities as an employed and self-employed person in that State came to an end; fourth, that neither Mr Baumbast nor the members of his family have become burdens on the public finances of the host Member State and, fifth, that both Mr Baumbast and his family have comprehensive sickness insurance in another Member State of the Union.
>
> 93. Under those circumstances, to refuse to allow Mr Baumbast to exercise the right of residence which is conferred on him by Article 18(1) EC by virtue of the application of the provisions of Directive 90/364 on the ground that his sickness insurance does not cover the emergency treatment given in the host Member State would amount to a disproportionate interference with the exercise of that right."

(d) *A free standing right*

The most liberal interpretation of art.21 TFEU sees it as a discrete provision founding the right to move and reside for those not catered for by the free movement provisions otherwise contained in the Treaties or secondary legislation. Opponents of such interpretation would doubtless maintain that the interpretation would render entirely otiose the phrase in art.21 TFEU that the right is "subject to the limitations and conditions laid down in this Treaty and by the measures adopted to give it effect". In fact the interpretation is more nuanced.

4–56

---

[69] *Baumbast and R. v Secretary of State for the Home Department* (C-413/99) [2002] E.C.R. I-7091, at [91].
[70] *Baumbast and R. v Secretary of State for the Home Department* (C-413/99) [2002] E.C.R. I-7091.

4–57 Such approach was first articulated by Advocate General Geelhoed in *Baumbast*.[71] Identifying the economically active and the economically non-active by reference to two discrete sets of rules,[72] Advocate General Geelhoed stated that art.21 TFEU added to such sets of rules "a general right of residence in favour of citizens of the European Union" which he described as "a fundamental right in favour of citizens of the European Union to move and reside freely within it".

4–58 In Advocate General Geelhoed's view art.21 TFEU has substantive significance in two respects. First, the unconditional nature of the first part of art.21(1) TFEU entails that the right of residence must be a recognisable right of substance for citizens. Whilst the provision lays down requirements to be met such requirements must be neither arbitrary, nor deprive the right of residence of its substantive content. Any limitations must respect the essence of the rights and freedoms, be proportionate and be made only if necessary and genuinely meeting objectives of general interest recognised by the Union. Secondly, the provision imposes an obligation on the EU legislature to ensure that a citizen of the European Union can actually enjoy the rights conferred on them under art.21 TFEU.

4–59 The approach is summarised by Advocate General Geelhoed[73] in these terms:

> "Finally, the unambiguous nature of Article [21(1) TFEU] entails that a person not entitled to a right of residence under other provisions of [EU] law can none the less acquire such a right by reliance on Article [21]. Since there is no single general and all-embracing set of rules concerning the exercise of the right of residence in Community law recourse must be had in cases for which the Community legislature has made no provision to Article [21 TFEU]. However, that does not mean that an unre-stricted right of residence is recognised in those—special—cases. The conditions and limitations imposed on that right by EC law must be applied by analogy as far as possible to persons who derive their right to reside directly from Article [21 TFEU]. The wording of the second part of Article [21(1) TFEU] forms the basis for that."

4–60 The first (and to date only) example of a case in which the CJEU has embraced this approach is *D'Hoop*[74] in which the CJEU considered the position of a Belgian national who had completed her secondary education in France before commencing university studies in Belgium. After she had completed her university studies she applied for a "tide-over allowance"—a social benefit intended for young unemployed people in search of their first job. The allowance was refused by the Belgian national employment office because Ms D'Hoop had completed her secondary education in France.

---

[71] *Baumbast and R v Secretary of State for the Home Department* (C-413/99) [2002] E.C.R. I-7091.
[72] art.39, et seq EC Treaty (now art.45, et seq TFEU) dealing with the economically active and Dirs 90/364, 90/365 and 93/96 dealing with the economically non-active—para.104.
[73] *Baumbast and R. v Secretary of State for the Home Department* (C-413/99) opinion July 5, 2001.
[74] *D'Hoop v Office national de l'emploi* (C-224/98) [2002] E.C.R. I-6191.

In assessing the provisions on Union citizenship the CJEU—as it had done   4–61
in *Grzelczyk*—emphasised both that Union citizenship was destined to be
the "fundamental status" of nationals of the Member States[75] and that the
situations falling within the scope of EU law included those involving the
exercise of the fundamental freedoms guaranteed by the Treaty "in particular those involving the freedom to move and reside within the territory
of the Member States, as conferred by Article [21 TFEU]".[76]

Of particular relevance for present purposes is the that the CJEU char-   4–62
acterised Ms D'Hoop as someone who had exercised "the opportunities
offered by the Treaty in relation to freedom of movement".[77] She had
exercised her fundamental right to move having undertaken her secondary
education in France. This was an entirely novel approach. Shortly stated
this is because there is no specific right recognised in the Treaties (or secondary legislation) to move for the purposes of secondary education.[78]
Whilst the decision of the ECJ in *Raulin*[79] requires equal treatment as
regards vocational training, the principle does not apply to general secondary education. Although art.12 of Regulation 1612/68 (now art.10 of
Regulation 492/2011) provides a discrete right for the children of workers to
be admitted to a Member State's "general education, apprenticeship and
vocational training courses" there is no indication that Ms D'Hoop was
exercising her own discrete right of access to secondary education as the
child of a worker. Thus—at least by implication—*D'Hoop*[80] can be characterised as the first case in which the ECJ treated art.21 TFEU itself as
founding the right to move and reside.

Furthermore, it is important to appreciate the significance of the ECJ's   4–63
finding that although not in force at such time the provisions on Union
citizenship could be taken into account enabling assessment to be made of
the present effects of a situation which had arisen previously.[81] It is clear
that without such finding and an ability to rely on art.18(1), Ms D'Hoop
could not have been characterised as having exercised Treaty opportunities
when she undertook her secondary education in France.

(e) *The future of art.21 TFEU*

As Advocate General Geelhoed has stated, art.21 TFEU provides the free   4–64
movement right for those not already covered by primary and secondary
legislation. In essence those not covered are twofold: children and the poor.

---

[75] *D'Hoop v Office national de l'emploi* (C-224/98), at [28]: as stated at para.31 of *Grzelczyk*, the ECJ stated that the status enabled those who find themselves in the same situation to enjoy within the scope *ratione materiae* of the Treaty the same treatment in law irrespective of their nationality, subject to such exceptions as are expressly provided for.
[76] *D'Hoop v Office national de l'emploi* (C-224/98), at [29], as the ECJ had stated in *Bickel and Franz* (C-274/96) [1998] E.C.R. I-7637, at [15–16], and *Grzelczyk*, at [33].
[77] *D'Hoop v Office national de l'emploi* (C-224/98) [2002] E.C.R. I-6191, at [30] and [33].
[78] Save for the art.12 right contained in Regulation 1612/68 considered below.
[79] *Raulin v Minister van Onderwijs en Wetenschappen* (C-357/89) [1992] E.C.R. I-1027.
[80] *D'Hoop v Office national de l'emploi* (C-224/98) [2002] E.C.R. I-6191.
[81] *D'Hoop v Office national de l'emploi* (C-224/98) [2002] E.C.R. I-6191, at [21–26].

(i) Children

4–65 As regards children, without art.21 TFEU they enjoy no specific free movement rights, other than as the consequence of being the children of parents exercising free movement rights[82] or students in vocational training.[83] In *D'Hoop*[84] the ECJ plainly remedied the lacuna, at least for children in secondary education. It did so by reference to the specific inclusion of art.149 in the EC Treaty (now art.165 TFEU) aimed at encouraging the mobility of students. Since art.165 applies to education generally and not only to secondary education, there is no reason why the CJEU's reasoning should not apply equally to children in primary education.

4–66 This leaves a potential lacuna only for those children who are not in education and do not have EU national parents.

4–67 This category of children was considered by the CJEU in *Chen*.[85] The case concerned a Chinese couple who decided that their second child should be born abroad. To this end Mrs Chen travelled to the United Kingdom and gave birth on September 16, 2000 to her daughter Catherine in Belfast, Northern Ireland, having been advised by lawyers that the child would thereby be Irish by birth. After the birth Mrs Chen moved to Cardiff with her child and applied to the UK authorities for residence permits which were refused.

4–68 The principal issue was whether the infant child could rely on the provisions of Directive 90/364 (providing the right of residence for the self-sufficient). It was argued by the Irish Government that because of her tender age the child was incapable of independently exercising the right to choose a place of residence in the United Kingdom and to establish herself there in the context of the Directive. The CJEU held that it was sufficient for nationals of Member States simply to "have" the necessary resources in order to benefit from the right of residence given by Directive 90/364. That Directive lays down no requirement whatsoever as to the origin of such resources.[86] (Nor, it should be noted, does the subsequent Directive 2004/38). Furthermore, as regards the child's mother and carer, the ECJ applied *Baumbast*[87] and held that unless Mrs Chen was able to reside with her daughter this would deprive the child's right of residence of any useful effect.[88]

4–69 The result in *Chen* is unsurprising. As regards sufficiency of resources, the Commission had long held the view that Directives 90/364 and 90/365 do not mean that the requirement must be satisfied by the beneficiaries' *own*

---

[82] See, for example, arts 10 and 12 of Regulation 1612/68.
[83] Directive 93/96 on the right of residence for students.
[84] *D'Hoop v Office national de l'emploi* (C-224/98) [2002] E.C.R. I-6191.
[85] *Man Lavette Chen and Kunqian Catherine Zhu v Secretary of State for the Home Department* (C-200/02) [2004] E.C.R. I-9925.
[86] *Man Lavette Chen and Kunqian Catherine Zhu v Secretary of State for the Home Department* (C-200/02) [2004] E.C.R. I-9925, para.30.
[87] *Baumbast and R. v Secretary of State for the Home Department* (C-413/99) [2002] E.C.R. I-7091.
[88] *Man Lavette Chen and Kunqian Catherine Zhu v Secretary of State for the Home Department* (C-200/02) [2004] E.C.R. I-9925, at [45].

Article 21 TFEU: The Right of Union Citizens to Move and Reside

resources, or indeed resources originating from any dependents.[89] There is no reason why the position should be different for an EU national child with resources, whatever the origin of such resources. The CJEU has since extended this ruling to all cases where an economically inactive EU citizen's resources are provided by a third party.[90]

As regards the position of the child's carer, the judgment in *Chen* reinforces the firmly established principles that family members facilitate the exercise of Treaty free movement rights and that a child will usually be unable to exercise free movement rights without being accompanied by a primary carer. The CJEU was clearly fortified in its views by the existence of the child's art.21 TFEU right to move and reside in another Member State. 4–70

This decision will undoubtedly be of considerable benefit to EU national children whose parents are not themselves EU nationals. The ECJ in *Chen* was clear that the primary carer of such children should have a right of residence. Such right of residence must include the right to work, which has long been recognised in secondary legislation as a corollary to the right of residence of family members. In assessing the ability of the child to meet the resources requirement of Directive 90/364 the income derived form any work by the carer should be included in considering the level of available resources. 4–71

(ii) *The poor*

The present position (children aside) is that those who are not economically self-sufficient or economically active do not benefit from free movement rights. Clearly this is a deliberate choice made by the EU institutions in determining the beneficiaries of free movement rights. 4–72

As discussed above, the "lawfully resident" and even just tolerated Union citizens are able, by virtue of arts 18 and 20 TFEU, to obtain a non-contributory benefit payable to own nationals on a non-discriminatory basis, thereby facilitating their further residence in other Member States. 4–73

It would undoubtedly be a considerable step forward for the CJEU to establish a free movement right for the poor from art.21(1) TFEU, although it is to be acknowledged that such a step would for some Member States be both particularly objectionable and a step too far. However, it remains to be seen how much longer the CJEU is prepared to countenance the regrettable situation in which the already socially excluded find themselves discriminated against further by EU law. 4–74

(iii) *Limitations and conditions*

If art.21 is to provide a free standing free movement right for those not already covered by EU law, there must plainly be limitations and conditions on the exercise of such right. Article 21(1) TFEU itself refers expressly to 4–75

---

[89] See Ch.9 at paras 9–12 to 9–18.
[90] *Commission v Belgium* (C-408/03) [2006] E.C.R. I-2647.

conditions and limitations and, as Advocate General Geelhoed observed, in respect of the "special cases" for which EU law has made no provision there is not an "unrestricted right of residence". There are (at least) two possible categories of limitations and conditions.

4–76 First, the limitations are likely to include some financial constraints. As a general principle it would doubtless be said that the exercise of Treaty free movement rights ought not place an unreasonable financial burden on Member States. Certainly such principle is one expressed (for example) in the preambles to the three directives concerning the economically inactive.[91] However, it is well settled that such principle could not be interpreted so as to exclude all access to any financial benefits. Indeed, such proposition is vouchsafed by the fact that *Sala*,[92] *Grzelczyk*[93] and *D'Hoop*[94] each concerned access to financial resources. Thus financial limitations will not *always* operate so as to defeat the exercise of the right to move and reside freely where the EU citizen who has exercised free movement rights is (or becomes) impecunious. The conditions and limitations already laid down in existing secondary legislation relating to the economically inactive (and now enshrined within Directive 2004/38) provide a useful yardstick in this respect, subject also to the interpretative gloss placed upon them by the CJEU (in, for example, *Baumbast*[95]).

4–77 Secondly, it is plain that the limitations justified on grounds of public policy, public security and public health—as provided expressly for example in relation to workers by art.45(3) TFEU—must apply to EU citizens exercising free movement rights.

---

[91] The preambles to Directives 90/364, 90/365 and 93/96 each contained the following recital: whereas the beneficiaries of the right of residence must not become an unreasonable burden on the public finances of the host Member State. See now recitals 10 and 16 of Directive 2004/38, and arts 7 and 14 of that Directive, and also the limitation on equal treatment set out in art.24(2) of that Directive.
[92] *Martinez Sala v Freistat Bayern* (C-85/96) [1998] E.C.R. I-2691.
[93] *Grzelczyk v Centre Public d'aide sociale d'Ottignies-Louvain-la-Neuve* (C-184/99) [2001] E.C.R. I-6193.
[94] *D'Hoop v Office national de l'emploi* (C-224/98) [2002] E.C.R. I-6191.
[95] *Baumbast and R. v Secretary of State for the Home Department* (C-413/99) [2002] E.C.R. I-7091.

Part Two
FREE MOVEMENT PROVISIONS FOR UNION CITIZENS AND THEIR FAMILY MEMBERS

CHAPTER 5

BENEFICIARIES OF FREE MOVEMENT PROVISIONS

This chapter considers who benefits from the TFEU provisions on free movement of persons. The primary focus is the identification of EU nationals although the chapter also examines which third country nationals have rights in the context of free movement law is also examined.

1. Citizenship of the Union

(a) *The Union citizen*

The historical and conceptual basis of citizenship of the Union has been discussed in Ch.4. Article 20 TFEU provides: 5–01

> "1. Citizenship of the Union is hereby established. Every person holding the nationality of a Member State shall be a citizen of the Union. Citizenship of the Union shall be additional to and not replace national citizenship.
>
> 2. Citizens of the Union shall enjoy the rights and be subject to the duties provided for in the Treaties, They shall have inter alia:
> (a) the right to move and reside freely within the territory of the Member States;
> (b) the right to vote and to stand as candidates in elections to the European Parliament and municipal elections in their Member State or residence, under the same conditions as nationals of that State:
> (c) the right to enjoy, in the territory of a third country in which the Member State of which they are nationals is not represented, the protection of the diplomatic and consular authorities of any Member State on the same conditions as the nationals of that State;
> (d) the right to petition the European Parliament, to apply to the European Ombudsman, and to address the institutions and advisory bodies of the Union in any of the Treaty languages and to obtain a reply in the same language."

Union citizenship is dependent on holding the nationality of one of the Member States. In other words, anyone who is a national of a Member State is considered to be a Union citizen but the European Union itself cannot confer status on a non-national of a Member State. Such an approach concords with the well defined principle of international law that the granting of nationality is the ultimate act of State sovereignty,[1] relating to notions of diplomatic and consular protection which only a State is considered able to provide. Since the European Union is not equitable to a nation state, and has not replaced the State in terms of international 5–02

---

[1] Nottebolm, Case (*Leichtenstein v Guatemala*) I.C.J. Reports (1995), p.4

5–03 The specific and detailed rights and duties conferred on Union citizens are laid down in the TFEU including the right to move and reside freely within the territory of the Member States, (art.21(1)), to stand for election and vote in any Member State in which they reside (art.22(1)), to work, provide and received services and establish themselves in any Member State, the right not to be subjected to discrimination, and to the rights contained in the Charter.

(b) *Nationals of Member States*

(i) *Who is a national?*

5–04 Nationality of the Member States is determined by reference to domestic law of the individual Member States alone. As the CJEU held in *Micheletti*[3]:

"Under international law, it is for each Member State, having due regard to EU law, to lay down the conditions for the acquisition and loss of nationality".

5–05 It is possible for a Member State to change its laws relating to the acquisition of nationality without reference to any EU or other body. The fact that it is much easier to acquire the nationality of some Member States[4] as compared others[5] does not alter the position in EU law.

5–06 Moreover, it is also permissible for Member States to define which of their nationals are to be considered Union citizens for the purposes of EU law. For most Member States this has no relevance at all and all of their nationals are to be treated as Union citizens and accordingly acquire full free movement rights within the European Union. However for the Member States such as the United Kingdom, which wish to preclude some of their nationals from obtaining the benefits from EU law, the European Union must be put on notice by means of a declaration.[6]

5–07 This and other such declarations by Member States were generally made at the time of the Member State joining the European Union and were understood to define who nationals of Member State were for the purposes of Treaty provisions such as the provision on freedom of establishment contained in art.49 TFEU which refers to "nationals of a Member State".

---

[2] *Matthews v UK* [1999] 28 E.H.R.R. 361; *TI v UK* [2000] I.N.L.R. 221.
[3] *Micheletti v Delegacion del Gobierno en Cantabria* (C-369/90) [1992] E.C.R. I-4239.
[4] Greece, and Ireland notwithstanding an amendment to the Constution of the Republic of Ireland in 2004 whereby those born in the island of Ireland whose parents were not Irish nationals were no longer Irish nationals.
[5] Germany and France.
[6] The UK's declaration means that the following are to be considered as "nationals" for the purpose of EU law: (a) British citizens; (b) British subjects with the right of abode in the UK; and (c) British Dependent Territories citizens who acquire that citizenship as a result of a connection to Gibraltar, January 28, 1983; [1983] O.J. C23; Cmnd 9062 (1983).

When the Maastricht Treaty developed the concept of the Union citizen in art.17 EC Treaty (now art.20 TFEU) there was debate as to whether the declarations were valid for interpretation of that provision. 5–08

In *Hung*,[7] the UK courts referred a question to the CJEU on the interpretation of "every person holding the nationality of a Member State" in art.17 EC Treaty (now art.20 TFEU). Without reference to the full court, the President of the CJEU (First Chamber) ruled that in order to determine whether a person was a national of a Member State for the purposes of EU law, it was necessary to refer to any declarations made by the government of that Member State on the definition of the term "nationals", thereby confirming that EU citizenship could be limited by declaration in the same way as "national of a Member State" was. 5–09

In *Kaur*,[8] the CJEU was also referred questions on the validity of the UK declaration and whether art.17 EC Treaty (now art.20 TFEU) conferred any rights on persons who were not defined as "nationals" under the terms of such a declaration. The CJEU was categorical in its response that Union citizenship was conferred only on "nationals of Member States" and the declarations entered by the United Kingdom defining who its "nationals" are for the purposes of EU law valid and unchallengeable.[9] 5–10

(ii) *Internal situations/own nationals*

Prior to the creation of Union citizenship, the CJEU had repeatedly held that in order for nationals of Member States to benefit from the rules relating to free movement and rights of residence contained in the Treaty and secondary legislation, they must generally be outside their own Member State.[10] As the following chapters discuss, Union citizens who exercise their Treaty rights to move and reside in another Member State, acquire a number of rights as a result. These include the right to install family members and the right, in certain circumstances, to tax and social benefits. 5–11

It might be thought that the creation of the concept of Union citizenship would bring in its wake without much delay benefits to all Union citizens, even those in their own Member States who had not exercised Treaty rights. The CJEU was tentative in its approach to the newly created citizenship right and internal situations. In *Uecker and Jacquet*,[11] the CJEU confirmed that art.17 EC Treaty[12] had not been intended to extend the material scope to include internal situations. The case of *Zambrano*[13] however has, for the first 5–12

---

[7] *The Queen v Secretary of State for the Home Department ex parte Cheung Chui Hung* (C-256/99) (2001) unreported, July 12, 2001 ECJ.
[8] *The Queen v Secretary of State for the Home Department ex parte Kaur* (C-192/99) [2001] E.C.R. 1-1237.
[9] The CJEU did not grapple with the discriminatory treatment of British nationals originating from East Africa reinforced by the United Kingdom's declaration. For a critique of the *Kaur* decision in this context see Professor Guild, "The Legal Elements of European Identity" (Arnhem: Kluwer Law International, 2004), pp.75–76.
[10] *Morson and Jhanjan v State of the Netherlands* (35 & 36/82) [1982] E.C.R. 3723, at [16]; *Zaoui v Cramif* (C-147/87) [1987] E.C.R. 5511.
[11] *Uecker and Jacquet v Land Nordrhein-Westfalen* (C-64 & 65/96) [1997] E.C.R. I-3171.
[12] Now art.20 TFEU.
[13] *Ruiz Zambrano v Office National de l'Emploi (ONEM)* (C-34/09) [2011] E.C.R. I-0000.

time, given real substance to the notion of citizenship of the Union. The CJEU found that a decision by the Belgian authorities refusing to give residence rights to the Colombian parents of a Belgian child, all of whom lived in Belgium, was an unlawful restriction on the rights enjoyed by the child under art.20 TFEU as a citizen of the Union. The removal of the parents to Colombia would have resulted in the child having to leave Belgium with them, a state of affairs the Court considered amounted to a restriction on the child's right to reside in the territory of the European Union.

5–13   *McCarthy*[14] came from the CJEU fast on the heels of *Zambrano*. It was asked to respond to the question essentially whether a person of dual Irish and UK nationality who resided at all material times in the UK came within the scope of EU law. The Court in clear terms summarised the case as follows:

> "25. There is no indication in the order for reference, in the case-file or in the observations submitted to the Court that Mrs McCarthy has ever exercised her right of free movement within the territory of the Member States, either individually or as a family member of a Union citizen who has exercised such a right. Likewise, Mrs McCarthy is applying for a right of residence under European law even though she does not argue that she is or has been a worker, self-employed person or self-sufficient person."

5–14   One might have expected following *Zambrano* that the absence of any cross border element to Mrs McCarthy's circumstances would be otiose. While acknowledging the "fundamental status" of Union citizenship and with express reference to *Zambrano*, the Court concluded that there was no question of her substantial rights being compromised in that there was no restriction on her right to reside in any Member State. The Court thus derives from the absence of practical restriction on the right to reside the conclusion that the challenged restriction did not infringe EU free movement law. There was no question of interfering or limiting in any way the freedom of Mrs McCarthy from moving within the Union in the company of her husband. This rational for the decision focuses on a factual distinction from *Zambrano* where the impugned restriction would lead to constructive removal from the European Union of a citizen of the Union. The Court went on to provide a further basis for its conclusions: the absence of any cross border element either historic or potential kept the circumstances outside the scope of Union law. It remained a purely internal situation.

5–15   In *Dereci*[15] the CJEU considered the refusal by the Austrian authorities to grant residence permits to family members of Austrian nationals in the light of its decisions in *Zambrano* and *McCarthy*. In a rather more illuminating decision than *Zambrano* the Court explained that art.20 TFEU will only found a right of residence for family members of Unions citizens living in

---

[14] *McCarthy (Shirley) v Secretary of State for the Home Department* (C -434/09) [2011] E.C.R. I-0000.
[15] *Dereci and others v Bundesministerium für Inneres* (C-256/11) [2012] E.C.R. I-0000. The case was considered under the accelerated procedure under art.23a of the Statute of the Court of Justice of the European Union and the first paragraph of art.104a of the Rules of Procedure of the Court following the decision of the CJEU in *Zambrano*.

their own Member State where the consequence of refusal would be that the Union citizen would have to leave the EU altogether. The CJEU held:

> "66. It follows that the criterion relating to the denial of the genuine enjoyment of the substance of the rights conferred by virtue of European Union citizen status refers to situations in which the Union citizen has, in fact, to leave not only the territory of the Member State of which he is a national but also the territory of the Union as a whole.
>
> 67. That criterion is specific in character inasmuch as it relates to situations in which, although subordinate legislation on the right of residence of third country nationals is not applicable, a right of residence may not, exceptionally, be refused to a third country national, who is a family member of a Member State national, as the effectiveness of Union citizenship enjoyed by that national would otherwise be undermined."

The Court went onto explain that it was not enough for a Union citizen to assert that it was desirable to have his family member living with him in his own Member State. It would be for the national court to consider on the facts whether denial of residence to that family member would result in the Union citizen having to leave the European Union. Only in those circumstances would the situation of the Union citizen be regarded as not purely internal and art.20 TFEU be able to be invoked to found a claim that the family member should be able to remain in the Member State in question.   **5–16**

The outcome of these three cases read together is that as a general rule the situation of Union citizens in the territory of their own Member States will be regarded as purely internal and therefore outside the scope of the TFEU. However, there are situations where the actions or decisions of a Member State will have the consequences that Union citizens deprived of the benefits of their citizenship such as where they would have to leave the EU altogether. In the case of the denial of residence to third country family members of a EU citizen it is necessary to examine whether the Union citizen could remain without their family or indeed live in another Member State with the family.[16]   **5–17**

(iii) *Other exceptions to the "internal situations" rule*

In addition to the exception to the internal situations rule identified in *Zambrano* and *Dereci* where the person would be deprived of the benefit of their Union citizenship by an action or decision taken by their own Member State, there are other exceptions: **5–18**

(a) where the Union citizen has exercised Treaty rights outside their own Member State: "the Surinder Singh" principle; and

---

[16] It is not without consequence that all the family members in *Dereci* would arguably fall within the scope of art.2(2) of Directive 2004/38 if they moved with the Union citizen to another Member State whereas the parents of the children in *Zambrano* would not. In the former case there is the possibility of the family moving within the EU and relying on Directive 2004/38 whereas in the latter there is no such possibility.

(b) in other areas where EU provisions are transposed into domestic law and will apply to own nationals, for instance, provisions relating to sex discrimination in employment that apply to all EU nationals irrespective as to whether they have exercised free movement.

"Returning" nationals: The first cases

5–19 EU free movement law is principally concerned with the removal of obstacles that would deter a Union citizen from exercising the right to move and reside in another Member State.[17] The landmark case of *Surinder Singh*[18] established that a national of a Member State must not be deterred from exercising free movement rights by facing conditions on return to the national's own Member State which are more restrictive than EU law. The conditions in that case related to the right of entry and residence of the third country national spouse of a British citizen on the couple's return to the United Kingdom following a two-year period of residing in Germany where the British citizen had worked. The CJEU held that the third country national spouse should attain at least the same rights as if accompanying the EU national to another Member State.

5–20 Since the CJEU's judgment in *Surinder Singh* focused on the specific regulation and directives relating to the free movement of workers, some national authorities attempted to limit the application of the *Surinder Singh* principle to nationals who exercise their rights of free movement as workers for a substantial period of time in another Member State. However, the CJEU has now extended this principle to students[19], the self-employed and service providers.[20] The principle must apply equally to all free movers.

5–21 Furthermore since the CJEU's decision in *Carpenter*[21] there is no requirement for the EU national to exercise the right to live in another Member State before invoking EU law in their own Member State, provided that the EU national can show that failure to grant an equivalent to the EU law right in question would constitute an obstacle to the fundamental right of free movement. Mr Carpenter, a British citizen residing in the United Kingdom with his third country national spouse, argued that his situation and that of his spouse were covered by EU law as he provided services, albeit on a short-term periodic basis, in other Member States whilst retaining his residence in the United Kingdom. The CJEU concluded that as Mr Carpenter was availing himself of the right to provide services guaranteed by art.49 EC Treaty[22] his situation was covered by EU law. The fact that Mr Carpenter remained established in the United Kingdom, his own Member State, did not affect the outcome. The Court recalled its own decisions where it had found that the rights flowing from art.49 could be relied on by a provider in the State in which they are established, if the services are provided for persons established in other Member States.

---

[17] *Watson and Belman* (C-118/75) [1976] E.C.R. 1185, at [16].
[18] *The Queen v Immigration Appeal Tribunal ex p. Surinder Singh* (C-370/90) E.C.R. 1-4265.
[19] *D'Hoop v Office National de l'Emploi* (C-224/98) [2002] E.C.R.1-6191.
[20] *Carpenter v Secretary of State for the Home Department* (C-60/00) [2000] E.C.R. 1-6279.
[21] *Carpenter v Secretary of State for the Home Department* (C-60/00) [2000] E.C.R. 1-6279.
[22] Now art.56 TFEU.

(c) *The situation of dual nationals*

5–22 It is well established that a dual national of two Member States may still rely on their second nationality to obtain rights under Community law in a Member State of which they may also be a national, irrespective of whether the person has ever resided in the second Member State.[23] Those rights might include the right to non-discrimination as well as general free movement rights. The CJEU has confirmed that these principles will apply even in situations where a dual national has never exercised free movement rights outside the Member State of which he is also a national.

5–23 In *Avello*,[24] the CJEU examined the situation of dual Spanish and Belgian national children who were born and lived all their lives in Belgium. Their father brought an action in the Belgium courts in respect of the failure of the Belgian authorities to allow the alteration of the children's surnames in accordance with Spanish practices. The three Governments which intervened in the case argued that as the children had been born in Belgium and never moved outside of it, their dispute with the Belgian authorities was "wholly internal" and thus outside the scope of EU law. The CJEU concluded that as the children had the nationality of a Member State other than the one they resided in, their situation was inextricably linked with the exercise of free movement rights by their father, a Spanish national with whom they resided, and thus EU law must apply to their situation. They were entitled to have their names registered in Belgium in a form usually aopted in Spain. Otherwise, the CJEU pointed out, the children's freedom of movement as a result of possessing a form of their names not in line with practice in Spain might be hindered. The Court concentrated on the fact that the children were nationals of one Member State residing in another Member State, regardless of where they were born.[17] The Court did not make any reference to the link between the exercise of free movement rights by their father and the rights of residence of the children. The Court made it clear that by refusing to treat the children as Spanish nationals the Belgium authorities would be in effect adding additional conditions for the recognition of that nationality. *Avello* thus clearly confirms that dual nationals may benefit from EU law even where they have not exercised free movement rights and were born and reside in one of the Member States of their nationality.

5–24 *McCarthy*,[25] as discovered above, concerned a dual British/Irish national who had always lived in UK and did not work nor was she self-sufficient. She argued that refusal to allow her husband to reside in the UK with her was a breach of her Treaty rights as she was also an Irish national. The Court disagreed finding that where a Union citizen resides in her own Member State and where the action or decision by that Member State does not prevent her from enjoying her free movement rights or rights as a Union citizen then the Treaty will have no application to her situation.

---

[23] *Saldanha v Hiross Holding* (C-122/96) [1997] E.C.R. 1-5325.
[24] *Garcia Avello v Belgium* (C-148/02).
[25] *McCarthy (Shirley) v Secretary of State for the Home Department* (C -434/09) [2011] E.C.R. I-0000.

5-25 The Court distinguished the position in *Avello* by explaining that if the Union citizens in that case had ended up with different surnames under different legal systems it may cause serious problems in their professional and private lives in having diplomas or other documents recognised in either Member State of which they were nationals.

5-26 The end result is that dual nationals can benefit from Treaty provisions in their own Member States. However, if they are to derive any benefit from arts 20 or 21 TFEU when they reside in a Member State of which they are nationals, just as persons with only one nationality living in their own Member States, they have to demonstrate that the action or decision of their Member State deprives them of enjoyment of their rights as Union citizens or impedes the exercise of free movement rights.

5-27 In the context of free movement, however, the real sting in the *McCarthy* judgment comes from the conclusion that Directive 2004/38 has no application for the situation of dual nationals who reside (and always have resided) in a Member State of which they are nationals.[26] Thus, the dual French/British national for example, cannot benefit from the comparatively generous family reunion provisions under Directive 2004/38 in the UK if that person has never resided elsewhere in the EU. The only way such benefit could be derived would be to renounce their British citizenship, a step that most would seek to avoid by exercising free movement rights elsewhere in the EU.

(d) *Third country nationals*

5-28 As a general rule, third country nationals are not direct beneficiaries of EU free movement law save in certain prescribed circumstances, namely where they are:

(a) family members of EU nationals;

(b) those who claim international protection including those in need of subsidiary protection including refugees and Stateless persons; and

(c) employees of national companies.

(i) *Family members of EU nationals*

5-29 One of the immediate benefits for EU nationals exercising their rights of free movement is that they have the right to install their family members with them. As Directive 2004/38 makes clear, the right to install family members exists irrespective of the nationality of the family members. The rights of family members are considered in Ch.9.

---

[26] art.3(1) of Directive 2004/38 refers to all Union nationals who "move to" or "reside in" a Member State "other" than that which they are nationals as being beneficiaries. The CJEU also noted a number of ways in which it was apparent from the Directive that "residence" is linked to the exercise of free movement of persons.

(ii) *Those in need of international protection*

Detailed consideration of the conferred rights on this category of persons is outside the scope of this book. However. some reference is made to them in Ch.3 when discussing the impact of human rights law on the EU legal system.

5–30

(iii) *Employees of national companies*

Companies established in one Member State will often want their employees to carry out work in other Member States. These workers may be third country nationals, thus not enjoying any rights of free movement themselves to reside in or move around the Union. In *Rush Portuguesa*,[27] the CJEU held that a company established in a Member State had the right to transfer its existing labour force including third country nationals to another Member State for the limited purpose of participating in a project being carried out there by the company. The Posted Workers Directive[28] aims to ensure the transnational provision of services under conditions of fair competition and of protected workers' rights. It applies to third country nationals and workers from Member States. The CJEU in *Laval*[29] however upheld as lawful a practice whereby Latvian workers transferred to work in Sweden (who had entered into a collective agreement in Latvia in respect of wages) could be paid by their employer in Sweden the reduced wages they were entitled to be paid under the collective agreement in Latvia. Thus, posted workers may be paid less than local workers would be paid for the same work.

5–31

Particular arrangements are in place in respect of posted workers from Switzerland. On June 1, 2002 an Agreement between the EU Member States and the Swiss Confederation on the Free Movement of Persons came into force. In general terms the agreement confers on Swiss nationals and their family members the same free movement rights as those enjoyed by EEA nationals and their family members.

5–32

Enlargement of the European Union

On May 1, 2004 Cyprus, the Czech Republic, Estonia, Hungary, Latvia, Lithuania, Malta, Poland, the Slovak Republic, and Slovenia became Members of the European Union.

5–33

The scale of development created by the Treaty of Accession 2003 went far beyond the previous four accession treaties which taken together in more than a 30-year period accounted for a total of nine new Member States. However, the figure would have been 11 had applications to join made by Norway and Switzerland in 1992 not proved abortive (the former after a

5–34

---

[27] *Rush Portuguesa Lda v ONI* (C-113/89) [1990] E.C.R. I-1417.
[28] Directive 96/71/EC of the European Parliament and of the Council of December 16, 1996 concerning the posting of workers in the framework of the provision of services, O.J. L018 January 21, 1997.
[29] *Laval un Partneri Ltd v Svenska Byggnadsarbetareforbundet* (C-341/05) [2007] E.C.R. I-11767.

referendum in which 52.2 per cent voted against membership). The Treaty of Accession 2005 enabled Bulgaria and Romania to become full members in 2007.

5–35 A landmark meeting of the European Council in Copahagen in June 1993 produced the famous "Copehagan criteria" which required that a successful candidate for membership must have achieved:

(a) stability of institutions guaranteeing democracy, the rule of law, human rights and respect for and protection of minorities;

(b) the existence of a functioning market economy as well as the capacity to cope with competitive pressure and market forces within the Union; and

(c) the ability to take on the obligation of membership including adherence to the aims of political, economic and monetary union.

5–36 The Treaty of Accession 2003 provided that prescribed measures in Annexes to the Treaty shall apply in respect of the new accession states.[30] There is one annex dedicated to each accession State that provide that transitional arrangements may be adopted in respect of the freedom of movement of persons between the new accession States and existing Member States. Existing Member States enjoyed a period of up to five years within which they could apply national law exclusively to nationals of the new Member States who sought to enter there to work. This amounted to a derogation for a transition limited period from arts 1–6 of Regulation 1612/68 which provided for freedom of movement of workers between Member States.[31] The transition period ended on April 30, 2011 in respect of the States which joined in 2004.

5–37 The Treaty of Accession 2005 enabled similar restrictions to be adopted in respect of workers and their families from Bulgaria and Romania[32] on accession.[33] By way of derogation, Member States are entitled, during the transitional period, to apply national measures in regulating access of Bulgarian and Romanian nationals to their labour market for two years from the date of accession.[34] Bulgarian and Romanian nationals already working in a Member State for at least 12 months at the date of accession are entitled to continued access to the labour market of that Member State only for the transitional period. The transitional period in the first instance was for two years from the date of accession, after which for another three years the period may be extended by Member States. In the event of "serious

---

[30] Treaty of Accession 2003 art.24, O.J. L236, September 23, 2003.
[31] See Ch.24, below, as to how the UK government exercised its derogation which ended in 2010.
[32] See Ch.24, below, on how the UK has exercised the right to derogate in respect of Bulgaria and Romania.
[33] art.20 Treaty of Accession 2005, O.J. L157, June 21, 2005.
[34] Annexes VI and VIII to the Treaty of Accession 2005.

disturbances in its labour market" the transitional period may be extended to seven years from the date of accession. Bulgaria and Romania are entitled to maintain equivalent restrictions on access to their labour market workers from the Member States during the transitional period.

CHAPTER 6

WORKERS

This chapter identifies the concept of "workers" in the context of the free movement of persons.

1. INTRODUCTION

(a) *Fundamental importance of free movement for workers*

The freedom of movement for workers was one of the foundations of the EC Treaty.[1] This was reflected by arts 2 and 3(1)(c) EC Treaty which provided that, for the purpose of establishing a common market and the promotion of the harmonious development of economic activities between Member States, obstacles to the free movement of persons between Member States shall be abolished.[2] Assuming that economic activities are being undertaken, the freedom applies to all workers of all Member States regardless of occupation. Such free movement provision contrasts the narrower rights of free movement contained in the 1951 Treaty Establishing the European Coal and Steel Community (ECSC) and the Treaty establishing the European Atomic Energy Community (EAEC) which concerned economic integration in the fields of coal, steel and nuclear energy and gave limited free movement rights only in those sectors.[3]

6–01

(b) *Treaty provisions on workers*

Post-Lisbon Treaty provisions on workers are contained in Ch.1 (Workers) of Title IV (Free movement of persons, services and capital) TFEU. Article 45 TFEU provides the principal means by which the abolition of obstacles to free movement of workers is achieved. Article 45(1) states that freedom of

6–02

---

[1] In the original text of the Treaty (as done in Rome on March 25, 1957) "Part Two" of the Treaty (which included the Title III provisions on free movement of persons, services and capital) was entitled "Foundations of the Community". The title was dropped in 1992 when amendments made by the Treaty on European Union substituted the title (for "Part Three") "Community Policies".

[2] Post the Lisbon Treaty art.3 TEU now provides that the Union shall offer its citizens "an area of freedom, security and justice without internal frontiers, in which the free movement of persons is ensured in conjunction with appropriate measures with respect to external border controls, asylum, immigration and the prevention and combating of crime". And art.26 TFEU provides that "(1) The Union shall adopt measures with the aim of establishing or ensuring the functioning of the internal market, in accordance with the relevant provisions of the Treaties" and that "(2) The internal market shall comprise an area without internal frontiers in which the free movement of goods, persons, services and capital is ensured in accordance with the provisions of the Treaties".

[3] See art.69 ECSC and art.96 EAEC, see further Ch.1.

movement for workers shall be secured within the Union. As art.45(2) TFEU makes clear, the abolition of any discrimination based on nationality between workers is of fundamental importance.[4] Such importance is reflected by the principle that the concepts which define "the field of application" of the freedom of movement for workers "may not be interpreted restrictively".[5] Article 45 TFEU itself gives meaning to the concept of "freedom of movement for workers" by the specific identification of the rights to accept employment offers made, to move freely within Member States for such purpose and to stay in Member States, both for employment and after having been employed:

Article 45 TFEU

1. Freedom of movement for workers shall be secured within the Union.

2. Such freedom of movement shall entail the abolition of any discrimination based on nationality between workers of the Member States as regards employment, remuneration and other conditions of work and employment.

3. It shall entail the right, subject to limitations justified on grounds of public policy, public security or public health:

(a) to accept offers of employment actually made;
(b) to move freely within the territory of Member States for this purpose;
(c) to stay in a Member State for the purpose of employment in accordance with the provisions governing the employment of nationals of that State laid down by law, regulation or administrative action;
(d) to remain in the territory of a Member State after having been employed in that State, subject to conditions which shall be embodied in implementing regulations to be drawn up by the Commission.

4. The provisions of this article shall not apply to employment in the public service.

6–03 Article 46 TFEU requires the European Parliament and the Council (after consultation with the Economic and Social Committee) to issue directives or make regulations to bring about the freedom of movement for workers as defined in art.45 TFEU.

6–04 Article 47 TFEU requires that Member States shall, within the framework of a joint programme, encourage the exchange of young workers. Finally, art.48 TFEU requires the European Parliament and the Council to adopt such measures in the field of social security as are necessary to provide freedom of movement for workers (and to this end shall make arrangements to secure for employed and self-employed migrant workers and their

---

[4] See Ch.11.
[5] *Levin v Staatssecretaris van Justitie* (53/81) [1982] E.C.R. 1035, at [13]. See also, for example, *Lawrie-Blum v Land Baden-Württemberg* (66/85) [1986] E.C.R. 2121, at [16]: "since it defines the scope of that fundamental freedom, the community concept of a 'worker' must be interpreted broadly."

INTRODUCTION

dependents, aggregation of periods to be taken into account for acquiring and retaining benefits and the payment of benefits).[6]

(c) *Secondary legislation*

6–05 The Treaty obligation to issue directives or make regulations (now art.47 TFEU) resulted inititally in the late 1960s in two principal measures implementing the rights of free movement for workers (Regulation 1612/68 (freedom of movement for workers within the Community) and Directive 68/360 (abolition of restrictions on movement and residence within the Community for workers of Member States and their families). Articles 10 and 11 of Regulation 1612/68 and Directive 68/360 were repealed with effect from April 30, 2006 to be replaced by provisions contained in Directive 2004/38/EC of April 29, 2004 ("Citizens' Directive"). Regulation 1612/68 has now been replaced by Regulation 492/2011.[7] The recitals in the preamble to Regulation 492/2011 are replete with statements emphasising the fundamental importance of the freedom of movement for workers. Recital (4) for example states as follows:

> "Freedom of movement constitutes a fundamental right of workers and their families. Mobility of labour within the Union must be one of the means by which workers are guaranteed the possibility of improving their living and working conditions and promoting their social advancement, while helping to satisfy the requirements of the economies of the Member States. The right of all workers in the Member States to pursue the activity of their choice within the Union should be affirmed."

(d) *The Union concept of worker*

6–06 The interpretation of who is a worker for the purposes of the free movement provisions is a matter of European Union law which, in light of the fundamental importance of the field in which such interpretation arises, must not be interpreted restrictively.[8] Moreover the Union concept of worker for these purposes must not take flavour from national concepts. This principle was established over 40 years ago in *Hoekstra*[9] where the CJEU considered the interpretation of the concept of "wage-earner or assimilated worker" in

---

[6] Regulation 883/2004 (on the co-ordination of social security schemes). For discussion of social security measures see Ch.12. Note the new provision post-Lisbon contained in art.48 TFEU enabling a Council member to have a draft legislative Act referred to the European Council where it would affect "important aspects of its social security system, including its scope, cost or financial structure, or would affect the financial balance of that system". This leads to initial suspension of the ordinary legislative procedure whilst the European Council considers the matter before either sending the matter back to the Council (in which case the suspension is terminated and the ordinary legislative procedure is resumed), taking no action, or requesting the Commission to submit a new proposal (in which case the Act originally proposed is deemed not to have been adopted).
[7] Regulation (EU) No.492/2011 of the European Parliament and of the Council of April 5, 2011 on freedom of movement for workers within the Union (largely reflecting its predecessor although arts 10 and 12 of Regulation 1612/68 had been repealed by art.38(1) Directive 2004/38/EC of April 29, 2004 ("Citizens' Directive") with effect from April 30, 2006).
[8] See *Levin v Staatssecretaris van Justitie* (53/81) [1982] E.C.R. 1035, at [13].
[9] *Hoekstra v The Netherlands* (75/63) [1964] E.C.R. 177.

a provision concerning social security for migrant workers.[10] As the CJEU stated,[11] if the definition were a matter within the competence of national law, "it would be possible for each Member State to modify the meaning of the concept of 'migrant worker' and to eliminate at will the protection afforded by the treaty to certain categories of person". The CJEU has constantly emphasised that the definition of worker has a Union meaning which must not be interpreted narrowly ever since.[12]

(e) *Union concept of worker depends on context*

6–07   There is no single definition of worker in European Union law. Rather the definition varies according to the area in which it is to be applied. For example, as recognised by the CJEU in *Sala*,[13] the definition of worker used in the art.45 TFEU context does not *necessarily* coincide with the definition applied in relation to measures adopted by the European Parliament and the Council under art.48 TFEU in the field of social security, notwithstanding that the focus of both is the freedom of movement for workers.

2. THE DEFINITION OF WORKER

(a) *Generally*

6–08   In *Lawrie-Blum*,[14] the CJEU identified the three essential criteria which determine whether there is an employment relationship and, in turn, whether the person concerned is a worker for the purposes of art.45 TFEU:

- First, the person must perform services of some economic value. As will be seen this requirement has come to be qualified by the CJEU[15] which has emphasised that such services must be effective and genuine (and not marginal and ancillary).

- Secondly, the performance of such services must be for and under the direction of another person.

- Thirdly, in return, the person concerned must receive remuneration.

---

[10] Council Regulation No.3 concerning social security for migrant workers O.J. 561/58.
[11] *Hoekstra v The Netherlands* (75/63) [1964] E.C.R. 177, at [3].
[12] See, for example, *Levin v Staatssecretaris van Justitie* (53/81) [1982] E.C.R. 1035, "the term 'worker' in Article 48 [now Art.45 TFEU] has a community meaning". See also, *Kurz v Land Baden-Württemberg* (C-188/00) [2002] E.C.R. I-10691 in the context of the Turkish Association Agreement (where reference is made to the interpretation of the concept of worker under Union law for the purposes of determining the scope of the same concept under the Agreement).
[13] *Martinez Sala v Freistaat Bayern* (C-85/96) [1998] E.C.R. I-2691, at [31]. See also, for example, *Ioannis Vougioukas v Idryma Koinonikon Asfalisseon* (C-443/93) *(IKA)* [1995] and *Christine Dodl and Petra Oberhollenzer v Tiroler Bebietskrankenkasse* (C-543/03). E.C.R. I-4033 in which the meaning of civil servants was distinguished from persons in public service.
[14] *Lawrie-Blum v Land Baden-Württemberg* (66/85) [1986] E.C.R. 2121. The CJEU has consistently applied the *Lawrie-Blum* principles ever since. See, for example, *Collins* (C-138/02) [2004] E.C.R. I-2703, at [26] *Trojani* (C-456/02) [2004] E.C.R. I-7573, at [15] and *Raccanelli v Max-Planck-Gesellschaft zur Forderung der Wissenschaften E.V*, (C-94/07), at [33].
[15] *Levin v Staatssecretaris van Justitie* (53/81) [1982] E.C.R. 1035.

These requirements are exhaustive. As the CJEU has stated, "Community law does not impose any additional conditions for a person to be classifiable as a worker".[16]

(b) *Services of economic value*

The CJEU has put a gloss on the meaning of the requirement that the person must perform services of some economic value. In *Levin*[17] the CJEU stated that the rules on freedom of movement for workers "cover only the pursuit of effective and genuine activities, to the exclusion of activities on such a small scale as to be regarded as purely marginal and ancillary."[18] The CJEU plainly had in mind the application of a de minimis principle. The implication is that small-scale activities which are purely marginal and ancillary do not engage the free movement provisions because (in the words of the CJEU in *Levin*) these apply only to those "who pursue or are desirous of pursuing an economic activity."[19] This is readily explicable because the pursuance of an economic activity is the indispensable prerequisite of the free movement provisions for the economically active.[20] Unfortunately the application of this apparently straightforward de minimis principle has in one circumstance proved problematic to apply.[21] 6–09

The question of whether services have economic value should be analysed from the perspective of the employer. Assuming then that the activity has some economic value to someone else, if the scale of the activity is such that it is not so small as to be marginal and ancillary, the activity will be effective and genuine and the requirement satisfied. 6–10

As observed by the CJEU in *Lawrie-Blum*, in which the position of trainee teachers was considered, since they were required to give lessons to pupils, they provided a service of some economic value. Plainly without the trainee teachers the school would have been required to pay others to give lessons. See further paras 6–30 to 6–39, below. 6–11

(c) *Services for and under the direction of another person*

The second requirement means that the services must be carried out in the context of a relationship of subordination. Thus for example in *Asscher*,[22] Mr Asscher, the director of a company of which he was also the sole shareholder was not a worker since there was no subordination. However, 6–12

---

[16] *Brown v Secretary of State for Scotland* (197/86) [1988] E.C.R. 3205, at [22].
[17] *Levin v Staatssecretaris van Justitie* (53/81) [1982] E.C.R. 1035.
[18] *Levin v Staatssecretaris van Justitie* (53/81) [1982] E.C.R. 1035, at [17].
[19] *Levin v Staatssecretaris van Justitie* (53/81) [1982] E.C.R. 1035.
[20] See *Walrave and Koch v Association Union Cycliste Internationale, Koninklijke Nederlandsche Wielren Unie et Federación Española Ciclismo* (36/74) [1974] E.C.R. 1405, at [4] and *Dona v Mantaro* (13/76) [1976] E.C.R. 1333, at [12]: "... the practice of sport is subject to community law only in so far as it constitutes an economic activity within the meaning of Article 2 of the Treaty".
[21] See para.6–40 et seq.
[22] *Asscher v Staatssecretaris van Financiën* (C-107/94) [1996] E.C.R. I-3089.

he was found to be pursuing an activity as a self-employed person under art.49 TFEU and thus was entitled to benefit from the free movement provisions in any event. Indeed, in this respect, the question of whether a person who performs services for remuneration does so under the direction of another person and is thus a worker will be unlikely to cause much practical difficulty. As in *Asscher* if the person is not a worker they will likely be self-employed and will benefit from free movement provisions in any event.

(d) *Remuneration*

6–13   Whilst remuneration is an essential element it is interpreted broadly. Remuneration need not be at a particular level, nor even in the form of wages as such. The "level" of wages was considered in *Levin*[23] in which the CJEU rejected an argument that remuneration had to reach a particular level so as to enable the person to be a worker (subject to the activity being effective and genuine and not purely marginal and ancillary).[24]

6–14   Nor does the nature of the remuneration matter. In *Ex p. Agegate*[25] the CJEU considered whether Spanish fishermen working on board British vessels were workers when paid as "share fishermen" (namely on the basis of the proceeds of sale of their catches). The CJEU emphasised that the identification of an employment relationship was to be examined

> "on the basis of all the factors and circumstances characterizing the arrangements between the parties, such as, for example, the sharing of the commercial risks of the business, the freedom for a person to choose his own working hours and to engage his own assistants".

The sole fact that remuneration was on a collectively determined paid "share" basis could not deprive the fishermen of their status as workers.

6–15   The breadth of approach taken to remuneration is well shown by the decision of the CJEU in *Steymann*.[26] The case concerned a German national living in the Netherlands as a member of the Bhagwan Community (which supplied its material needs by means of commercial activities, including running a discothéque, a bar and a launderette). Mr Steymann contributed to the life of the Bhagwan Community by doing plumbing work on its premises and general household duties. He also took part in the Bhagwan Community's commercial activity. For its part the Bhagwan Community provided for the material needs of its members (which included the payment

---

[23] See *Levin v Staatssecretaris van Justitie* (53/81) [1982] E.C.R. 1035.
[24] See also, *Trojani v Centre public d'aide sociale de Bruxelles (CPAS)* (C-456/02), September 7, 2004.
[25] *The Queen v Ministry of Agriculture, Fisheries and Food, Ex p. Agegate Ltd* (3/87) [1989] E.C.R. 4459. The question referred related to the transitional arrangements contained in arts 55 and 56 of the Act concerning the Accession of Spain and Portugal to the European Communities of 1985. These provisions introduced a derogation from the principle of the free movement of workers (excluding the application to Spanish workers of arts 1 to 6 of Regulation 1612/68 until January 1, 1993).
[26] *Steymann v Staatssecretaris van Justitie* (196/87) [1988] E.C.R. 6159.

of pocket money), irrespective of the nature and the extent of their activities. The CJEU considered that this was remuneration which was to be regarded as "an indirect quid pro quo" for the work carried out by the members of the Bhagwan Community.[27]

(e) *Application of principles*

(i) *Level of productivity*

Services will still have some economic value even where the "productivity" of the person concerned is low, or indeed even if remuneration is largely provided by subsidies from public funds. As the CJEU stated in *Bettray* "neither the level of productivity nor the origin of the funds from which the remuneration is paid can have any consequence in regard to whether or not the person is to be regarded as a worker".[28]

6–16

(ii) *Part-time work*

A consequence of the irrelevance of the level of productivity is that a person who works part-time can still be a worker. In *Levin*[29] the CJEU considered the position of a part-time British national worker resident in the Netherlands married to a third country national. It was argued by the Dutch (and Danish) Governments that the provisions of art.45 TFEU could only be relied on by those in receipt of a wage

6–17

> "at least commensurate with the means of subsistence considered as necessary by the legislation of the member state in which they work, or who work at least for the number of hours considered as usual in respect of full-time employment in the sector in question".

These arguments were rejected robustly by the CJEU, not least since it is impermissible to define the European Union concept of worker by reference to national laws.[30] Emphasising the fundamental nature of the freedom of movement for workers and the need for broad interpretation, the CJEU noted the importance of part-time work for a large number of persons "as an effective means of improving their living conditions" and stated that

6–18

> "the effectiveness of community law would be impaired and the achievement of the objectives of the Treaty .... jeopardized if the enjoyment of rights conferred by the principle of freedom of movement for workers were reserved solely to persons engaged in full-time employment".[31]

The CJEU applied these principles in *Ruzius-Wilbrink* and *Rinner-Kuhn* in recognising women working part-time (respectively for 18 and 10 hours a

6–19

---

[27] *Steymann v Staatssecretaris van Justitie* (196/87) [1988] E.C.R. 6159, at [14].
[28] *Bettray v Staatssecretaris van Justitie* (344/87) [1989] E.C.R. 1621, at [15].
[29] *Levin v Staatssecretaris van Justitie* See (53/81) [1982] E.C.R. 1035.
[30] See *Hoekstra v Netherlands* (75/63) [1964] E.C.R. 117, at [11].
[31] See *Hoekstra v Netherlands* (75/63) [1964] E.C.R. 117, at 15.

week) as workers.[32] In *Kempf*[33] a German national resident in the Netherlands who worked as a part-time music teacher for 12 hours a week was also a worker. And in *Megner and Scheffel*[34] (two cleaners working a 10-hour working week for remuneration not exceeding one seventh of the amount required for subsistence) the CJEU rejected the argument that persons in minor employment were not workers because their earnings were insufficient to satisfy their needs and emphasised that the facts did not prevent them being workers. Moreover it is to be emphasised that it is irrelevant whether part-time work is the *principal* activity of the person concerned. Such a person may for example undertake part-time work whilst a student. Whether such person is a worker is answered by reference to the principles here discussed: the relevant questions are not changed by reason only of the person's status as a student.

6–20 In spite of the clarity of the principles laid down in the judgments as regards part-time workers, references continue to be made by national courts to the CJEU. A good example is *Genc*[35] concerning a Turkish national whose right of residence under the Turkish Association Agreement depended on her being a "worker' where she worked for 5.5 hours a week and received a salary of some €175 (thus working for only approximately 14 per cent of the collectively agreed working time of a full-time worker for income only approximately 25 per cent of the amount determined under the national law of Germany to be necessary for subsistence). At para.26 of its judgment the CJEU states:

> "Although the fact that a person works for only a very limited number of hours in the context of an employment relationship may be an indication that the activities performed are marginal and ancillary (Case C-357/89 *Raulin* [1992] ECR I-1027, paragraph 14), the fact remains that, independently of the limited amount of the remuneration for and the number of hours of the activity in question, the possibility cannot be ruled out that, following an overall assessment of the employment relationship in question, that activity may be considered by the national authorities to be real and genuine, thereby allowing its holder to be granted the status of 'worker' within the meaning of Article [45 TFEU]."

The CJEU went on to emphasise the need in making such overall assessment to consider factors relating not only to the number of working hours and the level of remuneration, but also to Ms Genc's right to 28 days' paid leave, to the continued payment of her wages in the event of sickness, to the fact that her contract of employment was subject to the relevant collective agreement and that she had worked for the same undertaking for almost four years. In the CJEU's view such factors were "capable of constituting an indication that the professional activity in question is real and genuine".[36]

---

[32] *Ruzius-Wilbrink v Bestuur van de Bedrijfsvereniging voor Overheidsdiensten* (102/88) [1989] E.C.R. 4311; *Rinner-Kuhn v FWW Spezial-Gebrudereinigung GmbH & Co. KG.* (171/88) [1989] E.C.R. 2743.
[33] *Kempf v Staatssecretaris van Justitie* (139/85) [1986] E.C.R. 1741.
[34] *Megner and Scheffel* (C-444/93) [1995] E.C.R. I-4741.
[35] *Hava Genc v Land Berlin* (C-14/09).
[36] At para.28.

And in *R v (ota Payir, Aykuz and Ozturk) v Secretary of State for the Home Department*,[37] cases considered in the context of the Turkish Association Agreement, the CJEU confirmed that au pairs and students could be workers, albeit necessarily only working part-time because their hours were limited by the national immigration law and the conditions attached to their stay.   **6–21**

(iii) *Contracts for employment with variable conditions*

Those who undertake work for certain employers may perform services on an irregular basis as and when required to do so by their employer. Such relationships are plainly of employment rather than self-employment since it is the employer who dictates when and under what terms the person will work. Thus, for example, an interpreter contracted to an agency supplying court translators may work for a variable number of hours as and when required. Are such persons workers?   **6–22**

The CJEU considered such contracts in *Raulin*[38] in which a French national living in Holland signed an eight-month "on-call contract" (*oproepcontract*) to provide services as an "on-call worker" (*oproepkracht*)[39] under which she had worked for 60 hours as a waitress in a 16-day period. The CJEU considered whether the nature of the activities of an on-call worker prevented such a person from being a worker and whether the fact that such a person exercised or sought to exercise an economic activity for only a short time was relevant to the question of whether such activities are purely marginal and ancillary.   **6–23**

The CJEU held that the nature of the contract could not by reason of the conditions of employment preclude the person's being a worker, nor could the fact that the person had worked only for a short period of time. However, in considering whether the activity was effective and genuine and not marginal and ancillary the national court was entitled to take account of "the irregular nature and limited duration of the services actually performed under a contract for occasional employment." Furthermore,   **6–24**

> "the fact that the person concerned worked only a very limited number of hours in a labour relationship may be an indication that the activities exercised are purely marginal and ancillary".[40]

---

[37] *Payir and others* (C-294/06) E.C.R. I-203.
[38] *Raulin v Minister van Onderwijs en Wetenschappen* (C-357/89) [1992] E.C.R. I-1027.
[39] The CJEU describes the particular contract (para.9 of *Raulin v Minister van Onderwijs en Wetenschappen* (C-357/89) [1992] E.C.R. I-1027, above) in these terms: "It is apparent from the reference for a preliminary ruling that under Netherlands law an oproepcontract is a means of recruiting workers in sectors, such as the hotel trade, where the volume of work is subject to seasonal variations. Under such a contract, no guarantee is given as to the hours to be worked and, often, the person involved works only a very few days per week or hours per day. The employer is liable to pay wages and grant social advantages only in so far as the worker has actually performed work. Furthermore, the Netherlands Government stated at the hearing that under such an oproepcontract the employee is not obliged to heed the employer's call for him to work".
[40] *Raulin v Minister van Onderwijs en Wetenschappen* (C-357/89) [1992] E.C.R. I-1027, at [14–15].

6–25   The answer to the question posed as to whether such person is a worker is that there is nothing in the nature of such contracts which *prevents* a person being considered a worker for the purposes of the free movement provisions, subject always to the requirement of the activities performed being effective and genuine and not marginal and ancillary. In other words to be merely "signed on" with an agency cannot make the person a worker if no meaningful activities are actually performed. As regards fixed term contracts, the CJEU has made clear that "the fact that employment is of short duration cannot, in itself exclude that employment from the scope of [Article 45 TFEU]".[41]

(iv) *Receipt of supplementary funds irrelevant*

6–26   The consequence of the rejection by the CJEU in *Levin* of the arguments that a worker is required to work for a minimum number of hours and to earn a minimum amount[42] is that the means used by part-time workers to supplement their income will not deprive them of their status as workers. Thus it was irrelevant in *Levin* that the part-time worker's funds were supplemented by the income from the employment of a member of her family. The position is the same where "public funds" are used to supplement income earned as a part-time worker. Thus in *Kempf* where the part-time music teacher supplemented his income with benefits payable from public funds available to workers, the CJEU held that provided the effective and genuine nature of his work was established, it was irrelevant that his income was supplemented by assistance from public funds.[43] This approach reflects the decision in *Bettray*[44] in which remuneration financed largely by subsidies from public funds was held by the CJEU to be irrelevant to the question of whether the person concerned was a worker.

(v) *Nature of activities irrelevant*

6–27   The nature of the activities (for example whether they are said to offend public morality) is irrelevant to the question of whether a person may be a worker. This however does not mean that a worker could not face exclusion if the activities of the worker posed a genuine and sufficiently serious threat affecting one of the fundamental interests of society such that a Member State is able to invoke the public policy proviso.[45] Thus, in *Jany*,[46] the fact that the women were working as prostitutes could not affect the conclusion that the women were carrying out economic activities.

---

[41] *Franca Ninni-Orasche v Bundesminister für Wissenschaft* (C-413/01) November 6, 2003, at [25].
[42] See further para.7–13 et seq.
[43] *Kempf v Staatssecretaris van Justitie* (139/85) [1986] E.C.R. 1741, at [14].
[44] *Bettray v Staatssecretaris van Justitie* (344/87) [1989] E.C.R. 1621, at [15].
[45] *Adoui and Cornuaille* (115 & 116/81) [1982] E.C.R. 1665, at [8]; *Calfa* (C-348/96) [1999] E.C.R. I-11, at [21]. See also Ch.13.
[46] *Jany v Staatssecretaris van Justite* (C-268/99) [2001] E.C.R. I-8615. The cases concerned Czech and Polish women working in the Netherlands who sought to benefit from the Association Agreements as self-employed prostitutes.

(vi) *Motives irrelevant*

There is no requirement that a person who carries out economic activities must have some subjective intention to do so in order to be defined as a worker. In *Levin*,[47] the CJEU robustly rejected an argument that free movement rights could be denied to a worker whose objectives were not the pursuit of an economic activity. The rights could be relied on only by those who "actually pursue or seriously wish to pursue activities as employed persons."[48] But this did not mean:

6–28

> "that the enjoyment of this freedom may be made to depend upon the aims pursued by a national of a Member State in applying for entry upon and residence in the territory of another member state, provided that he there pursues or wishes to pursue an activity which ... is ... an effective and genuine activity as an employed person".

Once this condition is satisfied the motives which may have prompted the worker to seek employment in the Member State concerned are "of no account and must not be taken into consideration".[49] This will be the case even where it is alleged that the person has "sought abusively to create a situation enabling her to claim the status of worker". According to the CJEU, "the issue of abuse of rights can have no bearing".[50] The correctness of this principle was reaffirmed by the CJEU in *Akrich*.[51]

6–29

(vii) *Students, trainees, apprentices and au-pairs*

Whether a person is a worker *whilst* a student is answered by reference to whether genuine and effective services of some economic value are performed under the direction of another person for remuneration. The relevant questions are not changed by reason only of the person's status as a student. But is the position different where the activities relied on themselves constitute the studies (or training or apprenticeship)? For example, is a student whose studies involve the performance of activities as a trainee teacher to be regarded as a worker?

6–30

The answer to such questions is provided by the decision of the CJEU in *Lawrie-Blum*[52] in which a British citizen who had passed exams to be a teacher at the University of Freiburg was subsequently refused admission (on the ground of her nationality) to do her teacher training ("a period of preparatory service" which would have qualified her for appointment as a teacher in a "Gymnasium"). The essential issue was whether the activities undertaken during the period of preparatory service as a trainee teacher were work (and Mrs Lawrie-Blum ought thus to be regarded as a worker able to benefit from non-discrimination). The German Government argued

6–31

---

[47] *Levin v Staatssecretaris van Justitie* (53/81) [1982] E.C.R. 1035.
[48] *Levin v Staatssecretaris van Justitie* (53/81) [1982] E.C.R. 1035, at [20–23]. The CJEU refers to art.39 EC Treaty and provisions of Regulation 1612/68 and Directive 68/360.
[49] *Levin v Staatssecretaris van Justitie* (53/81) [1982] E.C.R. 1035.
[50] *Franca Ninni-Orasche v Bundesminister für Wissenschaft* (C-413/01) November 6, 2003, at [31].
[51] *Secretary of State for the Home Department v Akrich* (C-109/01) [2003] I-9607, at [55–56].
[52] *Lawrie-Blum v Land Baden-Württemberg* (66/85) [1986] E.C.R. 2121.

that since a trainee teacher's activity was a matter of education policy it was not an "economic activity" within the meaning of art.2 EC Treaty[53] and that the period of preparatory service should be regarded as the last stage of professional training (as opposed to work).

6–32 The CJEU robustly rejected such arguments. The broad Union concept of worker must be defined in accordance with the objective criteria to which reference has already been made. During the entire period of preparatory service the trainee teacher:

> "is under the direction and supervision of the school to which he is assigned. It is the school that determines the services to be performed by him and his working hours and it is the school's instructions that he must carry out and its rules that he must observe. During a substantial part of the preparatory service he is required to give lessons to the school's pupils and thus provides a service of some economic value to the school. The amounts which he receives may be regarded as remuneration for the services provided and for the duties involved in completing the period of preparatory service. Consequently, the three criteria for the existence of an employment relationship are fulfilled".[54]

6–33 Further, the fact that teachers' preparatory service ("like apprenticeships in other occupations") could be seen as practical preparation directly related to the actual pursuit of the occupation in point was not a bar to such a person being a worker "if the service is performed under the conditions of an activity as an employed person". Nor indeed could the objection be sustained that "services performed in education do not fall within the scope of the EEC Treaty because they are not of an economic nature." As the CJEU stated, "all that is required for the application of Article 48 [now Art.45 TFEU] is that the activity should be in the nature of work performed for remuneration, irrespective of the sphere in which it is carried out."[55] As the CJEU stated in answering the question "a trainee teacher who, under the direction and supervision of the school authorities, is undergoing a period of service in preparation for the teaching profession during which he provides services by giving lessons and receives remuneration must be regarded as a worker."

6–34 In light of *Lawrie-Blum* it is clear that the activities undertaken by persons who are students, trainees or apprentices may be "work" and that such persons may be regarded as "workers".

---

[53] art.2 EC Treaty refered to the implementation of common policies or activities referred to in arts 3 and 4. Article 3(1)(q) refered to "a contribution to education and training of quality and to the flowering of the cultures of the Member States".
[54] *Lawrie-Blum v Land Baden-Württemberg* (66/85) [1986] E.C.R. 2121, at [18].
[55] The CJEU further stated that "the nature of the legal relationship between employee and employer, whether involving public law status or a private law contract, is immaterial" as was the fact (by reference to *Levin v Staatssecretaris van Justitie* (53/81) [1982] E.C.R. 1035) that "trainee teachers give lessons for only a few hours a week and are paid remuneration below the starting salary of a qualified teacher" which did not prevent them from being regarded as workers.

Despite the clarity of the position established almost 20 years ago, the CJEU has been required to restate it on a number of occasions. For example, in *USRAFF*[56] (which concerned the characterisation of a period of practical vocational training undertaken in France by an Irish national studying vocational training at a technical college in Ireland) the CJEU stated that   6–35

> "the fact that a person performs those services under a traineeship contract does not prevent him from being regarded as a worker, if he pursues an activity which is effective and genuine and if the essential characteristics of the employment relationship are fulfilled".

The CJEU made the same point in relation to vocational training in *Kurz*[57] (albeit in the context of a Turkish Association Agreement case). Moreover in *Gunaydin*[58] (another Turkish Association Agreement case) the CJEU considered the position of a Turkish national being trained in Germany by Siemens for the specific purpose of taking up a post in a Siemens subsidiary in Turkey. The CJEU concluded that the mere fact that the employment had been designed solely to qualify Mr Gunaydin to work elsewhere did not deprive it of the character of employment on normal principles.

As regards au-pairs, their ability to be considered as workers is beyond doubt, both on normal principles and in light of *Watson and Belman*.[59] The case concerned an au pair employed as a family help who looked after children in return for board and lodging. Advocate General Trabucchi stated that the au pair "would undoubtedly come into one of the categories of person upon whom the Treaty confers the right to move within the Community". The Advocate General continued: 6–36

> "as this would in fact be work performed for a consideration (board and lodging), she could be classified as coming within a master and servant relationship or if this were not the case she would at least come under the alternative heading of provision of services".[60]

Although the CJEU did not specifically rule on the issue, the CJEU's decision was predicated on the au pair falling within the scope of the Treaty. The only basis on which an au pair could not be considered a worker would be if the au pair was not genuine and effective in the activities undertaken. Certainly there is nothing intrinsic in the nature of the relationship, the activities carried out or the form of remuneration which could negate the possibility of an au pair's being a worker.   6–37

More recently in *R v (ota Payir, Aykuz and Ozturk) v Secretary of State for the Home Department*,[61] cases considered in the context of the Turkish   6–38

---

[56] *Union de Recouvrement des Cotisations de Sècuritè Sociale et d'Allocations Familiales de la Savoie (URSSAF) v Hostellerie Le Manoir SARL* (C-27/91) [1991] E.C.R. I-5531. See also, *Raccanelli v Max-Planck-Gesellschaft zur Forderung der Wissenschaften E.V* (C-94/07) (concerning a researcher preparing a doctoral thesis).
[57] *Kurz v Land Baden-Württemberg* (C-188/00) [2002] E.C.R. I-10691, at [34].
[58] *Gunaydin v Freistaat Bayern* (C-36/96) [1997] E.C.R. I-5179.
[59] *Watson and Belmann* (118/75) [1976] E.C.R. 1185.
[60] *Watson and Belmann* (118/75) [1976] E.C.R. 1185, per A.G. Trabucchi, p.1202.
[61] *Payir and others* (C-294/06) [2008] E.C.R. I-203.

Association Agreement, the CJEU confirmed that au pairs (and students) could be workers in holding that the migrants' immigration status (having been given entry to the United Kingdom (respectively) as an au pair and students) could not deprive them of their status as workers.[62]

6–39 In sum it matters not whether the activities in question are characterised as studies, training, vocational training, an apprenticeship, work as an au-pair, or otherwise. Anyone carrying out such activities may be a worker if performing genuine and effective activities of some economic value under the direction of someone else for remuneration. Although such proposition might be considered somewhat trite, it is not always reflected by the practices of some Member States.[63]

(viii) *Rehabilitative employment*

6–40 In *Bettray*,[64] the CJEU considered the position of a German national drug addict living in the Netherlands who worked in rehabilitative employment under a scheme which provided work "for maintaining, restoring or improving" the capacity for work of those who for an indefinite period are unable to work under normal conditions. Since Mr Bettray performed services under the direction of another person in return for which he received remuneration, the CJEU concluded that the essential features of an employment relationship were present. However, his work was not an effective and genuine economic activity if:

> "merely a means of rehabilitation or reintegration for the persons concerned and the purpose of the paid employment, which is adapted to the physical and mental possibilities of each person, is to enable those persons sooner or later to recover their capacity to take up ordinary employment or to lead as normal as possible a life".

6–41 A conceptual difficulty with such reasoning (focussing as it does on the benefit to the worker) is that it has nothing whatsoever to do with the "scale" of Mr Bettray's activities (namely whether so small as to be marginal and ancillary and thus not an economic activity). Indeed, it is difficult to see how the rehabilitative nature of the activities and the fact that they are aimed at enabling those working under the scheme to "recover their capacity to take up ordinary employment" can deprive them of being economic activities where the criteria for determining the existence of an employment relationship are otherwise met.

6–42 The CJEU's focus on the benefit to the worker is inappropriate as a basis to conclude that the work is not genuine and effective. The motives which may have prompted a person to undertake activities are irrelevant to the question whether what is done is work. Moreover, such approach is, by implication at least, inconsistent with the approach taken by the CJEU in *Lawrie-Blum* where the fact that the trainee teacher gave lessons during the last stage of professional training which could be seen as "practical preparation directly

---

[62] See further Ch.18, below.
[63] See in relation to the UK, Ch.24.
[64] *Bettray v Staatssecretaris van Justitie* (344/87) [1989] E.C.R. 1621.

related to the actual pursuit of the occupation in point" was not a bar to her being a worker if the service was performed "under the conditions of an activity as an employed person".[65]

In fact *Bettray* is explicable because activities aimed "*merely* as a means of rehabilitation or reintegration" of the person performing them which are of no value to the employer will not be able to be characterised as work simply because the person undertakes the task under the direction of someone else and is remunerated. Although there may be *some* economic value in the activities undertaken, from the perspective of the employer they will likely be at best marginal and ancillary. Rather the relationship is more akin to an act of benevolence on the part of the employer. **6–43**

Bettray has not been applied to preclude *any* activity of a rehabilitative nature being considered as work. In *Birden*[66] the CJEU considered the position of a Turkish national who worked as a semi-skilled odd-job man under a sponsored social assistance scheme which provided temporary work opportunities to "improve the integration into working life of the person seeking assistance".[67] The fact that Mr Birden performed "as a subordinate, services for his employer in return for which he receives remuneration, thus satisfying the essential criteria of the employment relationship"[68] and that his work was not marginal and ancillary[69] were not affected by *Bettray* which the CJEU in *Birden* distinguished (this despite the rehabilitative nature of the employment). **6–44**

The issue of rehabilitative employment was considered by the CJEU again in *Trojani*[70] in which a French national carried out chores for some 30 hours a week in a Salvation Army hostel in Brussels where he lived as part of a rehabilitation project. In return the hostel provided him with food, lodgings and an allowance of €25 per week. In his opinion Advocate General Geelhoed[71] interprets the decision in *Bettray* as based on the CJEU's view that the aim of the activities was solely reintegration and not the carrying out of any real economic activity. The Advocate General considered Mr Trojani's relationship with the Salvation Army to be one of care rather than work wherein a service was being provided to Mr Trojani rather than to the Salvation Army. Thus his activity had no (or virtually no) economic value. **6–45**

It would be curious if the national court were to characterise 30 hours' work doing chores as marginal and ancillary from the perspective of the Salvation **6–46**

---

[65] *Lawrie Blum v Land-Baden-Württemberg* (66/85) [1986] E.C.R. 2121, at [19].
[66] *Birden v Stadtgemeinde Bremen* (C-1/97) [1998] E.C.R. I-7447. The case arose in the context of the Turkish Association Agreement.
[67] The issue was whether he was "a duly registered member of the labour force" within the meaning of art.6(1) of Decision 1/80 of the EEC-Turkey Association Council.
[68] *Birden v Stadtgemeinde Bremen* (C-1/97) [1998] E.C.R. I-7447, at [26].
[69] *Birden v Stadtgemeinde Bremen* (C-1/97) [1998] E.C.R. I-7447, at [27]. He worked for 38.5 hours a week receiving net pay of DM 2155.70.
[70] *Trojani v Centre public d'aide socialle de Bruxelles (CPAS)* (C-456/02).
[71] A.G. Geelhoed's Opinion, February 19, 2004.

Army. The CJEU in its decision referred to *Bettray* as being particular on its facts.[72] The CJEU confirmed that the nature of remuneration received by Mr Trojani was not a bar to him being considered a worker. The CJEU left it to the national court to determine if in the circumstances the nature of his activities were real and genuine. Part of the national court's enquiry would require it to ascertain "whether the services actually performed by Mr Trojani are capable of being regarded as forming part of the normal labour market. For that purpose, account may be taken of the status and practices of the hostel, the content of the social reintegration programme, and the nature and details of performance of the services".[73] It is certainly clear that the CJEU does not regard the fact that activities are of a rehabilitative nature as being something which in itself will necessarily prevent them being effective and genuine.

(f) *Work seekers*

(i) *Introduction*

6–47 Consideration has been given to persons whose activities may make them workers. But what of those who have never worked? Article 45 TFEU itself provides the right to move freely within Member States "to accept offers of employment actually made". However, it would plainly undermine the fundamental freedom of movement for workers were freedom of such movement restricted to those who have sought and actually found work (thus requiring them to have job offers before moving to other Member States). The position of work seekers is now dealt with in secondary legislation following the coming into force in 2006 of Directive 2004/38 (also referred to as the Citizens' Directive).

(ii) *Scope of rights for work seekers in Directive 2004/38*

6–48 Article 14(4)(b) of Directive 2004/38 provides as follows:

Article 14

Retention of the right of residence

4. By way of derogation from paragraphs 1 and 2 and without prejudice to the provisions of Chapter VI, an expulsion measure may in no case be adopted against Union citizens or their family members if:

(a) the Union citizens are workers or self-employed persons, or
(b) the Union citizens entered the territory of the host Member State in order to seek employment. In this case, the Union citizens and their family members may not be expelled for as long as the Union citizens can provide evidence that they are continuing to seek employment and that they have a genuine chance of being engaged.

---

[72] *Trojani v centre public d'aide sociale de Bruxelles (CPAS)* (C-456/02) September 7, 2004, at [19].
[73] *Trojani v centre public d'aide sociale de Bruxelles (CPAS)* (C-456/02) September 7, 2004, at [24].

This provision contains on its face no temporal limitation whatsoever as to the period for which a person can be a work seeker. In practice however the right will unlikely be indefinite since a Member State would doubtless argue that the longer a person remains unemployed, the less it could be said that the person could "have a genuine chance of being engaged". All cases will be fact sensitive and it should be borne in mind having regard to the fundamental importance given to the freedom of movement for workers that any restrictions on the exercise of the right must be interpreted strictly. Moreover, as made clear in recital (9) of the preamble to the Directive 2004/38[74] work seekers are deliberately given more favourable treatment than other Union citizens exercising the initial right of residence given by art.6(1) Directive 2004/38. And in recital (16) the lack of distinction between workers and work seekers is emphasised by the statement that "in no case should an expulsion measure be adopted against workers, self-employed persons or job-seekers as defined by the CJEU save on grounds of public policy or public security".

6–49

Article 14(1) provides (as regards the art.6 three-month right of residence without conditions for Union citizens and their family members) that such right endures "as long as they do not become an unreasonable burden on the social assistance system of the host Member State". Article 14(2) provides that the rights of residence provided for in arts 7, 12 and 13 for Union citizens and their family members endure "as long as they meet the conditions set out therein". In order to ensure that the work seekers have a right of residence art.14(4) is thus expressly "by way of derogation from paragraphs 1 and 2". And moreover the inclusion of art.14(4)(a) for workers and the self-employed shows the favoured status that they enjoy as against other free movers. However, the right of residence for such workers, the self-employed and work seekers is subject to the possibility of expulsion under the provisions of Chapter VI of Directive 2004/38 (that is on grounds of public policy, public security or public health. Finally, it is to be noted also that art.7(3)(b) and (c) of Directive 2004/38 makes provision for a person "registered as a job seeker with the relevant employment office" in certain circumstances to retain the status of worker. This is discussed below at para.6–58.

6–50

(iii) *The case law developments*

In *Antonissen*,[75] the CJEU expressly rejected the argument that art.45 TFEU limited the right to free movement solely to those accepting offers of employment actually made. Such interpretation could not be upheld since it would exclude the right of a national of a Member State to move freely and to stay in the territory of other Member States in order to seek employment there. It did so by reference to freedom of movement for workers as one of

6–51

---

[74] Recital (9) states:
"Union citizens should have the right of residence in the host Member State for a period not exceeding three months without being subject to any conditions or any formalities other than the requirement to hold a valid identity card or passport, without prejudice to a more favourable treatment applicable to job-seekers as recognized by the case-law of the Court of Justice."
[75] *The Queen v Immigration Appeal Tribunal Ex p. Antonissen* (C-292/89) [1991] E.C.R. I-745.

the foundations of the Union and the consequential need for a broad interpretation to be given to such freedom.[76] As made clear in *Levin*[77] the free movement rights may be enjoyed not only by those who actually pursue activities as employed persons, but also those who "seriously wish" to pursue such activities.[78] And in *Royer*[79] the CJEU refers to the right to "look for" and pursue such activities.

6–52   In *Antonissen*, the domestic court had held that Mr Antonissen, who had been seeking employment in the United Kingdom for more than six months, could no longer be treated as a Union worker.[80] The UK Government and the Commission had argued that persons could only be workseekers for three months. The CJEU rejected strict temporal limitations. The scope of the right of free movement for work seekers was expressed by the CJEU in these terms:

> "It is not contrary to the provisions of Community law governing the free movement of workers for the legislation of a Member State to provide that a national of another Member State who entered the first State in order to seek employment may be required to leave the territory of that State (subject to appeal) if he has not found employment there after six months, unless the person concerned provides evidence that he is continuing to seek employment and that he has genuine chances of being engaged".[81]

6–53   *Antonissen* thus identified the scope of the right of freedom of movement for work seekers. Member States could prescribe a period of six months within which work should be obtained, although this is not to be enforced if after such time as evidence is provided that the person concerned continues to seek employment and has genuine chances of being engaged.[82] As can be seen from the content of art.14(4) of Directive 2004/38 provision largely codified the case law developments of the CJEU.

---

[76] *The Queen v Immigration Appeal Tribunal Ex p. Antonissen* (C-292/89) [1991] E.C.R. I-745, at [11].
[77] *Levin v Staatssecretaris van Justitie* (53/81) [1982] E.C.R. 1035.
[78] *Levin v Staatssecretaris van Justitie* (53/81) [1982] E.C.R. 1035, at [20].
[79] *Procureur de Roi v Royer* (48/75) [1976] E.C.R. 497, in which the CJEU described the right to enter the territory of other Member States and to reside there "for the purposes intended by the Treaty" as including the right "in particular to look for or pursue an occupation or activities as employed or self employed persons" (para.31).
[80] *The Queen v Immigration Appeal Tribunal Ex p. Antonissen* (C-292/89) [1991] E.C.R. I-745, at [5]: The Immigration Appeal Tribunal based this part of its decision on para.143 of the Statement of Changes in Immigration Rules (HC 169), adopted pursuant to the Immigration Act 1971, under which "a national of a Member State may be deported if, after six months from admission to the United Kingdom, he has not yet found employment or is not carrying on any other occupation".
[81] *The Queen v Immigration Appeal Tribunal Ex p. Antonissen* (C-292/89) [1991] E.C.R. I-745, at [22].
[82] This was confirmed by the CJEU in *Collins v Secretary of State for Work and Pensions* (C-138/02) [2004] 2 C.M.L.R. 8, at [37]. However, the principle could not avail Mr. Tsiotras who remained unemployed for several years and "for whom it [was] objectively impossible to find employment": *Tsiotras v Landeshauptstadt Stuttgart* (C-171/91) [1993] E.C.R. I-2925.

(g) *Previous employment*

(i) *Generally*

The position considered above of work seekers who have never worked for whom the content of the right is about access to employment contrasts the position of persons who have worked previously but have ceased working. As a general rule (as stated by the CJEU in *Sala*[83]): "once the employment relationship has ended, the person concerned as a rule loses his status of worker".

6–54

However, there may be various reasons why a person ceases working (including redundancy, retirement, retraining or the wish to embark on full-time studies). Some such situations are dealt with by expressly secondary legislation giving rights of residence in specific circumstances. Such rights derive from art.45(3)(d) TFEU which identifies the scope of the right of freedom of movement as entailing the right to remain in a Member State "after having been employed in that State".

6–55

Article 16 Directive 2004/38 provides a right of permanent residence after Union citizens have remained legally resident in a host Member State for five years, although (reflective of art.45(3)(d) TFEU) for workers (and the self-employed) the right of permanent residence is given earlier in certain circumstances provided for in art.17 of Directive 2004/38. First, those who retire when they have been working in that Member State for at least the preceding 12 months and have resided there continuously for more than three years.[84] Secondly, those who have resided continuously in the host Member State for more than two years and stop working there as a result of permanent incapacity to work.[85] And thirdly, those who, after three years of continuous employment and residence in the host Member State, work in an employed or self-employed capacity in another Member State, while retaining their place of residence in the host Member State, to which they return, as a rule, each day or at least once a week.[86] The details are considered in Ch.10. The first two examples are of persons who cease to work and will have lost their status as workers.

6–56

On the other hand there are circumstances in which the status of worker is able (in the words of the CJEU in *Sala*[87]) to "produce certain effects after the relationship has ended". Are those circumstances limited to the specific instances in the secondary legislation already referred to above where rights (principally of residence) are expressly given on cessation of employment (for example, on retirement or permanent incapacity as catered for now in art.17(a) and (b) of Directive 2004/38), or are such circumstances wider? The answer to this question is undoubtedly that the secondary legislation does not represent the full extent of such circumstances. In a number of cases the CJEU has acknowledged that even although no longer employed, persons

6–57

---

[83] *Martinez Sala v Freistat Bayern* (C-85/96) [1998] E.C.R. I-2691, at [32].
[84] art.17.1(a) Directive 2004/38/EC of April 29, 2004.
[85] art.17.1(b) Directive 2004/38/EC of April 29, 2004.
[86] art.17.1(c) Directive 2004/38/EC of April 29, 2004.
[87] *Martinez Sala v Freistat Bayern* (C-85/96) [1998] E.C.R. I-2691, at [32].

may nevertheless continue to be considered workers. By the same token it is not always easy to identify precisely why the CJEU has reached its conclusion, although in broad terms such situations have largely arisen where, despite cessation of employment, the person concerned can be regarded as having retained the objective status of worker. Moreover, art.7 of Directive 2004/38 also deals with certain situations in which in spite of not working, a Union citizen worker (or self-employed person) will nevertheless retain the status of worker (or self-employed person). That provision is considered next, before turning to consider the case law developments in paras 6–59 to 6–65 below (which preceded Directive 2004/38).

(ii) *Article 7 of Directive 2004/38*

6–58 Article 7 lays down the requirements under which Union citizens (and their family members) have the right of residence in other Member States for more than three months. That right is given (by art.7.1(a)) to workers (and self-employed persons). For certain persons, however, who objectively may have ceased to be workers, they nevertheless retain that status (and therefore the right of residence given in art.7.1(a)) in the circumstances provided for in art.7(3)(a)–(d) of Directive 2004/38:

> "3. For the purposes of paragraph 1(a), a Union citizen who is no longer a worker or self-employed person shall retain the status of worker or self-employed person in the following circumstances:
>
> (a) he/she is temporarily unable to work as the result of an illness or accident;
> (b) he/she is in duly recorded involuntary unemployment after having been employed for more than one year and has registered as a job-seeker with the relevant employment office;
> (c) he/she is in duly recorded involuntary unemployment after completing a fixed-term employment contract of less than a year or after having become involuntarily unemployed during the first twelve months and has registered as a jobseeker with the relevant employment office. In this case, the status of worker shall be retained for no less than six months;
> (d) he/she embarks on vocational training. Unless he/she is involuntarily unemployed, the retention of the status of worker shall require the training to be related to the previous employment."

(iii) *Case law developments*

Status of worker not lost immediately

6–59 The objective status of worker is obviously not lost *immediately* on cessation of employment. Just as European Union law recognises the right of those who have never worked to be treated as workers whilst they seek employment, so where persons have worked previously they will always have a reasonable period within which to seek and obtain further employment by reference to the principles discussed above.[88] For such persons where national law provisions give benefits to own nationals, Union law will require workers of other Member States to be treated in the same way, although not in an employment relationship. However, in this context the assessment of national authorities will determine whether the person can be

---

[88] See paras 6–47 to 6–53.

said to retain the objective status of worker. It may be for instance that after a certain period of time a Member State does not characterise a person who has ceased economic activity as a worker. It would take extreme circumstances for Union law to characterise the national of another Member State as retaining the objective status of worker where national law no longer did, even in respect of its own nationals.

An example of a case in which someone retained the objective status of worker where the employment relationship had recently ended is *Meints*.[89] The case concerned an agricultural worker whose contract of employment was terminated as a result of the setting aside of land belonging to his former employer. The CJEU held that Mr Meints was entitled to a payment made to agricultural workers whose contract of employment was terminated because payment depended on the prior existence of his recently ended employment relationship which was thus intrinsically linked to his objective status as worker.[90] **6–60**

Those previously employed and capable of taking further employment

More than 40 years ago in *Hoekstra*[91] the CJEU interpreted the concept of "wage earner or assimilated worker"[92] in a case involving a woman who had stopped working. The CJEU held that a protected worker was not exclusively someone in current employment, but extended logically "to the worker who, having left his job, is capable of taking another". Mrs Hoekstra was thus protected by Union law as a worker even though she was no longer in employment. National law provided the unemployed the possibility to participate in a social security system on the grounds of previous possession of the status of "worker" and capability of re-acquiring that status. **6–61**

Available for work and prepared to take it up

The national legislation of some Member States would appear to treat own nationals as retaining the objective status of workers through the combination of being available for work and being prepared to take it up. In Belgium, for example, a general subsistence allowance known as the "minimex" is payable to all those in need who are prepared to accept work (unless pre-vented by the person's state of health or compelling social reasons[93]). In *Hoeckx*[94] and *Scrivner*[95] the CJEU stated the principle that migrant workers are entitled to all benefits: **6–62**

---

[89] *Meints v Minister van Landbouw, Natuurbeheer en Visserij* (C-57/96) [1997] E.C.R. I-6689.
[90] *Meints v Minister van Landbouw, Natuurbeheer en Visserij* (C-57/96) [1997] E.C.R. I-6689, at [41].
[91] *Hoekstra v The Netherlands* (75/63) [1964] E.C.R. 177.
[92] Within the meaning of Council Regulation 3 concerning social security for migrant workers J.O. 58.
[93] *Scrivner and Cole v Centre public d'aide sociale de Chastre* (122/84) [1985] E.C.R. 1027, at [20].
[94] *Hoeckx v Openbaar Centrum voor Maatschappelijk Welzijn, Kalmthout* (249/83) [1985] E.C.R. 973, at [20].
[95] *Scrivner and Cole v Centre public d'aide sociale de Chastre* (122/84) [1985] E.C.R. 1027, at [24].

"generally granted to national workers primarily because of their objective status as workers or by virtue of the mere fact of their residence on the national territory and whose extension to workers who are nationals of other member states therefore seems likely to facilitate the mobility of such workers within the community".

6–63 The facts of *Hoeckx* are striking because the Dutch national had been unemployed for some two years and in receipt of unemployment benefits in both France and Belgium before the minimex was refused. However, *Hoeckx* does not help in identifying why a person unemployed for such a period retained the status of worker since the matter was not in dispute.

Workers undertaking retraining

6–64 A further example of a situation in which the status of worker is retained arises where a person who has ceased employment undertakes some form of professional or vocational training. In *Lair*,[96] the CJEU stated that workers who have exercised their freedom of movement are entitled in the same way as national workers to all the advantages available to such workers "for improving their professional qualifications and promoting their social advancement." This will be the position even although they are no longer in employment, provided a relationship existed between the previous occupational activity and the course of study.[97] Such a person will be regarded as having retained the status of a worker.[98]

Objective status of worker must be linked to previous employment

6–65 Although a person who has ceased to work may retain the status of worker for the purpose of receipt of a particular benefit related to the past employment, such status may not be retained for all other purposes. In *Leclere*,[99] a Belgian national who had been employed as a frontier worker in Luxembourg until 1981 when he was a victim of an accident at work was in receipt of an invalidity pension paid by the Luxembourg social services. As such he was protected against any discrimination affecting rights acquired during his former employment relationship. However, since not currently engaged in an employment relationship, he could not claim to acquire new rights having no links with his former occupation. In particular, having had a child *after* he had stopped working he could not claim the benefit of allowances provided for workers on the birth of a child by the legislation of the Member State responsible for paying his pension.

---

[96] *Lair v Universitaat Hannover* (39/86) [1988] E.C.R. 3161. See also, *Brown v Secretary of State for Scotland* (C-197/86) [1988] E.C.R. 3205; *Raulin v Minister van Onderwijs en Wetenschappen* (C-357/89) [1992] E.C.R. I-1027; *Bernini v Netherlands Minstry of Education and Science* (C-3/90) [1992] E.C.R. I-1027.
[97] Although such a link cannot be required where the migrant has involuntarily become unemployed and is obliged to undertake occupational retraining in another field of activity— *Lair v Universitaat Hannover* (39/86) [1988] E.C.R. 3161, at [37].
[98] *Lair v Universitaat Hannover* (39/86) [1988] E.C.R. 3161, at [39].
[99] *Leclere and Deaconescu v Caisse nationale des prestations familiales* (C-43/99) [2001] E.C.R. I-4265.

(iv) *Summary*

As can be seen, art.7(3) reflects much of the case law which preceded it and to this extent it can be regarded as codification of that case law. However, the fact of codification will not mean that no other situations could arise in which the status of worker might not be retained. In most cases the way in which national law treats own national workers will be of primary importance. This is because at the heart of most situations is the proposition that it would be discriminatory and contrary to Union law to treat own nationals and free movers differently in terms of benefits and advantages given by national law to those who have been in employment. This is discussed in detail in Ch.11.

6–66

(h) *Frontier workers*

Frontier workers are defined as those who reside in one Member State whilst working in the territory of *another* Member State. The various provisions[100] similarly define the necessary frequency of return from the State of employment to the State of residence as being "as a rule, each day or at least once a week". In *Bergemann*,[101] the CJEU refers to those who

6–67

> "return regularly and frequently, in other words 'daily or at least once a week' to their state of residence [as those who] may be regarded as having the status of frontier workers".

This did not include a worker who "after having transferred his residence to a Member State other than the State of employment, no longer returns to that State".

In *Hartmann*[102] the CJEU considered the situation of a German national who moved his permanent residence to Austria for reasons not connected to his employment whilst holding the same job in Germany as a frontier worker. Could Mr Hartmann as a frontier worker claim the status of migrant worker for the purposes of Regulation 1612/68?[103] It was argued by the Governments of Germany, the Netherlands and the United Kingdom, as well as the Commission, that only the movement of a person to another Member State for the purpose of carrying on an occupation should be regarded as an exercise of the right of freedom of movement for workers. Therefore, Mr Hartmann, who never left his employment in the Member State of which he is a national and merely transferred his residence to the Member State of his spouse, could not benefit from the provisions on freedom of movement for workers. The CJEU rejected these arguments. Seen in the context of its decision in *Ritter-Coulais*[104] (where the CJEU had

6–68

---

[100] art.1(b) of Regulation 1408/71, art.2 of Regulation 1251/70, art.17.1(c) Directive 2004/38.
[101] *Bergemann v Bundesanstalt für Arbeit* (236/87) [1988] E.C.R. 5125.
[102] *Gertraud Hartmann v Freistaat Bayern* (C-212/05).
[103] Now replaced by Regulation (EU) No.492/2011 of the European Parliament and of the Council of April 5, 2011 on freedom of movement for workers within the Union.
[104] *Ritter-Coulais* (C-152/03) [2006] E.C.R. I-1711 (applying *De Groot* (C-385/00) [2002] E.C.R. I-11819, at [76]; *Schilling and Fleck-Schilling* (C-209/01) [2003] E.C.R. I-13389, at [23]; and *Van Pommeren-Bourgondiën* (C-277/03) [2005] E.C.R. I-0000, at [19, 44 and 45]).

observed that any national of a Member State, irrespective of his place of residence and his nationality, who has exercised the right to freedom of movement for workers and who has been employed in a Member State other than that of residence falls within the scope of that provision), it followed that Mr Hartmann, who worked in a Member State other than that of his actual place of residence, fell within the scope of art.45 TFEU. The fact that he had settled in Austria for reasons not connected with his employment

> "does not justify refusing him the status of migrant worker which he acquired as from the time when, following the transfer of his residence to Austria, he made full use of his right to freedom of movement for workers by going to Germany to carry on an occupation there".

(i) *The public service exception*

(i) *Generally*

6–69 By art.45(4) TFEU "the provisions of this article shall not apply to employment in the public service". The exception protects the legitimate interest of Member States in reserving for their own nationals a range of posts connected with the exercise of powers conferred by public law and with the protection of general interests. However, the scope of the exception is not so wide as to exclude *all* public service employment. Moreover, where those exercising free movement rights *are* admitted to the public service the provision cannot be used to justify discriminatory treatment (for example, as regards remuneration or other conditions of employment[105]). As stated by the CJEU in *Sotgiu*[106] the very fact that they have been admitted shows that the interests which justify the exceptions to the principle of non-discrimination permitted by art.45(4) TFEU "are not at issue".

(ii) *Scope of the exception*

6–70 The importance of the principle that Union concepts in this field must not be interpreted by reference to national concepts has already been underlined. This is particularly important in construing the scope of this exception. As stated by the CJEU in *Commission v Belgium*:[107]

> "recourse to provisions of the domestic legal systems to restrict the scope of the provisions of community law would have the effect of impairing the unity and efficacy of that law and consequently cannot be accepted. That rule, which is fundamental to the existence of the community, must also apply in determining the scope and bounds of Article 48(4) of the Treaty [now Art.45(4) TFEU]... It is necessary to ensure that the effectiveness and scope of the provisions of the Treaty on freedom of movement of workers and equality of treatment of nationals of all Member States shall not be restricted by interpretations of the concept of public

---

[105] See *Commission v Italy* (225/85) [1987] E.C.R. 2625.
[106] *Sotgiu v Deutsche Bundespost* (152/73) [1974] E.C.R. 153.
[107] *Commission v Belgium No. 1* (149/79) [1980] E.C.R. 3881, at [19]. See similarly, *Commission v France* (307/84) [1986] E.C.R. 1725, where the CJEU pointed out that access to certain posts may not be limited by reason of the fact that in a given Member State persons appointed to such posts have the status of civil servants since this would enable the Member States to determine at will the posts covered by the exception.

service which are based on domestic law alone and which would obstruct the application of community rules".

6–71 As to the actual posts removed from the ambit of art.45(1) TFEU, the CJEU in *Commission v Belgium* defined them as those which involved

"direct or indirect participation in the exercise of powers conferred by public law and duties designed to safeguard the general interests of the state or of other public authorities".

Such posts were thought by the CJEU to presume on the part of those occupying them the existence of a "special relationship of allegiance" to the State and "reciprocity of rights and duties which form the foundation of the bond of nationality".[108]

6–72 In theory at least the application of such principles could strike a fair balance between the legitimate interest of Member States identified above and the requirement that the effectiveness and scope of the free movement provisions are not restricted by interpretations of public service based on national law. Unfortunately however the actual posts found to fall within art.45(4) TFEU by the CJEU in *Commission v Belgium (No. 2)*[109] are so widely cast as to suggest that in practice the application of the principles is more difficult. Such posts are:

"head technical office supervisor, principal supervisor, works supervisor, stock controller and night watchman with the municipality of Brussels and architect with the municipalities of Brussels and Auderghem".

Whilst the CJEU also found that certain other jobs fell outside art.45(4) TFEU (including railway shunters and signallers, drivers, plate-layers, various unskilled workers with the local railways as well as posts for hospital nurses, night-watchmen, plumbers, carpenters and electricians), it is difficult to see (for example) why a stock controller or night-watchman could be thought to be doing something which involved any special relationship of allegiance or reciprocity of rights and duties forming the foundation of the bond of nationality.

6–73 A more appropriate approach is shown by *Lawrie-Blum*[110] where the CJEU appeared concerned to limit the scope of application of art.45(4) EC Treaty. By reference to the "fundamental principle that workers in the community should enjoy freedom of movement and not suffer discrimination" the CJEU cites the importance of construing the provision

---

[108] *Commission v Belgium (No.1)* (149/79) [1980] E.C.R. 3881, at [10].
[109] *Commission v Belgium (No. 2)* (149/79) [1982] E.C.R. 1845. When judgment was initially given on December 17, 1980 the CJEU stated (at para.23) that it had insufficient information to enable "a sufficiently accurate appraisal to be made of the actual nature of the duties involved so as to make it possible to identify, in the light of the foregoing considerations, those of the posts which do not come within the concept of public service within the meaning of Article 48(4) of the Treaty [now Art.45(4) TFEU]".
[110] *Lawrie-Blum v Land Baden-Württemberg* (66/85) [1986] E.C.R. 2121.

"in such a way as to limit its scope to what is strictly necessary for safeguarding the interests which that provision allows the member states to protect".

Even if as argued by the German Government a trainee teacher exercises powers conferred by public law in the course of activities which contribute towards the safeguarding of the general interests of the State or of other public authorities, this did not mean that the "very strict conditions" were fulfilled in the case of a trainee teacher. In *Allüe*,[111] the CJEU similarly held that employment as a foreign-language assistant at a university was not employment in the public service.

---

[111] *Alluë & Coonan v Universite degli studi di Venzia* (33/88) [1989] E.C.R. 1591.

Chapter 7

ESTABLISHMENT AND SERVICES

This chapter examines the Treaty provisions and subsidiary legislation on the freedom of establishment and the freedom to provide and receive services.

1. Treaty Provisions and Subsidiary Legislation on Establishment

(a) *General Treaty aims and relationship with provisions on workers*

The Treaty on the Functioning of the European Union contains a specific provision on the freedom of establishment in art.49 consistent with the general aim of promoting free movement of persons. The provision ensures that Member States accord to the nationals of other Member States the same treatment, as regards establishment, as it accords to its own nationals: **7–01**

Article 49 TFEU

Within the framework of the provisions set out below, restrictions on the freedom of establishment of nationals of a Member State in the territory of another Member State shall be prohibited. Such prohibition shall also apply to restrictions on the setting-up of agencies, branches or subsidiaries by nationals of any Member State established in the territory of any Member State.

Freedom of establishment shall include the right to take up and pursue activities as self-employed persons and to set up and manage undertakings, in particular companies or firms within the meaning of the second paragraph of Article 54, under the conditions laid down for its own nationals by the law of the country where such establishment is effected, subject to the provisions of the Chapter relating to capital.

Article 45 TFEU relating to workers and art.49 TFEU are based on the same principle that the restrictions on the freedom of movement of persons should be abolished. In this context entry into and residence in the territory of Member States are covered by European Union law. **7–02**

The right of establishment contained in art.49 TFEU applies to all natural persons and to companies. The first paragraph of art.49 TFEU prohibits restrictions on the freedom of establishment by nationals of a Member State in the territory of another Member State, including the setting up of agencies, branches or subsidiaries. The second paragraph of art.49 TFEU provides the direct right of establishment which includes the right to take up and pursue activities as a self-employed person as well as the right to set up and manage undertakings. **7–03**

(b) *Secondary legislation*

7–04 Directive 73/148 previously implemented the right of establishment for nationals of the Member States.[1] Repealed with effect from April 30, 2006 by art.38 of Directive 2004/38,[2] most of the provisions of Directive 73/148 are now contained in Directive 2004/38. Article 7(1) of Directive 2004/38 provides for the right of residence for longer than three months for the self-employed person. The rights of residence for those exercising the right of establishment are discussed in Ch.11.

2. CONCEPT OF ESTABLISHMENT

7–05 Article 49 TFEU provides that the freedom of establishment includes, on the one hand, the right to take up and pursue activities as self-employed persons, and, on the other hand, the setting up and managing of undertakings. According to the CJEU:

> "The concept of establishment within the meaning of the Treaty is therefore a very broad one, allowing a Community national to participate, on a stable and continuous basis, in the economic life of a Member State other than his State of origin and to profit therefrom, so contributing to economic and social interpenetration within the Community in the sphere of activities as self-employed persons".[3]

(a) *Definition of economic activity*

7–06 In order to engage in the economic life of a Member State, a person or legal entity would plainly need to be engaged in economic activity. As is the case with workers considered in Ch.6 above, activities of those exercising the freedom of establishment must be genuine and effective rather than marginal and ancillary. Further the activities must include the provision of services in return for some form of remuneration.[4]

7–07 Consistent with the broad interpretation given to free movement rights, the CJEU has found persons to be engaged in "economic activity" in a wide variety of situations. They will include where they have been engaged in sports activities, provided that they are professional or semi-professional sportsmen in gainful employment or providing a remunerated service.[5] They will also include those who where they have carried out activities as members of a community based on religion or other form of philosophy where the services which the community provides to its members may be regarded

---

[1] [1973] O.J. L172/14.
[2] Directive 2004/38/EC on the right of citizens of the Union and their family members to move and reside freely within the territory of the Member States.
[3] *Gebhard v Consiglio dell'Ordine degli Avvocati e Procuratori di Milano* (C-55/94) [2001] E.C.R. I-4165, at [24] and *Commission v Austria*, (C-161/07) December 22, 2009, at [24].
[4] *Jany v Staatssecretaris van Justitie* (C-268/99) [2001] E.C.R. I-8615.
[5] *Union Royal Belge des Societes de Football Association ASBL v Bosman* (C-415/93) [1995] E.C.R. 4353, at [73].

as being an indirect remuneration for their work.[6] They will even include prostitutes, "satisfy[ing] a request by the beneficiary in return for consideration without producing or transferring material goods".[7]

(b) *Cross-border character*

In order to provide a European Union law nexus to a situation, the activity cannot be purely internal, but must have a cross-border character. If there is no element of the activity which goes beyond a purely national setting, the provisions of Union law will not be applicable.[8] 7–08

Internal situations are discussed in Ch.5 above. The two exceptions to the purely internal rule, namely those returning to their own Member State and those with dual nationality, apply equally to establishment cases as they do elsewhere. 7–09

In respect of returning nationals, the CJEU has confirmed that even where a national of a particular Member State acquires a vocational qualification in another Member State which is recognised under European Union law, that person is to be treated in accordance with the principles of Union law on return to the State of origin.[9] 7–10

The provisions in the Treaty on the Functioning of the European Union relating to freedom of establishment are directed mainly at ensuring that nationals and companies of other Member States are not treated differently compared with own nationals and own companies in the host Member State. However, the provisions are not limited to treatment in a host Member State. Those provisions have also been interpreted as prohibiting the Member State of origin from hindering the establishment in another Member State of one of its nationals or a company incorporated under its legislation.[10] 7–11

(c) *Stable and continuous nature of economic activity*

According to the case law of the CJEU, the concept of establishment within the meaning of the TFEU requires the pursuit of an economic activity through a fixed establishment in another Member State without a foreseeable limit as to its duration.[11] 7–12

This is to be contrasted with the provision of services, which does not include an activity carried out on a permanent basis or, in any event, 7–13

---

[6] *Steymann v Staatssecretaris van Justitie* (196/87) [1988] E.C.R. 6159, at [13].
[7] *Jany v Staatssecretaris van Justitie* (C-268/99) [2001] E.C.R. I-8615, at [48].
[8] *Criminal Proceedings Against Eleonora Neno* (C-54/88) [1990] E.C.R. I-3537, at [11].
[9] *Kraus v Land Baden-Württemberg* (C-19/92) [1993] E.C.R. I-1663, at [15].
[10] *Union Royal Belge des Societes de Football Association ASBL v Bosman* (C-415/93) [1995] E.C.R. 4353, at [97].
[11] *The Queen v Secretary of State for Transport Ex p. Factortame Ltd* (C-221/89) [1991] E.C.R. I-3905, at [20].

without a foreseeable limit to its duration.[12] It is thus the stable and continuous basis on which the services are carried out in the other Member State which distinguishes a situation of establishment from one concerned with the mere provision of services.

7–14 However, even where the activities are apparently temporary in nature, whether or not they constitute establishment has to be determined in the light not only of the duration of the provision of the service, but also of its regularity and continuity. If carried out on a frequent basis or over a significant period of time, the provider of the services may need to obtain some form of infrastructure, such as office space, in the host Member State in order to carry out these services.[13] Obtaining permanent infrastructure would be thus regarded as establishment even if the provision of services is not continuous.

3. Establishment of Persons

7–15 Establishment is granted to natural persons who are nationals of Member States as well as companies. The definition of a Union national for the purpose of benefiting from free movement rights is discussed in Ch.5 above. Subject to the exceptions and conditions laid down in art.49 TFEU, the provisions permit all types of self-employed activity to be taken up and pursued on the territory of any other Member State.

7–16 Self-employment is defined in European Union law as existing where

> "economic activities are carried out by a person outside any relationship of subordination with regard to the conditions of work or remuneration and under his own personal responsibility".[14]

7–17 According to the case law of the CJEU there is nothing to prevent an employee of a company in one Member State working in a self-employed capacity in another Member State.[15] Furthermore, there is nothing to prevent a person being established as self-employed in two different Member States. This would be the case for example where a member of a profession establishes a second professional base in another Member State.[16]

7–18 Freedom of establishment is to be exercised under the conditions laid down for a host Member State's own nationals by the law of that Member State.[17] If own nationals do not have to have any specific qualifications in order to carry out a particular activity in a Member State, then nationals of other

---

[12] *Steymann v Staatssecretaris van Justitie* (196/87) [1988] E.C.R. 6159, at [16].
[13] *Gebhard v Consigol dell' Ordine degli Advocat AE Procuratori di Milano* (C-55/94) [1995] E.C.R. I-4165, at [27].
[14] *Jany v Staatssecretaris van Justitie* (C-268/99) [2001] E.C.R. I-8615, at [37].
[15] *Ramrath v Minister of Justice* (C-106/91) [1992] E.C.R. I-3351, at [26].
[16] *Gebhard v Consigol dell' Ordine degli Advocat AE Procuratori di Milano* (C-55/94) [1995] E.C.R. I-4165, at [24].
[17] *Gebhard v Consigol dell' Ordine degli Advocat AE Procuratori di Milano* (C-55/94) [1995] E.C.R. I-4165, at [33].

Member States cannot be required to comply with any additional rules or regulations in order to carry out these same activities.[18] The recognition of the qualifications obtained in other Member States is somewhat contentious and potentially stands in the way of the freedom of establishment of persons. As discussed in Ch.11 below, it is for this reason that there are detailed European Union law rules relating to the mutual recognition of qualifications and diplomas in a wide range of professional areas.

7–19 As described in Ch.6, work seekers in another Member State have free movement rights which flow from art.45 TFEU such that their right of residence must be recognised for a reasonable period of time, and at least six months. This reference to six months was a reflection of the decision of the CJEU in *Antonissen*[19] and although not subject to decision of the CJEU it might have been thought that such principle would apply similarly to those wishing to establish themselves in another Member State who required a period of time in order to set themselves up.

7–20 The decision in *Antonissen* is now codified by art.14(4) of Directive 2004/38 which is considered at paras 6–48 to 6–50. However, the art.14.4(b) protection from expulsion applies only to Union citizens who entered a host Member State "in order to seek employment" (in which case such Union citizen and family members could not be expelled "for as long as the Union citizens can provide evidence that they are continuing to seek employment and that they have a genuine chance of being engaged"). This is somewhat surprising but would seem to tell against what might otherwise have been assumed would be the position for those wishing to establish themselves as self-employed persons. Both the work seeker and the person seeking to establish themselves in employment seek to do at heart the same thing, that is to engage in economic activity in a host Member State in the exercise of rights of free movement. Seen in this context it seems very odd that the individual free mover's status in European Union law should depend solely on the characterisation of an employment relationship. It is suggested that whilst art.14(4)(b) plainly codifies the *Antonissen* decision for workers, it should not been seen as representing the limit of European Union law. Establishment is plainly an organic process and a broad interpretation of the term establishment should mean that art.14(4)(b) will apply equally to those who are seeking to establish themselves in self-employment.

4. ESTABLISHMENT OF COMPANIES

7–21 The right of establishment under the TFEU is equally provided to legal persons, namely undertakings or companies. This is generally, although not necessarily, exercised by the setting-up of agencies, branches or subsidiaries.

---

[18] *Gebhard v Consigol dell' Ordine degli Advocat AE Procuratori di Milano* (C-55/94) [1995] E.C.R. I-4165, at [34].
[19] *The Queen v Immigration Appeal Tribunal Ex p. Antonissen* (C-292/89) [1991] E.C.R. I-745.

The CJEU tends to define the concept of establishment by reference to the setting up of either undertakings or agencies somewhat interchangeably.[20]

(a) *Primary establishment—head office*

7–22 A company's "primary establishment" is normally its head office where centralised decisions are made and where key management functions occur. In the context of freedom of establishment a company may wish to move its primary establishment to another Member State.

7–23 If a company is to make its primary establishment in another Member State this would involve the transfer of central management and control of a company to another Member State. In the *Daily Mail* case, the CJEU considered that the transfer of central management and control of a company to another Member State could amount to establishment of the company in that second Member State. This would be the case where the company locates its centre of decision-making in the second Member State since this would constitute genuine and effective economic activity.[21]

(b) *Secondary establishment—branches, subsidiaries and agencies*

7–24 As the CJEU has held on a number of occasions, freedom of establishment is not confined to the right to create a single establishment within the Union but includes the freedom to set up and maintain, subject to the observance of professional rules of conduct, more than one place of work within the territory of the Member States.[22] Where, however, a branch is established in another Member State art.49 TFEU does not preclude legislation of that second Member State which makes registration, in the register of companies, of the branch subject to the payment of an advance on the anticipated cost of the publication of the objects of the company as set out in its instrument of constitution.[23]

7–25 The fact that the right of establishment for a company is capable of being exercised by the setting up of agencies, branches or subsidiaries is supported by the express provision to that effect in art.49 TFEU. A company may also exercise its right of establishment by taking part in the incorporation of a company in another Member State.[24]

---

[20] See, for instance, *Segers v Bestuur van de Bedrijfsvereniging voor Bank* (79/85) [1986] E.C.R. 2375 and *Commission v France* (270/53) [1986] E.C.R. 273.
[21] *The Queen v HM Treasury and Commissioners of Inland Revenue, Ex p. Daily Mail and General Trust plc* (81/87) [1988] E.C.R. 5483, at [12].
[22] See *Ordre des avocats au barreau de Paris v Klopp* (107/83) [1984] E.C.R. 2971; see also, *Inasti v Kemmler* (C-53/95) [1996] E.C.R. I-703.
[23] *Innoventif Limited* (C-453/04) [2006] I-04929.
[24] *The Queen v HM Treasury and Commissioners of Inland Revenue, Ex p. Daily Mail and General Trust plc* (81/87) [1988] E.C.R. 5483, at [17].

Furthermore, the merger of companies established in different Member States can also engage freedom of establishment rights. In *Sevic Systems Aktiengesellschaft*[25] the CJEU held that a refusal to register a merger between companies established in Germany and Luxembourg (because German law provided only for mergers between legal entities established in Germany) was contrary to European Union law. Cross-border merger operations which constituted particular methods of exercise of the freedom of establishment are important for the proper functioning of the internal market and therefore amongst those economic activities in respect of which Member States are required to comply with the freedom of establishment laid down by art.49 TFEU.[26]

7–26

(c) *Nationality of the company*

The nationality of a company is determined by the law of the individual Member States. This is not a matter governed by European Union law which at the present time does not include rules relating to the incorporation and functioning of companies. Such national laws vary greatly as regards the means of incorporation. The Treaty on the Functioning of the European Union takes a flexible approach by treating all such factors which could be said to connect a company to that State as equal. Thus Union law draws no distinction between, for example, the registered office, central administration and principle place of business of a company. This flexibility is necessary to take account of the variety in national legislation.[27]

7–27

However, there are problems which are yet to be resolved regarding the differences in national legislation concerning the factors connecting a company to a particular Member State. Such differences can result in difficulties. Where, for example, incorporation rules in one Member State treat the location of a company's head office as determinative of incorporation, that company might not able to establish itself in another Member State by simply moving its head office, if incorporation laws are different in that other Member State.

7–28

(d) *Nationality of the employees*

The nationality of the employees is irrelevant to the question of the establishment of a legal person, whether it be a company or a subsidiary. However, if the employees are third country nationals and the company wishes to transfer those employees on a permanent basis to a branch or subsidiary in another Member State, such transfer will be governed by national immigration laws as regards those third country nationals. As

7–29

---

[25] (C-411/03)–Matter concerning companies register relating to *Sevic Systems Aktiengesellschaft*.
[26] Judgment at para.19; such difference in treatment between companies, according to whether the merger was internal or cross-border in nature, constituted a restriction on freedom of establishment that could not be justified on imperative grounds in the public interest.
[27] *The Queen v HM Treasury and Commissioners of Inland Revenue, Ex p. Daily Mail and General Trust plc* (81/87) [1988] E.C.R. 5483, at [21].

described below,[28] a company established in one Member State will have the right to "post" a third country national employee on a temporary basis in order to perform services there. The Posted Workers Directive regulates the legal framework of such transfers as regards working conditions and applicable employment legislation to safeguard the rights of those employees.[29]

5. Meaning of Freedom of Establishment "Without Restrictions"

7–30 The concept of establishment is a very broad one, allowing Union citizens to participate in the economic life of a host Member State and to profit therefrom (in the words of the CJEU)

> "so contributing to economic and social interpenetration within the European Union in the sphere of activities of self-employed persons."[30]

At heart the enjoyment of the right of freedom of establishment without restrictions conferred by art.49 TFEU on Union citizens is about the right for them to take up and pursue activities as self-employed persons and to set up and manage undertakings

> "under the same conditions as are laid down by the law of the Member State of establishment for its own nationals".[31]

In other words, Member States must not provide in their laws any conditions for the pursuit of activities by persons exercising their right of establishment which differ from those laid down for its own nationals.[32] As will be seen, the obligation goes further if the same conditions nevertheless result in effect in differential treatment.

7–31 In *Commission v Austria*[33] the CJEU considered an obligation under Austrian law which required nationals of eight of the new Member States joining the Union in 2004 who wished to register a partnership or company in the commercial register to obtain a certificate determining that they were self-employed, or a work permit exemption certificate. The Commission contended that this constituted an unjustified restriction on the exercise of the freedom of establishment. The CJEU considered that the Austrian legislation infringed the prohibition on restrictions contained in art.49 TFEU by laying down laws on nationals of the eight new Member States which differed from those laid down for its own nationals. Austria had

---

[28] At paras 7–61 to 7–67.
[29] Directive 96/71/EC of the European Parliament and of the Council of December 16, 1996 concerning the posting of workers in the framework of the provision of services [1997] O.J. L18/1.
[30] *Centro di Musicologia Walter Stauffer* (C-386/04) [2006] E.C.R. I-8203, at [18].
[31] See *Centros* (C-212/97) [1999] E.C.R. I-1459, at [19], and *Denkavit Internationaal and Denkavit France* (C-170/05) [2006] E.C.R. I-11949, at [20].
[32] *Commission v France* (270/83) [1986] E.C.R. 273, at [24].
[33] *Commission v Austria* (C-161/07) December 22, 2009.

sought to justify the discriminatory treatment on public policy grounds, a contention given short shrift by the CJEU:

> 37. (T)he Republic of Austria has merely invoked in a general manner the danger of circumvention by supposed 'bogus self-employed persons' of the transitional rules governing the freedom of movement for workers coming from the eight new Member States, without putting forward any precise evidence capable of establishing that the potential infringement of those rules constitutes a genuine and sufficiently serious threat to a fundamental interest of society.
>
> 38. Furthermore, even supposing that that danger of circumvention of the rules is liable to cause such interference with public policy, it must be held that the defendant Member State has not established to the requisite legal standard either that the objective concerning the proper working of the labour market which is pursued by the legislation in question makes it necessary to put in place a general system of prior authorisation, applying to all economic operators concerned from the eight new Member States, or that that objective cannot be achieved by measures less restrictive of the freedom of establishment.

The prohibition on restrictions is not however limited to the sort of situation where different laws or practices are applied in a discriminatory manner. It will include measures taken by a Member State which although applied to own nationals and those exercising their right of establishment alike, adversely affect the latter. As the CJEU explained in *Commission v Spain*,[34] art.49 TFEU:

> "precludes any national measure which, even though it is applicable without discrimination on grounds of nationality, is liable to hinder or to render less attractive the exercise by EU citizens of the freedom of establishment that is guaranteed by the Treaty".

The CJEU continued:

> "64. In that context, it should be borne in mind that the concept of 'restriction' ... covers measures taken by a Member State which, although applicable without distinction, affect access to the market for undertakings from other Member States and thereby hinder intra-Community trade (see, to that effect, Case C-442/02 *CaixaBank France* [2004] ECR I-8961, paragraph 11; Case C-518/06 *Commission* v *Italy* [2009] ECR I-3491, paragraph 64; and, by analogy, Case C-110/05 *Commission* v *Italy* [2009] ECR I-519, paragraph 37).
>
> 65. National legislation which makes the establishment of an undertaking from another Member State conditional upon the issue of prior authorisation falls within that category, since it is capable of hindering the exercise by that undertaking of freedom of establishment, by preventing it from freely pursuing its activities through a fixed place of business (see Joined Cases C-570/07 and C-571/07 *Blanco Pérez and Chao Gómez* [2010] ECR I-0000, paragraph 54)."

---

[34] *Commission v Spain* (C-400/08) March 24, 2011, at [63]. See also, *Commission* v *Netherlands* (C-299/02) [2004] E.C.R. I-9761, at [15], and *Commission* v *Greece* (C-140/03) [2005] E.C.R. I-3177, at [27].

6. Treaty Provisions and Subsidiary Legislation on Service Provision and Recipients of Services

Article 56 TFEU

7–33   Within the framework of the provisions set out below, restrictions on freedom to provide services within the Union shall be prohibited in respect of nationals of Member States who are established in a Member State other than that of the person for whom the services are intended.

7–34   The European Parliament and the Council, acting in accordance with the ordinary legislative procedure, may extend the provisions of the Chapter to nationals of a third country who provide services and who are established within the Union.

Article 57 TFEU

7–35   Services shall be considered to be "services" within the meaning of the Treaties where they are normally provided for remuneration, in so far as they are not governed by the provisions relating to freedom of movement for goods, capital and persons.

7–36   "Services" shall in particular include:

(a) activities of an industrial character;
(b) activities of a commercial character;
(c) activities of craftsmen; and
(d) activities of the professions.

Without prejudice to the provisions of the Chapter relating to the right of establishment, the person providing a service may, in order to do so, temporarily pursue their activity in the Member State where the service is provided, under the same conditions as are imposed by that State on its own nationals.

(a) General Treaty aims and relationship with establishment provisions

7–37   The situation of a Union national who moves to another Member State in order to pursue an economic activity there is governed by the TFEU provisions on free movement of workers, the right of establishment, or the provision of services. The CJEU has described them as mutually exclusive.[35] The TFEU provides that persons or companies established in one Member State should be able to provide their services in other Member States.

7–38   The CJEU considers that the provisions in the TFEU relating to the provision of services are subordinate to those relating to the right of establishment.[36] The first paragraph of art.57 TFEU makes clear that a person will only fall within the scope of the provisions relating to services if they are not governed by the provisions relating to freedom of movement for goods,

---

[35] *Gebhard v Consigol dell' Ordine degli Advocat AE Procuratori di Milano* (C-55/94) [1995] E.C.R. I-4165, at [20].
[36] *Gebhard v Consigol dell' Ordine degli Advocat AE Procuratori di Milano* (C-55/94) [1995] E.C.R. I-4165, at [22].

capital and persons. According to the CJEU within the context of Title IV of the Treaty on the Functioning of the European Union ("free movement of persons, services and capital"), the free movement of persons includes the movement of workers within the Union and freedom of establishment within the territory of the Member States.[37] If a person falls within the scope of the Treaty provisions relating to establishment they will be precluded from benefiting from the provisions relating to the provision of services.[38]

It is often advantageous for persons providing services in another Member State to characterise their activities as "provision of services" as opposed to "establishment" since this might avoid professional rules of conduct which would be applicable if they were established within that State. Thus for example the architect travelling to another Member State to advise on the completion of a building project will likely avoid having to comply with the rules of any professional body governing the conduct of architects in that second Member State by merely providing services on a temporary basis. European Union law does not prevent a Member State from adopting measures to ensure a person who is directing their services principally towards that Member State from circumventing its laws relating to establishment. In the case of dispute as to the legality of such measures, they fall to be determined in accordance with art.49 TFEU relating to establishment. 7–39

There are four basic conditions to be met for a person or company to benefit from the European Union law provisions relating to service provision. First, the service provision must be a form of economic activity. Secondly, there must be a cross-border element in that the service provider should be established in one Member State and providing services in another Member State. Thirdly, the service provision must be of a temporary nature. Finally, the service provider, if a natural person, must be an EU national and, if a company, must be incorporated under the legislation of a Member State. These conditions are considered in detail below.[39] 7–40

(b) *Articles 56–62 TFEU*

Article 56 TFEU prohibits the restriction on the right of freedom of movement in order to provide services. The wording of art.56 assumes that the provider and the recipient of the service are "established" in two different Member States.[40] Article 62 TFEU makes clear that the provisions of arts 51–54 TFEU are extended to the provisions on the provision of services. Through art.54 TFEU the right to freedom of movement in order to provide services is extended to companies. 7–41

---

[37] *Luisi and Carbone v Minstero del Tesoro* (C-286/82 & 26/83) [1984] E.C.R. 377, at [9].
[38] *Gebhard v Consigol dell' Ordine degli Advocat AE Procuratori di Milano* (C-55/94) [1995] E.C.R. I-4165, at [22].
[39] See paras 7–47 to 7–58.
[40] *Gebhard v Consigol dell' Ordine degli Advocat AE Procuratori di Milano* (C-55/94) [1995] E.C.R. I-4165, at [22].

Establishment and Services

7-42   Article 57 TFEU provides that the person providing a service may temporarily pursue their activity in the host Member State, on the same conditions as own nationals are permitted to provide services.

(c) *Secondary legislation*

7-43   Directive 73/148[41] previously implemented the Treaty provisions relating to the free movement of persons for the purposes of provision of services. Repealed with effect from April 30, 2006 by art.38 of Directive 2004/38,[42] some of the provisions of Directive 73/148 are now contained in the Directive 2004/38. However, Directive 2004/38 is silent as regards service provision itself. It is to be noted that art.6 of Directive 2004/38 gives all Union citizens (and their family members) a right of residence in other Member States for up to three months (without any conditions or formalities) making ample provision for persons to exercise their free movement rights to provide services in light of the necessary temporary nature of service provision and its subordination to the right of establishment.

7-44   Directive 73/148 was significant also because of the reference in its preamble to the fact that the freedom to provide services entailed that persons providing and *receiving services* have the right of residence for the time during which the services are being provided. The free movement rights of those receiving services are plainly also catered for by art.6 of Directive 2004/38, even though that directive is silent as regards *recipients* of services (as it is as regards providers of services). And as mentioned in the following paragraph, *recipients* are catered for also by the Services Directive.

7-45   Directive 2006/123/EC (the "Services Directive")[43] came into force on December 28, 2006 to be implemented by Member States before December 28, 2009. The Services Directive removes legal and administrative barriers to trade in the services sector which (in the words of the preamble[44])

> "is essential in order to strengthen the integration of the peoples of Europe and to promote balanced and sustainable economic and social progress".

The Services Directive requires the simplification by Member States of procedures and formalities that service providers need to comply with, in particular by removing unjustified and disproportionate burdens and by substantially facilitating both the establishment of businesses and cross-border provision of services. The Services Directive also strengthens the rights of recipients of services, for example by prohibiting discriminatory conditions based on the nationality or residence of the service recipient, such

---

[41] Council Directive 73/148 of May 21, 1973 on the abolition of restrictions on movement and residence within the Community for nationals of Member States with regard to establishment and services [1973] O.J. L-172/14.
[42] Directive 2004/38/EC on the right of citizens of the Union and their family members to move and reside freely within the territory of the Member States.
[43] Directive 2006/123/EC of the European Parliament and the Council of December 12, 2006 on services in the internal market.
[44] para.1.

as discriminatory tariffs. Detailed consideration of the Services Directive is beyond the scope of this book. However, the express applicability of the directive to recipients of services (covering also third country nationals who already benefit from European Union acts) is of particular significance in the free movement context.

It is to be emphasised that these provisions do not cover the situation of employees of companies established in one Member State wishing to provide services in another Member State. The conditions relating to the entry and residence of those "posted" employees are discussed below.[45] 7–46

7. SERVICE PROVIDERS

(a) *Economic activity*

The first paragraph of art.57 of the Treaty on the Functioning of the European Union provides that activities are to be considered "services" within the meaning of the chapter on services in TFEU where they are normally provided for remuneration. Whilst art.57 TFEU expressly states that "services" include four types of activity, this list is not exhaustive and indeed any activity which is economic in character would fulfil the requirements of art.57. 7–47

Service provision will fall within the scope of TFEU where the specific activity is one which is normally provided for remuneration. The essential characteristic of remuneration is that it constitutes consideration for the service in question, and is normally agreed upon between the provider and recipient of the service. Where there is no remuneration for the service, it will not fulfil the conditions in the Treaty. Thus, for example, the provision of State education or State-provided health services would not constitute service provision within the meaning of the Treaty. 7–48

In *Humbel*,[46] the CJEU considered whether the position of State education constituted service provision. The CJEU held that the essential characteristic of economic activity was not fulfilled. This was because the State was not seeking to engage in gainful economic activity but it was fulfilling social and cultural obligations. Secondly, the State education system is in general funded from the public purse and not by the pupils or their carers. However, State education is to be distinguished from private education, which is capable of fulfilling the economic activity condition since it is aimed at producing a commercial benefit.[47] 7–49

The fact that a service provides entertainment or recreation to the recipient does not deprive it of its economic character, nor does the fact that profits made are for charity or public benefit. In this context in the case of 7–50

---

[45] See paras 7–61 to 7–70.
[46] *Belgium v Humbel and Adele* (C-263/86) [1988] E.C.R. 5365, at [17–19].
[47] *Wirth v Landefhauptstadt Hannover* (C-109/92) [1993] E.C.R. I-6447.

Schindler[48] the CJEU considered that running a lottery could constitute service provision within the meaning of the Treaty. It held that the entertainment or recreational nature of a lottery did not take it outside the scope of the provision of services, nor did the fact that in most Member States the profits made from lotteries could be used only for certain public interest purposes. Moreover, the provision of games of chance over the internet will also engage the freedom to provide services where such providers are established in Member States. As such restrictions on the provision of such services in Member States (even if those restrictions apply without distinction to national providers of services and to those from other Member States) may breach art.56 TFEU when they are liable to prohibit, impede or render less advantageous the activities of a service provider established in another Member State where it lawfully provides similar services.[49] However, as shown by the decision of the CJEU in *Bwin International Ltd v Departamento de Jagos da Santa Casa da Misericordia de Lisboa*[50] national legislation on games of chance is an area in which there are significant moral, religious and cultural differences between the Member States and in which it is for each Member State to determine, in accordance with its own scale of values, what is required in order to ensure that the interests in question are protected. As noted by the CJEU,

> "the Member States are ... free to set the objectives of their policy on betting and gambling and, where appropriate, to define in detail the level of protection sought".[51]

Whilst any restrictive measures must be proportionate,[52] the CJEU in *Bwin International Ltd v Departamento de Jagos da Santa Casa da Misericordia de Lisboa* concluded that art.56 TFEU did not preclude the Portuguese legislation prohibiting operators (which like *Bwin* are established in other Member States in which they lawfully provide similar services), from offering games of chance via the internet within Portugal.[53]

---

[48] *HM Customs and Excise v Schindler* (C-275/92) [1994] E.C.R. I-1039.
[49] See, to that effect, *Säger* (C-76/90) [1991] ECR I-4221, at [12], and *Corsten* (C-58/98) [2000] E.C.R. I-7919, at [33]).
[50] (C-42/07).
[51] At para.59.
[52] *Placanica* (C-360/04) [2007] E.C.R. I-1891 at [48].
[53] See paras 55–73 where the CJEU explains why the legislation (which gave exclusive rights to the Gaming Department of Santa Casa to organise games of chance) was justified, noting inter alia that the main objective of the legislation was "the fight against crime, more specifically the protection of consumers of games of chance against fraud on the part of operators" and that "games of chance involve a high risk of crime or fraud, given the scale of the earnings and the potential winnings on offer to gamblers". For an example of a case in which a national monopoly on sports betting was found not to be justified see the joined cases of *Markus Stoss and others v Wetteraukreis* and *Kulpa Automatenservice Asperg GmbH and others v Land Baden-Württemberg* (C-316/07, C-358/07 to C-360/07, C-409/07 and C-410/07) where the CJEU considered that the public monopoly of the organisation of sporting bets and lotteries in Germany did not pursue the objective of combating the dangers of gambling in a consistent and systematic manner. See also, *Societe Zeturf Ltd v Premier minister* (C-212/08) (clarifying the conditions under which a Member State that was seeking to ensure a particularly high level of consumer protection in the gambling sector may be justified in granting exclusive rights to a single body, subject to strict control by the public authorities, and thereby restricting the freedom to provide services).

7–51 The condition that the service is normally provided for remuneration is not a requirement that the service is paid for by those for whom it is performed. For instance in *Bond van Adverteerders*[54] the CJEU considered that services provided by cable network operators were capable of falling within the Treaty provisions relating to services. This was despite the fact that the service that they provide to broadcasters, namely relaying their programmes, are not generally paid for by the broadcasters themselves but by their subscribers.

(b) *Cross-border element*

7–52 The CJEU has consistently held that the provisions of the Treaty on the Functioning of the European Union on freedom to provide services cannot apply to activities all of which are confined within one Member State. As with the Treaty provisions relating to free movement of persons and the freedom of establishment, those relating to the free movement of services do not apply to purely internal situations in a Member State.[55] Thus there must be a cross-border element to the provision of services. Where such element is present (by for example, the intended provision of services in Germany by a private inspection body of organically-farmed products[56]), Germany cannot require of the service provider that it maintain an establishment there since this would run directly contrary to the freedom to provide services by rendering impossible the provision, in Germany, of the services in question by private bodies established only in other Member States. Nor, indeed, can national legislation in a "receiving" Member State in any way prohibit, impede or render less attractive the provision of services in that Member State lest it will breach art.49 TFEU (subject only to the possibility of justification).[57]

7–53 However, the requirement of the cross-border element can be satisfied without the person or company physically moving across the border to provide the service. The offer of services by telephone to potential recipients in other Member States, for instance, and the provision of those services

---

[54] *Bond van Aderteerders v Netherlands State* (C-352/85) [1988] E.C.R. 2085, at [16].
[55] *Reiseburo Broede v Sandke* (C-3/95) [1996] E.C.R. I-6511; *Gervais* (C-17/94) [1995] E.C.R. I-4353.
[56] *Commission v Germany* (C-404/05) [2007] E.C.R. I-10239, and see to same effect *Commission v Austria* (C-393/05) E.C.R. [2007] I-10195.
[57] See, for example, *Commission v Italy* (C-465/05); as stated at para.18, "national measures which restrict the exercise of the fundamental freedoms guaranteed by the Treaty can be justified only if they satisfy four conditions: they must apply in a non-discriminatory manner; they must be justified by overriding reasons relating to the general interest; they must be suitable for securing the attainment of the objective which they pursue; and they must not go beyond what is necessary in order to attain that objective (see Case C-424/97 *Haim* [2000] E.C.R. I-5123, paragraph 57 and the case-law cited, and *Commission v Greece*, paragraph 49)". See also Case *Commission v France* (C-389/05) (by allowing only authorised artificial insemination centres, with exclusive rights over determined geographical areas, and persons holding an inseminator's licence, the issue of which was subject to the conclusion of an agreement with one of those centres, to provide the service of artificial insemination of bovine animals, France had failed to fulfil its obligations under arts 49 and 56 TFEU).

without actually moving from the Member State in which the provider is established, will fall within the scope of the Treaty.[58]

7–54 Further, the condition of the cross-border element may be fulfilled by either the provider or the recipient of the service moving across a border. Article 56 TFEU is aimed at abolishing restrictions on freedom to provide services by nationals established in one Member State to persons established in other Member States. It may be that in order for those services to be provided, the provider of services would go to the Member State where the recipient of the service is established or the recipient of the service would go to the Member State where the provider of the service is established.[59] Moreover, this is reflected also by the Services Directive[60] which (in para.36 of the preamble) states that the concept of provider

> "should not be limited solely to cross-border service provision within the framework of the free movement of services but should also cover cases in which an operator establishes itself in a Member State in order to develop its service activities there".

(c) *Temporary character*

7–55 Except where the person or company is established, service provision is concerned with the *temporary* pursuit of economic activity in a State. The emphasis on temporary for the purposes of the service provisions in the TFEU means that not every cross-border provision of services will fall within the scope of art.56 TFEU. Where a person has a stable and permanent establishment in both the Member States concerned, only art.49 TFEU concerning the right of establishment is relevant.[61] An activity carried out on a permanent basis, or in any event without a foreseeable limit to its duration does not fall within the scope of the Treaty provisions relating to services.

7–56 The CJEU has held that the temporary nature of the provision of services is to be determined in light of its "duration, regularity, periodicity and continuity".[62]

(d) *Nationality of natural persons*

7–57 In order to benefit from the Treaty provisions relating to provision of services and the secondary legislation giving effect to those provisions, the service provider must be an EU national. The beneficiaries of free movement provisions are considered in Ch.5.

---

[58] *Alpine Investments BV v Minister van Financien* (C-384/93) [1995] E.C.R. I-1141.
[59] *Luisi and Carbone v Minstero del Tesoro* (C-286/82 & 26/83) [1984] E.C.R. 377.
[60] Directive 2006/123/EC of the European Parliament and the Couuncil of December 12, 2006 on services in the internal market.
[61] *Inasti v Kemmler* (C-53/95) [1996] E.C.R. I-703, at [8].
[62] *Gebhard v Consigol dell' Ordine degli Advocat AE Procuratori di Milano* (C-55/94) [1995] E.C.R. I-4165, at [39].

In *Svensson*,[63] the CJEU held the nationality of the intended recipient of the services to be irrelevant to the application of the Treaty provisions on services. According to art.56 TFEU the requirement is only that the recipient is established in another Member State. Although the judgment is somewhat unclear, the nationality of the intended recipient is only relevant when examining the rights of the recipient.

7–58

8. COMPANIES AS SERVICE PROVIDERS

(a) *Nationality of company*

Article 62 TFEU applies the provisions relating to establishment contained in arts 51–54 TFEU to service provision. This has the consequence that companies established in one Member State benefit from the freedom to provide services in another. The nationality of a company is discussed above.[64] The essential requirement is that the company is established and incorporated in a Member State. Under the Treaty provisions on services as extended to companies, it is the freedom to provide services in other Member States, in addition to setting up secondary establishments there,[65] which is of principal interest. Such freedom to provide services implies the abolition of any discrimination against a service provider on account of its nationality or the fact that it is established in a Member State other than that in which the service is provided.[66] In *Commission v Germany*[67] the CJEU considered the discriminatory impact of a bilateral agreement between Germany and Poland[68] under which Germany issued work permits to Polish workers posted[69] temporarily to Germany on works contracts between Polish employers and "an undertaking from the other side" which—as a matter of administrative practice with regard to the application of the agreement—was interpreted as referring *only* to German companies. The effect of this administrative practice was that only undertakings with their registered office or a permanent establishment in Germany could conclude works contracts with a Polish undertaking and thus benefit, by providing services in Germany, from the quota for Polish workers guaranteed under the German-Polish Agreement, notwithstanding the transitional provisions in the Act of Accession. The CJEU considered that this was direct discrimination against service providers established in Member States other than the Federal Republic of Germany who wish to conclude a works contract with a Polish undertaking in order to provide services in Germany. The CJEU held that in applying its discriminatory administrative practice (which could not be justified) Germany had failed to fulfil its obligations under art.56 TFEU.

7–59

---

[63] *Svensson and Gustavsson v Ministre du Logement et de L'Urganisme* (C-484/93) [1995] E.C.R. I-3955.
[64] See paras 7–27 to 7–28.
[65] See paras 7–24 to 7–25 on secondary establishments above.
[66] See, inter alia, *Commission v Germany* (C-490/04), at [83] and the case-law cited.
[67] *Commission (supported by Poland) v Germany* (C-546/07) E.C.R. [2010] I-00438.
[68] Concluded prior to Poland's accession.
[69] As to posted workers generally see paras 7–61 to 7–70, below.

7–60　It can be difficult to distinguish between the provision of services by a company on the one hand and the creation of a secondary establishment by such company on the other. However, it will be the temporary nature of the provision of services that will bring the company's activities within the scope of the Treaty provisions on services. Where a company obtains infrastructure such as office space in another Member State this will tend to suggest more permanent establishment with the consequence that the activity will likely fall within the scope of the establishment provisions in the Treaty rather than the service provisions.

(b) *Personnel of company*

7–61　It is not a requirement of the TFEU provisions that the employees of the company providing the services are EU nationals. If they are EU nationals then they may benefit from a free movement right under Treaty provisions themselves and gain a right of entry and residence in other Member States as workers under art.7(1)(a) of Directive 2004/38. However, the significance of the provisions relating to services under the Treaty on the Functioning of the European Union is that companies which transfer employees who are third country nationals are entitled to do so as a matter of European Union law.

7–62　Employees who are transferred to another Member State for the purpose of providing a service in that State on behalf of a company are known as "posted workers". In a landmark decision in the case of *Rush Portuguese*,[70] the CJEU held that a company established in one Member State is entitled to transfer its third country national workforce to another Member State for the duration of a project to be carried out there.

7–63　*Rush Portuguese* was a building works company with its registered office in Portugal. It entered into a sub-contract with a French company for works to be carried out on several different sites in France. In order to carry out the contract *Rush Portuguese* transferred some of its Portuguese work force to France. The case occurred during the transitional period of Portuguese membership of the European Union and therefore Portuguese workers were not able to rely on free movement rights during that time.[71] The French authorities therefore required that *Rush Portuguese* employees obtained work permits. However, *Rush Portuguese* could still rely on art.56 TFEU because the transitional provisions applied only to derogation from Regulation 1612/68 relating to access to the labour force for workers.[72] The CJEU held that arts 56 and 57 TFEU meant that a company established in Portugal and providing services in the construction industry in France must be able to move its own work force from Portugal for the duration of the contract. The French authorities were therefore not permitted to impose

---

[70] *Rush Portuguesa Lda v ONI* (C-113/89) [1990] E.C.R. I-1417.
[71] For further discussion about transititional provisions on accession see Ch.5.
[72] The same derogation applied as regards the 10 Member States who joined the EU with effect from May 1, 2004 and the further two joining on January 1, 2007. See Ch.5.

conditions such as the obtaining of work permits on the *Rush Portuguese* work force.

Although *Rush Portuguese* occurred during the transitional period of Portugal's entry to the Union, the principles established in it apply to any company registered in a Member State wishing to provide services in another Member State. This right to post workers belongs to the company and not the employee. It is dependent on the employee being posted by the company to another Member State to fulfil a contract. 7–64

The CJEU judgment in *Vander Elst*[73] makes clear that it is a condition precedent to the application of the principle that the employee can move under the umbrella of the service providing company that the employee should have been lawfully and "habitually employed" by that company prior to being posted (although not necessarily in another Member State[74]). The nationality of the employee is irrelevant. In *Vander Elst* the employer was established in Belgium as a specialist demolition business. Some of his employees were Moroccan nationals who were legally resident and permitted to work in Belgium. The employer sent Belgian and Moroccan staff to fulfil a contract on a demolition site in France. The French authorities stated that the Moroccans required work permits. The CJEU held that the requirement to obtain a work permit in such situation went beyond the permissible restrictions on service provision under the TFEU. The CJEU considered that work permits are intended to regulate access to the French labour market and are therefore not necessary for employees of a company who would be temporarily present only and who would return to the home State of the company on completion of the work. 7–65

Following the CJEU's decisions in *Rush Portuguese* and *Vander Elst*, the Posted Workers Directive[75] was adopted in 1996. The objective of the Directive is to avoid social dumping between companies from the various Member States and to ensure that minimum rights are guaranteed for workers posted by their employers to work in another Member State. The basic principle is that working conditions and pay in a Member State should 7–66

---

[73] *Vander Elst v Office des Migrations Internationales* (C-43/93) [1994] E.C.R. I-03803.
[74] On the facts of both *Vander Elst* and *Rush Portuguesa* the employees had been employed in the Member State in which their employers were established. However, the test of "habitual employment" could be satisfied if the posted worker had been previously employed by the company in one of its branches in a non-EU Member State provided that the company itself is established in a Member State (other than the Member State to which the worker is to be posted). More difficult is the question of how long an employee must work for the employer prior to posting in order to be regarded as being in "habitual employment". This will turn on the facts of each case and depend on various factors including importantly the terms of the employment contract and the length of time that the employee has been employed. It is suggested that the test could be satisfied in a matter of months. In *Commission v Luxembourg* (C-445/03) and *Commission v Germany* Case (C-244/04) the CJEU considered situations in which Luxembourg and Germany imposed on service providers established in another Member State wishing to deploy in their territories third country national workers, the requirement that they had worked for the undertaking for *six* and *12* months respectively. In both cases the CJEU held the restriction to be unlawful.
[75] Directive 96/71 concerning the posting of workers in the framework of the provision of services [1997] O.J. L18/1.

be applicable both to workers from that State, and those from other Member States posted to work there.[76] The Directive covers undertakings established in a Member State which, in the framework of the transnational provision of services, post workers to the territory of another Member State. It does not, however, set out the rights of companies to move staff, or the entry or residence conditions that apply to such workers. (These are taken from the guidelines of the CJEU in the two landmark cases.)

7–67   In *Commission v Luxembourg*[77] the CJEU considered the Commission's claim that Luxembourg had failed to fulfil its obligations under art.56 TFEU by requiring an individual or collective work permit from a service provider established in another Member State (where that provider sought to post lawfully resident third country national workers to Luxembourg), by making the issue of that permit subject to considerations connected to the job market, the existence of a contract of indefinite duration and of previous employment with the same provider for at least six months and by requiring that the provider give a minimum bank guarantee of LUF 60,000 (€1,487.36). The CJEU considered it "indisputable" that the conditions to be satisfied were, because of the administrative and financial burdens that they represented, liable to impede the planned deployment and, consequently, the provision of services by the undertaking.[78] Referring to *Vander Elst* the CJEU recalled that to require a work permit was a restriction on the freedom to provide services. The CJEU went on to consider whether the restrictions were justified by a public-interest objective and (if so) necessary in order effectively and by appropriate means to pursue such an objective. Luxembourg had relied on reasons of social welfare and stability in the labour market as justification. Whilst acknowledging that overriding public interest reasons which had been recognised by the CJEU included the protection of workers,[79] the present work licensing mechanism was not an appropriate means since it involved "formalities and periods ... liable to discourage the free provision of services through the medium of workers who are nationals of non-member countries".[80] The CJEU continued:

> 31. A measure which would be just as effective whilst being less restrictive than the measure at issue here would be an obligation imposed on a service-providing undertaking to report beforehand to the local authorities on the presence of one or

---

[76] See, for example, *Commission v Germany* (C-341/02) (in which the CJEU declared that by failing to recognise certain allowances and supplements paid by employers established in other Member States to their employees in the construction industry who are posted to Germany as constituent elements of the minimum wage Germany had failed to fulfill its obligations under art.3 of Directive 96/71/EC) and *Commission v Luxembourg* (C-319/06) (in which the CJEU held that having inter alia failed fully to transpose art.3(1)(a), Luxembourg had failed to fulfil its obligations under art.3(1) of Directive 96/71, read in conjunction with art.10 thereof, and arts 49 EC and 50 EC). See also, *Commission v Germany* (C-490/04) (Germany failed to fulfil its obligations under art. 56 TFEU by requiring foreign undertakings to pay into German holiday pay fund for their posted workers, to have employment contracts and other documents translated into German and to give prior notification each time a worker started a new job on a building site at the request of the user of his services).
[77] *Commission v Luxembourg* (C-445/03) [2004] E.C.R. I-10191.
[78] para.23 ibid. (see, to that effect, (C-49/98), (C-50/98), (C-52/98) to (C-54/98) and (C-68/98 to C-71/98) *Finalarte* [2001] E.C.R. I-7831, at [30]).
[79] See *Finalarte* (above) and *Portugaia Construções* (C-164/99) [2002] E.C.R. I-787.
[80] At para.30.

more deployed workers, the anticipated duration of their presence and the provision or provisions of services justifying the deployment. It would enable those authorities to monitor compliance with Luxembourg social welfare legislation during the deployment while at the same time taking account of the obligations by which the undertaking is already bound under the social welfare legislation applicable in the Member State of origin.

32. Moreover, making the granting of a collective work permit subject to the requirement that an employment contract of indefinite duration must have been in existence between the workers and their undertaking of origin for at least six months before their deployment to Luxembourg goes beyond what is required for the objective of social welfare protection as a necessary condition for providing services through the deployment of workers who are nationals of non-member countries.

As regards Luxembourg's concern of flooding of the labour market with third country national workers, posted workers do not purport to gain access to the labour market as they return to their country of origin or residence after the completion of their work. Whilst a Member State can check whether the posting undertaking is not availing itself of the freedom to provide services for a purpose other than the accomplishment of the service in question, such checks must

7–68

> "observe the limits imposed by Community law and in particular those stemming from the freedom to provide services, which cannot be rendered illusory and whose exercise may not be made subject to the discretion of the authorities".[81]

The CJEU was unhesitatingly of the view that Luxembourg had failed to fulfil its obligations under art.56 TFEU.

In *Commission v Germany*[82] the CJEU again considered a work visa regime applied to posted workers. The detailed conditions of the regime (to be checked in advance by the German diplomatic posts in the "posting" State) included prior employment for at least a year of the third country national worker, the lawfulness of such prior employment and the employee's membership of a social security scheme. The German Government had sought to justify the conditions on grounds relating to the prevention of abuse of the freedom to provide services, the protection of workers and legal certainty. The checks were said to be justified since they were intended to implement the requirement of European Union law that the workers concerned were "lawfully and habitually" employed in the provider's Member State of establishment, within the meaning of the judgment in *Vander Elst*, before being posted in Germany. Again the CJEU was unhesitatingly of the view that Germany had failed to fulfil its obligations under art.56 TFEU. The CJEU declared that, by not confining itself to making the posting of third country national workers subject to a simple prior declaration by the

7–69

---

[81] At para.40.
[82] *Commission v Germany* (C-244/04) [2006] I-00885.

undertaking and by requiring that they have been employed for at least a year by that undertaking, the Federal Republic of Germany has failed to fulfil its obligations under art.49 EC.[83]

7–70 In summary, the ability of an EU national company to post its employees to other Member States in the exercise of its freedom to provide services can have the consequence of giving some third country national employees an ability to move within the Union with a degree of freedom. However, such employees must have been lawfully and habitually employed by the company (even if not in another Member State[84]) and it is to be emphasised that Member States will be entitled to take steps (so long as they do no render the company's exercise of its right illusory) to guard against abuse. As such the ability of an EU national company to post its workers will not provide a solution to the immigration problems of a third country national who is unlawfully present in a Member State.[85]

9. Recipients of Services

(a) Concept of recipients of services

7–71 As outlined above,[86] art.6 of Directive 2004/38 plainly enables Union citizens and their family members to receive services throughout the Union in the exercise of their right of residence for up to three months without conditions or formalities. As discussed below, this on any view significantly reduces the importance of the concept in free movement terms. Further, the Services Directive includes within its scope the recipients as well as the providers of services. And moreover, the CJEU has consistently stated that Union citizens have the right to enter the territory of other Member States in the exercise of the freedom to provide services which "is enjoyed both by providers and by recipients of services".[87] In order to enable services to be provided, the person providing the service may go to the Member State where the recipient is established. Alternatively, the recipient may go to the Member State in which the provider of the service is established in order to receive the service. The movement of the service provider to another Member State is expressly provided for in art.57 TFEU. However, the CJEU has held that the movement of the recipient of services is a "necessary corollary" of the right contained in art.57 TFEU "which fulfils the objective

---

[83] See also, *Commission v Belgium* (C-219/08) (a requirement that the service provider furnished a simple prior declaration certifying that the situation of the workers concerned was lawful was a measure which, in principle, did not exceed what was necessary to prevent the abuse to which the implementation of the freedom to provide services may give rise).
[84] See fn.74, above.
[85] For example, a third country national unlawfully present in the UK could not establish a company in Ireland and rely on that company's right to provide services in the UK to employ them in the UK as a "posted worker" and thereby solve their immigration problems. The authors are aware that this was a suggestion being made by some immigration firms in the UK in 2008–2009. See *R (ota Lee Linglow and others) v SSHO* [2010] EWCA Civ 4.
[86] See para.7–44.
[87] *Vander Elst v Office des Migrations Internationales* (C-43/93), at [13].

(b) *Personal scope of recipients of services*

Previously in order to obtain the right of entry and residence provided for in (the now repealed) Directive 73/148 and the protection against discrimination envisaged by the Treaty, the recipient of services had to be a Union citizen or the family member of such a person. The Directive itself was quite clear on this issue[89] and the CJEU had never extended free movement rights to third country nationals (other than as family members). 7–72

However, as noted already the Services Directive[90] changes this making clear in para.36 of the preamble that the concept of recipient "should also cover third country nationals who already benefit from rights conferred upon them by [Union] acts". Moreoever, the risk of ambiguity lies in the fact that the nationality of the recipient of services is not relevant if it is the *provider's* rights that are under consideration, since those rights are only dependant on the provider of services providing them to a person established in another Member State[91] (the nationality of the recipient being irrelevant). 7–73

There is no restriction on the type of services that the recipient should be travelling to receive in the other Member State. In the case of *Luisi and Carbone*[92] the CJEU held that tourists, persons receiving medical treatment and persons travelling for the purposes of education or business are to be regarded as recipients of services. In *Bickel and Franz*[93] the CJEU reiterated that a person visiting another Member State falls within the scope of art.56 TFEU on the following grounds: 7–74

> "Article [56 TFEU] therefore covers all nationals of Member States who, independently of freedoms guaranteed by the Treaty, visit another Member State where they *intend or are likely to receive services*".

The CJEU's statement would appear to negate any need for a visitor to establish the particular services that will be received in the course of any visit.

Since an essential element of service provision is remuneration, a person will not be regarded as a recipient of services unless the service which is being received is paid for. Such payment need not be made by the recipient directly. However, in *Humbel*, the CJEU held that state school education did not fulfil the requirements of the Treaty since it was not "normally for 7–75

---

[88] *Luisi and Carbone v Minstero del Tesoro* (C-286/82 & 26/83) [1984] E.C.R. 377.
[89] art.1.
[90] Directive 2006/123/EC of the European Parliament and the Council of December 12, 2006 on services in the internal market.
[91] See paras 7–52 to 7–54, above.
[92] *Luisi and Carbone v Minstero del Tesoro* (C-286/82 & 26/83) [1984] E.C.R. 377.
[93] *Bickel and Franz* (C-274/96) [1998] E.C.R. I-7637 (at para.15).

remuneration", even if parents do make some financial contribution to the school.[94]

7–76　Finally, in reality it is to be emphasised that for Union citizens and their family members art.6 of Directive 2004/38 renders the concept of "recipients of services" largely meaningless for free movement purposes. The right of entry for up to three months without conditions or formalities given by art.6 means that the *purpose* for which such persons travel to other Member States is simply irrelevant (although such right of residence endures only as long as such persons "do not become an unreasonable burden on the social assistance system of the host Member State"[95]). And moreover, that is not to say that recipients of services would not have an interest in such benefits given to them by the Services Directive (such as the prohibition of discriminatory conditions based on the nationality or residence of the service recipient).

---

[94] *Belgium v Humbel* (C-263/86) [1988] E.C.R. 5365. See para.7–49, above.
[95] art.14 of Directive 2004/38.

CHAPTER 8

THE ECONOMICALLY INACTIVE

This chapter considers the position of those who exercise their right to free movement without engaging in economic activity. Three categories are considered: the self-sufficient person exercising a general right of residence; the retired person and the student. Together these free movers are referred to as the economically inactive.

1. INTRODUCTION: BEYOND THE ECONOMICALLY ACTIVE

The foundations of the European Economic Community as reflected by the Treaty of Rome were principally concerned with the free movement of persons who wished to further the aim of the EEC through economic activity. Thus the Treaty itself only referred to free movement rights for workers and the self-employed. Secondary legislation gave effect those free movement rights.[1] 8–01

In 1979 the Commission first put forward a proposal to extend the right of residence to other categories of person who were not engaged in any economic activity. Ten years later the original proposal culminated in the adoption by the European Council on June 28, 1990 of Directives 90/364 on the right of residence, 90/365 on the right of residence of employees and self-employed persons who have ceased their occupational activity, and 90/366 on the right of residence for students.[2] 8–02

This extension in secondary legislation of the categories of persons entitled to the right of residence has been formally enshrined at Treaty level with the insertion of art.8a into the Maastricht Treaty (subsequently art.18 EC Treaty and now art.21 Treaty on the Functioning of the European Union), which states that 8–03

> "every citizen of the Union shall have the right to ... reside freely within the territory of the Member States, subject to the limitations and conditions laid down in [the Treaties] and by the measures adopted to give [them] effect."[3]

Indeed as the European Commission points out whilst the right of a national of a Member State to reside in the territory of another Member State of the European Community was originally subject to that person engaging in an economic activity in that State: 8–04

---

[1] Previously Regulation 1612/68, Directives 68/360, 64/221, 73/148; see now Regulation 492/2011 and provisions of Directive 2004/38/EC of April 29, 2004 ("Citizens' Directive").
[2] This was later replaced by Directive 93/96.
[3] Words in square brackets reflect amendments in art.21 TFEU.

"such a state of affairs could not be allowed to continue indefinitely, because it did not fully comply with one of the objectives laid down in Article 3c of the Treaty of Rome ('the abolition, as between Member States, of obstacles to the free movement of ... persons'), nor did it meet the political aspiration expressed at the Paris Summit in 1974 to move towards a 'citizens' Europe'".

8–05 Prior to the legislative extension of free movement rights to the economically inactive, the CJEU had in fact already begun to recognise their rights, particularly where students were concerned. In 1985 the CJEU considered that the mobility of students for vocational training was so important to the aims of the Treaty that, despite the fact that a student did not satisfy the requirements of existing free movement legislation in so far as she could not be considered a worker, such a person should fall within the scope of the Treaty.[4]

2. General Requirement of the Provisions Relating to the Economically Inactive

8–06 As discussed in Ch.4, art.21 TFEU grants to all EU nationals the right to move and reside in other Member States. However, the provision makes such right subject to the limitations and conditions laid down in the Treaties and secondary legislation. The secondary legislation concerning the economically inactive includes an express condition regarding self-sufficiency which makes clear that a person wishing to exercise the right to move as an economically inactive person must be self-sufficient. Furthermore, such a person is required to obtain comprehensive sickness insurance.

8–07 As discussed in detail in Ch.4 the extent to which the limitations and conditions contained this secondary legislation can be maintained following inclusion of art.21 in the Treaty on the Functioning of the European Union is continually evolving.

8–08 The decisions of the CJEU in the cases of *Baumbast*[5] and *Grzelczk*[6] make clear that the limitations and conditions placed on the economically inactive remain relevant and have not been made entirely redundant by art.21 TFEU. However, the CJEU has categorically rejected the suggestion that failure to meet all the conditions laid down in the legislation relating to the economically inactive should automatically lead to the end of the right of residence. The conditions now laid down in Directive 2004/38[7] therefore cannot be treated as absolutes that must be strictly met at all times by all beneficiaries of Directive 2004/38.

---

[4] *Gravier v City of Liege* (293/83) [1985] E.C.R. 593.
[5] *Baumbast and R. v the Secretary of State for the Home Department* (C-413/99) [2002] E.C.R. I-7091.
[6] *Grzelczyk v Centre Public d'Aide Sociale d'Ottignies-Louvain-la-Neuve* (C-184/99) [2001] E.C.R. I-6193.
[7] Directive 2004/38/EC of April 29, 2004 ("Citizens' Directive") repealing Directives 90/364, 90/365 and 93/96.

In *Grzelczyk*,[8] for instance, the CJEU recognised that a Member State could **8–09** conclude that a student applying for social assistance no longer met the conditions to which their right of residence was subject and could accordingly require them to leave. However, the CJEU held that such a decision must be made "within the limits imposed by [European Union] law" and that "in no case may such measures become the automatic consequence of a student who is a national of another Member State having recourse to the host Member State's social assistance system".

In *Baumbast*[9] the CJEU was referred a question by an English tribunal **8–10** about the right of residence of a Union citizen who had not met the requirement in Directive 90/364 to have sickness insurance for all risks.[10] The CJEU concluded that it would be a disproportionate interference with the exercise of the right of residence for the host Member State to withhold a residence permit on the ground that the healthcare insurance of the person concerned did not cover emergency treatment. The CJEU held that any decision about withholding a residence permit must be made in compliance with the limits imposed by European Union law and in accordance with the general principles of Union law, in particular the proportionality principle.

At the present stage of development of European Union law the inclusion of **8–11** art.21 TFEU has not abolished all limitations or conditions on the freedom of movement. However, the application of any such limitations or conditions is subject to the general principles of European Union law and furthermore to judicial review. The principle of proportionality and the language of Directive 2004/38 for the economically inactive permit Member States to ensure that the beneficiaries do not become "unreasonable burdens". However, Member States must accept a:

> "certain degree of financial solidarity between nationals of a host Member State and nationals of other Member States, particularly if the difficulties which a beneficiary of the right of residence encounters are temporary".[11]

(a) *The concept of self-sufficiency*

(i) *The general right of residence and the retired*

Articles 7 and 8 of Directive 2004/38 include the following provisions **8–12** relating to the general right of residence and the retired:

---

[8] *Grzelczyk v Centre Public d'Aide Sociale d'Ottignies-Louvain-la-Neuve* (C-184/99) [2001] E.C.R. I-6193.
[9] *Baumbast and R. v the Secretary of State for the Home Department* (C-413/99) [2002] E.C.R. I-7091.
[10] See now art.7 Directive 2004/38/EC of April 29, 2004 ("Citizens' Directive") referring to "comprehensive sickness insurance cover".
[11] *Grzelczyk v Centre Public d'Aide Sociale d'Ottignies-Louvain-la-Neuve* (C-184/99) [2001] E.C.R. I-6193, at [44].

Article 7

Right of residence for more than three months

1. All Union citizens shall have the right of residence on the territory of another Member State for a period of longer than three months if they:

   b) have sufficient resources for themselves and their family members not to become a burden on the social assistance system of the host Member State during their period of residence and have comprehensive sickness insurance cover in the host Member State;

Article 8

Administrative formalities for Union citizens

4. Member States may not lay down a fixed amount which they regard as 'sufficient resources', but they must take into account the personal situation of the person concerned. In all cases this amount shall not be higher than the threshold below which nationals of the host Member State become eligible for social assistance, or, where this criterion is not applicable, higher than the minimum social security pension paid by the host Member State.

8–13　Prior to repeal by Directive 2004/38, the secondary legislation dealt in separate directives with the general right of residence (Directive 90/364) and the retired (Directive 90/365). As regards the test of self-sufficiency to be met Directive 2004/38 draws no such distinction. However, as will be seen in measuring the threshold of self-sufficiency[12] this legislative history is reflected by the references to both the threshold below which nationals become eligible for social assistance in the host Member State and the minimum social security pension paid by the host Member State (the former applying to those previously catered for by Directive 90/364, the latter covering those previously catered for by Directive 90/365). It is in this context that we maintain the distinction, albeit of little significance.

8–14　The concept of self-sufficiency is explained in Directive 2004/38 itself.[13] Article 7(1)(b) gives the right of residence for longer than three months[14] to Union citizens who "have sufficient resources for themselves and their family members not to become a burden on the social assistance system of the host Member State during their period of residence". Article 8(4) states that Member States may not lay down a fixed amount which they regard as "sufficient resources", but "they must take into account the personal situation of the person concerned" and "in all cases this amount shall not be higher than the threshold below which nationals of the host Member State become eligible for social assistance, or, where this criterion is not applicable, higher than the minimum social security pension paid by the host Member State." (As indicated, the criterion would not be applicable where the person seeking to enjoy the right of residence is retired.) This naturally

---

[12] art.8.4 of Directive 2004/38.
[13] Directive 2004/38/EC of April 29, 2004. Directive 90/364 (the general right of residence) and Directive 90/365 (retired persons) were repealed by Directive 2004/38 (art.38.2).
[14] art.6 provides a right of residence for Union citizens (and their family members) for up to three months "without any conditions or any formalities other than the requirement to hold a valid identity card or passport".

makes the level of resources required variable from one Member State to another since levels at which social assistance is granted or social security pension paid are not uniform across the Member States. This lack of uniformity is not surprising in the light of both the lack of social security harmonisation at EU level[15] and the variable cost of living across the Member States.

8–15 In *Commission v Italy*[16] the CJEU considered a situation where Italy granted more favourable treatment to persons who had previously been gainfully employed falling within the scope of Directive 90/365 (retired persons) than to beneficiaries of Directive 90/364 (the general right of residence). Italy had required the families of those falling within the general right of residence Directive to demonstrate that they had more resources than families falling within the retired persons Directive.[17] Overruling the Commission, the CJEU held that this differentiation was permissible since Member States have a degree of discretion in setting the amounts required. According to the CJEU the higher amount required for those falling within the general right of residence was not excessive. This is a somewhat surprising decision in view of the principle of equal treatment. The CJEU considered that the difference was permissible, based on its view that the Member State had not exceeded its "latitude" in having in place a regime that is more favourable to the family members of retired persons than to the beneficiaries of Directive 90/364. However, at issue under both Directives was the same question: were resources sufficient to avoid the person becoming a burden on the host Member State's social security system. It is difficult to see how the sufficiency of resources can vary as between different groups of people, particularly given the need for both to have in place comprehensive sickness insurance (which would meet a concern that retired people may need more resources in the event of becoming more susceptible to illness, being older). The "latitude" to be given to a Member State must relate to that State's assessment of the necessary level of resources for anyone to survive in their State. There is no reason why that assessment should differ as between either Directive's beneficiaries.

8–16 Repeal of Directives 90/364 and 90/365 and their substitution with art.7 of Directive 2004/38 perhaps makes this particular problem more theoretical than real, particularly since the only Member State which provided for differentiation was Italy. Italy had in any event amended its legislation to abolish the differentiation before the CJEU gave judgment in *Commission v Italy*. However, art.8(4) on its face draws distinction between the thresholds by reference to the point at which nationals of the host Member State become eligible for social assistance on the one hand and (if not an applicable criterion) the minimum social security pension paid by the host Member State on the other. If such thresholds are different in a Member

---

[15] For further discussion see Ch.12.
[16] *Commission v Italy* (C-424/98) [2000] E.C.R. I-4001.
[17] The Commission has understood the different level of resources required to be one third more. According to the CJEU, this calculation by the Commission was wrong. Italian legislation in fact required resources three times higher in respect of beneficiaries of Directive 90/364. See *Commission v Italy* (C-424/98) [2000] E.C.R. I-4001, at [22].

8–17 Directive 2004/38 is silent as to what the *source* of the resources referred to therein might be. Resources could come from the income of a spouse or child accompanying the Union citizen or indeed from any other family member, whether accompanying the Union citizen or not. The accompanying spouse and dependent children are entitled to take up employment or self-employment in the host Member State even where they are not Union citizens. The income derived from such activity can be included in considering the resources of the family as a whole.

State then this would create precisely the situation vouchsafed by the CJEU in *Commission v Italy*.

8–18 The Commission has taken issue with a number of Member States which have required that the Union citizen has sufficient resources of their own or originating only from a spouse or a child in interpreting Directives 90/364 and 90/365 prior to their repeal[18] The Commission considered that this added a supplementary condition to the Directives that did not exist on their face. The Commission considered (plainly correctly in view of subsequent case law developments considered below) that this was contrary to those Directives which did not exclude the possibility of sufficient resources coming from a third person such as a parent or unmarried partner. One Member State, Sweden, even went so far as to require that the sufficient resources be personal to the EU national and that such requirement could not be satisfied by reference to the resources provided by any family member, whether a spouse or child, or any other third party. Following intervention by the Commission, Sweden removed this condition from its legislation.[19]

8–19 The position as regards the permissible *source* of resources is beyond doubt following the decisions of the CJEU in *Zhu and Chen*[20] and *Commission v Belgium*.[21] In *Zhu and Chen* the CJEU considered the terms of art.1(1) of Directive 90/364 which required the Union citizen to "*have* sufficient resources" (the phrase being identical to that contained in art.7(1)(b) of Directive 2004/38). At paras 30 and 31 of its judgment the CJEU stated:

> "30. According to the very terms of Article 1(1) of Directive 90/364, it is sufficient for the nationals of Member States to 'have' the necessary resources, and that provision lays down no requirement whatsoever as to their origin.
>
> 31. The correctness of that interpretation is reinforced by the fact that provisions laying down a fundamental principle such as that of the free movement of persons must be interpreted broadly."

The CJEU therefore held that an interpretation of the condition concerning the sufficiency of resources to mean that the person concerned must have

---

[18] By issuing reasoned opinions, prior to taking action before the CJEU, Second Commission Report to the Council and Parliament on the implementation of Directives 90/364, 90/365 and 93/96 (right of residence), COM (2003) 101 final, p.12.
[19] See *Commission v Italy* (C-424/98) [2000] E.C.R. I-4001.
[20] *Zhu and Chen* (C-200/02) [2004] E.C.R. I- 9925.
[21] *Commission v Belgium* (C-408/03) [2006] E.C.R. I-02647.

such resources[22] and may not rely on the resources of a member of the family accompanying them

> "would add to that condition, as formulated in that directive, a requirement as to the origin of the resources which, not being necessary for the attainment of the objective pursued, namely the protection of the public finances of the Member States, would constitute a disproportionate interference with the exercise of the fundamental right of freedom of movement and of residence upheld by Article 18 EC [now art.21 TFEU]".[23]

Thus the condition is met where the financial resources are provided by a member of the family of the citizen of the Union.

In *Commission v Belgium* the CJEU considered whether the same conclusion would arise where a citizen of the Union intends to rely on the income of a partner who resides in the host Member State. The case also concerned Directive 90/364. The Commission's complaint was that whilst Belgium took into account the personal resources of the Union citizen or the resources of the spouse or child of that citizen, it excluded consideration of other third parties in the absence of a legal link obliging the third party to provide for the beneficiary. Belgium sought to justify the existence of such a legal link on the basis that 8–20

> "if account were taken of the income of a person whose link with the citizen of the Union was not legally defined and could, therefore, be severed easily, the risk of that citizen becoming a burden for the social security system of the host Member State after a certain time would be all the greater".[24]

The CJEU was unimpressed. The CJEU considered the requirement of such legal link to be disproportionate in going beyond what was necessary to protect the public finances in the host Member State. According to the CJEU, the loss of sufficient resources is always an underlying risk, whether those resources are personal or come from a third party, even where that third party has undertaken to support the holder of the residence permit financially. Thus,

> "the source of those resources has no automatic effect on the risk of such a loss arising, as the materialisation of such a risk is the result of a change of circumstances."

In sum the factual enquiry is whether the persons concerned "have" sufficient resources, without regard to the source of such resources. As was stated by the CJEU in *Zhu and Chen*, the provision lays down "no requirement *whatsoever* as to their origin" (emphasis added). Indeed, in the Opinion of Advocate General Mengozzi in *Eind*[25] "therefore, even a social security benefit may, in the abstract, represent a source of 'sufficient 8–21

---

[22] As suggested by the UK and Irish governments.
[23] At para.33.
[24] At para.45.
[25] *Minister voor Vreemdelingenzaken en Integratie v Rachel Nataly Geradina Eind* (C-291/05) [2007] E.C.R. I-10719.

resources'".[26] As pointed out by the Commission,[27] the notion of "sufficient resources" must be interpreted in the light of the objective of the Directive, which is to facilitate free movement, as long as the beneficiaries of the right of residence do not become an unreasonable burden on the social assistance system of the host Member State. Finally, it is to be recalled that following the decision of the CJEU in *Zambrano v Office National de l'Emploi*[28] it is not just the Union citizens' spouse and children whose income from work might be relied on to establish the sufficiency of resources. In that case the Union citizens were children with Belgian nationality dependant on their third country national father. The CJEU held that art.20 TFEU was to be interpreted as precluding a Member State from refusing a third country national (upon whom their minor European Union citizens are dependent) a right of residence in the Member State of residence and nationality of those children, and from refusing to grant a work permit to that third country national, in so far as such decisions deprive those children of the genuine enjoyment of the substance of the rights attaching to the status of European Union citizen. Although this is about citizenship rights nevertheless following *Zambrano* there can be no doubt that parents should be permitted to work, and their income taken into account to establish self-sufficiency, if to do otherwise would mean the Union citizen would be forced to leave the EU altogether.

(ii) *Students*

8–22 The concept of self-sufficiency for students is articulated differently. Article 7(1)(c) of Directive 2004/38 (as with art.7(1)(b) considered above) refers expressly to the requirement that they "have sufficient resources for themselves and their family members not to become a burden on the social assistance system of the host Member State during their period of residence". And the limitation contained in art.8(4) similarly applies to students since it lays down an approach to be taken to the interpretation of "sufficient resources" rather than any particular category of person enjoying such right of residence. However, whereas the enquiry of persons exercising the general right of residence will focus on whether they have sufficient resources (as seen, if not personally at least available to them), for students they must "*assure* the relevant national authority, by means of a declaration or by such equivalent means as they may choose, that they have sufficient resources" (emphasis added).[29]

---

[26] However, in Advocate General Mengozzi's opinion (at para.141)
"in the case of a benefit paid to one of its nationals by the State from which, under the same article, a right of residence is claimed, that benefit cannot be taken into consideration in the abovementioned context if the grant of it presupposes that the beneficiary is resident in the territory of that State".
[27] COM/2009/0313 final, Communication from the Commission to the European Parliament and the Council on guidance for better transposition and application of Directive 2004/38/EC on the right of citizens of the Union and their family members to move and reside freely within the territory of the Member States.
[28] *Ruiz Zambrano v Office National de l'Emploi (ONEM)* (C-34/09) [2011] E.C.R. I-0000.
[29] art.7(1)(c) Directive 2004/38 refers. See further Ch.10.

(b) *Sickness insurance*

8–23 For those exercising the general right of residence (including the retired) (art.7(1)(b)) and for students (art.7(1)(c)) of Directive 2004/38 requires that the Union citizens themselves and their families "have comprehensive sickness insurance cover in the host Member State". The repealed directives[30] had referred to the need to be covered by sickness insurance in respect of *all* risks in the host Member State. Certainly the change in wording ought not to be interpreted any more onerously than was the requirement that *all* risks be covered (which on its face was arguably a higher standard). As pointed out by the Commission,[31] any insurance cover, private or public, contracted in the host Member State or elsewhere, is acceptable in principle, as long as it provides comprehensive coverage and does not create a burden on the public finances of the host Member State. In protecting their public finances while assessing the comprehensiveness of sickness insurance cover, Member States must act in compliance with the limits imposed by Community law and in accordance with the principle of proportionality.[32]

8–24 Whilst Directive 2004/38 does not specify the exact form that this sickness insurance should take nor the meaning of "comprehensive", a form of sickness insurance which provides cover for *general* health risks should suffice, particularly when it is borne in mind that emergency treatment will be covered by the provisions of Regulation 883/2004.[33] This interpretation is supported by the CJEU in *Baumbast*.[34] The European Health Insurance Card offers such comprehensive cover when the Union citizen concerned does not move residence to the host Member State and has the intention to return, e.g. studies or posting to another Member State.[35] And pensioners fulfil the condition of comprehensive sickness insurance cover if they are entitled to health treatment on behalf of the Member State which pays their pension.[36]

8–25 Under the reciprocal arrangements for the provision of health care contained in Regulation 883/04, the beneficiaries of that Regulation are guaranteed the right to receive sickness benefits in kind provided by the

---

[30] Directives 90/364 and 90/365.
[31] COM/2009/0313 final, Communication from the Commission to the European Parliament and the Council on guidance for better transposition and application of Directive 2004/38/EC on the right of citizens of the Union and their family members to move and reside freely within the territory of the Member State (para.2.3.2).
[32] *Baumbast and R. v the Secretary of State for the Home Department* (C-413/99) [2002] E.C.R. I-7091.
[33] Replacing Regulation 1408/71; see Title III, Chapter 1 (sickness, maternity and equivalent paternity benefits), art.19 Regulation 883/2004. See Ch.13.
[34] *Baumbast and R. v the Secretary of State for the Home Department* (C-413/99) [2002] E.C.R. I-7091 (considering Regulation 1408/71).
[35] COM/2009/0313 final, Communication from the Commission to the European Parliament and the Council on guidance for better transposition and application of Directive 2004/38/EC on the right of citizens of the Union and their family members to move and reside freely within the territory of the Member States (para.2.3.2).
[36] COM/2009/0313 final, Communication from the Commission to the European Parliament and the Council on guidance for better transposition and application of Directive 2004/38/EC on the right of citizens of the Union and their family members to move and reside freely within the territory of the Member States (para.2.3.2).

institution of the Member State of residence at the expense of the Member State of origin. The beneficiaries include workers and those who were in employment previously. In these circumstances it would be unnecessary for the beneficiaries of the Regulation to obtain the sickness insurance required by the Directives on economically inactive persons.[37]

8–26 For those who do not benefit from Regulation 883/04, there would be a need to obtain sickness insurance. However, a failure to obtain a sickness insurance which covers *all* risks could not automatically result in the denial of the right of residence since such a result could "amount to a disproportional interference with the exercise of that right".[38]

3. THE GENERAL RIGHT OF RESIDENCE

8–27 In order to enjoy the general right of residence as a self-sufficient economically inactive person, Union citizens need only demonstrate that they have sufficient resources to avoid becoming a burden on the social assistance system of the host Member State and comprehensive sickness insurance cover there.

8–28 Directive 90/364, which had introduced the general right of residence for the economically self-sufficient but inactive, was intended to provide those EU nationals who were not covered by the provisions of any other Treaty provision or secondary legislation with rights of residence. Although now replaced by provisions in Directive 2004/38 discussed above, it is to be noted that the Directive's implementation was both largely successful in the Member States and non-contentious.

4. THE RETIRED PERSON

8–29 There are two categories of retired person covered by European Union law. The first category includes persons who have reached retirement age in a host Member State having been a worker or self-employed person in that state for the preceding 12 months and having resided in that State continuously for at least three years. Previously dealt with in Regulation 1251/70 (for workers) and Directive 75/34 (for the self-employed), they are provided for now by art.17 of Directive 2004/38.[39] This category of retired person is dealt with in detail in Ch.10.

---

[37] art.19(1) of Regulation 1408/71 [see now Title III, chapter 1 of Regulation 883/04] provided for the repayment of health care costs by the Member State of origin to the host Member State. See *Baumbast and R. v the Secretary of State for the Home Department* (C-413/99) [2002] E.C.R. I-7091.

[38] *Baumbast and R. v The Secretary for the Home Department* (C-413/99) [2002] E.C.R. I-7091, at [93].

[39] Directive 75/34 was repealed by art.38.2 of Directive 2004/38 with effect from April 30, 2006; Directive 2004/38 did not repeal Regulation 1251/70. This was repealed (also with effect from April 30, 2006) by Comission Regulation (EC) No 635/2006 of April 25, 2006.

The second category includes persons who have ceased their economic activity either as employed or self-employed persons, but who may not have resided in the territory of another Member State before retirement. Such persons were previously covered by Directive 90/365 and are now provided for in arts 7 and 8 of Directive 2004/38 discussed above. In order to qualify for the right of residence they must have sufficient resources in the sense there described. If pensioners and not persons to whom a minimum subsistence benefit would be payable, the level of necessary resources will be determined by reference to the minimum level of social security pension payable in the host Member State. This contrasts the previous position under Directive 90/365 which required that receipt be of an invalidity or early retirement pension, or old age benefit or of a pension in respect of an industrial accident or disease. They must also be covered by comprehensive sickness insurance in the host Member State. 8–30

This right of residence is obviously very beneficial to those Union citizens and their family members who have retired and who wish to enjoy their retirement away from their own Member State. It is most advantageous to those Union citizens in receipt of benefits from Member States where the rates of benefit are relatively high and who wish to move to a Member State where the cost of living is low. In contrast Union citizens in receipt of benefits from a Member State where such benefit rates are relatively low, may find it difficult to fulfil the requirements (without additional resources) if they move to a State where the cost of living is high. 8–31

5. STUDENTS

(a) *Generally*

Secondary legislation relating to workers provides for two categories of persons who enjoy educational rights: children of workers[40] and workers themselves who enter into vocational training.[41] Furthermore, art.7(1)(c) of Directive 2004/38 (replacing Directive 93/96) provides the right of residence for students who fall outside the ambit of the two provisions relating to workers. This section examines both those students falling under Directive 2004/38[42] and those whose rights flow from other provisions of European Union law. It is to be emphasised that whereas Directive 93/96 had applied only to those who attended an educational establishment for the principal purpose of following a vocational training course,[43] art.7(1)(c) of Directive 2004/38 is now extremely broadly cast in applying for enrolment at an educational establishment for the principal purpose of following a course of study, including vocational training. 8–32

---

[40] art.10 of Regulation 492/2011, previously art.12 of Regulation 1612/68.
[41] art.7(3) of Regulation 492/2011, previously art.7(3) of Regulation 1612/68.
[42] Directive 2004/38/EC on the right of citizens of the Union and their family members to move and reside freely within the territory of the Member States repealing Directive 93/96.
[43] art.1 of Directive 93/96 referred.

8–33　Even before Directive 93/96 was adopted, the CJEU had recognised a right of residence for students who wished to enter into vocational training in another Member State more generally than in the circumstances provided for in Regulation 1612/68. In *Gravier*,[44] a French student in Belgium challenged the requirement of an enrolment fee for non-Belgians. She had no family members in Belgium and thus no rights of residence there, apart from her claim as a student to such a right. The CJEU stated:

> "Article 128 of the Treaty [now Art.166 TFEU] provides that the Council is to lay down general principles for implementing a common vocational training policy capable of contribution to the harmonious development both of the national economies and of the common market ... It constitutes, moreover, an indispensable element of the activities of the Community, whose objectives include, *inter alia*, the free movement of persons, the mobility of labour, and the improvement of the living standards of workers. Access to vocational training is in particular likely to promote free movement of persons throughout the Community...It follows from all the foregoing that the conditions of access to vocational training fall within the scope of the Treaty".[45]

8–34　In *Raulin*,[46] the CJEU held that the principle of non-discrimination deriving from arts 12 and 150 EC Treaty [now arts 18 and 166 TFEU] meant that a Union citizen who had been admitted to a vocational training course in another Member State must have a right of residence in that State for the duration of the course.

8–35　In *Bidar*[47] the CJEU held that assistance, whether in the form of subsidised loans or of grants, provided to students lawfully resident in the host Member State to cover their maintenance costs fell within the scope of application of the Treaty for the purposes of the prohibition of discrimination laid down in the first paragraph of art.12 EC Treaty (now art.18 TFEU).

8–36　Furthermore, as regards students the Maastricht Treaty introduced a new chapter into the Treaty concerning "social policy, education, vocational training and youth". Article 126 of the Maastricht Treaty (now art.165 TFEU) makes clear that Community action is to be aimed at "encouraging mobility of students and teachers". In order to contribute to the achievement of the objectives, the Council is called on to "adopt incentive measures".

---

[44] *Gravier v City of Liege* (293/83) [1985] E.C.R. 593.
[45] *Gravier v City of Liege* (293/83) [1985] E.C.R. 593, at [19]–[25].
[46] *Raulin v Minister for Education and Science* (357/89) [1992] E.C.R. I-1071.
[47] *R (on the application of Dany Bidar) v London Borough of Ealing* (C-209/03) [2005] E.C.R. I-02119.

(b) *Specific provisions relating to the right of residence of students*

(i) *Children of workers*

Article 10 of Regulation 492/2011[48] provides that where a Union citizen is or has been employed in the territory of another Member State the child of that EU national must be admitted to that State's general educational, apprenticeship and vocational training courses under the same conditions as the nationals of that State. **8–37**

The CJEU has stated that this provision exists to ensure that a child of a worker has the possibility of going to school and pursuing further education in the host Member State and able to complete that education successfully.[49] This is consistent with the general aim of Regulation 1612/68 (now Regulation 492/2011), namely that free movement for workers requires "the best possible conditions for the integration of the Community worker's family in the society of the host Member State."[50] **8–38**

The corollary of the right to education for the children of workers is the right of residence for those children. That right of residence continues even once the worker ceases economic activity, or ceases to reside in the territory of the host Member State. **8–39**

Based on a narrow reading of the CJEU's judgment in the case of *Echternach and Moritz*,[51] some Member States considered that the right to remain beyond the worker was limited to circumstances where education could not be continued in the Member State of origin of the worker because of lack of co-ordination of diplomas or some other reason.[52] In *Baumbast* the CJEU rejected this argument stating that the right of residence for children of workers in education exists independently of the workers remaining in the host Member State and irrespective as to whether education could be continued elsewhere.[53] And moreover in *Ibrahim*[54] the CJEU went further and held that the *parent* (as the primary carer of a child of a Union citizen who works or has worked in the host Member State) can also claim a right of residence on the sole basis of art.12 of Regulation 1612/68 (now art.10 of Regulation 492/2011) without such a right being conditional on their having sufficient resources and comprehensive sickness insurance cover in that State. **8–40**

---

[48] art.10 of Regulation 492/2011 replaced art.12 of Regulation 1612/68.
[49] *Echternach and Moritz* (C-389-390/87) [1989] E.C.R. 723, at [21].
[50] *Di Leo v Land Berlin* (C-308/89) [1990] E.C.R. I-4185, at [13].
[51] *Echternach and Moritz* (C-389-390/87) [1989] E.C.R. 723, at [21].
[52] See the German Government's argument recited at para.42 of *Baumbast and R. v Secretary of State for the Home Department* (C-413/99) [2002] E.C.R. I-7091.
[53] *Baumbast and R. v Secretary of State for the Home Department* (C-413/99) [2002] E.C.R. I-7091, at [63].
[54] *London Borough of Harrow v Nimco Hassan Ibrahim and Secretary of State for the Home Department* (C-310/08) [2010] E.C.R. 01065.

8–41 Where a parent has ceased to work and reside in another Member State prior to the birth of a child, the child derives no benefit from art.10 of Regulation 492/2011 in that Member State.[55]

8–42 The right of residence for the children of a Union citizen worker exists irrespective of their nationality. Thus even where the children of a Union citizen worker are nationals of third countries they will have independent rights of residence. This is consistent with the fact that any descendents of an Union citizen worker, irrespective of nationality, have the right to install themselves with the worker.[56] The CJEU has held that the right to be admitted to the education system of the host Member State must apply to the same descendants.[57]

(ii) *Workers undertaking vocational training*

8–43 Article 7(3) of Regulation 492/2011 provides that EU national workers in the territory of another Member State shall have access to training in vocational schools and retraining centres under the same conditions as national workers.

8–44 The CJEU has interpreted the term "vocational schools" relatively restrictively. It has found that the fact that a teaching establishment provides some vocational training is not sufficient to enable it to be regarded as a vocational school within the meaning of that provision. According to the CJEU the term vocational school has a narrower meaning and refers solely to establishments providing only teaching between periods of employment or teaching which is closely connected with employment, particularly during apprenticeship. It rejected a suggestion that universities could be regarded as "vocational schools".[58]

8–45 This restrictive definition is somewhat surprising in light of the fact that the CJEU has acknowledged consistently that universities are capable of providing

> "studies which prepare for a qualification for a particular profession, trade or employment or which provide the necessary training and skills for such a profession, trade or employment"

and that this would constitute "vocational training" for the purposes of art.166 TFEU which applies to Union citizens generally as opposed to the narrower class of workers.[59]

8–46 Article 7(3)(d) of Directive 2004/38 also makes specific provision for workers (and self-employed persons) embarking on vocational training. The provision enables a person who is no longer working having embarked on

---

[55] *Brown v Secretary of State for Scotland* (197/86) [1988] E.C.R. 3205.
[56] art.7(1)(d) of Directive 2004/38 (and art.2 defining "family member").
[57] *Baumbast and R. v Secretary of State for the Home Department* (C-413/99) [2002] E.C.R. I-7091, at [56].
[58] *Brown v Secretary of State for Scotland* (197/86) [1988] E.C.R. 3205, at [13].
[59] *Gravier v City of Liege* (293/83) [1985] E.C.R. 593.

vocational training to retain the status of worker if the training is "related to the previous employment". However, there is no need for the vocational training to be linked with the previous employment if the person concerned is involuntarily employed. The effect of the provision is that the person concerned will retain the right of residence given by art.7.1(a) to those who are workers.

(iii) *Directive 2004/38*

Article 7(1)(c) of Directive 2004/38[60] provides that Union citizens who are enrolled at a private or public establishment, accredited or financed by the host Member State on the basis of its legislation or administrative practice, for the principal purpose of following a course of study, including vocational training, have a right of residence in that host Member State. Students must also have comprehensive sickness insurance cover in the host Member State. Also they must *assure* the relevant national authority ("by means of a declaration or by such equivalent means as they may choose") that they have sufficient resources for themselves and their family members not to become a burden on the social assistance system of the host Member State during their period of residence.

8–47

The difference between the requirement in art.7(1)(c) of Directive 2004/38 for students to provide a declaration of means (as opposed to having to prove means as must those falling into category art.7(1)(b) of Directive 2004/38) is significant. It reflects a more flexible attitude towards students and the Commission has taken action against Member States which require more than a declaration from students. In *Commission v Italy*[61] the CJEU upheld the Commission's view that the system of (now repealed) Directive 93/96 on the right of residence for students differs from that of the (now repealed) Directives 90/364 and 90/365 with regard to sufficient resources. The CJEU noted that Directive 93/96 contained no requirement regarding a given amount or moreover the furnishing of evidence thereof in the form of specific documents. In the circumstances the CJEU concluded that a Member State could not require a student benefiting from this Directive 93/96 to provide evidence or a guarantee of a given amount of resources, nor to provide certain specific documents. The Member State must be satisfied with a declaration or equivalent, at the choice of the student, even where the student is accompanied by family members. Although now repealed and replaced by art.7(1)(c) of Directive 2004/38, the scheme remains the same as regards the assurance required to be given by students. And moreover art.8(4) precludes host Member States from laying down a fixed amount which they regard as sufficient resources and emphasises that the personal situation of the person concerned is to be taken into account (effectively giving legislative force to the decision in *Commission v Italy*).

8–48

---

[60] Directive 2004/38/EC on the right of citizens of the Union and their family members to move and reside freely within the territory of the Member States.
[61] *Commission v Italy* (C-424/98) [2000] E.C.R. I-04001.

CHAPTER 9

FAMILY MEMBERS

This chapter considers the right of EU national free movers to install family members and the interpretation that the CJEU has given to the principle of family unity.

1. INTRODUCTION

(a) *General European Union law principles*

(i) *Importance of family life*

European Union law has always respected the notion of family life within the context of free movement provisions. It recognises that without the right to family reunion, EU nationals would be deterred from exercising free movement rights.[1] 9–01

In Directive 2004/38[2] itself the importance of family members is reinforced at Recital (5): 9–02

> "The right of all Union citizens to move and reside freely within the territory of the Member States should, if it is to be exercised under objective conditions of freedom and dignity, be also granted to their family members, irrespective of nationality."

Recital (6) of the Preamble emphasises the maintenance of the unity of the family in the broader sense.

The CJEU has repeatedly emphasised the importance of ensuring protection for the family life of nationals of Member States in order to eliminate obstacles to the exercise of the fundamental freedoms guaranteed by the TFEU (formerly the EC Treaty).[3] Furthermore, the CJEU has made clear that the integration of EU nationals and their family members into the life of the Member State in which they are resident is a fundamental objective of European Union law.[4] 9–03

---

[1] *The Queen v the Immigration Appeal Tribunal Ex p. Surinder Singh* (C-3709/90) [1992] E.C.R. I-4265, at [20].
[2] Directive 2004/38/EC.
[3] *Carpenter v Secretary of State for the Home Department* (60–00) [2002] E.C.R. I-6279, at [38].
[4] *Di Leo v Land Berlin* (C-308/89) [1990] E.C.R. I-4185:
"the aim of Regulation 1612/68, namely freedom of movement for workers, requires for such freedom to be guaranteed in compliance with the principles of liberty and dignity, the best possible conditions or the integration of the European Union worker's family in the society of the host country". (para.13). Such aim is replicated in Directive 2004/38.

9–04   In light of these principles the CJEU has considered in *MRAX*[5] that it would be contrary to European Union law to send back a third country national married to an EU national who arrives at the border of a Member State without the appropriate visa, where he is able to prove his identity and the conjugal ties and there is no evidence to establish that he represents a risk to the requirements of public policy, public security or public health.[6] The CJEU also considered that it would unlawful to refuse to recognise the right of residence of a third country national married to a national of a Member State where the third country national had entered the territory of the Member State unlawfully.[7]

(ii) *Interpretation of family reunion provisions*

9–05   In *Diatta*,[8] the CJEU made clear "having regard to its context and the objectives which it pursues, that provision [Art.10 of Reg. 1612/68] cannot be construed restrictively". Demonstrating its flexible attitude to the interpretation of family reunion provisions the CJEU held that in order to benefit from the right of residence, family members wishing to install themselves with a worker were not required to live permanently with the worker.[9]

9–06   The Advocate General's opinion in the case of *Baumbast*[10] referred to a right of residence in favour of the "spouse and other members of the family of a migrant worker". He considered that the terms of the Regulation should not be defined restrictively in light of the principles identified and was of the view that the CJEU must have regard to both social and European Union law developments:

> "If no account were taken of those developments the relevant rules of law risk losing their effectiveness".[11]

9–07   In *Metock* the CJEU again emphasised that the context and objectives of Directive 2004/38 meant that the provisions of that Directive cannot be interpreted restrictively and must not deprive them of their effectiveness. In the case of spouses this meant that there could be not extra requirements imposed on them other than a legal relationship with the EU national. In particular, a requirement of legal residence or a requirement that the relationship was formed prior to the EU national moving to the host Member State would be inconsistent with the necessity of not taking a restrictive approach.[12]

---

[5] *Mouvement contre le Racisme, l'Antisémitisme et la Xénophobie ASBL (MRAX) v Belgian State* (C-459/99) [2002] E.C.R. I-6591.
[6] *Mouvement contre le Racisme, l'Antisémitisme et la Xénophobie ASBL (MRAX) v Belgian State* (C-459/99) [2002] E.C.R. I-6591, at [61].
[7] *Metock and others v Minister for Justice, Equality and Law Reform* (C-127/08) July 25, 2008.
[8] *Diatta v Land Berlin* (267/83) [1985] E.C.R. 567, at [17].
[9] *Diatta v Land Berlin* (267/83) [1985] E.C.R. 567, at [18].
[10] A.G. Geelhoed in *Baumbast and R. v Secretary of State for the Home Department* (C-413/99) delivered on July 5, 2001, at [19].
[11] A.G. Geelhoed in *Baumbast and R. v Secretary of State for the Home Department* (C-413/99) delivered on July 5, 2001, at [19].
[12] *Metock v Minister for Justice, Equality and Law Reform* (C-127/08) July 25, 2008, at [93].

INTRODUCTION

(b) *Inter-relationship with the right to family life in human rights law*

(i) *Generally*

9–08 In a series of cases decided since 2001 the CJEU has emphasised the importance of ensuring protection for the right to respect for family life of nationals of the Member States in order to eliminate obstacles to the exercise of the fundamental freedoms guaranteed by the EC Treaty (now the TFEU).[13]

9–09 In Ch.3 the inter-relationship between human rights law, in particular the European Convention on Human Rights (ECHR), and European Union law was examined. Those principles have particular application in the field of the free movement of persons and the right to respect for family life in that context. The CJEU has consistently held that free movement provisions must be interpreted in conformity with art.8 ECHR and the fundamental right to respect for family life contained in that provision.[14]

9–10 Added to this is the incorporation of the Charter of Fundamental Rights of the European Union ("the Charter") which strengthens the right to respect for family life in the context of free movement law.[15] The CJEU has indicated that the approach to art.7 of the Charter which contains the right to respect for private and family life will be the same as that taken to art.8(1) ECHR.[16] However, the CJEU has also held that nothing in the Charter precludes the grant of wider protection by European Union law.[17]

(ii) *The scope of protection afforded by art.8 ECHR and art.7 of the Charter*

9–11 It must be recalled that the right to respect for family life contained in art.8(1) ECHR is not an absolute right and thus the right of non-nationals to enter a country is not guaranteed by the ECHR. However, the only permissible interferences with the art.8(1) rights are those outlined in art.8(2). Article 7 of the Charter itself contains no exceptions although it does include similar, but less extensive exceptions in European Union law to the enjoyment of rights given by the TFEU.[18] Assuming there is family life under art.8(2) ECHR the State must establish a legitimate aim for the interference with the individual's right which in the present context will likely be sought to be justified by reference to the need to have fair and firm immigration control in the context of the maintenance of public order. However, the State must establish also that any interference is proportionate when the State's interest in the interference in the family life is balanced

---

[13] *Carpenter v Secretary of State for the Home Department* (60–00) [2002] E.C.R. I-6279, at [38]. *Metock v Minister for Justice, Equality and Law Reform* (C-127/08) July 25, 2008.
[14] *Commission v Germany* (249/86) [1989] E.C.R. 1263, at [10]. See also, A.G.'s opinion in *Mouvement contre le Racisme, l'Antisémitisme et la Xénophobie ASBL (MRAX) v Belgian State* (C-459/99) [2002] E.C.R. I-6591.
[15] The relationship between the Charter and Directive 2004/38 in the context of family members of EU nationals will be considered in *Yoshikazu Iida v City of Ulm* (C-40/11).
[16] *PPU McB.* (C-400/10) [2010] E.C.R. I-0000, at [53] and *Dereci and others v Bundesministerium für Inneres* (C-256/11) [2012] E.C.R. I-0000, at [70].
[17] *PPU McB.* (C-400/10) [2010] E.C.R. I-0000, at [53].
[18] As to which see Ch.13.

against the effect that the measure would have on the individual's rights to respect for that family life.

9–12 The State's negative obligations under art.8 are well established and preclude a State from taking action, including expulsion or removals, which will disproportionately interfere with a person's right to the enjoyment of family life.[19] In assessing what is proportionate it will be necessary to examine whether there are obstacles to the family life being enjoyed outside the contracting State. In this context it is to be recalled that the European Court of Human Rights (ECtHR) has even considered language and cultural difficulties as impediments to family life being enjoyed elsewhere.[20] The ECHR thus imposes negative obligations on States to refrain from such interferences.

9–13 Additionally however art.1 also demands that States "secure" the rights protected by the ECHR. The European Court of Human Rights has therefore held in many cases that States are under a positive obligation to take steps to ensure that Convention rights are protected, not just to refrain from negative interferences. The State is obliged to have in place laws that grant individuals the legal status, rights and privileges required to ensure, for example, that their family life is properly respected.[21]

9–14 Article 8 also carries positive obligations for the State to protect all aspects of family life.[22] The judgments of the European Court of Human Rights in cases such as *Sen v Netherlands*[23] and *Rodrigues da Silva and Hoogkamer v the Netherlands*[24] highlight that the State has a positive obligation to facilitate family life which goes beyond protecting the family life that already exists in the territory of a State, but includes an obligation to permit the reunion of family members who have been living apart and to foster family life in the best possible environment. In this context the failure to meet this obligation must be weighed against the State's legitimate aims which will include immigration control.

9–15 The significance of art.7 of the Charter being an unqualified right with no equivalent to art.8(2) ECHR included is yet to be examined by the CJEU. However, as already indicated there is nothing to prevent wider protection being granted under the Charter than under the ECHR.

(iii) *The CJEU's approach to art.8 ECHR*

9–16 In a situation where an EU Member State denies entry or residence to the family member of an EU national exercising EU free movement rights it is not difficult to argue that to exclude the family member would be a breach of European Union law when read compatibly with the ECHR and the

---

[19] See most recently *Yildiz v Austria (Application no. 37295/97)*, judgment of October 31, 2002, ECtHR.
[20] *Boultif v Switzerland (Application no. 54273/00)*, judgment of August 2, 2001, ECtHR.
[21] *Marckx v Belgium* (1979) 2 E.H.R.R. 330, at [36].
[22] *Marckx v Belgium* (1979) 2 E.H.R.R. 330.
[23] *Sen v Netherlands (Application no. 31465/96)*, judgment of December 20, 2001 ECtHR.
[24] Application no. 50435/99, January 31, 2006, para.38 ECtHR.

INTRODUCTION

Charter, irrespective of whether European Union law alone would force that conclusion. For the EU national, it would constitute a breach of fundamental rights of free movement if the only way to enjoy family life is by leaving the host Member State. Similarly it would be a breach of European Union law if the only way to enjoy free movement rights were without family members being present. In other words European Union law would not force an EU national to choose between the enjoyment of family life and the continued exercise of TFEU rights to freedom of movement.[25]

This approach has been affirmed by the CJEU in *Carpenter*[26] which concerned the spouse of a provider of services. The CJEU found that notwithstanding that the spouse had infringed the immigration laws of the United Kingdom she was entitled to reside in the territory with the provider of services. In doing so, the CJEU read art.49 EC Treaty (now art.56 TFEU) in light of the fundamental right to respect for family life so as to infer a right of residence for the family member.

In *MRAX*,[27] the CJEU ruled that a Member State could not refuse to issue a residence permit to a third country national married to a national of a Member State who entered the territory of that Member State lawfully on the sole ground that the visa expired before the application was made for a residence permit.[28]

9–17

The protection of family life and the free movement of EU citizens are wholly interlinked. As the CJEU emphasised in *Eind* for instance Union law recognises the importance of ensuring protection for family life of nationals of the Member States "in order to eliminate obstacles to the exercise of the fundamental freedoms guaranteed by the Treaty".[29]

9–18

---

[25] The CJEU's decision in the case of *McCarthy (Shirley) v Secretary of State for the Home Department* (C-434/09) [2011] E.C.R. I-0000 might be suggested to qualify this in so far as the CJEU found that the failure to grant residence to a third country national spouse did not have the effect of depriving the EU citizen of her genuine enjoyment of the substance of her rights as an EU citizen. However, at no time had she in fact exercised free movement rights under the Treaty, she was residing in the Member State of which she was a national and there was no finding that the failure to grant her husband residence would interfere with the effective enjoyment of her rights as a Union citizen. Given the Grand Chamber's decision in *Zambrano* the result will be different for an EU citizen who can demonstrate that the exclusion or failure to grant residence (or even the right to work) to a family member does in fact impact on the effective enjoyment of EU law rights, even if the EU citizen is residing in its own Member State. This was confirmed in *Dereci and others v Bundesministerium für Inneres* (C-256/11) [2012] E.C.R. I-0000, another case in which Union citizens asserted the right to have with them third country family members in their own Member State (contrary to the usual principle that EU law will not apply in the Member State of which the Union citizen is a national). See further Ch.5.
[26] *Carpenter v Secretary of State for the Home Department* (60–00) [2002] E.C.R. I-6279, at [38].
[27] *Mouvement contre le Racisme, l'Antisémitisme et la Xénophobie ASBL (MRAX) v Belgium* (C-459/99) [2002] E.C.R. I-6591.
[28] The ECJ also held that a non-EU national spouse who had entered the territory of a Member State unlawfully was not grounds for exclusion or refusal of residents permit.
[29] *Minister voor Vreemdelingenzaken en Integratie v RNG Eind* (C-291/05) December 11, 2007, at [44].

9-19 In the first case on family members after the coming into force of Directive 2004/38 the CJEU firmly placed the protection of family life at the centre of its approach to the Directive. The Court found that it was not permissible for a Member State to refuse to issue a residence permit to a third country national spouse of an EU national on the basis that the relationship had been formed after the EU national had entered the Member State or that the third country national had not been lawfully resident in another Member State previously. The Court recalled the importance of ensuring the protection of family life in its own case law even prior to Directive 2004/38 coming into force and emphasised that Directive 2004/38 had the objective of strengthening the rights of EU citizens.[30]

9-20 All of these cases illustrate the determination of the CJEU to ensure the protection of the family life of Member State nationals in order to eliminate obstacles to the exercise of the fundamental freedoms guaranteed by the Treaty, even in the face of contrary domestic legislation.

9-21 There has been some criticism of the CJEU's approach to the ECHR and suggestion that it has given undue weight to the rights of the individuals as opposed to that of the State. However, such criticism is not warranted if the decisions of the CJEU are seen in light of the above observations and the fact that family members are seen in European Union law as being capable of "facilitating" free movement in so far as they may offer support,[31] care[32] and in some cases financial ability to exercise that free movement right. In the words of the CJEU in *Carpenter*:

> "It is clear that the separation of Mr and Mrs Carpenter would be detrimental to their family life and, therefore, to the conditions under which Mr Carpenter exercises a fundamental freedom. That freedom could not be fully effective if Mr Carpenter were to be deterred from exercising it by obstacles raised in his country origin to the entry and residence of his spouse".[33]

9-22 The CJEU has yet to give substantive consideration to a free movement case under art.7 of the Charter. However, given the lack of qualification in art.7 of the Charter it is more than likely that the CJEU would maintain its *Carpenter* approach in a case where fundamental freedoms or fundamental rights as a Union citizen are at stake.

(c) *Which family members can be installed with the Union citizen?*

9-23 The right to install family members is set out in detail in Directive 2004/38. Not all family members are treated in the same way by the Directive. There are "core" family members, defined in art.2(2) of the Directive who have the

---

[30] *Metock and others v Minister for Justice, Equality and Law Reform* (C-127/08) July 25, 2008, at [56–59].
[31] *Carpenter v Secretary of State for the Home Department* (60/00) [2002] E.C.R. I-6279.
[32] *Baumbast and R. v Secretary of State for the Home Department* (C-413/99) [2002] E.C.R. I-7091.
[33] See *Carpenter v Secretary of State for the Home Department* (60/00) [2002] E.C.R. I-6279, at [39].

automatic right to accompany and join EU nationals. Article 3(2) then provides for other family members who have the right to have their entry and residence "facilitated". Not all EU citizens exercising free movement have the right to install the same core family members.[34] Students have a more qualified set of family members they can install with them than the economically active and economically self-sufficient EU nationals.

Those family members who have the automatic right to accompany and join an EU citizen exercising free movements are: 9–24

(a) the spouse;

(b) the partner with whom the Union citizen has contracted a registered partnership, on the basis of the legislation of a Member State, if the legislation of the host Member State treats registered partnerships as equivalent to marriage and in accordance with the conditions laid down in the relevant legislation of the host Member State (the registered partner);

(c) the direct descendants who are under the age of 21 or are dependants and those of the spouse or registered partner; and

(d) the dependent direct relatives in the ascending line and those of the spouse or registered partner.

Relatives in the ascending line of students do not have the automatic right to accompany and install themselves with the EU national student. Their entry and residence is to be "facilitated" in the same way as for all other family members of EU nationals exercising free movement rights.[35] 9–25

Those other family members, provided for in art.3(2) are: 9–26

(a) any other family members, irrespective of their nationality, not falling under the definition in art.2(2) who, in the country from which they have come, are dependants or members of the household of the Union citizen having the primary right of residence, or where serious health grounds strictly require the personal care of the family member by the Union citizen; and

(b) the partner with whom the Union citizen has a durable relationship, duly attested.[36]

The difference between art.2(2) family members and art.3(2) family members is one of procedure. Article 2(2) family members have the automatic right accompany or join the EU citizen as a matter of EU law. This would be enforceable directly without reference to any domestic regulations or implementation and providing that the family member could prove his relationship with the EU citizen entry, residence would have to be granted 9–27

---

[34] This reflects differences in previous secondary legislation see Regulation 1612/68 (workers), Directive 90/364 (general rights of residence), and Directive 93/96 (students) now repealed or amended by Directive 2004/38.
[35] art.7(4) of Directive 2004/38.
[36] art.3(2) of Directive 2004/38.

automatically subject only to exclusion on public policy, public health or public security grounds. An art.2(2) family member cannot be required to obtain a residence card to prove their right of residence for instance or at least only administrative penalties (on a non-discriminatory basis) may follow for failing to obtain a residence card.[37]

9–28   Article 3(2) family members are to have their entry and residence facilitated by the Member State and thus need the Member State to grant them entry or residence. Thus art.3(2) family members may be required (if such requirement is set out in national legislation) to obtain the residence card to prove that they have been granted the right to remain. The procedure for obtaining such recognition may vary from one Member State to another. However, this does not mean that the *substantive requirements* imposed on family members under art.3(2) can vary from one Member State to another such as requiring them to fulfil additional conditions other than those provided for in art.3(2)(a) by for example requiring that they meet a condition that they must be widowed or orphaned to be considered under the provision. Nor does this mean that Member States can choose to restrict the type of family member to be considered under art.3(2)(a) so as to exclude all cousins or siblings.[38] If Member States were to exclude a particular category of family member this would render meaningless the requirement placed on Member States by the phrase "shall facilitate" and would read additional words into the term "other family member".

9–29   Some Member States may be taking a contrary approach and consider the requirement to facilitate entry and residence of art.3(2)(a) family members as optional or one which they can qualify or severely restrict. The CJEU will consider the position of art.3(2) family members in the future.[39] However, in the meantime the Commission's guidance on the Directive gives no hint whatsoever that it was intended that Member States would have the scope to restrict the type of family members they were required to admit or wholly alter the substantive requirements they could place on applicant family members.[40] The flexibility comes only in the procedure they can adopt

---

[37] See, for instance, *Movement contre le Racisme l'Antisémitisme et la Xénophobie ASBL (MRAX)* (C-459/99) [2002] E.C.R. I-6591.
[38] As the Commission states quite emphatically in its report to the European Parliament "Article 3(2)(a) does not lay down any restrictions as to the degree of relatedness when referring to '**other family members**'. See Communication from the Commission to the European Parliament and the Council on guidance for better transposition and application of Directive 2004/38/EC on the right of citizens of the Union and their family members to move and reside freely within the territory of the Member States COM/2009/0313 final."
[39] *Rahman v the Secretary of State for the Home Department* (C-83/11).
[40] The Commission refers to the discretion of the Member States only in laying down criteria by which to judge whether to grant rights of entry and residence, see Communication from the Commission to the European Parliament and the Council on guidance for better transposition and application of Directive 2004/38/EC on the right of citizens of the Union and their family members to move and reside freely within the territory of the Member States COM/2009/0313 final. There is a considerable difference between having discretion to lay down criteria by which it is judged whether the substantive requirements of art.3(2) are met and being able to impose additional substantive requirements on applicants. If the latter had been intended surely art.3(2)(a) would simply have stated "any other family member provided for in national legislation" rather than describing the circumstances of the family member that should lead to entry or residence being facilitated.

although Member States are nevertheless required under the Directive to undertake an extensive examination of the personal circumstances of the family member and justify any denial of entry or residence.[41] Advocate General Bot's opinion in the *Rahman* case[42] tends to suggest that the approach suggested above (at paras 9–28 and 9–29) is correct. As he states:

> "It follows that a Member State may not reduce the scope, either directly, by deciding, for example, to exclude from the facilitation measures family members in the direct line beyond a certain degree of relationship, or even collaterals, or the partner with whom the Union citizen has a durable relationship, or indirectly, by laying down conditions which have the purpose or effect of excluding certain categories of beneficiaries. It would not seem possible, for example, to make the rights accorded to the partner with whom the citizen has a durable relationship subject to a requirement of a registered partnership or to a condition of the partnership being treated as equivalent to marriage, as appears in Article 2(2)(b) of Directive 2004/38."

2. Spouses and Register Partners

(a) *Legal spouse*

(i) *Meaning of spouse*

9–30 Marriages validly contracted anywhere in the world must be in principle recognised for the purpose of the application of the Directive. This is potentially with two caveats. The Commission takes the view that Member States are not obliged to recognise either forced marriages[43] or polygamous marriages.[44] In relation to the latter it is interesting to note that Directive 2004/38 is silent on polygamous marriages whereas Directive 2003/86 on the right to family reunification[45] specifically refers to polygamous marriages and prevents the principal from bringing two spouses into a Member State. The legislature would surely have included a similar provision in Directive 2004/38 if it were agreed on excluding polygamous marriages.

9–31 The CJEU case law suggests that the term "spouse" refers to "a marital relationship only". Thus relationships outside legal marriage cannot be regarded as "spouses" for the purposes of European Union law.[46] Articles

---

[41] See wording of art.3(2) of Directive 2004/38. The formalities and procedures involved in obtaining entry and residence for all family members is discussed in detail in Ch.10.
[42] *Rahman v Secretary of State for the Home Department*, Opinion of March 27, 2012, para.67. See also, paras 79, 85 and 101.
[43] This is different from arranged marriages. Forced marriages would contravene international law, namely art.16(2) of the Universal Declaration of Human Rights or art.16(1)(b) of the Convention to Eliminate All Forms of Discrimination Against Women.
[44] The Commission states "Member States are not obliged to recognise polygamous marriages, contracted lawfully in a third country, which may be in conflict with their own legal order" in its Communication from the Commission to the European Parliament and the Council on guidance for better transposition and application of Directive 2004/38/EC on the right of citizens of the Union and their family members to move and reside freely within the territory of the Member States COM/2009/0313 final".
[45] "This Directive relates to the family reunion rights of third country nationals."
[46] *Reed v the Netherlands* (59/85) [1986] E.C.R. 1283.

2(2) and 3(2)(b) of Directive 2004/38 go some way to remedying this by making provision for registered partnerships and durable relationships. In the case of registered partnerships this is only really to the extent that the CJEU had already provided for in *Reed*[47] whereby Member States are obliged to recognise such relationships if they do for their own nationals. Registered partnerships and durable relationships are discussed further below.

(ii) *Divorce and separation*

9–32 It is the corollary of the very narrow definition of the term "spouse" (relating to the technical legal status of a couple) that, for as long as they remain legally married, they should be regarded as spouses. This includes situations where the couple have separated and even intend to divorce. It is only when the marriage is finally dissolved in law that they can no longer be regarded as spouses for the purposes of European Union law.

9–33 In *Diatta*,[48] the couple in question had separated and were living in different accommodation. The German authorities sought to deport Ms Diatta, a Sengalese national, on the basis that she had no right of residence in European Union law. The German authorities pointed to the fact that the couple intended to divorce and in that art.10(3) of Regulation 1612/68 refers to the requirement that the EU national has adequate accommodation for his family members.[49]

9–34 The CJEU held that a marriage could not be regarded as dissolved until it had been terminated by the relevant authorities and that the requirement that the EU national has adequate accommodation on installing his family members could not be translated into a requirement that they remain living together.

9–35 Article 13 of Directive 2004/38 provides for the retention of a right of residence for family members in the event of: divorce or annulment of marriage in certain circumstances (namely where the marriage has lasted at least three years, one of which was in the host Member State), where there is domestic violence, or where there are children of the marriage and agreements or court orders necessitating the presence of parents in the host Member State. Those conditions are discussed in Ch.10.

(b) *Registered partnerships*

9–36 The inclusion of registered partnerships in the definition of a family member in art.2(2) of Directive 2004/38 was undoubtedly welcome. However, there are a number of qualifications to the recognition of rights of registered partnerships which undermine the effectiveness of the provision. First, the registered partnership must be on the basis of legislation of a Member State,

---

[47] *Reed v the Netherlands* (C-59/85) [1986] E.C.R. 1283.
[48] *Diatta v Land Berlin* (267/83) [1985] E.C.R. 567.
[49] It should be noted that the art.10(3) of Regulation 1612/68 is not repeated in Directive 2004/38.

and secondly only Member States which treat registered partnerships as equivalent to marriage are obliged to recognise registered partnerships from other Member States.

This undoubtedly creates a wide discrepancy in the way in which registered partners will be treated across the European Union since more than a third of Member States do not treat registered partnerships as being equivalent to marriage.[50] If a Member State does not treat registered partnerships as equivalent to marriage then the partner will have to be considered under art.3(2) of the Directive as a "durable relationship". Plainly where a couple have entered into a registered partnership they should readily satisfy the requirements of being in a durable relationship "duly attested".[51] Any contrary conclusion would suggest some form of discrimination contrary to the Charter of Fundamental Rights and the demands of Recital 31 of the Preamble to the Directive. 9–37

Where a Member State recognises registered partnerships as equivalent to marriage it should recognise both same sex and hetrosexual registered partnerships or marriages contracted lawfully in other Member States whether that is the approach in that State. Recital 31 of the Preamble to the Directive provides that Member States should implement the Directive without discrimination on grounds of sex or sexual orientation. 9–38

With the increase in numbers of registered partnerships in the EU but the lack of universal acceptance and the lack of requirement in the Directive for Member States to recognise registered partnerships there is an ever-growing number of EU nationals and their partners who are disadvantaged as compared to their heterosexual, married equivalents. They will continue to be disadvantaged for so long as there are any States which refuse to recognise their partnerships and such disadvantage creates a real obstacle to free movement. Whilst States are bound to "facilitate entry and residence" of those in durable relationships, this is not an automatic right of entry and residence that spouses enjoy. Procedural impediments may impact in a significant way upon the decision to move within the European Union. 9–39

It is necessary therefore to consider ways in which European Union law solutions to these problems might be found. It is arguable that the time has come for the CJEU to re-interpret the term "spouse" to include registered partnerships, despite the Council's failure to do so. The decision in *Reed* was given over 20 years ago and it is undoubtedly arguable that in the light of legal and social developments over the last 20 years, the term "spouse" should be given a more liberal meaning. The CJEU is mindful of such developments and has been prepared to make similar developments in relation to transsexuals.[52] 9–40

---

[50] According to the European Commission as at October 2011 the following states did not recognise registered partnerships as equivalent to marriage: Bulgaria, Cyprus, Estonia, Greece, Ireland, Italy, Latvia, Liechtenstein, Malta, Poland, Romania and Slovakia.
[51] See below for further discussion of "durable relationships under art.3(2) of Directive 2004/38.
[52] See paras 9–42 to 9–45, below.

9–41 However, there is undoubtedly a risk that the CJEU would reject that argument even today. In 2001 the CJEU did not consider that legal and social developments could support the conclusion that a consensus had been reached amongst the Member States.[53] Further Directive 2004/38 was only agreed in 2004 and the approach taken to registered partnerships undoubtedly reflected a degree of disagreement between Member States.

(c) *Transsexuals*

(i) *European Union law*

9–42 In *S v Cornwall County Council*[54] the CJEU held that the right not to be discriminated on grounds of sex constitutes a fundamental human right and must be extended to discrimination arising from gender reassignment. Such discrimination, in the CJEU's view, would constitute a failure to respect dignity and freedom. The CJEU did not determine whether a relationship involving a transsexual is equivalent to marriage for the purposes of European Union law until recently.

9–43 The case of *KB*[55] concerned a British citizen who worked for the National Health Service (NHS) for 20 years, during which time she paid contributions to the NHS pension scheme. The scheme provided for a survivor's pension to be payable to a member's surviving spouse. "Spouse" meant the person to whom the scheme member had been married. KB argued that her partner, R, who had undergone female-to-male gender reassignment surgery, should be entitled to receive the widower's pension. United Kingdom legislation, however, prevented transsexuals from marrying on the basis of their acquired gender.

9–44 The CJEU rejected an argument that restricting the widower's pensions to married couples only was contrary to European Union law. The CJEU held that the decision to restrict certain benefits to married couples, while excluding all persons who lived together without being married from accessing such benefits, was either a matter for the legislature to decide or a matter of the interpretation of domestic legal rules for the national courts. Individuals affected could not claim that there was discrimination on grounds of sex, prohibited by European Union law. There was, however, inequality of treatment which related to the couple's inability to marry. The CJEU relied on the decision of the European Court of Human Rights in *Goodwin*[56] to conclude that the legislation making it impossible for transsexuals to marry on the basis of their acquired gender was incompatible with the EC Treaty (now TFEU). In *Goodwin*, the European Court of Human Rights had held that since it was impossible for a transsexual to marry a person of the sex to which he or she belonged prior to gender reassignment surgery, the United Kingdom was in breach of the right to marry in art.12

---

[53] See *D. v Council* (C-122/99P) [2001] E.C.R. I-4319.
[54] *S v Cornwall County Council* (C-13/94) [1996] E.C.R. I-2143, paras 21–22.
[55] *KB v (1) National Health Service Pensions Agency (2) Secretary of State for Health* (C-117/01) judgment of January 7, 2004.
[56] *Goodwin v United Kingdom* [2002] 35 E.H.R.R. 18, ECtHR.

ECHR. Thus the pensions legislation was incompatible with the EC Treaty (now TFEU).

The consequence of this case is that it is contrary to European Union law for Member States to prohibit transsexuals from marrying, whereas the failure to treat transsexuals as equal married and unmarried couples is not in contradiction with EU law.

9–45

(ii) *The future*

It is now established in EU law that the failure to permit transsexual couples to marry is contrary to the Treaty and in breach of human rights law. If Member States fail to legalise marriages of transsexuals on the basis of their acquired gender, the consequence must be that they give legal recognition to relationships akin to marriage.

9–46

In most Member States there remains a legal bar to marriage of a transsexual on the basis of acquired gender. However, the failure of national laws to reflect societal changes should not prevent the couples being regarded as spouses for the purposes of European Union law when national law would be so clearly in conflict with arts 8 and 12 ECHR.

9–47

In the context of free movement law, absent the ability of transsexuals to marry on the basis of their acquired gender, this would have to mean that the term "spouse" is interpreted as including the stable relationship of a transsexual and their partner, where on the basis of the acquired gender they are of the opposite sex. The failure to do so amounts to discrimination on the grounds of sex and is a breach of the ECHR and therefore a breach of EU law.[57]

9–48

The CJEU's decision in *KB*[58] has made clear that such breach of the ECHR is incompatible with European Union law. This is consistent with its other jurisprudence that European Union law must be compatible with ECHR obligations.[59]

9–49

(d) *Sham marriages/registered partnerships*

Article 35 of Directive 2004/38 provides that Member States may adopt measures to deal with cases of fraud including marriages of convenience. Consistent with its jurisprudence in other areas, the CJEU has held that European Union law will not act as a front for fraudulent conduct. In the case of *Surinder Singh*[60] the CJEU recalled that European Union law

9–50

---

[57] See Ch.3 on the relationship between the ECHR and EU law.
[58] *KB v (1) National Health Service Pensions Agency (2) Secretary of State for Health* (C-117/01) judgment of January 7, 2004.
[59] *Carpenter v Secretary of State for the Home Department* (60/00) [2002] E.C.R. I-6279.
[60] *R. v the IAT and the Secretary of State for the Home Department Ex p. Surinder Singh* (C-370/90) [1992] E.C.R. I-4265.

does not prevent national authorities from preventing abuse. In *Akrich*[61] the CJEU held that:

> "there would be an abuse if the facilities afforded by European Union law in favour of migrant workers and their spouses were invoked in the context of marriages of convenience entered into in order to circumvent the provisions relating to entry and residence of nationals of non-Member States".

9–51 Recital 28 of Directive 2004/38 defines marriages of convenience for the purposes of the Directive as marriages contracted for the sole purpose of enjoying the right of free movement and residence under the Directive that someone would not have otherwise.[62] A marriage cannot be considered as a marriage of convenience simply because it brings an immigration advantage or indeed any other advantage.

9–52 According to the Commission the quality of the relationship is immaterial to the application of art.35. The Commission in its 2009 report to the European Parliament suggests a number of factors including that the couple do not speak a mutually understood language or that there is a history of abuse that could trigger investigation.[63]

3. Descendants

(a) *Under the age of 21*

9–53 There is no definition of descendants to be found in the case law of the CJEU. However, it should include all blood children, whether legitimate or not. It includes grandchildren and great-grandchildren. It is notable that the age of 21 is the relevant age for the purposes of European Union law below which descendants are in effect treated automatically as dependants. This may differ from national rules which define children as under 18 (or in some cases as even younger). European Union law will prevail in the case of conflict with national rules.

9–54 Whereas previous secondary legislation tended to refer to the principal's right to install his spouse and their children or descendants, thus requiring the CJEU to clarify that this must include the children of the EU national's spouse,[64] art.2(2) of Directive 2004/38 makes this express.

---

[61] *Secretary of State for the Home Department v Akrich* (C-109/01) judgment of September 23, 2003, at [57].
[62] This is to be contrasted with certain Member State's domestic interpretation of such concepts which question more deeply the motivation for marriage.
[63] Communication from the Commission to the European Parliament and the Council on guidance for better transposition and application of Directive 2004/38/EC on the right of citizens of the Union and their family members to move and reside freely within the territory of the Member State, COM/2009/0313 final. Emphasis is placed in the report on the need for decisions to be made on an individual basis rather than based simply on automatic inferences. A number of factors indicating that a marriage is likely to be genuine are also included.
[64] *Baumbast and R.v Secretary of State for the Home Department* (C-413/99) [2002] E.C.R.I-7091.

DESCENDANTS

(b) *Dependency*

The concept of dependency is one which has a European Union law meaning. The established case law can be summarised by reference to *Lebon*[65] in which the CJEU held that the factors for assessing dependency are

9–55

> "... the provision of support by the worker, without there being any need to determine the reasons for recourse to the worker's support". Accordingly the assessment of whether there is a relationship of dependency is simply a factual one, namely whether the principal provides support to the dependant[66].

A broad approach has been adopted by the CJEU in defining the status of dependants and the relationship of dependency will not be affected by the fact that the EU national does not "wholly or largely support" the dependant.[67]

It is an assessment of the financial and social situation which determines the issue, although there is in fact no need for an EU national to be financially independant. As the CJEU held in the case of *Lebon*, it would be discriminatory and contrary to the aims of European Union law if a person was automatically excluded from being considered as dependent on the principal if the dependant was in receipt of social security benefits. If the dependant was so automatically excluded, EU nationals might be disadvantaged vis-à-vis own nationals in that they might feel unable to claim social security benefits to which they are entitled.

9–56

The status of dependent family members does not presuppose a right to maintenance. There is no need to examine whether the family members concerned would in theory be able to support themselves, for example, by taking up paid employment.[68]

9–57

In its judgments on the concept of dependency, the Court has not referred to any level of standard of living for determining the need for financial support by the EU citizen.[69]

9–58

The Directive does not lay down any requirement as to the minimum duration of the dependency or the amount of material support provided, as long as the dependency is genuine. As stipulated in Recital 6 to the Directive, physical as well as financial dependence is relevant.

9–59

In *Jia* the CJEU considered that "dependent on them" means that:

9–60

---

[65] *Centre public d'aide sociale de Courcelles v Lebon* (316/85) [1987] E.C.R. 2811.
[66] *Zhu and Chen* (C-200/02) [2004] E.C.R. I-9925, at [43].
[67] J. Handoll, *Free Movement of Persons in the EU* (Chichester: John Wiley and Sons, 1995), p.251. The Dutch Government in the case of *Lebon* argued that a worker would have show that they wholly or largely supported the dependant. The CJEU did not accept that argument and instead held that even where the worker was unable to provide financial support to the dependant, that did not undermine the relationship of dependency.
[68] See *Jia v Migrationsverket* (C-1/05) January 9, 2007, at [36].
[69] See, for instance, *Jia v Migrationsverket* (C-1/05) January 9, 2007.

"members of the family of a Community national established in another Member State within the meaning of art.43 EC [now art.49 TFEU) need the material support of that Community national or their spouse in order to meet their essential needs in the State of origin of those family members or the State from which they have come at the time when they apply to join the Community national".[70]

Justification for this position came from the reference in art.4(3) of Directive 68/360 that proof of the status of the dependent relative is to be provided by a document issued by the competent authority of the "State of origin or the State whence they came", testifying that the relative concerned is dependent on the worker or their spouse. However, no such reference is made to such documents in Directive 2004/38 as regards direct descendants or ascendants. Indeed art.10(2)(d) is noteably silent on what documentary evidence is required as compared with art.10(2)(e) which stipulates that other dependant family members must provide documents from their country of origin or country from which they are arriving.

(c) *Adopted and foster children*

9–61 Since art.2(2) refers to descendants as opposed to children, there is the potential problem that the latter could be read restrictively to exclude children who are not blood descendants of either the EU national or their spouse. This might arise in the case of adopted or foster children.

9–62 Interestingly even where the legislation refers to descendants, the CJEU often uses the term "children" as if they are were interchangeable. However, there is no guidance from the CJEU on adopted children. In *Diatta*,[71] the CJEU reiterated that the family provisions could not be interpreted restrictively. The Advocate General's opinion in the case of *Baumbast*[72] referred to a right of residence in favour of the "spouse and other members of the family of a migrant worker." He considered that the terms of the regulation should not be defined restrictively. He was of the view that the CJEU must be able to take into account social and legal developments, otherwise "the relevant rules of law risk losing their effectiveness".[73]

9–63 It is axiomatic that if EU law wishes to facilitate the free movement of workers and their families then adopted children must be included. The philosophy which invariably underlines judgments of the CJEU, in particular when interpreting the scope of TFEU provisions and subordinate legislation, is the recognition that at their core such provisions reflect fundamental principles and thus fall to be widely and purposively construed. Certainly the CJEU has tended to eschew a literal reading of provisions where to do so would conflict with the underlying principles which any such

---

[70] *Jia v Migrationsverket* (C-1/05) January 9, 2007, at [43].
[71] *Diatta v Land Berlin* (267/83) [1985] E.C.R. 567, at [17].
[72] A.G. Geelhoed in *Baumbast and R. v Secretary of State for the Home Department* (C-413/99) [2002] E.C.R. I-7091, at [19].
[73] A.G. Geelhoed in *Baumbast and R. v Secretary of State for the Home Department* (C-413/99) [2002] E.C.R. I-7091, at [20].

provisions are intended to implement. As the Commission pointed out in its report to the European Parliament, adopted children are fully protected by art.8 of the European Convention on Human Rights.[74]

4. Relatives in the Ascending Line

The notion of relatives in the ascending line covers not only the father and mother of the worker and the spouse or registered partner, but also grandparents and great grandparents. It includes step-parents and adoptive parents.[75] The age of the relative in the ascending line is irrelevant.   9–64

It is to be recalled that art.2.2 refers to such relatives being "dependent" on the EU national or their spouse. The definition of dependency is the same as that attaching to descendants and thus may include emotional as well as financial dependency.   9–65

5. Other Family Members

Under art.3(2) of Directive 2004/38 Member States are directed to facilitate the entry and residence of family members other than those included in art.2(2). The obligations on the State to "facilitate" are discussed in Ch.10.   9–66

(a) *Other dependants*

The concept of "family member" is not defined in European Union law and the CJEU has yet to make a substantive ruling on this provision.   9–67

Any relative would plainly be capable of being included. The Commission's guide for the public refers to siblings, cousins, aunts and uncles and other relatives as being included. However if the concept is to be read in conformity with the ECHR it must include de facto relationships beyond the biological relationships. In such cases the nature and stability of the relationship ought to be taken into account.[76]   9–68

The concept of dependency in EU law is discussed above.[77] There is a difference in proof required for other family members to obtain residence cards as compared with dependants who fall under art.2(2). In the former case a document issued by authorities in the country of origin or country   9–69

---

[74] ECtHR cases *X v Belgium and Netherlands* (July 10, 1975), *X v France* (October 5, 1982) as well as *X, Y and Z v UK* (April 22, 1997). See Communication from the Commission to the European Parliament and the Council on guidance for better transposition and application of Directive 2004/38/EC on the right of citizens of the Union and their family members to move and reside freely within the territory of the Member States, COM/2009/0313 final.
[75] See by analogy in the context of EC-Turkey Association Agreement case of *Engin Ayaz v Land Baden-Württemberg* (C-275/02) September 30, 2004.
[76] *Olsson v Sweden No.2* (Application no. 13441/87) judgment of November 27, 1992, ECtHR.
[77] See paras 9–55 to 9–61.

from where they are arriving certifying their dependence is required.[78] It is difficult to see that this changes the nature of the dependency, as opposed to just the proof required to prove it. It is an EU law concept which for consistency and taking an unrestrictive approach to interpretation[79] should have the same meaning as under art.2(2).[80]

(b) *Living as part of the household*

9–70 Alternative to the other family members being dependent on the EU national, they may be living as part of the household. This provision has yet to receive the attention of the CJEU. However, it is an alternative to dependency and might be applied for instance in cases of parents or grandparents who do not fall under art.2 of Directive 2004/38.

(c) *Serious health grounds*

9–71 As a further alternative the family member may require the personal care of the EU citizen for serious health grounds. As with "living as part of the household" in addition to wider family members, close family members who do not meet the requirements of art.2(2) may benefit from this provision.

9–72 What "serious health grounds" might include is not defined in the Directive nor has the CJEU considered this particular provision yet. The provision might assist in cases where past dependency cannot be demonstrated but where the family member has recently suffered a serious health problem or whether the family member's previous carer is no longer able to provide the care required.

(d) *Durable relationships*

9–73 Article 3(2)(b) of Directive 2004/38 introduced into secondary legislation for the first time the possibility of a partner in durable relationship with an EU national being capable of joining or accompanying the EU national in the exercise of free movement rights. The provision refers to the durable relationship being duly attested.

9–74 The inclusion of durable relationship is plainly to be welcomed in a modern age where couples do not necessarily feel the need to formalise their relationships in law and accords with the approach taken by the European Court of Human Rights on de facto relationships.

---

[78] See further in Ch.11 below.
[79] See, for instance, *Metock v Minister for Justice, Equality and Law Reform* (C-127/08), July 25, 2008, at [93].
[80] This is subject of a reference to the European Court of Justice by a UK Immigration Tribunal in the case of *Muhammed Rahman and others v the Secretary of State for the Home Department* (C-83/11). See A-G Bots discussion of dependency at paras 98–108 of his opinion, March 27, 2012.

"As to the notion of 'family life', the Court first reiterates its well-established case law, according to which the notion of family under art.8 of the Convention is not confined to marriage-based relationships and may encompass other de facto 'family' ties where the parties are living together out of wedlock (see, among others, *Schalk and Kopf v Austria*, no. 30141/04, § 94, ECHR 2010-..., and *Keegan v Ireland*, May 26, 1994, § 44, Series A no. 290)".[81]

9–75 The concept of "durable relationship" is not defined in the Directive. It will plainly cover same and different sex couples who are in a relationship not formalised in law. The provision will also cover those who have contracted a registered partnership in Member States where registered partnerships are not recognised. The term durable must mean stable and lasting. That might be attested by proof of future commitment such as joint purchase of a property or other financial commitment. The birth of a child to the couple would generally demonstrate its durable nature as would some kind of cohabitation agreement.

9–76 The temptation of some Member States has been to set a minimum period of cohabitation such as two years before the relationship will be considered durable. As the Commission has pointed out in its report to the European Parliament "the requirement of durability of the relationship must be assessed in the light of the objective of the Directive to maintain the unity of the family in a broad sense". The Commission cautions that Member States would need to be able to take into account other relevant aspects such as mortgages given the requirement to take account of personal circumstances under art.3(2).[82]

(e) *Beyond the scope of the Directive*

9–77 Although European Union law would appear to grant to EU nationals exercising free movement rights the right to be accompanied by a broad range of family members, it is still possible to envisage circumstances where the family member in question cannot be easily fitted into the scope of the particular free movement provision in question, for instance the non-dependent descendant over the age of 21 or the non-dependant parent. The question then arises of whether European Union law would nevertheless provide an ability for that family member to be installed.

9–78 The answer is to be found in the CJEU's decisions in cases such as *Baumbast*[83] and *Zambrano*,[84] where the CJEU has held that a family member can facilitate the exercise of a free movement right and that to exclude that

---

[81] *Alim v Russia*, Application no. 39417/07, September 27, 2011, at [49].
[82] Communication from the Commission to the European Parliament and the Council on guidance for better transposition and application of Directive 2004/38/EC on the right of citizens of the Union and their family members to move and reside freely within the territory of the Member States, COM/2009/0313 final, see also Recital (6) of the Preamble to Directive 2004/38/EC.
[83] *Baumbast and R v Secretary of State for the Home Department* (C-413/99) [2002] E.C.R. I-7091.
[84] *Gerardo Ruiz Zambrano v Office National de l'Emploi (ONEM)* (C-34/09) [2011] E.C.R. I-0000.

family member would either constitute an obstacle to free movement or that the exclusion of a family member could deprive an EU citizen of effective enjoyment of citizenship rights.

9–79 In *Baumbast* the persons exercising free movement rights were children of an EU national worker in education.[85] The children were dependent on their non-EU national mother. The CJEU accepted that the children's rights could found a right of residence for their mother, an ascendant upon whom they were dependent during the exercise of their free movement rights. This was despite the fact that they could point to no Regulation or Directive upon which to found such a right. The CJEU stated:

> "The right conferred by Article 12 of Regulation No 1612/68[86] on the child of a migrant worker to pursue, under the best possible conditions, his education in the host Member State necessarily implies that that child has the right to be accompanied by the person who is his primary carer and, accordingly, that that person is able to reside with him in that Member State during his studies. To refuse to grant permission to remain to a parent who is the primary carer of the child exercising his right to pursue his studies in the host Member State infringes that right".[87]

9–80 The CJEU made reference to the right to family life protected by art.8 ECHR as being a fundamental right to which the European Union law would give effect. Applying these principles more widely if a person (not necessarily an EU national) with rights under Directive 2004/38 requires the presence of third country family member in order to exercise those rights then, even if the family member is not provided for in arts 2 or 3 of the Directive, that family member should nevertheless be given rights of residence.[88]

9–81 *Zambrano* concerns the rights of EU nationals whether or not they are free movers.[89] In *Zambrano* the CJEU considered the situation of Belgian children born and residing in Belgium with Colombian national parents who were denied permission to reside or work. Relying directly on art.20 TFEU the parents argued that the failure to grant them residence and permission to work deprived their EU citizen children the benefit of their citizenship. The CJEU reiterated that citizenship of the Union is intended to be the

---

[85] Pursuant to art.12 of Regulation 1612/68 (now art.10 of Regulation 492/2011). See now decision of the CJEU in *Man Lavette Chen and Kunqian Catherine Zhu v Secretary of State for the Home Department* (C-200/02) October 19, 2004. See also, *London Borough of Harrow v Nimco Ibrahim* (C-310/08), February 23, 2010. It is important to note that art.12 of Regulation 1612/68 (now art.10 of Regulation 492/2011) survives the implementation of Directive 2004/38 and thus children of former EU national workers who are in education in a Member State are entitled to have installed with them their primary carer parents.
[86] Now art.10 of Regulation 492/2011.
[87] *Baumbast and R v Secretary of State for the Home Department* (C-413/99) [2002] E.C.R. I-7091, at [73]. Further questions have been referred to the CJEU on the nature of the relationship between the child and the primary carer in *Ajoke and Others v Secretary of State for the Home Department* (C-529/11).
[88] Rights of residence are considered more in Ch.10. However, reading *Baumbast* together with *Zambrano* if the effective enjoyment of rights by the principal requires the family member to be able to work then the permission to work must be granted with permission to reside.
[89] *Gerardo Ruiz Zambrano v Office National de l'Emploi (ONEM)* (C-34/09) [2011] E.C.R. I-0000.

fundamental status of nationals of the European Union and stated that any national measure that has the effect of depriving citizens of the Union genuine enjoyment of their rights would be contrary to art.20. According to the CJEU this would be the case following

> "a refusal to grant a right of residence to a third country national with dependent minor children in the Member State where those children are nationals and reside, and also a refusal to grant such a person a work permit".[90]

The CJEU assumed that the children would otherwise have to leave the territory of the Union in order to accompany their parents.

It would seem that the conditions necessary for the deployment of the *Zambrano* principles are that if an EU national can demonstrate that the family member's presence is necessary for the enjoyment of citizenship rights and that without the family member the EU national would have to leave the EU altogether, then the family member should be given rights of residence.[91] This is even the case where the EU national is not exercising rights under Directive 2004/38. 9–82

It is interesting in this context to consider whether an EU national is also entitled as a matter of European Union law to install child-carers who may not be family members in any strict sense. It is certainly arguable that European Union law would entitle the EU national to install such persons, if to fail to do so would represent an obstacle to free movement rights. Single parent EU nationals, for instance, who require a carer to look after the children whilst they are at work, might argue that failure by a Member State to grant the right of residence to that child-carer either prevents the EU nationals from exercising the free movement right, or interferes with the EU nationals' right to respect for family life, if the inability to be accompanied by the carer means that the children would have to leave the European Union. This is a choice which in *Carpenter* the CJEU considered unacceptable as a matter of European Union law when read in conjunction with the ECHR.[92] 9–83

---

[90] *Gerardo Ruiz Zambrano v Office National de l'Emploi (ONEM)* (C-34/09) [2011] E.C.R. I-0000, at [44].
[91] In *McCarthy (Shirley) v Secretary of State for the Home Department* (C-434/09) [2011] E.C.R. I-0000 the CJEU found that a dual Irish/British national would not be deprived of her Union citizenship rights if her husband could not reside with her in the UK. The Court's judgment is somewhat opaque but in essence it appears that as a dual national of two Member States the Court was not convinced that she would be deprived of enjoyment of the right of residence in the EU as a whole by measures taken to exclude her husband in one Member State. In *Dereci and others v Bundesministerium für Inneres* (C-256/11) [2012] E.C.R. I-0000, the CJEU explained that it was not enough for a Union citizen to assert that it was desirable to have his family member living with him in his own Member State. It would be for the national court to consider on the facts whether denial of residence to that family member would result in the Union citizen having to leave the European Union. The same principles would apply where the Union citizen was residing in a Member State that was not their own and wished to have with them a family member who did not fall within the scope of arts 2 and 3 of Directive 2004/38.
[92] *Carpenter v Secretary of State for the Home Department* (C-60/00) [2002] E.C.R. I-6279.

9–84 That argument could similarly be deployed in the case of EU national children whose effective enjoyment of their citizenship rights would be interfered with if their primary carer could not reside lawfully in the Member State.

(f) *Without the EU national*

9–85 While the rights granted to family members in the Directive are generally dependent upon their family relationship, the Directive grants protection to family members in the event of death of the Union citizen, divorce, annulment of marriage or termination of a registered partnership by calling for the adoption of measures

> "to ensure that in such circumstances family members already residing within the territory of the host member state retain their right of residence exclusively on a personal basis".[93]

It also grants a right of permanent residence to family members after having resided in a State for a continuous period of five years. Once the family members have achieved permanent residence their residence is no longer dependant on their relationship with the EU national.[94] These provisions are considered further in Ch.10.

---

[93] See Recital 15 of the Preamble to Directive 2004/38 and arts 12 and 13 of the Directive.
[94] See Recital 17 of the Preamble to Directive 2004/38 and arts 16–18 of the Directive.

Chapter 10

RIGHTS OF ENTRY AND RESIDENCE

This chapter examines the scope of the rights of entry and residence enjoyed by Union citizens who exercise free movement rights and their family members.

1. Introduction

(a) *Right of entry and residence as a corollary of right to move*

The right of entry residence in other Member States is the corollary of the fundamental principles contained in the Treaty on the European Union and the Treaty on the Functioning of the European Union, for the purpose of establishing a common market and the promotion of the harmonious development of economic activities between Member States. Obstacles to the free movement of persons between Member States shall be abolished.[1] Plainly this would be impossible without the right to enter into and reside in other Member States. 10–01

(b) *Deriving the right of residence from the Treaty*

The CJEU has constantly emphasised that it is the TFEU[2] itself (or, depending on the case, by the provisions adopted to implement it) which is the source of the right to enter into and reside in the territory of another Member State. This has important ramifications, notably that breaches of formalities, whether of specific provisions of the relevant directives or the national law of Member States relating to entry and residence, will not justify denial of the right. This principle was firmly established in *Royer*[3] in which a French national faced criminal proceedings and expulsion arising from his illegal entry into and residence in Belgian territory where his wife, also a French national, ran a café and dance hall. As the CJEU stated, the regulations and directives determine "the scope and detailed rules for the exercise of rights conferred directly by the Treaty".[4] Since the right of residence is acquired independently of the issue of a residence permit, the grant of the permit itself does not give rise to rights at all but is simply a measure "to prove the individual position of a national of another Member State with regard to provisions of Community law."[5] Further, the issue of 10–02

---

[1] See *Watson and Belmann* (118/75) [1976] E.C.R. 1185, at [16a].
[2] The Treaty on the Functioning of the European Union which replaced the EC Treaty.
[3] *Procureur de Roi v Royer* (48/75) [1976] E.C.R 497. See also, for example, *R. v Immigration Appeal Tribunal and Surinder Singh Ex p. Secretary of State for Home Department* (370/90) [1992] E.C.R. I-4265 where at [17] the CJEU refers to the right to enter and reside in the territory of other Member States in order to pursue an economic activity there as envisaged by Arts 39 and 43 EC Treaty as a right which such persons "derive directly from ... the Treaty".
[4] *Procureur de Roi v Royer* (48/75) [1976] E.C.R. 497.
[5] *Procureur de Roi v Royer* (48/75) [1976] E.C.R. 497.

the permit has merely declaratory effect.[6] Whilst the TFEU itself thus confers the right of residence directly on all those within its ambit, the various directives and regulations (to adopt the words of the CJEU in *Royer*[7]) give "closer articulation" to such right.

(c) *Human rights and proportionality*

10–03 Even where the Treaty and secondary legislation do not directly confer a right of residence, the CJEU has in recent years through the use of human rights and the principle of proportionality inferred a right of residence, particularly in relation to third country national family members. This is most apparent where not to recognise such right would create an obstacle to the exercise of fundamental freedoms under the Treaty.

10–04 For example, in *Carpenter*[8] the CJEU held that art.49 EC Treaty [now art.56 TFEU], read in the light of the fundamental right to respect for family life, gave the right of residence in the United Kingdom to a third country national spouse of a British citizen who was providing services to recipients established in other Member States.

10–05 Further in *Baumbast*[9] the CJEU held that by direct application of art.18(1) of the EC Treaty[10] a right of residence in the United Kingdom was conferred on a German national who no longer enjoyed a right of residence as a worker. Whilst the exercise of such right is subject to the limitations and conditions laid down by the TFEU and by the measures adopted to give it effect,

> "the competent authorities and, where necessary, the national courts must ensure that those limitations and conditions are applied in compliance with the general principles of Community law and, in particular, the principle of proportionality".[11]

Such limitations and conditions include the requirements that a person has sufficient resources to avoid becoming a burden on the social assistance system of the host Member State during their period of residence and that they are covered by sickness insurance in respect of all risks.[9] As to the latter condition, an adjudicator had found that Mr Baumbast was not covered for emergency treatment. However, in light of the circumstances of the case the CJEU held that:

---

[6] See *Sagulo, Brenca and Bakhouche* (8/77) [1977] E.C.R. 1495 and see also *R. v Pieck* (157/79) [1980] E.C.R. 2171.
[7] *Procureur de Roi v Royer* (48/75) [1976] E.C.R 497.
[8] *Carpenter v Secretary of State for the Home Department* (C-60/00) [2002] E.C.R. I-6279, at [46].
[9] *Baumbast and R. v Secretary of State for the Home Department* (C-413/99) [2002] E.C.R. I-7091, at [80–94].
[10] Now art.21(1) of the TFEU.
[11] *Baumbast and R v Secretary of State for the Home Department* (C-413/99) [2002] E.C.R. I-7091, at [94].

Specific Rights of Residence for EU Nationals

"to refuse to allow Mr Baumbast to exercise the right of residence which is conferred on him by Article 18(1) E.C. Treaty [now Article 21(1) TFEU] by virtue of the application of the provisions of Directive 90/364 on the ground that his sickness insurance does not cover the emergency treatment given in the host Member State would amount to a disproportionate interference with the exercise of that right".[12]

2. Specific Rights of Residence for EU Nationals and their Family Members under Directive 2004/38

(a) *The rights of residence for up to three months*

All Union citizens have the right of residence on the territory of the Member States for up to three months without any conditions or formalities other than the requirement to hold a valid identity card or passport.[13] Non-EU national family members of the Union citizen who are accompanying or joining a Union citizen may also reside in the host Member State for up to three months without formality or conditions. Such family member would need to produce only valid passport and evidence of the relationship with the Union citizen.[14]

10–06

(b) *The rights of residence for more than three months*

Under art.7(1) of Directive 2004/38 Union citizens have the right of residence for longer than three months if they are:

10–07

(a) workers or self-employed persons,

(b) have sufficient resources for themselves and their family members not to become a burden on the social assistance system of the host Member State during their period of residence and if they have comprehensive sickness insurance cover in the host Member State,

(c) are enrolled at a private or public establishment for the purpose of following a course of study and if they have comprehensive sickness insurance cover and assure the relevant State authorities that they have sufficient resources for themselves and their family members not to become a burden on the social assistance system of the host Member State, and

(d) the family member accompanying or joining a Union citizen satisfies (a), (b) or (c) above.

---

[12] *Baumbast and R v Secretary of State for the Home Department*, at [93].
[13] art.6(1) of Directive 2004/38. Recital 10 of the Preamble to the Directive states that "persons exercising their right of residence should not, however, become an unreasonable burden on the social assistance system of the host Member State during an initial period of residence".
[14] art.6(2) of Directive 2004/38.

10–08 The right of residence is granted also to non-EU national family members accompanying or joining a Union citizen who satisfies (a), (b) or (c) above.[15] However, students falling under (c) have a more qualified set of family members who have the right of residence. Dependants in the ascending line of students are to have their residence facilitated by the host Member State like other family members under art.3(2) of Directive 2004/38.[16]

(c) *Retained right of residence*

10–09 There are three different ways in which rights of residence may be retained under the Directive:

(i) For Union citizens who are workers or self-employed persons:

Under art.7(3) of Directive 2004/38 a person will retain the status of worker or self-employed person in circumstances specified in art.7(3) namely where they are temporarily unable to work as a result of illness or accident, where they are involuntarily unemployed subject to various conditions or if they have embarked on vocation training subject to various conditions.

(ii) For family members where the Union citizen dies or departs from the Member State:

(a) If the family member is an EU national then the death or departure of the Union citizen who had been exercising free movement rights will not affect his rights of residence.[17]

(b) If the family member is a non-EU national then the death of the Union citizen will not result in the loss of right of residence for the family member providing that he has been residing in the host Member State for at least one year as a family member.[18] The right of residence is retained on an exclusively personal basis and cannot be passed on to other family members.

(c) If the family member is a child or parent of a the child of an Union citizen then the Union citizen's departure from the host Member State or his death will not result in a loss of right of residence for that family member if the child is enrolled in an educational establishment until the completion of their studies.[19]

---

[15] art.7(2) of Directive 2004/38.
[16] art.7(4) of Directive 2004/38.
[17] art.12(1) of Directive 2004/38. Permanent residence for this category will not be achieved until the person is able to fulfil the condition of being a free mover as set out in art.7(1), namely economically active or self-sufficient or a student or become as a family member of one.
[18] art.12(2) of Directive 2004/38. Permanent residence for this category will not be achieved until the person is a worker, self-employed person or has sufficient resources not to be a burden on the social assistance system of the host Member State.
[19] art.12(3) of Directive 2004/38. There are no specific requirements to be met for this category to achieve permanent residence. This provision needs to be read alongside art.12 of Regulation 1612/68 (which survives the coming into force of Directive 2004/38 but is now replaced by art.10 of Regulation 492/2011) and which makes similar provision for children of former workers but where the worker is still living in the host Member State; see *London Borough of Harrow v Nimco Hassan Ibrahim* (C-310/08) February 23, 2010.

(iii) For family members in the event of divorce, annulment of marriage or termination of registered partnership:
  (a) If the family member is an EU national then divorce, annulment of a marriage or termination of a registered partnership will not affect their right of residence.[20]
  (b) If the family member is a non-EU national then in certain circumstances the ex-spouse or ex-registered partner will retain a right of residence[21] in the host Member State where:
   - The marriage or partnership has lasted three years prior to the initiation of divorce, annulment or termination of the partnership, one of which was in the host Member State.[22]
   - By agreement or court order the non-EU national ex-spouse or partner has custody of the Union citizen's children.[23]
   - There are particularly difficult circumstances such as domestic violence.[24]
   - By agreement or court order the non-EU national has a right of access to a minor child provided that the court has ruled that the access must be in the host Member State.[25]

(d) *Right to permanent residence*

(i) *Permanent residence after five years*

Article 16(1) of Directive 2004/38 provides that as a general rule Union citizens who have resided legally for a continuous period of five years in the host Member State will have the right of permanent residence. Non-EU family members who are have legally resided with the Union citizen in the host Member State for a continuous period of five years similarly have a permanent right of residence.[26]

(ii) *Persons no longer working in the host Member State*

Union citizen workers or self-employed persons can obtain the permanent right of residence earlier than five years if:

(a) They retire, either in line with pension law or take early retirement, having worked in the preceding 12 months in the host Member State and having resided there for more than three years.[27]

---

[20] art.13(1) of Directive 2004/38. Permanent residence for this category will not be achieved until the person is able to fulfil the condition of being a free mover as set out in art.7(1), namely being economically active or self-sufficient or a student or becomes a family member of one.
[21] Family members retain their right of residence under this category exclusively on a personal basis. Permanent residence for this category will not be achieved until the person is a worker, self-employed person or has sufficient resources not to be a burden on the social assistance system of the host Member State.
[22] art.13(2)(a) of Directive 2004/38.
[23] art.13(2)(b) of Directive 2004/38.
[24] art.13(2)(c) of Directive 2004/38.
[25] art.13(2)(d) of Directive 2004/38.
[26] art.16(2) of Directive 2004/38.
[27] art.17(1)(a) of Directive 2004/38.

(b) They stop working due to permanent incapacity having resided in the host Member State for two years (or less if the incapacity is a result of an accident at work or occupational disease resulting in a benefit payable in full or part by an institution in the host Member State).[28]

(c) They stop working in the host Member State after three years continuous employment, work in another Member State but return to the host Member State to reside there at least once a week.[29]

The family members of Union citizen workers or self employed persons can obtain the permanent right of residence earlier than five years and even where the Union citizen has not acquired permanent residence status if:

(a) The Union citizen was a worker or self-employed person who dies whilst still working having at the time of death resided continuously on the territory of the Member State for two years or where the death results from an accident at work or an occupational disease.[30]

(b) The family member is the spouse who lost the nationality of that Member State following marriage to the worker or self-employed person, that Union citizen having died while still working in the Member State.[31]

(iii) *Family members of Union citizens*

10–12 Certain non-EU family members of Union citizens will acquire the right of permanent residence after legally residing in the host Member State for five years where:

(a) The Union citizen has died and the family resided in the host Member State for at least one year before the Union citizen's death providing the family member is economically active or self-sufficient.[32]

(b) The family member is one of those who benefits from a retained right of residence following divorce, annulment of marriage or termination of registered partnership under art.13(2) of Directive 2004/38 providing that the family member is economically active or self-sufficient.[33]

3. Formalities

10–13 Identified below for each free mover and the types of family member are the particular documents which are required in order to establish the rights of entry and residence. In this section consideration is given to the principles which have been developed by the CJEU in the context of formalities, the

---

[28] art.17(1)(b) of Directive 2004/38.
[29] art.17(1)(c) of Directive 2004/38.
[30] art.17(4)(a) and 17(4)(b) of Directive 2004/38.
[31] art.17(4)(c) of Directive 2004/38.
[32] art.18 of Directive 2004/38 referring to art.12(2) family members.
[33] art.18 of Directive 2004/38, see para.10–09 above.

possible consequences of failure to comply with formalities, time limits, fees and visas.

It is to be noted at the outset that the formalities are the same in respect of all free movers covered by Directive 2004/38.[34] Articles 4 and 5 set out the administrative requirements in relation to exit and entry for both Union citizens and their family members, art.6 sets out the requirements for residence up to three months for both Union citizens and their family members, art.8 lays down the administrative formalities for Union citizens, and arts 9 to 11 lay down the administrative formalities for third country national family members. **10–14**

(a) *Declaratory effect of residence documents and visas*

The principles established by the CJEU in *Royer*[35] about the right of residence deriving from the EC Treaty itself and the declaratory effect of residence permits have already been emphasised. For Mr Royer, a French national who had failed to comply with formalities concerning his entry and residence in Belgium, these principles meant that neither his temporary imprisonment for such failures nor his expulsion could be justified. **10–15**

However, these principles have much wider impact as shown by the decision in *MRAX*[36] where the CJEU considered the position of a third country national marrying a worker in Belgium after having entered and remained unlawfully in Belgium. The Belgian Government argued that it was entitled both to refuse a residence permit to a third country national and to expel such person, lest art.3 of both Directives 68/360 and 73/148 (which enabled visas to be required of third country national family members) would be rendered "meaningless and entirely redundant". The CJEU disagreed. Just as the issue of a residence permit to a national of a Member State is simply a measure to prove the person's position with regard to provisions of Union law, so "the same finding must be made" in relation to such third country national whose right of residence exists irrespective of the issue of a residence permit.[37] Refusal of a permit and expulsion based solely on failure to comply with legal formalities concerning the control of aliens "would impair the very substance of the right of residence directly conferred by Community law and would be manifestly disproportionate to the gravity of the infringement."[38] Thus where a third country national is able to provide proof of identity and marriage to a national of a Member State[39] neither **10–16**

---

[34] Formerly provided for in Directive 68/360 for workers and Directive 73/148 for those exercising the right of establishment and freedom to receive and provide services.
[35] *Procureur de Roi v Royer* (48/75) [1976] E.C.R 497.
[36] *Mouvement contre le Racisme, l'Antisèmitisme et la Xènophobie ASBL (MRAX) v Belgian State* (C-459/99) [2002] E.C.R. I-6591.
[37] *Procureur de Roi v Royer* (48/75) [1976] E.C.R 497.
[38] *Mouvement contre le Racisme, l'Antisèmitisme et la Xènophobie ASBL (MRAX) v Belgian State* (C-459/99) [2002] E.C.R. I-6591, at [78].
[39] As effectively was required (respectively) by arts 4 and 6 of Directives 68/360 and 73/148 and now required by arts 5 and 10 of Directive 2004/38.

refusal of a permit nor expulsion "on the sole ground that he has entered the territory of the Member State concerned unlawfully" is permitted.[40]

10–17 There is nothing to suggest that the coming into force of Directive 2004/38 changed that position. In *Metock* the CJEU confirmed its case law in *MRAX* and emphasised that Recital 3 in the preamble to the Directive set out the aim to strengthen the right of free movement and residence for all Union citizens, "so that Union citizens cannot derive less rights from that directive than from the instruments of secondary legislation which it amends or repeals".[41]

(b) *Member States cannot ask for more than permitted in legislation*

10–18 It is a fundamental principle that Member States cannot ask more of those exercising rights of entry and residence than is prescribed in the provisions themselves. Indeed Recital 14 in the Preamble to Directive 2004/38 makes clear that the documents required by authorities for the issuing of residence documentation is comprehensively set out in the Directive

"in order to avoid divergent administrative practices or interpretations constituting an undue obstacle to the exercise of the right of residence by Union citizens and their family members".

10–19 Thus for example in relation to the right of entry of Union citizens referred to in art.3 of Directive 2004/38 Member States may require only the production of a valid identity document or passport.[42] In relation to the entry of family members the Commission makes clear in its guidance that Member States may require only the presentation of a valid passport and evidence of the family link.[43] Accordingly "no additional documents, such as a proof of accommodation, sufficient resources, an invitation letter or return ticket, can be required".[44]

---

[40] *Mouvement contre le Racisme, l'Antisèmitisme et la Xènophobie ASBL (MRAX) v Belgian State* (C-459/99) [2002] E.C.R. I-6591, at [80].

[41] para.59 of *Metock v Minister for Justice, Equality and Law Reform* (C-127/08) July 25, 2008. *Metock* is an important decision of the CJEU for two reasons. First, it ensures that Directive 2004/38 could not be interpreted in a more restrictive way or be used to denigrate the rights of EU nationals and their family members than was the case under previous secondary legislation. Secondly, it specifically overturned its own decision in *Akrich* (C-109/01) [2003] E.C.R. I-9607 which had caused a good deal of confusion at the very least and provided a potentially potent formula for Member States to restrict the rights of EU citizens and their family members on the grounds of lack of prior lawful residence.

[42] *Commission v Belgium* (321/87) [1989] E.C.R. 997 considered a similar provision in art.3 of Directive 68/360.

[43] Such as marriage certificate and also proof of dependency, serious health grounds, durability of partnerships, where applicable.

[44] See Communication from the Commission to the European Parliament and the Council on guidance for better transposition and application of Directive 2004/38/EC on the right of citizens of the Union and their family members to move and reside freely within the territory of the Member States, COM/2009/0313 final.

10–20 In *Commission v Netherlands*[45] an action was brought by the Commission for a declaration that the Netherlands had failed to fulfil the obligations imposed by Directives 68/360 and 73/148[46] by maintaining in force legislation requiring citizens of Member States to answer questions posed by border officials about the purpose and duration of their journey and the financial means at their disposal. The Dutch Government argued that the Directives applied only to those with a right of residence by virtue of the EU Treaties and that Member States were entitled to carry out spot checks at frontiers to investigate whether nationals have such right of residence. The CJEU granted the declaration, emphasising the general right to enter enjoyed by nationals of Member States in the exercise of the various freedoms. The condition that a valid identity document or passport be produced could not be supplemented by a requirement proving inclusion in any particular category covered by the directives. Nor more generally could the obligation to answer questions put by frontier officials be a pre-condition for entry. The lawfulness of control on entry is limited to assessing whether the identity document produced is valid.

10–21 It is clear that art.5 enables Member States to require only the production of an identity card or passport. A Member State may not impose any further border checks or require any further documentation as a pre-condition to admission.[47] This principle was confirmed in *Commission v Belgium*[48] although at first blush the decision might be thought to dilute the principle.

10–22 The case concerned the carrying out of checks at the border of a person's residence permit in order to ensure compliance with the obligation imposed by Belgian law to carry such permit. The Belgian government argued that inspection of residence permits was not a frontier control but part of a general system of police checks carried out habitually throughout Belgian territory to which all inhabitants are liable which may "incidentally" be carried out at the same time as the frontier control. The Commission on the other hand argued that the controls carried out at the time of entry added to the requirement of a production of an identity card. The CJEU did not consider the checks to be inconsistent with art.3. In particular there was no dispute that the controls were carried out "sporadically and unsystematically" and further that they were part of a system of internal control exercised by Belgium over all its inhabitants. As regards such internal controls the CJEU held:

> "The controls at issue are not a condition for the exercise of the right of entry into Belgian territory and it is undisputed that Community law does not prevent Belgium from checking, within its territory, compliance with the obligation imposed on persons enjoying a right of residence under Community law to carry

---

[45] *Commission v Netherlands* (C-68/89) [1991] E.C.R. I-2637.
[46] Now replaced by Directive 2004/38.
[47] See further Communication from the Commonwealth to the European Parliament and the Canal on guidance for better transportation and application of Directive 2004/38/EC on the right of citizens of the Union and their family members to move and reside freely within the territory of the Member States, COM/2009/0313 final.
[48] *Commission v Belgium* (321/87) [1989] E.C.R. 997.

their residence or establishment permits at all times, where an identical obligation is imposed upon Belgian nationals as regards their identity card".[49]

10–23   It was crucial to the CJEU's decision that the checks were in fact part of a system of internal control. Such checks if carried out at the border outside of such system of internal control would constitute a barrier to the free movement of persons and be unlawful if carried out in a systematic, arbitrary or unnecessarily restrictive manner.

10–24   Directive 2004/38 takes the "shall require no more" principle even further to make clear that even in cases where an EU national or their family member cannot produce a valid identity document this should not lead to automatic exclusion. Instead such persons are to be "given a reasonable opportunity to obtain the necessary documents ... or prove by other means that they are covered by the right of free movement and residence."[50]

(c) *Failure to comply with formalities*

10–25   It is very clear from Directive 2004/38, reflective of the decisions of the CJEU in *Royer*[51] and *MRAX*,[52] where the person concerned is able to fulfil the relevant conditions laid down that failure to comply with formalities will not in itself justify interference with the rights of either entry or residence, whether by refusal and return at the border,[53] or by expulsion thereafter[54] (nor indeed could any such failure in itself constitute a threat to public policy). This is because such measures would negate the very rights conferred and guaranteed by the TFEU.[55] Article 25 of the Directive makes clear that the possession of residence documents "may under no circumstances be made a precondition for the exercise of a right... as entitlement to rights may be attested by any other means of proof".

10–26   Furthermore, the corollary to the principle that Member States cannot ask for more than is permitted in the provisions themselves is that all forms of punishment will be prohibited for disregard of a provision which is incompatible with Union law. This was the position in the case of the national law provisions considered by the CJEU in *Sagula*[56] which required workers to possess a general residence permit instead of the document provided for in Directive 68/360.[57]

---

[49] *Commission v Belgium* (321/87) [1989] E.C.R. 997, at [12].
[50] art.5(4) of Directive 2004/38.
[51] *Procureur de Roi v Royer* (48/75) [1976] E.C.R. 497.
[52] *Mouvement contre le Racisme, l'Antisèmitisme et la Xènophobie ASBL (MRAX) v Belgian State* (C-459/99) [2002] E.C.R. I-6591.
[53] art.5(4) of Directive 2004/38.
[54] art.9(3) of Directive 2004/38 states that failure to comply with the requirement to apply for residence card may make the person concerned liable to proportionate and non-discriminatory sanctions.
[55] See also, *R. v Pieck* (157/79) [1980] E.C.R. 2171, particularly at [18].
[56] *Sagula* (8/77) [1977] E.C.R. 1495.
[57] Directive 68/360 is replaced by Directive 2004/38.

On the other hand this principle does not preclude the application of sanctions to those exercising free movement rights for infringement of national provisions which have been adopted in conformity with EU law provisions.[58] And moreover, as stated by the CJEU in *Royer*:[59]

10–27

> "Community law does not prevent the member states from providing, for breaches of national provisions concerning the control of aliens, any appropriate sanctions—other than measures of expulsion from the territory—necessary in order to ensure the efficacy of those provisions".

What are the possible sanctions for breaches of formalities? In *Pieck*[60] the CJEU confirmed the entitlement of national authorities to impose penalties in respect of such breaches "comparable to those attaching to minor offences by nationals". However, penalties would not be justified if so disproportionate to the gravity of the infringement that they become an obstacle to the free movement of persons. This would be especially so if the penalty included imprisonment. In practice this means that breaches of formalities may be punishable by fines, provided always that they are at a level which is proportionate to the gravity of the offence.

10–28

(d) *Time-limits for providing visas and residence permits*

Directive 2004/38 is silent as to the period of time within which Member States are required to issue visas, although Member States are obliged to afford third country national family members with "every facility to obtain the necessary visas". Such visas are to be issued "as soon as possible and on the basis of an accelerated procedure".[61] The Commission considers that anything longer than four weeks would be unreasonable.[62]

10–29

Registration certificates for EU citizens, whether they are the person exercising free movement rights or the family member, are to be issued "immediately".[63] Non-EU national family members are to apply for a residence card and this is to be issued within six months of application. A certificate of application for a residence card is to be issued immediately.[64]

10–30

Permanent residence certificates for Union citizens are to be issued "as soon as possible".[65] Permenant residence cards for non-EU national family members are to be issued within six months of application.[66]

10–31

---

[58] art.8(2) (for Union citizens) and art.9(3) (for third country nationals) of Directive 2004/38 refers to "proportionate and non-discriminatory sanctions" for failure to obtain the relevant registration certificate or residence card.
[59] *Procureur de Roi v Royer* (48/75) [1976] E.C.R. 497, at [42].
[60] *R. v Pieck* (157/79) [1980] E.C.R. 2171, at [19].
[61] art.5(2) of Directive 2004/38.
[62] See Communication from the Commission to the European Parliament and the Council on guidance for better transposition and application of Directive 2004/38/EC on the right of citizens of the Union and their family members to move and reside freely within the territory of the Member States, COM/2009/0313 final.
[63] art.8(2) of Directive 2004/38.
[64] art.10(1) of Directive 2004/38.
[65] art.19(1) of Directive 2004/38.
[66] art.20(1) of Directive 2004/38.

10–32 The obligation to issue registration certificates "as soon possible" is not defined by reference to any period of time. However, it is clear that such documents must be issued promptly and without delay since delay could impair the very substance of rights given by Union law by hindering their exercise. Furthermore, any unreasonable or excessive delay would be disproportionate and unlawful.

10–33 None of the formalities raise particularly difficult questions: on the contrary, most are straightforward matters. The six months permitted in the Directive for the issue of residence cards and permanent residence cards is a maximum period and Member States should be routinely responding more speedily to applications.

10–34 These propositions clearly reflect the views of the Commission which states:

> "the deadline must be interpreted in light of art.10 of the EC Treaty [now art.3a TEU] and the maximum period of six months is justified only in cases where examination of the application involves public policy considerations".[67]

(e) *Time limits imposed on applicants to comply with administrative formalities*

10–35 For EU citizens the deadline imposed by Member States for registration may not be less than three months from the date of arrival.[68] For non-EU citizen family members the deadline for submitting the residence card application is also to be not less than three months from date of arrival.[69] In both cases failure to comply with any requirement to apply for residence documentation may only make the person concerned liable to proportionate and non-discriminatory sanctions.

10–36 As pointed out by the Commission in proceedings instituted against Belgium:[70]

> "[T]he fact that the administrative procedures for the grant of the residence permit have not been complied with may not lead to a penalty such as refusal to grant the right of residence or removal from the territory, which would effectively deny the actual right of residence conferred by the Treaty. The notification of an order to leave the territory may be based not on exclusively administrative grounds, but on facts leading to the conclusion that the person concerned does not fulfil the conditions set for his right of residence by one of the relevant directives".

The CJEU agreed with the Commission that it was incompatible with Union law for national authorities to serve automatic notice of an order to leave

---

[67] See Communication from the Commission to the European Parliament and the Council on guidance for better transposition and application of Directive 2004/38/EC on the right of citizens of the Union and their family members to move and reside freely within the territory of the Member States COM/2009/0313 final.
[68] art.8(2) of Directive 2004/38.
[69] art.9(2) of Directive 2004/38.
[70] *Commission v Belgium* (C-408/03) O.J. November 15, 2003.

the territory of the host Member State because of a failure to provide documents to the authorities within a prescribed period of time.[71]

(f) *Fees*

Directive 2004/38 distinguishes between fees for residence documents and visas. Visas for non-EU national family members are to be issued free of charge.[72] Article 25(2) contains a general prohibition on the charging for residence documents other than a fee not exceeding that imposed on nationals for the issuing of similar documents.

10–37

(g) *Visas*

(i) *EU Nationals*

As discussed, EU nationals exercising free movement rights must be allowed to enter the territory simply on production of a valid identity card or passport.[73] The provisions expressly provide further that no "entry visa or equivalent document" may be demanded of such EU nationals. In *Pieck*[74] the British Government argued that the phrase meant exclusively a document issued before the traveller arrives at the frontier in the form of an endorsement on a passport or of a separate document, but not an endorsement stamped on a passport at the time of arrival giving permission to enter. The CJEU rejected the argument. The phrase covers

10–38

> "any formality for the purpose of granting leave to enter the territory of a Member State which is coupled with a passport or identity card check at the frontier, whatever may be the place or time at which that leave is granted and in whatever form it may be granted."[75]

(ii) *Non-EU national family members*

The position for family members who are not nationals of Member States is different. The provisions do enable entry visas or equivalent documents to be demanded of third country nationals, although Member States are obliged to afford to such persons "every facility for obtaining any necessary visas." Plainly this obligation falls to be broadly construed consistent with fundamental nature of the rights being exercised both by the EU national and their family members. It would certainly not be met by the offer of an

10–39

---

[71] *Commission v Belgium* (C-408/03) March 23, 2006 at [68–70]. The CJEU was not persuaded by arguments put forward by the Belgian Government that the notice to leave would not be acted upon immediately. The service of such an order would be liable to deter citizens of the Union from exercising their freedom of movement.
[72] art.5(2) of Directive 2004/38.
[73] art.5(1) of Directive 2004/38.
[74] *R. v Pieck* (157/79) [1980] E.C.R. 2171, in which case a Dutch national working in Wales whose passport on entry was stamped "given leave to enter the United Kingdom for six months" was prosecuted for having knowingly remained beyond the six months given.
[75] Further, to require such endorsement would offend the principle that Member States cannot ask for more than is permitted in the legislation discussed above. Following *Pieck*, the UK's legislation was changed: by s.7 of Immigration Act 1988 those exercising Treaty rights do not require "leave to enter or remain".

interview at an embassy for consideration to be given to an application for a visa some months away. Reflective of the decision of the CJEU in *MRAX*,[76] art.5(4) of Directive 2004/38 makes specific provision for the third country national family member who arrives at the border without a visa and there is, to all intents and purposes, little practical difference, at least in terms of the right of entry, between their position and that of the EU national.

10–40 The first question considered by the CJEU in *MRAX* was whether the provisions of the Directives, read in the light of the principles of proportionality and non-discrimination and the right to respect for family life, allowed a Member State at the border to send back a foreign national married to a Community national who seeks to enter without being in possession of either an identity document or a visa. The CJEU acknowledged that the exercise of the right of entry could be made conditional on possession of a visa. However the obligation to accord every facility would be denied its "full effect" unless visas were issued without delay and as far as possible at the place of entry into the national territory.[77] Further, in view of the importance attached to the protection of family life it would be disproportionate and prohibited:

> "to send back a third country national married to a national of a Member State where he is able to prove his identity and the conjugal ties and there is no evidence to establish that he represents a risk to the requirements of public policy, public security or public health within the meaning of art.10 of Directive 68/360 and art.8 of Directive 73/148 [now art.27 of Directive 2004/38]".[78]

10–41 In sum the position is as follows, Member States are entitled to make the exercise of the right of entry for family members conditional on possession of a visa. In practical terms this may mean that the third country national who tries to travel without a visa could face difficulties because of carrier sanctions. For those family members who do make it to the border without documents but are able to prove their identity and relationship, this potential pre-condition is irrelevant since they will not (subject to the public policy proviso) be able to be returned. This does not mean, however, that they might not be liable to lesser sanctions than being returned for having failed to obtain necessary visas. The CJEU has suggested that such lesser sanctions could take the form of administrative fines.

10–42 Family members may be required to provide confirmation of the family relationship. However, obtaining visas cannot be made subject to any requirements beyond such confirmation. Thus, for example, evidence of

---

[76] *Mouvement contre le Racisme, l'Antisèmitisme et la Xènophobie ASBL (MRAX) v Belgium* (C-459/99) [2002] E.C.R. I-6591.
[77] *Mouvement contre le Racisme, l'Antisèmitisme et la Xènophobie ASBL (MRAX) v Belgium* (C-459/99) [2002] E.C.R. I-6591.
[78] *Mouvement contre le Racisme, l'Antisèmitisme et la Xènophobie ASBL (MRAX) v Belgium* (C-459/99) [2002] E.C.R. I-6591.

means of support must not be required of the third country national spouse of a worker or work seeker.[79]

(h) *Residence documents*

In respect of each category of free mover the documentation required to be produced by both principal and family member in order to obtain the relevant residence document is considered below. The documents themselves are issued as proof of the right of residence and are required to take particular forms.

10–43

The corollary to the proposition that residence documents are declaratory of the underlying rights to which they relate is that possession of a residence document cannot be taken to be proof positive of the existence of a right to remain. Thus, for example, an EU citizen who is the holder of a registration certificate cannot claim that he has a right to reside in the host Member State merely for possessing such registration certificate if he cannot point to an underlying right to reside based on the TFEU or a relevant provision under Directive 2004/38 or any other secondary legislation. The CJEU confirmed this position in the case of *Dias* where an EU citizen sought to argue that her residence had been lawful as a matter of EU law during a period of residence in a host Member State when she was in possession of a residence permit[80] but she had not been there in exercise of any EU law right.[81]

10–44

The list of documents that can be required of persons applying for residence documents (either registration certificates or residence cards) is "comprehensively specified" in arts 8 and 10 of Directive 2004/38. This is deliberately so as to avoid divergent practices amongst Member States or differences in interpretation.[82] Member States therefore cannot require more supporting documentation for the issuing of either a registration certificate or a residence card than is set out in the Directive.

10–45

(i) *Registration certificates*

Article 8(3) of Directive 2004/38 lays down the requirements for obtaining registration certificates for Union citizens exercising free movement rights. Article 8(5) of Directive 2004/38 lays down the requirements for obtaining registration certificates for EU nationals who are family members of EU

10–46

---

[79] See Communication from the Commission to the European Parliament and the Council on guidance for better transposition and application of Directive 2004/38/EC on the right of citizens of the Union and their family members to move and reside freely within the territory of the Member States COM/2009/0313 final.

[80] Issued under previous secondary legislation, Directive 68/360 now replaced by Directive 2004/38 but there is no reason to suggest that a different approach would be taken to a residence document issued under Directive 2004/38.

[81] *Secretary of State for Work and Pensions v Maria Dias* (C-325/09) July 21, 2011. The purpose of establishing the lawfulness of her residence was to determine whether she had completed five years' legal residence for the purpose of attaining the right to permanent residence under art.16 of Directive 2004/38. The CJEU concluded that the residence was not lawful but could be considered a period of absence under art.16(4) thereby enabling her to count periods of residence before and after in order to establish her right to permanent residence.

[82] Recital 14 of the Preamble to Directive 2004/38.

citizens exercising free movement rights. In both cases Member States may require production of a valid identity card or passport. However, the person might no longer have the actual identity card or passport with which he entered the territory of the host Member State.[83]

Validity

10–47 The registration certificate issued to Union citizens and their EU national family members are not time limited. However after five years' legal residence they are entitled to have a document certifying their right to permanent residence.[84]

(ii) *Residence cards*

10–48 Article 10(2) of Directive 2004/38 sets out the documents that should be required by Member States in order to issue a residence card to a non-EU national family member. Other than the ability of EU national family members to produce either an identity card or a passport whereas the non-EU national family member must produce a passport, the documents required of all family members are the same.

Validity

10–49 Article 11(1) of Directive 2004/38 stipulates that residence cards will be valid for five years unless the period of residence for the Union citizen is envisaged to be for less than five years.

10–50 Article 11(2) makes clear that the validity of the residence card cannot be affected by temporary absences for less than six months in a year, or by absences for compulsory military service or by absences for 12 consecutive months for important reasons such as pregnancy and childbirth, serious illness, study or vocational training or posting in another Member State or third country.

10–51 As with EU national family members, non-EU national family members are entitled after five years' lawful residence in the host Member State to permanent residence and may therefore apply for a "permanent residence card".[85]

(i) *Permanent residence documents*

10–52 The administrative formalities for obtaining permanent residence documents for EU citizens, their EU national family members or their non-EU national family members are notably minimal. Article 19 of Directive 2004/

---

[83] See *Giagounidis v Stadt Reutlingen* (C-376/89) [1991] E.C.R. I-1069. In that case the CJEU was considering art.4 of Directive 68/360 (now repealed by Directive 2004/38) which referred to the identity document on which the person entered the Member State being produced. The CJEU held that it would be contrary to the principle of freedom of movement for workers if issue of the residence permit were to be made conditional "on production of that same document".
[84] art.19 of Directive 2004/38. See further on permanent residence below.
[85] art.20 of Directive 2004/38. See further on permanent residence below.

38 simply refers to Union citizens who are entitled to permanent residence being issued with a document certifying permanent residence by the Member State "after having verified duration of residence". Article 20 of Directive 2004/38 states that non-EU national family members who are entitled to permanent residence, shall be issued with a permanent residence card on application.

Validity

The Directive does not prescribe a length of time that permanent registration certificates should be valid for. Permanent residence cards for non-EU national family members are automatically renewable every 10 years. Their validity will not be affected by interruptions in residence for periods not exceeding two consecutive years.[86]   **10–53**

4. Obtaining and Retaining Specific Residence Documents

(a) *Registration certificates as a worker or self-employed person*

Obtaining a registration certificate

The right of residence for workers and self-employed persons is set out in art.7(1)(a) of Directive 2004/38. The definition of a worker is discussed at length in Ch.6 and the right of establishment is discussed in Ch.7.   **10–54**

For a registration certificate to be issued to a worker or self-employed person a Member State may only require that the Union citizen presents a valid identity card or passport, a confirmation of engagement from the employer, or a certificate of employment or proof of self-employment.[87]   **10–55**

Retaining a registration certificate

Where a Union citizen is no longer a worker or self-employed person he may nevertheless retain the status of a worker or self-employed person if: **10–56**

(a) he is temporarily unable to work as a result of illness or an accident,

(b) he is involuntarily unemployed which is duly recorded, having been employed for more than a year and having registered as a job seeker with the employment office,

(c) he is involuntarily unemployed which is duly recorded, after less than 12 months employment, and having registered as a job seeker with the employment office. The status can be retained for no less than six months, and

(d) he embarks on vocational training. Unless they are involuntarily unemployed, the training should relate to the previous employment.[88]

---

[86] art.20(3) of Directive 2004/38.
[87] art.8(3) of Directive 2004/38.
[88] art.7(3) of Directive 2004/38.

An expulsion measure may never been the consequence of a worker or self-employed person having recourse to the social assistance system of the host Member State.[89]

Work seekers

10–57   The right of free movement extends not only to those pursuing economic activities as workers, but includes those who wish to pursue such activities.[90]

10–58   Article 14(4) makes clear that an expulsion measure may never be taken against a Union citizen who entered the territory of the host Member State in order to seek employment. In such case the Union citizen and his family members cannot be expelled for as long as the Union citizen can provide evidence that he is continuing to seek employment and has a genuine chance of being employed.

10–59   This provision does not go as far as to suggest that Member States must issue registration certificates to work seekers. However, the absence of such provision cannot mean that the right of residence enjoyed by work seekers is not required to be recognised by Member States. To the contrary, at the very least in Member States whose national laws require persons to register their presence within three months and where the absence of a residence document may give rise to penalties (as is the case for example in Belgium), EU law would require the issue of confirmation of the right to reside. Failure to recognise the right of residence by such Member States would fundamentally undermine the right of free movement otherwise enjoyed. At the same time in Member States which would not so penalise work seekers (as would be the case for example in the United Kingdom) the right must still be recognised without issuing a registration certificate.

(b) *Self-sufficient persons*

Obtaining a registration certificate

10–60   Article 7(1)(b) of the Directive provides that Member States shall grant the right of residence to nationals of Member States who have sufficient resources for themselves and their family members to avoid becoming a burden on the social assistance system of the host Member State during their period of residence and who have comprehensive sickness insurance. For the purpose of issuing the registration certificate the Member State may require only the presentation of a valid identity card or passport and proof that the person meets the conditions laid down in art.7(1)(b).[91]

10–61   Article 8(4) provides that Member States must not stipulate a fixed amount which they regard as "sufficient resources" but instead must take account of the personal situation of the person concerned. In any event this amount

---

[89] art.14(4)(a) of Directive 2004/38.
[90] *The Queen v Immigration Appeal Tribunal, Ex p. Antonissen* (C-292/89) [1991] E.C.R. 745, at [21].
[91] art.8(3) of Directive 2004/38.

cannot be higher than the threshold below which the nationals of the host Member State become eligible for social assistance or higher than the minimum social security pension paid by the host Member State.

As made clear in *Commission v Belgium* resources from a third person must be accepted.[92] The resources do not have to be periodic such as an income and can be in the form of accumulated capital. The evidence of sufficient resources cannot be limited.[93] **10–62**

The Commission successfully brought an action against the Netherlands which had national rules in place insisting that Union citizens demonstrated that they had sufficient resources for a year before a residence document would be issued. The CJEU found that it was contrary to EU law for Member States to require proof of lasting means of support for residence documents to be issued.[94] **10–63**

Any insurance cover, private or public, contracted in the host Member State or elsewhere, is acceptable in principle, as long as it provides comprehensive coverage. **10–64**

Pensioners fulfil the condition of comprehensive sickness insurance cover if they are entitled to health treatment on behalf of the Member State which pays their pension.[95] **10–65**

The European Health Insurance Card offers such comprehensive cover when the EU citizens concerned do not move their place of residence to the host Member State and have the intention to return to another Member State.[96] **10–66**

In *Baumbast* the CJEU made clear that before refusing to issue a residence document on the basis that a Union citizen is not in possession of sickness insurance cover, Member States must act in compliance with the limits imposed by Community law and in accordance with the principle of proportionality.[97] **10–67**

Retaining the registration certificate

In assessing whether an individual whose resources can no longer be regarded as sufficient and who was granted the minimum subsistence benefit is or has become an unreasonable burden, the authorities of the Member States must carry out a proportionality test. The Commission has identified from Recital 16 of Directive 2004/38 three sets of criteria for the purpose of determining whether a person is an unreasonable burden on the Member State: **10–68**

---

[92] *Commission v Belgium* (C-408/03), at [30], et seq.
[93] *Commission v Italy* (C-424/98), at [37].
[94] *Commission v Netherlands* (C-398/06) April 10, 2008.
[95] Regulation (EC) No. 883/04 which replaced Regulation (EC) 1408/71.
[96] See Regulation 883/04.
[97] *Baumbast* (C-413/99) at [89–94].

(1) Duration

- For how long is the benefit being granted?
- Outlook: is it likely that the EU citizen will get out of the safety net soon?
- How long has the residence lasted in the host Member State?

(2) Personal situation

- What is the level of connection of the EU citizen and their family members with the society of the host Member State?
- Are there any considerations pertaining to age, state of health, family and economic situation that need to be taken into account?

(3) Amount

- Total amount of aid granted?
- Does the EU citizen have a history of relying heavily on social assistance?
- Does the EU citizen have a history of contributing to the financing of social assistance in the host Member State?

10–69   Article 14(3) of the Directive makes clear that expulsion cannot be the automatic consequence of a Union citizen's recourse (or their family member's) to the social assistance system. In the view of the Commission only receipt of social assistance benefits can be considered relevant to determining whether the person concerned is a burden on the social assistance system.[98]

10–70   The Commission sought a declaration from the CJEU that Belgium had failed in its obligation under Directive 90/364 (now Directive 2004/38) by making the right of residence subject to the condition that persons have sufficient personal resources for the entirety of their stay.[99] The Commission emphasised the flexibility of the Directive which was intended to allow citizens of the Union to move easily within the territory of the Member States without having to prove that they have means of subsistence of their own for the entire duration of their stay. The Commission submitted:

> "However, the system of the Belgian authorities seeks to introduce additional guarantees in order to avoid ab initio the citizen of the Union becoming a burden on the social assistance system, which is inherently contrary to the spirit of Directive 90/364/EEC".

The CJEU agreed with the Commission.

---

[98] See Commission Communication from the Commission to the European Parliament and the Council on guidance for better transposition and application of Directive 2004/38/EC on the right of citizens of the Union and their family members to move and reside freely within the territory of the Member States, COM/2009/0313 final.
[99] *Commission v Belgium* (C-408/03) [O.J. C257/37].

(c) *Students*

Obtaining a registration certificate

10–71 The rights of residence for Union citizens studying in the Member States are set out in art.7(1)(c) of Directive 2004/38. The student must assure the Member State by means of declaration or by such alternative means as the student may choose that are at least equivalent, that the student has sufficient resources to avoid becoming a burden on the social assistance system of the host Member State during their period of residence. The student must also be enrolled at an educational establishment accredited or financed by the host Member State and covered by sickness insurance "in respect of all risks in the host Member State".

10–72 Article 8(3) lays down the documents that can be required of a Union citizen student. These are a valid identity card or passport, proof of enrollment at an accredited establishment, evidence of comprehensive sickness insurance and a declaration or equivalent means that the student has sufficient resources not to become a burden on the social assistance system in the host Member State. Article 8(3) stipulates that Member States may not require this declaration to refer to any specific amount of resources.

10–73 In *Commission v Italy*[100] proceedings were brought against Italy because students were being required to prove their ability to support themselves, rather than provide the relevant assurance by means of the declaration prescribed in art.1 of Directive 93/96.[101] The CJEU stated that such practice was unlawful. It was evident from the wording of art.1 that the conditions for obtaining the right of residence did not include any requirement to have resources of a specific amount, evidenced by specific documents. Member States cannot require more than is laid down by the Directive (here the assurance by declaration or alternative means of sufficiency of resources, rather than evidence of any such resources themselves).

10–74 In practice students at the outset of their stay may find difficulties in proving their means; it is for this reason that the Directive requires only an assurance by way of declaration. It is to be noted, however, that neither enrolment nor sickness insurance is a matter in respect of which an assurance can be given. Rather the Directive refers to the establishment of the facts that the student is enrolled and is covered.[102]

Retaining the registration certificate

10–75 Article 14(2) of Directive 2004/38 makes clear that Union citizens have the right of residence as long as they meet the conditions set out in art.7(1)(c). For a student that would plainly mean that if he were to end his studies then they could not longer qualify under that provision. He could become a worker, self-employed person or a self-sufficient person (or a family member of a Union citizen who qualifies) but would then have to qualify under the

---

[100] *Commission v Italy* (C-424/98) [2000] E.C.R. I-4001.
[101] Now replaced by art.7(1)(c) of Directive 2004/38 but the same declaration is sought.
[102] *Commission v Italy* (C-424/98) [2000] E.C.R. I-4001, at [44].

relevant provisions of art.7(1). As with self-sufficient persons, recourse to the social security system of the host Member State cannot automatically result in expulsion.

(d) *Permanent registration certificate for Union citizens after five years' residence*

Obtaining the permanent registration certificate

10–76 Recital 17 of the Preamble to Directive 2004/38 makes clear that permanent residence is a key element to promoting social cohesion and giving Union citizenship greater meaning.

10–77 Article 16 provides that as a general rule Union citizens who have lawfully resided in a Member State for five years continuously will gain the right to permanent residence. This will be evidenced by a permanent registration certificate.

10–78 The administrative formalities for obtaining permanent residence documents, for EU citizens, their EU national family members or their non-EU national family members are notably minimal. Article 19 of Directive 2004/38 simply refers to Union citizens who are entitled to permanent residence being issued with a document certifying permanent residence by the Member State "after having verified duration of residence".

10–79 Article 16(3) sets out periods of absence that will not be taken as breaking the continuity of residence. Temporary absences of a total of six months per year are permitted, as are longer absences for compulsory military service or one absence of 12 months continuously for

> "important reasons such as pregnancy and childbirth, serious illness, study or vocation training, or a posting in another Member State or a third country".

The reasons given justifying a 12-month continuous absence is not an exhaustive list.

10–80 The CJEU has considered the term "lawful residence" and whether it means only lawful residence in accordance with Directive 2004/38, thereby excluding residence under previous secondary legislation.[103] The Court concluded that all lawful residence, whether before Directive 2004/38 came into force or after, would be counted as part of the five year requirement. Thus a Union citizen who had lawfully resided in the host Member State since April 2005 (namely one year prior to Directive 2004/38 coming into force) and continued to lawfully reside in the Member State thereafter would be eligible for permanent registration certificate in April 2010. The Court took the decision on the basis that the aim of the Directive was to provide stability and social cohesion for Union citizens and to encourage integration.

---

[103] *Secretary of State for Work and Pensions v Lassal* (C-162/09) October 7, 2010.

In *Ziolkowski*[104] the CJEU considered whether lawful residence under national law alone would be included in "lawful residence" under art.16 of Directive 2004/38. In the case the two Polish nationals had lived in Germany since the late 1980s and had been granted residence on humanitarian grounds. Neither of them was self-sufficient or economically active. The CJEU concluded that "lawful residence" for the purpose of art.16 of the Directive had to mean residence in accordance with art.7 of the Directive. In other words the applicants would need to demonstrate that during the relevant period they were self-sufficient or economically active. The CJEU further considered whether residence of an accession State national prior to accession to the EU would be included as lawful residence. The Court concluded that periods of residence completed by a national of a non-Member State in the territory of a Member State before the accession of the non-Member State to the European Union must be taken into account for the purpose of the acquisition of the right of permanent residence under art.16(1) of Directive 2004/38, provided those periods were completed in compliance with the conditions laid down in art.7(1) of the Directive.

10–81

"Lawful residence" for the purposes of art.16 of Directive 2004/38 will not however include periods of residence where a Union citizen is in possession of a EU residence document but where they are not in fact exercising any EU law right to reside there.[105]

10–82

According to art.21 of Directive 2004/38 "continuity of residence" may be attested by any means of proof in use in the host Member State. Further continuity of residence will be broken by any expulsion decision that is enforced. Thus a Union citizen who is deported from the host Member State before having acquired the right of permanent residence will be deemed to have broken continuous residence. If the Union Citizen returns to the host Member State subsequently he will need to start accruing his five years' legal residence from the time of return.

10–83

Retaining the right of permanent residence

Once the right to permanent residence is acquired it will only be lost by absences for longer than two years.[106] This means that a Union citizen who worked in a Member State for five years, could leave that Member State for up to two years, return to the Member State and obtain a permanent registration certificate without being eligible for a registration certificate as a worker, self-employed or self-sufficient person.

10–84

The CJEU has also found that a Union citizen who acquires the right to permanent residence after five years lawful residence will not lose that right by residing in the same host Member State without being lawfully resident there. Thus in the case of *Dias* the applicant was entitled to a permanent registration certificate where she had resided in accordance with EU law for five years previously but thereafter had remained in the Member State in

10–85

---

[104] *Ziolkowski* (C-424/10) and *Szeja v Land Berlin* (C-425/10) December 21, 2011.
[105] *Secretary of State for Work and Pensions v Maria Dias* (C-325/09) July 21, 2011.
[106] art.16(4) of Directive 2004/38.

possession of a EU residence permit even though she did not fulfil the conditions of being entitled to such a permit.[107]

(e) Permanent registration certificates after less than five years' residence

10–86 Under art.17(1) of Directive 2004/38 workers or self-employed persons can obtain the permanent right of residence earlier than five years if:

(a) They retire, either in line with pension law or take early retirement, having worked in the preceding 12 months in the host Member State and having resided there for more than three years.[108]

(b) They stop working due to permanent incapacity having resided in the host Member State for two years (or less if the incapacity is a result of an accident at work or occupational disease resulting in a benefit payable in full or part by an institution in the host Member State).[109]

(c) They stop working in the host Member State after three years continuous employment, work in another Member State but return to the host Member State to reside at least once a week.[110]

10–87 For the purposes of calculating how long a person has been in employment, art.17(1) of Directive 2004/38 makes clear that periods of involuntary unemployment duly recorded by the employment office, periods not worked for "reasons not of the person's own making" and absences from work or cessation of work due to illness or accident shall be regarded as periods of employment.

10–88 Article 19 simply provides that Member States will issue permanent registration certificates to any Union citizen eligible for permanent residence "after having verified duration of residence". No other requirements are made.

(f) Family members

(i) Generally

10–89 The rights of residence identified above extend to family members. This is entirely unsurprising in view of the importance given by European Union law to respect for family life in order to eliminate obstacles to the exercise of the fundamental freedoms guaranteed by the TFEU. Importantly, family members not only have the right to reside, but also the right to take up economic activity in the host Member State.[111]

---

[107] *Secretary of State for Work and Pensions v Maria Dias* (C-325/09) July 21, 2011.
[108] art.17(1)(a) of Directive 2004/38.
[109] art.17(1)(b) of Directive 2004/38.
[110] art.17(1)(c) of Directive 2004/38.
[111] See art.23 of Directive 2004/38.

Obtaining and Retaining Specific Residence Documents

The family members are to be issued with registration certificates if they are EU nationals themselves. If they are non-EU nationals they are to be issued with residence cards. **10–90**

The difference between the two in terms of validity is described above at paras 10–46 to 10–49. The definition of various family members is discussed in Ch.9. **10–91**

Article 8(5)(a), (b) and (c) sets out the documents that may be required of any family member who wishes to be issued with a registration certificate. Article 10(2)(a), (b) and (c) sets out the documents that may be required of any non-EU national who wishes to be issued with a residence card. **10–92**

The requirements are the same save that EU nationals may produce either a valid passport or identity card whereas non-EU nationals may only produce a passport. Both should provide evidence of their relationship with the Union citizen exercising rights under the Directive and the registration certificate of that Union citizen or other proof of the residence of the Union citizen. **10–93**

The form that the evidence of the family member's relationship with the Union citizen should take is not prescribed in the Directive. **10–94**

(ii) *Spouses and registered partnerships*

The definition of a spouse is discussed in Ch.9. Since Member States are obliged to recognise a validly contracted marriage from any country in the world, a marriage certificate issued by the competent authority from the country in which the marriage was contracted must be evidence of the relationship. **10–95**

All registered partnerships contracted in other Member States must be recognised and therefore a certificate attesting to the registered partnership will be evidence of that relationship. However, whether the registered partner has an automatic right of residence or whether it is for the host Member State to grant residence depends on whether the host Member State treats registered partnerships as equivalent to marriage. If it does, then the registered partner has an automatic right of residence with the Union citizen. In host Member States where nationals are not required to obtain residence documents the EU national partner might not be concerned to obtain a registration certificate. **10–96**

If the Member State does not treat registered partnerships as equivalent to marriage then the partner will need to have a positive decision from the host Member State recognising the relationship.[112] It is highly unlikely that a Member State could justify the denial of residence to a registered partner unless there was clear evidence that the relationship had broken down and was therefore not "durable". **10–97**

---

[112] Under art.3(2)(b) of Directive 2004/38 as a partner in a durable relationship. Such partners need to have their entry and residence "facilitated" by the host Member State.

(iii) *Family members directly in the ascending and descending line of the Union citizen and spouse or registered partner*

10–98 In addition to the documents generally required of family members by art.8(5)(a), (b) and (c) and art.10(2)(a), (b) and (c), persons in the ascending and descending lines are required to provide "documentary evidence that the conditions laid down therein are met".[113] Those conditions are thus of dependency.

10–99 Proving the family relationship in this category is not generally a problem if a valid birth certificate from a competent authority is produced. However, a problem may occur relating to adoption, where some Member States do not recognise the adoption proceedings in certain non-EU countries. Such Member States may not accept a child adopted as having complied with the documentary requirements where the document is produced by a country whose adoption proceedings are not recognised. Such an approach is in contravention of EU law. The principles relating to formalities are dealt with above. It is a basic principle that Member States cannot ask for more than is prescribed.

10–100 Evidence of dependency may be adduced by any appropriate means, as confirmed by the CJEU in the cases of *Oulane* and *Jia*.[114] Thus Member States cannot insist that the evidence is produced in a particular form or emanates from a particular source or authority. On the other hand the CJEU made clear in *Jia* that a mere undertaking from the Union citizen that the family member is dependent on them may not be sufficient to meet the documentary requirements.[115]

(iv) *Other family members falling under art.3(2)(a)*

10–101 It is to be recalled that family members falling under art.3(2)(a) need to have their residence facilitated by the host Member State. This will mean that their residence must be granted by the host Member State, as opposed to being merely recognised.

10–102 This does not mean, however, that Member States have carte blanche to require additional documents or impose additional conditions on those family members. Such an approach would run counter to Recital 14 to the Preamble to the Directive which states that the documentary evidence requirements for obtaining residence documents should be specified in the Directive to avoid divergent practices amongst Member States.

10–103 However, the reference in art.3(2) to Member States needing to facilitate entry and residence must mean that it is for the Member State to assess if the conditions of art.3(2)(a) are met and to lay down criteria against which an assessment will be made. Family members falling under art.3(2)(a) are

---

[113] art.8(5)(d) and art.10(2)(d) of Directive 2004/38.
[114] *Oulane* (C-215/03), at [53] and *Jia* (C-1/05) at [41].
[115] *Jia* (C-1/05), at [42].

unlikely to be able assert a right of residence in the absence of a registration certificate or residence card issued by the host Member State.[116]

Family members falling under art.3(2)(a) like all family members must produce their passports (or identity cards in the case of EU nationals), evidence of their relationship to the Union citizen and evidence of the Union citizen's residence in the host Member State. They must further produce: **10–104**

> "a document issued by the relevant authority in the country of origin or country from which they are arriving certifying that they are dependants or members of the household of the Union citizen, or proof of the existence of serious health grounds which strictly require the personal care of the family member by the Union citizen".[117]

The host Member State in considering an application from a family member falling under this category is required to undertake "an extensive examination of the personal circumstances" of the applicant and to justify any denial of entry or residence. **10–105**

The importance ascribed by European Union law to art.8 ECHR in this context must always be borne in mind. The existence of family life is a question of fact which can be established between more distant relatives than those catered for by art.2(2) of the Directive.[118] **10–106**

(g) *Remaining beyond the Union citizen*

In the situations considered above the right of residence of family members is derivative of the right of the Member State national exercising free movement rights. **10–107**

As a general rule such rights will expire when the Union citizen ceases to exercise free movement rights, ceases to reside in the territory of the host Member State or, in the case of spouses, the relationship is permanently dissolved. However, as outlined in para.10–09 above there are a number of instances under Directive 2004/38 in which the family member will retain rights of residence and even gain the right of permanent residence in the event of the death or departure of the Union citizen or on divorce, annulment of marriage or dissolution of a registered partnership. **10–108**

(i) *Where the Union citizen dies or departs from the Member State*

(a) If the family member is an EU national then the death or departure of the Union citizen who had been exercising free movement rights will **10–109**

---

[116] The approach to be taken to art.3(2) family members is to be examined by the CJEU in the case of *Muhammad Rahman* (C-83/11). See A-G Bot's opinion in the case.
[117] art.8(5)(e) of Directive 2004/38 (EU national family members) and art.10(2)(e) of Directive 2004/38 (non-EU national family members).
[118] See further, A-G Bot's opinion in *Rahman* (C-83/11) March 27, 2011.

Rights of Entry and Residence

not affect the family member's rights of residence.[119] Before such family member can acquire the permanent right of residence he must become economically active or self-sufficient or a student within the meaning of the Directive, or become the family member of another Union citizen fulfilling those conditions.

(b) If the family member is a non-EU national then the death of the Union citizen will not result in the loss of right of residence for the family member providing he has been residing in the host Member State for at least one year as a family member.[120] The right of residence is retained on an exclusively personal basis and cannot be passed on to other family members.

(c) If the family member is a child or parent of a the child of an Union citizen then the Union citizen's departure from the host Member State or their death will not result in a loss of right of residence for that family member if the child is enrolled in an educational establishment until the completion of their studies.[121]

10–110 The family members of Union citizen workers or self-employed persons can obtain the permanent right of residence earlier than five years and even where the Union citizen has not acquired permanent residence status if:

(a) the Union citizen was a worker or self-employed person who dies whilst still working having at the time of death resided continuously on the territory of the Member State for two years or where the death results from an accident at work or an occupational disease[122], and

(b) the family member is the spouse who lost the nationality of that Member State following marriage to the worker or self-employed person, that Union citizen having died while still working in the Member State.[123]

Evidential problems

10–111 In all of these cases there may be an evidential gap that cannot be filled by the family member where it is difficult for the family member to prove in the absence of the Union citizen that the latter was exercising a free movement right before death or departure from the host Member State. Due regard will need to be had for the objectives of the Directive of preserving family

---

[119] art.12(1) of Directive 2004/38. Permanent residence for this category will not be achieved until the person is able to fulfil the condition of being a free mover as set out in art.7(1), namely economically active or self-sufficient or a student or become as a family member of one.

[120] art.12(2) of Directive 2004/38. Permanent residence for this category will not be achieved until the person is able show that they are a worker, self-employed person or has sufficient resources not to be a burden on the social assistance system of the host Member State.

[121] art.12(3) of Directive 2004/38. There are no specific requirements to be met for this category to achieve permanent residence. This provision gives protection generally to the children of EU citizens who are in education and to their primary carers giving effect and wider application to the CJEU's decision in the case of *Baumbast*. That case concerned the rights of the children of former workers to continue their education in the host Member State pursuant to art.12 of Regulation 1612/68 (now art.10 of Regulation 492/2011).

[122] art.17(4)(a) and 17(4)(b) of Directive 2004/38.

[123] art.17(4)(c) of Directive 2004/38.

life and human dignity.[124] In this context a burden must lay on the authorities of the host Member State to provide whatever information they may have on the activities of the late or departed Union citizen.

The disappeared or disengaged Union citizen

There is a lacuna in the Directive where the Union citizen ceases to be in contact with their family so that it cannot be proven that they have left the host Member State. Further, there is no provision in the Directive for the instance where the Union citizen ceases to exercise free movement rights in the host Member State but nevertheless remains there. The children of such Union citizens are unprotected by the Directive unless they can themselves fulfil conditions under art.7(1) of the Directive. **10–112**

For the cases where the Union citizen was a worker, his children will be entitled to continue in education accompanied by any non-EU national parent by virtue of art.12 of Regulation 1612/68. That provision was not repealed by Directive 2004/38 (although it is now replaced by art.10 of Regulation 492/2011) and has been found by the CJEU in the case of *Ibrahim* to protect the children and carer parents of former workers even where that worker remains in the host Member State but outside the scope of Directive 2004/38.[125] **10–113**

(ii) *Family members in the event of divorce, annulment of marriage or termination of registered partnership*

(a) If the family member is an EU national then divorce, annulment of a marriage or termination of a registered partnership will not affect his right of residence.[126] **10–114**

(b) If the family member is a non-EU national then in circumstances the ex-spouse or ex-registered partner will retain a right of residence[127] in the host Member State where:

   (i) the marriage or partnership has lasted three years prior to the initiation of divorce, annulment or termination of the partnership, one of which was in the host Member State,[128]
   (ii) by agreement or court order the non-EU national ex-spouse or partner has custody of the Union citizen's children,[129]
   (iii) there are particularly difficult circumstances such as domestic violence,[130] or

---

[124] Recitals 5 and 15 of the Preamble to Directive 2004/38.
[125] *London Borough of Harrow v Nimco Ibrahim* (C-310/08) February 23, 2010.
[126] art.13(1) of Directive 2004/38. Permanent residence for this category will not be achieved until the person is able to fulfil the condition of being a free mover as set out in art.7(1), namely being economically active, self-sufficient, a student, or becomes a family member of one.
[127] Family members retain their right of residence under this category exclusively on a personal basis. Permanent residence for this category will not be achieved until the person is a worker, self-employed person or has sufficient resources not to be a burden on the social assistance system of the host Member State.
[128] art.13(2)(a) of Directive 2004/38.
[129] art.13(2)(b) of Directive 2004/38.
[130] art.13(2)(c) of Directive 2004/38.

(iv) by agreement or court order the non-EU national has a right of access to a minor child provided that the court has rules that the access must be in the host Member State.[131]

Evidential problems

10–115 As with death or departure of the Union citizen, a breakdown in the relationship between a couple may mean that the Union citizen is simply not willing to provide the evidence needed to prove that, for instance the Union citizen is working in the host Member State. Principles of proportionality as well as the general aims of the Directive should mean that the host Member State at least shares the evidential burden by disclosing whatever information its authorities may have.

Children born outside of marriage

10–116 There is undoubtedly a lacuna in the Directive for the parents of children born outside of marriage or a registered partnership. If the non-EU national parent has custody or access to the children but the couple were not previously married or in a registered partnership that parent would appear to fall outside the scope of art.13(2) of the Directive. In such instance reliance might be placed on the Charter of Fundamental Rights and the specific reference in Recital 31 of the Preamble to the Directive to the prohibition against discrimination on grounds of "birth". The European Court of Human Rights has consistently found discrimination against illegitimately born children to be contrary to art.14 of the European Convention on Human Rights.[132] Given the CJEU's approach to the protection of family life in general, a powerful argument could be made that parents of children born outside marriage should get the same protection as those under granted under art.13(b) and (d) of Directive 2004/38.[133]

10–117 That argument would be made all the more powerful by the demonstration that the presence of the non-EU national parent in the host Member State is necessary for the continued exercise of free movement rights by the Union citizen. Such might be the case for instance where the non-EU national parent with custody of the child might otherwise take the child out of the EU thereby forcing the Union citizen to also leave the EU.

---

[131] art.13(2)(d) of Directive 2004/38.
[132] *PM v the United Kingdom* July 19, 2005, A 198–205; *Inze v Austria*, Judgment of October 28, 1987, 10 EHRR 394; and *Pla and Puncernau v Andora*, Appl. No. 69498/01, Judgment of July 13, 2004.
[133] See cases such as *Baumbast* ((C-413/99) September 17, 2002) and *Carpenter v Secretary of State for the Home Department* (C-60/00) [2002] E.C.R. I-6279.

CHAPTER 11

DISCRIMINATION AND OTHER OBSTACLES TO FREEDOM OF MOVEMENT

The principal focus of this chapter is the examination of the principle of equal treatment as it applies to those benefiting from free movement rights in the Treaty on the Functioning of the European Union and secondary legislation. Other obstacles to the exercise of free movement rights are also considered including the failure to recognise professional qualifications.

1. General Principle of Non-discrimination in the European Union Law Context

(a) *Introduction*

The general principle of non-discrimination in the context of European Union law finds articulation in art.18 Treaty on the Functioning of the European Union which provides as follows: 11–01

> "Within the scope of application of the Treaties, and without prejudice to any special provisions contained therein, any discrimination on grounds of nationality shall be prohibited".

"Treaties" refers both to the Treaty on the Treaty on European Union (TEU) and the Treaty on the Functioning of the European Union (TFEU).[1]

The importance of the principle in the European Union legal order is apparent not only from its articulation in art.18 TFEU, but also from the fact that it is repeated throughout the TFEU and secondary legislation. Thus for example in relation to workers, art.45(2) TFEU provides expressly that the freedom of movement of workers shall entail   11–02

> "the abolition of any discrimination based on nationality between workers of the Member States as regards employment, remuneration and other conditions of work and employment".

---

[1] art.1 TEU states that "The Union shall be founded on the present Treaty and on the Treaty on the Functioning of the European Union (hereinafter referred to as 'the Treaties'). Those two Treaties shall have the same legal value. The Union shall replace and succeed the European Community".

11–03 Moreover, the principle is seen by the CJEU as one of the fundamental principles of European Union law.[2] At its core the principle of equality requires that similar situations shall not be treated differently unless differentiation is objectively justified.

(b) *The scope and application of art.18 TFEU*

(i) *Discrimination on grounds of nationality*

11–04 Immediately apparent from the text of art.18 TFEU is that it is discrimination on grounds of *nationality* which is prohibited (rather than discrimination on *any* grounds such as those listed—albeit by way of example—in arts 2 Universal Declaration of Human Rights ("UDHR") and 14 European Convention on Human Rights ("ECHR")). This is unsurprising since it is the free movement rights of *nationals* of the Member States which is one of the four fundamental principles of the TFEU.

11–05 Moreover, the *nationality* limitation does not mean that discrimination on other grounds is of no interest in the context of the European Union legal order. To the contrary, art.19 TFEU makes provision for the Council to take "appropriate action to combat discrimination based on sex, racial or ethnic origin, religion or belief, disability, age or sexual orientation". As seen in Ch.3, the wider non-discrimination obligations of the ECHR must be enjoyed not only by Union citizens but also third country nationals who find themselves within the territories of the Member States. Further, testament to the substantial interest taken by the Commission in discrimination is demonstrated by its activities undertaken in the context of the Action Programme to combat discrimination.[3]

(ii) *Discrimination within the scope of application of the Treaty*

11–06 It must be emphasised that the prohibition on discrimination in art.18 TFEU applies only "within the scope of application" of the TFEU. In order to determine whether discrimination falls within the scope (or as it is sometimes described the "sphere") of application of the TFEU there are two matters which must be established. First, that the circumstances of the individual fall within the personal scope of the provisions of the TFEU; second that the subject-matter of any dispute is one falling within the material scope of application of the TFEU. As frequently articulated in decisions of the CJEU the ability to invoke art.18 TFEU depends on the

---

[2] *Albert Ruckdeschel & Co. et Hansa-Lagerhaus Ströh & Co. v Hauptzollamt Hamburg-St Annen; Diamalt AG v Hauptzollamt Itzehoe* (117/76) [1977] E.C.R. 1753. The CJEU was considering the prohibition contained in art.34(2) of the EC Treaty [now art.40 TFEU] on discrimination between producers or consumers in the context of the common organisation of agricultural markets. As the CJEU stated
"This does not alter the fact that the prohibition of discrimination laid down in [art. 34(2)] is merely a specific enunciation of the general principle of equality which is one of the fundamental principles of Community law".

[3] See, for example, http://www.ec.europa.eu/justice/fdad/cms/stopdiscrimination?langid=en [Accessed February 2012].

relevant facts falling within the scope *ratione personae* and the scope *ratione materiae* of the Treaty.

Those falling within the personal scope of the TFEU include the free movers who are the subject-matter of the preceding chapters of this book. It will include also Union citizens lawfully residing in another Member State (see *Martinez-Sala*[4]) and Union citizens visiting another Member State (see *Bickel and Franz*[5]). The latter fall within the scope of the TFEU because they are recipients of services.[6] 11–07

Since the inclusion of art.20 in the TFEU establishing citizenship of the Union, all Union citizens residing in other Member States will benefit from the protection of art.18 TFEU.[7] The detail is considered in Ch.4. In short, a Union citizen need not establish that residence in another Member State is founded on the exercise of a free movement right in European Union law in order to so benefit.[8] 11–08

Far more difficult however is the question of material scope, namely whether the subject matter in dispute is something to which European Union law principles should be applied. This will be dependant on various factors, including the nature of the activity of the Union citizen and the reason why the Union citizen is residing in another Member State. The Union citizen whose presence in another Member State arises because of the exercise of a free movement right must be accorded every facility to enjoy that free movement right. Such Union citizen must be treated on a par with own nationals in all respects. The scope of that obligation is considered in detail from para.11–25 below. 11–09

In *Elsen*[9] the CJEU held that Member States are required to act in manner which is not 11–10

> "disadvantageous to Union citizens who have exercised their right to move and reside freely in the Member States as guaranteed in art.8A of the EC Treaty [now art.21 TFEU]".

For those exercising free movement rights the material scope is by no means limited to access to financial benefits on a non-discriminatory basis. In *Bickel and Franz*[10] (following its earlier decision in *Mutsch*[11]) the CJEU held that measures which would enhance the exercise of the right to move and reside freely in another Member State fell within the material scope of art.18. The CJEU held that the use of a given language to communicate with

---

[4] *Martinez Sala v Freistaat Bayern* (C-85/96) [1998] E.C.R. I-2691.
[5] *Bickel and Franz* (C-274/96) [1998] E.C.R. I-7637.
[6] Indeed art.6 of Directive 2004/38 provides for the free movement of all Union citizens for up to three months.
[7] *Trojani v Centre public d'aide sociale de Bruxelles (CPAS)* (C-456/02) September 7, 2004, at [39–46].
[8] See paras 41–25 to 41–29 for discussion of the meaning of residence in this context.
[9] *Elsen v Bundesversicherungsandstalt für Angestellte* (C-135/99) [2000] E.C.R. I-10409, at [34].
[10] *Bickel and Franz* (C-274/96) [1998] E.C.R. I-7637.
[11] *Ministere Public v Mutsch* (137/84) [1985] E.C.R. 2681.

the administrative and judicial authorities of a Member State on the same footing as nationals was a measure that would enhance the exercise of the right to move and freely reside in another Member State.

11–11 On the other hand, for the Union citizen whose residence is not derived from European Union law, material scope is more limited. The CJEU has been prepared to require Member States to provide all Union citizens with non discriminatory access to minimum forms of social assistance.[12] Further, in *Avello*[13] the CJEU held that the material scope of art.18 TFEU included national rules governing the use of surnames for lawfully resident Union citizen children. To benefit from wider material scope Union citizens will likely need to establish more Union law nexus to their situation. For further discussion of material scope in these contexts see Ch.4.

(c) *Inter-relationship with other non-discrimination provisions*

11–12 As regards the economically active, the TFEU provisions and secondary legislation providing for their free movement include specific non-discrimination provisions. For instance, in relation to workers the combination of art.45(2) TFEU and Regulation 492/2011 (considered in detail below) make comprehensive provision guaranteeing equality of treatment for workers. Where such provision is made art.18 TFEU may be superfluous, or indeed only be necessary where the discrimination alleged falls outside the scope of art.45(2) or Regulation 492/2011.

11–13 Directive 2004/38 on the free movement rights of EU citizens makes extensive reference to non-discrimination principles. The preamble to the Directive 2004/38 refers to the principle in Recitals (20) and (31) in these terms:

> "(20) In accordance with the prohibition of discrimination on grounds of nationality, all Union citizens and their family members residing in a Member State on the basis of this Directive should enjoy, in that Member State, equal treatment with nationals in areas covered by the Treaty, subject to such specific provisions as are expressly provided for in the Treaty and secondary law.
>
> (31) This Directive respects the fundamental rights and freedoms and observes the principles recognised in particular by the Charter of Fundamental Rights of the European Union. In accordance with the prohibition of discrimination contained in the Charter, Member States should implement this Directive without discrimination between the beneficiaries of this Directive on grounds such as sex, race, colour, ethnic or social origin, genetic characteristics, language, religion or beliefs, political or other opinion, membership of an ethnic minority, property, birth, disability, age or sexual orientation."

---

[12] See *Martinez Sala v Freistaat Bayern* (C-85/96) [1998] E.C.R. I-2691 (child raising allowance) and *Trojani v Centre public d'aide sociale de Bruxelles (CPAS)* (C-456/02) September 7, 2004 (minimex).
[13] *Avello v Etat Belge* (C-148/02) [2004] 1 C.M.L.R. 1.

Article 24 of the Directive states: 11–14

> "Subject to such specific provisions as are expressly provided for in the Treaty and secondary law, all Union citizens residing on the basis of this Directive in the territory of the host Member State shall enjoy equal treatment with the nationals of that Member State within the scope of the Treaty."

Perhaps of most significance is the additional protection given to third country family members in art.24(1): 11–15

> "The benefit of this right shall be extended to family members who are not nationals of a Member State and who have the right of residence or permanent residence."

The potential overlap between art.18 and specific European Union law provisions dealing expressly with non-discrimination for particular free movers was recognised in *Ameyde*[14] where the CJEU stated in the context of the inter-relationship between art.18 TFEU and arts 49 and 56 TFEU that: 11–16

> "Article 7 of the Treaty [now art.18 TFEU] prohibits in general terms all discrimination based on nationality. In the respective spheres of the right of establishment and the freedom to provide services Articles 52 and 59 EC Treaty [now art.49 and 56 TFEU] guarantee the application of the principle laid down by Article 7. It follows therefore that if rules are compatible with Articles 52 and 59 [now art.49 and 56 TFEU] they are also compatible with Article 7". [now art.18 TFEU][15]

In *Kremlis*[16] the CJEU stated (without analysis) that art.18 TFEU "applies independently *only* to situations governed by Community law in regard to which the Treaty lays down no specific prohibition of discrimination".[17] The same point was reiterated by the CJEU in *Scholz*[18] in which the CJEU considered an allegation of discrimination made relying on arts 182 and 45 TFEU and arts 1 and 3 of Regulation 1612/68.[19] At para.6 of its decision the CJEU stated: 11–17

> "It should be borne in mind, first of all, that Article 7 of the Treaty [now art.18 TFEU], which prohibits any discrimination on grounds of nationality, does not apply independently where the Treaty lays down, as it does in Article 48(2) [now art.45(2) TFEU] in relation to the free movement of workers, a specific prohibition of discrimination (see the judgment in Case 305/87 *Commission v Greece* [1989] ECR 1476, at paragraphs 12 and 13). In addition, Articles 1 and 3 of Regulation No 1612/68 merely clarify and give effect to the rights already

---

[14] S.r.l. Ufficio Henry van Ameyde v S.r.l. Ufficio centrale italiano di assistenza assicu-rativa automobilisti in circolazione internazionale (UCI) (90/76) [1977] E.C.R. 1091.
[15] para.27.
[16] Kremlis v Greece (305/87) [1989] E.C.R. 1476 (a case in which proceedings were brought by the Commission against Greece for a declaration that, by maintaining in force and applying certain provisions of its legislation with regard to the conclusion, by nationals of other Member States, of legal acts in respect of immovable property the Hellenic Republic had failed to fulfil its obligations under arts 12, 39, 43 and 49 EC Treaty).
[17] para.13 (emphasis added).
[18] Scholz v Opera Universitaria di Cagliari, Cinzia Porcedda (C-419/92) [1994] E.C.R. I-505.
[19] Now arts 1 and 3 Regulation 492/2011.

conferred by Article 48 of the Treaty [now art.45 TFEU]. Accordingly, that provision alone is relevant to this case".

11–18 The breadth of the specific non-discrimination provisions in the Treaty on the Functioning of the European Union for the economically active will mean that reliance on art.18 TFEU may be unnecessary. Plainly such provisions must always be interpreted at least as broadly as art.18 TFEU.

(d) *Indirect discrimination*

11–19 European Union law does not just prohibit direct discrimination. As stated in art.18 TFEU itself, *any* discrimination is prohibited. Indirect discrimination arises where a provision is likely to affect Union citizens in the exercise of their Treaty rights disproportionately. It may arise where a condition is imposed which is sought to be justified on the basis that it applies both to those exercising Treaty rights and own nationals, but where the ability of those exercising Treaty rights to satisfy any such condition is intrinsically more difficult.

11–20 For example if a residence requirement is attached to the grant of a particular benefit, whilst not impossible for Union citizens to satisfy such criterion, they are certainly more unlikely to be able to do so than own nationals, especially if they are "new" free movers, or have only recently exercised such rights.[20] As explained by the CJEU, such a residence requirement could be justified only if based on objective considerations independent of the nationality of the persons concerned and if proportionate to the legitimate aim of the national provisions. It is important to emphasise—as made clear by the CJEU in *Flynn*[21]—that it is not necessary to prove that the provision does in practice affect a substantially higher proportion of migrant workers. It will be enough that a provision is *liable* to have such an effect.[22]

(e) *Justification*

11–21 A finding of discrimination on grounds of nationality however will not in and of itself mean that art.18 TFEU has been contravened. As is repeatedly stated by the CJEU discrimination may be justified. However, justification in practice is not a simple matter for a Member State to establish. To do so the Member State will have to demonstrate that any condition is:

"based on objective considerations independent of the nationality of the persons concerned and is proportionate to the legitimate aim of the national provisions

---

[20] See, for example, *O'Flynn v Chief Adjudication Officer* (C-237/94) [1996] E.C.R. I-2617, at [20–21] and *Collins v Secretary of State for Work and Pensions* (C-138/02) judgment of March 23, 2004, not yet reported.
[21] *O'Flynn v Chief Adjudication Officer* (C-237/94) [1996] E.C.R. I-2617.
[22] See also, *Michael Neukirchinger v Bezirkshauptmannschaft Grieskirchen* (C-382/08) January 25, 2011 where a residence requirement imposed in legislation on balloon ride providers is found to be discriminatory contrary to the TFEU.

(see, to that effect, Case C-15/96 *Schöning-Kougebetopoulou* [1998] E.C.R. I-47, para.21)".[23]

The importance of the principle of proportionality cannot be overstated. The principle applies even where a measure appears to be able to be justified on objective considerations. It like any discriminatory measure must be proportionate to the legitimate aim of the national provisions. Thus in the case of *Bickel and Franz*[24] whilst the CJEU recognised that the protection of an ethno-cultural minority might constitute a legitimate aim, it did not consider that the aim would be undermined if the rules in issue, namely those concerned with the use of language in criminal proceedings, were extended to cover nationals of other Member States exercising their free movement rights.   11–22

The principles of objective justification and proportionality are well-established in international human rights law. Under the ECHR, the effect of the discrimination is weighed against its aims to determine whether the two are proportionate. If the disadvantage suffered is excessive in relation to the legitimate aim pursued, then the discrimination is unjustified and thus illegal. Part of the analysis involves inquiring as to whether a less restrictive alternative exists: if it does, such alternative must be used.   11–23

This strict level of scrutiny has also been applied to discrimination on the grounds of nationality in European Union law. Discrimination is only permissible if based on public policy, public security and public health grounds. Such grounds have been narrowly interpreted by the CJEU. The application of the principle is discussed in Ch.13.   11–24

2. OBSTACLES TO THE FREE MOVEMENT OF WORKERS

(a) *Introduction*

Article 45(2) TFEU gives specific articulation of the principle of non-discrimination in relation to workers providing that the freedom of movement of workers   11–25

> "shall entail the abolition of any discrimination based on nationality between workers of the Member States as regards employment, remuneration and other conditions of work and employment".

The principle is referred to in provisions of secondary legislation, principally in Regulation 492/2011 which implements and facilitates the right of freedom of movement for workers laid down in art.45 TFEU.

---

[23] See *Bickel and Franz* (C-274/96) [1998] E.C.R. I-7637, at [27].
[24] *Bickel and Franz* (C-274/96) [1998] E.C.R. I-7637.

(b) *The provisions of Regulation 492/2011*

11–26 The fundamental importance of the principle to Regulation 492/2011[25] is clear from its preamble in which more than half of the recitations deal expressly with the importance of non-discrimination.

11–27 Article 1 of Regulation 492/2011 (entitled "Eligibility for Employment") is concerned with the ability of Union citizen workers to access the work forces of other Member States. For example by art.6(1) the engagement and recruitment of a national of one Member State for a post in another Member State must not depend on medical, vocational or other criteria which are discriminatory on grounds of nationality.[26]

11–28 Article 2 of Regulation 492/2011 (entitled "Employment and Equality of Treatment") identifies the specific rights in respect of which equality of treatment must be enjoyed. They include (in art.7(1)) a statement of the references in art.45(2) TFEU to the general prohibition of discrimination on grounds of nationality as regards employment, remuneration and other conditions of work and employment. Article 7(1) provides as follows:

> "A worker who is a national of a Member State may not, in the territory of another Member State, be treated differently from national workers by reason of his nationality in respect of any conditions of employment and work, in particular as regards remuneration, dismissal, and should he become unemployed, reinstatement or re-employment".

11–29 By art.7(2) workers from other Member States must enjoy the same "social and tax advantages" as national workers. This provision goes some way to eliminating potential obstacles to the free movement of workers. In light of both, its importance and the extent of consideration given to it by the CJEU, art.7(2) is considered in detail below.

11–30 Article 7(3) makes similar provision as regards access to "training in vocational schools and retraining centres". Article 7(4) provides that discriminatory conditions in collective or individual agreements or regulations concerning "eligibility for employment, employment, remuneration and other conditions of work or dismissal" will be null and void.

---

[25] Regulation 492/2011 of April 5, 2011 on freedom of movement for workers within the Union replaced Regulation 1612/68. Regulation 492/2011 is a consolidating regulation and does not change the rights formerly contained in Regulation 1612/68.

[26] It will be recalled that where the European Union has sought to prevent the nationals of *new* Member States from enjoying the right of free movement for workers from accession it has prevented access to the labour forces of existing Member States by suspending the art. provisions. See Ch.5. In relation to Bulgaria and Romania who joined from 2007, arts 1 and 2 of the Annex in respect of each such Member State requires the "present member States" to apply national law measures for a two-year period "by way of derogation from Articles 1 to 6 of Regulation 1612/68". A similar approach (as regards derogation from arts 1–6 of Regulation 1612/68) was taken when Portugal joined (see art.216(1) of that Act of Accession). And also as regards the accession of Greece (the transitional provisions of arts 44–47 of the Act concerning the conditions of accession of the Hellenic Republic suspended, until December 31, 1987, the operation of arts 1–6 (and arts 13–23) of Regulation 1612/68).

Article 8 deals with non-discriminatory treatment as regards trade union membership, workers' representative bodies and such like (although with "public law" exceptions reflecting art.45(4) TFEU which states that art.45 does not apply to employment in the public services). Article 9 spells out the non-discrimination obligation as regards "all the rights and benefits accorded to national workers in matters of housing, including ownership of the housing he needs", including benefits and priorities given in relation to "housing lists". 11–31

(c) *Personal scope*

(i) *Workers*

Workers are unambiguously within the personal scope of the Treaty on the Functioning of the European Union. The question "who *is* a worker" is considered in detail in Ch.6. It is important to emphasise that whilst as a general rule a person loses the status as a worker once the employment relationship has ended,[27] a person's status as a worker may endure in various circumstances despite the fact that such person is no longer in an employment relationship. Those circumstances are considered in Ch.6 and include that: 11–32

(a) the status of worker is not lost immediately on cessation of employment;

(b) the status may be retained where the person has previously worked and remains capable of taking further employment;

(c) the status may be retained where the person is available for work and capable of taking it up; and

(d) the status may be retained where workers undertake retraining.

Where in spite of cessation of employment the person retains worker status such person remains within the personal scope of the Treaty for the purposes of the non-discrimination provisions. 11–33

It is also to be noted that frontier workers fall within the scope of Regulation 492/2011 and as such are protected from discrimination under art.7(2) and elsewhere in the Regulation in the Member State in which they work, rather than reside.[28] 11–34

(ii) *Work seekers*

As regards work seekers, until *Collins*[29] a distinction was drawn between work seekers and workers in terms of their access to social and tax advantages on a non-discriminatory basis. In *Lebon*[30] the CJEU considered 11–35

---

[27] See *Martinez Sala v Freistat Bayern* (85/96) [1998] E.C.R. I-2691, at [32].
[28] *Gertraud Hartmann v Freistaat Bayern* (C-212/05) July 18, 2007.
[29] *Collins v Secretary of State for Work and Pensions* (C-138/02), judgment of March 23, 2004, [2004] E.C.R. I-02703.
[30] *Centre public d'aide sociale de Courcelles v Lebon* (316/85) [1987] E.C.R. 2811.

whether equal treatment with regard to social and tax advantages in art.7(2) of Regulation 1612/68[31] applied to work seekers.[32]

The CJEU held that the right did not apply to work seekers:

> "It must be pointed out that the right to equal treatment with regard to social and tax advantages applies only to workers. Those who move in search of employment qualify for equal treatment only as regards access to employment in accordance with Article 48 of the EEC Treaty [now art.45 TFEU] and Articles 2 and 5 of Regulation No 1612/68".[33]

11–36 The CJEU reached the same conclusion in *Commission v Belgium*[34] which concerned the dependent children of workers living in Belgium seeking "tideover allowances".[35] The CJEU rejected the Commission's argument that tideover allowances fell within the scope of the rules on free access to employment (as provided for in art.3(1) of Regulation 1612/68[36]). The CJEU did so on the basis that the payment of the allowances constituted "active measures in the sphere of unemployment insurance" which were as such "linked to unemployment falling outside the field of access to employment in the strict sense".

11–37 However, these decisions are no longer good law following the decision of the CJEU in *Collins*[37] which concerned a dual Irish/American national who—after an absence of 17 years from the United Kingdom—returned there in May 1998 in order to find work in the social services sector. As expressly acknowledged by the CJEU by reference to *Lebon*[38] and *Commission v Belgium*,[39] the right to equal treatment enjoyed by work seekers seeking benefits of a financial nature applied only as regards *access* to employment, but not as regards the social and tax advantages otherwise enjoyed by workers. Moreover, the provisions of Regulation 492/2011[40] dealing with such access did not expressly refer to benefits of a financial nature. Despite these facts CJEU stated:

> "in view of the establishment of citizenship of the Union and the interpretation in the case-law of the right to equal treatment enjoyed by citizens of the Union, it is

---

[31] Now art.7(2) of Regulation 492/2011.
[32] The position of work seekers is considered in Ch.6.
[33] *Centre public d'aide sociale de Courcelles v Lebon* (316/85) [1987] E.C.R. 2811, at [26].
[34] *Commission v Belgium* (C-278/94) [1996] E.C.R. I-4307. See also, *Saada Zaoui v Caisse règionale d'assurance maladie de l'Ile-de-France (CRAMIF)* (147/87) [1987] E.C.R. 5511, where the CJEU held that the Community rules on freedom of movement for workers would not apply to workers who have never exercised the right and that accordingly a member of the family of a worker cannot rely on Regulation 1612/68 (now Regulation 492/2011) to claim the same social advantages as workers who are nationals of that State when the worker has never exercised the right to freedom of movement within the Community.
[35] These are grants provided to young people who have just completed their studies and are seeking their first employment allowing recipients to be regarded as "wholly unemployed and on benefit" within the meaning of the rules on employment and unemployment.
[36] Now art.3(1) of Regulation 492/2011.
[37] *Collins v Secretary of State for Work and Pensions* (137/84) judgment of March 23, 2004.
[38] *Centre public d'aide sociale de Courcelles v Lebon* (316/85) [1987] E.C.R. 2811.
[39] *Commission v Belgium* (C-278/94) [1996] E.C.R. I-4307.
[40] Formerly Regulation 1612/68.

no longer possible to exclude from the scope of Article 48(2) of the Treaty [now Art.45(2) TFEU]—which expresses the fundamental principle of equal treatment, guaranteed by Article 6 of the Treaty [now art.18 TFEU]—a benefit of a financial nature intended to facilitate access to employment in the labour market of a Member State. [...] The interpretation of the scope of the principle of equal treatment in relation to access to employment must reflect this development, as compared with the interpretation followed in *Lebon* and in Case C-278/94 *Commission v Belgium*."[41]

The principles set out in *Collins* were further affirmed by the CJEU in *Ioannidis*.[42]

The position now is clear: the principle of equal treatment for work seekers applies both as regards matters relating to access to employment in art.1 of Regulation 492/2011 and to social and tax advantages contained in art.2. No longer can any distinction be drawn between workers and work seekers. **11–38**

(d) *Material scope*

Plainly matters falling within the scope of Regulation 492/2011 are within the material scope of the Treaty on the Functioning of the European Union for the purposes of the prohibition against discrimination. Identification of such matters is for the most part straightforward. The provisions in art.7(1), (3) and (4) of Regulation 492/2011 are self-defining. For example, discriminatory conditions of employment as regards remuneration prohibited by art.7(1) need no further explanation. The same, however, cannot be said for art.7(2). In particular considerable attention has been given by the CJEU to the meaning of the phrase "social advantage" in art.7(2). The art.7(2) provision is considered below. **11–39**

(i) *Article 7(2) social advantages*

Article 7(2) is a provision unique to workers and is important in the elimination of obstacles to the right of free movement for workers. Generally the provision has been interpreted by the CJEU in a broad manner, consistent with the aim of ensuring that Union citizen workers who move around the European Union are not disadvantaged vis-à-vis own national workers. The failure to give Union citizen workers the same rights and benefits as own national workers would constitute an obstacle to free movement. **11–40**

The concept of social advantage was considered by the CJEU in *Even*.[43] The case concerned the payment of a pension to a French national living in Belgium who sought to obtain a benefit payable to Belgian workers who had fought in the Allied Forces during the Second World War and had suffered incapacity for work attributable to an act of war. He argued that the refusal **11–41**

---

[41] *Centre public d'aide sociale de Courcelles v Lebon* (316/85) [1987] E.C.R. 2811, at [63 and 64].
[42] *Office national de l'emploi v Ioannis Ioannidis* (C-258/04) September 15, 2005.
[43] *Even v Office National des Pensions pour Travailleurs Salariés* (207/78) [1979] E.C.R. 2019.

of such a benefit constituted discrimination on the grounds of nationality. The CJEU described the concept as follows:

> "It follows from all its provisions and from the objective pursued that the advantages which this Regulation extends to workers who are nationals of other Member States are all those which, whether or not linked to a contract of employment, are generally granted to national workers primarily because of their objective status as workers or by virtue of the mere fact of their residence on the national territory and the extension of which to workers who are nationals of other member states therefore seems suitable to facilitate their mobility within the community."[44]

11–42 Further in *Lair*[45] the CJEU described social advantage in the following terms:

> "In addition to the specific right mentioned in Article 7 (1) of [Regulation 1612/68[46]] not to be treated differently from national workers in respect of any conditions of employment and work, in particular as regards reinstatement or re-employment, 'social advantages' include all other advantages by means of which the migrant worker is guaranteed, in the words of the third recital in the preamble to the regulation, the possibility of improving his living and working conditions and promoting his social advancement."

11–43 There are many examples of rights or benefits which have been recognised as social advantages by the CJEU. These include:[47]

- benefits guaranteeing a minimum subsistence allowance dependent on residence qualification;[48]
- grants for training with a view to entry to university;[49]

---

[44] para.22. The definition has been consistently repeated ever since: see, inter alia, *Reina and Reina v Landeskreditbank Baden-Württemberg* (65/81) [1982] E.C.R. 33 and *Mutsch* (137/84) [1985] E.C.R. 2681. On the facts in *Even* the CJEU held that the benefit was not a social advantage: based on a scheme of national recognition it could not be considered as an advantage granted to a national worker by reason primarily of their status of worker or residence on the national territory.

[45] *Lair v Univeritaat Hannover* (39/86) [1988] E.C.R. 3161.

[46] Now Regulation 492/2011 art.7(1).

[47] The list is not intended to be exhaustive but gives a flavour of the breadth of what has been treated by the CJEU as social advantages.

[48] *Hoeckx v Openbaar Centrum voor Maatschappelijk Welzijn* (249/83) [1985] E.C.R. 973 and *Scrivner and Cole v Centre Public d'aide Sociale de Chastre* (122/84) [1985] E.C.R. 1027 in which the CJEU held that the minimum means of subsistence was a social advantage which could not be denied to a migrant worker or members of his family who were members of another Member State resident within the territory of the granting State, nor could it be subject to a residence qualification which was not imposed on nationals of the granting State.

[49] *Lair v Univeritaat Hannover* (39/86) [1988] E.C.R. 3161. The CJEU held also that art.12 of the EC Treaty (now art.18 TFEU) applied only to that portion of State-given assistance which related to payment of registration and other fees, in particular tuition fees: see to the same effect *Brown v Secretary of State for Scotland* (197/86) [1998] E.C.R. 3205. In *The Queen on the application of Dany Bidar v London Borough of Ealing and the Secretary of State for Education* (C-209/03) March 15, 2005 the CJEU considered that grants for maintenance (in the form of student loans) fall within art.12 of the EC Treaty (now art.18 TFEU).

- a scholarship to study in another Member State granted under a bilateral agreement reserving access for nationals of the two Member State Parties to the agreement;[50]
- benefit in the form of a single payment paid under a compensation scheme for agricultural workers whose contracts of employment have been terminated as a result of the setting aside of land;[51]
- child raising allowances;[52]
- childbirth loans given interest free by a credit institution incorporated under public law;[53]
- childbirth and maternity allowances;[54]
- provisions guaranteeing a minimum wage;[55]
- the right to require that legal proceedings take place in a specific language;[56]
- disability allowance in the form of a benefit for disabled adults for the assistance of a third person;[57]

and

- the possibility of a migrant workers obtaining permission for an unmarried companion to reside.[58]

These cases show the breadth of the CJEU's approach, both to the interpretation of social advantages in general and the meaning of "facilitating mobility" in particular. **11–44**

In *Reina*[59] for example the CJEU held that interest-free childbirth loans were social advantages. The CJEU emphasised that the concept of social advantage encompassed not only benefits granted to own nationals as of right, but also those granted on a discretionary basis.[60] Further, in *Mutsch*[61] the CJEU had held that the right to require that criminal proceedings take place in a language other than the language normally used in proceedings before the Court which tries a worker was a social advantage. The CJEU reached its conclusion on the basis that: **11–45**

---

[50] *Annunziata Matteucci v Communautè Française of Belgium and Commissariat gènèral aux relations internationals* (235/87) [1988] E.C.R. 5589.
[51] *Meints v Minister van Landbouw, Natuurbeheer en Visserij* (C-57/96) [1997] E.C.R. I-6689.
[52] *Martinez Sala v Freistaat Bayern* (C-85/96) [1998] E.C.R. I-2691.
[53] *Reina and Reina v Landeskreditbank Baden-Württemberg* (65/81) [1982] E.C.R. 33.
[54] *Commission v Luxembourg* (C-111/91) [1993] E.C.R. I-817.
[55] *Commission v Luxembourg* (C-299/01) [2002] E.C.R. I-5899.
[56] *Mutsch* (137/84) [1985] E.C.R. 2681.
[57] *Schmid v Belgium State* (C-310/91) [1993] E.C.R. I-3011.
[58] *Reed v Netherlands* (59/85) [1986] E.C.R. 1283.
[59] *Reina and Reina v Landeskreditbank Baden-Württemberg* (65/81) [1982] E.C.R. 33.
[60] *Reina and Reina v Landeskreditbank Baden-Württemberg* (65/81) [1982] E.C.R. 33, at [17]. The German Government had tried to argue that the benefit was not a social advantage because it was payable only on a demographic basis to counteract the decline in birth rate.
[61] *Mutsch* (137/84) [1985] E.C.R. 2681.

> "The right to use his own language in proceedings before the courts of the Member State in which he resides, under the same conditions as national workers, plays an important role in the integration of a migrant worker and his family into the host country, and thus in achieving the objective of free movement for workers".[62]

11–46 The non-discrimination provisions are enjoyed also by the family members of a worker, but only where those family members are dependent on the worker. In *Inzirillo*[63] the CJEU held that an allowance for disabled adults granted to own nationals must be granted to the worker's disabled adult dependants. The rationale for extending the availability of social advantages to family members dependent on the worker is that if a worker's dependent family member was to be deprived of a social benefit, the worker might be induced to leave the host Member State. In *Deak*[64] the CJEU explained the principles as follows:

> "The principle of equal treatment laid down in Article 7 of Reg. No 1612/68 is also intended to prevent discrimination against descendents of a worker who are dependent on him ... A worker anxious to ensure for his children the enjoyment of the social benefits provided for by the legislation of the Member States for the support of young persons seeking employment would be induced not to remain in the Member State where he had established himself and found employment if that state could refuse to pay the benefits in question to his children because of their foreign nationality ... That result would run counter to the objective of the principle of freedom of movement for workers within the community, bearing in mind *inter alia* the right granted under that principle to employed persons and to members of their families to remain within the territory of a Member State ...".

11–47 It is however to be noted that the extension of the principle to family members is "indirect", that is the right is not a discrete one given to the family member as such. Rather it is one enjoyed only through the principal on whom the family member is dependent. This was stated expressly by the CJEU in *Deak*.

11–48 It is important to bear in mind that the right is restricted to one of equality of treatment. When relying on the art.7(2), conditions that are imposed on own nationals in order to obtain a benefit might also be applied to Union citizen workers. An EU national worker for instance who wishes to install a domestic helper (a third country national who is not a family member) to look after his children while at work, claiming that this is a social advantage which is afforded to own nationals, will have to meet the conditions laid down in national legislation. This not someone who would obviously fall under art.3(2) of Directive 2004/38.

---

[62] *Mutsch* (137/84) [1985] E.C.R. 2681, at [16].
[63] *Inzirillo v Caisse d'allocations familiales de l'arrondissement de Lyon* (C-63/76) [1976] E.C.R. 2057, at [21–22].
[64] *Office National de l'emploi v Deak* (94/84) [1985] E.C.R. 1873, at [22–26].

(ii) *Article 7(2) tax advantages*

11–49 The non-discrimination provision in art.7(2) includes "tax advantages". However, it has very rarely been used by individuals wishing to obtain any such advantages. The CJEU has yet to explain the concept of tax advantages or their application to a case in any detail. As with social advantages, the concept should be broadly construed and would include any matter relating to taxation,[65] direct or indirect, and social security contributions.[66] European Union national workers must not be placed in a worse situation than own nationals vis-á-vis the amount of tax they must pay or the conditions under which they must pay it. Furthermore, they should be able to access all of the tax incentive and rebate schemes that own national workers can. Since issues of taxation inter-relate with issues surrounding conditions of remuneration, which is specifically provided for in the principal non-discrimination provision relating to workers (art.45(2) TFEU), it is unsurprising that the CJEU has mainly considered alleged discrimination on tax issues under art.45 TFEU itself.[67]

(e) *Prohibited forms of discrimination*

11–50 The prohibition in European Union law of discrimination against workers prohibits direct discrimination such as where a Member State limits employment in a particular sector (not covered by art.45(4) TFEU) to own nationals. However, the prohibition applies more widely and includes indirect forms of discrimination by the application of other criteria which lead to the same result.

11–51 The prohibition against indirect discrimination has been consistently restated by the CJEU. In *Sotgiu*[68] one of the questions concerned whether art.7(1) and (4) of Regulation 1612/68[69] were to be interpreted as containing a prohibition not only against treating workers differently because they are nationals of another Member State, but also against treating them differently because they are resident in another Member State. The CJEU held:

> "The rules regarding equality of treatment, both in the Treaty and in Article 7 of Regulation No 1612/68, forbid not only overt discrimination by reason of nationality but also all covert forms of discrimination which, by the application of other criteria of differentiation, lead in fact to the same result. This interpretation, which is necessary to ensure the effective working of one of the fundamental principles of the community, is explicitly recognized by the fifth recital of the preamble to Regulation No 1612/68 which requires that equality of treatment of workers shall be ensured 'in fact and in law'. It may therefore be that criteria such as place of origin or residence of a worker may, according to circumstances, be tantamount, as regards their practical effect, to discrimination on the grounds of nationality, such as is prohibited by the Treaty and the Regulation".

---

[65] See, for instance, *Schumacker* (C-279/93) [1995] E.C.R. I-225 and *Biehl* (C-175/88) [1990] E.C.R. I-1779.
[66] *F.C. Terhoeve v Inspecteur van der Belastingdienst Particulieren* (C-18/95) [1999] E.C.R. I-345.
[67] *F.C. Terhoeve v Inspecteur van der Belastingdienst Particulieren* (C-18/95) [1999] E.C.R. I-345.
[68] *Sotgiu v Deutsche Bundespost* (152/73) [1974] E.C.R. 153.
[69] Now art.7(1) and 7(4) of Regulation 492/2011.

11–52 The principle of indirect discrimination was further described by the CJEU in *O'Flynn*[70] as follows:

> "[A] provision of national law must be regarded as indirectly discriminatory if it is intrinsically liable to affect migrant workers more than national workers and if there is a consequent risk that it will place the former at a particular disadvantage. ... It is not necessary in this respect to find that the provision in question does in practice affect a substantially higher proportion of migrant workers. It is sufficient that it is liable to have such an effect. Further, the reasons why a migrant worker chooses to make use of his freedom of movement within the Community are not to be taken into account in assessing whether a national provision is discriminatory. The possibility of exercising so fundamental a freedom as the freedom of movement of persons cannot be limited by such considerations, which are purely subjective".

11–53 A form of indirect discrimination could be where national law imposes a residence condition for the payment of a particular benefit in respect of all applicants, both European Union migrant workers and own nationals alike. Whilst perhaps not at first blush discriminatory such condition would generally be regarded as discriminatory by the CJEU if it was more difficult for a migrant worker to fulfil it than an own national. A similar condition was considered by the CJEU in its decision in *Collins*[71] which concerned an application made for job seekers allowance where the national law provision introduced a difference in treatment according to whether the person involved was "habitually resident" in the United Kingdom. Identifying whether such provision—which on its face applied equally to all nationals—was discriminatory the CJEU stated:

> "Since that requirement is capable of being met more easily by the State's own nationals, the 1996 Regulations place at a disadvantage Member State nationals who have exercised their right of movement in order to seek employment in the territory of another Member State (see, to this effect, Case C-237/94 *O'Flynn* [1996] E.C.R. I-2617, para. 18, and Case C-388/01 *Commission v Italy* [2003] E.C.R. I-721, paras 13 and 14)".[72]

11–54 In *Ioannidis*[73] the CJEU considered Belgian legislation leading to a difference in treatment between citizens who have completed their secondary education in Belgium and those who have completed it in another Member State with only the former having a right to a tideover allowance. The CJEU found that such condition could place nationals of other Member States at a disadvantage. Inasmuch as it links the grant of that allowance to the requirement that the applicant has obtained the required diploma in Belgium, that condition can be met more easily by Belgian nationals. As such it was found to be discriminatory contrary to art.39 EC Treaty (now art.45 TFEU) and art.7(2) of Regulation 1612/68 (now Regulation 492/2011).

---

[70] *O'Flynn v Chief Adjudication Officer* (C-237/94) [1996] E.C.R. I-2617, at [20–21].
[71] *Collins v Secretary of State for Work and Pensions* (C-138/02) judgment of March 23, 2004.
[72] *Collins v Secretary of State for Work and Pensions* (C-138/02) judgment of March 23, 2004, at [65].
[73] *Office National de l'emploi v Ioannis Ioannidis* (C-258/04) September 15, 2005.

In *Hartmann*[74] the CJEU found a condition in German legislation that a child-raising benefit would only be granted to workers who resided in Germany could be indirectly discriminatory against migrant workers, in particular frontier workers such as Mr Hartmann.

11–55

(f) *Justification*

A finding of discrimination on grounds of nationality against a worker however will not in and of itself mean that the prohibition has been contravened. As discussed above, discrimination may be justified if based on objective considerations independent of the nationality of the worker concerned and if proportionate to the legitimate aim of the national provisions.

11–56

The CJEU's analysis in this respect in *Collins*[75] is instructive. Basing its decision on *D'Hoop*[76] the CJEU stated that it was legitimate for the national legislature to wish to ensure the existence of a genuine link between an applicant for an allowance in the nature of a social advantage within the meaning of art.7(2) of Regulation 1612/68 and the geographic employment market in question (as was the case with job-seekers' allowance). Moreover, the UK authorities could seek to determine the existence of such a link by establishing that the person concerned has, for a reasonable period, in fact genuinely sought work. The CJEU continued:

11–57

> "However, while a residence requirement is, in principle, appropriate for the purpose of ensuring such a connection, if it is to be proportionate it cannot go beyond what is necessary in order to attain that objective. More specifically, its application by the national authorities must rest on clear criteria known in advance and provision must be made for the possibility of a means of redress of a judicial nature. In any event, if compliance with the requirement demands a period of residence, the period must not exceed what is necessary in order for the national authorities to be able to satisfy themselves that the person concerned is genuinely seeking work in the employment market of the host Member State".[77]

3. OBSTACLES TO ESTABLISHMENT

(a) *Definition of restrictions of freedom of establishment*

Article 49 TFEU precludes any national measure which is liable to hamper or render less attractive the exercise of the right of establishment by Union citizens.[78] That said Member States are entitled to regulate, within certain limits, the conditions for all traders or persons carrying out a particular activity. However, those who seek to establish themselves from other

11–58

---

[74] *Gertraud Hartmann v Freistaat Bayern* (C-212/05) July 18, 2007.
[75] *Collins v Secretary of State for Work and Pensions* (138/02), judgment of March 23, 2004.
[76] *D'Hoop v Office National de l'emploi* (C-224/98) [2002] E.C.R. I-6191.
[77] para.72.
[78] *Semeroro Casa Uno Srl v Sindaco del Comune di Erbusco* (C-418/93) [1996] E.C.R. I-2975, at [32].

Member States must not be placed at a disadvantage or treated differently from the Member State's own nationals.[79]

11–59 Furthermore, even where national measures are not applied in a discriminatory way, they may still have the effect of hindering nationals of other Member States in the exercise of their right of establishment. For instance national rules which take no account of the knowledge and qualifications acquired by a person in another Member State might represent such an obstacle to free movement and would therefore be prohibited by art.49 TFEU.[80] In *Commission v Spain* the CJEU found that although the Commission had not shown laws restricting the establishment of large (as opposed to medium or small) retail establishments were discriminatory on grounds of nationality, they did overall constitute a restriction on the freedom of establishment protected by art.49 TFEU.[81]

11–60 The rights conferred by art.49 TFEU are unconditional and a Member State cannot make respect for them subject to a condition of reciprocity.[82]

11–61 Although art.49 TFEU is primarily aimed at ensuring that nationals and companies of other Member States are treated in the same way as own nationals and companies in the host Member State, it also prohibits the Member State of origin from hindering establishment in another Member State. The CJEU has considered that measures which prohibit undertakings from leaving the Member State of origin would render the rights guaranteed by art.49 TFEU meaningless.[83] With respect to natural persons, the right to leave the Member State of origin is expressly provided for in Directive 2004/38.[84] The right does not extend to companies.[85]

11–62 A national of a Member State who acquires professional qualifications in another Member State which are recognised by European Union law must be able to carry out professional services in the same way as any other Union citizen. Excluding own nationals from such benefit would constitute a restriction on establishment which is contrary to art.49 TFEU.[86]

(b) *Prohibited discrimination based on nationality*

11–63 Article 49 TFEU ensures that all Union citizens who establish themselves in another Member State, even where that establishment is only secondary, receive the same treatment as nationals of that Member State. The provision

---

[79] *Kraus v Land Baden-Württemburg* (C-19/92) [1993] E.C.R. 1663, at [32].
[80] *Vlassopoulou v Ministerium vor Justiz Bundes und Europaangelgenheiten BadenWürttemburg* (C-340/89) [1991] E.C.R. I-2357, at [15].
[81] *Commission v Spain* (C-400/08), March 24, 2011.
[82] *Commission v Italy* (C-58/90) [1991] E.C.R. I-4193.
[83] *Union Royal Belge des Societes de Football Association ASBL v Bosman* (C-415/93) [1995] E.C.R. I-4353.
[84] See art.4 of the Directive 2004/38/EC.
[85] *The Queen v HM Treasury and Commissioners of Inland Revenue Ex p. Daily Mail and General Trust PLC* (81/87) [1988] E.C.R. 5483.
[86] *J Knoors v Secretary of State for Economic Affairs* (115/78) [1979] E.C.R. 399, at [24].

prohibits, as a restriction on the freedom of establishment, any discrimination on grounds of nationality.

According to the CJEU's case law the principle of equal treatment, of which art.49 TFEU embodies specific instances, prohibits not only overt discrimination by reason of nationality but also more covert forms of discrimination through the application of other criteria of differentiation.[87] **11–64**

For instance a requirement that the owners and charterers of a vessel and, in the case of a company, the shareholders and directors, be resident and domiciled in the Member State in which the vessel is to be registered results in discrimination on grounds of nationality. This is not justified by the rights and obligations which the Member State may claim are created by the grant of a national flag to a vessel. Plainly it is much easier for nationals of the Member State to satisfy the requirement of being domiciled in that State since the majority of them will be resident and domiciled there, whereas nationals of other Member States would, in most cases, have to move their residence in order to comply with the legislation.[88] **11–65**

In certain instances the discriminatory treatment is very well disguised. The CJEU has held that the difference in treatment as regards access to sickness insurance between directors of a company formed under national law and those of a company formed under the law of another Member State, amounted to discrimination on grounds of nationality. The CJEU considered that such discrimination against employees of a company was contrary to the provision of art.49 TFEU since it indirectly restricted the freedom of establishment of the company itself.[89] **11–66**

The case of *Gebroeder Beentjes*[90] concerned a company which submitted a tender for a public works contract in connection with a land consolidation operation. One of the conditions for tender required the tenderer to employ long-term unemployed persons. The CJEU held that an obligation to employ long-term unemployed persons could infringe the prohibition of discrimination if it became apparent that such a condition could be satisfied only by tenderers from the State concerned or that tenderers from other Member States would have difficulties in complying with it. **11–67**

(c) *Non-prohibited restrictions*

(i) *Non-discriminatory measures*

Some restrictions on freedom of establishment may, in certain instances, be justified. Such restrictions must, however, fulfil certain general conditions: they must be applied in a non-discriminatory manner (see exceptions below); they must be justified by imperative requirements in the general **11–68**

---

[87] *Halliburton Services BV v Staatssecretaris van Financiën* (C-1/93) [1994] E.C.R. I-1137, at [15].
[88] *The Queen v Secretary of State for Transport Ex p. Factortame Ltd* (C-221/89) [1991] E.C.R. I-3905, at [32].
[89] *Serges* (79/85) [1986] E.C.R. 2375.
[90] *Gebroeders Beentjes* (31/87) [1988] E.C.R. 4635.

11–69 In *Kraus*[92] the CJEU considered that even though a measure was not discriminatory it could still be contrary to art.49 TFEU as it was liable to hamper or to render less attractive the exercise of fundamental freedoms guaranteed by the Treaty on the Functioning of the European Union. The restriction would only be permissible if it pursued a legitimate objective compatible with the TFEU and was justified by pressing reasons of public interest.[93] It would also be necessary for the Member State to demonstrate that the national rules are both appropriate for ensuring the attainment of the objective and proportionate.[94]

The preceding text continues: interest; they must be suitable for securing the attainment of the objective which they pursue; and they must not go beyond what is necessary in order to attain that objective.[91]

11–70 In the *Commission v Italy*[95] the CJEU held that imposing a duty of secrecy on the staff of companies, which if breached would lead to criminal sanctions, was not justified. The CJEU considered that the Italian Government had sufficient legal powers at its disposal to be able to adapt the performance of contracts to protect the confidential nature of the data in question in a manner which was less restrictive.

(ii) *Discriminatory measures*

11–71 There are two exceptions to the general rule that restrictions on freedom of establishment should be exercised in non-discriminatory manner: first in relation to participation in the exercise of official authority and secondly where public policy, public security or public health justifies such a discriminatory measure.

11–72 It is to be noted that the first paragraph of art.51 TFEU excludes from the application of the provisions on freedom of establishment activities which in a Member State are connected, even occasionally, with the exercise of official authority. However, the CJEU has made clear that the derogation provided for in art.51 TFEU must be restricted to activities which in themselves are directly and specifically connected with the exercise of official authority.[96]

11–73 The CJEU does not consider that professional activities involving regular contact with national courts to be connected with the exercise of official authority.[97] Nor does it consider the function of an internal auditor to be connected with the exercise of official authority.[98]

---

[91] *Gebhard v Consigol dell' Ordine degli Advocat AE Procuratori di Milano* (C-55/94) [1995] E.C.R. I-4165, at [37].
[92] *Kraus v Land Baden-Württemberg* (C-19/92) [1993] E.C.R. 1663, at [32].
[93] *Thieffry v Counseil de l'Ordre des Avocats a la Cour de Paris* (71/76) [1977] E.C.R. 765, at [12–15].
[94] *Kraus v Land Baden-Württemberg* (C-19/92) [1993] E.C.R. 1663, at [32].
[95] *Commission v Italy* (3/88) [1989] E.C.R. 4035, at [11].
[96] *Thijssen v Controledienst voor de verzekeringen* (C-42/92) [1993] E.C.R. I-4047, at [8].
[97] *Reyners v Belgium* (2/74) [1974] E.C.R. 631, at [51].
[98] *Thijssen v Controledienst voor de verzekeringen* (C-42/92) [1993] E.C.R. I-4047, at [18].

MUTUAL RECOGNITION OF DIPLOMAS/TRAINING

Other than where activities are connected with official authority, discriminatory measures may only be justified on grounds of public policy, public security and public health. These are discussed in detail in Ch.13. It is to be noted that these grounds do not include economic aims[99] and thus anti-competitive measures or those that protect a Member State's market will not be permissible. **11–74**

4. MUTUAL RECOGNITION OF DIPLOMAS/TRAINING

(i) General Treaty provisions relating to mutual recognition of qualifications

In order to make it easier for persons to take up and pursue self-employed activities, art.53 TFEU provides that the European Parliament and the Council will issue directives concerning the mutual recognition of diplomas and other formal qualifications. Article 53 TFEU further provides that the European Parliament and the Council shall issue directives for the **11–75**

> "coordination of the provisions laid down by law, regulation or administrative action in Member States concerning the taking-up and pursuit of activities as self-employed persons".

The chapter in the Treaty relating to establishment thus provides a "general programme" and the directives provided for in art.53 TFEU are intended to accomplish two functions. The first is the elimination of obstacles to the freedom of establishment and the second is the introduction into the law of Member States of a set of provisions intended to facilitate the effective exercise of this freedom.[100] **11–76**

The CJEU has held that the provision is directed towards reconciling freedom of establishment with the application of national professional rules justified by the general interest of States, in particular rules relating to organisation, qualifications, professional ethics, supervision and liability. **11–77**

Where a directive has not been adopted for a particular profession under art.53 TFEU, a person subject to European Union law cannot be denied the practical benefit of the freedom of establishment. **11–78**

There is no specific provision in the Treaties directing the European Parliament and the Council to make legislation relating to the mutual recognition of professional qualifications for employed persons. However, the system for mutual recognition of qualifications provided for by Directive 2005/36/EC[101] described below expressly applies to both the employed as **11–79**

---

[99] *Stichting Collective Antennevorrziening Gouda v Commissariaat voor de Media* (288/89) [1991] E.C.R. I-4007, at [11].
[100] *Reyners v Belgium* (2/74) [1974] E.C.R. 631.
[101] Directive 2005/36/EC of the European Parliament and of the Council of September 7, 2005 on the recognition of professional qualifications.

well as the self-employed.[102] The first recital in the preamble to Directive 2005/36/EC[103] moreover expresses the objective in clear terms.

> Pursuant to art.3(1)(c) of the [EC] Treaty, the abolition, as between Member States, of obstacles to the free movement of persons and services is one of the objectives of the Community. For nationals of the Member States, this includes, in particular, the right to pursue a profession, in a self-employed or employed capacity, in a Member State other than the one in which they have obtained their professional qualifications. In addition, art.47(1) of the Treaty [now art.53 TFEU] lays down that directives shall be issued for the mutual recognition of diplomas, certificates and other evidence of formal qualifications.

(ii) Mutual recognition in secondary legislation

11–80 Three Directives were initially adopted to provide a general system of mutual recognition of diplomas and education. The first (Directive 89/48[104]) was adopted in 1988 to enable higher-education professional diplomas gained in one Member State to be recognised in another Member State where the profession is regulated. The second (Directive 92/51[105]) was intended to supplement Directive 89/48, by extending the system of mutual recognition to those professions for which the required level of training was not as high or as long in duration as under Directive 89/48. The third (Directive 1999/42[106]) was intended to simplify and collate a whole range of transitional directives on the mutual recognition of diplomas in commerce, industry and craft trades and to supplement the two general system directives. Numerous amendments were made to this general scheme by subsequent directives.[107] In addition to the general system referred to above there were some 12 sectoral Directives[108] (also amended on occasions[109]) which covered the seven professions of doctor, nurse, dentist, veterinary surgeon, midwife, pharmacist and architect, together with two additional Directives[110] relating to the authorisation to practice as a lawyer.[111]

---

[102] art.2.1 of Directive 2005/36/EC of the European Parliament and of the Council of September 7, 2005 on the recognition of professional qualifications.
[103] Directive 2005/36/EC of the European Parliament and of the Council of September 7, 2005 on the recognition of professional qualifications.
[104] Council Directive 89/48 of December 21, 1988 [1989] O.J. L19/16.
[105] Council Directive 92/51 of June 18, 1992 [1992] O.J. L209/25.
[106] Directive 99/42 of the European Parliament and of the Council of June 7, 1999 [1999] O.J. L201/77.
[107] See, for example, Council Directive 2001/19 [2001] O.J. L206/1 (amending Council Directives 89/48 and 92/51).
[108] Council Directives 93/16, 77/452, 77/453, 78/686, 78/687, 8/1026, 78/1027, 80/154, 80/155, 85/432, 85/433 and 85/384.
[109] See, for example, Council Directive 2001/19 [2001] O.J. L206/1 amending Council Directives 77/452/EEC, 77/453/EEC, 78/686/EEC, 78/687/EEC, 78/1026/EEC, 78/1027/EEC, 80/154/EEC, 80/155/EEC, 85/384/EEC, 85/432/EEC, 85/433/EEC and 93/16/EEC concerning the professions of nurse responsible for general care, dental practitioner, veterinary surgeon, midwife, architect, pharmacist and doctor.
[110] Directives 77/249 and 98/5.
[111] The mutual recognition of qualifications were covered by the general system set out in Directives 89/48.

Unsurprisingly against such background in 2002 the Commission proposed **11–81**
a unifying Directive to replace all the sectoral Directives, as well as the three
Directives relating to the general system for mutual recognition.[112] While
maintaining the guarantees afforded by each of the existing recognition
systems, the Commission's proposal aimed to create a single, consistent legal
framework based on further liberalisation of the provision of services, more
automatic recognition of qualifications and greater flexibility in the procedures for updating the Directive. The Commission was concerned that free
movement of workers in an enlarged European Union required a simpler
and clearer system for the recognition of professional qualifications in order
to increase labour market flexibility and to help improve public services.

The resultant Directive 2005/36/EC[113] on the recognition of professional **11–82**
qualifications came into force on October 20, 2007 the date by which under
art.63 Member States were required to bring into force the "laws, regulations and administrative provisions necessary" to comply with the Directive.
There is large scale repeal of previous directives.[114] As acknowledged in
recital (9) of the preamble to the Directive, the previous directives were
amended on "several occasions" and "their provisions should be reorganised and rationalised by standardising the principles applicable". Nevertheless, there have already been numerous amendments made to the
Directive.[115]

The purpose of Directive 2005/36/EC (which is spelt out in art.1) is to **11–83**
establish the rules according to which a Member State (which makes access
to or pursuit of a regulated profession[116] in its territory dependent on
possession of specific professional qualifications) is required to recognise
professional qualifications obtained in other Member States so as to enable
the holder of such qualifications access to and pursuit of that profession.
The scope of those covered by the Directive is spelt out by art.2.1:

---

[112] Proposal for a Directive of the European Parliament and of the Council of March 7, 2002 on the recognition of professional qualifications, COM (2002) 119 final [2002] O. J. C181E.

[113] Directive 2005/36/EC of the European Parliament and of the Council of September 7, 2005 on the recognition of professional qualifications.

[114] See art.62: "Directives 77/452/EEC, 77/453/EEC, 78/686/EEC, 78/687/EEC, 78/1026/EEC, 78/1027/EEC, 80/154/EEC, 80/155/EEC, 85/384/EEC, 85/432/EEC, 85/433/EEC, 89/48/EEC, 92/51/EEC, 93/16/EEC and 1999/42/EC are repealed with effect from 20 October 2007."

[115] "Free movement of professionals" (at *http://www.ec.europa.eu/internal_market/qualifications/index_en.htm*) provides links to all documents relating to the law governing the recognition of professional qualifications. Note that the consolidated versions of Directive 2005/36/EC are not official documents but are meant "purely as a documentation tool" for which the institutions assume no liability as regards content.

[116] art.3(1) states that regulated profession means "a professional activity or group of professional activities, access to which, the pursuit of which, or one of the modes of pursuit of which is subject, directly or indirectly, by virtue of legislative, regulatory or administrative provisions to the possession of specific professional qualifications". In Joined Cases (*Josep Penarroja Fa* (C-372/09 and C-373/09)) March 17, 2011, the CJEU concluded that the duties of court expert translators, as discharged by experts enrolled in a register such as the national register of court experts maintained by the Cour de cassation in France, were not covered by the definition of "regulated profession" set out in art.3(1)(a) of Directive 2005/36.

"This Directive shall apply to all nationals of a Member State wishing to pursue a regulated profession in a Member State, including those belonging to the liberal professions, other than that in which they obtained their professional qualifications, on either a self- employed or employed basis."

11–84 It is not proposed to examine the provisions of Directive 2005/36/EC in detail.[117] In summary the Directive provides for a special scheme for temporary mobility. In such situations, professionals can in principle work on the basis of a declaration made in advance. The Directive also applies to professionals wishing to establish themselves in another Member State as an employed or self-employed person on a permanent basis (other than that in which they obtained their professional qualifications). The Directive sets out three systems for the recognition of qualifications, namely automatic recognition for professions for which the minimum training conditions have been harmonised, a general system for other regulated professions, and third recognition on the basis of professional experience for certain professional activities. The Directive also includes provisions on knowledge of languages and professional and academic titles.

11–85 Temporary mobility is dealt with in Title II of the Directive. The temporary and occasional nature of the activities of a self-employed or employed person is assessed on a case-by-case basis, in light of the duration of the activity, its frequency, regularity and continuity. The host country may require a written declaration, made in advance, including certain information. The Directive's scoreboard provides a snapshot of the declaration system in operation in the various Member States. However, if the profession in question has public health or safety implications and does not benefit from automatic recognition under Chapter III of Title III of the Directive, the host country may check the professional qualifications before the services are first provided, on condition that it complies with the principle of proportionality. The host country may provide for automatic temporary registration or pro forma membership on the basis of the declaration made in advance. The public social security bodies must also be informed in advance, or, in an urgent case, afterwards, of the services provided. Lastly, the host country may require the service provider to supply the recipient of the service with certain information.

11–86 The system of automatic recognition of professional qualifications applies throughout the Union for seven professions (known as the "sectoral" professions). These are architects, dentists, doctors, midwives, nurses, pharmacists and veterinary surgeons. In *Poland v European Parliament*[118] Poland claimed that arts 33(2) and 43(3) Directive 2005/36 setting out separate rules on the recognition of acquired rights applying to Polish qualifications of nurses and midwives should be declared invalid because of inadequate reasons given to justify such derogation. The CJEU rejected the claim. In the absence of evidence according to which the circumstances justifying the introduction, in the previously applicable directives, of differential treatment

---

[117] Much of what follows is taken from the Commission's website: *http://www.ec.europa.eu/internal_market/qualifications/index_en.htm*.
[118] *Poland v European Parliament* (C-460/05).

concerning certain situations would have changed, it was not necessary for specific reasons to be added to provisions which in Directive 2005/36 were limited to confirming the content of previously applicable provisions.

The general system for the recognition of evidence of training for the purposes of establishment in another Member State is dealt with in Chapter 1 of Title III of the Directive. Professional qualifications are grouped under five levels so that they can be compared. Qualifications are recognised if the migrant's level of professional qualification is at least equivalent to the level immediately below that required in the host country. Recognition must also be granted to migrants whose profession is not regulated in the country of origin but who have worked full-time in that profession for two years. **11–87**

There have been problems with the transposition of the Directive into the national laws of Member States. The Commission has successfully brought proceedings against various Member States (Austria, France, Germany, Greece, Luxembourg, the United Kingdom, and Northern Ireland[119]) seeking (and obtaining) declarations that such countries had not fulfilled their obligations under the Directive by failing to transpose its provisions into national law within the required time period namely by October 20, 2007. **11–88**

Furthermore, there have been a number of cases considered by the CJEU in which the Commission has alleged that the practice of various Member States (Austria, Belgium, Germany and Greece[120]) as regards notaries of limiting access to the profession of notary to Member State nationals was contrary to both art.49 TFEU and Directive 89/48 (repealed and replaced by Directive 2005/36 by the time the cases came to be considered). The CJEU held in such cases that the nationality conditions required by those Member States for access to the profession of notary constituted discrimination on grounds of nationality prohibited by art.49 TFEU of restrictions on the right of establishment. In so holding, the CJEU rejected the argument advanced by the Member States that the activities of notaries were connected with the exercise of official authority within the meaning of art.51 TFEU[121] and therefore outwith the ambit of art.49. The CJEU did so because on analysis of the activities performed by notaries in the various Member States it was not considered that such activities involved a direct and specific connection with the exercise of official authority. As regards alleged failure to implement Directive 2005/36 (and/or its predecessor Directive 89/48), the CJEU did consider such actions admissible because the obligations arising under each directive are analogous. However, on the **11–89**

---

[119] *Commission v Austria* (C-477/08); *Commission v France* (C-468/08); *Commission v Germany* (C-505/08); *Commission v Greece* (C-465/08); *Comission v Luxembourg* (C-51/08); and *Commission v United Kingdom and Northern Ireland* (C-556/08).
[120] *Commission v Austria* (C-53/08); *Commission v Belgium* (C-47/08); *Commission v Germany* (C-54/08); and *Commisison v Greece* (C-61/08). See also, *Commission v Portugal* (C-52/08) in which the same conclusion was reached as regards the lack of sufficiently clear obligation to transpose, although no finding made about unlawful discrimination under art.49 TFEU.
[121] art.51 TFEU states: "The provisions of this Chapter shall not apply, so far as any given Member State is concerned, to activities which in that State are connected, even occasionally, with the exercise of official authority."

merits the complaints failed, essentially because there had not been a sufficiently clear obligation for the Member States to transpose either Directive with respect to the profession of notary. There were a number of reasons for this lack of clarity, not least that until such cases the CJEU had not ruled on the inapplicability of art.51 to notaries. And moreover in recital (41) in the preamble to Directive 2005/35 the European Union legislature had been careful to state that the Directive was "without prejudice" to the application of arts 45(4) and 51 TFEU "concerning notably notaries".

5. Obstacles to Service Provision

11-90 As with the freedom of establishment, the TFEU provisions relating to the freedom to provide services are aimed at the abolition of restrictions on that freedom. At the heart of art.56 TFEU is the requirement that measures discriminating, directly or indirectly, between nationals of other Member States and the nationals of the host Member State are abolished.[122] Discrimination on grounds of nationality is discussed in detail in relation to establishment above. The same principles apply in relation to service provision.

11-91 In the context of service provision the CJEU has found that the requirement that the service provider resides in the host Member State when this is not imposed on own nationals is discriminatory.[123] The CJEU has also found that rules which limit the right to play in football matches as professional or semi-professional players solely to the nationals of the Member State in question are discriminatory and incompatible with the Treaty, except where the rules exclude foreign players for sporting reasons as opposed to economic ones.[124] This would be the case, for example, in matches played between national teams from different countries where played in the words of the CJEU, for reasons of "sporting interest".[125]

11-92 A requirement that an undertaking is established in the host Member State strikes at the heart of the freedom to provide services and is thus contrary to the TFEU. As stated by the CJEU in *Commission v Germany*:[126]

> "It is clear from settled case-law that the freedom to provide services implies, in particular, the abolition of any discrimination against a service provider on account of its nationality or the fact that it is established in a Member State other than that in which the service is provided (see, inter alia, C-490/04 *Commission v Germany*, paragraph 83 and the case-law cited). The requirement that an undertaking create a permanent establishment or branch in the Member State in which the services are provided runs directly counter to the freedom to provide services since it renders impossible the provision of services, in that Member State, by undertakings established in other Member States (see, to that effect, inter alia,

---

[122] *Criminal Proceedings against Lopez Brea and M Carlos Hidaglo Palacios* (C-330/90) and (C-331/90) [1992] E.C.R. I-323.
[123] *Cowan v Trèsor Public* (C-186/87) [1989] E.C.R. 195.
[124] *Dona v Mantero* (13/76) [1976] E.C.R. 1333.
[125] *Dona v Mantero* (13/76) [1976] E.C.R. 1333, at [14].
[126] *Commission v Germany* (C-546/07) January 21, 2010.

Case 205/84 *Commission v Germany* [1986] ECR 3755, paragraph 52; Case C-279/00 *Commission v Italy* [2002] ECR I-1425, paragraph 17; and Case C-496/01 *Commission v France* [2004] ECR I-2351, paragraph 65)".

Furthermore, the CJEU has stated that art.56 TFEU requires not only the elimination of discrimination against a person providing services on grounds of nationality, but also the abolition of any restriction when its effect is liable to prohibit or otherwise impede the activities of providers of services established in another Member State where they lawfully provide similar services. Such a restriction would be prohibited by art.56 TFEU even if it is applied without distinction to national providers of services and those from other Member States.[127]   **11–93**

In *Seco*[128] for instance, the CJEU held that the obligation to pay the employer's share of social security contributions imposed on persons providing services within the national territory if extended to persons established in another Member State could create a barrier to free movement. Such persons might already be liable to pay social security contributions in their own Member State and thus the provision of services in another Member State might lead to a heavier social security contributions' burden than a person would be liable to if established in one Member State and providing services in that Member State alone.   **11–94**

In the context of the freedom to provide and receive services the CJEU has consistently found that: **11–95**

> "Article 49 EC (now Article 56 TFEU) precludes the application of any national rules which have the effect of making the provision of services between Member States more difficult than the provision of services purely within a Member State".[129]

As with any restriction on the free movement rights contained within the TFEU, a restriction on the provision of services by nationals or companies from other Member States will only be permissible if it falls within one of express exemptions laid down in art.52 TFEU, namely public policy, public security or public health.[130]   **11–96**

---

[127] *Sager v Dennemeyer & Co Ltd* (C-76/90) [1991] E.C.R. I-4221.
[128] *Sociètè anonyme de droit français Seco et sociètè anonyme de droit francais Desquenne & Giral v Etablissement d'assurance contre la vieillesse et l'invalidite* (62/81) and (63/81) [1982] E.C.R. 223.
[129] See *Aikaterini Stamatelaki v PDD Organismos Asfaliseos Eleftheron Epangelmation (OAEE)* (C-444/05), April 19, 2007.
[130] See Ch.13.

DISCRIMINATION AND OTHER OBSTACLES TO FREEDOM OF MOVEMENT

6. OBSTACLES TO THE EXERCISE OF FREE MOVEMENT BY THE ECONOMICALLY INACTIVE

(a) *Introduction*

11–97 Prior to the Maastricht Treaty there was no specific Treaty provision for the freedom of movement for the economically inactive. As outlined in Ch.8 the rights of free movement for the economically inactive were created by secondary legislation. Article 21 TFEU now provides the Treaty basis for the free movement of the economically inactive. This right, which is one of the consequences of the creation through the Maastricht Treaty of Union Citizenship, is discussed in detail in Ch.4.

11–98 Whereas previously secondary legislation providing for the free movement of the economically inactive contained no express non-discrimination provision, Directive 2004/38 which includes the economically inactive does through Article 24.[131] That provision is tempered by a derogation in respect of access to social assistance particularly for the economically inactive.

> "2. By way of derogation from paragraph 1, the host Member State shall not be obliged to confer entitlement to social assistance during the first three months of residence or, where appropriate, the longer period provided for in Article 14(4)(b), nor shall it be obliged, prior to acquisition of the right of permanent residence, to grant maintenance aid for studies, including vocational training, consisting in student grants or student loans to persons other than workers, self-employed persons, persons who retain such status and members of their families."

As is discussed below that derogation should be read in the light of the CJEU's approach to access to social assistance and student finance under the TFEU.

11–99 The economically inactive whose free movement rights are founded upon the provisions of Directive 2004/38 plainly fall within the personal scope of the TFEU and therefore will be able to rely on the non-discrimination provision contained in art.18 TFEU.[132] Even those Union citizens whose situation is not covered by any secondary legislation will nonetheless also benefit from the non-discrimination provision in art.18 TFEU. They will do so through the application of art.21 TFEU.

(b) *Application to the economically inactive*

11–100 The self-sufficient and the retired do not in practice appear to have faced obstacles to their free movement or indeed discrimination.[133] Were they to do so since they plainly fall within the personal scope of the Treaty on the

---

[131] See above, para.11–14, art.24 of Directive 2004/38 and references in the Preamble to the Directive to non-discrimination principles.
[132] See, for example, *D'Hoop v Office National de l'emploi* (C-224/98) [2002] E.C.R. I-6191.
[133] *Pusa v Osuuspankkien Keskinäinen Vakuutusyhtiö* (C-224/02) April 29, 2004, however did concern discrimination against a retired Finnish national living in Spain in respect of taxation on his pension.

Functioning of the European Union, the question of whether any such discrimination would be contrary to the prohibition contained in art.18 TFEU would (subject to justification) depend on whether the subject-matter fell within the TFEU's material scope.

The position is different however as regards students in respect of whom experience has shown that Member States can be less receptive. Doubtless such concern is founded on the fear that the students who are required by art.7(1)(c) of Directive 2004/38 merely to declare their self-sufficiency will in fact cease to be able to maintain themselves and become a burden on the public finances of host Member States. Thus in practice it has generally been the position of students which has exercised the CJEU in the context of non-discrimination. **11–101**

In *Grzelczyk*,[134] for example, a student who had ceased fully to comply with the requirements of Directive 93/96 (prior to repeal by Directive 2004/38[135]) was held by the CJEU to be entitled to receipt of "the minimex" (a non-contributory minimum subsistence allowance) without discrimination. However, it is right to point out that his ability to do so—given that he no longer fulfilled the Directive 93/96 conditions in every respect—depended on the willingness of the CJEU to use art.21 TFEU to interpret the conditions generously. Mr Grzelczyk had previously fulfilled the conditions of Directive 93/96 in that he supported himself through taking on various jobs and obtaining credit facilities. It was only at the beginning of his fourth and final year of study that he applied for the minimex. **11–102**

It has long been the position that Member States will be obliged as the consequence of the prohibition on discrimination contained in art.18 TFEU to pay tuition fees for Union citizens where such fees are paid for own nationals. In *Bidar*[136] the CJEU revised its previous position that maintenance grants and loans for students would be outside the scope of EU law.[137] Now the position is that where Union citizen students were sufficiently integrated in the host Member State, they should have access to maintenance grants and loans on a non-discriminatory basis as compared with own nationals. **11–103**

---

[134] *Grzelczyk v Centre Public d'aide sociale d'Ottignies-Louvain-la-Neuve* (C-184/99) [2001] E.C.R. I-6193.
[135] See art.7(1)(c) of Directive 2004/38/EC.
[136] *The Queen v London Borough of Ealing and Secretary of State for Education Ex p. Bidar* (C-209/03). The UK legislation had required that students had "settled status" in the UK before they could access maintenance loans. Since settled status would not be granted to an EU national student, irrespective of their integration into the UK, that requirement was found to be discriminatory.
[137] See *Lair v Universitat Hannover* (C-39/86) [1998] E.C.R. 316 and *Brown v Secretary of State for Scotland* (C-197/86) [1988] E.C.R. 3205.

CHAPTER 12

ACCESS TO SOCIAL SECURITY

This chapter provides an outline and general guide to social security provisions in European Union law.

1. INTRODUCTION

There are two basic mechanisms for EU nationals exercising their free movement rights to access social security and other social and tax benefits in their host Member State. The first is through specific social security provisions laid down now in Regulation 883/2004[1] read alongside Regulation 987/09[2] which provides detailed procedural and administrative arrangements for the implementation of the former. The second is through the application of general provisions of EU law in particular non-discrimination provisions, both in the TFEU and in secondary legislation on free movement. The CJEU has developed a wealth of case law based on the general non-discrimination provision in the EC Treaty art.12 (now art.18 TFEU), a feature in many areas of EU law including social security law and practice.

12–01

The Administrative Commission for the Co-ordination of Social Security assists the national authorities applying Regulation 883/2004.[3] It is composed of representatives from Member States and its purpose is to assist with the interpretation of the Regulation and foster co-operation in social security systems between Member States. Its role is a limited one in that decisions it makes are not binding on anyone.

12–02

(a) *Regulation 883/2004*

Regulation 883/2004 replaced Regulation 1408/71 after a protracted negotiation period. It was finally implemented on May 1, 2010. Importantly, EU provisions on social security do not replace the different national social security systems with a single European System. This type of harmonisation remains an unachievable goal, given the divergence in social security systems across the Member States and the varying standards and costs of living within them. In general, EU law attempts to co-ordinate these systems of social security not to harmonise them: see *Borowitz*[4] where the CJEU held in respect of Regulation 1408/71:

12–03

"(it) does not set up a common scheme of social security but allows different national schemes to exist and its sole objective is to coordinate those national schemes".

---

[1] O.J. L166/1, April 30, 2004.
[2] O.J. L284/1, October 30, 2009.
[3] art.71 Regulation 883/2004.
[4] (C-21/87) [1988] E.C.R. 3715, at [23]; *Chuck* (C-331/06) [2008] E.C.R. I-1957, at [27].

12–04 This chapter provides an outline and general guide to social security provisions. However, in view of the detail and complexity of the provisions, a textbook such as this cannot provide an in-depth analysis of all the provisions or indeed how they are applied in the different Member States.

12–05 Regulation 883/2004 seeks, as did its predecessor Regulation 1408/71, to solve a number of problems that result from differences in social security systems across the Member States. In some Member States, social security is based on residence whereas in others it is based on the exercise of economic activity. Union law aims to ensure that the overarching aim of freedom of movement is facilitated by the social security systems of Member States not the opposite while at the same time seeking to ensure that windfalls are avoided by persons being able to benefit from two separate schemes, for example, by being entitled to claim benefits in two separate Member States at the same time.

12–06 All 30 EEA States and Switzerland[5] have different social security systems and in the absence of harmonisation of those systems the aim is to co-ordinate them so as to achieve the aims of free movement within the Union. Regulation 987/09 sets out the procedures needed to implement Regulation 883/2204. It reforms and simplifies the means by which EEA States exchange information in electronic form which previously was cored out by paper-based communication. The concept of "document" is thus extended by Regulation 987/09 to include an electronic exchange.[6]

(b) *Underlying principles*

12–07 Regulation 883/2004 draws on the following explicit and implicit principles contained in EU law and that of the Member States:

(i) the principle of non-discrimination;
(ii) the aggregation principle; and
(iii) the principle of subsidiarity.

The first principle permeates the whole Regulation and acts not only as an underlying principle but as a gatekeeper to prevent restrictive practices based on impermissible differentiations such as nationality. The second principle is directed at ensuring that periods of insurance and residence with

---

[5] The Regulation is applicable in the following countries: Austria, Belgium, Bulgaria, Cyprus, the Czech Republic, Denmark, Estonia, Finland, France, Germany, Greece, Hungary, Ireland, Italy, Latvia, Lithuania, Luxembourg, Malta, the Netherlands, Poland, Portugal, Romania, Slovakia, Slovenia, Spain, Sweden, and the United Kingdom. Regulation 1408/71 continues to apply in Norway, Iceland, Liechtenstein and Switzerland until the current agreements with EEA and Switzerland are amended and to nationals of non-EU countries, legally resident in the territory of the EU until the European Council reaches an agreement on the extension of the new regulations (there is no published agreement yet). Also during a transitory period (10 years), the provisions of Regulation 1408/71 will continue to apply to existing situations as long as the factual elements of the existing situation have not changed, unless the employee explicitly requests that the new Regulation is applied.
[6] art.1(2)(c) Regulation 987/09.

accrued rights under social security regulations and practice in any Member State must be included when calculating entitlements in other Member States. The third principle recognises the desirability in certain circumstances of leaving to Member States the content and method of enforcing some common aims. The aim of ensuring a basic social security system—which would be part of EU law and The Charter of Fundamental Freedoms—is left almost exclusively to Member States. Indeed, there might be some argument for stating that the principle of exclusivity is more apposite to describe what has developed in social security law and practice in that the content of the social security system of each Member State is within the exclusive competence of each State.

(c) *Non-discrimination, equal treatment*

12–08 While deferring to Member States on the content of social security provisions, the non-discriminatory provisions retain their vibrancy in undermining any such provision based on nationality. Article 18 TFEU prohibits discrimination based on nationality in all areas within the scope of application of the Treaty. Article 4 of Regulation 883/2004 mirrors this provision. It provides:

> "Unless otherwise provided for by this Regulation, persons to whom this Regulation applies shall enjoy the same benefits and be subject to the same obligations under the legislation of any Member State as the nationals thereof."

12–09 Article 24 Directive 2004/38 states:

> "1. Subject to specific provisions as are expressly provided for in the Treaty and secondary law, all Union citizens residing on the basis of this Directive in the territory of the host Member State shall enjoy equal treatment with the nationals of that Member State within the scope of the Treaty. The benefit of this right shall be extended to family members who are not nationals of a Member State and who have the right of residence or permanent residence".

12–10 The combination of these provisions is a powerful tool in seeking to challenge decisions hindering freedom of movement of persons within the Union. The CJEU has frequently been called upon to adjudicate on the "lawfulness" of provisions which were arguably discriminatory on the grounds of nationality. Thus, in *Rinner Kuhn*[7] a provision in Luxembourg law which provided that maternity benefit should be paid to persons resident in Luxembourg for one year was considered. The Court, unsurprisingly, held that the requirement was indirectly discriminatory in that it was more readily met by nationals of Luxembourg than other Member States. In *Toia*[8] the CJEU considered a case where the French authorities had a requirement for benefit in respect of women with large families. It required that five of the children of the family must be French, while not requiring the mother be

---

[7] *Ingrid Rinner-Kuhn v FWW Spezial-Gebauderemigung GMbH and Co. KG* (C-171/88) [1989] E.C.R. 2743.
[8] *Toia* (C-237/78) [1979] E.C.R. 2645. *Caisse régionale d'assurance maladie de Lille (CRAM) v Diamante Palermo, née Toia.*

French. In the circumstances, there was not direct discrimination. However, the CJEU held that there was indirect discrimination in that it was a requirement likely to be met most easily by a French woman. Attempts by the French government to justify the difference in treatment on the basis that the offending provision promoted the aim of boosting the birth rate in France were rejected by the Court.

12-11　In *Petersen*[9] the CJEU was asked in a preliminary ruling from a court in Austria to determine whether a benefit at issue in respect of an German national residing in Austria was an "invalidity benefit" or "unemployment benefit". The Court held it was an unemployment benefit notwithstanding that its form indicated it was an invalidity benefit. The importance of the case arises however from a further point. The Austrian government paid the benefit to residents of Austria only and so a person who had resided there but moved to another Member State would not qualify for it, albeit he satisfied all the other substantive requirements for its payment. The benefit was not exportable. While the Court noted that unemployment benefits were generally not exportable, in that case the person had been a worker in Austria and was a worker in Germany after leaving Austria. As such benefits arising as a result of his historic employment in Austria must be exportable so that he can continue to benefit from them when exercising the right of free movement. The requirement of residence in Austria to receive the benefit was held to be discriminatory which had not been justified by the Austrian government.

12-12　In *Lucy Stewart*[10] the CJEU was asked if a residence requirement on the date of application for the payment of a benefit by the UK (found by the CJEU to be an invalidity benefit) was lawful. It concluded that such payments were exportable and that as the applicant had been entitled to it when she resided in the UK, her entitlement continued after she moved to and resided in Spain. While the Court did not rely expressly on non-discrimination provisions—relying instead on the wording of art.10 of Regulation 1408/71—it clearly concluded that the residence requirement was unlawful as it offended the fundamental freedoms guaranteed by the Union including the right to move without discrimination. In this case, the UK government submitted to the CJEU adopted the reasoning of the Supreme Court in *Patmalniece*[11] that differential treatment could be justified if based on the need to display social integration as exhibited by a right to reside

---

[9] *Jörn Petersen v Landesgeschäftsstelle des Arbeitsmarktservice Niederösterreich* (C-228/07) [2008] E.C.R. I-6989.
[10] *Lucy Stewart v Secretary of State for Pensions* (C-503/09) July 21, 2001.
[11] *Patmalniece v Secretary of State for Work and Pensions* [2009] EWCA Civ 62 where the Supreme Court considered the lawfulness of a requirement of a right to reside in the UK in order to be entitled to State pension credit. The argument put to the Court was that the requirement was directly discriminatory. It was accepted by the UK government that the provision was indirectly discriminatory but that it was justified. The Supreme Court concluded that the reasons for the residence requirement related to the permissible object of economic or social integration which could be achieved by nationals of any of the Member States and while it was indirectly discriminatory it was objectively justified for the same reason. The Court did not consider a reference to the CJEU was necessary for the reason that whether discriminatory treatment was justified was a matter for domestic law.

requirement. The CJEU concluded that such integration need not be shown by a residence requirement only and in the circumstances was disproportionate.

It would be wrong to consider that the non-discrimination provisions in EU law are without limitations in their scope and effect. Article 24 of Directive 2004/38 contains the following important qualification as regards social security benefits:

> "2. By way of derogation from paragraph 1, the host Member State shall not be obliged to confer entitlement to social assistance during the first three months of residence or, where appropriate, the longer period provided for in Article 14(4)(b), nor shall it be obliged, prior to acquisition of the right of permanent residence, to grant maintenance aid for studies, including vocational training, consisting in student grants or student loans to person other than workers, self-employed persons, person who retain such status and members of their families."

12–13

The effect of this provision is that Member States are not obliged to grant social assistance to EU citizens and their family members except for workers and the self-employed or to "workers" seeking employment. While in a Member State in a temporary capacity, other Member State nationals are not entitled to social assistance of the host State. Once permanent residence is achieved, the provisions on equal treatment will always apply and the person with such residence will be entitled to the same social assistance as nationals of the host State.

12–14

Article 3(5) Regulation 883/2004 provides that the provisions of that Regulation do not extend to social and medical assistance. This provision and art.24(2) are derogations and in the circumstances they should be construed restrictively.[12] The CJEU concluded in *Vatsouras and Koupatantze*:

12–15

> "Benefits of a financial nature which, independently of their status under national law, are intended to facilitate access to the labour market cannot be regarded as constituting 'social assistance' within the meaning of Directive 2004/38".[13]

Such an approach to the derogations are a powerful argument in seeking to enable the abolition of restrictions on free movement of persons throughout the Union. It should prove particularly beneficial when arguing that the refusal to grant benefits to the economically inactive—in circumstances where they are paid to economically inactive own nationals—breaches EC law. With the development of the concept of citizenship of the Union, as discussed above at Ch.4 and the developing case law such as *Ruiz Zambrano* the scope for the provision of benefits to own nationals only or even to persons only with close integration into the host State is diminishing.

---

[12] See A. Valcke, "Five years of the Citizens Directive in the UK—Part 2" (2011) 24, *Journal of Immigration, Asylum and Nationality Law* 4, 331–357.
[13] *Athanasios Vatsouras and Josif Koupatantze v Arbeitsgemeinschaft (ARGE) Nürnberg 900* (C-22/08 & C-23/08) [2009] E.C.R. I-4585.

12–16 The limitations as to what Regulation 883/2004 achieves can be seen from the case of *European Commission v Kingdom of Spain*[14] which considered provisions in Regulation 1408/71, similar in terms to art. of Regulation 883/2004, which provided that qualifying persons were entitled to necessary benefits while on a temporary stay in a Member State other than the usual one of residence or where a stay in a Member State was for the purpose of obtaining certain medical treatment subject to prior authorisation. Like under Regulation 883/2004, the costs of the benefits or treatment could be recouped by the body providing them from the Member State of residence. Spanish regulations did not provide for the payment to another Member State the cost of treatment in that State over and above what it would cost in Spain while on a temporary stay there. It was argued that this infringed the freedom to provide and receive services throughout the Union. No issue arose as to discrimination. The CJEU decided that the approach of the Spanish authorities was not unlawful as to hold otherwise would require Member States to fund the most expensive treatments to all insured persons within its competence. That was not required by the Regulation or the provisions as regards the freedom to receive services. This reflects earlier jurisprudence of the CJEU where it held that the risk of serious undermining the financial balance of a social security system may in particular circumstances may constitute a justification even for discriminatory provisions: see *ITC*.[15]

(d) *Structure and content of Regulation 883/2004*

(i) *Who benefits*

12–17 Article 2 provides that the Regulation shall apply to all nationals of a Member State, Stateless persons and refugees residing in a Member State who are or have been subject to the legislation of one or more Member States and to their family members and their survivors. Regulation 1408/71 was more restrictive in that it stated that it applied to insured employed and self-employed nationals of Member States and their family members, students and their family members, civil servants and refugees and Stateless persons.[16] The wider scope provided for in Regulation 883/2004 has no obvious impact for the reason that the extent of any benefit provided for in the Regulation depends on the prior determination of Member States. Only if persons are actually entitled to receive benefits in one or more Member States can they receive the same or similar benefits in other Member States under Regulation 883/2004. However, with the expanding importance afforded to equal treatment, restrictions imposed by Member States so as to preclude non-nationals from benefits are subject to ever increasing scrutiny. In light of art.2 of Regulation 883/2004, the scope for a broader application of social security regulations and practice remains open.

---

[14] *Commission v Spain* (C-211/08) [2010] 3 C.M.L.R. 48.
[15] *I.T.C. Innovative Technology Center GMbH v Bundesagentur für Arbeit* (C-208/05) [2007] E.C.R. 1-181.
[16] art.2 Regulation 1408/71.

INTRODUCTION

A person will usually only be subject to the legislation of one Member State at a time. Generally speaking a person will be insured in the Member State where professional activity is exercised. Exceptions to this rule apply to those who are temporarily posted abroad by an employer. Persons who work in more than one Member State will be insured in the Member State in which they reside.

12–18

(ii) *Content of the Regulation*

The Regulation is in six parts or "Titles". Article 1 of Title 1 contains definitions of core terms in the Regulation such as "insured person", "activity as an employed person" , "activity as a self-employed person" and "member of the family" and "residence". Article 2 provides that the scope of the Regulation extends to nationals of Member States, Stateless persons and refugees residing in a Member State as well as their family members. Article 3 outlines the personal scope of the Regulation to include:

12–19

(a) sickness benefit;

(b) maternity and paternity benefit;

(c) invalidity benefits;

(d) old-age benefits;

(e) survivors benefits;

(f) benefits in respect of accidents at work and occupational diseases;

(g) death grants;

(h) unemployment benefits;

(i) pre-retirement benefits; and

(j) family benefits.

Articles 5 and 6 reflect the core rational of the Regulation:

12–20

(i) recognition of equivalent benefits and relevant events across Member States, and

(ii) the right to access and retain social security advantages arising from the said events.

Article 10 stipulates that the enjoyment of overlapping benefits is not conferred by the Regulation.

(iii) *Time limits*

Title 2 stipulates which legislation or Member State is responsible for the payment of benefits to qualifying persons. Employed or self-employed persons are subject to the legislative scheme of the State in which they pursue their activity (art.11). Employed or self-employed persons in a Member State posted to another Member State shall remain subject to the legislative scheme as long as the anticipated posting does not exceed 24 months. Article 13(1) provides that in circumstances where an employed

12–21

person is engaged in two or more Member States, the legislative scheme in the Member State of residence shall apply provided the person engages in "a substantial part of his activities in the Member State of residence". If the person does not exercise a substantial part in the State of residence then they fall under the scheme in operation in the State where their employer is registered. Similar arrangements are made in respect of the self-employed (art.13(2)). Article 14 provides that a person may be required to participate in one insurance scheme only.

(iv) *Specific benefits and payments*

Sickness and maternity benefits

12–22 Title 3, section 1 concerns sickness, maternity and equivalent paternity payments. Article 17 provides that insured persons and their family members who reside in a Member State other than the state where they are insured would be entitled to benefits in kind. Article 21 extends the right to cash benefits. Sickness benefits in cash are benefits normally intended to replace income which is lost through sickness. In some Member States national legislation provides that wages will be paid for a period of time once a person becomes incapacitated. The CJEU regards these payments as sickness benefits in cash. Sickness benefits in cash are paid according to the legislation of the Member State in which the person is insured, regardless of place of residence.

12–23 Sickness benefits in kind comprise medical and dental care. They are provided according to the legislation of the Member State in which the person resided rather than the place of insurance. If the person is resident in a Member State other than where he is insured, he is entitled to all the benefits in kind provided under the legislation of the Member State in which he resided, even where that might be more generous than that of the Member State in which he is insured.

12–24 In cases where a person is temporarily staying in a Member State other than where he is insured, for example staying there as a visitor, he is entitled to benefits in kind "necessary on medical grounds during the stay" (art.19). Article 25 of Regulation 987/2009 identifies the benefits as those that "become necessary on medical grounds with a view to preventing an insured person from being forced to return, before the end of the planned duration of stay" to his usual State of residence. The CJEU has held that the concept "necessary treatment" cannot be interpreted as,

> "meaning that those benefits are limited solely to cases where the treatment provided has become necessary because of a sudden illness. In particular the circumstances that the treatment necessitated by developments in the insured person's state of health during his temporary stay in another Member State may be linked to a pre-existent pathology of which he is aware, such as chronic illness, cannot suffice to prevent him from enjoying the benefit of [these] provisions."[17]

---

[17] *Idryma Koinonikon Asfaliseon [IKA] v Ioannidis* (C-326/00) [2003] E.C.R. I-1703.

Drawing on this case, the Administrative Commission published Decision No.53 that entitlement to unplanned treatment during a temporary stay in another Member State "includes benefits in conjunction with chronic or existing illnesses as well as in conjunction with pregnancy and childbirth".[18]

12–25

It is not unusual for EU nationals to move to other Member States specifically to obtain medical treatment there. This will be provided but only if prior authorisation is obtained for this (art.17). This is extended to qualifying persons and their family members during the course of a "stay" in another Member State (art.18). Article 19 provides that entitlements to benefits on medical grounds travel with the person and their family members.

12–26

Pensions

Section 2 of Title 3 provides detailed guidance as to pensions. In an increasingly ageing population in Europe and increased tendency to retire to Member States other than usual place of residence, old age pensions are among the most important social security benefits. A person and their family member who is entitled to a pension in any Member State is entitled to payment of that pension in any other Member State of residence.[19] The pension will be calculated according to the insurance record in the Member State where the entitlement arose.[20] In respect of survivors benefits, the same rules apply as to pensions for surviving spouses as to old-age pensioners. Articles 22 to 30 provide for the continuing of pension payments in circumstances where those entitled to such in one or more Member States moves to another.

12–27

Benefits in kind

Articles 32 to 35 provide for the maintenance of receipt of benefits in kind as persons move within the Union. Article 32 provides that family members independent rights to benefits take priority over derived rights unless the former arise from residence only in the Member State providing them. Article 33 provides for the allocation of the expense involved in the provision of benefits such as a prosthesis or other substantial benefits in kind between the institutions of the Member State where the person was insured before they moved and the institutions to where they reside: the former must bear the expense. Article 34 provides that long-term care benefits payable in the Member State of residence can be restricted to what would be payable in the original Member State. Articles 35 and 41 provide that reimbursements between Member States for payments of benefits in kind should be effected through the Implementing Regulation. Articles 36 to 38 provide for the provision of benefits in kind in respect of accidents at work and occupational diseases.

12–28

---

[18] O.J. (C-106/40), April 24, 2010.
[19] art.23.
[20] art.25.

Death and survivors benefits

12–29 Articles 42 and 43 provide that a person who dies in a Member State is entitled to any grant he would be entitled to in the insured Member State. When an insured person or member of his family dies in a Member State other than where he is insured, he is deemed to have died in the State of insurance. Death grants are to be paid in accordance with the legislation of the insured state.

Invalidity benefits

12–30 Articles 44 to 49 provide for the payment of invalidity benefits across Member States. These benefits are variable across Member States. In some they are only paid to those who are actually insured at the time when the invalidity occurs, at a rate which is independent of the insurance period. In others, pensions are paid to those who were insured and the amount depends on the length of insurance period. As a general rule, on becoming incapacitated a worker exercising free movement rights must not be in an inferior position when compared with someone who has always lived and worked in one single country. If a person has been insured in several Member States, the calculation of the amount of period payable is determined differently according to whether the person was insured in Member States where the amount of pension depends on the length of insurance periods or where the amount of pension is independent of the length of insurance periods. The result may be that the person ends up with two separate pensions on the basis of the payments being split between the two States according to the length of time spent in each Member State.

Unemployment benefits

12–31 Articles 61 to 65 provide for the co-ordination of unemployment benefits. If a person becomes unemployed in a Member State, that State is obliged to take account of periods of insurance or employment completed in any other Member State. However, these are to be taken account of only if before the unemployed claimed the benefit they were insured, employed or self-employed in the Member State requested to make the payment. The payment amount shall be made exclusively on the basis of the unemployed person's last salary while employed or self-employed. An unemployed person in a Member State who is entitled to unemployment benefit there and who migrates to seek employment in another Member State shall retain his entitlement for a period of three months provided he was registered in the former State as available for work and registers in the latter State as the same.

(v) *Administrative provisions*

12–32 Title 4 provides for the composition of an Administrative Commission and sets out its objects. Title 5 contains miscellaneous provisions for the exchange of information and protection of personal data. Title 6 sets out technical and transitional provisions.

2. Conclusions

Plainly, as there is so much divergence between the social security systems between Member States there remains the possibility of real obstacles being placed in the path of qualifying persons within the Union from moving freely between Member States. Regulation 883/2004 seeks to simplify that which was contained in Regulation 1408/71 with the aim of ensuring that entitlement to benefits built up in any Member State is exportable to a current State of residence. Further, the Regulation ensures that benefits can be aggregated albeit they may have been earned in a number of Member States. While the Regulation does not prescribe that benefits termed "social assistance" must be paid by a Member State to all European nationals within its borders, even that is subject to ongoing challenge as it tends to be discriminatory in circumstances where such benefits are paid only to nationals or to those who have close ties with the relevant Member State.

12–33

CHAPTER 13

EXCLUSION AND EXPULSION

This chapter examines the rights of free movers and other Union citizens when they face exclusion or expulsion from the territories of the Member States.

1. INTRODUCTION

European Union law clearly provides the right of Union citizens and their family members to enter and reside in the territories of other Member States under certain conditions. This right plainly impacts on the sovereign right of Member States to control their borders. Where the Union citizens and their family members can demonstrate a European Union law free movement right, their entry and stay can be interfered with only on very limited grounds of public policy, public security and public health and subject to strict provisions of EU law. Where Union citizens and their family members have the right of permanent residence in a Member State expulsion can only be on "serious grounds of public policy or public security". Union citizens who have resided in a host Member State for 10 years and minors (except if necessary for the best interests of the child) can only be expelled on "imperative grounds of public security".[1] The meaning of these provisions and the protection enjoyed by such persons from exclusion and expulsion are considered in sections 2–4, below. Where on the other hand Union citizens and their family members can establish no European Union law nexus to their situation in a host Member State, that Member State may be entitled to take expulsion or exclusion measures on a broader basis. Such measures are considered in section 5, below.

13–01

2. EU LAW PROVISIONS ON THE EXPULSION AND EXCLUSION OF FREE MOVERS

Article 45.3 of the TFEU makes clear that the right to move within the Member States and remain in other Member States for the purposes of employment is "subject to limitations justified on grounds of public policy, public security or public health". Likewise art.52 TFEU permits Member States to have in place measures for the special treatment of self-employed nationals of other Member States on grounds of public policy, public security or public health.[2] Such measures are referred to as "special treatment" because they offend the basic principles of free movement and

13–02

---

[1] See art.28 Directive 2004/38/EC on the right of citizens of the Union and their family members to move and reside freely within the territory of the Member States (the "Citizens Directive").
[2] The CJEU has held that the slight difference in wording between the arts 39(3) and 46 EC Treaty (now arts 45.3 and 52 TFEU) should not make any difference to the application of these provisions. See *Procureur de Roiv Royer* (C-48/75) [1976] E.C.R. 497.

because they cannot be used against own nationals, making them discriminatory.

13–03   Chapter VI of Directive 2004/38[3] contains detailed provisions on the application by Member States of special measures taken against Union citizens and their family members on grounds of public policy, public security or public health. Directive 2004/38 repeals Directive 64/221[4] as noted in recital 22 of the of the preamble:

> "in order to ensure a tighter definition of the circumstances and procedural safeguards subject to which Union citizens and their family members may be denied leave to enter or may be expelled".

In recital 23 it is acknowledged that expulsion can "seriously harm" those who have become "genuinely integrated into the host Member State" and for this reason states that the scope for such measures should be limited "in accordance with the principle of proportionality to take account of the degree of integration of the persons concerned, the length of their residence in the host Member State, their age, state of health, family and economic situation and the links with their country of origin".

13–04   Chapter VI applies to any action taken on public policy, security or health grounds which affect the rights of persons coming under the Directive to enter and reside freely in the host Member State under the same conditions as the nationals of that State.[5] Although Member States retain the freedom to determine for themselves their own requirements of public policy and public security in accordance with their national needs, when doing so in the context of the application of the Directive they must interpret those requirements strictly so that their scope is not determined unilaterally by each Member State without control by the institutions of the European Union.[6]

13–05   Reflective of the constant case law of the CJEU, Directive 2004/38 includes the following provisions in art.27:

> "General principles
>
> 1. Subject to the provisions of this Chapter, Member States may restrict the freedom of movement and residence of Union citizens and their family members, irrespective of nationality, on grounds of public policy, public security or public health. These grounds shall not be invoked to serve economic ends.
>
> 2. Measures taken on grounds of public policy or public security shall comply with the principle of proportionality and shall be based exclusively on the personal

---

[3] Directive 2004/38/EC on the right of citizens of the Union and their family members to move and reside freely within the territory of the Member States.
[4] Council Directive 64/221/EEC of February 25, 1964 on the co-ordination of special measures concerning the movement and residence of foreign nationals, which are justified on grounds of public policy, public security or public health.
[5] *Rutili* (C-36/75), at [8–21] and *Bouchereau* (C-30/77), at [6–24].
[6] *Ministerul Administratiei si Internelor—Directia Generala de Pasapoarte Bucuresti v Gheorghe Jipa* (C-33/07), at [23].

conduct of the individual concerned. Previous criminal convictions shall not in themselves constitute grounds for taking such measures.

The personal conduct of the individual concerned must represent a genuine, present and sufficiently serious threat affecting one of the fundamental interests of society. Justifications that are isolated from the particulars of the case or that rely on considerations of general prevention shall not be accepted."

13–06 Where an individual's personal conduct represents a threat that is serious enough to warrant expulsion, the host Member State must carry out the proportionality assessment to decide whether the measure can be justified on grounds of public policy or public security taking into account all relevant considerations including those spelt out in art.28:

"Protection against expulsion

1. Before taking an expulsion decision on grounds of public policy or public security, the host Member State shall take account of considerations such as how long the individual concerned has resided on its territory, his/her age, state of health, family and economic situation, social and cultural integration into the host Member State and the extent of his/her links with the country of origin."

13–07 As is clear from the foregoing in view of their discriminatory application as well as the fact that they create obstacles to free movement, these measures have to be justified by the Member State using them by reference to the very restrictive definitions of all three grounds for such measures. As with any measure which restricts one of the fundamental freedoms guaranteed by the TFEU, measures taken pursuant to arts 45(3) and 52 TFEU will be justified only if they comply with the principle of proportionality:

"In that respect, such a measure must be appropriate for securing the attainment of the objective which it pursues and must not go beyond what is necessary in order to attain it".[7]

As seen, this principle is now referred to expressly in arts 27 and 28 of Directive 2004/38.

13–08 Apart from grounds of public policy, public security or public health, there are no other grounds for the exclusion or expulsion of either a Union citizen exercising Treaty rights or that Union citizen's family members, regardless of nationality. In other circumstances the right of States to exclude or expel non-nationals is both recognised by international law and jealously guarded by States. In the European Union context, however, this right cannot be applied to Union citizens and their families unless the strict requirements of the TFEU and secondary legislation are met. The importance of the fundamental shift caused by the impact of European Union law on the exercise by States of powers otherwise seen as reflective of their own sovereignty cannot be overstated. Indeed there is at times a tendency by national authorities and courts to fail properly to reflect the importance of the EU

---

[7] *Gebhard v Consigol dell' Ordine degli Advocat AE Procuratori di Milano* (C-55/94) [1995] E.C.R. I-4165, at [37].

law context in this area. However antithetical to notions of national sovereignty, Member States' obligations to properly reflect principles of EU law must always remain at the forefront of the minds of decision makers.

13–09 Member States have not substantively co-ordinated criminal legislation, although post the Lisbon Treaty more and more areas will be co-ordinated.[8] Subject to this criminal legislation co-ordination is a matter for individual Member States. Member States continue in principle to be free to determine their own public policy and public security needs. However, European Union law sets limits on the exercise by Member States of this power where such exercise interferes with the fundamental freedoms set down in the TFEU.[9]

3. Grounds for Exclusion/Expulsion of Free Movers

(a) *General observations*

(i) *Grounds for taking special measures against Union citizens*

13–10 The secondary legislation implementing the provisions of the TFEU as well as interpretation of this legislation by the CJEU have provided a number of principles to guide Member States on the application of the three grounds for taking special measures against Union citizens exercising free movement rights under the TFEU. First, a decision leading to the expulsion or exclusion of a Union citizen exercising or wishing to exercise a Treaty right in another Member State may only be made on grounds of public policy, public security or public health. These concepts are very narrowly defined.[10] Decisions based upon them must be both strictly justified, and proportionate to the objective which they pursue.[11]

13–11 Secondly, a decision to expel or exclude a Union citizen must be limited to circumstances relating to the conduct of the individual concerned only[12] and not based on general considerations of public interest (such as the fight against drugs or organised crime).

13–12 Thirdly, a Member State employing expulsion or exclusion measures would need to demonstrate that the use of such measures does not amount to the taking of arbitrary measures against nationals of other Member States.

---

[8] The Treaty on the Functioning of the European Union does contain provisions on police co-operation in Ch.5 of Title V (Area of Freedom, Security and Justice) (and judicial co-operation in criminal matters in Ch.4 of Title V). There have been some adopted measures including Directive 2010/64/EU of the European Parliament and of the Council of October 20, 2010 on the right to interpretation and translation in criminal proceedings; Directive 2011/36/EU of the European Parliament and of the Council of April 5, 2011 on preventing and combating trafficking in human beings and protecting its victims and there are a number of proposed measures under consideration such as a directive on right to information in criminal proceedings.
[9] *Cowan v Trésor Public* (186/87) [1989] E.C.R. 195.
[10] See, for instance, *Van Duyn v Home Office* (41/74) [1974] E.C.R. 1337.
[11] *Rutili v Ministre de l'interieur* (36/75) [1975] E.C.R. 1219.
[12] art.27.2 of Directive 2004/38, see also *Procureur de Roi v Royer* (48/75) [1976] E.C.R. 497.

Thus it will be necessary for the Member State in question to demonstrate that it takes genuine and effective measures against its own nationals in order to combat the conduct justifying the expulsion or exclusion.[13]

Fourthly, the threat must exist at the moment when the restrictive measure is adopted by the Member State or reviewed by the courts.[14] This is particularly important if a lengthy period of time has elapsed between the date of the expulsion order and that of the review of that decision by the competent court (where the passage of time may point to the cessation or the substantial diminution of the present threat which the conduct of the person concerned constitutes to the requirements of public policy).

13–13

(ii) *Economic reasons for expulsion*

As art.27(1) of Directive 2004/38 makes clear, the three grounds for expulsion or exclusion cannot be invoked "to serve economic ends". In practice this will mean that the Member States will be unable to justify expulsion or exclusion against EU nationals and their family members simply on the basis that they are an economic burden on the Member State, if those persons have retained a right of residence under the TFEU or secondary legislation. This is emphasised also by recital 16 of the preamble to Directive 2004/38 which makes clear that an expulsion measure should not be the automatic consequence of recourse to the social assistance system of a Member State which should examine whether it is a case of temporary difficulties and take into account the duration of residence, the personal circumstances and the amount of aid granted in order to consider whether the beneficiary has become an unreasonable burden.[15] Further, the failure to meet administrative requirements laid down by Member States for registration or taxation of employment or self-employed activities will not constitute grounds for expulsion or exclusion.[16]

13–14

(iii) *Failure to comply with formalities*

As outlined in Ch.10 above, the mere failure to comply with immigration formalities such as obtaining visas or residence permits is not a basis for exclusion or expulsion under the TFEU or Directive 2004/38.[17] Furthermore, a Member State may not *refuse* visas to third country national spouses on the sole ground that they are persons for whom alerts were entered in the Schengen Information System, without first verifying whether the presence of those persons constitutes a genuine, present and sufficiently serious threat to one of the fundamental interests of society.[18]

13–15

---

[13] See, for instance, *Criminal Proceedings Against Calfa* (C-348/96) [1999] E.C.R. I-11.
[14] *Orfanopoulos and Oliveri* (C-482/01) and (C-493/01), at [82].
[15] The principle laid down by recital 16 is reflective of case law of the CJEU. See, for example, *Grzelczyk v Centre public d'aide social d'Ottignies-Louvain-la-Neuve* (C-184/99) [2001] E.C.R. I-6193 and *Trojani v Centre Public d'aide social de Bruxelles (CPAS)* (C-456/02), September 7, 2004 (discussed below at para.14–40).
[16] *Roux v Belgium* (C-363/89) [1991] E.C.R. I-273.
[17] *Procureur de Roi v Royer* (48/75) [1976] E.C.R. 497; *Mouvement contre le Racisme, l'Antisemitisme et la Xenophobie ASBL (MRAX) v Belgium State* (C-459/99) [2002] E.C.R. I-6591.
[18] See *Commission of the European Communities v Spain* (C-157/03) [2005] E.C.R. I-2911.

(iv) *Restrictions on free movement within a Member State*

13–16 Instead of expulsion or exclusion, a Member State may take administrative measures limiting a Union citizen's right of residence to a part of the territory. However, there is no distinction in the principles that are applied to a measure restricting movement within the territory as against those applicable in expulsion cases. Such measures may only be taken if, by reason of the seriousness of the individual's conduct, he could otherwise be liable to expulsion or exclusion from the whole of the territory of that Member State.[19]

(vi) *The proportionality assessment*

13–17 Articles 27 and 28 of Directive 2004/38 highlight the importance of the proportionality assessment. Such assessment was hitherto required to be undertaken as an obligation flowing from European Union law principles and case law developments of the CJEU, rather than secondary legislation. Article 27(2) provides that measures taken on grounds of public policy or public security

> "shall comply with the principle of proportionality" and art.28(1) lists factors to be considered before taking an expulsion decision. The list is indicative rather than exhaustive (stating that the Member State shall take account of considerations *such as* ...). As described by the Commission,[20] Member States must identify protected interests and in light of them carry out analysis of "the characteristics of the threat".

The personal and family situation of the individual concerned must be assessed carefully to ascertain whether the measure is appropriate and strictly necessary to achieve the objective pursued, or whether less stringent measures could suffice. According to the Commission, the following factors (outlined in art.28(1)) should be taken into account:[21]

- degree of social danger resulting from the presence of the person concerned on the territory of that Member State;
- nature of the offending activities, their frequency, cumulative danger and damage caused;
- time elapsed since acts committed and behaviour of the person concerned *(NB: also good behaviour in prison and possible release on parole could be taken into account)*;

---

[19] *Ministre de l'Intèrieur v Olazabal* (C-100/01) [2002] E.C.R. I-10981, at [45].
[20] See Communication from the Commission to the European Parliament and the Council on guidance for better transposition and application of Directive 2004/38/EC on the right of citizens of the Union and their family members to move and reside freely within the territory of the Member States (COM(2009) 313 final) at para.3.3.
[21] See Communication from the Commission to the European Parliament and the Council on guidance for better transposition and application of Directive 2004/38/EC on the right of citizens of the Union and their family members to move and reside freely within the territory of the Member States, (COM(2009) 313 final) at para.3.3.

- impact of expulsion on the economic, personal and family life of the individual *(including on other family members who would have the right to remain in the host Member State)*;
- the seriousness of the difficulties which the spouse/partner and any of their children risk facing in the country of origin of the person concerned;
- strength of ties *(relatives, visits, language skills)*—or lack of ties—with the Member State of origin and with the host Member State *(for example, the person concerned was born in the host Member State or lived there from an early age)*;
- length of residence in the host Member State *(the situation of a tourist is different from the situation of someone who has lived for many years in the host Member State)*; and
- age and state of health.

(b) *Public policy*

(i) *General test to be applied in public policy cases*

"Public policy" is generally interpreted along the lines of preventing disturbance of the social order.[22] It is crucial that Member States distinguish clearly between public policy and public security: the latter cannot be extended to measures that should be covered by the former. Public policy is the ground most frequently invoked against Union citizens and their family members when expulsion or exclusion measures are contemplated. However, as the CJEU has made clear consistently, this ground is to be narrowly construed. The test for whether public policy grounds exist for such measures to be taken is that the personal conduct of the individual concerned must represent a genuine, present and sufficiently serious threat affecting one of the fundamental interests of society. This is spelt out in art.27(2) of Directive 2004/38 which goes on to state that justifications that are isolated from the particulars of the case or that rely on considerations of general prevention "shall not be accepted".[23]

13–18

Present association with an organisation may be taken into account in assessing an individual's personal conduct where the individual participates in the activities of the organization and identifies with its aims or designs. In the words of the CJEU in *Van Duyn*[24] such conduct "may be considered a

13–19

---

[22] See Communication from the Commission to the European Parliament and the Council on guidance for better transposition and application of Directive 2004/38/EC on the right of citizens of the Union and their family members to move and reside freely within the territory of the Member States (COM(2009) 313 final) at para.3.1. The phrase used in the CJEU's case law is the "perturbation of the social order" (see amongst others *Commisson v Netherlands* (C-50/06) at [43].
[23] art.27(2) of Directive 2004/38 builds on the test previously articulated by the CJEU in the case law which was that the individual must pose a "genuine and sufficiently serious threat affecting one of the fundamental interests of society" (see, for instance, *R. v Bouchereau* (30/77) [1977] E.C.R. 1999).
[24] *Yvonne van Duyn v Home Office* (C-41/74), at [17].

Exclusion and Expulsion

voluntary act of the person concerned and consequently as part of his personal conduct". Member States do not have to criminalise or to ban the activities of an organisation to be in a position to restrict rights, as long as "some administrative measures to counteract the activities of that organization are in place".[25] Past associations however cannot, in general, constitute present threat.

13–20 The CJEU has not imposed any minimum level of crime or offence which might justify measures to be taken on public policy grounds and thus to some extent an assessment of whether conduct is contrary to public policy is left to Member States. However, conduct can never be considered to be of a sufficiently serious nature to justify expulsion or exclusion of the national of another Member State where the host Member States does not take genuine and effective measures against its own nationals for that conduct.[26] In *Aladzhov*[27] the CJEU accepted the possibility that non-recovery of tax liabilities could fall within the scope of public policy. The case concerned a prohibition imposed on Mr Aladzhov from leaving Bulgaria (the country of his nationality) for non-payment of taxes of the company he managed (together with others). However, as emphasised by the CJEU this could only be the case where there was a genuine, present and sufficiently serious threat affecting one of the fundamental interests of society "related for example to the amount of the sums at stake or to what is required to combat tax fraud". Such measure could not be taken solely to serve economic ends and moreover such a prohibition would have to be appropriate to ensure achievement of the objective pursued and not go beyond what was necessary. All recovery of taxes serves economic ends and it seems therefore plain that the circumstances to justify any such decision would need to be extreme.

13–21 In *Adoui and Cornuaille*[28] the EU nationals were "waitresses in a bar which was 'suspect' from the point of view of morals".[29] The CJEU held that where own nationals in engaging in similar activities were not subject to any repressive measures, the expulsion of Union citizens could not be justified on public policy grounds.

(ii) *General deterrence*

13–22 Article 27(2) of Directive 2004/38 provides that any measures taken on grounds of public policy must be based exclusively on the personal conduct of the individual concerned. Previous criminal convictions shall not in themselves constitute grounds for expulsion or exclusion of Union citizens or their family members. The CJEU has read these two provisions (contained originally in art.3(1) and art.3(2) Directive 64/221) as meaning that the expulsion of a Union citizen cannot be justified on the grounds of

---

[25] *Yvonne van Duyn v Home Office* (C-41/74), at [18–19].
[26] See, for example, *Ministre de l'Interieur v Aitor Oteiza Olazabal* (C-100/01).
[27] (C-434/10), at [37]. *Petar Aladzhov v Zamestnik direktor na Stolichna direktsia na vatreshnite raboti kam Ministerstvo na vatreshnite raboti* (C-434/10).
[28] *Adoui and Cornuaille* (115/81) and (116/81) [1982] E.C.R. 1665.
[29] *R. v Bouchereau* (30/77) [1977] E.C.R. 1999, at [2]. The women concerned were French nationals working in Belgium as prostitutes.

general deterrence. In *Bonsignore*,[30] an Italian national residing in Germany had purchased a gun without a licence and had accidentally killed his own brother. He was found guilty of illegal possession of a weapon as well as causing death by negligence. The German authorities wanted to deport him for general deterrent reasons and not because he was likely to re-offend. The CJEU ruled that art.3(1) read together with art.3(2) barred Member States from expelling Union citizens in order to deter others from committing similar offences.

This principle is now spelt out in art.27(2) of Directive 2004/38 which states that "previous criminal convictions shall not in themselves constitute grounds for taking such measures". This does not mean that a previous conviction cannot be taken into account at all. Rather it means that it will be relevant only insofar as the circumstances which gave rise to it constituted evidence of personal conduct and a present threat to the requirements of public policy).[31] **13–23**

(iii) *Serious crime*

Even where in principle the offence committed is one which is so serious as to entitle a Member State to regard the person's continued presence as constituting a danger to society, it is only the individual's own conduct which may justify expulsion or exclusion. In *Calfa*[32] the CJEU considered a case (under Directive 64/221) where the Union citizen had committed a drugs offence which in Belgian law automatically led to deportation with a three-year ban on re-entry. The CJEU held that such automatic expulsion following a drugs offence, notwithstanding the danger to society that drugs represent, did not fulfil the requirements of Directive 64/221 since it does not take into account the personal conduct of the offender. **13–24**

When examining the individual's conduct Member States must be satisfied that the individual constitutes a *present* threat to the fundamental interests of society. Past conduct alone will not justify expulsion or exclusion. The CJEU has held that a finding that such a threat exists implies the existence of a "propensity to act in the same way in the future".[33] Thus regardless of the public interest that Member States might have in combating a particular crime, any measure taken against an individual must be on the basis of that individual posing a present threat.[34] The kind and number of previous convictions must form a significant element in an assessment of future **13–25**

---

[30] *Bonsignore v Oberstadtdirector der Stadt Köln* (C-67/74) [1975] E.C.R. 297.
[31] See *Orfanopoulos and Oliveri* (C-482/01) and (C-493/01) at [82] and [100] and *Commission v Netherlands* (C-50/06) at [42–45] and see further following section "serious crime".
[32] *Criminal Proceedings Against Calfa* (C-348/96) [1999] E.C.R. I-11.
[33] *Bonsignore v Stadt Köln* (67/74) [1975] E.C.R. 297.
[34] The Advocate General in the case of *R. v Bouchereau* (30/77) [1977] E.C.R. 1999, was of the opinion that in exceptional circumstances following a particularly heinous crime past con-duct alone might constitute such a threat to the requirements of public policy. The CJEU has never applied such reasoning.

conduct and particular regard must be had to the seriousness and frequency of the crimes committed. While the danger of re-offending is of considerable importance, a remote possibility of new offences is not sufficient.[35]

13–26 In the post-September 11 era when Member States are intent on combating terrorism, it might be tempting for them to invoke public policy reasons for expelling or excluding a person who has been convicted of a crime relating to terrorism. This is only be permissible if it can be demonstrated that there is a propensity to act in the same way in the future, regardless of any public sentiment towards those branded as terrorists or indeed any wish on the part of the Member State to deter others from engaging in terrorism.

13–27 This principle is shown by the decision of the CJEU in *Olazabal*[36] which concerned a member of ETA (whose activites constituted a threat to both public order and security). As regards Mr Olazabal himself who was convicted of conspiracy to disturb public order by "intimidation or terror", the CJEU applied exactly the same principles as with other public policy cases without dilution of such principles by reason of any reference to terrorism.

13–28 Furthermore in *Nazli*[37] the CJEU took this approach to the fight against drugs, which since the 1980s has been a major concern of Member States. The CJEU acknowledged the special measures which Member States may wish to employ to deal with this problem but held fast to the principle that an interference with the fundamental right of free movement can only be justified by reference to the individual's conduct and the threat that they pose:

> "While a Member State may consider that the use of drugs constitutes a danger for society such as to justify, in order to maintain public order, special measures against aliens who contravene its laws on drugs, the public policy exception, like all derogations from a fundamental principle of the Treaty, must nevertheless be interpreted restrictively, so that the existence of a criminal conviction can justify expulsion only in so far as the circumstances which gave rise to that conviction are evidence of personal conduct constituting a present threat to the requirements of public policy (see, most recently, Case C-348/96 *Calfa* [1999] E.C.R. I—11, paras 22,23 and 24).
>
> The Court has thus concluded that Community law precludes the expulsion of a national of a Member State on general preventive grounds, that is to say an expulsion ordered for the purpose of deterring other aliens (see, in particular, Case 67/74 *Bonsignore v Stadt Köln* [1975] ECR 297, paragraph 7), especially where that measure has automatically followed a criminal conviction, without any account being taken of the personal conduct of the offender or of the danger which that conduct represents for the requirements of public policy (*Calfa*, cited above, para. 27)".[38]

---

[35] See Opinion of Advocate General Stix-Hackl in *Orfanopoulos and Oliveri v Land Baden-Württemberg* (C-482/01) and (C-493/01) at [50]. As pointed out by the AG by way of example, the danger of re-offending would be greater in the case of a drug dependency where there is a risk that further criminal offences will be committed in order to fund it.
[36] *Ministre de l'Intèrieur v Olazabal* (C-100/01) [2002] E.C.R. I-10981.
[37] *Nazli v Stadt Nürnburg* (C-340/97) [2000] E.C.R. I-957.
[38] *Nazli v Stadt Nürnburg* (C-340/97) [2000] E.C.R. I-957, at [58–59].

Member States which jealously guard their rights both to control the entry 13–29
of non-nationals to their territories and to combat serious crime can find the
application of these principles difficult, at odds with their own domestic law
and even the application of international human rights instruments (where
past conduct may be sufficient to justify expulsion).[39] However, Member
States have long since forgone their absolute right to control their borders,
at least in respect of Union citizens and their family members who exercise
the free movement rights conferred by the TFEU and secondary legislation.
It is the exercise of such fundamental right of free movement which European
Union law protects in the present context by ensuring that derogation
from the right is permitted only in very limited circumstances and where
absolutely necessary.

(c) *Public security*

(i) *Meaning of public security*

"Public security" is generally interpreted to cover both internal and external 13–30
security "along the lines of preserving the integrity of the territory of a
Member State and its institutions".[40] In *Olazabal*[41] the CJEU considered
measures taken against a member of ETA which were motivated by the fact
that he formed part of "an armed and organised group whose activity
constitutes a threat to public order". The CJEU stated that "prevention of
such activity may, moreover, be regarded as falling within the maintenance
of public security".[42] It is understandable (in the context of ETA and Mr
Olazabal's conviction for conspiracy to disturb public order by intimidation
or terror) that the measures taken against him might fall also under the
public security limb in the sense in which the phrase is generally interpreted.
What though of other criminal conduct, for example serious drugs offences?

In *Tsakouridis*[43] the CJEU considered the position of a Greek national born 13–31
in Germany in 1978 who had had unlimited residence there from 2001. His
criminal record included conviction in 2007 on eight counts of illegal dealing
in substantial quantities of narcotics as part of an organised group for which
he was sentenced to six years and six months' imprisonment. One of the
questions referred was whether "imperative grounds of public security" in
art.28(3) of Directive 2004/38 was to be interpreted as meaning that

> "only irrefutable threats to the external or internal security of the Member State
> [could] justify an expulsion, that is, only to the existence of the State and its

---

[39] See, for example, *Boultif v Switzerland* (2001) 33 E.H.R.R. 50 where the European Court of Human Rights held that the seriousness of the crime committed by the individual, rather than their propensity to re-offend is a factor to be taken into account in assessing their rights under art.8 ECHR (right to respect for family and private life).
[40] See COM(2009) 313 final at para.3.1 and see inter alia *Sirdar* (C-273/97) [1999] E.C.R. I-7403, at [17]; *Kreil* (C-285/98) [2000] E.C.R. I-69, at [17]; *Albore* (C-423/98) [2000] E.C.R. I-5965, at [18]; and *Dory* (C-186/01) [2003] E.C.R. I-2479, at [32].
[41] *Minstre de l'Interieur v Olazabal* (C-100/01) [2002] E.C.R I-10981, at [35].
[42] i.e. in addition to the threat to public policy (in the French *ordre public*).
[43] *Land Baden-Württemberg v Panagiotis Tsakouridis* (C-145/09).

essential institutions, their ability to function, the survival of the population, external relations and the peaceful coexistence of nations".

Acknowledging that public security covers both a Member State's internal and external security,[44] the CJEU went on to observe that a threat to

"the functioning of the institutions and essential public services and the survival of the population, as well as the risk of a serious disturbance to foreign relations or to peaceful coexistence of nations, or a risk to military interests"

might also affect public security.[45] The CJEU continued:

"45 It does not follow that objectives such as the fight against crime in connection with dealing in narcotics as part of an organised group are necessarily excluded from that concept.

46 Dealing in narcotics as part of an organised group is a diffuse form of crime with impressive economic and operational resources and frequently with transnational connections. In view of the devastating effects of crimes linked to drug trafficking, Council Framework Decision 2004/757/JHA of 25 October 2004 laying down minimum provisions on the constituent elements of criminal acts and penalties in the field of illicit drug trafficking (OJ 2004 L 335, p. 8) states in recital 1 that illicit drug trafficking poses a threat to health, safety and the quality of life of citizens of the Union, and to the legal economy, stability and security of the Member States.

47 Since drug addiction represents a serious evil for the individual and is fraught with social and economic danger to mankind (see, to that effect, inter alia, Case 221/81 *Wolf* [1982] ECR 3681, paragraph 9, and Eur. Court H.R., *Aoulmi v France*, no. 50278/99, § 86, ECHR 2006-I), trafficking in narcotics as part of an organised group could reach a level of intensity that might directly threaten the calm and physical security of the population as a whole or a large part of it."

Thus in the CJEU's view art.28(3) of Directive 2004/38:

"must be interpreted as meaning that the fight against crime in connection with dealing in narcotics as part of an organised group is capable of being covered by the concept of 'imperative grounds of public security' which may justify a measure expelling a Union citizen who has resided in the host Member State for the preceding 10 years".

13–32 Notwithstanding the foregoing the existence of criminal convictions alone will be generally unlikely to engage public security. However, the loss of national sovereignty to the Union[46] is particularly keenly felt by some Member States in the context of the expulsion of those convicted of serious criminal offences. In view of the enhanced protection afforded by art.28(3) such Member States may find it increasingly tempting to seek to characterise other types of criminal behaviour as potentially falling within the concept of

---

[44] At para.43.
[45] At para.44 by reference to *Campus Oil and Others* (72/83) [1984] E.C.R. 2727, at [34] and [35]; *Werner* (C-70/94) [1995] E.C.R. I-3189, at [27]; *Albore*, at [22]; and *Commission v Greece* (C-398/98) [2001] E.C.R. I-7915, at [29].
[46] See above at para.13–08.

public security. It seems very likely that the CJEU will again consider such questions. At minimum, however, based on its reasoning in *Tsakouridis* any such criminal conduct would have to reach such a level of intensity that it might "directly threaten the calm and physical security of the population as a whole or a large part of it".[47]

(ii) *Approach*

All of the principles described above in relation to public policy apply equally to measures taken on public security grounds, including importantly the carrying out of the proportionality assessment. At the same time it remains important to maintain the distinction between the two concepts and public security cannot be extended to cover measures that should be covered by public policy. This is all the more important in light of the heightened protection given by art.28(3) of Directive 2004/38 which prevents the expulsion of certain Union citizens[48] except if the decision is based on "imperative grounds of public security". 13–33

(d) *Public health*

Article 29(1) of Directive 2004/38 states that the only diseases justifying measures restricting freedom of movement shall be the diseases 13–34

> "with epidemic potential as defined by the relevant instruments of the World Health Organisation and other infectious diseases or contagious parasitic diseases if they are the subject of protection provisions applying to nationals of the host Member State".

However, the potential for Member States to take special measures on public health grounds is time limited. Article 29(2) of Directive 2004/38 provides that diseases occurring after a three-month period from the date of arrival "shall not constitute grounds for expulsion from the territory". Article 29(3) provides that before three months have elapsed Member States may require persons entitled to the right of residence 13–35

> "to undergo, free of charge, a medical examination to certify that they are not suffering from any of the conditions referred to in paragraph 1".

However, there must be "serious indications" that this is necessary and moreover such medical examinations "may not be required as a matter of routine".

---

[47] In *PI v Oberbürgermeisterin der Stadt Remscheid* (C-348/09) the CJEU has been asked to rule whether "imperative grounds of public security" (in art.29(3)(a) of the Citizens Directive) covers sexual abuse of a 14-year-old minor, sexual coercion and rape. In the opinion of Advocate General Bot (at [44]) although "undoubtedly a threat in the family sphere, it [was] not ... established, by the nature of the act committed, that he is a threat to the security of the citizens of the Union" and "however repellent it may be, the act of incest does not seem to me to involve, as regards public security, the same kind of threat as that defined by the Court in [*Tsakouridis*]".

[48] Those who: (a) have resided in the host Member State for the previous 10 years; or (b) are a minor, except if the expulsion is necessary for the best interests of the child, as provided for in the United Nations Convention on the Rights of the Child of November 20, 1989.

4. SAFEGUARDS AGAINST EXCLUSION OR EXPULSION OF FREE MOVERS

(a) *Heightened protection from expulsion*

(i) *Introduction*

13–36 The preamble to Directive 2004/38 acknowledges that the expulsion of Union citizens and their family members on grounds of public policy or public security is a measure that can "seriously harm" those free movers who have "become genuinely integrated into the host Member State". For this reason the scope for such measures to be taken in all cases is limited in accordance with the principle of proportionality.[49] However, as also acknowledged in the preamble, "the greater the degree of integration ....., the greater the degree of protection against expulsion should be". Recital 24 of the preamble continues:

> "Only in exceptional circumstances, where there are imperative grounds of public security, should an expulsion measure be taken against Union citizens who have resided for many years in the territory of the host Member State, in particular when they were born and have resided there throughout their life. In addition, such exceptional circumstances should also apply to an expulsion measure taken against minors, in order to protect their links with their family, in accordance with the United Nations Convention on the Rights of the Child, of 20 November 1989."

Reflective of such sentiments art.28 of Directive 2004/38 makes provision for three circumstances in which enhanced protection from expulsion – in the form of a heightening of the threshold required to be reached in order to justify an expulsion decision—is given.

13–37 The concept of integration is plainly of importance to the heightened protection from expulsion. In *Dias*[50] the CJEU stated that "the integration objective which lies behind the acquisition of the right of permanent residence is based not only on territorial and time factors but also on qualitative elements, relating to the level of integration in the host Member State." In *PI*[51] (a reference concerning the heightened protection relied on by Mr I who had begun to abuse, sexually coerce and rape his ex-partner's daughter from the third year of his residence) Advocate General Both explains why in his view art.28(2) and (3) of Directive 2004/38 is to be interpreted as meaning that a Union citizen cannot rely on the right to enhanced protection against expulsion where it is shown that the citizen derives such right from offending conduct constituting a serious disturbance of the public policy of the host Member State. As he states in his Opinion:

---

[49] Recital 23 in preamble to Directive 2004/38.
[50] *Secretary of State for Work and Pensions v Maria Dias* (C-325/09) (concerning the acquisition after five years of permanent residence given by art.16 of the Citizens Directive—see generally Ch.10, above).
[51] *PI v Oberbürgermeisterin der Stadt Remscheid* (C-348/09), Advocate General Bot's Opinion of March 27, 2011.

> "60. Although the integration of a Union citizen is, in fact, based on territorial and time factors, it is also based on qualitative elements. Now, it seems clear to me that Mr I's conduct, which constitutes a serious disturbance of a public policy, shows a total lack of desire to integrate into the society in which he finds himself and some of whose fundamental values he so conscientiously disregarded for years. Today he relies on the consequences of having completed a period of 10 years which was not interrupted because his conduct remained hidden owing to the physical and moral violence horribly exercised on the victim for years.
>
> 61. An offence of that nature, just because it has lasted a long time, cannot create a right. Furthermore, Directive 2004/38 itself provides, in Article 35, that the Member States may adopt the necessary measures to refuse, terminate or withdraw any right conferred by the directive in the case of abuse of rights or fraud. In this case, it should be for the Court to draw the appropriate conclusions from such fraud."

It remains to be seen whether such an approach is adopted by the CJEU. Undoubtedly it is fraught with difficulty but more fundamentally undermines the system of protection against expulsion enshrined in the Directive (both in relation to expulsion and permanent residence). An attempt to review the quality of integration in every case as if this were a specific condition would be both difficult to administer and would rewrite the qualifying conditions to include that which is not there, in effect by treating integration as only a rebuttable presumption. Furthermore, such an approach undermines the concept of EU citizenship which insists that EU citizens are treated equally. Just as Member States have to find ways of dealing with own nationals, however deviant or undesirable, so they must also find a way to deal with EU citizens who have resided in their territory for lengthy periods.

13–38

(ii) *Permanent residents*

The first circumstance in which enhanced protection is enjoyed is provided by art.28.2 of Directive 2004/38 which states:

13–39

> "The host Member State may not take an expulsion decision against Union citizens or their family members, irrespective of nationality, who have the right of permanent residence on its territory, except on serious grounds of public policy or public security."

The right of permanent residence is given by art.16 of Directive 2004/38 to those Union citizens (and their third country national family members) who have resided legally for a continuous period of five years in the host Member State. The detail (for example, as regards the meaning of "legally resided" and the affect of temporary absences, etc.) is considered in Ch.10, but once acquired it can be lost "only through absence from the host Member State for a period exceeding two consecutive years". The enhanced protection enjoyed by those Union citizens and their third country national family members with permanent residence reflects their presumed level of integration into the host Member State. "Serious grounds" of public policy or public security must be shown by the host Member State to justify expulsion in such cases and consistent with principle and the constant case law of the CJEU the phrase must be narrowly and strictly construed. Moreover, it is to be emphasised that some real meaning must be given to the word "serious", which plainly is a significantly higher threshold than "normal" cases where expulsion is based on public policy or public security grounds. In such normal cases as made clear by the constant case law of the CJEU and art.25(2) of Directive 2004/38, in order to justify an expulsion decision the personal conduct of the individual concerned must represent "a genuine, present and sufficiently serious threat affecting one of the fundamental interests of society". This is a high threshold itself, heightened yet further by the additional epithet "serious" for those enjoying art.28(2) protection.

(iii) *Ten years' residence*

13–40 The second circumstance in which enhanced protection is enjoyed is provided by art.28(3)(a) of Directive 2004/38. The beneficiaries are Union citizens[52] who "have resided in the host Member State for the previous 10 years". An expulsion decision may not be taken against such Union citizens "except if the decision is based on imperative grounds of public security, as defined by Member States". It is to be emphasised that there is no requirement that the residence was in accordance with European Union law or otherwise. It is simple residence.

13–41 Article 28(3)(a) was considered by the CJEU in *Tsakouridis*[53] (discussed above at paras 13–31 to 13–32 in relation to the meaning of "public security"). The second question referred asked the CJEU under what conditions the art.28(3)(b) right to enhanced protection could be lost and whether the condition for the loss of the right of permanent residence in art.16(4) (namely absence for a period "exceeding two consecutive years") was to be applied mutatis mutandis in that context. Mr Tsakouridis is a Greek national who had lived in Germany all his life, although during the 10 years preceding the expulsion decision he had been on the island of Rhodes in Greece for seven months in 2004 and between October 2005 until his transfer to Germany on March 19, 2007 (following his arrest on Rhodes on November 19, 2006). Residence for the previous 10 years "considerably strengthens" the protection of Union citizens against expulsion, although as observed by the CJEU[54] art.28(3)(a) is "silent as to the circumstances which are capable of interrupting the period of 10 years' residence for the purposes of the acquisition of the right to enhanced protection". While recitals 23 and 24 in the preamble refer to special protection for the genuinely integrated (particularly when born there and when they have spent all their life there), as stated by the CJEU[55] the fact remains that, in view of the wording of art.28(3) "the decisive criterion is whether the Union citizen has lived in that Member State for the 10 years preceding the expulsion decision".

---

[52] Unlike the enhanced protection for those with permanent residence (which is enjoyed by Union citizens and their third country national family members), art.28.3 applies only to Union citizens.
[53] *Land Baden-Württemberg v Panagiotis Tsakouridis* (C-145/09).
[54] *Land Baden-Württemberg v Panagiotis Tsakouridis* (C-145/09), at [28–29].
[55] *Land Baden-Württemberg v Panagiotis Tsakouridis* (C-145/09), at [31].

As for the absences and whether they would prevent Mr Tsakouridis from enjoying the enhanced protection, in the words of the CJEU[56] 13–42

> "an overall assessment must be made of the person's situation on each occasion at the precise time when the question of expulsion arises".

The CJEU made clear[57] that all relevant factors would be considered "in particular the duration of each period of absence from the host Member State, the cumulative duration and the frequency of those absences, and the reasons why the person concerned left the host Member State".

At issue in this context is

> "whether those absences involve the transfer to another State of the centre of the personal, family or occupational interests of the person concerned".

The fact of a forced return to serve a term of imprisonment and the time spent in prison can be taken into account as part of the necessary overall assessment for determining

> "whether the integrating links previously forged with the host Member State have been broken".

The CJEU did not endorse the possibility raised by the referring court of applying the criteria in art.16(4) (absence exceeding two consecutive years) by analogy.[58] This is unsurprising since the necessary focus is not (only) absences of a particular length, but rather the far more nuanced and fact sensitive question of where the person has resided. As the CJEU stated in answering the questions, art.28(3)(a) is to be interpreted as meaning that, in order to determine whether a Union citizen has resided for the 10 years preceding ("the decisive criterion for granting enhanced protection") all relevant factors must be taken into account 13–43

> "in particular the duration of each period of absence from the host Member State, the cumulative duration and the frequency of those absences, and the reasons why the person concerned left the host Member State, reasons which may establish whether those absences involve the transfer to another State of the centre of the personal, family or occupational interests of the person concerned."

In most cases more relevant than absences per se, whether as regards number or duration, will likely be the consequences of such absences. Have "integrating links" previously forged with a host Member State been broken and transferred irrevocably elsewhere? If so, a person may be said to have ceased residing in a host Member State. In many cases however this may 13–44

---

[56] *Land Baden-Württemberg v Panagiotis Tsakouridis* (C-145/09), at [32].
[57] *Land Baden-Württemberg v Panagiotis Tsakouridis* (C-145/09), at [33–34].
[58] On the facts this would have benefited Mr Tsakouridis.

13–45 According to the Commission,[59] "as a rule, Member States are not obliged to take time actually spent behind bars into account when calculating the duration of residence under art.28 where no links with the host Member State are built." However, this is a general approach and depending on the circumstances of a person's incarceration different considerations could apply on the particular facts of an individual's case (where, for example, a person maintains links with the community from prison, or on day release or such like).

13–46 As regards the meaning of "imperative grounds of public security", according to the CJEU in *Tsakouidis*[60] the European Union legislature clearly intended to limit measures based on art.28(3) to

> "exceptional circumstances". The concept 'presupposes not only the existence of a threat to public security, but also that such a threat is of a particularly high degree of seriousness, as is reflected by the use of the words 'imperative reasons'".

On the basis of the necessary individual examination of cases an expulsion measure falling within art.28(3) can be justified:

> "only if, having regard to the exceptional seriousness of the threat, such a measure is necessary for the protection of the interests it aims to secure, provided that that objective cannot be attained by less strict means, having regard to the length of residence of the Union citizen in the host Member State and in particular to the serious negative consequences such a measure may have for Union citizens who have become genuinely integrated into the host Member State."[61]

(iv) *Minors*

13–47 The third circumstance in which enhanced protection is enjoyed is provided by art.28.3(b) of Directive 2004/38. This provides enhanced protection from expulsion to all Union citizens who are minors "except if the decision is based on *imperative grounds of public security*, as defined by Member States". However, such enhanced protection does not apply where the expulsion of a Union citizen minor is "necessary for the best interests of the child, as provided for in the United Nations Convention on the Rights of the Child of 20 November 1989".

---

[59] See Communication from the Commission to the European Parliament and the Council on guidance for better transposition and application of Directive 2004/38/EC on the right of citizens of the Union and their family members to move and reside freely within the territory of the Member States (COM(2009) 313 final) at para.3.4.
[60] *Land Baden-Württemberg v Panagiotis Tsakouridis* (C-145/09), at [32].
[61] *Land Baden-Württemberg v Panagiotis Tsakouridis* (C-145/09), at [50].

(b) *Notification of decision to expel or exclude*

13–48 Article 6 of Directive 2004/38 gives an initial right of residence for up to three months to Union citizens and their family members without any conditions or formalities. Union citizens remaining beyond three months[62] may be required to register with the relevant authorities by the host Member State. In accordance with art.8 of Directive 2004/38 the host Member State shall issue a "registration certificate" to Union citizens "immediately". For third country national family members a "residence card" is issued "no later than six months from the date on which they submit the application".[63] Article 27(3) of Directive 2004/38 makes provision for ascertaining whether a person represents a danger for public policy or public security when issuing such registration certificates (or in the absence of a registration system, not later than three months from the date of arrival of the person concerned on its territory or from the date of reporting their presence within the territory) or when issuing such residence cards. During such periods if the host Member State considers it "essential" to do so it may "request the Member State of origin and, if need be, other Member States to provide information concerning any previous police record the person concerned may have". However, such enquiries "shall not be made as a matter of routine". The Member States consulted must reply within two months.

13–49 Article 30(1) of Directive 2004/38 provides that Union citizens and their family members (irrespective of nationality) must be notified in writing of *any* decision taken restricting their freedom of movement and residence on grounds of public policy, public security or public health. This must be done "in such a way that they are able to comprehend its content and the implications for them". It must also be done in detail. In the words of art.30(2):

> "The persons concerned shall be informed, *precisely and in full*, of the public policy, public security or public health grounds on which the decision taken in their case is based, unless this is contrary to the interests of State security".

Interpreting the much less exacting requirement in art.6 of (now repealed) Directive 64/221,[64] the CJEU in *Rutili*[65] stated that the reasons given must be a "precise and comprehensive statement of the grounds for the decision, to enable him to prepare his defence".

13–50 The "State security" caveat in art.30(2) should be read also in light of art.346(a) TFEU which states that:

> "the provisions of the Treaties shall not preclude the application of the following [rule]: (a) no Member State shall be obliged to supply information the disclosure of which it considers contrary to the essential interests of its security".

---

[62] i.e. those exercising rights of free movement in accordance with art.7 of Directive 2004/38.
[63] arts 9 and 10 of Directive 2004/38.
[64] art.6 provided that the person concerned be "informed of the grounds of public policy, public security or public health upon which the decision taken ... [was] based".
[65] *Rutili v Ministre de l'interieur* (36/75) [1975] E.C.R. 1219, at [39].

Taken together it is plain that the obligation in public policy, security or health cases to provide reasons for decisions "precisely and in full" does not apply in national security cases. However, whether that could mean no reasons need to be given at all in such cases is altogether a different question and surely an unlikely consequence. First, national courts must be able to review cases in accordance with the right to an effective remedy, which is a general principle of European Union law reflected in art.47 of the EU Charter. Secondly and moreover, there must be some basis on which an appellant is to be able (in the words of the CJEU in *Rutili*) "to prepare his defence" which would be impossible at the extreme postulated.

13–51 Practices vary in Member States as to the extent to which reasons are given for decisions in national security cases. In the United Kingdom for example a "special advocate" system is employed whereby sensitive information not able to be communicated to the appellant is considered by a special advocate (vetted by the Security Service). This advocate is appointed to represent the interests of the appellant in closed hearings which the appellant is unable to attend.[66] The extent to which reasons need be given in such national security cases will be considered by the CJEU following a reference by the United Kingdom Court of Appeal[67] of the question whether the principle of effective judicial protection set out in art.30(2) (as interpreted in the light of art.346(1)(a) TFEU) requires that a judicial body considering an appeal ensures that the Union citizen concerned:

> "is informed of the essence of the grounds against him, notwithstanding the fact that the authorities of the Member State and the relevant domestic court, after consideration of the totality of the evidence against the European Union citizen relied upon by the authorities of the Member State, conclude that the disclosure of the essence of the grounds against him would be contrary to the interests of state security?"

13–52 Recipients of such decisions must obviously be able to appeal against them. This is expressly provided for in art.31 of Directive 2004/38 (see "Legal Remedies" below) but is plain also from art.30(3) which states that the notification

> "shall specify the court or administrative authority with which the person concerned may lodge an appeal, the time limit for the appeal and, where applicable, the time allowed for the person to leave the territory of the Member State".

---

[66] The Special Immigration Appeals Act 1997 established the Special Immigration Appeals Commission to hear appeals in national security cases. This was the UK government's response to the decision of the ECtHR in *Chahal v UK* [1996] 23 EHRR 413 which had deprecated the use of "national security" by the executive to free itself from effective control of the domestic courts and commended arrangements used in Canada which "both accommodate legitimate security concerns and yet accord the individual a substantial measure of protection" (at para.130). The system introduced and employed by the UK however has been extremely controversial.

[67] Reference for a preliminary ruling made on June 17, 2011 in *ZZ v Secretary of State for the Home Department* (C-300/11).

As regards leaving, except for case of "duly substantiated" urgency, the time allowed to leave the territory "shall be not less than one month from the date of notification". As observed by the Commission,[68]

> "the justification of an urgent removal must be genuine and proportionate. In assessing the need to reduce this time in cases of urgency, the authorities must take into account the impact of an immediate or urgent removal on the personal and family life of the person concerned *(e.g. need to give notice at work, terminate a lease, need to arrange for personal belongings to be sent to the place of new residence, the education of children, etc.).* Adopting an expulsion measure on imperative or serious grounds does not necessarily mean that there is urgency. The assessment of urgency must be clearly and separately substantiated."

(c) *Legal remedies*

13–53 Article 31 of Directive 2004/38 (entitled "Procedural safeguards") makes provision for legal remedies in respect of decisions taken on grounds of public policy, public security or public health. Article 31(1) provides that recipients of such decisions "shall have access to judicial and, where appropriate, administrative redress procedures in the host Member State to appeal against or seek review of any decision taken against them" on such grounds.

13–54 There is no automatic requirement that persons accessing such redress procedures be permitted to remain in the host Member State pending the hearing of the procedure itself. To the contrary, art.31(4) provides that Member States "may exclude the individual concerned from their territory pending the redress procedure". However, individuals must be able to apply to suspend enforcement of the exclusion decision pending appeal or judicial review. Where an application for an interim order to suspend enforcement is made, then art.31(2) provides that "*actual* removal from the territory may not take place until such time as the decision on the interim order has been taken.[69] There are three circumstances where removal will not be stayed: first, where the expulsion decision is based on a previous judicial decision; secondly, where the persons concerned have had previous access to judicial review; and thirdly where the expulsion decision is based on imperative grounds of public security under art.28(3).

13–55 Although not expressly referred to in art.31 of Directive 2004/38, it is plain from art.30.1 that the redress procedure must be to a court or administrative authority (see para.13–50, above referring to art.30(3) which states that the notification of decision "shall shall specify the court or administrative authority with which the person concerned may lodge an appeal"). This is an improvement over the previous position under Directive 64/221 where the scope of available remedies for those facing expulsion depended on the

---

[68] See COM(2009) 313 final at para.3.5.
[69] Even if unsuccessful, individuals will be able to attend the redress procedure to submit their defence in person unless appearance may cause serious troubles to public policy, public security or when the appeal concerns a denial of entry to the territory. See further below at para.13–57.

remedies available to nationals of the host Member State in respect of acts of the administration and "appeals" were to a "competent authority".[70]

13–56 As regards the necessary scope of appeals, art.31(3) provides that the redress procedures

> "shall allow for an examination of the legality of the decision, as well as of the facts and circumstances on which the proposed measure is based. They shall ensure that the decision is not disproportionate, particularly in view of the requirements laid down in Article 28".

It is plainly intended that appeals be required to examine the substantive legal and factual merits of decisions under challenge and that the court or reviewing authority be able to substitute its own decision for that of the original decision maker in the host Member State. In the words of the Commission,[71]

> "national courts may review the case in accordance with the right to an effective remedy, which is a general principle of Community law reflected in Article 47 of the EU Charter".

13–57 As already observed (see para.13–54, above) art.31(4) of Directive 2004/38 provides that those accessing redress procedures may be excluded from the territory of a host Member State pending the redress procedure. However, subject to two exceptions, Member States cannot prevent personal attendance at the redress procedure itself. The exceptions are: (1) that the person's appearance "may cause serious troubles to public policy or public security", or (2) that "the appeal or judicial review concerns a denial of entry to the territory". In the words of art.31(4), assuming neither exception applies then Member States "may not prevent the individual from submitting his/her defence in person". The necessary implication is that there must be a proper hearing (as opposed to some sort of "paper" exercise only).

13–58 Article 32 of Directive 2004/38 makes specific provision as regards the duration of exclusion orders. Considering the position under Directive 64/221 the CJEU had previously stated in *Shingara and Radiom* that providing a reasonable amount of time had elapsed, a person would be entitled to have a fresh application for entry or a residence permit examined.[72] Reflecting the sentiments expressed by the CJEU, art.32(1) states persons excluded on grounds of public policy or public security

---

[70] arts 8 and 9 of the (repealed) Directive 64/221 refer. Although the "competent authority" could not be the same as the one making the decision, the CJEU held in *Gallagher* (C-175/94) *R v SSHD, ex p Gallagher* [1995] E.C.R I-4253, at [17]) that the body making the decision to expel or refuse the residence permit could appoint the competent authority, provided that this authority performs its duties independently.

[71] See COM(2009) 313 final at para.3.6.

[72] See *R v Secretary of State for the Home Department, Ex p. Shingara and Radiom* (C-65/95) and (C-111/95) [1997] 3 C.M.L.R. 703. Although the CJEU did not explain what a "reasonable" amount of time would be, certainly following a change of circumstances the individual should be entitled to re-examination.

The Exclusion/Expulsion of Other EU Nationals

"may submit an application for lifting of the exclusion order after a reasonable period, depending on the circumstances, and in any event after three years from enforcement of the final exclusion order which has been validly adopted in accordance with Community law, by putting forward arguments to establish that there has been a material change in the circumstances which justified the decision ordering their exclusion".

Where such application is made the Member State concerned must reach a decision within six months. Pending consideration of any such application however such persons "shall have no right of entry to the territory of the Member State concerned" (art.32(2) refers).

5. The Exclusion/Expulsion of Other EU Nationals

The position for the Union citizen resident in another Member State who is not exercising a free movement right is different from that of the free mover.[73] Generally the host Member State is entitled to expel such Union citizen without reliance being able to be placed by that Union citizen on the protection provided by Directive 2004/38 discussed above. However, even those who would appear to be outside of the scope of the Directive by being economically inactive and becoming a burden on the social assistance system of the host Member State may gain some protection from the Directive.

13–59

Such limitations are foreshadowed by recital 16 in the preamble to Directive 2004/38 which states:

13–60

"As long as the beneficiaries of the right of residence do not become an unreasonable burden on the social assistance system of the host Member State they should not be expelled. Therefore, an expulsion measure should not be the automatic consequence of recourse to the social assistance system. The host Member State should examine whether it is a case of temporary difficulties and take into account the duration of residence, the personal circumstances and the amount of aid granted in order to consider whether the beneficiary has become an unreasonable burden on its social assistance system and to proceed to his expulsion. In no case should an expulsion measure be adopted against workers, self-employed persons or job-seekers as defined by the Court of Justice save on grounds of public policy or public security."

Article 14 of Directive 2004/38 provides for the "retention of the right of residence". Article 14(1) states that the right of residence given by art.6 is retained as long as the Union citizens and their family members "do not become an unreasonable burden on the social assistance system of the host Member State". The right of residence given by arts 7, 12 and 13 is retained so long as the Union citizens and their family members "meet the conditions set out therein".

13–61

Article 14(3) and (4) states:

13–62

---

[73] It is to be recalled that art.6 of Directive 2004/38 gives all Union citizens and their family members (including those who are third country nationals) an initial right of residence for up to three months without conditions or formalities.

"3. An expulsion measure shall not be the automatic consequence of a Union citizen's or his or her family member's recourse to the social assistance system of the host Member State.

4. By way of derogation from paragraphs 1 and 2 and without prejudice to the provisions of Chapter VI, an expulsion measure may in no case be adopted against Union citizens or their family members if:
(a) the Union citizens are workers or self-employed persons, or
(b) the Union citizens entered the territory of the host Member State in order to seek employment. In this case, the Union citizens and their family members may not be expelled for as long as the Union citizens can provide evidence that they are continuing to seek employment and that they have a genuine chance of being engaged."

13–63 Article 14(3) is a freestanding provision which is not linked to the exercise by the Union citizen of free movement rights. It establishes the general proposition in European Union law that on no account should recourse to a Member State's social security system automatically lead to expulsion. Since not linked to the exercise of free movement rights this will be the position even if it can be said that by having had such recourse the person no longer fulfils the relevant conditions attached to the exercise of the right. As will be seen, it reflects the decision of the CJEU in *Grzelczyk*[74] (which concerned a student whose recourse to social assistance meant that he had ceased to fulfil the conditions for students).

13–64 As for art.14(4), the protection reflects the fundamental importance given by European Union law to the exercise of free movement rights by those performing economic activity (whether as workers or self-employed persons) and those work seekers with a genuine chance of performing economic activity. The essence of the protection is that on no account can such persons ever be expelled by reason of recourse to public funds (although they can otherwise be expelled on public policy or public security grounds). This is readily understandable not only because of the fundamental importance attached to the exercise of free movement rights by those performing economic activity, but also by reason of the fact that (unlike students and other free movers exercising a general right of residence or the retired), such persons are not required in any event to establish that they have sufficient resources for themselves or their families in order to be workers or self-employed persons (see Chs 6 and 7).

13–65 Additional protection against expulsion is provided by art.15 of Directive 2004/38 (entitled "procedural safeguards"). Article 15(1) states that the procedures provided for by arts 30 and 31 of Directive 2004/38 (discussed above at paras 13–57 to 13–61) "shall apply by analogy to all decisions restricting free movement of Union citizens and their family members on grounds other than public policy, public security or public health". Article 15(2)–(3) provides as follows:

---

[74] *Grzelczyk v Centre public d'aide social d'Ottignies-Louvain-la-Neuve* (C-184/99) [2001] E.C.R. I-6193.

"2. Expiry of the identity card or passport on the basis of which the person concerned entered the host Member State and was issued with a registration certificate or residence card shall not constitute a ground for expulsion from the host Member State.

3. The host Member State may not impose a ban on entry in the context of an expulsion decision to which paragraph 1 applies."

13–66 This means that non-economically active Union citizens who are unambiguously unable to support themselves may face expulsion measures on the grounds that they no longer meet the conditions laid down in the secondary legislation applicable to their situation (although as seen expulsion cannot be the automatic consequence of recourse to the social assistance system of a Member State). Moreover, any such expulsion will be permissible only subject to other relevant international obligations (such as the Convention on Social and Medical Assistance and ECHR obligations). Further, such expulsion measures could be taken only within the limits imposed by European Union law, namely the principles of proportionality and procedural safeguards.

13–67 Principles of proportionality if properly applied could have an important impact on the exercise by a Member State of the power to expel a Union citizen who does not meet the limitations and conditions contained in secondary legislation. For instance, such principles would dictate that where a Union citizen was only *temporarily* unable to meet the conditions laid down in relevant secondary legislation, an automatic decision to expel would be contrary to European Union law. The position would be the same where only a *minor* condition was unable to be met.

13–68 For example, in *Grzelczyk*[75] a French national student who had been self-sufficient for the first three years of his studies in Belgium applied to the Belgian authorities for payment of the minimex, a minimum form of social assistance. Although the CJEU acknowledged that Union law would not prevent a Member State from taking the view that a student having recourse to social assistance no longer fulfilled the conditions of his right of residence, or from taking measures either to withdraw his residence permit or not renew it,

"in no case may such measures become the automatic consequence of a student ... having recourse to the host Member State's social assistance system".[76]

Further, in *Trojani*[77] the CJEU reiterated that it remains open to Member States to remove Union citizens who no longer fulfil the conditions of their

---

[75] *Grzelczyk v Centre public d'aide social d'Ottignies-Louvain-la-Neuve* (C-184/99) [2001] E.C.R. I-6193, at [43].
[76] *Grzelczyk v Centre public d'aide social d'Ottignies-Louvain-la-Neuve* (C-184/99) [2001] E.C.R. I-6193.
[77] *Trojani v Centre public d'aide social de Bruxelles (CPAS)* (C-456/02), September 7, 2004.

right of residence. Again, however any such measures must be "within the limits imposed by European Union law".[78]

13–69 In *Baumbast*[79] the CJEU took a similar approach where it appeared that Mr Baumbast did not have sickness insurance for *all* risks in compliance with the provisions of Directive 90/364. The CJEU considered that the fact that Mr Baumbast's sickness insurance did not cover emergency treatment could not result in a refusal to allow him to exercise his right of residence in the host Member State since such refusal would be disproportionate.

---

[78] *Trojani v Centre public d'aide social de Bruxelles (CPAS)* (C-456/02), September 7, 2004, at [45].
[79] *Baumbast and R. v Secretary of State for the Home Department* (C-413/99) [2002] E.C.R. I-7091, at [91–93].

Part Three
ASSOCIATION AGREEMENTS WITH THIRD COUNTRIES

CHAPTER 14

AGREEMENTS WITH THIRD COUNTRIES

This chapter examines the powers of the European Union to negotiate and enter into agreements with third countries. The resulting agreements are considered and particular emphasis is placed on any provisions which might impact on the free movement of persons.

1. Treaty Provision for Agreements with Third Countries

(i) General Power to conclude agreements

14–01 Title V of the Treaty on the Functioning of the European Union entitled "International Agreements" provides for the conclusion of agreements between the Union and third countries or international organisations. Article 216(1) makes general provision for the conclusion of such agreements

> "where the Treaties so provide or where the conclusion of an agreement is necessary in order to achieve, within the framework of the Union's policies, one of the objectives referred to in the Treaties, or is provided for in a legally binding Union act or is likely to affect common rules or alter their scope".

Article 216(2) states that "agreements concluded by the Union are binding upon the institutions of the Union and on its Member States". In this sense Member States act collectively to conclude agreements with third countries, notwithstanding any bilateral agreements they might have with those third countries.

(ii) Association agreements

14–02 Specific provision is made to conclude association agreements in art.217 TFEU:

> "The Union may conclude with one or more third countries or international organisations agreements establishing an association involving reciprocal rights and obligations, common action and special procedure."

(iii) Procedure

14–03 Article 218 TFEU sets out the procedure for the conclusion of all such Agreements. The principal role is played by the Council (acting throughout the procedure by qualified majority[1]) which authorises the opening of negotiations, adopts negotiating directives, authorises the signing of agreements and concludes them.[2] As regards decisions adopting agreements,

---
[1] art.218(8) TFEU.
[2] art.218(2)–(5) TFEU.

art.218(6)(a) provides that (save where agreements "relate exclusively to the common foreign and security policy") the Council shall adopt the decision concluding the agreement "after obtaining the consent of the European Parliament" in specified cases which include association agreements.[3] For other cases[4] the Council adopts the decision concluding the agreement after consulting the European Parliament.[5]

(iv) *Discussion*

14–04   Historically a wide range of agreements with third countries have been concluded under these provisions (or their predecessors contained in art.310 EC Treaty or art.238 Treaty of Rome). Agreements tend to be regional to the extent that although they are concluded between the Union (previously the Community) and an individual third State, the terms of such agreements tend to be replicated throughout the region reflective of the intentions of the Union as regards its relations with that particular region as a whole.

14–05   With increasing intensity since the early 1990s the European Union broadened its relations to include nearly all regions of the world and signed agreements and conventions with a wide range of partners. However, the content of these agreements varies enormously. The pre-Accession Agreement with Turkey (still in place) and (historically) the pre-Accession agreements with Bulgaria, Romania and the other eastern European States conferred considerable rights connected with the free movement of persons, whereas the EU-Central America Political Dialogue and Co-operation Agreements confer no rights at all in this field.

14–06   Of particular interest in the free movement field is the EEA Agreement which extends free movement provisions to nationals of Iceland, Norway and Liechtenstein and the Agreement with Switzerland which likewise extends free movement of person provisions to Swiss nationals. None of those countries has joined the European Union, although that prospect would be open to them. Legally therefore Iceland, Norway, Liechtenstein and Switzerland remain third countries to the European Union.

14–07   All of the countries of the Western Balkans have the prospect of joining the European Union (an objective endorsed in June 2005 by the European Council). The European Union is engaged with the Western Balkan countries in a stabilisation and association process which has the three main aims of stabilising the countries and encouraging their swift transition to a market economy, promoting regional co-operation and (finally) membership of the Union. The first such Stabilisation and Association Agreement (SAA) was with Macedonia which entered into force on April 1, 2004; the second (with Croatia) entered into force on February 1, 2005; the third (with Albania) entered into force on April 1, 2009, and the fourth (with Montenegro) entered into force on May 1, 2010. SAAs have also been signed

---

[3] art.218(6)(a)(i) TFEU.
[4] i.e. those not listed in art.218(6)(a) TFEU.
[5] art.218(6)(b) TFEU. Parliament is obliged to deliver its opinion within a time-limit set by the Council depending on the urgency of the matter. In the absence of an opinion within the time-limit set, the Council may act.

with Bosnia and Herzegovina (in June 2008) and Serbia (in December 2009).[6] At time of writing although the agreement with Bosnia and Herzegovina has been ratified by all Member States entry into force has been delayed due to the fact that Bosnia has yet to make the required constitutional amendments.[7] The SAA with Serbia has yet to be ratified by all Member States. Croatia is the closest to accession of these States. Accession negotiations with Croatia closed on June 30, 2011 and accession is anticipated on July 1, 2013.[8]

14–08 There are no provisions granting the right of free movement of persons contained in the Stabilisation and Association Agreements. Each is cast in broadly similar terms. Taking the Croatia Agreement by way of example, the furthest that the Agreement goes is to guarantee non-discrimination for workers from Croatia "legally employed" in the Member States (with an accompanying right of access to the Member State's labour market for the worker's "legally resident" spouse and children)[9] and the right of establishment for companies[10] which largely reflects similar provisions in the previous Association Agreements with Bulgaria and Romania. Unlike the position under Europe Agreements[11] however the right of establishment is not given to individuals (at least at the time of writing). There is also a right for companies to post "key personnel" to Member States in certain circumstances, as well as an extremely limited right for "natural persons" to enter Member States temporarily to negotiate contracts for the sale of services. These rights under the SAAs are discussed in detail in Ch.16.

14–09 Various other Association Agreements, such as the Euro-Mediterranean Agreements with the Maghreb countries[12] and the 10 partnership and cooperation agreements (PCAs) concluded with Russia, countries of Eastern Europe, the Southern Caucasus and Central Asia,[13] reflect a wish on the part of the European Union to have close economic relations with these

---

[6] For Kosovo there was in place a "Stabilisation and Association Tracking Mechanism—STM". This was the main instrument for political dialogue between the government of Kosovo and the European Commission in the framework of the EU's Stabilisation and Association Process from March 2003 until October 2009. In October 2009 the Commission adopted its communication "Kosovo—Fulfilling its European Perspective" and launched an intensified political dialogue, the Stabilisation and Association Process Dialogue (SAP Dialogue). The dialogue continues, although the Union is divided on how to continue whilst certain Member States (Spain, Slovakia, Cyprus, Romania, and Greece) do not recognise the Republic of Kosovo as an independent State.
[7] See article at *http://daily.tportal.hr/124423/Press-Bosnia-EU-relations-put-on-hold.html* [Accessed April 26, 2011].
[8] See *Europa* press release ("Statement by President Barroso on Croatia—Commission proposes to close the last 'Chapters' in the accession talks") at: *http://europa.eu/rapid/pressReleasesAction.do?reference = MEMO/11/397* [Accessed February 2012].
[9] art.45 refers.
[10] arts 48–49 refer.
[11] That is the pre-Accession Agreements with the Eastern European States which joined the Union in 2004 and 2007.
[12] Morocco, Algeria and Tunisia. The EU also has Association Agreements with Egypt, Israel, Jordan and Lebanon.
[13] Since the end of the 1990s the European Union has concluded 10 similar PCAs with Armenia, Azerbaijan, Georgia, Kazakhstan, Kyrgyzstan, Moldova, Russia, Ukraine, Uzbekistan and Tajikistan.

countries although it is not intended that they will become full Member States in the foreseeable future. These agreements contain non-discrimination provisions relating to workers lawfully present in the Member States similar to those contained in the SAAs with the Western Balkan countries.

14–10 Given the scope of this book it is not possible to discuss all of the various agreements with third countries. In the rest of Part Three it is the Association Agreement with Turkey which is of principal interest. This chapter examines more generally agreements with third countries which contain provisions relating to the free movement of persons.

2. EEA Agreement

(a) *Background*

14–11 The European Economic Area Agreement was signed on May 2, 1990 by seven countries: Austria, Iceland, Finland, Norway, Sweden, Switzerland, Liechtenstein, and the European Union.[14] With the exception of Switzerland and Liechtenstein the Agreement came into force on January 1, 1994. Austria, Sweden and Finland joined the European Union as full Member States on January 1, 1995.

14–12 The EEA was maintained because of the wish of the three remaining States—Norway, Iceland and Liechtenstein—to participate in the single market, while not assuming the full responsibilities of membership of the European Union. The Agreement gives them the right to be consulted by the Commission during the formulation of Union legislation, but not the right to have any say in the decision-making, which is retained exclusively by Member States. All new Union legislation in areas covered by the EEA is integrated into the Agreement through a Joint Committee Decision. The Agreement is concerned principally with "four freedoms"—freedom of movement of goods (but agriculture and fisheries are included in the Agreement only to a very limited extent), freedom of movement of persons, of services and of capital. There are also provisions relevant to these four freedoms in the areas of social policy, consumer protection, environment, company law and statistics which complete the extended internal market.

14–13 The implementation of the Agreement is achieved through a set of special institutional arrangements. The Agreement established a Joint Committee whose main function is to take decisions extending EU Regulations and Directives to the EEA States. In 2011 the Joint Committee made 164 such Decisions. The Community is represented in the Joint Committee by the Commission, and decisions are taken by agreement between the Union and the EEA States, which have to "speak with one voice".

---

[14] The EEA Agreement (see below) refers to "EFTA". Iceland, Liechtenstein, Norway and Switzerland are members of the European Free Trade Association (EFTA). The EFTA Convention established a free trade area among its Member States in 1960. In addition, the EFTA States have jointly concluded free trade agreements with a number of countries worldwide.

The EEA Council meets twice a year. Its members are the members of the General Affairs Council and one member of the Government of each of the EEA States and EU Member States. Its Presidency is held alternately for six months by a member of the EU Council and a member of an EEA State Government.

In addition to the obligation to accept European Union acquis in the fields of the four freedoms, the Agreement contains provisions to allow co-operation between the Union and the EEA States in a range of the Union's activities: in research and technological development, information services, the environment, education, social policy, consumer protection, small and medium-sized enterprises, tourism, the audio-visual sector and civil protection.

(b) *Free movement of persons*

Part III of the main EEA Agreement is entitled "Free movement of persons, services and capital". Article 28 of the Agreement provides for the free movement of workers from EEA States:

Article 28

1. Freedom of movement for workers shall be secured among EC Member States and EFTA States.

2. Such freedom of movement shall entail the abolition of any discrimination based on nationality between workers of EC Member States and EFTA States as regards employment, remuneration and other conditions of work and employment.

3. It shall entail the right, subject to limitations justified on grounds of public policy, public security or public health:

(a) to accept offers of employment actually made;
(b) to move freely within the territory of EC Member States and EFTA States for this purpose;
(c) to stay in the territory of an EC Member State or an EFTA State for the purpose of employment in accordance with the provisions governing the employment of nationals of that State laid down by law, regulation or administrative action;
(d) to remain in the territory of an EC Member State or an EFTA State after having been employed there.

Annex 5 extends the relevant secondary legislation on workers to EEA nationals.[15]

Article 31 of the Agreement abolishes all restrictions on the freedom of establishment for persons from EEA States:

---

[15] Updated Annex V (incorporating Directive 2004/38 amendments) are available at *http://www.efta.int/legal-texts/eea/annexes-to-the-agreement.aspx* [Accessed February 2012].

Article 31

1. Within the framework of the provisions of this Agreement, there shall be no restrictions on the freedom of establishment of nationals of an EC Member State or an EFTA State in the territory of any other of these States. This shall also apply to the setting up of agencies, branches or subsidiaries by nationals of any EC Member State or EFTA State established in the territory of any of these States.

Freedom of establishment shall include the right to take up and pursue activities as self-employed persons and to set up and manage undertakings, in particular companies or firms within the meaning of art.34, second paragraph, under the conditions laid down for its own nationals by the law of the country where such establishment is effected, subject to the provisions of Ch.4.

14–19 Article 36 abolishes all restrictions on the freedom of EEA nationals to provide services in the EU Member States. Annex 8 extends the relevant secondary legislation relating to establishment of persons and freedom to provide services to EEA nationals.[16]

14–20 All of the free movement provisions are reciprocal thereby extending these free movement rights to Union citizen nationals wishing to exercise them in the EEA States.[17] However, it should be noted that art.21 TFEU (which refers to citizens of the Union) is not extended to EEA States through the Agreement or any protocol to the Agreement. Thus whilst non-EU/EEA State nationals benefit from all free movement provisions that flow from the relevant secondary Union legislation, those rights that are said to derive directly from art.21 TFEU arguably are not extended to the three EEA States. In practice this will have very limited effect since the free movement rights contained in Directive 2004/38[18] are extensive covering workers, self-employed, retired persons and students and even those economically inactive (albeit that the last three categories must be self-sufficient). It remains to be seen whether the benefits of Union citizenship would be extended to EEA citizens in their own State (see *Zambrano*[19]).

---

[16] Updated Annex VII (incorporating Directive 2004/38 amendments) available at *http://www.efta.int/legal-texts/eea/annexes-to-the-agreement.aspx* [Accessed February 2012].

[17] art.5 of Protocol 15 provided transitional provisions relating to the free movement of workers between Liechtenstein and the EU permitting national rules relating to free movement to remain in place until 1998 and Liechtenstein to retain sectoral or quantative restrictions on the number of workers from the EU or indeed other EEA States that would be granted a right of residence until 1998.

[18] Directive 2004/38/EC on the right of citizens of the Union and their family members to move and reside freely within the territory of the Member States.

[19] *Gerardo Ruiz Zambrano v Office National de l'Emploi (ONEM)* (C-34/09) [2011] E.C.R. I-0000.

3. AGREEMENT WITH SWITZERLAND

(a) *Background*

As the result of a referendum in 1992, Switzerland never became part of the EEA. However, negotiations for agreements in seven sectors began in 1994. These are Free Movement of Persons, Trade in Agricultural Products, Public Procurement, Conformity Assessments, Air Transport, Transport by Road and Rail, and Swiss Participation in the 5th Framework Programme for Research. These were concluded and Agreements signed on June 21, 1999. On May 6, 2000 the Swiss approved the Agreements in a referendum. Ratification in all EU Member States was concluded in early 2002 and the seven Agreements entered into force on June 1, 2002.[20]

14–21

(b) *Free movement rights*

One of the agreements entering into force on June 1, 2002 was the Agreement between the European Union and its Member States and the Swiss Confederation on the free movement of persons.[21] Article 1 states:

14–22

Article 1

The objective of this Agreement, for the benefit of nationals of the Member States of the European Community and Switzerland, is:

(a) to accord a right of entry, residence, access to work as employed persons, establishment on a self-employed basis and the right to stay in the territory of the Contracting Parties;
(b) to facilitate the provision of services in the territory of the Contracting Parties, and in particular to liberalise the provision of services of brief duration;
(c) to accord a right of entry into, and residence in the territory of the Contracting Parties to persons without an economic activity in the host country;
(d) to accord he same living, employment and working conditions as those accorded to nationals.

The purposes of this Agreement are gradually to introduce over a 12-year period the free movement of persons (both the economically active and inactive)[22] and to liberalise free cross-border trade in certain services.[23] The free movement of persons is supplemented by the mutual recognition of professional diplomas[24] and the co-ordination of the social insurance systems of the contracting States.[25]

14–23

---

[20] Decision of the Council, and of the Commission as regards the Agreement on Scientific and Technological Cooperation, of April 4, 2002 on the conclusion of seven Agreements with the Swiss Confederation [2002] O.J. L114/1.
[21] [2002] O.J. L114/6.
[22] art.4.
[23] art.5.
[24] art.9.
[25] art.9.

14-24 Since the coming into force of the Agreement Union citizens or nationals of EEA States have enjoyed the right to stay in Switzerland and to engage in economic activity as a self-employed or as an employed person, although subject to significant restrictions. During the first five years these rights were linked to the conditions of the quota system, the priority of Swiss nationals and the control of working and wage conditions by the Labor Market Authority.[26] Additionally for the first two years after the entry into force of the Agreement all of the Contracting Parties were able to "maintain controls on the priority of workers integrated into the labour market".[27] Thereafter, the absolute prohibition of discrimination entered into force. Subject to these transitional provisions from entry into force of the Agreement Swiss nationals enjoyed free movement rights in the EU Member States. In addition, the Agreement gives the right both to be joined by family members (irrespective of the nationality of the individual family members)[28] and the right to purchase immoveable property without a permit for those domiciled in Switzerland.[29] Further, the requirements for frontier workers are significantly relaxed. The principle of equal treatment contained in art.15(1) of Annex I to the Agreement was considered by the CJEU recently in a case concerning a self-employed frontier worker.[30] And in *Bergström*[31] the CJEU considered a case relating to eligibility for income-related childcare benefit claimed by a Swedish national in Sweden on the basis of income earned in Switzerland where she had lived and worked prior to her return to Sweden some six months after the birth of the birth of her child.

14-25 The Agreement on the Free Movement of Persons provides for three categories of residence permit: the short-term residence permit (valid for a maximum of one year), the permanent residence permit (valid for five years), and the frontier worker permit.

4. Agreement with Turkey

(a) *Background*

14-26 The Association Agreement with Turkey ("the Ankara Agreement") was signed in 1963 as a first step towards accession of Turkey to the European Union. It replicated much of the Agreement with Greece and was only the second agreement that the Union had signed with a third country. It reflected the desire of the Union to be more closely linked economically with Turkey.

---

[26] art.10(1). Thereafter as sated in art.10(1) itself "from the beginning of the sixth year, all quantitative limits applicable to nationals of the Member States of the European Community shall be abolished".
[27] art.10(2).
[28] art.8(d).
[29] art.8(e).
[30] *Rico Graf and Rudolf Engel v LandratsamtWaldshut* (C-506/10) (October 6, 2011).
[31] *Försäkringskassan v Elisabeth Bergström* (C-257/10) (judgment December 15, 2011). The CJEU held that Sweden was obliged to take into account periods of employment completed in their entirety in the Swiss confederation.

14–27 The Ankara Agreement established a customs union in stages. An Additional Protocol to the Ankara Agreement was signed in 1970. It set down the timetable for the establishment of a full customs union of between 12 and 22 years. Free movement of persons was to be achieved in the same time.

14–28 Changing economic conditions and a military coup in Turkey in 1980 damaged relations between Turkey and the European Union. Although the timetable for the full free movement of persons has overrun, in 1987 Turkey made an application for full membership of the European Union. In December 2002 the European Council stated that the EU would open negotiations with Turkey "without delay" if Turkey fulfilled the Copenhagen criteria. Two years later the Union agreed to start negotiations which began in October 2005 with the opening of six chapters of the "acquis communitaire".[32] To accede to the Union Turkey must successfully complete negotiations with the European Commission on each of the 35 chapters of the acquis. Afterwards, the Member States must unanimously agree on granting Turkey membership to the Union. Turkey's membership is politically contentious and at time of writing remains some distance in the future.

(b) *Free movement of persons*

14–29 The provisions of the Ankara Agreement and its Protocol relating to the free movement of persons are discussed in detail in Chs 17–21 below. In short the Ankara Agreement and decisions of the Association Council confer rights on workers who are legally employed in the Member State to continued employment and residence subject to the satisfaction of certain conditions[33] and rights for their family members.[34] Additionally Turkish nationals seeking to establish themselves in business or to provide services benefit from a "standstill clause" which does not permit Member States to place greater restrictions on them than were in place at the time when the Member State became party to the Additional Protocol.[35]

5. Agreements with Western Balkan States

(a) *Background*

14–30 After a period of violent conflict in the western Balkans, the European Union attempted through its "Regional Approach"[36] to underpin the implementation of the Dayton/Paris and Erdut Agreements and bring basic stability and prosperity to the region. The prospect of the five Western

---

[32] Referred to as the EU acquis, and often shortened to acquis, this is the accumulated legislation, legal acts and court decisions which constitute the body of European Union law.
[33] See Ch.6 on workers.
[34] See Ch.9 on family members.
[35] See Ch.7 on establishment.
[36] Weekly Press Release of the European Commission "Enlargement Weekly", June 7, 2004. (See *http://www.europa.eu.int/comm/enlargement/docs/newsletter* [Accessed February 2012]).

Balkan countries—Albania, the former Yugoslav Republic of Macedonia, Bosnia and Herzegovina, Croatia and the Federal Republic of Yugoslavia— of eventually becoming full members of the European Union was offered explicitly at the Feira European Council in June 2000. The Commission and the Council recognised that such a prospect offered a real motivation for democratic, legal and economic reform in the region.

14–31 The November 24, 2000 Zagreb Summit initiated the stabilisation and association process by gaining the region's agreement to a clear set of objectives and conditions. In return for the European Union's offer of a prospect of accession on the basis of the Treaty on European Union, the 1993 Copenhagen criteria and an assistance programme to support that ambition, the countries of the region undertook to abide by the European Union's conditionality and use the Stabilisation and Association process in particular the Stabilisation and Association Agreements when signed, as the means to begin to prepare themselves for the demands of the perspective on accession to the European Union.

14–32 The Stabilisation and Association Agreements are both the cornerstone of the stabilisation and association process and a key step to its completion. The conclusion of Stabilisation and Association Agreements represents the Contracting Parties' commitment to complete over a transition period a formal association with the European Union. Such an association has a high political value. It is based on the gradual implementation of a free trade area and both legislative and economic reforms are aimed at ensuring that the western Balkan countries move towards EU standards. Just as with the Europe Agreements, the Stabilisation and Association Agreements are seen as preparatory steps to full EU membership.

14–33 Whilst each of the Stabilisation and Association Agreements are tailored to the circumstances of each country, each Agreement has the common purpose of achieving formal association with the European Union. The Agreements set up Association Councils at Ministerial level, with committees and subcommittees, to assist with the implementation of the Agreements.

14–34 There are four Stabilisation and Association Agreements (SAA) currently in force (see para.14–07 above). In order of entry into force these are with Macedonia (April 2004), Croatia (February 2005), Albania (April 2009), and Montenegro (May 2010). Two others (with Bosnia and Herzegovina and with Serbia) are signed but are not yet in force.[37]

14–35 At the present time Croatia is closest to becoming a member of the European Union. Croatia applied for EU membership in 2003. A particularly difficult matter was the question of relations with the International Criminal Tribunal for the former Yugoslavia (ICTY). Croatia's record of compliance

---

[37] At the time of writing the agreement with Bosnia and Herzegovina has been ratified by all Member States entry into force has been delayed due to the fact that Bosnia has yet to make the required constitutional amendments. The SAA with Serbia has yet to be ratified by all Member States.

in the past had been far from perfect, although by the beginning of 2004 this had improved considerably. On April 20, 2004 the Commission adopted its opinion on Croatia's application for membership to the European Union.[38] Accession negotiations opened on October 3, 2005 and the process of screening 35 acquis chapters was finalised on October 18, 2006. A border dispute with Slovenia had meant the subsequent stalling of negotiations until September 2009 when Slovenia announced that it would remove restraints on Croatia's negotiations with the EU without prejudice to the international mediation on the border dispute.[39] Member States decided on June 30, 2011 to close accession negotiations with Croatia allowing for the signature of the Accession Treaty by the end of 2011. The European Commission stated[40] that "following the ratification procedure in all Member States and Croatia, accession is foreseen for 1 July 2013". It is likely (as with most admissions to membership) that transitional provisions would remain in place before full freedom of movement is granted for workers.

(b) *Free movement provisions*

The content of all four Stabilisation and Association Agreements is substantially the same for free movement purposes. As the first agreement to enter into force, the Macedonia Agreement, is referred to in this chapter by way of example, although comments would apply equally to the agreements with Croatia, Albania and Montenegro. 14–36

There are no free movement provisions relating to workers in the Stabilisation and Association Agreement with Macedonia. However, art.44(1) of the Macedonia Agreement is a non-discrimination provision relating to Macedonian workers who are legally employed in the Member States of the European Union. Article 44(1) applies to legally employed Macedonian workers to protect them from discrimination compared to the Member state's own nationals as regards "working conditions, remuneration or dismissal". Provision is also made for the worker's legally resident spouse and children who must be given access to the labour market during the worker's "authorised stay of employment". 14–37

Article 44(1)[41] of the Macedonian Agreement replicates art.38(1) of the Europe Agreements when they were in force. (The Europe Agreements were pre-accession association agreements with Central and Eastern European States which joined the EU in 2004 and 2007.) Bearing in mind the aim of the Macedonian Agreement and its clear and unambiguous nature, there is no reason why it would not be interpreted exactly as art.38(1) of the Europe 14–38

---

[38] Commission of the European Communities, Brussels, April 20, 2004 COM (2004) 257 final, Croatia: Opinion on the application of Croatia for membership of the European Union.
[39] See "Slovenia unblocks Croatian EU bid" (*http://news.bbc.co.uk/1/hi/world/europe/8250441.stm*) [Accessed February 2012].
[40] *http://europa.eu/rapid/pressReleasesAction.do?reference=IP/11/824&format=HTML&aged=0&language=EN&guiLanguage=en* [Accessed February 2012].
[41] Or in turn art.45 (Croatia Agreement), art.46 (Albania Agreement), or art.49 (Montenegro Agreement).

Agreements has been interpreted. The provision is discussed in detail in Ch.16 below.

14–39 In relation to establishment, the Macedonian Agreement is more conservative than the Europe Agreements (i.e. the pre-accession agreements with those European States which joined the Union in 2004 and 2007). Establishment of Macedonian companies is provided for in art.48(3) of the Agreement[42]:

Article 48

3. The Community and its Member States shall grant, from the entry into force of this Agreement:

(i) as regards the establishment of companies from the former Yugoslav Republic of Macedonia, treatment no less favourable than that accorded by Member States to their own companies or to any company of any third country, whichever is the better;

(ii) as regards the operation of subsidiaries and branches of companies from the former Yugoslav Republic of Macedonia, established in their territory, treatment no less favourable than that accorded by Member States to their own companies and branches, or to any subsidiary and branch of any third country company, established in their territory, whichever is the better.

14–40 Article 48(1) provides reciprocal provisions for the establishment of companies from the Member States in Macedonia. The provision in art.48(3) replicates the form of the establishment provision previously contained in art.45(1) of the Europe Agreements, although the Europe Agreement provision was clearly wider in that it related to the establishment of persons.[43]

14–41 In the Macedonian Agreement the establishment of persons is not provided for, from the entry into force of the Agreement. Article 48(4) only provides that the Stabilisation and Association Council will examine whether to extend the establishment provisions contained in art.48(3) to persons who wish to take up activities as self-employed persons after five years from the entry into force of the Agreement.[44] That possibility will be examined

"in the light of the relevant European Court of Justice case law, and the situation of the labour market."

At the time when the Agreement was concluded and signed the CJEU's first judgments on the establishment provision in the Europe Agreements were not available[45] and this provision undoubtedly reflected uncertainty as to the

---

[42] Or in turn art.49 (Croatia Agreement), art.50 (Albania Agreement) or art.53 (Montenegro Agreement).

[43] See, for example, art.45(1) of the Europe Agreement establishing an association between the European Economic Communities and their Member States, of the one part, and Romania, of the other part [1994] O.J. L357.

[44] Or in turn art.49(4) (*four* years in the Croatia Agreement), art.50(4) (*five* years in the Albania Agreement), or art.53(4) (*four* years in the Montenegro Agreement).

[45] e.g. in *R. v Secretary of State for the Home Department Ex. p. Barkoci and Malik* (C-257/99) [2001] E.C.R. I-6557 and *R. v Secretary of State for the Home Department Ex. p. Kondova* (C-235/99) [2001] E.C.R. I-6427.

outcome of those proceedings. Nevertheless, it is somewhat unusual for a provision to make reference to the judgments of the CJEU in this way. It rather suggests that the parties to the Agreement were unsure themselves as to the scope of such an establishment provision. The subsequent agreements do not mention the case law of the CJEU but state (in virtually identical terms) that the Stabilisation and Association Council shall "establish the modalities to extend the above provisions to the establishment of nationals of both Parties to the Agreement to take up economic activities as self-employed persons". This has not happened at time of writing.

14–42 The right of establishment conferred on Macedonian companies in art.48 is enhanced by art.53(1) of the Macedonia Agreement[46] which gives those companies the right to post key personnel in the EU Member States if they are Macedonian nationals and are employed exclusively by the company or its subsidiary or branch.

14–43 Article 53(2) describes "key personnel" in terms similar to those previously provided for in the Europe Agreements. The details are discussed in Ch.16. It should be noted that the main difference between the key personnel provision in the Macedonian Agreement and that previously existing for the most part in the Europe Agreements is that the latter (for the most part[47]) provided that self-employed persons as well as companies had the right to deploy key personnel. As the Macedonian Agreement does not provide for the right of establishment for persons, it follows that persons can have no right to post key personnel.

14–44 Finally the Agreement provides for some co-ordination of social security systems for legally employed workers and their family members. Their periods of insurance in a Member State are to be taken into account when calculations of entitlement to old-age and invalidity pensions are made.[48]

6. AGREEMENTS WITH OTHER EUROPEAN AND CENTRAL ASIAN COUNTRIES

(a) *Background*

14–45 With the collapse of the former Soviet Union, the European Union decided to support the transition process towards market economies and democratic societies in countries of Eastern Europe and Central Asia. Thus, since the beginning of the 1990s, the European Union has developed a much more formal and political relationship with 13 countries of the region: Armenia, Azerbaijan, Belarus, Georgia, Kazakhstan, Kyrgystan, Moldova, Mongolia, Russia, Tajikistan, Turkmenistan, Ukraine and Uzbekistan. Building strong trading links is a major objective, but the overall aim is to foster

---

[46] Or in turn art.54(1) (Croatia Agreement), art.55(1) (Albania Agreement), or art.58(1) (Montenegro Agreement).
[47] The Slovakian Agreement for example confined the benefit of the key personnel provision to companies alone and did not entitle self-employed nationals to employ key personnel.
[48] art.46 of the Macedonian Stabilisation and Association Agreement (or in turn art.47 (Croatia Agreement), art.48 (Albania Agreement), or art.51 (Montenegro Agreement).

enduring political, economic and cultural links, so as to ensure peace and security.

14–46 Furthermore, with the European Union enlargement process moving eastwards, the number of EU countries sharing a border with the partner countries will indeed sharply increase. This certainly influences the dialogue between the European Union and countries from Eastern Europe and Central Asia.

14–47 The formalisation of bilateral relations between the European Union and individual partner countries has been achieved through the negotiation of Partnership and Co-operation Agreements that are now in force with all the Eastern European and Central Asian countries (with the exception of Mongolia, Turkmenistan and Belarus[49]). These nearly all entered into force on July 1, 1999 with the exception of the Agreements with Russia,[50] Moldova[51] and Ukraine.[52]

14–48 These Partnership and Co-operation Agreements are legal frameworks, based on the respect of democratic principles and human rights, setting out the political, economic and trade relationship between the European Union and its partner countries. Each Agreement is a 10-year bilateral Treaty signed and ratified by the European Union and the individual State.

(b) *Free movement provisions*

14–49 For free movement purposes all of the Partnership and Co-operation Agreements are substantially the same. The provisions of the Russian Partnership and Co-operation Agreement are used by way of example and comments made would apply equally to the agreements with the other countries.

14–50 It is perhaps unsurprising given the nature of the relationship between the European Union and these countries that there are no provisions granting any free movement rights for nationals of those countries.

14–51 There is a non-discrimination provision in relation to conditions of work, remuneration and dismissal for those Russian nationals who are lawfully working in a Member State. Article 23 states:

Article 23

1. Subject to the laws, conditions and procedures applicable in each Member State, the Community and its Member States shall ensure[53] that the treatment

---

[49] An Agreement was in fact signed in March 1995 with Belarus but it is not yet in force as it has not been ratified.
[50] December 1, 1997.
[51] July 1, 1998.
[52] March 1, 1998.
[53] Other agreements (for example with the Ukraine and Moldavia) use the phrase "shall endeavour to ensure". This however should make no difference to the declaration.

accorded to Russian nationals, legally employed in the territory of a Member State shall be free from any discrimination based on nationality, as regards working conditions, remuneration or dismissal, as compared to its own nationals.

This is very similar in wording to the non-discrimination provision which existed in the Europe Agreements (prior to accession most recently of Bulgaria and Romania). In *Simutenkov*[54] the CJEU considered a reference from a Spanish court on the interpretation of art.23 of the Russian Agreement in a case concerning a lawfully employed Russian footballer. The Spanish court asked whether art.23(1) of the Agreement precluded the application to Mr Simutenkov of a rule drawn up by the Spanish sports federation which provides that clubs may field in competitions at national level as only a limited number of players from countries which are not parties to the EEA Agreement. The question referred was not dissimilar to that in the case of *Kolpak*[55] in the context of the Slovakian Agreement. The CJEU first considered whether art.23(1) of the Russia Agreement had "direct effect". In its view the provision lay down a prohibition against discrimination "in clear, precise and unconditional terms" giving rise to "a precise obligation" as to results which could be relied on by an individual before a national court as a basis for requesting that court to disapply discriminatory provisions "without any further implementing measures being required to that end".[56] Such finding that the principle of non-discrimination was directly effective was not gainsaid by the fact that the purpose of the Russia Agreement was limited to establishing a partnership as opposed to providing for an association or future accession to the Union. As regards the scope of the non-discrimination provision, the CJEU considered its previous decision in the factually similar case of *Kolpak*. Although that case concerned the interpretation of a pre-accession agreement (the Slovakia Association Agreement), according to the CJEU it did not

14–52

> "in any way follow from the context or purpose of [the Russia] Partnership Agreement that it intended to give to the prohibition of 'discrimination based on nationality, as regards working conditions ... as compared to [the Member State's] own nationals' any meaning other than that which follows from the ordinary sense of those words".

The CJEU continued:

> 36. ...... Consequently, in a manner similar to the first indent of Article 38(1) of the Communities-Slovakia Association Agreement, Article 23(1) of the Communities-Russia Partnership Agreement establishes, for the benefit of Russian workers lawfully employed in the territory of a Member State, a right to equal treatment in working conditions of the same scope as that which, in similar terms, nationals of Member States are recognised as having under the EC Treaty, which precludes any limitation based on nationality, such as that in issue in the main proceedings,

---

[54] *Simutenkov v Abogado del Estado, Real Federacion Espanola de Futbol and Ministerio Fiscal* (C-265/03).
[55] *Deutscher Handballbund eV v Kolpak* (C-438/00) [2003] E.C.R. I-4135 (concerning a handball player).
[56] Judgment at paras 22–23.

as the Court established in similar circumstances in the above judgments in *Bosman*[57] and *Deutscher Handballbund*.[58]

Moreover, there was no objective justification for the difference in treatment between professional players who are nationals of a Member State or of a State which is a party to the EEA Agreement and, on the other, professional players who are Russian nationals. The CJEU thus held that art.23(1) of the Russia Agreement precluded the application of such a discriminatory rule as that drawn up by the Spanish sports federation.

14–53 Notwithstanding such welcome outcome, it is to be acknowledged that the provision is of limited benefit. As the CJEU has stated in relation to a similar provision in the Maghreb Agreements it does not relate to conditions of entry or residence to a Member State.[59]

14–54 Article 24 provides for some degree of co-ordination of social security systems enabling periods of employment to be included in calculations of invalidity and old-age pensions.

14–55 Additionally there is an establishment provision in each of the Agreements. Article 28 of the Russian Agreement is typical of the establishment provision in the Partnership and Co-operation Agreements:

Article 28

1. The Community and its Member States of the one part and Russia of the other part, shall grant to each other treatment no less favourable than that accorded to any third country, with regard to conditions affecting the establishment of companies in their territories and this in conformity with the legislation and regulations applicable in each Party.

14–56 It should be noted that this provision relates only to companies. Even more limiting is the fact that the provision protects the companies against discrimination compared with companies from "any third country" only, as opposed to companies from the contracting States themselves. In other words the provisions in the Partnership and Co-operation Agreements only ensure that companies from the relevant partner countries are not placed in a worse position than companies from any other third country. It is thus significantly weaker than the establishment provision for companies in either the Europe Agreements or the Macedonian Agreement.

7. Euro-Mediterranean Agreements

(a) Background

14–57 The Barcelona Declaration was adopted at the Conference of Euro-Mediterranean Foreign Ministers held in Barcelona in late November 1995. It stated the intention of the (then) 15 EU Member States and 12

---

[57] *Bosman* [1995] E.C.R. I-492 (C-415/93).
[58] *Deutscher Handballbund eV v Kolpak* (C-438/00) [2003] E.C.R. I-4135.
[59] *Nour Eddline El-Yassini v Secretary of State for Home Department* (C-416/96) [1999] E.C.R. I-1209.

Mediterranean Partners to establish a comprehensive Euro-Mediterranean partnership in order to turn the Mediterranean into a common area of peace, stability and prosperity through the reinforcement of political dialogue and security, an economic and financial partnership and a social, cultural and human partnership. This is to be achieved by means of the Euro-Mediterranean Association Agreements negotiated between the European Union and individual Mediterranean partners, to be complemented by Agreements between the partners themselves. Agreements have been signed and entered into force between the European Union and (in date order) Tunisia,[60] Morocco,[61] Israel,[62] Jordan,[63] Egypt,[64] Algeria,[65] and Lebanon.[66] An interim Association Agreement on Trade and Co-operation has been concluded between the Union and the PLO for the benefit of the Palestinian Authority. As regards Syria, negotiations are still under way.[67]

The original Co-operation Agreements between Morocco, Tunisia and Algeria (the Maghreb Agreements) were similar in terms. They have now been replaced by Euro-Mediterranean Agreements. No specific free movement rights have been included in the Euro-Mediterranean Agreements (as was the case with the Maghreb Agreements). However, the Euro Mediterranean Agreements with Tunisia, Morocco and Algeria each contain non-discrimination provisions in the field of employment and social security (as did the original Maghreb Agreements). Such provisions are not replicated in the other Euro-Mediterranean Agreements.[68] The purpose of the Maghreb and Euro-Mediterranean Agreements is to promote co-operation between the Maghreb countries. There is no intention on the part of the European Union that the Maghreb countries will join the Union at any time in the future.

14–58

---

[60] Decision 98/238/EC on March 1, 1998.
[61] Decision 2000/204/EC on March 1, 2000.
[62] Decision 2000/384/EC on June 1, 2000.
[63] Decision 2002/635/EC on May 1, 2002.
[64] Decision 2004/635/EC on June 1, 2004.
[65] Decision 2005/690/EC on September 1, 2005.
[66] Decision 2006/356/EC on April 1, 2006.
[67] Following the violent repression of anti-government protests in Syria from mid-March 2011, the EU took a number of restrictive measures against Syria: 1) an embargo on arms and equipment that can be used for internal repression, and 2) targeted sanctions (a travel ban and asset freeze) against those responsible for or associated with the repression (see *http://www.eeas.europa.eu/syria/index_en.htm* [Accessed February 2012]).
[68] The highpoint is the Egyptian Agreement which refers at art.62 to the fact that the parties "reaffirm the importance they attach to the fair treatment of their workers legally residing and employed in the territory of the other Party" and states that "the Member States and Egypt, at the request of any of them, agree to initiate talks on reciprocal bilateral agreements related to the working conditions and social security rights of Egyptian and Member State workers legally resident and employed in their respective territory". The Jordan Agreements (art.80(1)–(2)) states that "a regular dialogue shall be established between the Parties on all social issues of mutual interest" and that "this dialogue shall be used to seek ways and means to further progress as regards the movement of workers and the equal treatment and social integration of Jordanian and Community nationals legally residing in their host countries".
The Lebanon Agreement (art.64) has similar provion as regards dialogue as the Jordan Agreement.

(b) *Free movement provisions*

14–59 The main provision of interest in the field of free movement of persons is art.67(1) of the EC-Algeria Euro-Mediterranean Agreement (replicated in all the Maghreb Agreements but not the other Euro-Mediterranean Agreements) which states:

Article 67(1)

> Each Member State shall accord to workers of Algerian nationality employed in its territory treatment which is free from any discrimination based on nationality, as regards working conditions, remuneration and dismissal, relative to its own nationals.

14–60 The provision replicates the non-discrimination provision relating to workers in the Stabilisation and Association Agreements (with Macedonia, Croatia, Albania and Montenegro) and the Partnership and Co-operation Agreements (with all the Eastern European and Central Asian countries (except Mongolia, Turkmenistan and Belarus). The former are pre-accession agreements. The question is therefore whether art.67(1) would be interpreted consistently with the provisions in those other agreements.

14–61 In *El-Yassini*,[69] a Moroccan national attempted to rely on the non-discrimination provision in Art.40 of the Moroccan Agreement[70] to derive a right to remain in the United Kingdom where he had been lawfully resident and working previously as the spouse of a British citizen. The CJEU found that the non-discrimination provision in the Agreement was capable of direct effect and thus individuals can rely upon it in national courts. However, the CJEU considered that the narrow scope of the non-discrimination provision meant that it did not extend to rights of entry and stay in a Member State but only to the conditions under which a person is employed there. The Member State is thus not prohibited from refusing to extend a residence permit of a Moroccan national whom it previously authorised to enter its territory and to take up employment where the reason for granting entry and stay—in that case marriage—no longer exists. According to the CJEU,[71] the fact that this meant Mr El-Yassini had to terminate his employment before the end of his contract was "as a general rule" irrelevant. However, the situation would be different if the host Member State had granted the Moroccan migrant worker specific rights in relation to employment which were more extensive his right of residence. This would be the case if, for example, the person had a residence permit for a period shorter than the duration of their work permit. In such a case, refusal to extend the residence permit could be justified only on public policy, public security or public health grounds.

---

[69] *Nour Eddline El-Yassini v Secretary of State for Home Department* (C-416/96) [1999] E.C.R. I-1209.

[70] See now art.64 of the Moroccan Euro-Mediterranean Agreement.

[71] *Nour Eddline El-Yassini v Secretary of State for Home Department* (C-416/96) [1999] E.C.R. I-1209 at [63].

14–62 The wording of art.40 of the Moroccan Agreement is on its face restricted to conditions of work and remuneration. In *El Yassini*[72] the CJEU stated that, absent any provisions in the Agreement that equated to the provisions relating to workers in the Ankara Agreement or Decision 1/80 of the Council of Association to that Agreement, no such provisions could be inferred.[73] The decision is important for the interpretation of equivalent non-discrimination provisions in other agreements with non-accession countries. This is because the CJEU held that the fact that the Moroccan Agreement is not a pre-accession agreement did not prevent art.40 from having direct effect. Indeed the narrow interpretation of the scope of art.40 is not influenced by the fact that it is not a pre-accession agreement since none of the equivalent provisions in the pre-accession agreements have been interpreted to extend to conditions of entry and stay.[74] Such narrow interpretation does not deprive the non-discrimination provision of any purpose since the CJEU has interpreted conditions of work broadly.

14–63 In *Mohamed Gattoussi v Stadt Rüsselsheim*[75] the CJEU considered the non-discrimination provision in art.64(1) of the Euro-Mediterranean Agreement with Tunisia. The facts were similar to those in *El-Yassini*. Mr Gattoussi married a German citizen and on September 24, 2002 was granted a residence permit valid for three years. On being informed by Mr Gattoussi's wife that she had been living apart from her husband since April 1, 2004, the Mayor of Rüsselsheim on June 23, 2004 curtailed the period of validity of his residence permit and required him to leave Germany without delay or face deportation to Tunisia. The crucial factual difference compared to the situation of Mr El-Yassini however was that Mr Gattoussi had been granted a work permit of indefinite duration (and had worked on a one-year fixed contract that had subsequently been extended to March 31, 2005). Applying similar reasoning to that in *El-Yassini*, the CJEU reiterated that since the Euro-Mediterranean Agreement was not intended to secure any kind of freedom of movement for workers, a Member State could not be prohibited in principle from taking measures concerning the right to remain of a Tunisian national whom it has previously authorised to enter its territory and to engage in gainful employment there. Moreover, this position was not as a general rule altered by the consequential loss of employment. According to the CJEU, however, this did not mean that a Tunisian national could never rely on the prohibition of discrimination to contest a measure taken by a Member State in limitation of their right to remain. As the CJEU stated, it would be

---

[72] *Nour Eddline El-Yassini v Secretary of State for Home Department* (C-416/96) [1999] E.C.R. I-1209.
[73] The CJEU did state that the situation would be different if the Member State had granted the person concerned a residence permit for a period shorter than their work permit and if, before the expiry of the work permit, it refused to extend the residence permit without reference to reasons of public policy, public security or public health.
In the UK this would have little benefit given that it is usually the case that it is the person's immigration status which dictates their ability to work rather than other way round. It is very unlikely that the situation envisaged by the CJEU would therefore even arise.
[74] See, for example, *Deutscher Handballbund eV v Kolpak* (C-438/00) [2003] E.C.R. I-4135.
[75] *Mohamed Gattoussi v Stadt Rüsselsheim* (C-978/05).

"quite unacceptable for the Member States to deal with the principle of non-discrimination ... by using provisions of national law to limit its effectiveness".

And in *El-Yassini* the Court had already held that where rights given in relation to employment are more extensive than the rights of residence, then the Member State cannot then

"reopen the question of that worker's situation on grounds unrelated to the protection of a legitimate national interest such as public policy, public security or public health".

The CJEU continued:

"42. In the light of the principles of the protection of legitimate expectations and of legal certainty, the rule referred to in paragraph 40 applies a fortiori in cases, such as that before the national court, in which permission to remain has been limited by the host Member State retroactively.

43. It follows from all of the foregoing that, on a proper construction of Article 64(1) of the Euro-Mediterranean Agreement, that provision may have effects on the right of a Tunisian national to remain in the territory of a Member State in the case where that person has been duly permitted by that Member State to work there for a period extending beyond the period of validity of his permission to remain."

14–64 The Euro-Mediterranean Agreements with Tunisia, Morocco and Algeria further provide for non-discrimination of lawfully resident workers and their families in the social security field[76] (as did the previous Maghreb Agreements). As put in art.65(1) of the Tunisian Euro-Mediterranean Agreement (by way of example), the concept of social security covers the branches of social security dealing with sickness and maternity benefits, invalidity, old-age and survivors' benefits, industrial accident and occupational disease benefits and death, unemployment, and family benefits. The CJEU has also held that these provisions are capable of direct effect.[77] In *Echouikh*[78] the CJEU held that art.65(1) of the Moroccan Euro-Mediterranean Agreement had to be interpreted as precluding the host Member State from refusing to grant an armed services invalidity pension to a Moroccan national who had served in the French armed forces on the sole ground that the person concerned was of Moroccan nationality.

14–65 Finally, it is to be emphasised that the worker must be a national of the relevant country. In *Mesbah*[79] the CJEU considered a case involving a Moroccan family member of a worker who sought to rely on her son-in-law's Moroccan nationality to receive disability allowance based on the non-discrimination obligation extending to the family member of a Moroccan national worker. According to the order for reference, the son-in-law had acquired Belgian nationality by naturalisation some years previously and

---

[76] art.68 of the Algerian Euro-Mediterrean Agreement, art.65 of the Moroccan Euro-Mediterranean Agreement, and art.65 of the Tunisian Euro-Mediterranean Agreement.
[77] *Office National de l'Emploi v Kziber* (C-18/90) [1991] E.C.R. I-199.
[78] *Ameur Echouikh v Secretaire d'etat aux anciens combatants* (C-336/05) [2006] E.C.R. I-5223.
[79] *Belgian State v Fatna Mesbah* [1999] E.C.R. I-07955.

the national court had started from the premise that in the eyes of Belgian law he had thereby lost his Moroccan nationality. Even although under Moroccan law he retained the nationality of his State of origin, the CJEU held that EU law did not preclude Belgian law from treating him as a national of Belgium alone. The son-in-law's nationality was a matter for determination by the national court and unless that court considered him to be Moroccan, Mrs Mesbah could not rely on the non-discrimination provision.[80]

8. Agreements with African, Caribbean and Pacific Countries

(a) *Background*

14–66 Relations between the European Union and the African, Caribbean and Pacific States ("ACP States") have developed as a combination of aid, trade and political co-operation. These special EU-ACP relations date back to the Treaty of Rome. At that time, the first of today's ACP States (mainly in Africa) were dependent countries and territories of some of the founding Member States. According to art.131 of the Treaty of Rome their association with the European Union was made in order "to promote (their) economic and social development ... and to establish close economic relations between them and the Community as a whole".

14–67 Following independence in the 1960s, the first Yaoundé Convention was negotiated with 18 of these former French dependent countries and territories (1963). These States are referred to as the Associated African States and Madagascar (AASMs). Yaoundé II followed in 1969 to include Kenya, Tanzania and Uganda. Then, after the accession of the United Kingdom to the Community, came the first Lomé Convention, signed in 1975 (with 46 ACP States), Lomé II in 1979 (with 58 ACP States), Lomé III in 1984 (with 65 ACP States), and Lomé IV in 1989 (with 68 ACP States, extended in 1995 to 70 ACP States).

14–68 The Lomé Conventions set out the principles and objectives to co-operation between the European Union[81] and the ACP States. Their main characteristics were the partnership principle, the contractual nature of the relationship, and development of relations in matters of aid, trade and political co-operation. Moreover the Conventions emphasise the objective of lasting partnership between the European Union and the ACP States.

---

[80] *Belgian State v Fatna Mesbah* (C–179/98) is of interest also because of the broad definition applied to the term "members of the family" to include not only the worker's spouse and children, but also "other relatives of the worker, such as, in particular, relatives in the ascending line" and not only such relatives "confined to members of the same blood as the worker ... including those related by marriage" (at [44–46]).
[81] At the time the European Community.

14–69 In February 2000 the expiration of the Lomé Conventions provided the opportunity for a thorough review of the future of EU-ACP relations. The new EU-ACP Agreement was signed on June 23, 2000 in Cotonou, Benin.[82] The Agreement was concluded for a 20-year period from March 2000 to February 2020, and entered into force in April 2003. In June 2005 it was revised for the first time, with the revision entering into force on July 1, 2008. A second revision (which adapts the partnership to changes which had taken place over the previous decade[83]) was agreed on March 11, 2010.[84] The Cotonou Agreement is a global agreement, introducing changes and objectives while preserving the "acquis" of 25 years of ACP-EC co-operation. The Agreement is designed to establish a comprehensive partnership, based on three complementary pillars: development co-operation, economic and trade co-operation and the political dimension. At present, 79 ACP countries are signatories to the Cotonou Agreement.[85] The Agreement entered into force on April 1, 2003.

(b) *Free movement provisions*

14–70 Despite the extent and duration of co-operation between the European Union and the ACP States reflected by the wide ranging scope of the Conventions referred to above, these Agreements are all essentially trade and development agreements only. There is nothing in the Agreements which confers any rights relating to free movement of persons.

14–71 Article 13(3) of the Cotonou Agreement prohibits discrimination against workers of ACP countries legally employed in their territory:

> "The treatment accorded by each Member State to workers of ACP countries legally employed in its territory, shall be free from any discrimination based on nationality, as regards working conditions, remuneration and dismissal, relative to its own nationals. Further in this regard, each ACP State shall accord comparable non-discriminatory treatment to workers who are nationals of a Member State."

14–72 Attempts have been made to derive benefits from the equivalent non-discrimination provision in the Lomé Conventions. However the CJEU has held in the past that the non-discrimination provisions in the Lomé Conventions for instance did not prohibit different treatment between Union

---

[82] Partnership Agreement between the members of the African, Caribbean and Pacific Group of States of the one part, and the European Community and its Member States, of the other part, signed in Cotonou on June 23, 2000 [2000] O.J. L317/3.
[83] http://www.ec.europa.eu/europeaid/where/acp/overview/cotonou-agreement/index_en.htm [Accessed February 2012].
[84] http://www.ec.europa.eu/development/icenter/repository/second_revision_cotonou_agreement_20100311.pdf [Accessed February 2012].
[85] For a fuller description of the developments in EU-ACP relations see C. Björnskov and E. Krivonos, *From Lomé to Cotonou: The new EU-ACP Agreement*, Danish Institute of Agricultural and Fisheries Economics, IFPRI and University of Maryland (see further at http://www.ictsd.org/ issarea/ag/resources/RegEU.pdf [Accessed February 2012]).

citizens and ACP nationals or even between different ACP nationals.[86] That said, the non-discrimination provision in the first Lomé Convention had an express reservation which provided that Member States and the ACP States were not bound to accord such equal treatment.[87] The non-discrimination provision in the Contonou Agreement has no such reservation attached and there is no reason in principle why it would not be considered in the same way as the non-discrimination provisions in other agreements, such as the Partnership and Co-operation Agreements and Maghreb Agreements.[88]

9. ASSOCIATION AGREEMENT WITH CHILE

(a) Background

Two Political Dialogue and Co-operation Agreements have been negotiated between the European Community and countries in Central and Latin America (known collectively as MERCOSUR): one with the Andean Community and its member countries (Bolivia, Colombia, Ecuador, Peru and Venezuela); and the other with Central American countries (the Republics of Costa Rica, El Salvador, Guatemala, Honduras, Nicaragua and Panama). These Agreements are not association agreements, although they are seen as an intermediate step towards better trade relations. They are primarily aimed at political and economic dialogue. **14–73**

A separate Association Agreement exists however with Chile. The objective of establishing a political and economic Association Agreement between the European Union and Chile was formulated in the 1996 Framework Co-operation Agreement. This Agreement constituted the basis that allowed the Commission to present directives for negotiations to the Council in July 1998. At the first EU and Latin American and Caribbean Summit, which took place on June 28–29, 1999 in Rio de Janeiro, the Heads of State of MERCUSOR countries and Chile, as well as of the European Union, strongly reaffirmed the objective of establishing a political and economic association in their common declaration. **14–74**

The Association Agreement was signed on November 18, 2002. It has been in force since March 1, 2005. The Agreement covers the main aspects of the Union's relations with Chile.[89] The Agreement deals with trade (and more specifically trade in goods, government procurement, competition, services, **14–75**

---

[86] *Ratzanatsimba* (65/77) [1978] 1 C.M.L.R. 246. In *Poirrez v CAF de la Seine-Saint-Denis* (C-206/91) [1992] E.C.R. I-6685, which concerned access to disability benefits for the adoptive son from the Ivory Coast of a French national. The CJEU did not refer to the Lomé Conventions and considered that as the French national adoptive father had not exercised his free movement rights anywhere in the Community, his situation was purely internal and therefore not covered by Community law.
[87] art.65 of the first Lomé Covention signed in 1975.
[88] See comments above in relation to the Maghreb Agreements and *Nour Eddline El-Yassini v Secretary of State for Home Department* (C-416/96) [1999] E.C.R. I-1209.
[89] In September 2002 the Union and Chile also signed an Agreement on scientific and technoclogical co-operation, and in June 2005 adopted a Horizontal Agreement with Chile in the field of Air transport.

establishment, current payments and capital movements, and intellectual property rights), co-operation and political dialogue.

(b) *Free movement provisions*

14–76 Of principal interest in the Chilean Agreement is the inclusion of an establishment provision contained in Chapter III of Title III (Trade in Services and Establishment). Article 132 states:

Article 132

In the sectors inscribed in Annex X, and subject to any conditions and qualifications set out therein, with respect to establishment, each Party shall grant to legal and natural persons of the other Party treatment no less favourable than that it accords to its own legal and natural persons performing a like economic activity.

Annex X contains various limitations on establishment in certain industries or sectors in different Member States.

14–77 Article 134 (Final Provisions) contains a provision affirming the right of Contracting Parties to have in place their own laws relating to entry, stay, working conditions and establishment providing that such laws do not "nullify or impair" the rights contained in the Agreement.

14–78 The language of arts 132 and 134 is very similar to that which was contained in the establishment provisions in the (now redundant) Europe Agreements.[90] To that extent the provisions in the Chilean Agreement must be said to be "clear and precise" just as they were in the Europe Agreements. However, there is a vital difference between the Chilean Agreement and the Europe Agreements which relates to the future intentions of the European Union. Whilst the Chilean Agreement is intended as an instrument to forge better economic relations with the Union, the Europe Agreements were a tool to accession. This aspect of the Europe Agreements influenced considerably the manner in which their provisions were interpreted by the CJEU. It remains to be seen whether for instance the CJEU would afford a provision in the Chilean Agreement direct effect. Support for such possibility is undoubtedly to be found in the approach taken to, for example, art.23(1) of the Russia Agreement.[91] However, even if it did, it is inevitable that the interpretation of the scope of any such provision would likely be circumscribed by the Agreement's limited objectives.

---

[90] Namely the Bulgarian and Romanian Agreements prior to the accession of those countries to the Union.
[91] See above at paras 14–51 to 14–52.

CHAPTER 15

ASSOCIATION AGREEMENTS IN COMMUNITY LAW

This chapter examines the European Union law context of Association Agreements with third countries as an overview to both the Ankara Agreement and the Stabilisation and Association Agreements.

1. INTRODUCTION

The Ankara Agreement and the Stabilisation and Association Agreements are referred to collectively in this chapter as "the Association Agreements". Focus is placed on these Association Agreements because of the intention that the third countries party to the Agreements will eventually accede to the European Union. Furthermore, the Ankara Agreement confers certain rights of free movement on Turkish nationals, whilst the SAAs also confer some rights on nationals of Macedonia, Croatia, Albania and Montenegro (albeit more limited than those granted to Turkish nationals and than those previously given under the Europe Agreements to nationals of those Eastern European States which joined the Union in 2004 and 2007). The CJEU's case law arising from consideration of provisions of the Europe Agreements[1] is referred to below since the approach taken to those cases would undoubtedly also be taken to the interpretation of similar provisions in the SAAs. Other association and co-operation agreements are founded on different aims and therefore interpretation of their provisions may be different.[2] Furthermore, other association agreements appear not to make specific provisions regarding the free movement of persons and at best include a non-discrimination provision relating to conditions of work.[3]

15–01

2. MIXED AGREEMENTS

The Association Agreements are mixed agreements. European Union law recognises three types of international agreement: first, where obligations and fulfilment of the agreement lie exclusively with the European Union, secondly where competence falls exclusively to the Member States, and thirdly where competence is shared between the EU and the Member States. The Association Agreements fall into this third category since the

15–02

---

[1] That is the pre-accession agreements with those (mainly eastern European) States which joined the Union in 2004 and 2007.
[2] See, for example, in relation to the Moroccan Agreement, *Nour Eddline El-Yassini v Secretary of State for Home Department* (C-416/96) [1999] E.C.R. I-1209.
[3] Which in the context of the Maghreb Agreements has already been held by the CJEU to confer no rights as regards entry and residence of persons, see *Nour Eddline El-Yassini v Secretary of State for Home Department* (C-416/96) [1999] E.C.R. I-1209.

Agreements are concluded between the EU, the Member States and a third non-member country.

15–03 The CJEU first ruled that an association agreement could be a mixed agreement in *Demirel*.[4] That case concerned the interpretation of specific provisions of the Ankara Agreement. It considered that an agreement concluded by the Council under arts 300 and 310 EC Treaty (now replaced by arts 217 and 218 TFEU) is an act of one of the institutions of the European Union and "from its entry into force, the provisions of such an agreement form an integral part of the [Union] legal system".

15–04 The United Kingdom and German Governments had argued in *Demirel*[5] that in the case of mixed agreements the delineation between Union and Member State competence was clear, and that in areas where the Member State has entered into specific commitments with regard to the third country, the Member State had exclusive competence.

15–05 The CJEU rejected this delineation and stated that any matter which generally falls within the scope of the EC Treaty (now the Treaty on the Functioning of the European Union), would fall within "Community competence" (referred to hereafter as 'Union competence') since the Union would guarantee the commitment towards non-Member States in all the fields covered by the TFEU. The CJEU emphasised the need for a common approach to the interpretation of obligations under an agreement to ensure uniformity.[6] The CJEU has in effect described this relationship as one in which the Member States act as if agents for the Union in the fulfilment of obligations towards the third country:

> "in ensuring respect for commitments arising from an agreement concluded by the Community institutions, the Member States fulfil, within the Community system, an obligation in relation to the Community, which has assumed responsibility for the due performance of the agreement".[7]

15–06 Given this general approach it is unsurprising that, where issues of competence arise regarding any aspect of free movement of persons, the CJEU has maintained a firm grip on competence for the Union institutions.[8] This is regardless of the fact that the Association Agreements do not explicitly grant unfettered free movement rights for persons but refer to the ability of Member States to have in place national rules on conditions of entry and stay.[9]

---

[4] *Demirel v Stadt Schwäbisch Gmünd* (12/86) [1987] E.C.R. 3719.
[5] *Demirel v Stadt Schwäbisch Gmünd* (12/86) [1987] E.C.R. 3719.
[6] *Demirel v Stadt Schwäbisch Gmünd* (12/86) [1987] E.C.R. 3719, at [9].
[7] *Commission v Ireland* (C-13/00) [2002] E.C.R. I-2943, at [15].
[8] See *Sevince v Staatssecretaris van Justitite* (C-192/89) [1990] E.C.R. I-3461 which relates to interpretation of Member State obligations towards Turkish workers under the Ankara Agreement; see also, *R. v Secretary of State for the Home Department Ex p. Kondova* (C-235/99) [2001] E.C.R. I-6427 relating to the interpretation of Member State obligations towards a Polish self-employed national under the Europe Agreements.
[9] e.g. art.62 of the Macedonia Agreement.

The fact that a matter is said to fall within Union competence does not mean that European Union rules will automatically replace national rules. If an agreement stipulates that national rules may be applied, the CJEU will not stand in the way of the application and implementation of those national rules. However, the CJEU retains for itself and the Commission the role of supervising the implementation of the substantive provisions of the Agreements and ensuring uniformity and general adherence to European Union standards. **15–07**

When in force the Europe Agreements had provided a right of establishment for each pre-accession State's nationals and companies.[10] The SAAs provide the same right for companies, although not for individuals (see paras 14–39—14-43 above). However, the Europe Agreements referred to the fact that Member States may retain their own laws as regards entry and stay creating an inherent tension in the Agreements.[11] There is an identical provision in the SAAs.[12] The task of the CJEU has been to reconcile that tension and ensure that Member States' legislation is compatible with the Agreements. The judgments of the CJEU on the Europe Agreements even in areas concerned with national laws are replete with references to European Union law concepts and principles such as proportionality, non-discrimination and adherence to human rights.[13] The same approach would undoubtedly be taken to the SAAs. **15–08**

The CJEU has taken a very similar approach in other fields outside the free movement of persons in relation to agreements with third countries. In *Commission v Ireland*[14] the Irish authorities had failed to give effect to the Berne Convention, relating to the protection of literary and artistic works, the provisions of which Member States must adhere to under Protocol 28 of the EEA Agreement. The CJEU considered that since Union legislation touches upon broad areas of intellectual property and protection of databases and copyright, there was sufficient overlap such that there would be "a Community interest in ensuring that all Contracting Parties to the EEA Agreement adhere to that Convention". The CJEU held that as a consequence the Commission was charged with assessing compliance with the Berne Convention, subject to review by the CJEU.[15] **15–09**

3. THE AGREEMENTS AS A TOOL TO ACCESSION

The Ankara Agreement and the Stabilsation and Association Agreements are "pre-accession" agreements. The intention that the Turkey will eventually become a full Member State of the European Union is clearly stated in the Preamble to the Ankara Agreement. In the SAAs with Macedonia, **15–10**

---

[10] See, for example, in relation to Bulgaria art.45 of the EC-Bulgaria Association Agreement.
[11] art.59 of the Bulgaria Agreement.
[12] See, for example, art.62 of the Macedonia Agreement.
[13] See, for instance, judgment in *R. v Secretary of State for the Home Department Ex p. Gloszczuk and Gloszczuk* (C-63/99) [2001] E.C.R. I-6369, at [41], [84], and [85].
[14] *Commission v Ireland* (C-13/00) [2002] E.C.R. I-2943, at [15].
[15] *Commission v Ireland* (C-13/00) [2002] E.C.R. I-2943, at [21].

Croatia and Albania the Preambles each recall in the same terms the Union's readiness to integrate each State to the fullest possible extent "into the political and economic mainstream of Europe and its status as a potential candidate for EU membership". As described by the Commission,[16] the stabilisation and association process (the framework for EU negotiations with the Western Balkan countries) itself has as its third aim "eventual membership of the EU".

15–11 The use of an association agreement as a tool towards accession was first employed with Greece. The Union entered into an Association agreement in 1961. Two years later the Ankara Agreement was signed with Turkey. Article 28 contained a specific provision stating that parties to the Agreement would "examine the possibility of the accession of Turkey to the Community".[17] The Additional Protocol signed in 1970 sets out a specific programme of 12–22 years for the completion of a customs union and full free movement rights for workers.[18] If such progression had been made within the timetable set, Turkey would have secured a substantial proportion of the core benefits of full EU membership. As it is, progression has been hampered by civil and economic problems that have plagued Turkey since the early 1980s.

15–12 The accession to the European Union of the Central and Eastern European countries had been rumoured ever since the fall of the Berlin Wall in 1989. Mandates to negotiate association agreements to prepare those countries to accede to the European Union were issued in 1989 and by 1994 when the first two Association Agreements with Poland and Hungary were signed.[19] At the 1995 Madrid Council meeting a timetable for the accession of Central and Eastern European countries was laid down with the possibility of the first wave of applicant countries, being admitted as early as 2000. In fact the first wave did not take place until May 1, 2004 with eight of the countries, (together with Malta and Cyprus) becoming full members. Bulgaria and Romania were the last of the Central and Eastern European countries to join the European Union which happened on January 1, 2007.

15–13 As regards the SAAs, the European Union's policy towards the Western Balkans is described at paras 14–30—14–35 above. The prospect of eventually becoming full members of the European Union was offered at the Feira European Council in June 2000. In June 2003 the Thessalonika European Council meeting confirmed the Stabilisation and Association Process as the EU's policy for the Western Balkans with participating countries being eligible for EU accession. Croatia, Montenegro Macedonia and Albania are all candidate countries at time of writing.

---

[16] See http://www.ec.europa.eu/enlargement/enlargement_process/accession_process/how_does_a_country_join_the_eu/sap/index_en.htm [Accessed February 2012].
[17] art.28 of the Ankara Agreement.
[18] art.36 of the Additional Protocol to the Ankara Agreement, see Ch.18.
[19] These were followed in 1995 with Association Agreements signed with Bulgaria, Czech Republic, Romania and Slovakia and in 1998 with Agreements signed with Estonia, Latvia and Lithuania.

The importance of an association agreement being employed as a tool to accession is that it represents a statement of future intentions of the parties and an instrument to facilitate the gradual movement towards the objective of eventual accession. It is with this in mind that the CJEU will give provisions contained in such an agreement a purposive interpretation and so far as is possible construe provisions consistently with similar European Union law provisions.[20]

15–14

4. Jurisdiction of the CJEU

Article 267 Treaty on the Functioning of the European Union provides:

15–15

> The Court of Justice of the European Union shall have jurisdiction to give preliminary rulings concerning:
> (a) the interpretation of the Treaties[21];
> (b) the validity and interpretation of acts of the institutions, bodies, offices or agencies of the Union;
>
> Where such a question is raised before any court or tribunal of a Member State, that court or tribunal may, if it considers that a decision on the question is necessary to enable it to give judgment, request the Court to give a ruling thereon.
>
> Where any such question is raised in a case pending before a court or tribunal of a Member State against whose decisions there is no judicial remedy under national law, that court or tribunal shall bring the matter before the Court.
>
> If such a question is raised in a case pending before a court or tribunal of a Member State with regard to a person in custody, the Court of Justice of the European Union shall act with the minimum of delay.

The CJEU clearly regards any Agreement concluded under arts 217 and 218 TFEU as "an act of one of the institutions of the Union" (to paraphrase art.267(b) TFEU) and its provisions form "an integral part of the (European Union) legal system".[22] This gives the CJEU jurisdiction to give preliminary rulings concerning the validity and interpretation of an agreement concluded under arts 217 and 218 TFEU.

15–16

CJEU first considered its jurisdiction in relation to an association agreement in the case of *Haegeman*[23] which concerned the interpretation of the Association Agreement with Greece. The CJEU was of the unequivocal view that the Agreement, concluded under art.310 EC Treaty (now arts 217 and 218 TFEU), was "an act of one of the institutions of the Community" within the

15–17

---

[20] See, for instance, *Jany v Staatssecretaris van Justitite* (C-268/99) [2001] E.C.R. I-8615, where the CJEU interpreted provisions relating to exclusion on public policy, public security and public health in the Europe Agreements consistently with interpretation given to such provisions in Community law.
[21] "The Treaties" are the Treaty on European Union and the Treaty on the Functioning of the European Union (art.1 TEU).
[22] See *Demirel v Stadt Schwäbisch Gmünd* (12/86) [1987] E.C.R. 3719, at [7].
[23] *Haegeman v Belgium* (181/73) [1974] E.C.R. 449.

meaning of art.234 EC Treaty (now art.267 TFEU). In fact Belgium had not questioned the ability of the CJEU to give a preliminary ruling and the CJEU appears to have affirmed its own jurisdiction unprompted.

15–18 When the first case was referred to the CJEU on the interpretation of the Ankara Agreement some Member States were less convinced of the CJEU's jurisdiction, at least when it came to issues relating to the exercise of the Member States' own powers under the Ankara Agreement.[24] The United Kingdom and Germany argued that the provisions on freedom of movement for workers were dependant on the exercise of the Member States' own powers to permit entry and residence in the first instance.

15–19 The CJEU recalled its decision in *Haegeman* regarding the integral part in the European Union legal order that such agreements played. The CJEU rejected the suggestion that its jurisdiction could be ousted on the basis that it was for Member States to lay down the rules necessary to give effect in their territory to the provisions of the Agreement. The CJEU reached its decision on the basis that in fact Member States fulfil an obligation under the Agreement on behalf of the Union, since it is the Union which assumes "responsibility for the due performance of the agreement."[25]

15–20 In the next case referred to the CJEU regarding the Ankara Agreement, the question arose concerning the CJEU's jurisdiction to interpret decisions of the Council of Association. The Council of Association is a body established under each of the Association Agreements with the power to take decisions in order to attain the objectives laid down under the Agreements. The Council of Association established under arts 22 and 23 of the Ankara Agreement for instance has taken a number of decisions relating to the implementation of provisions in the Agreement on free movement of workers. In the context of these decisions the CJEU repeated its opinion (previously stated in respect of the Association Agreement with Greece and decisions of the Council of Association[26] established under it) that:

> "since they are directly connected with the Agreement to which they give effect, the decisions of the Council of Association, in the same way as the Agreement itself, form an integral part, as from their entry into force, of the Community legal system".[27]

15–21 It is apparent the CJEU considers that since it has jurisdiction to give preliminary rulings under art.267 TFEU on the Ankara Agreement itself, it must have jurisdiction to give rulings on the decisions of the body entrusted under the Agreement with the responsibility of giving effect to its provisions. Decisions of the Council of Association are in that sense akin to secondary legislation, such as Regulation 1612/68 giving effect to provisions of the TFEU.

---

[24] *Demirel v Stadt Schwäbisch Gmünd* (12/86) [1987] E.C.R. 3719, at [6].
[25] *Demirel v Stadt Schwäbisch Gmünd* (12/86) [1987] E.C.R. 3719, at [12].
[26] *Greece v Commission* (30/88) [1989] E.C.R. 449.
[27] *Sevince v Staatsecretaris Van Justitite* (C-192/89) [1990] E.C.R. I-3461, at [9].

Direct Effect

15–22 The concern of Member States to retain within their preserve the interpretation of the Association Agreements did not stop there. In 1992 in the case of *Kus*[28] the German Government requested the CJEU to reconsider its jurisdiction to give preliminary rulings on the interpretation of decisions of the Council of Association. The CJEU refused to do so on the basis that the German Government had failed to put forward any new reasons why its jurisdiction should be limited.

15–23 In relation to the (now redundant) Europe Agreements, the Member States appeared to have more readily accepted the CJEU's jurisdiction to interpret the Agreements. This may have reflected their confidence that the CJEU would not be able to confer any directly effective rights on individuals from the provisions of the Europe Agreements and therefore that the CJEU's interference would do little to obstruct their sovereign rights to control the entry and stay of non-EU nationals.[29] As regards Council of Association decisions, none "was" made of relevance to the free movement of persons under the Europe Agreements and therefore the jurisdiction of the CJEU in relation to such decisions did not arise. As regards the SAAs, rights given are even less than under the Europe Agreements (most obviously unlike under the Europe Agreements no individual right of establishment is given). As yet there have been no cases under the SAAs considered by the CJEU. Were there to be such cases the result would undoubtedly be the same as that under the Greek Association Agreement and the Ankara Agreement.

5. Direct Effect

15–24 The relationship between domestic and Community law is discussed in detail in Ch.2. The concept of direct effect is integral to that relationship. A detailed analysis of the concept of direct effect is contained in Ch.2. Shortly stated, the concept, established by the CJEU in *Van Gend en Loos*,[30] means that a provision of European Union law can be relied on directly by an individual before national authorities and courts.

15–25 In essence the criteria laid down in *Van Geed en Loos* identify whether a provision is capable as it stands of judicial enforcement. Provisions which lay down general objectives for instance will not be directly effective.

15–26 The CJEU has held that provisions of the Association Agreements are capable of being directly effective, although many will not be due to their programmatic or imprecise nature. As the CJEU has pointed out in relation

---

[28] *Kuz Landeshauptstadt* (C-237/91) [1992] E.C.R. I-6781.
[29] See para.15–24 et seq. below for a discussion about direct effect.
[30] *Van Gend en Loos v Nederlandse Administratie der Berlastingen* (26/62) [1963] E.C.R. 1.

to the Ankara Agreement, Association Agreements often set out aims of the association without establishing the detailed rules for the attainment of those aims. Further, a non-discrimination provision of the Russian Partnership and Co-operation Agreement (not a pre-accession agreement) was held to have direct effect by the CJEU in *Simutenkov*.[31]

15–27 In order to establish whether a provision has a direct effect the general approach of the CJEU is first to examine the provision in question to establish its precision and clarity; then to consider whether further implementation would be required in order for the provision to be able to be *relied* upon; and finally to consider whether there is anything in the general structure of an agreement or the general aims of an agreement which would prevent it from being capable of direct effect.

15–28 Very few of the provisions of the Ankara Agreement itself for instance have been held to be directly effective because of their structure and lack of specific rules. Article 12 of the Agreement (relating to free movement of workers)[32] was described by the CJEU as being essentially programmatic and lacking in sufficient precision to be capable of conferring directly effective rights on individuals.[33] By contrast art.41(1) of the Additional Protocol,[34] a standstill provision relating to establishment of persons, was held to be sufficiently precise and "unequivocal".[35] The CJEU noted its similarity in wording to art.53 of the Treaty of Rome (a provision now repealed by Amsterdam Treaty) which it had already held to have direct effect.

15–29 The CJEU has found that many of the decisions of the Council of Association, which give effect to the programmes set out in the Ankara Agreement, are capable of direct effect. In *Sevince*[36] the CJEU stated:

> "Decisions 2/76 and 1/80 were adopted by the Council of Association in order to implement Article 12 of the Agreement and Article 36 of the Additional Protocol which, in its judgment in *Demirel* the Court recognised as being intended essentially to set out a programme ... The fact that the above mentioned provisions of the Agreement and the Additional Protocol essentially set out a programme does not prevent the decisions of the Council of Association which give effect in specific respects to the programmes envisaged in the Agreement from having direct effect."

---

[31] *Simutenkov v Abogado del Estado, Real Federacion Espanola de Futbol and Ministerio Fiscal* (C-265/03) [2005] E.C.R. I-2579 according to the CJEU art.23(1) of the Russia Agreement lay down a prohibition against discrimination "in clear, precise and unconditional terms" giving rise to "a precise obligation" as to results which could be relied on by an individual before a national court as a basis for requesting that court to disapply discriminatory provisions "without any further implementing measures being required to that end" (at paras 22–23).
[32] "The Contracting Parties agree to be guided by Articles 48, 49 and 50 of the Treaty establishing the Community for the propose of progressively securing freedom of movement for workers between them".
[33] *Meryem Demirel v Stadt Schwäbisch Gmünd* (12/86) [1987] E.C.R. 3719, at [23].
[34] "The Contracting Parties shall refrain from introducing between themselves any new restrictions on the freedom of establishment and the freedom to provide services."
[35] *The Queen v Secretary of State for the Home Department, Ex p. Savas* (C-37/98) [2000] E.C.R. I-2927.
[36] *Sevince v Staatsecretaris Van Justitite* (C-192/89) [1990] E.C.R. I-3461, at [21].

This conclusion is not altered by the fact that the decisions of the Association Council provide that the procedures for applying the rights conferred on Turkish workers are to be established under national rules. According to the CJEU this is simply to clarify that Member States are obliged to take the necessary administrative measures for the implementation of the provisions. However, Member States are not permitted to restrict the application of the rights which the decisions of the Council of Association grant to Turkish workers.[37]

15–30

Furthermore, the CJEU has held that the fact that a decision of the Association Council is not officially published in the *Official Journal of the European Communities* does not deprive the individual of the rights contained within it.

15–31

In relation to the now redundant Europe Agreements, the CJEU found that some of its provisions were capable of direct effect. In the context of free movement of persons, the most significant provision relating to the freedom of establishment contained in the Europe Agreements was held to have direct effect.[38] The CJEU held that the establishment provision laid down in clear, precise and unconditional terms the prohibition against discrimination against those wishing to establish themselves from the third countries. No further implementation was required in order for a person to rely upon it in a national court. As stated above however this provision is not replicated as regards individuals under the SAAs.[39]

15–32

From the CJEU's perspective, the purpose of the Europe Agreements, namely to promote the expansion of trade and economic relations between the Contracting Parties with a view to facilitating accession of the third country to the Union, was compatible with the establishment provision having direct effect. The fact that the Central and Eastern European country in question required the Agreement to assist with its own economic development and the fact that there was somewhat of an imbalance in the obligations assumed by the Union towards the third country concerned do not prevent it from being capable of direct effect.[40]

15–33

The conclusion that a provision of an association agreement and indeed of a decision of a Council of Association has direct effect is highly significant. It means that individuals can rely upon the provision to create rights for themselves before national authorities without there being any need for national legislation to give effect to the provision. Given the variable approaches that Member States have taken to the implementation of the Association Agreements, this is very important to ensure that European Union law rights created by such Association Agreements are not denied to

15–34

---

[37] *Sevince v Staatsecretaris Van Justitite* (C-192/89) [1990] E.C.R. I-3461, at [22].
[38] art.45(1) of the E.C.-Bulgaria Association Agreement for instance.
[39] Note that companies have the right of establishment in Member States.
[40] *R. v Secretary of State for the Home Department Ex p. Barkoci and Malik* (C-257/99) [2001] E.C.R. I-6557, at [37].

individuals altogether. Although there have been no cases under the SAAs yet considered by the CJEU, the decision of the CJEU in *Simutenkov*[41] gives every confidence that the same approach as was taken under the Europe Agreements would be taken under the SAAs.

---

[41] *Simutenkov v Abogado del Estado, Real Federacion Espanola de Futbol and Ministerio Fiscal* (C-265/03) [2005] E.C.R. I-2579.

CHAPTER 16

WORKERS UNDER THE STABILISATION AND ASSOCIATION AGREEMENTS

This chapter examines the principal provisions contained in the Stabilisation and Association Agreements relating to workers. These include a non-discrimination provision, provisions relating to key personnel and a provision relating to the supply of services. The provisions are limited and do not grant the right of free movement for workers.

1. INTRODUCTION

Title V to each of the Stabilisation and Association Agreements includes the phrase "Movement of workers, establishment, supply of services". Chapter 1 of Title V refers to "Movement of workers". Despite the misleading title of Title V, it is notable that there are no free movement provisions specifically relating to workers in any of the SAAs. The provisions contained in the Ankara Agreement relating to the free movement of workers and the specific aim of gradual progression towards the attainment of that goal are not replicated in any provisions of the SAAs (nor were there any such provisions in the Europe Agreements with the Eastern European states that joined the Union in 2004 and 2007).[1] Initial access to the labour force is left firmly in the hands of the Member States. Indeed, there are no rights relating to the free movement of persons at all given under the SAAs. Under the Europe Agreements a right of entry and residence could at least be inferred from the right of establishment (given to both companies and individuals). In the SAAs by contrast the right of establishment is given only to companies. There is an obligation on each Stabilisation and Association Council after four or five years[2] to "establish the modalities" to extend right of establishment for companies to individuals "to take up economic activities as self-employed persons". Such time periods have passed as regards Croatia (four years in February 2009) and Macedonia (five years in April 2009), although such right of establishment has not been extended to individuals. As regards the "supply of services", the parties to the SAAs undertake to allow progressively the supply of services by Macedonian companies and nationals, with measures to achieve this to be taken by the relevant Stabilisation and Association Council.[3] Again, no measures have as yet been taken. There is

16–01

---

[1] Namely Czech Republic, Estonia, Hungary, Latvia, Lithuania, Poland, Slovenia, and Slovakia in 2004 and Bulgaria and Romania in 2007.
[2] See art.48(3) in the Macedonia Agreement (five years); art.49(4) in the Croatia Agreement (four years); art.50(4) in the Albania Agreement (five years); and art.53(4) in the Montenegro Agreement (four years).
[3] See art.55(3) in the Macedonia Agreement (measures to be taken as from the second stage of the transition period); art.56(3) in the Croatia Agreement (measures to be taken as from four years after the entry into force of the Agreement); art.57(3) in the Albania Agreement (measures to be taken as from five years after the entry into force of the Agreement); and art.59(3) in the Montenegro Agreement (measures to be taken after four years).

however a provision enabling Macedonian nationals to enter Member States temporarily for the purpose of negotiating for "the sale of services or entering into agreements to sell services" where those representatives will not be engaged in making direct sales to the general public or in supplying services themselves.[4]

16–02 The limitations of the SAAs (and the Europe Agreements before them) is perhaps indicative of the differences in the economic and social climates in which the SAAs and the Europe Agreements were negotiated when compared with the Ankara Agreement. During the 1960s and 1970s when the negotiations between Turkey and the European Community were taking place, the Member States were experiencing a significant economic boom which relied at least to some extent upon a large migrant labour force. By the early 1990s/2000s when the Europe Agreements and the SAAs were under negotiation, the Member States' economies were less buoyant and the political climate was one of protectionism, particularly where employment and migrant labour forces were concerned.

16–03 This protectionism of labour markets flowed through even to the accession of the Europe Agreement countries which have now joined the Union to the extent that free movement of workers (as opposed to any other persons) was delayed during the transitional period. There have been such transitional arrangements even when Spain and Portugal joined and there is no reason to suppose that the same approach will not be taken to the eventual succession of the countries with whom SAAs are in force.

16–04 There are only two provisions that might benefit workers from Macedonia, Croatia, Albania or Montenegro[5] in the SAAs with those countries. One provision relates to non-discrimination and the second relates to the movement of key personnel by companies registered in those countries.

2. Non-discrimination of Workers

(a) *Introduction*

16–05 Article 44 of the Macedonia Agreement contains the following non-discrimination provision relating to Macedonian workers. The Macedonia Agreement is used by way of example (as the first SAA which entered into force). The corresponding provisions of the other SAAs are to all intents and purposes the same.[6]

---

[4] art.55(2) in the Macedonia Agreement; art.56(2) in the Croatia Agreement; art.57(2) in the Albania Agreement; and art.59(2) in the Montenegro Agreement.
[5] Or in due course workers from Bosnia, Herzegovina and Serbia should the SAAs with those countries enter into force.
[6] See in turn art.45 (Croatia Agreement), art.46 (Albania Agreement), or art.49 (Montenegro Agreement).

Article 44

1. Subject to the conditions and modalities applicable in each Member State:

— treatment accorded to workers who are nationals of the former Yugoslav Republic of Macedonia and who are legally employed in the territory of a Member State shall be free of any discrimination based on nationality, as regards working conditions, remuneration or dismissal, compared to its own nationals;

— the legally resident spouse and children of a worker legally employed in the territory of a Member State, with the exception of seasonal workers and of workers coming under bilateral agreements, within the meaning of Article 45, unless otherwise provided by such agreements, shall have access to the labour market of that Member State, during the period of that worker's authorised stay of employment.

It is to be noted this non-discrimination provision relates to those workers of Macedonian nationality who are "legally employed" within a Member State. Moreover the non-discrimination provision is restricted in its scope in so far as it relates to conditions of work, remuneration and dismissal only. There is no reference to conditions of entry or stay and indeed the reference to those "legally employed" makes clear that workers wishing to benefit from the provision must have been granted permission to enter and work in the Member State already.[7]

(b) *Direct effect*

The analogous provision in the Europe Agreement with Poland was held by the CJEU to be directly effective in European Union law in *Pokrzeptowicz-Meyer*.[8] The CJEU noted that it was clear and precise and not subject in its implementation to the adoption of any subsequent measure. According to the CJEU: **16–06**

> "This rule of equal treatment lays down a precise obligation to produce a specific result and, by its nature, can be relied on by an individual to apply to a national court to set aside the discriminatory provisions of a Member State's legislation, without any further implementing measures being required for that purpose".[9]

The German Government had argued that the equivalent provision in the Polish Agreement was not unconditional since the provision is put into effect "subject to the conditions and modalities applicable in each Member State". The CJEU held that this proviso could not be interpreted in a way that permitted the Member States to make the principle of non-discrimination dependent on certain conditions being met or being diluted in anyway. In concluding that the provision was capable of direct effect, the CJEU had regard to the nature and purpose of the Europe Agreements **16–07**

---

[7] *Land Nordrhein-Westfalen v Pokrzeptowicz-Meyer* (C-162/00) [2002] E.C.R. I-1049, at [20].
[8] *Land Nordrhein-Westfalen v Pokrzeptowicz-Meyer* (C-162/00) [2002] E.C.R. I-1049.
[9] *Land Nordrhein-Westfalen v Pokrzeptowicz-Meyer* (C-162/00) [2002] E.C.R. I-1049, at [22].

which are aimed at promoting the expansion of trade and economic relations with a view to accession.

16–08 There cannot be the slightest doubt that art.44 of the Macedonia Agreement (and the corresponding provisions of the other SAAs[10]) are similarly directly effective in European Union law. Indeed, the similar provision in the Russian Partnership and Co-operation Agreement was held to have direct effect by the CJEU in *Simutenkov*[11] and (unlike the SAAs which in their preambles each acknowledge the relevant country as a potential candidate for EU membership) that agreement is only one limited to establishing a partnership.

(c) Relationship with national laws permitted by art.62

16–09 Article 62 of the Macedonia Agreement contains a general provision on the operation of national laws and regulations which must be applied when examining rights under the Agreement (which must not be "nullified or impaired" by the operation of such laws and regulations). Article 62 provides:

Article 62

> For the purpose of this Title, nothing in this Agreement shall prevent the Parties from applying their laws and regulations regarding entry and stay, employment, working conditions, establishment of natural persons and supply of services, provided that, in so doing, they do not apply them in such a manner as to nullify or impair the benefits accruing to any Party under the terms of a specific provision of this Agreement. This provision shall be without prejudice to the application of Article 61.

16–10 At first sight the inclusion of art.62 in the Agreement might suggest that the non-discrimination provision contained in art.44 can be diluted in some way by Member States since art.62 provides that they may have in place national laws concerning conditions of entry, stay, employment and working conditions. However, as the CJEU has made clear (in a case which concerned the analogous provision in the Europe Agreement with the Czech Republic[12]), all that follows from the provision is that whilst the authorities of the Member States remain competent to apply their own national laws and regulations regarding entry, stay, employment and working conditions of the relevant nationals, they do so subject to the conditions in relevant Agreement itself.

16–11 The fundamental obligation in the Stabilisation and Association Agreements (and the Europe Agreements when they were in force) is that of

---

[10] art.45 (Croatia Agreement), art.46 (Albania Agreement), or art.49 (Montenegro Agreement).
[11] *Simutenkov v Abogado del Estado, Real Federacion Espanola de Futbol and Ministerio Fiscal* (C-265/03) [2005] E.C.R. I-2579.
[12] See, for instance, *R. v Secretary of State for the Home Department Ex p. Barkoci and Malik* (C-257/99) [2001] E.C.R. I-6557.

non-discrimination in particular fields. Article 44 is concerned with non-discrimination in relation to conditions of work for those lawfully employed in the Member States. Although not present in the SAAs except as regards companies (rather than individuals—at least prior to action by the Stabilisation and Association Council, which has not hitherto happened) under the Europe Agreements there was also a non-discrimination provision as regards the right of establishment (which was broader in scope than that relating to workers because it related to rights of entry and stay as well as conditions of establishment).

It is plain that art.62 is not intended to make implementation or the effects of the principle of non-discrimination laid down in the first indent of art.44(1) of the Macedonia Agreement subject to the adoption of further national measures.[13] Article 44(1) would be rendered meaningless if Member States could have in place national measures which permitted discrimination against Macedonian nationals vis-à-vis their EU national equivalents. 16–12

(d) *Meaning of the non-discrimination provision*

The CJEU held that art.38 of the Europe Agreements had the same meaning as art.39(2) EC Treaty (now art.45(2) TFEU) which prohibits discrimination against non-Member State nationals.[14] There is no reason why the same approach would not be taken to the Stabilisation and Association Agreements, particularly in light of the decision of the CJEU in *Simutenkov*[15] interpreting the same provision in the Russian Partnership and Co-operation Agreement. The importance of this comparison between the SAAs and the Treaty on the Functioning of the European Union itself is that it extends the CJEU's case law on discrimination under art.45(2) TFEU to the interpretation of the SAAs. The case law of the CJEU makes clear that the *scope* of the non-discrimination provision in the Europe Agreements (and by analogy the SAAs) is the same as that contained in art.45(2) TFEU in that discrimination which relates to any condition of employment will be prohibited unless objectively justified. Conditions of employment are broadly interpreted and will include the type of activities that are carried out by the employee, as well as conditions of remuneration, other benefits and rewards. 16–13

In the contested area of sports rules, the CJEU held in *Bosman*[16] that rules governing the extent to which football clubs field their players for participation in official matches fell within the scope of [art.45(2) TFEU]. Such rules were said to concern "conditions of work" since participation in such matches is the essential purpose of a professional sportsman's activities. The 16–14

---

[13] See *Land Nordrhein-Westfalen v Pokrzeptowicz-Meyer* (C-162/00) [2002] E.C.R. I-1049, at [23].
[14] *Deutscher Handballbund eV v Kolpak* (C-438/00) [2003] E.C.R. I-4135.
[15] *Simutenkov v Abogado del Estado, Real Federacion Espanola de Futbol and Ministerio Fiscal* (C-265/03) [2005] E.C.R. I-2579.
[16] *Union Royale Belge des Sociétès de Football Association ASBL v Bosman* (C-415/93) [1995] E.C.R. I-4921.

CJEU thus held that art.45(2) TFEU must be read so as to prohibit sports rules which restrict the number of Union citizen players able to be fielded in an official match.

16–15 In *Kolpak*[17] the CJEU applied the same reasoning to a case concerning the application of rules restricting the number of non-EEA national handball players who could be chosen to play in an official match in Germany in relation to a Slovakian player lawfully employed in Germany. The CJEU considered that such rules had no objective justification and were thus discriminatory contrary to the Europe Agreements. If the rules had applied to matches between national teams there would have been objective justification for the discrimination. However, these rules applied to all official matches between clubs. As the CJEU had pointed out in *Bosman*, a club's links with the Member State in which it is established cannot be regarded as any more essential than are its links with its locality, town or region. The CJEU noted that there were no rules relating to the locality within the country that the player had to come from. The CJEU took the same approach in the similar case of *Simutenkov*[18] (considering a rule drawn up by the Spanish sports federation which provided that clubs could field in competitions at national level only a limited number of players from countries which are not parties to the EEA Agreement) in the context of the same non-discrimination provision in the Russian Partnership and Co-operation Agreement.

(e) *Indirect discrimination*

16–16 The principle of non-discrimination in European Union law protects individuals from both direct and indirect forms of discrimination. The CJEU has interpreted the principle of non-discrimination under art.45(2) TFEU as extending to situations of *indirect* discrimination. In *Spotti*[19] for instance the CJEU had held that art.45(2) TFEU precludes the application of a provision of national law imposing a limit on the duration of the employment relationship between universities and foreign-language assistants where there is, in principle, no such limit with regard to other workers. The CJEU based its finding on the fact that the great majority of foreign-language assistants were foreign nationals. The difference in treatment between them and other teachers with special duties, placed the foreign nationals at a disadvantage compared with German nationals. This constituted indirect discrimination, prohibited by art.45(2) TFEU, unless it was justified by objective reasons.

16–17 In *Pokrzeptowicz-Meyer*[20] the CJEU applied its interpretation of art.45(2) TFEU in *Spotti* to the Europe Agreements. The same approach would be

---

[17] *Deutscher Handballbund eV v Kolpak* (C-438/00) [2003] E.C.R. I-4135.
[18] *Simutenkov v Abogado del Estado, Real Federacion Espanola de Futbol and Ministerio Fiscal* (C-265/03).
[19] *Chiara Spotti v Freistaat Bayern* (C-272/92) [1993] E.C.R. I-5185.
[20] *Land Nordrhein-Westfalen v Beata Pokrzeptowicz-Meyer* (C-162/00) [2002] E.C.R. I-1049, at [39].

taken to the SAAs. The CJEU stated that there was no reason to give a more restrictive interpretation and thus, limitations on the duration of contracts for foreign language assistants constituted indirect discrimination against Polish nationals.

(f) *Scope of non-discrimination provision*

16–18 Whilst a broad interpretation is given to the non-discrimination provision, it is plainly limited in scope to conditions of work, remuneration and dismissal for those in legal employment. The concept of "legal employment" is discussed below. However, it is plain that the provision does not extend to conditions of entry or residence or access to the labour market. Decisions about whether to admit a Macedonian, Croatian, Albanian or Montenegran national to the labour force remains the sole preserve of the Member States, unaffected by European Union law. Likewise decisions regarding conditions of entry to the territory and continued residence fall within the jurisdiction of the Member States alone. A comparison with the Ankara Agreement and the decisions of its Council of Association demonstrates what measures could be taken to progress towards the free movement of workers. However, no such steps were taken by the Council of Association under the Europe Agreements, nor have any such steps been taken by the Stabilisation and Association Council. Thus no progress towards the free movement of workers can be inferred.[21]

16–19 An example of the sort of question which might arise in the context of the non-discrimination provision is whether a Macedonian national who obtained permission to work on the basis of an employment contract which excluded them from access to maternity leave, could rely on art.44(1) of the Macedonia Agreement in order subsequently to obtain maternity benefits or leave. The answer would have to be that such a Macedonian national must be afforded the same conditions of work as a national of the Member State in question and thus obtain maternity leave and benefits on the same basis as the own-national worker.

16–20 An example of a matter not covered by the scope of the non-discrimination on the other hand arose in the case of *Pavlov*[22] in which the CJEU found that a provision in the Austrian Lawyer's Code which precluded a Bulgarian national from being included in a list of trainee lawyers and, consequently,

---

[21] See, for instance, *Nour Eddline El-Yassini v Secretary of State for Home Department* (C-416/96) [1999] E.C.R. I-1209, where the CJEU examined a similar non-discrimination provision in the Moroccan Agreement and concluded the lack of provisions equivalent to those under the Ankara Agreement and the plain wording of the provision meant that its scope could not extend to conditions of entry or stay. It might be thought that since the Europe Agreements have different objectives than the Moroccan Agreement in so far as the latter is not a pre-accession agreement, this will generally affect the method of interpretation of a provision and that the Europe Agreements should be more generously interpreted. In fact the plain wording of the provision in the Europe Agreements and the lack of any other provisions setting out any rights in relation to the free movement of workers must preclude a different interpretation.
[22] *Gentcho Pavlov and Gregor Famnira v Ausschuss der Rechtsanwaltskammer Wien* (C-101/10) July 7, 2011.

to obtain a certificate of entitlement to appear in court did not breach the non-discrimination obligation in art.38(1) of the Bulgaria Agreement. This was because the provision did not extend to rules of access to the regulated profession of lawyer. As noted by the CJEU at para.27 of its decision:

> "Nothing in the Association Agreement with the Republic of Bulgaria allows it to be deduced from the first indent of Article 38(1), or other provisions of the Agreement, that the contracting parties intended to eliminate all discrimination based on nationality as regards access to regulated professions by Bulgarian nationals. It must also be borne in mind that that provision appears in Title IV, Chapter I of the Agreement, "Movement of workers", while regulated professions are mentioned in Article 47 of the Agreement, which appears in Title IV, Chapter II, "Establishment", and deals with access to regulated professions without imposing an obligation in that connection not to discriminate on grounds of nationality."

16–21 In the context of the Ankara Agreement the CJEU has found that the reasons for admitting a Turkish national to the labour force or the conditions under which such a worker is admitted are irrelevant for the purposes of obtaining the benefits of the provisions of the Ankara Agreement or decisions of the Council of Association.[23] There is no reason why the same approach would not be taken under the SAAs to the scope of the non-discrimination provision as has been taken previously under the Europe Agreements and the Ankara Agreement.

(g) *The meaning of "legally employed"*

16–22 Only those who are legally employed in a Member State obtain the benefits of art.44(1) of the Macedonia Agreement. Legal employment is not defined anywhere in the SAAs. Since Union citizens have the right to work in other Member States, the term has little relevance to Union citizens and therefore has not had to be interpreted by the CJEU in the context of the Treaty on the Functioning of the European Union. However, "legal employment" is a term referred to in Decision 1/80 of the Council of Association established under the Ankara Agreement[24] and has been the subject of interpretation by the CJEU.

16–23 Legal working is discussed in greater detail in Ch.18 in relation to workers under the Ankara Agreement. It must be appropriate to apply the CJEU's case law by analogy to Macedonian, Croatian, Albanian and Montenegran workers lawfully working in the Member States.[25] In short the worker must be in a *"stable and secure position"* as regards the legality of their residence in the Member State. The worker would need to have an undisputed right of

---

[23] See, for instance, *Gnaydin v Freistaat Bayern* (C-36/96) [1997] E.C.R. I-5197.
[24] For more detailed discussion, see Ch.22.
[25] Although art.6(1) of Decision 1/80 of the Council of Association under the Ankara Agreement additionally refers to the fact that Turkish workers who wish to benefit from that particular provision must be "duly registered as belonging to the labour force" as well as legally employed the CJEU has stated that the phrases are synonymous: see *Birden v Stadtgemeinde Bremen* (C-1/97) [1998] E.C.R. I-7747.

residence since any dispute as to the right of residence could lead to insecurity in the worker's situation. Thus a person who is working in a Member State with the permission of the authorities whilst awaiting the outcome of an application to remain[26] or of an appeal against the refusal of a residence permit would not fulfil the requirements of legal employment.[27]

The reasons why the worker is permitted to work, however, are not relevant to the question of whether the employment is "legal". If for instance work and residence permits were granted to a Macedonian national by virtue of their being the spouse of a national of the relevant Member State, rather than because of a desire to have them admitted to the labour force, this would not affect the worker's rights under art.44(1), even if the marriage subsequently dissolved.[28]   **16–24**

(h) *The meaning of "worker"*

Just as the notion of legal employment is nowhere defined in the SAAs, so there is no definition of workers to be found in those Agreements. However, the meaning of "worker" has been comprehensively considered by the CJEU, and in relation to the Ankara Agreement the CJEU has repeatedly emphasised that the concept of Turkish worker should take on the European Union law definition. The same approach should be taken to the interpretation of the term worker in the Stabilisation and Association Agreements (not least given the fact that these are agreements with the same underlying objective of ultimate accession to the European Union).   **16–25**

The European Union concept of worker is considered in Ch.6 and, in the context of the Ankara Agreement, in Ch.18. For present purposes it suffices to emphasise that the concept must be interpreted broadly and that the person must pursue an activity which is genuine and effective, to the exclusion of activities on such a small scale as to be regarded as purely marginal and ancillary. The essential feature of an employment relationship is that for a certain period of time a person performs services for and under the direction of another person in return for which remuneration is received.   **16–26**

(i) *Temporal effect of the non-discrimination provision for workers*

The question has arisen as to the temporal effect of the non-discrimination provision. Does the provision have any affect on conditions of work for instance where a contract for employment was entered into prior to the coming into force of the relevant SAA?   **16–27**

The CJEU has answered this question by reference to general principles of EU law applied in accession cases and where new legislation is brought into   **16–28**

---

[26] e.g. an application for asylum.
[27] *Kuz v Landeshauptstadt Wiesbaden* (C-237/91) [1992] E.C.R. I-6781.
[28] Although of course the dissolving of the marriage might affect the right of residence itself.

force. In *Pokrzeptowicz-Meyer*[29] it held that the non-discrimination provision contained in the Europe Agreements was a new rule which would apply with immediate effect from the date of coming into force of the relevant agreement to a fixed-term contract for employment. There is no reason why the same approach would not be taken to the SAAs. Thus it would apply to any situation arising after the date on which the Agreement comes into force.[30] It would not, however, apply to situations which arose prior to the coming into force of the Agreement. The CJEU dismissed arguments about legal certainty and the protection of the legitimate expectations of the persons concerned on the grounds that it was only the matters of law and fact which existed at the time of the conclusion of such contract which were to be applied to its operation. The CJEU held that such arguments had no application in the context of a non-discrimination provision which individuals should be able to rely upon immediately, regardless of when they entered into contracts of employment.

3. Family Members

16–29 In addition to making provision for non-discrimination in relation to workers, art.44 of the Macedonia Agreement also makes specific provision for the legally resident spouse and children of workers that are legally employed in Member States and who are given a right of access to the labour market. The relevant part of art.38(1) provides as follows:

> "1. Subject to the conditions and modalities applicable in each Member State:
>
> — the legally resident spouse and children of a worker legally employed in the territory of a Member State, with the exception of seasonal workers and of workers coming under bilateral agreements, within the meaning of Article 45, unless otherwise provided by such agreements, shall have access to the labour market of that Member State, during the period of that worker's authorised stay of employment."

16–30 This provision is predicated expressly on the legal residence of family members. However, the existence of a right of access to the labour market for family members at least implies that some national law provision must be made so as to enable workers legally employed in a Member State to be joined by such family members. Just as the existence of free movement rights generally implies as a corollary the right to enter and reside, so a right in certain circumstances to access the labour market ought similarly to imply at least the possibility of entry, lest the right given be rendered entirely meaningless. Such an interpretation is mandated also by human rights obligations, in particular the right to respect for family life contained in art.8 ECHR. As discussed in Chs 3 and 9, the fundamental importance of art.8 ECHR in the context of free movement rights has in recent years has been given particular prominence.

---

[29] *Land Nordrhein-Westfalen v Pokrzeptowicz-Meyer* (C-162/00) [2002] E.C.R. I-1049, at [39].
[30] In a Community law context see *Germany v Commission* (278/84) [1987] E.C.R. 1, at [36], and *Butterfly Music Srl v Carosello Edizioni Musicali e Discografiche Srl* (C-60/98) [1999] E.C.R. I-3939, at [25].

The CJEU has not considered the position of the family members of workers in the context of the SAAs (nor did it under the Europe Agreements). By contrast, the CJEU has considered the limited provision made for the family members of Turkish nationals exercising their rights under the Ankara Agreement. The provision in art.44(1) of the Macedonia Agreement is not dissimilar to that contained in art.7 of Decision 1/80 under the Ankara Agreement. It is acknowledged that the context is different because the Turkish worker attains rights of residence under the Ankara Agreement whereas the Macedonian workers do not attain any such comparable rights. However, to the extent that both family member provisions provide a right of access to the labour market the analysis of the CJEU in the context of the Ankara Agreement provides a useful benchmark for the assertion of the right to family unity in the present context. The family unity provisions under the Ankara Agreement are discussed in Ch.20.

4. KEY PERSONNEL

Article 48(3) of the Macedonia Agreements gives the right of establishment to companies[31] but not to individuals (albeit with the possibility of extension to individuals, but this is as yet to be provided for[32]). The SAAs differ in this respect from the position under the Europe Agreements which had provided such right of establishment for *both* companies and individuals. Such right of establishment conferred on Macedonian companies in art.48(3) is extended by art.53 which gives those companies the right to post "key personnel" to EU Member States. The key personnel provision applies only to *companies* establishing themselves in the territory of a Member State who wish to employ key personnel in that Member State. The SAAs also differ in this respect from the analogous provision in the Europe Agreements which had (for the most part[33]) conferred the power to post key employees on both companies and individuals. The provision in the Macedonia Agreement is reflected by identical provisions in the other SAAs.[34] The provisions are reciprocal in the sense that they confer the same rights on each party (the Member States and Macedonia), although for simplicity the discussion which follows considers the position of Macedonian companies exercising the right.

---

[31] Or in turn art.49 (Croatia Agreement), art.50 (Albania Agreement), or art.53 (Montenegro Agreement).

[32] See art.48(4) Macedonia Agreement which provides that the Stabilisation and Association Council will examine whether to extend the establishment provisions contained in art.48(3) to persons who wish to take up activities as self-employed persons after five years from the entry into force of the Agreement and the similar provisions in art.49(4) of the Croatia Agreement (after *four* years), art.50(4) of the Albania Agreement (after *five* years), and art.53(4) of the Montenegro Agreement (after *four* years). At time of writing there has been no such extension under any of the SAAs.

[33] The Slovakian Agreement, for example, confined the benefit of the key personnel provision to companies alone and did not entitle self-employed nationals to employ key personnel.

[34] See art.54(1) of the Croatia Agreement, art.55(1) of the Albania Agreement, or art.58(1) of the Montenegro Agreement.

Article 53

1. A Community company or a company from the former Yugoslav Republic of Macedonia established in the territory of the former Yugoslav Republic of Macedonia or the Community respectively shall be entitled to employ, or have employed by one of its subsidiaries or branches, in accordance with the legislation in force in the host country of establishment, in the territory of the former Yugoslav Republic of Macedonia and the Community respectively, employees who are nationals of the Community Member States and former Yugoslav Republic of Macedonia respectively, provided that such employees are key personnel as defined in paragraph 2 and that they are employed exclusively by companies, subsidiaries or branches. The residence and work permits of such employees shall only cover the period of such employment.

3. The entry into and the temporary presence within the territory of the Community or the former Yugoslav Republic of Macedonia of nationals of the former Yugoslav Republic of Macedonia and Community nationals respectively shall be permitted, when these representatives of companies are persons working in a senior position, as defined in paragraph 2(a) above, within a company, and are responsible for the setting up of a Community subsidiary or branch of a company from the former Yugoslav Republic of Macedonia or of a subsidiary or branch in the former Yugoslav Republic of Macedonia of a Community company in a Community Member State or in the former Yugoslav Republic of Macedonia respectively, when:

— those representatives are not engaged in making direct sales or supplying services, and
— the company has its principal place of business outside the Community or the former Yugoslav Republic of Macedonia, respectively, and has no other representative, office, branch or subsidiary in that Community Member State or former Yugoslav Republic of Macedonia respectively.

16–33 "Key personnel" are defined in art.53(2). They are referred to as "intra-corporate transferees" (defined as natural persons temporarily transferred in the pursuit of economic activities to the territory of a Member State by a company having its principal place of business in Macedonia with the transfer being to a branch or subsidiary of the Macedonian company[35]). The company posting the key personal must be a "legal person" and the person concerned must have been employed by it or have been a partner in it (other than as a majority shareholder) for at least the year immediately preceding the temporary posting. Such key personnel must fall within either sub-para.(a) or (b) of art.53(2):

"(a) persons working in a senior position with an organisation, who primarily direct the management of the establishment, receiving general supervision or direction principally from the board of directors or stockholders of the business or their equivalent including:

— directing the establishment of a department or sub-division of the establishment;
— supervising and controlling the work of other supervisory, professional or managerial employees;

---

[35] art.53(2)(c) of the Macedonia Agreement refers.

— having the authority personally to recruit and dismiss or recommend recruiting, dismissing or other personnel actions;

(b) persons working within an organisation who possess uncommon knowledge essential to the establishment's service, research equipment, techniques or management. The assessment of such knowledge may reflect, apart from knowledge specific to the establishment, a high level of qualification referring to a type of work or trade requiring specific technical knowledge, including membership of an accredited profession."

16–34   The key personnel employee must be a Macedonian national who is employed exclusively by the company, its subsidiary or branch. The employee cannot be a third country national. The employee must have been employed by the company for at least one year before transfer and the employee cannot therefore have been employed by another company or person in the year before transfer.

16–35   Article 53(3) makes provision for the entry into and temporary presence in Member States of Macedonian nationals if they are key personel working in a "senior position"[36] who are responsible for the setting up of a European Union subsidiary or branch of a Macedonian company. Such persons must however be engaged only in the setting up of such subsidiary or branch: they must not be "engaged in making direct sales or supplying services". Moreover, in such cases the company's principal place of business must be outside the European Union and it must have no other representative, office, branch or subsidiary in the Member State concerned.

16–36   The employment of key personnel must be in accordance with national rules of the Member State concerned. Article 62 of the Macedonia Agreement[37] provides that nothing in the Agreement prevents the parties from applying their laws and regulations regarding entry and stay. As made clear by art.53(1), the residence and work permits of such employees will be restricted in duration to cover only the period of such employment.

16–37   However, the ability of Member States to regulate conditions relating to "entry and stay, employment, working conditions, establishment of natural persons and supply of services" is not unfettered. The key personnel provision is subject to art.62 of the Macedonia Agreement which provides that national legal requirements must not "nullify or impair" the benefits accruing to any party under the terms of a specific provisions of the Agreement. Thus if an employee satisfied the definition of key personnel, the Member State could not refuse entry or stay to that employee other than on grounds of public policy, public security or public health.[38] The Member State could however require that the person obtains a visa prior to entering its territory.

---

[36] As defined in art.53(2)(a) of the Macedonian Agreement.
[37] See also art.63 of the Croatia Agreement, art.64 of the Albania Agreement or art.66 of the Montenegro Agreement.
[38] art.61(1) of the Macedonia Agreement (see also art.62(1) of the Croatia Agreement, art.63(1) of the Albania Agreement, and art.65(1) of the Montenegro Agreement).

16–38 There have been no cases to date on the interpretation of the key personnel provisions in the SAAs (or indeed were there any under the Europe Agreements). This may be reflective of their underutilisation, or perhaps the detail contained in the provision.

5. Supply of Services

16–39 Chapter III of Title V is entitled "Supply of Services in each SAA". The first Article in Ch.III in each SAA[39] records the parties' undertaking "to take the necessary steps to allow progressively the supply of services by (EU or Macedonian, Croatian, Albanian or Montenegrin) companies or nationals" which are established in a Party other than that of the person for whom the services are intended". This objective is to be achieved by each Stabilisation and Association Council which from a particular point in time is required to take the necessary implementation measures.[40] However, no such measures have been taken by the Stabilisation and Association Councils and so there is (as yet) no general right of free movement for individuals (or workers) to supply services.

16–40 However, there is a specific right given to individuals under the SAAs as regards service provision. The right is given by art.55(2) of the Macedonian Agreement:[41]

Article 55

2. In step with the liberalisation process mentioned in paragraph 1, the Parties shall permit the temporary movement of natural persons providing the service or who are employed by the service provider as key personnel as defined in Article 53, including natural persons who are representatives of a Community or the former Yugoslav Republic of Macedonia company or national and are seeking temporary entry for the purpose of negotiating for the sale of services or entering into agreements to sell services for that service provider, where those representatives will not be engaged in making direct sales to the general public or in supplying services themselves.

16–41 The individual can be either a service provider or employed as "key personel" (considered above). The right is given only for the temporary purpose of negotiating for the sale of services or entering into contracts to sell services. There can be no "direct sales" or services actually supplied. The right

---

[39] art.55 of the Macedonia Agreement, art.56 of the Croatia Agreement, art.57 of the Albania Agreement, or art.59 of the Montenegro Agreement.
[40] See art.55(3) in the Macedonia Agreement (measures to be taken as from the second stage of the transition period); art.56(3) in the Croatia Agreement (measures to be taken as from four years after the entry into force of the Agreement); art.57(3) in the Albania Agreement (measures to be taken as from five years after the entry into force of the Agreement); and art.59(3) in the Montenegro Agreement (measures to be taken after four years).
[41] See in similar terms art.56(2) in the Croatia Agreement; art.57(2) in the Albania Agreement; and art.59(2) in the Montenegro Agreement.

is therefore extremely limited. It is expressly not about the fulfillment in Member States of any such contracts or the actual provision of any services there.

CHAPTER 17

INTRODUCTION TO THE ANKARA AGREEMENT

This chapter provides the background to and identifies the key provisions of the EC-Turkey Association Agreement ("the Ankara Agreement") relating to the free movement of Turkish nationals.

1. BACKGROUND TO THE AGREEMENT

As discussed in Ch.15 above, the Ankara Agreement is one of the oldest Association Agreements. The beginning of Turkey's relations with the European Union dates to that country's application for European Community membership of July 31, 1959 immediately after Greece's application made on June 8 of the same year. After the rejection of that application the Ankara Agreement itself was signed on September 12, 1963[1] and the Additional Protocol on November 23, 1970.[2] Eventual accession of Turkey to the European Community was envisaged by the Agreement and indeed the Additional Protocol detailed a timescale of between 12 and 22 years for the establishment of the customs union and the free movement of workers.

17–01

However, in 1987 Turkey's application to join the European Community was rejected. The timetable for the free movement of workers has long overrun. Decision 1/95 of the EC-Turkey Association Council[3] implemented the final phase of the Customs Union but makes no reference to the free movement of persons.

17–02

At the December 2002 Copenhagen European Council meeting it was resolved that a decision would be made in December 2004 to open accession negotiations with Turkey "without delay" if recommended by the Commission that Turkey fulfils the Copenhagen political criteria. The European Commission recommended that the negotiations should begin in 2005, but also added various precautionary measures. The EU leaders agreed on December 16, 2004 to start accession negotiations with Turkey from October 3, 2005. Turkey's accession talks have since been stalled by a number of domestic and external problems. The issue of Cyprus continues to be a major obstacle to negotiations. Due to various setbacks and disagreements about the extent of Turkish reforms, negotiations again came to a halt in December 2006, with the EU freezing talks in eight of the 35 key areas under negotiation. In 2008 the European Council adopted a new Accession Partnership decision outlining key areas of negotiation.[4] With

17–03

---

[1] [1977] O.J. L361/29 and [1973] O.J. C113/2.
[2] [1977] O.J. L361/59 and [1973] O.J. C113/17.
[3] [1996] O.J. L35/1.
[4] 2008/157/EC: Council Decision of February 18, 2008 on the principles, priorities and conditions contained in the Accession Partnership with the Republic of Turkey and repealing Decision 2006/35/EC Official Journal L051, February 26, 2008 P. 0004 – 0018.

politicians and the public in Europe divided on Turkish accession it looks extremely unlikely that Turkey will accede to the European Union quickly.

17–04 Large-scale Turkish labour emigration to Europe started with an agreement signed by the Turkish and West German Governments in 1961. This agreement was made at a time of economic boom in West Germany. It aimed to provide the German economy with temporary unskilled labour (known as "guest workers"), while thinning the ranks of Turkey's unemployed. It was anticipated that these workers would return to Turkey with new skills and help the development of the Turkish economy from one based on agriculture to one based on industry. Turkey signed similar agreements with other European countries, including Austria, Belgium, the Netherlands, France, and Sweden. Many of these guest workers chose instead to settle in their host Member States and to bring their families to join them. Furthermore, it was often skilled labourers who took advantage of such agreements.

17–05 Today, it is estimated that there are over 3 million Turkish nationals living in European countries—a substantial increase from 600,000 in 1972. Turkish nationals represent the largest non-European national group living in Europe today.[5]

17–06 The Ankara Agreement and its Protocol has given rise to a considerable amount of litigation in the domestic courts leading to references to the CJEU. Member States appear to have been very slow in some cases to take on board the consequences of the Agreement despite the longevity of its existence. The CJEU for its part has been consistent in its ardent protection of the rights laid down for Turkish nationals and their families in the Agreement, its Protocol and the various decisions of the Association Council, and appears to be intolerant of any attempt to narrowly interpret or apply those rights.

2. The Structure and Content of the Ankara Agreement and the Additional Protocol

(a) The Ankara Agreement

17–07 The Ankara Agreement is divided into three Titles.

   (i) *Title I* sets out the principles of the Agreement. Articles 2–5 lay down three stages of the Association: a preparatory, a transitional and a final stage. Article 7 provides that the Contracting Parties should take all protective measures, whether general or particular, to ensure the fulfilment of the obligations arising under the Agreement and should refrain from any measure liable to jeopardise the attainment of the objectives of the Agreement.

---

[5] Eurostat (2004 and 2010) reported numbers vary greatly depending on the source.

(ii) *Title II* lays down the framework for the transitional stage of the Association. Under this title art.12 provides that the Contracting Parties agree to be guided by the relevant Treaty provisions relating to workers. Article 13 provides similarly that the contracting parties are to be guided by the relevant Treaty provisions relating to the freedom of establishment and art.14 contains the corresponding provision with regard to abolition of restrictions on freedom to provide services.

(iii) *Title III* contains the final provisions to the Agreement. Articles 22 and 23 provide for the establishment of a Council of Association comprising members of the governments of the Member States of the European Union, members of the Council and the Commission and members of the Turkish Government. The Association Council has the power to take decisions in order to attain the objectives laid down by the Agreement. Article 30 provides that the Protocols annexed to the Agreement should form an integral part of it.

There are financial protocols annexed to the Agreement and one additional protocol outlined below.

(b) *The Additional Protocol*

The Additional Protocol is divided into four titles, relating to specific free movement areas.

(i) *Title I* relates to the free movement of goods. It contains detailed provisions regarding the transitional phase of the customs union between the European Union and Turkey.

(ii) *Title II* is entitled "Movement of Persons and Services". Chapter 1 is concerned with workers and provides a programme for the progressive implementation of the free movement of workers between Turkey and the Member States of the European Union.[6] The Council of Association is empowered to decide on the rules necessary to achieve this aim. Article 39 provides that the Council of Association should adopt social security measures for Turkish workers moving within the European Union and for their family members who are resident within the European Union. Chapter II is concerned with the right of establishment, services and transport. Of particular importance is art.41(1) which contains a standstill provision relating to establishment and the freedom to provide services. Article 41(2) empowers the Council of Association to adopt rules and a timetable for the progressive abolition of restrictions on freedom of establishment and the freedom to provide services.

(iii) Title III contains provisions relating to the closer alignment of economic policies, underlining the essentially economic relationship that is formed through the Association Agreement between Turkey and the European Union.

---

[6] art.36.

(iv) Title IV contains the final provisions of the Protocol. Of particular interest is art.50 which provides that in fields covered by the Protocol, the arrangements applied by the European Union in respect of Turkey shall not give rise to "any discrimination between Turkish nationals or its companies". This non-discrimination provision is, however, extremely weak. It relates only to the equal treatment of Turkish nationals and Turkish companies, rather than discrimination as between Turkish nationals and Turkish companies on the one hand and nationals of the host Member State on the other. Article 60 permits Turkey to take economic protective measures in the case of serious disturbances to its economy.

3. The Objectives of the Ankara Agreement and its Protocol

17–09   As discussed in Ch.15 above, an examination of objectives of an association agreement is very important as an aid to interpretation of the agreement. The preamble to the Ankara Agreement and indeed some of the substantive provisions of both the Agreement and its protocol demonstrate very clear objectives, essentially that of eventual accession of Turkey to the European Union.

(a) Preamble to the Agreement

17–10   The preamble to the Ankara Agreement provides for the establishment of "ever closer bonds between the Turkish people and the peoples brought together in the European Economic Community." Further the Contracting Parties resolved to ensure a continuous improvement in living conditions in Turkey and in the Union through

> "accelerated economic progress and the harmonious expansion of trade and to reduce the disparity between the Turkish economy and the economies of the Member States of the Community".

The preamble also makes reference to the objective of facilitating the accession of Turkey to the Union at a later date.

17–11   As the CJEU has itself observed by reference to the fourth recital in the preamble and art.28 of the Ankara Agreement, the:

> "purpose of that Agreement is to establish an association designed to promote the development of trade and economic relations between the Contracting Parties, including in the area of self-employment, the progressive abolition of restrictions on freedom of establishment, so as to improve the living conditions of the Turkish people and facilitate the accession of the Republic of Turkey to the Community at a later date".[7]

---

[7] *R. v the Secretary of State for the Home Department Ex p. Savas* (C-37/98) [2000] E.C.R. I-2927, at [53].

These aims of the Ankara Agreement influence the manner in which the substantive provisions of the Agreement are interpreted in so far as the clear intentions of the Contracting Parties of both the economic development of Turkey and the ultimate accession to the European Union ensure that where possible provisions are given direct effect.[8]

Further, the aims of the Ankara Agreement and its Protocol as well as the decisions of the Association Council have meant that the CJEU has adopted very strict rules of interpretation affording Member States no scope to take a restrictive approach to provisions in the Agreement or elsewhere.[9] 17–12

(b) *Other provisions in the Agreement and its Protocol*

Article 2(1) states that the aim of the Agreement is: 17–13

> "to promote the continuous and balanced strengthening of trade and economic relations between the Parties, while taking full account of the need to ensure an accelerated development of the Turkish economy and to improve the level of employment and living conditions of the Turkish people."

The CJEU has emphasised that this provision means that the situation of Turkish nationals and citizens of the Union should be brought closer through progressive securing of free movement for workers and abolition of restrictions on the freedom of establishment and services.[10]

Article 9 of the Agreement lays down a general principle of non-discrimination on grounds of nationality which the CJEU has stated contributes further to facilitating the progressive integration of migrant Turkish workers and Turkish nationals who move for the purposes of establishment.[11] 17–14

Articles 12, 13 and 14 of the Ankara Agreement provide that the Contracting Parties agree to be guided by the relevant Treaty provisions relating to the free movement of the workers, freedom of establishment and the freedom to provide services. These provisions are discussed in more detail in Chs 18 and 19 below. However, they demonstrate the clear aim of the parties that Union law concepts should apply to the Agreement and that eventually full free movement of persons as provided for in the Treaty will be secured as between Turkey and the Member States of the Union. 17–15

---

[8] See, for instance, *R. v the Secretary of State for the Home Department Ex p. Savas* [2000] E.C.R. I-2927.
[9] See, for instance, *Pehlivan v Staatssecretaris van Justitie*, (C-484/07), June 16, 2011.
[10] *Commission v the Netherlands* (C-92/07) April 29, 2010, at [67]. However, in *Ziebell v Land Baden Württemberg* (C-371/08) December 8, 2011, the CJEU did emphasise the economic objective of the Agreement which differentiates it from the objective of the EU Treaties and provisions on citizenship in those Treaties (see paras 66–78). As a consequence not all the benefits of Union citizenship will be extended to Turkish natinals at this time, such as protection against expulsion on public policy grounds after 10 years' residence. See further Ch.21.
[11] *Commission v the Netherlands* (C-92/07) April 29, 2010, at [69].

17–16 Article 36 of the Additional Protocol provides a specific timetable in which the full free movement of workers was to have been achieved, although the detailed rules are left to the Council of Association to make. Although the timetable has overrun this does not undermine the general aims of the Contracting Parties to achieve that objective but rather illustrates the difficulties in negotiating and implementing international agreements with long-term aims.

17–17 No such specific timetable is provided for the abolition of restrictions on freedom of establishment or the freedom to provide services since this is left to the Council of Association. The lack of time table itself does not undermine the general aims of the Contracting Parties to secure those freedoms between Turkey and the European Union.

4. Decisions of the Association Council

(a) Decisions relating to free movement

17–18 There have been a number of decisions made by the Council of Association which relate to the implementation of objectives of the Ankara Agreement and the Additional Protocol.[12] Of principal importance in the field of free movement of persons are Council of Association Decisions 2/76, 1/80 and 3/80. Decisions of Association Councils may also be seen as agreements since such decisions, like Association Agreements themselves, are both acts agreed between the Union and its Member States and third States with implications for the EU legal order. They are directly connected with the agreement to which they give effect. The approach of the CJEU is therefore to consider the decisions, in the same way as the Agreement itself, an integral part of the EU legal system.[13]

(i) Decision 2/76

17–19 Decision 2/76 was the first decision relevant to the question of free movement of workers. Article 2 provided for continued employment for a Turkish worker in the same occupation after three years and free access to any paid employment after five years. Article 5 provided for priority to be accorded to Turkish nationals in the offering of employment to non-EC nationals. Article 7 provided a standstill clause, prohibiting Member States from introducing new restrictions on the conditions of access to employment for workers that are legally resident and employed in their territory. However, the Association Council adopted this Decision as a first step for a period of four years beginning on December 1, 1976. In light of its four-year

---

[12] See, for instance, Decision 2/2000 of the EC-Turkey Association Council of April 11, 2000 on the opening of negotiations aimed at the liberalisation of services and the mutual opening of procurement markets between the Community and Turkey [2000] O.J. L138/28; Decision 3/2000 of the EC-Turkey Association Council of April 11, 2000 on the establishment of Association Committee subcommittees [2000] O.J. L138/28.
[13] *Sevince* (C-192/89) [1990] E.C.R. I-3461, at [9].

duration the provisions contained in Decision 2/76 are of historic interest, except for the standstill clause which may continue to be of relevance.[14]

(ii) *Decision 1/80*

In contrast to Decision 2/76, Decision 1/80 has no time-limit on its applicability. Decision 1/80 entered into force on December 1, 1980. The provisions contained Decision 1/80 have been said by the CJEU to constitute "one stage further, guided by arts 48, 49 and 50 of the Treaty (now Arts 45, 46 and 47 TEFU), towards securing freedom of movement for workers".[15] In order to ensure compliance with that objective, the CJEU has held that it is "essential to transpose, so far as is possible, the principles enshrined in those articles to Turkish workers who enjoy the rights conferred by Decision 1/80."[16]

17–20

The CJEU has consistently held that the specific provisions of Decision 1/80 are capable of having direct effect. In *Sevince*,[17] the CJEU held that the fact that relevant provisions of the Ankara Agreement and the Additional Protocol essentially set out a programme

17–21

> "does not prevent the decisions of the Council of Association which give effect in specific respects to the programmes envisaged in the Agreement from having direct effect".[18]

It is not surprising that the decisions of the Association Council, and in particular Decision 1/80, have been the subject of the most litigation to date.

Of specific interest with regard to the free movement of workers is art.6(1) of Decision 1/80 which creates rights for Turkish workers legally employed in the territory of the Member States. The CJEU has repeatedly held that art.6(1) has direct effect. However, the rights provided for in art.6(1) only benefit those workers who fulfil the requirements in terms of legal employment, belonging to the labour force and duration of employment. This provision is discussed in detail in Ch.18.

17–22

Article 7 provides rights for members of the worker's family who may respond to offers of employment after three years subject to the priority of EU national workers and enjoy free access to the labour market after five years. Children who have completed vocational training are able to respond to an offer of employment irrespective of the length of time for which they have been resident in the Member State. This provision is discussed in detail in Ch.20 on family members.

17–23

Article 13 contains a standstill clause regarding the introduction of new restrictions on access to the labour market for workers legally resident and employed in the territory of the contracting States.

17–24

---

[14] See para.18–77, below.
[15] *Bozkurt v Staatssecretaris van Justitie* (C-434/93) [1995] E.C.R. I-1475.
[16] *Bozkurt v Staatssecretaris van Justitie* (C-434/93) [1995] E.C.R. I-1475, at [20].
[17] *Sevince v Staatssecretaris van Justitite* (C-192/89) [1990] E.C.R. I-3461.
[18] *Sevince v Staatssecretaris van Justitite* (C-192/89) [1990] E.C.R. I-3461, at [21].

(iii) Decision 3/80

17-25 Decision 3/80[19] aims to co-ordinate Member States' social security schemes with a view to enabling Turkish workers employed or formerly employed in the Community, members of their families and their survivors to qualify for benefits in the traditional branches of social security. Decision 3/80 refers specifically to Regulation 1408/71[20] on the application of social security schemes to employed persons and their families moving within the Community.

17-26 There is no specified date of entry into force of Decision 3/80 (unlike in Decision 1/80). However, the CJEU has held that the date of entry into force is the date on which it was adopted, namely September 19, 1980.

17-27 Whilst Decision 3/80 refers specifically to Regulation 1408/71, the former lacks the cumbersome implementing measures set out in Regulation 574/72[21] which were deemed necessary for the implementation of Regulation 1408/71. It is for this reason that the CJEU has held that the provisions of Decision 3/80 that refer to further implementing measures[22] do not have direct effect.

17-28 In its judgment in the case of *Taflan-Met*[23] the CJEU referred to the fact that the Commission had submitted a proposal for a Council Regulation implementing Decision 3/80 in 1983, which was based to a large extent on Regulation 574/72.[24] That proposal, however, has not yet been adopted by the Council depriving Decision 3/80 of much of its impact.

17-29 In *Kocak*[25] the CJEU held that the non-discrimination provision art.3(1) of Decision 3/80 was capable of direct effect. Under art.3(1), Turkish nationals who reside in one of the Member States and to whom Decision 3/80 applies, are to enjoy in that Member State the same social security benefits under the legislation of that Member State as do the nationals of that State. According to art.2, Decision 3/80 applies to Turkish nationals who are or have been subject to the legislation of one of the Member States and their family members resident in that Member State, as well as the survivors of these workers.

17-30 The detail of the social security provisions contained in Decision 3/80 is beyond the scope of this book. However, it is to be noted that the Council of Association has attempted through this decision to give effect to art.39(1) of

---

[19] (C110/60) [1983] O.J.
[20] Regulation (EC) No.883/2004 has replaced Regulation 1408/71.
[21] Council Regulation (EEC) No.574/72 of March 21, 1972 laying down the procedure for implementing Regulation (EEC) 1408/71.
[22] arts 12 and 13 of December 3/80 which consist of co-ordinating provisions relating to sickness and maternity benefits, invalidity benefits, old-age benefits and death benefits (pensions).
[23] *Talfan-Met, Altun-Baser, Andal-Bugdayci v Bestuur van de Sociale Verzekeringsbank* (C-277/94) [1996] E.C.R. I-4085.
[24] [1972] O.J. Spec. Ed.159.
[25] *Kocak v Landesversicherungsanstalt Overfranken und Mittelfranken* (C-102/98) and *Ramazan v Bundesknappschaft* (C-211/98) [2000] E.C.R. I-1287.

the Additional Protocol which directs the Council to adopt social security measures for Turkish workers.

(b) *The direct effect of decisions of the Council of Association*

Whether a provision in the decisions of the Council of Association is capable of creating directly effective rights in EU law is of importance. The Council of Association is specifically charged with responsibility for making rules in relation to the progressive securing of the free movement of persons. If those rules were not held to be directly effective, that aim might be undermined. 17–31

In principle there is no reason why a body created by an Association Agreement with representatives from all of the Contracting Parties involved could not make decisions that are directly effective in EU law. In the context of the Ankara Agreement the CJEU has repeated the view [previously held in respect of the Greek Association Agreement] that: 17–32

> "since they are directly connected with the Agreement to which they give effect, the decisions of the Council of Association, in the same way as the Agreement itself, form an integral part, as from their entry into force, of the Community legal system".[26]

The CJEU considers that since it has jurisdiction to give preliminary rulings on the Ankara Agreement itself, it must also have jurisdiction to give rulings on the interpretation of the decisions adopted by the authority established by the Agreement and entrusted with responsibility for its implementation.[27]

It is a function of art.267 TFEU (ex-art.234 EC Treaty) to ensure uniform application of all of the provisions forming part of the EU legal system, which would include decisions by the Association Council. The CJEU's jurisdiction is thereby fortified. 17–33

Despite the clarity with which the CJEU has declared its jurisdiction both in relation to the Ankara Agreement and to the decisions of the Association Council, Member States persisted until 1992[28] in requesting the CJEU to reconsider its jurisdiction to give rulings pursuant to art.267 TFEU. The CJEU has not been prepared to relinquish its jurisdiction. 17–34

In its case law the CJEU has held that arts 6(1), 6(2), 7(1), 7(2) and 13 of Decision 1/80 have direct effect. There is in principle no reason why any other provision of a decision of the Council of Association which is sufficiently precise and unconditional would not be capable of conferring directly effective rights on individuals. 17–35

---

[26] *Sevince v Staatssecretaris van Justitite* (C-192/89) [1990] E.C.R. I-3461, at [9].
[27] This is of course comparable with the situation under the TFEU itself where provisions need specifying through regulations and directives.
[28] *Kus v Landeshauptstadt Wiesbaden* (C-237/91) [1992] E.C.R. I-6781.

17–36 The CJEU is very clear on the need for certain terms contained in the provisions of the decisions of the Association Council to be interpreted and defined uniformly at European Union level.

> "in the light of the spirit and purpose of the provisions in question, and of their context, in order to ensure their consistent application in the Member States"[29].

---

[29] *Pehlivan v Staatssecretaris van Justitie* (C-484/07) June 16, 2011, at [44].

CHAPTER 18

WORKERS UNDER THE ANKARA AGREEMENT

This chapter examines the rights given by the Ankara Agreement to Turkish nationals legally employed in Member States. Although Member States retain control of the entry into their labour force of Turkish nationals, once admitted to the labour force the provisions confer significant rights.

1. INTRODUCTION: THE PROVISIONS

(a) *The Ankara Agreement and Additional Protocol*

Of principal importance in the context of the free movement of workers are art.12 of the Ankara Agreement and art.36 of the Additional Protocol. **18–01**

Article 12

The Contracting Parties agree to be guided by Articles 48, 49 and 50[1] of the Treaty establishing the Community for the purpose of progressively securing freedom of movement for workers between them.

Article 36

Freedom of movement for workers ... shall be secured by progressive stages in accordance with the principles set out in Article 12 of the Agreement of Association between the end of the twelfth and the twenty-second year after the entry into force of that Agreement.

The Council of Association shall decide on the rules necessary to that end.

Article 12 follows from the general aim of the Ankara Agreement to promote economic relations between Turkey and the European Union and the eventual accession of Turkey to the Union. It outlines an objective of the Contracting Parties to the Agreement and lays the foundation stone for the free movement of workers. The CJEU has held however that the general nature of the provision deprives it of direct effect.[2] Under art.36 of the Additional Protocol the aim of the free movement of workers was to be achieved between November 30, 1974 and November 30, 1986. **18–02**

In *Demirel*,[3] the CJEU held that art.12 of the Ankara Agreement, together with art.36 of the Additional Protocol, were essentially programmatic and not sufficiently precise and unconditional to be capable of governing directly the movement of workers. This is partly justified by the exclusive powers conferred on the Association Council to lay down the detailed rules to **18–03**

---

[1] Now arts 45, 46 and 47 TFEU.
[2] *Demirel v Stadt Schwäbisch Gmünd* (12/86) [1987] E.C.R. 3719, at [23].
[3] *Demirel v Stadt Schwäbisch Gmünd* (12/86) [1987] E.C.R. 3719.

achieve the aims of the provisions. The fact that the time framework set out in art.36 of the Protocol has now long overrun has not resulted in any legal measure making the provisions of art.12 directly effective. This is to be contrasted with the provisions of art.48 of the Treaty of Rome where the CJEU held that the end of the transitional period set out in the Treaty did confer rights on Union workers upon which they could rely directly.[4] Whilst the CJEU has not yet examined the specific question of the implication of the expiry of the time framework for the transitional stage, Advocate General Darmon suggested in his Opinion in *Demirel*[5] that the expiry of that time framework did not create any binding effect:

> "The passage of time, has no legal implications here. Progressive implementation depends on decisions of the Council of Association. The absence of such decisions in this field, reflecting the difficulties experienced by the Contracting Parties in reaching a consensus, precludes the application of provisions without a clearly circumscribed content. Any other solution would, indeed, be incompatible with the consensual nature of an international convention".

(b) *Relevant provisions of the Decisions of the Council of Association*

18–04 Decision 1/80 contains specific provisions relating to workers. The provisions contained within Decision 1/80 are said to constitute "one stage further, guided by Articles 48, 49 and 50 of the Treaty, towards securing freedom of movement for workers."[6] The Court has considered that this means:

> "In order to ensure compliance with that objective, it would seem to be essential to transpose, so far as is possible, the principles enshrined in those articles to Turkish workers who enjoy the rights conferred by Decision No 1/80."[7]

18–05 As illustrated by the cases of *Gürol*[8] and *Dogan*[9] the Court is inclined to interpret the provisions in Decision 1/80 in a manner which attains "the full the objective pursued" by those provisions.[10] Of specific interest with regard to the free movement of workers is art.6(1) of Decision 1/80, which provides:

> "1. Subject to Article 7 on free access to employment for members of his family, a Turkish worker duly registered as belonging to the labour force of a Member State:
>
> — shall be entitled in that Member State, after one year's legal employment, to renewal of his permit to work for the same employer, if a job is available;
> — shall be entitled in that Member State, after three years of legal employment and subject to the priority to be given to workers of Member States of the Community, to respond to another offer of employment, with an employer of

---

[4] *Van Duyn v Home Office* (41/74) [1974] E.C.R. 1337.
[5] *Demirel v Stadt Schwäbisch Gmünd* (12/86) [1987] E.C.R. 3719, at [23].
[6] *Bozkurt* (C-434/93) [1995] E.C.R. I-1475.
[7] *Bozkurt* (C-434/93) [1995] E.C.R. I-1475, at [20].
[8] *Gürol v Bezirksregierung Köln* (C-374/03) [2005] All E.R. (D) 86 (Jul).
[9] *Ergul Dogan v Sicherheitsdirektion für das Bundesland Vorarlberg* (C-383/03) July 7, 2005.
[10] *Gürol* (C-374/03) July 7, 2005, at [40].

his choice, made under normal conditions and registered with the employment services of that State, for the same occupation;
— shall enjoy free access in that Member State to any paid employment of his choice, after four years of legal employment."

18–06 The CJEU has repeatedly held that art.6(1) has direct effect.[11] As stated in *Kurz*,[12] Turkish nationals who satisfy its conditions are able therefore to rely directly

> "on the rights which the three indents of that provision confer on them progressively, according to the duration of their employment in the host Member State."

However, the rights provided for in art.6(1) only benefit those Turkish workers who fulfil the requirements in terms of legal employment, belonging to the labour force and time. The full implication of the provision is discussed below.

18–07 Article 6(2) makes provision for certain absences being incorporated into periods of legal employment (annual holidays, short periods of sickness, etc.) and for other longer absences which, although not able to be incorporated into periods of legal employment, do not affect rights already acquired. Article 6(3) provides that the procedures for applying arts 6(1) and (2) are those established under national law.

18–08 Article 7 makes provision for members of the worker's family to be able to respond to offers of employment after three years and to access the labour market freely after five years. Provision is also made for children who have completed vocational training to be able to respond to offers of employment, irrespective of the length of time they have been resident in the Member State.

18–09 Article 13 contains a standstill clause regarding the introduction of new restrictions on access to the employment of workers legally resident and employed in the territory of the contracting States.

2. THE WORKER'S RIGHT TO CONTINUED EMPLOYMENT

Introduction

18–10 Nothing in the Ankara Agreement itself or the decisions of the Council of Association confers rights of free movement on workers not already part of the labour force. However, Decision 1/80 is designed to promote the gradual integration in the host Member State of Turkish national workers with the objective of achieving progressive stages of freedom of movement for

---

[11] The CJEU has consistently so held since its decision in *Sevince v Staatssecretaris van Justitite* (C-192/89) [1990] E.C.R. I-3461 (see, for example, *Birden v Stadtgemeinde Bremen* (C-1/97) [1998] E.C.R. I-7747 and *Kurz v Land Baden-Württemberg* (C-188/00) [2002] E.C.R. I-691).
[12] *Kurz v Land Baden-Württemberg* (C-188/00) [2002] E.C.R. I-691, at [26].

workers.[13] To that end art.6(1) of Decision 1/80 does provide the right to continued employment to Turkish workers in certain circumstances. In order to benefit from those rights Turkish nationals must satisfy three conditions, namely:

(a) they must be workers;

(b) they must be in legal employment and duly registered as belonging to the labour force of the host Member State; and

(c) they must fulfil the requisite time periods.

Whilst the concept of worker is one familiar to European Union law, the other requirements are imposed only on Turkish nationals in the context of art.6 of Decision 1/80.

18-11 The conditions are interconnected and overlapping. This can be potentially confusing. For instance in *Birden*[14] the CJEU treated the condition of legal employment and being duly registered as belonging to the labour force as synonymous.[15] Despite this, the test of legal employment does indeed raise discrete questions from those considered when assessing whether a person is duly registered as belonging to the labour force. The overlap is reflected also in the fact that since its decision in *Sevince*,[16] the CJEU has consistently stated that legal employment presupposes a stable and secure situation as a member of the labour force, thereby merging the conditions treated as synonymous by the CJEU in *Birden*. Moreover, analysis of the relevant conditions is not helped by the fact that on occasions the CJEU has conflated its consideration of the various questions. Thus for example in *Günaydin*[17] having stated that the Turkish national was "undeniably" a worker duly registered as belonging to the labour force, the CJEU then examined whether the worker was

> "bound by an employment relationship covering a genuine and effective economic activity pursued for the benefit and under the direction of another person for remuneration".

18-12 At the heart of much of the case law in this area is the tension between, on the one hand, the wishes of certain Member States to recruit Turkish nationals to the labour force for finite periods under potentially strict conditions, and, on the other hand, the practical consequences of such recruitment giving rights to those Turkish nationals in the circumstances laid down in art.6. This creates a tension because there is no doubt that the art.6 rights go far beyond what will have been contemplated by the Member States when granting entry and permission to work to such Turkish nationals. The tension referred to is well shown by *Akyuz*[18] in which the UK Government attempted to argue that those granted entry as students could

---

[13] See, for instance, *Bekleyen v Land Berlin* (C-462/08) January 21, 2010 at [24–25].
[14] *Birden v Stadtgemeinde Bremen* (C-1/97) [1998] E.C.R. I-7747.
[15] See para.18–20, below.
[16] *Sevince v Staatssecretaris van Justitite* (C-192/89) [1990] E.C.R. I-3461, at [30].
[17] *Günaydin v Freistaat Bayern* (C-36/96) [1997] E.C.R. I-5143.
[18] *Payir, Akyuz and Ozturk v SSHD* (C-294/06) January 24, 2008.

not be workers or regarded as being duly registered as belonging to the labour force even if they are legally engaged in genuine and effective economic activity because they were not admitted to the UK for the purpose of work.

Despite such overlap each condition raises specific questions and it is necessary to examine each term. 18–13

(a) *The concept of "worker"*

Just as in the TFEU there is no definition of a European Union "worker", so there is no definition of a "Turkish worker" in the Ankara Agreement, its Protocol or the decisions of the Council of Association. However, the references to various TFEU provisions and the general commitment in the Ankara Agreement towards eventual accession of Turkey to the European Union indicate that the concept of "Turkish worker" should take on the European Union law definition. Such approach is further indicated by the CJEU's commitment to providing uniform and objective application of the provisions contained within the Ankara Agreement, the decisions adopted by the Council of Association, and the CJEU's attempts to interpret the decisions of the Council, as far as possible, in the light of TFEU provisions on the freedom of movement of workers. 18–14

In fact the CJEU has repeatedly concluded from the wording of art.12 of the Agreement and art.36 of the Protocol, as well as from the objective of Decision 1/80, that the principles enshrined in arts 45, 46 and 47 TFEU must be extended, so far as possible, to Turkish nationals who enjoy the rights conferred by Decision 1/80.[19] This has meant that reference is made to the interpretation of the concept of worker under European Union law for the purposes of determining the scope of the same concept employed in art.6(1) of Decision 1/80. 18–15

The Union concept of worker is considered in detail in Ch.6. The concept must be interpreted broadly. In order to be treated as a worker, a person must pursue an activity which is genuine and effective, to the exclusion of activities on such a small scale as to be regarded as purely marginal and ancillary. The essential feature of an employment relationship is that for a certain period of time a person performs services for and under the direction of another person in return for which remuneration is received. Neither the nature of the employment relationship under national law, nor the level of productivity of the person concerned, the origin of the funds 18–16

---

[19] See to that effect, inter alia, *Bozkurt v Staatssecretaris van Justitie* (C-434/93) [1995] E.C.R. I-1475, at [14], [19] and [20]; *Tetik v Land Berlin* (C-171/95) [1997] E.C.R. I-329, at [20] and [28]; *Birden v Stadtgemeinde Bremen* (C-1/97) at [23]; *Nazli* (C-340/97) [2000] E.C.R. I-957, at [50–55]; and *Kurz v Land Baden-Württemberg* (C-188/00) [2002] E.C.R. I-691, at [30].

from which the remuneration is paid or the limited amount of the remuneration can have any consequence in regard to whether or not the person is a worker for the purposes of Union law.[20]

18–17 In *Genc* the CJEU recalled that the fact that a worker's earnings do not cover all of his needs cannot preclude him from being a worker and that employment which yields an income lower than the minimum required for subsistence or normally does not exceed even 10 hours a week does not prevent the person in such employment from being regarded as a worker in Union law.

> "Although the fact that a person works for only a very limited number of hours in the context of an employment relationship may be an indication that the activities performed are marginal and ancillary (Case C-357/89 *Raulin* [1992] ECR I-1027, paragraph 14), the fact remains that, independently of the limited amount of the remuneration for and the number of hours of the activity in question, the possibility cannot be ruled out that, following an overall assessment of the employment relationship in question, that activity may be considered by the national authorities to be real and genuine, thereby allowing its holder to be granted the status of 'worker.'"[21]

The CJEU stated in an order to determine whether a person was a worker that it was necessary to take account of factors including the right to paid leave, the continued payment of wages in the event of sickness and the existence of a contract for employment over a period of four years with the same undertaking rather than merely focusing on levels of renumeration or numbers of working hours.[22]

18–18 In line with its case law on art.45 TFEU the CJEU stated in *Birden*[23] that:

> "A Turkish national such as Mr Birden, who is employed on the basis of a law such as the BSHG, performs, as a subordinate, services for his employer in return for which he receives remuneration, thus satisfying the essential criteria of the employment relationship ... That interpretation is not altered by the fact that the remuneration of the person concerned is provided using public funds since, by analogy with the case-law relating to Article 48 of the Treaty [now Art. 45 TFEU] neither the origin of the funds from which the remuneration is paid, nor the 'sui generis' nature of the employment relationship under national law and the level of productivity of the person concerned can have any consequence in regard to whether or not the person is to be regarded as a worker".

---

[20] See, in particular, *Lawrie-Blum* (66/85) [1986] E.C.R. 2121, at [16] and [17]; *Brown* (197/86) [1988] E.C.R. 3205, at [21]; *Bettray v Staatssecretaris van Justitite* (344/87) [1989] E.C.R. 1621, at [15] and [16]; *Raulin v Minnster van Onderwijs en Wetenschappen* (C-357/89) [1992] E.C.R. I-1027, at [10]; and *Bernini v Netherlands Ministry of Education and Science* (C-3/90) [1992] E.C.R. I-1071, at [14–17]; and, as regards art.6(1) of Decision 1/80, *Günaydin v Freistaat Bayern* (C-36/96) [1997] E.C.R. I-5143, at [31]; *Ertanir v Land Hessen* (C-98/96) [1997] E.C.R. I-5179, at [43]; *Birden v Stadtgemeinde Bremen* (C-1/97) [1998] E.C.R. I-7747, at [25] and [28]; and *Kurz v Land Baden-Württemberg* (C-188/00) [2002] E.C.R. I-691, at [32].
[21] *Genc v Land Berlin* (C-14/09) February 4, 2010, at [26].
[22] *Genc v Land Berlin* (C-14/09), February 4, 2010, at [27].
[23] *Birden v Stadtgemeinde Bremen* (C-1/97) [1998] E.C.R. I-7747, at [26] and [28].

The term "worker" includes trainees and apprentices, part-time workers, au-pairs and those engaged in employment schemes.[24]

Any person who pursues a genuine and effective economic activity for and under the direction of an employer and receives remuneration (whether in cash or kind) for that activity must be regarded as a worker for the purposes of Union law. It is not relevant that the person holds another status at the same time, even one which they might regard as their principal activity such as that of a student.[25] **18–19**

(b) *The concepts of "legal employment" and being "duly registered as belonging to the labour force"*

Introduction

At the core of the concepts of legal employment and being duly registered as belonging to the labour force are the following matters which must be established by the worker that: **18–20**

(i) his situation as a member of the labour force is stable and secure ("legal employment");

(ii) formal requirements have been complied with ("duly registered");

(iii) he is a member of the "labour force"; and

(iv) the employment can be located within the territory of the Member State or retains a sufficiently close link with that territory.

(i) *Stable and secure situation*

Since its decision in *Sevince*[26] the CJEU has repeatedly stated that the legality of employment (the phrase "legal employment" being repeated in each indent of art.6(1) of Decision 1/80) pre-supposes a stable and secure situation as a member of the labour force. Such requirement of legal employment does not necessarily presuppose the possession of residence documents or even a work permit.[27] However, legality of employment must be determined in the light of the legislation of the Member State governing the conditions under which the Turkish worker entered the national territory and is employed there. The worker must not be working in breach of any legal conditions of stay or have entered on false documentation and thereby entered into employment as the result of fraudulent conduct.[28] **18–21**

---

[24] *Payir, Akyuz and Ozturk v SSHD* (C-294/06) [2008] E.C.R. I-00203.
[25] See *Payir, Akyuz and Ozturk v SSHD* (C-294/06) [2008] E.C.R. I-00203, see also *Grzelczyk* (C-184/99) [2001] E.C.R. I-06193.
[26] *Sevince v Staatssecretaris van Justitite* (C-192/89) [1990] E.C.R. I-3461, at [30].
[27] See *Bozkurtz v Staatssecretaris van Justitite* (C-434/93) [1995] E.C.R. I-1475, at [14], [19] and [20]. The case concerned the position of a Turkish worker employed as an international lorry driver by a company incorporated under Netherlands law with its head office in the Netherlands where, in periods between journeys and during his leave, Mr Bozkurt lived. As an international lorry driver under Netherlands law Mr Bozkurt did not require either a work permit or residence permit.
[28] *Kol v Land Berlin* (C-285/95) [1997] E.C.R. I-3069.

18–22 The requirement of stability and security means that there must be an undisputed right of residence: plainly any dispute as to the existence of such right would lead to instability and lack of security in the worker's situation. Thus, a Turkish worker who is only able to work by virtue of making an appeal against the refusal of a residence permit will not be considered to fulfil the requirements of legal employment. This is equally the case where a first instance judgment upholds the right of residence, but where there is retroactive suspension of the residence permit ordered by a court through the exercise of an appeal against such first instance judgment. Further, the same would apply to a period of temporary residence given whilst an asylum claim is considered where during such period the Turkish national is permitted to work.

18–23 In *Sevince*,[29] the CJEU considered the position of a Turkish national refused a residence permit by the Dutch authorities who sought subsequently to rely—as periods of legal employment—on time spent working whilst he benefited from the suspensive effect of his appeal against refusal of the residence permit. The CJEU refused to treat such time as periods of legal employment for the purposes of art.6. The CJEU justified its decision refusing to recognise as periods of legal employment those periods during which the worker was legally able to continue in employment only because of the suspensory effect of an appeal on the basis that it was "inconceivable" that a Turkish worker should be able to "contrive to fulfil" the condition of legal employment in this manner, provided always that the court dismisses such an appeal.[30]

18–24 The decision of the CJEU in *Kus*[31] might seem even harsher than the decision in *Sevince*[32] since in *Kus* it was the authorities which appealed against a first instance decision to grant the residence permit. The CJEU justified the decision on the basis that if the national court subsequently refused the residence permit such refusal would have

> "no effect whatever and the person in question will be enabled to contrive to obtain the rights provided by ... Article 6(1) during a period when he did not fulfil the requisite conditions".[33]

The CJEU did acknowledge that if the right of residence was finally granted, then the worker must be deemed retrospectively to have had during the period in question a right of residence which was not provisional but fulfilled the requirement of being "stable and secure".[34]

18–25 The reasons for a Member State allowing a Turkish national to work and reside in its territory are not relevant to the question of whether employment is legal. As the CJEU has repeatedly stated, art.6(1) cannot be construed so

---

[29] *Sevince v Staatssecretaris van Justitite* (C-192/89) [1990] E.C.R. I-3461, at [30].
[30] See paras 31 and 32. See also, *Kus v Landeshauptstadt Wiesbaden* (C-23/91) [1992] E.C.R. I-6781.
[31] *Kus v Landeshauptstadt Wiesbaden* (C-23/91) [1992] E.C.R. I-6781.
[32] *Sevince v Staatssecretaris van Justitite* (C-192/89) [1990] E.C.R. I-3461, at [30].
[33] *Kus v Landeshauptstadt Wiesbaden* (C-23/91) [1992] E.C.R. I-6781, at [16].
[34] *Kus v Landeshauptstadt Wiesbaden* (C-23/91) [1992] E.C.R. I-6781, at [17].

as to allow a Member State to modify unilaterally the scope of the system of gradual integration of Turkish workers which is at the heart of the Ankara Agreement and Additional Protocol. Where a Turkish worker's employment is stable and secure the legality of such employment cannot be undermined by the terms on which the right of entry was first given. This is the case notwithstanding the exclusive competence of Member States to regulate both the entry of Turkish nationals into their territory and the circumstances in which they are permitted to take up first employment. This reflects the tension identified at para.18–11 above. Member States may suggest that the CJEU's interpretation of art.6 does encroach upon such competence since initial restrictions can become meaningless where after a year the Turkish worker begins to accumulate the rights given in art.6(1) irrespective of any initial limitations.

These principles have been applied in a case where work and residence permits were granted to a worker only after his marriage to a German national, even where the marriage is subsequently dissolved.[35] **18–26**

Similarly where the Turkish worker was allowed to enter the Member State to fulfil a specific labour requirement there, for example as a specialist chef.[36] Even the fact that a Turkish worker expressly accepted restrictions on his length of stay does not deprive him of the rights acquired under art.6(1). **18–27**

Indeed these principles have similarly been applied where the Turkish worker was granted employment and residence permits for the purpose of allowing him to pursue a training course at a factory in Germany.[37] **18–28**

The CJEU decided in the *Gunaydin* case that the fact that a Turkish worker declared his intention of returning to Turkey after having been employed in the Member State for the purpose of perfecting his vocational skills does not deprive him of the rights deriving from art.6(1) unless it is established by a national court that he made that declaration with the sole intention of deceiving the national authorities.[38] **18–29**

The motivation for the Member State granting the Turkish national permission to work is irrelevant. For instance, the fact that a student may have been granted permission to work for a "social objective" does not take away the lawful character of the activities performed and therefore cannot prevent them from being regarded as duly registered as belonging to the labour force.[39] **18–30**

---

[35] See *Kus v Landeshaupstadt Wiesbaden* (C-237/91) [1992] E.C.R. I-06781.
[36] *Ertanir* (C-98/96) [1997] E.C.R. I-5179.
[37] *Faik Gunaydin and others v Freistaat Bayern* (C-36/96) [1997] E.C.R. I-5143.
[38] *Gunaydin* (C-36/96) [1997] E.C.R. I-5143, at [54].
[39] *Payir, Akyuz and Ozturk v SSHD* (C-294/06) January 24, 2008, at [35]. Similarly au pairs granted permission to work for a limited number of hours with social objectives in mind may be nevertheless regarded as belonging to the labour force. It is obviously open to Member States to attempt to deny persons in such situations permission to work from the outset, but whether that would be either cost effective or politically expedient given the benefits to the State of having people in its territory working or compatible with general principles of discrimination if Turkish nationals were to be singled out is doubtful.

18-31 Even where conditions of residence are not met during the first year of employment and residence art.6(1) rights can nevertheless be derived if the Turkish worker is lawfully employed for a year. In *Unal*[40] the CJEU found that where a residence permit had been granted on condition that the Turkish worker cohabited with his partner but within a year that relationship had broken down, provided he had been working legally for a year and had entered the territory legally and had not obtained entry by fraud or been given a provisional residence permit, he fulfilled the conditions of the first indent of art.6(1). Whilst the Dutch Government had argued that he had failed to comply with a condition of his stay, namely cohabitation, in the CJEU's view since the residence permit granted to him had not been provisional, his employment was legal for the entire year. The Court found that it is the date on which the authorities decided not to renew his permit which was relevant, not the date on which he was no longer in compliance with his conditions of stay. The emphasis was placed on the fact there was nothing provisional about his residence and employment permit, he had complied with conditions of employment (although not residence), he had entered lawfully and without use of fraud.

(ii) *Formal requirements*

18-32 The Turkish worker must comply with any applicable formalities required by the national law of the Member State concerned. There is obvious overlap with the concept of legal employment which as already indicated requires compliance with the national law provisions governing the conditions under which the Turkish worker enters the national territory and is employed there. In *Birden*[41] however, the CJEU distinguished between the requirements of compliance with legislation governing entry into the territory and pursuit of employment there. On the facts in *Birden* the CJEU considered there to be no doubt that Mr Birden satisfied the requirements since he both legally entered and occupied a post "organised and financed by public authorities" of the Member State. The CJEU stated that being duly registered as belonging to the labour force that applied

> "to all workers who have complied with the requirements laid down by law and regulation in the Member State concerned and are thus entitled to pursue an occupation in its territory."[42]

Examples of requirements relating to the pursuit of employment could include the payment of income tax, contributions for health, pension, and unemployment insurance.

18-33 In *Unal* the CJEU emphasised the legality and conditions of employment that need to be complied with as opposed to conditions of residence. Where a Turkish worker legally enters the Member State (for family reunion purposes for instance), and where he is granted the right to work,

---

[40] *Baris Unal v Staatssecretaris van Justitie* (C-187/10) September 29, 2010.
[41] *Birden v Stadtgemeinde Bremen* (C-1/97) [1998] E.C.R. I-7747, at [48–51].
[42] *Birden v Stadtgemeinde Bremen* (C-1/97) [1998] E.C.R. I-7747, at [51].

the fact that it is subsequent to expiry of the residence permit that it transpires that he did not comply with a condition of residence (as opposed to employment) such as cohabitation does not retrospectively allow the Member State to deny him his rights under art.6(1). It would only be in a case of fraud which would allow a Member State to deny a Turkish worker rights under art.6(1).[43]

(iii) *The meaning of "labour force"*

Turkish national workers are additionally required to be members of the labour force. It is perhaps difficult to conceive of a scenario in which a Turkish national who is working in a Member State in a situation which is both stable and secure and who has complied with all formalities might nevertheless be able to be said not to be part of the labour force. The facts of *Birden*[44] however provide a useful example of the agreements in this area. Mr Birden's work as a semi skilled odd-job man with a cultural centre (which was work of a kind offered to a limited group of persons) was sponsored by the German authorities with public funds. The authorities required the payment of social security contributions and it was intended to enable him to enter or re-enter working life. It was argued by the German Government that the employment—which was essentially social in nature consisting of public utility work which in other circumstances would not be carried out—was intended to improve the integration into working life of a limited group of persons who were unable to compete with most other job seekers. Such persons were said to be distinguishable from workers as a whole and did not belong to the Germany's general labour force. The Commission similarly argued that being duly registered as belonging to the labour force referred only to the pursuit of

18–34

> "a normal economic activity on the labour market, as opposed to employment created artificially and financed by the public authorities such as that undertaken by Mr Birden".

The CJEU rejected the submission in these terms:[45]

18–35

> "The concept of 'being duly registered as belonging to the labour force' must be regarded as applying to all workers who have complied with the requirements laid down by law and regulation in the Member State concerned and are thus entitled to pursue an occupation in its territory. By contrast, contrary to the assertions of the German Government and the Commission, it cannot be interpreted as applying to the labour market in general as opposed to a specific market with a social objective supported by the public authorities".

The "labour force" to which the Turkish worker must belong is therefore broadly interpreted. It matters not whether the Turkish worker can be said to be part of the general workforce, or as in *Birden*, whether the Turkish worker is part of a specific sector labour force defined by specific

18–36

---

[43] *Unal v Staatssecretaris van Justitie* (C-187/10) September 29, 2011.
[44] *Birden v Stadtgemeinde Bremen* (C-1/97) [1998] E.C.R. I-7747.
[45] *Birden v Stadtgemeinde Bremen* (C-1/97) [1998] E.C.R. I-7747, at [51].

objectives.[46] This approach chimes with that taken in relation to legal employment whereby, as discussed above, the CJEU has made clear that the reasons for a Member State allowing a Turkish national to work and reside in its territory are not relevant to the question of whether the employment was legal.

18–37 Whether examined as an aspect of legal employment or being a duly registered member of the labour force, the CJEU has consistently refused to accept interpretations urged upon them by some Member States which would limit access to the rights contained in art.6(1) by reference to the nature of the employment or the original conditions on which it was given.

18–38 In *Kurz*,[47] the CJEU again examined a submission by the German Government seeking to limit the application of art.6(1) rights to certain types of worker (on the facts an apprentice was pursuing an activity of a purely temporary and specific nature). The CJEU rejected the submission that the worker was not duly registered as belonging to the labour force since his was not a "normal employment relationship" intended to bring about his future inclusion in the labour market in general. According to the CJEU there was no doubt that Mr Kurz (who was in legal employment in Germany for four years) was a Turkish worker who had complied with Germany's legislation governing entry into its territory and pursuit of employment. An interpretation limiting the applicability of art.6(1) to such a person (who on the facts was "just as integrated in the host Member State as a worker who has carried out comparable work for an equivalent period"[48]) would be inconsistent with the aim and broad logic of Decision 1/80.

(iv) *Employment located within territory or retaining sufficiently close link with that territory*

18–39 The CJEU has repeatedly stated[49] that being duly registered as belonging to the labour force requires that the employment relationship:

> "can be located within the territory of a Member State or retains a sufficiently close link with that territory, taking account in particular of the place where the Turkish national was hired, the territory on or from which the paid activity is pursued and the applicable national legislation in the field of labour and social security law".[50]

---

[46] See also, *Kus v Landeshauptstadt Wisbaden* (C-23/91) [1992] E.C.R. I-6781, at [43] ("... [T]he concept of being 'duly registered as belonging to the labour force of a Member State' cannot be interpreted as applying to the labour market in general as opposed to a restricted market with a specific objective").
[47] *Kurz v Land Baden-Württemberg* (C-188/00) [2002] E.C.R. I-691.
[48] *Kurz v Land Baden-Württemberg* (C-188/00) [2002] E.C.R. I-691, at [45].
[49] See, for instance, *Bozkurt v Staatssecretaris van Justitie* (C-434/93) [1995] E.C.R. I-1475, at [22] and [23]; *Günaydin* [1997] E.C.R. I-5143 (C-36/96) at [29]; *Ertanir v Land Hessen* (C-98/96) [1997] E.C.R. I-5179, at [39]; *Birden v Stadtgemeinde* (C-1/97); *Bremen* [1998] E.C.R. I-7747, at [33]; and *Kurz v Land Baden-Württemberg* (C-188/00) [2002] E.C.R. I-691, at [37].
[50] *Kurz v Land Baden-Württemberg* (C-188/00) [2002] E.C.R. I-691, at [37].

18–40 The requirement has been regarded by the CJEU as invariably met in a number of decisions and, subject to the example of persons whose work is not performed in the Member State concerned (as in the case of, for example, sailors or international lorry drivers considered below), rarely causes difficulty. In *Kurz*,[51] for example, the CJEU described the condition as "undoubtedly satisfied" where the worker had been hired and had pursued in the course of his apprenticeship a paid activity on the territory of the host Member State, and his employment had been subject to the legislation of that State.[52]

18–41 One example of potential dispute in relation to this condition is provided by *Bozkurt*[53] in which the principle identified above was first laid down. The case concerned a Turkish worker who, without the need to possess either a work or residence permit, lived in the Netherlands employed as an international lorry driver. One question considered by the CJEU was what criteria were to be used to determine whether Mr Bozkurt belonged to the labour force. The CJEU accepted that the same criteria should be applied to his situation as an international lorry driver as were applied by the CJEU in *Lopes de Veiga*[54] to the position of a Member State national seaman employed on board a ship flying the flag of another Member State. The intervening governments had argued that such interpretation, applicable in the context of full free movement rights conferred by the TFEU, would not be consistent with the modest objectives of an association agreement. The CJEU held that, so far as possible, it was essential to transpose the principles enshrined in the EC Treaty to Turkish workers enjoying the rights conferred by Decision 1/80.

18–42 The CJEU held that in deciding whether Mr Bozkurt's employment retained a sufficiently close link with the territory of the Netherlands, the national court would be required to take account in particular where he was hired, where his paid employment was based and the applicable national legislation in the field of employment and social security law.

---

[51] *Kurz v Land Baden-Württemberg* (C-188/00) [2002] E.C.R. I-691.
[52] See, for example, to like effect *Birden v Stadtgemeinde Bremen* (C-1/97) [1998] E.C.R. I-7747, at [34].
[53] *Bozkurt v Staatssecretaris van Justitie* (C-434/93) [1995] E.C.R. I-1475.
[54] *Lopes da Veiga v Staatsecretaris van Justitite* (C-9/88) [1989] E.C.R. 2989. The CJEU ruled that in the case of a worker who is a national of a Member State and who is permanently employed on board a ship flying the flag of another Member State (in that instance the Netherlands) in deciding whether the legal relationship of employment could be located within the territory of the Union or retained a sufficiently close link with that territory, for the purposes of the application of Regulation 1612/68 (now replaced by Directive 2004/38), it was for the national court to take into account the following: the fact that the applicant worked on board a vessel registered in the Netherlands in the employment of a shipping company established in the Netherlands, that he was hired in the Netherlands, that the employment relationship between him and his employer was subject to Netherlands law and, finally, that he was insured under the social security system of the Netherlands and paid income tax there.

(c) *Employment for one of three requisite time periods*

(i) *The specified time periods*

18–43 In order to qualify under art.6(1) of Decision 1/80 specific time periods of legal employment must have been fulfilled.

18–44 The first indent of art.6(1) provides that after one year's legal employment the worker is entitled to a renewal of their work permit "for the same employer". The aim of the first indent is to ensure continuity of employment with the same employer and is therefore only applicable where the worker requests an extension of his work permit in order to continue working for the same employer after the initial year.[55] Furthermore, the CJEU has stated that even where the Turkish worker has worked for one year without interruption but for different employers, he does not qualify under the first indent of art.6(1) and will only qualify when he has completed a full year's employment with one employer.[56] This is the case even where the national authorities have themselves authorised such changes of employment. Once a worker has fulfilled the first year's legal employment with one employer any attempts by the national authorities to limit renewal of a work permit would be incompatible with Decision 1/80.

18–45 The second indent provides that the Turkish worker may after three years, of legal employment, change employers and respond to any other offer of employment "for the same occupation".[57]

18–46 The third indent provides that after four years of legal employment the worker enjoys free access to any paid employment. This will include the right to seek employment for a "reasonable period".

(ii) *Annual holidays, absences, accidents, sickness and involuntary unemployment*

18–47 Since rights under art.6(1) are acquired on an incremental basis in accordance with the length of the paid legal employment it is necessary to understand what affect periods of absence from work might have on the acquisition of rights. Article 6(2) lays down the effect that various causes of interruption of employment has on the calculation of the time periods necessary to accrue rights.

18–48 Article 6(2) specifically states that "annual holidays and absences for reasons of maternity or accident at work or short periods of sickness shall be treated as legal employment." The CJEU has not defined what periods of time are envisaged by art.6(2) in precise terms and therefore it will be a question of fact and degree as to whether time taken off for illness

---

[55] See Directive 2001/23 on the approximation of laws of the Member States relating to the safeguarding of employees' rights in the event of transfer of undertakings, businesses or parts of undertakings or businesses [2001] O.J. L82/16). The Directive would indicate that where there has been a transfer of undertakings, for these purposes the employer remains the same even if the legal entity has changed.
[56] See *Eker* (C-386/95) [1997] E.C.R. I-2697.
[57] As yet there is no CJEU guidance on the meaning of "same occupation".

constitutes "short periods of sickness". In *Ertanir*[58] the CJEU further clarified that short periods without a valid residence or work permit do not affect the periods of legal employment referred to in art.6(1).

In the case of involuntary unemployment ("duly certified by the relevant authorities"[59]), art.6(2) provides—as in the case of long periods of absence due to sickness—that the inactive periods cannot be treated as periods of legal employment for the purposes of art.6(1). However, such periods of unemployment do not affect the rights which the worker has acquired as the result of preceding employment. Thus a worker who had been employed for three years and is made involuntarily unemployed for three months, will not have the three months taken into account when calculating periods of legal employment, but will not have to recommence the periods of employment under art.6(1) as if he had never previously been employed. The CJEU has not defined what periods of time are envisaged by art.6(2) in precise terms and so "long absences on account of sickness" will be a question of fact and degree. 18–49

In *Tetik*,[60] the CJEU described the second sentence in art.6(2) as relating to periods of inactivity due to long-term sickness or to involuntary unemployment when the failure to work was "not attributable to any misbehaviour on the part of the worker". Making the behaviour of the worker a relevant factor in this context was said by the CJEU to follow from the use of the adjective "unverschuldet" in the German version of Decision 1/80.[61] According to the CJEU: 18–50

> "The sole purpose of this latter provision is therefore to prevent a Turkish worker who recommences employment after having been forced to stop working because of long-term illness or unemployment through no fault of his own from being required, in the same way as a Turkish national who has never previously been in paid employment in the Member State in question, to recommence the periods of legal employment envisaged by the three indents of Article 6(1)."[62]

This aspect of the decision in *Tetik* is concerned with the circumstances in which a worker will have the clock reset for the purposes of establishing one, three or four years' legal employment following a period of involuntary unemployment (or sickness). Where that unemployment is not the fault of the worker, the CJEU has stated in effect that the worker should not be penalised by being treated as if he had never worked. The implication is at the very least that for the worker whose period of unemployment is attributable to misbehaviour the clock will have to be reset and previous periods of employment will count for nothing. The notion that fault on the part of the worker can have such a consequence is extremely problematic for a 18–51

---

[58] *Ertanir v Land Hessen* (C-98/96) [1997] E.C.R. I-5179, at [63–69].
[59] The failure by a Turkish worker to have involuntary absences certified was considered irrelevant by the CJEU in circumstances where more often than not it appeared the worker already had another employment contract or had real prospects of obtaining further employment shortly, *Sedef v Freie und Hansestadt Hamburg* (C-230/03) [2006] All E.R. (D) 07 (Jan).
[60] *Tetik v Land Berlin* (C-171/95) [1997] E.C.R. I-329.
[61] *Tetik v Land Berlin* (C-171/95) [1997] E.C.R. I-329, at [38].
[62] *Tetik v Land Berlin* (C-171/95) [1997] E.C.R. I-329, at [39].

number of reasons considered below. At the very least any assessment of "fault" must be determined in a manner which is fair and any decision taken must be proportionate.

18–52 If this were not the case, the consequences could be absurd. First, it would wholly disproportionate, for example, were a worker who was made unemployed as the result of a failure to pay an administrative fine resulting in a two-day prison sentence to be treated as being in the same position as someone who had never worked. Such person could have completed three years and 11 months of legal employment leaving them short by only one month of obtaining the right of free access to the labour market contained in the third indent of art.6(1). Plainly there must be scope for the application of some form of de minimis principle. Secondly, it will always be only too easy for an employer to attribute fault at the feet of an employee. This could have the draconian consequence of the employee's entire record of legal employment being discounted without any opportunity for the employee to counter the allegation, or any assessment at all being able to be made of the gravity of any alleged misconduct. The latter matter is particularly important since even if the conduct alleged has been carried out by the employee, its gravity must surely be such as to justify the consequence. Again this would call for the application of some form of de minimis principle.

18–53 By contrast with the foregoing, however, the position as regards misbehaviour is different where rights are already enjoyed on completion of such time periods.[63] Further, it is important to note that art.6(2) is only important for the calculation of time periods under art.6(1) and therefore the acquisition of rights under the three indents. However, once the Turkish worker satisfies the conditions laid down in the third indent of art.6(1) of Decision 1/80 and therefore already enjoys the unconditional right to free access to the paid employment of their choice, art.6(2) is no longer applicable.[64]

(iii) *Incapacity and retirement*

18–54 In *Bozkurt*,[65] the CJEU stated that underlying art.6 was the prerequisite that the worker is able to work. The CJEU pointed out that whilst art.6(2) envisages temporary breaks in employment and therefore periods of legal employment will include annual holidays, absences for reason of maternity or an accident at work or short periods of sickness, the provisions of art.6 presuppose fitness to continue working.

18–55 As stated above, where a worker is absent from work for long periods on account of sickness, the second sentence of art.6(2) stipulates that the "inactive" period cannot be treated as a period of legal employment, although the rights of the worker acquired as a result of previous employment cannot be affected. The CJEU has stated that this prevents a worker,

---

[63] See discussion from para.18–66 onwards of *Nazli v Stadt Nürnberg* (C-340/97) [2000] E.C.R. I-957.
[64] *Ergul Dogan v Sicherheitsdirektion für das Bundesland Vorarlberg* (C-383/03) July 7, 2005.
[65] *Bozkurt v Staatssecretaris van Justitie* (C-434/93) [1995] E.C.R. I-1475.

who recommences work after a long period of illness, from having to reset the clock in terms of time periods fulfilled under art.6(1) as a new arrival would.[66] However, in the case of permanent incapacity, the worker can no longer be considered as available for work and there is no reason to guarantee such worker the right of access to the labour force and an ancillary right of residence.

18–56 Turkish workers will not be able to benefit from the provisions of art.6 where they have "definitely ceased to belong to the labour force of a Member State"[67] whether by reason of reaching retirement age or becoming totally or permanently incapacitated for work. In the absence of any other right, the worker thus loses the right of residence.

(iv) Voluntary unemployment and other absences from the labour market

18–57 Once the third indent of art.6(1) is reached the question arises as to whether voluntary unemployment or absences for reasons other than envisaged under art.6(2) can affect rights acquired under art.6(1).

18–58 In *Tetik*,[68] the CJEU made specific reference to its own jurisprudence under art.45 TFEU in relation to those seeking employment. By reference to its decision in *Antonissen*[69] (a case concerning work seekers in the context of art.45 TFEU) the CJEU noted that:

> "Article 48... [now Art. 45 TFEU] requires that the person concerned be given a reasonable time in which to appraise himself, in the territory of the Member State which he has entered, of offers of employment corresponding to his occupational qualifications and to take, where appropriate, the necessary steps in order to be engaged."[70]

18–59 The CJEU went on to reiterate the relationship between Decision 1/80 and the EC Treaty. Whilst Decision 1/80 does not confer a right of entry into a Member State and thus cannot confer the right to enter and seek employment analogous to the situation under art.45 TFEU, the CJEU has held that a Turkish worker must be able, for a reasonable period, to seek new employment in the Member State and have a corresponding right of residence. The CJEU left it to the discretion of the Member State to determine how long a reasonable period for seeking employment would be but it may not deprive art.6 of its substance by "jeopardising in fact the Turkish worker's prospects of finding new employment".[71]

18–60 *Antonissen* provides an appropriate benchmark of what would be a reasonable period without jeopardising the prospects of finding new

---

[66] *Tetik v Land Berlin* (C-171/95) [1997] E.C.R. I-329, at [39].
[67] *Bozkurt v Staatssecretaris van Justitie* (C-434/93) [1995] E.C.R. I-1475, at [39].
[68] *Tetik v Land Berlin* (C-171/95) [1997] E.C.R. I-329.
[69] *The Queen v Immigration Appeal Tribunal Ex p. Antonissen* (C-292/89) [1991] E.C.R. I-745, at [13], [15] and [16].
[70] *Tetik v Land Berlin* (C-171/95) [1997] E.C.R. I-329, at [27].
[71] *Tetik v Land Berlin* (C-171/95) [1997] E.C.R. I-329, at [32].

employment. As pointed out by the CJEU in *Tetik*,[72] the principles enshrined in the TFEU worker provisions must so far as possible "inform the treatment of Turkish workers" in the context of Decision 1/80. In *Antonissen*, the CJEU held that Member States may prescribe a period of six months within which work should be obtained, although this should not to be enforced if after such time evidence is provided that the person concerned continues to seek employment and has genuine chances of being engaged. The same approach should be taken in the interpretation of the rights of residence of Turkish workers under art.6(1).[73]

18-61 In *Altun* the CJEU made clear that:

> "a Turkish worker is excluded from the labour force only if objectively he no longer has any chance of rejoining the labour force or has exceeded a reasonable time-limit for finding new employment after the end of the period of inactivity."[74]

18-62 The same approach is taken by the CJEU to periods of absence from the labour force due to imprisonment. In *Dogan* the CJEU made clear that absence from the labour force to serve a three-year prison sentence would not deprive him of the right of free access to the labour force on his release

> "provided that he does in fact try to find a new job and, if appropriate, registers with the employment services in order to find another job within a reasonable time"[75].

The rationale being that the absence from the labour force for the purpose of serving a prison sentence is only temporary and does not exclude the possibility of the worker continuing to work or look for work on release.

18-63 The only circumstances therefore that a person who has a period of inactivity may be denied continued rights under the third indent of art.6(1) is where he has "definitively ceased to be duly registered as belonging to the labour force" or "exceeded a reasonable time-limit for entering into a new employment relationship."[76]

(d) *The right of residence*

18-64 The CJEU has repeatedly held that the rights which art.6(1) of Decision 1/80 confers on Turkish workers in regard to employment

---

[72] *The Queen v Immigration Appeal Tribunal Ex p. Antonissen* (C-292/89) [1991] E.C.R. I-745, at [20] and [28].
[73] Six months is a benchmark repeated in the context of EU national workers retaining their status whilst looking for work if involuntarily unemployed during the first year of employment.
[74] *Altun v Stadt Boblingen* (C-337/07) December 18, 2008, at [25].
[75] *Ergul Dogan v Sicherheitsdirektion für das Bundesland Vorarlberg* (C-383/03) July 7, 2005, at [19].
[76] para.44. Subject also to the application of art.14(1) of Decision 1/80 (the "public policy, public security or public health" proviso which was the subject matter of the second question referred in *Nazli v Stadt Nurnberg* (C-340/97) [2000] E.C.R. I-957).

"necessarily imply the existence of a corresponding right of residence for the person concerned, since otherwise the right of access to the labour market and the right to work as an employed person would be deprived of all effect".[77]

Thus a worker qualifying under art.6(1) for extensions of employment in the Member State will have a corresponding right to remain in that Member State. Furthermore, as is clear from the decision of the CJEU in *Tetik*[78] such corresponding right of residence will exist for a reasonable period where the worker concerned becomes a work seeker. Indeed, the right of residence will continue to exist until a Turkish national has definitely ceased to belong to the labour force.

There is no requirement in art.6(1) that Turkish nationals must establish the legality of their employment by possession of any specific administrative document (such as a work permit or residence permit) in order to have their right of residence recognised. The CJEU has made it clear that: **18–65**

"the fact that (the worker's) residence permit was issued to him only for a fixed period is not relevant, since it is settled case-law that the rights conferred on Turkish workers by Article 6(1) of Decision 1/80 are accorded irrespective of whether or not the authorities of the host Member State have issued a specific administrative document, such as a work permit or residence permit."[79]

In this context such administrative documents are only "declaratory" of the existence of the worker's rights and do not constitute a condition of their existence. This is consistent with the position for workers in Union law in general.[80]

It is clear from the decision of the CJEU in *Nazli*[81] that rights accrued under art.6(1) will not be forfeited simply because of acts which are attributable to the worker's misbehaviour.[82] **18–66**

The CJEU has made clear that there are only two kinds of restrictions on the right of residence which are permissible for those who meet the conditions laid down in art.6(1). These are either by reference to art.14(1) that the presence of the worker constitutes a genuine and serious threat to public policy, public security or public health,[83] or where the person concerned has left the territory of the Member State for a significant length of time without legitimate reason. **18–67**

---

[77] See, most recently, *Birden v Stadtgemeinde Bremen* (C-1/97) [1998] E.C.R. I-7747, at [20]; *Günaydin v Freistaat Bayern* (C-36/96) [1997] E.C.R. I-5179. at [26]; and *Ertanir v Land Hessen* (C-98/96) [1997] E.C.R. I-5179, at [26].
[78] *Tetik v Land Berlin* (C-171/95) [1997] E.C.R. I-329.
[79] *Günaydin v Freistaat Bayern* (C-36/96) [1997] E.C.R. I-5179, at [26].
[80] *Sahin* (C-242/06) September 17, 2009 at [59].
[81] *Nazli v Stadt Nurnberg* (C-340/97) [2000] E.C.R. I-957.
[82] The position is to be contrasted with that where rights have yet to be accrued; see paras 18–51 to 18–52.
[83] See further, Ch.21, below. It should be noted that all Turkish workers will have the protection of art.14 of Decision 1/80.

18–68 According to the CJEU:

> "the exhaustive nature of the restrictions set out in the preceding paragraph would be undermined if the national authorities were able to make the interested person's right of residence subject to additional conditions as to the existence of interests capable of justifying residence or as to the nature of the employment (see, to that effect, *Altun* (C-337/07) [2008] E.C.R. I-0000, para.63)."[84]

(e) *The right of non-discrimination*

18–69 Equality of treatment is a fundamental principle of European Union law which lies at the heart of the exercise of free movement rights. The principle and its application is considered in Ch.11. In the Ankara Agreement art.9 provides a general non-discrimination provision:

> 'The Contracting Parties recognise that within the scope of this Agreement, and without prejudice to any special provisions which may be laid down pursuant to Article 8, any discrimination on grounds of nationality shall be prohibited in accordance with the principle laid down in Article 7 of the Treaty establishing the Community [now Article 18 TFEU]."

18–70 Further specific provision is made for Turkish national workers where the principle is articulated in art.10(1) of Decision 1/80 which provides as follows:

> "The Member States of the Community shall as regards remuneration and other conditions of work grant Turkish workers duly registered as belonging to their labour forces treatment involving no discrimination on the basis of nationality between them and Community workers".

The CJEU has emphasised the importance of these two non-discrimination provisions in *Commission v the Netherlands*, stating:

> "In that regard, the general principle of non-discrimination on grounds of nationality, laid down in Article 9 of the Association Agreement, and the application of that principle to the specific field of workers, in accordance with Article 10 of Decision No 1/80, contribute to facilitating the progressive integration of migrant Turkish workers and Turkish nationals who move for the purposes of establishment or in order to provide services in a Member State."[85]

In that case the CJEU found that charging Turkish national workers two thirds more than EU nationals for the issuing of residence documents was discriminatory and thus contrary to both art.9 of the Ankara Agreement and art.10 of Decision 1/80.[86]

---

[84] *Genc v Land Berlin* at [42–43].
[85] *Commission v the Netherlands* (C-92/07) April 29, 2010, at [68].
[86] In the same case the CJEU also concluded that charging self-employed Turkish nationals substantially more than EU nationals for the issuing of residence documents was also discrimination contrary to art.9 of the Ankara Agreement.

The non-discrimination provision in Decision 1/80 was considered by the **18–71**
CJEU in detail in *Wählergruppe Gemeinsam*.[87] The case concerned annulment of elections to a general assembly of workers because five Turkish workers (who fulfilled all the conditions in the third indent of art.6(1) of Decision 1/80) had their names deleted from a candidate list for elections to the general assembly of workers because they were not Austrian nationals.[88] Two questions were referred. The first concerned the scope of the prohibition of discrimination laid down by art.10(1), in particular whether "other conditions of work" in art.10(1) encompassed the right to stand as a candidate in elections to the bodies legally representing the interests of workers; the second whether the provision had direct effect in Union law.

The CJEU dealt first with the direct effect. As pointed out in Ch.17, a **18–72**
provision in an agreement concluded by the Union with a non-member has direct effect where, in light of its wording and the purpose and nature of the agreement, the provision contains a clear and precise obligation which is not subject to the adoption of any subsequent measure. The CJEU held that art.10(1) satisfied the test.[89]

In considering the scope of art.10(1) the CJEU reiterated the interpretative **18–73**
principle requiring the scope of rights in Decision 1/80 to be defined as far as possible by reference to the TFEU provisions relating to free movement of workers.[90] The CJEU stated that application of the principle was all the more justified because art.10(1) is formulated in terms "almost identical" to those in art.45(2) TFEU.[91] The CJEU held that:

> "in the context of Community law and, in particular, Article 48(2) of the Treaty [now Art. 45(2)], the Court has consistently held that national legislation which denies workers who are nationals of other Member States the right to vote and/or the right to stand as a candidate in elections held by bodies such as occupational guilds to which those workers are compulsorily affiliated, to which they must pay contributions, which are responsible for defending and representing workers' interests and which perform a consultative function in the legislative field is contrary to the fundamental principle of non-discrimination on the grounds of nationality (see *ASTI I* and *ASTI II*)".[92]

Thus the CJEU held that national legislation which required candidates to **18–74**
hold Austrian nationality in order to be eligible for election to a body representing and defending the interests of workers was incompatible with

---

[87] *Wählergruppe "Gemeinsam Zajedno/Birlikte Alternative und Grüne GewerkschafterInnen/UG"* (C-171/01) [2003] E.C.R. 4301.
[88] According to art.26(4) of Austria's Federal Constitution Law "All persons possessing Austrian nationality on the relevant date who have reached the age of 19 before 1 January of the year of the election shall be eligible for election".
[89] *Wählergruppe "Gemeinsam Zajedno/Birlikte Alternative und Grüne GewerkschafterInnen/UG"* (C-171/01) [2003] E.C.R. 4301, at [57].
[90] para.72; see also, *Nazli v Stadt Nurnberg* (C-340/97) [2000] E.C.R. I-957, at [50–55] and references therein.
[91] para.74.
[92] *Wählergruppe "Gemeinsam Zajedno/Birlikte Alternative und Grüne GewerkschafterInnen/UG"* (C-171/01) [2003] E.C.R. 4301, at [75]; *ASTI I* (C-213/90) [1991] E.C.R. I-3507; and *Commission v Luxembourg* (C-118/92) [1994] E.C.R. I-1891 (*ASTI II*).

art.10(1). According to the CJEU this interpretation was the only one consistent with the aims of Decision 1/80 to secure progressively freedom of movement for Turkish workers and to promote their integration into host Member States. In such a context, granting Turkish workers entitlement to the same conditions of work as those enjoyed by national workers was "an important step towards creating an appropriate framework for the gradual integration of migrant Turkish worker's."[93] As with the same phrase in art.45(2) TFEU, the art.10(1) reference to "conditions of work" was to be interpreted as having a broad scope providing for equal treatment "in all matters directly or indirectly related to the exercise of activity as an employee in the host Member State."[94]

18–75 This non-discrimination provision thus replicates those both in the TFEU itself and the Stabilisation and Association Agreements. In the context of those provisions their application has been most contested in relation to rules governing the number of foreign players fielded in national sporting events.[95] The non-discrimination provisions in other Agreements with third countries is discussed in Ch.16.[96]

(f) *The standstill clause*

18–76 Article 13 of Decision 1/80 contains the only provision dealing with access to employment for Turkish nationals (and thereby indicates the only limitation on the competence of Member States to regulate entry into their territories and access to first employment). Article 13 provides as follows:

> "The Member States of the Community and Turkey may not introduce new restrictions on the conditions of access to employment applicable to workers and members of their families legally resident and employed in their respective territories".

The provision in Decision 1/80 replaces that contained in art.7 of the Association Council Decision 2/76 which provided a standstill clause in relation to workers and employment, but did not include family members.

---

[93] *Wählergruppe "Gemeinsam Zajedno/Birlikte Alternative und Grüne Gewerk-schafterInnen/UG"* (C-171/01) [2003] E.C.R. 4301, at [79]. Note that the CJEU rejected expressly a submission made by the Austrian Government that art.10(1) was narrower in scope than the same term used in art.48(2) TFEU because the latter was clarified in specific terms by Regulation 1612/68, the first paragraph of art.8 of which expressly refers to trade-union and similar rights, whereas no such specific terms are used in the EC-Turkey Association Agreement, and because the aims of that Agreement were less ambitious than those of the Treaty. See the judgment at [81–94].
[94] *Wählergruppe "Gemeinsam Zajedno/Birlikte Alternative und Grüne GewerkschafterInnen/UG"* (C-171/01) [2003] E.C.R. 4301, at [85–88].
[95] See, for example, *Union Royal Belge des Societes de Football Association ASBL v Bosman* (C-415/93) [1995] E.C.R. 4353, at [73] and *Deutscher Handballbund eV v Kolpak* (C-438/00) May 8, 2003.
[96] The CJEU is asked to consider the application of art.10(1) of Decision 1/80 in the light of some of the case law on non-discrimination provisions in other agreements in the case of *Atilla Gülbahce v Freie und Hansestadt Hamburg* (C-268/11).

In *Sevince*,[97] the CJEU described the standstill clauses contained within Decisions 2/76 and 1/80 as "unequivocal" and to have direct effect in the Member States. As indicated the art.13 provision reproduced that made in Decision 2/76 as regards workers. Decision 2/76 had entered into force on December 20, 1976 and remained in force until the entry into force of Decision 1/80. Thus the relevant date for the purposes of "standstill" is December 20, 1976.[98] Turkish workers must enjoy the conditions of access to employment which existed at that time in Member States. It is not open to Member States to apply more restrictive conditions than were in force on December 20, 1976 as regards workers.[99]

18–77

The standstill clauses refer specifically to persons "legally resident and employed" in the Member States. The CJEU has repeatedly stated in relation to art.6(1) of Decision 1/80 that reference to persons already in legal employment means that Member States are able to control both entry into their territory of Turkish nationals and conditions of initial employment. It would appear from the wording of the standstill clauses that similar provisos exist. Member States are therefore able to apply whatever conditions of entry to the territory and first access to employment they wish.

18–78

It is clear from the case law of the CJEU that art.13 will apply to persons who do not yet qualify for the rights in relation to employment and residence under art.6(1) of Decision 1/80.[100] Thus a person who is "legally" resident in a Member State but who has not, for instance, gained the right to free access to the labour market under the third intent of art.6(1) will nevertheless be able to rely on art.13 to prevent a Member State applying more stringent conditions or procedures than had been in place historically to the renewal of a residence or work permit.

18–79

The benefit of the standstill clause is that Turkish nationals who are granted entry and access to the labour force by a Member State must have their subsequent stay and further access to employment regulated by the national laws in place at the time when Decision 2/76 came into force in the Member State if they are less restrictive than those in place at the present time. For the original Member States this was December 1976. The standstill clause applies to both substantive and procedural conditions.[101] Further, if a Member State has improved the conditions since that time for Turkish nationals, it cannot subsequently reverse that improvement even if that would mean a return to the situation in place at the time Decision 2/76 came into force.[102]

18–80

---

[97] *Sevince v Staatssecretaris Van Justitite* (C-192/89) [1990] E.C.R. 3461, at [30].
[98] Or the date on which the relevent Member State became a member of the EU as therefore party to the Ankara Agreement.
[99] However, the standstill clause relating to the family members was not part of Decision 2/76 and therefore family members may only enjoy conditions of access to employment which existed on the date of entry into force of Decision 1/80 (December 1, 1980).
[100] See *Abatay and others* (C-317/01) and (C-369/01) [2003] E.C.R. I-12301 and *Sahin* (C-242/06).
[101] See *Sahin v Minster voor Vreemdelingenzaken en Integratie* (C-242/06) September 17, 2009, at [62–65].
[102] See *Staatsseretaris van Justitie* (C-300/09) and (C-301/09) December 9, 2010, at [54–60].

18–81 Where those national laws are no more favourable than the provisions of art.6 of Decision 1/80, the clause will be of no practical benefit. If, however, the national laws contained more favourable conditions, then such a Turkish worker must obtain the benefit of them. For example, if in 1976 national law gave the right of permanent residence after two years' legal employment, but such national law provision had been changed in 1981 so as to require four years' legal employment to qualify for permanent residence, the more favourable provision could benefit a Turkish worker who had completed two years' legal employment.

18–82 The standstill clause does not prevent a Member State from introducing new rules that are applied equally to both Turkish nationals and EU citizens. Any other approach would be inconsistent with art.59 of the Additional Protocol which prohibits Member States from according to Turkish nationals more favourable treatment than that accorded to EU nationals in a comparable situation.[103]

---

[103] See *Sahin v Minster voor Vreemdelingenzaken en Integratie* (C-242/06) September 17, 2009 at [67–69].

CHAPTER 19

ESTABLISHMENT UNDER THE ANKARA AGREEMENT

This chapter examines the scope of the establishment provisions contained in the Ankara Agreement and its Protocol. The provision of principal importance is the standstill clause relating to establishment in the Additional Protocol.

1. PROVISIONS IN THE ANKARA AGREEMENT AND ADDITIONAL PROTOCOL

(a) *Ankara Agreement provisions relating to establishment and services*

Article 13 of the Ankara Agreement states: **19–01**

"The Contracting Parties agree to be guided by Arts 52 to 56 and Art.58[1] of the Treaty establishing the Community for the purpose of abolishing restrictions on the freedom of establishment between them".

Article 14 of the Agreement states: **19–02**

"The Contracting Parties agree to be guided by Arts 55, 56 and 58 to 65[2] of the Treaty establishing the Community for the purpose of abolishing restrictions on freedom to provide services between them."

Articles 13 and 14 of the Ankara Agreement provide the foundation stone for freedom of establishment and the freedom to provide services, in much the same way as the foundation stone for the freedom of movement of workers is laid down by art.12 of the Agreement. The provisions of arts 13 and 14 are further developed in art.41 of the Additional Protocol. **19–03**

The similarities between art.12, in relation to workers, and arts 13 and 14 would suggest that the decisions of the CJEU relating to art.12[3] of the Agreement are of interpretative value for arts 13 and 14. Certainly those provisions provide guidance as to the general aims of the Contracting Parties and to the interpretation of various concepts including the meaning of "establishment". **19–04**

(b) *Additional Protocol relating to establishment and services*

Article 41 of the Additional Protocol states: **19–05**

"(1) The Contracting Parties shall refrain from introducing between themselves any new restrictions on the freedom of establishment and the freedom to provide services.

---

[1] Now arts 49, 52–59 TFEU.
[2] Now arts 51, 52, 54 and 56–62 TFEU.
[3] Particularly *Demirel v Stadt Schwäbish Gmünd* (12/86) [1987] E.C.R. 3719.

(2) The Council of Association shall, in accordance with the principles set out in Articles 13 and 14 of the Agreement of Association, determine the timetable and rules for the progressive abolition by the Contracting Parties, between themselves, of restrictions on freedom of establishment and on freedom to provide services.

The Council of Association shall, when determining such timetable and rules for the various classes of activity, take into account corresponding measures already adopted by the Community in these fields and also the special economic and social circumstances of Turkey. Priority shall be given to activities making a particular contribution to the development of production and trade."

19–06 The provision in art.41(1) is known as a "standstill clause", prohibiting Member States from changing their legislation to make exercising freedom to establish or provide services more difficult. The effect of this provision is discussed below.

19–07 The remainder of art.41 is concerned with the progressive abolition of restrictions on freedom of establishment and on freedom to provide services under rules laid down by the Council of Association. It is notable that unlike the position in relation to workers, there have been no decisions of the Council of Association relating to establishment.

2. Right of Establishment and Right to Provide Services Under the Agreement

(a) *Entry and establishment*

19–08 As with workers, there is no express right contained within the Ankara Agreement or its Additional Protocol for Turkish nationals to establish themselves or to provide services in the territory of the Member States. Whilst arts 13 and 14 of the Ankara Agreement make reference to Treaty provisions in order to "guide" Contracting Parties on the abolition of restrictions in those areas, neither provision creates any directly effective right.

19–09 Indeed, as observed above, the wording of arts 13 and 14 is very similar to that contained in art.12 of the Ankara Agreement. In *Demirel*,[4] the CJEU expressly rejected a suggestion that art.12 was capable of directly governing the movement of workers or that any rights are created by the provision.[5]

19–10 Article 41(2) of the Additional Protocol charges the Council of Association with setting the timetable for the progressive abolition of restrictions on establishment and provision of services. Again this mirrors the provision relating to workers in art.36 of the Additional Protocol which charges the Council of Association with responsibility for securing the free movement of workers in progressive stages. The CJEU has stated that art.36 "essentially

---

[4] *Demirel v Stadt Schwäbish Gmünd* (12/86) [1987] E.C.R. 3719, at [23].
[5] *Demirel v Stadt Schwäbish Gmünd* (12/86) [1987] E.C.R. 3719, at [25].

serves to set out a programme" which does not create directly effective rights which individuals can rely upon.

The rights of Turkish workers are discussed in Ch.18. It is apparent that the rights of Turkish workers flow from decisions of the Council of Association (which are to be treated like secondary legislation). In relation to Turkish workers the Council of Association has passed a number of decisions setting out in some detail the rights that they achieve. However, such rights do not include the right of entry to the Member States in order to take up employment. Member States retain the right to make decisions regarding first entry and thereby prevent the free movement of Turkish workers into their territory if they so choose. **19–11**

The provisions in the Agreement which relate to establishment (and services) are similar to those relating to workers. In light of the approach taken to workers it would be impossible to suggest that the Agreement creates any right for Turkish nationals to enter the territory of a Member State with the purposes of establishment. The lack of any decisions of the Council of Association on establishment or the provision of services only reinforces that position. **19–12**

(b) *Lawful residence and establishment*

The case law relating to Turkish workers demonstrates that those lawfully resident and working in the territory of a Member State accumulate rights in relation to their continued employment and residence once they have been in legal employment for a specific period. Such rights are contained in art.6 of Decision 1/80 of the Council of Association. **19–13**

The CJEU has stated that these provisions and the principles flowing from them are established in the context of the interpretation of the provisions of the Ankara Agreement for the progressive achievement of free movement of Turkish workers. These principles must apply by analogy in the context of the provisions of the Agreement concerning the right of establishment. **19–14**

Thus whilst art.13 of the Ankara Agreement and art.41(2) of the Protocol are not capable of creating a directly effective right of establishment, they nevertheless create **19–15**

> "certain rights under Community law in relation to ... exercising self-employed activity, and, correlatively, in relation to residence, ...in so far as [the Turkish national's] position in a Member State concerned is regular".[6]

The CJEU has yet to examine what those rights might be. Moreover, the Council of Association has not provided interpretation through its **19–16**

---

[6] *The Queen v Secretary of State for the Home Department Ex p. Savas* (C-37/98) [2000] E.C.R. I-2927, at [65].

decisions. However, it is implicit from the CJEU's judgment in *Savas*[7] that a Turkish national lawfully resident and lawfully carrying out a genuine and effective self-employed activity in the territory of a Member State would have the right in EU law to continue in that self-employed activity and, as a corollary, extend their residence.[8] Anything less would render the CJEU's statement that a Turkish national can claim "certain rights in EU law in relation to exercising self-employed activity" otiose since it is difficult to envisage that rights in EU law could have any real meaning if at the very least the position of the lawfully established person were not protected.

3. The Standstill Provision

(a) *The concept of a standstill provision*

19–17 EU law has long recognised the concept of a standstill provision. Indeed, art.53 Treaty of Rome[9] contained such a standstill clause as a first step in the transitional period towards the progressive abolition of restrictions on establishment provided for in art.52 of the same Treaty (now art.49 TFEU). Whilst national laws still had some application to the situation of those wishing to establish themselves in other Member States, the Member States were directed to ensure that they did not make their national laws any more restrictive than those in existence at the time when the Treaty came into force.[10] Indeed, the provision also prevents a Member State from reverting back to less liberal measures than have been imposed during the transitional period by EU law. As stated by the CJEU in *Royer*:

---

[7] *The Queen v Secretary of State for the Home Department Ex p. Savas* (C-37/98) [2000] E.C.R. I-2927.

[8] At least one commentator has suggested that the analogy made by the CJEU between the position of Turkish workers and Turkish nationals in self-employed activity is very limited and that the rights pertaining to workers cannot be applied to the self-employed. This is because in the case of the self-employed the Council of Association has failed to implement any decision setting in motion the program towards progressive abolition of restrictions on establishment or freedom to provide services, and furthermore there are distinctions made as a matter of policy between employed and self-employed persons (see A. Ott, "The *Savas* case—Analogies between Turkish Self-Employed and Workers" (2000) *European Journal of Migration and Law* 2, 445–458). Such factors were also pointed to by the Advocate General in *Savas*. However valid these observations, the conclusion that the "rights" pertaining to self-employed persons are limited to the reliance on the standstill provision must be unsustainable in the light of the clear reference by the CJEU to "rights in Community law". A standstill clause does not create any rights per se in Community law. It must be arguable that the failure by the Council of Association to progress the abolition of restrictions on freedom of establishment does not render the provisions in arts 13 and 14 nugatory and that if they are to have any meaning then at the very least a Turkish national who is lawfully resident and engaged in self-employed activity in a Member State can expect to be afforded stability and security in so doing. That would represent a first step towards the abolition of restrictions on freedom of establishment. It would be surprising if no progression had been made towards that goal in the 40 or more years since the Ankara Agreement was agreed.

[9] Treaty of Rome 1957:
"Member States shall not introduce any new restrictions on the right of establishment in their territories of nationals of other Member States, save as otherwise provided in the Treaty".
The provision was transititional and is not replicated in subsequent Treaties.

[10] See, for instance, *Procureur de Roi v Royer* (C-48/75) [1976] E.C.R. 497, at [65–74].

"Article 53 ... of the Treaty prohibit[s] the introduction by a Member State of new restrictions on the establishment of nationals of other Member States and the freedom to provide services which has in fact been attained and that they prevent the Member States from reverting to less liberal provisions or practices in so far as the liberalization measures already adopted constitute the implementation of obligations arising from the provisions and objectives of the Treaty".[11]

In other words a standstill clause has the effect of preventing a Member State from reversing the progression imposed by EU law on domestic law at the same time as preventing the imposition of any greater controls or restrictions in domestic law. The situation of nationals of other Member States in the relevant field can thereby only improve over time (or at worse remain static).[12] **19–18**

The standstill provision contained in art.41(1) of the Additional Protocol to the Ankara Agreement is very similarly worded to art.53 of the Treaty of Rome. The provision has been interpreted by the CJEU in such as way as to give it the same effect as art.53.[13] A Member State is thus prevented from imposing any new measure, having the "object or effect" of making the establishment of a Turkish national in its territory subject to stricter conditions than those which applied at the time when the Additional Protocol entered into force for the particular Member State in question. **19–19**

The CJEU has found that the importance of the standstill clause in art.41(1) of the Additional Protocol is to place a bar on Member States from creating new obstacles on the ability of Turkish nationals to establish themselves in their territories so as not to undermine the general aim of the gradual securing of the freedom of establishment between the Member States and Turkey.[14] **19–20**

(b) *Applicability of the standstill clause*

The question of whether a provision of EU law has direct effect is of significance in terms of its applicability and consequences. If a provision has direct effect then all of those falling within its scope are able to rely upon it before national courts and authorities without the need for any transposition into domestic law. **19–21**

In *Savas*,[15] the CJEU had no difficulty in accepting the direct effect of art.41(1) of the Additional Protocol which "confers on individuals individual rights which national courts must safeguard". In *Abatay*,[16] the second **19–22**

---

[11] *Procureur de Roi v Royer* (C-48/75) [1976] E.C.R. 497, at [74].
[12] Improvements cannot subsequently be reversed or tempered in any way, *Staatssecretaris van Justitie v Oguz and Toprak* (C-300/09) and (C-301/09) December 9, 2010, at [54–60].
[13] See *The Queen v Secretary of State for the Home Department Ex p. Savas* (C-37/98) [2000] E.C.R. I-2927, at [69].
[14] See *Tum and Dari* (C-16/05) [2007] E.C.R. I-07415, at [51].
[15] See *The Queen v Secretary of State for the Home Department Ex p. Savas* (C-37/98) [2000] E.C.R. I-2927.
[16] *Abatay v Bundesanstalt für Arbeit* (C-317/01) and *Sahin v Bundesanstalt für Arbeit* (C-369/01) [2005] All E.R. (D) 342.

judgment concerning art.41(1) of the Additional Protocol, the CJEU confirmed that the provision has direct effect resulting from the fact that the provision, as with other standstill provisions under the Ankara Agreement,[17] lays down

> "clearly, precisely and unconditionally, unequivocal standstill clauses, which contain an obligation entered into by the Contracting Parties which amounts in law to a duty not to act".

19–23 This conclusion is reinforced when the purpose and subject-matter of the Ankara Agreement is examined. As with other provisions in the Ankara Agreement the CJEU affirmed that the essential object of the Agreement, namely to promote the development of trade and economic relations between the Contracting Parties, and Turkey lends support to the conclusion that this provision has direct effect in Community law.[18]

(c) *The scope of the standstill clause*

19–24 The CJEU has applied the provision in art.41(1) to any measure having the object or purpose of making the establishment, and as a corollary, the residence of a Turkish national in its territory subject to stricter conditions than those which applied at the time when the Member State became party to the Additional Protocol.

19–25 It is plain from the facts of *Savas*[19] that such a Turkish national does not have to be lawfully resident in the Member State in question in order to obtain the benefit of the standstill provision in art.41(1). Mr Savas had obtained lawful entry to the United Kingdom as a visitor for one month with his wife. By the time of his application to remain in the United Kingdom as a self-employed person he had overstayed that visa by some 11 years and was plainly unlawfully resident in the United Kingdom. Nevertheless, the CJEU held that it was the task of the national court to determine whether the domestic rules applied to Mr Savas were stricter than those rules that were applicable to self-employed persons at the time the United Kingdom became a party to the Additional Protocol.

19–26 The scope of the standstill provision in art.41(1) therefore extends to all Turkish nationals, whatever their legal status in the Member State in which they wish to establish themselves. No distinction in the application of the standstill clause can be made on the basis of whether the Turkish national is lawfully resident, unlawfully resident, or only a prospective resident wishing

---

[17] art.13 of December 1/80, see Ch.18, above.
[18] See *The Queen v Secretary of State for the Home Department Ex p. Savas* (C-37/98) [2000] E.C.R. I-2927.
[19] See *The Queen v Secretary of State for the Home Department Ex p. Savas* (C-37/98) [2000] E.C.R. I-2927, at [52–53].

to obtain entry to a particular Member State.[20] Further, the scope of the standstill provision applies to those who establish themselves in business, irrespective of whether they have permission from the Member State to do so.[21]

The effect of the provision is to ensure that any immigration laws or laws relating to conditions of establishment to which the Turkish national is made subject are no stricter than those that would have been applicable to a Turkish national in the same position at the time when the Additional Protocol came into force in the Member State in question.[22] The benefit of the provision extends to both substantive and procedural provisions, as well as any policies or practises in existence at the relevant time.[23] **19–27**

The benefits of such a provision can be significant. At the time at which the Additional Protocol came into force in a large number of the original Member States or those which joined in the 1960s and 1970s, Member States' immigration regimes were extremely liberal. In a quest to stimulate post-war economies in Western Europe, non-EU nationals who could bring skills and economic benefit to a Member State were encouraged to migrate. Domestic immigration laws and policies have undoubtedly become far harsher in the last three decades. Turkish nationals who wish to establish themselves in the territory of a Member State will likely be in a better position if they able to rely on the liberal immigration regimes of the 1960s and 1970s rather than current immigration laws. **19–28**

The scope of the standstill provision extends to "any new measure" which has the object or effect of making establishment more difficult for Turkish nationals. For instance such measures would include the imposition of new procedures involving a requirement to obtain certain permits,[24] as well as substantive provisions, such as the imposition of a new requirement to invest a certain sum of money in the Member State in question. **19–29**

---

[20] In *Tum and Dari* the UK Government attempted to argue that the standstill clause could not apply to conditions for first entry into the Member State on the basis that this would undermine the right of Member States to regulate first entry to their territory. The CJEU specifically rejected this argument finding that the duty not to act in a negative manner towards the entry of Turkish national to the Member State did not undermine the sovereign right of the State to control who enters its territory, see further, *Tum and Dari* (C-16/05) [2007] E.C.R. I-07415.

[21] See *Oguz v Secretary of State for the Home Department* (C-186/10), July 21, 2011, at [40–46] where the CJEU specifically rejects arguments put forward by the UK Government based on abuse of rights where a Turkish national lawfully resident in the UK enters into business in breach of a condition of his residence.

[22] In this regard the standstill provision in art.41(1) of the Additional Protocol is wider in scope that the standstill provision in art.13 of Decision 1/80 which is plainly restricted those already "legally resident" in the Member State.

[23] *Abatay v Bundesanstalt für Arbeit* (C-317/01) and *Sahin v Bundesanstalt für Arbei* (C-369/01) [2003] All E.R. (D) 342. See also, *Tum and Dari* (C-16/05) [2007] E.C.R. I-07415.

[24] See, for instance, *Abatay v Bundesanstalt für Arbeit* (C-317/01) and *Sahin v Bundesanstalt für Arbeit* (C-369/01) where the CJEU concluded that:

"Article 41(1) precludes the introduction into the national legislation of a Member State of a requirement of a work permit in order for an undertaking established in Turkey to provide services in the territory of that State, if such a permit was not already required at the time of the entry into force of the Additional Protocol", para.117.

19–30 In *Soysal* and *Savatli* the CJEU examined imposition of visa requirements on Turkish nationals wishing to provide services in the Member States and found them to be contrary to the standstill clause in art.41(1) if they did not exist in the Member State at the time the provision came into force there.[25] This is even the case where secondary EU legislation requires Member States to impose visas on Turkish nationals.[26] The CJEU emphasised that international agreements concluded by the EU have primacy over EU secondary legislation.

19–31 The implications of *Soysal* and *Savatli* are wide. There is no reason why its rationale cannot be applied to instances where Turkish nationals wish to visit a Member State for tourism, attend trade fairs, undertake short-term study, medical treatment or other short-term visits where services are provided or received by the Turkish national.[27] It is necessary, however, to establish what regime was in place in the particular Member State for Turkish nationals entering its territory at the time that the Additional Protocol to came into force in that State.[28] In some Member States (particularly more recent members of the EU) that regime might have included a visa requirement for Turkish nationals.

19–32 The standstill clause is not unlimited and there are circumstances in which the Member States are permitted to impose new rules on Turkish nationals wishing to establish themselves in business. In *Commission v the Netherlands* the CJEU indicated that the imposition of a fee or charge for residence documents for self-employed Turkish nationals would not necessarily be contrary to the standstill clause in art.41(1) if it were also imposed on EU nationals.[29] If such measures applied to EU nationals but were not also imposed on Turkish nationals, Turkish nationals would be placed in a more favourable position than EU nationals. This would be contrary to the requirement laid down in art.59 of the Additional Protocol, under which Turkey may not receive more favourable treatment than that which Member States grant to one another pursuant to the EC Treaty.[30]

---

[25] *Soysal and Savatli* (C-228/06) [2009] E.C.R. I-01031.
[26] Council Regulation No.539/2001 lists the third countries whose nationals must be in possession of visas when crossing the EU external borders. Under this regulation Turkish nationals require a visa to travel to the EU Member States subject to the Regulation (the UK has an opt-out of the Regulation).
[27] In the context of EU free movement law the CJEU has found that the freedom to provide services set out in the Treaty (now the TFEU) is to be enjoyed by both providers and recipients of services and the movement of recipients of services is a necessary corollary of the right contained in art.57 TFEU (ex-art.50 EC Treaty). Article 41 of the Additional Protocol refers back to art.13 of the Ankara Agreement which itself states that Contracting Parties are to be guided by the relevant Treaty provisions on freedom of establishment and freedom to provided services. The CJEU will consider the validity of visas for visitors in the case of *Leyla Ecem Demirkan v Federal Republic of Germany* (C-221/11).
[28] According to the EU observer (*http://EUobserver.com/7/115560*) article by G. Knaus and A. Stiglmayer, "Being fair to Turkey is in the EU's interest", when the Protocol entered into force in January 1973, 11 of today's Member States did not have a visa requirement for Turkish nationals.
[29] Subject to the fees being applied in a non-discriminatory way. See further below.
[30] *Commission v the Netherlands* (C-92/07) [2010] E.C.R. I-03683, at [60–62].

4. NON-DISCRIMINATION

Article 9 of the Ankara Agreement is a general non-discrimination provision. As discussed in Ch.18 on Turkish workers, this provision makes reference to TFEU principles. The provision has application to all Turkish nationals falling within the scope of the Agreement. This includes self-employed Turkish nationals.

19–33

In *Commission v the Netherlands* the CJEU considered the application of art.9 to self-employed Turkish nationals in the context of national rules on the fees for residence documents. The CJEU considered that charging Turkish nationals who wished to avail themselves of the freedom of establishment or freedom to provide services pursuant to the Ankara Agreement at least two thirds more than EU nationals was discrimination contrary to art.9 as the difference in fees was significant and could not be justified.[31]

---

[31] *Commission v the Netherlands* (C-92/07) [2010] E.C.R. I-03683. The introduction of fees was also contrary to the standstill clause art.41(1) of the Additional Protocol.

CHAPTER 20

FAMILY MEMBERS UNDER THE ANKARA AGREEMENT

This chapter examines the extent to which Turkish nationals exercising rights under the Ankara Agreement enjoy the right of family unity. Although specific provision is limited, the CJEU has recognised the right of family unity for such Turkish nationals.

1. Provision for Family Members in the Ankara Agreement and the Decisions of the Council of Association

(a) *The Agreement*

There is no reference to rights of family reunification for Turkish nationals in the Ankara Agreement or the Additional Protocol. The question of whether the rights of workers under the Ankara Agreement include the right to bring with them their spouse and children was included in the questions for reference in the case of *Demirel*.[1] The CJEU did not specifically answer the question, although it stated 20–01

> "There is at present no provision of Community law defining the conditions in which Member States must permit the family reunification of Turkish workers lawfully settled in the Community".[2]

Advocate General Darmon had stated in his Opinion that: 20–02

> "Although family reunification is certainly a necessary element in giving effect to the freedom of movement of workers, it does not become a right until the freedom which it presupposes has taken effect and a special provision on the matter has been adopted".[3]

Neither of these observations is particularly surprising since the Ankara Agreement does not confer any directly effective rights on Turkish workers itself. However, the reference in art.12 of the Agreement to the fact that Contracting Parties are to be guided by the provisions relating to workers in the EC Treaty is significant. Bearing in mind the importance that the CJEU places on the right to family unity in the context of free movement rights under the TFEU and the fact that lack of family reunification rights is seen by the CJEU as an unacceptable obstacle to the exercise of free movement rights, family unity must at least constitute an aim of the Agreement, even if it does not give rise to a right itself.[4] 20–03

---

[1] *Demirel v Stadt Schwäbisch Gmünd* (12/86) [1987] E.C.R. 3719, at [23].
[2] *Demirel v Stadt Schwäbisch Gmünd* (12/86) [1987] E.C.R. 3719, at [28].
[3] *Demirel v Stadt Schwäbisch Gmünd* (12/86) [1987] E.C.R. 3719, at 3745.
[4] See Ch.9 and *Carpenter v Secretary of State for the Home Department* (C-60/00) [2002] E.C.R. I-6279.

20–04 In respect of the free movement of workers and the freedom of establishment the Council of Association is charged under the Agreement with responsibility for deciding rules to give effect to the aim of gradually securing free movement in these areas. The absence of any specific reference to family unity in either the Agreement or the Additional Protocol means that there is no specific direction given to the Council of Association in this area. However, given the importance of family unity in the context of free movement rights, the Council of Association could be expected to decide rules in relation to this question in the context of effecting progression towards the free movement of workers and the freedom of establishment.

(b) *Decisions of the Council of Association*

20–05 In fact, the Council of Association has only made decisions in relation to workers and their family members in the free movement of persons context. Consistent with the guidance provided by secondary legislation relating to the free movement of EU national workers in the context of the TFEU, the Council of Association has made decisions relating to family unity. These provisions largely mirror the gradual progression towards free movement of workers contained in decisions of Council of Association, providing for access to the labour market only after certain conditions are fulfilled and retaining the right of Member States to control first entry to their territories.

20–06 It is art.7 of Decision 1/80 which is of principal interest in the context of free movement, although family members of Turkish workers additionally fall within the scope of Decision 3/80 relating to social security. There are no provisions in the decisions of the Association Council relating to the family members of those established in business.

2. THE RIGHTS OF FAMILY MEMBERS OF TURKISH WORKERS

20–07 The first paragraph of art.7 of Decision 1/80 provides:

"The members of the family of a Turkish worker duly registered as belonging to the labour force of a Member State, who have been authorised to join him:

— shall be entitled—subject to the priority to be given to workers of Member States of the Community—to respond to any offer of employment after they have been legally resident for at least three years in that Member State;
— shall enjoy free access to any paid employment of their choice provided they have been legally resident there for at least five years."

20–08 The CJEU has stated that art.7 is intended to promote family reunification in the host Member State. This is to accord with the general objective of Decision 1/80 to improve the treatment accorded to Turkish workers and their family members with a view to achieving gradual freedom of movement.[5]

---

[5] *Fatma Pehlivan v Staatssecretaris van Justitie* (C-484/07) June 16, 2011, at [45].

(a) *Direct effect of art.7 of Decision 1/80*

The CJEU has confirmed the direct effect of art.7 of Decision 1/80 on several occasions[6] which means that it can be directly relied upon by individuals before national courts and authorities. In conferring direct effect on the provision the CJEU has emphasised that art.7 contains social provisions which constitute a further stage in securing freedom of movement for workers on the basis of the relevant provisions in the TFEU. Having regard to the general aim of art.7 the CJEU in *Kadiman*[7] stated:

20–09

> "it must be emphasised that the purpose of that provision is to favour employment and residence of Turkish workers duly registered as belonging to the labour force of a Member State by ensuring that their family links are maintained there".[8]

The extent of the obligations placed on the Member States by the provision are discussed below, but at the heart of art.7 is a system "designed to create conditions conducive to family unity".[9] Such provision constitutes a very important stage in securing freedom of movement of workers, guided by the TFEU itself, and it is for this reason that the CJEU has held that it is essential to transpose as far as possible the principles enshrined in the TFEU.[10] Whilst this might not result in full rights of family unity at the present stage of development in the relationship between Turkey and the European Union, the provisions contained in art.7 must be interpreted as consistently as possible with EU law.

20–10

(b) *Right of entry for family members of workers*

As with Turkish workers, Decision 1/80 confers no explicit right of entry into the Member States for family members of Turkish workers. Indeed the CJEU has confirmed on a number of occasions that the power to lay down conditions of first entry of a family member into the territories of the Member States is retained by the Member States.[11] As the CJEU reiterated in *Ergat*:[12]

20–11

> "under Community law as it now stands, the Member States have retained the power to regulate both the entry into their territory of a member of the family of a Turkish worker and the conditions of his residence during the initial three-year period before he has the right to respond to any offer of employment."[13]

---

[6] See *Eroglu v Land Baden-Württemberg* (C-355/93) [1994] E.C.R. I-5113 and *Kadiman v State of Bavaria* (C-351/97) [1997] E.C.R. I-2133, see, most recently, *Ergat v Stadt Ulm* (C-329/97) [2000] E.C.R. I-1487.
[7] *Kadiman v State of Bavaria* (C-351/97) [1997] E.C.R. I-2133.
[8] *Kadiman v State of Bavaria* (C-351/97) [1997] E.C.R. I-2133, at [35].
[9] *Kadiman v State of Bavaria* (C-351/97) [1997] E.C.R. I-2133, at [37].
[10] *Kadiman v State of Bavaria* (C-351/97) [1997] E.C.R. I-2133, at [31].
[11] *Kadiman v State of Bavaria* (C-351/97) [1997] E.C.R. I-2133, at [33].
[12] *Ergat v Stadt Ulm* (C-329/97) [2000] E.C.R. I-1487.
[13] *Ergat v Stadt Ulm* (C-329/97) [2000] E.C.R. I-1487, at [42].

However, the clear principle of family unity that underpins the provision in the first paragraph of art.7 of Decision 1/80 means that the Member States' powers in this regard are not unfettered by EU law.

20–12 Although it is clearly for Member States to lay down the conditions under which family members may enter their territories to join Turkish workers duly registered as belonging to the labour force, the inclusion of art.7 does presume that Member States will in fact permit family unity of such workers. The CJEU held in *Kadiman*[14] that the system under art.7 was

> "designed to create conditions conducive to family unity in the host Member State, first by enabling family members to be with a migrant worker."[15]

20–13 Plainly apart from any obligations that may be created EU law, Member States retain the competence to determine which third country nationals can enter their territories. Seen in this context, it is curious that Member States would need such an "enabling" provision to permit family unity if the first indent of art.7 only leaves open the possibility for Member States to permit first entry. It must be implicit from the inclusion of art.7 in Decision 1/80 that it is anticipated that in view of the general objective of family unity that Member States would, subject to conditions of national law, facilitate family reunification in some form for Turkish workers lawfully resident in their territories.

20–14 Indeed it can be inferred from the CJEU's judgment in *Kadiman* that Member States should be facilitating entry to family members of workers integrated in their labour forces.

> "In view of its meaning and purpose, that provision cannot therefore be interpreted as merely requiring the host Member State to have authorised a family member to enter its territory to join a Turkish worker without at the same requiring the person concerned to continue actually to reside there with the migrant worker until he or she becomes entitled to enter the labour market".[16]

20–15 The Turkish worker can therefore claim no right in EU law to be joined by their family member under any particular conditions. However, an absolute bar to the entry of any family member of a Turkish national legally employed in the territory of a Member State would arguably contradict the general aims of the Ankara Agreement, the decisions of the Council of Association and the understanding of the position by the CJEU as reflected by its statements in *Kadiman*.

(c) *Right of residence for family members during the first three years*

20–16 The first indent of art.7 of Decision 1/80 provides that the family members of Turkish workers have the right to respond, subject to priority being given to own national workers, to any offer of employment after three years legal

---

[14] *Kadiman v State of Bavaria* (C-351/97) [1997] E.C.R. I-2133.
[15] *Kadiman v State of Bavaria* (C-351/97) [1997] E.C.R. I-2133, at [37].
[16] *Kadiman v State of Bavaria* (C-351/97) [1997] E.C.R. I-2133, at [38] (emphasis added).

residence. What rights then pertain to family members who have been granted entry to a Member State but who have not been legally resident for three years?

The CJEU has found that the aim of art.7 is to enable, during the first three years, family members to be with a Turkish worker with a view to thus furthering the employment and residence of the Turkish worker who is already legally integrated into the host Member State.[17] **20–17**

The CJEU has held that nothing in Decision 1/80 affects the power of Member States to attach conditions to the stay of family members of Turkish workers until they become entitled to respond to offers of employment after the initial period of three years' residence.[18] In particular, the CJEU has stated that the first paragraph of art.7 of Decision 1/80 does not preclude Member States from requiring that the family members of a Turkish worker live together for the period of three years prescribed by the first indent of that provision since the spirit and purpose of that provision is intended to preserve the unity of the family.[19] **20–18**

However, the Member State is not entitled to impose conditions other than those provided for in Decision 1/80. The CJEU has stated that since art.7 of Decision 1/80 has direct effect and given the primacy of EU law, Member States could not be permitted to unilaterally modify the system of gradually integrating Turkish workers into the host Member State's labour force. In *Pehlivan* the CJEU considered a Dutch law providing that a child of a Turkish worker who marries or forms a relationship during the first three years of residence in the Netherlands is automatically deemed to have broken the family link even if she continues to reside with the Turkish worker parent and is thus excluded from benefiting from art.7 of Decision 1/80. The Court found that such a rule went beyond the limits of measures which the Member State is authorised to adopt on the basis of Decision 1/80.[20] **20–19**

(d) *Right of residence of family members of workers after three years' residence*

(i) *Right of residence as a corollary of right to take up employment*

After three years of residence, art.7 seeks to deepen the integration of the Turkish worker's family into the host Member State by granting to the family member concerned the possibility of gaining access to the labour force. The CJEU has described the fundamental objective of the provision as being that of consolidating the position of those family members by **20–20**

---

[17] *Land Baden-Württemberg v Metin Bozkurt* (C-303/08) December 22, 2010.
[18] *Kadiman v State of Bavaria* (C-351/97) [1997] E.C.R. I-2133, at [33].
[19] The CJEU has certainly envisaged that there may be cases where the objective circumstances justified the failure of the family member concerned to live under the same roof as the Turkish worker in the host Member State, see *Pehlivan v Staatssecretaros van Justitie* (C-484/07) June 16, 2011, at [46].
[20] See *Pehlivan v Staatssecretaris van Justitie* (C-484/07) June 16, 2011, at [55–61].

giving them the means to earn their own living in the host Member State and therefore to establish a position which is independent of that the Turkish worker.[21]

20–21   Once the family member of a Turkish worker fulfils the conditions of art.7 there is an implied right of residence as a corollary of the right to respond to offers of employment since the right of residence is "essential to access to and the pursuit of any paid employment".[22] This position consistently taken by the CJEU in relation to art.7 is in line with its jurisprudence in relation to art.45 TFEU and art.6 of Decision 1/80.[23]

20–22   This right of residence will also include a reasonable period of grace when the person concerned is looking for employment in the Member State.[24] The length of such period is a matter for the host Member State, although it should not be so short as to impair the right.[25] The CJEU has referred to its case law in relation to EU nationals who are seeking work pursuant to Treaty rights when considering the position of family members of Turkish workers. The CJEU considers it appropriate to treat such family members in an equivalent way to EU nationals who have the right to seek work in the territory of other Member States.[26]

(ii) *Calculation of the three-year or five-year period*

20–23   The first indent of the first paragraph of art.7 refers to lawful residence for three years and the second indent to lawful residence for five years. The CJEU has stated that whilst the family member must in principle reside "uninterruptedly" during those three (or five) years with the Turkish worker, the notion is one which must be interpreted flexibly.[27] Accordingly absences from the family home for a reasonable period and for legitimate reasons such as to take holidays, are permissible and will not break continuity of residence.

20–24   Consistent with provisions in secondary legislation relating to EU national workers, breaks in residence of no longer than six months will not affect the right of residence.[28] So far as the calculation of the time periods under the first paragraph of art.7 is concerned, absences of up to six months must be treated as periods in which the family member concerned actually lived with

---

[21] para.34. *Bozkurt* (C-303/08) December 22, 2010, at [34]. Thus if the family member no longer resides with the Turkish worker, his rights under art.7 of Decision 1/80 once acquired are still protected, see *Ismail Derin v Landkreis Darmstadt-Dieburg* (C-325/05) [2007] E.C.R. I-06495, at [49–50].
[22] *Eroglu v Land Baden-Württemberg* (C-355/93) [1994] E.C.R. I-5113, at [20].
[23] *Akman v Oberkreisdirektor des Rheinisch-Bergischen-Kreises* (C-210/97) [1998] E.C.R. I-7519.
[24] *Eroglu v Land Baden-Württemberg* (C-355/93) [1994] E.C.R. I-5113, at [21].
[25] *Kus v Landeshauptstadt Wiesbaden* (C-237/91) [1992] E.C.R I-6781.
[26] See Ch.9 and see *Akman v Oberkreisdirektor des Rheinisch-Bergischen-Kreises* (C-210/97) [1998] E.C.R. I-7519.
[27] *Kadiman v State of Bavaria* (C-351/95) [1997] E.C.R. I-2133, at [48–49]. *Kadiman* was a case concerned with the first indent.
[28] cf. art.11 of Directive 2004/38 discussed in Ch.10 in relation to EU nationals.

the Turkish worker, provided that there is a legitimate reason for such an absence.[29]

Furthermore, although the first paragraph of art.7 refers to "lawful residence", short periods when the family member is not in possession of a valid residence document cannot affect the running of time for the purposes of the three-year period. In *Kadiman*[30] the former spouse of a Turkish worker was without a valid residence permit for a period of four months after her first residence permit was curtailed on the grounds that the couple were separated and a second permit was issued to her four months later when her husband declared that they would resume living together.[31] The CJEU concluded that the lack of residence permit during that period did not affect the calculation of the three-year time period under art.7.[32]

20–25

In the event of dispute as to the entitlement to rights under art.7 of Decision 1/80, and if the individual is unable to produce a valid residence permit for the relevant period, the CJEU has stated that she must prove by any other means that she was present on the territory of the Member State or that she only left it for legitimate reasons. This implies that emphasis is not to be placed on the legality of residence, but instead on the fact of residence for the relevant period (since presence on a territory cannot be equated in national laws with legal residence). This is at odds with the emphasis placed on legality of residence and employment under art.6(1) of Decision 1/80. However, it can be explained by the fact that in giving effect to principles of family unity, protection is given to families that have in fact resided together for three years, even if their situation was not at all times regularised by the host Member State and even if that Member State did not intend to create conditions conducive to family unity.

20–26

(iii) *Retaining the right to take up employment and residence*

Once a family member has remained in the territory of a Member State for three years and thereby satisfied the requirements of the first indent of the first paragraph of art.7, that family member acquires an EU law right to take up offers of employment, subject to the priority given to EU nationals in the labour market. After five years of residence (as provided in the second indent of the first paragraph of art.7), the family member of the Turkish worker attains unfettered access to the labour market.

20–27

It is important that once acquired the rights under art.7 of Decision 1/80 will only be lost in two circumstances. First, where on account of personal conduct the family member's presence in the host Member State constitutes a genuine and serious threat to public policy, public security or public health[33]. Secondly, where the person concerned has left the territory of the

20–28

---

[29] *Kadiman v State of Bavaria* (C-351/95) [1997] E.C.R. I-2133, at [49] and [50].
[30] *Kadiman v State of Bavaria* (C-351/95) [1997] E.C.R. I-2133.
[31] *Kadiman v State of Bavaria* (C-351/95) [1997] E.C.R. I-2133, at [15], [16] and [22].
[32] In fact the German authorities had not sought to argue that she was unlawfully resident during that period despite the lack of residence permit.
[33] See art.14 of Decision 1/80.

host Member State for a significant length of time without legitimate reason.[34]

20–29   Thus on satisfaction of three year's residence, a break in residence should not in principle affect the right under art.7 to take up offers of employment (and as a corollary to reside in the relevant Member State) since this is a right which has already been acquired. Where the person leaves the territory of the relevant Member State for a "significant" length of time without legitimate reason, the legal rights acquired under the first paragraph of art.7 will generally be lost.[35] In such instance the family member concerned can be expected to make a fresh application to re-join the Turkish worker in the relevant Member State.

20–30   The CJEU's interpretation of these principles is generous to the absent family member. In *Ergat*[36] the CJEU found a period of absence from Germany of one year to be irrelevant to the acquisition of rights under art.7 of Decision 1/80. This was because Mr Ergat had made an application for residence before departing based on his acquired rights under the provision. The CJEU did not consider it necessary to consider why he remained away from Germany for that year.[37] It was of some significance that the German authorities had not made his re-admission to Germany conditional upon the issue of a fresh authorisation to enter.

20–31   Further, the fact that a person applies for recognition of their right of residence acquired under art.7 of Decision 1/80 after the expiry of a previous residence permit does not affect the right of residence. This is consistent with general principles of EU law that residence permits issued pursuant to rights under EU law do not themselves confer the rights and that the lack of a residence permit does not affect the right of residence itself. As the CJEU stated in *Ergat*:

> "the issue of a residence permit does not constitute the basis of the right of residence which is conferred directly by Decision No 1/80, and that is so irrespective of whether the authorities of the host Member State have issued that particular document, which is merely evidence of the existence of that right".[38]

20–32   The fact that the family member no longer cohabits with the Turkish worker or is no longer in a relationship with the Turkish worker does not affect the family member's rights acquired under art.7 of Decision 1/80. In *Bozkurt* the CJEU considered that the divorce of spouses, if it takes place after the family member concerned has acquired rights under art.7 of Decision 1/80 is irrelevant to the continuing existence of those rights for the person entitled, even if, at the outset that person could have only secured those rights through their ex-spouse.[39]

---

[34] See *Bozkurt* (C-303/08) December 22, 2010, at [42]. See also, *Derin* (C-325/05) July 18, 2007.
[35] *Sezgin Ergat v Stadt Ulm* (C-329/97) [2000] E.C.R. I-1487, at [48].
[36] *Sezgin Ergat v Stadt Ulm* (C-329/97) [2000] E.C.R. I-1487.
[37] *Sezgin Ergat v Stadt Ulm* (C-329/97) [2000] E.C.R. I-1487, at [51].
[38] *Sezgin Ergat v Stadt Ulm* (C-329/97) [2000] E.C.R. I-1487, at [61].
[39] See *Bozkurt* (C-303/08) December 22, 2010, at [44].

The fact that the Turkish worker loses his job during the first three years of the family member's residence in the host Member State does not affect the acquisition of rights under the first paragraph of art.7 providing that the couple cohabited during that period and the family member was lawfully resident. The Turkish worker need only be "duly registered as belonging to the labour force", and a period of involuntary unemployment if there is a reasonable prospect of obtaining other employment will not prevent them belonging to the labour force.[40] **20–33**

The family member will not lose rights acquired under the first paragraph of art.7 of Decision 1/80 even following imprisonment for more than two years and thus preventing the family member from being able to join the labour force during that time.[41] **20–34**

Just as with art.6(1) of Decision 1/80 the reasons why the Turkish worker was granted entry and residence in the host Member State are irrelevant to the question of rights that flow. Thus the first paragraph of art.7 does not make the recognition of the right of access to employment in the host Member State and the right of residence of family members of a Turkish worker dependant on the circumstances in which the right of entry or residence were obtained by the Turkish worker.[42] This remains the case even if the Turkish worker originally made false statements in order to obtain entry or residence and the residence permit is subsequently withdrawn. Once the family member has attained rights under art.7, the Turkish worker's status, or how that status was obtained becomes irrelevant.[43] **20–35**

(iv) *Definition of the "family member"*

There is no definition of family member in the Agreement or any of the Council of Association decisions. The CJEU in *Ayaz*[44] described the scope of family members in the context of art.7 of Decision 1/80 as follows: **20–36**

> "[I]n the determination of the scope of 'member of the family' for the purposes of the first paragraph of Article 7 of Decision No 1/80, reference should be made to the interpretation given to that concept in the field of freedom of movement for workers who are nationals of the Member States of the Community and, more specifically, to the scope given to Article 10(1) of Regulation No 1612/68."

Family members at the very least must include:

---

[40] *Ibrahim Altun v Stadt Boblingen* (C-337/07) [2008] E.C.R. I-10323.
[41] See *Derin v Landkreis Darmstadt-Dieburg* (C-325/05) [2007] E.C.R. I-06495.
[42] In *Altun* the Turkish worker had obtained the right of residence and the right of access to the labour market as a political refugee. The CJEU found that this was irrelevant to acquisition of rights under art.7 of Decision 1/80, see *Altun* (C-337/07) [2008] E.C.R. I-10323, at [42–50].
[43] See *Altun* (C-337/07) [2008] E.C.R. I-10323.
[44] *Ayaz v Land Baden-Württemberg* (C-275/02), [2004] All E.R. (D) 188, at [45].

(a) spouses, their descendants under the age of 21 years or their dependants; and

(b) dependent relatives in the ascending line of the worker and their spouse.[45]

20–37 Beyond such relationships the CJEU has given a broad interpretation to the concept of "member of the family" in the context of art.7 of Decision 1/80. In *Eyüp*,[46] for example, the CJEU treated a divorcee who cohabited with her ex-husband as a "member of the family" with the result her residence during that period of cohabitation could be included in calculating her period of stay Austria and determining her art.7 rights. The interpretation of family members in EU law is discussed in Ch.9 above. Undoubtedly the CJEU's decision in *Eyüp* represents a significant move forward in recognising de facto family relationships. Furthermore, in *Ayaz*,[47] the CJEU interpreted family members to include those who are not blood relations such as step-children.

3. Children

(a) *Provisions in Decision 1/80 relating to children*

20–38 In addition to the rights acquired by family members of Turkish workers after certain periods of residence, the second paragraph of art.7 of Decision 1/80 confers specific rights on the children of Turkish workers to respond to offers of employment following the completion of a course of vocational training.

20–39 The second paragraph of art.7 of Decision 1/80 provides:

"Children of Turkish workers who have completed a course of vocational training in the host country may respond to any offer of employment there, irrespective of the length of time they have been resident in that Member State, provided one of their parents has been legally employed in the Member State concerned for at least three years."

20–40 Further, art.9 of Decision 1/80 provides:

"Turkish children residing legally with their parents, who are or have been legally employed in a Member State of the Community, will be admitted to courses of general education, apprenticeship and vocational training under the same educational entry qualifications as the children of nationals of the Member States.

---

[45] art.10 of Regulation 1612/68 (replaced by art.2 of Directive 2004/38). See *Mesbah* (C-179/98) [1999] E.C.R. I-7955, in which the CJEU held that the term "member of the family" of a Moroccan migrant worker, within the meaning of art.41(1) of the Moroccan Cooperation Agreement, extends to relatives in the ascending line of that worker and of his spouse who live with him in the host Member State. As the CJEU observed in *Ayuz*:
"that interpretation, given in respect of a cooperation agreement, must apply a fortiori with respect to an association agreement, which pursues a more ambitious objective." (para.47)
[46] *Eyüp v Landesgeschäftsstelle des Arbeitsmarktservice Vorarlberg* (C-65/98) [2000] E.C.R. I-4747.
[47] *Ayaz v Land Baden-Württemberg* (C-275/02) September 30, 2004, at [46].

Children

They may in that Member State be eligible to benefit from the advantages provided for under the national legislation in this area".

(b) *Children who have completed vocational training*

20–41 The right contained in art.7 to respond to employment offers which is conferred on children who have undertaken vocational training is silent as to the length of time for which any such vocational training must be undertaken. The second paragraph of art.7 extends the right to take up employment and as a corollary the right of residence to all children, whatever nationality, of Turkish workers. At least one parent must have been legally employed in the Member State for at least three years.

(i) *Reasons for granting entry to the child*

20–42 It is clear from the CJEU's decision in *Eroglu*[48] that the fact that the child of a Turkish worker was originally granted a right to enter and stay for the purposes of vocational training only cannot preclude that child from benefiting from rights under the second paragraph of art.7. Regardless of conditions of entry and stay, children of Turkish mothers who satisfy the conditions set out in the second paragraph of art.7, may respond to any offer of employment in the Member State concerned and, by the same token, rely on that provision to obtain the extension of their residence permits:

> "The fact that the right was not given to [children of Turkish workers] with a view to reuniting the family but, for example, for the purpose of study does not, therefore, deprive the child of a Turkish worker who satisfies the conditions of the second paragraph of Article 7 of the enjoyment of the rights conferred thereunder".[49]

20–43 This is consistent with the CJEU's view expressed in the context of Turkish workers benefitting from art.6 of Decision 1/80 that the intentions of the Member State in admitting a person are unimportant once the individual has acquired rights in EU law. Thus the operation of art.7 cannot be hindered by a lack of motivation of the part on the Member States to encourage family unity.

(ii) *Limitations on exercise of the right to take up employment*

20–44 There is no indication in art.7 that the temporal conditions of art.6(1) of Decision 1/80 have any relevance to children benefitting from art.7. Thus a child qualifying under the second paragraph of art.7 should be able to change occupation at any time under art.6(1), since there is no limitation on changes in employer or occupation contained in art.7.

20–45 It appears that there is not a time-limit within which the Turkish child qualifying under the second paragraph of art.7 has to take up employment. Thus in *Eroglu* the CJEU found that a Turkish national who had acquired the right to take up freely paid employment under the second indent of art.7

---

[48] *Eroglu v Land Baden-Württemberg* (C-355/93) [1994] E.C.R. I-5113.
[49] *Eroglu v Land Baden-Württemberg* (C-355/93) [1994] E.C.R. I-5113, at [22].

does not lose the right of residence even though at the age of 23 he had not been in paid employment since leaving school at the age of 16 and had only ever taken part in government job support schemes which he did not complete.[50]

(iii) *Remaining beyond worker*

20–46 Whilst the second paragraph of art.7 stipulates that at least one parent of the child must have been legally employed in the relevant Member State for at least three years, just as with the first paragraph of art.7, it does not exclude the possibility of the child remaining beyond the worker.

20–47 In the case of *Akman*[51] the CJEU held that in order to benefit from the provisions of the second paragraph of art.7, it is not necessary for the parent still to work or be resident in the Member State when the child wishes to gain access to the employment market there.

20–48 The rationale for this is that the second paragraph of art.7 is intended to provide specific treatment for children with a view to facilitating their entry into the employment market following completion of a course of vocational training, the objective being the achievement by progressive stages of freedom of movement for workers. The CJEU considered that the second paragraph of art.7 is not aimed at providing the conditions for family unity. It would thus be unreasonable to require that the Turkish worker should continue to reside in the host Member State even after the worker's employment relationship there has ceased in order to secure the child's position, when that child has already completed training and wishes to respond to an offer of employment.

20–49 In *Akman*[52] the German Government had argued that the child should only be allowed to take up employment under the strict restrictions of art.6(1) of Decision 1/80. The CJEU rejected this argument stating that such an interpretation of art.7 would negate the effectiveness of art.7.[53] Clearly art.6(1) applies to a child who has been legally employed in the Member State for a year and wishes to extend her contract with that employer but the second paragraph of art.7 goes further. In the CJEU's words it is a "special provision specifically conferring on [children of Turkish workers] more favourable conditions as regards employment" in Member States.[54]

20–50 In *Bekleyen* the CJEU rejected the argument of the Danish and Netherlands Governments that the right of access of the child of a Turkish worker to the employment market must be conditional upon there being a temporal concomitance between the employment or residence of one of the parents in the host Member State and the start of the child's vocational training. The CJEU noted that no condition of cohabitation exists in the wording of

---

[50] See *Hakan Er v Wetteraukreis* (C-453/07) [2008] E.C.R. I-07299.
[51] *Akman v Oberkreisdirektor des Rheinisch-Bergischen-Kreises* (C-210/97) [1998] E.C.R. I-7519.
[52] *Akman v Oberkreisdirektor des Rheinisch-Bergischen-Kreises* (C-210/97) [1998] E.C.R. I-7519.
[53] *Akman v Oberkreisdirektor des Rheinisch-Bergischen-Kreises* (C-210/97) [1998] E.C.R. I-7519, at [49].
[54] *Akman v Oberkreisdirektor des Rheinisch-Bergischen-Kreises* (C-210/97) [1998] E.C.R. I-7519.

the second paragraph of art.7 of Decision 1/80. Nor is there any condition that the parent must still be in employment when the child starts her vocational training. The CJEU found that the child could rely on her rights under the second paragraph of art.7 even where she had travelled back with her parents to Turkey and had returned on her own to the Member State in order to start a training course there.[55]

Just as the child of a Turkish worker is entitled to respond to employment offers and as a corollary reside even if the Turkish worker should leave the territory, the child is entitled to the same even if she becomes independent of her parents. As the CJEU observed *Derin* the right of access to employment enjoyed by members of a Turkish worker's family "is in fact specifically intended to consolidate their position in that State by offering them the chance to become independent".[56]   20–51

(c) *Children and education*

The provision in art.9 of Decision 1/80 reflects the right of access to general education conferred on the children of EU national workers by art.10 of Regulation 492/2011. Such access is seen as part of the integration of workers and their families to the host Member State.   20–52

The clear and unambiguous nature of the provision means that it has direct effect. The CJEU has observed that art.9 does not require the parents of the children to be legally employed when the children wish to exercise the rights thus conferred on them.[57] This is consistent with the interpretation of the equivalent provision relating to EU nationals.[58]   20–53

A child who has benefited from the provisions of art.9 may thereafter benefit from the provisions of the second paragraph of art.7 by responding to any offer of employment having completed vocational training. In order to benefit from the right given by art.9 of entry to the education system, children must be resident with their parents in the Member State (although the parents need not still be employed). Thereafter it would appear unnecessary for the parents to even reside in the Member State.   20–54

4. FAMILY MEMBERS OF THOSE ESTABLISHED IN BUSINESS

Given the lack of specific rights of establishment conferred on Turkish nationals beyond the standstill clause provided for in art.41(1) of the Additional Protocol, the lack of any detailed rights relating to family unity for those established in the territory of the Member States is unsurprising.   20–55

---

[55] See *Bekleyen v Land Berlin* (C-462/08) January 21, 2010.
[56] *Ismail Derin v Landkreis Darmstadt-Dieburg* (C-325/05) [2007] E.C.R. I-06495, at [50].
[57] *Akman v Oberkreisdirektor des Rheinisch-Bergischen-Kreises* (C-210/97) [1998] E.C.R. I-7519, at [41].
[58] See *Baumbast and R. v Secretary of State for the Home Department* (C-413/99) E.C.R. I-709. See discussion in Ch.9.

20–56 However, art.13 of the Agreement refers to the guidance given by EC Treaty [now TFEU] provisions relating to establishment of EU citizens and further the CJEU has placed emphasis on family unity as being fundamental to the TFEU provisions. This must mean that the scope of the standstill clause in art.41(1) of the Additional Protocol extends to rights of family reunification for those seeking to establish themselves in the territory of the Member States.[59]

20–57 Thus although a Turkish national established or seeking to establish himself in a Member State does not have the unequivocal right to be accompanied by family members conferred by the Ankara Agreement, any application for family reunification must be considered at least under conditions which are no more stringent than those reflected in national laws in place in the relevant Member State at the time when the Agreement came into force in that particular Member State.

---

[59] For further discussion of the standstill provision in art.41(1) of Additional Protocol, see Ch.19.

CHAPTER 21

EXPULSION UNDER THE ANKARA AGREEMENT

This chapter considers the application of the "public policy proviso" to Turkish nationals and their family members exercising rights under the Ankara Agreement. The rights enjoyed by workers in relation to expulsion are distinguishable from those enjoyed by Turkish nationals established in the Member States.

1. WORKERS AND THEIR FAMILY MEMBERS

(a) *Workers and their family members with accrued rights under arts 6 and 7 of Decision 1/80*

(i) *Measures taken on grounds of public policy, public security or public health*

21–01 Article 14(1) of Decision 1/80 provides in relation to workers that "the provisions of this section shall be applied subject to limitations justified on grounds of public policy, public security or public health". The public policy proviso is a concept well known to EU law which is considered in detail in Ch.13. Article 14(1) is identical to that contained in art.45(3) TFEU (ex-art.39(3) EC Treaty).

21–02 The interpretative principle requiring the scope of rights in Decision 1/80 to be defined as far as possible by reference to the TFEU provisions relating to free movement of workers[1] provides ample justification for applying the Union law meaning given to such identically worded proviso where expulsion is faced by Turkish workers exercising rights under Decision 1/80. Nevertheless in *Nazli*[2] one of the questions referred to the CJEU was whether the expulsion of a Turkish worker on general preventive grounds as a deterrent to other aliens was compatible with art.14(1) of Decision 1/80. The German Government argued that the prohibition of recourse to expulsion on general preventive grounds could not be derived from art.45(3) TFEU (ex-art.39 EC Treaty) and was introduced for EU nationals *only* by Directive 64/221.[3]

21–03 The CJEU in *Nazli* robustly rejected such approach. The CJEU had no difficulty whatsoever in applying the interpretative principle identified[4] and stated:

---

[1] *Nazli v Stadt Nürnberg* (C-340/97) [2000] E.C.R. I-957, at [50–55] and references therein. Directive 64/221 has now been replaced by Directive 2004/38. See Ch.13 on expulsion of EU citizens.
[2] *Nazli v Stadt Nürnberg* (C-340/97) [2000] E.C.R. I-957.
[3] Now repealed and replaced by Directive 2004/38/EC.
[4] *Nazli v Stadt Nürnberg* (C-340/97) [2000] E.C.R. I-957, at [50–55].

[385]

"It follows that, when determining the scope of the public policy exception provided for by Article 14(1) of Decision No 1/80, reference should be made to the interpretation given to that exception in the field of freedom of movement for workers who are nationals of a Member State of the Community. Such an approach is all the more justified because Article 14(1) is formulated in almost identical terms to Article 48(3) of the Treaty [now Article 45(3) TFEU]".[5]

21–04 The CJEU did not find it necessary to refer at all to Directive 64/221. The CJEU held that art.14(1) precluded the expulsion of a Turkish national enjoying a right granted by Decision 1/80 following a criminal conviction as a deterrent to other aliens where there was no reason to consider that they would commit other serious offences prejudicial to the requirements of public policy in the host Member State. The CJEU did so on the basis of the following principles which in light of *Nazli* must be applied to Turkish workers facing expulsion:[6]

(a) the concept of public policy presupposes the existence of a genuine and sufficiently serious threat to one of the fundamental interests of society;

(b) although Member States may consider the use of drugs to constitute a danger for society justifying special measures against aliens who contravene its laws on drugs, the public policy exception must nevertheless be interpreted restrictively so that the existence of a criminal conviction could justify expulsion only in so far as the circumstances which gave rise to that conviction are evidence of personal conduct constituting a present threat to the requirements of public policy[7]; and

(c) expulsion on general preventive grounds for the purpose of deterring others is not permitted, especially where applied automatically following a criminal conviction without any account being taken of the personal conduct of the offender or of the danger which that conduct represents for the requirements of public policy.

21–05 The importance of these principles cannot be overstated. They mean that a Turkish national can be denied the rights derived from Decision 1/80 only if expulsion is justified because of personal conduct indicating a specific risk of new and serious prejudice to the requirements of public policy, public security or public health.[8]

---

[5] *Nazli v Stadt Nürnberg* (C-340/97) [2000] E.C.R. I-957, at [56].
[6] *Nazli v Stadt Nürnberg* (C-340/97) [2000] E.C.R. I-957, at [57–59] and references there given.
[7] As acknowledged by the German national court in making the references to the CJEU in *Engin Ayuz v Land Baden-Württemberg* (C-275/02) [2004] E.C.R. I-08765, where personal contact did not indicate a specific risk "of new and serious prejudice to the requirements of public policy" expulsion of a person falling within the scope of Decision 1/80 would not be justified; see para.29.
[8] *Nazli v Stadt Nürnberg* (C-340/97) [2000] E.C.R. I-957, at [61]. See below para.21–09 however on the enhanced protection for EU Citizens under art.28(3) of Directive 2004/38 which will not apply to Turkish nationals.

21-06 Moreover in response to such specific question raised by the Berlin Administrative Court in *Bicakci*[9] the CJEU made an order on September 19, 2000 in which it ruled—without hearing argument[10]—that:

> "Article 14(1) ... is to be interpreted as precluding the expulsion of a Turkish national who enjoys a right granted directly by [Decision 1/80] when it is ordered, following a criminal conviction, as a deterrent to other aliens without the personal conduct of the person concerned giving reason to consider that he will commit other serious offences prejudicial to the requirements of public policy in the host Member State."

21-07 The same approach taken to Turkish workers facing expulsion applies to members of the worker's family who enjoy rights of residence under art.7 of Decision 1/80. This is clear because art.14(1) applies both to arts 6 and 7 of Decision 1/80.[11]

21-08 The question of whether the expulsion of a Turkish worker who had obtained a residence permit by fraud would be compatible with art.14(1) of Decision 1/80 was raised, although not answered, in the earlier case of *Kol*.[12] In that case the Turkish worker had obtained his residence permit only by means of inaccurate declarations for which he was convicted of fraud. Expulsion was sought as a preventative measure with a view to deterring others. In light of *Nazli*[13] the answer to the question about the compatibility with Decision 1/80 of a measure taken on such grounds must be that such expulsion would be prohibited. This does not mean however that a Turkish worker who obtains a residence permit by fraud cannot be expelled. To the contrary, such person will not have any accrued rights under art.6(1) of Decision 1/80 since—as held by the CJEU in *Kus*[14]—periods of employment in reliance on a fraudulently obtained residence permit cannot be regarded as legal employment for the purposes of art.6(1). In these circumstances the narrow interpretation to be given to the public policy proviso contained in art.14(1) is irrelevant to such person.

21-09 The relationship between art.14(1) of Decision 1/80 and art.28 of Directive 2004/38 was considered in *Ziebell*.[15] In that case the Turkish national had been lawfully resident in the host Member State for over 10 years. The CJEU concluded that the protection for EU nationals under art.28(3) of Directive 2004/38 permitting expulsion only on grounds of public security after 10 years' lawful residence did not apply to Turkish nationals. Although the Court recalled its constant jurisprudence that the provisions of Decision 1/80 must be interpreted as closely as possible to art.52 TFEU, it found that the enhanced protection regime in art.28(3) is not necessarily born out of art.52 alone but follows from the fundamental importance of Union

---

[9] *Bulent Recep Bicakci* (C-89/00) (O.J. 2000/C149/41).
[10] The CJEU invoked art.104(3) of the rules of procedure relating to identical questions.
[11] See, for instance, *Derin v Landkreis Darmstad-Dieburg* (C-325/07) July 18, 2007.
[12] *Kol v Land Berlin* (C-285/95) [1997] E.C.R. I-3069.
[13] *Nazli v Stadt Nürnberg* (C-340/97) [2000] E.C.R. I-957.
[14] *Kus v Landeshauptstadt Wiesbaden* (C-237/91) [1992] E.C.R. I-6781, at [26].
[15] *Ziebell v Land Baden-Württemberg* (C-371/08) December 8, 2011.

citizenship, born out of other provisions of the TFEU which do not apply to Turkish citizens.

(ii) *Appeals*

21–10 The corollary to the proposition that Turkish national workers enjoying rights of residence under arts 6 and 7 of Decision 1/80 may not be expelled save in the circumstances identified by the CJEU in *Nazli*,[16] must be the existence of some procedural guarantees to protect the individual from the arbitrary interference by a Member State with rights derived from EU law.

21–11 In the European Union context arts 30–33 of Directive 2004/38/EC provide procedural guarantees for persons exercising free movement rights—together with members of their families—who face expulsion. The provisions of Directive 2004/38/EC are considered in Ch.13. These should be regarded as the minimum guarantees to be afforded to Turkish workers in these circumstances. In *Dorr* the CJEU ruled that since the principles laid down in the EC Treaty (now art.45(3) TEFU) were to be extended as far as possible to Turkish workers falling under Decision 1/80 and since art.14(1) of Decision 1/80 was almost identical in wording to the Treaty provision (now art.45(3) TFEU), art.14(1) imposes limits on the competent national authorities analogous to those which applied to a measure expelling a national of a Member State. For the same reasons the principles enshrined in arts 8 and 9 of Directive 64/221 (now arts 30–33 of Directive 2004/38)[17] mean that any review or appeal must be capable of subjecting the merits of the underlying expulsion decision to proper scrutiny. Further, applicants for an appeal or review must be able to apply for a suspension of the exclusion order pending the appeal, subject to the exceptions set out in art.31 of Directive 2004/38.

(b) *Workers and their family members without accrued rights*

21–12 Workers and their family members who have yet to accrue rights otherwise contained in arts 6 and 7 will nevertheless potentially benefit from the standstill provision in art.13 of Decision 1/80 if legally resident (for example, a legally resident worker who has only worked for six months in the host Member State). Although art.13 prevents the introduction of new restrictions on the conditions of access to employment for both workers and their family members, *access* must plainly be interpreted broadly so as to include expulsion which by definition would prevent any access to employment.

---

[16] *Nazli v Stadt Nürnberg* (C-340/97) [2000] E.C.R. I-957.
[17] *Dorr and Unal* (C-136/03) [2005] E.C.R. I-04759.

2. Self-employed Turkish Nationals

(a) *The self-employed in a regular position*

21–13 If expulsion measures are taken against the six-month legally resident worker, they can be subject to measures that are no more stringent than were in place at the time when Decision 2/76 came into force in the host Member State. This is because the standstill provision in relation to workers was first introduced by art.7 of Decision 2/76, which as regards workers was repeated in identical terms in art.13 of Decision 1/80. The position for family members on the other hand is different. They can be subject to measures that are no more stringent than were in place at the time when Decision 1/80 came into force in the host Member State. This is because art.7 of Decision 2/76 made no mention whatsoever of family members. National law and practices in many Member States are likely to have been more benevolent in 1976 or 1980 (whichever applies) than they are today.

21–14 In this context, Turkish nationals in self-employment in Member States should be accorded the same protections and guarantees as are accorded to workers and their families when expulsion measures are taken against them. According to the CJEU in *Savas*,[18] Turkish nationals who are lawfully resident and lawfully carrying out a genuine and effective self-employed activity in the territory of a Member State have the Union law rights to continue in that self-employed activity and, as a corollary, extend their residence. Such persons must similarly enjoy the same protections against expulsion as are enjoyed by workers or indeed any EU national enjoying Union rights of free movement.

(b) *Self-employed covered by the standstill provision*

21–15 As explained in Ch.19, all Turkish nationals who wish to establish themselves in business are protected by the standstill provision in art.41(1) of the Additional Protocol. Whilst those in a regular position will have the right of continued residence and the corresponding protection against expulsion, other self-employed Turkish nationals attain only the right not to be subjected to any new restrictions on the freedom of establishment and the freedom to provide services.

21–16 Turkish nationals who are unlawfully present (which will include both those who have been admitted and remained beyond their permission and those who entered irregularly) cannot be subject to expulsion measures that are any more stringent than those in place when the Additional Protocol came into force in the host Member State.[19] Finally, Turkish nationals who seek entry in order to establish themselves must likewise receive at least such procedural guarantees as were afforded to business applicants at the time when the Additional Protocol came into force in the host Member State.

---

[18] *The Queen v Secretary of State for the Home Department Ex p. Savas* (C-37/98) [2000] E.C.R. I-2927.
[19] Namely 1973 for the original Member States, the date of accession for the others.

CHAPTER 22

INTRODUCTION TO UK LAW AND PRACTICE

This Part provides information and analysis on UK law and practice and the implementation of EU law provisions on the free movement of persons. It is intended to mirror the scheme of the book and be used alongside the main parts of this book which describe the position in EU law. It is divided into three parts: **22–01**

- Chapter 23 examines in brief the general implementation of Community law into UK legislation and the relationship between the UK courts and the CJEU.
- Chapter 24 examines the United Kingdom's implementation of EU law relating to the EU citizens and their family members covered in Part 2.
- Chapter 25 examines the United Kingdom's implementation of free movement provision contained in the Association Agreements covered in Part Three.

It is not necessary or intended to describe in detail legal provisions and practices in the United Kingdom which conform properly with EU law provision. The aim of this part of the book therefore is to focus on contentious areas where UK law and practice including case law appears to diverge from EU law. The focus will be on areas where there is doubt as to the correct interpretation of EU law with a view to identifying possible references to the CJEU from the national courts for an authoritative interpretation. **22–02**

The supremacy of EU law in the area of free movement must always be kept in mind as must the fact that most concepts, procedures and rights are spelt out in detail by EU law itself. In the case of divergence between EU Law and UK law and practice, the former will always prevail. As a matter of good practice, readers should always firstly have regard to the substantive EU law provisions applicable in any given situation. Certainly, it must never be assumed that UK law and practice accurately reflect EU law provisions or standards. Reading the decisions of some national courts at times gives the impression that national law standards have been applied at the expense of the dilution of EU principles. **22–03**

Finally, detailed explanation in this Part of EU law principles is necessarily extremely limited. It will always be important therefore to refer for substantive discussion of EU law matters to Parts 1–3 of this book. **22–04**

CHAPTER 23

INCORPORATION OF EUROPEAN UNION LAW INTO UK LAW

For the European Union law on the relationship between domestic law and EU law readers are referred to Chapter 2 in Part One of this book.

1. RELEVANT LEGISLATION

European Communities Act 1972 23–01

European Communities (Spanish and Portuguese Accession) Act 1985

European Communities (Amendment) Act 1986

European Communities (Amendment) Act 1993

European Economic Area Act 1993

European Union Accessions Act 1994

European Communities (Amendment) Act 1998

European Communities (Amendment) Act 2002

European Union (Accessions) Act 2003

European Union (Accessions) Act 2006

European Union (Amendment) Act 2008

European Union Act 2011

The Treaty of Lisbon (Changes in Terminology) Order 2011

2. THE LEGAL FRAMEWORK FOR UNION LAW IN THE UNITED KINGDOM

(a) *Introduction*

In UK law the foundation of the UK's relationship with the European Union is 23–02
the European Communities Act 1972 ("the 1972 Act"). On January 1, 1973 the UK became a member of the European Communities (the EEC, Euratom and ECSC) pursuant to the EEC Treaty of Accession 1972. Politically the United Kingdom's membership of the European Communities has not been easy. Despite the passing of the 1972 Act, membership has remained controversial. In 1975 a new Labour government recommended that the UK remained in the European Communities but that the matter be put to a referendum. In the only UK national referendum to be held to date on the UK's participation in the European project, the electorate voted to remain in the European Union.[1]

---

[1] 67.2% of the electorate voted to remain in the Community, 32.8% voted to leave. E.C.S. Wade and A.W. Bradley, *Constitutional and Administrative Law*, 10th edn (London: Longman, 1985).

INCORPORATION OF EU LAW INTO UK LAW

23–03 The 1972 Act (as amended) makes it possible for the UK to comply with its obligations arising from the EU Treaties. Section 1 of the Act defines the Community Treaties to which the Act relates. They originally included the Treaty of Rome and the Euratom Treaty, the Treaty of Accession, the Council decision relating to the United Kingdom's accession to the ECSC, and certain other treaties entered into by the Communities prior to the Act.

(b) Main provisions of the European Communities' Act 1972

(i) Treaties included in the Act

23–04 Section 1 has been subsequently amended by a series of Acts where Treaty amendments have occurred:

(a) European Communities (Spanish and Portuguese Accession) Act 1985 amends the 1972 Act to include Spain and Portugal in the Member States of the European Economic Community (as it was then known).

(b) European Communities (Amendment) Act 1986 was passed to incorporate the provisions of the Single European Act 1986 into the 1972 Act.

(c) European Communities (Amendment) Act 1993 was enacted following the Maastricht Treaty signed on February 7, 1992. Section 1 of the 1972 Act is amended to include the provisions of the Maastricht Treaty within its scope.

(d) European Economic Area Act 1993 incorporated the provisions of the European Economic Area Agreement signed in Oporto on May 2, 1992 such that the 1972 Act will apply to the EEA where appropriate.[2]

(e) European Union Accessions Act 1994 amended the definition of Treaties in s.1 of the 1972 Act so as to include the Treaty concerning the accession of Norway, Austria, Finland and Sweden to the European Union.

(f) European Communities (Amendment) Act 1998 makes consequential provisions following the amendments to the EU and EC Treaties made by the Amsterdam Treaty signed on October 2, 1997.

(g) European Communities (Amendment) Act 2002 amends the 1972 Act following amendments to the EU and EC Treaties by the Treaty of Nice signed on February 26, 2001.

(h) European Union (Accessions) Act 2003 makes consequential provisions following the accession of the Czech Republic, Estonia, Cyprus, the Republic of Latvia, Lithuania, Hungary, Malta, Poland, Slovenia and the Slovak Republic to the European Union, signed at Athens on April 16, 2003. The 2003 Act additionally makes special provision in relation to the entitlement of nationals of certain acceding States to enter or reside in the UK as workers.

---

[2] See Ch.14, paras 14–11 to 14–20 and the EEA Agreement.

The Legal Framework for Union Law in the United Kingdom

(i) European Union (Accessions) Act 2006 makes consequential provisions for the accession of Bulgaria and Romania on January 1, 2007.

(j) European Union (Amendment) Act 2008 gives effect to amendments brought about by the Treaty of Lisbon.

(ii) *Operation of EU law in the UK*

Section 2 of the 1972 Act is of paramount importance in ensuring the effective operation of EU law in the United Kingdom. Section 2(1) provides (as amended): 23–05

> "All such rights, powers, liabilities, obligations and restrictions from time to time created or arising by or under the Treaties, and all such remedies and procedures from time to time provided for by or under the Treaties, as in accordance with the Treaties are without further enactment to be given legal effect or used in the United Kingdom shall be recognised and available in law, and be enforced, allowed and followed accordingly; and the expression 'enforceable EU right' and similar expressions shall be read as referring to one to which this subsection applies".

Section 2(1) thus provides that all those provisions that under Union law are directly effective,[3] shall be directly effective in UK and given the force of law. The provision has both retroactive and prospective effect in that it applies to EU law made both before and after the coming into force of the 1972 Act. This provision gives effect to the doctrine of primacy of EU law over national law. 23–06

Those EU law provisions which do not have direct effect require implementation by the Member States.[4] Section 2(2) and (4) of the 1972 Act give broad powers for the passing of delegated legislation to implement EU legislation. 23–07

(iii) *Obligation on UK courts*

Section 3 of the 1972 Act relates to the use of Union law in UK courts. Section 3(1) provides that any question as to the interpretation or validity of a Union law provision shall be treated as a question of law. If not referred to the European Court of Justice such questions of law are to be decided in accordance with the principles laid down by the relevant decisions of the ECJ. Section 3(2) provides that all UK courts are to take judicial notice of the Union Treaties, the Official Journal of the European Union and any decisions of the CJEU. 23–08

---

[3] See Ch.2.
[4] See Ch.2 for discussion about direct effect in EU law.

3. REFERENCE TO THE CJEU FROM UK COURTS

(a) Circumstances in which a case will be referred from a UK court

23–09 The circumstances in which a court should refer a question for preliminary ruling to the CJEU are discussed in Ch.2 above. The UK courts, other than the Supreme Court which will for most cases be the final court of appeal for the purposes of art.267 TFEU (ex-art.234) are guided by the case of *Else*[5] in which Sir Thomas Bingham, M.R. stated:

> "I understand the correct approach in principle of a national court (other than a final court of appeal) to be quite clear: if the facts have been found and the Community law issue is critical to the court's final decision, the appropriate course is ordinarily to refer the issue to the Court of Justice unless the national court can with complete confidence resolve the issue itself. In considering whether it can with complete confidence resolve the issue itself the national court must be fully mindful of the differences between national and Community legislation, of the pitfalls which face a national court venturing into what may be an unfamiliar field, of the need for uniform interpretation throughout the Community and of the great advantages enjoyed by the Court of Justice in construing Community instruments.
>
> If the national court has any real doubt, it should ordinarily refer. I am not here attempting to summarise comprehensively the effect of such leading cases as *H P Bulmer Ltd v J Bollinger* ([1973] 2 All E.R. 1226) *Srl CILFIT v Ministry of Health* (C-283/81) and *R v Pharmaceutical Society of GB, Ex p. Association of Pharmaceutical Importers* ([1987] 3 CMLR 951), but I hope I am fairly expressing their essential point."

23–10 Practice Direction 11 of the Supreme Court sets out in very brief terms the circumstances that give rise to a reference to the Court of Justice and those that do not by reference to *CILFIT v Ministry of Health*.[6] The Practice Direction requires the court when refusing permission to appeal to give additional reasons where a question of EU law is involved. The Practice Direction notes the obligation on a court of last resort to refer a matter to the CJEU. The Practice Direction repeats the guidance in *CILFIT* not to refer in the following circumstances:

> "(a) where the question raised is irrelevant; (b) where the Community provision in question has already been interpreted by the Court of Justice; (c) where the question raised is materially identical with a question which has already been the subject of a preliminary ruling in a similar case; and (d) where the correct application of Community law is so obvious as to leave no scope for any reasonable doubt."

---

[5] *R v International Stock Exchange Ex p. Else Ltd* [1993] 1 All E.R. 420.
[6] *CILFIT v Ministry of Health* (C-283/81) [1982] E.C.R. 3415.

(b) *Which English courts or tribunals are entitled to refer questions to the CJEU*

Article 267(ex-art.234) TFEU provides that any court or tribunal may make a reference to the CJEU. The question of whether a referring body is a "court or tribunal" for the purposes of art.234(2) is a matter of EU, not national law.[7] In *Dorsch Consult*[8] the CJEU laid down the following criteria for determining whether a body is a court or tribunal for these purposes:

23–11

- whether the body concerned is established in law;
- whether it is permanent;
- whether it is independent;
- whether its jurisdiction is compulsory;
- whether its procedure is inter partes;
- whether it applies rules of law; and
- whether it is called upon to give judgment in proceedings intended to lead to a decision of a judicial nature.

In the immigration jurisdiction the CJEU has found that an adjudicator satisfied these requirements and thus can refer questions for reference to the CJEU.[9] Similarly questions for reference were accepted from the now defunct Immigration Appeal Tribunal.[10] Indeed there is no reason for a judge of the First Tier Tribunal or Upper Tribunal to refrain from inferring a question for reference if there are issues that are determinative of an appeal that cannot be answered by reference to the CJEU's existing case law. No practice directions exist for judges of the Immigration and Asylum Chamber on referring questions for the CJEU, which may be indicative of the infrequency with which this occurs.[11] Article 68(1) of the EC Treaty which restricted the power of courts to make a reference to the CJEU in prescribed matters of immigration and asylum law has been repealed by the Lisbon Treaty, so the constraints on the making of a reference for which it provided no longer apply. The TFEU makes no special provision for references on immigration and asylum matters.

23–12

---

[7] *Brockmeulen v Huisarts Registratie Commissie* (C-246/80) [1981] E.C.R. 2311.
[8] *Dorsch Consult Ingenieurgesellschaft mbH v Bundesbaugesellschaft Berlin mbH* (C-54/96) [1997] E.C.R. I-4961.
[9] *Nour Eddline El-Yassini v Secretary of State for the Home Department* (C-416/96) E.C.R. I-1209.
[10] *Akrich v Secretary of State for the Home Department* (C-109/01) [2003] E.C.R. I-9607.
[11] However, Blake J. in a speech on his taking over as President of the Upper Tribunal (Immigration and Asylum Chamber), February 11, 2010 stated in respect of references by the IAC:
"Although, it is not possible to predict when the reference will be made and by whom, in general it should only be done when really needed, and when the relevant factual basis for the ruling has been identified. Where it needs to be done, I am of the view that it should be done at the earliest opportunity rather than after the case has progressed to more than one level of review".

23–13 On a judicial review the High Court may make an order for reference providing the hearing is inter partes. Part 68 of the Civil Procedure Rules (CPR) sets out the rules in relation to the making of an order for reference by a court in England and Wales. A court may make the order of its own initiative or on an application by a party. An order may not, however, be made by a Master or district judge in the High Court or a district judge in the County Court. The CPR make clear that where an order for reference is made, unless the court orders otherwise the proceedings will be stayed until the CJEU has given a preliminary ruling on the question referred.

(c) *The final court*

23–14 In most civil matters, the Supreme Court will be the final court of appeal for the purposes of art.267 TFEU (ex-art.234 EC Treaty). However, with the introduction of s.13(6) of the Tribunals, Courts and Enforcement Act 2007 the final court is, at least, arguably the Upper Tribunal. That provision introduced restrictions on the scope to appeal to an appeal court decision of the Upper Tribunal: the appeal must raise an "important point of principle or practice" or display "some other compelling reason" for leave to be grant. The Court of Appeal in *PR(Sri Lanka)*[12] concluded that the particular facts of a case—such as the drastic impact of a wrong on an appellant—is not ground for treating that as a compelling reason. The effect is that for many cases the Upper Tribunal is a court of last resort and decisions of the Tribunal dismissing appeals or refusing leave to appeal to itself and to the Court of Appeal will be subject to the requirement of providing additional reasons if EU rights are involved.

(d) *Appeals against the making of a reference*

23–15 It is often agreed (or at least conceded) between the parties that a question should be referred by the court or tribunal in question to the CJEU. However, where a party is aggrieved by a question being referred, that party may appeal, although such appeals rarely succeed.[13]

(e) *Costs*

23–16 No order for costs is generally made by the CJEU in a preliminary reference. All CJEU judgments have a standard formula in the final paragraph of the reasoning in which the Court states that since the preliminary reference proceedings are, for the parties to the main proceedings, a step in the

---

[12] [2011] EWCA Civ 988.
[13] An appeal to the Court of Appeal against the decision to refer made by the High Court was successful in *R (on the application of A) v Secretary of State for the Home Department, ex p. A* [2002] EWCA Civ 1008.

proceedings pending before the national court, the decision on costs is a matter for that court. In the English courts the decision in *Fish Producers' Organisation*[14] makes clear that costs in respect of the reference generally follow the event.

Since in the immigration jurisdiction there are no provisions for the award of costs before the Immigration and Asylum Chamber, it is often beneficial for parties to seek references from these tribunals rather than waiting until the matter reaches the Court of Appeal or the Supreme Court.[15]   **23–17**

---

[14] *R. v Intervention Board for Agricultural Produce Ex p. Fish Producers' Organisation Ltd* [1993] 1 C.M.L.R. 707.
[15] This will not be affected by the limited scope of the immigration costs to successful applicants in respect of fees incurred for bringing appeals. See the First Tier Tribunal (Immigration and Asylum Chamber) Fees Order (SI 2011/2841).

CHAPTER 24

FREE MOVEMENT OF UNION CITIZENS AND THEIR FAMILIES

1. RELEVANT PRIMARY AND SECONDARY LEGISLATION

(a) *Incorporation of EU law into UK law*

Immigration Act 1971   24–01
Immigration Act 1988
Immigration (Swiss Free Movement of Persons) (No.3) Regulations 2002
The Accession (Immigration and Worker Registration) Regulations 2004
The Accession (Immigration and Worker Authorisation) Regulations 2006
The Immigration (European Economic Area) Regulations 2006
Immigration (European Economic Area) (Amendment) Regulations 2009
Immigration (European Economic Area) (Amendment) Regulations 2011

2. UK NATIONALS FOR THE PURPOSES OF EU LAW

In Ch.5 the beneficiaries of Community law are identified. It is permissible   24–02
for Member States to define which of their nationals are EU citizens for the purposes of EU law. For most Member States this has no relevance and all their nationals are treated as EU citizens and accordingly acquire full free movement rights within the European Union. However for the UK some of the categories of nationals are precluded from obtaining the benefits of EU law. In the UK Declaration accompanying the UK's Treaty of Accession, the Government defined the meaning of "national" for the purposes of the Treaties. A new declaration was made at the time of the British Nationality Act 1981 when much of British nationality law was changed.

The UK's Declaration means that the following are to be considered as   24–03
"nationals" for the purposes of EU law:

(a) British citizens;
(b) British subjects with the right of abode in the UK; and
(c) British Dependent Territories citizens who acquire that citizenship as a result of a connection to Gibraltar.[1]

---

[1] O.J. C23/1, January 28, 1983 (Cmnd. 9062/983). The term "British Dependent Territories Citizen" is now a reference to British Overseas Territories Citizens (with effect February 26, 2003, on passing of the British Overseas Territories Act 2002).

24-04 In *Kaur*[2] the CJEU was referred questions on the validity of the UK declaration[3] and whether art.17 of the EC Treaty conferred any rights on persons who were not defined as "nationals" under the terms of such a declaration. The CJEU was categorical in its response that EU citizenship was conferred only on "nationals of Member States" and the declarations entered by the UK defining who its "nationals" are for the purposes of EU citizenship were valid and unchallengeable.

3. General Scheme for EEA Nationals and their Family Members

(a) Introduction

24-05 As will be apparent from the discussion of the free movement of persons in EU law, Member States of the European Union, by being party to the EC Treaty, forego their sovereign right to control the entry and stay of nationals of other Member States who are exercising free movement rights contained within the EC Treaty and secondary legislation.[4] The only exception is where exclusion or expulsion is justified on grounds of public policy, public security and public health.[5]

24-06 This is reflected in UK law by the Immigration Act 1988 (the "1988 Act" as amended). Unlike other non-UK citizens, a person entitled to enter or remain in the UK "by virtue of an enforceable EU right or of any provision made under section 2(2) of the European Communities Act 1972"[6] does not require leave to enter or remain under the Immigration Act 1971 (the "1971 Act").

24-07 Thus the control by immigration officers and other agents of the Secretary of State on the movement of persons exercising Treaty rights is removed.[7] Section 7(2) of the 1988 Act provides that where EU nationals are not entitled to enter or remain in the UK pursuant to the Treaties, the Secretary of State may make an order giving them leave to enter for a limited period.

(b) *Immigration (European Economic Area) Regulations 2006*

(i) *Summary of provisions*

24-08 The EEA Regulations 2006 replaced the Immigration (European Economic Area) Regulations 2000 on April 30, 2006. The Regulations are not the ultimate source of rights as many provisions of the Directive are directly

---

[2] *The Queen on the application for the Home Department ex p. Kaur* (C-192/99) [2001] E.C.R. I-1237.
[3] The validity of the Declaration was questioned as it was made without any statutory authority or parliamentary approval.
[4] See Ch.5.
[5] See Ch.13.
[6] s.7(1) of the Immigration Act 1988.
[7] *Blaise Bahaten Metock v Ministry of Justice, Equality and Law Reform* (C-127/08) [2008] E.C.R. I-06241 resulting in amendment to EEA Regulation in the Immigration (EEA) (Amendment) Regulations 2011.

effective and where there is conflict between the Directive and the Regulations, the provisions of the Directive will prevail. The EEA Regulations 2006 have not faithfully transposed Directive 2004/38 as we shall see below so there is constant need to refer back to the Directive. A very recent example of this is seen in the failed attempt in the Regulations to impose a prior lawful residence requirement in another Member State on the part of a national of another Member State and their family member before they could reside in the UK.[8]

The domestic courts have not been as assiduous as they should be in identifying the core of EU rights and have too often adopted too narrow an interpretation of EU law. **24–09**

Part 1 of the Regulations begin with an interpretative section which outlines the beneficiaries of EU rights to reside (Regulation 2). They continue by defining what is meant by various terms in the Regulations including worker, self-employed person, self-sufficient person and student (Regulation 4). They proceed to introduce the concept of "qualified person" to cover the said persons (Regulation 6) Following on from this are definitions of family members (Regulation 7) and the Regulations introduce the concepts of extended family member and the family member who has retained the right of residence (Regulations 8, 10). All of these definitions are important as the Regulations proceed to provide for substantial rights to reside those categories of persons enjoy. **24–10**

Part 2 of the Regulations provide for an initial right of admission to the UK on the part of EEA nationals and their family members (Regulation 11) and for EEA family permits for qualifying family members (Regulation 12). Somewhat controversially, Regulation 12 required prior lawful residence in another Member State on the part of the family member with the EEA national in order to be granted a family permit. As noted in para.24–08, above, this requirement was held to be unlawful in *Metock* and Regulation 12 was amended to reflect this in the Immigration (EEA) (Amendment) Regulations 2011. Otherwise, the family member would have to meet the requirements of the immigration rules for third country nationals. Part 3 provides for an initial right to reside, followed by extended and permanent rights to Regulations 13, 14 and 15 to provide on the part of EEA nationals and family members. Part 4 of the Regulations provide for the exclusion and expulsion of EEA nationals and family members. The Regulations, reflecting the Directive, introduce progressively higher thresholds to justify exclusion and expulsion. The highest threshold for a Member State to reach is "on imperative grounds of public policy, public security or public health" which applies to those who enjoy permanent residence rights in the UK. "Serious grounds of public policy, public security or public health" applies in respect of those with permanent residence rights while those on "grounds of public policy, public security or public health" apply to all others. Part 5 provides for detailed tests to be met in order to justify exclusion or expulsion **24–11**

---

[8] See *Metock* where a similar requirement by Ireland was found to be an unlawful construction of the Directive.

(Regulation 21). Significantly, the impugned conduct must be personal to the affected person and the person concerned "must represent genuine, present and sufficiently serious threat affecting one of the fundamental interests of society". Part 6 provides for appeals including appeals by affected persons to the Immigration and Asylum Chamber of the First Tier Tribunal against an adverse decision made on EU law grounds relating to rights to enter and reside in the UK (Regulation 26).

(ii) *Limitation of the Regulations*

24–12   The Regulations are restrictive in that they do not contain a discretion to extend the scope of the right to reside beyond those included in the Regulations. The ensuing problem that arises from this is that there is no room under the Regulations for argument that persons who do not fall within the Regulations can nevertheless come within the scope of EU law and the rights of free movement in particular. An on-going example of this is the scope of art.20 TFEU which provides that citizens of Member States are citizens of the European Union. The CJEU in *Zambrano*[9] used art.20 in conjunction with the Charter on Fundamental Freedoms to hold that the Colombian national parents of a Belgian child could not be removed from Belgium as it would restrict or frustrate the right to reside under art.20. The Regulations do not conceive of any such free-standing right as declared by the CJEU on the basis of art.20. The UK Border Agency has indicated that they will amend the Regulations to incorporate the effect of *Zambrano*. No doubt, the incorporation will be very limited and will not give any clue as to further developments under art.20 TFEU. In the meantime, they have proposed the following interim arrangement whereby UKBA will issue a certificate of application to those who are able to show:

- evidence that the dependent national is a British citizen;
- evidence of the relationship between the applicant and the British citizen; and
- adequate evidence of dependency between the applicant and the British citizen.

24–13   This certificate will enable a person to work in the UK while their application is outstanding and will act as proof to employers of entitlement to work. This transitional arrangement is not a faithful reflection of the effect of *Zambrano*. The rational of *Zambrano* would include as benefitting from the case dependents on nationals of any Member State residing in any Member State. There seems no obvious reason why the answer of the CJEU would have been different if the children were citizens of Germany. In *Dereci*,[10] the CJEU interpreted as holding that the refusal to grant residence rights to a third country national family member of a national of a Member State in the State of said national, if its effect were to deny the Member State national from residing in his own State would be contrary to art.20 TFEU.

---

[9] *Gerardo Ruiz Zambrano v Office National de l'Emploi (ONEM)* (C-34/09) [2011] E.C.R. I-0000.
[10] *Dereci and others v Bundesministerium für Inneres* (C-256/11) [2012] E.C.R. I-0000.

(c) *Controversial points*

(i) *Family members*

The Regulations (Regulation 12) sought to restrict the rights of family members to reside to those who had lawfully resided with the EEA national in another Member State. That provision and a similar Irish provision not surprisingly came under sustained attack and eventually in a reference from the High Court in Dublin, *Metock*[11] the CJEU ruled that a similar provision in Irish law was unlawful and was not part of the qualifying requirements in the Citizen Directive. A similar provision is contained in the EEA Regulations in respect of extended family members (Regulation 8(2)) and was considered by the Court of Appeal to have survived *Metock*. The Court in *Metock* concluded that there was no justification for the requirement of prior residence as a family member in another EEA State before a family member could enter Ireland.

24–14

(d) *Extended family members*

In respect of extended family members as defined in the Regulations as "Other Family Members" (OFM) as meant in the Directive, the case law has proved tortuous. In *Bigia and others v Secretary of State for the Home Department*[12] the Court approved the following propositions contained in the previous case of *KS Sri Lanka*:

24–15

> "(i) The tight relationship between the exercise of rights by the Union citizen and the requirement that the OFM should be dependant in the country from which they have come strongly suggests that the relationship should have existed in the country from which the Union citizen has come and this have existed immediately before the Union citizen was accompanied or joined the OFM.
> (ii) The members of the household whose entry is to be facilitated will be members of the Union citizen's household immediately before the Union citizen leaves for another country.
> (iii) Even if the OFM cannot still be a member of the Union citizens' household at the member of application for entry to the EEA host Member State, both such membership and dependency should be very recent."

The effect of the requirement of prior lawful residence in another Member State with the relevant EEA national was also unlawful in respect of extended family members (Regulation 8). The Directive did not justify this requirement according to the Court of Appeal. However, prior residence in the household of the EEA national in any State remained a pre-condition for entry as an OFM or prior dependency in any State before entry remained a valid requirement. That was not the end of the matter however.

24–16

---

[11] *Metock v Minister for Justice, Equality and Law Reform* (C-127/08) [2008] I-06241.
[12] [2009] EWCA Civ 79.

The Upper Tribunal in the case of *MR and others (EEA extended family members) Bangladesh*[13] considered after reviewing the main domestic cases on extended family members that the case law was in a state of uncertainty and referred to the CJEU a number of questions which are significant for their scope. The Tribunal expressed doubt as to the rational for the admission of OFMs identified in *KS Sri Lanka* as being able to facilitate the exercise of free movement rights of EEA nationals. The Court of Appeal considered that there must be close proximity between the EEA national's free movement to the UK and the admission of OFMs. The Tribunal in *Aladesulu and Others*[14] (2006 Regulations, Regulation 8) maintained the scepticism as to this rational and considered the circumstances where a family relative had entered the UK some time before the EAA sponsor joined him there. The Regulations require that the OFM is "accompanying or...wants to join" the EEA national sponsor in the UK (Regulation 8(2)). At first sight it is difficult to see how in the circumstances the OFM could satisfy the requirement. However, the Tribunal concluded that the requirement should be construed in accordance with the way the CJEU construed a similar requirement in *Metock* in respect of family members. The Tribunal went on to note that the Regulations did not require lawful presence in the UK of OFM's in order to reside as relatives of an EEA sponsor.[15]

24–17 The power to admit OFMs is not an unfettered one in that the Regulations give a discretion to so do.

(e) *Right to permanent residence*

24–18 The right to permanent residence rights is provided for under art.16 of Directive 2004/38 and is transposed by Regulation 15. Five years prior continuous residence "in accordance with the Regulations" in the UK is required in order to obtain permanent residence. The Directive requires that an applicant has "resided legally for five years" in the host Member State. This provision not surprisingly raised the following two issues: (i) does residence before the commencement of the Regulations count towards the five years; and (ii) does residence that is lawful but not in exercise of Treaty rights count towards the five years?

---

[13] [2010] UKUT 449 (IAC). Advocate General Bot in his Opinion of March 27, 2012 in the case (C-83/11) before the CJEU concluded that art.3(2) of Directive 2004/38 precludes national legislation which limits the scope of that provision to other family members who resided in the same State as the Union national before the Union national came to the host Member State. Further, the notion of "dependant" does not imply that dependency existed shortly before the Union citizen moved to the host Member State. A rejection of an application from such extended family members must be based on an extensive examination of personal circumstances and be fully justified. He went on to conclude that national legislation may not automatically exclude certain categories of extended family members and in the assessment of which it should be admitted that the impact on the freedom of the Union citizen to reside in the applicable Member State is of great importance.

[14] UKUT 253 (IAC).

[15] At the time of writing it is understood that leave to appeal has been granted to the Court of Appeal in *Aladesulu*.

In *McCarthy v SSHD*[16] the Court of Appeal concluded that the requirement **24–19** "legally resided" meant in accordance with Community law not national law as that construction fitted with recital 17 to the Directive, which refers to five years continuous residence "in accordance with the conditions laid down in this Directive". The House of Lords however referred the matter to the Court of Justice. The Court of Appeal in *Dias* and *Lassal* gave the provisional view that periods of residence prior to April 2006 in accordance with European Union law then in place could be included for the qualifying five-year period.[17] The Court of Justice agreed.[18]

The CJEU in *Dias* also considered the question of whether a period of **24–20** residence which was exercised while holding an EC residence card as a worker under art.3 of Directive 90/364 but at a time when the holder was not a worker was legal residence. It held that such a period does not count towards five years' legal residence required under art.16 of the Directive.

(f) *Surrinder Singh principle*

Regulation 9 was designed to give effect to the right of a British national and **24–21** their spouse, whatever nationality, to enter the UK from another Member State where they were economically active. The foundations for the Regulations are found in *Surrinder Singh*[19] where the CJEU concluded:

> "When a Community national who availed himself or herself of those (Treaty) rights returns to his or her country of original, his or her spouse must enjoy at least the same rights of entry and residence as would be granted to him or her under Community law if his or her spouse chose to enter and resided in another Member State."

The Tribunal in *OB (EEA Regulations 2006—art.9(2)—Surrinder Singh* **24–22** *spouse) Morocco*[20] was faced with the situation where the British national resided in the Republic of Ireland with his third country spouse but had not worked for the 13 months preceding his re-entry to the UK with his spouse. The Tribunal concluded that such a break in employment did not preclude reliance on the regulation as to do otherwise would impede the exercise of Treaty rights and family life. The Tribunal went on to conclude that other factors such as periods of unemployment due to illness or due to pregnancy or child rearing did not break the link between the previous exercise of Treaty rights by way of working and right to re-enter the UK on the basis of EU law. Significantly, Regulation 9(2) does not repeat the requirement contained in EEA Regulations 2000 in respect of the same category of people to the effect that,

---

[16] [2008] EWCA Civ 641. See Ch.5 for findings of the CJEU, *McCarthy (Shirley) v Secretary of State for the Home Department* (C -434/09) [2011] E.C.R. I-0000.
[17] *Secretary of State for Work and Pensions v Dias* [2009] EWCA Civ 807; *Secretary of State for Work and Pensions v Lassal* [2009] EWCA Civ 157.
[18] *Secretary of State for Work and Pensions v Dias* (C-235/09) July 21, 2011 and *Lassal v Secretary of State for Work and Pensions* (C-162/09).
[19] (C-370/90) [1992] Imm. A.R. 565.
[20] [2010] UKUT 420 (IAC).

"the United Kingdom national did not leave the United Kingdom in order to enable his family member to acquire rights under these Regulations and thereby to evade the application of United Kingdom immigration law".

This requirement was always controversial and in light of *Akrich*[21] was clearly wrong.

(g) *Common law partners*

24–23 With developments regarding the concept of family life, the understanding of family life within the meaning of art.8 ECHR and, in the case of the UK, the enactment of the Civil Partnership Act 2004, it was no surprise that the Directive extended the scope of residence rights to include non-married partners (art.2(b)). The Regulations provide that the scope of the residence rights extend to anyone in a "durable relationship" with an EEA national. That is transposed faithfully by Regulation 8(5). However, the European Directorate Instructions add a gloss to the provision in requiring: (i) the EEA national and their spouse have lived together in a relationship akin to marriage, and (ii) they intend to live together permanently. These further requirements are obtained from immigration r.295A which outlines the requirements for leave to enter or remain for those in common law relationships. Neither the Directive or the Regulations provide for a two-year period or for any period of living together. Its absence in the Regulations might be fatal to any attempt to apply it in a particular case. Of course, the longer the relationship has lasted the easier it will be to prove that the relationship existed. But the inclusion of this and the requirement of having lived together as absolute would likely be found to breach EU law. The imperatives of the freedom to move and reside in accordance with the fundamental rights of the Treaty and the importance of family life in the Charter and art.8 ECHR would compel a court to conclude that the absolute nature of the extra requirements are unlawful.[22]

(h) *Change in circumstances—loss of EU status*

24–24 One area that raises difficulties are the provisions in relation to residence cards in respect of persons whose circumstances have changed disentitling them to the said card. Thus, is a person who was issued with a residence card, say for five years, on the basis of being the spouse of a qualified person but the EEA national is no longer qualified within the meaning of the Regulations. In the circumstances where the spouse of the EEA national has no right to reside under the Directive does the possession of the residence card still count for anything? It is clear from *Dias*[23] that such a person obtains no benefits from the Directive as the residence card is merely declaratory of rights under the Directive. The possession of the card merely goes to prove that there are benefits from Treaty rights. The Court of

---

[21] *Secretary of State for the Home Department v Hacene Akrich* (C-109/01) [2003] E.C.R. I-9607.
[22] See further Ch.9.
[23] *Secretary of State for Work and Pensions v Dias* (C-325/09) July 21, 2011.

Appeal in *Okofor*[24] reached the same view and went further and concluded that the possession of the residence card under the Regulations counted for nothing either in domestic law. The Court reached this conclusion with surprising confidence. It is of course open for a Member State to decide for itself as the Advocate General in *Dias* makes clear (para.121) "to provide for a rule according to which such periods are taken into account". Thus, contrary to what the court concluded in *Okafor* a period of residence based on domestic law alone cannot automatically be discarded as going towards the prescribed five-years' residence. It will be a matter of domestic law what, if any, significance is afforded to a period of residence not in line with the Directive but nevertheless on back of a residence card not revoked by the Secretary of State.[25]

(i) *Evidential problems*

The burden of proving the entitlement of residence rights under the Directive is on an applicant. This may be very difficult, even impossible, to do in circumstances of a hostile separation from the EEA spouse. The spouse may not be willing to respond to inquiries about his situation, if he is living in the UK and/or if he is exercising Treaty rights. Such issues may be very important when the third country national is seeking to argue that he has retained a right of residence in the UK or are entitled to permanent residence. The Court of appeal in *Amos v Secretary of State for the Home Department*[26] concluded that there was no duty on the Home Office to assist an applicant in the quest for proof. This conclusion must be considered in the light of the following factors: first, as the President of the Tribunal held in *Hussam Samsam*[27] the actual issue of a residence card is proof in itself that the underlying circumstances that would give rise to its issue did exist at the time and the Tribunal went as far as saying the following:

24–25

> "29..... It is plain that if the facts reveal that a person was not exercising Treaty rights then the existence of a residence card cannot assist. It is not conclusive proof. It may, however, be some evidence of past lawful status if there is some evidence to support the exercise of Treaty right, nothing to contradict and the historic position can (sic) be established with precision."

Secondly, an applicant should use all of the procedural advantages he has to force the Home Office into taking some action to assist the Tribunal. By virtue of the Asylum and Immigration (Procedure) Rules 2005 rr.45 and 51, an applicant can apply to the Tribunal for the Respondent to be compelled to provide evidence necessary for the fair determination of an appeal. Further s.36 of the Immigration, Asylum and Nationality Act 2006 provides for the sharing of information between the Secretary of State and other

24–26

---

[24] *Franklin M.C. Okafor v Secretary of State for the Home Department* [2011] EWCA Civ 499 (April 20, 2011).
[25] *Ziolkowski* (C-424/10) which has held that residence on the sole basis of national law does not count towards permanent residence under Directive 2004/38 rule unless the person satisfied the conditions of art.7(1) during that time.
[26] [2011] EWCA Civ 552.
[27] [2011] UKUT 165 (IAC).

specified bodies (including HMRC) for inter alia immigration purposes. Sections 40–42 of the UK Borders Act 2007 are to the same effect. These are important provisions that can assist an applicant in seeking to obtain evidence in possession of the Home Office or other government department that might be germane to an appeal.

24-27 The Regulations seek to give effect to the judgment of the CJEU in *Baumbast*.[28] Regulation 10 provides that a person who has custody of a child and whose status as a family member has ceased through the death or cessation of residence in the UK of the EEA national of whom the child was a family member is entitled to a right to reside.

(j) *Primary carers of children*

24-28 The Regulations seek to give effect to the judgment of the CJEU in *Baumbast and R*. Regulation 10 provides that a person who has custody of a child who is attending an educational course and whose status as a family member of an EEA nationals has ceased through the death or cessation of residence in the UK of the EEA national, is entitled to a right to reside. Article 10 of Regulation (EU) No.492/2011 (which replaced exactly similarly worded art.12 of Regulation (EEC) of April 25, 2011 provides that children of a national of a Member State are entitled to the same educational provision as that enjoyed by children of the State. Three points arise which have been the subject of litigation. First, the right to reside in a Member State of a third country national parent of such a child. The CJEU in cases *Ibrahim* and *Texeira* held that the primary carer of such a child enjoys a right to reside as long as the child is in full-time education. There is no requirement the parent should have sufficient resources and comprehensive sickness insurance cover in the UK in order to reside there (*Ibrahim* at [59]). The 2006 Regulations have not been amended to incorporate this newly declared right. However, that is not fatal for the reason that art.288 TFEU states that a Regulation is directly effective and so art.10 can be relied upon by a primary carer. Secondly, there is no requirement that the EU national parent of the child has left the relevant Member State. It is sufficient that he was or is a worker. Thirdly, can that child acquire permanent residence rights under EU law? At first blush it seems that he would under art.16 of the Directive once he "resided legally" in a Member State for five years in accordance with EU law. But the residence enjoyed by the child is not in accordance with the Directive and certainly not in accordance with the EEA Regulations 2006. The CJEU in *Dias* (see para.24–20, above) and *Ziolkowski* (see para.24–24, above) have held that residence under purely domestic law does not qualify for permanent residence rights under art.15 of the Citizens Directive unless the conditions of art.7 of that Directive are met. It remains an open question regarding whether residence under

---

[28] *Baumbast v Secretary of State for the Home Department* (C-413/99) [2002] E.C.R. I-7091.

Regulation 492/2011 satisfies the requirement of "lawful residence" within the meaning of art.16 of the Directive.[29]

(i) *Exclusion and expulsion*

Part 4 of the Regulations provide for the refusal of admission and exclusion of EEA nationals and family members and the revocation of a residence card. This part reflects arts 27–33 of Directive 2004/38 and includes the concepts of public policy, public security or public health, serious grounds of public policy, and imperative grounds of public policy as thresholds to be met in order to merit exclusion from the UK. The Regulations reflect the narrow grounds the Directive permits on which the restriction of free movement might be exercised. Such restrictions must not be for economic ends (Regulation 21(2), must comply with the principle of proportionality (Regulation 21(5)(c)), and must be based exclusively on the personal conduct of the person concerned (Regulation 21(5)(b)). Previous criminal convictions shall not in themselves constitute grounds for restriction of free movement (Regulation 21(5)(e)) and qualifying conduct for restrictive acts must represent a "genuine, present and sufficiently serious threat affecting one of the fundamental interests of society"). In respect of a person with permanent residence rights in the UK, the Regulations provide, again in line with the Directive, that serious grounds of public or security must be established (Regulation 21(3)) and in respect of an EEA national who has resided in the UK for 10 years, imperative grounds of public policy or security must be shown (Regulation 21(4)(4)). The Court of Appeal in *HR (Portugal) v Secretary of State for the Home Department*[30] held that residence within the meaning of Regulation 21 and art.28(3) of the Directive did not include time spent in prison, albeit Sedley L.J. warned that this proposition must be applied flexibly so as to permit adjustments to reflect subsequent acquittals or quashing of convictions. Not surprisingly, the issue was revisited by the Court of Appeal in *Cesar C v Secretary of State for the Home Department*.[31] The rational for the conclusion in *HR* was that enhanced degrees of integration evidenced by greater integration into society merited greater levels of protection. The argument put in *Cesar C* was that a short period of imprisonment set aside a long period of lawful residence could not act as a stop gap preventing reliance on the enhanced level of protection. The Court disagreed, concluding that as the fundamental protection afforded by the Regulation—that is, the restriction on free movement must meet the public policy threshold—the prevention of the reliance on the enhanced protection is proper. One can appreciate that there are many examples where the harshness of this approach may breach EU law. Plainly, the prisoner who is detained in open conditions and allowed into the community to work could argue that is exercising a high degree of integration into the community and so the fact of their imprisonment alone should not act as a break on a qualifying period for enhanced levels of

24–29

---

[29] See *Alarape and another* (art.12 of EC Regulation 1612/68) *Nigeria* [2011] UKUT 00413 where the Upper Tribunal has referred this issue to the CJEU: *Maria Texeira v London Borough of Lambeth* (C-480/08) [2010] E.C.R. I-1107; *London Borough of Harrow v Ibrahim* (C-310/08) [2010] E.C.R. I-1065.
[30] [2009] EWCA Civ 371.
[31] [2010] EWCA Civ 1406.

protection under the Regulation. It is an issue that might yet find its way to the CJEU for consideration.

24–30 The highest level of protection afforded by the Regulations is for those who have resided in the UK for 10 years. There must be imperative grounds of public security for any restriction. The Tribunal in *MG and VC*[32] concluded that imperative grounds do not include "ordinary risk to society arising from commission of further offences by a convicted criminal". It accepted the interpretation advanced by the Secretary of State that it related to the "commission or suspicion of terrorist offences". The Court of Appeal in *VP (Italy) v Secretary of State for the Home Department*[33] treated as correct a more recent formulation by the Tribunal to the effect that imperative grounds of public security might include factors beyond only national security considerations. In *Tsakouridis*[34] the CJEU considered whether dealing in narcotics as part of an organised group or gang fell within the scope of imperative grounds of public security. The CJEU found that it could in view of "the social and economic danger" such crime represents.

(k) *Accession*

(i) *Relevant legislation*

24–31 The Accession (immigration and Worker Registration) Regulations 2004 (SI 2004/121)

The Immigration (European Economic Area) and Accession (Amendment) Regulations 2004 (SI 2004/1236)

The Accession (Immigration and Worker Authorisation) Regulations 2006

The Immigration (European Economic Area) Regulations 2006

The Accession (Immigration and Worker Registration) (Revocation, Savings and Consequential Provisions) Regulations 2011

(ii) *General provisions*

24–32 The Accession (Immigration and Worker Registration) Regulations 2004 (the Accession Regulations 2004) amended the Immigration (European Economic Area) Regulations 2000 to include within their scope the then 10 new Member States as from May 1, 2004. The Accession Regulations 2006 brought within the scope of the Regulations 2006 nationals of the new Member States of Bulgaria and Romania. In compliance with the Treaties of Accession of 2003 and 2005, the EEA Regulations reflect the fact that free movement rights are generally extended to the nationals of all 12 Member States and their family members.

24–33 In accordance with the Treaty of Accession 2003, restrictive laws were put in place to provide for the special situation of workers from eight of the 10 new

---

[32] [2006] UKAIT 53.
[33] [2010] EWCA Civ 806.
[34] *Land Baden-Württemberg v Pangotis Tsakouridis* (C-145/09) [2010] E.C.R. T-0000.

Member States by way of the Accession Regulations 2004. These Regulations required workers from these 10 Member States to register their employment in the UK during the first year of their employment in order to be lawfully resident and they were not entitled to have their family members join them during that first year of legal residence in the UK. By the Accession (Immigration and Worker Registration) (Revocation, Savings and Consequential Provision) Regulations 2011 these restrictive Regulations were revoked with the effect that a person who was an accession national within the meaning of the 2004 Regulations requiring registration under those Regulations will be entitled to reside in the UK in accordance with the EEA Regulations 2006 (including their family members).[35]

Limitations were placed on workers from Bulgaria and Romania by way of the Accession Regulations 2006 except for those who were already in the UK on accession with leave and permission to work and highly skilled migrants. They provide that worker authorisation (that is, worker authorisation containing conditions as to nature of work that can be engaged in) must be obtained by all other workers from those two countries for legal residence during the accession period (from January 1, 2007 to December 31, 2011). By virtue of the Accession (Immigration and Worker Authorisation) (Amendment) Regulations 2011, the UK extended the transitional measures to December 31, 2013.

24-34

---

[35] The transitional provisions under the Accession Treaty had come to an end on April 30, 2011. The UK had applied national measures to workers from the accession States for the maximum time permitted under the Treaty.

Chapter 25

AGREEMENTS WITH THIRD COUNTRIES

For detailed discussion on the free movement provisions contained in the Agreements between the European Union and third counties readers are referred to Pt Three (Chs 14–21) of this book.

1. Swiss Agreement

(a) *Relevant legislation*

Immigration (Swiss Free Movement of Persons) (No.3) Regulations 2002   **25–01**

Immigration (European Economic Area) Regulations 2006

(b) *General provisions*

The provisions of the Immigration (European Economic Area) Regulations   **25–02**
2006 have generally been extended to Swiss nationals by the Agreement between the European Community and the Swiss Confederation on the Free Movement of Persons. The Immigration (Swiss Free Movement of Persons) (No.3) Regulations 2002 extended the scope of the Immigration (European Economic Area) Regulations 2000 to Swiss nationals. The Swiss Regulations were revoked by the Immigration Regulations 2006 except in so far as they concerned posted workers. The Regulations' 2006 definition of EEA States includes Switzerland and so Swiss nationals and their family members enjoy the full panoply of rights transposed by the Regulations. The Swiss Regulations provide that the following must be satisfied in order to issue entry clearance to a posted worker:

(a) the posted worker is lawfully resident in an EEA State including Switzerland for the this narrow purpose;
(b) the employee is lawfully and habitually employed by an employer who is temporarily providing a service in the UK;
(c) the employee will not take any other employment;
(d) the employee has been employed by their employer for at least 12 months; and
(e) the employee intends to leave the UK after they have spent 90 days in the UK in any calendar year.

2. EC-Turkey Association Agreement

(a) *Residence of Turkish workers under art.6 of Decision 1/80*

25–03 The provisions of art.6 of Decision 1/80 are not incorporated into the Immigration Rules. They are not referred to in the 2006 Regulations. The position of Turkish nationals under art.6 of Decision 1/80 is dealt with in the Immigration Directorate's Instructions[1] only. There is no possibility in UK immigration law of making an application for entry clearance to first enter the UK as a worker under the Ankara Agreement. This is reflective of art.6 of Decision 1/80 itself. All applicants will be applying to switch status in country, having entered the UK as a spouse, a work permit holder or in some other capacity and having been granted at least one year leave to remain with permission to work. Successful applicants under art.6 of Decision 1/80 are granted a further year's leave to remain. The current Immigration Directorate Instructions provide that the duration of leave granted to applicants who have acquired rights under the third indent are to be given leave consistent with their particular circumstances. Previous Immigration Directorate Instructions provided that such applicants were to be granted successive periods of 12 months leave only. That policy, at least in so far as it impacted on the individual applicant, was challenged successfully in the Administrative Court.[2] The court concluded that a grant of leave for eight months for a worker who has resident rights under the third indent was an unlawful restriction on free access to the labour market provided in Decision 1/80. While the court did not go as far as holding that an applicant with resident rights under the third indent must be granted indefinite leave to remain, it held that out as a possibility depending on the circumstances of the case.[3] Thus, if an applicant can establish that an offer of particular employment or even the opportunity to apply for a particular post is dependent for its success on their having indefinite leave to remain

---

[1] Immigration Directorate Instructions, Ch.6, section 6, "Business Applications under Turkish-EC Association Agreements (ECAA)", May 2011 available at *http://www.homeoffice/policy-andlaw/* [Accessed February 2012].

[2] See *R (on the application of Sema Bessuroglu) v Secretary of State for the Home Department* [2009] EWHC Admin 327.

[3] The ruling is reflected in the Immigration Directorate Instructions which provide:
"Third Indent
14.6. Applicants who fall within the third indent should be granted code 1 leave. There will be no specified employer/occupation on the endorsement as the worker will have free access to the labour force. In terms of duration of leave a balance needs to be struck between the rights of free access that have been accrued under the third indent and the fact that the applicant's right to reside is still dependent on them being duly registered as belonging to the labour force and that those rights can still be lost (see section 3.8).
Duration of leave in such cases should therefore take account of the length and stability of the applicant's employment in the UK and the evidence they can produce in support of their ongoing employment. Grants under the third indent should not normally exceed three years. Examples: An applicant who has acquired rights under the third indent and who has been working for the same employer continuously for two or more years and who produces evidence of the continuation of their employment may be granted leave for up to three years. An applicant who has acquired rights under the third indent and who has had periods of involuntary unemployment and can only produce evidence of short term future employment may be granted for a shorter period of between one and two years."

then a grant of limited leave would be an unlawful restriction on the free access to the labour market.

25–04 Although indefinite leave to remain is not referred to specifically in Decision 1/80 (and indeed it would not be as it is a creature of domestic law), art.6 does refer to "free access to any paid employment". The CJEU has consistently treated the right of residence as a direct corollary of the right to access the labour market. If this access to the labour market is to be truly "free", the requirement to apply for leave to remain on an annual basis could interfere with that right. This is particularly the case if the applicant's passport (containing the endorsement confirming permission to work) is retained by the Home Office during consideration of the application for months at a time making it difficult for the applicant to be able to prove to prospective employers that any employment would be lawful. Moreover, since non-EU national work permit holders can apply for indefinite leave to remain after five years residence in the UK[4] it is clearly discriminatory and contrary to the spirit of the Ankara Agreement for Turkish nationals to be treated in a manner which is plainly less favourable. Another way of making the argument is derived from the case of *Commission v Netherlands*[5] where the CJEU concluded that the imposition of a charge on the family member of a Turkish national to enter a Member State to join the Turkish national working there was contrary to the non-discrimination provisions in the Ankara Agreement (art.9 and art.13 of Decision 1/80). The comparator, the Court held, was family members of EEA nationals. If it is unlawful discrimination to impose charges on family members seeking to join Turkish workers in a Member State (charges that it does not impose on family members of EU nationals) then surely the failure to grant leave to a Turkish worker equivalent to an EU worker is discriminatory.

25–05 A further argument is that by virtue of the standstill clause in Decision 1/80 a Turkish worker in the UK should be granted indefinite leave after four years as was provided for in the 1976 Rules[6] (in respect of a worker in approved employment). Article 13 of Decision 1/80 provides:

> "The Member States of the Community and Turkey may not introduce new restrictions on the conditions of access to employment applicable to workers and members of their families legally resident and employed in their respective territories".

This provides an avenue into arguing that as the Rules in place in 1976 provided for the provision of indefinite leave to remain after four years in "approved employment" and the absence of a similar feature in the current rules is an unlawful restriction a Turkish national should be granted ILR after four years working.[7] The argument would meet obstacles in that the

---

[4] para.134 HC 395. This rules has limited relevance now as work permits ceased to be granted from November 2009, replaced by a Points Based System (PBS). The PBS comprised five tiers under which applications for leave from migrants had to be assessed. "Tier 2" replaced the old non-statutory scheme for work permit holders.
[5] *Commission v the Netherlands* (C-92/07) [2010] E.C.R. I-03683.
[6] The year Decision 1/80 was adopted.
[7] See para.28HC 81.

1976 Rules required "approved" employment (and it is not clear that employment under Decision 1/80 fits with that requirement) and further the phrase "access to employment" arguably does not cover the quality of right to reside one enjoys.[8] The former position of the Home Office supported by the Tribunal, to the effect that Turkish national au pairs and students do not benefit from the Agreement was considered by the CJEU in *Ozturk* and *Payir*.[9] The CJEU concluded that they did.

25–06 The absence of provision for Turkish national workers in the current Immigration Rules has potential for a further adverse consequence. Where a Turkish national seeks to vary leave in-country by relying on Decision 1/80 it could be argued there will be no appeal against refusal of such application because of s.88(2)(d) of the Nationality, Immigration and Asylum Act 2002. This section read with para.5 of the Immigration Rules prevents an appeal where the application was for a purpose not covered by the Immigration Rules.[10] The potential for such a blatant discriminatory consequence of the failure to incorporate the obligations arising under Decision 1/80 into the Immigration Rules cannot be justified.

(b) *Self-employed Turkish nationals*

(i) *General*

25–07 The Additional Protocol entered into force in the United Kingdom on January 1, 1973 when the UK entered the European Community as a full Member State and become party to all international agreements concluded by the Community under the Treaty.

25–08 Those wishing to establish themselves in business in the UK will therefore need to rely on the immigration laws and practice that were in place on January 1, 1973. This was primarily the Immigration Act 1971 and the Immigration Rules HC 509 (control on entry) and HC 510 (control after entry). Compared with the current immigration rules applicable to business persons (HC 395) the 1973 Immigration Rules HC 509 and 510 were extremely flexible and generous. In brief the principal differences are:

(a) there was no minimum level of investment under HC 510 or 509;

---

[8] See *OY (Ankara Agreement: standstill clause; worker's family) Turkey* [2006] UKAIT 00028.
[9] *Ezgi Payir, Burhan Akyuz, Birol Ozturk v Secretary of State for the Home Department* (C-294/06) [2008] E.C.R. I-00203.
[10] "15.1. Although the rights conferred under article 6(1) are not currently included in the Immigration Rules, section 88(2)(d) of the NIA Act 2002 – ineligible to appeal on the grounds that the reason for refusal is not covered by the Immigration Rules – does not apply. To the extent that the Rules are inconsistent with article 6(1) they are unlawful and any right of appeal cannot lawfully be excluded by section 88(2)(d).
15.2. Those who apply in time under the provisions of Decision 1/80 and are refused leave to remain have an in-country right of appeal by virtue of section 82 and section 92(2) of the NIA Act 2002.
15.3. Those who apply out of time under the provisions of Decision 1/80 and are refused leave to remain have no right of appeal as they are not covered by section 82(2) of the NIA Act 2002".

(b) there was no requirement to offer employment to a minimum number of people under HC 510 or 509; and

(c) there was no mandatory entry clearance requirement under HC 509 and passengers arriving without entry clearance would be given a period of leave to enter to have their application examined by the Home Office. The CJEU in *Savas* confirmed that this provision applied to all Turkish nationals resident in the Member States, whether or not that residence had become unlawful by virtue of the Turkish national overstaying a visa. In the case of Mr Savas, he had in fact been an overstayer for 11 years before seeking to rely on the standstill provision in the Additional Protocol. Despite so many years overstaying he was still entitled to be treated in accordance with rules that are no more stringent than those that were in place on January 1, 1973.

After *Savas*[11] the Home Office issued guidance in January 2003 stating that the standstill clause only applied to those who sought to lawfully switch in-country or overstayers, but not to port applicant asylum seekers on temporary admission, illegal entrants, or persons applying for entry clearance. Applicants on temporary admission, illegal entrants or those applying for entry clearance would have their applications considered under the current Immigration Rules (HC 395) and not the 1973 Rules. Thus the UK did not accept that the standstill provision could benefit anyone who had at one stage been given leave to enter or remain. Since only those few Turkish nationals obtain visas or leave to enter in other capacities, the Government was substantially limiting the benefit of the standstill provisions.

25–09

Whether the standstill provision (and therefore the 1973 Rules) could apply to on-entry and temporary admission cases was challenged in an action for judicial review in the two joined cases of *Tum and Dari*. At first instance Davies J. found that the standstill provision must apply to all Turkish nationals, whether or not they had been granted leave to enter in some other capacity. He therefore quashed decision letters which had refused business applications on the basis of the current immigration rules and held that the SSHD was obliged to apply the 1973 Rules to the applications.[12]

25–10

The Secretary of State appealed. By judgment dated May 25, 2004 the Court of Appeal dismissed the Secretary of State's appeal. In the leading judgment the Lord Chief Justice held that all Turkish nationals could obtain the benefit of the standstill clause, whether in the UK or outside (and including asylum seekers on temporary admission).[13] All such Turkish nationals should have their applications considered under the 1973 Rules. The only Turkish nationals excluded from the benefit of the standstill provision are those who committed fraud. The House of Lords, however, referred the

25–11

---

[11] *Savas v Secretary of State for the Home Department* (C-37/98) [2000] E.C.R. I-02927.
[12] *R (on the application of Veli Tum) v Secretary of State for the Home Department* [2003] EWHC 2745.
[13] *R (on the application of Veli Tum) v Secretary of State for the Home Department* [2004] EWCA Civ 788.

matter to the CJEU as it was not satisfied that the material issue was acte clair. The CJEU affirmed the conclusions of the Court of Appeal.[14]

25–12 Both the Court of Appeal and the CJEU in *Tum and Dari* made passing reference to the so-called fraud exception. These references opened the door for the Home Office whereby they directed themselves in general terms that the standstill clause could not be used to avail those who have engaged in fraud. These isolated comments led the Home Office to conclude, supported by tribunals and courts up to and including the Court of Appeal, that if an applicant's presence in the UK was tainted in any way by illegality or even impropriety such as having made a baseless asylum claim, having overstayed leave by even the smallest of margins, or having breached a condition of stay then the applicant was not entitled to the benefit of the standstill clause.[15] The rational for this approach tended towards one of two arguments:

(i) there was in EU law a developing abuse of rights principle which precluded a person from benefitting from EU law if to do so they engaged in acts contrary to the aims of the founding Treaties; and

(ii) the principle in that no one should benefit from their own wrongdoing precluded reliance on the standstill clause by Turkish nationals who were in the UK in breach of national law-no matter how minor the breach.

That the courts found the abuse principle so beguiling, as they did, is surprising as is the ease with which they applied it in cases where plainly the issue of abuse was not adequately explored.[16]

25–13 Shortly after the decision of the Court of Appeal in *Sonmez*, the Court itself granted permission to appeal to itself in *Oguz* where the very same issue had been determined by the Tribunal in line with *Sonmez*.[17] In *Oguz* before the CJEU, the Home Office advanced the following argument. Mr Oguz's presence in the UK was tainted by illegality as he commenced his business operations before he made his application to remain in the UK on that basis and he relied on the fruits of the business to establish the prospects of the business. The breach of condition of his leave to remain as a work permit holder only—with prohibition on engaging in business—and his reliance on the operating business precluded him from reliance on the standstill clause. Mr Oguz argued that the standstill clause was not an abuse sensitive clause at all, conferring no substantial rights and if abuse were to be an issue it had to be considered according to the relevant immigration rules or scheme which was in place in 1973. The Court agreed, stating that the standstill

---

[14] *The Queen on the application of Dari and Tum v Secretary of State for the Home Department* (C-16/05) [2007] E.C.R. I-07415.
[15] See *FS(Breach of Conditions: Ankara Agreement) Turkey* [2008] UKAIT 00066; *Sonmez v Secretary of State for the Home Department* [2009] EWCA Civ 582; *LF (Turkey)* [2007] EWCA Civ 1441.
[16] See, for example, *LF (Turkey) v Secretary of State for the Home Department* [2007] EWCA Civ 1441.
[17] *Tural Oguz v Secretary of State for the Home Department* [2010] EWCA Civ 311; *Tural Oguz v Secretary of State for the Home Department* (C-186/10) [2011] E.C.R. I-0000.

clause did not convey any substantial right but rather determined which domestic procedures or rules applied to a Turkish national seeking to set up a business in a Member State. Concerns such as abuse are substantive considerations that fell for consideration under the substantive procedures or rules that were held to apply.

The Home Office put in place Immigration Directorate Instructions in May 2005 seeking to reflect the up to date situation as understood at that time. They put forward fraudulent conduct as something which could in extreme circumstances allow for the complete rejection of an application without more evidence. Short of that, circumstances were postulated whereby, what was loosely termed, fraud had decreasing significance depending on the alleged wrongdoing and going to the situation where fraud was not present in any guise and a person with leave to enter/remain applied to switch to self-employment status. A feature of those Immigration Directorate Instructions was the apparent tolerance therein of applicants who began the operation of their business before they made their applications to switch or did so while the applications were pending before the Home Office.[18] That indulgence was removed in an instruction issued in July 2008 by which time the Tribunal and courts had emboldened the hand of the Home Office in its rather clumsy attempt to rely on their expanded and incorrect understanding of the abuse principle. It took a further three years and repeated misapplication of the correct understanding of the abuse principle as disclosed in *Oguz* before the sorry saga was brought to a conclusion. The Current Immigration Directorate Instructions are outdated in that they predate *Oguz*. They repeat the claim that those who are considered to have practised deception on entry to the UK or those who breach a condition of their stay may be refused by consideration only under the current immigration rules[19] a direction that is wholly at odds with *Oguz*.

25–14

The CJEU stated in *Oguz* that it is a matter for the substantive law of a Member State to apply its own law on abuse as it existed at the relevant date (in the case of the UK that is January 1, 1973). Paragraph 4 of HC 510 allowed such issues to be taken account of. It stated and the accompanying substantial rule for business applications state as follows.

25–15

> *"Businessmen and self-employed persons*
>
> *General Considerations*
>
> 4. The succeeding paragraphs set out the main categories of people who may be given limited leave to enter and who may seek variation of their leave, and the principles to be followed in dealing with their applications, or in initiating any variation of their leave. In deciding these matters account is to be taken of all the relevant facts; the fact that the applicant satisfies the formal requirements of these rules for stay or further stay, in the proposed capacity is not conclusive in his

---

[18] If it were established that such an indulgence was in place and was later resiled from, that would arguably constitute a new restriction on the freedom to set up in business contrary to the standstill clause: see Opinion of Advocate General Kokott, in *Oguz*.

[19] Immigration Directorate Instructions, Ch.6, section 6, para.2: "Business Applications under Turkish-EC Association Agreements (ECAA)", May 2011 available at *http://www.homeoffice/policyandlaw/* [Accessed February 2012].

favour. It will, for example be relevant whether the person has observed the time limit and conditions subject to which he was admitted; whether in the light of his character, conduct or associations it is undesirable to permit him to remain; whether he represents a danger to national security; or whether, if allowed to remain for the period he wishes to stay, he might not be returnable to another country.

21. People admitted as visitors may apply for the consent of the Secretary of State to their establishing themselves here for the purpose of setting up in business, whether on their own account or as partners in a new or existing business. Any such application is to be considered on merits. Permission will depend on a number of factors, including evidence that the applicant will be devoting assets of his own to the business, proportional to his interest in it, that he will be able to bear his share of any liabilities the business may incur, and that his share of the profits will be sufficient to support him and any dependants. The applicant's part in the business must not amount to disguised employment, and it must be clear that he will not have to supplement his business activities by employment for which a work permit is required. Where the applicant intends to join an existing business, audited accounts should be produced to establish its financial position, together with a written statement of the terms on which he is to enter into it; evidence should be sought that he will be actively concerned with its running and that there is a genuine need for his services and investment. Where the application is granted the applicant's stay may be extended for a period of up to 12 months, on a condition restricting his freedom to take employment. A person admitted as a businessman in the first instance may be granted an appropriate extension of stay if the conditions set out above are still satisfied at the end of the period for which he was admitted initially."

25–16 The open texture of those rules should be noted with care. They do not set out a number of requirements to be met but rather demand a rounded approach to be taken both on the substantial rule that is para.21 and the general rule that is para.4. No one factor in paras 21 or 4 should be considered either a pre-condition for success or rejection under the rules either. In *R v Secretary of State for the Home Department ex parte Joseph*[20] Goff J. stated in respect of the 1973 Rules:

"These rules, which are intended to provide guidance as to the practice to be followed, are not in my judgment to be construed too rigidly. Furthermore, the part of para.21 in question is preceded by a statement that the application is to be 'considered on merits'. When the paragraph goes on to provide that 'permission will depend upon a number of factors including' certain specified factors, the paragraph is not in my judgment specifying prerequisites for the grant of permission. It is specifying factors which must be taken into account, but failure to comply with any one of them will not necessarily be fatal to the application".

25–17 Much more recently, Blake J. stated in *EK*[21] that the 1973 Rules are "an open textured exercise in discretion" (para.23) and goes on:

"24. We would accept the submission that in a extreme case where the evidence demonstrated that the business for which the applicant had been given permission to remain was completely dormant or generated such marginal funds as to be incapable of supporting anybody in the United Kingdom, the Home Office might

---

[20] [1978] Imm. A.R. 70.
[21] *EK v Secretary of State for the Home Department* [2010] UKUT 425.

well be able to identify that consideration as a highly relevant factor to the exercise of discretion to grant or refuse indefinite leave to remain. Such a decision would not be expressed in terms of failing to satisfy a requirement of the Rules but the identification of a particular factor why discretion to grant indefinite leave was not considered appropriate. In such a case on appeal it would be open to the Immigration Judge to see whether discretion should have been exercised differently in all the circumstances of the case. In recognising this, a pragmatic application of the principles of the Rules is called for. It was certainly the case in 1972 and for a number of years thereafter that the Home Office recognised that a business often needed some time to turn a profit and losses in the early years were not inconsistent with a business that met the policy and purposes of the Rules in general. The case was always considered in the round. In cases of doubt a further extension of limited leave was often given."

The result of all this case law is that the following categories of Turkish national benefited from the standstill provision: **25–18**

(a) port applicants and persons on temporary admission;

(b) out of country applicants for entry clearance;

(c) illegal entrants;

(d) those with leave to enter or remain; and

(e) overstayers.

Each category is dealt with below in turn.

(ii) *Port applicants and persons on temporary admission*

Those who arrive at port or who are asylum seekers on temporary admission must be treated as if they are applying for leave to enter for business purposes. For those asylum seekers granted temporary admission this is the position regardless of the stage they have reached in the asylum procedure. It is to be noted that both Mr Tum and Mr Dari were asylum seekers subject to the third country procedure who would otherwise have been sent to Germany to have their asylum claims determined. Mr Tum had in fact obtained an injunction against removal. **25–19**

Paragraph 30 of the 1973 Immigration Rules (control on entry (HC 509)) provides that persons who are unable to provide entry clearance but who "nevertheless seem likely to be able to satisfy the requirements" should be admitted for a period of two months and advised to present their case to the Home Office. Thus there is no mandatory entry clearance requirement. Since, however, the question whether the requirements are likely to be satisfied will be judged by reference to the factors set out in the Rules for the issue of entry clearance, it is to those Rules (considered below) that reference should be made. **25–20**

(iii) *Applicants for entry clearance*

The requirements for obtaining entry clearance are set out in paras 31 and 32 of the Rules which provide as follows: **25–21**

A business person who is joining an established business must show that:
(a) they will be bringing money of their own to put into the business;
(b) they will be able to bear their share of the liabilities;
(c) that their share of the profits will be sufficient to support them and any dependants without recourse to employment;
(d) they will be actively concerned in the running of the business;
(e) there is a genuine need for their services and investment;
(f) audited accounts of the business of the previous years must be produced; and
(g) the partnership or directorship does not amount to disguised employment.

If the person wishes to establish a new business in the UK they must show that:

(a) they will be bringing into country sufficient funds to establish a business; and
(b) the business can realistically be expected to support them and any dependants without recourse to employment.

25–22 It is of particular importance to note that past immigration history is not a matter that can be taken into account by the entry clearance officer under to the 1973 control on entry Rules (HC 509). This is because unlike the position under para.320 of the current Rules (HC 395), the general considerations under which entry clearance could be refused in 1973 did not include provisions requiring that applications should be normally be refused on grounds of overstay, breach of conditions or the obtaining of leave by deception.

25–23 Persons who obtain entry clearance will be granted leave to enter for 12 months with a prohibition on employment.

(iv) *Illegal entrants*

25–24 Those who have entered illegally probably do not stand to benefit immediately from the standstill clause save that they could leave the UK and apply to re-enter on the basis of the 1973 Immigration Rules (control on entry). This is because even in 1973 illegal entrants could be removed pursuant to the Immigration Act 1971 Sch.2 para.8. Further, illegal entrants would find themselves subject to para.4 of HC 510 considerations and the fact of illegal entry would weigh heavily against being permitted to remain.

25–25 Since the 1973 Rules make no reference to refusals of entry clearance on the basis of past immigration history, a person formerly in the UK illegally could leave the UK and re-apply to enter without that person's immigration history acting as a barrier to entry.

(v) *Those with leave to enter or remain*

25–26 Those present in the UK with leave to enter or remain may apply to switch to remain on the basis of their business. The Home Office has long accepted this to be the position. Their application for in-country switching should be considered on the basis of the 1973 Immigration Rules: control after entry (HC 510). The relevant paragraphs (4 and 21) are already included in this chapter.

Successful applicants will be granted an extension of leave to remain for 12 months with a prohibition on employment. 25–27

(vi) *Overstayers*

Turkish nationals granted leave to enter but who have overstayed their lawful residence may apply for leave to remain as business persons. Their applications should be considered on the basis of the 1973 Immigration Rules: control after entry (HC 510) and they need to meet the same requirements as those applying to switch in-country. 25–28

Under s.3(5)(a) of the Immigration Act 1971 (as then in force) the Secretary of State was entitled to make a decision to make a deportation order on the basis that the person had failed to comply with a condition attached to their leave or that the person remained beyond the time limited by such leave. 25–29

However, if a decision to make a deportation order was taken, an in-country merits appeal was given by s.15(1)(a) of the Immigration Act 1971 (as was then in force). At such an appeal (unencumbered by thle provisions of the Immigration Act 1988 which in broad terms limited such an appeal to persons who had been in the UK for more than seven years) the adjudicator would have been able to balance all the factors, such as good character, business and personal contacts, and length of stay against the gravity of the breach of conditions or the overstaying. 25–30

Since these were the appeal provisions in force at the time, self-employed Turkish nationals facing removal at the present time for overstay or breach of conditions (as provided for by s.10(1)(a) of the Immigration and Asylum Act 1999) must benefit from the previously existing appeals regime. 25–31

3. THE STABILISATION AND ASSOCIATION AGREEMENTS (SAAs)

There are SAAs in force with Macedonia, Croatia, Albania and Montenegro. They are discussed in detail in Ch.14. Each is cast in broadly similar terms. Taking the Croatia Agreement by way of example, the furthest that the Agreement goes is to guarantee non-discrimination for workers from Croatia that are "legally employed" in the Member States (with an accompanying right of access to the Member State's labour market for the worker's "legally resident" spouse and children)[22] and the right of establishment for companies[23] which largely reflects similar provisions in the previous Association Agreements with Bulgaria and Romania. Unlike the position under European Agreements[24] however, the right of establishment is not given to individuals (at least at time of writing). There is also a right for companies to post "key personnel" to Member States in certain circumstances, as well as an extremely limited right for "natural persons" to 25–32

---

[22] art.45, Stabilisation and Association Agreement between the European Communities and their Member States on the one part and the Republic of Croatia on the other part.
[23] ibid., arts 48–49.
[24] See Ch.14.

enter Member States temporarily to negotiate contracts for the sale of services. Thus, no right to reside can be derived or inferred from the Agreements. There are no provisions in domestic law to transpose or reflect even the limited benefits derived from the Agreements in so far as freedom of movement is concerned

4. Partnership and Co-operation Agreements

25–33   The formalisation of bilateral relations between the European Union and individual partner countries in Easter Europe and Central Asia (Armenia, Azerbaijan, Belarus, Georgia, Kazakhstan, Kyrgystan, Moldova, Mongolia, Russia, Tajikistan, Turkmenistan, Ukraine and Uzbekistan) has been achieved through the negotiation of Partnership and Co-operation Agreements now in force with all the Eastern European and Central Asian countries (with the exception of Mongolia, Turkmenistan and Belarus). These nearly all entered into force on July 1, 1999 with the exception of the Agreements with Russia, Moldova and Ukraine.[25]

25–34   The Agreements contain a non-discrimination provision. However, as we have seen in Ch.14 this provision does not create any right to reside. Again, there are no provisions in domestic law to transpose or reflect the limited benefits conferred by these Agreements.

---

[25] Partnership and Co-operation Agreement between the European Communities and their Member States, of the one part, and the Republic of Armenia, the Republic of Azerbaijan, Georgia, the Republic of Kazakhstan, the Kyrgyz Republic, the Republic of Moldova, the Russian Federation, Ukraine, and the Republic of Uzbekistan, Tajikistan of the other part, respectively.

Part Four
APPENDICES

CONTENTS OF APPENDICES

PRIMARY EUROPEAN LEGISLATION

Appendix 1— Treaty on European Union (excerpts): arts 1–19 A1–01
Appendix 2— The Treaty on the Functioning of the European Union (excerpts): arts 18–22, 45–47, 49–52, 56–57, 216–218, 267 and 288 A2–01
Appendix 3— Directive 2004/38/EC of the European Parliament and of the Council A3–01
Appendix 4— Regulation (EU) No 492/2011 on freedom of movement for workers within the Union A4–01
Appendix 5— Regulation (EC) No 883/2004 of the European Parliament and of the Council of 29 April 2004 on the coordination of social security systems A5–01
Appendix 6— Agreement on the European Economic Area (excerpts): arts 28–35 A6–01
Appendix 7— Agreement between the European Community and its Member States, of the one part, and the Swiss Confederation, of the other, on the free movement of persons (excerpts): Preamble, arts 1–25, Annex I A7–01
Appendix 8— Agreement Establishing an Association between the European Economic Community and Turkey (excerpts): arts 7, 12–14 A8–01
Appendix 9— Additional protocol to the EU Turkey Agreement (excerpts): arts 36–41, 58–59 A9–01
Appendix 10— Decision No 1/80 of the Association Council of 19 September 1980 on the Development of the Association (excerpts): preamble, arts 7–19 A10–01
Appendix 11— Stabilisation and Association Agreement between the European Communities and their Member States, of the one part, and the former Yugoslav Republic of Macedonia, of the other part (excerpts): Preamble, arts 1, 44–57 and 61–63 A11–01

UK LAW

Appendix 12— European Communities Act 1972 c.68 (excerpts): ss.1–3 A12–01
Appendix 13— Immigration Act 1988 c.14 (excerpts): s.7 A13–01
Appendix 14— Immigration (European Economic Area) Regulations 2006 (SI 2006/1003) A14–01
Appendix 15— The Immigration (European Economic Area) (Amendment) Regulations 2011 (SI 2011/1247) A15–01
Appendix 16— The Accession (Immigration and Worker Authorisation) Regulations 2006 (SI 2006/3317) A16–01

CONTENTS OF APPENDICES

Appendix 17— The Accession (Immigration and Worker Registration) (Revocation, Savings and Consequential Provisions) Regulations 2011 (SI 2011/544)   A17–01

Appendix 18— Immigration (Swiss Free Movement of Persons) (No.3) Regulations 2002 (SI 2002/1241)   A18–01

PRIMARY LEGISLATION

APPENDIX 1

TREATY ON EUROPEAN UNION

Title I

Common Provisions

Article 1
(ex Article 1 TEU) (1)

By this Treaty, the HIGH CONTRACTING PARTIES establish among themselves a EUROPEAN UNION, hereinafter called 'the Union' on which the Member States confer competences to attain objectives they have in common.

This Treaty marks a new stage in the process of creating an ever closer union among the peoples of Europe, in which decisions are taken as openly as possible and as closely as possible to the citizen.

The Union shall be founded on the present Treaty and on the Treaty on the Functioning of theEuropean Union (hereinafter referred to as 'the Treaties'). Those two Treaties shall have the same legal value. The Union shall replace and succeed the European Community.

(1) These references are merely indicative. For more ample information, please refer to the tables of equivalences between the old and the new numbering of the Treaties.

Article 2

The Union is founded on the values of respect for human dignity, freedom, democracy, equality, the rule of law and respect for human rights, including the rights of persons belonging to minorities. These values are common to the Member States in a society in which pluralism, non-discrimination, tolerance, justice, solidarity and equality between women and men prevail.

Article 3
(ex Article 2 TEU)

1. The Union's aim is to promote peace, its values and the well-being of its peoples.

2. The Union shall offer its citizens an area of freedom, security and justice without internal frontiers, in which the free movement of persons is ensured in conjunction with appropriate measures with respect to external border controls, asylum, immigration and the prevention and combating of crime.

Appendix 1

3. The Union shall establish an internal market. It shall work for the sustainable development of Europe based on balanced economic growth and price stability, a highly competitive social market economy, aiming at full employment and social progress, and a high level of protection and improvement of the quality of the environment. It shall promote scientific and technological advance.

It shall combat social exclusion and discrimination, and shall promote social justice and protection, equality between women and men, solidarity between generations and protection of the rights of the child.

It shall promote economic, social and territorial cohesion, and solidarity among Member States.

It shall respect its rich cultural and linguistic diversity, and shall ensure that Europe's cultural heritage is safeguarded and enhanced.

4. The Union shall establish an economic and monetary union whose currency is the euro.

5. In its relations with the wider world, the Union shall uphold and promote its values and interests and contribute to the protection of its citizens. It shall contribute to peace, security, the sustainable development of the Earth, solidarity and mutual respect among peoples, free and fair trade, eradication of poverty and the protection of human rights, in particular the rights of the child, as well as to the strict observance and the development of international law, including respect for the principles of the United Nations Charter.

6. The Union shall pursue its objectives by appropriate means commensurate with the competences which are conferred upon it in the Treaties.

Article 4

1. In accordance with Article 5, competences not conferred upon the Union in the Treaties remain with the Member States.

2. The Union shall respect the equality of Member States before the Treaties as well as their national identities, inherent in their fundamental structures, political and constitutional, inclusive of regional and local self-government. It shall respect their essential State functions, including ensuring the territorial integrity of the State, maintaining law and order and safeguarding national security. In particular, national security remains the sole responsibility of each Member State.

3. Pursuant to the principle of sincere cooperation, the Union and the Member States shall, in full mutual respect, assist each other in carrying out tasks which flow from the Treaties.

The Member States shall take any appropriate measure, general or particular, to ensure fulfilment of the obligations arising out of the Treaties or resulting from the acts of the institutions of the Union.

The Member States shall facilitate the achievement of the Union's tasks and refrain from any measure which could jeopardise the attainment of the Union's objectives.

Article 5
(ex Article 5 TEC)

1. The limits of Union competences are governed by the principle of conferral. The use of Union competences is governed by the principles of subsidiarity and proportionality.

2. Under the principle of conferral, the Union shall act only within the limits of the competences conferred upon it by the Member States in the Treaties to attain the objectives set out therein. Competences not conferred upon the Union in the Treaties remain with the Member States.

3. Under the principle of subsidiarity, in areas which do not fall within its exclusive competence, the Union shall act only if and in so far as the objectives of the proposed action cannot be sufficiently achieved by the Member States, either at central level or at regional and local level, but can rather, by reason of the scale or effects of the proposed action, be better achieved at Union level.

The institutions of the Union shall apply the principle of subsidiarity as laid down in the Protocol on the application of the principles of subsidiarity and proportionality. National Parliaments ensure compliance with the principle of subsidiarity in accordance with the procedure set out in that Protocol.

4. Under the principle of proportionality, the content and form of Union action shall not exceed what is necessary to achieve the objectives of the Treaties.

The institutions of the Union shall apply the principle of proportionality as laid down in the Protocol on the application of the principles of subsidiarity and proportionality.

Article 6
(ex Article 6 TEU)

1. The Union recognises the rights, freedoms and principles set out in the Charter of Fundamental Rights of the European Union of 7 December 2000, as adapted at Strasbourg, on 12 December 2007, which shall have the same legal value as the Treaties.

The provisions of the Charter shall not extend in any way the competences of the Union as defined in the Treaties.

The rights, freedoms and principles in the Charter shall be interpreted in accordance with the general provisions in Title VII of the Charter governing its interpretation and application and with due regard to the explanations referred to in the Charter, that set out the sources of those provisions.

2. The Union shall accede to the European Convention for the Protection of Human Rights and Fundamental Freedoms. Such accession shall not affect the Union's competences as defined in the Treaties.

3. Fundamental rights, as guaranteed by the European Convention for the Protection of Human Rights and Fundamental Freedoms and as they result from the

constitutional traditions common to the Member States, shall constitute general principles of the Union's law.

Article 7
(ex Article 7 TEU)

1. On a reasoned proposal by one third of the Member States, by the European Parliament or by the European Commission, the Council, acting by a majority of four fifths of its members after obtaining the consent of the European Parliament, may determine that there is a clear risk of a serious breach by a Member State of the values referred to in Article 2. Before making such a determination, the Council shall hear the Member State in question and may address recommendations to it, acting in accordance with the same procedure.

The Council shall regularly verify that the grounds on which such a determination was made continue to apply.

2. The European Council, acting by unanimity on a proposal by one third of the Member States or by the Commission and after obtaining the consent of the European Parliament, may determine the existence of a serious and persistent breach by a Member State of the values referred to in Article 2, after inviting the Member State in question to submit its observations.

3. Where a determination under paragraph 2 has been made, the Council, acting by a qualified majority, may decide to suspend certain of the rights deriving from the application of the Treaties to the Member State in question, including the voting rights of the representative of the government of that Member State in the Council. In doing so, the Council shall take into account the possible consequences of such a suspension on the rights and obligations of natural and legal persons.

The obligations of the Member State in question under this Treaty shall in any case continue to be binding on that State.

4. The Council, acting by a qualified majority, may decide subsequently to vary or revoke measures taken under paragraph 3 in response to changes in the situation which led to their being imposed.

5. The voting arrangements applying to the European Parliament, the European Council and the Council for the purposes of this Article are laid down in Article 354 of the Treaty on the Functioning of the European Union.

Article 8

1. The Union shall develop a special relationship with neighbouring countries, aiming to establish an area of prosperity and good neighbourliness, founded on the values of the Union and characterised by close and peaceful relations based on cooperation.

2. For the purposes of paragraph 1, the Union may conclude specific agreements with the countries concerned. These agreements may contain reciprocal rights and obligations as well as the possibility of undertaking activities jointly. Their implementation shall be the subject of periodic consultation.

TREATY ON EUROPEAN UNION

TITLE II

PROVISIONS ON DEMOCRATIC PRINCIPLES

Article 9

In all its activities, the Union shall observe the principle of the equality of its citizens, who shall receive equal attention from its institutions, bodies, offices and agencies. Every national of a Member State shall be a citizen of the Union. Citizenship of the Union shall be additional to national citizenship and shall not replace it.

Article 10

1. The functioning of the Union shall be founded on representative democracy.

2. Citizens are directly represented at Union level in the European Parliament. Member States are represented in the European Council by their Heads of State or Government and in the Council by their governments, themselves democratically accountable either to their national Parliaments, or to their citizens.

3. Every citizen shall have the right to participate in the democratic life of the Union. Decisions shall be taken as openly and as closely as possible to the citizen.

4. Political parties at European level contribute to forming European political awareness and to expressing the will of citizens of the Union.

Article 11

1. The institutions shall, by appropriate means, give citizens and representative associations the opportunity to make known and publicly exchange their views in all areas of Union action.

2. The institutions shall maintain an open, transparent and regular dialogue with representative associations and civil society.

3. The European Commission shall carry out broad consultations with parties concerned in order to ensure that the Union's actions are coherent and transparent.

4. Not less than one million citizens who are nationals of a significant number of Member States may take the initiative of inviting the European Commission, within the framework of its powers, to submit any appropriate proposal on matters where citizens consider that a legal act of the Union is required for the purpose of implementing the Treaties.

The procedures and conditions required for such a citizens' initiative shall be determined in accordance with the first paragraph of Article 24 of the Treaty on the Functioning of the European Union.

Appendix 1

Article 12

National Parliaments contribute actively to the good functioning of the Union:

(a) through being informed by the institutions of the Union and having draft legislative acts of the Union forwarded to them in accordance with the Protocol on the role of national Parliaments in the European Union;

(b) by seeing to it that the principle of subsidiarity is respected in accordance with the procedures provided for in the Protocol on the application of the principles of subsidiarity and proportionality;

(c) by taking part, within the framework of the area of freedom, security and justice, in the evaluation mechanisms for the implementation of the Union policies in that area, in accordance with Article 70 of the Treaty on the Functioning of the European Union, and through being involved in the political monitoring of Europol and the evaluation of Eurojust's activities in accordance with Articles 88 and 85 of that Treaty;

(d) by taking part in the revision procedures of the Treaties, in accordance with Article 48 of this Treaty;

(e) by being notified of applications for accession to the Union, in accordance with Article 49 of this Treaty;

(f) by taking part in the inter-parliamentary cooperation between national Parliaments and with the European Parliament, in accordance with the Protocol on the role of national Parliaments in the European Union.

Title III

Provisions on the Institutions

Article 13

1. The Union shall have an institutional framework which shall aim to promote its values, advance its objectives, serve its interests, those of its citizens and those of the Member States, and ensure the consistency, effectiveness and continuity of its policies and actions.

The Union's institutions shall be:

— the European Parliament,
— the European Council,
— the Council,
— the European Commission (hereinafter referred to as 'the Commission'),
— the Court of Justice of the European Union,
— the European Central Bank,
— the Court of Auditors.

2. Each institution shall act within the limits of the powers conferred on it in the Treaties, and in conformity with the procedures, conditions and objectives set out in them. The institutions shall practice mutual sincere cooperation.

3. The provisions relating to the European Central Bank and the Court of Auditors and detailed provisions on the other institutions are set out in the Treaty on the Functioning of the European Union.

4. The European Parliament, the Council and the Commission shall be assisted by an Economic and Social Committee and a Committee of the Regions acting in an advisory capacity.

Article 14

1. The European Parliament shall, jointly with the Council, exercise legislative and budgetary functions. It shall exercise functions of political control and consultation as laid down in the Treaties. It shall elect the President of the Commission.

2. The European Parliament shall be composed of representatives of the Union's citizens. They shall not exceed seven hundred and fifty in number, plus the President. Representation of citizens shall be degressively proportional, with a minimum threshold of six members per Member State.

No Member State shall be allocated more than ninety-six seats.

The European Council shall adopt by unanimity, on the initiative of the European Parliament and with its consent, a decision establishing the composition of the European Parliament, respecting the principles referred to in the first subparagraph.

3. The members of the European Parliament shall be elected for a term of five years by direct universal suffrage in a free and secret ballot.

4. The European Parliament shall elect its President and its officers from among its members.

Article 15

1. The European Council shall provide the Union with the necessary impetus for its development and shall define the general political directions and priorities thereof. It shall not exercise legislative functions.

2. The European Council shall consist of the Heads of State or Government of the Member States, together with its President and the President of the Commission. The High Representative of the Union for Foreign Affairs and Security Policy shall take part in its work.

3. The European Council shall meet twice every six months, convened by its President. When the agenda so requires, the members of the European Council may decide each to be assisted by a minister and, in the case of the President of the Commission, by a member of the Commission. When the situation so requires, the President shall convene a special meeting of the European Council.

4. Except where the Treaties provide otherwise, decisions of the European Council shall be taken by consensus.

5. The European Council shall elect its President, by a qualified majority, for a term of two and a half years, renewable once. In the event of an impediment or serious misconduct, the European Council can end the President's term of office in accordance with the same procedure.

6. The President of the European Council:

(a) shall chair it and drive forward its work;
(b) shall ensure the preparation and continuity of the work of the European Council in cooperation with the President of the Commission, and on the basis of the work of the General Affairs Council;
(c) shall endeavour to facilitate cohesion and consensus within the European Council;
(d) shall present a report to the European Parliament after each of the meetings of the European Council.

The President of the European Council shall, at his level and in that capacity, ensure the external representation of the Union on issues concerning its common foreign and security policy, without prejudice to the powers of the High Representative of the Union for Foreign Affairs and Security Policy.

The President of the European Council shall not hold a national office.

Article 16

1. The Council shall, jointly with the European Parliament, exercise legislative and budgetary functions. It shall carry out policy-making and coordinating functions as laid down in the Treaties.

2. The Council shall consist of a representative of each Member State at ministerial level, who may commit the government of the Member State in question and cast its vote.

3. The Council shall act by a qualified majority except where the Treaties provide otherwise.

4. As from 1 November 2014, a qualified majority shall be defined as at least 55 % of the members of the Council, comprising at least fifteen of them and representing Member States comprising at least 65 % of the population of the Union.

A blocking minority must include at least four Council members, failing which the qualified majority shall be deemed attained.

The other arrangements governing the qualified majority are laid down in Article 238(2) of the Treaty on the Functioning of the European Union.

5. The transitional provisions relating to the definition of the qualified majority which shall be applicable until 31 October 2014 and those which shall be applicable

from 1 November 2014 to 31 March 2017 are laid down in the Protocol on transitional provisions.

6. The Council shall meet in different configurations, the list of which shall be adopted in accordance with Article 236 of the Treaty on the Functioning of the European Union. The General Affairs Council shall ensure consistency in the work of the different Council configurations. It shall prepare and ensure the follow-up to meetings of the European Council, in liaison with the President of the European Council and the Commission.

The Foreign Affairs Council shall elaborate the Union's external action on the basis of strategic guidelines laid down by the European Council and ensure that the Union's action is consistent.

7. A Committee of Permanent Representatives of the Governments of the Member States shall be responsible for preparing the work of the Council.

8. The Council shall meet in public when it deliberates and votes on a draft legislative act. To this end, each Council meeting shall be divided into two parts, dealing respectively with deliberations on Union legislative acts and non-legislative activities.

9. The Presidency of Council configurations, other than that of Foreign Affairs, shall be held by Member State representatives in the Council on the basis of equal rotation, in accordance with the conditions established in accordance with Article 236 of the Treaty on the Functioning of the European Union.

Article 17

1. The Commission shall promote the general interest of the Union and take appropriate initiatives to that end. It shall ensure the application of the Treaties, and of measures adopted by the institutions pursuant to them. It shall oversee the application of Union law under the control of the Court of Justice of the European Union. It shall execute the budget and manage programmes. It shall exercise coordinating, executive and management functions, as laid down in the Treaties. With the exception of the common foreign and security policy, and other cases provided for in the Treaties, it shall ensure the Union's external representation. It shall initiate the Union's annual and multiannual programming with a view to achieving interinstitutional agreements.

2. Union legislative acts may only be adopted on the basis of a Commission proposal, except where the Treaties provide otherwise. Other acts shall be adopted on the basis of a Commission proposal where the Treaties so provide.

3. The Commission's term of office shall be five years.

The members of the Commission shall be chosen on the ground of their general competence and European commitment from persons whose independence is beyond doubt.

In carrying out its responsibilities, the Commission shall be completely independent. Without prejudice to Article 18(2), the members of the Commission shall neither seek nor take instructions from any Government or other institution, body, office or entity. They shall refrain from any action incompatible with their duties or the performance of their tasks.

4. The Commission appointed between the date of entry into force of the Treaty of Lisbon and 31 October 2014, shall consist of one national of each Member State, including its President and the High Representative of the Union for Foreign Affairs and Security Policy who shall be one of its Vice-Presidents.

5. As from 1 November 2014, the Commission shall consist of a number of members, including its President and the High Representative of the Union for Foreign Affairs and Security Policy, corresponding to two thirds of the number of Member States, unless the European Council, acting unanimously, decides to alter this number.

The members of the Commission shall be chosen from among the nationals of the Member States on the basis of a system of strictly equal rotation between the Member States, reflecting the demographic and geographical range of all the Member States. This system shall be established unanimously by the European Council in accordance with Article 244 of the Treaty on the Functioning of the European Union.

6. The President of the Commission shall:

(a) lay down guidelines within which the Commission is to work;

(b) decide on the internal organisation of the Commission, ensuring that it acts consistently, efficiently and as a collegiate body;

(c) appoint Vice-Presidents, other than the High Representative of the Union for Foreign Affairs and Security Policy, from among the members of the Commission.

A member of the Commission shall resign if the President so requests. The High Representative of the Union for Foreign Affairs and Security Policy shall resign, in accordance with the procedure set out in Article 18(1), if the President so requests.

7. Taking into account the elections to the European Parliament and after having held the appropriate consultations, the European Council, acting by a qualified majority, shall propose to the European Parliament a candidate for President of the Commission. This candidate shall be elected by the European Parliament by a majority of its component members. If he does not obtain the required majority, the European Council, acting by a qualified majority, shall within one month propose a new candidate who shall be elected by the European Parliament following the same procedure.

The Council, by common accord with the President-elect, shall adopt the list of the other persons whom it proposes for appointment as members of the Commission. They shall be selected, on the basis of the suggestions made by Member States, in accordance with the criteria set out in paragraph 3, second subparagraph, and paragraph 5, second subparagraph.

The President, the High Representative of the Union for Foreign Affairs and Security Policy and the other members of the Commission shall be subject as a body to a vote of consent by the European Parliament. On the basis of this consent the Commission shall be appointed by the European Council, acting by a qualified majority.

8. The Commission, as a body, shall be responsible to the European Parliament. In accordance with Article 234 of the Treaty on the Functioning of the European Union, the European Parliament may vote on a motion of censure of the Commission. If such a motion is carried, the members of the Commission shall resign as a

body and the High Representative of the Union for Foreign Affairs and Security Policy shall resign from the duties that he carries out in the Commission.

Article 18

1. The European Council, acting by a qualified majority, with the agreement of the President of the Commission, shall appoint the High Representative of the Union for Foreign Affairs and Security Policy. The European Council may end his term of office by the same procedure.

2. The High Representative shall conduct the Union's common foreign and security policy. He shall contribute by his proposals to the development of that policy, which he shall carry out as mandated by the Council. The same shall apply to the common security and defence policy.

3. The High Representative shall preside over the Foreign Affairs Council.

4. The High Representative shall be one of the Vice-Presidents of the Commission. He shall ensure the consistency of the Union's external action. He shall be responsible within the Commission for responsibilities incumbent on it in external relations and for coordinating other aspects of the Union's external action. In exercising these responsibilities within the Commission, and only for these responsibilities, the High Representative shall be bound by Commission procedures to the extent that this is consistent with paragraphs 2 and 3.

Article 19

1. The Court of Justice of the European Union shall include the Court of Justice, the General Court and specialised courts. It shall ensure that in the interpretation and application of the Treaties the law is observed.

Member States shall provide remedies sufficient to ensure effective legal protection in the fields covered by Union law.

2. The Court of Justice shall consist of one judge from each Member State. It shall be assisted by Advocates-General.

The General Court shall include at least one judge per Member State. The Judges and the Advocates-General of the Court of Justice and the Judges of the General Court shall be chosen from persons whose independence is beyond doubt and who satisfy the conditions set out in Articles 253 and 254 of the Treaty on the Functioning of the European Union. They shall be appointed by common accord of the governments of the Member States for six years. Retiring Judges and Advocates-General may be reappointed.

3. The Court of Justice of the European Union shall, in accordance with the Treaties:

(a) rule on actions brought by a Member State, an institution or a natural or legal person;

(b) give preliminary rulings, at the request of courts or tribunals of the Member States, on the interpretation of Union law or the validity of acts adopted by the institutions;

(c) rule in other cases provided for in the Treaties.

APPENDIX 2

CONSOLIDATED VERSION OF THE TREATY ON THE FUNCTIONING OF THE EUROPEAN UNION

PART TWO

NON-DISCRIMINATION AND CITIZENSHIP OF THE UNION

Article 18
(ex Article 12 TEC)

Within the scope of application of the Treaties, and without prejudice to any special provisions contained therein, any discrimination on grounds of nationality shall be prohibited.

The European Parliament and the Council, acting in accordance with the ordinary legislative procedure, may adopt rules designed to prohibit such discrimination.

Article 19
(ex Article 13 TEC)

1. Without prejudice to the other provisions of the Treaties and within the limits of the powers conferred by them upon the Union, the Council, acting unanimously in accordance with a special legislative procedure and after obtaining the consent of the European Parliament, may take appropriate action to combat discrimination based on sex, racial or ethnic origin, religion or belief, disability, age or sexual orientation.

2. By way of derogation from paragraph 1, the European Parliament and the Council, acting in accordance with the ordinary legislative procedure, may adopt the basic principles of Union incentive measures, excluding any harmonisation of the laws and regulations of the Member States, to support action taken by the Member States in order to contribute to the achievement of the objectives referred to in paragraph 1.

Article 20
(ex Article 17 TEC)

1. Citizenship of the Union is hereby established. Every person holding the nationality of a Member State shall be a citizen of the Union. Citizenship of the Union shall be additional to and not replace national citizenship.

2. Citizens of the Union shall enjoy the rights and be subject to the duties provided for in the Treaties. They shall have, inter alia:

(a) the right to move and reside freely within the territory of the Member States;

(b) the right to vote and to stand as candidates in elections to the European Parliament and in municipal elections in their Member State of residence, under the same conditions as nationals of that State.

(c) the right to enjoy, in the territory of a third country in which the Member State of which they are nationals is not represented, the protection of the diplomatic and consular authorities of any Member State on the same conditions as the nationals of that State;

(d) the right to petition the European Parliament, to apply to the European Ombudsman, and to address the institutions and advisory bodies of the Union in any of the Treaty languages and to obtain a reply in the same language.

These rights shall be exercised in accordance with the conditions and limits defined by the Treaties and by the measures adopted thereunder.

Article 21
(ex Article 18 TEC)

1. Every citizen of the Union shall have the right to move and reside freely within the territory of the Member States, subject to the limitations and conditions laid down in the Treaties and by the measures adopted to give them effect.

2. If action by the Union should prove necessary to attain this objective and the Treaties have not provided the necessary powers, the European Parliament and the Council, acting in accordance with the ordinary legislative procedure, may adopt provisions with a view to facilitating the exercise of the rights referred to in paragraph 1.

3. For the same purposes as those referred to in paragraph 1 and if the Treaties have not provided the necessary powers, the Council, acting in accordance with a special legislative procedure, may adopt measures concerning social security or social protection. The Council shall act unanimously after consulting the European Parliament.

Article 22
(ex Article 19 TEC)

1. Every citizen of the Union residing in a Member State of which he is not a national shall have the right to vote and to stand as a candidate at municipal elections in the Member State in which he resides, under the same conditions as nationals of that State. This right shall be exercised subject to detailed arrangements adopted by the Council, acting unanimously in accordance with a special legislative procedure and after consulting the European Parliament; these arrangements may provide for derogations where warranted by problems specific to a Member State.

2. Without prejudice to Article 223(1) and to the provisions adopted for its implementation, every citizen of the Union residing in a Member State of which he is not a national shall have the right to vote and to stand as a candidate in elections to the European Parliament in the Member State in which he resides, under the same conditions as nationals of that State. This right shall be exercised subject to detailed arrangements adopted by the Council, acting unanimously in accordance with a special legislative procedure and after consulting the European Parliament; these

arrangements may provide for derogations where warranted by problems specific to a Member State.

Title IV

Free Movement of Persons, Services and Capital

Chapter 1

Workers

Article 45
(ex Article 39 TEC)

1. Freedom of movement for workers shall be secured within the Union.

2. Such freedom of movement shall entail the abolition of any discrimination based on nationality between workers of the Member States as regards employment, remuneration and other conditions of work and employment.

3. It shall entail the right, subject to limitations justified on grounds of public policy, public security or public health:

(a) to accept offers of employment actually made;
(b) to move freely within the territory of Member States for this purpose;
(c) to stay in a Member State for the purpose of employment in accordance with the provisions governing the employment of nationals of that State laid down by law, regulation or administrative action;
(d) to remain in the territory of a Member State after having been employed in that State, subject to conditions which shall be embodied in regulations to be drawn up by the Commission.

4. The provisions of this Article shall not apply to employment in the public service.

Article 46
(ex Article 40 TEC)

The European Parliament and the Council shall, acting in accordance with the ordinary legislative procedure and after consulting the Economic and Social Committee, issue directives or make regulations setting out the measures required to bring about freedom of movement for workers, as defined in Article 45, in particular:

(a) by ensuring close cooperation between national employment services;
(b) by abolishing those administrative procedures and practices and those qualifying periods in respect of eligibility for available employment, whether resulting from national legislation or from agreements previously concluded

between Member States, the maintenance of which would form an obstacle to liberalisation of the movement of workers;

(c) by abolishing all such qualifying periods and other restrictions provided for either under national legislation or under agreements previously concluded between Member States as imposed on workers of other Member States conditions regarding the free choice of employment other than those imposed on workers of the State concerned;

(d) by setting up appropriate machinery to bring offers of employment into touch with applications for employment and to facilitate the achievement of a balance between supply and demand in the employment market in such a way as to avoid serious threats to the standard of living and level of employment in the various regions and industries.

Article 47
(ex Article 41 TEC)

Member States shall, within the framework of a joint programme, encourage the exchange of young workers.

CHAPTER 2

RIGHT OF ESTABLISHMENT

Article 49
(ex Article 43 TEC)

Within the framework of the provisions set out below, restrictions on the freedom of establishment of nationals of a Member State in the territory of another Member State shall be prohibited. Such prohibition shall also apply to restrictions on the setting-up of agencies, branches or subsidiaries by nationals of any Member State established in the territory of any Member State.

Freedom of establishment shall include the right to take up and pursue activities as self-employed persons and to set up and manage undertakings, in particular companies or firms within the meaning of the second paragraph of Article 54, under the conditions laid down for its own nationals by the law of the country where such establishment is effected, subject to the provisions of the Chapter relating to capital.

Article 50
(ex Article 44 TEC)

1. In order to attain freedom of establishment as regards a particular activity, the European Parliament and the Council, acting in accordance with the ordinary legislative procedure and after consulting the Economic and Social Committee, shall act by means of directives.

2. The European Parliament, the Council and the Commission shall carry out the duties devolving upon them under the preceding provisions, in particular:

(a) by according, as a general rule, priority treatment to activities where freedom of establishment makes a particularly valuable contribution to the development of production and trade;

(b) by ensuring close cooperation between the competent authorities in the Member States in order to ascertain the particular situation within the Union of the various activities concerned;

(c) by abolishing those administrative procedures and practices, whether resulting from national legislation or from agreements previously concluded between Member States, the maintenance of which would form an obstacle to freedom of establishment;

(d) by ensuring that workers of one Member State employed in the territory of another Member State may remain in that territory for the purpose of taking up activities therein as self-employed persons, where they satisfy the conditions which they would be required to satisfy if they were entering that State at the time when they intended to take up such activities;

(e) by enabling a national of one Member State to acquire and use land and buildings situated in the territory of another Member State, in so far as this does not conflict with the principles laid down in Article 39(2);

(f) by effecting the progressive abolition of restrictions on freedom of establishment in every branch of activity under consideration, both as regards the conditions for setting up agencies, branches or subsidiaries in the territory of a Member State and as regards the subsidiaries in the territory of a Member State and as regards the conditions governing the entry of personnel belonging to the main establishment into managerial or supervisory posts in such agencies, branches or subsidiaries;

(g) by coordinating to the necessary extent the safeguards which, for the protection of the interests of members and others, are required by Member States of companies or firms within the meaning of the second paragraph of Article 54 with a view to making such safeguards equivalent throughout the Union;

(h) by satisfying themselves that the conditions of establishment are not distorted by aids granted by Member States.

Article 51
(ex Article 45 TEC)

The provisions of this Chapter shall not apply, so far as any given Member State is concerned, to activities which in that State are connected, even occasionally, with the exercise of official authority.

The European Parliament and the Council, acting in accordance with the ordinary legislative procedure, may rule that the provisions of this Chapter shall not apply to certain activities.

APPENDIX 2

Article 52
(ex Article 46 TEC)

1. The provisions of this Chapter and measures taken in pursuance thereof shall not prejudice the applicability of provisions laid down by law, regulation or administrative action providing for special treatment for foreign nationals on grounds of public policy, public security or public health.

2. The European Parliament and the Council shall, acting in accordance with the ordinary legislative procedure, issue directives for the coordination of the above-mentioned provisions.

CHAPTER 3

SERVICES

Article 56
(ex Article 49 TEC)

Within the framework of the provisions set out below, restrictions on freedom to provide services within the Union shall be prohibited in respect of nationals of Member States who are established in a Member State other than that of the person for whom the services are intended.

The European Parliament and the Council, acting in accordance with the ordinary legislative procedure, may extend the provisions of the Chapter to nationals of a third country who provide services and who are established within the Union.

Article 57
(ex Article 50 TEC)

Services shall be considered to be 'services' within the meaning of the Treaties where they are normally provided for remuneration, in so far as they are not governed by the provisions relating to freedom of movement for goods, capital and persons.

'Services' shall in particular include:

(a) activities of an industrial character;
(b) activities of a commercial character;
(c) activities of craftsmen;
(d) activities of the professions.

Without prejudice to the provisions of the Chapter relating to the right of establishment, the person providing a service may, in order to do so, temporarily pursue his activity in the Member State where the service is provided, under the same conditions as are imposed by that State on its own nationals.

Title V

International Agreements

Article 216

1. The Union may conclude an agreement with one or more third countries or international organisations where the Treaties so provide or where the conclusion of an agreement is necessary in order to achieve, within the framework of the Union's policies, one of the objectives referred to in the Treaties, or is provided for in a legally binding Union act or is likely to affect common rules or alter their scope.

2. Agreements concluded by the Union are binding upon the institutions of the Union and on its Member States.

Article 217
(ex Article 310 TEC)

The Union may conclude with one or more third countries or international organisations agreements establishing an association involving reciprocal rights and obligations, common action and special procedure.

Article 218
(ex Article 300 TEC)

1. Without prejudice to the specific provisions laid down in Article 207, agreements between the Union and third countries or international organisations shall be negotiated and concluded in accordance with the following procedure.

Article 267
(ex Article 234 TEC)

The Court of Justice of the European Union shall have jurisdiction to give preliminary rulings concerning:

(a) the interpretation of the Treaties;
(b) the validity and interpretation of acts of the institutions, bodies, offices or agencies of the Union;

Where such a question is raised before any court or tribunal of a Member State, that court or tribunal may, if it considers that a decision on the question is necessary to enable it to give judgment, request the Court to give a ruling thereon.

Where any such question is raised in a case pending before a court or tribunal of a Member State against whose decisions there is no judicial remedy under national law, that court or tribunal shall bring the matter before the Court.

Appendix 2

If such a question is raised in a case pending before a court or tribunal of a Member State with regard to a person in custody, the Court of Justice of the European Union shall act with the minimum of delay.

Chapter 2

Legal Acts of the Union, Adoption Procedures and Other Provisions

Section 1

The Legal Acts of the Union

Article 288
(ex Article 249 TEC)

To exercise the Union's competences, the institutions shall adopt regulations, directives, decisions, recommendations and opinions.

A regulation shall have general application. It shall be binding in its entirety and directly applicable in all Member States.

A directive shall be binding, as to the result to be achieved, upon each Member State to which it is addressed, but shall leave to the national authorities the choice of form and methods.

A decision shall be binding in its entirety. A decision which specifies those to whom it is addressed shall be binding only on them.

Recommendations and opinions shall have no binding force.

Appendix 3

DIRECTIVE 2004/38/EC OF THE EUROPEAN PARLIAMENT AND OF THE COUNCIL OF 29 APRIL 2004
on the right of citizens of the Union and their family members to move and reside freely within the territory of the Member States amending Regulation (EEC) No 1612/68 and repealing Directives 64/221/EEC, 68/360/EEC, 72/194/EEC, 73/148/EEC, 75/34/EEC, 75/35/EEC, 90/364/EEC, 90/365/EEC and 93/96/EEC

(Text with EEA relevance)

THE EUROPEAN PARLIAMENT AND THE COUNCIL OF THE EUROPEAN UNION,

Having regard to the Treaty establishing the European Community, and in particular Articles 12, 18, 40, 44 and 52 thereof,

Having regard to the proposal from the Commission[1],

Having regard to the Opinion of the European Economic and Social Committee[2],

Having regard to the Opinion of the Committee of the Regions[3],

Acting in accordance with the procedure laid down in Article 251 of the Treaty[4],

Whereas:

(1) Citizenship of the Union confers on every citizen of the Union a primary and individual right to move and reside freely within the territory of the Member States, subject to the limitations and conditions laid down in the Treaty and to the measures adopted to give it effect.

(2) The free movement of persons constitutes one of the fundamental freedoms of the internal market, which comprises an area without internal frontiers, in which freedom is ensured in accordance with the provisions of the Treaty.

(3) Union citizenship should be the fundamental status of nationals of the Member States when they exercise their right of free movement and residence. It is therefore necessary to codify and review the existing Community instruments dealing separately with workers, self-employed persons, as well as students and other inactive persons in order to simplify and strengthen the right of free movement and residence of all Union citizens.

(4) With a view to remedying this sector-by-sector, piecemeal approach to the right of free movement and residence and facilitating the exercise of this right, there needs to be a single legislative act to amend Council Regulation (EEC) No

---

[1] OJ C 270 E, 25.9.2001, p. 150.
[2] OJ C 149, 21.6.2002, p. 46.
[3] OJ C 192, 12.8.2002, p. 17.
[4] Opinion of the European Parliament of 11 February 2003 (OJ C 43 E, 19.2.2004, p. 42), Council Common Position of 5 December 2003 (OJ C 54 E, 2.3.2004, p. 12) and Position of the European Parliament of 10 March 2004 (not yet published in the Official Journal).

Appendix 3

1612/68 of 15 October 1968 on freedom of movement for workers within the Community[5], and to repeal the following acts: Council Directive 68/360/EEC of 15 October 1968 on the abolition of restrictions on movement and residence within the Community for workers of Member States and their families[6], Council Directive 73/148/EEC of 21 May 1973 on the abolition of restrictions on movement and residence within the Community for nationals of Member States with regard to establishment and the provision of services[7], Council Directive 90/364/EEC of 28 June 1990 on the right of residence[8], Council Directive 90/365/EEC of 28 June 1990 on the right of residence for employees and self-employed persons who have ceased their occupational activity[9] and Council Directive 93/96/EEC of 29 October 1993 on the right of residence for students[10].

(5) The right of all Union citizens to move and reside freely within the territory of the Member States should, if it is to be exercised under objective conditions of freedom and dignity, be also granted to their family members, irrespective of nationality. For the purposes of this Directive, the definition of "family member" should also include the registered partner if the legislation of the host Member State treats registered partnership as equivalent to marriage.

(6) In order to maintain the unity of the family in a broader sense and without prejudice to the prohibition of discrimination on grounds of nationality, the situation of those persons who are not included in the definition of family members under this Directive, and who therefore do not enjoy an automatic right of entry and residence in the host Member State, should be examined by the host Member State on the basis of its own national legislation, in order to decide whether entry and residence could be granted to such persons, taking into consideration their relationship with the Union citizen or any other circumstances, such as their financial or physical dependence on the Union citizen.

(7) The formalities connected with the free movement of Union citizens within the territory of Member States should be clearly defined, without prejudice to the provisions applicable to national border controls.

(8) With a view to facilitating the free movement of family members who are not nationals of a Member State, those who have already obtained a residence card should be exempted from the requirement to obtain an entry visa within the meaning of Council Regulation (EC) No 539/2001 of 15 March 2001 listing the third countries whose nationals must be in possession of visas when crossing the external borders and those whose nationals are exempt from that requirement[11] or, where appropriate, of the applicable national legislation.

(9) Union citizens should have the right of residence in the host Member State for a period not exceeding three months without being subject to any conditions or any formalities other than the requirement to hold a valid identity card or passport, without prejudice to a more favourable treatment applicable to job-seekers as recognised by the case-law of the Court of Justice.

---

[5] OJ L 257, 19.10.1968, p. 2. Regulation as last amended by Regulation (EEC) No 2434/92 (OJ L 245, 26.8.1992, p. 1).
[6] OJ L 257, 19.10.1968, p. 13. Directive as last amended by the 2003 Act of Accession.
[7] OJ L 172, 28.6.1973, p. 14.
[8] OJ L 180, 13.7.1990, p. 26.
[9] OJ L 180, 13.7.1990, p. 28.
[10] OJ L 317, 18.12.1993, p. 59.
[11] OJ L 81, 21.3.2001, p. 1. Regulation as last amended by Regulation (EC) No 453/2003 (OJ L 69, 13.3.2003, p. 10).

(10) Persons exercising their right of residence should not, however, become an unreasonable burden on the social assistance system of the host Member State during an initial period of residence. Therefore, the right of residence for Union citizens and their family members for periods in excess of three months should be subject to conditions.

(11) The fundamental and personal right of residence in another Member State is conferred directly on Union citizens by the Treaty and is not dependent upon their having fulfilled administrative procedures.

(12) For periods of residence of longer than three months, Member States should have the possibility to require Union citizens to register with the competent authorities in the place of residence, attested by a registration certificate issued to that effect.

(13) The residence card requirement should be restricted to family members of Union citizens who are not nationals of a Member State for periods of residence of longer than three months.

(14) The supporting documents required by the competent authorities for the issuing of a registration certificate or of a residence card should be comprehensively specified in order to avoid divergent administrative practices or interpretations constituting an undue obstacle to the exercise of the right of residence by Union citizens and their family members.

(15) Family members should be legally safeguarded in the event of the death of the Union citizen, divorce, annulment of marriage or termination of a registered partnership. With due regard for family life and human dignity, and in certain conditions to guard against abuse, measures should therefore be taken to ensure that in such circumstances family members already residing within the territory of the host Member State retain their right of residence exclusively on a personal basis.

(16) As long as the beneficiaries of the right of residence do not become an unreasonable burden on the social assistance system of the host Member State they should not be expelled. Therefore, an expulsion measure should not be the automatic consequence of recourse to the social assistance system. The host Member State should examine whether it is a case of temporary difficulties and take into account the duration of residence, the personal circumstances and the amount of aid granted in order to consider whether the beneficiary has become an unreasonable burden on its social assistance system and to proceed to his expulsion. In no case should an expulsion measure be adopted against workers, self-employed persons or job-seekers as defined by the Court of Justice save on grounds of public policy or public security.

(17) Enjoyment of permanent residence by Union citizens who have chosen to settle long term in the host Member State would strengthen the feeling of Union citizenship and is a key element in promoting social cohesion, which is one of the fundamental objectives of the Union. A right of permanent residence should therefore be laid down for all Union citizens and their family members who have resided in the host Member State in compliance with the conditions laid down in this Directive during a continuous period of five years without becoming subject to an expulsion measure.

(18) In order to be a genuine vehicle for integration into the society of the host Member State in which the Union citizen resides, the right of permanent residence, once obtained, should not be subject to any conditions.

(19) Certain advantages specific to Union citizens who are workers or self-employed persons and to their family members, which may allow these persons to acquire

a right of permanent residence before they have resided five years in the host Member State, should be maintained, as these constitute acquired rights, conferred by Commission Regulation (EEC) No 1251/70 of 29 June 1970 on the right of workers to remain in the territory of a Member State after having been employed in that State[12] and Council Directive 75/34/EEC of 17 December 1974 concerning the right of nationals of a Member State to remain in the territory of another Member State after having pursued therein an activity in a self-employed capacity[13].

(20) In accordance with the prohibition of discrimination on grounds of nationality, all Union citizens and their family members residing in a Member State on the basis of this Directive should enjoy, in that Member State, equal treatment with nationals in areas covered by the Treaty, subject to such specific provisions as are expressly provided for in the Treaty and secondary law.

(21) However, it should be left to the host Member State to decide whether it will grant social assistance during the first three months of residence, or for a longer period in the case of job-seekers, to Union citizens other than those who are workers or self-employed persons or who retain that status or their family members, or maintenance assistance for studies, including vocational training, prior to acquisition of the right of permanent residence, to these same persons.

(22) The Treaty allows restrictions to be placed on the right of free movement and residence on grounds of public policy, public security or public health. In order to ensure a tighter definition of the circumstances and procedural safeguards subject to which Union citizens and their family members may be denied leave to enter or may be expelled, this Directive should replace Council Directive 64/221/EEC of 25 February 1964 on the coordination of special measures concerning the movement and residence of foreign nationals, which are justified on grounds of public policy, public security or public health[14].

(23) Expulsion of Union citizens and their family members on grounds of public policy or public security is a measure that can seriously harm persons who, having availed themselves of the rights and freedoms conferred on them by the Treaty, have become genuinely integrated into the host Member State. The scope for such measures should therefore be limited in accordance with the principle of proportionality to take account of the degree of integration of the persons concerned, the length of their residence in the host Member State, their age, state of health, family and economic situation and the links with their country of origin.

(24) Accordingly, the greater the degree of integration of Union citizens and their family members in the host Member State, the greater the degree of protection against expulsion should be. Only in exceptional circumstances, where there are imperative grounds of public security, should an expulsion measure be taken against Union citizens who have resided for many years in the territory of the host Member State, in particular when they were born and have resided there throughout their life. In addition, such exceptional circumstances should also apply to an expulsion measure taken against minors, in order to protect their links with their family, in accordance with the United Nations Convention on the Rights of the Child, of 20 November 1989.

(25) Procedural safeguards should also be specified in detail in order to ensure a high level of protection of the rights of Union citizens and their family members

---

[12] OJ L 142, 30.6.1970, p. 24.
[13] OJ L 14, 20.1.1975, p. 10.
[14] OJ 56, 4.4.1964, p. 850. Directive as last amended by Directive 75/35/EEC (OJ 14, 20.1.1975, p. 14).

in the event of their being denied leave to enter or reside in another Member State, as well as to uphold the principle that any action taken by the authorities must be properly justified.

(26) In all events, judicial redress procedures should be available to Union citizens and their family members who have been refused leave to enter or reside in another Member State.

(27) In line with the case-law of the Court of Justice prohibiting Member States from issuing orders excluding for life persons covered by this Directive from their territory, the right of Union citizens and their family members who have been excluded from the territory of a Member State to submit a fresh application after a reasonable period, and in any event after a three year period from enforcement of the final exclusion order, should be confirmed.

(28) To guard against abuse of rights or fraud, notably marriages of convenience or any other form of relationships contracted for the sole purpose of enjoying the right of free movement and residence, Member States should have the possibility to adopt the necessary measures.

(29) This Directive should not affect more favourable national provisions.

(30) With a view to examining how further to facilitate the exercise of the right of free movement and residence, a report should be prepared by the Commission in order to evaluate the opportunity to present any necessary proposals to this effect, notably on the extension of the period of residence with no conditions.

(31) This Directive respects the fundamental rights and freedoms and observes the principles recognised in particular by the Charter of Fundamental Rights of the European Union. In accordance with the prohibition of discrimination contained in the Charter, Member States should implement this Directive without discrimination between the beneficiaries of this Directive on grounds such as sex, race, colour, ethnic or social origin, genetic characteristics, language, religion or beliefs, political or other opinion, membership of an ethnic minority, property, birth, disability, age or sexual orientation,

HAVE ADOPTED THIS DIRECTIVE:

CHAPTER I

GENERAL PROVISIONS

Article 1—Subject

This Directive lays down:

(a) the conditions governing the exercise of the right of free movement and residence within the territory of the Member States by Union citizens and their family members;

(b) the right of permanent residence in the territory of the Member States for Union citizens and their family members;

(c) the limits placed on the rights set out in (a) and (b) on grounds of public policy, public security or public health.

Appendix 3

Article 2—Definitions

For the purposes of this Directive:

1) "Union citizen" means any person having the nationality of a Member State;

2) "Family member" means:

   (a) the spouse;
   (b) the partner with whom the Union citizen has contracted a registered partnership, on the basis of the legislation of a Member State, if the legislation of the host Member State treats registered partnerships as equivalent to marriage and in accordance with the conditions laid down in the relevant legislation of the host Member State;
   (c) the direct descendants who are under the age of 21 or are dependants and those of the spouse or partner as defined in point (b);
   (d) the dependent direct relatives in the ascending line and those of the spouse or partner as defined in point (b);

3) "Host Member State" means the Member State to which a Union citizen moves in order to exercise his/her right of free movement and residence.

Article 3—Beneficiaries

1. This Directive shall apply to all Union citizens who move to or reside in a Member State other than that of which they are a national, and to their family members as defined in point 2 of Article 2 who accompany or join them.

2. Without prejudice to any right to free movement and residence the persons concerned may have in their own right, the host Member State shall, in accordance with its national legislation, facilitate entry and residence for the following persons:

(a) any other family members, irrespective of their nationality, not falling under the definition in point 2 of Article 2 who, in the country from which they have come, are dependants or members of the household of the Union citizen having the primary right of residence, or where serious health grounds strictly require the personal care of the family member by the Union citizen;

(b) the partner with whom the Union citizen has a durable relationship, duly attested.

The host Member State shall undertake an extensive examination of the personal circumstances and shall justify any denial of entry or residence to these people.

DIRECTIVE 2004/38/EC

CHAPTER II

RIGHT OF EXIT AND ENTRY

Article 4—Right of exit

1. Without prejudice to the provisions on travel documents applicable to national border controls, all Union citizens with a valid identity card or passport and their family members who are not nationals of a Member State and who hold a valid passport shall have the right to leave the territory of a Member State to travel to another Member State.

2. No exit visa or equivalent formality may be imposed on the persons to whom paragraph 1 applies.

3. Member States shall, acting in accordance with their laws, issue to their own nationals, and renew, an identity card or passport stating their nationality.

4. The passport shall be valid at least for all Member States and for countries through which the holder must pass when travelling between Member States. Where the law of a Member State does not provide for identity cards to be issued, the period of validity of any passport on being issued or renewed shall be not less than five years.

Article 5—Right of entry

1. Without prejudice to the provisions on travel documents applicable to national border controls, Member States shall grant Union citizens leave to enter their territory with a valid identity card or passport and shall grant family members who are not nationals of a Member State leave to enter their territory with a valid passport.

No entry visa or equivalent formality may be imposed on Union citizens.

2. Family members who are not nationals of a Member State shall only be required to have an entry visa in accordance with Regulation (EC) No 539/2001 or, where appropriate, with national law. For the purposes of this Directive, possession of the valid residence card referred to in Article 10 shall exempt such family members from the visa requirement.

Member States shall grant such persons every facility to obtain the necessary visas. Such visas shall be issued free of charge as soon as possible and on the basis of an accelerated procedure.

3. The host Member State shall not place an entry or exit stamp in the passport of family members who are not nationals of a Member State provided that they present the residence card provided for in Article 10.

4. Where a Union citizen, or a family member who is not a national of a Member State, does not have the necessary travel documents or, if required, the necessary visas, the Member State concerned shall, before turning them back, give such persons every reasonable opportunity to obtain the necessary documents or have them

brought to them within a reasonable period of time or to corroborate or prove by other means that they are covered by the right of free movement and residence.

5. The Member State may require the person concerned to report his/her presence within its territory within a reasonable and non-discriminatory period of time. Failure to comply with this requirement may make the person concerned liable to proportionate and non-discriminatory sanctions.

Chapter III

Right of Residence

Article 6—Right of residence for up to three months

1. Union citizens shall have the right of residence on the territory of another Member State for a period of up to three months without any conditions or any formalities other than the requirement to hold a valid identity card or passport.

2. The provisions of paragraph 1 shall also apply to family members in possession of a valid passport who are not nationals of a Member State, accompanying or joining the Union citizen.

Article 7—Right of residence for more than three months

1. All Union citizens shall have the right of residence on the territory of another Member State for a period of longer than three months if they:

(a) are workers or self-employed persons in the host Member State; or

(b) have sufficient resources for themselves and their family members not to become a burden on the social assistance system of the host Member State during their period of residence and have comprehensive sickness insurance cover in the host Member State; or

(c) — are enrolled at a private or public establishment, accredited or financed by the host Member State on the basis of its legislation or administrative practice, for the principal purpose of following a course of study, including vocational training; and
— have comprehensive sickness insurance cover in the host Member State and assure the relevant national authority, by means of a declaration or by such equivalent means as they may choose, that they have sufficient resources for themselves and their family members not to become a burden on the social assistance system of the host Member State during their period of residence; or

(d) are family members accompanying or joining a Union citizen who satisfies the conditions referred to in points (a), (b) or (c).

2. The right of residence provided for in paragraph 1 shall extend to family members who are not nationals of a Member State, accompanying or joining the Union citizen

in the host Member State, provided that such Union citizen satisfies the conditions referred to in paragraph 1(a), (b) or (c).

3. For the purposes of paragraph 1(a), a Union citizen who is no longer a worker or self-employed person shall retain the status of worker or self-employed person in the following circumstances:

(a) he/she is temporarily unable to work as the result of an illness or accident;

(b) he/she is in duly recorded involuntary unemployment after having been employed for more than one year and has registered as a job-seeker with the relevant employment office;

(c) he/she is in duly recorded involuntary unemployment after completing a fixed-term employment contract of less than a year or after having become involuntarily unemployed during the first twelve months and has registered as a job-seeker with the relevant employment office. In this case, the status of worker shall be retained for no less than six months;

(d) he/she embarks on vocational training. Unless he/she is involuntarily unemployed, the retention of the status of worker shall require the training to be related to the previous employment.

4. By way of derogation from paragraphs 1(d) and 2 above, only the spouse, the registered partner provided for in Article 2(2)(b) and dependent children shall have the right of residence as family members of a Union citizen meeting the conditions under 1(c) above. Article 3(2) shall apply to his/her dependent direct relatives in the ascending lines and those of his/her spouse or registered partner.

Article 8—Administrative formalities for Union citizens

1. Without prejudice to Article 5(5), for periods of residence longer than three months, the host Member State may require Union citizens to register with the relevant authorities.

2. The deadline for registration may not be less than three months from the date of arrival. A registration certificate shall be issued immediately, stating the name and address of the person registering and the date of the registration. Failure to comply with the registration requirement may render the person concerned liable to proportionate and non-discriminatory sanctions.

3. For the registration certificate to be issued, Member States may only require that

— Union citizens to whom point (a) of Article 7(1) applies present a valid identity card or passport, a confirmation of engagement from the employer or a certificate of employment, or proof that they are self-employed persons;
— Union citizens to whom point (b) of Article 7(1) applies present a valid identity card or passport and provide proof that they satisfy the conditions laid down therein;
— Union citizens to whom point (c) of Article 7(1) applies present a valid identity card or passport, provide proof of enrolment at an accredited establishment and of comprehensive sickness insurance cover and the declaration or equivalent means referred to in point (c) of Article 7(1). Member States may not require this declaration to refer to any specific amount of resources.

Appendix 3

4. Member States may not lay down a fixed amount which they regard as "sufficient resources", but they must take into account the personal situation of the person concerned. In all cases this amount shall not be higher than the threshold below which nationals of the host Member State become eligible for social assistance, or, where this criterion is not applicable, higher than the minimum social security pension paid by the host Member State.

5. For the registration certificate to be issued to family members of Union citizens, who are themselves Union citizens, Member States may require the following documents to be presented:

(a) a valid identity card or passport;

(b) a document attesting to the existence of a family relationship or of a registered partnership;

(c) where appropriate, the registration certificate of the Union citizen whom they are accompanying or joining;

(d) in cases falling under points (c) and (d) of Article 2(2), documentary evidence that the conditions laid down therein are met;

(e) in cases falling under Article 3(2)(a), a document issued by the relevant authority in the country of origin or country from which they are arriving certifying that they are dependants or members of the household of the Union citizen, or proof of the existence of serious health grounds which strictly require the personal care of the family member by the Union citizen;

(f) in cases falling under Article 3(2)(b), proof of the existence of a durable relationship with the Union citizen.

Article 9—Administrative formalities for family members who are not nationals of a Member State

1. Member States shall issue a residence card to family members of a Union citizen who are not nationals of a Member State, where the planned period of residence is for more than three months.

2. The deadline for submitting the residence card application may not be less than three months from the date of arrival.

3. Failure to comply with the requirement to apply for a residence card may make the person concerned liable to proportionate and non-discriminatory sanctions.

Article 10—Issue of residence cards

1. The right of residence of family members of a Union citizen who are not nationals of a Member State shall be evidenced by the issuing of a document called "Residence card of a family member of a Union citizen" no later than six months from the date on which they submit the application. A certificate of application for the residence card shall be issued immediately.

2. For the residence card to be issued, Member States shall require presentation of the following documents:

(a) a valid passport;

(b) a document attesting to the existence of a family relationship or of a registered partnership;

(c) the registration certificate or, in the absence of a registration system, any other proof of residence in the host Member State of the Union citizen whom they are accompanying or joining;

(d) in cases falling under points (c) and (d) of Article 2(2), documentary evidence that the conditions laid down therein are met;

(e) in cases falling under Article 3(2)(a), a document issued by the relevant authority in the country of origin or country from which they are arriving certifying that they are dependants or members of the household of the Union citizen, or proof of the existence of serious health grounds which strictly require the personal care of the family member by the Union citizen;

(f) in cases falling under Article 3(2)(b), proof of the existence of a durable relationship with the Union citizen.

Article 11—Validity of the residence card

1. The residence card provided for by Article 10(1) shall be valid for five years from the date of issue or for the envisaged period of residence of the Union citizen, if this period is less than five years.

2. The validity of the residence card shall not be affected by temporary absences not exceeding six months a year, or by absences of a longer duration for compulsory military service or by one absence of a maximum of twelve consecutive months for important reasons such as pregnancy and childbirth, serious illness, study or vocational training, or a posting in another Member State or a third country.

Article 12—Retention of the right of residence by family members in the event of death or departure of the Union citizen

1. Without prejudice to the second subparagraph, the Union citizen's death or departure from the host Member State shall not affect the right of residence of his/her family members who are nationals of a Member State.

Before acquiring the right of permanent residence, the persons concerned must meet the conditions laid down in points (a), (b), (c) or (d) of Article 7(1).

2. Without prejudice to the second subparagraph, the Union citizen's death shall not entail loss of the right of residence of his/her family members who are not nationals of a Member State and who have been residing in the host Member State as family members for at least one year before the Union citizen's death.

Before acquiring the right of permanent residence, the right of residence of the persons concerned shall remain subject to the requirement that they are able to show that they are workers or self-employed persons or that they have sufficient resources for themselves and their family members not to become a burden on the social assistance system of the host Member State during their period of residence and have comprehensive sickness insurance cover in the host Member State, or that they are

Appendix 3

members of the family, already constituted in the host Member State, of a person satisfying these requirements. "Sufficient resources" shall be as defined in Article 8(4). Such family members shall retain their right of residence exclusively on a personal basis.

3. The Union citizen's departure from the host Member State or his/her death shall not entail loss of the right of residence of his/her children or of the parent who has actual custody of the children, irrespective of nationality, if the children reside in the host Member State and are enrolled at an educational establishment, for the purpose of studying there, until the completion of their studies.

Article 13—Retention of the right of residence by family members in the event of divorce, annulment of marriage or termination of registered partnership

1. Without prejudice to the second subparagraph, divorce, annulment of the Union citizen's marriage or termination of his/her registered partnership, as referred to in point 2(b) of Article 2 shall not affect the right of residence of his/her family members who are nationals of a Member State.

Before acquiring the right of permanent residence, the persons concerned must meet the conditions laid down in points (a), (b), (c) or (d) of Article 7(1).

2. Without prejudice to the second subparagraph, divorce, annulment of marriage or termination of the registered partnership referred to in point 2(b) of Article 2 shall not entail loss of the right of residence of a Union citizen's family members who are not nationals of a Member State where:

(a) prior to initiation of the divorce or annulment proceedings or termination of the registered partnership referred to in point 2(b) of Article 2, the marriage or registered partnership has lasted at least three years, including one year in the host Member State; or

(b) by agreement between the spouses or the partners referred to in point 2(b) of Article 2 or by court order, the spouse or partner who is not a national of a Member State has custody of the Union citizen's children; or

(c) this is warranted by particularly difficult circumstances, such as having been a victim of domestic violence while the marriage or registered partnership was subsisting; or

(d) by agreement between the spouses or partners referred to in point 2(b) of Article 2 or by court order, the spouse or partner who is not a national of a Member State has the right of access to a minor child, provided that the court has ruled that such access must be in the host Member State, and for as long as is required.

Before acquiring the right of permanent residence, the right of residence of the persons concerned shall remain subject to the requirement that they are able to show that they are workers or self-employed persons or that they have sufficient resources for themselves and their family members not to become a burden on the social assistance system of the host Member State during their period of residence and have comprehensive sickness insurance cover in the host Member State, or that they are members of the family, already constituted in the host Member State, of a person satisfying these requirements. "Sufficient resources" shall be as defined in Article 8(4).

Such family members shall retain their right of residence exclusively on personal basis.

Article 14—Retention of the right of residence

1. Union citizens and their family members shall have the right of residence provided for in Article 6, as long as they do not become an unreasonable burden on the social assistance system of the host Member State.

2. Union citizens and their family members shall have the right of residence provided for in Articles 7, 12 and 13 as long as they meet the conditions set out therein.

In specific cases where there is a reasonable doubt as to whether a Union citizen or his/her family members satisfies the conditions set out in Articles 7, 12 and 13, Member States may verify if these conditions are fulfilled. This verification shall not be carried out systematically.

3. An expulsion measure shall not be the automatic consequence of a Union citizen's or his or her family member's recourse to the social assistance system of the host Member State.

4. By way of derogation from paragraphs 1 and 2 and without prejudice to the provisions of Chapter VI, an expulsion measure may in no case be adopted against Union citizens or their family members if:

(a) the Union citizens are workers or self-employed persons, or

(b) the Union citizens entered the territory of the host Member State in order to seek employment. In this case, the Union citizens and their family members may not be expelled for as long as the Union citizens can provide evidence that they are continuing to seek employment and that they have a genuine chance of being engaged.

Article 15—Procedural safeguards

1. The procedures provided for by Articles 30 and 31 shall apply by analogy to all decisions restricting free movement of Union citizens and their family members on grounds other than public policy, public security or public health.

2. Expiry of the identity card or passport on the basis of which the person concerned entered the host Member State and was issued with a registration certificate or residence card shall not constitute a ground for expulsion from the host Member State.

3. The host Member State may not impose a ban on entry in the context of an expulsion decision to which paragraph 1 applies.

Appendix 3

Chapter IV

Right of Permanent Residence

Section I

Eligibility

Article 16—General rule for Union citizens and their family members

1. Union citizens who have resided legally for a continuous period of five years in the host Member State shall have the right of permanent residence there. This right shall not be subject to the conditions provided for in Chapter III.

2. Paragraph 1 shall apply also to family members who are not nationals of a Member State and have legally resided with the Union citizen in the host Member State for a continuous period of five years.

3. Continuity of residence shall not be affected by temporary absences not exceeding a total of six months a year, or by absences of a longer duration for compulsory military service, or by one absence of a maximum of twelve consecutive months for important reasons such as pregnancy and childbirth, serious illness, study or vocational training, or a posting in another Member State or a third country.

4. Once acquired, the right of permanent residence shall be lost only through absence from the host Member State for a period exceeding two consecutive years.

Article 17—Exemptions for persons no longer working in the host Member State and their family members

1. By way of derogation from Article 16, the right of permanent residence in the host Member State shall be enjoyed before completion of a continuous period of five years of residence by:

(a) workers or self-employed persons who, at the time they stop working, have reached the age laid down by the law of that Member State for entitlement to an old age pension or workers who cease paid employment to take early retirement, provided that they have been working in that Member State for at least the preceding twelve months and have resided there continuously for more than three years.

If the law of the host Member State does not grant the right to an old age pension to certain categories of self-employed persons, the age condition shall be deemed to have been met once the person concerned has reached the age of 60;

(b) workers or self-employed persons who have resided continuously in the host Member State for more than two years and stop working there as a result of permanent incapacity to work.

If such incapacity is the result of an accident at work or an occupational disease entitling the person concerned to a benefit payable in full or in part by an institution in the host Member State, no condition shall be imposed as to length of residence;

(c) workers or self-employed persons who, after three years of continuous employment and residence in the host Member State, work in an employed or self-employed capacity in another Member State, while retaining their place of residence in the host Member State, to which they return, as a rule, each day or at least once a week.

For the purposes of entitlement to the rights referred to in points (a) and (b), periods of employment spent in the Member State in which the person concerned is working shall be regarded as having been spent in the host Member State.

Periods of involuntary unemployment duly recorded by the relevant employment office, periods not worked for reasons not of the person's own making and absences from work or cessation of work due to illness or accident shall be regarded as periods of employment.

2. The conditions as to length of residence and employment laid down in point (a) of paragraph 1 and the condition as to length of residence laid down in point (b) of paragraph 1 shall not apply if the worker's or the self-employed person's spouse or partner as referred to in point 2(b) of Article 2 is a national of the host Member State or has lost the nationality of that Member State by marriage to that worker or self-employed person.

3. Irrespective of nationality, the family members of a worker or a self-employed person who are residing with him in the territory of the host Member State shall have the right of permanent residence in that Member State, if the worker or self-employed person has acquired himself the right of permanent residence in that Member State on the basis of paragraph 1.

4. If, however, the worker or self-employed person dies while still working but before acquiring permanent residence status in the host Member State on the basis of paragraph 1, his family members who are residing with him in the host Member State shall acquire the right of permanent residence there, on condition that:

(a) the worker or self-employed person had, at the time of death, resided continuously on the territory of that Member State for two years; or

(b) the death resulted from an accident at work or an occupational disease; or

(c) the surviving spouse lost the nationality of that Member State following marriage to the worker or self-employed person.

Article 18—Acquisition of the right of permanent residence by certain family members who are not nationals of a Member State

Without prejudice to Article 17, the family members of a Union citizen to whom Articles 12(2) and 13(2) apply, who satisfy the conditions laid down therein, shall acquire the right of permanent residence after residing legally for a period of five consecutive years in the host Member State.

Appendix 3

Section II

Administrative Formalities

Article 19—Document certifying permanent residence for Union citizens

1. Upon application Member States shall issue Union citizens entitled to permanent residence, after having verified duration of residence, with a document certifying permanent residence.

2. The document certifying permanent residence shall be issued as soon as possible.

Article 20—Permanent residence card for family members who are not nationals of a Member State

1. Member States shall issue family members who are not nationals of a Member State entitled to permanent residence with a permanent residence card within six months of the submission of the application. The permanent residence card shall be renewable automatically every ten years.

2. The application for a permanent residence card shall be submitted before the residence card expires. Failure to comply with the requirement to apply for a permanent residence card may render the person concerned liable to proportionate and non-discriminatory sanctions.

3. Interruption in residence not exceeding two consecutive years shall not affect the validity of the permanent residence card.

Article 21—Continuity of residence

For the purposes of this Directive, continuity of residence may be attested by any means of proof in use in the host Member State. Continuity of residence is broken by any expulsion decision duly enforced against the person concerned.

Chapter V

Provisions Common to the Right of Residence and the Right of Permanent Residence

Article 22—Territorial scope

The right of residence and the right of permanent residence shall cover the whole territory of the host Member State. Member States may impose territorial restrictions on the right of residence and the right of permanent residence only where the same restrictions apply to their own nationals.

Directive 2004/38/EC

Article 23—Related rights

Irrespective of nationality, the family members of a Union citizen who have the right of residence or the right of permanent residence in a Member State shall be entitled to take up employment or self-employment there.

Article 24—Equal treatment

1. Subject to such specific provisions as are expressly provided for in the Treaty and secondary law, all Union citizens residing on the basis of this Directive in the territory of the host Member State shall enjoy equal treatment with the nationals of that Member State within the scope of the Treaty. The benefit of this right shall be extended to family members who are not nationals of a Member State and who have the right of residence or permanent residence.

2. By way of derogation from paragraph 1, the host Member State shall not be obliged to confer entitlement to social assistance during the first three months of residence or, where appropriate, the longer period provided for in Article 14(4)(b), nor shall it be obliged, prior to acquisition of the right of permanent residence, to grant maintenance aid for studies, including vocational training, consisting in student grants or student loans to persons other than workers, self-employed persons, persons who retain such status and members of their families.

Article 25—General provisions concerning residence documents

1. Possession of a registration certificate as referred to in Article 8, of a document certifying permanent residence, of a certificate attesting submission of an application for a family member residence card, of a residence card or of a permanent residence card, may under no circumstances be made a precondition for the exercise of a right or the completion of an administrative formality, as entitlement to rights may be attested by any other means of proof.

2. All documents mentioned in paragraph 1 shall be issued free of charge or for a charge not exceeding that imposed on nationals for the issuing of similar documents.

Article 26—Checks

Member States may carry out checks on compliance with any requirement deriving from their national legislation for non-nationals always to carry their registration certificate or residence card, provided that the same requirement applies to their own nationals as regards their identity card. In the event of failure to comply with this requirement, Member States may impose the same sanctions as those imposed on their own nationals for failure to carry their identity card.

Appendix 3

Chapter VI

Restrictions on the Right of Entry and the Right of Residence on Grounds of Public Policy, Public Security or Public Health

Article 27—General principles

1. Subject to the provisions of this Chapter, Member States may restrict the freedom of movement and residence of Union citizens and their family members, irrespective of nationality, on grounds of public policy, public security or public health. These grounds shall not be invoked to serve economic ends.

2. Measures taken on grounds of public policy or public security shall comply with the principle of proportionality and shall be based exclusively on the personal conduct of the individual concerned. Previous criminal convictions shall not in themselves constitute grounds for taking such measures.

The personal conduct of the individual concerned must represent a genuine, present and sufficiently serious threat affecting one of the fundamental interests of society. Justifications that are isolated from the particulars of the case or that rely on considerations of general prevention shall not be accepted.

3. In order to ascertain whether the person concerned represents a danger for public policy or public security, when issuing the registration certificate or, in the absence of a registration system, not later than three months from the date of arrival of the person concerned on its territory or from the date of reporting his/her presence within the territory, as provided for in Article 5(5), or when issuing the residence card, the host Member State may, should it consider this essential, request the Member State of origin and, if need be, other Member States to provide information concerning any previous police record the person concerned may have. Such enquiries shall not be made as a matter of routine. The Member State consulted shall give its reply within two months.

4. The Member State which issued the passport or identity card shall allow the holder of the document who has been expelled on grounds of public policy, public security, or public health from another Member State to re-enter its territory without any formality even if the document is no longer valid or the nationality of the holder is in dispute.

Article 28—Protection against expulsion

1. Before taking an expulsion decision on grounds of public policy or public security, the host Member State shall take account of considerations such as how long the individual concerned has resided on its territory, his/her age, state of health, family and economic situation, social and cultural integration into the host Member State and the extent of his/her links with the country of origin.

2. The host Member State may not take an expulsion decision against Union citizens or their family members, irrespective of nationality, who have the right of permanent residence on its territory, except on serious grounds of public policy or public security.

Directive 2004/38/EC

3. An expulsion decision may not be taken against Union citizens, except if the decision is based on imperative grounds of public security, as defined by Member States, if they:

(a) have resided in the host Member State for the previous ten years; or

(b) are a minor, except if the expulsion is necessary for the best interests of the child, as provided for in the United Nations Convention on the Rights of the Child of 20 November 1989.

Article 29—Public health

1. The only diseases justifying measures restricting freedom of movement shall be the diseases with epidemic potential as defined by the relevant instruments of the World Health Organisation and other infectious diseases or contagious parasitic diseases if they are the subject of protection provisions applying to nationals of the host Member State.

2. Diseases occurring after a three-month period from the date of arrival shall not constitute grounds for expulsion from the territory.

3. Where there are serious indications that it is necessary, Member States may, within three months of the date of arrival, require persons entitled to the right of residence to undergo, free of charge, a medical examination to certify that they are not suffering from any of the conditions referred to in paragraph 1. Such medical examinations may not be required as a matter of routine.

Article 30—Notification of decisions

1. The persons concerned shall be notified in writing of any decision taken under Article 27(1), in such a way that they are able to comprehend its content and the implications for them.

2. The persons concerned shall be informed, precisely and in full, of the public policy, public security or public health grounds on which the decision taken in their case is based, unless this is contrary to the interests of State security.

3. The notification shall specify the court or administrative authority with which the person concerned may lodge an appeal, the time limit for the appeal and, where applicable, the time allowed for the person to leave the territory of the Member State. Save in duly substantiated cases of urgency, the time allowed to leave the territory shall be not less than one month from the date of notification.

Article 31—Procedural safeguards

1. The persons concerned shall have access to judicial and, where appropriate, administrative redress procedures in the host Member State to appeal against or seek review of any decision taken against them on the grounds of public policy, public security or public health.

2. Where the application for appeal against or judicial review of the expulsion decision is accompanied by an application for an interim order to suspend enforcement of that decision, actual removal from the territory may not take place until such time as the decision on the interim order has been taken, except:

— where the expulsion decision is based on a previous judicial decision; or

— where the persons concerned have had previous access to judicial review; or

— where the expulsion decision is based on imperative grounds of public security under Article 28(3).

3. The redress procedures shall allow for an examination of the legality of the decision, as well as of the facts and circumstances on which the proposed measure is based. They shall ensure that the decision is not disproportionate, particularly in view of the requirements laid down in Article 28.

4. Member States may exclude the individual concerned from their territory pending the redress procedure, but they may not prevent the individual from submitting his/her defence in person, except when his/her appearance may cause serious troubles to public policy or public security or when the appeal or judicial review concerns a denial of entry to the territory.

Article 32—Duration of exclusion orders

1. Persons excluded on grounds of public policy or public security may submit an application for lifting of the exclusion order after a reasonable period, depending on the circumstances, and in any event after three years from enforcement of the final exclusion order which has been validly adopted in accordance with Community law, by putting forward arguments to establish that there has been a material change in the circumstances which justified the decision ordering their exclusion.

The Member State concerned shall reach a decision on this application within six months of its submission.

2. The persons referred to in paragraph 1 shall have no right of entry to the territory of the Member State concerned while their application is being considered.

Article 33—Expulsion as a penalty or legal consequence

1. Expulsion orders may not be issued by the host Member State as a penalty or legal consequence of a custodial penalty, unless they conform to the requirements of Articles 27, 28 and 29.

2. If an expulsion order, as provided for in paragraph 1, is enforced more than two years after it was issued, the Member State shall check that the individual concerned is currently and genuinely a threat to public policy or public security and shall assess whether there has been any material change in the circumstances since the expulsion order was issued.

Chapter VII

Final Provisions

Article 34—Publicity

Member States shall disseminate information concerning the rights and obligations of Union citizens and their family members on the subjects covered by this Directive, particularly by means of awareness-raising campaigns conducted through national and local media and other means of communication.

Article 35—Abuse of rights

Member States may adopt the necessary measures to refuse, terminate or withdraw any right conferred by this Directive in the case of abuse of rights or fraud, such as marriages of convenience. Any such measure shall be proportionate and subject to the procedural safeguards provided for in Articles 30 and 31.

Article 36—Sanctions

Member States shall lay down provisions on the sanctions applicable to breaches of national rules adopted for the implementation of this Directive and shall take the measures required for their application. The sanctions laid down shall be effective and proportionate. Member States shall notify the Commission of these provisions not later than ......* and as promptly as possible in the case of any subsequent changes.

Article 37—More favourable national provisions

The provisions of this Directive shall not affect any laws, regulations or administrative provisions laid down by a Member State which would be more favourable to the persons covered by this Directive.

Article 38—Repeals

1. Articles 10 and 11 of Regulation (EEC) No 1612/68 shall be repealed with effect from ......*.

2. Directives 64/221/EEC, 68/360/EEC, 72/194/EEC, 73/148/EEC, 75/34/EEC, 75/35/EEC, 90/364/EEC, 90/365/EEC and 93/96/EEC shall be repealed with effect from ....*.

---

* Two years from the date of entry into force of this Directive.

3. References made to the repealed provisions and Directives shall be construed as being made to this Directive.

Article 39—Report

No later than......* the Commission shall submit a report on the application of this Directive to the European Parliament and the Council, together with any necessary proposals, notably on the opportunity to extend the period of time during which Union citizens and their family members may reside in the territory of the host Member State without any conditions. The Member States shall provide the Commission with the information needed to produce the report.

Article 40—Transposition

1. Member States shall bring into force the laws, regulations and administrative provisions necessary to comply with this Directive by ......**.

When Member States adopt those measures, they shall contain a reference to this Directive or shall be accompanied by such a reference on the occasion of their official publication. The methods of making such reference shall be laid down by the Member States.

2. Member States shall communicate to the Commission the text of the provisions of national law which they adopt in the field covered by this Directive together with a table showing how the provisions of this Directive correspond to the national provisions adopted.

Article 41—Entry into force

This Directive shall enter into force on the day of its publication in the Official Journal of the European Union.

Article 42—Addressees

This Directive is addressed to the Member States.

Done at Strasbourg, 29 April 2004.

---

* Four years from the date of entry into force of this Directive.
** Two years from the date of entry into force of this Directive.

APPENDIX 4

REGULATION (EU) NO 492/2011 OF THE EUROPEAN PARLIAMENT AND OF THE COUNCIL OF 5 APRIL 2011
on freedom of movement for workers within the Union
(codification)
(Text with EEA relevance)

THE EUROPEAN PARLIAMENT AND THE COUNCIL OF THE EUROPEAN UNION,

Having regard to the Treaty on the Functioning of the European Union, and in particular Article 46 thereof,

Having regard to the proposal from the European Commission,

After transmission of the draft legislative act to the national parliaments,

Having regard to the opinion of the European Economic and Social Committee[1],

Acting in accordance with the ordinary legislative procedure[2],

Whereas:

(1) Regulation (EEC) No 1612/68 of the Council of 15 October 1968 on freedom of movement for workers within the Community[3] has been substantially amended several times.[4] In the interests of clarity and rationality the said Regulation should be codified.

(2) Freedom of movement for workers should be secured within the Union. The attainment of this objective entails the abolition of any discrimination based on nationality between workers of the Member States as regards employment, remuneration and other conditions of work and employment, as well as the right of such workers to move freely within the Union in order to pursue activities as employed persons subject to any limitations justified on grounds of public policy, public security or public health.

(3) Provisions should be laid down to enable the objectives laid down in Articles 45 and 46 of the Treaty on the Functioning of the European Union in the field of freedom of movement to be achieved.

(4) Freedom of movement constitutes a fundamental right of workers and their families. Mobility of labour within the Union must be one of the means by which workers are guaranteed the possibility of improving their living and working conditions and promoting their social advancement, while helping to satisfy the requirements of the economies of the Member States. The right of all workers in the Member States to pursue the activity of their choice within the Union should be affirmed.

---

[1] OJ C 44, 11.2.2011, p. 170.
[2] Position of the European Parliament of 7 September 2010 (not yet published in the Official Journal) and decision of the Council of 21 March 2011.
[3] OJ L 257, 19.10.1968, p. 2.
[4] See Annex I.

Appendix 4

(5) Such right should be enjoyed without discrimination by permanent, seasonal and frontier workers and by those who pursue their activities for the purpose of providing services.

(6) The right of freedom of movement, in order that it may be exercised, by objective standards, in freedom and dignity, requires that equality of treatment be ensured in fact and in law in respect of all matters relating to the actual pursuit of activities as employed persons and to eligibility for housing, and also that obstacles to the mobility of workers be eliminated, in particular as regards the conditions for the integration of the worker's family into the host country.

(7) The principle of non-discrimination between workers in the Union means that all nationals of Member States have the same priority as regards employment as is enjoyed by national workers.

(8) The machinery for vacancy clearance, in particular by means of direct cooperation between the central employment services and also between the regional services, as well as by coordination of the exchange of information, ensures in a general way a clearer picture of the labour market. Workers wishing to move should also be regularly informed of living and working conditions.

(9) Close links exist between freedom of movement for workers, employment and vocational training, particularly where the latter aims at putting workers in a position to take up concrete offers of employment from other regions of the Union. Such links make it necessary that the problems arising in this connection should no longer be studied in isolation but viewed as interdependent, account also being taken of the problems of employment at the regional level. It is therefore necessary to direct the efforts of Member States toward coordinating their employment policies,

HAVE ADOPTED THIS REGULATION:

Chapter I

Employment, Equal Treatment and Workers' Families

Section 1

Eligibility for Employment

Article 1

1. Any national of a Member State shall, irrespective of his place of residence, have the right to take up an activity as an employed person, and to pursue such activity, within the territory of another Member State in accordance with the provisions laid down by law, regulation or administrative action governing the employment of nationals of that State.

2. He shall, in particular, have the right to take up available employment in the territory of another Member State with the same priority as nationals of that State.

Article 2

Any national of a Member State and any employer pursuing an activity in the territory of a Member State may exchange their applications for and offers of employment, and may conclude and perform contracts of employment in accordance with the provisions in force laid down by law, regulation or administrative action, without any discrimination resulting therefrom.

Article 3

1. Under this Regulation, provisions laid down by law, regulation or administrative action or administrative practices of a Member State shall not apply:

(a) where they limit application for and offers of employment, or the right of foreign nationals to take up and pursue employment or subject these to conditions not applicable in respect of their own nationals; or

(b) where, though applicable irrespective of nationality, their exclusive or principal aim or effect is to keep nationals of other Member States away from the employment offered.

The first subparagraph shall not apply to conditions relating to linguistic knowledge required by reason of the nature of the post to be filled.

2. There shall be included in particular among the provisions or practices of a Member State referred to in the first subparagraph of paragraph 1 those which:

(a) prescribe a special recruitment procedure for foreign nationals;

(b) limit or restrict the advertising of vacancies in the press or through any other medium or subject it to conditions other than those applicable in respect of employers pursuing their activities in the territory of that Member State;

(c) subject eligibility for employment to conditions of registration with employment offices or impede recruitment of individual workers, where persons who do not reside in the territory of that State are concerned.

Article 4

1. Provisions laid down by law, regulation or administrative action of the Member States which restrict by number or percentage the employment of foreign nationals in any undertaking, branch of activity or region, or at a national level, shall not apply to nationals of the other Member States.

2. When in a Member State the granting of any benefit to undertakings is subject to a minimum percentage of national workers being employed, nationals of the other Member States shall be counted as national workers, subject to Directive 2005/36/EC of the European Parliament and of the Council of 7 September 2005 on the recognition of professional qualifications.[5]

---

[5] OJ L 255, 30.9.2005, p. 22.

Appendix 4

Article 5

A national of a Member State who seeks employment in the territory of another Member State shall receive the same assistance there as that afforded by the employment offices in that State to their own nationals seeking employment.

Article 6

1. The engagement and recruitment of a national of one Member State for a post in another Member State shall not depend on medical, vocational or other criteria which are discriminatory on grounds of nationality by comparison with those applied to nationals of the other Member State who wish to pursue the same activity.

2. A national who holds an offer in his name from an employer in a Member State other than that of which he is a national may have to undergo a vocational test, if the employer expressly requests this when making his offer of employment.

SECTION 2

EMPLOYMENT AND EQUALITY OF TREATMENT

Article 7

1. A worker who is a national of a Member State may not, in the territory of another Member State, be treated differently from national workers by reason of his nationality in respect of any conditions of employment and work, in particular as regards remuneration, dismissal, and, should he become unemployed, reinstatement or re-employment.

2. He shall enjoy the same social and tax advantages as national workers.

3. He shall also, by virtue of the same right and under the same conditions as national workers, have access to training in vocational schools and retraining centres.

4. Any clause of a collective or individual agreement or of any other collective regulation concerning eligibility for employment, remuneration and other conditions of work or dismissal shall be null and void in so far as it lays down or authorises discriminatory conditions in respect of workers who are nationals of the other Member States.

Article 8

A worker who is a national of a Member State and who is employed in the territory of another Member State shall enjoy equality of treatment as regards membership of trade unions and the exercise of rights attaching thereto, including the right to vote and to be eligible for the administration or management posts of a trade union. He

Regulation (EU) No 492/2011

may be excluded from taking part in the management of bodies governed by public law and from holding an office governed by public law. Furthermore, he shall have the right of eligibility for workers' representative bodies in the undertaking.

The first paragraph of this Article shall not affect laws or regulations in certain Member States which grant more extensive rights to workers coming from the other Member States.

Article 9

1. A worker who is a national of a Member State and who is employed in the territory of another Member State shall enjoy all the rights and benefits accorded to national workers in matters of housing, including ownership of the housing he needs.

2. A worker referred to in paragraph 1 may, with the same right as nationals, put his name down on the housing lists in the region in which he is employed, where such lists exist, and shall enjoy the resultant benefits and priorities.

If his family has remained in the country whence he came, they shall be considered for this purpose as residing in the said region, where national workers benefit from a similar presumption.

Section 3

Workers' Families

Article 10

The children of a national of a Member State who is or has been employed in the territory of another Member State shall be admitted to that State's general educational, apprenticeship and vocational training courses under the same conditions as the nationals of that State, if such children are residing in its territory.

Member States shall encourage all efforts to enable such children to attend these courses under the best possible conditions.

Appendix 4

Chapter II

Clearance of Vacancies and Applications for Employment

Section 1

Cooperation between the Member States and with the Commission

Article 11

1. The Member States or the Commission shall instigate or together undertake any study of employment or unemployment which they consider necessary for freedom of movement for workers within the Union.

The central employment services of the Member States shall cooperate closely with each other and with the Commission with a view to acting jointly as regards the clearing of vacancies and applications for employment within the Union and the resultant placing of workers in employment.

2. To this end the Member States shall designate specialist services which shall be entrusted with organising work in the fields referred to in the second subparagraph of paragraph 1 and cooperating with each other and with the departments of the Commission.

The Member States shall notify the Commission of any change in the designation of such services and the Commission shall publish details thereof for information in the Official Journal of the European Union.

Article 12

1. The Member States shall send to the Commission information on problems arising in connection with the freedom of movement and employment of workers and particulars of the state and development of employment.

2. The Commission, taking the utmost account of the opinion of the Technical Committee referred to in Article 29 ('the Technical Committee'), shall determine the manner in which the information referred to in paragraph 1 of this Article is to be drawn up.

3. In accordance with the procedure laid down by the Commission taking the utmost account of the opinion of the Technical Committee, the specialist service of each Member State shall send to the specialist services of the other Member States and to the European Coordination Office referred to in Article 18 such information concerning living and working conditions and the state of the labour market as is likely to be of guidance to workers from the other Member States. Such information shall be brought up to date regularly.

The specialist services of the other Member States shall ensure that wide publicity is given to such information, in particular by circulating it among the appropriate employment services and by all suitable means of communication for informing the workers concerned.

Section 2

Machinery for Vacancy Clearance

Article 13

1. The specialist service of each Member State shall regularly send to the specialist services of the other Member States and to the European Coordination Office referred to in Article 18:

(a) details of vacancies which could be filled by nationals of other Member States;
(b) details of vacancies addressed to third countries;
(c) details of applications for employment by those who have formally expressed a wish to work in another Member State;
(d) information, by region and by branch of activity, on applicants who have declared themselves actually willing to accept employment in another country.

The specialist service of each Member State shall forward this information to the appropriate employment services and agencies as soon as possible.

2. The details of vacancies and applications referred to in paragraph 1 shall be circulated according to a uniform system to be established by the European Coordination Office referred to in Article 18 in collaboration with the Technical Committee.

This system may be adapted if necessary.

Article 14

1. Any vacancy within the meaning of Article 13 communicated to the employment services of a Member State shall be notified to and processed by the competent employment services of the other Member States concerned.

Such services shall forward to the services of the first Member State the details of suitable applications.

2. The applications for employment referred to in point (c) of the first subparagraph of Article 13(1) shall be responded to by the relevant services of the Member States within a reasonable period, not exceeding 1 month.

3. The employment services shall grant workers who are nationals of the Member States the same priority as the relevant measures grant to nationals vis-à-vis workers from third countries.

Appendix 4

Article 15

1. The provisions of Article 14 shall be implemented by the specialist services. However, in so far as they have been authorised by the central services and in so far as the organisation of the employment services of a Member State and the placing techniques employed make it possible:

(a) the regional employment services of the Member States shall:

    (i) on the basis of the information referred to in Article 13, on which appropriate action will be taken, directly bring together and clear vacancies and applications for employment;
    (ii) establish direct relations for clearance:

- of vacancies offered to a named worker,
- of individual applications for employment sent either to a specific employment service or to an employer pursuing his activity within the area covered by such a service,
- where the clearing operations concern seasonal workers who must be recruited as quickly as possible;

(b) the services territorially responsible for the border regions of two or more Member States shall regularly exchange data relating to vacancies and applications for employment in their area and, acting in accordance with their arrangements with the other employment services of their countries, shall directly bring together and clear vacancies and applications for employment.

If necessary, the services territorially responsible for border regions shall also set up cooperation and service structures to provide:

- users with as much practical information as possible on the various aspects of mobility, and
- management and labour, social services (in particular public, private or those of public interest) and all institutions concerned, with a framework of coordinated measures relating to mobility,

(c) official employment services which specialise in certain occupations or specific categories of persons shall cooperate directly with each other.

2. The Member States concerned shall forward to the Commission the list, drawn up by common accord, of services referred to in paragraph 1 and the Commission shall publish such list for information, and any amendment thereto, in the *Official Journal of the European Union*.

Article 16

Adoption of recruiting procedures as applied by the implementing bodies provided for under agreements concluded between two or more Member States shall not be obligatory.

REGULATION (EU) No 492/2011

SECTION 3

MEASURES FOR CONTROLLING THE BALANCE OF THE LABOUR MARKET

Article 17

1. On the basis of a report from the Commission drawn up from information supplied by the Member States, the latter and the Commission shall at least once a year analyse jointly the results of Union arrangements regarding vacancies and applications.

2. The Member States shall examine with the Commission all the possibilities of giving priority to nationals of Member States when filling employment vacancies in order to achieve a balance between vacancies and applications for employment within the Union. They shall adopt all measures necessary for this purpose.

3. Every 2 years the Commission shall submit a report to the European Parliament, the Council and the European Economic and Social Committee on the implementation of Chapter II, summarising the information required and the data obtained from the studies and research carried out and highlighting any useful points with regard to developments on the Union's labour market.

SECTION 4

EUROPEAN COORDINATION OFFICE

Article 18

The European Office for Coordinating the Clearance of Vacancies and Applications for Employment ('the European Coordination Office'), established within the Commission, shall have the general task of promoting vacancy clearance at Union level. It shall be responsible in particular for all the technical duties in this field which, under the provisions of this Regulation, are assigned to the Commission, and especially for assisting the national employment services.

It shall summarise the information referred to in Articles 12 and 13 and the data arising out of the studies and research carried out pursuant to Article 11, so as to bring to light any useful facts about foreseeable developments on the Union labour market; such facts shall be communicated to the specialist services of the Member States and to the Advisory Committee referred to in Article 21 and the Technical Committee.

Article 19

1. The European Coordination Office shall be responsible, in particular, for:

(a) coordinating the practical measures necessary for vacancy clearance at Union level and for analysing the resulting movements of workers;

(b) contributing to such objectives by implementing, in cooperation with the Technical Committee, joint methods of action at administrative and technical levels;

(c) carrying out, where a special need arises, and in agreement with the specialist services, the bringing together of vacancies and applications for employment for clearance by those specialist services.

2. It shall communicate to the specialist services vacancies and applications for employment sent directly to the Commission, and shall be informed of the action taken thereon.

Article 20

The Commission may, in agreement with the competent authority of each Member State, and in accordance with the conditions and procedures which it shall determine on the basis of the opinion of the Technical Committee, organise visits and assignments for officials of other Member States, and also advanced programmes for specialist personnel.

CHAPTER III

COMMITTEES FOR ENSURING CLOSE COOOPERATION BETWEEN THE MEMBER STATES IN MATTERS CONCERNING THE FREEDOM OF MOVEMENT OF WORKERS AND THEIR EMPLOYMENT

SECTION 1

THE ADVISORY COMMITTEE

Article 21

The Advisory Committee shall be responsible for assisting the Commission in the examination of any questions arising from the application of the Treaty on the Functioning of the European Union and measures taken in pursuance thereof, in matters concerning the freedom of movement of workers and their employment.

Article 22

The Advisory Committee shall be responsible in particular for:

(a) examining problems concerning freedom of movement and employment within the framework of national manpower policies, with a view to coordinating the employment policies of the Member States at Union level, thus contributing to the development of the economies and to an improved balance of the labour market;

(b) making a general study of the effects of implementing this Regulation and any supplementary measures;

(c) submitting to the Commission any reasoned proposals for revising this Regulation;

(d) delivering, either at the request of the Commission or on its own initiative, reasoned opinions on general questions or on questions of principle, in particular on exchange of information concerning developments in the labour market, on the movement of workers between Member States, on programmes or measures to develop vocational guidance and vocational training which are likely to increase the possibilities of freedom of movement and employment, and on all forms of assistance to workers and their families, including social assistance and the housing of workers.

Article 23

1. The Advisory Committee shall be composed of six members for each Member State, two of whom shall represent the Government, two the trade unions and two the employers' associations.

2. For each of the categories referred to in paragraph 1, one alternate member shall be appointed by each Member State.

3. The term of office of the members and their alternates shall be 2 years. Their appointments shall be renewable.

On expiry of their term of office, the members and their alternates shall remain in office until replaced or until their appointments are renewed.

Article 24

The members of the Advisory Committee and their alternates shall be appointed by the Council, which shall endeavour, when selecting representatives of trade unions and employers' associations, to achieve adequate representation on the Committee of the various economic sectors concerned.

The list of members and their alternates shall be published by the Council for information in the Official Journal of the European Union.

Article 25

The Advisory Committee shall be chaired by a member of the Commission or his representative. The Chairman shall not vote. The Committee shall meet at least twice a year. It shall be convened by its Chairman, either on his own initiative, or at the request of at least one third of the members.

Secretarial services shall be provided for the Committee by the Commission.

Appendix 4

Article 26

The Chairman may invite individuals or representatives of bodies with wide experience in the field of employment or movement of workers to take part in meetings as observers or as experts. The Chairman may be assisted by expert advisers.

Article 27

1. An opinion delivered by the Advisory Committee shall not be valid unless two thirds of the members are present.

2. Opinions shall state the reasons on which they are based; they shall be delivered by an absolute majority of the votes validly cast; they shall be accompanied by a written statement of the views expressed by the minority, when the latter so requests.

Article 28

The Advisory Committee shall establish its working methods by rules of procedure which shall enter into force after the Council, having received an opinion from the Commission, has given its approval. The entry into force of any amendment that the Committee decides to make thereto shall be subject to the same procedure.

Section 2

The Technical Committee

Article 29

The Technical Committee shall be responsible for assisting the Commission in the preparation, promotion and follow-up of all technical work and measures for giving effect to this Regulation and any supplementary measures.

Article 30

The Technical Committee shall be responsible in particular for:

(a) promoting and advancing cooperation between the public authorities concerned in the Member States on all technical questions relating to freedom of movement of workers and their employment;

(b) formulating procedures for the organisation of the joint activities of the public authorities concerned;

(c) facilitating the gathering of information likely to be of use to the Commission and the undertaking of the studies and research provided for in this Regulation, and encouraging exchange of information and experience between the administrative bodies concerned;

(d) investigating at a technical level the harmonisation of the criteria by which Member States assess the state of their labour markets.

Article 31

1. The Technical Committee shall be composed of representatives of the Governments of the Member States. Each Government shall appoint as member of the Technical Committee one of the members who represent it on the Advisory Committee.

2. Each Government shall appoint an alternate from among its other representatives—members or alternates—on the Advisory Committee.

Article 32

The Technical Committee shall be chaired by a member of the Commission or his representative. The Chairman shall not vote. The Chairman and the members of the Committee may be assisted by expert advisers.

Secretarial services shall be provided for the Committee by the Commission.

Article 33

The proposals and opinions formulated by the Technical Committee shall be submitted to the Commission, and the Advisory Committee shall be informed thereof. Any such proposals and opinions shall be accompanied by a written statement of the views expressed by the various members of the Technical Committee, when the latter so request.

Article 34

The Technical Committee shall establish its working methods by rules of procedure which shall enter into force after the Council, having received an opinion from the Commission, has given its approval. The entry into force of any amendment which the Committee decides to make thereto shall be subject to the same procedure.

Appendix 4

Chapter IV

Final Provisions

Article 35

The rules of procedure of the Advisory Committee and of the Technical Committee in force on 8 November 1968 shall continue to apply.

Article 36

1. This Regulation shall not affect the provisions of the Treaty establishing the European Atomic Energy Community which deal with eligibility for skilled employment in the field of nuclear energy, nor any measures taken in pursuance of that Treaty.

Nevertheless, this Regulation shall apply to the category of workers referred to in the first subparagraph and to members of their families in so far as their legal position is not governed by the above-mentioned Treaty or measures.

2. This Regulation shall not affect measures taken in accordance with Article 48 of the Treaty on the Functioning of the European Union.

Chapter III

Committees for Ensuring Close Cooperation Between the Member States in Matters Concerning the Freedom of Movement of Workers and Their Employment

Section 1

Article 27

1. An opinion delivered by the Advisory Committee shall not be valid unless two thirds of the members are present.

2. Opinions shall state the reasons on which they are based; they shall be delivered by an absolute majority of the votes validly cast; they shall be accompanied by a written statement of the views expressed by the minority, when the latter so requests.

Article 28

The Advisory Committee shall establish its working methods by rules of procedure which shall enter into force after the Council, having received an opinion from the Commission, has given its approval. The entry into force of any amendment that the Committee decides to make thereto shall be subject to the same procedure.

SECTION 2

THE TECHNICAL COMMITTEE

Article 29

The Technical Committee shall be responsible for assisting the Commission in the preparation, promotion and follow-up of all technical work and measures for giving effect to this Regulation and any supplementary measures.

Article 30

The Technical Committee shall be responsible in particular for:

(a) promoting and advancing cooperation between the public authorities concerned in the Member States on all technical questions relating to freedom of movement of workers and their employment;

(b) formulating procedures for the organisation of the joint activities of the public authorities concerned;

(c) facilitating the gathering of information likely to be of use to the Commission and the undertaking of the studies and research provided for in this Regulation, and encouraging exchange of information and experience between the administrative bodies concerned;

(d) investigating at a technical level the harmonisation of the criteria by which Member States assess the state of their labour markets.

Article 31

1. The Technical Committee shall be composed of representatives of the Governments of the Member States. Each Government shall appoint as member of the Technical Committee one of the members who represent it on the Advisory Committee.

2. Each Government shall appoint an alternate from among its other representatives—members or alternates—on the Advisory Committee.

APPENDIX 4

Article 32

The Technical Committee shall be chaired by a member of the Commission or his representative. The Chairman shall not vote. The Chairman and the members of the Committee may be assisted by expert advisers.

Secretarial services shall be provided for the Committee by the Commission.

Article 33

The proposals and opinions formulated by the Technical Committee shall be submitted to the Commission, and the Advisory Committee shall be informed thereof. Any such proposals and opinions shall be accompanied by a written statement of the views expressed by the various members of the Technical Committee, when the latter so request.

Article 34

The Technical Committee shall establish its working methods by rules of procedure which shall enter into force after the Council, having received an opinion from the Commission, has given its approval. The entry into force of any amendment which the Committee decides to make thereto shall be subject to the same procedure.

CHAPTER IV

FINAL PROVISIONS

Article 35

The rules of procedure of the Advisory Committee and of the Technical Committee in force on 8 November 1968 shall continue to apply.

Article 36

1. This Regulation shall not affect the provisions of the Treaty establishing the European Atomic Energy Community which deal with eligibility for skilled employment in the field of nuclear energy, nor any measures taken in pursuance of that Treaty.

Nevertheless, this Regulation shall apply to the category of workers referred to in the first subparagraph and to members of their families in so far as their legal position is not governed by the above-mentioned Treaty or measures.

2. This Regulation shall not affect measures taken in accordance with Article 48 of the Treaty on the Functioning of the European Union.

REGULATION (EU) No 492/2011

ANNEX I

REPEALED REGULATION WITH LIST OF ITS SUCCESSIVE AMENTMENTS

Council Regulation (EEC) No 1612/68 (OJ L 257, 19.10.1968, p. 2)

Council Regulation (EEC) No 312/76 (OJ L 39, 14.2.1976, p. 2)

Council Regulation (EEC) No 2434/92 (OJ L 245, 26.8.1992, p. 1)

Directive 2004/38/EC of the European Parliament and of the Council (OJ L 158, 30.4.2004, p. 77)   Only Article 38(1)

ANNEX II

CORRELATION TABLE

Regulation (EEC) No 1612/68	This Regulation
Part I	Chapter I
Title I	Section 1
Article 1	Article 1
Article 2	Article 2
Article 3(1), first subparagraph	Article 3(1), first subparagraph
Article 3(1), first subparagraph, first indent	Article 3(1), first subparagraph, point (a)
Article 3(1), first subparagraph, second indent	Article 3(1), first subparagraph, point (b)
Article 3(1), second subparagraph	Article 3(1), second subparagraph
Article 3(2)	Article 3(2)
Article 4	Article 4
Article 5	Article 5
Article 6	Article 6
Title II	Section 2
Article 7	Article 7
Article 8(1)	Article 8
Article 9	Article 9
Title III	Section 3
Article 12	Article 10
Part II	Chapter II

Appendix 4

Title I	Section 1
Article 13	Article 11
Article 14	Article 12
Title II	Section 2
Article 15	Article 13
Article 16	Article 14
Article 17	Article 15
Article 18	Article 16
Title III	Section 3
Article 19	Article 17
Title IV	Section 4
Article 21	Article 18
Article 22	Article 19
Article 23	Article 20
Part III	Chapter III
Title I	Section 1
Article 24	Article 21
Article 25	Article 22
Article 26	Article 23
Article 27	Article 24
Article 28	Article 25
Article 29	Article 26
Article 30	Article 27
Article 31	Article 28
Title II	Section 2
Article 32	Article 29
Article 33	Article 30
Article 34	Article 31
Article 35	Article 32
Article 36	Article 33
Article 37	Article 34
Part IV	Chapter IV
Title I	—
Article 38	—

Regulation (EU) No 492/2011

Article 39	Article 35
Article 40	—
Article 41	—
Title II	—
Article 42(1)	Article 36(1)
Article 42(2)	Article 36(2)
Article 42(3), first subparagraph, first and second indents	Article 36(3), first subparagraph
Article 42(3), second subparagraph	Article 36(3), second subparagraph
Article 43 Article 44	Article 37 Article 38
Article 45	—
Article 46	Article 39
Article 47	Article 40
—	Article 41
Article 48	Article 42
—	Annex I
—	Annex II

Appendix 5

(Acts whose publication is obligatory)

REGULATION (EC) NO 883/2004 OF THE EUROPEAN PARLIAMENT AND OF THE COUNCIL OF 29 APRIL 2004 ON THE COORDINATION OF SOCIAL SECURITY SYSTEMS
(Text with relevance for the EEA and for Switzerland)

THE EUROPEAN PARLIAMENT AND THE COUNCIL OF THE EUROPEAN UNION,

Having regard to the Treaty establishing the European Community, and in particular Articles 42 and 308 thereof,

Having regard to the proposal from the Commission presented after consultation with the social partners and the Administrative Commission on Social Security for Migrant Workers[1],

Having regard to the Opinion of the European Economic and Social Committee[2],

Acting in accordance with the procedure laid down in Article 251 of the Treaty[3],

Whereas:

(1) The rules for coordination of national social security systems fall within the framework of free movement of persons and should contribute towards improving their standard of living and conditions of employment.

(2) The Treaty does not provide powers other than those of Article 308 to take appropriate measures within the field of social security for persons other than employed persons.

(3) Council Regulation (EEC) No 1408/71 of 14 June 1971 on the application of social security schemes to employed persons, to self-employed persons and to members of their families moving within the Community[4] has been amended and updated on numerous occasions in order to take into account not only developments at Community level, including judgments of the Court of Justice, but also changes in legislation at national level. Such factors have played their part in making the Community coordination rules complex and lengthy. Replacing, while modernising and simplifying, these rules is therefore essential to achieve the aim of the free movement of persons.

(4) It is necessary to respect the special characteristics of national social security legislation and to draw up only a system of coordination.

---

[1] OJ C 38, 12.2.1999, p. 10 and OJ C ... (proposal).
[2] OJ C 75, 15.3.2000, p. 29.
[3] Opinion of the European Parliament of 3 September 2003 (not yet published in the Official Journal). Council Common Position of 26 January 2004 (OJ C 79 E, 30.3.2004, p. 15) and Position of the European Parliament of 20 April 2004 (not yet published in the Official Journal). Decision of the Council of 26 April 2004.
[4] OJ L 149, 5.7.1971, p. 2. Regulation as last amended by Regulation (EC) No 1386/2001 of the European Parliament and of the Council (OJ L 187, 10.7.2001, p. 1).

(5) It is necessary, within the framework of such coordination, to guarantee within the Community equality of treatment under the different national legislation for the persons concerned.

(6) The close link between social security legislation and those contractual provisions which complement or replace such legislation and which have been the subject of a decision by the public authorities rendering them compulsory or extending their scope may call for similar protection with regard to the application of those provisions to that afforded by this Regulation. As a first step, the experience of Member States who have notified such schemes might be evaluated.

(7) Due to the major differences existing between national legislation in terms of the persons covered, it is preferable to lay down the principle that this Regulation is to apply to nationals of a Member State, stateless persons and refugees resident in the territory of a Member State who are or have been subject to the social security legislation of one or more Member States, as well as to the members of their families and to their survivors.

(8) The general principle of equal treatment is of particular importance for workers who do not reside in the Member State of their employment, including frontier workers.

(9) The Court of Justice has on several occasions given an opinion on the possibility of equal treatment of benefits, income and facts; this principle should be adopted explicitly and developed, while observing the substance and spirit of legal rulings.

(10) However, the principle of treating certain facts or events occurring in the territory of another Member State as if they had taken place in the territory of the Member State whose legislation is applicable should not interfere with the principle of aggregating periods of insurance, employment, self-employment or residence completed under the legislation of another Member State with those completed under the legislation of the competent Member State. Periods completed under the legislation of another Member State should therefore be taken into account solely by applying the principle of aggregation of periods.

(11) The assimilation of facts or events occurring in a Member State can in no way render another Member State competent or its legislation applicable.

(12) In the light of proportionality, care should be taken to ensure that the principle of assimilation of facts or events does not lead to objectively unjustified results or to the overlapping of benefits of the same kind for the same period.

(13) The coordination rules must guarantee that persons moving within the Community and their dependants and survivors retain the rights and the advantages acquired and in the course of being acquired.

(14) These objectives must be attained in particular by aggregating all the periods taken into account under the various national legislation for the purpose of acquiring and retaining the right to benefits and of calculating the amount of benefits, and by providing benefits for the various categories of persons covered by this Regulation.

(15) It is necessary to subject persons moving within the Community to the social security scheme of only one single Member State in order to avoid overlapping of the applicable provisions of national legislation and the complications which could result therefrom.

(16) Within the Community there is in principle no justification for making social security rights dependent on the place of residence of the person concerned;

REGULATION (EC) No 883/2004

nevertheless, in specific cases, in particular as regards special benefits linked to the economic and social context of the person involved, the place of residence could be taken into account.

(17) With a view to guaranteeing the equality of treatment of all persons occupied in the territory of a Member State as effectively as possible, it is appropriate to determine as the legislation applicable, as a general rule, that of the Member State in which the person concerned pursues his activity as an employed or self-employed person.

(18) In specific situations which justify other criteria of applicability, it is necessary to derogate from that general rule.

(19) In some cases, maternity and equivalent paternity benefits may be enjoyed by the mother or the father and since, for the latter, these benefits are different from parental benefits and can be assimilated to maternity benefits *strictu sensu* in that they are provided during the first months of a new-born child's life, it is appropriate that maternity and equivalent paternity benefits be regulated jointly.

(20) In the field of sickness, maternity and equivalent paternity benefits, insured persons, as well as the members of their families, living or staying in a Member State other than the competent Member State, should be afforded protection.

(21) Provisions on sickness, maternity and equivalent paternity benefits were drawn up in the light of Court of Justice case-law. Provisions on prior authorisation have been improved, taking into account the relevant decisions of the Court of Justice.

(22) The specific position of pension claimants and pensioners and the members of their families makes it necessary to have provisions governing sickness insurance adapted to this situation.

(23) In view of the differences between the various national systems, it is appropriate that Member States make provision, where possible, for medical treatment for family members of frontier workers in the Member State where the latter pursue their activity.

(24) It is necessary to establish specific provisions regulating the non-overlapping of sickness benefits in kind and sickness benefits in cash which are of the same nature as those which were the subject of the judgments of the Court of Justice in Case C-215/99 *Jauch* and C-160/96 *Molenaar*, provided that those benefits cover the same risk.

(25) In respect of benefits for accidents at work and occupational diseases, rules should be laid down, for the purpose of affording protection, covering the situation of persons residing or staying in a Member State other than the competent Member State.

(26) For invalidity benefits, a system of coordination should be drawn up which respects the specific characteristics of national legislation, in particular as regards recognition of invalidity and aggravation thereof.

(27) It is necessary to devise a system for the award of old-age benefits and survivors' benefits where the person concerned has been subject to the legislation of one or more Member States.

(28) There is a need to determine the amount of a pension calculated in accordance with the method used for aggregation and pro-rata calculation and guaranteed by Community law where the application of national legislation, including rules concerning reduction, suspension or withdrawal, is less favourable than the aforementioned method.

(29) To protect migrant workers and their survivors against excessively stringent application of the national rules concerning reduction, suspension or withdrawal, it is necessary to include provisions strictly governing the application of such rules.

(30) As has constantly been reaffirmed by the Court of Justice, the Council is not deemed competent to enact rules imposing a restriction on the overlapping of two or more pensions acquired in different Member States by a reduction of the amount of a pension acquired solely under national legislation.

(31) According to the Court of Justice, it is for the national legislature to enact such rules, bearing in mind that it is for the Community legislature to fix the limits within which the national provisions concerning reduction, suspension or withdrawal are to be applied.

(32) In order to foster mobility of workers, it is particularly appropriate to facilitate the search for employment in the various Member States; it is therefore necessary to ensure closer and more effective coordination between the unemployment insurance schemes and the employment services of all the Member States.

(33) It is necessary to include statutory pre-retirement schemes within the scope of this Regulation, thus guaranteeing both equal treatment and the possibility of exporting pre-retirement benefits as well as the award of family and health-care benefits to the person concerned, in accordance with the provisions of this Regulation; however, the rule on the aggregation of periods should not be included, as only a very limited number of Member States have statutory pre-retirement schemes.

(34) Since family benefits have a very broad scope, affording protection in situations which could be described as classic as well as in others which are specific in nature, with the latter type of benefit having been the subject of the judgments of the Court of Justice in Joined Cases C-245/94 and C-312/94 *Hoever and Zachow* and in Case C-275/96 *Kuusijärvi*, it is necessary to regulate all such benefits.

(35) In order to avoid unwarranted overlapping of benefits, there is a need to lay down rules of priority in the case of overlapping of rights to family benefits under the legislation of the competent Member State and under the legislation of the Member State of residence of the members of the family.

(36) Advances of maintenance allowances are recoverable advances intended to compensate for a parent's failure to fulfil his legal obligation of maintenance to his own child, which is an obligation derived from family law. Therefore, these advances should not be considered as a direct benefit from collective support in favour of families. Given these particularities, the coordinating rules should not be applied to such maintenance allowances.

(37) As the Court of Justice has repeatedly stated, provisions which derogate from the principle of the exportability of social security benefits must be interpreted strictly. This means that they can apply only to benefits which satisfy the specified conditions. It follows that Chapter 9 of Title III of this Regulation can apply only to benefits which are both special and non-contributory and listed in Annex X to this Regulation.

(38) It is necessary to establish an Administrative Commission consisting of a government representative from each Member State, charged in particular with dealing with all administrative questions or questions of interpretation arising from the provisions of this Regulation, and with promoting further cooperation between the Member States.

(39) The development and use of data-processing services for the exchange of information has been found to require the creation of a Technical Commission, under the aegis of the Administrative Commission, with specific responsibilities in the field of data-processing.

(40) The use of data-processing services for exchanging data between institutions requires provisions guaranteeing that the documents exchanged or issued by electronic means are accepted as equivalent to paper documents. Such exchanges are to be carried out in accordance with the Community provisions on the protection of natural persons with regard to the processing and free movement of personal data.

(41) It is necessary to lay down special provisions which correspond to the special characteristics of national legislation in order to facilitate the application of the rules of coordination.

(42) In line with the principle of proportionality, in accordance with the premise for the extension of this Regulation to all European Union citizens and in order to find a solution that takes account of any constraints which may be connected with the special characteristics of systems based on residence, a special derogation by means of an Annex XI—"DENMARK" entry, limited to social pension entitlement exclusively in respect of the new category of non-active persons, to whom this Regulation has been extended, was deemed appropriate due to the specific features of the Danish system and in the light of the fact that those pensions are exportable after a ten-year period of residence under the Danish legislation in force (Pension Act).

(43) In line with the principle of equality of treatment, a special derogation by means of an Annex XI—"FINLAND" entry, limited to residence-based national pensions, is deemed appropriate due to the specific characteristics of Finnish social security legislation, the objective of which is to ensure that the amount of the national pension cannot be less than the amount of the national pension calculated as if all insurance periods completed in any Member State were completed in Finland.

(44) It is necessary to introduce a new Regulation to repeal Regulation (EEC) No 1408/71. However, it is necessary that Regulation (EEC) No 1408/71 remain in force and continue to have legal effect for the purposes of certain Community acts and agreements to which the Community is a party, in order to secure legal certainty.

(45) Since the objective of the proposed action, namely the coordination measures to guarantee that the right to free movement of persons can be exercised effectively, cannot be sufficiently achieved by the Member States and can therefore, by reason of the scale and effects of that action, be better achieved at Community level, the Community may adopt measures in accordance with the principle of subsidiarity as set out in Article 5 of the Treaty. In accordance with the principle of proportionality as set out in that article, this Regulation does not go beyond what is necessary, in order to achieve that objective,

HAVE ADOPTED THIS REGULATION:

Appendix 5

Title I

General Provisions

Article 1—Definitions

For the purposes of this Regulation:

(a) "activity as an employed person" means any activity or equivalent situation treated as such for the purposes of the social security legislation of the Member State in which such activity or equivalent situation exists;

(b) "activity as a self-employed person" means any activity or equivalent situation treated as such for the purposes of the social security legislation of the Member State in which such activity or equivalent situation exists;

(c) "insured person", in relation to the social security branches covered by Title III, Chapters 1 and 3, means any person satisfying the conditions required under the legislation of the Member State competent under Title II to have the right to benefits, taking into account the provisions of this Regulation;

(d) "civil servant" means a person considered to be such or treated as such by the Member State to which the administration employing him is subject;

(e) "special scheme for civil servants" means any social security scheme which is different from the general social security scheme applicable to employed persons in the Member State concerned and to which all, or certain categories of, civil servants are directly subject;

(f) "frontier worker" means any person pursuing an activity as an employed or self-employed person in a Member State and who resides in another Member State to which he returns as a rule daily or at least once a week;

(g) "refugee" shall have the meaning assigned to it in Article 1 of the Convention relating to the Status of Refugees, signed in Geneva on 28 July 1951;

(h) "stateless person" shall have the meaning assigned to it in Article 1 of the Convention relating to the Status of Stateless Persons, signed in New York on 28 September 1954;

(i) "member of the family" means

   (1) (i) any person defined or recognised as a member of the family or designated as a member of the household by the legislation under which benefits are provided;

   (ii) with regard to benefits in kind pursuant to Title III, Chapter 1 on sickness, maternity and equivalent paternity benefits, any person defined or recognised as a member of the family or designated as a member of the household by the legislation of the Member State in which he resides;

   (2) If the legislation of a Member State which is applicable under sub-paragraph (1) does not make a distinction between the members of the family and other persons to whom it is applicable, the spouse, minor children, and dependent children who have reached the age of majority shall be considered members of the family;

(3) If, under the legislation which is applicable under subparagraphs (1) and (2), a person is considered a member of the family or member of the household only if he lives in the same household as the insured person or pensioner, this condition shall be considered satisfied if the person in question is mainly dependent on the insured person or pensioner;

(j) "residence" means the place where a person habitually resides;

(k) "stay" means temporary residence;

(l) "legislation" means, in respect of each Member State, laws, regulations and other statutory provisions and all other implementing measures relating to the social security branches covered by Article 3(1);

This term excludes contractual provisions other than those which serve to implement an insurance obligation arising from the laws and regulations referred to in the preceding subparagraph or which have been the subject of a decision by the public authorities which makes them obligatory or extends their scope, provided that the Member State concerned makes a declaration to that effect, notified to the President of the European Parliament and the President of the Council of the European Union. Such declaration shall be published in the Official Journal of the European Union;

(m) "competent authority" means, in respect of each Member State, the Minister, Ministers or other equivalent authority responsible for social security schemes throughout or in any part of the Member State in question;

(n) "Administrative Commission" means the commission referred to in Article 71;

(o) "Implementing Regulation" means the Regulation referred to in Article 89;

(p) "institution" means, in respect of each Member State, the body or authority responsible for applying all or part of the legislation;

(q) "competent institution" means:

  (i) the institution with which the person concerned is insured at the time of the application for benefit; or
  (ii) the institution from which the person concerned is or would be entitled to benefits if he or a member or members of his family resided in the Member State in which the institution is situated; or
  (iii) the institution designated by the competent authority of the Member State concerned; or
  (iv) in the case of a scheme relating to an employer's obligations in respect of the benefits set out in Article 3(1), either the employer or the insurer involved or, in default thereof, the body or authority designated by the competent authority of the Member State concerned;

(r) "institution of the place of residence" and "institution of the place of stay" mean respectively the institution which is competent to provide benefits in the place where the person concerned resides and the institution which is competent to provide benefits in the place where the person concerned is staying, in accordance with the legislation administered by that institution or, where no such institution exists, the institution designated by the competent authority of the Member State concerned;

(s) "competent Member State" means the Member State in which the competent institution is situated;

(t) "period of insurance" means periods of contribution, employment or self-employment as defined or recognised as periods of insurance by the legislation under which they were completed or considered as completed, and all periods

Appendix 5

treated as such, where they are regarded by the said legislation as equivalent to periods of insurance;

(u) "period of employment" or "period of self-employment" mean periods so defined or recognised by the legislation under which they were completed, and all periods treated as such, where they are regarded by the said legislation as equivalent to periods of employment or to periods of self-employment;

(v) "period of residence" means periods so defined or recognised by the legislation under which they were completed or considered as completed;

(w) "pension" covers not only pensions but also lump-sum benefits which can be substituted for them and payments in the form of reimbursement of contributions and, subject to the provisions of Title III, revaluation increases or supplementary allowances;

(x) "pre-retirement benefit" means: all cash benefits, other than an unemployment benefit or an early old-age benefit, provided from a specified age to workers who have reduced, ceased or suspended their remunerative activities until the age at which they qualify for an old-age pension or an early retirement pension, the receipt of which is not conditional upon the person concerned being available to the employment services of the competent State; "early old-age benefit" means a benefit provided before the normal pension entitlement age is reached and which either continues to be provided once the said age is reached or is replaced by another old-age benefit;

(y) "death grant" means any one-off payment in the event of death excluding the lump-sum benefits referred to in subparagraph (w);

(z) "family benefit" means all benefits in kind or in cash intended to meet family expenses, excluding advances of maintenance payments and special childbirth and adoption allowances mentioned in Annex I.

Article 2—Persons covered

1. This Regulation shall apply to nationals of a Member State, stateless persons and refugees residing in a Member State who are or have been subject to the legislation of one or more Member States, as well as to the members of their families and to their survivors.

2. It shall also apply to the survivors of persons who have been subject to the legislation of one or more Member States, irrespective of the nationality of such persons, where their survivors are nationals of a Member State or stateless persons or refugees residing in one of the Member States.

Article 3—Matters covered

1. This Regulation shall apply to all legislation concerning the following branches of social security:

(a) sickness benefits;
(b) maternity and equivalent paternity benefits;
(c) invalidity benefits;

(d) old-age benefits;

(e) survivors' benefits;

(f) benefits in respect of accidents at work and occupational diseases;

(g) death grants;

(h) unemployment benefits;

(i) pre-retirement benefits;

(j) family benefits.

2. Unless otherwise provided for in Annex XI, this Regulation shall apply to general and special social security schemes, whether contributory or non-contributory, and to schemes relating to the obligations of an employer or shipowner.

3. This Regulation shall also apply to the special non-contributory cash benefits covered by Article 70.

4. The provisions of Title III of this Regulation shall not, however, affect the legislative provisions of any Member State concerning a shipowner's obligations.

5. This Regulation shall not apply to social and medical assistance or to benefit schemes for victims of war or its consequences.

Article 4—Equality of treatment

Unless otherwise provided for by this Regulation, persons to whom this Regulation applies shall enjoy the same benefits and be subject to the same obligations under the legislation of any Member State as the nationals thereof.

Article 5—Equal treatment of benefits, income, facts or events

Unless otherwise provided for by this Regulation and in the light of the special implementing provisions laid down, the following shall apply:

(a) where, under the legislation of the competent Member State, the receipt of social security benefits and other income has certain legal effects, the relevant provisions of that legislation shall also apply to the receipt of equivalent benefits acquired under the legislation of another Member State or to income acquired in another Member State;

(b) where, under the legislation of the competent Member State, legal effects are attributed to the occurrence of certain facts or events, that Member State shall take account of like facts or events occurring in any Member State as though they had taken place in its own territory.

Article 6—Aggregation of periods

Unless otherwise provided for by this Regulation, the competent institution of a Member State whose legislation makes:

Appendix 5

— the acquisition, retention, duration or recovery of the right to benefits,
— the coverage by legislation, or
— the access to or the exemption from compulsory, optional continued or voluntary insurance,

conditional upon the completion of periods of insurance, employment, self-employment or residence shall, to the extent necessary, take into account periods of insurance, employment, self-employment or residence completed under the legislation of any other Member State as though they were periods completed under the legislation which it applies.

Article 7—Waiving of residence rules

Unless otherwise provided for by this Regulation, cash benefits payable under the legislation of one or more Member States or under this Regulation shall not be subject to any reduction, amendment, suspension, withdrawal or confiscation on account of the fact that the beneficiary or the members of his family reside in a Member State other than that in which the institution responsible for providing benefits is situated.

Article 8—Relations between this Regulation and other coordination instruments

1. This Regulation shall replace any social security convention applicable between Member States falling under its scope. Certain provisions of social security conventions entered into by the Member States before the date of application of this Regulation shall, however, continue to apply provided that they are more favourable to the beneficiaries or if they arise from specific historical circumstances and their effect is limited in time. For these provisions to remain applicable, they shall be included in Annex II. If, on objective grounds, it is not possible to extend some of these provisions to all persons to whom the Regulation applies this shall be specified.

2. Two or more Member States may, as the need arises, conclude conventions with each other based on the principles of this Regulation and in keeping with the spirit thereof.

Article 9—Declarations by the Member States on the scope of this Regulation

1. The Member States shall notify the Commission of the European Communities in writing of the declarations referred to in Article 1(l), the legislation and schemes referred to in Article 3, the conventions entered into as referred to in Article 8(2) and the minimum benefits referred to in Article 58, as well as substantive amendments made subsequently. Such notifications shall indicate the date of entry into force of the laws and schemes in question or, in the case of the declarations provided for in Article 1(l), the date from which this Regulation will apply to the schemes specified in the declarations by the Member States.

2. These notifications shall be submitted to the Commission of the European Communities every year and published in the Official Journal of the European Union.

REGULATION (EC) No 883/2004

Article 10—Prevention of overlapping of benefits

Unless otherwise specified, this Regulation shall neither confer nor maintain the right to several benefits of the same kind for one and the same period of compulsory insurance.

TITLE II

DETERMINATION OF THE LEGISLATION APPLICABLE

Article 11—General rules

1. Persons to whom this Regulation applies shall be subject to the legislation of a single Member State only. Such legislation shall be determined in accordance with this Title.

2. For the purposes of this Title, persons receiving cash benefits because or as a consequence of their activity as an employed or self-employed person shall be considered to be pursuing the said activity. This shall not apply to invalidity, old-age or survivors' pensions or to pensions in respect of accidents at work or occupational diseases or to sickness benefits in cash covering treatment for an unlimited period.

3. Subject to Articles 12 to 16:

(a) a person pursuing an activity as an employed or self-employed person in a Member State shall be subject to the legislation of that Member State;

(b) a civil servant shall be subject to the legislation of the Member State to which the administration employing him is subject;

(c) a person receiving unemployment benefits in accordance with Article 65 under the legislation of the Member State of residence shall be subject to the legislation of that Member State;

(d) a person called up or recalled for service in the armed forces or for civilian service in a Member State shall be subject to the legislation of that Member State;

(e) any other person to whom subparagraphs (a) to (d) do not apply shall be subject to the legislation of the Member State of residence, without prejudice to other provisions of this Regulation guaranteeing him benefits under the legislation of one or more other Member States.

4. For the purposes of this Title, an activity as an employed or self-employed person normally pursued on board a vessel at sea flying the flag of a Member State shall be deemed to be an activity pursued in the said Member State. However, a person employed on board a vessel flying the flag of a Member State and remunerated for such activity by an undertaking or a person whose registered office or place of business is in another Member State shall be subject to the legislation of the latter Member State if he resides in that State. The undertaking or person paying the remuneration shall be considered as the employer for the purposes of the said legislation.

Appendix 5

Article 12—Special rules

1. A person who pursues an activity as an employed person in a Member State on behalf of an employer which normally carries out its activities there and who is posted by that employer to another Member State to perform work on that employer's behalf shall continue to be subject to the legislation of the first Member State, provided that the anticipated duration of such work does not exceed twenty-four months and that he is not sent to replace another person.

2. A person who normally pursues an activity as a self-employed person in a Member State who goes to pursue a similar activity in another Member State shall continue to be subject to the legislation of the first Member State, provided that the anticipated duration of such activity does not exceed twenty-four months.

Article 13—Pursuit of activities in two or more Member States

1. A person who normally pursues an activity as an employed person in two or more Member States shall be subject to:

(a) the legislation of the Member State of residence if he pursues a substantial part of his activity in that Member State or if he is employed by various undertakings or various employers whose registered office or place of business is in different Member States, or

(b) the legislation of the Member State in which the registered office or place of business of the undertaking or employer employing him is situated, if he does not pursue a substantial part of his activities in the Member State of residence.

2. A person who normally pursues an activity as a self-employed person in two or more Member States shall be subject to:

(a) the legislation of the Member State of residence if he pursues a substantial part of his activity in that Member State; or

(b) the legislation of the Member State in which the centre of interest of his activities is situated, if he does not reside in one of the Member States in which he pursues a substantial part of his activity.

3. A person who normally pursues an activity as an employed person and an activity as a self-employed person in different Member States shall be subject to the legislation of the Member State in which he pursues an activity as an employed person or, if he pursues such an activity in two or more Member States, to the legislation determined in accordance with paragraph 1.

4. A person who is employed as a civil servant by one Member State and who pursues an activity as an employed person and/or as a self-employed person in one or more other Member States shall be subject to the legislation of the Member State to which the administration employing him is subject.

5. Persons referred to in paragraphs 1 to 4 shall be treated, for the purposes of the legislation determined in accordance with these provisions, as though they were pursuing all their activities as employed or self-employed persons and were receiving all their income in the Member State concerned.

Regulation (EC) No 883/2004

Article 14—Voluntary insurance or optional continued insurance

1. Articles 11 to 13 shall not apply to voluntary insurance or to optional continued insurance unless, in respect of one of the branches referred to in Article 3(1), only a voluntary scheme of insurance exists in a Member State.

2. Where, by virtue of the legislation of a Member State, the person concerned is subject to compulsory insurance in that Member State, he may not be subject to a voluntary insurance scheme or an optional continued insurance scheme in another Member State. In all other cases in which, for a given branch, there is a choice between several voluntary insurance schemes or optional continued insurance schemes, the person concerned shall join only the scheme of his choice.

3. However, in respect of invalidity, old age and survivors' benefits, the person concerned may join the voluntary or optional continued insurance scheme of a Member State, even if he is compulsorily subject to the legislation of another Member State, provided that he has been subject, at some stage in his career, to the legislation of the first Member State because or as a consequence of an activity as an employed or self-employed person and if such overlapping is explicitly or implicitly allowed under the legislation of the first Member State.

4. If the legislation of any Member State makes admission to voluntary insurance or optional continued insurance conditional upon residence in that Member State, the equal treatment of residence in another Member State as provided under Article 5(b) shall apply only to persons who have been subject, at some earlier stage, to the legislation of the first Member State on the basis of an activity as an employed or self-employed person.

Article 15—Auxiliary staff of the European Communities

Auxiliary staff of the European Communities may opt to be subject to the legislation of the Member State in which they are employed, to the legislation of the Member State to which they were last subject or to the legislation of the Member State whose nationals they are, in respect of provisions other than those relating to family allowances, provided under the scheme applicable to such staff. This right of option, which may be exercised once only, shall take effect from the date of entry into employment.

Article 16—Exceptions to Articles 11 to 15

1. Two or more Member States, the competent authorities of these Member States or the bodies designated by these authorities may by common agreement provide for exceptions to Articles 11 to 15 in the interest of certain persons or categories of persons.

2. A person who receives a pension or pensions under the legislation of one or more Member States and who resides in another Member State may at his request be exempted from application of the legislation of the latter State provided that he is not subject to that legislation on account of pursuing an activity as an employed or self-employed person.

Appendix 5

Title III

Special Provisions Concerning the Various Categories of Benefits

Chapter 1

Sickness, Maternity and Equivalent Paternity Benefits

Section 1

Insured Persons and Members of Their Families, Except Pensioners and Members of Their Families

Article 17—Residence in a Member State other than the competent Member State

An insured person or members of his family who reside in a Member State other than the competent Member State shall receive in the Member State of residence benefits in kind provided, on behalf of the competent institution, by the institution of the place of residence, in accordance with the provisions of the legislation it applies, as though they were insured under the said legislation.

Article 18—Stay in the competent Member State when residence is in another Member State—Special rules for the members of the families of frontier workers

1. Unless otherwise provided for by paragraph 2, the insured person and the members of his family referred to in Article 17 shall also be entitled to benefits in kind while staying in the competent Member State. The benefits in kind shall be provided by the competent institution and at its own expense, in accordance with the provisions of the legislation it applies, as though the persons concerned resided in that Member State.

2. The members of the family of a frontier worker shall be entitled to benefits in kind during their stay in the competent Member State, unless this Member State is listed in Annex III. In this event, the members of the family of a frontier worker shall be entitled to benefits in kind in the competent Member State under the conditions laid down in Article 19(1).

Article 19—Stay outside the competent Member State

1. Unless otherwise provided for by paragraph 2, an insured person and the members of his family staying in a Member State other than the competent Member State shall be entitled to the benefits in kind which become necessary on medical grounds during their stay, taking into account the nature of the benefits and the expected length of the stay. These benefits shall be provided on behalf of the competent institution by the institution of the place of stay, in accordance with the provisions of the

legislation it applies, as though the persons concerned were insured under the said legislation.

2. The Administrative Commission shall establish a list of benefits in kind which, in order to be provided during a stay in another Member State, require for practical reasons a prior agreement between the person concerned and the institution providing the care.

Article 20—Travel with the purpose of receiving benefits in kind—Authorisation to receive appropriate treatment outside the Member State of residence

1. Unless otherwise provided for by this Regulation, an insured person travelling to another Member State with the purpose of receiving benefits in kind during the stay shall seek authorisation from the competent institution.

2. An insured person who is authorised by the competent institution to go to another Member State with the purpose of receiving the treatment appropriate to his condition shall receive the benefits in kind provided, on behalf of the competent institution, by the institution of the place of stay, in accordance with the provisions of the legislation it applies, as though he were insured under the said legislation. The authorisation shall be accorded where the treatment in question is among the benefits provided for by the legislation in the Member State where the person concerned resides and where he cannot be given such treatment within a time-limit which is medically justifiable, taking into account his current state of health and the probable course of his illness.

3. Paragraphs 1 and 2 shall apply mutatis mutandis to the members of the family of an insured person.

4. If the members of the family of an insured person reside in a Member State other than the Member State in which the insured person resides, and this Member State has opted for reimbursement on the basis of fixed amounts, the cost of the benefits in kind referred to in paragraph 2 shall be borne by the institution of the place of residence of the members of the family. In this case, for the purposes of paragraph 1, the institution of the place of residence of the members of the family shall be considered to be the competent institution.

Article 21—Cash benefits

1. An insured person and members of his family residing or staying in a Member State other than the competent Member State shall be entitled to cash benefits provided by the competent institution in accordance with the legislation it applies. By agreement between the competent institution and the institution of the place of residence or stay, such benefits may, however, be provided by the institution of the place of residence or stay at the expense of the competent institution in accordance with the legislation of the competent Member State.

2. The competent institution of a Member State whose legislation stipulates that the calculation of cash benefits shall be based on average income or on an average contribution basis shall determine such average income or average contribution basis exclusively by reference to the incomes confirmed as having been paid, or contribution bases applied, during the periods completed under the said legislation.

Appendix 5

3. The competent institution of a Member State whose legislation provides that the calculation of cash benefits shall be based on standard income shall take into account exclusively the standard income or, where appropriate, the average of standard incomes for the periods completed under the said legislation.

4. Paragraphs 2 and 3 shall apply mutatis mutandis to cases where the legislation applied by the competent institution lays down a specific reference period which corresponds in the case in question either wholly or partly to the periods which the person concerned has completed under the legislation of one or more other Member States.

Article 22—Pension claimants

1. An insured person who, on making a claim for a pension, or during the investigation thereof, ceases to be entitled to benefits in kind under the legislation of the Member State last competent, shall remain entitled to benefits in kind under the legislation of the Member State in which he resides, provided that the pension claimant satisfies the insurance conditions of the legislation of the Member State referred to in paragraph 2. The right to benefits in kind in the Member State of residence shall also apply to the members of the family of the pension claimant.

2. The benefits in kind shall be chargeable to the institution of the Member State which, in the event of a pension being awarded, would become competent under Articles 23 to 25.

Section 2

Pensioners and Members of Their Families

Article 23—Right to benefits in kind under the legislation of the Member State of residence

A person who receives a pension or pensions under the legislation of two or more Member States, of which one is the Member State of residence, and who is entitled to benefits in kind under the legislation of that Member State, shall, with the members of his family, receive such benefits in kind from and at the expense of the institution of the place of residence, as though he were a pensioner whose pension was payable solely under the legislation of that Member State.

Article 24—No right to benefits in kind under the legislation of the Member State of residence

1. A person who receives a pension or pensions under the legislation of one or more Member States and who is not entitled to benefits in kind under the legislation of the Member State of residence shall nevertheless receive such benefits for himself and the members of his family, insofar as he would be entitled thereto under the legislation of the Member State or of at least one of the Member States competent in respect of his pensions, if he resided in that Member State. The benefits in kind shall be provided at

the expense of the institution referred to in paragraph 2 by the institution of the place of residence, as though the person concerned were entitled to a pension and benefits in kind under the legislation of that Member State.

2. In the cases covered by paragraph 1, the cost of benefits in kind shall be borne by the institution as determined in accordance with the following rules:

(a) where the pensioner is entitled to benefits in kind under the legislation of a single Member State, the cost shall be borne by the competent institution of that Member State;

(b) where the pensioner is entitled to benefits in kind under the legislation of two or more Member States, the cost thereof shall be borne by the competent institution of the Member State to whose legislation the person has been subject for the longest period of time; should the application of this rule result in several institutions being responsible for the cost of benefits, the cost shall be borne by the institution applying the legislation to which the pensioner was last subject.

Article 25—Pensions under the legislation of one or more Member States other than the Member State of residence, where there is a right to benefits in kind in the latter Member State

Where the person receiving a pension or pensions under the legislation of one or more Member States resides in a Member State under whose legislation the right to receive benefits in kind is not subject to conditions of insurance, or of activity as an employed or self-employed person, and no pension is received from that Member State, the cost of benefits in kind provided to him and to members of his family shall be borne by the institution of one of the Member States competent in respect of his pensions determined in accordance with Article 24(2), to the extent that the pensioner and the members of his family would be entitled to such benefits if they resided in that Member State.

Article 26—Residence of members of the family in a Member State other than the one in which the pensioner resides

Members of the family of a person receiving a pension or pensions under the legislation of one or more Member States who reside in a Member State other than the one in which the pensioner resides shall be entitled to receive benefits in kind from the institution of the place of their residence in accordance with the provisions of the legislation it applies, insofar as the pensioner is entitled to benefits in kind under the legislation of a Member State. The costs shall be borne by the competent institution responsible for the costs of the benefits in kind provided to the pensioner in his Member State of residence.

APPENDIX 5

Article 27—Stay of the pensioner or the members of his family in a Member State other than the Member State in which they reside—Stay in the competent Member State— Authorisation for appropriate treatment outside the Member State of residence

1. Article 19 shall apply mutatis mutandis to a person receiving a pension or pensions under the legislation of one or more Member States and entitled to benefits in kind under the legislation of one of the Member States which provide his pension(s) or to the members of his family who are staying in a Member State other than the one in which they reside.

2. Article 18(1) shall apply mutatis mutandis to the persons described in paragraph 1 when they stay in the Member State in which is situated the competent institution responsible for the cost of the benefits in kind provided to the pensioner in his Member State of residence and the said Member State has opted for this and is listed in Annex IV.

3. Article 20 shall apply mutatis mutandis to a pensioner and/or the members of his family who are staying in a Member State other than the one in which they reside with the purpose of receiving there the treatment appropriate to their condition.

4. Unless otherwise provided for by paragraph 5, the cost of the benefits in kind referred to in paragraphs 1 to 3 shall be borne by the competent institution responsible for the cost of benefits in kind provided to the pensioner in his Member State of residence.

5. The cost of the benefits in kind referred to in paragraph 3 shall be borne by the institution of the place of residence of the pensioner or of the members of his family, if these persons reside in a Member State which has opted for reimbursement on the basis of fixed amounts. In these cases, for the purposes of paragraph 3, the institution of the place of residence of the pensioner or of the members of his family shall be considered to be the competent institution.

Article 28—Special rules for retired frontier workers

1. A frontier worker who retires is entitled in case of sickness to continue to receive benefits in kind in the Member State where he last pursued his activity as an employed or self-employed person, insofar as this is a continuation of treatment which began in that Member State. The term "continuation of treatment" means the continued investigation, diagnosis and treatment of an illness.

2. A pensioner who, in the five years preceding the effective date of an old-age or invalidity pension has been pursuing an activity as an employed or self-employed person for at least two years as a frontier worker shall be entitled to benefits in kind in the Member State in which he pursued such an activity as a frontier worker, if this Member State and the Member State in which the competent institution responsible for the costs of the benefits in kind provided to the pensioner in his Member State of residence is situated have opted for this and are both listed in Annex V.

3. Paragraph 2 shall apply mutatis mutandis to the members of the family of a former frontier worker or his survivors if, during the periods referred to in paragraph 2, they were entitled to benefits in kind under Article 18(2), even if the frontier worker died before his pension commenced, provided he had been pursuing an

activity as an employed or self-employed person as a frontier worker for at least two years in the five years preceding his death.

4. Paragraphs 2 and 3 shall be applicable until the person concerned becomes subject to the legislation of a Member State on the basis of an activity as an employed or self-employed person.

5. The cost of the benefits in kind referred to in paragraphs 1 to 3 shall be borne by the competent institution responsible for the cost of benefits in kind provided to the pensioner or to his survivors in their respective Member States of residence.

Article 29—Cash benefits for pensioners

1. Cash benefits shall be paid to a person receiving a pension or pensions under the legislation of one or more Member States by the competent institution of the Member State in which is situated the competent institution responsible for the cost of benefits in kind provided to the pensioner in his Member State of residence. Article 21 shall apply mutatis mutandis.

2. Paragraph 1 shall also apply to the members of a pensioner's family.

Article 30—Contributions by pensioners

1. The institution of a Member State which is responsible under the legislation it applies for making deductions in respect of contributions for sickness, maternity and equivalent paternity benefits, may request and recover such deductions, calculated in accordance with the legislation it applies, only to the extent that the cost of the benefits under Articles 23 to 26 is to be borne by an institution of the said Member State.

2. Where, in the cases referred to in Article 25, the acquisition of sickness, maternity and equivalent paternity benefits is subject to the payment of contributions or similar payments under the legislation of a Member State in which the pensioner concerned resides, these contributions shall not be payable by virtue of such residence.

SECTION 3

COMMON PROVISIONS

Article 31—General provision

Articles 23 to 30 shall not apply to a pensioner or the members of his family who are entitled to benefits under the legislation of a Member State on the basis of an activity as an employed or self-employed person. In such a case, the person concerned shall be subject, for the purposes of this Chapter, to Articles 17 to 21.

Appendix 5

Article 32—Prioritising of the right to benefits in kind – Special rule for the right of members of the family to benefits in the Member State of residence

1. An independent right to benefits in kind based on the legislation of a Member State or on this Chapter shall take priority over a derivative right to benefits for members of a family. A derivative right to benefits in kind shall, however, take priority over independent rights, where the independent right in the Member State of residence exists directly and solely on the basis of the residence of the person concerned in that Member State.

2. Where the members of the family of an insured person reside in a Member State under whose legislation the right to benefits in kind is not subject to conditions of insurance or activity as an employed or self-employed person, benefits in kind shall be provided at the expense of the competent institution in the Member State in which they reside, if the spouse or the person caring for the children of the insured person pursues an activity as an employed or self-employed person in the said Member State or receives a pension from that Member State on the basis of an activity as an employed or self-employed person.

Article 33—Substantial benefits in kind

1. An insured person or a member of his family who has had a right to a prosthesis, a major appliance or other substantial benefits in kind recognised by the institution of a Member State, before he became insured under the legislation applied by the institution of another Member State, shall receive such benefits at the expense of the first institution, even if they are awarded after the said person has already become insured under the legislation applied by the second institution.

2. The Administrative Commission shall draw up the list of benefits covered by paragraph 1.

Article 34—Overlapping of long-term care benefits

1. If a recipient of long-term care benefits in cash, which have to be treated as sickness benefits and are therefore provided by the Member State competent for cash benefits under Articles 21 or 29, is, at the same time and under this Chapter, entitled to claim benefits in kind intended for the same purpose from the institution of the place of residence or stay in another Member State, and an institution in the first Member State is also required to reimburse the cost of these benefits in kind under Article 35, the general provision on prevention of overlapping of benefits laid down in Article 10 shall be applicable, with the following restriction only: if the person concerned claims and receives the benefit in kind, the amount of the benefit in cash shall be reduced by the amount of the benefit in kind which is or could be claimed from the institution of the first Member State required to reimburse the cost.

2. The Administrative Commission shall draw up the list of the cash benefits and benefits in kind covered by paragraph 1.

3. Two or more Member States, or their competent authorities, may agree on other or supplementary measures which shall not be less advantageous for the persons concerned than the principles laid down in paragraph 1.

REGULATION (EC) No 883/2004

Article 35—Reimbursements between institutions

1. The benefits in kind provided by the institution of a Member State on behalf of the institution of another Member State under this Chapter shall give rise to full reimbursement.

2. The reimbursements referred to in paragraph 1 shall be determined and effected in accordance with the arrangements set out in the Implementing Regulation, either on production of proof of actual expenditure, or on the basis of fixed amounts for Member States the legal or administrative structures of which are such that the use of reimbursement on the basis of actual expenditure is not appropriate.

3. Two or more Member States, and their competent authorities, may provide for other methods of reimbursement or waive all reimbursement between the institutions coming under their jurisdiction.

CHAPTER 2

BENEFITS IN RESPECT OF ACCIDENTS AT WORK AND OCCUPATIONAL DISEASES

Article 36—Right to benefits in kind and in cash

1. Without prejudice to any more favourable provisions in paragraph 2 of this Article, Articles 17, 18(1), 19(1) and 20(1) shall also apply to benefits relating to accidents at work or occupational diseases.

2. A person who has sustained an accident at work or has contracted an occupational disease and who resides or stays in a Member State other than the competent Member State shall be entitled to the special benefits in kind of the scheme covering accidents at work and occupational diseases provided, on behalf of the competent institution, by the institution of the place of residence or stay in accordance with the legislation which it applies, as though he were insured under the said legislation.

3. Article 21 shall also apply to benefits falling within this Chapter.

Article 37—Costs of transport

1. The competent institution of a Member State whose legislation provides for meeting the costs of transporting a person who has sustained an accident at work or is suffering from an occupational disease, either to his place of residence or to a hospital, shall meet such costs to the corresponding place in another Member State where the person resides, provided that that institution gives prior authorisation for such transport, duly taking into account the reasons justifying it. Such authorisation shall not be required in the case of a frontier worker.

2. The competent institution of a Member State whose legislation provides for meeting the costs of transporting the body of a person killed in an accident at work to the place of burial shall, in accordance with the legislation it applies, meet such

costs to the corresponding place in another Member State where the person was residing at the time of the accident.

Article 38—Benefits for an occupational disease where the person suffering from such a disease has been exposed to the same risk in several Member States

When a person who has contracted an occupational disease has, under the legislation of two or more Member States, pursued an activity which by its nature is likely to cause the said disease, the benefits that he or his survivors may claim shall be provided exclusively under the legislation of the last of those States whose conditions are satisfied.

Article 39—Aggravation of an occupational disease

In the event of aggravation of an occupational disease for which a person suffering from such a disease has received or is receiving benefits under the legislation of a Member State, the following rules shall apply:

(a) if the person concerned, while in receipt of benefits, has not pursued, under the legislation of another Member State, an activity as an employed or self-employed person likely to cause or aggravate the disease in question, the competent institution of the first Member State shall bear the cost of the benefits under the provisions of the legislation which it applies, taking into account the aggravation;

(b) if the person concerned, while in receipt of benefits, has pursued such an activity under the legislation of another Member State, the competent institution of the first Member State shall bear the cost of the benefits under the legislation it applies without taking the aggravation into account. The competent institution of the second Member State shall grant a supplement to the person concerned, the amount of which shall be equal to the difference between the amount of benefits due after the aggravation and the amount which would have been due prior to the aggravation under the legislation it applies, if the disease in question had occurred under the legislation of that Member State;

(c) the rules concerning reduction, suspension or withdrawal laid down by the legislation of a Member State shall not be invoked against persons receiving benefits provided by institutions of two Member States in accordance with subparagraph (b).

Article 40—Rules for taking into account the special features of certain legislation

1. If there is no insurance against accidents at work or occupational diseases in the Member State in which the person concerned resides or stays, or if such insurance exists but there is no institution responsible for providing benefits in kind, those benefits shall be provided by the institution of the place of residence or stay responsible for providing benefits in kind in the event of sickness.

2. If there is no insurance against accidents at work or occupational diseases in the competent Member State, the provisions of this Chapter concerning benefits in kind shall nevertheless be applied to a person who is entitled to those benefits in the event

of sickness, maternity or equivalent paternity under the legislation of that Member State if that person sustains an accident at work or suffers from an occupational disease during a residence or stay in another Member State. Costs shall be borne by the institution which is competent for the benefits in kind under the legislation of the competent Member State.

3. Article 5 shall apply to the competent institution in a Member State as regards the equivalence of accidents at work and occupational diseases which either have occurred or have been confirmed subsequently under the legislation of another Member State when assessing the degree of incapacity, the right to benefits or the amount thereof, on condition that:

(a) no compensation is due in respect of an accident at work or an occupational disease which had occurred or had been confirmed previously under the legislation it applies; and

(b) no compensation is due in respect of an accident at work or an occupational disease which had occurred or had been confirmed subsequently, under the legislation of the other Member State under which the accident at work or the occupational disease had occurred or been confirmed.

Article 41—Reimbursements between institutions

1. Article 35 shall also apply to benefits falling within this Chapter, and reimbursement shall be made on the basis of actual costs.

2. Two or more Member States, or their competent authorities, may provide for other methods of reimbursement or waive all reimbursement between the institutions under their jurisdiction.

CHAPTER 3

DEATH GRANTS

Article 42—Right to grants where death occurs in, or where the person entitled resides in, a Member State other than the competent Member State

1. When an insured person or a member of his family dies in a Member State other than the competent Member State, the death shall be deemed to have occurred in the competent Member State.

2. The competent institution shall be obliged to provide death grants payable under the legislation it applies, even if the person entitled resides in a Member State other than the competent Member State.

3. Paragraphs 1 and 2 shall also apply when the death is the result of an accident at work or an occupational disease.

APPENDIX 5

Article 43—Provision of benefits in the event of the death of a pensioner

1. In the event of the death of a pensioner who was entitled to a pension under the legislation of one Member State, or to pensions under the legislations of two or more Member States, when that pensioner was residing in a Member State other than that of the institution responsible for the cost of benefits in kind provided under Articles 24 and 25, the death grants payable under the legislation administered by that institution shall be provided at its own expense as though the pensioner had been residing at the time of his death in the Member State in which that institution is situated.

2. Paragraph 1 shall apply mutatis mutandis to the members of the family of a pensioner.

CHAPTER 4

INVALIDITY BENEFITS

Article 44—Persons subject only to type A legislation

1. For the purposes of this Chapter, "type A legislation" means any legislation under which the amount of invalidity benefits is independent of the duration of the periods of insurance or residence and which is expressly included by the competent Member State in Annex VI, and "type B legislation" means any other legislation.

2. A person who has been successively or alternately subject to the legislation of two or more Member States and who has completed periods of insurance or residence exclusively under type A legislations shall be entitled to benefits only from the institution of the Member State whose legislation was applicable at the time when the incapacity for work followed by invalidity occurred, taking into account, where appropriate, Article 45, and shall receive such benefits in accordance with that legislation.

3. A person who is not entitled to benefits under paragraph 2 shall receive the benefits to which he is still entitled under the legislation of another Member State, taking into account, where appropriate, Article 45.

4. If the legislation referred to in paragraph 2 or 3 contains rules for the reduction, suspension or withdrawal of invalidity benefits in the case of overlapping with other income or with benefits of a different kind within the meaning of Article 53(2), Articles 53(3) and 55(3) shall apply mutatis mutandis.

Article 45—Special provisions on aggregation of periods

The competent institution of a Member State whose legislation makes the acquisition, retention or recovery of the right to benefits conditional upon the completion of periods of insurance or residence shall, where necessary, apply Article 51(1) mutatis mutandis.

Regulation (EC) No 883/2004

Article 46—Persons subject either only to type B legislation or to type A and B legislation

1. A person who has been successively or alternately subject to the legislation of two or more Member States, of which at least one is not a type A legislation, shall be entitled to benefits under Chapter 5, which shall apply mutatis mutandis taking into account paragraph 3.

2. However, if the person concerned has been previously subject to a type B legislation and suffers incapacity for work leading to invalidity while subject to a type A legislation, he shall receive benefits in accordance with Article 44, provided that:

— he satisfies the conditions of that legislation exclusively or of others of the same type, taking into account, where appropriate, Article 45, but without having recourse to periods of insurance or residence completed under a type B legislation, and

— he does not assert any claims to old-age benefits, taking into account Article 50(1).

3. A decision taken by an institution of a Member State concerning the degree of invalidity of a claimant shall be binding on the institution of any other Member State concerned, provided that the concordance between the legislation of these Member States on conditions relating to the degree of invalidity is acknowledged in Annex VII.

Article 47—Aggravation of invalidity

1. In the case of aggravation of an invalidity for which a person is receiving benefits under the legislation of one or more Member States, the following provisions shall apply, taking the aggravation into account:

(a) the benefits shall be provided in accordance with Chapter 5, applied mutatis mutandis;

(b) however, where the person concerned has been subject to two or more type A legislations and since receiving benefit has not been subject to the legislation of another Member State, the benefit shall be provided in accordance with Article 44(2).

2. If the total amount of the benefit or benefits payable under paragraph 1 is lower than the amount of the benefit which the person concerned was receiving at the expense of the institution previously competent for payment, that institution shall pay him a supplement equal to the difference between the two amounts.

3. If the person concerned is not entitled to benefits at the expense of an institution of another Member State, the competent institution of the Member State previously competent shall provide the benefits in accordance with the legislation it applies, taking into account the aggravation and, where appropriate, Article 45.

APPENDIX 5

Article 48—Conversion of invalidity benefits into old-age benefits

1. Invalidity benefits shall be converted into old-age benefits, where appropriate, under the conditions laid down by the legislation or legislations under which they are provided and in accordance with Chapter 5.

2. Where a person receiving invalidity benefits can establish a claim to old-age benefits under the legislation of one or more other Member States, in accordance with Article 50, any institution which is responsible for providing invalidity benefits under the legislation of a Member State shall continue to provide such a person with the invalidity benefits to which he is entitled under the legislation it applies until paragraph 1 becomes applicable in respect of that institution, or otherwise for as long as the person concerned satisfies the conditions for such benefits.

3. Where invalidity benefits provided under the legislation of a Member State, in accordance with Article 44, are converted into old-age benefits and where the person concerned does not yet satisfy the conditions laid down by the legislation of one or more of the other Member States for receiving those benefits, the person concerned shall receive, from that or those Member States, invalidity benefits from the date of the conversion.

Those invalidity benefits shall be provided in accordance with Chapter 5 as if that Chapter had been applicable at the time when the incapacity for work leading to invalidity occurred, until the person concerned satisfies the qualifying conditions for old-age benefit laid down by the national legislations concerned or, where such conversion is not provided for, for as long as he is entitled to invalidity benefits under the latter legislation or legislations.

4. The invalidity benefits provided under Article 44 shall be recalculated in accordance with Chapter 5 as soon as the beneficiary satisfies the qualifying conditions for invalidity benefits laid down by a type B legislation, or as soon as he receives old-age benefits under the legislation of another Member State.

Article 49—Special provisions for civil servants

Articles 6, 44, 46, 47 and 48 and Article 60(2) and (3) shall apply mutatis mutandis to persons covered by a special scheme for civil servants.

CHAPTER 5

OLD-AGE AND SURVIVORS' PENSIONS

Article 50—General provisions

1. All the competent institutions shall determine entitlement to benefit, under all the legislations of the Member States to which the person concerned has been subject, when a request for award has been submitted, unless the person concerned expressly requests deferment of the award of old-age benefits under the legislation of one or more Member States.

2. If at a given moment the person concerned does not satisfy, or no longer satisfies, the conditions laid down by all the legislations of the Member States to which he has been subject, the institutions applying legislation the conditions of which have been satisfied shall not take into account, when performing the calculation in accordance with Article 52(1) (a) or (b), the periods completed under the legislations the conditions of which have not been satisfied, or are no longer satisfied, where this gives rise to a lower amount of benefit.

3. Paragraph 2 shall apply mutatis mutandis when the person concerned has expressly requested deferment of the award of old-age benefits.

4. A new calculation shall be performed automatically as and when the conditions to be fulfilled under the other legislations are satisfied or when a person requests the award of an old-age benefit deferred in accordance with paragraph 1, unless the periods completed under the other legislations have already been taken into account by virtue of paragraph 2 or 3.

Article 51—Special provisions on aggregation of periods

1. Where the legislation of a Member State makes the granting of certain benefits conditional upon the periods of insurance having been completed only in a specific activity as an employed or self-employed person or in an occupation which is subject to a special scheme for employed or self-employed persons, the competent institution of that Member State shall take into account periods completed under the legislation of other Member States only if completed under a corresponding scheme or, failing that, in the same occupation, or where appropriate, in the same activity as an employed or self-employed person. If, account having been taken of the periods thus completed, the person concerned does not satisfy the conditions for receipt of the benefits of a special scheme, these periods shall be taken into account for the purposes of providing the benefits of the general scheme or, failing that, of the scheme applicable to manual or clerical workers, as the case may be, provided that the person concerned had been affiliated to one or other of those schemes.

2. The periods of insurance completed under a special scheme of a Member State shall be taken into account for the purposes of providing the benefits of the general scheme or, failing that, of the scheme applicable to manual or clerical workers, as the case may be, of another Member State, provided that the person concerned had been affiliated to one or other of those schemes, even if those periods have already been taken into account in the latter Member State under a special scheme.

3. Where the legislation of a Member State makes the acquisition, retention or recovery of the right to benefits conditional upon the person concerned being insured at the time of the materialisation of the risk, this condition shall be regarded as having been satisfied in the case of insurance under the legislation of another Member State, in accordance with the procedures provided for in Annex XI for each Member State concerned.

Article 52—Award of benefits

1. The competent institution shall calculate the amount of the benefit that would be due:

(a) under the legislation it applies, only where the conditions for entitlement to benefits have been satisfied exclusively under national law (independent benefit);

(b) by calculating a theoretical amount and subsequently an actual amount (pro-rata benefit), as follows:

  (i) the theoretical amount of the benefit is equal to the benefit which the person concerned could claim if all the periods of insurance and/or of residence which have been completed under the legislations of the other Member States had been completed under the legislation it applies on the date of the award of the benefit. If, under this legislation, the amount does not depend on the duration of the periods completed, that amount shall be regarded as being the theoretical amount;

  (ii) the competent institution shall then establish the actual amount of the pro-rata benefit by applying to the theoretical amount the ratio between the duration of the periods completed before materialisation of the risk under the legislation it applies and the total duration of the periods completed before materialisation of the risk under the legislations of all the Member States concerned.

2. Where appropriate, the competent institution shall apply, to the amount calculated in accordance with subparagraphs 1(a) and (b), all the rules relating to reduction, suspension or withdrawal, under the legislation it applies, within the limits provided for by Articles 53 to 55.

3. The person concerned shall be entitled to receive from the competent institution of each Member State the higher of the amounts calculated in accordance with sub-paragraphs 1(a) and (b).

4. Where the calculation pursuant to subparagraph 1(a) in one Member State invariably results in the independent benefit being equal to or higher than the pro-rata benefit, calculated in accordance with subparagraph 1(b), the competent institution may waive the pro-rata calculation, under the conditions provided for in the Implementing Regulation. Such situations are set out in Annex VIII.

Article 53—Rules to prevent overlapping

1. Any overlapping of invalidity, old-age and survivors' benefits calculated or provided on the basis of periods of insurance and/or residence completed by the same person shall be considered to be overlapping of benefits of the same kind.

2. Overlapping of benefits which cannot be considered to be of the same kind within the meaning of paragraph 1 shall be considered to be overlapping of benefits of a different kind.

3. The following provisions shall be applicable for the purposes of rules to prevent overlapping laid down by the legislation of a Member State in the case of overlapping of a benefit in respect of invalidity, old age or survivors with a benefit of the same kind or a benefit of a different kind or with other income:

(a) the competent institution shall take into account the benefits or incomes acquired in another Member State only where the legislation it applies provides for benefits or income acquired abroad to be taken into account;

(b) the competent institution shall take into account the amount of benefits to be paid by another Member State before deduction of tax, social security contributions and other individual levies or deductions, unless the legislation it applies provides for the application of rules to prevent overlapping after such deductions, under the conditions and the procedures laid down in the Implementing Regulation;

(c) the competent institution shall not take into account the amount of benefits acquired under the legislation of another Member State on the basis of voluntary insurance or continued optional insurance;

(d) if a single Member State applies rules to prevent overlapping because the person concerned receives benefits of the same or of a different kind under the legislation of other Member States or income acquired in other Member States, the benefit due may be reduced solely by the amount of such benefits or such income.

Article 54—Overlapping of benefits of the same kind

1. Where benefits of the same kind due under the legislation of two or more Member States overlap, the rules to prevent overlapping laid down by the legislation of a Member State shall not be applicable to a pro-rata benefit.

2. The rules to prevent overlapping shall apply to an independent benefit only if the benefit concerned is:

(a) a benefit the amount of which does not depend on the duration of periods of insurance or residence,

or

(b) a benefit the amount of which is determined on the basis of a credited period deemed to have been completed between the date on which the risk materialised and a later date, overlapping with:

   (i) a benefit of the same type, except where an agreement has been concluded between two or more Member States to avoid the same credited period being taken into account more than once, or
   (ii) a benefit referred to in subparagraph (a).

The benefits and agreements referred to in subparagraphs (a) and (b) are listed in Annex IX.

Article 55—Overlapping of benefits of a different kind

1. If the receipt of benefits of a different kind or other income requires the application of the rules to prevent overlapping provided for by the legislation of the Member States concerned regarding:

(a) two or more independent benefits, the competent institutions shall divide the amounts of the benefit or benefits or other income, as they have been taken into account, by the number of benefits subject to the said rules;

however, the application of this subparagraph cannot deprive the person concerned of his status as a pensioner for the purposes of the other Chapters of this Title under the conditions and the procedures laid down in the Implementing Regulation;

(b) one or more pro-rata benefits, the competent institutions shall take into account the benefit or benefits or other income and all the elements stipulated for applying the rules to prevent overlapping as a function of the ratio between the periods of insurance and/or residence established for the calculation referred to in Article 52(1)(b)(ii);

(c) one or more independent benefits and one or more pro-rata benefits, the competent institutions shall apply mutatis mutandis subparagraph (a) as regards independent benefits and subparagraph (b) as regards pro-rata benefits.

2. The competent institution shall not apply the division stipulated in respect of independent benefits, if the legislation it applies provides for account to be taken of benefits of a different kind and/or other income and all other elements for calculating part of their amount determined as a function of the ratio between periods of insurance and/or residence referred to in Article 52(1)(b)(ii).

3. Paragraphs 1 and 2 shall apply mutatis mutandis where the legislation of one or more Member States provides that a right to a benefit cannot be acquired in the case where the person concerned is in receipt of a benefit of a different kind, payable under the legislation of another Member State, or of other income.

Article 56—Additional provisions for the calculation of benefits

1. For the calculation of the theoretical and pro-rata amounts referred to in Article 52(1)(b), the following rules shall apply:

(a) where the total length of the periods of insurance and/or residence completed before the risk materialised under the legislations of all the Member States concerned is longer than the maximum period required by the legislation of one of these Member States for receipt of full benefit, the competent institution of that Member State shall take into account this maximum period instead of the total length of the periods completed; this method of calculation shall not result in the imposition on that institution of the cost of a benefit greater than the full benefit provided for by the legislation it applies. This provision shall not apply to benefits the amount of which does not depend on the length of insurance;

(b) the procedure for taking into account overlapping periods is laid down in the Implementing Regulation;

(c) if the legislation of a Member State provides that the benefits are to be calculated on the basis of incomes, contributions, bases of contributions, increases, earnings, other amounts or a combination of more than one of them (average, proportional, fixed or credited), the competent institution shall:

   (i) determine the basis for calculation of the benefits in accordance only with periods of insurance completed under the legislation it applies;
   (ii) use, in order to determine the amount to be calculated in accordance with the periods of insurance and/or residence completed under the legislation of the other Member States, the same elements determined or recorded for the periods of insurance completed under the legislation it applies;

in accordance with the procedures laid down in Annex XI for the Member State concerned.

2. The provisions of the legislation of a Member State concerning the revalorisation of the elements taken into account for the calculation of benefits shall apply, as appropriate, to the elements to be taken into account by the competent institution of that Member State, in accordance with paragraph 1, in respect of the periods of insurance or residence completed under the legislation of other Member States.

Article 57—Periods of insurance or residence of less than one year

1. Notwithstanding Article 52(1)(b), the institution of a Member State shall not be required to provide benefits in respect of periods completed under the legislation it applies which are taken into account when the risk materialises, if:

— the duration of the said periods is less than one year,

and

— taking only these periods into account no right to benefit is acquired under that legislation.

For the purposes of this Article, "periods" shall mean all periods of insurance, employment, self-employment or residence which either qualify for, or directly increase, the benefit concerned.

2. The competent institution of each of the Member States concerned shall take into account the periods referred to in paragraph 1, for the purposes of Article 52(1)(b)(i).

3. If the effect of applying paragraph 1 would be to relieve all the institutions of the Member States concerned of their obligations, benefits shall be provided exclusively under the legislation of the last of those Member States whose conditions are satisfied, as if all the periods of insurance and residence completed and taken into account in accordance with Articles 6 and 51(1) and (2) had been completed under the legislation of that Member State.

Article 58—Award of a supplement

1. A recipient of benefits to whom this Chapter applies may not, in the Member State of residence and under whose legislation a benefit is payable to him, be provided with a benefit which is less than the minimum benefit fixed by that legislation for a period of insurance or residence equal to all the periods taken into account for the payment in accordance with this Chapter.

2. The competent institution of that Member State shall pay him throughout the period of his residence in its territory a supplement equal to the difference between the total of the benefits due under this Chapter and the amount of the minimum benefit.

Appendix 5

Article 59—Recalculation and revaluation of benefits

1. If the method for determining benefits or the rules for calculating benefits are altered under the legislation of a Member State, or if the personal situation of the person concerned undergoes a relevant change which, under that legislation, would lead to an adjustment of the amount of the benefit, a recalculation shall be carried out in accordance with Article 52.

2. On the other hand, if, by reason of an increase in the cost of living or changes in the level of income or other grounds for adjustment, the benefits of the Member State concerned are altered by a percentage or fixed amount, such percentage or fixed amount shall be applied directly to the benefits determined in accordance with Article 52, without the need for a recalculation.

Article 60—Special provisions for civil servants

1. Articles 6, 50, 51(3) and 52 to 59 shall apply mutatis mutandis to persons covered by a special scheme for civil servants.

2. However, if the legislation of a competent Member State makes the acquisition, liquidation, retention or recovery of the right to benefits under a special scheme for civil servants subject to the condition that all periods of insurance be completed under one or more special schemes for civil servants in that Member State, or be regarded by the legislation of that Member State as equivalent to such periods, the competent institution of that State shall take into account only the periods which can be recognised under the legislation it applies.

If, account having been taken of the periods thus completed, the person concerned does not satisfy the conditions for the receipt of these benefits, these periods shall be taken into account for the award of benefits under the general scheme or, failing that, the scheme applicable to manual or clerical workers, as the case may be.

3. Where, under the legislation of a Member State, benefits under a special scheme for civil servants are calculated on the basis of the last salary or salaries received during a reference period, the competent institution of that State shall take into account, for the purposes of the calculation, only those salaries, duly revalued, which were received during the period or periods for which the person concerned was subject to that legislation.

Chapter 6

Unemployment Benefits

Article 61—Special rules on aggregation of periods of insurance, employment or self-employment

1. The competent institution of a Member State whose legislation makes the acquisition, retention, recovery or duration of the right to benefits conditional upon the completion of either periods of insurance, employment or self-employment shall,

to the extent necessary, take into account periods of insurance, employment or self-employment completed under the legislation of any other Member State as though they were completed under the legislation it applies.

However, when the applicable legislation makes the right to benefits conditional on the completion of periods of insurance, the periods of employment or self-employment completed under the legislation of another Member State shall not be taken into account unless such periods would have been considered to be periods of insurance had they been completed in accordance with the applicable legislation.

2. Except in the cases referred to in Article 65(5)(a), the application of paragraph 1 of this Article shall be conditional on the person concerned having the most recently completed, in accordance with the legislation under which the benefits are claimed:

— periods of insurance, if that legislation requires periods of insurance,

— periods of employment, if that legislation requires periods of employment, or

— periods of self-employment, if that legislation requires periods of self-employment.

Article 62—Calculation of benefits

1. The competent institution of a Member State whose legislation provides for the calculation of benefits on the basis of the amount of the previous salary or professional income shall take into account exclusively the salary or professional income received by the person concerned in respect of his last activity as an employed or self-employed person under the said legislation.

2. Paragraph 1 shall also apply where the legislation administered by the competent institution provides for a specific reference period for the determination of the salary which serves as a basis for the calculation of benefits and where, for all or part of that period, the person concerned was subject to the legislation of another Member State.

3. By way of derogation from paragraphs (1) and (2), as far as the frontier workers covered by Article 65(5)(a) are concerned, the institution of the place of residence shall take into account the salary or professional income received by the person concerned in the Member State to whose legislation he was subject during his last activity as an employed or self-employed person, in accordance with the Implementing Regulation.

Article 63—Special provisions for the waiving of residence rules

For the purposes of this Chapter, Article 7 shall apply only in the cases provided for by Articles 64 and 65 and within the limits prescribed therein.

Article 64—Unemployed persons going to another Member State

1. A wholly unemployed person who satisfies the conditions of the legislation of the competent Member State for entitlement to benefits, and who goes to another Member State in order to seek work there, shall retain his entitlement to

unemployment benefits in cash under the following conditions and within the following limits:

(a) before his departure, the unemployed person must have been registered as a person seeking work and have remained available to the employment services of the competent Member State for at least four weeks after becoming unemployed. However, the competent services or institutions may authorise his departure before such time has expired;

(b) the unemployed person must register as a person seeking work with the employment services of the Member State to which he has gone, be subject to the control procedure organised there and adhere to the conditions laid down under the legislation of that Member State. This condition shall be considered satisfied for the period before registration if the person concerned registers within seven days of the date on which he ceased to be available to the employment services of the Member State which he left. In exceptional cases, the competent services or institutions may extend this period;

(c) entitlement to benefits shall be retained for a period of three months from the date when the unemployed person ceased to be available to the employment services of the Member State which he left, provided that the total duration for which the benefits are provided does not exceed the total duration of the period of his entitlement to benefits under the legislation of that Member State; the competent services or institutions may extend the period of three months up to a maximum of six months;

(d) the benefits shall be provided by the competent institution in accordance with the legislation it applies and at its own expense.

2. If the person concerned returns to the competent Member State on or before the expiry of the period during which he is entitled to benefits under paragraph 1(c), he shall continue to be entitled to benefits under the legislation of that Member State. He shall lose all entitlement to benefits under the legislation of the competent Member State if he does not return there on or before the expiry of the said period, unless the provisions of that legislation are more favourable. In exceptional cases the competent services or institutions may allow the person concerned to return at a later date without loss of his entitlement.

3. Unless the legislation of the competent Member State is more favourable, between two periods of employment the maximum total period for which entitlement to benefits shall be retained under paragraph 1 shall be three months; the competent services or institutions may extend that period up to a maximum of six months.

4. The arrangements for exchanges of information, cooperation and mutual assistance between the institutions and services of the competent Member State and the Member State to which the person goes in order to seek work shall be laid down in the Implementing Regulation.

Article 65—Unemployed persons who resided in a Member State other than the competent State

1. A person who is partially or intermittently unemployed and who, during his last activity as an employed or self-employed person, resided in a Member State other than the competent Member State shall make himself available to his employer or to the employment services in the competent Member State. He shall receive benefits in

accordance with the legislation of the competent Member State as if he were residing in that Member State. These benefits shall be provided by the institution of the competent Member State.

2. A wholly unemployed person who, during his last activity as an employed or self-employed person, resided in a Member State other than the competent Member State and who continues to reside in that Member State or returns to that Member State shall make himself available to the employment services in the Member State of residence. Without prejudice to Article 64, a wholly unemployed person may, as a supplementary step, make himself available to the employment services of the Member State in which he pursued his last activity as an employed or self-employed person.

An unemployed person, other than a frontier worker, who does not return to his Member State of residence, shall make himself available to the employment services in the Member State to whose legislation he was last subject.

3. The unemployed person referred to in the first sentence of paragraph 2 shall register as a person seeking work with the competent employment services of the Member State in which he resides, shall be subject to the control procedure organised there and shall adhere to the conditions laid down under the legislation of that Member State. If he chooses also to register as a person seeking work in the Member State in which he pursued his last activity as an employed or self-employed person, he shall comply with the obligations applicable in that State.

4. The implementation of the second sentence of paragraph 2 and of the second sentence of paragraph 3, as well as the arrangements for exchanges of information, cooperation and mutual assistance between the institutions and services of the Member State of residence and the Member State in which he pursued his last occupation, shall be laid down in the Implementing Regulation.

5.
(a) The unemployed person referred to in the first and second sentences of paragraph 2 shall receive benefits in accordance with the legislation of the Member State of residence as if he had been subject to that legislation during his last activity as an employed or self-employed person. Those benefits shall be provided by the institution of the place of residence.

(b) However, a worker other than a frontier worker who has been provided benefits at the expense of the competent institution of the Member State to whose legislation he was last subject shall firstly receive, on his return to the Member State of residence, benefits in accordance with Article 64, receipt of the benefits in accordance with (a) being suspended for the period during which he receives benefits under the legislation to which he was last subject.

6. The benefits provided by the institution of the place of residence under paragraph 5 shall continue to be at its own expense. However, subject to paragraph 7, the competent institution of the Member State to whose legislation he was last subject shall reimburse to the institution of the place of residence the full amount of the benefits provided by the latter institution during the first three months. The amount of the reimbursement during this period may not be higher than the amount payable, in the case of unemployment, under the legislation of the competent Member State. In the case referred to in paragraph 5(b), the period during which benefits are provided under Article 64 shall be deducted from the period referred to in the second sentence of this paragraph. The arrangements for reimbursement shall be laid down in the Implementing Regulation.

7. However, the period of reimbursement referred to in paragraph 6 shall be extended to five months when the person concerned has, during the preceding 24 months, completed periods of employment or self-employment of at least 12 months in the Member State to whose legislation he was last subject, where such periods would qualify for the purposes of establishing entitlement to unemployment benefits.

8. For the purposes of paragraphs 6 and 7, two or more Member States, or their competent authorities, may provide for other methods of reimbursement or waive all reimbursement between the institutions falling under their jurisdiction.

Chapter 7

Pre-Retirement Benefits

Article 66—Benefits

When the applicable legislation makes the right to pre-retirement benefits conditional on the completion of periods of insurance, of employment or of self-employment, Article 6 shall not apply.

Chapter 8

Family Benefits

Article 67—Members of the family residing in another Member State

A person shall be entitled to family benefits in accordance with the legislation of the competent Member State, including for his family members residing in another Member State, as if they were residing in the former Member State. However, a pensioner shall be entitled to family benefits in accordance with the legislation of the Member State competent for his pension.

Article 68—Priority rules in the event of overlapping

1. Where, during the same period and for the same family members, benefits are provided for under the legislation of more than one Member State the following priority rules shall apply:

(a) in the case of benefits payable by more than one Member State on different bases, the order of priority shall be as follows: firstly, rights available on the basis of an activity as an employed or self-employed person, secondly, rights available on the basis of receipt of a pension and finally, rights obtained on the basis of residence;

REGULATION (EC) No 883/2004

(b) in the case of benefits payable by more than one Member State on the same basis, the order of priority shall be established by referring to the following subsidiary criteria:

   (i) in the case of rights available on the basis of an activity as an employed or self-employed person: the place of residence of the children, provided that there is such activity, and additionally, where appropriate, the highest amount of the benefits provided for by the conflicting legislations. In the latter case, the cost of benefits shall be shared in accordance with criteria laid down in the Implementing Regulation;
   (ii) in the case of rights available on the basis of receipt of pensions: the place of residence of the children, provided that a pension is payable under its legislation, and additionally, where appropriate, the longest period of insurance or residence under the conflicting legislations;
   (iii) in the case of rights available on the basis of residence: the place of residence of the children.

2. In the case of overlapping entitlements, family benefits shall be provided in accordance with the legislation designated as having priority in accordance with paragraph 1. Entitlements to family benefits by virtue of other conflicting legislation or legislations shall be suspended up to the amount provided for by the first legislation and a differential supplement shall be provided, if necessary, for the sum which exceeds this amount. However, such a differential supplement does not need to be provided for children residing in another Member State when entitlement to the benefit in question is based on residence only.

3. If, under Article 67, an application for family benefits is submitted to the competent institution of a Member State whose legislation is applicable, but not by priority right in accordance with paragraphs 1 and 2 of this Article:

(a) that institution shall forward the application without delay to the competent institution of the Member State whose legislation is applicable by priority, inform the person concerned and, without prejudice to the provisions of the Implementing Regulation concerning the provisional award of benefits, provide, if necessary, the differential supplement mentioned in paragraph 2;

(b) the competent institution of the Member State whose legislation is applicable by priority shall deal with this application as though it were submitted directly to itself, and the date on which such an application was submitted to the first institution shall be considered as the date of its claim to the institution with priority.

Article 69—Additional provisions

1. If, under the legislation designated by virtue of Articles 67 and 68, no right is acquired to the payment of additional or special family benefits for orphans, such benefits shall be paid by default, and in addition to the other family benefits acquired in accordance with the abovementioned legislation, under the legislation of the Member State to which the deceased worker was subject for the longest period of time, insofar as the right was acquired under that legislation. If no right was acquired under that legislation, the conditions for the acquisition of such right under the legislations of the other Member States shall be examined and benefits provided in decreasing order of the length of periods of insurance or residence completed under the legislation of those Member States.

2. Benefits paid in the form of pensions or supplements to pensions shall be provided and calculated in accordance with Chapter 5.

CHAPTER 9

SPECIAL NON-CONTRIBUTORY CASH BENEFITS

Article 70—General provision

1. This Article shall apply to special non-contributory cash benefits which are provided under legislation which, because of its personal scope, objectives and/or conditions for entitlement, has characteristics both of the social security legislation referred to in Article 3(1) and of social assistance.

2. For the purposes of this Chapter, "special non-contributory cash benefits" means those which:

(a) are intended to provide either:

   (i) supplementary, substitute or ancillary cover against the risks covered by the branches of social security referred to in Article 3(1), and which guarantee the persons concerned a minimum subsistence income having regard to the economic and social situation in the Member State concerned;

   or

   (ii) solely specific protection for the disabled, closely linked to the said person's social environment in the Member State concerned,

and

(b) where the financing exclusively derives from compulsory taxation intended to cover general public expenditure and the conditions for providing and for calculating the benefits are not dependent on any contribution in respect of the beneficiary. However, benefits provided to supplement a contributory benefit shall not be considered to be contributory benefits for this reason alone,

and

(c) are listed in Annex X.

3. Article 7 and the other Chapters of this Title shall not apply to the benefits referred to in paragraph 2 of this Article.

4. The benefits referred to in paragraph 2 shall be provided exclusively in the Member State in which the persons concerned reside, in accordance with its legislation. Such benefits shall be provided by and at the expense of the institution of the place of residence.

Regulation (EC) No 883/2004

Title IV

Administrative Commission and Advisory Committee

Article 71—Composition and working methods of the Administrative Commission

1. The Administrative Commission for the Coordination of Social Security Systems (hereinafter called "the Administrative Commission") attached to the Commission of the European Communities shall be made up of a government representative from each of the Member States, assisted, where necessary, by expert advisers. A representative of the Commission of the European Communities shall attend the meetings of the Administrative Commission in an advisory capacity.

2. The rules of the Administrative Commission shall be drawn up by mutual agreement among its members.

Decisions on questions of interpretation referred to in Article 72(a) shall be adopted under the voting rules established by the Treaty and shall be given the necessary publicity.

3. Secretarial services for the Administrative Commission shall be provided by the Commission of the European Communities.

Article 72—Tasks of the Administrative Commission

The Administrative Commission shall:

(a) deal with all administrative questions and questions of interpretation arising from the provisions of this Regulation or those of the Implementing Regulation, or from any agreement concluded or arrangement made thereunder, without prejudice to the right of the authorities, institutions and persons concerned to have recourse to the procedures and tribunals provided for by the legislation of the Member States, by this Regulation or by the Treaty;

(b) facilitate the uniform application of Community law, especially by promoting exchange of experience and best administrative practices;

(c) foster and develop cooperation between Member States and their institutions in social security matters in order, inter alia, to take into account particular questions regarding certain categories of persons; facilitate realisation of actions of crossborder cooperation activities in the area of the coordination of social security systems;

(d) encourage as far as possible the use of new technologies in order to facilitate the free movement of persons, in particular by modernising procedures for exchanging information and adapting the information flow between institutions for the purposes of exchange by electronic means, taking account of the development of data processing in each Member State; the Administrative Commission shall adopt the common structural rules for data processing services, in particular on security and the use of standards, and shall lay down provisions for the operation of the common part of those services;

(e) undertake any other function falling within its competence under this Regulation and the Implementing Regulation or any agreement or arrangement concluded thereunder;

Appendix 5

(f) make any relevant proposals to the Commission of the European Communities concerning the coordination of social security schemes, with a view to improving and modernising the Community "acquis" by drafting subsequent Regulations or by means of other instruments provided for by the Treaty;

(g) establish the factors to be taken into account for drawing up accounts relating to the costs to be borne by the institutions of the Member States under this Regulation and to adopt the annual accounts between those institutions, based on the report of the Audit Board referred to in Article 74.

Article 73—Technical Commission for Data Processing

1. A Technical Commission for Data Processing (hereinafter called the "Technical Commission") shall be attached to the Administrative Commission. The Technical Commission shall propose to the Administrative Commission common architecture rules for the operation of data-processing services, in particular on security and the use of standards; it shall deliver reports and a reasoned opinion before decisions are taken by the Administrative Commission pursuant to Article 72(d). The composition and working methods of the Technical Commission shall be determined by the Administrative Commission.

2. To this end, the Technical Commission shall:

(a) gather together the relevant technical documents and undertake the studies and other work required to accomplish its tasks;

(b) submit to the Administrative Commission the reports and reasoned opinions referred to in paragraph 1;

(c) carry out all other tasks and studies on matters referred to it by the Administrative Commission;

(d) ensure the management of Community pilot projects using data-processing services and, for the Community part, operational systems using data-processing services.

Article 74—Audit Board

1. An Audit Board shall be attached to the Administrative Commission. The composition and working methods of the Audit Board shall be determined by the Administrative Commission.

The Audit Board shall:

(a) verify the method of determining and calculating the annual average costs presented by Member States;

(b) collect the necessary data and carry out the calculations required for establishing the annual statement of claims of each Member State;

(c) give the Administrative Commission periodic accounts of the results of the implementation of this Regulation and of the Implementing Regulation, in particular as regards the financial aspect;

(d) provide the data and reports necessary for decisions to be taken by the Administrative Commission under Article 72(g);
(e) make any relevant suggestions it may have to the Administrative Commission, including those concerning this Regulation, in connection with subparagraphs (a), (b) and (c);
(f) carry out all work, studies or assignments on matters referred to it by the Administrative Commission.

Article 75—Advisory Committee for the Coordination of Social Security Systems

1. An Advisory Committee for the Coordination of Social Security Systems (hereinafter referred to as "Advisory Committee") is hereby established, comprising, from each Member State:

(a) one government representative;
(b) one representative from the trade unions;
(c) one representative from the employers' organisations.

For each of the categories referred to above, an alternate member shall be appointed for each Member State.

The members and alternate members of the Advisory Committee shall be appointed by the Council. The Advisory Committee shall be chaired by a representative of the Commission of the European Communities. The Advisory Committee shall draw up its rules of procedure.

2. The Advisory Committee shall be empowered, at the request of the Commission of the European Communities, the Administrative Commission or on its own initiative:

(a) to examine general questions or questions of principle and problems arising from the implementation of the Community provisions on the coordination of social security systems, especially regarding certain categories of persons;
(b) to formulate opinions on such matters for the Administrative Commission and proposals for any revisions of the said provisions.

TITLE V

MISCELLANEOUS PROVISIONS

Article 76—Cooperation

1. The competent authorities of the Member States shall communicate to each other all information regarding:

(a) measures taken to implement this Regulation;
(b) changes in their legislation which may affect the implementation of this Regulation.

2. For the purposes of this Regulation, the authorities and institutions of the Member States shall lend one another their good offices and act as though implementing their own legislation. The administrative assistance given by the said authorities and institutions shall, as a rule, be free of charge. However, the Administrative Commission shall establish the nature of reimbursable expenses and the limits above which their reimbursement is due.

3. The authorities and institutions of the Member States may, for the purposes of this Regulation, communicate directly with one another and with the persons involved or their representatives.

4. The institutions and persons covered by this Regulation shall have a duty of mutual information and cooperation to ensure the correct implementation of this Regulation.

The institutions, in accordance with the principle of good administration, shall respond to all queries within a reasonable period of time and shall in this connection provide the persons concerned with any information required for exercising the rights conferred on them by this Regulation.

The persons concerned must inform the institutions of the competent Member State and of the Member State of residence as soon as possible of any change in their personal or family situation which affects their right to benefits under this Regulation.

5. Failure to respect the obligation of information referred to in the third sub-paragraph of paragraph 4 may result in the application of proportionate measures in accordance with national law. Nevertheless, these measures shall be equivalent to those applicable to similar situations under domestic law and shall not make it impossible or excessively difficult in practice for claimants to exercise the rights conferred on them by this Regulation.

6. In the event of difficulties in the interpretation or application of this Regulation which could jeopardise the rights of a person covered by it, the institution of the competent Member State or of the Member State of residence of the person concerned shall contact the institution(s) of the Member State(s) concerned. If a solution cannot be found within a reasonable period, the authorities concerned may call on the Administrative Commission to intervene.

7. The authorities, institutions and tribunals of one Member State may not reject applications or other documents submitted to them on the grounds that they are written in an official language of another Member State, recognised as an official language of the Community institutions in accordance with Article 290 of the Treaty.

Article 77—Protection of personal data

1. Where, under this Regulation or under the Implementing Regulation, the authorities or institutions of a Member State communicate personal data to the authorities or institutions of another Member State, such communication shall be subject to the data protection legislation of the Member State transmitting them. Any communication from the authority or institution of the receiving Member State as well as the storage, alteration and destruction of the data provided by that Member State shall be subject to the data protection legislation of the receiving Member State.

2. Data required for the application of this Regulation and the Implementing Regulation shall be transmitted by one Member State to another Member State in accordance with Community provisions on the protection of natural persons with regard to the processing and free movement of personal data.

Article 78—Data processing

1. Member States shall progressively use new technologies for the exchange, access and processing of the data required to apply this Regulation and the Implementing Regulation. The Commission of the European Communities shall lend its support to activities of common interest as soon as the Member States have established such data-processing services.

2. Each Member State shall be responsible for managing its own part of the data-processing services in accordance with the Community provisions on the protection of natural persons with regard to the processing and the free movement of personal data.

3. An electronic document sent or issued by an institution in conformity with this Regulation and the Implementing Regulation may not be rejected by any authority or institution of another Member State on the grounds that it was received by electronic means, once the receiving institution has declared that it can receive electronic documents. Reproduction and recording of such documents shall be presumed to be a correct and accurate reproduction of the original document or representation of the information it relates to, unless there is proof to the contrary.

4. An electronic document shall be considered valid if the computer system on which the document is recorded contains the safeguards necessary in order to prevent any alteration, disclosure or unauthorised access to the recording. It shall at any time be possible to reproduce the recorded information in an immediately readable form. When an electronic document is transferred from one social security institution to another, appropriate security measures shall be taken in accordance with the Community provisions on the protection of natural persons with regard to the processing and the free movement of personal data.

Article 79—Funding of activities in the social security field

In connection with this Regulation and the Implementing Regulation, the Commission of the European Communities may fund in full or in part:

(a) activities aimed at improving exchanges of information between the social security authorities and institutions of the Member States, particularly the electronic exchange of data;

(b) any other activity aimed at providing information to the persons covered by this Regulation and their representatives about the rights and obligations deriving from this Regulation, using the most appropriate means.

APPENDIX 5

Article 80—Exemptions

1. Any exemption from or reduction of taxes, stamp duty, notarial or registration fees provided for under the legislation of one Member State in respect of certificates or documents required to be produced in application of the legislation of that Member State shall be extended to similar certificates or documents required to be produced in application of the legislation of another Member State or of this Regulation.

2. All statements, documents and certificates of any kind whatsoever required to be produced in application of this Regulation shall be exempt from authentication by diplomatic or consular authorities.

Article 81—Claims, declarations or appeals

Any claim, declaration or appeal which should have been submitted, in application of the legislation of one Member State, within a specified period to an authority, institution or tribunal of that Member State shall be admissible if it is submitted within the same period to a corresponding authority, institution or tribunal of another Member State. In such a case the authority, institution or tribunal receiving the claim, declaration or appeal shall forward it without delay to the competent authority, institution or tribunal of the former Member State either directly or through the competent authorities of the Member States concerned. The date on which such claims, declarations or appeals were submitted to the authority, institution or tribunal of the second Member State shall be considered as the date of their submission to the competent authority, institution or tribunal.

Article 82—Medical examinations

Medical examinations provided for by the legislation of one Member State may be carried out at the request of the competent institution, in another Member State, by the institution of the place of residence or stay of the claimant or the person entitled to benefits, under the conditions laid down in the Implementing Regulation or agreed between the competent authorities of the Member States concerned.

Article 83—Implementation of legislation

Special provisions for implementing the legislation of certain Member States are referred to in Annex XI.

Article 84—Collection of contributions and recovery of benefits

1. Collection of contributions due to an institution of one Member State and recovery of benefits provided by the institution of one Member State but not due may be effected in another Member State in accordance with the procedures and with the guarantees and privileges applicable to the collection of contributions due to the corresponding institution of the latter Member State and the recovery of benefits provided by it but not due.

2. Enforceable decisions of the judicial and administrative authorities relating to the collection of contributions, interest and any other charges or to the recovery of benefits provided but not due under the legislation of one Member State shall be recognised and enforced at the request of the competent institution in another Member State within the limits and in accordance with the procedures laid down by the legislation and any other procedures applicable to similar decisions of the latter Member State. Such decisions shall be declared enforceable in that Member State insofar as the legislation and any other procedures of that Member State so require.

3. Claims of an institution of one Member State shall in enforcement, bankruptcy or settlement proceedings in another Member State enjoy the same privileges as the legislation of the latter Member State accords to claims of the same kind.

4. The procedure for implementing this Article, including costs reimbursement, shall be governed by the Implementing Regulation or, where necessary and as a complementary measure, by means of agreements between Member States.

Article 85—Rights of institutions

1. If a person receives benefits under the legislation of one Member State in respect of an injury resulting from events occurring in another Member State, any rights of the institution responsible for providing benefits against a third party liable to provide compensation for the injury shall be governed by the following rules:

(a) where the institution responsible for providing benefits is, under the legislation it applies, subrogated to the rights which the beneficiary has against the third party, such subrogation shall be recognised by each Member State;

(b) where the institution responsible for providing benefits has a direct right against the third party, each Member State shall recognise such rights.

2. If a person receives benefits under the legislation of one Member State in respect of an injury resulting from events occurring in another Member State, the provisions of the said legislation which determine the cases in which the civil liability of employers or of their employees is to be excluded shall apply with regard to the said person or to the competent institution.

Paragraph 1 shall also apply to any rights of the institution responsible for providing benefits against employers or their employees in cases where their liability is not excluded.

3. Where, in accordance with Article 35(3) and/or Article 41(2), two or more Member States or their competent authorities have concluded an agreement to waive reimbursement between institutions under their jurisdiction, or, where reimbursement does not depend on the amount of benefits actually provided, any rights arising against a liable third party shall be governed by the following rules:

(a) where the institution of the Member State of residence or stay accords benefits to a person in respect of an injury sustained in its territory, that institution, in accordance with the provisions of the legislation it applies, shall exercise the right to subrogation or direct action against the third party liable to provide compensation for the injury;

(b) for the application of (a):

(i) the person receiving benefits shall be deemed to be insured with the institution of the place of residence or stay, and
(ii) that institution shall be deemed to be the institution responsible for providing benefits;

(c) Paragraphs 1 and 2 shall remain applicable in respect of any benefits not covered by the waiver agreement or a reimbursement which does not depend on the amount of benefits actually provided.

Article 86—Bilateral agreements

As far as relations between, on the one hand, Luxembourg and, on the other hand, France, Germany and Belgium are concerned, the application and the duration of the period referred to in Article 65(7) shall be subject to the conclusion of bilateral agreements.

Title VI

Transitional and Final Provisions

Article 87—Transitional provisions

1. No rights shall be acquired under this Regulation for the period before its date of application.

2. Any period of insurance and, where appropriate, any period of employment, self-employment or residence completed under the legislation of a Member State prior to the date of application of this Regulation in the Member State concerned shall be taken into consideration for the determination of rights acquired under this Regulation.

3. Subject to paragraph 1, a right shall be acquired under this Regulation even if it relates to a contingency arising before its date of application in the Member State concerned.

4. Any benefit which has not been awarded or which has been suspended by reason of the nationality or place of residence of the person concerned shall, at the request of that person, be provided or resumed with effect from the date of application of this Regulation in the Member State concerned, provided that the rights for which benefits were previously provided have not given rise to a lump-sum payment.

5. The rights of a person to whom a pension was provided prior to the date of application of this Regulation in a Member State may, at the request of the person concerned, be reviewed, taking into account this Regulation.

6. If a request referred to in paragraph 4 or 5 is submitted within two years from the date of application of this Regulation in a Member State, the rights acquired under this Regulation shall have effect from that date, and the legislation of any Member State concerning the forfeiture or limitation of rights may not be invoked against the persons concerned.

7. If a request referred to in paragraph 4 or 5 is submitted after the expiry of the two-year period following the date of application of this Regulation in the Member State concerned, rights not forfeited or not time-barred shall have effect from the date on which the request was submitted, subject to any more favourable provisions under the legislation of any Member State.

8. If, as a result of this Regulation, a person is subject to the legislation of a Member State other than the one determined in accordance with Title II of Regulation (EEC) No 1408/71, that legislation shall continue to apply as long as the relevant situation remains unchanged, unless the person concerned requests that he be subject to the legislation applicable under this Regulation. The request shall be submitted within three months after the date of application of this Regulation to the competent institution of the Member State whose legislation is applicable under this Regulation if the person concerned is to be subject to the legislation of that Member State as of the date of application of this Regulation. If the request is made after the time limit indicated, the changeover shall take place on the first day of the following month.

9. Article 55 of this Regulation shall apply only to pensions not subject to Article 46c of Regulation (EEC) No 1408/71 on the date of application of this Regulation.

10. The provisions of the second sentences of Article 65(2) and (3) shall be applicable to Luxembourg at the latest two years after the date of application of this Regulation.

11. Member States shall ensure that appropriate information is provided regarding the changes in rights and obligations introduced by this Regulation and the Implementing Regulation.

Article 88—Updating of the Annexes

The Annexes of this Regulation shall be revised periodically.

Article 89—Implementing Regulation

A further Regulation shall lay down the procedure for implementing this Regulation.

Article 90—Repeal

1. Council Regulation (EEC) No 1408/71 shall be repealed from the date of application of this Regulation.

However, Regulation (EEC) No 1408/71 shall remain in force and shall continue to have legal effect for the purposes of:

(a) Council Regulation (EC) No 859/2003 of 14 May 2003 extending the provisions of Regulation (EEC) No 1408/71 and Regulation (EEC) No 574/72 to nationals of third countries who are not already covered by those provisions solely on the ground of their nationality[5], for as long as that Regulation has not been repealed or modified;

---

[5] OJ L 124, 20.5.2003, p. 1.

Appendix 5

(b) Council Regulation (EEC) No 1661/85 of 13 June 1985 laying down the technical adaptations to the Community rules on social security for migrant workers with regard to Greenland[6], for as long as that Regulation has not been repealed or modified;

(c) the Agreement on the European Economic Area[7] and the Agreement between the European Community and its Member States, of the one part, and the Swiss Confederation, of the other part, on the free movement of persons[8] and other agreements which contain a reference to Regulation (EEC) No 1408/71, for as long as those agreements have not been modified in the light of this Regulation.

2. References to Regulation (EEC) No 1408/71 in Council Directive 98/49/EC of 29 June 1998 on safeguarding the supplementary pension rights of employed and self-employed persons moving within the Community[9] are to be read as referring to this Regulation.

Article 91—Entry into force

This Regulation shall enter into force on the twentieth day after its publication in the Official Journal of the European Union.

It shall apply from the date of entry into force of the Implementing Regulation.

This Regulation shall be binding in its entirety and directly applicable in all Member States.

Done at Strasbourg, 29.4.2004.

Annex I

Advances of Maintenance Payments and Special Childbirth and Adoption Allowances
(Article 1(z))

I. Advances of maintenance payments

A. BELGIUM

Advances of maintenance allowances under the law of 21 February 2003 creating a maintenance payments agency within the federal public service, Finance Department

B. DENMARK

Advance payment of child support laid down in the Act on Child Benefits

---

[6] OJ L 160, 20.6.1985, p. 7.
[7] OJ L 1, 3.1.1994, p. 1.
[8] OJ L 114, 30.4.2002, p. 6. Agreement as last amended by Decision No 2/2003 of the EU-Swiss Committee (OJ L 187, 26.7.2003, p. 55).
[9] OJ L 209, 25.7.1998, p. 46.

Advance payment of child support consolidated by Law No 765 of 11 September 2002

C. GERMANY

Advances of maintenance payments under the German law on advances of maintenance payments (Unterhaltsvorschussgesetz) of 23 July 1979

D. FRANCE

Family support allowance paid to a child one of whose parents or both of whose parents are in default or are unable to meet their maintenance obligations or the payment of a maintenance allowance laid down by a court decision

E. AUSTRIA

Advances of maintenance payments under the Federal Law on the grant of advances of child maintenance (Unterhaltsvorschussgesetz 1985 – UVG)

F. PORTUGAL

Advances of maintenance payments (Act No 75/98, 19 November, on the guarantee of maintenance for minors)

G. FINLAND

Maintenance allowance under the Security of Child Maintenance Act (671/1998)

H. SWEDEN

Maintenance allowance under the Maintenance Support Act (1996:1030)

II. Special childbirth and adoption allowances

A. BELGIUM

Childbirth allowance and adoption grant

B SPAIN

Single payment birth grants

C. FRANCE

Birth or adoption grants as part of the "early childhood benefit"

D. LUXEMBOURG

Antenatal allowances

Childbirth allowances

APPENDIX 5

E. FINLAND

Maternity package, maternity lump-sum grant and assistance in the form of a lump sum intended to offset the cost of international adoption pursuant to the Maternity Grant Act

Annex II

Provisions of Conventions Which Remain in Force and Which, Where Applicable, are Restricted to the Persons Covered Thereby
(Article 8(1))

The content of this Annex shall be determined by the European Parliament and by the Council in accordance with the Treaty as soon as possible and at the latest by the date of application of this Regulation referred to in Article 91.

Annex III

Restriction of Rights to Benefits in Kind for Members of the Family of a Frontier Worker
(Article 18(2))

DENMARK

SPAIN

IRELAND

NETHERLANDS

FINLAND

SWEDEN

UNITED KINGDOM

Regulation (EC) No 883/2004

Annex IV

More Rights for Pensioners Returning to the Competent Member State
(Article 27(2))

BELGIUM

GERMANY

GREECE

SPAIN

FRANCE

ITALY

LUXEMBOURG

AUSTRIA

SWEDEN

Annex V

More rights for former frontier workers who return to their previous Member State of activity as an employed or self-employed person (applicable only if the Member State in which the competent institution responsible for the costs of the benefits in kind provided to the pensioner in his Member State of residence is situated also appears on the list)
(Article 28(2))

BELGIUM

GERMANY

SPAIN

FRANCE

LUXEMBOURG

AUSTRIA

PORTUGAL

APPENDIX 5

ANNEX VI

IDENTIFICATION OF TYPE A LEGISLATION WHICH SHOULD BE SUBJECT TO
SPECIAL COORDINATION
(Article 44(1))

A. GREECE

Legislation relating to the agricultural insurance scheme (OGA), under Law No 4169/1961

B. IRELAND

Part II, Chapter 15 of the Social Welfare (Consolidation) Act, 1993

C. FINLAND

Invalidity pensions determined according to the National Pensions Act of 8 June 1956 and awarded under the transitional rules of the National Pensions Act (547/93) National pensions to persons who are disabled or become disabled at an early age (the National Pensions Act (547/93))

D. SWEDEN

Income-related sickness benefit and activity compensation (Act 1962:381 as amended by Act 2001:489)

E. UNITED KINGDOM

(a) Great Britain
    Sections 30A(5), 40, 41 and 68 of the Contributions and Benefits Act 1992.
(b) Northern Ireland
    Sections 30A(5), 40, 41 and 68 of the Contributions and Benefits (Northern Ireland) Act 1992.

REGULATION (EC) No 883/2004

ANNEX VII

CONCORDANCE BETWEEN THE LEGISLATIONS OF MEMBER STATES ON CONDITIONS RELATING TO THE DEGREE OF INVALIDITY
(Article 46(3) of the Regulation)

BELGIUM

Member State	Schemes administered by institutions of Member States which have taken a decision recognising the degree of invalidity	Schemes administered by Belgian institutions on which the decision is binding in cases of concordance				
		General scheme	Miners' scheme		Mariners' scheme	Ossom
			General invalidity	Occupational invalidity		
FRANCE	1. General scheme:					
	– Group III (constant attendance)	Concordance	Concordance	Concordance	Concordance	No concordance
	– Group II	Concordance	Concordance	Concordance	Concordance	No concordance
	– Group I	Concordance	Concordance	Concordance	Concordance	No concordance
	2. Agricultural scheme					
	– Total, general invalidity	Concordance	Concordance	Concordance	Concordance	No concordance
	– Two-thirds general invalidity	Concordance	Concordance	Concordance	Concordance	No concordance
	– Constant attendance	Concordance	Concordance	Concordance	Concordance	No concordance
	3. Miners' scheme:					
	– Partial, general invalidity	Concordance	Concordance	Concordance	Concordance	No concordance
	– Constant attendance	Concordance	Concordance	Concordance	Concordance	No concordance
	– Occupational invalidity	No concordance	No concordance	Concordance	No concordance	No concordance
	4. Mariners' scheme:					
	– General invalidity	Concordance	Concordance	Concordance	Concordance	No concordance
	– Constant attendance	Concordance	Concordance	Concordance	Concordance	No concordance
	– Occupational invalidity	No concordance	No concordance	No concordance	No concordance	No concordance
ITALY	1. General scheme:					
	– Invalidity					
	– manual workers	No concordance	Concordance	Concordance	Concordance	No concordance
	– Invalidity – clerical staff	No concordance	Concordance	Concordance	Concordance	No concordance
	2. Mariners' scheme:					
	– Unfitness for seafaring	No concordance	No concordance	No concordance	No concordance	No concordance
LUXEM-BOURG[1]	Workers' invalidity – manual workers	Concordance	Concordance	Concordance	Concordance	No concordance
	Invalidity – clerical staff	Concordance	Concordance	Concordance	Concordance	No concordance

[1] Entries concerning concordance between Luxembourg and France or Belgium will be the subject of technical re-examination taking account of the changes which have been made to national legislation in Luxembourg.

APPENDIX 5

FRANCE

Schemes administered by French institutions on which the decision is binding in cases of concordances

Member State	Schemes administered by institutions of Member States which have taken a decision recognising the degree of invalidity	General scheme			Agricultural scheme				Miners' scheme			Mariners' scheme	
		Group I	Group II	Group III Constant attendance	2/3 Invalidity	Total invalidity	Constant attendance	2/3 General invalidity	Constant attendance	Occupational invalidity	2/3 General invalidity	Total occupational invalidity	Constant attendance
BELGIUM	1. General scheme	Concordance	No concordance	No concordance	Concordance	No concordance	No concordance	Concordance	No concordance	No concordance	No concordance	No concordance	No concordance
	2. Miners' scheme – partial general invalidity	Concordance	No concordance	No concordance	Concordance	No concordance	No concordance	Concordance	No concordance	No concordance	No concordance	No concordance	No concordance
	– occupational invalidity	No concordance	No concordance	No concordance	No concordance	No concordance	No concordance	No concordance	No concordance	Concordance[2]	No concordance	No concordance	No concordance
	3. Mariners' scheme	Concordance[1]	No concordance	No concordance	Concordance[1]	No concordance	No concordance	Concordance[1]	No concordance	No concordance	No concordance	No concordance	No concordance
ITALY	1. General scheme – invalidity – manual workers	Concordance	No concordance	No concordance	Concordance	No concordance	No concordance	Concordance	No concordance	No concordance	No concordance	No concordance	No concordance
	– invalidity – clerical staff	Concordance	No concordance	No concordance	Concordance	No concordance	No concordance	Concordance	No concordance	No concordance	No concordance	No concordance	No concordance
	2. Mariners' scheme – unfitness for seafaring	No concordance	No concordance	No concordance	No concordance	No concordance	No concordance	No concordance	No concordance	No concordance	No concordance	No concordance	No concordance
LUXEMBOURG[3]	Invalidity – manual workers	Concordance	No concordance	No concordance	Concordance	No concordance	No concordance	Concordance	No concordance	No concordance	No concordance	No concordance	No concordance
	Invalidity – clerical staff	No concordance	No concordance	No concordance	No concordance	No concordance	No concordance	No concordance	No concordance	No concordance	No concordance	No concordance	No concordance

(1) In so far as the invalidity recognised by the Belgian institutions is general invalidity.
(2) Only if the Belgian institution has recognised that the worker is unfit for work underground or at ground level.
(3) Entries concerning concordance between Luxembourg and France or Belgium will be the subject of technical re-examination taking account of the changes which have been made to national legislation in Luxembourg.

REGULATION (EC) No 883/2004

ITALY

Member State	Schemes administered by institutions of Member States which have taken a decision recognising the degree of invalidity	Schemes administered by Italian institutions on which the decision is binding in cases of concordance		
		General scheme		Mariners Unfit for navigation
		Manual workers	Clerical staff	
BELGIUM	1. General scheme	No concordance	No concordance	No concordance
	2. Miners' scheme			
	– partial general invalidity	Concordance	Concordance	No concordance
	– occupational invalidity	No concordance	No concordance	No concordance
	3. Mariners' scheme	No concordance	No concordance	No concordance
FRANCE	1. General scheme			
	– Group III (constant attendance)	Concordance	Concordance	No concordance
	– Group II	Concordance	Concordance	No concordance
	– Group I	Concordance	Concordance	No concordance
	2. Agricultural scheme			
	– total general invalidity	Concordance	Concordance	No concordance
	– partial general invalidity	Concordance	Concordance	No concordance
	– constant attendance	Concordance	Concordance	No concordance
	3. Miners' scheme			
	– partial general invalidity	Concordance	Concordance	No concordance
	– constant attendance	Concordance	Concordance	No concordance
	– occupational invalidity	No concordance	No concordance	No concordance
	4. Mariners' scheme			
	– partial general invalidity	No concordance	No concordance	No concordance
	– constant attendance	No concordance	No concordance	No concordance
	– occupational invalidity			

APPENDIX 5

LUXEMBOURG[1]

Member State	Schemes administered by institutions of Member States which have taken a decision recognising the degree of invalidity	Schemes administered by Luxembourg institutions on which the decision is binding in cases of concordance	
		Invalidity – manual workers	Invalidity – clerical staff
BELGIUM	1. General scheme	Concordance	Concordance
	2. Miners' scheme :		
	– partial general invalidity	No concordance	No concordance
	– occupational invalidity	No concordance	No concordance
	3. Mariners' scheme	Concordance[1]	No concordance[1]
FRANCE	1. General scheme :		
	– Group III (constant attendance)	Concordance	Concordance
	– Group II	Concordance	Concordance
	– Group I	Concordance	Concordance
	2. Agricultural scheme:		
	– total general invalidity	Concordance	Concordance
	– two-thirds general invalidity	Concordance	Concordance
	– constant attendance	Concordance	Concordance
	3. Miners' scheme:		
	– two-thirds general invalidity	Concordance	Concordance
	– constant attendance	Concordance	Concordance
	– total general invalidity	No concordance	No concordance
	4. Mariners' scheme:		
	– partial general invalidity	Concordance	Concordance
	– constant attendance	Concordance	concordance
	– occupational invalidity	No concordance	No concordance

[1] In so far as the invalidity recognised by the Belgian institution is general invalidity.

---

[1] Entries concerning concordance between Luxembourg and France or Belgium will be the subject of technical re-examination taking account of the changes which have been made to national legislation in Luxembourg.

Regulation (EC) No 883/2004

Annex VIII

Cases in Which the Independent Benefit is Equal To or Higher Than the Pro-rata Benefit
(Article 52(4))

A. DENMARK

All applications for pensions referred to in the law on social pensions, except for pensions mentioned in Annex IX

B. FRANCE

All applications for pension benefits or survivor's benefits under supplementary retirement schemes for employees or self-employed workers, with the exception of applications for old-age or widow's pensions under the supplementary retirement scheme for professional cabin crew in civil aviation

C. IRELAND

All applications for retirement pensions, old-age (contributory) pensions, widow's (contributory) pension and widower's (contributory) pension

D. NETHERLANDS

Where a person is entitled to a pension on the basis of the Netherlands' law on general old-age insurance (AOW)

E. PORTUGAL

Invalidity, old-age and survivors' pension claims, except for the cases where the total periods of insurance completed under the legislation of more than one Member State are equal to or longer than 21 calendar years, the national periods of insurance are equal to, or less than, 20 years, and the calculation is made under Article 11 of Decree-Law No 35/2002, 19 February, which defines the rules for the determination of the pension amount. In such cases, by applying more favourable pension formation rates, the amount resulting from the pro-rata calculation may be higher than that resulting from the independent calculation.

F. SWEDEN

Earnings-related old-age pension (Act 1998:674), earnings-related survivor's pension in the form of adjustment pension and child's pension allowance when the death occurred before 1 January 2003 and widow's pension (Act 2000:461 and Act 2000:462)

G. UNITED KINGDOM

All applications for retirement pension, widows' and bereavement benefits determined pursuant to the provisions of Title III, Chapter 5 of the Regulation, with the exception of those for which:

(a) during a tax year beginning on or after 6 April 1975:

Appendix 5

   (i) the party concerned had completed periods of insurance, employment or residence under the legislation of the United Kingdom and another Member State; and
   (ii) one (or more) of the tax years referred to in (i) was not considered a qualifying year within the meaning of the legislation of the United Kingdom;

(b) the periods of insurance completed under the legislation in force in the United Kingdom for the periods prior to 5 July 1948 would be taken into account for the purposes of Article 52(1)(b) of the Regulation by application of the periods of insurance, employment or residence under the legislation of another Member State.

Annex IX

Benefits and Agreements Which Allow the Application of Article 54

I. Benefits referred to in Article 54(2)(a) of the Regulation, the amount of which is independent of the length of periods of insurance or residence completed

A. BELGIUM

Benefits relating to the general invalidity scheme, the special invalidity scheme for miners and the special scheme for merchant navy mariners

Benefits on insurance for self-employed persons against incapacity to work

Benefits relating to invalidity in the overseas social insurance scheme and the invalidity scheme for former employees of the Belgian Congo and Ruanda-Urundi

B. DENMARK

The full Danish national old-age pension acquired after 10 years' residence by persons who will have been awarded a pension by 1 October 1989

C. GREECE

Benefits under Law No 4169/1961 relating to the agricultural insurance scheme (OGA)

D. SPAIN

Survivors' pensions granted under the general and special schemes, with the exception of the Special Scheme for Civil Servants

E. FRANCE

Invalidity pension under the general social security system or under the agricultural workers scheme

Widower's or widow's invalidity pension under the general social security system or under the agricultural workers scheme where it is calculated on the basis of the deceased spouse's invalidity pension settled in accordance with Article 52(1)(a)

REGULATION (EC) No 883/2004

F. IRELAND

Type A Invalidity Pension

G. NETHERLANDS

The law of 18 February 1966 on invalidity insurance for employees, as amended (WAO)

The law of 24 April 1997 on invalidity insurance for self-employed persons, as amended (W AZ)

The law of 21 December 1995 on general insurance for surviving dependants (ANW)

H. FINLAND

National pensions to persons who are born disabled or become disabled at an early age (National Pensions Act 547/93)

National pensions determined according to the National Pensions Act of 8 June 1956 and awarded under the transitional rules of the National Pensions Act (547/93)

The additional amount of the child's pension in accordance with the Survivors Pension Act of 17 January 1969

I. SWEDEN

Earnings-related survivor's pension in the form of child's pension allowance and adjustment pension when the death occurred on 1 January 2003 or later when the deceased was born in 1938 or later (Act 2000:461)

II. Benefits referred to in Article 54(2)(b) of the Regulation, the amount of which is determined by reference to a credited period deemed to have been completed between the date on which the risk materialised and a later date

A. GERMANY

Invalidity and survivors' pensions, for which account is taken of a supplementary period

Old-age pensions, for which account is taken of a supplementary period already acquired

B. SPAIN

The pensions for retirement or retirement for permanent disability (invalidity) under the Special Scheme for Civil Servants due under Title I of the consolidated text of the Law on State Pensioners if at the time of materialisation of the risk the beneficiary was an active civil servant or treated as such; death and survivors' (widows'/widowers', orphans' and parents') pensions due under Title I of the consolidated text of the Law on State Pensioners if at the time of death the civil servant was active or treated as such

C. ITALY

Italian pensions for total incapacity for work (inabilità)

Appendix 5

D. LUXEMBOURG

Invalidity and survivors' pensions

E. FINLAND

Employment pensions for which account is taken of future periods according to the national legislation

F. SWEDEN

Sickness benefit and activity compensation in the form of guarantee benefit (Act 1962:381)

Survivor's pension calculated on the basis of assumed insurance periods (Act 2000:461 and 2000:462)

Old-age pension in the form of guarantee pension calculated on the basis of assumed periods previously counted (Act 1998:702)

III. Agreements referred to in Article 54(2)(b)(i) of the Regulation intended to prevent the same credited period being taken into account two or more times:

The Social Security Agreement of 28 April 1997 between the Republic of Finland and the Federal Republic of Germany

The Social Security Agreement of 10 November 2000 between the Republic of Finland and the Grand Duchy of Luxembourg

Nordic Convention of 15 June 1992 on social security

Annex X

Special Non-contributory Cash Benefits
(Article 70(2)(c))

The content of this Annex shall be determined by the European Parliament and by the Council in accordance with the Treaty as soon as possible and at the latest before the date of application of this Regulation as referred to in Article 91.

Annex XI

Special provisions for the application of the legislation of the Member States
(Article 51(3), 56(1) and 83)

The content of this Annex shall be determined by the European Parliament and by the Council in accordance with the Treaty as soon as possible and at the latest before the date of application of this Regulation as referred to in Article 91.

APPENDIX 6

AGREEMENT ON THE EUROPEAN ECONOMIC AREA

PART III

FREE MOVEMENT OF PERSONS, SERVICES AND CAPITAL

CHAPTER 1

WORKERS AND SELF-EMPLOYED PERSONS

Article 28

1. Freedom of movement for workers shall be secured among EC Member States and EFTA States.

2. Such freedom of movement shall entail the abolition of any discrimination based on nationality between workers of EC Member States and EFTA States as regards employment, remuneration and other conditions of work and employment.

3. It shall entail the right, subject to limitations justified on grounds of public policy, public security or public health:

(a) to accept offers of employment actually made;
(b) to move freely within the territory of EC Member States and EFTA States for this purpose;
(c) to stay in the territory of an EC Member State or an EFTA State for the purpose of employment in accordance with the provisions governing the employment of nationals of that State laid down by law, regulation or administrative action;
(d) to remain in the territory of an EC Member State or an EFTA State after having been employed there.

4. The provisions of this Article shall not apply to employment in the public service.

5. Annex V contains specific provisions on the free movement of workers.

Article 29

In order to provide freedom of movement for workers and self-employed persons, the Contracting Parties shall, in the field of social security, secure, as provided for in Annex VI, for workers and self-employed persons and their dependants, in particular:

(a) aggregation, for the purpose of acquiring and retaining the right to benefit and of calculating the amount of benefit, of all periods taken into account under the laws of the several countries;

(b) payment of benefits to persons resident in the territories of Contracting Parties.

Article 30

In order to make it easier for persons to take up and pursue activities as workers and self-employed persons, the Contracting Parties shall take the necessary measures, as contained in Annex VII, concerning the mutual recognition of diplomas, certificates and other evidence of formal qualifications, and the coordination of the provisions laid down by law, regulation or administrative action in the Contracting Parties concerning the taking up and pursuit of activities by workers and self-employed persons.

CHAPTER 2

RIGHT OF ESTABLISHMENT

Article 31

1. Within the framework of the provisions of this Agreement, there shall be no restrictions on the freedom of establishment of nationals of an EC Member State or an EFTA State in the territory of any other of these States. This shall also apply to the setting up of agencies, branches or subsidiaries by nationals of any EC Member State or EFTA State established in the territory of any of these States.

Freedom of establishment shall include the right to take up and pursue activities as self-employed persons and to set up and manage undertakings, in particular companies or firms within the meaning of Article 34, second paragraph, under the conditions laid down for its own nationals by the law of the country where such establishment is effected, subject to the provisions of Chapter 4.

2. Annexes VIII to XI contain specific provisions on the right of establishment.

Article 32

The provisions of this Chapter shall not apply, so far as any given Contracting Party is concerned, to activities which in that Contracting Party are connected, even occasionally, with the exercise of official authority.

Article 33

The provisions of this Chapter and measures taken in pursuance thereof shall not prejudice the applicability of provisions laid down by law, regulation or administrative action providing for special treatment for foreign nationals on grounds of public policy, public security or public health.

Article 34

Companies or firms formed in accordance with the law of an EC Member State or an EFTA State and having their registered office, central administration or principal place of business within the territory of the Contracting Parties shall, for the purposes of this Chapter, be treated in the same way as natural persons who are nationals of EC Member States or EFTA States.

'Companies or firms' means companies or firms constituted under civil or commercial law, including cooperative societies, and other legal persons governed by public or private law, save for those which are non-profit-making.

Article 35

The provisions of Article 30 shall apply to the matters covered by this Chapter.

Appendix 7

AGREEMENT BETWEEN THE EUROPEAN COMMUNITY AND ITS MEMBER STATES, OF THE ONE PART, AND THE SWISS CONFEDERATION, OF THE OTHER, ON THE FREE MOVEMENT OF PERSONS

THE SWISS CONFEDERATION, of the one part, and A7–01

THE EUROPEAN COMMUNITY,

THE KINGDOM OF BELGIUM,

THE KINGDOM OF DENMARK,

THE FEDERAL REPUBLIC OF GERMANY,

THE HELLENIC REPUBLIC,

THE KINGDOM OF SPAIN,

THE FRENCH REPUBLIC,

IRELAND,

THE ITALIAN REPUBLIC,

THE GRAND DUCHY OF LUXEMBOURG,

THE KINGDOM OF THE NETHERLANDS,

THE REPUBLIC OF AUSTRIA,

THE PORTUGUESE REPUBLIC,

THE REPUBLIC OF FINLAND,

THE KINGDOM OF SWEDEN,

THE UNITED KINGDOM OF GREAT BRITAIN AND NORTHERN IRELAND, of the other part, hereinafter referred to as 'the Contracting Parties',

Convinced that the free movement of persons between the territories of the Contracting Parties is a key factor in the harmonious development of their relations,

Resolved to bring about the free movement of persons between them on the basis of the rules applying in the European Community,

Have decided to conclude this Agreement:

Appendix 7

I. Basic Provisions

Article 1

Objective

The objective of this Agreement, for the benefit of nationals of the Member States of the European Community and Switzerland, is:

(a) to accord a right of entry, residence, access to work as employed persons, establishment on a self-employed basis and the right to stay in the territory of the Contracting Parties;

(b) to facilitate the provision of services in the territory of the Contracting Parties, and in particular to liberalise the provision of services of brief duration;

(c) to accord a right of entry into, and residence in, the territory of the Contracting Parties to persons without an economic activity in the host country;

(d) to accord the same living, employment and working conditions as those accorded to nationals.

Article 2

Non-discrimination

Nationals of one Contracting Party who are lawfully resident in the territory of another Contracting Party shall not, in application of and in accordance with the provisions of Annexes I, II and III to this Agreement, be the subject of any discrimination on grounds of nationality.

Article 3

Right of entry

The right of entry of nationals of one Contracting Party into the territory of another Contracting Party shall be guaranteed in accordance with the provisions laid down in Annex I.

Article 4

Right of residence and access to an economic activity

The right of residence and access to an economic activity shall be guaranteed unless otherwise provided in Article 10 and in accordance with the provisions of Annex I.

Article 5

Persons providing services

1. Without prejudice to other specific agreements between the Contracting Parties specifically concerning the provision of services (including the Government Procurement Agreement in so far as it covers the provision of services), persons providing services, including companies in accordance with the provisions of Annex I, shall have the right to provide a service in the territory of the other Contracting Party for a period not exceeding 90 days' of actual work in a calendar year.

2. Providers of services shall have the right of entry into and residence in, the territory of the other Contracting Party:

(a) where they have the right to provide a service under paragraph 1 or by virtue of the provisions of an agreement mentioned in paragraph 1;

(b) or, if the conditions specified in (a) are not fulfilled, where they have received authorisation to provide a service from the competent authorities of the Contracting Party concerned.

3. Nationals of a Member State of the European Community or Switzerland entering the territory of a Contracting Party solely to receive services shall have the right of entry and residence.

4. The rights referred to in this Article shall be guaranteed in accordance with the provisions laid down in Annexes I, II and III. The quantitative limits of Article 10 may not be relied upon as against persons referred to in this Article.

Article 6

Right of residence for persons not pursuing an economic activity

The right of residence in the territory of a Contracting Party shall be guaranteed to persons not pursuing an economic activity in accordance with the provisions of Annex I relating to non-active people.

Article 7

Other rights

The Contracting Parties shall make provision, in accordance with Annex I, for the following rights in relation to the free movement of persons:

(a) the right to equal treatment with nationals in respect of access to, and the pursuit of, an economic activity, and living, employment and working conditions;

(b) the right to occupational and geographical mobility II. which enables nationals of the Contracting Parties to move freely within the territory of the host state and to pursue the occupation of their choice;

(c) the right to stay in the territory of a Contracting Party after the end of an economic activity;

(d) the right of residence for members of the family, irrespective of their nationality;

(e) the right of family members to pursue an economic activity, irrespective of their nationality;

(f) the right to acquire immovable property in so far as this is linked to the exercise of rights conferred by this Agreement;

(g) during the transitional period, the right, after the end of an economic activity or period of residence in the territory of a Contracting Party, to return there for the purposes of pursuing an economic activity and the right to have a temporary residence permit converted into a permanent one.

Article 8

Coordination of social security systems

The Contracting Parties shall make provision, in accordance with Annex II, for the coordination of social security systems with the aim in particular of:

(a) securing equality of treatment;

(b) determining the legislation applicable;

(c) aggregation, for the purpose of acquiring and retaining the right to benefits, and of calculating such benefits, all periods taken into consideration by the national legislation of the countries concerned;

(d) paying benefits to persons residing in the territory of Contracting Parties;

(e) fostering mutual administrative assistance and cooperation between authorities and institutions.

Article 9

Diplomas, certificates and other qualifications

In order to make it easier for nationals of the Member States of the European Community and Switzerland to gain access to and pursue activities as employed and self-employed persons and to provide services, the Contracting Parties shall take the necessary measures, in accordance with Annex III, concerning the mutual recognition of diplomas, certificates and other qualifications, and coordination of the laws, regulations and administrative provisions of the Contracting Parties on access to and pursuit of activities as employed and self-employed persons and the provision of services.

Agreement between the European Community and its Member States

II. General and Final Provisions

Article 10

Transitional provisions and development of the Agreement

1. For five years after the entry into force of the Agreement, Switzerland may maintain quantitative limits in respect of access to an economic activity for the following two categories of residence: residence for a period of more than four months and less than one year and residence for a period equal to, or exceeding, one year. There shall be no restriction on residence for less than four months.

From the beginning of the sixth year, all quantitative limits applicable to nationals of the Member States of the European Community shall be abolished.

2. For a maximum period of two years, the Contracting Parties may maintain the controls on the priority of workers integrated into the regular labour market and wage and working conditions applicable to nationals of the other Contracting Party, including the persons providing services referred to in Article 5. Before the end of the first year, the Joint Committee shall consider whether these restrictions need to be maintained. It may curtail the maximum period of two years. The controls on the priority of workers integrated into the regular labour market shall not apply to providers of services liberalised by a specific agreement between the Contracting Parties concerning the provision of services (including the Agreement on certain aspects of government procurement in so far as it covers the provision of services).

3. On entry into force of this Agreement and until the end of the of the fifth year, each year Switzerland shall reserve, within its overall quotas, for employed and self-employed persons of the European Community at least 15 000 new residence permits valid for a period equal to, or exceeding, one year and 115 500 valid for more than four months and less than one year.

4. Notwithstanding the provisions of paragraph 3, the Contracting Parties have agreed on the following arrangements: if, after five years and up to 12 years after the entry into force of the Agreement, the number of new residence permits of either of the categories referred to in paragraph 1 issued to employed and self-employed persons of the European Community in a given year exceeds the average for the three preceding years by more than 10 %, Switzerland may, for the following year, unilaterally limit the number of new residence permits of that category for employed and self-employed persons of the European Community to the average of the three preceding years plus 5 %. The following year, the number may be limited to the same level.

Notwithstanding the provisions of the previous subparagraph, the number of new residence permits issued to employed and self-employed persons of the European Community may not be limited to fewer than 15 000 per year valid for a period equal to, or exceeding, one year and 115 500 per year valid for more than four months and less than one year.

5. The transitional provisions of paragraphs 1 to 4, and in particular those of paragraph 2 concerning the priority of workers integrated into the regular labour market and controls on wage and working conditions, shall not apply to employed and self-employed persons who, at the time of this Agreement's entry into force, are authorised to pursue an economic activity in the territory of the Contracting Parties.

Appendix 7

Such persons shall in particular enjoy occupational and geographical mobility. The holders of residence permits valid for less than one year shall be entitled to have their permits renewed; the exhaustion of quantitative limits may not be invoked against them. The holders of residence permits valid for a period equal to, or exceeding, one year shall automatically be entitled to have their permits extended. Such employed and self-employed persons shall therefore enjoy the rights to free movement accorded to established persons in the basic provisions of this Agreement, and in particular Article 7 thereof, from its entry into force.

6. Switzerland shall regularly and promptly forward to the Joint Committee any useful statistics and information, including measures implementing paragraph 2. A Contracting Party may request a review of the situation within the Joint Committee.

7. No quantitative limits may be applied to frontier workers.

8. The transitional provisions on social security and the retrocession of unemployment insurance contributions are laid down in the Protocol to Annex II.

Article 11

Processing of appeals

1. The persons covered by this Agreement shall have a right of appeal to the competent authorities in respect of the application of the provisions of this Agreement.

2. Appeals must be processed within a reasonable period of time.

3. Persons covered by this Agreement shall have the opportunity to appeal to the competent national judicial body in respect of decisions on appeals, or the absence of a decision within a reasonable period of time.

Article 12

More favourable provisions

This Agreement shall not preclude any more favourable national provisions which may exist for both nationals of the Contracting Parties and their family members.

Article 13

Standstill

The Contracting Parties undertake not to adopt any further restrictive measures vis-à-vis each other's nationals in fields covered by this Agreement.

Article 14

Joint Committee

1. A Joint Committee composed of representatives of the Contracting Parties is hereby established. It shall be responsible for the management and proper application of the Agreement. To that end it shall issue recommendations. It shall take decisions in the circumstances provided for in the Agreement The Joint Committee shall reach its decisions by mutual agreement.

2. In the event of serious economic or social difficulties, the Joint Committee shall meet, at the request of either Contracting Party, to examine appropriate measures to remedy the situation. The Joint Committee may decide what measures to take within 60 days of the date of the request. This period may be extended by the Joint Committee. The scope and duration of such measures shall not exceed that which is strictly necessary to remedy the situation. Preference shall be given to measures that least disrupt the working of this Agreement.

3. For the purposes of proper implementation of the Agreement, the Contracting Parties shall regularly exchange information and, at the request of either of them, shall consult each other within the Joint Committee.

4. The Joint Committee shall meet as and when necessary and at least once a year. Either Party may request the convening a meeting. The Joint Committee shall meet within 15 days of a request under paragraph 2.

5. The Joint Committee shall establish its rules of procedure which shall contain, inter alia, provisions on the convening of meetings, the appointment of the chairman and the chairman's term of office.

6. The Joint Committee may decide to set up any working party or group of experts to assist it in the performance of its duties.

Article 15

Annexes and Protocols

The Annexes and Protocols to this Agreement shall form an integral part thereof. The Final Act shall contain the declarations.

Article 16

Reference to Community law

1. In order to attain the objectives pursued by this Agreement, the Contracting Parties shall take all measures necessary to ensure that rights and obligations equivalent to those contained in the legal acts of the European Community to which reference is made are applied in relations between them.

2. Insofar as the application of this Agreement involves concepts of Community law, account shall be taken of the relevant case-law of the Court of Justice of the European Communities prior to the date of its signature. Case-law after that date shall

be brought to Switzerland's attention. To ensure that the Agreement works properly, the Joint Committee shall at the request of either Contracting Party, determine the implications of such case-law.

Article 17

Development of law

1. As soon as one Contracting Party initiates the process of adopting a draft amendment to its domestic legislation, or as soon as there is a change in the case-law of authorities against whose decisions there is no judicial remedy under domestic law in a field governed by this Agreement, it shall inform the shall not affect the double taxation agreements' definition of other Contracting Party through the Joint Committee.

2. The Joint Committee shall hold an exchange of views on the implications of such an amendment for the proper functioning of the Agreement.

Article 18

Revision

If a Contracting Party wishes to have this Agreement revised, it shall submit a proposal to that effect to the Joint Committee. Amendments to this Agreement shall enter into force after the respective internal procedures have been completed, with the exception of amendments to Annexes II and III, which shall be adopted by decision of the Joint Committee and may enter into force immediately after that decision.

Article 19

Settlement of disputes

1. The Contracting Parties may bring a matter under dispute which concerns the interpretation or application of this Agreement to the Joint Committee.

2. The Joint Committee may settle the dispute. Any information which might be of use in making possible an in-depth examination of the situation with a view to finding an acceptable solution shall be supplied to the Joint Committee. To this end, the Joint Committee shall consider every possible means to maintain the good functioning of this Agreement.

Article 20

Relationship to bilateral social security agreements

Unless otherwise provided for under Annex II, bilateral social security agreements between Switzerland and the Member States of the European Community shall be suspended on the entry into force of this Agreement, in so far as the latter covers the same subject-matter.

Article 21

Relationship to bilateral agreements on double taxation

1. The provisions of bilateral agreements between Switzerland and the Member States of the European Community on double taxation shall be unaffected by the provisions of this Agreement. In particular, the provisions of this Agreement shall not affect the double taxation agreements' definition of 'frontier workers'.

2. No provision of this Agreement may be interpreted in such a way as to prevent the Contracting Parties from distinguishing, when applying the relevant provisions of their fiscal legislation, between taxpayers whose situations are not comparable, especially as regards their place of residence.

3. No provision of this Agreement shall prevent the Contracting Parties from adopting or applying measures to ensure the imposition, payment and effective recovery of taxes or to forestall tax evasion under their national tax legislation or agreements aimed at preventing double taxation between Switzerland, of the one part, and one or more Member States of the European Community, of the other part, or any other tax arrangements.

Article 22

Relationship to bilateral agreements on matters other than social security and double taxation

1. Notwithstanding the provisions of Articles 20 and 21 this Agreement shall not affect agreements linking Switzerland of the one part, and one or more Member States of the European Community, of the other part, such as those concerning private individuals, economic operators, cross- border cooperation or local frontier traffic, in so far as they are compatible with this Agreement.

2. In the event of incompatibilities between such agreements and this Agreement, the latter shall prevail.

Article 23

Acquired rights

In the event of termination or non-renewal, rights acquired by private individuals shall not be affected. The Contracting Parties shall settle by mutual agreement what action is to be taken in respect of rights in the process of being acquired.

Article 24

Territorial scope

This Agreement shall apply, on the one hand, to the territory of Switzerland and, on the other hand, to the territories in which the Treaty establishing the European Community is applicable and under the conditions laid down by that Treaty.

Appendix 7

Article 25

Entry into force and duration

1. This Agreement shall be ratified or approved by the Contracting Parties in accordance with their own procedures. It shall enter into force on the first day of the second month following the last notification of deposit of the instruments of ratification or approval of all seven of the following agreements:

Agreement on the free movement of persons

Agreement on air transport

Agreement on the carriage of passengers and goods by road and rail

Agreement on trade in agricultural products

Agreement on the mutual recognition of conformity assessment

Agreement on certain aspects of government procurement

Agreement on scientific and technological cooperation.

2. This Agreement shall be concluded for an initial period of seven years. It shall be renewed indefinitely unless the European Community or Switzerland notifies the other Contracting Party to the contrary before the initial period expires. In the event of such notification, paragraph 4 shall apply.

3. The European Community or Switzerland may terminate this Agreement by notifying its decision to the other Party. In the event of such notification, the provisions of paragraph 4 shall apply.

4. The seven Agreements referred to in paragraph 1 shall cease to apply six months after receipt of notification of non renewal referred to in paragraph 2 or termination referred to in paragraph 3.

Annex I

Free Movement of Persons

I. General Provisions

Article 1

Entry and exit

1. The Contracting Parties shall allow nationals of the other Contracting Parties and members of their family within the meaning of Article 3 of this Annex and posted persons within the meaning of Article 17 of this Annex to enter their territory simply upon production of a valid identity card or passport.

No entry visa or equivalent requirement may be demanded save in respect of members of the family and posted workers within the meaning of Article 17 of this Annex who do not have the nationality of a Contracting Party. The Contracting

Party concerned shall grant these persons every facility for obtaining any necessary visas.

2. The Contracting Parties shall grant nationals of the Contracting Parties, and members of their family within the meaning of Article 3 of this Annex and posted workers within the meaning of Article 17 of this Annex, the right to leave their territory simply upon production of a valid identity card or passport. The Contracting Parties may not demand any exit visa or equivalent requirement from nationals of the other Contracting Parties.

The Contracting Parties, acting in accordance with their laws, shall issue to such nationals, or renew, an identity card or passport, which shall state in particular the holder's nationality.

The passport must be valid at least for all the Contracting Parties and for the countries through which the holder must pass when travelling between them. Where the passport is the only document on which the holder may lawfully leave the country, its period of validity may not be less than five years.

Article 2

Residence and economic activity

1. Without prejudice to the provisions for the transitional period, which are laid down in Article 10 of this Agreement and Chapter VII of this Annex, nationals of a Contracting Party shall have the right to reside and pursue an economic activity in the territory of the other Contracting Party under the procedures laid down in Chapters II to IV. That right shall be substantiated through the issue of a residence permit or, for persons from frontier zones, by means of a special permit.

Nationals of a Contracting Party shall also have the right to visit another Contracting Party or to remain there after a period of employment of less than one year in order to seek employment and to reside there for a reasonable amount of time, which may be up to six months, to allow them to find out about the employment opportunities corresponding to their professional qualifications and, if necessary, take the appropriate steps to take up employment. Those seeking employment shall have the right, in the territory of the Contracting Party concerned, to receive the same assistance as employment agencies in that state grant to its own nationals. They may be excluded from social security schemes for the duration of such residence.

2. Nationals of the Contracting Parties not pursuing any economic activity in the host State who do not have a right of residence pursuant to other provisions of this Agreement shall, provided they fulfil the preconditions laid down in Chapter V, have a right of residence. That right shall be substantiated through the issue of a residence permit.

3. The residence or special permit granted to nationals of the Contracting Parties shall be issued and renewed free of charge or on payment of a sum not exceeding the charges or taxes which nationals are required to pay for the issue of identity cards. The Contracting Parties shall take the necessary measures to simplify the formalities and procedures for obtaining those documents as far as possible.

4. The Contracting Parties may require nationals of the other Contracting Parties to report their presence in the territory.

Article 3

Members of the family

1. A person who has the right of residence and is a national of a Contracting Party is entitled to be joined by the members of his family. An employed person must possess housing for his family which is regarded as of normal standard for national employed persons in the region where he is employed, but this provision may not lead to discrimination between national employed persons and employed persons from the other Contracting Party.

2. The following shall be regarded as members of the family, whatever their nationality:

(a) his spouse and their relatives in the descending line who are under the age of 21 or are dependent;
(b) his relatives in the ascending line and those of his spouse who are dependent on him;
(c) in the case of a student, his spouse and their dependent children.

The Contracting Parties shall facilitate the admission of any member of the family not covered by the provisions of this paragraph under (a), (b) and (c), if that person is a dependant or lives in the household of the national of a Contracting Party in the country of provenance.

3. When issuing a residence permit to members of the family of a national of a Contracting Party, the Contracting Parties may require only the documents listed below:

(a) the document by virtue of which they entered the territory;
(b) a document issued by the competent authority of the state of origin or provenance proving their relationship;
(c) for dependants, a document issued by the competent authority of the state of origin or provenance certifying that they are dependants of the person referred to in paragraph 1 or that they live in his household in that state.

4. The period of validity of a residence permit issued to a member of the family shall be the same as that of the permit issued to the person on whom he is dependent.

5. The spouse and the dependent children or children aged under 21 of a person having a right of residence shall have the right to take up an economic activity whatever their nationality.

6. The children of a national of a Contracting Party, whether or not he is pursuing or has pursued an economic activity in the territory of the other Contracting Party, shall be admitted to general education, apprenticeships and vocational training courses on the same basis as nationals of the host state, if those children are living in its territory.

The Contracting Parties shall promote initiatives to enable such children to follow the abovementioned courses under the best conditions.

Article 4

Right to stay

1. Nationals of a Contracting Party and members of their family shall have the right to stay in the territory of another Contracting Party after their economic activity has finished.

2. In accordance with Article 16 of the Agreement, reference is made to Regulation (EEC) No 1251/70 (OJ L 142, 1970, p. 24)[1] and Directive 75/34/EEC (OJ L 14, 1975, p. 10)[1].

Article 5

Public order

1. The rights granted under the provisions of this Agreement may be restricted only by means of measures which are justified on grounds of public order, public security or public health.

2. In accordance with Article 16 of the Agreement, reference is made to Directives 64/221/EEC (OJ L 56, 4.4.1964, p. 850/64)[1], 72/194/EEC (OJ L 121, 26.5.1972, p. 32)[1] and 75/35/EEC (OJ L 14, 20.1.1975, p. 14)[1].

II. Employed Persons

Article 6

Rules regarding residence

1. An employed person who is a national of a Contracting Party (hereinafter referred to as 'employed person') and is employed for a period of one year or more by an employer in the host state shall receive a residence permit which is valid for at least five years from its date of issue. It shall be extended automatically for a period of at least five years. When renewed for the first time, its period of validity may be limited, but not to less than one year, where its holder has been involuntarily unemployed for more than 12 consecutive months.

2. An employed person who is employed for a period of more than three months but less than one year by an employer in the host state shall receive a residence permit for the same duration as his contract.

An employed person who is employed for a period of up to three months does not require a residence permit.

3. When issuing residence permits, the Contracting Parties may not require an employed person to produce more than the following documents:

(a) the document by virtue of which he entered their territory;

---

[1] As in force at the date of signing the Agreement.

(b) a contractual statement from the employer or a written confirmation of engagement.

4. A residence permit shall be valid throughout the territory of the issuing state.

5. Breaks in residence of less than six consecutive months and absences for the purposes of fulfilling military service obligations shall not affect the validity of the residence permit.

6. A valid residence permit may not be withdrawn from an employed person merely on the grounds that he is no longer working, either because he has become temporarily unable to work owing to an accident or illness, or because he is involuntarily unemployed as certified by the competent employment office.

7. Completion of the formalities for obtaining a residence permit shall not prevent an applicant immediately taking up employment under the contract he has concluded.

Article 7

Employed frontier workers

1. An employed frontier worker is a national of a Contracting Party who has his residence in the territory of a Contracting Party and who pursues an activity as an employed person in the territory of the other Contracting Party, returning to his place of residence as a rule every day, or at least once a week.

2. Frontier workers shall not require a residence permit.

The competent authorities of the state of employment may nevertheless issue the frontier worker with a special permit for a period of at least five years or for the duration of his employment where this is longer than three months and less than one year. It shall be extended for at least five years provided that the frontier worker furnishes proof that he is actually pursuing an economic activity.

3. Special permits shall be valid throughout the territory of the issuing state.

Article 8

Occupational and geographical mobility

1. Employed persons shall have the right to occupational and geographical mobility throughout the territory of the host state.

2. Occupational mobility shall include changes of employer, employment or occupation and changing from employed to self-employed status. Geographical mobility shall include changes in the place of work and residence.

Article 9

Equal treatment

1. An employed person who is a national of a Contracting Party may not, by reason of his nationality, be treated differently in the territory of the other Contracting Party from national employed persons as regards conditions of employment and working conditions, especially as regards pay, dismissal, or reinstatement or re-employment if he becomes unemployed.

2. An employed person and the members of his family referred to in Article 3 of this Annex shall enjoy the same tax concessions and welfare benefits as national employed persons and members of their family.

3. He shall also be entitled on the same basis and on the same terms as national employed persons to education in vocational training establishments and in vocational retraining and occupational rehabilitation centres.

4. Any clause in a collective or individual agreement or in any other collective arrangements concerning access to employment, employment, pay and other terms of employment and dismissal, shall be automatically void insofar as it provides for or authorises discriminatory conditions with respect to foreign employed persons who are nationals of the Contracting Parties.

5. An employed person who is a national of a Contracting Party and is employed in the territory of the other Contracting Party shall enjoy equal treatment in terms of membership of trade union organisations and exercise of union rights, including the right to vote and right of access to executive or managerial positions within a trade union organisation; he may be precluded from involvement in the management of public law bodies and from holding an office governed by public law. He shall, moreover, have the right to be eligible for election to bodies representing employees in an undertaking.

These provisions shall be without prejudice to laws or regulations in the host state which confer more extensive rights on employed persons from the other Contracting Party.

6. Without prejudice to the provisions of Article 26 of this Annex, an employed person who is a national of a Contracting Party and employed in the territory of the other Contracting Party shall enjoy all the rights and all the advantages accorded to national employed persons in terms of housing, including ownership of the housing he needs.

Such a worker shall have the same right as nationals to register on the housing lists in the region in which he is employed, where such lists exist; he shall enjoy the resultant benefit, and priorities.

If his family has remained in his state of provenance, it shall be considered for this purpose as residing in the said region, where national workers benefit from a similar presumption.

Appendix 7

Article 10

Public service employment

A national of a Contracting Party pursuing an activity as an employed person may be refused the right to take up employment in the public service which involves the exercise of public power and is intended to protect the general interests of the state or other public bodies.

Article 11

Cooperation in relation to employment services

The Contracting Parties shall cooperate, within the EURES (European Employment Services) network, in particular in setting up contacts, matching job vacancies and applications and exchanging information on the state of the labour market and living and working conditions.

III. Self-Employed Persons

Article 12

Rules regarding residence

1. A national of a Contracting Party wishing to become established in the territory of another Contracting Party in order to pursue a self-employed activity (hereinafter referred to as a 'self-employed person') shall receive a residence permit valid for a period of at least five years from its date of issue, provided that he produces evidence to the competent national authorities that he is established or wishes to become so.

2. The residence permit shall be extended automatically for a period of at least five years, provided that the self-employed person produces evidence to the competent national authorities that he is pursuing a self-employed economic activity.

3. When issuing residence permits, the Contracting Parties may not require self-employed persons to produce more than the following:

(a)   the document by virtue of which he entered their territory;

(b)   the evidence referred to in paragraphs 1 and 2.

4. A residence permit shall be valid throughout the territory of the issuing state.

5. Breaks in residence of less than six consecutive months and absences for the purposes of fulfilling military service obligations shall not affect the validity of the residence permit.

6. Valid residence permits may not be withdrawn from persons referred to in paragraph 1 merely because they are no longer working owing to temporary incapacity as a result of illness or accident.

Agreement between the European Community and its Member States

Article 13

Self-employed frontier workers

1. A self-employed frontier worker is a national of a Contracting Party who is resident in the territory of a Contracting Party and who pursues a self-employed activity in the territory of the other Contracting Party, returning to his place of residence as a rule every day or at least once a week.

2. Self-employed frontier workers shall not require a residence permit.

The relevant authorities of the state concerned may nevertheless issue a self-employed frontier worker with a special permit valid for at least five years provided that he produces evidence to the competent national authorities that he is pursuing or wishes to pursue a self-employed activity. The permit shall be extended for at least five years, provided that the frontier worker produces evidence that he is pursuing a self-employed activity.

3. Special permits shall be valid throughout the territory of the issuing state.

Article 14

Occupational and geographical mobility

1. Self-employed persons shall have the right to occupational and geographical mobility throughout the territory of the host state.

2. Occupational mobility shall include change of occupation and changing from self-employed to employed status. Geographical mobility shall include changes in the place of work and residence.

Article 15

Equal treatment

1. As regards access to a self-employed activity and the pursuit thereof, a self-employed worker shall be afforded no less favourable treatment in the host country than that accorded to its own nationals.

2. The provisions of Article 9 of this Annex shall apply mutatis mutandis to the self-employed persons referred to in this Chapter.

Article 16

Exercise of public authority

A self-employed person may be denied the right to pursue an activity involving, even on an occasional basis, the exercise of public authority.

IV. Provision of Services

Article 17

Persons providing services

With regard to the provision of services, the following shall be prohibited under Article 5 of this Agreement:

(a) any restriction on the cross-frontier provision of services in the territory of a Contracting Party not exceeding 90 days of actual work per calendar year;

(b) any restriction on the right of entry and residence in the cases covered by Article 5(2) of this Agreement concerning:

    (i) persons providing services who are nationals of the Member States of the European Community or Switzerland and are established in the territory of a Contracting Party other than that of the person receiving services;

    (ii) employees, irrespective of their nationality, of persons providing services, who are integrated into one Contracting Party's regular labour market and posted for the provision of a service in the territory of another Contracting Party without prejudice to Article 1.

Article 18

The provisions of Article 17 of this Annex shall apply to companies formed in accordance with the law of a Member State of the European Community or Switzerland and having their registered office, central administration or principal place of business in the territory of a Contracting Party.

Article 19

A person providing services who has the right or has been authorised to provide a service may, for the purposes of its provision, temporarily pursue his activity in the state in which the service is provided on the same terms as those imposed by that state on its own nationals, in accordance with the provisions of this Annex and Annexes II and III.

Article 20

1. Persons referred to in Article 17(b) of this Annex who have the right to provide a service shall not require a residence permit for periods of residence of 90 days or less. Such residence shall be covered by the documents referred to in Article 1, by virtue of which they entered the territory.

2. Persons referred to in Article 17(b) of this Annex who have the right or have been authorised to provide a service for a period exceeding 90 days shall receive, to substantiate that right. a residence permit for a period equal to that of the provision of services.

3. The right of residence shall apply throughout the territory of Switzerland or the Member State of the European Community concerned.

4. For the purposes of issuing residence permits, the Contracting Parties may not require of the persons referred to in Article 17(b) of this Annex more than:

(a)   the document by virtue of which they entered the territory;

(b)   evidence that they are providing or wish to provide a service.

Article 21

1. The total duration of provision of services under Article 17(a) of this Annex, whether continuous or consisting of successive periods of provision, may not exceed 90 days of actual work per calendar year.

2. The provisions of paragraph 1 shall be without prejudice to the discharge by the person providing a service of his legal obligations under the guarantee given to the person receiving the service or to cases of force majeure.

Article 22

1. The provisions of Articles 17 and 19 of this Annex shall not apply to activities involving, even on an occasional basis, the exercise of public authority in the Contracting Party concerned.

2. The provisions of Articles 17 and 19 of this Annex and measures adopted by virtue thereof shall not preclude the applicability of laws, regulations and administrative provisions providing for the application of working and employment conditions to employed persons posted for the purposes of providing a service. In accordance with Article 16 of this Agreement, reference is made to Directive 96/71/EC of 16 December 1996 concerning the posting of workers in the framework of the provision of services (OJ L 18, 21.1.1997, p. 1)[2].

3. The provisions of Articles 17(a) and 19 of this Annex shall be without prejudice to the applicability of the laws, regulations and administrative provisions prevailing in all Contracting Parties at the time of this Agreement's entry into force in respect of:

(i)   the activities of temporary and interim employment agencies;

(ii) financial services where provision is subject to prior authorisation in the territory of a Contracting Party and the provider to prudential supervision by that Contracting Party's authorities.

4. The provisions of Articles 17(a) and 19 of this Annex shall be without prejudice to the applicability of the Contracting Parties' respective laws, regulations and administrative provisions concerning the provision of services of 90 days of actual work or less required by imperative requirements in the public interest.

---

[2] As in force at the date of signing the Agreement.

APPENDIX 7

Article 23

Persons receiving services

1. A person receiving services within the meaning of Article 5(3) of this Agreement shall not require a residence permit for a period of residence of three months or less. For a period exceeding three months, a person receiving services shall be issued with a residence permit equal in duration to the service. He may be excluded from social security schemes during his period of residence.

2. A residence permit shall be valid throughout the territory of the issuing state.

V. PERSONS NOT PURSUING AN ECONOMIC ACTIVITY

Article 24

Rules regarding residence

1. A person who is a national of a Contracting Party not pursuing an economic activity in the state of residence and having no right of residence pursuant to other provisions of this Agreement shall receive a residence permit valid for at least five years provided he proves to the competent national authorities that he possesses for himself and the members of his family:

(a) sufficient financial means not to have to apply for social assistance benefits during their stay;

(b) all-risks sickness insurance cover[3].

The Contracting Parties may, if they consider it necessary, require the residence permit to be revalidated at the end of the first two years of residence.

2. Financial means shall be considered sufficient if they exceed the amount below which nationals, having regard to their personal situation and, where appropriate, that of their family, can claim social security benefits. Where that condition cannot be applied, the applicant's financial means shall be regarded as sufficient if they are greater than the level of the minimum social security pension paid by the host state.

3. Persons who have been employed for less than one year in the territory of a Contracting Party may reside there provided they comply with the conditions set out in paragraph 1 of this Article. The unemployment benefits to which they are entitled under national law which is, where appropriate, complemented by the provisions of Annex II, shall be considered to be financial means within the meaning of paragraphs 1(a) and 2 of this Article.

4. A student who does not have a right of residence in the territory of the other Contracting Party on the basis of any other provision of this Agreement shall be issued with a residence permit for a period limited to that of the training or to one year, if the training lasts for more than one year, provided he satisfies the national authority concerned, by means of a statement or, if he chooses, by any other at least

---

[3] In Switzerland, sickness insurance for persons who do not elect to make it their domicile must include accident and maternity cover.

equivalent means. that he has sufficient financial means to ensure that neither he, his spouse nor his dependent children will make any claim for social security of the host state during their stay, and provided he is registered in an approved establishment for the purpose of following, as his principal activity, a vocational training course and has all-risks sickness insurance cover. This Agreement does not regulate access to vocational training or maintenance assistance given to the students covered by this Article.

5. A residence permit shall automatically be extended for at least five years provided that the eligibility conditions are still met. Residence permits for students shall be extended annually for a duration equal to the remaining training period.

6. Breaks in residence of less than six consecutive months and absences for the purposes of fulfilling military service obligations shall not affect the validity of the residence permit.

7. A residence permit shall be valid throughout the territory of the issuing state.

8. The right of residence shall obtain for as long as beneficiaries of that right fulfil the conditions laid down in paragraph 1.

VI. Purchase of Immovable Property

Article 25

1. A national of a Contracting Party who has a right of residence and his principal residence in the host state shall enjoy the same rights as a national as regards the purchase of immovable property. He may set up his principal residence in the host state at any time in accordance with the relevant national rules irrespective of the duration of his employment. Leaving the host state shall not entail any obligation to dispose of such property.

2. The national of a Contracting Party who has a right of residence but does not have his principal residence in the host state shall enjoy the same rights as a national as regards the purchase of immovable property needed for his economic activity. Leaving the host state shall not entail any obligation to dispose of such property. He may also be authorised to purchase a second residence or holiday accommodation. This Agreement shall not affect the rules applying to pure capital investment or business of unbuilt land and apartments.

3. A frontier worker shall enjoy the same rights as a national as regards the purchase of immovable property for his economic activity and as a secondary residence. Leaving the host state shall not entail any obligation to dispose of such property. He may also be authorised to purchase holiday accommodation. This Agreement shall not affect the rules applying in the host state to pure capital investment or business of unbuilt land and apartments.

Appendix 7

VII. Transitional Provisions and Development of the Agreement

Article 26

General provisions

1. When the quantitative restrictions laid down in Article 10 of this Agreement are applied, the provisions contained in this Chapter shall supplement or replace the other provisions of this Annex, as the case may be.

2. When the quantitative restrictions laid down in Article 10 of this Agreement are applied, the pursuit of an economic activity shall be subject to the issue of a residence and/or a work permit.

Article 27

Rules relating to the residence of employed persons

1. The residence permit of an employed person who has an employment contract for a period of less than one year shall be extended for up to a total of 12 months provided that the employed person furnishes proof to the competent national authorities that he is able to pursue an economic activity. A new residence permit shall be issued provided that the employed person furnishes proof that he is able to pursue an economic activity and that the quantitative limits laid down in Article 10 of this Agreement have not been reached. There shall be no obligation to leave the country between two employment contracts in accordance with Article 24 of this Annex.

2. During the period referred to in Article 10(2) of this Agreement, a Contracting Party may require that a written contract or draft contract be produced before issuing a first residence permit.

3.
(a) Persons who have previously held temporary jobs in the territory of the host state for at least 30 months shall automatically have the right to take up employment for an unlimited duration[4]. They may not be denied this right on the grounds that the number of residence permits guaranteed has been exhausted.

(b) Persons who have previously held seasonal employment in the territory of the host state for a total of not less than 50 months during the last 15 years and do not meet the conditions of entitlement to a residence permit in accordance with the provisions of subparagraph (a) above shall automatically have the right to take up employment for an unlimited duration.

---

[4] They shall not be subject to the priority accorded to workers integrated into the regular labour market or monitoring of compliance with wage and employment conditions in a particular sector or place.

Article 28

Employed frontier workers

1. An employed frontier worker is a national of a Contracting Party who has his normal place of residence in the frontier zones of Switzerland or neighbouring states and who pursues an activity as an employed person in the frontier zones of another Contracting Party returning as a rule to his principal residence every day, or at least once a week. For the purposes of this Agreement, frontier zones shall mean the zones defined in the agreements concluded between Switzerland and its neighbours concerning movement in frontier zones.

2. The special permit shall be valid throughout the frontier zone of the issuing state.

Article 29

Employed persons' right to return

1. An employed person who, on the date this Agreement entered into force, was holding a residence permit valid for at least one year and who has then left the host country shall be entitled to preferential access to the quota for a new residence permit within six years of his departure provided he proves that he is able to pursue an economic activity.

2. A frontier worker shall have the right to a new special permit within six years of the end of his previous employment over an uninterrupted period of three years, subject to verification of his pay and working conditions if he is employed for the two years following the Agreement's entry into force, provided he proves to the competent national authorities that he is able to pursue an economic activity.

3. Young persons who have left the territory of a Contracting Party after residing there for at least five years before the age of 21 shall have the right for a period of four years to return to that country and pursue an economic activity.

Article 30

Employed persons' occupational and geographical mobility

1. An employed person holding a residence permit valid for less than one year shall, for the twelve months following the commencement of his employment, have the right to occupational and geographical mobility. The right to change from employed to self-employed status shall also be allowed subject to compliance with Article 10 of this Agreement.

2. Special permits issued to employed frontier workers shall confer the right to occupational and geographical mobility within all the frontier zones of Switzerland or its neighbouring states.

Appendix 7

Article 31

Rules relating to the residence of self-employed persons

A national of a Contracting Party wishing to become established in the territory of another Contracting Party in order to pursue a self-employed activity (hereinafter referred to as a 'self-employed worker') shall receive a residence permit valid for a period of six months. He shall receive a residence permit valid for at least five years provided that he proves to the competent national authorities before the end of the six-month period that he is pursuing a self-employed activity. If necessary, the six-month period may be extended by a maximum of two months if there is a genuine likelihood that he will produce such proof.

Article 32

Self-employed frontier workers

1. A self-employed frontier worker is a national of a Contracting Party who is ordinarily resident in the frontier zones of Switzerland or neighbouring states and who pursues a self-employed activity in the frontier zones of the other Contracting Party returning as a rule to his principal residence in principle every day or at least once a week. For the purposes of this Agreement. frontier zones shall mean the zones defined in the agreements concluded between Switzerland and its neighbouring states concerning movement in frontier zones.

2. A national of a Contracting Party who wishes in his capacity as a frontier worker to pursue a self-employed activity in the frontier zones of Switzerland or its neighbouring states shall receive a preliminary six-month special permit in advance. He shall receive a special permit for a period of at least five years provided that he proves to the competent national authorities, before the end of that six-month period. that he is pursuing a self-employed activity. If necessary, the six-month period may be extended by a maximum of two months if there is a genuine likelihood that he will produce such proof.

3. Special permits shall be valid throughout the frontier zone of the issuing state.

Article 33

Self-employed persons' right to return

1. A self-employed person who has held a residence permit valid for a period of at least five years and who has left the host state shall have the right to a new permit within six years of his departure provided he has already worked in the host country for an uninterrupted period of three years and proves to the competent national authorities that he is able to pursue an economic activity.

2. A self-employed frontier worker shall have the right to a new special permit within a period of six years of the termination of previous activity lasting for an uninterrupted period of four years provided he proves to the competent national authorities that he is able to pursue an economic activity.

3. Young persons who have left the territory of a Contracting Party after residing there for at least five years before the age of 21 shall have the right for a period of four years to return to that country and pursue an economic activity.

Article 34

Self-employed persons' occupational and geographical mobility

Special permits issued to self-employed frontier workers shall confer the right to occupational and geographical mobility within the frontier zones of Switzerland or its neighbouring states. Preliminary six-month residence permits issued in advance (in the case of frontier workers, special permits) shall confer the right only to geographical mobility.

Appendix 8

AGREEMENT ESTABLISHING AN ASSOCIATION BETWEEN THE EUROPEAN ECONOMIC COMMUNITY AND TURKEY

(signed at Ankara, 12 September 1963)

Preamble

HIS MAJESTY THE KING OF THE BELGIANS,

THE PRESIDENT OF THE FEDERAL REPUBLIC OF GERMANY,

THE PRESIDENT OF THE FRENCH REPUBLIC,

THE PRESIDENT OF THE ITALIAN REPUBLIC,

HER ROYAL HIGHNESS THE GRAND DUCHESS OF LUXEMBOURG,

HER MAJESTY THE QUEEN OF THE NETHERLANDS,

and

THE COUNCIL OF THE EUROPEAN ECONOMIC COMMUNITY,

of the one part, and

THE PRESIDENT OF THE REPUBLIC OF TURKEY,

of the other part,

DETERMINED to establish ever closer bonds between the Turkish people and the peoples brought together in the European Economic Community;

RESOLVED to ensure a continuous improvement in living conditions in Turkey and in the European Economic Community through accelerated economic progress and the harmonious expansion of trade, and to reduce the disparity between the Turkish economy and the economies of the Member States of the Community;

MINDFUL both of the special problems presented by the development of the Turkish economy and of the need to grant economic aid to Turkey during a given period;

RECOGNIZING that the support given by the European Economic Community to the efforts of the Turkish people to improve their standard of living will facilitate the accession of Turkey to the Community at a later date;

RESOLVED to preserve and strengthen peace and liberty by joint pursuit of the ideals underlying the Treaty establishing the European Economic Community;

HAVE DECIDED to conclude an Agreement establishing an Association between the European Economic Community and Turkey in accordance with Article 238 of the Treaty establishing the European Economic Community, and to this end have designated as their Plenipotentiaries:

Appendix 8

Article 7

The Contracting Parties shall take all appropriate measures, whether general or particular, to ensure the fulfilment of the obligations arising from this Agreement.

They shall refrain from any measures liable to jeopardize the attainment of the objectives of this Agreement.

Chapter 3

Other Economic Provisions

Article 12

The Contracting Parties agree to be guided by Articles 48, 49 and 50 of the Treaty establishing the Community for the purpose of progressively securing freedom of movement for workers between them.

Article 13

The Contracting Parties agree to be guided by Articles 52 to 56 and Article 58 of the Treaty establishing the Community for the purpose of abolishing restrictions on freedom of establishment between them.

Article 14

The Contracting Parties agree to be guided by Articles 55, 56 and 58 to 65 of the Treaty establishing the Community for the purpose of abolishing restrictions on freedom to provide services between them.

Appendix 9

FROM ADDITIONAL PROTOCOL AND FINANCIAL PROTOCOL SIGNED ON 23 NOVEMBER 1970, ANNEXED TO THE AGREEMENT ESTABLISHING THE ASSOCIATION BETWEEN THE EUROPEAN ECONOMIC COMMUNITY AND TURKEY AND ON MEASURES TO BE TAKEN FOR THEIR ENTRY INTO FORCE — FINAL ACT — DECLARATIONS

Title II

Movement of Persons and Services

Chapter I

Workers

Article 36

Freedom of movement for workers between Member States of the Community and Turkey shall be secured by progressive stages in accordance with the principles set out in Article 12 of the Agreement of Association between the end of the twelfth and the twenty-second year after the entry into force of that Agreement.

The Council of Association shall decide on the rules necessary to that end.

Article 37

As regards conditions of work and remuneration, the rules which each Member State applies to workers of Turkish nationality employed in the Community shall not discriminate on grounds of nationality between such workers and workers who are nationals of other Member States of the Community.

Article 38

While freedom of movement for workers between Member States of the Community and Turkey is being brought about by progressive stages, the Council of Association may review all questions arising in connection with the geographical and occupational mobility of workers of Turkish nationality, in particular the extension of work and residence permits, in order to facilitate the employment of those workers in each Member State.

To that end, the Council of Association may make recommendations to Member States.

A9–01

Appendix 9

Article 39

1. Before the end of the first year after the entry into force of this Protocol the Council of Association shall adopt social security measures for workers of Turkish nationality moving within the Community and for their families residing in the Community.

2. These provisions must enable workers of Turkish nationality, in accordance with arrangements to be laid down, to aggregate periods of insurance or employment completed in individual Member States in respect of old-age pensions, death benefits and invalidity pensions, and also as regards the provision of health services for workers and their families residing in the Community. These measures shall create no obligation on Member States to take into account periods completed in Turkey.

3. The abovementioned measures must ensure that family allowances are paid if a worker's family resides in the Community.

4. It must be possible to transfer to Turkey old-age pensions, death benefits and invalidity pensions obtained under the measures adopted pursuant to paragraph 2.

5. The measures provided for in this Article shall not affect the rights and obligations arising from bilateral agreements between Turkey and Member States of the Community, in so far as these agreements provide more favourable arrangements for Turkish nationals.

Article 40

The Council of Association may make recommendations to Member States and Turkey for encouraging the exchange of young workers; the Council of Association shall be guided in the matter by the measures adopted by Member States in implementation of Article 50 of the Treaty establishing the Community.

Chapter II

Right of Establishment, Services and Transport

Article 41

1. The Contracting Parties shall refrain from introducing between themselves any new restrictions on the freedom of establishment and the freedom to provide services.

2. The Council of Association shall, in accordance with the principles set out in Articles 13 and 14 of the Agreement of Association, determine the timetable and rules for the progressive abolition by the Contracting Parties, between themselves, of restrictions on freedom of establishment and on freedom to provide services.

The Council of Association shall, when determining such timetable and rules for the various classes of activity, take into account corresponding measures already adopted by the Community in these fields and also the special economic and social circumstances of Turkey. Priority shall be given to activities making a particular contribution to the development of production and trade.

Article 58

In the fields covered by this Protocol:

— the arrangements applied by Turkey in respect of the Community shall not give rise to any discrimination between Member States, their nationals or their companies or firms;

— the arrangements applied by the Community in respect of Turkey shall not give rise to any discrimination between Turkish nationals or Turkish companies or firms.

Article 59

In the fields covered by this Protocol Turkey shall not receive more favourable treatment than that which Member States grant to one another pursuant to the Treaty establishing the Community

Appendix 10

DECISION NO 1/80 OF THE ASSOCIATION COUNCIL OF 19 SEPTEMBER 1980 ON THE DEVELOPMENT OF THE ASSOCIATION

THE ASSOCIATION COUNCIL,

Having regard to the Agreement establishing an Association between the European Economic Community and Turkey,

WHEREAS the revitalization and development of the Association must, as agreed on 5 February 1980, cover the entire range of current Association problems; whereas the search for solutions to these problems must take account of the specific nature of the Association links between the Community and Turkey;

WHEREAS in the agricultural sector, the elimination of customs duties applicable to Turkish products imported into the Community will make for the achievement of the desired result and for the alleviation of Turkey's concern as to the effects of the enlargement of the Community; whereas, moreover, Article 33 of the Additional Protocol should be implemented as a prior condition for the introduction of free movement of agricultural products; whereas the arrangements provided for must be implemented with due regard for the principles and mechanisms of the common agricultural policy;

WHEREAS, in the social field, and within the framework of the international commitments of each of the Parties, the above considerations make it necessary to improve the treatment accorded workers and members of their families in relation to the arrangements introduced by Decision No 2/76 of the Association Council; whereas, furthermore, the provisions relating to social security should be implemented as should those relating to the exchange of young workers;

WHEREAS development of the Association justifies the establishment of such economic, technical and financial co-operation as will help to attain the objectives of the Association Agreement, in particular by means of a Community contribution to the economic development of Turkey in various sectors,

HAS DECIDED AS FOLLOWS:

Article 7

The members of the family of a Turkish worker duly registered as belonging to the labour force of a Member State, who have been authorized to join him:

— shall be entitled-subject to the priority to be given to workers of Member States of the Community—to respond to any offer of employment after they have been legally resident for at least three years in that Member State;
— shall enjoy free access to any paid employment of their choice provided they have been legally resident there for at least five years.

Children of Turkish workers who have completed a course of vocational training in the host country may respond to any offer of employment there, irrespective of the length of time they have been resident in that Member State, provided one of their parents has been legally employed in the Member State concerned for at least three years.

Article 8

1. Should it not be possible in the Community to meet an offer of employment by calling on the labour available on the employment market of the Member States and should the Member States, within the framework of their provisions laid down by law, regulation or administrative action, decide to authorize a call on workers who are not nationals of a Member State of the Community in order to meet the offer of employment, they shall endeavour in so doing to accord priority to Turkish workers.

2. The employment services of the Member State shall endeavour to fill vacant positions which they have registered and which the duly registered Community labour force has not been able to fill with Turkish workers who are registered as unemployed and legally resident in the territory of that Member State.

Article 9

Turkish children residing legally in a Member State of the Community with their parents who are or have been legally employed in that Member State, shall be admitted to courses of general education, apprenticeship and vocational training under the same educational entry qualifications as the children of nationals of that Member State. They may in that Member State be eligible to benefit from the advantages provided for under the national legislation in this area.

Article 10

1. The Member States of the Community shall as regards remuneration and other conditions of work grant Turkish workers duly registered as belonging to their labour forces treatment involving no discrimination on the basis of nationality between them and Community workers.

2. Subject to the application of Articles 6 and 7, the Turkish workers referred to in paragraph 1 and members of their families shall be entitled, on the same footing as Community workers, to assistance from the employment services in their search for employment.

Article 11

Nationals of the Member States duly registered as belonging to the labour force in Turkey, and members of their families who have been authorized to join them, shall enjoy in that country the rights and advantages referred to in Articles 6, 7, 9 and 10 if they meet the conditions laid down in those Articles.

Decision No 1/80

Article 12

Where a Member State of the Community of Turkey experiences or is threatened with disturbances on its employment market which might seriously jeopardize the standard of living or level of employment in a particular region, branch of activity or occupation, the State concerned may refrain from automatically applying Articles 6 and 7. The State concerned shall inform the Association Council of any such temporary restriction.

Article 13

The Member States of the Community and Turkey may not introduce new restrictions on the conditions of access to employment applicable to workers and members of their families legally resident and employed in their respective territories.

Article 14

1. the provisions of this section shall be applied subject to limitations justified on grounds of public policy, public security or public health.

2. They shall not prejudice the rights and obligations arising from national legislation or bilateral agreements between Turkey and the Member States of the Community where such legislation or agreements provide for more favourable treatment for their nationals.

Article 15

1. So as to be in a position to ensure the harmonious application of the provisions of this section and determine that they are applied in such a way as to exclude the danger of disturbance of the employment markets, the Association Committee shall periodically exchange information in order to improve mutual knowledge of the economic and social situation, including the state of and outlook for the labour market in the Community and in Turkey. It shall each year present a report on its activities to the Association Council.

2. The Association Committee shall be authorized to enlist the assistance of an ad hoc Working Party in order to implement paragraph 1.

Article 16

1. The provisions of this section shall apply from 1 December 1980.

2. From 1 June 1983, the Association Council shall, particularly in the light of the reports on activities referred to in Article 15 examine the results of application of the provisions of this section with a view to preparing solutions which might apply as from 1 December 1983.

Section 2

Social and Cultural Advancement and the Exchange of Young Workers

Article 17

The Member States and turkey shall co-operate, in accordance with their domestic situations and their legal systems, in appropriate schemes to promote the social and cultural advancement of Turkish workers and the members of their family, in particular literacy campaigns and courses in the language of the host country, activities to maintain links with Turkish culture and access to vocational training.

Article 18

The Association Committee shall prepare a recommendation to be forwarded by the Association Council to the Member States of the Community and Turkey with a view to the implementation of any action that may enable young workers who have received their basic training in their own country to complement their vocational training by participating in in-service training, under the conditions set out in Article 40 of the Additional Protocol.

It shall monitor the actual implementation of this provision.

Chapter III

Economic and Technical Co-operation

Article 19

Co-operation shall be established between the Contracting Parties in order to contribute to the development of Turkey by complementing the country's own efforts to strengthen the economic ties between Turkey and the Community on as broad a basis as possible and to the mutual benefit of the Parties.

APPENDIX 11

STABILISATION AND ASSOCIATION AGREEMENT BETWEEN THE EUROPEAN COMMUNITIES AND THEIR MEMBER STATES, OF THE ONE PART, AND THE FORMER YUGOSLAV REPUBLIC OF MACEDONIA, OF THE OTHER PART

THE KINGDOM OF BELGIUM,

THE KINGDOM OF DENMARK,

THE FEDERAL REPUBLIC OF GERMANY,

THE HELLENIC REPUBLIC,

THE KINGDOM OF SPAIN,

THE FRENCH REPUBLIC,

IRELAND,

THE ITALIAN REPUBLIC,

THE GRAND DUCHY OF LUXEMBOURG,

THE KINGDOM OF THE NETHERLANDS,

THE REPUBLIC OF AUSTRIA,

THE PORTUGUESE REPUBLIC,

THE REPUBLIC OF FINLAND,

THE KINGDOM OF SWEDEN,

THE UNITED KINGDOM OF GREAT BRITAIN AND NORTHERN IRELAND,

Contracting Parties to the Treaty establishing the European Community, the Treaty establishing the European Coal and Steel Community, the Treaty establishing the European Atomic Energy Community, and the Treaty on European Union

hereinafter referred to as 'Member States', and

THE EUROPEAN COMMUNITY, THE EUROPEAN COAL AND STEEL COMMUNITY, THE EUROPEAN ATOMIC ENERGY COMMUNITY,

hereinafter referred to as the 'Community',

of the one part, and

THE FORMER YUGOSLAV REPUBLIC OF MACEDONIA,

hereinafter referred to as 'the former Yugoslav Republic of Macedonia',

of the other part,

CONSIDERING the strong links between the Parties and the values that they share, their desire to strengthen those links and establish a close and lasting relationship based on reciprocity and mutual interest, which should allow the former Yugoslav Republic of Macedonia to further strengthen and extend the relations established previously, in particular through the Cooperation Agreement signed on 29 April 1997 by way of Exchange of Letters, which entered into force on 1 January 1998,

Appendix 11

CONSIDERING that the relationship between the Parties in the field of inland transport should continue to be governed by the Agreement between the European Community and the former Yugoslav Republic of Macedonia in the field of transport, signed on 29 June 1997, which entered into force on 28 November 1997,

CONSIDERING the importance of this Agreement, in the framework of the Stabilisation and Association process with the countries of south-eastern Europe, to be further developed by an EU Common strategy for this region, in the establishment and consolidation of a stable European order based on cooperation, of which the European Union is a mainstay, as well as in the framework of the Stability Pact,

CONSIDERING the commitment of the Parties to contribute by all means to the political, economic and institutional stabilisation in the former Yugoslav Republic of Macedonia as well as in the region, through the development of civic society and democratisation, institution building and public administration reform, enhanced trade and economic cooperation, the strengthening of national and regional security, as well as increased cooperation in justice and home affairs,

CONSIDERING the commitment of the Parties to increasing political and economic freedoms as the very basis of this Agreement, as well as their commitment to respect human rights and the rule of law, including the rights of persons belonging to national minorities, and democratic principles through free and fair elections and a multiparty system,

CONSIDERING the commitment of the Parties to the principles of free market economy and the readiness of the Community to contribute to the economic reforms in the former Yugoslav Republic of Macedonia,

CONSIDERING the commitment of the Parties to the full implementation of all principles and provisions of the UN Charter, of the OSCE, notably those of the Helsinki Final Act, the concluding documents of the Madrid and Vienna Conferences, the Charter of Paris for a New Europe, and of the Cologne Stability Pact for south-eastern Europe, so as to contribute to regional stability and cooperation among the countries of the region,

DESIROUS of establishing regular political dialogue on bilateral and international issues of mutual interest, including regional aspects,

CONSIDERING the commitment of the Parties to free trade, in compliance with the rights and obligations arising out of the WTO,

CONVINCED that the Stabilisation and Association Agreement will create a new climate for economic relations between them and above all for the development of trade and investment, factors crucial to economic restructuring and modernisation,

BEARING IN MIND the commitment by the former Yugoslav Republic of Macedonia to approximate its legislation to that of the Community,

TAKING ACCOUNT of the Community's willingness to provide decisive support for the implementation of reform, and to use all available instruments of cooperation and technical, financial and economic assistance on a comprehensive indicative multi-annual basis to this endeavour,

CONFIRMING that the provisions of this Agreement that fall within the scope of Part III, Title IV of the Treaty establishing the European Community bind the United Kingdom and Ireland as separate Contracting Parties, and not as part of the European Community, until the United Kingdom or Ireland (as the case may be) notifies the former Yugoslav Republic of Macedonia that it has become bound as part of the European Community in accordance with the Protocol on the position of the United Kingdom and Ireland annexed to the Treaty on European Union and the

Treaty establishing the European Community. The same applies to Denmark, in accordance with the Protocol annexed to those Treaties on the position of Denmark,

RECALLING the European Union's readiness to integrate to the fullest possible extent the former Yugoslav Republic of Macedonia into the political and economic mainstream of Europe and its status as a potential candidate for EU membership on the basis of the Treaty on European Union and fulfilment of the criteria defined by the European Council in June 1993, subject to successful implementation of this Agreement, notably regarding regional cooperation,

HAVE AGREED AS FOLLOWS:

Article 1

1. An Association is hereby established between the Community and its Member States of the one part and the former Yugoslav Republic of Macedonia of the other part.

2. The aims of this Association are:

— to provide an appropriate framework for political dialogue, allowing the development of close political relations between the Parties,

— to support the efforts of the former Yugoslav Republic of Macedonia to develop its economic and international cooperation, also through the approximation of its legislation to that of the Community,

— to promote harmonious economic relations and develop gradually a free trade area between the Community and the former Yugoslav Republic of Macedonia,

— to foster regional cooperation in all the fields covered by this Agreement.

TITLE V

MOVEMENT OF WORKERS, ESTABLISHMENT, SUPPLY OF SERVICES, CAPITAL

CHAPTER 1

MOVEMENT OF WORKERS

Article 44

1. Subject to the conditions and modalities applicable in each Member State:

— treatment accorded to workers who are nationals of the former Yugoslav Republic of Macedonia and who are legally employed in the territory of a Member State shall be free of any discrimination based on nationality, as regards working conditions, remuneration or dismissal, compared to its own nationals,

— the legally resident spouse and children of a worker legally employed in the territory of a Member State, with the exception of seasonal workers and of workers coming under bilateral agreements, within the meaning of Article 45, unless otherwise provided by such agreements, shall have access to the labour market of that Member State, during the period of that worker's authorised stay of employment.

2. The former Yugoslav Republic of Macedonia shall, subject to conditions and modalities in that country, accord the treatment refereed to in paragraph 1 to workers who are nationals of a Member State and are legally employed in its territory as well as to their spouse and children who are legally resident in the said country.

Article 45

1. Taking into account the labour market situation in the Member States, subject to their legislation and to compliance with the rules in force in the Member States in the area of mobility of workers:

— the existing facilities of access to employment for workers of the former Yugoslav Republic of Macedonia accorded by Member States with bilateral agreements should be preserved and if possible improved,

— the other Member States shall examine the possibility of concluding similar agreements.

2. The Stabilisation and Association Council shall examine the granting of other improvements, including facilities for access to professional training, in accordance with the rules and procedures in force in the Member States, and taking into account the labour market situation in the Member States and in the Community.

Article 46

Rules shall be laid down for the coordination of social security system for workers with the nationality of the former Yugoslav Republic of Macedonia, legally employed in the territory of a Member State, and for the members of their families legally resident there. To that effect, a decision of the Stabilisation and Association Council, which should not affect any rights or obligations arising from bilateral agreements where the latter provide for more favourable treatment, will put the following provisions in place:

— all periods of insurance, employment or residence completed by such workers in the various Member States shall be added together for the purpose of pensions and annuities in respect of old age, invalidity and death and for the purpose of medical care for such workers and such family members,

— any pensions or annuities in respect of old age, death, industrial accident or occupational disease, or of invalidity resulting therefrom, with the exception of non-contributory benefits, shall be freely transferable at the rate applied by virtue of the law of the debtor Member State or States,

— the workers in question shall receive family allowances forthe members of their families as defined above.

The former Yugoslav Republic of Macedonia shall accord to workers who are nationals of a Member State and legally employed in its territory, and to members of their families legally resident there, treatment similar to that specified in the second and third indents of the first paragraph.

Chapter II

Establishment

Article 47

For the purposes of this Agreement:

(a) a 'Community company' or a 'company of the former Yugoslav Republic of Macedonia' respectively shall mean a company set up in accordance with the laws of a Member State or of former Yugoslav Republic of Macedonia respectively and having its registered office or central administration or principal place of business in the territory of the Community or former Yugoslav Republic of Macedonia respectively.

However, should the company, set up in accordance with the laws of a Member State or of the former Yugoslav Republic of Macedonia respectively, have only its registered office in the territory of the Community or the former Yugoslav Republic of Macedonia respectively, the company shall be considered a Community or a company from the former Yugoslav Republic of Macedonia respectively if its operations possess a real and continuous link with the economy of one of the Member States or the former Yugoslav Republic of Macedonia respectively;

(b) 'subsidiary' of a company shall mean a company which is effectively controlled by the first company;

(c) 'branch' of a company shall mean a place of business not having legal personality which has the appearance of permanency, such as the extension of a parent body, has a management and is materially equipped to negotiate business with third Parties so that the latter, although knowing that there will if necessary be a legal link with the parent body, the head office of which is abroad, do not have to deal directly with such parent body but may transact business at the place of business constituting the extension;

(d) 'establishment' shall mean:
   (i) as regards nationals, the right to set up undertakings, in particular companies, which they effectively control. Business undertakings by nationals shall not extend to seeking or taking employment in the labour market or confer a right of access to the labour market of another Party;
   (ii) as regards Community or the former Yugoslav Republic of Macedonia companies, the right to take up economic activities by means of the setting up of subsidiaries and branches in the former Yugoslav Republic of Macedonia or in the Community respectively;

(e) 'operations' shall mean the pursuit of economic activities;

(f) 'economic activities' shall in principle include activities of an industrial, commercial and professional character and activities of craftsmen;

(g) 'Community national' and 'national of the former Yugoslav Republic of Macedonia' shall mean respectively a natural person who is a national of one of the Member States or of the former Yugoslav Republic of Macedonia;

(h) with regard to international maritime transport, including inter-modal operations involving a sea leg, nationals of the Member States or of the former Yugoslav Republic of Macedonia established outside the Community or of the former Yugoslav Republic of Macedonia respectively, and shipping companies established outside the Community or the former Yugoslav Republic of Macedonia and controlled by nationals of a Member State or the nationals of the former Yugoslav Republic of Macedonia respectively, shall also be beneficiaries of the provisions of this Chapter and Chapter III, if their vessels are registered in that Member State or in the former Yugoslav Republic of Macedonia respectively, in accordance with their respective legislation;

(i) 'financial services' shall mean those activities described in Annex VI. The Stabilisation and Association Council may extend or modify the scope of that Annex.

Article 48

1. The former Yugoslav Republic of Macedonia shall grant, upon entry into force of this Agreement:

(i) as regards the establishment of Community companies treatment no less favourable than that accorded to its own companies or to any third country company, whichever is the better, and

(ii) as regards the operation of subsidiaries and branches of Community companies in the former Yugoslav Republic of Macedonia, once established, treatment no less favourable than that accorded to its own companies and branches or to any subsidiary and branch of any third country company, whichever is the better.

2. The former Yugoslav Republic of Macedonia shall not adopt any new regulations or measures which introduce discrimination as regards the establishment of Community companies on its territory or in respect of their operation, once established, by comparison with its own companies.

3. The Community and its Member States shall grant, from the entry into force of this Agreement:

(i) as regards the establishment of companies from the former Yugoslav Republic of Macedonia, treatment no less favourable than that accorded by Member States to their own companies or to any company of any third country, whichever is the better;

(ii) as regards the operation of subsidiaries and branches of companies from the former Yugoslav Republic of Macedonia, established in their territory, treatment no less favourable than that accorded by Member States to their own companies and branches, or to any subsidiary and branch of any third country company, established in their territory, whichever is the better.

4. Five years after the entry into force of this Agreement, and in the light of the relevant European Court of Justice case law, and the situation of the labour market, the Stabilisation and Association Council will examine whether to extend the above

provisions to the establishment of nationals of both Parties to this Agreement to take up economic activities as self-employed persons.

5. Notwithstanding the provisions of this Article:

(a) subsidiaries and branches of Community companies shall have, from the entry into force of this Agreement, the right to use and rent real property in the former Yugoslav Republic of Macedonia;

(b) subsidiaries of Community companies shall also have the right to acquire and enjoy ownership rights over real property as the companies of the former Yugoslav Republic of Macedonia and as regards public goods/goods of common interest, including natural resources, agricultural land and forestry, the same rights as enjoyed by companies of the former Yugoslav Republic of Macedonia, where these rights are necessary for the conduct of the economic activities for which they are established;

(c) by the end of the first stage of transitional period the Stabilisation and Association Council shall examine the possibility of extending the rights under (b) to branches of the Community companies.

Article 49

1. Subject to the provisions of Article 48, with the exception of financial services described in Annex VI, each Party may regulate the establishment and operation of companies and nationals on its territory, insofar as these regulations do not discriminate against companies and nationals of the other Party in comparison with its own companies and nationals.

2. In respect of financial services, notwithstanding any other provisions of this Agreement, a Party shall not be prevented from taking measures for prudential reasons, including for the protection of investors, depositors, policy holders or persons to whom a fiduciary duty is owned by a financial service supplier, or to ensure the integrity and stability of the financial system.

Such measures shall not be used as a means of avoiding the Party's obligations under the Agreement.

3. Nothing in the Agreement shall be construed to require a Party to disclose information relating to the affairs and accounts of individual customers or any confidential or proprietary information in the possession of public entities.

Article 50

1. The provisions of this Chapter shall not apply to air transport services, inland waterways transport services and maritime cabotage services.

2. The Stabilisation and Association Council may make recommendations for improving establishment and operations in the areas covered by paragraph 1.

Appendix 11

Article 51

1. The provisions of Articles 48 and 49 do not preclude the application by a Party of particular rules concerning the establishment and operation in its territory of branches of companies of another Party not incorporated in the territory of the first Party, which are justified by legal or technical differences between such branches as compared to branches of companies incorporated in its territory or, as regards financial services, for prudential reasons.

2. The difference in treatment shall not go beyond what is strictly necessary as a result of such legal or technical differences or, as regards financial services, for prudential reasons.

Article 52

In order to make it easier for Community nationals and nationals of the former Yugoslav Republic of Macedonia to take up and pursue regulated professional activities in the former Yugoslav Republic of Macedonia and Community respectively, the Stabilisation and Association Council shall examine which steps are necessary for the mutual recognition of qualifications. It may take all necessary measures to that end.

Article 53

1. A Community company or a company from the former Yugoslav Republic of Macedonia established in the territory of the former Yugoslav Republic of Macedonia or the Community respectively shall be entitled to employ, or have employed by one of its subsidiaries or branches, in accordance with the legislation in force in the host country of establishment, in the territory of the former Yugoslav Republic of Macedonia and the Community respectively, employees who are nationals of the Community Member States and former Yugoslav Republic of Macedonia respectively, provided that such employees are key personnel as defined in paragraph 2 and that they are employed exclusively by companies, subsidiaries or branches. The residence and work permits of such employees shall only cover the period of such employment.

2. Key personnel of the abovementioned companies, herein referred to as 'organisations', are 'intra-corporate transferees' as defined in (c) of this paragraph in the following categories, provided that the organisation is a legal person and that the persons concerned have been employed by it or have been partners in it (other than as majority shareholders), for at least the year immediately preceding such movement:

(a) persons working in a senior position with an organisation, who primarily direct the management of the establishment, receiving general supervision or direction principally from the board of directors or stockholders of the business or their equivalent including:

— directing the establishment of a department or sub-division of the establishment,

- supervising and controlling the work of other supervisory, professional or managerial employees,
- having the authority personally to recruit and dismiss or recommend recruiting, dismissing or other personnel actions;

(b) persons working within an organisation who possess uncommon knowledge essential to the establishment's service, research equipment, techniques or management. The assessment of such knowledge may reflect, apart from knowledge specific to the establishment, a high level of qualification referring to a type of work or trade requiring specific technical knowledge, including membership of an accredited profession;

(c) an 'intra-corporate transferee' is defined as a natural person working within an organisation in the territory of a Party, and being temporarily transferred in the context of pursuit of economic activities in the territory of the other Party; the organisation concerned must have its principal place of business in the territory of a Party and the transfer be to an establishment (branch, subsidiary) of that organisation, effectively pursuing like economic activities in the territory of the other Party.

3. The entry into and the temporary presence within the territory of the Community or the former Yugoslav Republic of Macedonia of nationals of the former Yugoslav Republic of Macedonia and Community nationals respectively shall be permitted, when these representatives of companies are persons working in a senior position, as defined in paragraph 2(a) above, within a company, and are responsible for the setting up of a Community subsidiary or branch of a company from the former Yugoslav Republic of Macedonia or of a subsidiary or branch in the former Yugoslav Republic of Macedonia of a Community company in a Community Member State or in the former Yugoslav Republic of Macedonia respectively, when:

- those representatives are not engaged in making direct sales or supplying services, and
- the company has its principal place of business outside the Community or the former Yugoslav Republic of Macedonia, respectively, and has no other representative, office, branch or subsidiary in that Community Member State or former Yugoslav Republic of Macedonia respectively.

Article 54

During the first four years following the date of entry into force of this Agreement, the former Yugoslav Republic of Macedonia may introduce measures which derogate from the provisions of this Chapter as regards the establishment of Community companies and nationals of certain industries which:

- are undergoing restructuring, or are facing serious difficulties, particularly where these entail serious social problems in the former Yugoslav Republic of Macedonia, or
- face the elimination or a drastic reduction of the total market share held by the former Yugoslav Republic of Macedonia companies or nationals in a given sector or industry in the former Yugoslav Republic of Macedonia, or
- are newly emerging industries in the former Yugoslav Republic of Macedonia.

Such measures:

(i) shall cease to apply at the latest two years after the end of the first stage of the transitional period;
(ii) shall be reasonable and necessary in order to remedy the situation, and
(iii) shall not introduce discrimination concerning the activities of Community companies or nationals already established in the former Yugoslav Republic of Macedonia at the time of introduction of a given measure, by comparison with companies or nationals from the former Yugoslav Republic of Macedonia.

While devising and applying such measures, the former Yugoslav Republic of Macedonia shall grant preferential treatment wherever possible to Community companies and nationals, and in no case treatment less favourable than that accorded to companies or nationals from any third country. Prior to the adoption of these measures, the former Yugoslav Republic of Macedonia shall consult the Stabilisation and Association Council and shall not put them into effect before a one month period has elapsed following the notification to the Stabilisation and Association Council of the concrete measures to be introduced by the former Yugoslav Republic of Macedonia, except where the threat of irreparable damage requires the taking of urgent measures, in which case the former Yugoslav Republic of Macedonia shall consult the Stabilisation and Association Council immediately after their adoption.

Upon the expiry of the fourth year following the entry into force of this Agreement the former Yugoslav Republic of Macedonia may introduce or maintain such measures only with the authorisation of the Stabilisation and Association Council and under conditions determined by the latter.

CHAPTER III

SUPPLY OF SERVICES

Article 55

1. The Parties undertake in accordance with the following provisions to take the necessary steps to allow progressively the supply of services by Community or the former Yugoslav Republic of Macedonia companies or nationals which are established in a Party other than that of the person for whom the services are intended.

2. In step with the liberalisation process mentioned in paragraph 1, the Parties shall permit the temporary movement of natural persons providing the service or who are employed by the service provider as key personnel as defined in Article 53, including natural persons who are representatives of a Community or the former Yugoslav Republic of Macedonia company or national and are seeking temporary entry for the purpose of negotiating for the sale of services or entering into agreements to sell services for that service provider, where those representatives will not be engaged in making direct sales to the general public or in supplying services themselves.

3. As from the second stage of the transition period, the Stabilisation and Association Council shall take the measures necessary to implement progressively the provisions of paragraph 1. Account shall be taken of the progress achieved by the Parties in the approximation of their laws.

Article 56

1. The Parties shall not take any measures or actions which render the conditions for the supply of services by Community and the former Yugoslav Republic of Macedonia nationals or companies which are established in a Party other than that of the person for whom the services are intended significantly more restrictive as compared to the situation existing on the day preceding the day of entry into force of the Agreement.

2. If one Party is of the view that measures introduced by the other Party since the entry into force of the Agreement result in a situation which is significantly more restrictive in respect of supply of services as compared with the situation existing at the date of entry into force of the Agreement, such first Party may request the other Party to enter into consultations.

Article 57

With regard to supply of transport services between the Community and the former Yugoslav Republic of Macedonia, the following provisions shall apply:

1. with regard to inland transport, the relationship between the Parties is governed by the Agreement between the European Community and the former Yugoslav Republic of Macedonia in the field of transport entered into force on 28 November 1997. The Parties confirm the importance they attach to the correct application of this Agreement;

2. with regard to international maritime transport the Parties undertake to apply effectively the principle of unrestricted access to the market and traffic on a commercial basis.

(a) The above provision does not prejudice the rights and obligations under the United Nations Code of Conduct for Liner Conferences, as applied by one or the other Party to this Agreement. Non-conference liners will be free to operate in competition with a conference as long as they adhere to the principle of fair competition on a commercial basis;

(b) the Parties affirm their commitment to a freely competitive environment as being an essential of the dry and liquid bulk trade.

3. In applying the principles of paragraph 2, the Parties shall:

(a) not introduce cargo-sharing clauses in future bilateral agreements with third countries, other than in those exceptional circumstances where liner shipping companies from one or other Party to this Agreement would not otherwise have an effective opportunity to ply for trade to and from the third country concerned;

(b) prohibit cargo-sharing arrangements in future bilateral agreements concerning dry and liquid bulk trade;

(c) abolish, upon the entry into force of this Agreement, all unilateral measures and administrative, technical and other obstacles that could have restrictive or discriminatory effects on the free supply of services in international maritime transport.

4. With a view to ensuring a coordinated development and progressive liberalisation of transport between the Parties adapted to their reciprocal commercial needs, the conditions of mutual market access in air transport shall be dealt with by special agreements to be negotiated between the Parties after the entry into force of this Agreement.

5. Prior to the conclusion of the agreement referred to in paragraph 4, the Parties shall not take any measures or actions which are more restrictive or discriminatory as compared with the situation existing prior to the entry into force of this Agreement.

6. During the transitional period, the former Yugoslav Republic of Macedonia shall adapt its legislation, including administrative, technical and other rules, to that of the Community existing at any time in the field of air and inland transport insofar as it serves liberalisation purposes and mutual access to markets of the Parties and facilitates the movement of passengers and of goods.

In step with the common progress in the achievement of the objectives of this Chapter, the Stabilisation and Association Council shall examine ways of creating the conditions necessary for improving freedom to provide air and inland transport services.

CHAPTER V

GENERAL PROVISIONS

Article 61

1. The provisions of this Title shall be applied subject to limitations justified on grounds of public policy, public security or public health.

2. They shall not apply to activities that in the territory of either Party are connected, even occasionally, with the exercise of official authority.

Article 62

For the purpose of this Title, nothing in this Agreement shall prevent the Parties from applying their laws and regulations regarding entry and stay, employment, working conditions, establishment of natural persons and supply of services, provided that, in so doing, they do not apply them in such a manner as to nullify or impair the benefits accruing to any Party under the terms of a specific provision of this Agreement.

This provision shall be without prejudice to the application of Article 61.

Article 63

Companies which are controlled and exclusively owned jointly by the former Yugoslav Republic of Macedonia companies or nationals and Community companies or nationals shall also be covered by the provisions of this Title.

UK LAW

Appendix 12

EUROPEAN COMMUNITIES ACT 1972

CHAPTER 68

An Act to make provision in connection with the enlargement of the European Communities to include the United Kingdom, together with (for certain purposes) the Channel Islands, the Isle of Man and Gibraltar. [17th October 1972]

Annotations:

Modifications etc. (not altering text)

C1 Act: transfer of certain functions (1.7.1999) by S.I. 1999/672, arts. 1(2), 2, Sch. 1; S.I. 1998/3178, art. 2(1)

PART I

GENERAL PROVISIONS

1 Short title and interpretation

(1) This Act may be cited as the European Communities Act 1972. A12–01

(2) In this Act ...[F1]—

"the Communities" means the European Economic Community, the European Coal and Steel Community and the European Atomic Energy Community;

"the Treaties" or [[F2] the EU Treaties] means, subject to subsection (3) below, the pre-accession treaties, that is to say, those described in Part I of Schedule 1 to this Act, taken with—

(a) the treaty relating to the accession of the United Kingdom to the European Economic Community and to the European Atomic Energy Community, signed at Brussels on the 22nd January 1972; and
(b) the decision, of the same date, of the Council of the European Communities relating to the accession of the United Kingdom to the European Coal and Steel Community; [[F3] and
(c) the treaty relating to the accession of the Hellenic Republic to the European Economic Community and to the European Atomic Energy Community, signed at Athens on 28th May 1979; and
(d) the decision, of 24th May 1979, of the Council relating to the accession of the Hellenic Republic to the European Coal and Steel Community;][[F4] and
[[F5](e) the decisions of the Council of 7th May 1985, 24th June 1988, 31st October 1994, 29th September 2000 and 7th June 2007 on the Communities' system of own resources;]][[F6] and
(g) the treaty relating to the accession of the Kingdom of Spain and the Portuguese Republic to the European Economic Community and to the European Atomic Energy Community, signed at Lisbon and Madrid on 12th June 1985; and

Appendix 12

(h) the decision, of 11th June 1985, of the Council relating to the accession of the Kingdom of Spain and the Portuguese Republic to the European Coal and Steel Community;][F7 and

(j) the following provisions of the Single European Act signed at Luxembourg and The Hague on 17th and 28th February 1986, namely Title II (amendment of the treaties establishing the Communities) and, so far as they relate to any of the Communities or any Community institution, the preamble and Titles I (common provisions) and IV (general and final provisions);][F8 and

(k) Titles II, III and IV of the Treaty on European Union signed at Maastricht on 7th February 1992, together with the other provisions of the Treaty so far as they relate to those Titles, and the Protocols adopted at Maastricht on that date and annexed to the Treaty establishing the European Community with the exception of the Protocol on Social Policy on page 117 of Cm 1934][F9 and

(l) the decision, of 1st February 1993, of the Council amending the Act concerning the election of the representatives of the European Parliament by direct universal suffrage annexed to Council Decision 76/787/ECSC, EEC, Euratom of 20th September 1976.][F10 and

(m) the Agreement on the European Economic Area signed at Oporto on 2nd May 1992 together with the Protocol adjusting that Agreement signed at Brussels on 17th March 1993][F11 and

(n) the treaty concerning the accession of the Kingdom of Norway, the Republic of Austria, the Republic of Finland and the Kingdom of Sweden to the European Union, signed at Corfu on 24th June 1994;][F12 and

(o) the following provisions of the Treaty signed at Amsterdam on 2nd October 1997 amending the Treaty on European Union, the Treaties establishing the European Communities and certain related Acts—

    (i) Articles 2 to 9,
    (ii) Article 12, and
    (iii) the other provisions of the Treaty so far as they relate to those Articles,

and the Protocols adopted on that occasion other than the Protocol on Article J.7 of the Treaty on European Union;][F13 and

(p) the following provisions of the Treaty signed at Nice on 26th February 2001 amending the Treaty on European Union, the Treaties establishing the European Communities and certain related Acts—

    (i) Articles 2 to 10, and
    (ii) the other provisions of the Treaty so far as they relate to those Articles,

and the Protocols adopted on that occasion;][F14 and

(q) the treaty concerning the accession of the Czech Republic, the Republic of Estonia, the Republic of Cyprus, the Republic of Latvia, the Republic of Lithuania, the Republic of Hungary, the Republic of Malta, the Republic of Poland, the Republic of Slovenia and the Slovak Republic to the European Union, signed at Athens on 16th April 2003;][F15 and

(r) the treaty concerning the accession of the Republic of Bulgaria and Romania to the European Union, signed at Luxembourg on 25th April 2005;][F16 and

(s) the Treaty of Lisbon Amending the Treaty on European Union and the Treaty Establishing the European Community signed at Lisbon on 13th December 2007 (together with its Annex and protocols), excluding any provision that relates to, or in so far as it relates to or could be applied in relation to, the Common Foreign and Security Policy;]

European Communities Act 1972

and [**F17** any other treaty entered into by the EU (except in so far as it relates to, or could be applied in relation to, the Common Foreign and Security Policy)] , with or without any of the member States, or entered into, as a treaty ancillary to any of the Treaties, by the United Kingdom;

and any expression defined in Schedule 1 to this Act has the meaning there given to it.

(3) If Her Majesty by Order in Council declares that a treaty specified in the Order is to be regarded as one of [**F18** the EU Treaties] as herein defined, the Order shall be conclusive that it is to be so regarded; but a treaty entered into by the United Kingdom after the 22nd January 1972, other than a pre-accession treaty to which the United Kingdom accedes on terms settled on or before that date, shall not be so regarded unless it is so specified, nor be so specified unless a draft of the Order in Council has been approved by resolution of each House of Parliament.

(4) For purposes of subsections (2) and (3) above, "treaty" includes any international agreement, and any protocol or annex to a treaty or international agreement.

Annotations:

Amendments (Textual)

- **F1** Words repealed by Interpretation Act 1978 (c. 30, SIF 115:1), s. 25, Sch. 3.
- **F2** Words in s. 1(2) substituted (1.12.2009) by European Union (Amendment) Act 2008 (c. 7), s. 3, Sch. Pt. 1; S.I. 2009/314, art. 2.
- **F3** S. 1(2)(c)(d) inserted by European Communities (Greek Accession) Act 1979 (c. 57, SIF 29:5), s. 1.
- **F4** S. 1(2)(e) and the word "and"immediately preceding it substituted (4.12.2001) by 2001 c. 22, s. 1 (the replaced para. (e) having itself previously been substituted for paras. (e) and (f)).
- **F5** S. 1(2)(e) substituted (19.2.2008) by European Communities (Finance) Act 2008 (c. 1), s. 1.
- **F6** S. 1(2)(g)(h) inserted by European Communities (Spanish and Portuguese Accession) Act 1985 (c. 75, SIF 29:5), s. 1.
- **F7** Words inserted by European Communities (Amendment) Act 1986 (c. 58, SIF 29:5), s. 1.
- **F8** S. 1(2)(k) and the word "and"immediately preceding it inserted (23.7.1992) by 1993, c. 32, s. 1(1)(7); resolution of House of Lords dated 27.7.1993; resolution of House of Commons dated 23.7.1993.
- **F9** S. 1(2)(l) and the word "and"immediately preceding it inserted (5.11.1993) by 1993 c. 41, s. 3(2).
- **F10** S. 1(2)(m) and the word "and"immediately preceding it added (5.11.1993) by 1993 c. 51, s. 1.
- **F11** S. 1(2)(n) and the preceding "and"inserted (3.11.1994) by 1994 c. 38, s. 1.
- **F12** S. 1(2)(o) and the preceding "and"inserted (11.6.1998) by 1998 c. 21, s. 1.
- **F13** S. 1(2)(p) and word "and"immediately preceding inserted (26.2.2002) by 2002 c. 3, s. 1(1).
- **F14** S. 1(2)(q) and preceding word inserted (13.11.2003) by European Union (Accessions) Act 2003 (c. 35), s. 1(1).
- **F15** S. 1(2)(r) inserted (16.2.2006) by European Union (Accessions) Act 2006 (c. 2), s. 1(1).
- **F16** S. 1(2)(s) and preceding word added (19.6.2008) by European Union (Amendment) Act 2008 (c. 7), s. 2.
- **F17** Words in s. 1(2) substituted (1.12.2009) by European Union (Amendment) Act 2008 (c. 7), s. 3, Sch. Pt. 1; S.I. 2009/3143, art. 2.
- **F18** Words in s. 1(3) substituted (1.12.2009) by European Union (Amendment) Act 2008 (c. 7), s. 3, Sch. Pt. 1; S.I. 2009/3143, art. 2.

Modifications etc. (not altering text)

- **C2** S. 1(2): Power to amend definitions conferred by (26.2.2002) by 2002 c. 3, s. 1(1)(2)
- **C3** S. 1(2)(l) and the word "and" preceding it continue to be inserted (24.10.2002) by 2002 c. 24, s. 15, Sch. 3 para. 1

2 General implementation of Treaties

(1) All such rights, powers, liabilities, obligations and restrictions from time to time created or arising by or under the Treaties, and all such remedies and procedures from time to time provided for by or under the Treaties, as in accordance with the Treaties are without further enactment to be given legal effect or used in the United Kingdom shall be recognised and available in law, and be enforced, allowed and followed accordingly; and the expression [[F19] "enforceable EU right"] and similar expressions shall be read as referring to one to which this subsection applies.

(2) Subject to Schedule 2 to this Act, at any time after its passing Her Majesty may by Order in Council, and any designated Minister or department may [[F20] by order, rules, regulations or scheme], make provision—

(a) for the purpose of implementing any [[F21] EU obligation] of the United Kingdom, or enabling any such obligation to be implemented, or of enabling any rights enjoyed or to be enjoyed by the United Kingdom under or by virtue of the Treaties to be exercised; or

(b) for the purpose of dealing with matters arising out of or related to any such obligation or rights or the coming into force, or the operation from time to time, of subsection (1) above;

and in the exercise of any statutory power or duty, including any power to give directions or to legislate by means of orders, rules, regulations or other subordinate instrument, the person entrusted with the power or duty may have regard to the [[F22] objects of the EU] and to any such obligation or rights as aforesaid.

In this subsection "designated Minister or department" means such Minister of the Crown or government department as may from time to time be designated by Order in Council in relation to any matter or for any purpose, but subject to such restrictions or conditions (if any) as may be specified by the Order in Council.

(3) There shall be charged on and issued out of the Consolidated Fund or, if so determined by the Treasury, the National Loans Fund the amounts required to meet any [[F23] EU obligation] to make payments to [[F24] the EU or a member State] , or any [[F23]EU obligation] in respect of contributions to the capital or reserves of the European Investment Bank or in respect of loans to the Bank, or to redeem any notes or obligations issued or created in respect of any such [[F23]EU obligation] and, except as otherwise provided by or under any enactment,—

(a) any other expenses incurred under or by virtue of the Treaties or this Act by any Minister of the Crown or government department may be paid out of moneys provided by Parliament; and

(b) any sums received under or by virtue of the Treaties or this Act by any Minister of the Crown or government department, save for such sums as may be required for disbursements permitted by any other enactment, shall be paid into the Consolidated Fund or, if so determined by the Treasury, the National Loans Fund.

(4) The provision that may be made under subsection (2) above includes, subject to Schedule 2 to this Act, any such provision (of any such extent) as might be made by Act of Parliament, and any enactment passed or to be passed, other than one contained in this part of this Act, shall be construed and have effect subject to the foregoing provisions of this section; but, except as may be provided by any Act passed after this Act, Schedule 2 shall have effect in connection with the powers

European Communities Act 1972

conferred by this and the following sections of this Act to make Orders in Council [F25 or orders, rules, regulations or schemes].

(5) ...F26 and the references in that subsection to a Minister of the Crown or government department and to a statutory power or duty shall include a Minister or department of the Government of Northern Ireland and a power or duty arising under or by virtue of an Act of the Parliament of Northern Ireland.

(6) A law passed by the legislature of any of the Channel Islands or of the Isle of Man, or a colonial Law (within the meaning of the M1Colonial Laws Validity Act 1865) passed or made for Gibraltar, if expressed to be passed or made in the implementation of the Treaties and of the obligations of the United Kingdom thereunder, shall not be void or inoperative by reason of any inconsistency with or repugnancy to an Act of Parliament, passed or to be passed, that extends to the Island or Gibraltar or any provision having the force and effect of an Act there (but not including this section), nor by reason of its having some operation outside the Island or Gibraltar; and any such Act or provision that extends to the Island or Gibraltar shall be construed and have effect subject to the provisions of any such law.

Annotations:

Amendments (Textual)

F19 Words in s. 2(1) substituted (1.12.2009) by European Union (Amendment) Act 2008 (c. 7), ss. 3, 8, Sch. Pt. 1; S.I. 2009/3143, art. 2.
F20 Words in s. 2(2) substituted (8.1.2007) by Legislative and Regulatory Reform Act 2006 (c. 51), ss. 27(1)(a), 33.
F21 Words in s. 2(2)(a) substituted (1.12.2009) by European Union (Amendment) Act 2008 (c. 7), ss. 3, 8, Sch. Pt. 1; S.I. 2009/3143, art. 2.
F22 Words in s. 2(2) substituted (1.12.2009) by European Union (Amendment) Act 2008 (c. 7), ss. 3, 8, Sch. Pt. 1; S.I. 2009/3143, art. 2.
F23 Words in s. 2(3) substituted (1.12.2009) by European Union (Amendment) Act 2008 (c. 7), ss. 3, 8, Sch. Pt. 1; S.I. 2009/3143, art. 2.
F24 Words in s. 2(3) substituted (1.12.2009) by European Union (Amendment) Act 2008 (c. 7), ss. 3, 8, Sch. Pt. 1; S.I. 2009/3143, art. 2.
F25 Words in s. 2(4) substituted (8.1.2007) by Legislative and Regulatory Reform Act 2006 (c. 51), ss. 27(1)(b), 33.
F26 Words repealed by Northern Ireland Constitution Act 1973 (c. 36 SIF 29:3), Sch. 6 Pt. I.

Modifications etc. (not altering text)

C4 S. 2 extended (1.7.1999) by 1998 c. 46, s. 125, Sch. 8 para. 15(2); S.I. 1998/3178, art. 2(1)
S. 2 modified (1.7.1999) by 1998 c. 46, s. 125, Sch. 8 para. 15(3); S.I. 1998/3178, art. 2(1)
S. 2: power to make certain corresponding provisions conferred (27.7.1999) by 1999 c. 24, s. 2, Sch. 1 Pt. I para. 20(1)(d)
C5 S. 2(2) extended (27.9.1993) by 1993 c. 36, s. 70(2)
C6 S. 2(2) extended (5.11.1993) by 1993 c. 51, s. 2(5)
S. 2(2) extended (1.12.1998) by 1998 c. 38, s. 29(2); S.I. 1998/2789, art. 2
S. 2(2) amended (1.7.1999) by S.I. 1999/1750, arts. 1(1), 3, Sch. 2; S.I. 1998/3178, art. 2(1) (with art. 7(4))
S. 2(2) modified (30.11.2000) by 2000 c. 37, s. 81(2)
C7 S. 2(2): Transfer of certain functions (27.3.2002) by S.I. 2002/794, art. 3(11)
C8 S. 2(2) power made exercisable concurrently (15.2.2006) by The Scotland Act 1998 (Transfer of Functions to the Scottish Ministers etc.) Order 2006 {S.I. 2006/304}, {art. 3} (with art. 5)
C9 S. 2(2) extended (3.5.2007) by Government of Wales Act 2006, (c. 32), {s. 59(1)}, (with Sch. 11 para. 22) the amending provision coming into force immediately after "the 2007 election" (held on 3.5.2007) subject to s. 161(4)(5) of the amending Act, which provides for certain provisions to come into force for specified purposes immediately after the end of "the initial period" (which ended with the day of the first appointment of a First Minister on 25.5.2007) - see ss. 46, 161(1)(4)(5) of the amending Act.

Appendix 12

C10 S. 2(2)(a)(b) excluded (N.I.) by Northern Ireland Constitution Act 1973 (c. 36, SIF 29:3), s. 2(2), Sch. 2 para. 3

C11 Reference in s. 2(5) to "that subsection" means s. 2(2) of this Act. Reference to a Minister of the Government of Northern Ireland to be construed, as respects the discharge of functions, as a reference to the head of a Northern Ireland department: Northern Ireland Constitution Act 1973 (c. 36, SIF 29:3), Sch. 5 para. 7(2)

Marginal Citations

M1 1865 c. 63(26:1).

3 Decisions on, and proof of, Treaties and [F27EU instruments] etc.

(1) For the purposes of all legal proceedings any question as to the meaning or effect of any of the Treaties, or as to the validity, meaning or effect of any [F28EU instrument] , shall be treated as a question of law (and, if not referred to the European Court, be for determination as such in accordance with the principles laid down by and any relevant [F29decision of [F30the European Court])].

(2) Judicial notice shall be taken of the Treaties, of the [F31Official Journal of the European Union] and of any decision of, or expression of opinion by, the [F32the European Court] on any such question as aforesaid; and the Official Journal shall be admissible as evidence of any instrument or other act thereby communicated of [F33the EU] or of any [F34EU institution] .

(3) Evidence of any instrument issued by a [F35EU institution] , including any judgment or order of [F36the European Court] , or of any document in the custody of a [F35EU institution] , or any entry in or extract from such a document, may be given in any legal proceedings by production of a copy certified as a true copy by an official of that institution; and any document purporting to be such a copy shall be received in evidence without proof of the official position or handwriting of the person signing the certificate.

(4) Evidence of any [F37EU instrument] may also be given in any legal proceedings—

(a) by production of a copy purporting to be printed by the Queen's Printer;

(b) where the instrument is in the custody of a government department (including a department of the Government of Northern Ireland), by production of a copy certified on behalf of the department to be a true copy by an officer of the department generally or specially authorised so to do;

and any document purporting to be such a copy as is mentioned in paragraph (b) above of an instrument in the custody of a department shall be received in evidence without proof of the official position or handwriting of the person signing the certificate, or of his authority to do so, or of the document being in the custody of the department.

(5) In any legal proceedings in Scotland evidence of any matter given in a manner authorised by this section shall be sufficient evidence of it.

Annotations:

Amendments (Textual)

F27 Words in s. 3 heading substituted (1.12.2009) by European Union (Amendment) Act 2008 (c. 7), ss. 3, 8, Sch. Pt. 1; S.I. 2009/3143, art. 2.

F28 Words in s. 3(1) substituted (1.12.2009) by European Union (Amendment) Act 2008 (c. 7), ss. 3, 8, Sch. Pt. 1; S.I. 2009/3143, art. 2.

F29 Words substituted by European Communities (Amendment) Act 1986 (c. 58, SIF 29:5), s. 2(a).
F30 Words in s. 3(1) substituted (1.12.2009) by European Union (Amendment) Act 2008 (c. 7), ss. 3, 8, Sch. Pt. 1; S.I. 2009/3143, art. 2.
F31 Words in s. 3(2) substituted (1.12.2009) by European Union (Amendment) Act 2008 (c. 7), ss. 3, 8, Sch. Pt. 1; S.I. 2009/3143, art. 2.
F32 Words in s. 3(2) substituted (1.12.2009) by European Union (Amendment) Act 2008 (c. 7), ss. 3, 8, Sch. Pt. 1; S.I. 2009/3143, art. 2.
F33 Words in s. 3(2) substituted (1.12.2009) by European Union (Amendment) Act 2008 (c. 7), ss. 3, 8, Sch. Pt. 1; S.I. 2009/3143, art. 2.
F34 Words in s. 3(2) substituted (1.12.2009) by European Union (Amendment) Act 2008 (c. 7), ss. 3, 8, Sch. Pt. 1; S.I. 2009/3143, art. 2.
F35 Words in s. 3(3) substituted (1.12.2009) by European Union (Amendment) Act 2008 (c. 7), ss. 3, 8, Sch. Pt. 1; S.I. 2009/3143, art. 2.
F36 Words in s. 3(3) substituted (1.12.2009) by European Union (Amendment) Act 2008 (c. 7), ss. 3, 8, Sch. Pt. 1; S.I. 2009/3143, art. 2.
F37 Words in s. 3(4) substituted (1.12.2009) by European Union (Amendment) Act 2008 (c. 7), ss. 3, 8, Sch. Pt. 1; S.I. 2009/3143, art. 2.

Modifications etc. (not altering text)

C12 Sections 3(2)-(5) extended (5.11.1993) by 1993 c. 51, s. 4
S. 3(4) extended (1.7.1999) by 1998 c. 46, s. 125, Sch. 8 para. 15(4); S.I. 1998/3178, art. 2
S. 3(3)(4): power to modify conferred (2.12.1999) by 1998 c. 47, s. 7(2); S.I 1999/3208, art. 2

Appendix 13

IMMIGRATION ACT 1988

CHAPTER 14

7 Persons exercising Community rights and nationals of member States

(1) A person shall not under the principal Act require leave to enter or remain in the United Kingdom in any case in which he is entitled to do so by virtue of an enforceable Community right or of any provision made under section 2(2) of the European Communities Act 1972.

(2) The Secretary of State may by order made by statutory instrument give leave to enter the United Kingdom for a limited period to any class of persons who are nationals of member States but who are not entitled to enter the United Kingdom as mentioned in subsection (1) above; and any such order may give leave subject to such conditions as may be imposed by the order.

(3) References in the principal Act to limited leave shall include references to leave given by an order under subsection (2) above and a person having leave by virtue of such an order shall be treated as having been given that leave by a notice given to him by an immigration officer within the period specified in paragraph 6(1) of Schedule 2 to that Act.

A13–01

APPENDIX 14

THE IMMIGRATION (EUROPEAN ECONOMIC AREA) REGULATIONS 2006

SI 2006 No. 1003

Made	*30th March 2006*
Laid before Parliament	*4th April 2006*
Coming into force	*30th April 2006*

The Secretary of State, being a Minister designated[1] for the purposes of section 2(2) of the European Communities Act 1972[2] in relation to measures relating to rights of entry into, and residence in, the United Kingdom, in exercise of the powers conferred upon him by that section, and of the powers conferred on him by section 109 of the Nationality, Immigration and Asylum Act 2002[3], makes the following Regulations:

PART 1

INTERPRETATION ETC

Citation and commencement

1. These Regulations may be cited as the Immigration (European Economic Area) Regulations 2006 and shall come into force on 30th April 2006. **A14–01**

General interpretation

2.—(1) In these Regulations—
　"the 1971 Act" means the Immigration Act 1971[4];
　"the 1999 Act" means the Immigration and Asylum Act 1999[5];
　"the 2002 Act" means the Nationality, Immigration and Asylum Act 2002;
　"civil partner"[6] does not include a party to a civil partnership of convenience;
　"decision maker" means the Secretary of State, an immigration officer or an entry clearance officer (as the case may be);
　"document certifying permanent residence" means a document issued to an EEA national, in accordance with regulation 18, as proof of the holder's permanent right of residence under regulation 15 as at the date of issue;
　"EEA decision" means a decision under these Regulations that concerns a person's—

　(a) entitlement to be admitted to the United Kingdom;

---

[1] S.I. 2000/1813.
[2] 1972 c.68.
[3] 2002 c.41.
[4] 1971 c. 77.
[5] 1999 c. 33.
[6] Civil partner has the meaning given by Schedule 1 to the Interpretation Act 1978 (c. 30) as amended by paragraph 59 of Schedule 27 to the Civil Partnership Act 2004 (c.33).

Appendix 14

(b) entitlement to be issued with or have renewed, or not to have revoked, a registration certificate, residence card, document certifying permanent residence or permanent residence card; or

(c) removal from the United Kingdom;

"EEA family permit" means a document issued to a person, in accordance with regulation 12, in connection with his admission to the United Kingdom;

"EEA national" means a national of an EEA State;

"EEA State" means—

(a) a member State, other than the United Kingdom;
(b) Norway, Iceland or Liechtenstein; or
(c) Switzerland;

"entry clearance" has the meaning given in section 33(1) of the 1971 Act[7];

"entry clearance officer" means a person responsible for the grant or refusal of entry clearance;

"immigration rules" has the meaning given in section 33(1) of the 1971 Act;

"military service" means service in the armed forces of an EEA State;

"permanent residence card" means a card issued to a person who is not an EEA national, in accordance with regulation 18, as proof of the holder's permanent right of residence under regulation 15 as at the date of issue;

"registration certificate" means a certificate issued to an EEA national, in accordance with regulation 16, as proof of the holder's right of residence in the United Kingdom as at the date of issue;

"relevant EEA national" in relation to an extended family member has the meaning given in regulation 8(6);

"residence card" means a card issued to a person who is not an EEA national, in accordance with regulation 17, as proof of the holder's right of residence in the United Kingdom as at the date of issue;

"spouse" does not include a party to a marriage of convenience;

"United Kingdom national" means a person who falls to be treated as a national of the United Kingdom for the purposes of the Community Treaties.

(2) Paragraph (1) is subject to paragraph 1(a) of Schedule 4 (transitional provisions).

Continuity of residence

3.—(1) This regulation applies for the purpose of calculating periods of continuous residence in the United Kingdom under regulation 5(1) and regulation 15.

(2) Continuity of residence is not affected by —

(a) periods of absence from the United Kingdom which do not exceed six months in total in any year;

(b) periods of absence from the United Kingdom on military service; or

(c) any one absence from the United Kingdom not exceeding twelve months for an important reason such as pregnancy and childbirth, serious illness, study or vocational training or an overseas posting.

(3) But continuity of residence is broken if a person is removed from the United Kingdom under regulation 19(3).

---

[7] Section 33(1) is amended by paragraph 5 of the Schedule to the Immigration Act 1988 (c.14).

The Immigration (European Economic Area) Regulations 2006

"Worker", "self-employed person", "self-sufficient person" and "student"

4.—(1) In these Regulations —

(a) "worker" means a worker within the meaning of Article 39 of the Treaty establishing the European Community[8];

(b) "self-employed person" means a person who establishes himself in order to pursue activity as a self-employed person in accordance with Article 43 of the Treaty establishing the European Community;

(c) "self-sufficient person" means a person who—

   (i) sufficient resources not to become a burden on the social assistance system of the United Kingdom during his period of residence; and
   (ii) comprehensive sickness insurance cover in the United Kingdom;

(d) "student" means a person who—

   (i) is enrolled at a private or public establishment, included on the Department for Education and Skills' Register of Education and Training Providers[9] or financed from public funds, for the principal purpose of following a course of study, including vocational training;
   (ii) has comprehensive sickness insurance cover in the United Kingdom; and
   (iii) assures the Secretary of State, by means of a declaration, or by such equivalent means as the person may choose, that he has sufficient resources not to become a (a) OJ No. C325, 24.12.02, p. 51. (b) The Register of Education and Training Providers is maintained by, and is available on the website of, the Department for Education and Skills. 5 burden on the social assistance system of the United Kingdom during his period of residence.

(2) For the purposes of paragraph (1)(c), where family members of the person concerned reside in the United Kingdom and their right to reside is dependent upon their being family members of that person—

(a) the requirement for that person to have sufficient resources not to become a burden on the social assistance system of the United Kingdom during his period of residence shall only be satisfied if his resources and those of the family members are sufficient to avoid him and the family members becoming such a burden;

(b) the requirement for that person to have comprehensive sickness insurance cover in the United Kingdom shall only be satisfied if he and his family members have such cover.

(3) For the purposes of paragraph (1)(d), where family members of the person concerned reside in the United Kingdom and their right to reside is dependent upon their being family members of that person, the requirement for that person to assure the Secretary of State that he has sufficient resources not to become a burden on the social assistance system of the United Kingdom during his period of residence shall only be satisfied if he assures the Secretary of State that his resources and those of the family members are sufficient to avoid him and the family members becoming such a burden.

---

[8] OJ No. C325, 24.12.02, p. 51.
[9] The Register of Education and Training Providers is maintained by, and is available on the website of, the Department for Education and Skills.

(4) For the purposes of paragraphs (1)(c) and (d) and paragraphs (2) and (3), the resources of the person concerned and, where applicable, any family members, are to be regarded as sufficient if they exceed the maximum level of resources which a United Kingdom national and his family members may possess if he is to become eligible for social assistance under the United Kingdom benefit system.

"Worker or self-employed person who has ceased activity"

5.—(1) In these Regulations, "worker or self-employed person who has ceased activity" means an EEA national who satisfies the conditions in paragraph (2), (3), (4) or (5).

(2) A person satisfies the conditions in this paragraph if he—

(a) terminates his activity as a worker or self-employed person and—

   (i) has reached the age at which he is entitled to a state pension on the date on which he terminates his activity; or
   (ii) in the case of a worker, ceases working to take early retirement;

(b) pursued his activity as a worker or self-employed person in the United Kingdom for at least twelve months prior to the termination; and

(c) resided in the United Kingdom continuously for more than three years prior to the termination.

(3) A person satisfies the conditions in this paragraph if—

(a) he terminates his activity in the United Kingdom as a worker or self-employed person as a result of a permanent incapacity to work; and

(b) either—

   (i) he resided in the United Kingdom continuously for more than two years prior to the termination; or
   (ii) the incapacity is the result of an accident at work or an occupational disease that entitles him to a pension payable in full or in part by an institution in the United Kingdom.

(4) A person satisfies the conditions in this paragraph if—

(a) he is active as a worker or self-employed person in an EEA State but retains his place of residence in the United Kingdom, to which he returns as a rule at least once a week; and

(b) prior to becoming so active in that EEA State, he had been continuously resident and continuously active as a worker or self-employed person in the United Kingdom for at least three years.

(5) A person who satisfies the condition in paragraph (4)(a) but not the condition in paragraph (4)(b) shall, for the purposes of paragraphs (2) and (3), be treated as being active and resident in the United Kingdom during any period in which he is working or self-employed in the EEA State.

(6) The conditions in paragraphs (2) and (3) as to length of residence and activity as a worker or self-employed person shall not apply in relation to a person whose spouse or civil partner is a United Kingdom national.

(7) For the purposes of this regulation—

(a) periods of inactivity for reasons not of the person's own making;
(b) periods of inactivity due to illness or accident; and
(c) in the case of a worker, periods of involuntary unemployment duly recorded by the relevant employment office,

shall be treated as periods of activity as a worker or self-employed person, as the case may be.

"Qualified person"

6.—(1) In these Regulations, "qualified person" means a person who is an EEA national and in the United Kingdom as—

(a) a jobseeker;
(b) a worker;
(c) a self-employed person;
(d) a self-sufficient person; or
(e) a student.

(2) A person who is no longer working shall not cease to be treated as a worker for the purpose of paragraph (1)(b) if—

(a) he is temporarily unable to work as the result of an illness or accident;
(b) he is in duly recorded involuntary unemployment after having been employed in the United Kingdom, provided that he has registered as a jobseeker with the relevant employment office and—
   (i) he was employed for one year or more before becoming unemployed;
   (ii) he has been unemployed for no more than six months; or
   (iii) he can provide evidence that he is seeking employment in the United Kingdom and has a genuine chance of being engaged;
(c) he is involuntarily unemployed and has embarked on vocational training; or
(d) he has voluntarily ceased working and embarked on vocational training that is related to his previous employment.

(3) A person who is no longer in self-employment shall not cease to be treated as a self employed person for the purpose of paragraph (1)(c) if he is temporarily unable to pursue his activity as a self-employed person as the result of an illness or accident.

(4) For the purpose of paragraph (1)(a), "jobseeker" means a person who enters the United Kingdom in order to seek employment and can provide evidence that he is seeking employment and has a genuine chance of being engaged.

Family member

7.—(1) Subject to paragraph (2), for the purposes of these Regulations the following persons shall be treated as the family members of another person—

(a) his spouse or his civil partner;
(b) direct descendants of his, his spouse or his civil partner who are—
   (i) under 21; or
   (ii) dependants of his, his spouse or his civil partner;

(c) dependent direct relatives in his ascending line or that of his spouse or his civil partner;

(d) a person who is to be treated as the family member of that other person under paragraph (3).

(2) A person shall not be treated under paragraph (1)(b) or (c) as the family member of a student residing in the United Kingdom after the period of three months beginning on the date on which the student is admitted to the United Kingdom unless—

(a) in the case of paragraph (b), the person is the dependent child of the student or of his spouse or civil partner; or

(b) the student also falls within one of the other categories of qualified persons mentioned in regulation 6(1).

(3) Subject to paragraph (4), a person who is an extended family member and has been issued with an EEA family permit, a registration certificate or a residence card shall be treated as the family member of the relevant EEA national for as long as he continues to satisfy the conditions in regulation 8(2), (3), (4) or (5) in relation to that EEA national and the permit, certificate or card has not ceased to be valid or been revoked.

(4) Where the relevant EEA national is a student, the extended family member shall only be treated as the family member of that national under paragraph (3) if either the EEA family permit was issued under regulation 12(2), the registration certificate was issued under regulation 16(5) or the residence card was issued under regulation 17(4).

"Extended family member"

8.—(1) In these Regulations "extended family member" means a person who is not a family member of an EEA national under regulation 7(1)(a), (b) or (c) and who satisfies the conditions in paragraph (2), (3), (4) or (5).

(2) A person satisfies the condition in this paragraph if the person is a relative of an EEA national, his spouse or his civil partner and—

(a) the person is residing in an EEA State in which the EEA national also resides and is dependent upon the EEA national or is a member of his household;

(b) the person satisfied the condition in paragraph (a) and is accompanying the EEA national to the United Kingdom or wishes to join him there; or

(c) the person satisfied the condition in paragraph (a), has joined the EEA national in the United Kingdom and continues to be dependent upon him or to be a member of his household.

(3) A person satisfies the condition in this paragraph if the person is a relative of an EEA national or his spouse or his civil partner and, on serious health grounds, strictly requires the personal care of the EEA national his spouse or his civil partner.

(4) A person satisfies the condition in this paragraph if the person is a relative of an EEA national and would meet the requirements in the immigration rules (other than those relating to entry clearance) for indefinite leave to enter or remain in the United Kingdom as a dependent relative of the EEA national were the EEA national a person present and settled in the United Kingdom.

The Immigration (European Economic Area) Regulations 2006

(5) A person satisfies the condition in this paragraph if the person is the partner of an EEA national (other than a civil partner) and can prove to the decision maker that he is in a durable relationship with the EEA national.

(6) In these Regulations "relevant EEA national" means, in relation to an extended family member, the EEA national who is or whose spouse or civil partner is the relative of the extended family member for the purpose of paragraph (2), (3) or (4) or the EEA national who is the partner of the extended family member for the purpose of paragraph (5).

Family members of United Kingdom nationals

9.—(1) If the conditions in paragraph (2) are satisfied, these Regulations apply to a person who is the family member of a United Kingdom national as if the United Kingdom national were an EEA national.

(2) The conditions are that—

(a) the United Kingdom national is residing in an EEA State as a worker or self-employed person or was so residing before returning to the United Kingdom; and

(b) if the family member of the United Kingdom national is his spouse or civil partner, the parties are living together in the EEA State or had entered into the marriage or civil partnership and were living together in that State before the United Kingdom national returned to the United Kingdom.

(3) Where these Regulations apply to the family member of a United Kingdom national the United Kingdom national shall be treated as holding a valid passport issued by an EEA State for the purpose of the application of regulation 13 to that family member.

"Family member who has retained the right of residence"

10.—(1) In these Regulations, "family member who has retained the right of residence" means, subject to paragraph (8), a person who satisfies the conditions in paragraph (2), (3), (4) or (5).

(2) A person satisfies the conditions in this paragraph if—

(a) he was a family member of a qualified person when the qualified person died;

(b) he resided in the United Kingdom in accordance with these Regulations for at least the year immediately before the death of the qualified person; and

(c) he satisfies the condition in paragraph (6).

(3) A person satisfies the conditions in this paragraph if—

(a) he is the direct descendant of—

   (i) a qualified person who has died;
   (ii) a person who ceased to be a qualified person on ceasing to reside in the United Kingdom; or
   (iii) the person who was the spouse or civil partner of the qualified person mentioned in sub-paragraph (i) when he died or is the spouse or civil partner of the person mentioned in sub-paragraph (ii); and

Appendix 14

(b) he was attending an educational course in the United Kingdom immediately before the qualified person died or ceased to be a qualified person and continues to attend such a course.

(4) A person satisfies the conditions in this paragraph if the person is the parent with actual custody of a child who satisfies the condition in paragraph (3).

(5) A person satisfies the conditions in this paragraph if—

(a) he ceased to be a family member of a qualified person on the termination of the marriage or civil partnership of the qualified person;

(b) he was residing in the United Kingdom in accordance with these Regulations at the date of the termination;

(c) he satisfies the condition in paragraph (6); and

(d) either—

   (i) prior to the initiation of the proceedings for the termination of the marriage or the civil partnership the marriage or civil partnership had lasted for at least three years and the parties to the marriage or civil partnership had resided in the United Kingdom for at least one year during its duration;

   (ii) the former spouse or civil partner of the qualified person has custody of a child of the qualified person;

   (iii) the former spouse or civil partner of the qualified person has the right of access to a child of the qualified person under the age of 18 and a court has ordered that such access must take place in the United Kingdom; or

   (iv) the continued right of residence in the United Kingdom of the person is warranted by particularly difficult circumstances, such as he or another family member having been a victim of domestic violence while the marriage or civil partnership was subsisting.

(6) The condition in this paragraph is that the person—

(a) is not an EEA national but would, if he were an EEA national, be a worker, a selfemployed person or a self-sufficient person under regulation 6; or

(b) is the family member of a person who falls within paragraph (a).

(7) In this regulation, "educational course" means a course within the scope of Article 12 of Council Regulation (EEC) No. 1612/68 on freedom of movement for workers[10].

(8) A person with a permanent right of residence under regulation 15 shall not become a family member who has retained the right of residence on the death or departure from the United Kingdom of the qualified person or the termination of the marriage or civil partnership, as the case may be, and a family member who has retained the right of residence shall cease to have that status on acquiring a permanent right of residence under regulation 15.

---

[10] OJ No. L 257, 19.10.68, p. 2 (OJ/SE 1st series 1968, vol II, p. 475.

THE IMMIGRATION (EUROPEAN ECONOMIC AREA) REGULATIONS 2006

PART 2

EEA RIGHTS

Right of admission to the United Kingdom

11.—(1) An EEA national must be admitted to the United Kingdom if he produces on arrival a valid national identity card or passport issued by an EEA State.

(2) A person who is not an EEA national must be admitted to the United Kingdom if he is a family member of an EEA national, a family member who has retained the right of residence or person with a permanent right of residence under regulation 15 and produces on arrival—

(a) a valid passport; and

(b) an EEA family permit, a residence card or a permanent residence card.

(3) An immigration officer may not place a stamp in the passport of a person admitted to the United Kingdom under this regulation who is not an EEA national if the person produces a residence card or permanent residence card.

(4) Before an immigration officer refuses admission to the United Kingdom to a person under this regulation because the person does not produce on arrival a document mentioned in paragraph (1) or (2), the immigration officer must give the person every reasonable opportunity to obtain the document or have it brought to him within a reasonable period of time or to prove by other means that he is—

(a) an EEA national;

(b) a family member of an EEA national with a right to accompany that national or join him in the United Kingdom; or

(c) a family member who has retained the right of residence or a person with a permanent right of residence under regulation 15.

(5) But this regulation is subject to regulations 19(1) and (2).

Issue of EEA family permit

12.—(1) An entry clearance officer must issue an EEA family permit to a person who applies for one if the person is a family member of an EEA national and—

(a) the EEA national—

(i) is residing in the UK in accordance with these Regulations; or
(ii) will be travelling to the United Kingdom within six months of the date of the application and will be an EEA national residing in the United Kingdom in accordance with these Regulations on arrival in the United Kingdom; and

(b) the family member will be accompanying the EEA national to the United Kingdom or joining him there and—

(i) is lawfully resident in an EEA State; or
(ii) would meet the requirements in the immigration rules (other than those relating to entry clearance) for leave to enter the United Kingdom as the family member of the EEA national or, in the case of direct descendants

or dependent direct relatives in the ascending line of his spouse or his civil partner, as the family member of his spouse or his civil partner, were the EEA national or the spouse or civil partner a person present and settled in the United Kingdom.

(2) An entry clearance officer may issue an EEA family permit to an extended family member of an EEA national who applies for one if—

(a) the relevant EEA national satisfies the condition in paragraph (1)(a);
(b) the extended family member wishes to accompany the relevant EEA national to the United Kingdom or to join him there; and
(c) in all the circumstances, it appears to the entry clearance officer appropriate to issue the EEA family permit.

(3) Where an entry clearance officer receives an application under paragraph (2) he shall undertake an extensive examination of the personal circumstances of the applicant and if he refuses the application shall give reasons justifying the refusal unless this is contrary to the interests of national security.

(4) An EEA family permit issued under this regulation shall be issued free of charge and as soon as possible.

(5) But an EEA family permit shall not be issued under this regulation if the applicant or the EEA national concerned falls to be excluded from the United Kingdom on grounds of public policy, public security or public health in accordance with regulation 21.

Initial right of residence

13.—(1) An EEA national is entitled to reside in the United Kingdom for a period not exceeding three months beginning on the date on which he is admitted to the United Kingdom provided that he holds a valid national identity card or passport issued by an EEA State.

(2) A family member of an EEA national residing in the United Kingdom under paragraph (1) who is not himself an EEA national is entitled to reside in the United Kingdom provided that he holds a valid passport.

(3) But—

(a) this regulation is subject to regulation 19(3)(b); and
(b) an EEA national or his family member who becomes an unreasonable burden on the social assistance system of the United Kingdom shall cease to have the right to reside under this regulation.

Extended right of residence

14.—(1) A qualified person is entitled to reside in the United Kingdom for so long as he remains a qualified person.

(2) A family member of a qualified person residing in the United Kingdom under paragraph (1) or of an EEA national with a permanent right of residence under regulation 15 is entitled to reside in the United Kingdom for so long as he remains the family member of the qualified person or EEA national.

The Immigration (European Economic Area) Regulations 2006

(3) A family member who has retained the right of residence is entitled to reside in the United Kingdom for so long as he remains a family member who has retained the right of residence.

(4) A right to reside under this regulation is in addition to any right a person may have to reside in the United Kingdom under regulation 13 or 15.

(5) But this regulation is subject to regulation 19(3)(b).

Permanent right of residence

15.—(1) The following persons shall acquire the right to reside in the United Kingdom permanently—

(a) an EEA national who has resided in the United Kingdom in accordance with these Regulations for a continuous period of five years;

(b) a family member of an EEA national who is not himself an EEA national but who has resided in the United Kingdom with the EEA national in accordance with these Regulations for a continuous period of five years;

(c) a worker or self-employed person who has ceased activity;

(d) the family member of a worker or self-employed person who has ceased activity;

(e) a person who was the family member of a worker or self-employed person where—
   (i) the worker or self-employed person has died;
   (ii) the family member resided with him immediately before his death; and
   (iii) the worker or self-employed person had resided continuously in the United Kingdom for at least the two years immediately before his death or the death was the result of an accident at work or an occupational disease;

(f) a person who—
   (i) has resided in the United Kingdom in accordance with these Regulations for a continuous period of five years; and
   (ii) was, at the end of that period, a family member who has retained the right of residence.

(2) Once acquired, the right of permanent residence under this regulation shall be lost only through absence from the United Kingdom for a period exceeding two consecutive years.

(3) But this regulation is subject to regulation 19(3)(b).

Part 3

Residence Documentation

Issue of registration certificate

16.—(1) The Secretary of State must issue a registration certificate to a qualified person immediately on application and production of—

(a) a valid identity card or passport issued by an EEA State;

(b) proof that he is a qualified person.

(2) In the case of a worker, confirmation of the worker's engagement from his employer or a certificate of employment is sufficient proof for the purposes of paragraph (1)(b).

(3) The Secretary of State must issue a registration certificate to an EEA national who is the family member of a qualified person or of an EEA national with a permanent right of residence under regulation 15 immediately on application and production of—

(a) a valid identity card or passport issued by an EEA State; and

(b) proof that the applicant is such a family member.

(4) The Secretary of State must issue a registration certificate to an EEA national who is a family member who has retained the right of residence on application and production of—

(a) a valid identity card or passport; and

(b) proof that the applicant is a family member who has retained the right of residence.

(5) The Secretary of State may issue a registration certificate to an extended family member not falling within regulation 7(3) who is an EEA national on application if—

(a) the relevant EEA national in relation to the extended family member is a qualified person or an EEA national with a permanent right of residence under regulation 15; and

(b) in all the circumstances it appears to the Secretary of State appropriate to issue the registration certificate.

(6) Where the Secretary of State receives an application under paragraph (5) he shall undertake an extensive examination of the personal circumstances of the applicant and if he refuses the application shall give reasons justifying the refusal unless this is contrary to the interests of national security.

(7) A registration certificate issued under this regulation shall state the name and address of the person registering and the date of registration and shall be issued free of charge.

(8) But this regulation is subject to regulation 20(1).

Issue of residence card

17.—(1) The Secretary of State must issue a residence card to a person who is not an EEA national and is the family member of a qualified person or of an EEA national with a permanent right of residence under regulation 15 on application and production of—

(a) a valid passport; and

(b) proof that the applicant is such a family member.

(2) The Secretary of State must issue a residence card to a person who is not an EEA national but who is a family member who has retained the right of residence on application and production of—

(a) a valid passport; and

(b) proof that the applicant is a family member who has retained the right of residence.

(3) On receipt of an application under paragraph (1) or (2) and the documents that are required to accompany the application the Secretary of State shall immediately issue the applicant with a certificate of application for the residence card and the residence card shall be issued no later than six months after the date on which the application and documents are received.

(4) The Secretary of State may issue a residence card to an extended family member not falling within regulation 7(3) who is not an EEA national on application if—

(a) the relevant EEA national in relation to the extended family member is a qualified person or an EEA national with a permanent right of residence under regulation 15; and

(b) in all the circumstances it appears to the Secretary of State appropriate to issue the residence card.

(5) Where the Secretary of State receives an application under paragraph (4) he shall undertake an extensive examination of the personal circumstances of the applicant and if he refuses the 13 application shall give reasons justifying the refusal unless this is contrary to the interests of national security.

(6) A residence card issued under this regulation may take the form of a stamp in the applicant's passport and shall be entitled "Residence card of a family member of an EEA national" and be valid for—

(a) five years from the date of issue; or

(b) in the case of a residence card issued to the family member or extended family member of a qualified person, the envisaged period of residence in the United Kingdom of the qualified person, whichever is the shorter.

(7) A residence card issued under this regulation shall be issued free of charge.

(8) But this regulation is subject to regulation 20(1).

Issue of a document certifying permanent residence and a permanent residence card

18.—(1) The Secretary of State must issue an EEA national with a permanent right of residence under regulation 15 with a document certifying permanent residence as soon as possible after an application for such a document and proof that the EEA national has such a right is submitted to the Secretary of State.

(2) The Secretary of State must issue a person who is not an EEA national who has a permanent right of residence under regulation 15 with a permanent residence card no later than six months after the date on which an application for a permanent residence card and proof that the person has such a right is submitted to the Secretary of State.

Appendix 14

(3) Subject to paragraph (5) and regulation 20(3), a permanent residence card shall be valid for ten years from the date of issue and must be renewed on application.

(4) A document certifying permanent residence and a permanent residence card shall be issued free of charge.

(5) A document certifying permanent residence and a permanent residence card shall cease to be valid if the holder ceases to have a right of permanent residence under regulation 15.

Part 4

Refusal of Admission and Removal etc

Exclusion and removal from the United Kingdom

19.—(1) A person is not entitled to be admitted to the United Kingdom by virtue of regulation 11 if his exclusion is justified on grounds of public policy, public security or public health in accordance with regulation 21.

(2) A person is not entitled to be admitted to the United Kingdom as the family member of an EEA national under regulation 11(2) unless, at the time of his arrival—

(a) he is accompanying the EEA national or joining him in the United Kingdom; and

(b) the EEA national has a right to reside in the United Kingdom under these Regulations.

(3) Subject to paragraphs (4) and (5), a person who has been admitted to, or acquired a right to reside in, the United Kingdom under these Regulations may be removed from the United Kingdom if—

(a) he does not have or ceases to have a right to reside under these Regulations; or

(b) he would otherwise be entitled to reside in the United Kingdom under these Regulations but the Secretary of State has decided that his removal is justified on the grounds of public policy, public security or public health in accordance with regulation 21.

(4) A person must not be removed under paragraph (3) as the automatic consequence of having recourse to the social assistance system of the United Kingdom.

(5) A person must not be removed under paragraph (3) if he has a right to remain in the United Kingdom by virtue of leave granted under the 1971 Act unless his removal is justified on the grounds of public policy, public security or public health in accordance with regulation 21.

Refusal to issue or renew and revocation of residence documentation

20.—(1) The Secretary of State may refuse to issue, revoke or refuse to renew a registration certificate, a residence card, a document certifying permanent residence or a permanent residence card if the refusal or revocation is justified on grounds of public policy, public security or public health.

(2) The Secretary of State may revoke a registration certificate or a residence card or refuse to renew a residence card if the holder of the certificate or card has ceased to have a right to reside under these Regulations.

(3) The Secretary of State may revoke a document certifying permanent residence or a permanent residence card or refuse to renew a permanent residence card if the holder of the certificate or card has ceased to have a right of permanent residence under regulation 15.

(4) An immigration officer may, at the time of a person's arrival in the United Kingdom—

(a) revoke that person's residence card if he is not at that time the family member of a qualified person or of an EEA national who has a right of permanent residence under regulation 15, a family member who has retained the right of residence or a person with a right of permanent residence under regulation 15;

(b) revoke that person's permanent residence card if he is not at that time a person with a right of permanent residence under regulation 15.

(5) An immigration officer may, at the time of a person's arrival in the United Kingdom, revoke that person's EEA family permit if—

(a) the revocation is justified on grounds of public policy, public security or public health; or

(b) the person is not at that time the family member of an EEA national with the right to reside in the United Kingdom under these Regulations or is not accompanying that national or joining him in the United Kingdom.

(6) Any action taken under this regulation on grounds of public policy, public security or public health shall be in accordance with regulation 21.

Decisions taken on public policy, public security and public health grounds

21.—(1) In this regulation a "relevant decision" means an EEA decision taken on the grounds of public policy, public security or public health.

(2) A relevant decision may not be taken to serve economic ends.

(3) A relevant decision may not be taken in respect of a person with a permanent right of residence under regulation 15 except on serious grounds of public policy or public security.

(4) A relevant decision may not be taken except on imperative grounds of public security in respect of an EEA national who—

(a) has resided in the United Kingdom for a continuous period of at least ten years prior to the relevant decision; or

(b) is under the age of 18, unless the relevant decision is necessary in his best interests, as provided for in the Convention on the Rights of the Child adopted by the General Assembly of the United Nations on 20th November 1989[11].

---

[11] Cmd 1976.

Appendix 14

(5) Where a relevant decision is taken on grounds of public policy or public security it shall, in addition to complying with the preceding paragraphs of this regulation, be taken in accordance with the following principles—

(a) the decision must comply with the principle of proportionality;
(b) the decision must be based exclusively on the personal conduct of the person concerned;
(c) the personal conduct of the person concerned must represent a genuine, present and sufficiently serious threat affecting one of the fundamental interests of society;
(d) matters isolated from the particulars of the case or which relate to considerations of general prevention do not justify the decision;
(e) a person's previous criminal convictions do not in themselves justify the decision.

(6) Before taking a relevant decision on the grounds of public policy or public security in relation to a person who is resident in the United Kingdom the decision maker must take account of considerations such as the age, state of health, family and economic situation of the person, the person's length of residence in the United Kingdom, the person's social and cultural integration into the United Kingdom and the extent of the person's links with his country of origin.

(7) In the case of a relevant decision taken on grounds of public health—

(a) a disease that does not have epidemic potential as defined by the relevant instruments of the World Health Organisation[12] or is not a disease to which section 38 of the Public Health (Control of Disease) Act 1984[13] applies (detention in hospital of a person with a notifiable disease) shall not constitute grounds for the decision; and
(b) if the person concerned is in the United Kingdom, diseases occurring after the three month period beginning on the date on which he arrived in the United Kingdom shall not constitute grounds for the decision.

Part 5

Procedure in Relation to EEA Decisions

Person claiming right of admission

22.—(1) This regulation applies to a person who claims a right of admission to the United Kingdom under regulation 11 as—

(a) a person, not being an EEA national, who is a family member of an EEA national, a family member who has retained the right of residence or a person with a permanent right of residence under regulation 15; or

---

[12] The relevant instrument of the World Health Organisation for these purposes is currently the International Health Regulations (2005).
[13] 1984 c.22; section 38 applies to a "notifiable disease", as defined in section 10 of the Act and has been applied to an additional list of diseases by the Public Health (Infectious Diseases) Regulations S.I. 1988/1546.

The Immigration (European Economic Area) Regulations 2006

(b) an EEA national, where there is reason to believe that he may fall to be excluded from the United Kingdom on grounds of public policy, public security or public health.

(2) A person to whom this regulation applies is to be treated as if he were a person seeking leave to enter the United Kingdom under the 1971 Act for the purposes of paragraphs 2, 3, 4, 7, 16 to 18 and 21 to 24 of Schedule 2 to the 1971 Act[14] (administrative provisions as to control on entry etc), except that—

(a) the reference in paragraph 2(1) to the purpose for which the immigration officer may examine any persons who have arrived in the United Kingdom is to be read as a reference to the purpose of determining whether he is a person who is to be granted admission under these Regulations;

(b) the references in paragraphs 4(2A), 7 and 16(1) to a person who is, or may be, given leave to enter are to be read as references to a person who is, or may be, granted admission under these Regulations; and

(c) a medical examination is not be carried out under paragraph 2 or paragraph 7 as a matter of routine and may only be carried out within three months of a person's arrival in the United Kingdom.

(3) For so long as a person to whom this regulation applies is detained, or temporarily admitted or released while liable to detention, under the powers conferred by Schedule 2 to the 1971 Act, he is deemed not to have been admitted to the United Kingdom.

Person refused admission

23.—(1) This regulation applies to a person who is in the United Kingdom and has been refused admission to the United Kingdom—

(a) because he does not meet the requirement of regulation 11 (including where he does not meet those requirements because his EEA family permit, residence card or permanent residence card has been revoked by an immigration officer in accordance with regulation 20); or

(b) in accordance with regulation 19(1) or (2).

(2) A person to whom this regulation applies, is to be treated as if he were a person refused leave to enter under the 1971 Act for the purpose of paragraphs 8, 10, 10A, 11, 16 to 19 and 21 to 24 of Schedule 2 to the 1971 Act, except that the reference in paragraph 19 to a certificate of entitlement, entry clearance or work permit is to be read as a reference to an EEA family permit, residence card or a permanent residence card.

---

[14] The relevant parts of Schedule 2 were amended by Schedule 6 to the Criminal Justice Act 1972 (c. 71), paragraphs 2 and 3 of Schedule 4 to the British Nationality Act 1981 (c. 61), paragraphs 6, 8, 9 and 10 of the Schedule to the Immigration Act 1988 (c. 14), paragraphs 5, 7, 10 and 11 of Schedule 2, and Schedule 4 to the Asylum and Immigration Act 1996 (c. 49), paragraph 70 of Schedule 13 to the Access to Justice Act 1999 (c. 22), section 140 of and paragraphs 43, 56, 58 to 63 of Schedule 14, and Schedule 16 to the 1999 Act, sections 63, 64 and 73 of and paragraphs 3 and 4 of Schedule 7 to the 2002 Act, paragraph 149 of Schedule 8 to the Courts Act 2003 (c. 39), paragraph 1 of Schedule 2 to the Asylum and Immigration (Treatment of Claimants, etc) Act 2004 (c. 19), and S.I. 1993/1813.

Appendix 14

Person subject to removal

24.—(1) This regulation applies to a person whom it has been decided to remove from the United Kingdom in accordance with regulation 19(3).

(2) Where the decision is under regulation 19(3)(a), the person is to be treated as if he were a person to whom section 10(1)(a) of the 1999 Act[15] applied, and section 10 of that Act (removal of certain persons unlawfully in the United Kingdom) is to apply accordingly.

(3) Where the decision is under regulation 19(3)(b), the person is to be treated as if he were a person to whom section 3(5)(a) of the 1971 Act[16] (liability to deportation) applied, and section 5 of that Act[17] (procedure for deportation) and Schedule 3 to that Act[18] (supplementary provision as to deportation) are to apply accordingly.

(4) A person who enters or seeks to enter the United Kingdom in breach of a deportation order made against him pursuant to paragraph (3) shall be removable as an illegal entrant under Schedule 2 to the 1971 Act and the provisions of that Schedule shall apply accordingly.

(5) Where such a deportation order is made against a person but he is not removed under the order during the two year period beginning on the date on which the order is made, the Secretary of State shall only take action to remove the person under the order after the end of that period if, having assessed whether there has been any material change in circumstances since the deportation order was made, he considers that the removal continues to be justified on the grounds of public policy, public security or public health.

(6) A person to whom this regulation applies shall be allowed one month to leave the United Kingdom, beginning on the date on which he is notified of the decision to remove him, before being removed pursuant to that decision except—

(a) in duly substantiated cases of urgency;

(b) where the person is detained pursuant to the sentence or order of any court;

(c) where a person is a person to whom regulation 24(4) applies.

---

[15] Section 10 is amended by sections 73 to 75 of and Schedule 9 to the 2002 Act.

[16] Section 3(5) is amended by paragraphs 43 and 44 of Schedule 14 to the 1999 Act.

[17] Section 5 is amended by paragraph 2 of Schedule 4 to the British Nationality Act 1981 (c. 61), paragraph 2 of the Schedule to the Immigration Act 1988 (c. 14), paragraph 2 of Schedule 2 to the Asylum and Immigration Act 1996 (c. 49) and paragraph 37 of Schedule 27 to the Civil Partnership Act 2004 (c. 33).

[18] Schedule 3 is amended by paragraphs 1 and 2 of Schedule 10 to the Criminal Justice Act 1982 (c.48), paragraph 10 of Schedule 10 to the Immigration Act 1988 (c.14), paragraph 13 of Schedule 2 to the Asylum and Immigration Act 1996 (c.49), section 54 of, and paragraphs 43 and 68 of Schedule 14 to, the 1999 Act, paragraphs 7 and 8 of Schedule 7 to the 2002 Act, paragraph 150 of Schedule 8, and Schedule 10, to the Courts Act 2003 (c.39), and section 34 of the Asylum and Immigration (Treatment of Claimants, etc) Act 2004 (c.19).

The Immigration (European Economic Area) Regulations 2006

Part 6

Appeals under these Regulations

Interpretation of Part 6

25.—(1) In this Part—

"Asylum and Immigration Tribunal" has the same meaning as in the 2002 Act;

"Commission" has the same meaning as in the Special Immigration Appeals Commission Act 1997[19];

"the Human Rights Convention" has the same meaning as "the Convention" in the Human Rights Act 1998[20]; and

"the Refugee Convention" means the Convention relating to the Status of Refugees done at Geneva on 28th July 1951[21] and the Protocol relating to the Status of Refugees done at New York on 31st January 1967[22].

(2) For the purposes of this Part, and subject to paragraphs (3) and (4), an appeal is to be treated as pending during the period when notice of appeal is given and ending when the appeal is finally determined, withdrawn or abandoned.

(3) An appeal is not to be treated as finally determined while a further appeal may be brought; and, if such a further appeal is brought, the original appeal is not to be treated as finally determined until the further appeal is determined, withdrawn or abandoned.

(4) A pending appeal is not to be treated as abandoned solely because the appellant leaves the United Kingdom.

Appeal rights

26.—(1) Subject to the following paragraphs of this regulation, a person may appeal under these Regulations against an EEA decision.

(2) If a person claims to be an EEA national, he may not appeal under these Regulations unless he produces a valid national identity card or passport issued by an EEA State.

(3) If a person claims to be the family member or relative of an EEA national he may not appeal under these Regulations unless he produces—

(a) an EEA family permit; or

(b) other proof that he is related as claimed to an EEA national.

(4) A person may not bring an appeal under these Regulations on a ground certified under paragraph (5) or rely on such a ground in an appeal brought under these Regulations.

---

[19] 1997 c. 68.
[20] 1998 c. 42.
[21] Cmd 9171.
[22] Cmnd 3906.

(5) The Secretary of State or an immigration officer may certify a ground for the purposes of paragraph (4) if it has been considered in a previous appeal brought under these Regulations or under section 82(1) of the 2002 Act[23].

(6) Except where an appeal lies to the Commission, an appeal under these Regulations lies to the Asylum and Immigration Tribunal.

(7) The provisions of or made under the 2002 Act referred to in Schedule 1 shall have effect for the purposes of an appeal under these Regulations to the Asylum and Immigration Tribunal in accordance with that Schedule.

Out of country appeals

27.—(1) Subject to paragraphs (2) and (3), a person may not appeal under regulation 26 whilst he is in the United Kingdom against an EEA decision—

(a) to refuse to admit him to the United Kingdom;

(b) to refuse to revoke a deportation order made against him;

(c) to refuse to issue him with an EEA family permit; or

(d) to remove him from the United Kingdom after he has entered or sought to enter the United Kingdom in breach of a deportation order.

(2) Paragraph (1)(a) does not apply where—

(a) the person held an EEA family permit, a registration certificate, a residence card, a document certifying permanent residence or a permanent residence card on his arrival in the United Kingdom or can otherwise prove that he is resident in the United Kingdom;

(b) the person is deemed not to have been admitted to the United Kingdom under regulation 22(3) but at the date on which notice of the decision to refuse to admit him is given he has been in the United Kingdom for at least 3 months;

(c) the person is in the United Kingdom and a ground of the appeal is that, in taking the decision, the decision maker acted in breach of his rights under the Human Rights Convention or the Refugee Convention, unless the Secretary of State certifies that that ground of appeal is clearly unfounded.

(3) Paragraph (1)(d) does not apply where a ground of the appeal is that, in taking the decision, the decision maker acted in breach of the appellant's rights under the Human Rights Convention or the Refugee Convention, unless the Secretary of State certifies that that ground of appeal is clearly unfounded.

Appeals to the Commission

28.—(1) An appeal against an EEA decision lies to the Commission where paragraph (2) or (4) applies.

(2) This paragraph applies if the Secretary of State certifies that the EEA decision was taken—

(a) by the Secretary of State wholly or partly on a ground listed in paragraph (3); or

---

[23] Section 82(1) is amended by section 26 of the Asylum and Immigration (Treatment of Claimants etc) Act 2004 (c.19).

(b) in accordance with a direction of the Secretary of State which identifies the person to whom the decision relates and which is given wholly or partly on a ground listed in paragraph (3).

(3) The grounds mentioned in paragraph (2) are that the person's exclusion or removal from the United Kingdom is—

(a) in the interests of national security; or

(b) in the interests of the relationship between the United Kingdom and another country.

(4) This paragraph applies if the Secretary of State certifies that the EEA decision was taken wholly or partly in reliance on information which in his opinion should not be made public—

(a) in the interests of national security;

(b) in the interests of the relationship between the United Kingdom and another country; or

(c) otherwise in the public interest.

(5) In paragraphs (2) and (4) a reference to the Secretary of State is to the Secretary of State acting in person.

(6) Where a certificate is issued under paragraph (2) or (4) in respect of a pending appeal to the Asylum and Immigration Tribunal the appeal shall lapse.

(7) An appeal against an EEA decision lies to the Commission where an appeal lapses by virtue of paragraph (6).

(8) The Special Immigration Appeals Commission Act 1997 shall apply to an appeal to the Commission under these Regulations as it applies to an appeal under section 2 of that Act to which subsection (2) of that section applies (appeals against an immigration decision) but paragraph (i) of that subsection shall not apply in relation to such an appeal.

Effect of appeals to the Asylum and Immigration Tribunal

29.—(1) This Regulation applies to appeals under these Regulations made to the Asylum and Immigration Tribunal.

(2) If a person in the United Kingdom appeals against an EEA decision to refuse to admit him to the United Kingdom, any directions for his removal from the United Kingdom previously given by virtue of the refusal cease to have effect, except in so far as they have already been carried out, and no directions may be so given while the appeal is pending.

(3) If a person in the United Kingdom appeals against an EEA decision to remove him from the United Kingdom, any directions given under section 10 of the 1999 Act or Schedule 3 to the 1971 Act for his removal from the United Kingdom are to have no effect, except in so far as they have already been carried out, while the appeal is pending.

(4) But the provisions of Part I of Schedule 2, or as the case may be, Schedule 3 to the 1971 Act with respect to detention and persons liable to detention apply to a person appealing against a refusal to admit him or a decision to remove him as if there were

in force directions for his removal from the United Kingdom, except that he may not be detained on board a ship or aircraft so as to compel him to leave the United Kingdom while the appeal is pending.

(5) In calculating the period of two months limited by paragraph 8(2) of Schedule 2 to the 1971 Act for—

(a) the giving of directions under that paragraph for the removal of a person from the United Kingdom; and

(b) the giving of a notice of intention to give such directions,

any period during which there is pending an appeal by him under is to be disregarded.

(6) If a person in the United Kingdom appeals against an EEA decision to remove him from the United Kingdom, a deportation order is not to be made against him under section 5 of the 1971 Act while the appeal is pending.

(7) Paragraph 29 of Schedule 2 to the 1971 Act (grant of bail pending appeal) applies to a person who has an appeal pending under these Regulations as it applies to a person who has an appeal pending under section 82(1) of the 2002 Act.

PART 7

GENERAL

Effect on other legislation

30. Schedule 2 (effect on other legislation) shall have effect.

Revocations, transitional provisions and consequential amendments

31.—(1) The Regulations listed in column 1 of the table in Part 1 of Schedule 3 are revoked to the extent set out in column 3 of that table, subject to Part 2 of that Schedule and to Schedule 4.

(2) Schedule 4 (transitional provisions) and Schedule 5 (consequential amendments) shall have effect.

SCHEDULE 1   Regulation 26(7)

APPEALS TO THE ASYLUM AND IMMIGRATION TRIBUNAL

The following provisions of, or made under, the 2002 Act have effect in relation to an appeal under these Regulations to the Asylum and Immigration Tribunal as if it were an appeal against an immigration decision under section 82(1) of that Act:

section 84(1)[24], except paragraphs (a) and (f);

---

[24] Section 84(1) is amended by S.R. 2003/341.

The Immigration (European Economic Area) Regulations 2006

sections 85 to 87;

sections 103A to 103E;

section 105 and any regulations made under that section; and

section 106 and any rules made under that section[25].

SCHEDULE 2   Regulation 30

Effect on Other Legislation

Leave under the 1971 Act

1.—(1) In accordance with section 7 of the Immigration Act 1988[26], a person who is admitted to or acquires a right to reside in the United Kingdom under these Regulations shall not require leave to remain in the United Kingdom under the 1971 Act during any period in which he has a right to reside under these Regulations but such a person shall require leave to remain under the 1971 Act during any period in which he does not have such a right.

(2) Where a person has leave to enter or remain under the 1971 Act which is subject to conditions and that person also has a right to reside under these Regulations, those conditions shall not have effect for as long as the person has that right to reside.

Persons not subject to restriction on the period for which they may remain

2.—(1) For the purposes of the 1971 Act and the British Nationality Act 1981[27], a person who has a permanent right of residence under regulation 15 shall be regarded as a person who is in the United Kingdom without being subject under the immigration laws to any restriction on the period for which he may remain.

(2) But a qualified person, the family member of a qualified person and a family member who has retained the right of residence shall not, by virtue of that status, be so regarded for those purposes.

Carriers' liability under the 1999 Act

3. For the purposes of satisfying a requirement to produce a visa under section 40(1)(b) of the 1999 Act[28] (charges in respect of passenger without proper documents), "a visa of the required kind" includes an EEA family permit, a residence card or a permanent residence card required for admission under regulation 11(2).

Appeals under the 2002 Act and previous immigration Acts

4.—(1) The following EEA decisions shall not be treated as immigration decisions for the purpose of section 82(2) of the 2002 Act (right of appeal against an immigration decision)—

---

[25] Sections 85 to 87 and 105 to 106 are amended by, and sections 103A to 103E are inserted by, section 26 of the Asylum and Immigration (Treatment of Claimants etc) Act 2004 (c.19).
[26] 1988 c.14.
[27] 1981 c. 61.
[28] Section 40 was substituted by paragraph 13 of Schedule 8 to the 2002 Act.

Appendix 14

- (a) a decision that a person is to be removed under regulation 19(3)(a) by way of a direction under section 10(1)(a) of the 1999 Act (as provided for by regulation 24(2));
- (b) a decision to remove a person under regulation 19(3)(b) by making a deportation order under section 5(1) of the 1971 Act (as provided for by regulation 24(3));
- (c) a decision to remove a person mentioned in regulation 24(4) by way of directions under paragraphs 8 to 10 of Schedule 2 to the 1971 Act.

(2) A person who has been issued with a registration certificate, residence card, a document certifying permanent residence or a permanent residence card under these Regulations or a registration certificate under the Accession (Immigration and Worker Registration) Regulations 2004[29], or a person whose passport has been stamped with a family member residence stamp, shall have no right of appeal under section 2 of the Special Immigration Appeals Commission Act 1997 or section 82(1) of the 2002 Act. Any existing appeal under those sections of those Acts or under the Asylum and Immigration Appeals Act 1993[30], the Asylum and Immigration Act 1996[31] or the 1999 Act shall be treated as abandoned.

(3) Subject to paragraph (4), a person may appeal to the Asylum and Immigration Tribunal under section 83(2) of the 2002 Act against the rejection of his asylum claim where—

- (a) that claim has been rejected, but
- (b) he has a right to reside in the United Kingdom under these Regulations.

(4) Paragraph (3) shall not apply if the person is an EEA national and the Secretary of State certifies that the asylum claim is clearly unfounded.

(5) The Secretary of State shall certify the claim under paragraph (4) unless satisfied that it is not clearly unfounded.

(6) In addition to the national of a State which is a contracting party to the Agreement referred to in section 84(2) of the 2002 Act, a Swiss national shall also be treated as an EEA national for the purposes of section 84(1)(d) of that Act.

(7) An appeal under these Regulations against an EEA decision (including an appeal made on or after 1st April 2003 which is treated as an appeal under these Regulations under Schedule 4 but not an appeal made before that date) shall be treated as an appeal under section 82(1) of the 2002 Act against an immigration decision for the purposes of section 96(1)(a) of the 2002 Act.

(8) Section 120 of the 2002 Act shall apply to a person if an EEA decision has been taken or may be taken in respect of him and, accordingly, the Secretary of State or an immigration officer may by notice require a statement from that person under subsection (2) of that section and that notice shall have effect for the purpose of section 96(2) of the 2002 Act.

(9) In sub-paragraph (1), "family member residence stamp" means a stamp in the passport of a family member of an EEA national confirming that he is the family

---

[29] S.I 2004/1219, amended by S.I. 2004/1236 and S.I. 2005/2400.
[30] 1993 c. 23.
[31] 1996 c. 49.

The Immigration (European Economic Area) Regulations 2006

member of an accession State worker requiring registration with a right of residence under these Regulations as the family member of that worker; and in this sub-paragraph "accession State worker requiring registration" has the same meaning as in regulation 2 of the Accession (Immigration and Worker Registration) Regulations 2004.

SCHEDULE 3

Regulation 31(2)

REVOCATIONS AND SAVINGS

PART 1

TABLE OF REVOCATIONS

(1) Regulations revoked	(2) References	(3) Extent of revocation
The Immigration (European Economic Area) Regulations 2000	S.I. 2000/2326	The whole Regulations
The Immigration (European Economic Area) (Amendment) Regulations 2001	S.I. 2001/865	The whole Regulations
The Immigration (Swiss Free Movement of Persons) (No. 3) Regulations 2002	S.I. 2002/1241	The whole Regulations
The Immigration (European Economic Area) (Amendment) Regulations 2003	S.I. 2003/549	The whole Regulations
The Immigration (European Economic Area) (Amendment No. 2) Regulations 2003	S.I. 2003/3188	The whole Regulations
The Accession (Immigration and Worker Registration) Regulations 2004	S.I. 2004/1219	Regulations 3 and 6
The Immigration (European Economic Area) and Accession (Amendment) Regulations 2004	S.I. 2004/1236	Regulation 2
The Immigration (European Economic Area) (Amendment) Regulations 2005	S.I. 2005/47	The whole Regulations
The Immigration (European Economic Area) (Amendment) (No. 2) Regulations 2005	S.I. 2005/671	The whole Regulations

APPENDIX 14

PART 2

SAVINGS

1. The—

(a) Immigration (Swiss Free Movement of Persons) (No. 3) Regulations 2002[32] are not revoked insofar as they apply the 2000 Regulations to posted workers; and

(b) the 2000 Regulations and the Regulations amending the 2000 Regulations are not revoked insofar as they are so applied to posted workers; and, accordingly, the 2000 Regulations, as amended, shall continue to apply to posted workers in accordance with the Immigration (Swiss Free Movement of Persons) (No. 3) Regulations 2002.

2. In paragraph 1, "the 2000 Regulations" means the Immigration (European Economic Area) Regulations 2000[33] and "posted worker" has the meaning given in regulation 2(4)(b) of the Immigration (Swiss Free Movement of Persons) (No. 3) Regulations 2002.

SCHEDULE 4 Regulation 31(2)

TRANSITIONAL PROVISIONS

Interpretation

1. In this Schedule—

(a) the "2000 Regulations" means the Immigration (European Economic Area) Regulations 2000[34] and expressions used in relation to documents issued or applied for under those Regulations shall have the meaning given in regulation 2 of those Regulations;

(b) the "Accession Regulations" means the Accession (Immigration and Worker Registration) Regulations 2004[35].

Existing documents

2.—(1) An EEA family permit issued under the 2000 Regulations shall, after 29th April 2006, be treated as if it were an EEA family permit issued under these Regulations.

(2) Subject to paragraph (4), a residence permit issued under the 2000 Regulations shall, after 29th April 2006, be treated as if it were a registration certificate issued under these Regulations.

---

[32] S.I. 2002/1241.
[33] S.I. 2000/2326, amended by S.I. 2001/865, S.I. 2003/549, S.I. 2003/3188, S.I. 2005/47 and S.I. 2005/671.
[34] S.I. 2000/2326, amended by S.I. 2001/865, S.I. 2003/549, S.I. 2003/3188, S.I. 2005/47 and S.I. 2005/671.
[35] S.I. 2004/1219, amended by S.I. 2004/1236 and 2005/2400.

The Immigration (European Economic Area) Regulations 2006

(3) Subject to paragraph (5), a residence document issued under the 2000 Regulations shall, after 29th April 2006, be treated as if it were a residence card issued under these Regulations.

(4) Where a residence permit issued under the 2000 Regulations has been endorsed under the immigration rules to show permission to remain in the United Kingdom indefinitely it shall, after 29th April 2006, be treated as if it were a document certifying permanent residence issued under these Regulations and the holder of the permit shall be treated as a person with a permanent right of residence under regulation 15.

(5) Where a residence document issued under the 2000 Regulations has been endorsed under the immigration rules to show permission to remain in the United Kingdom indefinitely it shall, after 29th April 2006, be treated as if it were a permanent residence card issued under these Regulations and the holder of the permit shall be treated as a person with a permanent right of residence under regulation 15.

(6) Paragraphs (4) and (5) shall also apply to a residence permit or residence document which is endorsed under the immigration rules on or after 30th April 2006 to show permission to remain in the United Kingdom indefinitely pursuant to an application for such an endorsement made before that date.

Outstanding applications

3.—(1) An application for an EEA family permit, a residence permit or a residence document made but not determined under the 2000 Regulations before 30 April 2006 shall be treated as an application under these Regulations for an EEA family permit, a registration certificate or a residence card, respectively.

(2) But the following provisions of these Regulations shall not apply to the determination of an application mentioned in sub-paragraph (1)—

(a) the requirement to issue a registration certificate immediately under regulation 16(1); and

(b) the requirement to issue a certificate of application for a residence card under regulation 17(3).

Decisions to remove under the 2000 Regulations

4.—(1) A decision to remove a person under regulation 21(3)(a) of the 2000 Regulations shall, after 29th April 2006, be treated as a decision to remove that person under regulation 19(3)(a) of these Regulations.

(2) A decision to remove a person under regulation 21(3)(b) of the 2000 Regulations, including a decision which is treated as a decision to remove a person under that regulation by virtue of regulation 6(3)(a) of the Accession Regulations, shall, after 29th April 2006, be treated as a decision to remove that person under regulation 19(3)(b) of these Regulations.

(3) A deportation order made under section 5 of the 1971 Act by virtue of regulation 26(3) of the 2000 Regulations shall, after 29th April 2006, be treated as a deportation made under section 5 of the 1971 Act by virtue of regulation 24(3) of these Regulations.

Appeals

5.—(1) Where an appeal against an EEA decision under the 2000 Regulations is pending immediately before 30th April 2006 that appeal shall be treated as a pending appeal against the corresponding EEA Decision under these Regulations.

(2) Where an appeal against an EEA decision under the 2000 Regulations has been determined, withdrawn or abandoned it shall, on and after 30th April 2006, be treated as an appeal against the corresponding EEA decision under these Regulations which has been determined, withdrawn or abandoned, respectively.

(3) For the purpose of this paragraph—

(a) a decision to refuse to admit a person under these Regulations corresponds to a decision to refuse to admit that person under the 2000 Regulations;

(b) a decision to remove a person under regulation 19(3)(a) of these Regulations corresponds to a decision to remove that person under regulation 21(3)(a) of the 2000 Regulations;

(c) a decision to remove a person under regulation 19(3)(b) of these Regulations corresponds to a decision to remove that person under regulation 21(3)(b) of the 2000 Regulations, including a decision which is treated as a decision to remove a person under regulation 21(3)(b) of the 2000 Regulations by virtue of regulation 6(3)(a) of the Accession Regulations;

(d) a decision to refuse to revoke a deportation order made against a person under these Regulations corresponds to a decision to refuse to revoke a deportation order made against that person under the 2000 Regulations, including a decision which is treated as a decision to refuse to revoke a deportation order under the 2000 Regulations by virtue of regulation 6(3)(b) of the Accession Regulations;

(e) a decision not to issue or renew or to revoke an EEA family permit, a registration certificate or a residence card under these Regulations corresponds to a decision not to issue or renew or to revoke an EEA family permit, a residence permit or a residence document under the 2000 Regulations, respectively.

Periods of residence under the 2000 Regulations

6.—(1) Any period during which a person carried out an activity or was resident in the United Kingdom in accordance with the 2000 Regulations shall be treated as a period during which the person carried out that activity or was resident in the United Kingdom in accordance with these Regulations for the purpose of calculating periods of activity and residence under these Regulations.

THE IMMIGRATION (EUROPEAN ECONOMIC AREA) REGULATIONS 2006

SCHEDULE 5   Regulation 31(2)

CONSEQUENTIAL AMENDMENTS

Statutory Instruments

The Channel Tunnel (International Arrangements) Order 1993

1.—(1) The Channel Tunnel (International Arrangements) Order 1993[36] is amended as follows.

(2) In Schedule 4, in paragraph 5—

(a) at the beginning of the paragraph, for "the Immigration (European Economic Area) Regulations 2000" there is substituted "the Immigration (European Economic Area) Regulations 2006";

(b) in sub-paragraph (a), for "regulation 12(2)" there is substituted "regulation 11(2)" and for "residence document or document proving family membership" there is substituted "residence card or permanent residence card";

(c) for sub-paragraph (b) there is substituted—

"(b) in regulations 11(4) and 19(2) after the word "arrival" and in regulations 20(4) and (5) after the words "United Kingdom" insert "or the time of his production of the required documents in a control zone or a supplementary control zone".

The Travel Restriction Order (Prescribed Removal Powers) Order 2002

2.—(1) The Travel Restriction Order (Prescribed Removal Powers) Order 2002[37] is amended as follows.

(2) In the Schedule, for "Immigration (European Economic Area) Regulations 2000 (2000/2326)" in the first column of the table there is substituted "Immigration (European Economic Area) Regulations 2006" and for "Regulation 21(3)" in the corresponding row in the second column of the table there is substituted "Regulation 19(3)".

The Immigration (Notices) Regulations 2003

3.—(1) The Immigration (Notices) Regulations 2003[38] are amended as follows.

(2) In regulation 2, in the definition of "EEA decision"—

---

[36] S.I. 1993/1813, amended by S.I. 1994/1405, S.I. 1996/2283, S.I. 2000/913, S.I. 2000/1775, S.I. 2001/178, S.I. 2001/418, S.I. 2001/1544, S.I. 2000/3707 and S.I. 2003/2799.
[37] S.I. 2002/313.
[38] S.I. 2003/658.

Appendix 14

(a) at the end of paragraph (b), "or" is omitted;

(b) in paragraph (c), after "residence document;", there is inserted "or"; and

(c) after paragraph (c), there is inserted—

"(d) on or after 30th April 2006, entitlement to be issued with or have renewed, or not to have revoked, a registration certificate, residence card, document certifying permanent residence or permanent residence card;"

The Nationality, Immigration and Asylum Act 2002 (Juxtaposed Controls) Order 2003

4.—(1) The Nationality, Immigration and Asylum Act 2002 (Juxtaposed Controls) Order 2003[39] is amended as follows.

(2) In article 11(1), for sub-paragraph (e) there is substituted—

"(e) the Immigration (European Economic Area) Regulations 2006.".

(3) In Schedule 2, in paragraph 5—

(a) at the beginning of the paragraph, for "the Immigration (European Economic Area) Regulations 2000" there is substituted "the Immigration (European Economic Area) Regulations 2006";

(b) in sub-paragraph (a), for "in regulation 2, at the beginning insert" there is substituted "in regulation 2(1), after the definition of "civil partner" insert";

(c) in sub-paragraph (b), for "regulation 12(2)" there is substituted "regulation 11(2)" and for "residence document or document proving family membership" there is substituted "residence card or permanent residence card";

(d) for sub-paragraph (c) there is substituted—

"(c) in regulations 11(4) and 19(2) after the word "arrival" and in regulations 20(4) and (5) after the words "United Kingdom" insert "or the time of his production of the required documents in a Control Zone".

The Immigration and Asylum Act 1999 (Part V Exemption: Relevant Employers) Order 2003

5.—(1) The Immigration and Asylum Act 1999 (Part V Exemption: Relevant Employers) Order 2003[40] is amended as follows.

(2) In Article 2, in the definition of "EEA national" and "family member of an EEA national", for "Immigration (European Economic Area) Regulations 2000" there is substituted "Immigration (European Economic Area) Regulations 2006".

---

[39] S.I. 2003/2818.
[40] S.I. 2003/3214.

The Immigration (European Economic Area) Regulations 2006

The Immigration (Restrictions on Employment) Order 2004

6.—(1) The Immigration (Restrictions on Employment) Order 2004[41] is amended as follows.

(2) In Part 1 of the Schedule (descriptions of documents for the purpose of article 4(2)(a) of the Order)—

(a) for paragraph 4 there is substituted—

"4. A registration certificate or document certifying permanent residence within the meaning of regulation 2 of the Immigration (European Economic Area) Regulations 2006, including a document which is treated as a registration certificate or document certifying permanent residence by virtue of Schedule 4 to those Regulations.";

(b) for paragraph 5 there is substituted—

"5. A residence card or a permanent residence card within the meaning of regulation 2 of the Immigration (European Economic Area) Regulations 2006, including a document which is treated as a residence card or a permanent residence card by virtue of Schedule 4 to those Regulations".

The Accession (Immigration and Worker Registration) Regulations 2004

7.—(1) The Accession (Immigration and Worker Registration) Regulations 2004[42] are amended as follows.

(2) In regulation 1(2) (interpretation)—

(a) after paragraph (b) there is inserted—

"(ba) "the 2006 Regulations" means the Immigration (European Economic Area) Regulations 2006;";

(b) in paragraph (j), for "regulation 3 of the 2000 Regulations" these is substituted "regulation 4 of the 2006 Regulations".

(3) In regulation 2 ("accession State worker requiring registration")—

(a) for paragraph (6)(b) there is substituted—

"(b) a family member of a Swiss or EEA national (other than an accession State worker requiring registration) who has a right to reside in the United Kingdom under regulation 14(1) or 15 of the 2006 Regulations;";

(b) paragraph (9)(a) is omitted;

(c) for paragraph (9)(c) there is substituted—

"(c) "family member" has the same meaning as in regulation 7 of the 2006 Regulations.".

---

[41] S.I. 2004/755.
[42] S.I. 2004/1219; amended by S.I. 2004/1236 and S.I. 2005/2400.

Appendix 14

(4) In regulation 4 (right of residence of work seekers and workers from relevant acceding States during the accession period)—

(a) in paragraph (1), before "Council Directive" there is inserted "Council Directive 2004/38/EC of the European Parliament and of the Council on the right of citizens of the Union and their family members to move and reside freely within the territory of the Member States[43], insofar as it takes over provisions of";

(b) in paragraph (3), for "2000 Regulations" there is substituted "2006 Regulations";

(c) in paragraph (4), for "An" there is substituted "A national of a relevant accession State who is seeking employment and an" and for "2000 Regulations" there is substituted "2006 Regulations".

(5) For regulation 5 (application of 2000 Regulations in relation to accession State worker requiring registration) there is substituted—

"*Application of 2006 Regulations in relation to accession State worker requiring registration*

5.—(1) The 2006 Regulations shall apply in relation to a national of a relevant accession State subject to the modifications set out in this regulation.

(2) A national of a relevant accession State who is seeking employment in the United Kingdom shall not be treated as a jobseeker for the purpose of the definition of "qualified person" in regulation 6(1) of the 2006 Regulations and an accession State worker requiring registration shall be treated as a worker for the purpose of that definition only during a period in which he is working in the United Kingdom for an authorised employer.

(3) Subject to paragraph (4), regulation 6(2) of the 2006 Regulations shall not apply to an accession State worker requiring registration who ceases to work.

(4) Where an accession State worker requiring registration ceases working for an authorised employer in the circumstances mentioned in regulation 6(2) of the 2006 Regulations during the one month period beginning on the date on which the work begins, that regulation shall apply to that worker during the remainder of that one month period.

(5) An accession State worker requiring registration shall not be treated as a qualified person for the purpose of regulations 16 and 17 of the 2006 Regulations (issue of registration certificates and residence cards)."

---

[43] OJ L 158, 30.4.2004, p.77 (the full title of the Directive is Council Directive 2004/38/EC of the European Parliament and the Council on the rights of citizens of the Union and their family members to move and reside freely within the territory of the member States amending Regulation (EEC) No. 1612/68 and repealing Directives 64/221/EEC, 68/360/EEC, 72/194/EEC, 75/34/EEC, 90/364/EEC, 90/365/EEC and 93/96/EEC).

The Immigration (European Economic Area) Regulations 2006

The Asylum and Immigration Tribunal (Procedure) Rules 2005

8.—(1) The Asylum and Immigration Tribunal (Procedure) Rules 2005[44] are amended as follows.

(2) In regulation 18(1)(b), after "('the 2000 Regulations')" there is inserted "or, on or after 30th April 2006, paragraph 4(2) of Schedule 2 to the Immigration (European Economic Area) Regulations 2006 ('the 2006 Regulations')".

(3) In regulation 18(2), after "2000 Regulations" there is inserted "or paragraph 4(2) of Schedule 2 to the 2006 Regulations".

---

[44] S.I. 2005/230.

Appendix 15

THE IMMIGRATION (EUROPEAN ECONOMIC AREA) (AMENDMENT) REGULATIONS 2011

SI 2011 No. 1247

Made	9th May 2011
Laid before Parliament	12th May 2011
Coming into force	2nd June 2011

The Secretary of State, being a Minister designated[1] for the purpose of section 2(2) of the European Communities Act 1972[2] in relation to measures relating to rights of entry into, and residence in, the United Kingdom, in exercise of the powers conferred by that section makes the following Regulations:

Citation, commencement and interpretation

1.—(1) These Regulations may be cited as the Immigration (European Economic Area) (Amendment) Regulations 2011 and shall come into force on 2 June 2011.

(2) In these Regulations, "the 2006 Regulations" means the Immigration (European Economic Area) Regulations 2006.[3]

Amendment of the 2006 Regulations

2.—(1) The 2006 Regulations are amended as follows.

(2) In regulation 4, for paragraph (4) substitute—

"(4) For the purposes of paragraphs (1)(c) and (d) and paragraphs (2) and (3), the resources of the person concerned and, where applicable, any family members, are to be regarded as sufficient if—

(a) they exceed the maximum level of resources which a United Kingdom national and his family members may possess if he is to become eligible for social assistance under the United Kingdom benefit system; or
(b) paragraph (a) does not apply but, taking into account the personal situation of the person concerned and, where applicable, any family members, it appears to the decision maker that the resources of the person or persons concerned should be regarded as sufficient."

(3) In regulation 8, at paragraph 2(a) for "an EEA State" substitute "a country other than the United Kingdom".

(4) In regulation 12, for paragraph (1)(b) substitute—

"(b) the family member will be accompanying the EEA national to the United Kingdom or joining the EEA national there.".

---

[1] S.I. 2000/1813.
[2] 1972 c.68.
[3] S.I. 2006/1003, amended by S.I. 2009/1117 and S.I. 2011/544.

Appendix 16

THE ACCESSION (IMMIGRATION AND WORKER AUTHORISATION) REGULATIONS 2006

SI 2006 No. 3317

Made 13th December 2006
Coming into force 1st January 2007

The Secretary of State, being a Minister designated[1] for the purposes of section 2(2) of the European Communities Act 1972[2] in relation to measures relating to the right of entry into, and residence in, the United Kingdom and access to the labour market of the United Kingdom, in exercise of the powers conferred upon him by that section, and in exercise of the powers conferred upon him by section 2 of the European Union (Accessions) Act 2006[3], makes the following Regulations, a draft of which has been approved by resolution of each House of Parliament:

Part 1

General

Citation, commencement, interpretation and consequential amendments

1.—(1) These Regulations may be cited as the Accession (Immigration and Worker Authorisation) Regulations 2006 and shall come into force on 1st January 2007.

(2) In these Regulations—

(a) "the 1971 Act" means the Immigration Act 1971[4] ;

(b) "the 2006 Regulations" means the Immigration (European Economic Area) Regulations 2006[5] ;

(c) "accession period" means the period beginning on 1st January 2007 and ending on 31st December 2011;

(d) "accession State national subject to worker authorisation" has the meaning given in regulation 2;

(e) "accession worker authorisation document" shall be interpreted in accordance with regulation 9(2);

(f) "authorised category of employment" means a category of employment listed in the first column of the table in Schedule 1;

(g) "authorised family member" has the meaning given in regulation 3;

---

[1] S.I. 2000/1813 and S.I. 2004/706.
[2] 1972 c.68.
[3] 2006 c.2.
[4] 1971 c.77.
[5] S.I. 2006/1003.

Appendix 16

(h) "civil partner" does not include a party to a civil partnership of convenience[6];

(i) "EEA State" means—

    (i) a member State, other than the United Kingdom;
    (ii) Norway, Iceland or Liechtenstein;
    (iii) Switzerland;

(j) "employer" means, in relation to a worker, the person who directly pays the wage or salary of that worker;

(k) "family member" shall be interpreted in accordance with regulation 7 of the 2006 Regulations;

(l) "highly skilled person" has the meaning given in regulation 4;

(m) "immigration rules" means the rules laid down as mentioned in section 3(2) of the 1971 Act applying on 1st January 2007[7];

(n) "letter of approval under the work permit arrangements" has the meaning given in paragraph 1(b) of Schedule 1;

(o) "registration certificate" means a certificate issued in accordance with regulation 16 of the 2006 Regulations;

(p) "relevant requirements" means, in relation to an authorised category of employment, the requirements set out in the second column of the table in Schedule 1 for that category;

(q) "Sectors Based Scheme" has the meaning given in paragraph 1(f) of Schedule 1;

(r) "spouse" does not include a party to a marriage of convenience;

(s) "student" has the meaning given in regulation 4(1)(d) of the 2006 Regulations;

(t) "worker" means a worker within the meaning of Article 39 of the Treaty establishing the European Community[8], and "work" and "working" shall be construed accordingly.

(3) Schedule 2 (consequential amendments) shall have effect.

"Accession State national subject to worker authorisation"

2.—(1) Subject to the following paragraphs of this regulation, in these Regulations "accession State national subject to worker authorisation" means a national of Bulgaria or Romania.

(2) A national of Bulgaria or Romania is not an accession State national subject to worker authorisation if he has leave to enter or remain in the United Kingdom under the 1971 Act and that leave is not subject to any condition restricting his employment.

(3) A national of Bulgaria or Romania is not an accession State national subject to worker authorisation if he was legally working in the United Kingdom on 31st December 2006 and had been legally working in the United Kingdom without interruption throughout the period of 12 months ending on that date.

---

[6] "Civil partner" has the meaning given by Schedule 1 to the Interpretation Act 1978 (c.30), as amended by paragraph 59 of Schedule 27 to the Civil Partnership Act 2004 (c.33).
[7] Immigration Rules H.C. 395, laid before Parliament on 23 May 1994 (as amended).
[8] OJ No. C325, 24.12.02, p.51.

The Accession (Immigration and Worker Authorisation) Regs 2006

(4) A national of Bulgaria or Romania who legally works in the United Kingdom without interruption for a period of 12 months falling partly or wholly after 31st December 2006 shall cease to be an accession State national subject to worker authorisation at the end of that period of 12 months.

(5) A national of Bulgaria or Romania is not an accession State national subject to worker authorisation during any period in which he is also a national of—

(a) the United Kingdom; or

(b) an EEA State, other than Bulgaria or Romania.

(6) A national of Bulgaria or Romania is not an accession State national subject to worker authorisation during any period in which he is the spouse or civil partner of a national of the United Kingdom or of a person settled in the United Kingdom.

(7) A national of Bulgaria or Romania is not an accession State national subject to worker authorisation during any period in which he has a permanent right of residence under regulation 15 of the 2006 Regulations.

(8) A national of Bulgaria or Romania is not an accession State national subject to worker authorisation during any period in which he is a family member of an EEA national who has a right to reside in the United Kingdom under the 2006 Regulations, unless that EEA national is—

(a) an accession State national subject to worker authorisation; or

(b) a student who is not an accession State national subject to worker authorisation solely by virtue of falling within paragraph (10).

(9) A national of Bulgaria or Romania is not an accession State national subject to worker authorisation during any period in which he is a highly skilled person and holds a registration certificate that includes a statement that he has unconditional access to the United Kingdom labour market.

(10) A national of Bulgaria or Romania is not an accession State national subject to worker authorisation during any period in which he is in the United Kingdom as a student, does not work for more than 20 hours a week and holds a registration certificate that includes a statement that he is a student who has access to the United Kingdom labour market for 20 hours a week.

(11) A national of Bulgaria or Romania is not an accession State national subject to worker authorisation during any period in which he is a posted worker.

(12) For the purposes of paragraphs (3) and (4) of this regulation—

(a) a person working in the United Kingdom during a period falling before 1st January 2007 was working legally in the United Kingdom during that period if—

   (i) he had leave to enter or remain in the United Kingdom under the 1971 Act for that period, that leave allowed him to work in the United Kingdom, and he was working in accordance with any condition on that leave restricting his employment; or

Appendix 16

      (ii) he was entitled to reside in the United Kingdom for that period under the Immigration (European Economic Area) Regulations 2000[9] or the 2006 Regulations without the requirement for such leave;

(b) a person working in the United Kingdom on or after 1st January 2007 is legally working during any period in which he—

      (i) falls within paragraphs (5) to (10); or
      (ii) holds an accession worker authorisation document and is working in accordance with the conditions set out in that document;

(c) a person shall be treated as having worked in the United Kingdom without interruption for a period of 12 months if he was legally working in the United Kingdom at the beginning and end of that period and any intervening periods in which he was not legally working in the United Kingdom do not, in total, exceed 30 days.

(13) In this regulation—

(a) "posted worker" means a worker who is posted to the United Kingdom, within the meaning of Article 1(3) of Directive 96/71/EC concerning the posting of workers[10], by an undertaking established in an EEA State;

(b) the reference to a person settled in the United Kingdom shall be interpreted in accordance with section 33(2A)[11] of the 1971 Act.

Authorised family member

3.—(1) For the purposes of these Regulations a person shall be treated as an authorised family members if he is the family member of—

(a) an accession State national subject to worker authorisation who has a right to reside in the United Kingdom under regulation 14(1) of the 2006 Regulations, unless that national only has a right to reside under that regulation by virtue of his status as a worker and he is working as an au pair, a seasonal agricultural worker or under the Sectors Based Scheme; or

(b) a student who is not an accession State national subject to worker authorisation solely by virtue of falling within regulation 2(10).

(2) The spouse or civil partner of a person who has leave to enter or remain in the United Kingdom under the 1971 Act that allows him to work in the United Kingdom shall also be treated as an authorised family member.

"Highly skilled person"

4.—(1) In these Regulations "highly skilled person" means a person who—

---

[9] S.I. 2000/2326; amended by S.I. 2001/865, S.I. 2003/549, S.I. 2003/3188, S.I.2005/47 and S.I. 2005/671.

[10] O.J. L 018, 21.1.1997, p.1 (the full title of the Directive is Council Directive 96/71/EC of the European Parliament and of the Council of 16 December 1996 concerning the posting of workers in the framework of the provision of services).

[11] Section 33(2A) was inserted by paragraph 7(b) of Schedule 4 to the British Nationality Act 1981 (c. 61).

The Accession (Immigration and Worker Authorisation) Regs 2006

(a) meets the criteria specified by the Secretary of State for the purpose of paragraph 135A(i)[12] of the immigration rules (entry to the United Kingdom under the Highly Skilled Migrant Programme) and applying on 1st January 2007, other than the criterion requiring a proficiency in the English language; or

(b) has been awarded one of the following qualifications and applies for a registration certificate or submits a registration certificate to the Secretary of State under regulation 7(4) within 12 months of being awarded the qualification—

   (i) a Higher National Diploma or degree awarded by a relevant institution in Scotland; or
   (ii) a degree with second class honours or above in a subject approved by the Department for Education and Skills for the purpose of participation in the Science and Engineering Graduates Scheme[13], or a master's degree or doctorate in any subject, awarded by a relevant institution in England, Wales or Northern Ireland.

(2) In paragraph (1)(b), "relevant institution" means an institution that is financed from public funds or included on the Department for Education and Skills' Register of Education and Training Providers[14] on 1st January 2007.

Derogation from provisions of Community law relating to workers

5. Regulations 6, 7 and 9 derogate during the accession period from Article 39 of the Treaty establishing the European Communities, Articles 1 to 6 of Regulation (EEC) No. 1612/68 on freedom of movement for workers within the Community[15] and Council Directive 2004/38/EC[16] on the right of citizens of the Union and their family members to move and reside freely within the territory of the Member States.

Part 2

Immigration

Right of residence of an accession State national subject to worker authorisation

6.—(1) An accession State national subject to worker authorisation shall, during the accession period, only be entitled to reside in the United Kingdom in accordance with the 2006 Regulations, as modified by this regulation.

(2) An accession State national subject to worker authorisation who is seeking employment in the United Kingdom shall not be treated as a jobseeker for the purpose of the definition of "qualified person" in regulation 6(1) of the 2006

---

[12] Paragraph 135A(i) was inserted by immigration rules changes on 1st April 2003 (HC 538). The specified criteria are published by Work Permits UK, part of the Home Office, and are available on the Home Office website (www.workingintheuk.gov.uk).

[13] Details of the Science and Engineering Graduates Scheme are available on the Home Office website (www.workingintheuk.gov.uk).

[14] The Register of Education and Training Providers is maintained by, and is available on the website of, the Department for Education and Skills (www.dfes.gov.uk/providersregister).

[15] O.J. L 257, 19.10.1968, p.2.

[16] OJ L 158, 30.4.2004, p.77 (the full title of the Directive is Council Directive 2004/38/EC of the European Parliament and the Council of 29 April 2004 on the right of citizens of the Union and their family members to move and reside freely within the territory of the member States amending Regulation (EEC) No. 1612/68 and repealing Directives 64/221/EEC, 68/360/EEC, 72/194/EEC, 75/34/EEC, 90/364/EEC, 90/365/EEC and 93/96/EEC).

Regulations and such a person shall be treated as a worker for the purpose of that definition only during a period in which he holds an accession worker authorisation document and is working in accordance with the conditions set out in that document.

(3) Regulation 6(2) of the 2006 Regulations shall not apply to an accession State national subject to worker authorisation who ceases to work.

Issuing registration certificates and residence cards to nationals of Bulgaria and Romania and their family members during the accession period

7.—(1) Subject to paragraph (2), an accession State national subject to worker authorisation shall not be treated as a qualified person for the purposes of regulations 16 and 17 of the 2006 Regulations (issue of registration certificates and residence cards) during the accession period unless he falls within sub-paragraphs (c), (d) or (e) of regulation 6(1) of the 2006 Regulations.

(2) The Secretary of State shall issue a registration certificate to an accession State national subject to worker authorisation on application if he is satisfied that the applicant—

(a) is seeking employment in the United Kingdom; and

(b) is a highly skilled person.

(3) Where the Secretary of State issues a registration certificate during the accession period to a Bulgarian or Romanian national under paragraph (2) or in any case where he is satisfied that the Bulgarian or Romanian national is not an accession State national subject to worker authorisation, the registration certificate shall include a statement that the holder of the certificate has unconditional access to the United Kingdom labour market.

(4) A Bulgarian or Romanian national who holds a registration certificate that does not include a statement that he has unconditional access to the United Kingdom labour market may, during the accession period, submit the certificate to the Secretary of State for the inclusion of such a statement.

(5) The Secretary of State shall re-issue a certificate submitted to him under paragraph (4) with the inclusion of a statement that the holder has unconditional access to the United Kingdom labour market if he is satisfied that the holder—

(a) is a highly skilled person; or

(b) has ceased to be an accession State national subject to worker authorisation other than solely by virtue of falling within regulation 2(10).

(6) A registration certificate issued to a Bulgarian or Romanian student during the accession period shall include a statement that the holder of the certificate is a student who has access to the United Kingdom labour market for 20 hours a week, unless it includes a statement under paragraph (3) or (5) that the holder has unconditional access to the United Kingdom labour market.

(7) But this regulation is subject to regulation 20 of the 2006 Regulations (power to refuse to issue and to revoke registration certificates).

The Accession (Immigration and Worker Authorisation) Regs 2006

Transitional provisions to take account of the application of the 2006 Regulations to nationals of Bulgaria and Romania and their family members on 1st January 2007

8.—(1) Where before 1st January 2007 directions have been given for the removal of a Bulgarian or Romanian national or the family member of such a national under paragraphs 8 to 10A of Schedule 2 to the 1971 Act[17] or section 10 of the 1999 Act, those directions shall cease to have effect on and after that date.

(2) Where before 1st January 2007 the Secretary of State has made a decision to make a deportation order against a Bulgarian or Romanian national or the family member of such a national under section 5(1) of the 1971 Act—

(a) that decision shall, on and after 1st January 2007, be treated as if it were a decision under regulation 19(3)(b) of the 2006 Regulations; and

(b) any appeal against that decision, or against the refusal of the Secretary of State to revoke the deportation order, made under section 63 of the 1999 Act or section 82(2)(j) or (k) of the 2002 Act before 1st January 2007, shall, on or after that date, be treated as if it had been made under regulation 26 of the 2006 Regulations.

(3) In this regulation—

(a) "the 1999 Act" means the Immigration and Asylum Act 1999[18];

(b) "the 2002 Act" means the Nationality, Immigration and Asylum Act 2002[19];

(c) any reference to the family member of a Bulgarian or Romanian national is a reference to a person who on 1st January 2007 acquires a right to reside in the United Kingdom under the 2006 Regulations as the family member of a Bulgarian or Romanian national.

PART 3

ACCESSION STATE WORKER AUTHORISATION

Requirement for an accession State national subject to worker authorisation to be authorised to work

9.—(1) An accession State national subject to worker authorisation shall only be authorised to work in the United Kingdom during the accession period if he holds an accession worker authorisation document and is working in accordance with the conditions set out in that document.

(2) For the purpose of these Regulations, an accession worker authorisation document is—

---

[17] Paragraphs 8 to 10 have been amended by the Schedule to the Immigration Act 1988 (c.14), Schedule 2 to the Asylum and Immigration Act 1996 (c. 49) and Schedule 7 to the Nationality, Immigration and Asylum Act 2002 (c.41), and paragraph 10A was inserted by section 73 of the 2002 Act.

[18] 1999 c. 33; section 63 of the 1999 Act was repealed by Schedule 9 to the Nationality, Immigration and Asylum Act 2002 but continues to have effect in relation to appeals made before 1st April 2003.

[19] 2002 c. 41.

Appendix 16

(a) a passport or other travel document endorsed before 1st January 2007 to show that the holder has leave to enter or remain in the United Kingdom under the 1971 Act, subject to a condition restricting his employment in the United Kingdom to a particular employer or category of employment;

(b) a seasonal agricultural work card, except where the holder of the card has a document mentioned in sub-paragraph (a) giving him leave to enter the United Kingdom as a seasonal agricultural worker; or

(c) an accession worker card issued in accordance with regulation 11.

(3) But a document shall cease to be treated as an accession worker authorisation document under paragraph (2)—

(a) in the case of a document mentioned in paragraph (2)(a), at the end of the period for which leave to enter or remain is given;

(b) in the case of a seasonal agricultural work card, at the end of the period of six months beginning with the date on which the holder of the card begins working for the agricultural employer specified in the card;

(c) in the case of an accession worker card, on the expiry of the card under regulation 11(7).

(4) For the purpose of this regulation—

(a) "seasonal agricultural work card" means a Home Office work card issued by the operator of a seasonal agricultural workers scheme approved by the Secretary of State for the purpose of paragraph 104(ii) of the immigration rules;

(b) the reference to a travel document other than a passport is a reference to a document which relates to a national of Bulgaria or Romania and which is designed to serve the same purpose as a passport.

Application for an accession worker card

10.—(1) An application for an accession worker card may be made by an accession State national subject to worker authorisation who wishes to work for an employer in the United Kingdom if—

(a) the employment concerned falls within an authorised category of employment; or

(b) the applicant is an authorised family member.

(2) The application shall be in writing and shall be made to the Secretary of State.

(3) The application shall state—

(a) the name, address, and date of birth of the applicant;

(b) the name and address of the employer for whom the applicant wishes to work; and

(c) unless the applicant is an authorised family member, the authorised category of employment covered by the application.

(4) The application shall be accompanied by—

(a) the applicant's national identity card or passport; and

(b)   two passport size photographs of the applicant.

(5) Where the applicant is not an authorised family member, the application shall, in addition to the documents required by paragraph (4), be accompanied by—

(a)   where the relevant requirements for the authorised category of employment specified in the application require the applicant to hold a letter of approval under the work permit arrangements, that letter;

(b)   where sub-paragraph (a) does not apply, a letter from the employer specified in the application confirming that the applicant has an offer of employment with the employer; and

(c)   any other proof that the applicant wishes to provide to establish that he meets the relevant requirements.

(6) Where the applicant is an authorised family member, the application shall, in addition to the documents required by paragraph (4), be accompanied by—

(a)   a letter from the employer specified in the application confirming that the applicant has an offer of employment with the employer; and

(b)   proof that the applicant is an authorised family member.

(7) In this regulation "address" means, in relation to an employer which is a body corporate or partnership, the head or main office of that employer.

Issuing an accession worker card etc

11.—(1) Subject to paragraph (2), the Secretary of State shall issue an accession worker card pursuant to an application made in accordance with regulation 10 if he is satisfied that the applicant is an accession State national subject to worker authorisation who—

(a)   is an authorised family member; or

(b)   meets the relevant requirements for the authorised category of employment covered by the application.

(2) The Secretary of State shall not issue an accession worker card if he has decided to remove the applicant from the United Kingdom under regulation 19(3)(b) of the 2006 Regulations (removal on grounds of public policy, public security or public health).

(3) An accession worker card issued under this regulation to an authorised family member shall include a condition restricting the applicant's employment to the employer specified in the application.

(4) An accession worker card issued under this regulation pursuant to an application that was accompanied by a letter of approval under the work permit arrangements shall include the following conditions—

(a)   a condition restricting the applicant's employment to the employer specified in the application and any secondary employer; and

(b)   a condition restricting him to the type of employment specified in the letter of approval under the work permit arrangements.

(5) In any other case, an accession worker card issued under this regulation shall include the following conditions—

(a)   a condition restricting the applicant's employment to the employer specified in the application; and

(b)   a condition restricting him to the authorised category of employment specified in the application.

(6) An accession worker card issued under this regulation shall include a photograph of the applicant and shall set out—

(a)   the name, nationality and date of birth of the applicant;

(b)   the name and address of the employer specified in the application;

(c)   the conditions required by paragraph (3), (4) or (5), as the case may be; and

(d)   the date on which the card was issued.

(7) An accession worker card shall expire if the holder of the card ceases working for the employer specified in the application.

(8) Where the Secretary of State is not satisfied as mentioned in paragraph (1) or where paragraph (2) applies, he shall refuse the application and issue a notice of refusal setting out the reasons for the refusal.

(9) An accession worker card or notice of refusal issued under this regulation shall be sent to the applicant by post together with the identity card or passport that accompanied the application.

(10) In this regulation, "secondary employer" means, in relation to an applicant, an employer who is not specified in his application and who employs the applicant for no more than 20 hours a week when the applicant is not working for the employer who is specified in the application.

Unauthorised employment of accession State national—employer offence

12.—(1) Subject to paragraphs (2) and (3), an employer who employs an accession State national subject to worker authorisation during the accession period shall be guilty of an offence if—

(a)   the employee does not hold an accession worker authorisation document; or 9

(b)   the employee's accession worker authorisation document is subject to conditions that preclude him from taking up the employment.

(2) Subject to paragraph (4), in proceedings under this regulation it shall be a defence to prove that before the employment began there was produced to the employer a document that appeared to him to be a registration certificate issued to the worker and—

(a)   the registration certificate contained a statement that the worker has unconditional access to the United Kingdom labour market; or

(b)   the registration certificate contained a statement that the worker is a student who has access to the United Kingdom labour market for 20 hours a week and the employer has not employed that worker for more than 20 hours a week.

(3) Subject to paragraph (4), in proceedings under this regulation it shall be a defence to prove that before the employment began there was produced to the employer a document that appeared to him to be an accession worker authorisation document that authorised the worker to take up the employment.

(4) The defence afforded by paragraph (2) and (3) shall not be available in any case where the employer—

(a) did not take and retain a copy of the relevant document; or
(b) knew that his employment of the worker constituted an offence under this regulation.

(5) A person guilty of an offence under this regulation shall be liable on summary conviction to a fine not exceeding level 5 on the standard scale.

(6) Where an offence under this regulation committed by a body corporate is proved to have been committed with the consent or connivance of, or to be attributable to any neglect on the part of—

(a) any director, manager, secretary or other similar officer of the body corporate; or
(b) any person purporting to act in such a capacity,

he, as well as the body corporate, shall be guilty of an offence and shall be liable to be proceeded against and punished accordingly.

(7) Where the affairs of a body corporate are managed by its members, paragraph (6) shall apply in relation to acts and defaults of a member in connection with his functions of management as if he were a director of the body corporate.

(8) Where an offence under this regulation is committed by a partnership (other than a limited partnership) each partner shall be guilty of an offence and shall be liable to be proceeded against and punished accordingly.

(9) Paragraph (6) shall have effect in relation to a limited partnership as if—

(a) a reference to a body corporate were a reference to a limited partnership; and
(b) a reference to an officer of the body corporate were a reference to a partner.

(10) An offence under this regulation shall be treated as—

(a) a relevant offence for the purpose of sections 28B and 28D of the 1971 Act[20] (search, entry and arrest);
(b) an offence under Part III of that Act (criminal proceedings) for the purposes of sections 28E, 28G and 28H[21] of that Act (search after arrest); and
(c) an offence referred to in section 28AA[22] of that Act (arrest with warrant).

---

[20] Section 28B was inserted by section 129 of the Immigration and Asylum Act 1999 (c.33) and section 28D was inserted by section 131 of that Act; both sections have been amended by sections 144 and 150 of the Nationality, Immigration and Asylum Act 2002 (c.41).
[21] Sections 28E, 28G and 28 H were inserted by sections 132, 134 and 135 of the Immigration and Asylum Act 1999(c.33) respectively.
[22] Section 28AA was inserted by section 152 of the Nationality, Immigration and Asylum Act 2002 (c. 41).

Appendix 16

Unauthorised working by accession State national – employee offence

13.—(1) Subject to paragraph (2), an accession State national subject to worker authorisation who works in the United Kingdom during the accession period shall be guilty of an offence if—

(a) he does not hold an accession worker authorisation document; or

(b) he is working in breach of the conditions set out in his accession worker authorisation document.

(2) A person guilty of an offence under this regulation shall be liable on summary conviction to a fine not exceeding level 5 on the standard scale or imprisonment for not more than three months, or both.

(3) A constable or immigration officer who has reason to believe that a person has committed an offence under this regulation may give that person a notice offering him the opportunity of discharging any liability to conviction for that offence by payment of a penalty in accordance with the notice.

(4) The penalty payable in pursuance of a notice under paragraph (3) is £1000 and shall be payable to the Secretary of State.

(5) Where a person is given a notice under paragraph (3) in respect of an offence—

(a) no proceedings may be instituted for that offence before the expiration of the period of twenty one days following the date of the notice; and

(b) he may not be convicted of that offence if before the expiration of that period he pays the penalty in accordance with the notice.

(6) A notice under paragraph (3) must give such particulars of the circumstances alleged to constitute the offence as are necessary for giving reasonable information of the offence.

(7) A notice under paragraph (3) must also state—

(a) the period during which, by virtue of paragraph (5), proceedings will not be instituted for the offence;

(b) the amount of the penalty; and

(c) that the penalty is payable to the Secretary of State at the address specified in the notice.

(8) Without prejudice to payment by any other method, payment of a penalty in pursuance of a notice under paragraph (3) may be made by pre-paying and posting a letter containing the amount of the penalty (in cash or otherwise) to the Secretary of State at the address specified in the notice.

(9) Where a letter is sent in accordance with paragraph (8) payment is to be regarded as having been made at the time at which that letter would be delivered in the ordinary course of post.

Deception—employee offence

14.—(1) A person is guilty of an offence if, by means which include deception by him, he obtains or seeks to obtain an accession worker card.

The Accession (Immigration and Worker Authorisation) Regs 2006

(2) A person guilty of an offence under this regulation shall be liable on summary conviction to a fine not exceeding level 5 on the standard scale or imprisonment for not more than three months, or both.

Offences under regulations 13 and 14—search, entry and arrest

15. An offence under regulation 13 or 14 shall be treated as—

(a) a relevant offence for the purpose of sections 28B and 28D of the 1971 Act (search, entry and arrest);

(b) an offence under Part III of that Act (criminal proceedings) for the purpose of sections 28E, 28G and 28H of that Act (search after arrest); and

(c) an offence under section 24(1)(b) of that Act for the purpose of sections 28A, 28CA and 28FA[23] of that Act (arrest without warrant, entry of business premises to arrest and search for personal records).

SCHEDULE 1   Regulation 1(2)

Authorised Categories of Employment and Relevant Requirements

Authorised category of employment	Relevant requirements in relation to authorised category of employment
Authorised categories of employment requiring a letter of approval under the work permit arrangements	
Employment under the Sectors Based Scheme	The applicant— (1) holds a letter of approval under the work permit arrangements issued under the Sectors-Based Scheme; and (2) is capable of undertaking the employment specified in that letter.
Training or work experience	The applicant— (1) holds a letter of approval under the work permit arrangements issued under the Training and Work Experience Scheme; and (2) is capable of undertaking the training or work experience as specified in that letter.
Work permit employment	The applicant— (1) holds a letter of approval under the work permit arrangements issued in relation to work permit employment; and

---

[23] Section 28A was inserted by section 128 of the Immigration and Asylum Act 1999 (c.33) and amended by sections 144 and 150 of the Nationality, Immigration and Asylum Act 2002 (c.41); sections 28CA and 28FA were inserted by sections153 and 154 of the Nationality, Immigration and Asylum Act 2002 respectively.

APPENDIX 16

Authorised category of employment	Relevant requirements in relation to authorised category of employment
	(2) is capable of undertaking the employment specified in that letter.
Other authorised categories of employment	
Airport based operational ground staff of an overseas air line	The applicant has been transferred to the United Kingdom by an overseas-owned airline operating services to and from the United Kingdom to take up duty at an international airport as station manager, security manager or technical manager.
Au pair placement	The applicant— (1) has and intends to take up an offer of an au pair placement; (2) is aged between 17 to 27 inclusive; (3) is unmarried and is not in a civil partnership; and (4) is without dependants.
Domestic worker in a private household	The applicant— (1) is over 18; (2) has been employed for at least a year outside the United Kingdom as a domestic worker under the same roof as his employer or in a household that the employer uses for himself on a regular basis; and (3) intends to be so employed by that employer in the United Kingdom.
Minister of religion, missionary or member of a religious order	The applicant— (1) if a minister of religion— (a) has either been working for at least one year as a minister of religion in any of the five years immediately prior to the date on which the application for the worker accession card is made or, where ordination is prescribed by a religious faith as the sole means of entering the ministry, has been ordained as a minister of religion following at least one year's full time or two years' part time training for the ministry; and (b) holds an International English Language Testing System Certificate issued to him to certify that he has achieved level 4 competence in spoken English, and the Certificate is dated not more than two

Authorised category of employment	Relevant requirements in relation to authorised category of employment
	years prior to the date on which the application for an accession worker card is made; (2) if a missionary, has been trained as a missionary or has worked as a missionary and is being sent or has been sent to the United Kingdom by an overseas organisation; (3) if a member of a religious order, is living or coming to live in a community maintained by the religious order of which he is a member and, if intending to teach, does not intend to do so save at an establishment maintained by his order; and (4) intends to work in the United Kingdom as a minister of religion, missionary or for the religious order of which he is a member.
Overseas government employment	The applicant intends to work in the United Kingdom for an overseas government or the United Nations or other international organisation of which the United Kingdom is a member.
Postgraduate doctors, dentists and trainee general practitioners	The applicant— (1) is a graduate from a medical or dental school who is eligible for provisional or limited registration with the General Medical Council or General Dental Council and intends to work in the United Kingdom as a doctor or dentist as part of his training; or (2) is a doctor, dentist or trainee general practitioner eligible for full or limited registration with the General Medical Council or the General Dental Council and intends to work in the United Kingdom as part of his postgraduate training or general practitioner training in a hospital or the Community Health Services.

Appendix 16

Authorised category of employment	Relevant requirements in relation to authorised category of employment
Private servant in a diplomatic household	The applicant— (1) is over 18; and (2) intends to work in the United Kingdom as a private servant in the household of a member of staff of a diplomatic or consular mission who enjoys diplomatic privileges and immunity within the meaning of the Vienna Convention on Diplomatic Relations[24].
Representative of an overseas newspaper, news agency or broadcasting organisation	The applicant has been engaged by an overseas newspaper, news agency or broadcasting organisation outside the United Kingdom and is being posted to the United Kingdom by that newspaper, agency or organisation to act as its representative.
Sole representative	The applicant— (1) has been employed outside the United Kingdom as a representative of a firm that has its headquarters and principal place of business outside the United Kingdom and has no branch, subsidiary or other representative in the United Kingdom; (2) intends to work as a senior employee with full authority to take operational decisions on behalf of the overseas firm for the purpose of representing it in the United Kingdom by establishing and operating a registered branch or wholly owned subsidiary of that overseas firm; and (3) is not a majority shareholder in that overseas firm.
Teacher or language assistant	The applicant intends to work at an educational establishment in the United Kingdom under an exchange scheme approved by the Department for Education and Skills, the Scottish or Welsh Office of Education or the Department of Education, Northern Ireland, or administered by the British Council's Education and Training Group.

---

[24] Cmnd. 2565.

Authorised category of employment	Relevant requirements in relation to authorised category of employment
Overseas qualified nurses	The applicant— (1) has obtained confirmation from the Nursing and Midwifery Council that he is eligible for admission to the Overseas Nurses Programme; and (2) has been offered and intends to take up a supervised practice placement through an education provider that is recognised by the Nursing and Midwifery Council or a midwifery adaptation programme placement in a setting approved by that Council.

1. In this Schedule—

(a) "au pair placement" means an arrangement whereby a young person—

   (i) comes to the United Kingdom for the purpose of learning English;
   (ii) lives for a time as a member of an English speaking family with appropriate opportunities for study; and
   (iii) helps in the home for a maximum of 5 hours per day in return for an allowance and with two free days per week;

(b) "letter of approval under the work permit arrangements" means a letter issued by the Secretary of State under the work permit arrangements stating that employment by the employer specified in the letter of the person so specified for the type of employment so specified satisfies the labour market criteria set out in those arrangements;

(c) "member of a religious order" means a person who lives in a community run by that order;

(d) "minister of religion" means a religious functionary whose main regular duties comprise the leading of a congregation in performing the rites and rituals of the faith and in preaching the essentials of the creed;

(e) "missionary" means a person who is directly engaged in spreading a religious doctrine and whose work is not in essence administrative or clerical;

(f) "Sectors Based Scheme" means the scheme established by the Secretary of State for the purpose of paragraph 135I(i)[25] of the immigration rules (requirements for leave to enter the United Kingdom for the purpose of employment under the Sectors Based Scheme);

(g) "Training and Work Experience Scheme" means the scheme established by the Secretary of State for the purpose of paragraph 116(i) of the immigration rules (requirement for leave to enter the United Kingdom for approved training or work experience);

(h) "work permit arrangements" means the arrangements published by the Secretary of State[26] setting out the labour market criteria to be applied for the

---

[25] Paragraph 135I was inserted by immigration rules changes on 30th May 2003 (Cm 5829).
[26] These arrangements are published by Work Permits UK, part of the Home Office, and are available on the Home Office website (www.workingintheuk.gov.uk).

purpose of issuing the work permits referred to in paragraphs 116(i) (Training and Work Experience Scheme) and 128(i) of the immigration rules and the immigration employment document referred to in paragraph 135I(i) (Sectors Based Scheme) of the immigration rules;

(i) "work permit employment" means a category of employment covered by the work permit arrangements, other than employment covered by the Sectors Based Scheme and the Training and Work Experience Scheme.

SCHEDULE 2   Regulation 1(3)

CONSEQUENTIAL AMENDMENTS

The Accession (Immigration and Worker Registration) Regulations 2004

1.—(1) The Accession (Immigration and Worker Registration) Regulations 2004[27] are amended as follows.

(2) In regulation 2 ("accession State worker requiring registration")—

(a) for paragraph (5)(b) there is substituted—

"(b) another EEA State, other than a relevant accession State or Bulgaria or Romania;";

(b) for paragraph (6)(b) there is substituted—

"(b) a family member of a Swiss or EEA national who has a right to reside in the United Kingdom under the 2006 Regulations, other than the family member of—

(i) a national of a relevant accession State who only has a right to reside under regulation 13 of those Regulations and would be an accession State worker requiring registration if he began working in the United Kingdom;
(ii) an accession State worker requiring registration who only has a right to reside under regulation 14 of those Regulations by virtue of being treated as a worker for the purpose of the definition of "qualified person" in regulation 6(1) of those Regulations; or
(iii) an accession State national subject to worker authorisation or a student who is not an accession State national subject to worker authorisation solely by virtue of falling within regulation 2(10) of the 2006 Accession Regulations;";

(c) in paragraph (9), before paragraph (b) there is inserted—

"(aa) "2006 Accession Regulations" means the Accession (Immigration and Worker Authorisation) Regulations 2006 and "accession State national subject to worker authorisation" has the meaning given in regulation 2 of those Regulations;".

---

[27] S.I. 2004/1219; the relevant amending instruments are S.I. 2004/1236 and S.I. 2006/1003.

The Accession (Immigration and Worker Authorisation) Regs 2006

The 2006 Regulations

2.—(1) The 2006 Regulations are amended as follows.

(2) In Schedule 2 (effect on other legislation)—

(a) in paragraph 1 (leave under the 1971 Act)—

  (i) at the beginning of sub-paragraph (2) there is inserted "Subject to sub-paragraph (3),";
  (ii) after sub-paragraph (2) there is inserted—

  "(3) Where the person mentioned in sub-paragraph (2) is an accession State national subject to worker authorisation working in the United Kingdom during the accession period and the document endorsed to show that the person has leave is an accession worker authorisation document, any conditions to which that leave is subject restricting his employment shall continue to apply.

  (4) In sub-paragraph (3)—

  (a) "accession period" has the meaning given in regulation 1(2)(c) of the Accession (Immigration and Worker Authorisation) Regulations 2006;
  (b) "accession State national subject to worker authorisation" has the meaning given in regulation 2 of those Regulations; and
  (c) "accession worker authorisation document" has the meaning given in regulation 9(2) of those Regulations.";

(b) in paragraph 4 (appeals under the Nationality, Immigration and Asylum Act 2002 and previous immigration Acts)—

  (i) in sub-paragraph (2), after "Accession (Immigration and Worker Registration) Regulations 2004," there is inserted "or an accession worker card under the Accession (Immigration and Worker Authorisation) Regulations 2006,";

(c) in sub-paragraph (9), after "accession State worker requiring registration" where it first occurs there is inserted "or an accession State national subject to worker authorisation working in the United Kingdom" and at the end of the sub-paragraph there is inserted "and "accession State national subject to worker authorisation" has the meaning given in 16 regulation 2 of the Accession (Immigration and Worker Authorisation) Regulations 2006".

(3) Paragraph 7(3)(a) of Schedule 5 (consequential amendments) is omitted.

Appendix 17

THE ACCESSION (IMMIGRATION AND WORKER REGISTRATION) (REVOCATION, SAVINGS AND CONSEQUENTIAL PROVISIONS) REGULATIONS 2011

SI 2011 No. 544

Made 24th February 2011
Laid before Parliament 10th March 2011
Coming into force 1st May 2011

The Secretary of State, being a Minister designated[1] for the purposes of section 2(2) of the European Communities Act 1972[2] in relation to measures relating to the rights of entry into, and residence in, the United Kingdom and access to the labour market of the United Kingdom, in exercise of the powers conferred by that section, makes the following Regulations:

Citation, commencement and interpretation

1.—(1) These Regulations may be cited as the Accession (Immigration and Worker Registration) (Revocation, Savings and Consequential Provisions) Regulations 2011 and shall come into force on 1st May 2011.

(2) In these Regulations—

"the 2004 Regulations" means the Accession (Immigration and Worker Registration) Regulations 2004[3];
"the 2006 Regulations" means the Immigration (European Economic Area) Regulations 2006[4].

Revocation of the 2004 Regulations

2. Subject to regulation 3, the 2004 Regulations are revoked.

Saving provisions

3.—(1) The 2004 Regulations shall continue to have effect as follows.

(2) Subject to paragraph 3, regulation 8 of the 2004 Regulations shall continue to have effect until 30th April 2012.

(3) For regulation 8(5)(a) of those Regulations, substitute "(a) was an accession State worker requiring registration at the date on which the applicant began working for that employer; and".

---

[1] S.I. 2000/813 in relation to measures relating to the rights of entry into, and residence in, the United Kingdom and S.I. 2004/706 in relation to measures relating to access to the labour market in the United Kingdom.
[2] 1972 c.68.
[3] S.I. 2004/1219 as amended by S.I. 2006/1003, S.I. 2006/3317, S.I. 2007/475, S.I. 2007/928, S.I. 2007/3012, S.I. 2009/892 and S.I. 2009/2426.
[4] S.I. 2006/1003 as amended by S.I. 2009/1117.

Appendix 17

(4) The 2004 Regulations shall continue to have effect to the extent necessary for the purposes of regulation 7A of the 2006 Regulations as inserted into the 2006 Regulations by regulation 5 of, and Schedule 2 to, these Regulations.

Revocation of other instruments

4. The Regulations listed in column 1 of the table in Schedule 1 are revoked to the extent set out in column 3 of that table.

Consequential amendments to the 2006 Regulations

5. The 2006 Regulations are amended as set out in Schedule 2.

SCHEDULE 1   Regulation 4

REVOCATIONS

Table of Revocations

(1) Regulations revoked	(2) References	(3) Extent of revocation
The Immigration (European Economic Area) Regulations 2006	S.I. 2006/1003	Paragraph 7 of Schedule 5
The Accession (Immigration and Worker Authorisation) Regulations 2006	S.I. 2006/3317	Paragraph 1 of Schedule 2
The Accession (Immigration and Worker Authorisation) (Amendment) Regulations 2007	S.I. 2007/475	Regulation 3
The Accession (Immigration and Worker Registration) (Amendment) Regulations 2007	S.I. 2007/928	The whole Regulations.
The Accession (Worker Authorisation and Worker Registration) (Amendment) Regulations 2007	S.I. 2007/3012	Regulation 3
The Accession (Immigration and Worker Registration) (Amendment) Regulations 2009	S.I. 2009/892	The whole Regulations.
The Accession (Worker Authorisation and Worker Registration) (Amendment) Regulations 2009	S.I. 2009/2426	Regulation 3

SCHEDULE 2

Regulation 5

AMENDMENTS TO THE 2006 REGULATIONS

1. In regulation 2(1), after ""the 2002 Act" means the Nationality, Immigration and Asylum Act 2002;" insert—

""the Accession Regulations" means the Accession (Immigration and Worker Registration) Regulations 2004;".

2. In regulation 5(7), for "For the purposes of this regulation—", substitute "Subject to regulation 7A(3), for the purposes of this regulation—".

3. In regulation 6(2), for "A person who is no longer working shall not cease to be treated as a worker for the purpose of paragraph (1)(b) if—", substitute "Subject to regulation 7A(4), a person who is no longer working shall not cease to be treated as a worker for the purpose of paragraph (1)(b) if—".

4. After regulation 7, insert—

"**Application of the Accession Regulations**

7A.—(1) This regulation applies to an EEA national who was an accession State worker requiring registration on 30th April 2011 ('an accession worker').

(2) In this regulation— "accession State worker requiring registration" has the same meaning as in regulation 1(2)(d) of the Accession Regulations; "legally working" has the same meaning as in regulation 2(7) of the Accession Regulations.

(3) In regulation 5(7)(c), where the worker is an accession worker, periods of involuntary unemployment duly recorded by the relevant employment office shall be treated only as periods of activity as a worker—

(a) during any period in which regulation 5(4) of the Accession Regulations applied to that person; or
(b) when the unemployment began on or after 1st May 2011.

(4) Regulation 6(2) applies to an accession worker where he—

(a) was a person to whom regulation 5(4) of the Accession Regulations applied on 30th April 2011; or
(b) became unable to work, became unemployed or ceased to work, as the case maybe, on or after 1st May 2011.

(5) For the purposes of regulation 15, an accession worker shall be treated as having resided in accordance with these Regulations during any period before 1st May 2011 in which the accession worker—

(a) was legally working in the United Kingdom; or
(b) was a person to whom regulation 5(4) of the Accession Regulations applied.

(6) Subject to paragraph (7), a registration certificate issued to an accession worker under regulation 8 of the Accession Regulations shall, from 1st May 2011, be treated as if it was a registration certificate issued under these Regulations where

the accession worker was egally working in the United Kingdom for the employer specified in that certificate on—

(a) 30th April 2011; or
(b) the date on which the certificate is issued where it is issued after 30th April 2011.

(7) Paragraph (6) does not apply—

(a) if the Secretary of State issues a registration certificate in accordance with regulation 16 to an accession worker on or after 1st May 2011; and
(b) from the date of registration stated on that certificate.

5. For regulation 16(8), substitute "But this regulation is subject to regulations 7A(6) and 20(1)."

Appendix 18

THE IMMIGRATION (SWISS FREE MOVEMENT OF PERSONS) (NO. 3) REGULATIONS 2002*

SI 2002 No. 1241

Made 1st May 2002
Laid 9th May 2002
Coming into force 1st June 2002

The Secretary of State, being a Minister designated for the purposes of section 2(2) of the European Communities Act 1972[1] in relation to measures relating to rights of entry into, and residence in, the United Kingdom[2], in exercise of the powers conferred on him by that section, hereby makes the following Regulations:

Citation, commencement and interpretation

1.—(1) These Regulations may be cited as the Immigration (Swiss Free Movement of Persons) (No. 3) Regulations 2002 and shall come into force on 1st June 2002.

(2) The "2000 Regulations" means the Immigration (European Economic Area) Regulations 2000[3].

Application of 2000 Regulations to Swiss nationals, their family members and posted workers

2.—(1) The 2000 Regulations shall apply in relation to a Swiss national, and to any person related to that national, as if the Swiss national were an EEA national and Switzerland an EEA state.

(2) The 2000 Regulations shall also apply to a posted worker.

(3) In the application of the 2000 Regulations to a Swiss national or to any person related to a Swiss national or to a posted worker those Regulations shall have effect subject to the modifications set out in the Schedule to these Regulations.

(4) In this regulation—

(a) "EEA national" and "EEA state" have the same meaning as in regulation 2(1) of the 2000 Regulations;

(b) "posted worker" has the same meaning as in regulation 3(1) of the 2000 Regulations, as modified by the Schedule to these Regulations;

(c) a person is related to a Swiss national if that person—

---

* Schedule 3 Pt 2 to the Immigration (European Economic Area) Regulations 2006 revoked these Regulations and the Immigration (European Economic Area) Regulations 2000 except in so far as they apply to posted workers.
[1] 1972 c. 68.
[2] S.I. 2000/1813.
[3] S.I. 2000/2326; amended by S.I. 2001/865.

APPENDIX 18

(i) is a family member of that Swiss national (as determined in accordance with regulation 6 of the 2000 Regulations); or
(ii) would satisfy any of the conditions in regulation 10(4) of the 2000 Regulations in relation to the Swiss national if the Swiss national were an EEA national.

SCHEDULE   Regulation 2(3)

MODIFICATION OF 2000 REGULATIONS IN THEIR APPLICATION TO SWISS NATIONALS

1. In regulation 2(1),

(a) after the definition of "the 1999 Act" insert—

""control zone" and "supplementary control zone" have the same meaning as in the Channel Tunnel (International Arrangements) Order 1993[4] ";

(b) after the definition of "military service" insert—

""posted worker authorisation" means a document issued to a person, in accordance with regulation 13A, in connection with his admission to the United Kingdom;";

(c) after the definition of "Regulation 1251/70" insert—

""required documents" means the documents referred to in regulation 12(3);".

2. In regulation 3 of the 2000 Regulations—

(a) after paragraph (1)(b) insert—

"(ba) "posted worker" means a person who is not an EEA national and—

(i) is the employee of a Swiss national or Swiss company that provides or seeks to provide services in the United Kingdom;
(ii) is posted to the United Kingdom for the purpose of providing those services on behalf of his employer; and
(iii) prior to the posting, is integrated into the regular labour market of an EEA State,

and, for the purpose of this definition, "services" has the same meaning as in Article 50 of the EC Treaty, and "Swiss company" means a company that is formed in accordance with the law of Switzerland and has its registered office, central administration or principal place of business in Switzerland;";

(b) delete paragraph (1)(f);

(c) for paragraph (2) substitute—

"(2) For the purposes of paragraph (1)(e)—

(a) resources are to be regarded as sufficient if they exceed the level in respect of which the recipient would qualify for social assistance;

---

[4] S.I. 1993/1813; amendments relevant to these Regulations are made by S.I. 2001/1544 and 2001/3707.

(b) where the person concerned has been employed in the United Kingdom for less than one year, any unemployment benefit to which he is entitled by virtue of having paid national insurance contributions shall be treated as the resources of that person.".

3. At the end of regulation 7 insert "and, in the case of a posted worker, a valid posted worker authorisation".

4. At the end of regulation 9 insert "and posted workers".

5. In regulation 10, delete paragraph (5).

6. In regulation 12, after paragraph (2) insert—

"(3) Subject to regulation 21(1) and (2A), a posted worker must be admitted to the United Kingdom if he produces, on arrival—

(a) a valid passport; and
(b) a valid posted worker authorisation.

(4) Any passport, identity card, family permit, residence document, posted worker authorisation or document proving family membership which is required to be produced under this regulation as a condition for admission to the United Kingdom may, for the same purpose, be required to be produced in a control zone or a supplementary control zone.".

7. After regulation 13 insert—

"13A Issue of posted worker authorisation

(1) A person may apply to an entry clearance officer for a posted worker authorisation authorising him to enter and reside in the United Kingdom in a calendar year if—

(a) he is to be posted to the United Kingdom by his employer during that calendar year;
(b) he will be a posted worker on arrival in the United Kingdom; and
(c) he has not already been authorised to enter and reside in the United Kingdom under this regulation for 90 days or more in that calendar year.

(2) A posted worker authorisation issued under paragraph (1) shall specify the period during which the posted worker is authorised to enter and reside in the United Kingdom.

(3) A person who applies under paragraph (1) shall be entitled to be issued in relation to any calendar year with a single posted worker authorisation which individually, or with a number of authorisations which collectively, authorise him to enter and reside in the United Kingdom for at least 90 days in that calendar year.

(4) Paragraph (3) shall not apply if the applicant falls to be excluded from the United Kingdom on grounds of public policy, public security or public health.".

8. In regulation 14, after paragraph (3) insert—

"(4) A posted worker is entitled to reside in the United Kingdom without the requirement for leave to remain under the 1971 Act for as long as he has a valid

APPENDIX 18

posted worker authorisation and the period of authorised entry and residence specified in that authorisation has not expired.".

9. In regulation 15, after paragraph (2) insert—

"(2A) Subject to regulation 16A and 22 (1), the Secretary of State must issue a residence document to a posted worker on application and production of—

(a) a valid passport; and
(b) a valid posted worker authorisation".

10. In regulation 16—

(a) in paragraph (1)—

   (i) in sub-paragraph (b), after "worker who is employed" insert ", or self-employed person who is established,";
   (ii) delete sub-paragraph (c);

(b) delete paragraph (2).

11. After regulation 16 insert—

"Where no requirement to issue residence document

16A. The Secretary of State is not required to issue a residence document to a posted worker if the period of authorised entry and residence specified in his posted worker authorisation is 90 days or less.".

12. Delete regulation 17.

13. In regulation 18—

(a) delete paragraph (3);
(b) in paragraph (6) delete "a retired person or".

14. After regulation 20 insert—

"Duration of residence document granted to a posted worker

20A. In the case of a posted worker the validity of the resident document may be limited to the period of authorised entry and residence specified in his posted worker authorisation.".

15. In regulation 21—

(a) in paragraph (2), after "arrival" insert "or the time of his production of the required documents in a control zone or supplementary control zone";
(b) after paragraph (2) insert—

"(2A) A person is not entitled to be admitted to the United Kingdom by virtue of regulation 12(3) if, at the time of his arrival, he is not a posted worker.";

(c) in paragraph (3)(b), after "such a person" insert "or a posted worker";
(d) after paragraph (3) insert—

"(4) A person who was admitted to the United Kingdom as a posted worker may be removed from the United Kingdom if—

(a) he ceases to be a posted worker or the period of authorised entry and residence specified in his posted worker authorisation has expired; and
(b) he is not a qualified person or the family member of a qualified person.".

16. In regulation 22—

(a) in paragraph (2), after paragraph (b) insert—

"or

(c) the person to whom the residence document was issued was admitted to the United Kingdom as a posted worker and—

(i) he has ceased to be a posted worker; and
(ii) he is not a qualified person or the family member of a qualified person.";

(b) in paragraph (3), after "EEA national" insert ", or the time of his production of the required documents in a control zone or supplementary control zone," and at the end of that paragraph insert "or a posted worker";

(c) in paragraph (4), after "United Kingdom" insert ", or the time of his production of the required documents in a control zone or supplementary control zone,";

(d) after paragraph (4) insert—

"(5) An immigration officer may, at the time of a person's arrival in the United Kingdom, or the time of his production of the required documents in a control zone or supplementary control zone, revoke that person's posted worker authorisation if—

(a) the revocation is justified on the grounds of public policy, public security or public health; or
(b) the person is not at that time a posted worker.".

17. In regulation 24(1), after paragraph (a) insert—

"(aa) a posted worker; or".

18. In regulation 25—

(a) in paragraph (1)—

(i) in sub-paragraph (a), after "EEA family permit" insert "or posted worker authorisation";
(ii) in sub-paragraph (b), for "or (2)" insert ", (2) or (2A)";

(b) in paragraph (3)—

(i) in sub-paragraph (b), after "EEA family permit" insert ", posted worker authorisation";
(ii) in sub-paragraph (c), after "EEA family permit" insert ", posted worker authorisation".

19. In regulation 26—

(a) in paragraph (1), at the end insert "or (4)";
(b) in paragraph (2), after "regulation 21(3)" insert "or regulation 21(4)".

20. In regulation 30(3)(c), after "EEA family permit" insert "or posted worker authorisation".

21. For regulation 35 and 36 substitute—

"**Transitional provisions**

35.—(1) Where before 1st June 2002 a qualified person or the family member of a qualified person has been given limited leave to enter or remain in the United Kingdom under section 3 of the 1971 Act[5] subject to conditions, those conditions shall cease to have effect on and after that date.

(2) Where before 1st June 2002 directions have been given for the removal of a qualified person or the family member of a qualified person under paragraphs 8 to 10 of Schedule 2 to the 1971 Act[6] or section 10 of the 1999 Act, those directions shall cease to have effect on and after that date.

(3) Where before 1st June 2002 the Secretary of State has made a decision to make a deportation order against a qualified person or the family member of a qualified person under section 5(1) of the 1971 Act—

(a) that decision shall, on and after 1st June 2002, be treated as if it were a decision under regulation 21(3)(b); and
(b) any appeal against that decision, or against the refusal by the Secretary of State to revoke the deportation order, made under section 63 of the 1999 Act before 1st June 2002 shall, on and after that date, be treated as if it had been made under regulation 29.

(4) Any reference in this regulation to a qualified person or to the family member of a qualified person is a reference to a person who becomes a qualified person or the family member of a qualified person, as the case may be, on or after 1st June 2002 by virtue of these Regulations.".

22. The modifications of the 2000 Regulations set out in paragraph 5 of Schedule 4 to the Channel Tunnel (International Arrangements) Order 1993[7] shall not apply.

---

[5] Section 3 had been amended by the British Nationality Act 1981 (c. 61), the Immigration Act 1998 (c. 14), the Asylum and Immigration Act 1996 (c. 49) and the 1999 Act.
[6] Paragraphs 8 to 10 have been amended by the Immigration Act 1988 (c. 14) and the Asylum and Immigration Act 1996 (c. 49).
[7] S.I. 1993/1813; paragraph 5 of Schedule 4 was inserted by S.I. 2001/3707.

INDEX

LEGAL TAXONOMY
FROM SWEET & MAXWELL

This index has been prepared using Sweet and Maxwell's Legal Taxonomy. Main index entries conform to keywords provided by the Legal Taxonomy except where references to specific documents or non-standard terms (denoted by quotation marks) have been included. These keywords provide a means of identifying similar concepts in other Sweet & Maxwell publications and online services to which keywords from the Legal Taxonomy have been applied. Readers may find some minor differences between terms used in the text and those which appear in the index.

Abuse of rights
see **Fraud**
Access to social security
see **Benefits (entitlement)**
Accession
see also **Enlargement**
association agreements, 14–28, 14–30—14–33, 14–35, 15–01, 15–10—15–14
Croatia, 14–35
stabilisation and association agreements, 14–30—14–33, 14–35
Treaty of Accession 2003
freedom of movement, 5–36
scale of development, 5–34
transitional arrangements, 5–36
Treaty of Accession 2005
freedom of movement, 5–37
transitional arrangements, 5–37
Turkey, 14–28, 17–03, 17–10
Actions for annulment
Court of Justice of the European Union, 2–15, 2–18
Adopted children
dependency, 9–61—9–63
Agents
freedom of establishment, 7–01, 7–03, 7–21, 7–25
ACP States
economic partnership agreements
Cotonou Agreement, 14–69
economic and social development, 14–66
EU relationship, 14–66, 14–68, 14–69
freedom of movement, 14–70—14–72
Lomé Conventions, 14–67—14–69
non-discrimination provisions, 14–71, 14–72
Yaoundé Conventions, 14–67
Agreements with third countries
see **Association agreements; Economic partnership agreements; Partnership and co–operation agreements; Political dialogue and co–operation agreements;**
Stabilisation and association agreements
Agreements with Western Balkan States
see **Stabilisation and association agreements**
Albania
accession 15–10
stabilisation and association agreement
economic and political rights, 2–09, 15–10
equal treatment, 16–19
families, 16–29—16–31
freedom of establishment, 14–39—14–44
freedom of movement, 14–36—14–44, 16–20, 16–32
freedom to provide services, 16–39
non-discrimination provisions, 14–60, 16–05, 16–08, 16–09, 16–12, 16–17, 16–18, 25–32
regional co-operation, 2–09, 14–07, 14–34, 15–01
rights of entry and residence, 16–01, 16–04, 16–05, 16–18, 16–21
social security systems, 14–44
supply of services, 16–39
workers, 16–04, 16–23
Algeria
association agreement
political and economic co–operation, 2–09
regional co-operation, 14–57
Euro–Mediterranean agreement
free movement of workers, 14–59
non-discrimination provisions, 14–64
regional co-operation, 14–57, 14–58
Ankara Agreement
accession, 14–28, 17–03, 17–10
Additional Protocol
economic policies, 17–08, 18–01
free movement of goods, 17–08
free movement of persons and services, 17–08, 18–01, A9–01
freedom of establishment, 19–05, 19–10, A9–01

[687]

Index

more favourable treatment, A9–01
non-discrimination provision, 17–08, A9–01
residence documents, A9–01
social security, A9–01
young workers, A9–01
children
  access to education, 20–53, 20–54
  lawful residence, 20–41
  meaning of children, 20–37
  offers of employment, 20–39, 20–40, 20–42
  remaining beyond worker, 20–47—20–52
  right to take up employment, 20–39, 20–40, 20–42, 20–45, 20–46
  rights of entry and residence, 20–43, 20–44, 20–46
  vocational training, 20–39—20–43, 20–49, 20–51, 20–55
content, 17–07, A8–01
Council of Association Decisions
  agriculture, A10–01
  development, A10–01
  direct effect, 17–31—17–36
  economic and technical co-operation, A10–01
  families, 20–05—20–07
  freedom of movement, 17–18—17–30, A10–01
  social provisions, A10–01
  workers, 18–04—18–09, A10–01
customs union, 14–27
deportation
  accrued rights, 21–01—21–12
  appeals, 21–10
  criminal conviction, 21–04, 21–06
  denial of rights, 21–05
  deterrence, 21–02, 21–04, 21–06
  drug offences, 21–04
  enhanced protection, 21–09
  families, 21–07
  general preventive grounds, 21–02
  interpretation principle, 21–02, 21–03
  justification, 21–05
  national security, 21–01, 21–09
  personal conduct, 21–05
  public health, 21–01
  public policy, 21–01, 21–04, 21–05
  self-employed workers, 21–13—21–16
  standstill clause, 21–15, 21–16
  workers, 21–01, 21–07, 21–08
economic relations, 14–26, 17–08, 17–10, 17–11, 17–13, 18–02
families
  calculation of residence periods, 20–24—20–27
  children, 20–39—20–52
  Council of Association Decisions, 20–05—20–07
  direct effect, 20–10, 20–11
  family reunification, 20–01—20–04, 20–09
  family unity, 20–11, 20–49, 20–56
  freedom of establishment, 20–56—20–58
  general provision, 16–31
  gradual freedom of movement, 20–09
  legal residence, 20–08
  registered workers, 20–08, 20–10
  retaining right to take up employment, 20–28—20–36
  rights of entry, 20–12—20–16
  rights of residence (after three years), 20–21—20–36
  rights of residence (taking up employment), 20–21—20–23, 20–51
  rights of residence (first three years), 20–17—20–20
freedom of establishment
  abolition of restrictions, 19–08, 19–10, A8–01
  Additional Protocol, 19–05, 19–10
  families, 20–56—20–58
  general provision, 17–15, 17–17, 19–01, 19–03, 19–05, 19–08
  lawful residence, 19–13—19–16
  meaning of establishment, 19–04
  non-discrimination, 19–33, 19–34
  rights of entry and residence, 19–11, 19–12
  standstill clause, 19–17, 19–20
freedom of movement
  general provision, 14–29, 15–01, 17–13, 17–15, 17–16
  workers, 18–01—18–04, A8–01
freedom to provide services
  abolition of restrictions, 19–08, 19–10, A8–01
  Additional Protocol, 17–08
  general provision, 17–15, 17–17, 19–02—19–05, 19–07, 19–08
  non-discrimination provision, 19–33, 19–34
  standstill clause, 19–17
generally, 2–09, 14–57, 17–01—17–06
interpretation, 17–06, 17–12
non-discrimination provisions
  Additional Protocol, 17–08
  application, 19–33, 19–34
  duly registered workers, 18–70
  equal treatment, 18–69
  freedom of establishment, 19–33, 19–34
  freedom to provide services, 19–33, 19–34
  general provisions, 17–14, 18–69, 18–70
  interpretation, 18–73, 18–75
  nationality grounds, 17–14, 18–70—18–74
  self-employed workers, 19–34
  standstill clause, 18–76—18–82
objectives, 17–09—17–11, 17–18
obligations, A8–01
protection of rights, 17–06
right to continued employment
  absence due to imprisonment, 18–62

[688]

INDEX

absence from work, 18–47, 18–48
annual leave, 18–48
compliance with formalities, 18–20, 18–32
conditions, 18–10, 18–11, 18–13, 18–33
contracts of employment, 18–17
duly registered workers, 18–20, 18–32, 18–63
earnings level, 18–17
employment within EU Member State, 18–20, 18–39—18–42
gradual integration, 18–10
hours worked, 18–17
incapacity, 18–54
involuntary unemployment, 18–49—18–53
jobseekers, 18–59
legal employment, 18–20
maternity leave, 18–48
member of labour force, 18–20, 18–34—18–38
recruitment issues, 18–12
retirement, 18–54, 18–56
right of non-discrimination, 18–69—18–75
rights of entry and residence, 18–59, 18–64—18–68
sick leave, 18–48, 18–50, 18–51, 18–54, 18–55
specified time periods, 18–43—18–45
stable and secure situation, 18–20—18–31
voluntary unemployment, 18–57—18–60
wages, 18–17
self-employed workers (United Kingdom)
Ankara Agreement, 25–07
appeals, 25–31, 25–30
business applications, 25–13—25–17
deportation orders, 25–29, 25–30
entry clearance, 25–09, 25–10, 25–15, 25–18, 25–21—25–23, 25–26
fraud, 25–12—25–14
freedom of establishment, 25–08, 25–15
illegal immigrants, 25–09, 25–18, 25–24
immigration, 25–08, 25–09, 25–14
leave to remain, 25–18, 25–26
overstayers, 25–18, 25–28—25–31
port applicants, 25–18, 25–19
standstill clause, 25–09—25–13, 25–18
temporary admission, 25–09—25–11, 25–18, 25–19
standstill clause
application, 19–21, 19–23
effect, 19–18
prohibiting legislative change, 19–06, 19–17—19–19
restrictions on establishment, 19–17, 19–20
scope, 19–24—19–32
trade relations, 17–10, 17–11, 17–13
workers
access to employment, 18–05

concept of worker, 18–14—18–19
Council of Association Decisions, 18–04—18–09
duly registered workers, 18–20, 18–32, 18–63, 18–70
freedom of movement, 18–01—18–04
workers in United Kingdom
access to labour markets, 25–03—25–05
acquired rights, 25–03
au pairs, 25–05
entry clearance, 25–03
families, 25–04
immigration, 25–06
leave to remain, 25–03, 25–04
less favourable treatment, 25–04
standstill clause, 25–05
students, 25–05
Annual leave
right to continued employment, 18–48
Appeals
Ankara Agreement, 25–341, 25–30
Court of Justice of the European Union, 2–22, 23.12, 23–15, 23–17
deportation, 13–52, 13–54, 13–56, 13–57
immigration, 24–11
Armenia
partnership and co-operation agreements
economic co-operation, 2–10
freedom of movement, 14–45
political relationship, 14–45, 25–33
Association Agreements
see also **Economic partnership agreements; Partnership and co–operation agreements**
accession, 15–01, 15–10—15–14
Algeria
non-discrimination, 14–64
political and economic co–operation, 2–09
regional co-operation, 14–57
Ankara Agreement
see also **Ankara Agreement**
content, 17–07
economic relations, 14–26, 17–08, 17–10, 17–11, 17–13, 18–02
interpretation, 17–06, 17–12
objectives, 17–09—17–11, 17–18
protection of rights, 17–06
Bulgaria
association agreements, 15–08, 25–32
immigration, 24–31, 24–33
Chile
EU co–operation, 14–73
freedom of movement, 14–74—14–76
trade relations, 14–73
compatible national laws, 15–08, 15–09
Czech Republic, 16–10
Egypt, 2–09
EU competence
exclusive competence, 15–04
generally, 15–05—15–07
shared competence, 15–02, 15–03

[689]

Index

Euro–Mediterranean agreements
  Algeria, 14–57—14–59, 16–64
  direct effect, 14–61
  freedom of movement, 14–58, 14–59
  generally, 14–09
  inter-State co-operation, 14–58
  Israel, 14–57
  Jordan, 14–57
  Lebanon, 14–57
  non-discrimination provisions, 14–58, 14–60—14–65
  residence documents, 14–61, 14–63
  rights of entry and residence, 14–61
freedom of movement, 14–10
Israel
  association agreements, 2–09
  economic and political, co-operation, 2–09
Jordan
  association agreements, 2–09
  economic and political, co-operation, 2–09
Lebanon
  association agreements, 2–09
  economic and political, co-operation, 2–09
Maghreb countries, 14–09, 14–53
mixed agreements, 15–02—15–09
Morocco, 2–09
Poland, 16–06, 16–07
pre-accession agreements, 14–05
regional agreements, 14–04, 14–05
Romania, 15–08
stabilisation and association agreements
  see also **Stabilisation and association agreements**
  direct discrimination, 16–16
  direct effect, 16–06, 16–08
  equal treatment, 16–07
  freedom of establishment, 14–37, 14–39—14–43, 16–01, 16–11, 16–32
  freedom of movement, 14–08, 14–36, 14–37, 16–01
  freedom to provide services, 16–39—16–41
  indirect discrimination, 16–16
  limitations, 16–02
  meaning of discrimination, 16–13—16–15
  national laws, 16–09, 16–10, 16–12
  temporal effect, 16–27
  workers, 16–18—16–26
process, 14–31, 14–323
reforms, 14–32
regional co-operation, 14–07, 14–30
Switzerland
  acquired rights, A7–01
  air transport, 14–21
  appeals, A7–01
  conformity assessments, 14–21
  development of land, A7–01
  dispute resolution, A7–01
  double taxation, A5–01
  economic activity, A7–01
  economically inactive persons, A7–01
  entry into force, A7–01
  equal treatment, 14–24, A7–01
  families, 14–24, A7–01
  formalities, A7–01
  freedom of movement, 14–21—14–23, A7–01
  freedom to provide services, A7–01
  frontier workers, 14–24, 14–25, A7–01
  immovable property, A7–01
  lawful and habitual employment, 25–02
  more favourable provisions, A7–01
  mutual recognition principle, A7–01
  non-discrimination provisions, 14–24, A7–01
  objective, A7–01
  posted workers, 25–02, A7–01
  public order, A7–01
  public procurement, 14–21
  public service exception, A7–01
  reference to EU law, A7–01
  residence documents, 14–25, A7–01
  revision, A7–01
  rights of entry and residence, A7–01
  road and rail transport, 14–21
  self-employed workers, A7–01
  service providers, A7–01
  social security, A7–01
  special permits, A7–01
  standstill clause, A7–01
  territorial scope, A7–01
  trade in agricultural products, 14–21
  United Kingdom, 25–01, 25–02
  workers, 14–24, A7–01
Treaty on the Functioning of the European Union
  general power, 14–01, 14–02
  qualified majority procedure, 14–03
  reciprocal rights, 14–02
Tunisia
  association agreements, 2–09
  economic and political co-operation, 2–09
Turkey
  see also **Ankara Agreement**
  content, 17–07
  economic relations, 14–26, 17–08, 17–10, 17–11, 17–13, 18–02
  interpretation, 17–06, 17–12
  objectives, 17–09—17–11, 17–18
  obligations, A8–01
  protection of rights, 17–06
  workers
    key personnel, 16–32—16–38
Association Councils
  decisions
    access to employment, A10–01
    development, A10–01
    direct effect, 17–31—17–36

INDEX

economic and technical co–operation, A10–01
families, 20–05—20–07, A10–01
freedom of movement, 17–18—17–30, A10–01
workers, 18–04—18–09, A10–01
Asylum
asylum seekers, 3–23, 3–24
EU law, 1–22, 1–24, 1–25
Availability for employment
discrimination, 11–32
previous employment, 6–61, 6–62
status of worker, 11–32
Azerbaijan
partnership and co-operation agreements
economic co-operation, 2–10
freedom of movement, 14–45
political relationship, 14–45, 25–33

Belarus
partnership and co-operation agreements
economic relations, 2–10, 14–09, 14–45
freedom of movement, 14–49
Benefits (entitlement)
see also **Social Security**
accidents at work, A5–01
benefits in kind, 12–22—12–24, 12–28, A5–01
cash benefits, A5–01
death grants, 12–19, 12–29, A5–01
derogations, 12–13—12–15
economic and social benefits, A5–01
family benefits, A5–01
insurance period, A5–01
invalidity benefits, 12–19, 12–29, A5–01
maintenance, A5–01
maternity benefit, 12–10, 12–19, 12–22, A5–01
medical treatment, 12–15, 12–24—12–26, A5–01
overlapping benefits, A5–01
paternity benefit, 12–19, 12–22, A5–01
pensions, 12–19, 12–27, A5–01
recovery of benefits, A5–01
residence requirement, 12–12, A5–01
sickness benefit, 12–19, 12–22, 12–23, A5–01
social assistance, 12–15
survivors' benefits, 12–19, 12–29, A5–01
unemployment benefits, 12–11, 12–19, 12–31, A5–01
Border controls
duration of journey, 10–20
financial means, 10–20
purpose of journey, 10–20
Schengen Agreement, 1–18
spot checks, 10–20, 10–22, 10–23
Bosnia and Herzegovina
stabilisation and association agreements, 14–07, 2–09
Branches
freedom of establishment, 7–01, 7–03, 7–21, 7–24, 7–25, A11–01

Bulgaria
association agreements, 15–08, 25–32
immigration, 24–31, 24–33

Carers
non-EU parents
free movement of children 4–66—4–71
right to reside, 4–24—4–27
Central Asia
bilateral relations, 14–47
EU enlargement, 14–46
EU relationship, 14–45
freedom of movement, 14–49—14–56
partnership and co-operation agreements, 14–47, 14–48
trade relations, 14–45
Charter of Fundamental Rights of the European Union 2000
citizens' rights, 3–07
equality, 3–07
European Convention on Human Rights relationship, 3–09
evaluation, 3–13
families, 9–10, 9–11, 9–15, 9–22
general provisions, 3–07
human dignity, 3–07, 3–08, 3–12
human rights protection, 3–01, 3–03, 3–05—3–07
justice, 3–07
limitations, 3–10
non-discrimination, 2–66
prohibition of torture, 3–07, 3–12
right to life, 3–07
right to respect for family and private life, 3–07
subsidiarity, 3–10, 3–11
Children
adopted children, 9–61—9–63
Ankara Agreement
access to education, 20–53, 20–54
lawful residence, 20–41
meaning of children, 20–37
offers of employment, 20–39, 20–40, 20–42
remaining beyond worker, 20–47—20–52
right to take up employment, 20–39, 20–40, 20–42, 20–45, 20–46
rights of entry and residence, 20–43, 20–44, 20–46
vocational training, 20–39—20–43, 20–49, 20–51, 20–55
blood children, 9–53
carers, 4–66—4–71, 9–79, 9–83, 24–27
foster children, 9–61
grandchildren, 9–53
great-grandchildren, 9–53
non-EU parents, 4–66—4–69, 4–71
rights of entry and residence, 4–68, 4–69, 8–32, 8–37—8–42
Chile
association agreements
EU co-operation, 14–73

[691]

freedom of movement, 14–74—14–76
trade relations, 14–73
Citizens Directive 2004/38
see **Directive 2004/38 (Citizens' Directive)**
Citizenship
basis, 5–01, 5–02
deprivation of rights, 4–43
diplomatic protection, 5–01, A2–01
freedom of establishment, 5–03
freedom of movement
discrete rights, 4–02
economic free movement rights, 4–17—4–19
economically inactive persons, 4–05
EU nationals, 4–01
exercise of rights, 4–12, 4–13, 4–16, 4–17, 4–21, 4–34, A2–01
general right, 4–05, 4–06
limitations and conditions, A2–01
retirement, 4–05
students, 4–05
historical background, 4–03—4–08
introduction, 4–01, 4–02
lawful residence, 4–25—4–29, 4–73
membership of supranational body, 4–01, 4–35
national citizenship
EU citizenship link, 4–11, 4–36—4–42, 5–01
EU nationals, 5–02, 5–04—5–10
rights of nationals, 4–01, 4–02, 4–08
naturalisation, 4–39—4–41
non-discrimination
equal treatment, 4–12, 4–13, 4–20
financial issues, 4–33
freedom of movement, 4–12, 4–13, 4–16—4–19, 4–21, 4–34
legitimate aim, 4–31
proportionality, 4–31
protection, 4–14—4–17, 4–30, 4–33, 4–51, 5–03
right to petition, 5–01, A2–01
right to provide services, 5–03
right to receive services, 5–03
right to work, 5–03
rights and benefits, 4–10, 4–32
social policy, 4–32
social security measures, A2–01
voting rights, 5–01, 5–03, A2–01
Civil partnerships
differential treatment, 9–37
Directive 2004/38, 9–36, 9–41
disadvantages, 9–39
durable relationships, 9–37
equivalent to marriage, 9–36—9–38, 10–97
increasing numbers, 9–39
partners accompanying and joining EU nationals, 9–24
recognition, 9–36, 9–38, 9–39
reinterpretation, 9–40
rights, 9–36

rights of entry and residence, 10–96, 10–97, A3–01
Companies
freedom of establishment
branches, 7–01, 7–03, 7–21, 7–24, 7–25
employees, 7–29
incorporation rules, 7–28
Macedonia, A11–01
mergers, 7–26
movement to another EU State, 7–22, 7–23
nationality, 7–27, 7–28
primary establishment, 7–22, 7–23
secondary establishment, 7–24, 7–25
subsidiary companies, 7–01, 7–03, 7–21, 7–25
freedom to provide services
employees, 7–61
nationality, 7–59
permanent residence, 7–60
posted workers, 7–46, 7–62—7–64
provision of services, 7–41, 7–59, 7–60
secondary establishment, 7–60
temporary provision, 7–60
"Copenhagen criteria"
EU accession
functioning market economy, 5–35
political, economic and monetary union, 5–35
protection of minorities, 5–35
stability of institutions, 5–35
Turkey, 14–28
Western Balkan States, 14–31
Cotonou Agreement
EU relations, 14–69
Council of the European Union
agreements with non-EU countries, 1–54
decision-making, 1–57
function, 1–36, 1–37, 1–53, 1–55
organisation, 1–51, 1–52
policy-making, 1–53, 1–55
powers, 1–53—1–55
Presidency of the Council, 1–56
voting, 1–57—1–60
Court of Auditors
function, 1–38
Court of Justice of the European Union
annulment actions, 2–15, 2–18
appeals, 2–22, 23–15
Civil Service Tribunal, 2–13
composition, 2–13
costs, 23–16, 23–17
damages actions, 2–20, 2–21
direct actions, 2–14, 2–15
direct effect, 15–24—15–34
employment disputes, 2–21
failure to act complaints, 2–19
family-related cases, 9–16—9–22
final court, 23–14
function, 1–15, 1–38
General Court, 2–13
human rights, 3–14—3–22

immigration appeals, 23–12, 23–17
individual complaints, 2–14, 2–15
infringement proceedings, 2–14, 2–16, 2–17
judicial authority, 2–13
judicial review proceedings, 23–13
jurisdiction, 15–15—15–23
national court decisions, 23–09
preliminary rulings
  availability, 2–26, 15–15
  damages, 2–24
  excluded cases, 23–10
  procedure, 2–24, 2–26, 23–09, 23–10
  subject matter, 2–25
  uniform interpretation, 23–09
  UK courts, 23–11, 23–12
provisional legal protection, 2–23
Croatia
  accession negotiations, 14–35
  International Criminal Court for the Former Yugoslavia, 14–35
  regional co-operation, 2–09, 14–07, 14–08, 14–34, 15–01
  rights of entry and residence, 16–01, 16–04
  relationship with Slovenia, 14–35
  stabilisation and association agreements
    equal treatment, 16–19
    families, 16–29—16–31
    freedom of establishment, 14–39—14–44
    freedom of movement, 14–36—14–44, 16–20, 16–32
    freedom to provide services, 16–39
    non-discrimination provisions, 16–05, 16–08, 16–09, 16–12, 16–17
    regional co-operation, 2–09, 14–07, 14–34, 15–01
    rights of entry and residence, 16–01, 16–04, 16–05, 16–18, 16–21
    social security systems, 14–44
    United Kingdom, 25–32
Customs union
  Treaty of Lisbon 2007, 1–34
  Treaty on the Functioning of the European Union
    custom duties, A2–01
    free movement of workers, A2–01
    generally, A2–01
    import formalities, A2–01
Czech Republic
  association agreements, 16–10

Damages
  damage caused by EU staff, 2–15, 2–20
  failure to implement Directive, 2–52
  preliminary rulings, 2–24
Decisions
  binding effect, 2–54
  secondary legislation, 2–03, 2–07,
Dependants
  children, 9–79, 9–81, 9–83, 9–84
  cohabitation, 9–74
  dependency
    assessment, 9–55, 9–56

concept, 9–55, 9–58
duration, 9–59
financial dependency, 9–59
health grounds, 9–71, 9–72
material support, 9–60
physical dependency, 9–59
Directive 2004/38, 9–66
durable relationships, 9–73—9–76
exclusion, 9–77, 9–78, 9–81
living as part of household, 9–70
living without EU national, 9–85
outside EU law, 9–77—9–84
rights of entry and residence, 9–79—9–82
workers in education, 9–78—9–79
Deportation
deportation orders, 13–58, 25–29, 25–30
Directive 2004/38
  general provisions, 13–03—13–05
  national security, 13–31, 13–33, 13–49, 13–64
  notification, 13–49
  public health, 13–35, 13–49, 13–64
  public policy, 13–18, 13–23, 13–49, 13–64
  remedies, 13–53—13–55, 13–57, 13–58
economic reasons, 13–14
EU law, 13–02
EU nationals
  Directive 2004/38, 13–59, 13–60
  economic activity, 13–63
  economically inactive persons, 13–59, 13–65
  jobseekers, 13–61
  proportionality, 13–66, 13–67
  protection, 13–61—13–64
  resident in another EU State, 13–59
  rights of entry and residence, 13–59, 13–60
  self-employed workers, 13–61, 13–63
  sickness insurance, 13–68
  social security systems, 13–61, 13–62, 13–65, 13–67
  sufficient resources, 13–63, 13–67
  workers, 13–61, 13–63
fundamental freedoms, 13–07, 13–09
immigration formalities, 13–15
individuals
  degree of integration, 13–03, 13–06, 13–36, 13–41
  meaning of integration, 13–37, 13–38
  links with country of origin, 13–03, 13–06
  personal circumstances, 13–03, 13–06
  personal conduct, 13–05, 13–06, 13–11
  serious harm, 13–03, 13–36
introduction, 13–01
justification, 13–07
national security
  Ankara Agreement, 21–01, 21–04, 21–05, 21–09
  criminal convictions, 13–31, 13–32
  Directive 2004/38, 13–31, 13–33, 13–49, 13–64

[693]

drug offences, 13–31
European Economic Area Regulations 2006, 24–11, 24–28
generally, 13–01—13–08
imperative grounds, 13–31, 13–33, 13–46, 13–54
internal and external security, 13–30, 13–31
meaning, 13–30—13–32
notification, 13–50, 13–51
proportionality, 13–33
sovereignty, 13–32
United Kingdom, 24–05, 24–11, 24–28
notification
  appeals, 13–52
  comprehensive statements, 13–49
  Directive 2004/38, 13–49
  national security cases, 13–50, 13–51
  precise information, 13–39, 13–50
  sensitive information, 13–50, 13–51
  urgent cases, 13–52
police record, 13–47
proportionality
  EU nationals 13–66, 13–67
  national security, 13–33
  proportionality assessment, 13–03, 13–05—13–07, 13–17
  remedies, 13–56
  safeguards, 13–36
  special measures, 13–10
public health
  Ankara Agreement, 21–01, 21–04, 21–05, 21–09
  Directive 2004/38, 13–35, 13–49, 13–64
  epidemics, 13–34
  European Economic Area Regulations 2006, 24–11, 24–28
  generally, 13–01—13–08
  medical examinations, 13–35
  time limits, 13–35
  special measures, 13–35
  United Kingdom, 24–05, 24–11, 24–28
public policy
  Ankara Agreement, 21–01, 21–04, 21–05, 21–09
  association with organisations, 13–19
  danger to society, 13–24
  deterrence, 13–22, 13–23
  Directive 2004/38, 13–18, 13–23, 13–49, 13–64
  disturbance of social order, 13–18, 13–27
  drug offences, 13–28
  European Economic Area Regulations 2006, 24–11, 24–28
  generally, 13–01—13–08
  level of crime, 13–20
  national security distinguished, 13–18
  personal conduct, 13–18, 13–19, 13–25
  present threat, 13–25
  serious crime, 13–24—13–29
  serious threats, 13–18, 13–29
  terrorism, 13–26, 13–27

  United Kingdom, 24–05, 24–11, 24–28
registration certificates, 13–47
remedies
  access to justice, 13–53
  appeals, 13–54, 13–56, 13–57
  defence in person, 13–57
  Directive 2004/38, 13–53—13–55, 13–57, 13–58
  interim orders, 13–54
  judicial authority, 13–55
  judicial review, 13–54, 13–57
  personal attendance, 13–57
  proportionality, 13–56
  redress, 13–53—13–57
  right to effective remedy, 13–56
restrictions on freedom of movement, 13–05, 13–06, 13–49
safeguards
  Directive 2004/38, 13–64
  indefinite leave to remain, 13–39
  minors, 13045
  proportionality, 13–36
  protection, 13–06, 13–07, 13–36, 13–41, 13–42
  ten years residence, 13–40—13–46
self–employed workers, 13–02
sovereignty, 13–01, 13–08, 13–09
special measures
  arbitrariness, 13–12
  equivalent national measures, 13–12, 13–20, 13–21
  existence of threat, 13–13
  justification, 13–10
  personal conduct, 13–11
  proportionality, 13–10
  public health, 13–35
special treatment, 13–02
Direct effect
conferral of rights, 2–37
direct applicability distinguished, 2–40
Directives, 2–50, 2–51, 2–53
enforcement, 2–38
horizontal direct effect, 2–39, 2–53
unconditional provisions, 2–37
vertical direct effect, 2–39
Directive 2004/38 (Citizens' Directive)
abuse of rights, A3–01
civil partnerships, 9–36, 9–41, A3–01
deportation
  deportation orders, A3–01
  EU nationals, 13–59, 13–60
  general provisions, 13–03—13–05
  national security, 13–31, 13–33, 13–49, 13–64, A3–01
  notification, 13–49
  public health, 13–35, 13–49, 13–64, A3–01
  public policy, 13–18, 13–23, 13–49, 13–64, A3–01
  remedies, 13–53—13–55, 13–57, 13–58
  safeguards, 13–64, A3–01

INDEX

economically inactive persons
  restrictions, 8–11
  retirement, 8–12
  rights of entry and residence, 8–12—8–15
  self-sufficiency, 8–12—8–14, 8–16, 8–17
  sickness insurance, 8–23, 8–24
  source of resources, 8–17
  students, 8–32, 8–37—8–46
equal treatment, A3–01
families, A3–01
freedom of establishment
  rights of entry and residence, 7–04
  self-employed workers, 7–04
freedom to provide services
  receipt of services, 7–71, 7–76
  service providers, 7–43
fundamental freedoms, A3–01
immigration
  civil partnerships, 24–23
  deportation, 24–11
  EEA Regulations 2006, 24–08, 24–12, 24–22
  family members, 24–10, 24–11
  family permits, 24–11
  national security, 24–11
  permanent residence, 24–18
  prior lawful residence, 24–16
  public health, 24–11
  public policy, 24–11
  self-employed persons, 24–10
  self-sufficient persons, 24–10
  students, 24–10
  workers, 24–10
jobseekers
  families, 6–48, 6–50
  more favourable treatment, 6–49
  prohibition on expulsion, 6–48, 6–49, 7–20
  rights of entry and residence, 6–48, 6–50, 6–56, 6–58, A3–01
non-discrimination provisions, A3–01
proportionality, A3–01
rights of entry and residence
  beyond EU citizen, A3–01
  declaration of means, 8–47
  degree of integration, A3–01
  economically inactive persons, 8–12—8–15
  families, A3–01
  formalities, 10–14, 10–17, 10–18, 10–25, 10–44, 10–45, A3–01
  involuntary unemployment, A3–01
  jobseekers, 6–48, 6–50, 6–56, 6–58, A3–01
  permanent residence, A3–01
  registration certificates, 10–76—10–83, A3–01
  self-employed workers, A3–01
  social assistance, A3–01
  students, 8–32, 8–37—8–46
  sufficient resources, A3–01

vocational training, 8–32, 8–46, 8–47
workers, A3–01
sham marriages, 9–48, 9–49, A3–01
Union citizenship, A3–01
Directives
binding effect, 2–48—2–52
direct effect, 2–49, 2–50, 2–51, 2–53
individual rights, 2–52
national implementation, 2–52
Discrimination
Ankara Agreement
  Additional Protocol, 17–08
  application, 19–33, 19–34
  duly registered workers, 18–70
  equal treatment, 18–69
  freedom of establishment, 19–33, 19–34
  freedom to provide services, 19–33, 19–34
  general provisions, 17–14, 18–69, 18–70
  interpretation, 18–73, 18–75
  nationality grounds, 17–14, 18–70—18–74
  self-employed workers, 19–34
  standstill clause, 18–76—18–82
citizenship
  equal treatment, 4–12, 4–13, 4–20
  financial issues, 4–33
  freedom of movement, 4–12, 4–13, 4–16—4–19, 4–21, 4–34
  legitimate aim, 4–31
  proportionality, 4–31
  protection, 4–14—4–17, 4–30, 4–33, 4–51, 5–03
differential treatment, 11–03, 11–54
direct discrimination
  nationality grounds, 12–10
  prohibition, 11–19
  service providers, 7–59
  workers, 11–50
economically inactive persons
  Directive 2004/38, 9–54, 11–99, 11–101
  freedom of movement, 11–97—11–99
  non-discrimination provisions, 11–98, 11–99, 11–102, 11–103
  retirement, 11–100
  self-sufficiency, 11–100, 11–101
  social assistance, 11–98
  students, 11–101—11–103
equal treatment
  case law, 11–61, 11–64
  conditions of work, 11–28
  differential treatment, 11–03
  employment, 11–28
  family members, 11–46
  Freedom of Movement Directive 2004/38, 11–14, 11–48
  fundamental principle, 11–03
  nationality grounds, 11–28
  remuneration, 11–28
free movement of workers
  eligibility for employment, 11–26, 11–27
  equal treatment, 11–28

[695]

Index

generally, 11–25
jobseekers, 11–35—11–38
social and tax advantages, 11–29
trade union membership, 11–31
vocational training, 11–30
workers, 11–32—11–34
freedom of establishment
  differential treatment, 11–58, 11–66
  discrimination on nationality grounds, 11–59, 11–63—11–67
  discriminatory measures, 11–71—11–74
  equal treatment, 11–61, 11–64
  fundamental freedoms, 11–69
  justification, 11–68
  national measures, 11–59
  non-discriminatory measures, 11–68—11–70
  professional services, 11–62
  restrictions, 11–58—11–62, 11–68, 11–71
  right of establishment, 11–58, 11–59
  secondary establishment, 11–63
  unconditional rights, 11–60
freedom to provide services
  national security exemption, 11–96
  non-discrimination requirement, 11–90—11–93
  public health exemption, 11–96
  public policy exemption, 11–96
  receipt of services, 11–95
  residence requirement, 11–91
  restrictions, 11–90—11–92, 11–96
  service providers, 11–91, 11–94
general principle
  equality, 11–03
  introduction, 11–01 — 11–03
  material scope, 11–06, 11–09, 11–10, 11–11
  personal scope, 11–06, 11–07
  relationship with other non-discrimination provisions, 11–12—11–18
  Treaty on the Functioning of the European Union, 11–01, 11–02, 11–04—11–11
human rights, 2–65
indirect discrimination
  benefits (entitlement), 11–20, 11–53—11–55, 12–10
  case law, 11–51, 11–53, 11–55, 12–10
  differential treatment, 11–51
  exercise of Treaty rights, 11–19
  migrant workers, 11–20, 11–52
  prohibition, 11–09, 11–51
  residence requirement, 11–20, 11–51, 11–53
justification, 11–03, 11–21—11–24, 11–56, 11–57, 11–68
material scope
  families, 11–46—11–48
  remuneration, 11–39
  social advantages, 11–39—11–45
  tax advantages, 11–49
mutual recognition principle
  evidence of training, 11–87
  freedom of establishment, 7–18, 11–76—11–78
  general system, 11–75, 11–76, 11–81
  national professional rules, 11–77
  professional qualifications, 11–80, 11–82—11–84, 11–88, 11–89
  self-employed workers, 11–79
  temporary mobility, 11–85, 11–86
  workers, 11–79
national security, 11–24
nationality grounds
  benefits (entitlement), 11–66, 12–10
  case law, 11–59, 11–64—11–67
  conditions of work, 11–28
  employment, 11–28
  equal treatment, 11–64
  general prohibition, 11–04, 11–05, 11–16
  justification, 11–21, 11–24, 11–56
  remuneration, 11–28
  residence and domicile, 11–65
non-discrimination principle, 2–63—2–66, 11–01—11–03
personal scope
  entitlement to protection, 11–06—11–08
  jobseekers, 11–35—11–38
  workers, 11–32—11–34
prohibited forms, 11–50, 11–51
proportionality, 11–22, 11–57
public health, 11–24
public policy, 11–24
relationship with non-discrimination provisions, 11–11, 11–13—11–18
stabilisation and association agreements
  direct discrimination, 16–16
  direct effect, 16–06, 16–08
  equal treatment, 16–07
  freedom of establishment, 16–11
  generally, 14–37, 16–05
  indirect discrimination, 16–16
  meaning of discrimination, 16–13—16–15
  national laws, 16–09, 16–10, 16–12
  temporal effect, 16–27
  workers, 16–18—16–26
third country family members, 11–15

Dual nationality
citizenship, 5–26
freedom of establishment, 7–09
freedom of movement, 5–24, 5–26, 5–27
rights and benefits, 5–13, 5–55—5–27

Eastern Europe
bilateral relations, 14–47
EU enlargement, 14–46
EU relationship, 14–45
freedom of movement, 14–49—14–56
partnership and co-operation agreements, 14–47, 14–48
trade relations, 14–45

Index

EC Treaty
  amendment, 1–16
  common market, 1–10, 1–11
  economic and monetary union, 1–10
  freedom of movement
    capital, 1–12
    goods, 1–12
    persons, 1–12, 1–14
    services, 1–12
  fulfilment of obligations, 1–13
  generally, 1–03
  internal market, 1–11, 1–16
  non-discrimination, 1–13
Economic partnership agreements
  ACP States
    Cotonou Agreement, 14–69
    economic and social development, 14–66
    freedom of movement, 14–70—14–72
    EU relationship, 14–66, 14–68, 14–69
    Lomé Conventions, 14–67—14–69
    non-discrimination provisions, 14–71, 14–72
    Yaoundé Conventions, 14–67
Economically inactive persons
  deportation, 13–59, 13–65
  Directive 2004/38
    discrimination, 11–99, 11–101
    restrictions, 8–11
    retirement, 8–12
    rights of entry and residence, 8–12, 8–14
    self-sufficiency, 8–12—8–14, 8–16, 8–17
    sickness insurance, 8–23, 8–24
    source of resources, 8–17
  discrimination
    Directive 2004/38, 11–99, 11–101
    freedom of movement, 11–97—11–99
    non-discrimination provisions, 11–98, 11–99, 11–102, 11–103
    retirement, 11–100
    self-sufficiency, 11–100, 11–101
    social assistance, 11–98
    students, 11–101—11–103
  freedom of movement, 8–01, 8–04, 8–05, 11–97—11–99
  limitations and conditions, 8–07—8–09, 8–11
  proportionality, 8–10, 8–11
  residence documents, 8–10
  retirement
    continuous residence, 8–29
    discrimination, 11–100
    family members, 8–31
    invalidity pensions, 8–30
    non-residence, 8–30
    previously employed persons, 8–29
    rights of entry and residence, 8–31
    self-sufficiency, 8–12, 8–15
    sickness insurance, 8–30
    social security, 8–30, 8–31
    sufficient resources, 8–30
  rights of entry and residence, 8–02—8–04, 8–08—8–11
  self-sufficiency
    discrimination, 11–100, 11–101
    Free Movement Directive 2004/38, 8–12—8–14, 8–16, 8–17
    requirement, 8–06
    retirement, 8–12, 8–15
    rights of entry and residence, 8–12—8–15, 8–22, 8–27, 8–28
    social assistance, 8–12—8–16, 8–22
    source of resources, 8–17—8–20
    sufficient resources, 8–12, 8–14, 8–18, 8–19, 8–21, 8–22
  sickness insurance, 8–06, 8–10, 8–12, 8–23—8–26
  students, 8–02, 8–05, 8–09, 8–22
  vocational training, 8–02
Employees
  freedom to provide services
    EU nationals, 7–61
    lawfully and habitually employed, 7–65
    minimum rights, 7–66
    posted workers, 7–46, 7–62—7–64
    protection, 7–67, 7–69
    social dumping, 7–66
    work permits, 7–65, 7–67
  nationality, 7–29
Enlargement
  accession treaties
    Treaty of Accession 2003, 5–34, 5–36
    Treaty of Accession 2005, 5–37
  Copenhagen criteria
    functioning market economy, 5–35
    political, economic and monetary union, 5–35
    protection of minorities, 5–35
    stability of institutions, 5–35
    Turkey, 14–28
    Western Balkan States, 14–31
  freedom of movement, 5–36, 5–37
  generally, 1–05
  new Member States, 5–33, 5–34
  Turkey, 14–28, 17–03, 17–10
Equal treatment
  association agreements
    Ankara Agreement, 18–69
    Switzerland, 14–24
  citizenship, 4–12, 4–13, 4–20
  discrimination
    case law, 11–61, 11–64
    conditions of work, 11–28
    differential treatment, 11–03
    employment, 11–28
    family members, 11–46
    Freedom of Movement Directive 2004/38, 11–14, 11–48
    fundamental principle, 11–03
    nationality grounds, 11–28
    remuneration, 11–28
  free movement of workers, 11–28
  freedom of establishment, 7–01, 7–11, 11–16, 11–64
  human rights, 2–65, 2–66

[697]

jobseekers, 11–35, 11–37, 11–38
social security, 12–09, 12–17
stabilisation and association agreements,
  16–07, 16–19
EU citizenship
see **Citizenship**
EU general principles
  direct effect, 2–36—2–40, 2–50, 2–51,
    2–53
  fundamental rights, 2–68
  indirect effect, 2–55—2–57
  interpretation of national law, 2–56, 2–57
  introduction, 2–27, 2–28
  legal certainty, 2–61
  legitimate expectation, 2–61, 2–62
  non-discrimination, 2–63—2–66,
    11–01—11–03
  proportionality, 2–59, 2–60
  sincere co-operation, 2–30
  supremacy of EU law, 2–29—2–35
EU institutions
  Council of the European Union, 1–36,
    1–37, 1–52—1–60
  Court of Auditors, 1–38
  Court of Justice of the European Union,
    1–15, 1–38
  European Commission, 1–15, 1–37, 1–45,
    1–62—1–79
  European Council, 1–36
  European Parliament, 1–37, 1–39, 1–40,
    1–41—1–43, 1–45, 1–47—1–50
  framework, 1–35
EU law
  agreements with third countries
    association agreements, 2–09
    freedom of movement, 2–12
    partnership and co-operation
      agreements, 2–10
    trade agreements, 2–11
  direct effect
    conferral of rights, 2–37
    direct applicability distinguished, 2–40
    Directives, 2–49, 2–50, 2–51, 2–53
    enforcement, 2–38
    horizontal direct effect, 2–39, 2–53
    unconditional provisions, 2–37
    vertical direct effect, 2–39
  Decisions
    binding effect, 2–54
    secondary legislation, 2–03, 2–07,
  Directives
    binding effect, 2–48—2–52
    direct effect, 2–49, 2–50, 2–51, 2–53
    individual rights, 2–52
    national implementation, 2–52
  discrimination
    differential treatment, 11–03
    equal treatment, 11–03
    justification, 11–03
    nationality grounds, 11–04, 11–05,
      11–16, 11–21, 11–24, 11–28, 11–56
  non-discrimination principle, 2–63—
    2–66, 11–01—11–03
  human rights
    asylum, 3–23, 3–24
    immigration, 3–23
    protection, 2–64—2–66, 3–01
    refugees, 3–23, 3–24
    subsidiary protection, 3–24
  principles
    direct effect, 2–36—2–40, 2–50, 2–51,
      2–53
    fundamental rights, 2–68
    indirect effect, 2–55—2–57
    interpretation of national law, 2–56, 2–57
    introduction, 2–27, 2–28
    legal certainty, 2–61
    legitimate expectation, 2–61, 2–62
    non-discrimination, 2–63—2–66,
      11–01—11–03
    proportionality, 2–59, 2–60
    sincere co-operation, 2–30
    supremacy of EU law, 2–29—2–35
  secondary legislation
    asylum, 3–23, 3–24
    Decisions, 2–03, 2–07, 2–54
    Directives, 2–03, 2–06
    freedom of movement, 2–04
    immigration, 3–23
    Recommendations and Opinions, 2–03
    refugees, 3–23, 3–24
    Regulations, 2–03, 2–05
  sources of law
    generally, 2–01
    secondary legislation, 2–03
    treaties, 1–03, 1–04, 1–06, 2–02, 2–41—
      2–47
  treaties
    direct applicability, 2–44, 2–45
    direct effect, 2–42, 2–43
    individual rights, 2–41, 2–43
    national implementation, 2–46—2–53
EU nationals
  determination of status, 5–04, 5–06—5–10
  dual nationals
    freedom of movement, 5–24, 5–26, 5–27
    rights and benefits, 5–13, 5–22—5–26
  freedom of establishment, 7–15
  freedom to provide services, 7–33, 7–37,
    7–40, 7–61, 7–72
  internal situations rule
    dual nationals, 5–22, 5–23, 7–09
    exceptions, 5–18
    family members, 5–11—5–17
    returning nationals, 5–19, 7–09, n7–10
    self-employed workers, 5–20
    service providers, 5–20, 5–21
    students, 5–20
  outside Member State, 5–11
  social security, 12–17
  visas, 10–38
Euro–Mediterranean Agreements
  see also **Association Agreements**

INDEX

Algeria
    association agreements, 2–09, 14–57
    discrimination on nationality grounds, 14–59
    family members, 14–64
    free movement of workers, 14–59, 14–60, 14–64
    non-discrimination provisions, 14–59, 14–60, 14–64
    political and economic co-operation, 2–09
    regional co-operation, 14–57, 14–58
association agreements
    political and economic co-operation, 2–09
    regional co-operation, 14–57
Barcelona Declaration, 14–57
direct effect, 14–61
freedom of movement, 14–58, 14–59
generally, 14–09
inter-State co-operation, 14–58
Morocco
    family members, 14–64
    free movement of workers, 14–61, 14–62, 14–64
    non-discrimination provisions, 14–61, 14–64
non-discrimination provisions, 14–58, 14–60—14–64
residence documents, 14–61, 14–63
rights of entry and residence, 14–61
Tunisia
    family members, 14–64
    free movement of workers, 14–63, 14–64
    non-discrimination provisions, 14–63, 14–64
European Atomic Energy Community Treaty
    freedom of movement, 1–09
    generally, 1–08
European Coal and Steel Community Treaty
    freedom of movement, 1–07
European Commission
    appointment, 1–66
    consultation process, 1–70
    external trade relations, 1–79
    function
        EU law enforcement, 1–68, 1–75—1–78
        international representation, 1–68, 1–79
        policy implementation, 1–73, 1–74
        programmes of action, 1–62
        proposing legislation, 1–69—1–72
    international agreements, 1–79
    membership, 1–64—1–66
    organisation, 1–64, 1–67
European Communities Act 1972
    direct effect of EU Law, 23–06, 23–07
    general provisions, A12–01
    interpretation, A12–01
    operation of Community law, 23–05—23–07
    obligation on UK courts, 23–08

treaties
    amendments, 23–04
    decisions, A12–01
    implementation, A12–01
European Convention on Human Rights 1950
see also **Charter of Fundamental Rights**
    importance, 3–03
    negative obligations, 9–12
    non-discrimination, 2–65
    positive obligations, 9–13, 9–14
    respect for private and family life
        exceptions, 9–11
        existence of family life, 10–106
        fundamental right, 9–80, 10–04, 16–30
        immigration, 9–11
        justification, 9–11
        negative obligations, 9–11, 9–12
        positive obligations, 9–13
        proportionality, 9–12
        protection, 3–07, 9–08, 9–09, 9–11—9–13
        public order, 9–11
        transsexual marriage, 9–47
    right to marry, 9–47
European Council
    function, 1–36
European Economic Area
    EEA Council, 14–14
    EU co-operation, 14–15
    European Economic Area Agreement
        companies, A6–01
        freedom of establishment, 14–18, A6–01
        freedom of movement, 14–06, 14–16—14–20
        freedom to provide services, 14–19
        institutional arrangements, 14–13
        Member States, 14–11
        mutual recognition principle, A6–01
        national security, A6–01
        non-discrimination, A6–01
        public health, A6–01
        public policy, A6–01
        public service exemption, A6–01
        reciprocal rights, 14–20
        relationship with EU law, 14–12
        self-employed workers, A6–01
        social security, A6–01
        workers, A6–01
European Economic Area Regulations 2006
    beneficiaries of EU rights, 24–10
    carers, 24–27
    common law partners, 24–22
    deportation
        criminal conviction, 24–28
        enhanced protection, 24–28
        generally, 24–11
        national security, 24–28, 24–29
        personal conduct, 24–28
        proportionality, 24–28
        public health, 24–28
        public policy, 24–28
        terrorism, 24–29

families, 24–14—24–17, 24–20, 24–21, 24–26
immigration appeals, 24–11
indefinite leave to remain, 24–18
limitation, 24–12
prior lawful residence, 24–08, 24–16
rights of entry and residence, 24–11, 24–14, 24–20, 24–22, 24–26

European Parliament
budgetary powers, 1–41, 1–49, 1–50
democratic supervision, 1–41, 1–46—1–48
function, 1–37, 1–41
legislation, 1–41, 1–42, 1–43, 1–45
location, 1–40
membership, 1–39
plenary sessions, 1–40

European Union
asylum, 1–22, 1–24, 1–25, 3–23, 3–24
co-operation
  intergovernmental, 1–03, 1–04
  justice and home affairs, 1–04, 1–22, 1–24
  policing and judicial co-operation, 1–22
enlargement
  freedom of movement, 5–36, 5–37
  generally, 1–05
  new Member States, 5–33, 5–34
immigration, 1–22, 1–24, 1–25
introduction, 1–01—1–06
Member States, 1–02—1–04
population, 1–02
reforms, 1–06
three pillars
  common foreign and security policy, 1–21
  freedom of movement, 1–04, 1–20
  justice and home affairs, 1–04, 1–22
treaties, 1–03, 1–04, 1–06

Exclusion and expulsion
see **Deportation**

Egypt
association agreement, 2–09, 14–57

Families
see also **Marriage**; **Spouses**
accompanying and joining EU nationals
  civil partnerships, 9–24
  core family members, 9–23
  dependants, 9–24, 9–26
  direct descendants, 9–24
  Directive 2004/38, 9–23—9–29
  EU law, 9–27, 9–75
  health grounds, 9–26
  relatives in ascending line, 9–25
  residence cards, 9–27
  spouses, 9–24
  students' relatives, 9–25
descendants
  adopted children, 9–61—9–63
  blood children, 9–53
  children, 9–62, 9–79, 9–81, 9–83, 9–84
  Directive 2004/38, 9–54
  foster children, 9–61
  grandchildren, 9–53
  great-grandchildren, 9–53
  right to install, 9–54
  under 21 years, 9–53, 9–54
Directive 2004/38
  accompanying and joining EU nationals, 9–23—9–29
  family life, 9–19
  family unity, 9–02
  freedom of movement, 9–02
  right to install family members, 9–73
  rights of entry and residence, 9–02, A3–01
durable relationships
  freedom of movement, 9–73—9–76
  treatment of civil partners, 9–37, 9–39
human rights
  case law, 9–16—9–22
  Charter of Fundamental Rights, 9–10, 9–11, 9–15, 9–22
  freedom of movement, 9–16, 9–18, 9–22
  fundamental freedoms, 9–08, 9–18, 9–20, 9–22
  interference with individual's rights, 9–11
  legitimate aim, 9–11
  residence documents, 9–17, 9–19
other family members
  durable relationships, 9–73—9–76
  living as part of household, 9–70
  non-dependants, 9–77—9–84
  other dependants, 9–67—9–69
  serious health grounds, 9–71—9–72
  without EU national, 9–85
principles
  family life, 9–01—9–04
  family reunification, 9–01, 9–05—9–07, 9–14
  freedom of movement, 9–02, 9–16, 9–18, 9–22
  proportionality, 9–12
  relatives in ascending line, 9–25, 9–64, 9–65
respect for private and family life
  exceptions, 9–11
  existence of family life, 10–106
  fundamental right, 9–80, 10–04, 16–30
  immigration, 9–11
  justification, 9–11
  negative obligations, 9–11, 9–12
  positive obligations, 9–13
  proportionality, 9–12
  protection, 3–07, 9–08, 9–09, 9–11—9–13
  public order, 9–11
  transsexual marriage, 9–47
rights of entry and residence
  annulment of marriage, 10–114
  ascending and descending line, 10–98, 10–99
  children born outside marriage, 10–116, 10–117
  civil partnerships, 10–96, 10–97
  divorce, 10–114

[700]

INDEX

EU nationals, 5–11, 5–15, 5–16, 10–90, 10–93
evidence of dependency, 10–100
evidence of family link, 10–19, 10–94, 10–99
evidential problems, 10–111, 10–115
generally, 10–03, 10–89—10–94
identity cards, 10–93, 10–104
non-EU nationals, 10–90, 10–93
other family members, 10–101—10–105
passports, 10–93, 10–104
registration certificates, 10–90—10–93, 10–103
remaining beyond EU national, 10–107—10–110
residence cards, 10–103
right to respect for private and family life, 10–106
spouses, 10–95

Fraud
Ankara Agreement
deportation, 21–08
self-employed workers, 25–11—25–15
stable and secure employment, 18–21, 18–33
sham marriages, 9–50—9–51

Freedom of establishment
agents, 7–01, 7–03, 7–21, 7–25
citizenship, 5–03
companies
branches, 7–01, 7–03, 7–21, 7–24, 7–25
employees, 7–29
incorporation rules, 7–28
mergers, 7–26
movement to another EU State, 7–22, 7–23
nationality, 7–27, 7–28
primary establishment, 7–22, 7–23
secondary establishment, 7–24, 7–25
subsidiary companies, 7–01, 7–03, 7–21, 7–25
concept, 7–05, 7–30
Directive 2004/38
rights of entry and residence, 7–04
self-employed workers, 7–04
discrimination
differential treatment, 11–58, 11–66
discrimination on nationality grounds, 11–59, 11–63—11–67
discriminatory measures, 11–71—11–74
equal treatment, 7–01, 7–11, 11–61, 11–64
fundamental freedoms, 11–69
justification, 11–68
national measures, 11–59
non-discriminatory measures, 11–68—11–70
professional services, 11–62
restrictions, 11–58—11–62, 11–68, 11–71
right of establishment, 11–58, 11–59
secondary establishment, 11–63
unconditional rights, 11–60

economic activity
cross-border activity, 7–08—7–11
duration, 7–13—7–14
meaning, 7–05—7–07
permanent infrastructure, 7–14
self-employed workers, 7–16
stable and continuous nature, 7–12—7–14
EU nationals, 7–15
internal situations rule
dual nationality, 7–09
returning nationals, 7–09, 7–10
jobseekers, 7–19, 7–20
management of undertakings, 7–01, 7–03, 7–05, 7–30
mutual recognition principle, 7–18
national laws, 7–18
natural persons, 7–03, 7–15
prohibition on restrictions, 7–01—7–03, 7–11
rights of entry and residence, 7–04
second professional base, 7–17
self-employed workers, 7–01, 7–03—7–05, 7–15—7–17, 7–20, 7–30
"without restrictions"
differential treatment, 7–30
hindrance to trade, 7–32
national laws, 7–30—7–32
prior authorisation, 7–32
prohibition on restrictions, 7–01—7–03, 7–11, 7–32
unjustified restriction, 7–31

Freedom of movement
children, 4–65, 4–70
in education, 4–65
non-EU parents, 4–66–4–71
citizenship
non-discrimination, 4–12, 4–13, 4–16—4–19, 4–21, 4–34
rights of entry and residence, 4–01, 4–02, 4–05—4–07
economically inactive persons, 8–01, 8–04, 8–05
enlargement, 5–36, 5–37
families
Directive 2004/38, 9–02
human rights, 9–16, 9–18, 9–22
legal framework
agreements with third countries, 2–12
secondary legislation, 2–04
Single European Act 1986, 1–17
Treaty of Rome, 1–12, 1–14
poor people, 4–72, 4–74
social security
access to social security, 12–01
complexity, 12–04
differing systems, 12–05, 12–06, 12–33
national systems, 12–03
social and tax benefits, 12–01
third country nationals, 5–28, 5–29
workers
applications for employment, A4–01

[701]

clearance of vacancies, A4–01
committes for ensuring close cooperation between Member States, A4–01
Directives, 6–03, 6–05
employment, A4–01
equal treatment, A4–01
exchange of young workers, 6–04
families, 6–05, A4–01
importance, 6–01, 6–02, 6–05, 6–06
interpretation, 6–02, 6–06
limitations, 6–02
migrant workers, 6–06
national concepts, 6–06, 6–18, 6–70
Regulations, 6–03, 6–05, A4–01
removal of obstacles, 6–02
social security, 6–04

Freedom to provide services
companies
  employees, 7–61
  nationality, 7–59
  permanent residence, 7–60
  posted workers, 7–46, 7–62—7–64
  provision of services, 7–41, 7–59, 7–60
  secondary establishment, 7–60
  temporary provision, 7–60
cross-border element, 7–40
discrimination
  national security exemption, 11–96
  non-discrimination requirement, 11–90—11–93
  public health exemption, 11–96
  public policy exemption, 11–96
  receipt of services, 11–95
  residence requirement, 11–91
  restrictions, 11–90—11–92, 11–96
  service providers, 11–91, 11–94
economic activity, 7–40
employees
  EU nationals, 7–61
  lawfully and habitually employed, 7–65
  minimum rights, 7–66
  posted workers, 7–46, 7–62—7–64
  protection, 7–67, 7–69
  social dumping, 7–66
  work permits, 7–65, 7–67
EU nationals, 7–33, 7–37, 7–40, 7–61
Free Movement Directive 2004/38, 7–43, 7–71, 7–76
freedom of establishment, 7–37—7–39, 7–43
meaning of services, 7–35, 7–36
prohibition of restrictions, 7–33, 7–41
provision of services
  companies, 7–41, 7–59, 7–60
  discrimination, 11–91, 11–95
recipients of services
  business travellers, 7–74
  concept, 7–71
  Directive 2004/38, 7–71, 7–76education, 7–74
  EU nationals, 7–72
  medical treatment, 7–74
  recipient established in another EU State, 7–71
  recipient travels to another EU State, 7–71, 7–74
  rights of entry and residence, 7–44
  services for remuneration, 7–75
  third country nationals, 7–72
  tourists, 7–74
rights of entry and residence, 7–43
Services Directive 2006/123, 7–45, 7–71, 7–73
services for remuneration, 7–35, 7–47, 7–48, 7–51, 7–75
temporary provision, 7–40, 7–42, 7–43

Frontier workers
discrimination, 11–34
frequency of return, 6–67
meaning, 6–67
migrant workers, 6–68
protection, 11–34
rights of entry and residence, 6–67, 6–68, A7–01

Georgia
partnership and co-operation agreements
  economic relations, 2–10, 14–09, 14–45
  freedom of movement, 14–49

Human rights
see also **Charter of Fundamental Rights**
Agency for Fundamental Rights, 3–02
Court of Justice of the European Union, 3–14—3–22
equal treatment, 2–65, 2–66
EU law
  asylum, 3–23, 3–24
  immigration, 3–23
  refugees, 3–23, 3–24
  subsidiary protection, 3–24
families
  case law, 9–16—9–22
  Charter of Fundamental Rights, 9–10, 9–11, 9–15, 9–22
  family reunification, 9–14
  freedom of movement, 9–16, 9–18, 9–22
  fundamental freedoms, 9–08, 9–18, 9–20, 9–22
  interference with individual's rights, 9–11
  legitimate aim, 9–11
  residence documents, 9–17, 9–19
fundamental rights, 1–33, 2–68
non-discrimination, 2–65
prohibition of torture, 3–07, 3–12
respect for private and family life
  exceptions, 9–11
  existence of family life, 10–106
  fundamental right, 9–80, 10–04, 16–30
  immigration, 9–11
  justification, 9–11
  negative obligations, 9–11, 9–12
  positive obligations, 9–13
  proportionality, 9–12

protection, 3–07, 9–08, 9–09, 9–11—9–13
public order, 9–11
transsexual marriage, 9–47
right to life, 3–07
right to marry, 9–47
rights of entry and residence, 10–03, 10–04
subsidiarity, 3–10, 3–11
transsexuals
   gender reassignment, 9–42, 9–43
   protection, 9–42, 9–44, 9–46—9–49
Universal Declaration of Human Rights, 2–63

Immigration
Accession (Immigration and Worker Authorisation) Regulations 2006
   accession State nationals, A16–01
   accession worker cards, A16–01
   authorised categories of employment, A16–01
   Bulgarian nationals, A16–01
   deportation orders, A16–01
   families, A16–01
   highly skilled persons, A16–01
   offences, A16–01
   registration certificates, A16–01
   residence cards, A16–01
   Romanian nationals, A16–01
   unauthorised employment, A16–01
   unauthorised working, A16–01
   worker authorisation, A16–01
Accession (Immigration and Worker Registration) Regulations 2011, A17–0
Directive 2004/38
   civil partnerships, 24–23
   deportation, 24–11
   EEA Regulations 2006, 24–08, 24–12, 24–22
   family members, 24–10, 24–11
   family permits, 24–11
   national security, 24–11
   permanent residence, 24–18
   prior lawful residence, 24–16
   public health, 24–11
   public policy, 24–11
   self-employed persons, 24–10
   self-sufficient persons, 24–10
   students, 24–10
   workers, 24–10
EU law, 1–22, 1–24, 1–25, 3–23
human rights, 3–23
Immigration Act 1988, A13–01
Immigration (EEA) (Amendment) Regulations 2011, A15–01
Immigration (EEA) Regulations 2006
   admissions procedure, A14–01
   appeals, A14–01
   continuity of residence, A14–01
   deportation, A14–01
   economically inactive persons, A14–01
   families, A14–01
   interpretation, A14–01
   permanent residence, A14–01
   registration certificates, A14–01
   residence card, A14–01
   rights of entry and residence, A14–01
   self-employed persons, A14–01
   self-sufficient persons, A14–01
   students, A14–01
   workers, A14–01
Immigration (Swiss Free Movement of Persons)(No3) Regulations 2002
   families, A18–01
   posted workers, A18–01
   residence documents, A18–01
   Swiss nationals, A18–01
part-time employment, 6–21
rights of entry and residence, A13–01
United Kingdom
   accession legislation, 24–30—24–33
   Bulgarian nationals, 24–31, 24–33
   certificates of application, 24–12, 24–13
   dependency, 24–12
   Directive 2004/38, 24–08, 24–11, 24–15, 24–16, 24–18, 24–22, 24–23
   evidence, 24–24, 24–25
   families, 24–10, 24–11, 24–13, 24–14
   human rights, 24–22
   indefinite leave to remain, 24–18
   involuntary unemployment, 24–21
   judicial interpretation, 24–09
   lawful residence, 24–08
   loss of EU status, 24–23
   rights of entry and residence, 24–05—24–07, 24–10—24–12, 24–19
   Romanian nationals, 24–31, 24–33

Indefinite leave to remain
after five years, 10–10
annulment of marriage, 10–12
death of family member, 10–11, 10–12
deportation, 13–39, 24–18
divorce, 10–12
non-EU family members, 10–12
permanent incapacity, 10–11

International trade
General Agreement on Tariffs and Trade, 2–11
World Trade Organisation, 2–11

Israel
association agreements, 2–09
economic and political co-operation, 2–09
Euro-Mediterranean agreements, 14–57

Jobseekers
access to employment, 11–36, 11–37
case law, 6–51—6–53
continuing to seek employment, 6–48, 6–53
deportation, 13–61
Directive 2004/38
   families, 6–48, 6–50
   more favourable treatment, 6–49
   prohibition on expulsion, 6–48, 6–49, 7–20

INDEX

rights of entry and residence, 6–48, 6–50, 6–56, 6–58
equal treatment, 11–35, 11–37, 11–38
freedom of establishment, 7–19, 7–20
genuine chance of employment, 6–48
introduction, 6–27
rights of entry and residence, 6–48, 6–50, 6–56, 6–58, 7–19
seeking employment, 6–51
social and tax advantages, 11–35, 11–57
social security, 12–14
time limits, 6–49, 6–52, 6–53

Jordan
association agreements, 2–09
economic and political, co-operation, 2–09
Euro-Mediterranean agreements, 14–57

Kazakhstan
partnership and co-operation agreements
economic relations, 2–10, 14–09, 14–45
freedom of movement, 14–49

Kyrgystan
partnership and co-operation agreements
economic relations, 2–10, 14–09, 14–45
freedom of movement, 14–49

Lebanon
association agreements, 2–09
economic and political, co-operation, 2–09
Euro-Mediterranean agreements, 14–57

Lomé Conventions
EU relations, 14–67—14–69

Maastricht Treaty
see **Treaty on European Union**

Macedonia
stabilisation and association agreements
economic and political rights, 2–09, A11–01
equal treatment, 16–19
families, 16–29—16–31
freedom of establishment, 14–39—14–44, A11–01
freedom of movement, 14–36—14–44, 16–20, 16–32, A11–01
freedom to provide services, 16–39
non-discrimination provisions, 16–05, 16–08, 16–09, 16–12, 16–17, 25–32, A11–01
objectives, A11–01
regional co-operation, 2–09, 14–07, 14–34, 15–01, A11–01
rights of entry and residence, 16–01, 16–04, 16–05, 16–18, 16–21
social security systems, 14–44
United Kingdom, 25–32

Marriage
annulment, 9–35, 10–09, 10–12, 10–114, A3–01
breakdown of marriage
dissolution, 9–32, 9–34

divorce, 9–32, 9–33, 9–35, 10–09, 10–12, 10–114, A3–01
separation, 9–32, 9–33
forced marriage, 9–30
polygamous marriages, 9–30
sham marriages
common language, 9–52
Directive 2004/38, 9–50, 9–51
history of abuse, 9–52
immigration, 9–51
marriage of convenience, 9–50, 9–51
transsexuals, 9–42, 9–45—9–48
valid marriage, 9–30

Moldova
partnership and co-operation agreements
economic relations, 2–10, 14–09, 14–45
freedom of movement, 14–49

Montenegro
stabilisation and association agreements
equal treatment, 16–19
families, 16–29—16–31
freedom of movement, 14–36—14–44, 16–20, 16–32
freedom to provide services, 16–39
non-discrimination provisions, 16–05, 16–08, 16–09, 16–12, 16–17
regional co-operation, 2–09, 14–07, 14–34, 15–01
rights of entry and residence, 16–01, 16–04, 16–05, 16–18, 16–21
social security systems, 14–44

Morocco
association agreements
political and economic co-operation, 2–09
regional co-operation, 14–57
Euro-Mediterranean agreements
family members, 14–64
free movement of workers, 14–61, 14–62, 14–64
non-discrimination provisions, 14–61, 14–64

Mutual recognition principle
evidence of training, 11–87
freedom of establishment, 7–18, 11–76—11–78
general system, 11–75, 11–76, 11–81
national professional rules, 11–77
professional qualifications, 11–80, 11–82—11–84, 11–88, 11–89
self-employed workers, 11–79
temporary mobility, 11–85, 11–86
workers, 11–79

National security
deportation
Ankara Agreement, 21–01, 21–04, 21–05, 21–09
criminal convictions, 13–31, 13–32
Directive 2004/38, 13–31, 13–33, 13–49, 13–64
drug offences, 13–31

[704]

European Economic Area Regulations 2006, 24–11, 24–28
  generally, 13–01—13–08
  imperative grounds, 13–31, 13–33, 13–46, 13–54
  internal and external security, 13–30, 13–31
  meaning, 13–30—13–32
  notification, 13–50, 13–51
  proportionality, 13–33
  safeguards, A3–01
  sovereignty, 13–32
  United Kingdom, 24–05, 24–11, 24–28
  discrimination, 11–24, 11–96
  freedom to provide services, 11–96
Nationality
  see also **EU nationals**
  acquisition, 5–05
  citizenship, 5–06—5–10
  domestic law, 5–04
  dual nationals
    citizenship, 5–26
    free movement of persons, 5–13, 5–22—5–26
    freedom of establishment, 7–09
    rights and benefits, 5–13, 5–22—5–27
  own nationals
    equal treatment of non-nationals, 4–18—4–24, 4–73
    internal situations rule, 5–11—5–17
  third country nationals
    employees of national companies, 5–28, 5–31, 5–32
    families of EU nationals, 5–28
    freedom of movement, 5–28, 5–29
    protection, 5–28, 5–30
    refugees, 5–28
Non-discrimination
  see **Discrimination**

Partnership and Co-operation Agreements
  see also **Association Agreements**
  Armenia
    economic co-operation, 2–10
    political relationship, 14–45, 25–33
  Azerbaijan
    economic co-operation, 2–10
    political relationship, 14–45, 25–33
  direct effect, 14–52
  economic relations, 2–09, 14–09, 14045
  freedom of establishment, 14–55
  Georgia
    economic co-operation, 2–10, 14–09, 14–45
    freedom of movement, 14–49
  Kazakhstan
    economic co-operation, 2–10, 14–09, 14–45
    freedom of movement, 14–49
  legal framework, 14–47, 14–48

  Moldova
    economic co-operation, 2–10, 14–09, 14–45
    freedom of movement, 14–49
    no less favourable treatment, 14–56
    non-discrimination provisions, 14–51, 14–52, 25–34
    rights of entry and residence, 14–53, 25–34
  Russia
    bilateral relations, 14–47, 25–33
    economic co-operation, 2–10, 14–09, 14–45
    freedom of movement, 14–49
    non-discrimination, 14–51—14–53
    social security systems, 14–54
  Tajikistan
    economic co-operation, 2–10, 14–09, 14–45
    freedom of movement, 14–49
  Ukraine
    economic co-operation, 2–10, 14–09, 14–45
    freedom of movement, 14–49
  United Kingdom
    Central Asian countries, 25–33
    Eastern European countries, 25–33
    non-discrimination provision, 25–34
    rights of entry and residence, 25–34
  Uzbekistan
    economic co-operation, 2–10, 14–09, 14–45
    freedom of movement, 14–49
Part-time workers
  au pairs, 6–21
  collective agreements, 6–20
  immigration, 6–21
  importance, 6–18
  minor employment, 6–19
  paid leave, 6–20
  principal activity, 6–19
  sickness benefits, 6–20
  students, 6–21
  working hours, 6–17, 6–19, 6–20
Passports
  rights of entry and residence, 10–19—10–21, 10–93, 10–104, A3–01
"Permanent residence"
  after five years, 10–10
  annulment of marriage, 10–12
  death of family member, 10–11, 10–12
  divorce, 10–12
  non-EU family members, 10–12
  permanent incapacity, 10–11
Poland
  association agreements, 16–06, 16–07
Political Dialogue and Co-operation agreements
  Andean Community, 14–73
  Central American Countries, 14–73
  MERCOSUR countries, 14–73
"Poor people"
  freedom of movement, 4–72, 4–74

rights of entry and residence, 4–73
Posted workers
  freedom to provide services, 7–46, 7–62—
    7–64
  Swiss Association Agreement, 25–02
Preliminary rulings
  availability, 2–26, 15–15
  damages, 2–24
  excluded cases, 23–10
  procedure, 2–24, 2–26, 23–09, 23–10
  subject matter, 2–25
  uniform interpretation, 23–09
  United Kingdom courts, 23–11, 23–12
Primary carers
  see **Carers**
Principles of EU law
  see **General principles of EU law**
Proportionality
  deportation
    EU nationals 13–66, 13–67
    national security, 13–33
    proportionality assessment, 13–03,
      13–05—13–07, 13–17
    remedies, 13–56
    safeguards, 13–36
    special measures, 13–10
  EU law, 2–59, 2–60
  European Economic Area Agreement,
    24–28
  non-discrimination, 4–31, 11–22, 11–57
  rights of entry and residence, 4–55, 10–03,
    10–05, 10–40
Providers of services
  see **Service provision**
Public health
  deportation
    Ankara Agreement, 21–01, 21–04, 21–05,
      21–09
    Directive 2004/38, 13–35, 13–49, 13–64
    epidemics, 13–34
    European Economic Area Regulations
      2006, 24–11, 24–28
    generally, 13–01—13–08
    medical examinations, 13–35
    safeguards, A3–01
    special measures, 13–35
    time limits, 13–35
    United Kingdom, 24–05, 24–11, 24–28
  discrimination, 11–24, 11–96
  freedom to provide services, 11–96
Public policy
  deportation
    Ankara Agreement, 21–01, 21–04, 21–05,
      21–09
    association with organisations, 13–19
    danger to society, 13–24
    deterrence, 13–22, 13–23
    Directive 2004/38, 13–18, 13–23, 13–49,
      13–64
    disturbance of social order, 13–18, 13–27
    drug offences, 13–28

    European Economic Area Regulations
      2006, 24–11, 24–28
    generally, 13–01—13–08
    level of crime, 13–20
    national security distinguished, 13–18
    personal conduct, 13–18, 13–19, 13–25
    present threat, 13–25
    safeguards, A3–01
    serious crime, 13–24—13–29
    serious threats, 13–18, 13–29
    terrorism, 13–26, 13–27
    United Kingdom, 24–05, 24–11, 24–28
  discrimination, 11–24, 11–96
  freedom to provide services, 11–96
  rights of entry and residence, 4–77
Public security
  see **National security**

"Recipients of services"
  business travellers, 7–74
  concept, 7–71
  Directive 2004/38, 7–71, 7–76
  education, 7–74
  EU nationals, 7–72
  medical treatment, 7–74
  recipient establishing in another EU State,
    7–71
  recipient travels to another EU State 7–71,
    7–74
  rights of entry and residence, 7–44
  services for remuneration, 7–75
  third country nationals, 7–72
  tourists, 7–74
Refugees
  freedom of movement, 5–28
  human rights, 3–23, 3–24
  social security entitlement, 12–17
Residence
  lawful residence, 4–25—4–29, 4–73,
    10–80—10–82
Residence documents
  economically inactive persons, 8–10
  families, 9–17, 9–19
  rights of entry and residence, 10–02, 10–15,
    10–16, 10–22
Retained rights of residence
  see **Rights of entry and residence**
Retirement
  continuous residence, 8–29
  family members, 8–31
  invalidity pensions, 8–30
  non-residence, 8–30
  previously employed persons, 8–29
  rights of entry and residence, 8–31
  self-sufficiency, 8–12, 8–15
  sickness insurance, 8–30
  social security, 8–30, 8–31
  sufficient resources, 8–30
Right of establishment
  see **Freedom of establishment**

INDEX

Rights of entry and residence
see also **Border controls; Permanent residence**
children, 4–64—4–71, 8–32, 8–37—8–42
citizenship, 4–01, 4–02
economically inactive persons, 8–02—8–04, 8–08—8–15
entitlement, 4–06, 5–01, 5–03
equal treatment, A3–01
families
  annulment of marriage, 10–114
  ascending and descending line, 10–98, 10–99
  children born outside marriage, 10–116, 10–117
  civil partnerships, 10–96, 10–97
  divorce, 10–114
  EU nationals, 5–11, 5–15, 5–16, 10–90, 10–93
  evidence of dependency, 10–100
  evidence of family link, 10–19, 10–94, 10–99
  evidential problems, 10–111, 10–115
  generally, 10–03, 10–89—10–94
  identity cards, 10–93, 10–104
  non-EU nationals, 10–90, 10–93
  other family members, 10–101—10–105
  passports, 10–93, 10–104
  registration certificates, 10–90—10–93, 10–103, A3–01
  remaining beyond EU national, 10–107—10–110
  residence cards, 10–103, A3–01
  right to respect for private and family life, 9–08—9–15, 10–106
  spouses, 10–95
financial constraints, 4–76
formalities
  breaches, 10–02, 10–28
  compliance, 10–13, 10–25—10–28, 10–36
  Directive 2004/38, 10–14, 10–17, 10–18, 10–25, 10–44, 10–45 divergences, 10–18
  documentation, 10–13, 10–18—10–21, 10–24, 10–43—10–45, 10–52, 10–53
  evidence of family link, 10–19, 10–94, 10–99
  identity cards, 10–19—10–21, 10–24, 10–72, 10–93, 10–104
  passports, 10–19—10–21, 10–72, 10–93, 10–104, A3–01
  proof of right, 10–15, 10–43, 10–44
  registration certificates, 10–30, 10–44—10–47, A3–01
  residence cards, 10–30, 10–33, 10–35, 10–45, 10–48—10–51, 10–103, A3–01
  residence certificates, 10–31
  residence documents, 10–02, 10–15, 10–16, 10–22, 10–36, 10–44
  sanctions, 10–27, 10–28
  time limits, 10–29—10–36

visas, 10–13, 10–16, 10–29
free standing rights, 4–56—4–63, 4–75
freedom of establishment, 7–04
fundamental principle, 10–01
human rights, 10–03
illegal entry and residence, 10–02
internal controls, 10–22, 10–23
interpretative obligation, 4–45, 4–48—4–55
introduction, 4–44, 4–45
jobseekers, 6–48, 6–50, 6–56, 6–58, 7–19
limitations and conditions, 4–45, 4–48, 4–50, 4–53, 4–75—4–77
loss of residence rights, 10–09, 10–84—10–85
more than three months
  educational courses, 10–07
  relatives in ascending line, 10–08
  self-employed workers, 10–07
  sickness insurance, 10–07
  students, 10–08
  sufficient resources, 10–07
  workers, 10–07, A3–01
non-EU nationals, 10–06, 10–08, 10–09, 10–12
poor people, 4–64, 4–72—4–74
proportionality, 4–55, 10–03, 10–05, 10–40
public policy, 4–77
registration certificates
  continuity of residence, 10–83
  family members, 10–90—10–92, 10–103
  jobseekers, 10–57—10–59
  lawful residence, 10–80—10–82
  obtaining, 10–54, 10–55, 10–60—10–67, 10–71—10–74, 10–76—10–83
  permanent registration certificates, 10–53, 10–76—10–88
  requirement, 10–30, 10–44—10–46
  retaining, 10–56, 10–68—10–70, 10–75, 10–84—10–88
  self-employed workers, 10–54—10–56
  self-sufficient persons, 10–60—10–70
  validity, 10–47
  workers, 10–54—10–56, A3–01
restrictive interpretation, 4–45—4–47
retained right of residence
  annulment of marriage, 10–09, A3–01
  death of family member, 10–09
  divorce, 10–09, A3–01
  domestic violence, 10–09
  illness or accident, 10–09
  involuntary unemployment, 10–09, A3–01
  self-employed workers, 10–09, A3–01
  vocational training, 10–09
  workers, 10–09, A3–01
right to respect for private and family life
  exceptions, 9–11
  existence of family life, 10–106
  fundamental right, 9–80, 10–04, 16–30
  immigration, 9–11
  justification, 9–11
  negative obligations, 9–11, 9–12

positive obligations, 9–13
proportionality, 9–12
protection, 9–08, 9–09, 9–11—9–13
public order, 9–11
transsexual marriage, 9–47
self-sufficiency
  comprehensive insurance, 10–64, 10–66
  sickness insurance, 10–60, 10–65
  social assistance, 10–60, 10–68, 10–69
  sufficient resources, 10–61—10–63, 10–70, A3–01
sickness insurance, 10–05, 10–60, 10–65, 10–72, 10–74
social assistance, 10–05, 10–60, 10–68, 10–69, 10–71
source of right, 10–02
students, 8–32—8–34, 8–43—8–46, 10–71—10–74
tax and social benefits, 5–11
third country nationals, 10–03, 10–04, 10–14, 10–16
up to three months, 10–06, A3–01
vocational training, 8–33, 8–34, 8–43—8–46

Right to private and family life
Charter of Fundamental Rights, 3–05, 3–07, 9–10
development of law, 3–22
Directive 2004/38, 3–24
exceptions, 9–11
existence of family life, 10–106
fundamental right, 9–80, 10–04, 16–30
immigration, 9–11
justification, 9–11
negative obligations, 9–11, 9–12
positive obligations, 9–13
proportionality, 9–12
protection, 3–07, 9–08, 9–09, 9–11—9–13
public order, 9–11
transsexual marriage, 9–47

Romania
association agreements, 15–08. 25–32
immigration, 24–31, 24–33

Russia
partnership and co-operation agreements
  bilateral relations, 14–47, 25–33
  economic co-operation, 2–10, 14–09, 14–45
  freedom of movement, 14–49
  non-discrimination, 14–51—14–53

Schengen Agreement
border free area, 1–18

Self-employed workers
deportation, 13–02, 13–61, 13–63
freedom of establishment, 7–01, 7–03, 7–05, 7–15—7–17, 7–20, 7–30
meaning, 6–22
rights of entry and residence, 10–07, 10–09
social security, 12–14
Turkish workers
  Ankara Agreement, 25–07

appeals, 25–31, 25–30
business applications, 25–13—25–17
deportation orders, 25–29, 25–30
entry clearance, 25–09, 25–10, 25–15, 25–18, 25–21—25–23, 25–26
fraud, 25–12—25–14
freedom of establishment, 25–08, 25–15
illegal immigrants, 25–09, 25–18, 25–24
immigration, 25–08, 25–09, 25–14
leave to remain, 25–18, 25–26
overstayers, 25–18, 25–28—25–31
port applicants, 25–18, 25–19
standstill clause, 25–09—25–13, 25–18
temporary admission, 25–09—25–11, 25–18, 25–19

Self-sufficiency
see **Rights of entry and residence**

Serbia
stabilisation and association agreements
  economic and political rights, 2–09
  regional co-operation, 14–07

Service provision
freedom to provide services
  companies, 7–41, 7–59, 7–60
  discrimination, 11–91, 11–94

Sham marriages
common language, 9–52
Directive 2004/38, 9–50, 9–51
history of abuse, 9–52
immigration, 9–51
marriage of convenience, 9–50, 9–51

Sickness insurance
deportation 13–68
economically inactive persons, 8–06, 8–10, 8–12, 8–23—8–26
rights of entry and residence, 10–05, 10–07, 10–72, 10–74
self-sufficient persons, 10–60, 10–65
students, 8–47

Single European Act 1986
freedom of movement, 1–17
internal market, 1–17

Social security
access to social security
  aggregation principle, 12–07, 12–33, A5–01
  citizenship, A2–01
  determinable or applicable legislation, A5–01
  differing systems, 12–05, 12–06, 12–33
  exchange of information, 12–06, A–01
  freedom of movement, 12–01, 12–05, 12–06, 12–10
  funding of activities, A5–01
  harmonisation, 12–03—12–06
  non-discrimination provisions, 12–01, 12–07—12–13, 12–33
  occupational diseases, A5–01
  personal data, A5–01
  procedural arrangements, 12–01
  residence requirement, 12–12
  social and tax benefits, 12–01

INDEX

subsidiarity, 12–07
time limits, 12–21
administrative arrangements, 12–01
Administrative Commission for Co-ordination of Social Security, 12–02, 12–32, A5–01
beneficiaries
 civil servants, A5–01
 collection of contributions, A5–01
 EU nationals, 12–17, A5–01
 families, 12–17, A5–01
 frontier workers, A5–01
 jobseekers, 12–14
 pensioners, A5–01
 posted workers, A5–01
 refugees, 12–17, A5–01
 residence rules, A5–01
 retirement, A5–01
 self-employed workers, 12–14, A5–01
 stateless persons, 12–17
 workers, 12–14, A5–01
complexity, 12–04
discrimination
 equal treatment, 12–09, 12–17, A5–01
 indirect discrimination, 12–10
 nationality grounds, 12–10
entitlement (benefits)
 accidents at work, A5–01
 benefits in kind, 12–22—12–24, 12–28, A5–01
 cash benefits, A5–01
 death grants, 12–19, 12–29, A5–01
 derogations, 12–13—12–15
 economic and social benefits, A5–01
 family benefits, A5–01
 insurance period, A5–01
 invalidity benefits, 12–19, 12–29, A5–01
 maintenance, A5–01
 maternity benefit, 12–10, 12–19, 12–22, A4–01
 medical treatment, 12–15, 12–24—12–26, A5–01
 overlapping benefits, A5–01
 paternity benefit, 12–19, 12–22, A5–01
 pensions, 12–19, 12–27, A5–01
 recovery of benefits, A4–01
 residence requirement, 12–12, A5–01
 sickness benefit, 12–19, 12–22, 12–23, A5–01
 social assistance, 12–15
 survivors' benefits, 12–19, 12–29, A5–01
 unemployment benefits, 12–11, 12–19, 12–31, A5–01
European Economic Area, 12–06
freedom of movement
 access to social security, 12–01
 social and tax benefits, 12–01
 Social Security Systems Regulation 883/2004, 12–05, 12–06, 12–10
 subsidiarity, 12–07
insurance provisions, 12–18
national systems, 12–03, A5–01

proportionality, A5–01
Social Security Systems Regulation 883/2004
 bilateral agreements, A5–01
 content, 12–19
 entry into force, A5–01
 implementation, 12–06, A5–01
 limitations, 12–16
subsidiarity, A5–01
Spouses
marriage breakdown
 annulment, 9–35, 10–09, 10–12, 10–114
 dissolution, 9–32, 9–34
 divorce, 9–32, 9–33, 9–35, 10–09, 10–12, 10–114
 separation, 9–32, 9–33
meaning, 9–30
rights of entry and residence, 10–95
Stabilisation and Association Agreements
see also **Association Agreements**
Albania
 economic and political rights, 2–09, 15–10
 equal treatment, 16–19
 families, 16–29—16–31
 freedom of establishment, 14–39—14–44
 freedom of movement, 14–36—14–44, 16–20, 16–32
 freedom to provide services, 16–39
 non-discrimination provisions, 14–60, 16–05, 16–08, 16–09, 16–12, 16–17, 16–18, 25–32
 regional co-operation, 2–09, 14–07, 14–34, 15–01
 rights of entry and residence, 16–01, 16–04, 16–05, 16–18, 16–21
 social security systems, 14–44
 supply of services, 16–39
 workers, 167–04, 16–23
Bosnia and Herzegovina
 economic and political rights, 2–09
 regional co-operation, 14–07
Copenhagen criteria, 14–31
Croatia
 economic and political rights, 2–09
 equal treatment, 16–19
 families, 16–29—16–31
 freedom of establishment, 14–39—14–44
 freedom of movement, 14–36—14–44, 16–20, 16–32
 freedom to provide services, 16–39
 non-discrimination provisions, 16–05, 16–08, 16–09, 16–12, 16–17, 25–32
 regional co-operation, 2–09, 14–07, 14–34, 15–01
 rights of entry and residence, 16–01, 16–04, 16–05, 16–18, 16–21
 social security systems, 14–44
EU accession, 14–30—14–33
families
 access to labour market, 16–29
 legal residence, 16–29, 16–30

[709]

INDEX

right to respect for private and family life, 16–30
rights of entry and residence, 16–30
freedom of establishment, 14–37, 14–39—14–43, 16–01, 16–11, 16–32
freedom of movement, 14–08, 14–36, 14–37, 16–01
freedom to provide services, 16–39—16–41
limitations, 16–02
Macedonia
　economic and political rights, 2–09, A11–01
　equal treatment, 16–19
　families, 16–29—16–31
　freedom of establishment, 14–39—14–44, A11–01
　freedom of movement, 14–36—14–44, 16–20, 16–32, A11–01
　freedom to provide services, 16–39
　non-discrimination provisions, 16–05, 16–08, 16–09, 16–12, 16–17, 25–32, A11–01
　objectives, A11–01
　regional co-operation, 2–09, 14–07, 14–34, 15–01, A11–01
　rights of entry and residence, 16–01, 16–04, 16–05, 16–18, 16–21
　social security systems, 14–44
Montenegro
　economic and political rights, 2–09
　equal treatment, 16–19
　families, 16–29—16–31
　freedom of establishment, 14–39—14–44
　freedom of movement, 14–36—14–44, 16–20, 16–32
　freedom to provide services, 16–39
　non-discrimination provisions, 16–05, 16–08, 16–09, 16–12, 16–17, 25–32
　regional co-operation, 2–09, 14–07, 14–34, 15–01
　rights of entry and residence, 16–01, 16–04, 16–05, 16–18, 16–21
　social security systems, 14–44
non-discrimination provisions
　direct discrimination, 16–16
　direct effect, 16–06, 16–08
　equal treatment, 16–07
　freedom of establishment, 16–11
　generally, 14–37, 16–05
　indirect discrimination, 16–16
　meaning of discrimination, 16–13—16–15
　national laws, 16–09, 16–10, 16–12
　temporal effect, 16–27
　workers, 16–18—16–26
process, 14–31, 14–323
reforms, 14–32
regional co-operation, 14–07, 14–30
Serbia
　economic and political rights, 2–09
　regional co-operation, 14–07

United Kingdom
　access to labour market, 25–32
　freedom of establishment, 25–32
　freedom to provide services, 25–32
　key personnel, 25–32
　non-discrimination provisions, 25–32
workers
　freedom of establishment, 16–01, 16–11
　freedom of movement, 16–01
　non-discrimination provisions, 16–05—16–16, 16–18—16–26
　protectionism, 16–03
　rights of entry and residence, 16–01
Students
discrimination, 11–101—11–103
economically inactive persons, 8–02, 8–05, 8–09, 8–22, 8–32—8–36
educational rights
　children of workers, 8–32
　mobility, 8–36
　non-discrimination, 8–34
　student grants, 8–35
　vocational training, 8–32—8–36
family members, 8–47
internal situations rule, 5–20
part-time employment, 6–21
rights of entry and residence
　children of workers, 8–37—8–42
　more than three months, 10–08
　vocational training, 8–33, 8–34, 8–43—8–46
self-sufficiency, 8–22
sickness insurance, 8–47
social assistance, 8–47
sufficient resources, 8–47, 10–71—10–74
workers, 6–30, 6–34, 6–39
Subsidiarity
decision-making process, 1–72
human rights protection, 3–10, 3–11
social security systems, A5–01
Supremacy of EU law
EU law, 2–29—2–35, 22–03
Switzerland
Association Agreement
　acquired rights, A7–01
　air transport, 14–21
　appeals, A7–01
　conformity assessments, 14–21
　development of land, A7–01
　dispute resolution, A7–01
　double taxation, A7–01
　economic activity, A7–01
　economically inactive persons, A7–01
　entry into force, A7–01
　equal treatment, 14–24, A7–01
　families, 14–24, A7–01
　formalities, A7–01
　freedom of movement, 14–21—14–23, A7–01
　freedom to provide services, A7–01
　frontier workers, 14–24, 14–25, A7–01
　immovable property, A7–01

[710]

Index

invalidity benefits, A7–01
lawful and habitual employment, 25–02
more favourable provisions, A7–01
mutual recognition principle, A7–01
non-discrimination provisions, 14–24, A7–01
objective, A7–01
posted workers, 25–02, A7–01
public order, A7–01
public procurement, 14–21
public service exception, A7–01
reference to EU law, A7–01
residence documents, 14–25, A7–01
revision, A7–01
rights of entry and residence, A7–01, A7–01, A7–01
road and rail transport, 14–21
self-employed workers, A7–01
service providers, A7–01
social security, A7–01
special permits, A7–01
standstill clause, A7–01
territorial scope, A7–01
trade in agricultural products, 14–21
United Kingdom, 25–01, 25–02
workers, 14–24, A7–01
Immigration (Swiss Free Movement of Persons)(No3) Regulations 2002
families, A18–01
posted workers, A18–01
residence documents, A18–01
Swiss nationals, A18–01

Tajikistan
partnership and co-operation agreements
economic co-operation, 2–10, 14–45
freedom of movement, 14–49
Terrorist offences
deportation, 24–29, 13–26, 13–27
Trade agreements
see **International trade**
Trainees
workers, 6–30—6–35, 6–39
Transsexuals
discrimination, 9–42, 9–44, 9–48
EU law, 9–42—9–45, 9–48
human rights
gender reassignment, 9–42, 9–43
protection, 9–42, 9–44, 9–46—9–49
respect for private and family life, 9–47
right to marry, 9–47
marriage, 9–42, 9–45—9–48
pension rights, 9–43, 9–44
Treaties
accession treaties
Treaty of Accession 2003, 5–34, 5–36
Treaty of Accession 2005, 5–37
compliance, 23–03
EU law
direct applicability, 2–44, 2–45
direct effect, 2–42, 2–43
individual rights, 2–41, 2–43

foundation treaties, 1–03, 1–04, 1–06
national implementation, 2–46—2–53
Treaty Establishing the European Economic Community
see **EC Treaty**
Treaty of Accession 2003
freedom of movement, 5–36
scale of development, 5–34
transitional arrangements, 5–36
Treaty of Accession 2005
freedom of movement, 5–37
transitional arrangements, 5–37
Treaty of Amsterdam 1997
asylum, 1–24, 1–25
citizenship, 4–09
generally, 1–06, 1–23
immigration, 1–24, 1–25
justice and home affairs, 1–24
Treaty of Lisbon 2007
competition rules, 1–34
customs union, 1–34
defence policy, 1–30
double majority voting, 1–30
enhanced co-operation, 1–30
EU competences, 1–34
foreign and security policy, 1–30
free movement of workers, 6–02
fundamental rights, 1–33
generally, 1–06, 1–29
High Representative for Foreign Affairs, 1–32
institutional changes, 1–30
qualified majority voting, 1–30
Vice-President of the Commission, 1032
withdrawal provision, 1–31
Treaty of Nice 2001
enhanced co-operation, 1–27
generally, 1–06
institutional changes, 1–26—1–28
qualified majority voting, 1–27
Treaty of Rome
see **EC Treaty**
Treaty on European Union
area of freedom, security and justice, A1–01
decision-making, A1–01
democratic principles, A1–01
equality principle, 3–01, A1–01
EU institutions, A1–01
external relations, A1–01
freedom of movement, A1–01
fundamental freedoms, A1–01
generally, 2–02
human rights, 3–01, A1–01
indirect effect, 2–55
international agreements, A1–01
legal acts of the Union, A1–01
objectives, A1–01
relations between Member States, A1–01
rule of law, A1–01
sincere co-operation, 2–30
supremacy doctrine, 2–29

[711]

INDEX

three pillars
  common foreign and security policy, 1–21
  freedom of movement, 1–04, 1–20
  justice and home affairs, 1–04, 1–22
Treaty on the Functioning of the European Union
  actions
    actions for annulment, 2–15, 2–18
    appeals, 2–22
    damages, 2–20
    EU staff, 2–21
    failure to act, 2–19
  association agreements
    general power, 14–01, 14–02
    qualified majority procedure, 14–03
    reciprocal rights, 14–02
  binding nature, 2–44, 2–48, 2–54
  children, 4–64
  citizenship
    dual nationals, 5–26
    EU nationals, 4–01, 4–09, 4–10, 5–01—5–03
    families, 5–17
    freedom of movement, 4–06, 4–07, A2–01
    non-discrimination, 4–14—4–16
    reciprocal rights, 14–20
    right to vote, A2–01
  codification, 2–28
  customs union
    custom duties, A2–01
    free movement of workers, A2–01
    generally, A2–01
    import formalities, A2–01
  deportation
    national security, 11–96, 13–02
    public health, 11–96, 13–02
    public policy, 11–96, 13–02
  freedom of establishment
    agents, A2–01
    branches, A2–01
    citizenship, 5–07
    companies, 7–01—7–03, 7–24, 7–26, 7–59
    differential treatment, 7–30
    economic activity, 7–05, 7–11, 7–12, 7–40
    EU nationals, 7–15
    freedom to provide services, 7–37
    movement of capital, A2–01
    national laws, A2–01
    non-discrimination, 11–58, 11–59, 11–61—11–64, 11–69
    public service exemption, A2–01
    self-employed workers, A2–01
    subsidiaries, A2–01
    unjustified restriction, 7–31
  freedom of movement
    citizenship, 4–06, 4–07, A2–01
    economically inactive persons, 8–03, 8–06, 8–07, 11–97, 11–102
    generally, 2–67
    interpretation, 4–45—4–55
    jobseekers, 6–27
    non-discrimination, 4–12, 4–13, 4–16—4–19, 4–21, 4–34, 6–02
    public service exception, 6–69—6–72, 12–31, A2–01
    self-employed workers, 6–12
    vocational training, 8–34, 8–36, 8–45
    workers, 6–02—6–05, 6–07, 6–08, 6–20, 6–25, 6–51, 6–55, 6–56
  freedom to provide services
    meaning of services, A2–01
    non-discrimination, 11–90, 11–93, 11–95
    prohibition of restrictions, 7–33, 7–35, 7–37, 7–38, 7–41, 7–42, 7–47, 7–48, A2–01
    service providers, 7–50, 7–52, 7–55, 7–67
    temporal provision, A2–01
  generally, 2–20
  lawful residence, 4–25—4–29, 4–73
  legal certainty, 2–61
  mutual recognition principle, 11–75, 11–76, 11–678
  non-discrimination
    citizenship, 4–02, 4–12—4–24, 4–30—4–33, 4–51
    direct discrimination, 16–16
    economically inactive persons, 11–99, 11–100, 11–103
    equal treatment, 4–12, 4–13, 4–20, 4–30, 11–37
    freedom of movement, 4–06, 4–07, 4–12, 4–13, 4–16—4–19, 4–21, 4–34, 6–02
    generally, 11–01, 11–02, 11–04—11–19, 11–21, 11–25, 11–28
    harmonisation, A2–01
    indirect discrimination 16–16
    prohibited activity, A2–01
    social security, 12–08,
    students, 8–35
  poor persons, 4–72—4–74
  preliminary rulings, 2–24
  proportionality, 13–07
  provisional legal protection, 2–22, 2–23
  rights of entry and residence
    free standing rights, 4–56—4–63, 4–75
    generally, 4–06, 4–30, 5–15, 7–19, 10–02, 10–44, A2–01
    interpretation, 4–45—4–59, 4–62
    limitations and conditions, 4–45, 4–48, 4–50, 4–53, 4–75—4–77, 8–06
    proportionality, 4–55
  supremacy doctrine, 2–29
  Union competences, 2–03
Tunisia
  association agreements
    political and economic co-operation, 2–09
    regional co-operation, 14–57
  Euro-Mediterranean agreements
    family members, 14–64
    free movement of workers, 14–63, 14–64

Index

non–discrimination provisions, 14–63, 14–64
Turkey
  Ankara Agreement
  see also **Ankara Agreement**
    content, 17–07
    economic relations, 14–26, 17–08, 17–10, 17–11, 17–13, 18–02
    interpretation, 17–06, 17–12
    objectives, 17–09—17–11, 17–18
    protection of rights, 17–06
  EU accession application, 14–28, 17–03
  labour emigration, 17–04, 17–05
Turkmenistan
  partnership and co-operation agreements
    economic relations, 2–10, 14–09, 14–45
    freedom of movement, 14–49

Ukraine
  partnership and co-operation agreements
    economic relations, 2–10, 14–09, 14–45
    freedom of movement, 14–49
United Kingdom
  see also **European Economic Area Regulations 2006**
  association agreements
    Bulgaria, 25–32
    Romania, 25–32
    Switzerland, 25–01, 25–02
  deportation
    criminal convictions, 24–28
    national security, 24–05, 24–11, 24–28
    personal conduct, 24–28
    proportionality, 24–28
    public health, 24–05, 24–11, 24–28
    public policy, 24–05, 24–11, 24–28
  EU law (freedom of movement)
    divergence, 22–02, 22–03
    EEA nationals, 24–11, 24–14, 24–16
    EU nationals, 24–04
    families, 24–10, 24–11, 24–13
    immigration law, 24–05—24–07
    implementation, 22–01
    incorporation, 23–01—23–08, 24–01
    interpretation, 22–02—22–04
    relevant nationals, 24–04
    rights of entry and residence, 24–05—24–07, 24–10, 24–12
    self-employed workers, 24–10
    self-sufficiency, 24–10
    sovereignty, 24–05
    students, 24–10
    supremacy principle, 22–03
    workers, 24–10
  EU law (incorporation)
    freedom of movement, 23–01—23–08, 24–01
    legal framework, 23–02—23–08
    legislation, 23–01
  European Communities Act 1972
    compliance with EU Treaties, 23–03
    direct effect of Community Law, 23–06, 23–07
    EC/EU membership, 23–02
    effective operation of Community law, 23–05—23–07
    implementation of Community Law, 23–07
    interpretation of Community Law, 23–08
    judicial notice of Community Law, 23–08
    treaty amendments, 23–04
    treaty implementation, A12–01
  immigration law
    accession legislation, 24–30—24–33
    Bulgarian nationals, 24–31, 24–33
    certificates of application, 24–12, 24–13
    dependency, 24–12
    Directive 2004/38, 24–08, 24–11, 24–15, 24–16, 24–18, 24–22, 24–23
    evidence, 24–24, 24–25
    families, 24–10, 24–11, 24–13, 24–14
    human rights, 24–22
    indefinite leave to remain, 24–18
    involuntary unemployment, 24–21
    judicial interpretation, 24–09
    lawful residence, 24–08
    loss of EU status, 24–23
    rights of entry and residence, 24–05—24–07, 24–10—24–12, 24–19
    Romanian nationals, 24–31, 24–33
  partnership and co-operation agreements
    Central Asian countries, 25–33
    Eastern European countries, 25–33
    non-discrimination provision, 25–34
    rights of entry and residence, 25–34
  referrals to Court of Justice of the European Union
    adjudicators, 23–12
    appeals, 23–15
    costs, 23–16, 23–17
    eligibility to refer, 23–11, 23–12
    excluded cases, 23–10
    final court, 23–14
    immigration cases, 23–12, 23–17
    judicial review proceedings, 23–13
    preliminary rulings, 23–09, 23–10
    uniform interpretation, 23–09
  Swiss Association Agreement
    lawful and habitual employment, 25–02
    legislation, 25–01, 25–02
    posted workers, 25–02
  self-employed Turkish workers
    Ankara Agreement, 25–07
    appeals, 25–31, 25–30
    business applications, 25–13—25–17
    deportation orders, 25–29, 25–30
    entry clearance, 25–09, 25–10, 25–15, 25–18, 25–21—25–23, 25–26
    fraud, 25–12—25–14
    freedom of establishment, 25–08, 25–15
    illegal immigrants, 25–09, 25–18, 25–24
    immigration, 25–08, 25–09, 25–14
    leave to remain, 25–18, 25–26

INDEX

overstayers, 25–18, 25–28—25–31
port applicants, 25–18, 25–19
standstill clause, 25–09—25–13, 25–18
temporary admission, 25–09—25–11, 25–18, 25–19
stabilisation and association agreements
  access to labour market, 25–32
  freedom of establishment, 25–32
  freedom to provide services, 25–32
  key personnel, 25–32
  non-discrimination provisions, 25–32
Turkish workers (Ankara Agreement)
  access to labour markets, 25–03—25–05
  acquired rights, 25–03
  au pairs, 25–05
  entry clearance, 25–03
  families, 25–04
  immigration, 25–06
  leave to remain, 25–03, 25–04
  less favourable treatment, 25–04
  standstill clause, 25–05
  students, 25–05
Universal Declaration of Human Rights
non-discrimination, 2–63
Unmarried couples
durable relationships
  freedom of movement, 9–73—9–76
  treatment of civil partners, 9–37, 9–39
family members, 9–26
Unmarried partners
see **Unmarried couples**
Uzbekistan
partnership and co-operation agreements
  economic relations, 2–10, 14–09, 14–45
  freedom of movement, 14–49

Visas
EU nationals, 10–38
non-EU nationals, 10–39—10–42
rights of entry and residence, 10–13, 10–16, 10–29
time limits, 10–29
Vocational training
Directive 2004/38, 8–32, 8–46,
discrimination, 11–30
economically inactive persons, 8–02
rights of entry and residence, 8–33, 8–34, 10–09
Voting
double majority voting, 1–30
qualified majority voting, 1–27, 1–30
voting rights, 5–01, 5–03

Western Balkan States
see **Stabilisation and Association Agreements**
Work seekers
see **Jobseekers**
Workers
see also **Jobseekers**; **Part–time workers**
apprentices, 6–30, 6–33, 6–34, 6–39
au pairs, 6–21, 6–36—6–39

deportation, 13–61, 13–63
discrimination
  nationality grounds, 6–02, 11–04, 11–05, 11–16, 11–21, 11–24, 11–28, 11–56
  personal scope, 11–32—11–34
  termination of employment, 11–32, 11–33
freedom of movement
  applications for employment, A4–01
  clearance of vacancies, A4–01
  committes for ensuring close cooperation between Member States, A4–01
  Directives, 6–03, 6–05
  employment, A4–01
  equal treatment, A4–01 exchange of young workers, 6–04
  families, 6–05, A4–01
  importance, 6–01, 6–02, 6–05, 6–06
  interpretation, 6–02, 6–06
  limitations, 6–02
  migrant workers, 6–06
  national concepts, 6–06, 6–18, 6–70
  Regulations, 6–03, 6–05, A4–01
  removal of obstacles, 6–02
  social security, 6–04
freedom to provide services
  EU nationals, 7–61
  minimum rights, 7–66
  protection, 7–67, 7–69
  posted workers, 7–46, 7–62—7–64
  work permits, 7–65, 7–67
frontier workers
  discrimination, 11–34
  frequency of return, 6–67
  meaning, 6–67
  migrant workers, 6–68
  protection, 11–34
  residence, 6–67, 6–68
irregular work, 6–22—6–24
meaning, 6–07, 6–08, 11–32
motive for work, 6–28, 6–29
nature of work, 6–27
on-call workers, 6–23
previous employment
  availability for work, 6–62
  capability to take further employment, 6–61
  case law, 6–59—6–66
  generally, 6–54
  retraining, 6–64
  rights of entry and residence, 6–55, 6–56
  status of worker, 6–54, 6–57, 6–59, 6–60, 6–62—6–66
productivity, 6–16, 6–17
public service exception
  discriminatory treatment, 6–69, 6–73
  generally, 6–69
  legitimate interest, 6–69, 6–72
  scope, 6–70—6–73
rehabilitative employment, 6–40—6–42
remuneration, 6–08, 6–13—6–16, 6–39

[714]

rights of entry and residence
   more than three months, 10–07, A3–01
   previous employment, 6–55, 6–56
   registration certificates, 10–54—10–56
   retained rights, 10–09
self-employed workers, 6–22
services of economic value, 6–08—6–11, 6–16, 6–30
services under another's direction, 6–08. 6–12, 6–39
social security, 12–14

status of worker, 6–54, 6–57, 6–59, 6–60, 6–62—6–66, 11–32, 11–33
students, 6–30, 6–34, 6–39
supplementary funds, 6–26
termination of employment, 11–32, 11–33
trainees, 6–30—6–35, 6–39
variable employment conditions, 6–22—6–25
workers in education, 9–78—9–79

Yaoundé Conventions
   EU relations, 14–67